AUTHOR'S LETTER

Dear Colleague:

Hundreds of faculty across the globe have adopted *International Business: The New Realities* because of its comprehensive coverage of key, contemporary issues—globalization, technology, governments' evolving role, globalization of finance, the service sector, small and medium-size enterprises, and emerging markets, such as the BRIC countries (Brazil, Russia, India, and China).

The Third Edition has been completely revised and continues to reflect the new realities of today's international business environment for tomorrow's managers:

New **emphasis on sustainability, ethics, and corporate social responsibility.** In each chapter, we examine the link between business and social issues. The Third Edition highlights conscientious business and the importance of responsibly meeting humanity's needs throughout the text.

Practical treatment of managerial issues. The class-tested Third Edition bridges the gap between scholarly knowledge and real-world practice. Our applied, managerial approach is supported by theory and fundamentals from international business, economics, and related fields.

Accessible style and visually appealing. Lucid writing and explanations facilitate learning and teaching. Our many exhibits and tables illustrate difficult or complex topics. Vignettes and cases appeal to students, featuring firms and subjects like Apple, Diesel, Disney, Harley-Davidson, H&M, and the global movie industry.

Comprehensive support material. The *Instructor's Manual* to accompany the Third Edition is one of the most comprehensive and practical resources in the field. Our large collection of videos covers fascinating topics, such as born global firms, emerging markets, survival of the euro, and China's emergent roles. Our test bank has been honed and expanded over three editions.

MyManagementLab. MyManagementLab makes it easier for you to add meaningful assessment to your course. Whether you're interested in testing your students on simple recall of concepts & theories or if you'd like to gauge how well your students can apply their newly minted knowledge to real-world scenarios, MyManagementLab offers a variety of assessment questions to fit your needs.

Additional improvements to the Third Edition include numerous new closing cases; improved explanatory frameworks; enhanced treatment of *culture*; more than 180 new or updated exhibits; and new vignettes in each chapter—*Ethical Connections* and *Country Realities*.

As you review *International Business: The New Realities*, we hope you will agree it provides instructors and students with a fully integrated learning program designed expressly to frame the new realities of international business.

Thank you for considering the Third Edition of *International Business: The New Realities* for your course!

Sincerely,
S. Tamer Cavusgil
Gary Knight
John R. Riesenberger

Discover New Realities of International Business

- **Motivate and prepare future managers to grasp the contemporary developments in international business** critical to their success—globalization, technology, governments' evolving roles, globalization of finance, the service sector, the success of small and medium-size enterprises, and emerging markets.

- **New Country Realities** found in the margin of each chapter relate the chapter material to a factual description on a given country, or set of countries.

- **New emphasis on sustainability, ethics, and corporate social responsibility** raises student awareness of firms' roles as good corporate citizens.

- **Expanded geographic coverage of emerging markets and developing economies,** including more emphasis on Africa and other developing regions, provides students an improved understanding of the changing landscape of international business as it relates to emerging markets and developing economies.

- **Reorganized Culture chapter** examines culture models and perspectives more systematically, provides enhanced explanations of key concepts and models related to culture, and expands coverage of religion and its role in culture and business. The new opening vignette examines the role of culture in Google's entry into China.

Personalize Learning

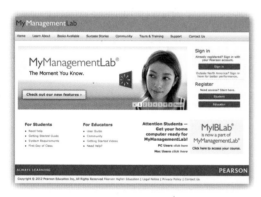

- **MyManagementLab** delivers online assessment and preparation material that helps students actively study and prepare material for class. Chapter-by-chapter activities, including pre-tests and post-tests and video and critical-thinking exercises, focus on what students need to learn and to review in order to succeed.

- **The Pearson eText** lets students access their textbook any time, anywhere, and any way they want—including online or downloading to iPad.

- A **personalized study plan** for each student promotes better critical thinking skills and helps students succeed in the course and beyond.

Engage Students

- **You Can Do It** (formerly *Recent Grad in IB*) profiles in selected chapters highlight IB graduates working in exciting international careers to motivate today's students to travel, learn another language, and be open to working internationally.

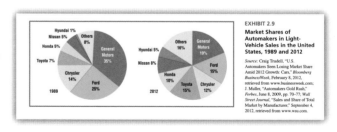

EXHIBIT 2.9
Market Shares of Automakers in Light-Vehicle Sales in the United States, 1989 and 2012
Source: Craig Trudell, "U.S. Automakers Seen Losing Market Share Amid 2012 Growth: Cars," *Bloomberg BusinessWeek*, February 8, 2012, retrieved from www.businessweek.com; J. Muller, "Automakers Gold Rush," *Forbes*, June 8, 2009, pp. 70–77; *Wall Street Journal*, "Sales and Share of Total Market by Manufacturer," September 4, 2012, retrieved from www.wsu.com.

- **Numerous videos** support the major themes of the program, including Globalization and the Growth of International Business, Internationalization of Born Globals and Other Small and Medium Enterprises, and more.

- **More than 180 new and updated exhibits and graphics** more effectively illustrate complex or interesting material enhancing reading and retention for the student.

- **Balanced coverage of multinational enterprises, small- and medium-sized enterprises, and born globals** provide students the much needed familiarity with the variety of firms active in international business today.

- Large, easy to read, colorful **maps** throughout the text help students improve their understanding of world geography.

Explore Theory and Application

- **Practical treatment of managerial issues** bridges the gap between scholarly knowledge and real-world practice. The applied, managerial approach is coupled with theory and fundamentals from international business, economics, and related fields.

- **New Ethical Connections feature** illustrates dilemmas that managers encounter at the boundary of ethical norms and business practice. Students can apply the CKR Ethical Framework from Chapter 5 to address ethical dilemmas presented in each chapter.

- **Deeper focus on economics** via more detailed explanations of key concepts based in micro- and macro-economic theory and numerous new exhibits illustrate important phenomena.

- **All chapters have been thoroughly updated to reflect the latest trends and facts** impacting the world economy and global business, such as the recession or stagnant economic conditions, emergent regulation, and more.

- **New organizing framework to start each chapter** provides an outline that summarizes the major topics and how they relate to each other, enriching the readability and flow.

- **New or revised vignettes and closing cases** capture the latest trends relevant to each chapter. New Opening Stories include the Globalization of Facebook, Google in China, Corporate Social Responsibility at Coca-Cola, Apple's Advantages, and Huawei's Investments in Africa.

- **GlobalEDGE™ Internet Exercises** in each chapter provide instructors a basis for student assignments and projects. GlobalEDGE™ was developed under the direction of co-author S. Tamer Cavusgil while at Michigan State University.

Support Instructors

- **AACSB tagging** accompanies all end of chapter exercises to help instructors identify which AACSB learning goals that exercise supports and to help measure whether students are grasping the course content that aligns with AACSB guidelines. All Testbank items are tagged as well.

- **Instructor's Manual,** authored by Marta Szabo White of Georgia State University and winner of numerous teaching awards, goes beyond the traditional, limited chapter outline and end-of-chapter answers to provide a variety of additional resources for each chapter such as exercises, critical-thinking assignments, debate topics, and research assignments.

- **Test Item File,** authored by an assessment expert with extensive experience in test authoring, includes 100 questions per chapter, all reviewed and edited to ensure accuracy and appropriateness. TestGen Test Generating software is also available.

- **Newly prepared PowerPoint** slides and an **Image Library** containing all of the exhibits from the textbook are available electronically for instructors to download.

why do you need this new edition?

14 good reasons why you should buy this new third edition of *International Business!*

1 Engaging online resources to help you succeed! MyManagementLab provides you with online study resources to help make your study time even more effective.

2 All chapters have been thoroughly updated to reflect the latest trends and facts impacting the world economy and global business, such as the worldwide recession, government intervention, and more.

3 Greater attention to sustainability and corporate social responsibility, as well as the role of corporate governance, to reflect companies, non-profit organizations, and governments increasing focus on sustainability.

4 More emphasis on Africa and other developing regions, as well as key emerging markets to improve your understanding of the changing landscape of international business. Among the emerging markets, particular focus is given to BRICS and the next tier of growth markets, given their huge role in global trade, investment, and politics.

5 More detailed explanations of key concepts based in micro- and macro-economic theory and numerous new exhibits to provide you with a critical foundation for describing nations, organizations, and economic phenomena.

6 Each chapter opens with an organizing framework that systematically explains the major topics and how they relate to each other, enriching readability and flow.

7 More than 180 new and updated exhibits throughout this edition illustrate complex or interesting material more effectively.

8 Each chapter features a new vignette, *Ethical Connections*, which illustrates dilemmas that managers encounter at the boundary of ethical norms and business practice.

9 Each chapter includes a new feature, *Country Realities*, which relates the chapter material to a factual description of a given country, or set of countries.

10 Eight new *Opening Stories* and *Global Trends* vignettes, reflect contemporary trends such as The Globalization of Facebook, Google in China, Corporate Social Responsibility at Coca-Cola, Apple's Advantages, and Huawei's Investments in Africa.

11 Reorganized Chapter 4 examines culture models and perspectives more systematically, provides enhanced explanations of key concepts and models related to culture, and expands coverage of religion and its role in culture and business.

12 Chapter 12 features a new Closing Case on Lenovo, with an emerging market focus.

13 Chapter 15 features a new Closing Case on the failed global merger of DaimlerChrysler.

14 You Can Do It features in selected chapters replace Recent Grad in IB feature in the last edition. These highlight IB graduates now working in exciting international careers. We hope this feature will motivate you to travel, learn another language, and be open to working internationally!

International Business

The New Realities

Third Edition

International Business

The New Realities

Third Edition

S. Tamer Cavusgil
Georgia State University

Gary Knight
Willamette University

John R. Riesenberger
Thunderbird School of Global Management

PEARSON

Boston   Columbus   Indianapolis   New York   San Francisco   Upper Saddle River   Amsterdam
Cape Town   Dubai   London   Madrid   Milan   Munich   Paris   Montréal   Toronto   Delhi
Mexico City   São Paulo   Sydney   Hong Kong   Seoul   Singapore   Taipei   Tokyo

Editor in Chief: Stephanie Wall
Senior Editor: Kristin Ellis-Levy
Editorial Project Manager: Sarah Holle
Editorial Assistant: Bernard Ollila, IV
Director of Marketing: Maggie Moylan
Senior Marketing Manager: Erin Gardner
Senior Managing Editor: Judy Leale
Senior Production Project Manager: Ann Pulido
Operations Specialist: Cahtleen Petersen
Creative Director: Blair Brown

Art Director: Steve Frim
Interior and Cover Design: Black
    Horse Designs
Media Editor: Denise Vaughn
Media Project Manager: Lisa Rinaldi
Full-Service Project Management and Composition:
    Integra
Printer/Binder: RRD/Jefferson City
Cover Printer: Lehigh-Phoenix Color/Hagerstown
Text Font: 10/12, Times LT Std Roman

Credits and acknowledgments borrowed from other sources and reproduced, with permission, in this textbook appear on the appropriate page within text.

Microsoft and/or its respective suppliers make no representations about the suitability of the information contained in the documents and related graphics published as part of the services for any purpose. All such documents and related graphics are provided "as is" without warranty of any kind. Microsoft and/or its respective suppliers hereby disclaim all warranties and conditions with regard to this information, including all warranties and conditions of merchantability, whether express, implied or statutory, fitness for a particular purpose, title and non-infringement. In no event shall Microsoft and/or its respective suppliers be liable for any special, indirect or consequential damages or any damages whatsoever resulting from loss of use, data or profits, whether in an action of contract, negligence or other tortious action, arising out of or in connection with the use or performance of information available from the services.

The documents and related graphics contained herein could include technical inaccuracies or typographical errors. Changes are periodically added to the information herein. Microsoft and/or its respective suppliers may make improvements and/or changes in the product(s) and/or the program(s) described herein at any time. Partial screen shots may be viewed in full within the software version specified.

Microsoft® and Windows® are registered trademarks of the Microsoft Corporation in the U.S.A. and other countries. This book is not sponsored or endorsed by or affiliated with the Microsoft Corporation.

Many of the designations by manufacturers and sellers to distinguish their products are claimed as trademarks. Where those designations appear in this book, and the publisher was aware of a trademark claim, the designations have been printed in initial caps or all caps.

Library of Congress Cataloging-in-Publication Data

Cavusgil, S. Tamer.
  International business : the new realities / S. Tamer Cavusgil, Gary Knight, John R. Riesenberger.—3rd ed.
    p. cm.
  ISBN-13: 978-0-13-299126-1
  ISBN-10: 0-13-299126-8
  1. International business enterprises—Management.   I. Knight, Gary A.   II. Riesenberger,
John R., 1948-   III. Title.
  HD62.4.C389 2014
  658'.049—dc23

                                                        2012043910

10 9 8 7 6 5 4 3 2 1

ISBN 13: 978-0-13-299126-1
ISBN 10:   0-13-299126-8

About the Authors

S. Tamer Cavusgil
Georgia State University, Fuller E. Callaway Professorial Chair, Executive

Director, Center for International Business Education and Research, J. Mack Robinson College of Business

Professor Cavusgil has been mentoring students, executives, and educators in international business for the past three decades. A native of Turkey, Professor Cavusgil's professional work has taken him to numerous other emerging markets.

Professor Cavusgil has authored more than 200 refereed journal articles and three dozen books, including *Doing Business in Emerging Markets* (Sage, 2nd Edition). His work is among the most cited contributions in international business. He is the founding editor of the *Journal of International Marketing* and *Advances in International Marketing*. He serves on the editorial review boards of leading professional journals. He is the recipient of numerous awards for his teaching, scholarship, and institutional leadership.

Professor Cavusgil is an elected Fellow of the Academy of International Business, a distinction earned by a select group of intellectual leaders in international business. He also served as Vice President of the AIB, and on the Board of Directors of the American Marketing Association. Michigan State University bestowed him with its highest recognition for contributions to the international mission: the Ralph H. Smuckler Award for Advancing International Studies. He was named International Trade Educator of the Year in 1996 by the National Association of Small Business International Trade Educators (NASBITE). At Michigan State University, he also earned the distinction of University Distinguished Faculty, the highest award given to a faculty member. In 2007, he was named an Honorary Fellow of the Sidney Sussex College at the University of Cambridge.

Professor Cavusgil holds MBA and PhD degrees in business from the University of Wisconsin. Previously, he held positions at the Middle East Technical University in Turkey, University of Wisconsin–Whitewater, Bradley University, and Michigan State University. He also served as Senior Fulbright Scholar to Australia and taught at Monash University and other Australian institutions. He served as a visiting Professor at Manchester Business School and was Gianni and Joan Montezemolo Visiting Chair at the University of Cambridge, the United Kingdom.

Gary Knight
Willamette University, Professor of Global Management

Helen Simpson Jackson Chair in International Management

Professor Knight has extensive experience in international business in the private sector. In his position as Export Manager for a medium-sized enterprise, he directed the firm's operations in Canada, Europe, Japan, and Mexico, supervising the business activities of some fifty distributors in these regions. Previously, he worked for several years in Tokyo, Japan.

Professor Knight has developed several study abroad programs in business in Asia and Europe. He has been an invited speaker at numerous institutions worldwide. He has won several awards for research and teaching, including best teacher in the MBA program and the Hans Thorelli Best Paper Award for his article "Entrepreneurship and Strategy: The SME Under Globalization." His research emphasizes international business strategy, international services, emerging markets, and internationalization of small and medium-sized firms.

Professor Knight is a member of the Academy of International Business. He has co-authored five books and more than 100 refereed articles in academic journals and conference proceedings, including *Journal of International Business Studies, Journal of World Business, International Executive,* and *Management International Review.* He has been ranked one of the top fifteen most prolific scholars in the United States, and one of the top thirty worldwide, in the six leading international business journals. He is on the editorial review boards of several international journals. The U.S. House of Representatives invited Professor Knight to provide expert testimony on global commerce and small business.

For 15 years Professor Knight was professor, and Director of the Program in International Business, at Florida State University. He earned his MBA at the University of Washington and PhD at Michigan State University, both in international business. Earlier degrees were in Finance and Modern Languages. He also attended the University of Paris in France and Sophia University in Japan and is fluent in French, Japanese, and Spanish.

John R. Riesenberger
Thunderbird School of Global Management, Clinical Professor of Executive Development, Corporate Learning Group

Professor Riesenberger's teaching and research activities center on leadership and global project management. His passion is to help students develop the managerial skills frequently required of new graduates entering careers in international business.

Professor Riesenberger is an accomplished author, consultant, and international executive with senior executive positions in major pharmaceutical firms, with C-suite experience in biotechnology firms and pharmaceutical agencies. Professor Riesenberger's international business career spans over three decades in the global pharmaceutical industry. He has conducted business transactions in twenty-one countries.

Currently, he also serves as the President of Consilium Partners, Inc., a pharmaceutical consulting firm with clients in pharmaceutical, biotechnology, and pharmaceutical agency firms.

He worked for 30 years with Pharmacia & Upjohn and The Upjohn Company as a senior international executive. His experience covered a diverse range of divisional, geographic, and functional accountabilities. His most recent position was Vice President, Global Business Management. He also served as Corporate Vice President and Chief Commercialization Officer for a biotechnology firm and as the Executive Vice President of a pharmaceutical science agency.

Professor Riesenberger served as a member of the Global Advisory Board of the *American Marketing Association.* He serves as an Executive in Residence at the Michigan State University Center for International Business Education and Research. He served on the Editorial Review Board of *The Journal of International Marketing.* He served as Chairman, Industry Advisory Board, "Value of Marketing Program," SEI Center for the Advanced Studies in Management, The Wharton School of the University of Pennsylvania. He is the former Chairman of the Pharmaceutical Manufacturing Association Marketing Practices Committee. Professor Riesenberger is the coauthor, with Robert T. Moran, of *The Global Challenge: Building the New Worldwide Enterprise* (McGraw-Hill, London).

Professor Riesenberger holds a Bachelor of Science degree in Economics-Business and an MBA in Management from Hofstra University. He attended the Harvard Business School's International Senior Management Program.

> Brief Contents

> Contents

xii

Contents

Information Technology 35
Communications 38
Manufacturing 39
Transportation 39
Societal Consequences of Market Globalization 39
■ Global Trend: Globalization and E-Business in the Online World 40
Contagion: Rapid Spread of Monetary or Financial Crises 40
Loss of National Sovereignty 41
Offshoring and the Flight of Jobs 42
Effect on the Poor 42
Effect on Sustainability and the Natural Environment 43
Effect on National Culture 46
Globalization and Africa 47
Firm-Level Consequences of Market Globalization: Internationalization of the Firm's Value Chain 47
■ Closing Case: Debating the Merits of Globalization 49
■ Chapter Essentials: Key Terms 50 Summary 50 Test Your Comprehension 51 Apply Your Understanding 52
globalEDGE™ Internet Exercises 52

3 Organizational Participants That Make International Business Happen 55

> The Emergence of Born Global Firms 54
Four Types of Participants in International Business 56
Participants Arranged by Value-Chain Activity 57
Illustrating the International Value Chain Using Dell Inc. 58
Focal Firms in International Business 59
The Multinational Enterprise (MNE) 60
Small and Medium-Sized Enterprises 62
Born Global Firms 62
International Entry Strategies of Focal Firms 63
A Framework for Classifying International Entry Strategies 63
Other Types of International Entry Strategies 64
Distribution Channel Intermediaries in International Business 66
Intermediaries Based in the Foreign Market 67
Intermediaries Based in the Home Country 68
Online Intermediaries 70
Facilitators in International Business 70
■ Global Trend: Online Retailers Surge Ahead 71
Governments in International Business 73
■ Closing Case: DHL, FedEx, and UPS: Shifting Fortunes in the Global Logistics Services Industry 74
■ Chapter Essentials: Key Terms 75 Summary 76 Test Your Comprehension 77 Apply Your Understanding 77
globalEDGE™ Internet Exercises 78

> Preface

This Book Supports Association to Advance Collegiate Schools of Business (AACSB) International Accreditation

In every chapter, next to each end-of-chapter exercise, we provide a specific AACSB tagging logo to help instructors identify which AACSB learning goals that activity supports. We also provide AACSB tagging for all the questions in the Test Item File that accompanies the textbook.

WHAT ARE AACSB LEARNING STANDARDS? One of the criteria for AACSB accreditation is the quality of the curricula. Although no specific courses are required, the AACSB expects a curriculum to include learning experiences in such areas as:

- Communication abilities
- Ethical understanding and reasoning abilities
- Analytic skills
- Use of information technology
- Dynamics of the global economy
- Multicultural and diversity understanding
- Reflective thinking skills

These seven categories are AACSB Learning Standards. Questions that test skills relevant to these standards are tagged with the appropriate standard. For example, a question testing the moral questions associated with externalities would receive the ethical understanding and reasoning abilities tag.

HOW CAN I USE THESE TAGS? Tagged exercises help you measure whether students are grasping the course content that aligns with AACSB guidelines noted previously. In addition, the tagged exercises may help to identify potential applications of these skills. This, in turn, may suggest enrichment activities or other educational experiences to help students achieve these goals.

Supplements

All of the following supplements can be downloaded from our Instructor Resource Center. Request your user name and password from your Pearson Sales Representative. www.pearsonhighered.com/irc

If you ever need assistance, our dedicated technical support team is ready to help with the media supplements that accompany this text. Visit http://247pearsoned.custhelp.com for answers to frequently asked questions and user support.

INSTRUCTOR'S MANUAL Authored by Marta Szabo White, professor at Georgia State University and winner of numerous teaching awards, the Instructor's Manual offers much more than just the traditional, limited chapter outline and answers to the end-of-chapter materials. In addition to these basic items, each chapter includes a variety of resources such as exercises, critical-thinking assignments, debate topics, and research assignments.

TEST ITEM FILE The Test Item File is authored by experts with extensive experience in assessment and test creation. The number of questions per chapter has been increased in this edition from seventy five to one hundred. Each question has been carefully reviewed and edited to ensure accuracy and appropriateness.

Test questions are annotated with the following information:

- Learning Objectives from the main text
- Difficulty level: Easy for straight recall, Moderate for some analysis, or Analytical for complex analysis
- Skill: concept, application, critical thinking or synthesis

For each question that tests a standard from the Association to Advance Collegiate Schools of Business (AACSB), we use one of the following annotations:

- Communication abilities
- Ethical understanding and reasoning abilities
- Analytic skills
- Use of information technology
- Dynamics of the global economy
- Multicultural and diversity understanding
- Reflective thinking skills

TESTGEN TEST GENERATING SOFTWARE This easy-to-use software allows instructors to custom design, save, and generate classroom tests. Instructors can edit, add, or delete questions from the test bank, analyze test results, and organize a database of tests and student results. It provides many flexible options for organizing and displaying tests, along with a search-and-sort feature. TestGen can be downloaded from www.pearsonhighered.com/educator.

POWERPOINT SLIDES Fully updated PowerPoints offer helpful instructional support by highlighting and clarifying key concepts.

IMAGE LIBRARY All of the exhibits from the textbook are available electronically for instructors to download, print, display in class, or produce customized materials.

DVD Library

Videos illustrating the most important subject topics are available in two formats:

DVD – available for in classroom use by instructors, includes videos mapped to Pearson textbooks. MyLab – available for instructors and students, provides round the clock instant access to videos and corresponding assessment and simulations for Pearson textbooks.

Contact your local Pearson representative to request access to either format.

COURSESMART ETEXTBOOKS ONLINE CourseSmart eTextbooks were developed for students looking to save on required or recommended textbooks. Students simply select their eText by title or author and purchase immediate access to the content for the duration of the course using any major credit card. With a CourseSmart eText, students can search for specific keywords or page numbers, take notes online, print out reading assignments that incorporate lecture notes, and bookmark important passages for later review. For more information or to purchase a CourseSmart eTextbook, visit www.coursesmart.com.

Acknowledgments

Our Reviewers

Through numerous drafts of the manuscript, we received guidance and insights at several critical junctures from many trusted reviewers who provided specific recommendations on how to improve and refine the content, presentation, and organization. Their contributions were invaluable in crystallizing our thinking. We extend our gratitude to:

Anil Agarwal, University of Arizona
Raj Aggarwal, University of Akron
Anshu Arora, Savannah State University
Richard Ajayi, University of Central Florida
Hamid Ali, Chicago State University
Allen Amason, University of Georgia
Gary Anders, Arizona State University
Robert Armstrong, University of North Alabama
Mathias Arrfelt, Arizona State University
Bulent Aybar, Southern New Hampshire University
Nizamettin Aydin, Suffolk University
Peter Banfe, Ohio Northern University
Eric Baumgardner, Xavier University
Mack Bean, Franklin Pierce University
Lawrence Beer, Arizona State University
Enoch Beraho, South Carolina State University
David Berg, University of Wisconsin–Milwaukee
Jean Boddewyn, Baruch College, City University of New York
Henry Bohleke, Owens Community College
Santanu Borah, University of Northern Alabama
Darrell Brown, Indiana University, Purdue University, Indianapolis
Linda Brown, Scottsdale Community College
Diana Bullen, Mesa Community College
Nancy Bush, Wingate University
Kirt Butler, Michigan State University
Michael Campo, Regis University
Tom Cary, City University, Seattle
Kalyan Chakravarty, California State University, Northridge
Aruna Chandra, Indiana State University
Kent Cofoid, Seminole State College
Tim Curran, University of South Florida
Madeline Calabrese Damkar, California State University–East Bay
Donna Davisson, Cleveland State University
Seyda Deligonul, St. John Fisher College
Peter Dowling, Latrobe University, Australia
Juan España, National University

Bradley Farnsworth, University of Michigan, Ann Arbor
Aysun Ficici, Southern New Hampshire University
John Finley, Columbus State University
Ian Gladding, Lewis University
Jorge Gonzalez, University of Texas–Pan American
Tom Head, Roosevelt University
Bruce Heiman, San Francisco State University
David Hrovat, Northern Kentucky University
Douglas Johansen, Jacksonville University
Paul Jones, Regis University
Ali Kara, Pennsylvania State University–University Park
Bruce Keillor, Youngstown University
Daekwan Kim, Florida State University
Ki Hee Kim, William Patterson University
Konghee Kim, St. Cloud State University
Ahmet Kirca, Michigan State University
Leonard Kloft, Wright State University
Peter Knight, Santa Clara University
Anthony Koh, University of Toledo
Stephanie Kontrim-Baumann, Missouri Baptist University
Tatiana Kostova, University of South Carolina
Chuck Kwok, University of South Carolina
Ann Langlois, Palm Beach Atlantic University
Romas Laskauskas, Stevenson University
Yikuan Lee, San Francisco State University
Bijou Lester, Drexel University
Phil Lewis, Eastern Michigan University
Charles Main, Northern Arizona University
Minghua Li, Franklin Pierce University
Bob McNeal, Alabama State University, Montgomery
Janis Miller, Clemson University
Barbara Moebius, Waukesha County Technical College
Bruce Money, Brigham Young University
Bill Murray, University of San Francisco
Paul Myer, University of Maine
Matthew B. Myers, University of Tennessee
Max Grunbaum Nagiel, Daytona State College

Kuei-Hsien Niu, Sacramento State University

Bernard O'Rourke, Caldwell College

Braimoh Oseghale, Fairleigh Dickinson University

Jeffrey W. Overby, Belmont University

Susan Peterson, Scottsdale Community College

Iordanis Petsas, University of Scranton

Zahir Quraeshi, Western Michigan University

Roberto Ragozzino, University of Central Florida

Brandon Randolph-Seng, Texas Tech University

Michelle Reina, Wisconsin Lutheran College

Michael Rubach, University of Central Arkansas

Carol Sanchez, Grand Valley State University

Hakan Saraoglu, Bryant University

Jeff Sarbaum, University of North Carolina at Greensboro

Amit Sen, Xavier University

Deepak Sethi, Old Dominion University

Karen Sneary, Northwestern Oklahoma State University

Kurt Stanberry, University of Houston-Downtown

John Stanbury, George Mason University

William Streeter, Olin Business School, Washington University in Saint Louis

Philip Sussan, University of Central Florida

Charles Ray Taylor, Villanova University

Deanna Teel, Houston Community College

Gladys Torres-Baumgarten, Ramapo College of New Jersey

Kimberly Townsend, Syracuse University

Thuhang Tran, Middle Tennessee State University

Joseph Trendowski, Old Dominion University

Sameer Vaidya, Texas Wesleyan University

Chandu Valluki, St. Mary's University of Minnesota

Cheryl Van Deusen, University of North Florida

Linn Van Dyne, Michigan State University

Davina Vora, State University of New York at New Paltz

William Walker, University of Houston

Paula Weber, St. Cloud State University

Mindy West, Arizona State University

Sidney Wheeler, Embry-Riddle Aeronautical University

Marta Szabo White, Georgia State University

Richard Wilson, Hofstra University

Yim-Yu Wong, San Francisco State University

Jennifer Woolley, Santa Clara University

Alan Wright, Troy University

Attila Yaprak, Wayne State University

Betty Yobaccio, Bryant University

Pierre Yourougou, Whitman School of Management, Syracuse University

Bashar Zakaria, California State University, Sacramento

Anatoly Zhuplev, Loyola Marymount University

Focus Group Participants

We were also fortunate that so many colleagues generously gave their time and offered perspectives on our teaching resources. We met with these colleagues in person, teleconferenced with them, or otherwise received their input. The insights and recommendations of these educators were instrumental in the design and format of our teaching system. We extend our gratitude and thanks to the following reviewers and colleagues:

David Ahlstrom, The Chinese University of Hong Kong

Yusaf Akbar, Southern New Hampshire University

Victor Alicea, Normandale Community College

Gail Arch, Curry College

Anke Arnaud, University of Central Florida

Choton Basu, University of Wisconsin–Whitewater

Eric Baumgardner, Xavier University

Mark Bean, Franklin Pierce College

Enoch Beraho, South Carolina State University

Paula Bobrowski, Auburn University

Teresa Brosnan, City University, Bellevue

Darrell Brown, Indiana University, Purdue University–Indianapolis

Nichole Castater, Clark Atlanta University

Aruna Chandra, Indiana State University

Mike C. H. (Chen-Ho) Chao, Baruch College, City University of New York

David Chaplin, Waldorf College

Dong Chen, Loyola Marymount University

Chen Oi Chin, Lawrence Technological University

Patrick Chinon, Syracuse University

Farok J. Contractor, Rutgers University

Angelica Cortes, University of Texas–Pan American

Michael Deis, Clayton State University
Les Dlabay, Lake Forest College
Gary Donnelly, Casper College
Gideon Falk, Purdue University–Calumet
Marc Fetscherin, Rollins College
Charles Fishel, San Jose State University
Frank Flauto, Austin Community College
Georgine K. Fogel, Salem International University
Frank Franzak, Virginia Commonwealth University
Debbie Gilliard, Metropolitan State College
Robert Goddard, Appalachian State University
Andy Grein, Baruch College, City University of New York
Andrew C. Gross, Cleveland State University
David Grossman, Goucher College
Seid Hassan, Murray State University
Wei He, Indiana State University
Xiaohong He, Quinnipiac University
Christina Heiss, University of Missouri–Kansas City
Pol Herrmann, Iowa State University
Guy Holburn, University of Western Ontario
Anisul Islam, University of Houston–Downtown
Basil Janavaras, Minnesota State University
Raj Javalgi, Cleveland State University
Ruihua Jiang, Oakland University
Yikuan Jiang, California State University–East Bay
James Kennelly, Skidmore College
Ken Kim, University of Toledo
Leonard Kloft, Wright State University
Anthony C. Koh, The University of Toledo
Ann Langlois, Palm Beach Atlantic University
Michael La Rocco, University of Saint Francis
Romas A. Laskauskas, Villa Julie College
Shaomin Li, Old Dominion University
Ted London, University of Michigan
Peter Magnusson, Saint Louis University
Charles Mambula, Suffolk University
David McArthur, Utah Valley State College
Ofer Meilich, Bradley University

Lauryn Migenes, University of Central Florida
Mortada Mohamed, Austin Community College
Robert T. Moran, Thunderbird
Carolyn Mueller, Stetson University
Kelly J. Murphrey, Texas A&M University
Lilach Nachum, Baruch College, CUNY
William Newburry, Florida International University
Stanley Nollen, Georgetown University
Augustine Nwabuzor, Florida A&M University
Bernard O'Rourke, Caldwell College
David Paul, California State University–East Bay
Christine Cope Pence, University of California Riverside
Heather Pendarvis-McCord, Bradley University
Kathleen Rehbein, Marquette University
Liesl Riddle, George Washington University
John Rushing, Barry University
Mary Saladino, Montclair State University
Carol Sanchez, Grand Valley State University
Camille Schuster, California State University–San Marcos
Eugene Seeley, Utah Valley State College
Deepak Sethi, Old Dominion University
Mandep Singh, Western Illinois University
Rajendra Sinhaa, Des Moines Area Community College
John E. Spillan, Pennsylvania State University–DuBois
Uday S. Tate, Marshall University
Janell Townsend, Oakland University
Sameer Vaidya, Texas Wesleyan University
Robert Ware, Savannah State University
Marta Szabo White, Georgia State University
Steve Williamson, University of North Florida
Lynn Wilson, Saint Leo University
Attila Yaprak, Wayne State University
Rama Yelkur, University of Wisconsin–Eau Claire
Minyuan Zhao, University of Michigan
Christopher Ziemnowicz, Concord University

Our Colleagues, Doctoral Students, and Practitioners

Numerous individuals have contributed to our thinking over the years. Through conversations, conferences, seminars, and writings, we have greatly benefited from the views and experience of international business educators and professionals from around the world. The senior author also had many rich conversations with the doctoral students whom he mentored over the years. Their names appear below if they have not been previously mentioned. Directly or indirectly, their thoughtful ideas and suggestions have had a significant impact on the development of this book. Our appreciation goes to many individuals, including:

John Abbott, The Upjohn Company
Billur Akdeniz, University of New Hampshire
Catherine N. Axinn, Ohio University
Nizam Aydin, Suffolk University
Ted Bany, The Upjohn Company
Christopher Bartlett, Harvard Business School
Simon Bell, University of Melbourne
Daniel C. Bello, Georgia State University
Muzaffer Bodur, Bogazici University
Jacobus Boers, Georgia State University
Nakiye Boyacigiller, Sabanci University
John Brawley, The Upjohn Company
David Bruce, Georgia State University
Susan Caolo, Georgia State University
Pedro Carrillo, Georgia State University
Erin Cavusgil, University of Michigan–Flint
Brian Chabowski, University of Tulsa
Emin Civi, University of New Brunswick, St. John, Canada
Mourad Dakhli, Georgia State University
Tevfik Dalgic, University of Texas at Dallas
Guillermo D'Andrea, Universidad Austral–Argentina
Angela da Rocha, Universidad Federal do Rio de Janeiro, Brazil
Fernando Doria, Georgia State University
Rick Della Guardia, The Upjohn Company
Deniz Erden, Bogazici University
Felicitas Evangelista, University of Western Sydney, Australia
Cuneyt Evirgen, Sabanci University
Carol Finnegan, University of Colorado at Colorado Springs
Harold Fishkin, The Upjohn Company
Michael Fishkin, Stony Brook University
Richard Fletcher, University of Western Sydney, Australia
Esra Gencturk, Ozyegin University
Pervez Ghauri, Kings College London
Tracy Gonzalez-Padron, University of Colorado at Colorado Springs
Qian Gu, Georgia State University
Bill Hahn, Science Branding Communications
Tomas Hult, Michigan State University
Destan Kandemir, Bilkent University
Ilke Kardes, University of Applied Sciences, Dusseldorf, Germany
George Kaufman, The Upjohn Company
Ihsen Ketata, Georgia State University
Irem Kiyak, Michigan State University
Tunga Kiyak, Michigan State University
Yener Kandogan, University of Michigan–Flint
Phillip Kotler, Northwestern University
John Lavaca, Pearson Prentice Hall

Tiger Li, Florida International University
Karen Loch, Georgia State University
Mushtaq Luqmani, Western Michigan University
Robert McCarthy, The Upjohn Company
Ellen Miller, The Upjohn Company
Myron Miller, Michigan State University (ret.)
Vincent Mongello, The Upjohn Company
Robert T. Moran, Thunderbird
G. M. Naidu, University of Wisconsin–Whitewater (ret.)
John R. Nevin, University of Wisconsin
Gregory Osland, Butler University
Aysegul Ozsomer, Koc University
Ed Perper, Science Branding Communications
Morys Perry, University of Michigan–Flint
Vivas Reyes, Georgia State University
Alex Rialp, Universidad Autonoma de Barcelona, Spain
Tony Roath, University of Bath
Carol Sanchez, Grand Valley State University
Michael Savitt, The Upjohn Company
Peter Seaver, The Upjohn Company
Linda Hui Shi, University of Victoria
Rudolf R. Sinkovics, The University of Manchester
Carl Arthur Solberg, Norwegian School of Management, Norway
Elif Sonmez-Persinger, Eastern Michigan University
Douglas Squires, The Upjohn Company of Canada
Barbara Stoettinger, Wirtschaftuniversitaet Wein, Austria
Detmar Straub, Georgia State University
Berk Talay, University of Massachusetts Lowell
Cherian Thachenkary, Georgia State University
David Tse, University of Hong Kong
Mithat Uner, Gazi University
Nukhet Vardar, Yeditepe University
Marta Szabo White, Georgia State University
Fang Wu, University of Texas–Dallas
Shichun (Alex) Xu, University of Tennessee
Goksel Yalcinkaya, University of New Hampshire
Attila Yaprak, Wayne State University
Ugur Yavas, East Tennessee State University
Sengun Yeniyurt, Rutgers University
Poh-Lin Yeoh, Bentley College
Eden Yin, University of Cambridge
Chun Zhang, University of Vermont
Shaoming Zou, University of Missouri

Our Pearson Team

This book would not have been possible without the tireless efforts of many dedicated professionals at our publisher, Pearson. We are especially grateful to Stephanie Wall, Editor-in-Chief; Kris Ellis-Levy, Senior Editor; Sarah Holle, Editorial Project Manager; Bernard Ollila, Editorial Assistant; Erin Gardner, Marketing Manager; Gianna Sandi, Marketing Assistant; and Ann Pulido, Production Project Manager. Our appreciation goes to many other individuals at Prentice Hall, including: Linda Albelli, Steve Deitmer, Paul Corey, Maggie Moylan, Judy Leale, and Ashley Santora.

International Business

The New Realities

Third Edition

Source: Antony Souter/Dorling Kindersley Limited

Facebook: A Global Phenomenon

Globalization refers to intense economic, political, and personal interconnectedness between countries, companies, and consumers. Facebook exemplifies the globalization of business and converging lifestyles worldwide. Founded in 2004, by Mark Zuckerberg and his Harvard University classmates, Facebook is a social networking service. It has a dual identity—a vehicle for our personal lives and a for-profit business.

One of every eight people on the planet, roughly one billion users, has a Facebook account. Membership is growing rapidly. Facebook's top competitors are Google and Microsoft.

While half of all U.S. residents have a Facebook account, some 70 percent of Facebook users live outside the United States and speak over 75 languages. Globally, users spend more than 700 billion minutes on Facebook every month.

Facebook has a vision of a web tied together through personal relationships and recommendations. It is a social networking platform that enables individuals to share information with the idea of empowering them, mapping the social relationships among them, and creating a new system for exchanging information that many find indispensible.

CHAPTER 1

Introduction: What Is International Business?

 LEARNING OBJECTIVES *In this chapter, you will learn about the following:*

1. Key concepts in international business
2. How international business differs from domestic business
3. Who participates in international business
4. Why firms internationalize
5. Why you should study international business

MyManagementLab®
⭐ **Improve Your Grade!**
Over 10 million students improved their results using the Pearson MyLabs.
Visit **mymanagementlab.com** for simulations, tutorials, and end-of-chapter problems.

Facebook managers have used foreign direct investment to establish offices around the world. Facebook is especially popular in France, Italy, Japan, and the United Kingdom. It is the fastest growing social networking site in Indonesia, and is establishing a loyal user base throughout Africa.

At present, Facebook earns all its revenue from advertising. It is fast becoming the place where brand advertisers go to raise awareness of their products. Part of the success secret is that Facebook knows so much about its users—the site contains precise information on user interests, who voluntarily upload

such data. The information is priceless to brand managers in a world of targeted advertising. Some governments fear the Facebook database and the ease with which it can be used to form networks and spread information. In fact, China, Egypt, Iran, Pakistan, Saudi Arabia, and other countries have banned its use at one time or another.

Millions of people use Facebook to make friends in other countries. In India, Facebook is popular with business executives, who use the site to track down and keep up with friends from their youth. In France, people use Facebook to connect with their contemporaries, just as the French government erects barriers to protect France from what it considers cultural invasion. In Sweden, IKEA used the Facebook photo tagging option to promote the opening of a new store. Sweden is densely populated, and Facebook deepens ties among people who are often already connected through mutual friends.

In Japan, users access Facebook via their cell phones as they travel between home and office on the nation's massive commuter train network. Marketers set up their own communities to interact with members. In Australia, Facebook fans use the site not only for social networking, but also for social dating, and are a prime target for firms marketing youth-oriented services. In Poland, Facebook is popular with the upwardly mobile set, young people with rising incomes who perceive Facebook users as better educated, successful urban dwellers. Firms use Facebook for display ads and targeted advertising to attract upwardly mobile managers.

The Facebook phenomenon illustrates how converging lifestyles, modern communications technology, and imaginative entrepreneurship are facilitating the emergence of global enterprises.

SOURCES: "Facebook," *New York Times*, January 11, 2011 (www.nytimes.com); L. Grossman, "2010 Person of the Year: Mark Zuckerberg," *Time*, December 27, 2010—January 3, 2011, pp. 45–69; J. Neff, "Once Skeptics, Brands Drink the Facebook Kool-Aid," *Advertising Age*, February 22, 2010, p. 40; K. Patel, V. Vescovi, and A. Rocca, "Profiling the Facebooks of the World," *Advertising Age*, June 14, 2010, p. 6; S. Richmond and W. Heaven, "Will Facebook Conquer the World?," *The Telegraph*, January 4, 2011 (www.telegraph.co.uk); P. Srivastava, "The Gregarious Web," *Business Today*, October 21, 2007, p. 226; Ashlee Vance, "Where Everybody Knows Your Name," *Bloomberg Businessweek*, March 26–April 1, 2012, pp. 40–41; H. Warlaumont, "Social Networks and Globalization: Facebook, YouTube and the Impact of Online Communities on France's Protectionist Policies," *French Politics*, July, 2010, pp. 204–214; Hoover.com profile of Facebook; G. Fowler, "Facebook: One Billion and Counting," *Wall Street Journal*, October 4, 2012, retrieved from www.wsj.com.

International business
Performance of trade and investment activities by firms across national borders.

As revealed in the opening story, international business touches our daily experiences. **International business** refers to the performance of trade and investment activities by firms across national borders. Because it emphasizes crossing national boundaries, we also refer to international business as *cross-border business*. Firms organize, source, manufacture, market, and conduct other value-adding activities on an international scale. They seek foreign customers and engage in collaborative relationships with foreign business partners. While international business is performed mainly by individual firms, governments and international agencies also conduct international business activities.[1] Firms and nations exchange many physical and intellectual assets, including products, services, capital, technology, know-how, and labor. In this book, we are mainly concerned with the international business activities of the individual firm.

International business is characterized by six major elements illustrated in Exhibit 1.1. Firms' growing international activities give rise to the globalization of markets. As they venture abroad, companies undertake international trade and investment activities. Operating internationally entails various types of risks that occur to a lesser degree, or not at all, in the home country. International business is conducted by a distinctive collection of participants, including firms, distribution channel intermediaries, and facilitators. When they expand abroad, firms employ any of several international entry strategies, including exporting and direct investment. We explore each of the six dimensions in detail in this chapter.

While international business has been around for centuries, it has gained much momentum and complexity over the past three decades. Firms seek international market opportunities more today than ever before. Like Facebook, international business affects the everyday lives of people worldwide. Daily activities such as shopping, listening to music, watching a movie, or surfing the Internet involve transactions that connect you to the global economy. International business gives you access to products and services from around the world and profoundly affects your quality of life and economic well-being.

Globalization of markets
Ongoing economic integration and growing interdependency of countries worldwide.

Internationalization
The tendency of companies to systematically increase the international dimension of their business activities.

The Facebook phenomenon is a notable expression of ongoing economic integration and growing interdependency of countries worldwide, known as the **globalization of markets**. **Internationalization** refers to the tendency of companies to systematically increase the international dimension of their business activities. Globalization is a macro trend of intense economic interconnectedness among the nations of the world. It is associated with the internationalization

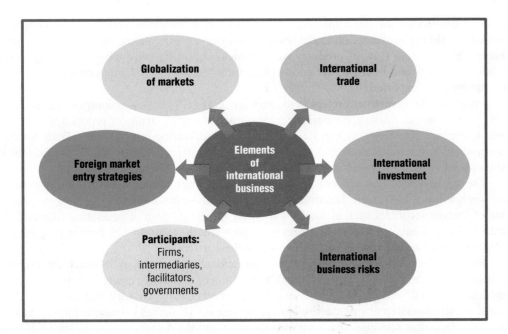

EXHIBIT 1.1

Elements of International Business

of countless firms and dramatic growth in the volume and variety of cross-border transactions in goods, services, and capital flows. It has led to widespread diffusion of products, technology, and knowledge worldwide.

The globalization of markets is evident in several related trends:

- *Unprecedented growth of international trade.* In 1960, cross-border trade was modest—about $100 billion per year. Today, it accounts for a substantial proportion of the world economy, with world exports amounting to some $14 trillion annually— that is, $14,000,000,000,000![2]
- *Trade between nations, accompanied by substantial flows of capital, technology, and knowledge.*
- *Development of highly sophisticated global financial systems and mechanisms* that facilitate the cross-border flow of products, money, technology, and knowledge.
- *Greater collaboration among nations* through multilateral regulatory agencies such as the World Trade Organization (WTO; www.wto.org) and the International Monetary Fund (IMF; www.imf.org).

Globalization both compels and facilitates companies to expand abroad. Simultaneously, company internationalization has become easier than ever before. A few decades ago, international business was largely the domain of large, multinational companies. Recent developments have created a more level playing field that allows all types of firms to benefit from active participation in international business. In this book, you will read about the international activities of smaller firms, along with those of large, multinational enterprises. While international business once was conducted mainly by firms that manufacture products, this is no longer the case. Companies in the services sector are also internationalizing, in such industries as banking, engineering, insurance, and retailing.

 What Are the Key Concepts in International Business?

International business refers mainly to international trade and investment. **International trade** describes the exchange of products and services across national borders. Trade involves both products (merchandise) and services (intangibles). Exchange can be through **exporting**, an entry strategy involving the sale of products or services to customers located abroad, from a base in the home country or a third country. Exchange also can take the form

International trade
Exchange of products and services across national borders, typically through exporting and importing.

Exporting
Sale of products or services to customers located abroad, from a base in the home country or a third country.

Importing or global sourcing
Procurement of products or services from suppliers located abroad for consumption in the home country or a third country.

International investment
The transfer of assets to another country or the acquisition of assets in that country.

International portfolio investment
Passive ownership of foreign securities such as stocks and bonds for the purpose of generating financial returns.

Foreign direct investment (FDI)
An internationalization strategy in which the firm establishes a physical presence abroad through acquisition of productive assets such as capital, technology, labor, land, plant, and equipment.

of **importing** or **global sourcing**—the procurement of products or services from suppliers located abroad for consumption in the home country or a third country. While exporting represents the outbound flow of products and services, importing is an inbound activity. Both finished products and intermediate goods (for example, raw materials and components) can be imported and exported.

International investment refers to the transfer of assets to another country or the acquisition of assets in that country. Economists refer to such assets as *factors of production* and they include capital, technology, managerial talent, and manufacturing infrastructure. Trade implies that products and services cross national borders. By contrast, investment implies the firm itself crosses borders to secure ownership of assets located abroad.

The two essential types of cross-border investment are international portfolio investment and foreign direct investment. **International portfolio investment** refers to the passive ownership of foreign securities such as stocks and bonds for the purpose of generating financial returns. It does not entail active management or control over these assets. The foreign investor has a relatively short-term interest in the ownership of these assets.

Foreign direct investment (FDI) is an internationalization strategy in which the firm establishes a physical presence abroad through acquisition of productive assets such as land, plant, equipment, capital, and technology. It is a foreign-market entry strategy that gives investors partial or full ownership of a productive enterprise typically dedicated to manufacturing, marketing, or management activities. Investing such resources abroad is generally for the long term and involves extensive planning.

The Nature of International Trade

Overall, export growth has outpaced the growth of domestic production during the last few decades, illustrating the fast pace of globalization. Exhibit 1.2 contrasts the growth of total world exports to the growth of total world *gross domestic product (GDP)* since 1970. GDP is defined as the total value of products and services produced in a country in the course of a year. Following a 27-year boom, world trade declined in 2009 due to the global recession. The hardest hit imports were consumer goods, cars, and car parts. However, trade revived and returned to normal levels by 2012. Trade was a key factor reducing the impact of the global recession.[3] Overall, however, in the past few decades world exports have grown more than thirty-fold, while world GDP grew only ten-fold.

To illustrate this point, consider the journey of a shirt sold in France. Initially, the cotton to produce the shirt is exported from the United States to China. After the shirt is manufactured in China, it is exported to France. Eventually, after the French owner discards her used shirt, it is

EXHIBIT 1.2

Comparing the Growth Rates of World GDP and World Exports

Sources: Based on World Bank, *World Development Indicators,* World Bank, Washington DC, 2012, (www.worldbank.org); World Trade Organization, *International Trade Statistics,* World Trade Organization, Geneva, 2012 (www.wto.org); UNCTAD, *World Investment Report,* United Nations, New York, 2012, (www.unctad.org).

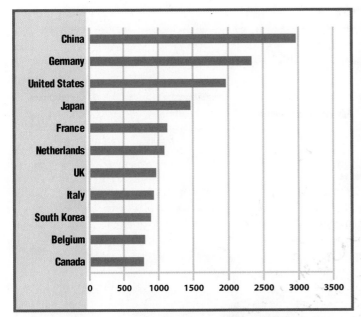

(a) Total annual value of products trade (exports + imports) in billions of US dollars

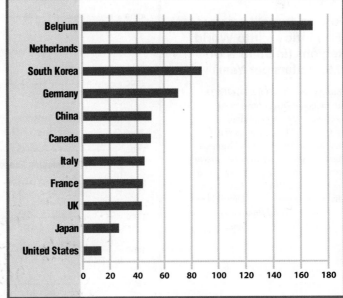

(b) Total annual value of products trade (exports + imports) as a percentage of nation's GDP

EXHIBIT 1.3

Leading Countries in International Merchandise Trade

Sources: Based on World Bank, World Development Indicators, World Bank, Washington, DC, 2011 (www.worldbank.org); World Trade Organization, Statistics Database, World Trade Organization, Geneva, 2011 (www.wto.org); UNCTAD, World Investment Report, United Nations, New York, 2011 (www.unctad.org).

exported once again and sold on the used clothing market in Africa. In total, the value generated in exporting the shirt greatly exceeds the cost to produce it.

Much of the difference in the growth of exports versus GDP is due to advanced (or developed) economies such as Canada and the United States now sourcing many of the products they consume from low-cost manufacturing locations such as China and Mexico. This has resulted largely from the rapid integration of world economies, fueled by advances in information and transportation technologies, the decline of trade barriers, the liberalization of markets, and the remarkable growth of emerging market economies.

Exhibit 1.3 identifies the nations that lead in the exporting and importing of products (but not services)—that is, international merchandise trade. Panel (a) shows the total value of products traded in billions of U.S. dollars. Panel (b) shows the annual value of products traded as a percentage of each nation's GDP. During the recent global recession, China surpassed the United States to become the world's leading exporter. China is the leading country in terms of the absolute value of total merchandise trade. Trade accounts for about 51 percent of China's GDP. Merchandise trade is a much larger component of economic activity in countries such as Belgium (169 percent), the Netherlands (139 percent), and South Korea (88 percent). These percentages show that some countries depend very heavily on international trade relative to the value of all goods and services they produce domestically.

Singapore, Hong Kong, and Malaysia are known as *entrepôt* economies. *Entrepôt* is from the French for "intermediate depot." Such countries import a large volume of products, some of which they process into higher value-added products and some they simply re-export to other destinations. For example, Singapore is a major *entrepôt* for petroleum products received from the Middle East, which it then exports to China and other destinations in Asia.

The Nature of International Investment

In this text, of the two types of investment flows—portfolio investment and foreign direct investment—we are concerned primarily with FDI, because it is the ultimate stage of internationalization and encompasses the widest range of international business involvement. FDI is the foreign entry strategy practiced by the most internationally active firms. Companies usually undertake FDI for the long term and retain partial or complete ownership of the assets they acquire.

In most cases, firms engage in FDI abroad to establish:

1. A factory or other facility to produce products or services,
2. A sales or representative office to conduct marketing or distribution activities, or
3. A regional headquarters.

EXHIBIT 1.4

Foreign Direct Investment (FDI) Inflows into World Regions (in Billions of U.S. Dollars per Year)

Sources: Based on OECD, *OECD International Direct Investment Statistics 2011*, Organisation for Economic Co-operation and Development; International Monetary Fund, *Coordinated Direct Investment Survey*, International Monetary Fund, Washington, 2010; UNCTAD, *World Investment Report 2011*, United Nations; World Bank, *World Bank Development Indicators 2011*, World Bank.

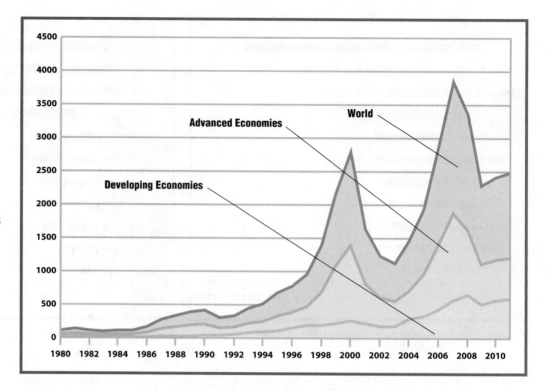

In the process, the firm establishes a new legal business entity, subject to the regulations of the host government in the country where the entity is established.

FDI is especially common among large, resourceful companies with substantial international operations. For example, many European and U.S. firms have invested in China, India, and Russia to establish plants to manufacture or assemble products, taking advantage of low-cost labor and other resources in these countries. At the same time, companies from these rapidly developing economies have begun to invest in Western markets. For example, in 2008, the Turkish company Yildiz acquired the premium chocolate maker Godiva from U.S.-based Campbell Soup Company in a deal valued at $850 million. More recently, Ford invested some $3 billion to build a new car factory in Mexico to manufacture Fiesta automobiles.

Exhibit 1.4 illustrates the dramatic growth of FDI into various world regions since the 1980s. The exhibit reveals that the dollar volume of FDI has grown immensely since the 1980s, especially in advanced economies such as Japan, Europe, and North America. FDI inflows were interrupted in 2001 as investors panicked following the September 11 terrorist attacks in the United States. The inflows were interrupted again in 2008 by the global recession. But the overall trend remains strong and growing over time. Particularly significant is the growth of FDI into *developing economies*, which are nations with lower incomes, less-developed industrial bases, and less investment capital than the advanced economies. Most of the developing economies are located in parts of Africa, Asia, and Latin America. Despite lower income levels, developing economies collectively comprise a substantial and growing proportion of international trade and investment.

Services as Well as Products

Historically, international trade and investment were mainly the domain of companies that make and sell products—tangible merchandise such as clothing, computers, and cars. Today, firms that produce *services* (intangibles) are key international business players as well. Services are deeds, performances, or efforts performed directly by people working in banks, consulting firms, hotels, construction companies, retailers, and countless other firms in the services sector. International trade in services accounts for about one-quarter of all international trade and is growing rapidly. In recent years, services trade has been growing faster than products trade.

Facebook in the opening story is a leading services firm that has internationalized rapidly. If you own a house, your mortgage may be underwritten by the Dutch bank ABN Amro. Perhaps you eat lunch in a cafeteria owned by the French firm Sodexho, which manages the food and

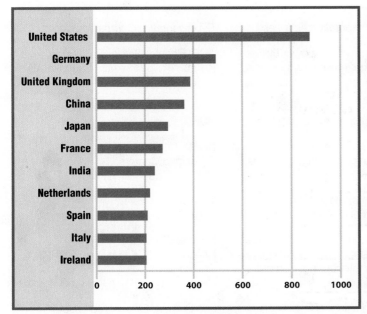

(a) Total annual value of services trade (exports + imports) in billions of US dollars

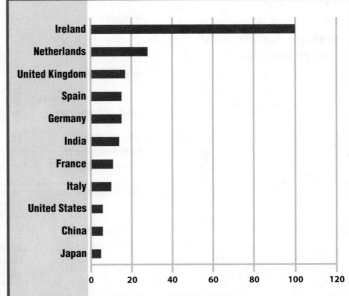

(b) Total annual value of services trade (exports + imports) as a percentage of nation's GDP

EXHIBIT 1.5

Leading Countries in International Services Trade

Sources: Based on World Bank, World Development Indicators, World Bank, Washington, DC, 2011 (www.worldbank.org); World Trade Organization, Statistics Database, World Trade Organization, Geneva, 2011 (www.wto.org); UNCTAD, World Investment Report, United Nations, New York, 2011 (www.unctad.org).

beverage operations on numerous university campuses. Recently, the U.S.-based diet center operator Jenny Craig has made a big push to enter France. About one in three French citizens is now overweight, opening a big market for Jenny Craig's diet counseling. The average customer in France is an obese 46-year-old woman.[4]

Exhibit 1.5 identifies the leading countries in total international services trade, including both exports and imports. Panel (a) shows the total annual value of services trade in billions of U.S. dollars. Panel (b) shows the total annual value of services trade as a percentage of each nation's GDP. As with products, larger advanced economies account for most world services trade. This is expected, because services typically comprise more than two-thirds of the GDPs of these countries. Recently the emerging markets of China and India have gained strong reputations in this area. Ireland has emerged as the leader in world services trade, as a percentage of GDP. Compare the value of merchandise trade in Exhibit 1.3 with the value of services trade in Exhibit 1.5 for each country. Although services trade is growing rapidly, the value of merchandise trade is still much larger. One reason is that services face greater challenges and barriers in cross-border trade than merchandise goods.

Not all services can be exported. For example, you cannot export the construction work to build a house, repair work done on your car, or the experience of eating a meal in a restaurant. Although some services can be digitized and moved across borders, most service providers can operate internationally only by establishing a physical presence abroad through direct investment. Firms employ FDI to set up restaurants, retail stores, and other physical facilities through which they sell trillions of dollars worth of services abroad every year.

There are numerous industries in the services sector with strong potential for internationalization. The giant Internet retailer eBay earned more than $11 billion in 2011, of which more than 50 percent came from international sales. The company expects most future revenue growth will come from abroad. When developing its business in India, eBay acquired the Mumbai-based e-retailer Baazee. This acquisition followed eBay's expansion into China, Korea, and Europe.[5] Exhibit 1.6 illustrates the diversity of service sectors that are internationalizing, extending their reach beyond the countries where they are based. If you are considering a career in international business, keep these industries in mind.

The International Financial Services Sector

International banking and financial services are among the most internationally active service industries. Explosive growth of investment and financial flows has led to the emergence of capital markets worldwide. It resulted from two main factors: the internationalization of banks and the

EXHIBIT 1.6

Service Industry Sectors that Are Rapidly Internationalizing

Source: Based on International Trade Administration, Washington, DC: U.S. Department of Commerce.

Industry	Representative Activities	Representative Companies
Architectural, construction, and engineering	Construction, power utilities, design, engineering services, for airports, hospitals, dams	ABB, Bechtel Group, Halliburton, Kajima, Philip Holzman, Skanska AB
Banking, finance, and insurance	Banks, insurance, risk evaluation, management	Bank of America, CIGNA, Barclays, HSBC, Ernst & Young
Education, training, and publishing	Management training, technical training, language training	Berlitz, Kumon Math & Reading Centers, NOVA, Pearson, Elsevier
Entertainment	Movies, recorded music, Internet-based entertainment	Time Warner, Sony, Virgin, MGM
Information services	E-commerce, e-mail, funds transfer, data interchange, data processing, computer services	Infosys, EDI, Hitachi, Qualcomm, Cisco
Professional business services	Accounting, advertising, legal, management consulting	Leo Burnett, EYLaw, McKinsey, A.T. Kearney, Booz Allen Hamilton
Transportation	Aviation, ocean shipping, railroads, trucking, airports	Maersk, Santa Fe, Port Authority of New Jersey, SNCF (French railroads)
Travel and tourism	Transportation, lodging, food and beverage, aircraft travel, ocean carriers, railways	Carlson Wagonlit, Marriott, British Airways

massive flow of money across national borders into pension funds and portfolio investments. In the developing economies, banks and other financial institutions have fostered economic activity by increasing the availability of local investment capital, which stimulates the development of financial markets and encourages locals to save money.

International banking is flourishing in the Middle East. For example, the return on equity in Saudi Arabia often exceeds 20 percent (compared to 15 percent in the United States and much less in France and Germany). Citibank, Deutsche Bank, BNP Paribas, and other international banks are thriving because of higher oil prices, a boom in consumer banking, and low taxes. National Commercial Bank, the biggest bank in the region, calculates that non-interest-bearing deposits comprise nearly 50 percent of total deposits in Saudi Arabia. Banks lend this free money to companies and consumers at high margins. By structuring loans as partnerships, they comply with Islamic rules that forbid banks to pay interest.[6]

Many international banks experienced turmoil following the 2008 collapse of the United States housing mortgage market. The crisis spread worldwide because many American mortgages had been "securitized," bundled and sold as investment instruments in financial markets worldwide. In 2012, several nations in the European Union experienced debt crises, which affected the stability of the region's single currency, the euro. These events coincided with a sharp decline in the global financial sector, forcing banks worldwide to lay off thousands of workers.[7]

How Does International Business Differ from Domestic Business?

Firms that engage in international business operate in countries characterized by distinctive economic, cultural, and political conditions. For example, the economic environment of Colombia differs sharply from that of Germany. The legal environment of Saudi Arabia does not resemble that of Japan. The cultural environment of China is very distinct from that of Kenya. Not only does the firm find itself in unfamiliar surroundings, it encounters many *uncontrollable variables*—factors over which management has little control. These factors introduce new or elevated business risks. As exemplified by Facebook in the opening story, distinctive conditions in each country require firms to adapt their products and approaches, from country to country.

The Four Risks in Internationalization

Globalization is not without risks. Our global economy is more integrated than ever, and, like a virus, economic problems can spread quickly across porous national borders. The recent global financial crisis originated in the United States and quickly moved to other countries.[8] Canada experienced a recession due to its intense trading relationship with the United States. Mexico's exports to the United States declined substantially, worsening Mexico's already high unemployment rate. Job losses also ensued in Japan and other Asian countries. The economies of both China and India, the world's most populous countries, slowed significantly due to the crisis. In short, integration and interdependency of national economies quickly spread the crisis throughout the world. It affected most firms and individuals in an increasingly interconnected world. We address globalization and the global financial crisis in more detail in Chapter 2.

When they undertake international business, companies are routinely exposed to four major types of risk, as illustrated in Exhibit 1.7: cross-cultural risk, country risk, currency risk, and commercial risk. The firm must manage these risks to avoid financial loss or product failures.

Cross-cultural risk occurs when a cultural misunderstanding puts some human value at stake. Cross-cultural risk arises from differences in language, lifestyles, mind-sets, customs, and religion. Values unique to a culture tend to be long-lasting and transmitted from one generation to the next. These values influence the mind-set and work style of employees and the shopping patterns of buyers. Foreign customer characteristics differ significantly from those of buyers in the home market. Language is a critical dimension of culture. In addition to facilitating communication, language is a window on people's value systems and living conditions. For example, Inuit (Eskimo) languages have various words for snow, while the South American Aztecs used the same basic word stem for snow, ice, and cold. When translating from one language to another,

Cross-cultural risk
A situation or event where a cultural misunderstanding puts some human value at stake.

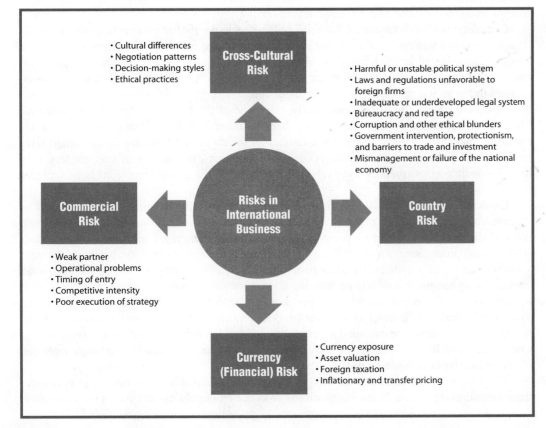

EXHIBIT 1.7

The Four Risks of International Business

it is often difficult to find words that convey the same meanings. For example, a one-word equivalent to *aftertaste* does not exist in many languages. Such challenges impede effective communication and cause misunderstandings. Miscommunication due to cultural differences gives rise to inappropriate business strategies and ineffective relations with customers. Cross-cultural risk most often occurs in encounters in foreign countries. However, the risk also can occur domestically, as when management meets with customers or business associates who visit company headquarters from abroad.

Ethical Connections

In the fashion industry, hundreds of factory workers die annually from dangerous working conditions. Consider the production of faded denim jeans. Every year thousands of garment workers develop deadly lung diseases from constant exposure to crystalline silica used to sandblast jeans to give them the worn, vintage look. Although illegal in Europe and the United States, such production methods are still widely used in low-income countries, from where the jeans are then exported to affluent consumers worldwide.

Source: G. Brown, "Fashion Kills: Industrial Manslaughter in the Global Supply Chain," *EHS Today*, September 2010, p. 59.

Country risk
Potentially adverse effects on company operations and profitability caused by developments in the political, legal, and economic environment in a foreign country.

Country risk (also known as *political risk*) refers to the potentially adverse effects on company operations and profitability caused by developments in the political, legal, and economic environment in a foreign country. Country risk includes the possibility of foreign government intervention in firms' business activities. For example, governments may restrict access to markets, impose bureaucratic procedures on business transactions, and limit the amount of income that firms can bring home from foreign operations. The degree of government intervention in commercial activities varies from country to country. For example, Singapore and Ireland are characterized by substantial economic freedom—that is, a fairly liberal economic environment. By contrast, the Chinese and Russian governments regularly intervene in business affairs.[9] Country risk also includes laws and regulations that potentially hinder company operations and performance. Critical legal dimensions include property rights, intellectual property protection, product liability, and taxation policies. Nations also experience potentially harmful economic conditions, often due to high inflation, national debt, and unbalanced international trade. Indeed, the global financial crisis plunged many nations into a deep recession in 2009.

Currency risk
Risk of adverse fluctuations in exchange rates.

Currency risk (also known as *financial risk*) refers to the risk of adverse fluctuations in exchange rates. Fluctuation is common for *exchange rates*—the value of one currency in terms of another. Currency risk arises because international transactions are often conducted in more than one national currency. For example, when U.S. fruit processor Graceland Fruit Inc. exports dried cherries to Japan, it is normally paid in Japanese yen.

When currencies fluctuate significantly, the value of the firm's earnings can be reduced. The cost of importing parts or components used in manufacturing finished products can increase dramatically if the value of the currency in which the imports are denominated rises sharply. Inflation and other harmful economic conditions experienced in one country may have immediate consequences for exchange rates due to the interconnectedness of national economies.

Commercial risk
Firm's potential loss or failure from poorly developed or executed business strategies, tactics, or procedures.

Commercial risk refers to the firm's potential loss or failure from poorly developed or executed business strategies, tactics, or procedures. Managers may make poor choices in such areas as the selection of business partners, timing of market entry, pricing, creation of product features, and promotional themes. While such failures also exist in domestic business, the consequences are usually more costly when committed abroad. For example, in domestic business a company may terminate a poorly performing distributor simply with advance notice. In foreign markets, however, terminating business partners can be costly due to regulations that protect local firms. Marketing inferior or harmful products, falling short of customer expectations, or failing to provide adequate customer service may damage the firm's reputation and profitability. Commercial risk is also often affected by currency risk because fluctuating exchange rates can affect various types of business deals.

The four types of international business risks are omnipresent; the firm may encounter them around every corner. Some international risks are extremely challenging. One example is the global financial crisis that emerged in 2008. The crisis spread to banks and insurance firms in Asia, Europe, and elsewhere. Many countries experienced deflation and severe declines in consumer confidence and spending power. The year 2009 saw sharp reductions in international commerce and shipping. The global economy saw little improvement through 2012, with financial crises prolonged by high government debt in the advanced economies, especially in Europe and the United States. Central banks worldwide sought to rally national economies by injecting billions of dollars into their financial systems.[10]

Although risk cannot be avoided, it can be anticipated and managed. Experienced international firms constantly assess their environments and conduct research to anticipate potential risks, understand their implications, and take proactive action to reduce their effects. This book is dedicated to providing you, the future manager, with a solid understanding of these risks as well as managerial skills and strategies to effectively counter them.

 ## Who Participates in International Business?

What types of organizations are active in international business? Among the most important are *focal firms*, the companies that directly initiate and implement international business activity. Two critical focal firms in international business are the multinational enterprise and the small and medium-sized enterprise.

Multinational Enterprise (MNE)

Multinational enterprises (also known as *multinational corporations*) historically have been the most important type of focal firm. A **multinational enterprise (MNE)** is a large company with substantial resources that performs various business activities through a network of subsidiaries and affiliates located in multiple countries. MNEs carry out research and development (R&D), procurement, manufacturing, and marketing activities wherever in the world the firm can reap the most advantages. For example, Alcon is a Swiss pharmaceutical firm that established major R&D facilities in the United States to take advantage of the country's superior know-how in the chemicals sector. Verizon Wireless has located much of its technical support operations in India, to take advantage of high-quality, low-cost customer support personnel located there. Royal Dutch Shell owns several oil refineries and nearly 2,000 gasoline stations in Canada. In addition to a home office or headquarters, the typical MNE owns a worldwide network of subsidiaries. It collaborates with numerous suppliers and independent business partners abroad (sometimes termed *affiliates*).

Typical MNEs include Barclays, Caterpillar, Disney, DHL, Four Seasons Hotels, Samsung, Unilever, Vodafone, and Nippon Life Insurance. In recent years, the largest MNEs have been firms in the oil industry (such as Exxon-Mobil and Royal Dutch Shell) and the automotive industry (General Motors and Honda), as well as retailing (Walmart). Exhibit 1.8 shows the geographic distribution of the world's largest MNEs, drawn from *Fortune*'s Global 500 list. As shown, these firms are concentrated in the advanced economies. The United States is home to 133 of the top 500 MNEs, a number that has declined over time as other countries' firms increase in size. Japan has the second-most MNEs (68 firms), closely followed by China (61). Europe is home to many top MNEs, in France (35 firms), Germany (34 firms), and the United Kingdom (30 firms). Collectively, the European Union countries have more top 500 firms than the United States.[11]

In recent years, large MNEs have begun to appear in emerging market countries, such as China, Mexico, and Russia. China currently hosts 61 of the top 500 MNEs, a number that has increased from only 11 countries in the course of just 10 years. Note that nearly all of China's top firms are state enterprises, that is, owned by the Chinese government, which provides them substantial advantages.[12]

The "new global challenger" firms from emerging markets are fast becoming key contenders in world markets. For example, the Mexican firm Cemex is one of the world's largest cement producers. In Russia, Lukoil has big ambitions in the global energy sector. China Mobile dominates the cell phone industry in Asia. The new global challengers make best use of home-country

Multinational enterprise (MNE) A large company with substantial resources that performs various business activities through a network of subsidiaries and affiliates located in multiple countries.

EXHIBIT 1.8

Geographic Distribution of the Headquarters of the World's 500 Largest MNEs

Sources: Based on *Forbes*, "The World's Biggest Public Companies" (2011), accessed on March 22, 2011 at http://
www.forbes.com/global2000/list/; *Fortune*, "Global 500" (2011), accessed on March 22, 2012 at http://money.cnn
.com/magazines/fortune/global500/2011/; UNCTAD, "Largest Transnational Corporations," accessed on 3/22/11
at www.unctad.org.

natural resources and low-cost labor to succeed in world markets. Thousands of firms from emerging markets have big global dreams and pose competitive challenges to companies from the advanced economies.

Although MNEs are among its leading participants, international business is not the domain of large, resourceful firms alone. Many **small and medium-sized enterprises (SMEs)** participate as well. An SME is a company with 500 or fewer employees, as defined in Canada and the United States. In the European Union, SMEs are defined as firms with 250 or fewer employees. In addition to accounting for smaller market shares of their respective industries, SMEs tend to have limited managerial and other resources and primarily use exporting to expand internationally. However, in most nations, SMEs constitute the great majority of all firms. With the globalization of markets, advances in various technologies, and other facilitating factors, many more SMEs are pursuing international opportunities. SMEs account for about one-third of exports from Asia and about a quarter of exports from the affluent countries in Europe and North America. In some countries—for example, Italy, South Korea, and China—SMEs contribute roughly 50 percent of total national exports.[13]

One type of contemporary international SME is the **born global firm**, a young entrepreneurial company that initiates international business activity very early in its evolution, moving rapidly into foreign markets. Born globals are found in advanced economies, such as Australia and Japan, and in emerging markets, such as China and India. International business requires specialized knowledge, commitment of resources, and considerable time to develop foreign business partnerships.

Small and medium-sized enterprise (SME) A company with 500 or fewer employees (as defined in Canada and the United States).

Born global firm A young entrepreneurial company that initiates international business activity very early in its evolution, moving rapidly into foreign markets.

How do SMEs succeed in international business despite resource limitations?

- Compared to large MNEs, smaller firms are often more innovative and adaptable and have quicker response times when it comes to implementing new ideas and technologies and meeting customer needs.
- SMEs are better able to serve niche markets around the world that hold little interest for MNEs.
- Smaller firms are usually avid users of information and communication technologies, including the Internet.
- As they usually lack substantial resources, smaller firms minimize overhead or fixed investments. They rely on external facilitators, such as FedEx and DHL, as well as independent distributors in foreign markets.
- Smaller firms tend to thrive on private knowledge that they possess or produce. They access and mobilize resources through their cross-border knowledge networks or their international social capital.[14]

In each chapter of this text, you will find a feature entitled *Global Trend*, profiling an important recent development in international business. The first *Global Trend* features Diesel, an SME that eventually grew into a large firm.

Governments and Nongovernmental Organizations (NGOs)

In addition to profit-seeking focal firms, governments are central participants in international trade and investment. The role of governments is so important that we devote later chapters to government intervention, political systems, and other government-related topics. In addition, numerous *nonprofit organizations* conduct cross-border activities. These include charitable groups and *nongovernmental organizations (NGOs)*. They work on behalf of special causes,

GLOBAL TREND

DIESEL: A Smaller Firm's Smashing International Success

The global youth culture loves Diesel jeans, Europe's hottest brand. Founded in Italy, Diesel began as an SME and grew to achieve annual sales of more than $500 million (U.S.), 85 percent of which comes from abroad. Diesel produces unusual but popular men's and women's casual wear, like $300 jeans in exotic shades and styles, that competes with Ralph Lauren and Tommy Hilfiger brands. Its style is futuristic. Company management sees the world as a single, borderless macro-culture, and Diesel staff includes an assortment of personalities from all parts of the globe who create an unpredictable, dynamic vitality and energy. The firm focuses on de-sign and marketing, leaving production to subcontractors.

Diesel has expanded distribution to de-partment stores and specialty retailers in over 80 countries, as well as to 400 company-owned stores from Paris to Miami to Tokyo.

Japan is currently Diesel's largest market. In 2010 Diesel opened its first stores in Mumbai, aiming to have more than 30 stores in India by 2015.

Controversial advertising has propelled it to enormous international success. Ads have featured sumo wrestlers kissing, a row of chimpanzees giving the fascist salute, and inflatable naked dolls in a board meet-ing with a hugely overweight CEO. Some people see the prankish campaigns, which poke fun at death, obesity, murder, and do-gooders, as politically incorrect. Under pressure from activists, Diesel withdrew ads that applauded smoking and gun owner-ship with slogans such as "145 cigarettes a day will give you that sexy voice and win new friends." Another ad featured nuns in blue jeans below the copy, "Pure, virginal 100 percent cotton. Soft and yet miracu-lously strong."

Diesel was one of the first firms to have a major Internet presence (www.diesel.com), selling jeans via an online virtual store. Its web advertising is also hip, with a powerful, mar-ket-friendly message that drives its popularity among youth worldwide. The firm introduces some 1,500 new designs every 6 months and employs a multicultural team of young designers who travel the globe for inspiration and weave their impressions into the next collection. Diesel is a classic success story in international business by a smaller firm.

Sources: Web site, http://www.diesel.com; Gail Edmondson, "Diesel Is Smoking But Can Its Provocative Ads Keep Sales Growth Hot?" *BusinessWeek*, February 10, 2003, p. 64; Diesel corporate profile at http://www.hoovers.com; Y. Moroz, "Adidas Refuels with Diesel Collaboration," *Retailing Today*, March 17, 2008, p. 4; Luisi Zargani, "Fresh Outlook At Diesel," *WWD: Women's Wear Daily*, May 9, 2011.

Source: Maciej Dakowicz/Alamy

The British Wellcome Trust funds nongovernmental organizations (NGOs) and research initiatives to work in collaboration with private businesses to develop remedies for diseases in Africa and other less developed areas.

such as education, research, health care, human development, and the natural environment, operating internationally either to conduct their activities or to raise funds. Examples of nonprofit organizations include the Bill and Melinda Gates Foundation and the British Wellcome Trust, both of which support health and educational initiatives. CARE is an international nonprofit organization dedicated to reducing poverty. Many MNEs operate charitable foundations that support various initiatives. GlaxoSmithKline (GSK), the giant pharmaceutical firm, operates a number of small country-based foundations in Canada, France, Italy, Romania, Spain, and the United States.

 ## Why Do Firms Internationalize?

There are multiple motives for international expansion. Some are strategic in nature, while others are reactive. An example of a strategic, or proactive, motive is to tap foreign market opportunities or acquire new knowledge. An example of a reactive motive is the need to serve a key customer that has expanded abroad. Nine specific motivations include:

1. *Seek opportunities for growth through market diversification.* Substantial market potential exists abroad. Many firms—for example, Facebook, Gillette, Siemens, Sony, Biogen—derive more than half of their sales from international markets.[15] In addition to offering sales opportunities that often cannot be matched at home, foreign markets can extend the marketable life of products or services that have reached maturity in the home market. One example is the internationalization of automatic teller machines (ATMs). The first ATMs were installed in London by Barclays Bank. The machines were next adopted in the United States and Japan. As growth of ATMs began to slow in these countries, they were marketed throughout the rest of the world. Today there are more than 2.3 million ATMs worldwide; a new one is installed somewhere every few minutes.

2. *Earn higher margins and profits.* For many types of products and services, market growth in mature economies is sluggish or flat. Competition is often intense, forcing firms to get by on slim profit margins. By contrast, most foreign markets may be underserved (typical of high-growth emerging markets) or not served at all (typical of developing economies). Less intense competition, combined with strong market demand, implies that companies can command higher margins for their offerings. For example, compared to their home markets, bathroom fixture manufacturers American Standard and Toto (of Japan) have found more favorable competitive environments in rapidly industrializing countries such as Indonesia, Mexico, and Vietnam. Just imagine the demand for bathroom fixtures in the thousands of office buildings and residential complexes going up from Taiwan to Turkey!

3. *Gain new ideas about products, services, and business methods.* International markets are characterized by tough competitors and demanding customers with various needs. Unique foreign environments expose firms to new ideas for products, processes, and business methods. The experience of doing business abroad helps firms acquire new knowledge for improving organizational effectiveness and efficiency. For example, just-in-time inventory techniques were refined by Toyota in Japan and then adopted by other manufacturers around the world. Numerous foreign suppliers learned about just-in-time from Toyota and then applied the method to manufacturing in their own countries.

4. *Better serve key customers that have relocated abroad.* In a global economy, many firms internationalize to better serve clients that have moved into foreign markets. For example, when Nissan opened its first factory in the United Kingdom, many Japanese auto parts suppliers followed, establishing their own operations there.

5. *Be closer to supply sources, benefit from global sourcing advantages, or gain flexibility in product sourcing.* Companies in extractive industries such as petroleum, mining, and forestry establish international operations where these raw materials are located. One example is the aluminum producer Alcoa, which established operations in Brazil, Guinea, Jamaica, and elsewhere to extract aluminum's base mineral bauxite from local mines. Some firms internationalize to gain flexibility from a greater variety of supply bases. Dell Computer has assembly facilities in Asia, Europe, and the Americas that allow management to quickly shift production from one region to another. This flexibility provides Dell with competitive advantages over less agile rivals—a distinctive capability that allows Dell to outperform competitors and skillfully manage fluctuations in currency exchange rates.

6. *Gain access to lower-cost or better-value factors of production.* Internationalization enables the firm to access capital, technology, managerial talent, and labor at lower costs, higher quality, or better value. For example, some Taiwanese computer manufacturers established subsidiaries in the United States to access low-cost capital. The United States is home to numerous capital sources in the high-tech sector, such as stock exchanges and venture capitalists, which have attracted many firms from abroad seeking funds. More commonly, firms venture abroad in search of skilled or low-cost labor. For example, the Japanese firm Canon relocated much of its production to China to profit from that country's inexpensive and productive workforce.

7. *Develop economies of scale in sourcing, production, marketing, and R&D.* Economies of scale reduce the per-unit cost of manufacturing due to operating at high volume. For example, the per-unit cost of manufacturing 100,000 cameras is much cheaper than the per-unit cost of making just 100 cameras. By expanding internationally, the firm greatly increases the size of its customer base, thereby increasing the volume of goods it produces. On a per-unit-of-output basis, the greater the volume of production, the lower the total cost. Economies of scale are also present in R&D, sourcing, marketing, distribution, and after-sales service.

8. *Confront international competitors more effectively or thwart the growth of competition in the home market.* International competition is substantial and increasing, with multinational competitors invading markets worldwide. The firm can enhance its competitive positioning by confronting competitors in international markets or preemptively entering a competitor's home markets to destabilize and curb its growth. One example is Caterpillar's entry into Japan to confront its main rival in the earthmoving equipment industry, Komatsu. Caterpillar's preemptive move hindered Komatsu's international expansion for at least a decade. Had it not acted proactively to stifle Komatsu's growth in Japan, Komatsu's home market, Caterpillar would certainly have had to face a more potent rival sooner.

9. *Invest in a potentially rewarding relationship with a foreign partner.* Firms often have long-term strategic reasons for venturing abroad. Joint ventures or project-based alliances with key foreign players can lead to the development of new products, early positioning in future key markets, or other long-term, profit-making opportunities. For example, Black and Decker entered a joint venture with Bajaj, an Indian retailer, to position itself for expected long-term sales in the huge Indian market. The French computer firm Groupe Bull partnered with Toshiba in Japan to gain insights for developing the next generation of information technology.

At the broadest level, companies internationalize to enhance competitive advantage and to seek growth and profit opportunities. Throughout this book, we explore the environment within which firms seek these opportunities, and we discuss the strategies and managerial skills necessary for achieving international business success.

Source: Tim Drape/Dorling Kindersley Limited

A vibrant workforce is driving economic development and buying power in emerging markets. Here consumers flock to a popular shopping street in Beijing, China.

International trade is encouraging faster diffusion of consumer products and brands around the world.

Why Study International Business?

There are many reasons to study international business. We can examine them from the perspectives of the global economy, the national economy, the firm, and you as a future manager.

Facilitator of the Global Economy and Interconnectedness

International business is transforming the world as never before. In the last 50 years, international trade and investment have experienced unprecedented growth. Since the 1980s, *emerging markets* have provided new impetus to worldwide economic interconnectedness. These fast-growth developing economies—some thirty countries, including Brazil, Russia, India, and China, the so-called BRICs—are experiencing substantial market liberalization, privatization, and industrialization, which are fueling global economic transformation. Located on every continent, they are gradually breaking away from the stagnation typical of developing economies. The emerging markets are home to the largest proportion of world population and participate increasingly in foreign trade. In the opening story, Facebook is doing business in numerous emerging markets, including China, India, and Poland.

Along with market globalization, *advances in technology* are another megatrend helping to transform the global economy. The rise of information and communication technologies, as well as production and process technologies, has dramatically reduced the cost of conducting business with customers around the world. E-commerce makes international business increasingly imperative for firms of all sizes and resource levels. Technological advances are allowing globalization to progress more rapidly. Globalization, in turn, is accelerating the development of the latest technologies.

Contributor to National Economic Well-Being

International business contributes to economic prosperity, helps countries use their resources more efficiently, and provides interconnectedness to the world economy and access to a range of products and services. Consequently, governments have become more willing to open their borders to foreign trade and investment.

International trade is a critical engine for job creation. It is estimated that every $1 billion increase in exports creates more than 20,000 new jobs. In the United States, cross-border trade directly supports at least 12 million jobs. One of every seven dollars of U.S. sales is made abroad. One of every three U.S. farm acres and one of every six U.S. jobs is producing for export markets. On average, exporting firms create jobs faster and provide better pay than nonexporting firms.[16]

There is a strong relationship between national prosperity and participation in international trade and investment. Nations once suffering from economic stagnation are now increasingly prosperous. For example, China, India, and Eastern European nations are active international traders. The proportion of affluent citizens in these countries is growing rapidly. In terms of material gain, households in many developing economies have recently experienced huge increases in the ownership of televisions, refrigerators, and other mass-produced products. While these gains are attributable to various causes, the benefits of free exchange of products, services, capital, and technology among nations are paramount.

Rising prosperity associated with international trade and investment helps improve literacy rates, nutrition, and health care in nations around the world. Trade and investment promote freedom and democracy and may reduce the likelihood of cross-border conflict. In an era of economic turmoil and strained global relations, international business is helping to decrease such tensions, by reducing world poverty and increasing interactions that help soothe relations among nations.[17]

Country Realities

The most popular countries for international business these days are China, India, and Brazil, known as "emerging markets." China's appeal stems from its huge consumer market. India is an excellent location to establish operations in the global services sector. Brazil is a gateway to the growing consumer market in Latin America and an important location for factories that manufacture various products.

Source: AT Kearney, *The 2011 AT Kearney FDI Confidence Index*, AT Kearney, Inc., at www.atkearney.com.

Cross-border business also helps integrate world economies. Development of the European Union (EU) is transforming Europe into a new powerhouse in global trade. The North American Free Trade Agreement (NAFTA) has integrated the economies of Canada, Mexico, and the United States into a giant market of roughly 450 million consumers. Following NAFTA's launch, the volume of trade among the three countries jumped dramatically. In Mexico, NAFTA led to substantially higher wages and higher employment rates.[18] Recently, a new accord was launched between the United States and Costa Rica, El Salvador, Guatemala, Honduras, Nicaragua, and the Dominican Republic. Known as the Dominican Republic Central American Free Trade Agreement (DR-CAFTA), it is invigorating the economies of the member countries.

A Competitive Advantage for the Firm

To sustain a competitive advantage in the global economy, firms must readily participate in cross-border business and acquire the necessary skills, knowledge, and competence. Procter & Gamble sells shampoo, disposable diapers, and other consumer products in more than 150 countries. MTV broadcasts its programming in some 140 countries. Nestlé sells its food and beverage products worldwide, obtaining nearly all its revenue from foreign operations. As these examples imply, going international offers countless opportunities for firms to grow and earn additional profits.

In addition, international business allows firms to maximize the efficiency of their operations. Companies secure cost-effective factor inputs by establishing manufacturing in emerging markets like Malaysia, Mexico, and Poland, or sourcing from foreign suppliers. For example, Microsoft cuts the costs of its operations by having much of its software written in India. Renault achieves efficiency by assembling cars at low-cost factories in Romania.

International business also allows firms to access critical resources that may be unavailable at home. It helps firms reduce the costs of new product development, after-sales service, and other critical business activities. Companies access foreign sources of information and knowledge that provide the basis for future R&D, improved production and administrative processes, and other innovations. Finally, internationalization broadens the firm's options for dealing with competitors. It offers opportunities to make globally strategic moves and countermoves that help the firm compete more effectively with rivals.[19]

A Competitive Advantage for You

While most international careers are based in one's home country, managers travel the world and meet people from various cultures and backgrounds. Traveling abroad leads to exciting challenges and learning experiences. Managers rising to the top of most of the world's leading corporations honed their managerial skills in international business. In this text you will learn about the merits of gaining international business proficiency, through the experiences of people like you, in a special feature called *Recent Grad in IB*. Read about Ashley Lumb, a recent graduate who is enjoying her early experiences in international business.

An Opportunity to Support Sustainability and Corporate Citizenship

As the world's population grows, so do pressures to meet consumer demand in a sustainable way. Increasingly, companies operate in environments characterized by limited resources, vulnerable human conditions, and stakeholder consciousness on issues that affect all society. In response to this trend, companies are increasing their awareness about the social and environmental implications of their actions. Rather than being caught off guard, firms increasingly develop socially responsible policies and practices. For example, Starbucks began selling coffee only from growers certified by the Rain Forest Alliance (www.rainforest-alliance.org), a nonprofit organization that promotes the interests of coffee growers

Source: Alex Robinson/Dorling Kindersley Limited

International business contributes to national economic well-being. Nations once suffering from economic stagnation are now increasingly prosperous. This trendy shopping mall is in Bangkok, Thailand.

ASHLEY LUMB

Ashley's Majors: Finance and International Business
Objectives: Adventure, international perspective, self-understanding, career growth, and the opportunity to learn foreign languages
Internships during college: Merrill Lynch
Jobs held since graduating:
- Junior Analyst at KPMG, London, England
- Marketing Representative, Vins Sans Frontieres, Nice, France
- Account Representative, The Ultimate Living Group, Monte Carlo, Monaco
- Marketing Associate, Made in Museum, Rome, Italy
- Advertising/Marketing Coordinator, Italian Vogue, New York, United States

In Ashley Lumb's senior year in college, a six-week study abroad program to Europe sparked a desire for an international career. Following graduation, Ashley interned as a Junior Analyst at KPMG in London, where she gained technical training and analytical skills. She wanted to work in the luxury goods industry in Europe and eventually took a six-month contract job at Vins Sans Frontieres. VSF enrolled Ashley in its wine courses at the company headquarters in the south of France. VSF imports wine from around the world and sells it exclusively to private yachts along the French Riviera. Ashley gained experience in various marketing methods. For example, VSF attends yacht trade fairs and hosts wine tastings. VSF's marketing reps like Ashley scour the ports from San Remo, Italy, to St. Tropez, France, daily, speaking with yacht chefs, stewards, or captains about wine and distributing wine catalogs.

Ashley then took up a position as a marketing associate at Made in Museum (MIM) in Rome, Italy. MIM specializes in the design, production, and delivery of authorized museum reproductions. It markets jewelry, sculptures, mosaics, and Etruscan pottery. Ashley organized the products into groups and restructured the inventory and Web site.

While in Italy, Ashley developed a passion for the fashion industry, so she decided to move to New York. Before leaving Italy, Ashley took a course at the prestigious Polimoda International Institute of Design and Marketing in Florence entitled "Business and Marketing in the Fashion Industry." In New York, Ashley worked at the headquarters of fashion houses Hermès and J. Crew. Subsequently, she leveraged the services of a bilingual recruiting agency, Euromonde Inc., to land a job at Italian Vogue magazine in Times Square to work as the U.S. advertising/marketing coordinator.

Ashley's Advice for an International Career

"Working abroad helped me sort through my career goals, as Europe offered a view into other industries that the U.S. lacked. I was able to experience different cultures and work environments and, although they might seem far apart, I saw a shared passion for exceptional products and dynamism. Back in the U.S., my international experience was an impressive asset to prospective employers; it is valued as proof of one's ability to handle challenging assignments and work with people from diverse cultures and backgrounds."

Success Factors

"The two most important factors in working abroad were hard work and networking. I cast a wide net and met many people, sent a lot of résumés, asked many questions, and researched the market. To keep myself afloat between assignments, I took some unglamorous jobs. Some days I wanted to give up and go home, but instead I just kept going.... Hard work and persistence are crucial."

Challenges

"The decision to work abroad carries some risks. After all, you're leaving much of what you know behind and stepping outside a clearly defined career path. The language barrier is always present. The work was usually in English, though I did pick up Italian and a bit of French through classes and immersing myself in the culture."

and the environment. Such multinational enterprises as Philips, Unilever, and Walmart follow business practices that promote sustainable development. McDonald's buys beef from farmers who meet special standards on animal welfare and environmental practices. Its outlets in Austria, Germany, Sweden, and the United Kingdom sell only organic milk.[20] Internationally active firms must embed corporate citizenship into their strategic decisions as well as their ongoing processes and practices. Ethics and responsible behavior in firms' international activities are of such importance that we devote Chapter 5 to this topic.

CLOSING CASE   Internationalization at Harley-Davidson

Founded in 1903, Harley-Davidson (Harley) is a U.S. motorcycle manufacturer that offers thirty-five models through a network of more than 1,500 dealers. Its annual revenues are about $6 billion, mainly from sales of the big bikes that made the firm famous. Harley earns three-quarters of its total sales in the United States, where it also manufactures almost all its bikes to ensure quality control. The firm makes four distinctive groups of models:

- **Standard.** Practical bikes used for low-cost commuting.
- **Performance.** Sleek, sport-style racing bikes built for speed and easy handling.
- **Custom.** Stylized bikes customized to customer tastes.
- **Touring.** Long-distance, large-capacity, comfort bikes that typically include cruise control, stereos, and luggage racks.

In the United States Harley competes primarily in the custom and touring segments, which account for around 85 percent of "heavyweight" sales. Its numerous competitors are all headquartered outside the United States and include Honda, Suzuki, Yamaha, and Kawasaki in Japan, and BMW, Ducati, and Triumph in Europe. New competitors are emerging from China.

Harley heavyweight bikes sell for $17,000 or more, which puts them beyond the reach of many buyers. The average age of a Harley buyer in the United States is nearly 50. One key to Harley's success is the Harley Owners Group (HOG), a club of loyal Harley owners with over one million members, including 100,000 in Europe. HOG is an important marketing tool for promoting sales. In the United States brand loyalty is fierce, and switching costs for Harley owners are high. Over time, the firm has created a mystique around its heavyweight bikes that helps drive sales. Indeed, many owners get Harley tattoos.

Threat of Foreign Competitors

Some year ago, Harley faced financial ruin. By the 1980s, Honda, Kawasaki, Suzuki, and Yamaha were selling millions of motorcycles in the United States and specializing in inexpensive, lightweight models. Initially Harley paid little attention to the competition and continued to focus on heavyweight bikes, but the market for lightweights continued to grow. Meanwhile, Harley had begun to experience major problems with the quality of its bikes and poor productivity in its factories. Over time, the firm's image suffered and sales declined sharply; Harley nearly went bankrupt.

Revival

The arrival of a new CEO marked the beginning of efforts to revive Harley. Ironically, it adopted Japanese-style management techniques, updating manufacturing methods, improving quality, and expanding model offerings. In its factories, Harley instituted just-in-time inventory systems and total quality management and empowered its production workers. Management increased marketing efforts, improved the dealer network, and undertook various cross-branding ventures. By the mid-1990s, management had repositioned Harley more strongly in the performance motorcycle market. The improvements paid off in sharp improvements in company image and in sales.

International Expansion

About the same time, Harley management resolved that future success would come from expansion into foreign markets. The firm had established a distribution network and local subsidiary in

Japan, and by 2005, it was selling more than 12,000 motorcycles there annually. It continued to sell heavyweight motorcycles in Japan at a price of more than $18,000, substantially more than Honda's standard lightweight model. In 2012, Harley generated about one-third of its total sales from international markets, up from 25 percent in 2006.

Harley also made significant inroads in Europe, a vast marketplace that is home to dozens of countries with diverse needs and tastes. In Europe, Performance bikes are the top seller by far, accounting for more than one-third of Harley sales. This is followed by Touring, Standard, and Custom bikes. In the United States, customers strongly prefer Custom and Touring bikes, which account for about half and one-third of U.S. sales, respectively. Performance and Standard models produce much smaller revenues in the United States. European tastes are distinctive, often differing by region. Some buyers prefer Italian styling, which is dominated by Ducati. Others prefer the German styling of BMW.

Compared to U.S. customers' tastes, European preferences are diverse. Freeways in much of Europe have high speed limits that necessitate high-performance bikes. Most Europeans do not relate to Harley's U.S. image of rugged individualism, freedom, and rebellion, and its big bikes are difficult to maneuver in narrow streets and impractical for daily commuting. Fortunately, Harley sells a broad range of bikes that suit diverse European tastes. To enhance its European presence, Harley launched an overseas branch of the HOG club. The company bought the Italian motorcycle firm MV Agusta Group for $109 million in 2008. However, economic conditions forced Harley to divest its interest in Agusta in 2010.

In addition to Europe and Japan, Harley management wants to target emerging markets. Brazil, Harley's biggest potential market in Latin America, is fraught with challenges. Initially Brazil's government imposed high import tariffs that doubled the cost of bikes to Brazilian buyers. To address this dilemma, Harley established an assembly plant in Brazil. Local assembly avoids import barriers and reduces costs thanks to the availability of low-cost workers.

Management also set its sights on China, home to 1.3 billion people, many of whom ride small motorcycles. While average wages are low, income levels are growing rapidly. Harley is concerned about piracy. Some Chinese entrepreneurs are known to counterfeit well-known foreign-branded products, especially those with big price tags. Moreover, many Chinese cities restrict motorcycle usage on local highways, to reduce noise and drive-by thefts. Harley also must overcome the perception in China that motorcycles are only for commuting; management wants to develop the market for leisure riding too.

Harley is also considering India, where millions of households have annual incomes over $80,000. Honda, Yamaha, and Kawasaki all have a strong presence there. Harley established a subsidiary near Delhi, but market entry has been delayed due to high trade barriers and local emissions regulations.

Harley's fastest-growing market outside the United States is Canada. But Canada still accounts for just 4 percent of total Harley sales. Harley holds a similar market share in Japan, but the country's economy is stagnant, and disposable income has declined. Australia is promising, but with a population of 20 million people, the market is limited. In Latin America, Brazil provides less than 2 percent of total sales. Low buying power in Latin America remains a challenge.

Environmental Sustainability Challenges

Like automobiles, motorcycles pollute the natural environment, and Harley is vulnerable to regulatory sanctions because it manufactures very large bikes. Most of Harley's greenhouse gas (GHG) emissions emanate from its manufacturing plants, and management is moving to reduce pollution, as well as energy and water usage, as part of an integrated sustainability strategy. The firm is also addressing climate change by preparing for the transition to a lower-carbon economy. These actions and its recycling program help align Harley's actions with stakeholder expectations and strengthen the brand. California and Taiwan have recently imposed rigorous new GHG standards on motorcycles. Japan and various European countries are developing similar new standards aimed at GHG reduction. Harley is attempting to stay ahead of evolving regulations. In Japan, the firm launched a motorcycle recycling program.

The Future

The recent global recession hurt Harley as discretionary income fell around the world. For management, a big question is how best to position the firm given declining demand worldwide. Management believes the keys to sustainable growth will be: (i) a heightened focus on foreign markets; (ii) an appeal to lighter-weight, performance-based markets; (iii) improved and larger dealer networks; and (iv) strategic control of distribution.

Harley also needs to balance production and sales for domestic and international markets. As the U.S. market slows, Harley's revenues are suffering. To diversify its revenue streams and reduce its dependence on U.S. sales, Harley wants to increase its international business. Its CEO believes the ideal sales mix is 60 percent in the United States and 40 percent internationally, but the company is struggling to achieve this goal.

AACSB: Reflective Thinking, Analytical Skills, Ethical Reasoning

Case Questions

1. What is the nature of the international business environments Harley faces? What types of risks does the firm face?
2. How can Harley benefit from expanding abroad? What types of advantages can the firm obtain? What advantages acquired abroad can help Harley improve its performance in its home market?
3. How can Harley effectively compete with rivals from Japan and Europe? What strategies should management apply to grow the firm's sales in those regions?
4. Competitors such as Lifan and Zongshen are beginning to emerge from China, where they enjoy competitive advantages like low-cost labor and extensive experience with emerging markets. How can Harley compete against such firms? Should Harley more aggressively pursue emerging markets such as Brazil, China, and India? If so, what strategies will help it succeed in those markets?
5. Evaluate Harley's environmental sustainability initiatives in the evolving regulatory environment on global greenhouse gas. What advantages does Harley gain by attempting to produce environmentally safe and sustainable products?

Sources: R. Hartley, "Harley Davidson—Creating an Enduring Mystique," in *Marketing Mistakes and Successes*, 11th ed. (New York: Wiley, 2009); Harley-Davidson: Sustainability Strategy Report (2009), retrieved from http://www.investor.harley-davidson.com; G. Athanassakos, R. Barel, and S. Karsan, Ivey Management Services: Harley Davidson, Inc. (London: Ivey School of Business, University of Western Ontario, 2008); EDGAR Online, Inc., Harley-Davidson, Form 10-K Annual Report, 12/31/11, retrieved from http://www.harley-davidson.com; J. Hagerty, "Harley Net Roars On U.S. Rebound," *Wall Street Journal*, July 20, 2011, p. B4; Harley-Davidson, Inc., Company Profile, Datamonitor, June 5, 2008; Harley Davidson corporate profile at http://www.hoovers.com; L. Lin, M. Clothier, and Y. Tian, "Why Harley Can't Rev Up in China," *Bloomberg Businessweek*, October 24, 2011, pp. 24–25; D. Mohsenian, R. Mukerji, and K. Grundy, Harley-Davidson. J.P. Morgan, *North America Equity Research*, October 7, 2008; A. Murugan, "Harley-Davidson: Market Entry Strategies in India," *The Icfai Journal of International Business* 3, no. 2 (2008): 49–66.

This case was prepared by Dr. Marta Szabo White, Georgia State University. Many thanks to Casey Long, Business Liaison Librarian at Georgia State University, for her proficiency and research assistance.

CHAPTER ESSENTIALS

Key Terms

born global firm   14
commercial risk   12
country risk   12
cross-cultural risk   11
currency risk   12
exporting   5

foreign direct investment (FDI)   6
globalization of markets   4
importing or global sourcing   6
international business   4
international investment   6
internationalization   4

international portfolio investment   6
international trade   5
multinational enterprise (MNE)   13
small and medium-sized enterprise (SMEs)   14

Summary

In this chapter, you learned about:

1. Key concepts in international business

International business refers to the performance of trade and investment activities by firms across national borders. **Globalization of markets** is the ongoing economic integration and growing interdependency of countries worldwide. International business is characterized by international trade and investment. International trade refers to exchange of products and services across national borders, typically through exporting and importing. **Exporting** is the sale of products or services to customers located abroad, from a base in the home country or a third country. **Importing** or **global sourcing** refers to procurement of products or services from foreign suppliers for consumption in the home country or a third country. **International investment** refers to international transfer or acquisition of ownership in assets. **International portfolio investment** is passive ownership of foreign securities such as stocks and bonds for the purpose of generating financial returns. **Foreign direct investment** is an internationalization strategy in which the firm establishes a physical presence abroad through acquisition of productive assets such as capital, technology, labor, land, plant, and equipment.

2. How international business differs from domestic business

International firms are constantly exposed to four major categories of risk that must be managed. **Cross-cultural risk** refers to a situation or event where some human value has been put at stake due to a cultural misunderstanding. **Country risk** refers to the potentially adverse effects on company operations and profitability caused by developments in the political, legal, and economic environment in a foreign country. **Currency risk** refers to the risk of adverse fluctuations in exchange rates. **Commercial risk** arises from the possibility of a firm's loss or failure from poorly developed or executed business strategies, tactics, or procedures. The risks are ever present in international business and firms take proactive steps to reduce their effects.

3. Who participates in international business

A key participant in international business is the **multinational enterprise (MNE)**, a large company with many resources whose business activities are performed by a network of subsidiaries located in multiple countries. Also active in international business are **small and medium-sized enterprises (SMEs)**, companies with 500 or fewer employees. **Born global firms** are entrepreneurial firms that initiate international business from or near their founding. Nongovernmental organizations (NGOs) are nonprofit organizations that pursue special causes and serve as an advocate for the arts, education, politics, religion, and research.

4. Why firms internationalize

Companies internationalize for various reasons. These include the ability to increase sales and profits, better serve customers, access lower-cost or superior production factors, optimize sourcing activities, develop economies of scale, confront competitors more effectively, develop rewarding relationships with foreign partners, and gain access to new ideas for creating or improving products and services.

5. Why you should study international business

There are many reasons to study international business. It enhances a firm's competitive positioning in the global market, facilitates development of the global economy and of the interconnectedness among nations, and contributes to national economic well-being. From a career standpoint, learning about international business will provide you with a competitive edge and enhance your ability to thrive in the job market. Firms have various opportunities for ethical corporate citizenship abroad.

Test Your Comprehension AACSB: Reflective Thinking

1. Distinguish between international business and globalization of markets.

2. What is the difference between exporting and foreign direct investment?

3. What makes international business different from domestic business?

4. What are the various types of risks that firms face when they conduct international business?

5. Who are the major participants in international business?

6. What is the difference between a multinational enterprise (MNE) and a small and medium-sized enterprise (SME)?

7. What are some of the key motivations for firms to engage in international business?

8. Why should you care about international business?

Apply Your Understanding   AACSB: Communication, Reflective Thinking, Ethical Reasoning

1. Richard Bendix is the marketing manager at a firm that makes and sells high-quality prefabricated houses. He believes that there is little difference between his home-country market and foreign markets, and that he can use the same methods for selling in Asia or Latin America as he does in his home country. Write a memo in which you explain to Richard the differences between domestic and international business. Explain the risks and other differences that Richard's firm will likely encounter if it expands abroad.

2. Suppose that after graduation you get a job with Cottonwood Corporation, a small firm that does business only in its domestic market. You have just completed coursework in international business, are aware of various business opportunities abroad, and believe that Cottonwood should internationalize. Write a memo to your boss in which you explain why your company should pursue international business. What are the benefits to Cottonwood of venturing abroad? Explain why firms internationalize.

3. You have become the president of the International Business Club at your school. You are trying to recruit new members and find that many students do not recognize the importance of international business or the career opportunities available to them. You decide to give a presentation on this theme. Prepare an outline of a presentation in which you explain what types of companies participate in international business, why students should study international business, and what career opportunities they might find.

 INTERNET EXERCISES
(http://www.globalEDGE.msu.edu)

AACSB: Communication, Use of Information Technology, Analytical Skills

Knowledge Portal

globalEDGE™ is a leading knowledge portal for professionals in international business. It is a gateway to specialized knowledge on countries, international business transactions, culture, and firm practice. globalEDGE™ was developed at Michigan State University under the direction of Professor S. Tamer Cavusgil. Consult the globalEDGE™ portal to complete the Internet exercises at the end of each chapter.

1. You can gain valuable insights into international business by examining how countries compare to each other. Various research groups and international agencies systematically examine economic, political, and other features of nations. Visit globalEDGE™ Knowledge Tools, scroll down and click on "Interactive Rankings." Then select "Countries." You will find dozens of criteria ranking countries based on: GDP per capita; Education—literacy rate; People—population total; People—population density; Health—mortality rate; Energy—electricity production; Infrastructure—mobile cellular subscriptions; Infrastructure—roads total network; Trade and Investment—foreign direct investment net inflows; and many other factors. Choose the ranking criteria that interest you most. Then, examine the following three countries: Germany, India, and South Africa. Based on your analysis, explain why they rank where they do. Do their relative positions make sense to you? Does each country seem like a good place to do business? Why or why not? Hint: Evaluate countries on a "per capita" basis by dividing each criterion by the country's population.

2. In this chapter, we reviewed the four major risks that firms face in international business: cross-cultural risk, country risk, currency risk, and commercial risk. Identify one or more countries that interest you, then visit globalEDGE™ and research the countries to uncover examples of each of the four types of risks. For example, China is characterized by various cultural differences and a national government that tends to intervene in business. Research by entering the country name into the search engine. Visit "Country Insights" and "Market Potential Index." Illustrate each risk with examples.

3. You have recently been hired by a smaller firm that is beginning to expand internationally. When first starting out, most firms choose exporting as their main foreign market entry strategy. However, no one in your firm knows how to conduct exporting. Therefore, your boss has given you an assignment: Prepare a presentation for your coworkers on how to engage in exporting. Using globalEDGE™, find and review a "Guide to Exporting" that you can use to create your presentation.

MyManagementLab

Go to **mymanagementlab.com** for Auto-graded writing questions as well as the following Assisted-graded writing question:

1-1. Mymanagementlab Only – comprehensive writing assignment for this chapter.

Bangalore: IT's Global Destination

Weekday evenings in Bangalore, thousands of young men and women commute by bus to call centers throughout the city, the fifth largest in India. As the business day begins in Eastern Canada and the United States, these young Indians put on their telephone headsets to begin the overnight shift. They assist North American customers with service problems regarding credit cards, product purchases, and Internet transactions. To put callers at ease, they often use Western-sounding names (e.g., Bill, Mary) and may receive language training that includes specific accents and cultural tips on callers' geographical locations.

Hundreds of thousands of Indians work in Bangalore writing software, designing chips, running computer systems, reading X-rays, processing mortgages, preparing tax forms, and tracing lost luggage for firms in Australia, China, Europe, Japan, and North America. The same trend is found in Delhi, Chennai, Hyderabad, and other emerging high-tech centers across India. Accenture, AOL, British Airways, Cisco, Philips, and Ernst & Young all have located operations in the country.

Millions of people now work in outsourced information technology (IT) services in India. In recent years, the sector

CHAPTER 2

Globalization of Markets and the Internationalization of the Firm

 LEARNING OBJECTIVES *In this chapter, you will learn about the following:*

1. Why globalization is not new
2. Market globalization: An organizing framework
3. Dimensions of market globalization
4. Drivers of market globalization
5. Technological advances
6. Societal consequences of market globalization
7. Firm-level consequences of market globalization: Internationalization of the firm's value chain

---

MyManagementLab®

⭐ **Improve Your Grade!**

Over 10 million students improved their results using the Pearson MyLabs. Visit **mymanagementlab.com** for simulations, tutorials, and end-of-chapter problems.

---

has enjoyed exponential growth. What is the attraction? First, Indians are paid roughly one-quarter of what Westerners receive for similar work, and in many cases they do a better job. Second, India is home to several million highly educated knowledge workers. Third, English is widely spoken. Finally, being located in a different time zone from Europe and the United States allows Indians to take advantage of time-sharing: When North Americans are ending their workday, Indians are arriving at the office to start theirs. Thanks to instant data transmission technologies, Europeans and North Americans can e-mail the projects they are working on to their Indian counterparts, who then submit the completed work by the next morning. For firms in the knowledge economy, welcome to the 24-hour workday.

Infosys (www.infosys.com) is India's leading software company. CEO Nandan Nilekani has a video conference room with wall-size flat screen TVs through which he regularly holds virtual meetings with suppliers around the world. The firm's U.S. designers can be on the screen speaking with their Indian software writers and their Asian manufacturers simultaneously. Above the screen are eight clocks that sum up the Infosys work-day: 24/7/365. The clocks are labeled U.S. West, U.S. East, London, India, Singapore, Hong Kong, Japan, and Australia.[1]

Nilekani explains that computers are becoming cheaper and commonplace around the world, and there has been an explosion of e-mail software and search engines like Google. Proprietary software can chop up any piece of work and send one part to Boston, one part to Bangalore, and one part to Beijing, making it easy for anyone to do remote development. Technology has created a platform for intellectual work that can be delivered from anywhere. It can be disaggregated, delivered, distributed, produced, and re-assembled. Emerging markets like India, Brazil, and China can compete equally for global knowledge work as never before.[2]

Ravi Patel is typical of the knowledge workers that Bangalore IT firms employ. He drives a Suzuki car, uses a Sony Ericsson mobile phone, and banks with Citibank. He hangs out with friends drinking Starbucks coffee or Bacardi and Sprite. He watches U.S. movies on a Samsung TV, brushes his teeth with Colgate, and owns a pair of Reeboks. At work Ravi drinks Coca-Cola, and uses an Acer computer with Microsoft software, a Lucent telephone, and a Mita copy machine.

Ravi's life illustrates the globalization of markets. Globalization has several implications:

- It is increasingly difficult to distinguish where you are in the world based on the products and services you consume.
- Important technologies can be developed in most locations worldwide.
- Jobs in the knowledge sector are being performed wherever the firm can extract maximal advantages, anywhere in the world.
- In the long run, by emphasizing free trade and global sourcing, globalization allows consumers worldwide to receive maximum quality at minimum price. Buyers in both producer and consumer nations can increase their income and quality of life.[3]

Meanwhile, Bangalore is also experiencing the downside of globalization. Before leading software companies made it their headquarters, it was considered one of India's most livable cities, with cheap housing and a rich cultural environment. But Bangalore may be choking on its own success: The arrival of hundreds of thousands of IT workers has brought congestion, pollution, high rents, a raucous nightlife, and Western values. Bangalore recently opened a new $500 million airport to support the city's rapid growth, even though fewer than 5 percent of Bangalore residents have ever been inside an airplane. And while a shortage of affordable housing has forced long-time residents out of the city or into slums, government construction projects focus on high-rise apartments for the wealthy.

SOURCES: A. Balakrishnan, "India's IT Industry: The End of the Beginning," *Social Research*, Spring 2011, pp. 1–20; D. Chadee, R. Raman, and S. Michailova, "Sources of Competitiveness of Offshore IT Service Providers in India: Towards a Conceptual Framework," *Competition & Change*, August 2011, pp. 196–220; *Country Monitor*, "Economic Structure and Context: Key Sectors," November 2011, pp. 22–24; Mehul Srivastava, "A Backlash Grows in Bangalore Over Tech Revolution," *BusinessWeek*, November 6, 2008; Thomas Friedman, "It's a Flat World, After All," *The New York Times Magazine*, April 2005.

Globalization of markets
Ongoing economic integration and growing interdependency of countries worldwide.

The chapter opening story highlights two megatrends that, more than any others, have altered the international business environment: technological advances and the globalization of markets. As explained in Chapter 1, **globalization of markets** refers to the gradual integration and growing interdependence of national economies. Globalization allows firms to view the world as an integrated marketplace that includes buyers, producers, suppliers, and governments in different countries. Market globalization is manifested by the production and marketing of branded products and services worldwide. Declining trade barriers and the ease with which international business transactions take place due to the Internet and other technologies are contributing to a gradual integration of most national economies into a unified global marketplace.

Ongoing *technological advances* characterize the other megatrend that has transformed contemporary business. Developments in information, manufacturing, and transportation technologies, as well as the emergence of the Internet, have facilitated rapid and early internationalization of countless firms, such as Neogen (www.neogen.com). The firm's founders developed diagnostic kits to test for food safety. Compared to test kits available from other firms, Neogen's products were more accurate, more efficient, and easier to use. As word spread about the superiority of its products, Neogen was able to internationalize quickly and acquired a worldwide clientele. Farmers use Neogen test kits to check for pesticide residue; veterinarians use them for pharmaceuticals, vaccines, and topicals; government agencies use them to test for *E. coli*. Today, Neogen is a successful international firm.

Modern technology is promoting a higher level of international business activity than ever before. For example, many companies in software, gaming, and entertainment maintain a presence only on the Web. Advances in transportation and communication technologies have greatly aided express delivery service providers such as DHL, UPS, and FedEx to serve clients around the world.

The twin trends of market globalization and technological advances permit firms to more readily engage in both marketing and *procurement* activities on a global scale. Companies sell their offerings worldwide and source raw materials, parts, components, and service inputs from suppliers around the globe. Such trends are transforming national economies. Growing world trade and foreign direct investment (FDI), coupled with the spread of technology, provide consumers and industrial buyers with a much wider choice of products and services. The competitive and innovative activities of internationally active firms are helping to reduce the prices people pay for products and services. Internationally active firms create jobs, contribute to higher living standards around the world.

Simultaneously, preferences for some consumer products appear to be converging across markets, exemplified by the universal popularity of certain music, entertainment, consumer electronics, and food. Globalization is helping disseminate values from liberalized economies about free trade and respect for intellectual property rights to an ever-widening international audience.[4]

 ## Why Globalization Is Not New

Globalization is not new; it has simply accelerated and acquired a more complex character in recent decades. In early history, civilizations in the Mediterranean, Middle East, Asia, Africa, and Europe all contributed to the growth of cross-border trade. Globalization evolved out of a common desire of civilizations, no matter where they developed, to reach out and touch one another.[5] It is a culmination of people's recognition, thousands of years ago, of the wonders of difference and discovery. Exchange with others gave societies the opportunity to expand and grow. Trade through the ages fostered civilization; without it, we would be a world of warring tribes bent on getting what we need through combat.[6] Cross-border trading opened the world to innovations and progress.

Phases of Globalization

We can identify four distinct phases in the evolution of market globalization since the 1800s. Each phase, as illustrated in Exhibit 2.1, was accompanied by revolutionary technological developments and international trends.

- *The first phase of globalization* began about 1830 and peaked around 1880.[7] International business became widespread due to the growth of railroads, efficient ocean transport, and the rise of large manufacturing and trading firms. Invention of the telegraph and telephone in the late 1800s facilitated information flows between and within nations and greatly aided early efforts to manage companies' supply chains.
- *The second phase of globalization* began around 1900 and was associated with the rise of electricity and steel production. This phase reached its height just before the Great Depression, a worldwide economic downturn that began in 1929. In 1900, Western Europe was the most industrialized world region. Europe's colonization of countries in Asia, Africa, and the Middle East led to establishment of some of the earliest subsidiaries of multinational

EXHIBIT 2.1 Phases of Globalization Since the Early 1800s

Phase of Globalization	Approximate Period	Triggers	Key Characteristics
First phase	1830 to late 1800s, peaking in 1880	Introduction of railroads and ocean transport	Rise of manufacturing: cross-border trade of commodities, largely by trading companies
Second phase	1900 to 1930	Rise of electricity and steel production	Emergence and dominance of early MNEs (mainly from Europe and North America) in manufacturing, extractive, and agricultural industries
Third phase	1948 to 1970s	Formation of General Agreement on Tariff and Trade (GATT); conclusion of World War II; Marshall Plan to reconstruct Europe	Focus by industrializing Western countries to reduce trade barriers; rise of MNEs from Japan; development of global capital markets; rise of global trade names
Fourth phase	1980s to present	Privatization of state enterprises in transition economies; revolution in information, communication, and transportation technologies; remarkable growth of emerging markets	Rapid growth in cross-border trade of products, services, and capital; rise of internationally active SMEs and services firms; rising prosperity of emerging markets

enterprises (MNEs). European companies such as BASF, Nestlé, Shell, Siemens, and British Petroleum had established foreign manufacturing plants by 1900.[8] In the years before World War I (pre-1914), many firms were already operating globally. The Italian manufacturer Fiat supplied vehicles to nations on both sides of the war.

- *The third phase of globalization* began after World War II. At war's end in 1945, substantial pent-up demand existed for consumer products, as well as for input goods to rebuild Europe and Japan. The United States was least harmed by the war and became the world's dominant economy. Substantial government aid helped stimulate economic activity in Europe. The pre-war years had been characterized by high tariffs and strict controls on currency and capital movements. After the war, leading industrialized countries, including Australia, the United Kingdom, and the United States, sought to reduce international trade barriers.

The Bretton Woods Conference of twenty-three nations in 1947 led to the *General Agreement on Tariffs and Trade (GATT)* and a series of negotiations that, over time, reduced barriers to international trade and investment. Participating governments recognized that liberalized trade would stimulate industrialization, modernization, and better living standards. The GATT eventually transformed into the **World Trade Organization** (WTO; www.wto.org), a multilateral governing body that grew to include 149 member nations. The WTO aims to regulate and ensure fairness and efficiency in global trade and investment. Global cooperation in the post-war era gave birth to other international organizations such as the International Monetary Fund and the World Bank.

Early multinationals from the third phase of globalization originated in the United States, Western Europe, and Japan. European firms like Unilever, Philips, Royal Dutch-Shell, and Bayer organized their businesses by establishing independent subsidiaries around the world, often in former colony countries. Many companies developed internationally recognized trade names, including Nestlé, Kraft, Kellogg, Lockheed, Caterpillar, Coca-Cola, Chrysler, and Levi's. Foreign subsidiaries of such companies operated as miniature, autonomous versions of the parent firm, selling much the same products in markets worldwide. Gradually, MNEs began to seek cost advantages by locating factories in developing countries with low labor costs. In the 1960s, trade liberalization and growing MNE activity led to substantial growth in international trade and investment. Recovered from World War II, MNEs in Europe

World Trade Organization (WTO)
A multilateral governing body empowered to regulate international trade and investment.

and Japan began to challenge the global dominance of U.S. multinationals. With the easing of trade barriers and currency controls, capital began to flow freely across national borders, leading to integration of global financial markets.[9]

- *The fourth phase of globalization* began in the early 1980s, which saw enormous growth in cross-border trade and investment. The phase was triggered by the development of personal computers, the Internet, and Web browsers; the collapse of the Soviet Union and ensuing market liberalization in Central and Eastern Europe; and industrialization and modernization in East Asian economies, including China.

Growing international prosperity began to reach emerging markets such as Brazil, India, and Mexico. The 1980s witnessed huge increases in FDI, especially in capital- and technology-intensive sectors. Technological advances in information, communications, and transportation made it feasible for the rise of internationally active small and medium-sized enterprises (SMEs) and for managers to organize far-flung operations around the world, geographically distant yet electronically interconnected. These technologies also facilitated the globalization of the service sector in such areas as banking, entertainment, tourism, insurance, and retailing. The merger of major firms once viewed as strongholds of national corporate power exemplified the growing integration of the world economy. Today, countless firms configure and coordinate trade and investment activities in a giant global marketplace.

 ## Market Globalization: An Organizing Framework

Exhibit 2.2 presents an organizing framework for examining market globalization. The exhibit makes a distinction between: (1) drivers or causes of globalization; (2) dimensions or manifestations of globalization; (3a) societal consequences of globalization; and (3b) firm-level consequences of globalization. In the exhibit, the double arrows illustrate the interactive nature of the relationship between market globalization and its consequences. As market globalization intensifies, individual firms respond to the challenges and new advantages that it brings.

Keep in mind firms do not expand abroad solely as a reaction to market globalization. As discussed in Chapter 1, they also internationalize proactively, in order to pursue new markets, find lower-cost inputs, or obtain other advantages. Often, adverse conditions in the home market, such as regulation or declining industry sales, push firms to boldly venture abroad. Firms that do so tend to be more successful in global competition than those that engage in international business as a reactive move.

Vodafone (www.vodafone.com), one of the leading wireless phone service providers, is a good example of firms pursuing internationalization as a strategic growth alternative. Its main offerings include telecommunications and data services, multimedia portals, cellular operations, satellite services, and retail shops. Vodafone has annual sales of $74 billion and more than 340 million customers worldwide. Founded in 1983 as a joint venture between a British and a U.S. firm, the company had set up mobile phone networks in Australia and Hong Kong and throughout Scandinavia by 1993. It then launched or bought stakes in operations throughout Africa, Asia, Europe, and the Americas. Vodafone has internationalized mainly via foreign direct investment. Today it has equity interests in more than twenty countries and owns a 45 percent stake in the U.S. provider Verizon Wireless.

Vodafone took advantage of such globalization trends as harmonization of communications technologies, convergence of buyer characteristics, and reduced trade and investment barriers. As emerging markets develop economically, they leapfrog older telecom technologies (typically landline systems) and embrace cell phone technology instead—a boon to Vodafone. In Turkey in 2008, the firm acquired Telsim, the country's second-biggest mobile phone operator. In 2011, the firm acquired a controlling interest in a major cell phone firm in India, a move that leveraged the country's rapid economic growth and need to upgrade its phone systems.

Vodafone's proactive global strategy emphasizes selling standardized products and services and pursuing standardized marketing programs across the globe. To minimize costs, many of its cell phones are essentially identical worldwide, with adaptations to accommodate local languages, regulations, and telephone standards. Vodafone's advertising aims at developing and maintaining a global brand that people recognize everywhere. Convergence of buyer lifestyles and incomes

DRIVERS OF MARKET GLOBALIZATION

- Worldwide reduction of barriers to trade and investment
- Market liberalization and adoption of free markets
- Industrialization, economic development, and modernization
- Integration of world financial markets
- Advances in technology

 DIMENSIONS OF MARKET GLOBALIZATION

- Integration and interdependence of national economies
- Rise of regional economic integration blocs
- Growth of global investment and financial flows
- Convergence of buyer lifestyles and preferences
- Globalization of production activities
- Globalization of services

 SOCIETAL CONSEQUENCES OF MARKET GLOBALIZATION

- Contagion: Rapid spread of financial or monetary crises from one country to another
- Loss of national sovereignty
- Offshoring and the flight of jobs
- Effect on the poor
- Effect on the natural environment
- Effect on national culture

 FIRM-LEVEL CONSEQUENCES OF MARKET GLOBALIZATION: INTERNATIONALIZATION OF THE FIRM'S VALUE CHAIN

- Countless new business opportunities for internationalizing firms
- New risks and intense rivalry from foreign competitors
- More demanding buyers who source from suppliers worldwide
- Greater emphasis on proactive internationalization
- Internationalization of firm's value chain

EXHIBIT 2.2

The Drivers and Consequences of Market Globalization

worldwide help facilitate the global approach. Management coordinates operations on a global scale and applies common business processes in procurement and quality control. The strategies of product standardization, global branding, and selling to customers worldwide owe much of their success to the globalization of markets. Vodafone's strategic internationalization allows the firm to benefit from economies of scale, which make its products more price-competitive.[10]

 ## Dimensions of Market Globalization

Globalization has been studied within various disciplines, including economics, anthropology, political science, sociology, and technology. In terms of international business, market globalization can be viewed simultaneously as a: (1) consequence of economic, technological, and government policy trends; (2) driver of economic, political, and social phenomena; and (3) driver and consequence of firm-level internationalization.

Globalization of markets is a multifaceted phenomenon, with six major dimensions:

1. *Integration and interdependence of national economies.* Internationally active firms devise multicountry operations through trade, investment, geographic dispersal of company resources, and integration and coordination of value-chain activities. A **value chain** is the sequence of value-adding activities performed by the firm in the course of developing, producing, marketing, and servicing a

Value chain

The sequence of value-adding activities performed by the firm in the course of developing, producing, marketing, and servicing a product.

product. The *aggregate* activities of such firms give rise to *economic integration.* Governments have facilitated this integration by lowering barriers to international trade and investment, harmonizing their monetary and fiscal policies within *regional economic integration* blocs (also known as *trade blocs*), and developing *supranational* institutions—the World Bank, International Monetary Fund, World Trade Organization, and others—that seek further reductions in trade and investment barriers.

2. *Rise of regional economic integration blocs.* Closely related to the first trend is the emergence since the 1950s of regional economic integration blocs. Examples include the North American Free Trade Agreement area (NAFTA), the Asia Pacific Economic Cooperation zone (APEC), and Mercosur in Latin America. These blocs consist of groups of countries within which trade and investment flows are facilitated through reduced trade and investment barriers. In more advanced arrangements, such as the "common market," barriers to the cross-border flow of factors of production (mostly labor and capital)

Source: © Jeff Greenberg/PhotoEdit

Advances in transportation and low freight costs have helped spur market globalization. This cargo ship is approaching the Port of Miami, Florida.

are removed. For example, the European Union (www.europa.eu), in addition to adopting free trade among its member countries, has harmonized fiscal and monetary policies and adopted common business regulations.

3. *Growth of global investment and financial flows.* In the process of conducting international transactions, firms and governments buy and sell large volumes of national currencies (such as dollars, euros, and yen). The free movement of capital around the world—the globalization of capital—extends economic activities across the globe and is fostering interconnectedness among world economies. Commercial and investment banking is a global industry. The bond market has gained worldwide scope, with foreign bonds representing a major source of debt financing for governments and firms. Information and communications networks facilitate heavy volumes of financial transactions every day, integrating national markets. Nevertheless, widespread integration can have negative effects. For example, when the United States experienced a banking crisis in 2008, the crisis quickly spread to Europe, Japan, and emerging markets, triggering a global recession.

4. *Convergence of consumer lifestyles and preferences.* Around the world, consumers spend their money and time in increasingly similar ways. Lifestyles and preferences are converging. Shoppers in Tokyo, New York, and Paris demand similar household goods, clothing, automobiles, and electronics. Teenagers everywhere are attracted to iPods, Levi's jeans, and BlackBerry cell phones. Major brands have gained a global following, encouraged by greater international travel, movies, global media, and the Internet, which expose people to products, services, and living patterns from around the world. Movies such as *Transformers* and *The Twilight Saga* receive much attention from a global audience. Convergence of preferences is also occurring in industrial markets, where professional buyers source raw materials, parts, and components that are increasingly *standardized*—that is, very similar in design and structure. Yet, even as converging tastes facilitate the marketing of highly standardized products and services to buyers worldwide, they also promote the loss of traditional lifestyles and values in individual countries.

5. *Globalization of production.* Intense global competition is forcing firms to reduce their costs of production and marketing. Companies strive to drive down prices through economies of scale, by standardizing what they sell, and by shifting manufacturing and procurement to foreign locations with inexpensive labor. For example, companies in the auto and textile industries have relocated their manufacturing to low labor-cost locations such as China, Mexico, and Eastern Europe.

6. *Globalization of services.* The services sector is undergoing widespread internationalization. First, banking, hospitality, retailing, and other service industries are rapidly expanding abroad. The real estate firm REMAX has established more than 5,000 offices in over fifty

Source: © Robert Harding Picture Library Ltd/Alamy

Google is one of many multinational enterprises that contribute to convergence of consumer lifestyles and preferences.

countries. Second, as noted in the opening story, firms increasingly outsource business processes and other services in the value chain to vendors located abroad. Finally, in a relatively new trend, many people go abroad to take advantage of low-cost services. For example, many U.S. consumers regularly travel to India, Latin America, and other international destinations to undergo medical procedures like cataract and knee surgeries. Several U.S. health insurance companies view international "medical tourism" as a means to reduce costs.[11]

 ## Drivers of Market Globalization

Various trends have converged in recent years as causes of market globalization. Five are particularly notable:

1. *Worldwide reduction of barriers to trade and investment.* The tendency of national governments to reduce trade and investment barriers has accelerated global economic integration. For example, tariffs on the import of automobiles, industrial machinery, and countless other products have declined nearly to zero in many countries, encouraging freer international exchange of goods and services. Falling trade barriers are facilitated by the WTO. After joining the WTO in 2001, China has made its market more accessible to foreign firms. Reduction of trade barriers is also associated with the emergence of regional economic integration blocs, a key dimension of market globalization.

2. *Market liberalization and adoption of free markets.* The collapse of the Soviet Union's economy in 1989 and China's free-market reforms marked the end of the 50-year Cold War and smoothed the integration of former command economies into the global economy. Numerous East Asian economies, stretching from South Korea to Malaysia and Indonesia, had already embarked on ambitious market-based reforms. India joined the trend in 1991. These events opened roughly one-third of the world to freer international trade and investment. China, India, and Eastern Europe have become some of the most cost-effective locations for producing goods and services worldwide. Privatization of previously state-owned industries in these countries has encouraged economic efficiency and attracted massive foreign capital into their national economies.

3. *Industrialization, economic development, and modernization.* Industrialization implies that emerging markets—rapidly developing economies in Asia, Latin America, and Eastern Europe—are moving from being low value-adding commodity producers, dependent on low-cost labor, to sophisticated competitive producers and exporters of premium products such as electronics, computers, and aircraft.[12] For example, Brazil is now a leading producer of private aircraft, and the Czech Republic excels in the manufacture of automobiles. As highlighted in the opening story, India has become a leading supplier of computer software. Economic development is enhancing standards of living and discretionary income in emerging markets. Perhaps the most important measure of economic development is *gross national income (GNI)* per head.[13] Exhibit 2.3 maps the levels of GNI worldwide. The exhibit reveals that Africa is home to the lowest-income countries, along with India and a few other countries in Asia and Nicaragua. These areas are also characterized by lower levels of market globalization. Modernization is increasing the attractiveness of emerging markets as investment targets and facilitating the spread of ideas, products, and services across the globe.

4. *Integration of world financial markets.* Financial market integration makes it possible for internationally active firms to raise capital, borrow funds, and engage in foreign currency transactions. Financial services firms follow their customers to foreign markets. Cross-border transactions are made easier partly as a result of the ease with which funds can be transferred between buyers and sellers, through a network of international commercial banks. For example, as an individual you can transfer funds to a friend in another country using the SWIFT network. Connecting more than 9,000 financial institutions in some 200 countries, the network facilitates global financial transactions. The globalization of finance contributes to firms' abilities to develop and operate world-scale production and marketing operations. It enables companies to pay suppliers and collect payments from customers worldwide.

5. *Advances in technology.* Technological advances are a remarkable facilitator of cross-border trade and investment. Let's elaborate on this important driver of globalization and company internationalization in detail.

 ## Technological Advances

Perhaps the most important driver of market globalization has been technological advances in information, communications, manufacturing, and transportation. While globalization makes internationalization imperative, technological advances provide the *means* for it to happen.

Initially, technology eases management of international operations, allowing firms to interact more efficiently with foreign partners and value-chain members than ever before. Companies continuously transmit information and communications that help ensure the smooth running of their operations worldwide. They use information technology to improve operational productivity, providing substantial competitive advantages.

In addition, technological advances have made international operations affordable for all types of firms, explaining why so many SMEs have internationalized in recent years. Panel (a) of Exhibit 2.4 shows the dramatic decrease in the cost of international communications, expressed as the cost of a 3-minute telephone call from London to New York. Panel (b) reveals the growth in Internet users in various regions since 2000. Africa has the fewest number of Internet users, while North America and Oceania/Australia have the most, reflecting the level of economic and infrastructural development in each region.

Managers use the latest technologies to manage international operations: iPads that combine laptop functionality with smartphone convenience; BlackBerry phones with cross-national WiFi capability that can take phone calls from anywhere on Earth; iPods for listening to audio downloads or mini Sony PlayStations for that ride home on the train after work.

Technological advances have spurred the development of new products and services that appeal to a global audience. Leading examples include Wii and the iPhone. Emerging markets and developing economies also benefit from technological advances, partly through technological leapfrogging. For example, Hungary and Poland went directly from old-style analog telecommunications (with rotary dial telephones) to cell phone technology, bypassing much of the early digital technology (push-button telephones) that characterized advanced economy telephone systems.

China and India are the new frontiers in technological advances. The chapter's opening story revealed how India excels in global Internet- and knowledge-based industries. Intel and Motorola, two leading technology companies, now generate substantial sales in China. Management predicts double-digit increases in demand for technology products in China far into the future.[14]

Technological advances have had the greatest impact in several key areas—information technology, communications, manufacturing, and transportation—which we review next.

Information Technology

Information technology (IT) is the science and process of creating and using information resources. Its effect on business has been revolutionary. The cost of computer processing fell by 30 percent per year during the past two decades and continues to fall. IT creates competitive advantages by giving companies new ways to outperform rivals.[15] For example, geographically distant subsidiaries of a multinational firm can be interconnected via intranets, facilitating the instant sharing of data, information, and experience across company operations worldwide. MNEs also use collaboration software that connects global product development teams located worldwide, enabling them to work together.

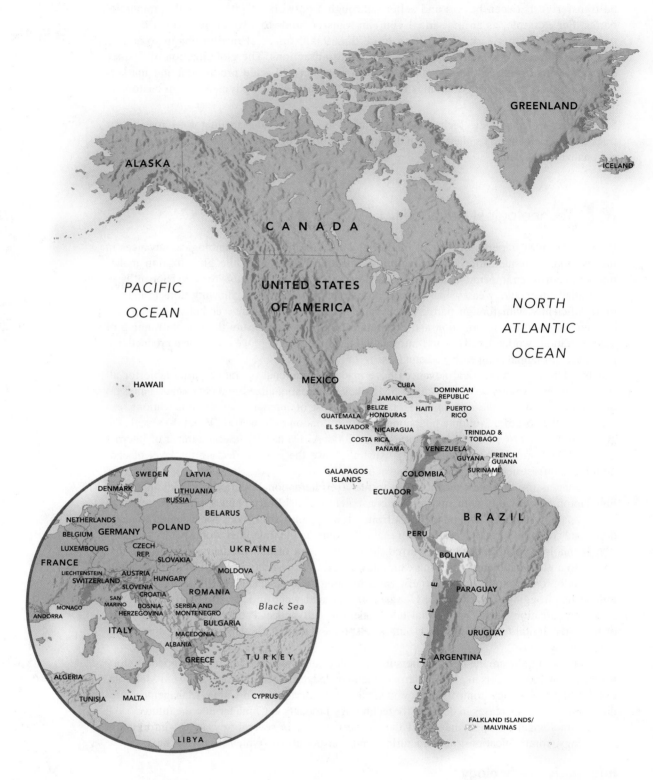

EXHIBIT 2.3

Gross National Income in U.S. Dollars

Source: Based on World Bank (2012); World Bank Development Indicator database, http://www.data.worldbank.org.

ARCTIC OCEAN

NORWAY
SWEDEN
FINLAND

RUSSIA

UNITED KINGDOM
IRELAND
ESTONIA
LATVIA
LITHUANIA
DENMARK
RUSSIA
BELARUS
NETHERLANDS
BELGIUM
GERMANY
POLAND
LUXEMBOURG
CZECH REP.
SLOVAKIA
UKRAINE
FRANCE
LIECH.
AUSTRIA
HUNGARY
MOLDOVA
SWITZ.
SLOVENIA
ROMANIA
MONACO
CROATIA
BOSNIA-
HERZEGOVINA
SERBIA AND
MONTENEGRO
BULGARIA
ANDORRA
ITALY
MACEDONIA
ALBANIA
GREECE
TURKEY

KAZAKHSTAN

MONGOLIA

NORTH KOREA
SOUTH KOREA
JAPAN

SPAIN
PORTUGAL
TUNISIA
CYPRUS
LEBANON
SYRIA
IRAQ
GEORGIA
ARMENIA
AZERBAIJAN
TURKMENISTAN
UZBEKISTAN
KYRGYZSTAN
TAJIKISTAN
AFGHANISTAN
IRAN

CHINA

PACIFIC OCEAN

MOROCCO
ALGERIA
LIBYA
EGYPT
ISRAEL
JORDAN
KUWAIT
QATAR
UNITED ARAB EMIRATES
OMAN
SAUDI ARABIA
PAKISTAN
NEPAL
BHUTAN
BANGLADESH
MYANMAR (BURMA)
LAOS
TAIWAN

WESTERN SAHARA
MAURITANIA
MALI
NIGER
CHAD
NORTH SUDAN
ERITREA
YEMEN
DJIBOUTI
SOMALIA
INDIA
SRI LANKA
THAILAND
VIETNAM
CAMBODIA
PHILIPPINES

SENEGAL
GAMBIA
GUINEA-BISSAU
GUINEA
SIERRA LEONE
LIBERIA
BURKINA FASO
GHANA
TOGO
BENIN
IVORY COAST
NIGERIA
CENTRAL AFRICAN REPUBLIC
CAMEROON
SOUTH SUDAN
ETHIOPIA
BRUNEI
MALAYSIA
SINGAPORE

EQUATORIAL GUINEA
GABON
CONGO REPUBLIC
CONGO DEMOCRATIC REPUBLIC (ZAIRE)
UGANDA
RWANDA
BURUNDI
KENYA
TANZANIA
INDIAN OCEAN
INDONESIA
PAPUA NEW GUINEA
SOLOMON ISLANDS

SOUTH ATLANTIC OCEAN

ANGOLA
ZAMBIA
MALAWI
MOZAMBIQUE
NAMIBIA
ZIMBABWE
BOTSWANA
MADAGASCAR
MAURITIUS
RÉUNION

AUSTRALIA

VANUATU
FIJI
NEW CALEDONIA

SWAZILAND
SOUTH AFRICA
LESOTHO

NEW ZEALAND

GNI in U.S. Dollars Per Capita, 2007

7,490 or more
2,350 - 7,490
1,110 - 2,350
430 - 1,110
less than 430
No data

EXHIBIT 2.4

Declining Cost of Global Communication and Growing Internet Penetration Rate (as a % of the region's population)

Sources: Based on IMF (2011), *World Economic Outlook*, Washington, DC: International Monetary Fund; United Nations International Telecommunications Union (2012), *Statistics & Database*, at www.itu .int; Internet World Stats (2012), *Internet Usage Statistics*, at http://www .internetworldstats.com.

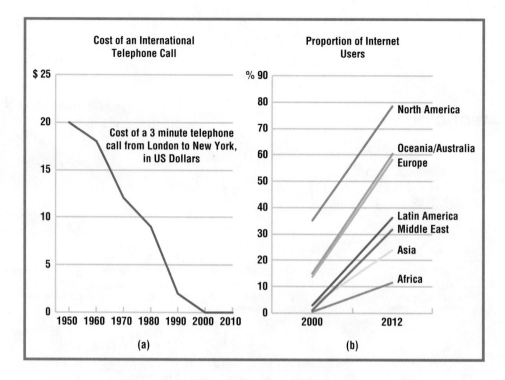

IT benefits smaller firms too, allowing them to design and produce customized products they can target to narrow, cross-national market niches. Google, Yahoo, and other online search engines provide easy access to unlimited data for researching markets, customers, competitors, and countries' economic conditions. At a higher level, IT supports managerial decision making, such as the selection of qualified foreign business partners, by allowing firms to quickly access key information and intelligence.

Communications

It took five months for Spain's Queen Isabella to learn about Columbus's voyage in 1492, two weeks for Europe to learn of President Lincoln's assassination in 1865, and only seconds for the world to witness the collapse of New York's World Trade Center towers in 2001. At one time, the only way to communicate with foreign suppliers was through slow postal services, expensive phone calls, and clunky telex machines. Today, scanners and fax machines send documents worldwide for practically nothing. Bank transactions are relatively costly when performed via ATM machines or telephones but are virtually free when handled online.

The Internet, and Internet-dependent systems such as intranets, extranets, and e-mail, connect millions of people worldwide. Today, the widest range of products and services—from auto parts to bank loans—is marketed online. Transmitting voices, data, and images is essentially costless, making Seoul, Stockholm, and San Jose next-door neighbors, instantly. South Korea has nearly 100 percent Internet access and among the fastest broadband networks worldwide. Koreans use their phones to pay bills, do banking, and watch news programs.

The Internet opens the global marketplace to SMEs and other firms that normally lack the resources to do international business. By establishing a presence on the Web, even tiny enterprises can take the first step in becoming multinational firms. Services as diverse as designing an engine, monitoring a security camera, selling insurance, and doing secretarial work are easier to export than car parts or refrigerators. The *Global Trend* feature highlights the emergence of e-commerce and its effect on company internationalization.

Source: © Gilles Paire/Fotolia

Increasing availability of cell phones in Africa has helped spur economic growth there.

EXHIBIT 2.5 The Death of Distance

In This Time Period...	Fastest Transportation Was Via...	At a Speed of...
1500 to 1840s	• Human-powered ships and horse-drawn carriages	10 miles per hour
1850 to 1900	• Steamships	36 miles per hour
	• Steam locomotive trains	65 miles per hour
Early 1900s to today	• Motor vehicles	75 miles per hour
	• Propeller airplanes	300–400 miles per hour
	• Jet aircraft	500–700 miles per hour

Source: Based on P. Dicken (1992), *Global Shift.* New York: Guilford, p. 104.

Ethical Connections

In six years, Nigeria increased its telecom infrastructure from just 500,000 phone lines to more than 30 million cellular subscribers. The result has been a dramatic rise in productivity and commerce, which helps improve living standards. Greater access to cell phones saves wasted trips, provides access to education and healthcare services, and facilitates communication between suppliers and customers. MNE telecom investment in Africa allows firms to fulfill social responsibilities and improve the lives of millions of poor people.

Countries need modern infrastructure in communications, such as reliable telephone systems, to support economic development. Mobile phones are the most transformative technology in developing economies. Cell phone infrastructure is inexpensive and relatively easy to install.[16]

Manufacturing

Computer-aided design (CAD) of products, robotics, and production lines managed and monitored by microprocessor-based controls have transformed manufacturing, mainly by reducing production costs. Revolutionary developments facilitate low-scale and low-cost manufacturing. Firms can make products cost-effectively even in short production runs. Such developments benefit international business by allowing firms to more efficiently adapt products to individual foreign markets, profitably target small national markets, and compete more effectively with foreign competitors that enjoy cost advantages.

Transportation

Managers consider the costs of transporting raw materials, components, and finished products when deciding to either export or manufacture abroad. If transport costs to an important market are high, management may decide to manufacture merchandise in the market by building a factory there. The development of fuel-efficient jumbo jets, giant ocean-going freighters, and low-cost shipping, often through the use of high-tech composites, have revolutionized international transportation. The "death of distance"[17] refers to the shrinkage of the geographic and cultural distances that long separated nations. Exhibit 2.5 reveals the progression of this trend. Technological advances in transportation have shrunk the world into a manageable marketplace.

In the 20-year period through 2012, the number of containers transported internationally increased by nearly five times, to about 175 million 20-foot equivalent units. Containers are the big boxes, usually 40 feet long (about 12 meters), loaded on top of ships, trucks, and rail cars that carry the world's cargo. Today, the typical ocean-going container ship holds more than 2,300 containers, double the average of the 1980s.[18] Consequently, the cost of transportation, as a proportion of the value of products shipped internationally, has declined dramatically. Thanks to cost-effective air travel, managers quickly travel the world.

 ## Societal Consequences of Market Globalization

Our discussion so far has highlighted the far-reaching, positive outcomes of market globalization. Major advances in living standards have been achieved in virtually all countries that have opened their borders to increased trade and investment. Nevertheless, the transition to a global

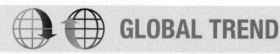

GLOBAL TREND

Globalization and E-Business in the Online World

Information technology and the Internet are transforming international business by allowing firms to conduct e-commerce online and to integrate e-business capabilities for activities such as sourcing and managing customer relations. E-business drives the firm's globalization efforts by helping it beat geography and time zones, and do business around the world all day, every day. E-business levels the playing field for all types of firms, large and small. Even new companies can be active abroad. Born global firms are among the most intensive users of the Web for global selling, procurement, and customer service.

E-business provides at least four types of benefits:

- *Increases productivity* and reduces costs in worldwide value-chain activities through online integration and coordination of production, distribution, and after-sale services.

- *Creates value for existing customers* by increasing the efficiency and effectiveness of links between customers and vendors. Online connectedness facilitates superior service and better communications with customers. It enhances the sharing of new ideas and best practices for serving customer needs.
- *Uncovers new sales opportunities* by boosting marketing capabilities and facilitating entrepreneurial initiatives. Using online technologies, firms routinely discover opportunities and new product ideas in the global marketplace.
- *Improves the flow of information and knowledge throughout the firm's worldwide operations*. The Internet enhances interaction with customers, suppliers, and partners worldwide. Managers can make instantaneous changes to strategies and tactics in value-chain activities. The firm can

accommodate real-time changes in market conditions almost as quickly as they occur.

Cisco uses e-business solutions to minimize costs and maximize operational effectiveness in its international supply chain. The firm uses the Internet to remain constantly linked to suppliers and distributors. This helps Cisco manage inventory, product specifications, purchase orders, and product life cycles. E-procurement systems help Cisco save money on transaction processing, reduce cycle times, and leverage supplier relations.

Customer relationship management is especially critical in foreign markets where buyers often favor local vendors. Internet-based systems provide real-time information, help forecast shifting short- and long-term market needs, and increase after-sales service effectiveness. E-commerce greatly enhances competitive advantages and performance objectives in the global marketplace.

---

marketplace poses challenges to individuals, organizations, and governments. Low-income countries have not been able to integrate with the global economy as rapidly as others. Poverty remains a major problem in Africa and populous nations like Brazil, China, and India. Let's turn to some of the unintended consequences of globalization.

Contagion: Rapid Spread of Monetary or Financial Crises

Starting in 2008, the world economy experienced a severe financial crisis and global recession, the worst in decades. The crisis was precipitated by excessively high prices in housing and commodities markets worldwide. As prices in real estate markets tumbled, home values crashed, leaving owners with mortgage debts greater than the value of their homes. Thousands of mortgages had been sold as investment vehicles on stock markets worldwide. As the value of these securities plunged or became uncertain, stock markets crashed.[19]

Exhibit 2.6 shows how GDP growth in advanced, developing, and emerging economies varies over time. It declined substantially during the global recession and financial crisis. One lesson of the exhibit is that, even following deep recessions, the global economy has always returned to net GDP growth.

Contagion

The tendency of a financial or monetary crisis in one country to spread rapidly to other countries, due to the ongoing integration of national economies.

The crisis began in the United States and, like a contagious disease, spread around the world. In international economics, **contagion** refers to the tendency for a financial or monetary crisis in one country to spread rapidly to other countries, due to integrated national economies.[20] Widespread borrowing by consumers to purchase homes and durable goods led to unsustainable overheating of the U.S. economy. Another cause of the financial crisis was inadequate regulation of the financial and banking sector in the United States. As we will see later in this text, having a strong legal and regulatory framework is critical to national economic well-being.[21]

Consumer confidence dwindled, triggering substantial declines in spending on cars, consumer electronics, home appliances, luxury goods, gasoline, bank loans, and new homes. Decreased spending, in turn, has been a drag on global commerce.[22] Trade has especially slowed or flattened in consumer durables, energy, financial services, new construction, and related industries. In 2009–2010, global growth declined sharply to levels not seen since World War II.

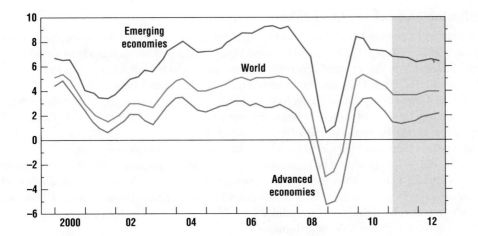

EXHIBIT 2.6

Percentage of Change in Annual GDP Growth

Source: Based on IMF, *World Economic Outlook* (Washington, DC: International Monetary Fund, September 2011). Accessed at http://www.imf.org/external/pubs/ft/weo/2011/02/pdf/text.pdf, 2/14/12.

Canada and Mexico slipped into recession partly due to their heavy reliance on trade and investment with the United States. Japan, Iceland, New Zealand, Singapore, Turkey, the United States, and most countries in the European Union all experienced significant recessions. Living standards were severely affected, and millions of people worldwide fell into deeper poverty. This occurred partly because developing economies depend on exports to, and direct investments from, the advanced economies that were hurt by the crisis. Major economic recovery beginning in 2012 helped drive economic growth in much of the world.[23]

The recent "European debt crisis" arose from various factors, especially the globalization of finance, real estate bubbles, easy money and credit conditions, and excessive spending by national governments. Beginning in 2010, the European Union provided rescue packages for Greece, Ireland, and Portugal, which found themselves unable to refinance their own debts.[24]

Loss of National Sovereignty

Sovereignty, the ability of a nation to govern its own affairs, is a fundamental principle that underlies global relations. One country's laws cannot be applied or enforced in another country. Globalization can threaten national sovereignty in various ways. MNE activities can interfere with the sovereign ability of governments to control their own economies, social structures, and political systems. Some corporations are bigger than the economies of many nations. Indeed, Walmart's internal economy—its total revenues—is larger than the GDP of most of the world's nations, such as Greece, Peru, and Thailand. Large multinationals can exert considerable influence on governments through lobbying or campaign contributions. They often lobby their government for, say, devaluation of the home currency, which gives them greater price competitiveness in export markets. MNEs influence the legislative process and extract special favors from government agencies.

At the same time, even the largest firms are constrained by *market forces*. In countries with many competing firms, one company cannot force customers to buy its products or force suppliers to supply it with raw materials and inputs. The resources that customers and suppliers control are the result of free choices made in the marketplace. Company performance depends on the firm's skill at winning customers, working with suppliers, and dealing with competitors. Corporate dominance of individual markets is rare. In reality, market forces generally dominate companies. Gradual integration of the global economy and increased global competition, combined with privatization of industries in various nations, are making some companies less powerful within their national markets.[25] For example, Ford, Chrysler, and General Motors once dominated the U.S. auto market. Today, many more firms compete in the United States, including Toyota, Honda, Hyundai, Nissan, and BMW.

Today, globalization and the spread of financial crises compel governments to pursue sound economic policies and managers to manage their firms more effectively. To minimize globalization's harm and reap its benefits, governments should strive for open and liberalized economic regimes. Specifically, governments should ensure the freedom to enter and compete in markets, protect private and intellectual property, enforce the rule of law, and support voluntary exchange through markets rather than through political processes. Banks and financial institutions should be regulated appropriately. Transparency in the affairs of business and regulatory agencies is critical.

Offshoring and the Flight of Jobs

Globalization has created countless new jobs and opportunities around the world, but it has also cost many people their jobs. Ford and General Motors have laid off thousands of workers in the United States, partly the result of competitive pressures posed by carmakers from Europe, Japan, and South Korea. Ford, GM, and Volkswagen have all transferred thousands of jobs from their factories in Germany to countries in Eastern Europe. This occurred partly because mandated shorter working hours (often just 35 hours per week) and generous benefits made Germany less competitive, while Eastern Europe offers abundant low-wage workers. Recognizing this, the German government loosened Germany's labor laws to conform to global realities.[26]

Offshoring is the relocation of manufacturing and other value-chain activities to cost-effective locations abroad. For example, the global accounting firm Ernst & Young relocated much of its accounting support work to the Philippines. Massachusetts General Hospital has its CT scans and X-rays interpreted by radiologists in India. Many IT support services for customers in Germany are based in the Czech Republic and Romania.[27]

Offshoring has resulted in job losses in numerous mature economies. The first wave of offshoring began in the 1960s and 1970s with the shift of U.S. and European manufacturing of cars, shoes, electronics, textiles, and toys to cheap-labor locations such as Mexico and Southeast Asia. The next wave began in the 1990s with the exodus of service-sector jobs in credit card processing, software code writing, accounting, health care, and banking services.

High-profile plant closures and relocation of manufacturing have received much media attention in recent years. Critics have labeled some MNEs as "runaway" or "footloose" corporations—quick to relocate production to countries that offer more favorable access to inputs. For example, Polaris, the U.S. manufacturer of snowmobiles and all-terrain vehicles, recently moved its Osceola, Wisconsin, factory to Mexico. Closure of the plant, which once provided 515 jobs, devastated the small Wisconsin community, population 2,085. Management shifted manufacturing to Mexico in order to reduce production costs.[28]

Simultaneously, however, MNEs create millions of jobs abroad, which help raise living standards. For example, United States MNEs now employ about one million workers in each of Canada, China, Mexico, and the United Kingdom.[29] In developing economies and emerging markets, such positions help raise living standards.

Effect on the Poor

MNEs are often criticized for paying low wages, exploiting workers, and employing child labor. Child labor is particularly troubling because it denies children educational opportunities. In 2012, the International Labor Organization (www.ilo.org) reported there are approximately 215 million children aged 5 to 14 at work around the world.[30]

Nike was criticized for paying low wages to shoe factory workers in Asia, some of whom work in sweatshop conditions. Critics complained that while founder Phil Knight is a billionaire and Nike shoes sell for $100 or more, Nike's suppliers often pay their workers only a few dollars per day.

Labor exploitation and sweatshop conditions are major concerns in many developing economies.[31] Nevertheless, consideration must be given to the other choices available to people in those countries. A low-paying job is usually better than no job at all. Studies suggest that banning products made using child labor may produce negative unintended consequences such as reduced living standards.[32] Legislation passed to reduce child labor in the formal economic sector (the sector regulated and monitored by public authorities) may have little effect on jobs in the informal economic sector, sometimes called the *underground economy*. In the face of persistent poverty, abolishing formal sector jobs does not ensure that children leave the workforce and go to school.

Source: Peter Cook/Dorling Kindersley

Media attention and consumer concern are helping to slowly improve wages and sweatshop conditions in developing economies, such as those in south Asia.

In many developing countries, work conditions tend to improve over time. The growth of the footwear industry in Vietnam translated into a fivefold increase in wages. While still low by advanced economy standards, growing wages are improving the lives of millions of workers and their families. For most countries, globalization tends to support a growing economy. Countries that liberalize international trade and investment enjoy faster per-capita economic growth. Developing economies that seek to integrate with the rest of the world tend to have faster per-capita GDP growth than those that fail to participate in the world economy.[33]

Exhibit 2.7 shows the GDP growth rate worldwide from 2003 to 2012. Note that most nations experienced positive growth. The world's fastest-growing large economies are China and India. Argentina, Panama, and Vietnam also have been on the fast-growth track. Most African countries continue to suffer low or negative GDP growth and alarming poverty.

Exhibit 2.8 reveals how global poverty is declining over time.[34] This exhibit illustrates the income status of people in developing economies, especially in East and South Asia, and Sub-Saharan Africa (that part of Africa below the Saharan Desert). It also shows the number of people living on $2.00 or $1.25 per day, which the World Bank considers the thresholds for "poverty" and "extreme poverty," respectively. In total, the number of people living in poverty in these areas has declined consistently for the past few decades, while the number of people living at higher income levels has been rising. Much of these improvements are due to international trade and investment activities.[35] Only Sub-Saharan Africa has shown little improvement in income status during this time.

Effect on Sustainability and the Natural Environment

Globalization promotes manufacturing and economic activity that results in pollution, habitat destruction, and deterioration of the ozone layer. Economic development and industrialization have long-term implications for sustaining the natural environment. In China, for example, economic development is attracting much inward FDI and stimulating the growth of numerous industries. But construction of factories, infrastructure, and modern housing can spoil previously pristine environments. In Eastern China, growing industrial demand for electricity led to construction of the Three Gorges Dam, which flooded agricultural lands and permanently altered the natural landscape. See the *Apply Your Understanding* exercise at the end of this chapter, which presents an Ethical Dilemma problem on the environmental damage done by a large oil company in Nigeria.

The evidence suggests that environmental destruction diminishes as economies develop, at least in the long run. As globalization stimulates rising living standards, people focus on improving their environment. Over time, governments pass legislation that promotes improved environmental conditions. For example, Japan endured polluted rivers and smoggy cities in the early decades of its economic development following World War II. As their economy grew, the Japanese passed tough environmental standards to restore natural environments.

Evolving company values and concern for corporate reputations have led many firms to reduce or eliminate practices that harm the environment.[36] In Mexico, for example, big automakers such as Ford

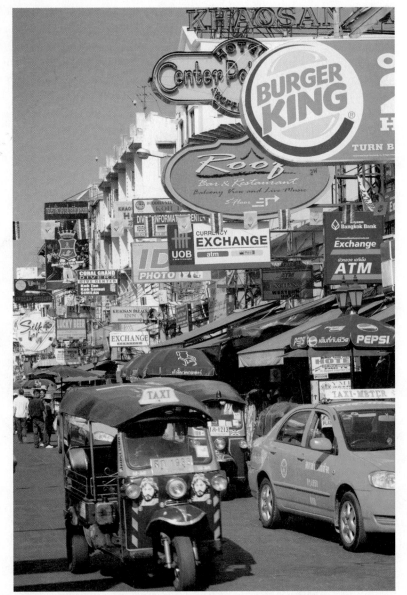

Source: Martin Richardson/Dorling Kindersley Limited

Western companies can influence food preferences, but cultural values tend to remain stable over time. This Burger King is in Bangkok, Thailand.

EXHIBIT 2.7

The Growth of World GDP, Average Annual GDP Growth Rate, 2003–2012 (Percent)

Source: Based on International Monetary Fund, World Economic Outlook Database, http://www.imf.org/external/pubs/ft/weo/2012/01/weodata/index.aspx.

ARCTIC OCEAN

NORWAY

SWEDEN

FINLAND

ESTONIA
LATVIA
LITHUANIA
RUSSIA
BELARUS

UNITED
KINGDOM
DENMARK

IRELAND

NETHERLANDS
POLAND
GERMANY
BELGIUM
LUXEMBOURG
CZECH
REP.
SLOVAKIA
UKRAINE
FRANCE
LIECH.
AUSTRIA
HUNGARY
MOLDOVA
SWITZ.
SLOVENIA
CROATIA
ROMANIA
MONACO
BOSNIA-
HERZEGOVINA
SERBIA AND
MONTENEGRO
BULGARIA
ANDORRA
ITALY
MACEDONIA
ALBANIA
SPAIN
GREECE
TURKEY
PORTUGAL

GEORGIA
ARMENIA
AZERBAIJAN
TURKMENISTAN

KAZAKHSTAN

MONGOLIA

NORTH
KOREA
SOUTH
KOREA
JAPAN

RUSSIA

UZBEKISTAN
KYRGYZSTAN
TAJIKISTAN

TUNISIA
CYPRUS
LEBANON
SYRIA
ISRAEL
IRAQ
JORDAN
KUWAIT

AFGHANISTAN

CHINA

PACIFIC
OCEAN

MOROCCO

ALGERIA

LIBYA

EGYPT

IRAN
PAKISTAN

NEPAL
BHUTAN

WESTERN
SAHARA

BAHRAIN
QATAR
UNITED ARAB
EMIRATES
SAUDI
ARABIA
OMAN

INDIA

BANGLADESH

MYANMAR
(BURMA)
LAOS

TAIWAN

MAURITANIA

MALI

NIGER

CHAD

NORTH
SUDAN

ERITREA
YEMEN

THAILAND
VIETNAM
CAMBODIA
PHILIPPINES

SENEGAL
GAMBIA
GUINEA-BISSAU
BURKINA
FASO
NIGERIA
DJIBOUTI
SOMALIA

GUINEA
SIERRA LEONE
IVORY
COAST
GHANA
TOGO
BENIN
CENTRAL
AFRICAN REPUBLIC
SOUTH
SUDAN
ETHIOPIA
LIBERIA

SRI
LANKA

BRUNEI
MALAYSIA
SINGAPORE

EQUATORIAL
GUINEA
GABON
CONGO
REPUBLIC
CONGO
DEMOCRATIC
REPUBLIC
(ZAIRE)
CAMEROON
UGANDA
KENYA
RWANDA
BURUNDI
TANZANIA

INDIAN
OCEAN

INDONESIA
PAPUA
NEW
GUINEA
SOLOMON
ISLANDS

ANGOLA
ZAMBIA
MALAWI
MOZAMBIQUE

SOUTH
ATLANTIC
OCEAN

NAMIBIA
ZIMBABWE
BOTSWANA
MADAGASCAR
MAURITIUS
RÉUNION

VANUATU
FIJI

AUSTRALIA

SWAZILAND
SOUTH
AFRICA
LESOTHO

NEW
CALEDONIA

NEW
ZEALAND

Average annual GDP growth
rate, 2000-2009 (%)

negative
less than -2.5

-2.5 to 0

no data available

positive
0 to 1

1 to 2

2 to 3

3 to 4

4 to 5

over 5

EXHIBIT 2.8

Number of People (in Billions) Living in Poverty

Source: World Bank, *World Development Indicators* (Washington, DC: World Bank, 2011).

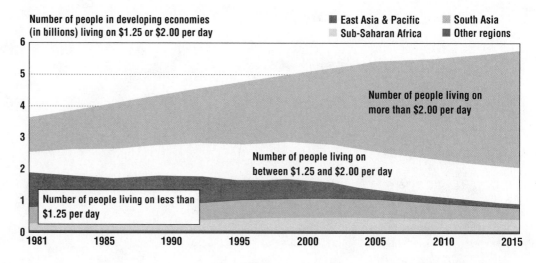

and General Motors have gradually improved their environmental standards. Benetton in Italy (clothing), Alcan in Canada (aluminum), and Kirin in Japan (beverages) are examples of firms that embrace practices that protect the environment, often at the expense of profits.[37] The Conservation Coffee Alliance, a consortium of companies, has committed approximately $2 million to environmentally friendly coffee cultivation in Central America, Peru, and Colombia.

Effect on National Culture

Globalization exerts strong pressures on national culture. Market liberalization opens the door to foreign companies, global brands, unfamiliar products, and new values. Consumers increasingly wear similar clothing, drive similar cars, watch the same movies, and listen to the same recording stars. Advertising leads to the emergence of societal values modeled on Western countries, especially the United States. Hollywood dominates the global entertainment industry. In this way, globalization can alter people's norms, values, and behaviors, which may tend to homogenize over time.

Critics call these trends the "McDonaldization" or the "Coca-Colonization" of the world. To combat such trends, some governments try to block cultural imperialism and prevent the erosion of local traditions. In Canada, France, and Germany, the public sector attempts to prevent U.S. ideals from diluting local traditions. Hollywood, McDonald's, and Disneyland are seen as Trojan horses that permanently alter food preferences, lifestyles, and other aspects of traditional life. For better or worse, however, such trends are probably inevitable in a globalizing world.

Information and communications technologies speed the homogenization of world cultures. People worldwide are exposed to movies, television, the Internet, and other information sources that promote lifestyles of people in the United States and other advanced economies. Appetites grow for Western products and services, which are seen to signal higher living standards. For example, despite low per-capita income, many Chinese buy consumer electronics such as cell phones and TV sets. Global media have a pervasive effect on local culture, gradually shifting it toward a universal norm.

The flow of cultural influence often goes both ways. Cafe Spice (http://www.cafespice .com) is an Indian food company whose founder hails from Mumbai. The firm is transforming American tastes by selling curry dishes and other Indian favorites in cafeterias and supermarkets. Cafe Spice is making Indian cuisine mainstream in the United States.[38] As the influence of the Chinese economy grows over time, Western countries will likely adopt some of China's cultural norms, too. Chinese restaurants and some Chinese traditions are already a way of life in much of the world. Similar influences can be seen from Latin America and other areas in the developing world.

While a degree of cultural imperialism may be at work, it is offset by the countertrend of local nationalism. Although some tangibles are becoming more universal, people's behaviors and mind-sets remain relatively stable over time. Religious differences are as strong as ever. Language differences are steadfast across national borders. As globalization standardizes superficial aspects of life across national cultures, people resist these forces by insisting on their national identity and taking steps to protect it. This is evident, for example, in Belgium, Canada, and France, where laws were passed to protect national language and culture.

Globalization and Africa

Africa is home to the poorest countries. The majority of its 1 billion people live on less than $2 a day. It is the area least integrated into the world economy and accounts for less than 3 percent of world trade. Although it has abundant natural resources, Africa remains underdeveloped due to such factors as inadequate commercial infrastructure, lack of access to foreign capital, high illiteracy, government corruption, wars, and the spread of AIDS.

Experience of the past half-century suggests that traditional methods of trying to help Africa— mainly foreign aid provided by advanced economies—have achieved little success. Despite billions of dollars of aid to Africa, per-capita income has not increased significantly.[39]

In recent years, experts have suggested that the most effective way to alleviate African poverty is to employ business-based models.[40] After decades of stagnation, several sub-Saharan African countries have experienced significant economic growth thanks to increasing international trade in commodities. For example, Africa is a major supplier of petroleum to Europe and the United States. Angola is among the top oil suppliers to China. There is a ripple effect to economic development. As certain sectors in Africa have boomed in recent years, foreign banks, retailers, and MNEs have set up operations in the continent. In formerly war-torn Rwanda, countless business opportunities have emerged in sectors as diverse as mining, tourism, telecommunications, and real estate. China and India are beating out U.S. firms and quickly increasing their business dealings in Africa. Chinese companies are investing billions of dollars in the continent. International trade and investment are helping to address many of Africa's most pressing development needs.[41] It will take many more years before Africa achieves a critical mass of infrastructure and business culture sufficient to substantially raise average incomes across the continent.

Firm-Level Consequences of Market Globalization: Internationalization of the Firm's Value Chain

The globalization of markets has opened up countless new business opportunities for internationalizing firms. As illustrated in Exhibit 2.9, globalization also means that firms face intense rivalry from foreign competitors. This exhibit shows that in 1989 General Motors, Ford, and Chrysler together held nearly three-quarters of the market share in light vehicle sales in the United States. By 2012, the percentage had fallen to 46 percent, as the market shares of competitors such as Toyota, Hyundai, and others rose dramatically. Indeed, Toyota is number one in some vehicle categories in the United States.

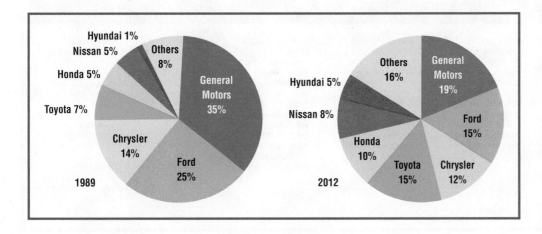

EXHIBIT 2.9

Market Shares of Automakers in Light-Vehicle Sales in the United States, 1989 and 2012

Sources: Based on Craig Trudell, "U.S. Automakers Seen Losing Market Share Amid 2012 Growth: Cars," *Bloomberg BusinessWeek*, February 8, 2012, retrieved from www.businessweek.com; J. Muller, "Automakers Gold Rush," *Forbes*, June 8, 2009, pp. 70–77; *Wall Street Journal*, "Sales and Share of Total Market by Manufacturer," September 4, 2012, retrieved from www.wsu.com.

Globalization results in more demanding buyers who shop for the best deals worldwide. A purely domestic focus is no longer viable for firms in most industries. Managers should replace parochial attitudes with a more cosmopolitan orientation. Internationalization may take the form of global sourcing, exporting, or investment in key markets abroad. Proactive firms seek a simultaneous presence in major trading regions, especially Asia, Europe, and North America.

The most direct implication of market globalization is on the firm's value chain. Market globalization compels firms to organize their sourcing, manufacturing, marketing, and other value-adding activities on a global scale. In a typical value chain, the firm conducts research and product development (R&D), purchases production inputs, and assembles or manufactures a product or service. Next, the firm performs marketing activities such as pricing, promotion, and selling, followed by distribution of the product in targeted markets and after-sales service. The value-chain concept is useful in international business because it helps clarify what activities are performed *where* in the world. For example, exporting firms perform most "upstream" value-chain activities (R&D and production) in the home market and most "downstream" activities (marketing and after-sales service) abroad.

Each value-adding activity in the firm's value chain is subject to internationalization; that is, it can be performed abroad instead of at home. Exhibit 2.10 portrays a value chain in a typical international firm. As examples in the exhibit suggest, companies have considerable latitude regarding where in the world they locate or configure key value-adding activities. The most typical reasons for locating value-chain activities in particular countries are to reduce the costs of R&D and production or to gain closer access to customers. Through offshoring, the firm relocates a major value-chain activity by establishing a factory or other subsidiary abroad. A related trend is global outsourcing, in which the firm delegates performance of a value-adding activity to an external supplier or contractor located abroad. We discuss these trends in greater detail in Chapter 17.

In the same month that German carmaker BMW launched a new factory in South Carolina, an aging textile plant a few miles away, Jackson Mills, closed its doors and shed thousands of workers. Globalization created a new reality for both these firms. By establishing operations in the United States, BMW found it could manufacture cars cost-effectively while more readily accessing the huge U.S. market. In the process, BMW created thousands of high-paying, better-quality jobs for U.S. workers. Simultaneously, Jackson Mills had discovered it could source textiles of comparable quality more cost-effectively from suppliers in Asia. Globalization drove these firms to relocate key value-adding activities to the most advantageous locations around the world.

EXHIBIT 2.10

Examples of How Firms' Value-Chain Activities Can Be Internationalized

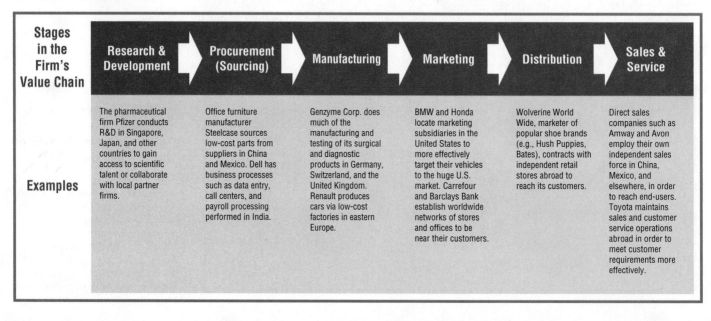

CLOSING CASE   Debating the Merits of Globalization

Recently, a university sponsored a roundtable on the broader implications of international business. The participants were an anti-international business activist, a business executive with extensive international dealings, and a government trade official. Excerpts from the exchange present the diverse perspectives of market globalization held by different interest groups.

Activist

"One problem with international business is that it often ignores human rights and basic labor standards. Low-wage factories abroad create substandard working conditions. The activities of multinational companies not only result in job losses here at home, but also in low wages and exploited workers around the world. Just think of the sweatshops in Asia that make imported clothing. Think of the autoworkers in Mexico who live in horrible conditions and make only a few dollars a day. Also consider the poverty caused worldwide by the recent global financial and economic crisis."

Business Executive

"Our country needs to participate in the global economy. Companies that export provide better-paying jobs, have more profits, pay higher taxes, and stimulate purchases from local suppliers. Foreign companies that invest here create new jobs, enhance local living standards, and pressure our firms to stay competitive in a challenging global marketplace. Exporters pay higher wages and provide better benefits than nonexporting firms. Many companies need access to foreign markets because of the huge, upfront research and development costs they accumulate. One more pill is cheap; it's the cost of research to find a cure for AIDS that is prohibitive. I think it's a pretty strong argument for the human basis of doing international business. Companies need big markets to amortize the costs of big projects. Africa is getting decimated by AIDS. But pharmaceutical firms can't do the necessary R&D unless they can amortize those costs over a huge, global marketplace. In the long run, uninterrupted international commerce is good."

Trade Official

"The current administration believes in the value of free trade. The government strongly supported NAFTA, and this has already had a positive effect on the economy through increasing exports to Mexico, creating jobs, and leading to improved investment opportunities. Countries are forging ahead with international trade ties. Canada has completed a free trade agreement with Chile. Economic ties lead to cultural ties and more peaceful relations. Also, it is hard for our government to promote freedom and democracy around the world if we are not promoting free trade."

Activist

"We cannot overlook the detrimental effects of globalization on the natural environment. The more we trade internationally, the more irreparable harm will be done to the environment. International business means more environmentally damaging development. Companies internationalize so they can become more efficient. But if countries have weak environmental standards, then factories will be built with minimal environmental standards."

Business Executive

"If we trade internationally, then living standards will increase everywhere. As living standards rise, awareness of and care for the environment will also increase. International business is good for the world because it creates wealth. The more affluent the people, the more they will care about their environment and pass laws to protect it. We are also becoming more responsive to concerns over social responsibility and environmental degradation. We have shown that a good economy and a clean environment are not mutually exclusive. We can have it both ways: a clean planet and a better economic quality of life."

Trade Official

"I think part of the solution is to negotiate trade agreements that take environmental factors into account. International trade that runs roughshod over legitimate environmental concerns is counterproductive and defeats the political agendas of most governments around the world. It is clear that international trade must take environmental concerns into account."

Activist

"International trade interferes with the sovereignty of national governments. When General Motors is the nation's biggest company, like it is in Canada, it is harder for governments to manage policies regarding taxes, monetary policy, social issues, and exchange rates. And who are we, trying to impose our own cultural standards on the world? When I travel in Asia or Latin America, I see McDonald's all over the place. They see Western powers exploiting globalization, harming the economic, cultural, and environmental interests of the rest of the world.

"Global corporations claim they spread modern technologies around the world. But technology is good only if you have access to it. In most of Africa, you have no on-ramp to the Internet. You need access to a computer, which is awfully difficult or impossible in countries where people make only a few dollars a day. When you're paid such a low wage, how can you afford technology? How can you afford to see a doctor? Globalization is widening the gap between rich and poor. As inequality grows, people have less and less in common. Multinational companies exploit poor countries and expose their people to harmful competition. Infant industries in developing economies can't make it when they're confronted with the power of giant multinational firms."

Business Executive

"Companies increasingly recognize the importance of being good global citizens. Motorola has profited from its business in China, but it also contributes to developing educational systems in that country. There are a lot more literate people, especially literate women, in China than ever before. Japanese MNEs invest in the communities where they do business. Companies are not all evil; they do a lot of good for the world, too. Bill Gates is going to do more than any government to get people computers and get them hooked up on the Internet. He has created the world's biggest fund to combat diseases of the poor. He and Warren Buffett are tackling many of these diseases. GlaxoSmithKline is working with the World Health Organization to find a cure for Elephantiasis, a terrible disease that ravages people in Africa."

Trade Official

"Globalization is complex and it's hard to tease out what is bad and what is good. Globalization has made rapid progress; global poverty has declined. Social indicators for many poor countries show improvement over several decades. It's true that income disparities have increased dramatically over the last 50 years while international trade has integrated the world economy. The world has experienced a generally rising tide in terms of people's standard of living. People everywhere are better off than they were 50 years ago. There are some exceptions to this, especially during recessions, but it's better to live in a world where 20 percent of the people are affluent and 80 percent are poor, than a world in which nearly 100 percent of the people are poor, as was the case throughout most of history. There is a strong role for government in all this. Countries benefit from trade, but governments are responsible for protecting citizens from the negative or unintended consequences that trade may bring."

Activist

"Governments have not done enough to regulate the excesses of capitalism. We saw this clearly in the global financial and economic crises, from which the world is still recovering."

AACSB: Reflective Thinking Skills, Ethical Understanding and Reasoning Abilities

Case Questions

1. Do you think globalization and MNE activity are creating problems for the world? What kinds of problems can you identify? What are the unintended consequences of international business?

2. Summarize the arguments in favor of globalization made by the business executive. What is the role of technology in supporting company performance in a globalizing business environment?

3. What are the roles of state and federal governments in dealing with globalization? What is government's role in protecting citizens from the potential negative effects of foreign MNEs conducting business in your country? What kinds of government actions would you recommend?

4. What is the role of education in: (i) addressing the problems raised in the roundtable; (ii) creating societies in which people can deal effectively with public policy issues; and (iii) creating citizens who can compete effectively in the global marketplace?

Sources: Uri Dadush and William Shaw, *Juggernaut: How Emerging Powers Are Reshaping Globalization* (Washington, DC: Carnegie Endowment for International Peace, 2010); Luke Martell, *The Sociology of Globalization* (Malden, MA: Polity Press, 2010); OECD, statistics on globalization, retrieved from http://www.stats.oecd.org; S. Sethi, "Globalization and the Good Corporation," *Journal of Business Ethics* 87 (April 2009): 1–2; "The Globalization Website," retrieved from Emory University Globalization Web site, http://www.sociology.emory.edu/globalization/index.html; Matthew Sparke, *Introducing Globalization: Ties, Tensions, and Integration in a Divided World* (Hoboken, NJ: Wiley-Blackwell, 2012).

CHAPTER ESSENTIALS

MyManagementLab

Go to **mymanagementlab.com** to complete the problems marked with this icon ⭐.

Key Terms

contagion 40	value chain 32
globalization of markets 28	World Trade Organization (WTO) 30

Summary

In this chapter, you learned about:

1. Why globalization is not new

Globalization of markets refers to the gradual integration and growing interdependence of national economies. Early civilizations in the Mediterranean, Middle East, Asia, Africa, and Europe all contributed to the growth of cross-border trade. International trade was triggered by world events and technological discoveries. Globalization has progressed in phases, particularly since the early 1800s. The current phase was stimulated particularly by the rise of IT, the Internet, and other advanced technologies. The **World Trade Organization** is a multilateral governing body empowered to regulate international trade and investment.

2. Market globalization: An organizing framework

Market globalization can be modeled in terms of its drivers, dimensions, societal consequences, and firm-level consequences. As market globalization intensifies, firms are compelled to respond to challenges and exploit new advantages. Many firms proactively pursue internationalization as a strategic move. They become more aggressive at identifying foreign market opportunities, seeking partnerships with foreign firms, and building organizational capabilities to enhance their competitive advantage.

3. Dimensions of market globalization

Market globalization refers to the growing integration of the world economy from the international business activities of countless firms. It represents a growing global interconnectedness of buyers, producers, suppliers, and governments. Globalization has fostered a new dynamism in the world economy, the emergence of regional economic integration blocs, growth of global investment and financial flows, the convergence of buyer lifestyles and needs, and the globalization of both production and services. At the business enterprise level, market globalization amounts to reconfiguration of company **value chains**—the sequence of value-adding activities including sourcing, manufacturing, marketing, and distribution—on a global scale.

4. Drivers of market globalization

Market globalization is driven by several factors, including falling trade and investment barriers; market liberalization and adoption of free market economics in formerly closed economies; industrialization and economic development, especially among emerging markets; integration of world financial markets; and technological advances.

5. Technological advances

Advances in technology are particularly important in driving market globalization. The most important advances in technology have occurred in information technology, communications, the Internet, manufacturing, and transportation. These systems help create an interconnected network of customers, suppliers, and intermediaries worldwide. They have made the cost of international business affordable for all types of firms.

6. Societal consequences of market globalization

There is much debate about globalization's benefits and harm. Globalization was a major factor in the recent global recession and financial crisis. Critics complain that globalization interferes with national sovereignty, the ability of a state to govern itself without external intervention. Globalization is associated with *offshoring*, the relocation of value-chain activities to foreign locations where they can be performed at less cost by subsidiaries or independent suppliers. Globalization tends to decrease poverty, but it may also widen the gap between the rich and the poor. Unrestricted industrialization may harm the natural environment. Globalization is also associated with the loss of cultural values unique to each nation. Trade and investment can help address many of Africa's development needs.

7. Firm-level consequences of market globalization: Internationalization of the firm's value chain

Market globalization compels firms to organize their sourcing, manufacturing, marketing, and other value-adding activities on a global scale. Each value-adding activity can be performed in the home country or abroad. Firms choose where in the world they locate or configure key value-adding activities. Firms internationalize value-chain activities to reduce the costs of R&D and production, or to gain closer access to customers.

Test Your Comprehension

1. Define market globalization. What are the underlying dimensions of this megatrend?

2. Is globalization a recent phenomenon? Describe the phases of globalization.

3. Summarize the six dimensions of globalization. Which of these do you think is the most visible manifestation of globalization?

4. Describe the five drivers of globalization.

5. What is the role of the World Trade Organization?

⭐ **6.** What effect does globalization have on national sovereignty, employment, the poor, the natural environment, and national culture?

⭐ **7.** What are the implications of globalization for company internationalization?

Apply Your Understanding AACSB: Communication Abilities, Reflective Thinking Skills, Ethical Understanding and Reasoning Abilities, Use of Information Technology, Analytic Skills

1. Imagine you are studying for your international business class at a local coffee shop. The manager notices your textbook and remarks, "I don't get all that foreign business stuff. I don't pay much attention to it. I'm a local guy running a small business. Thank goodness I don't have to worry about any of that." The manager's comments make you realize there is much more to business than just local concerns. What is the likely value chain of a coffee shop? For example, how did the varieties of coffee beans get there? What is the likely effect of market globalization on coffee shops? Do technological advances play any role in the shop's value chain? Does globalization imply any negative consequences for the worldwide coffee industry? Justify your answer.

2. Globalization provides numerous advantages to businesses and consumers around the world. At the same time, some critics believe globalization is harming various aspects of

life and commerce. In what ways is globalization good for firms and consumers? In what ways is globalization harmful to firms and consumers?

3. *Ethical Dilemma:* Northern Energy, Inc. (Northern) is a large oil company with production and marketing operations worldwide. You are a recently hired manager at Northern's subsidiary in Nigeria, which provides jobs to hundreds of Nigerians and supports many local merchants and suppliers. Suppose Northern's drilling and refining practices have severely damaged the natural environment in Nigeria, polluting the air, land, and water. As a result, Northern has faced violent protests and much negative publicity in Nigeria. Develop suggestions on how Northern should address these issues. Keep in mind that top management is reluctant to invest significant new resources in Nigeria, given the firm's weakening business performance there.

 globalEDGE INTERNET EXERCISES
(http://www.globalEDGE.msu.edu)

AACSB: Reflective Thinking Skills, Ethical Understanding and Reasoning Abilities, Use of Information Technology, Analytic Skills

Refer to Chapter 1, page 24, for instructions on how to access and use globalEDGE™.

1. The KOF Swiss Economic Institute prepares the annual *KOF Index of Globalization*, which ranks the most globalized countries (enter "KOF Index of Globalization" at globalEDGE™ or other search engine). The index uses three different dimensions to measure globalization: *economic globalization*, *political globalization*, and *social globalization*. Visit the index and explain what each dimension represents, and why each is important for a nation to achieve a substantial presence in the global economy.

2. Service-sector jobs are increasingly outsourced to lower-cost locations abroad. The globalEDGE™ Web site has various resources that detail the nature and location of jobs that have been transferred abroad. Some experts believe the resulting foreign investment and increased demand in lower-cost countries will cause wages to rise in those countries, eliminating cost advantages from offshoring and narrowing the income gap between developed economies and low-cost countries. In other words, offshoring will help to reduce global poverty. Others believe that manufacturing jobs will be consistently moved to low-cost countries, making China and India the world's center of innovation and production. What do you think? Find three articles on outsourcing at globalEDGE™ by doing a search using the keywords "global outsourcing" or "offshoring," and write a report on the most likely

consequences of these trends for your country, its workers, and consumers.

3. A key characteristic of globalization is the increasingly integrated world economy. MNEs and many nations have a vested interest in maintaining the globalization trend. If the trend were somehow reversed, participants in international business, such as exporters, would likely suffer big economic losses. In many ways, globalization's role in the world economy is critical. But just how big is the global economy? What is the extent of international trade relative to the size of the global economy? What is the proportion of international trade in the GDPs of each of the following countries: Australia, Canada, Sweden, United Kingdom, and the United States? Consult globalEDGE™ to address these questions.

4. Globalization refers to the reduction barriers to trade and investment, which is facilitating the internationalization of countless firms. Globalization is quickening and affecting firms around the world. Globalization is associated with various issues and challenges that confront firms as they undertake international business. Among the major issues are the condition of the global economy; indebtedness of national governments; power shifts to emerging markets; and country risk in the developing economies. Visit globalEDGE™ and enter the key word "globalization." Explore the information and Web sites that emerge from your search. Write a report on the most important contemporary issues that firms are facing as they undertake international business.

MyManagementLab

Go to **mymanagementlab.com** for Auto-graded writing questions as well as the following Assisted-graded writing questions:

2-1. In what areas have technological advances had their greatest effect on facilitating world trade and investment?

2-2. What are the pros and cons of globalization?

2-3. Mymanagementlab Only – comprehensive writing assignment for this chapter.

The Emergence of Born Global Firms

Geo Search Ltd. is a Japanese company that develops high-technology equipment to help engineers survey ground surfaces for cavities and build safe roads, airports, and underground utility lines. At the request of the United Nations, Geo Search (www.geosearch.co.jp) designed the world's first land-mine detector, called Mine Eye. The firm had an immediate international market because there are millions of mines buried in countries like Afghanistan, Cambodia, and Libya. The firm works with nongovernmental organizations (NGOs) to search for mines worldwide. Removing land mines is risky, particularly plastic mines that cannot be found with metal detectors. Geo Search's electromagnetic radar can distinguish between mines and other objects buried underground. Images appear in three dimensions on a liquid crystal display, and there is no need to touch the ground surface.

Geo Search is one of an increasing number of small and medium-sized enterprises (SMEs) active in international business. SMEs make up the majority of all firms in a typical country and often account for more than 50 percent of national economic activity. Compared to large multinational

CHAPTER 3

Organizational Participants That Make International Business Happen

 LEARNING OBJECTIVES *In this chapter, you will learn about the following:*

1. Four types of participants in international business
2. Participants arranged by value-chain activity
3. Focal firms in international business
4. International entry strategies of focal firms
5. Distribution channel intermediaries in international business
6. Facilitators in international business
7. Governments in international business

MyManagementLab®

⭐ **Improve Your Grade!**

Over 10 million students improved their results using the Pearson MyLabs. Visit **mymanagementlab.com** for simulations, tutorials, and end-of-chapter problems.

---

enterprises (MNEs), historically the most common types of international firms, the typical SME has far fewer financial and human resources. In the past, international business was often beyond their reach. But globalization and technological advances have made venturing abroad much less expensive, creating a commercial environment in which many more small firms do international business than ever before. In the past two decades, companies that internationalize at or near their founding, *born global firms*, have been springing up all over the world.

Management in born global firms targets products and services to a dozen or more countries within a few years after launching the firm. By internationalizing as early and rapidly as they do, these firms develop a borderless corporate culture. Despite the limited resources that characterize young firms, their agility and flexibility help them serve both foreign and domestic customers well.

Born globals internationalize early for various reasons. Some specialize in a product category for which demand in the home market is too small. Management may perceive big demand for the firm's products abroad or have a strong international orientation. Neogen Corporation (www.neogen.com) is a U.S. born global that makes chemicals to kill harmful bacteria and toxins in food crops. Because certain toxins are more common abroad, Neogen was able to internationalize shortly after its founding.

The widespread emergence of born globals shows that any firm, regardless of its size, age, or resource base, can participate actively in international business. Today, born globals and other SME exporters make up a sizable proportion of internationally active firms.

SOURCES: S. Tamer Cavusgil and Gary Knight, *Born Global Firms: The New International Enterprise* (New York: Business Expert Press, 2009); Terence Fan and Phillip Phan, "International New Ventures: Revisiting the Influences Behind The 'Born-Global' Firm," *Journal of International Business Studies* 38, no. 7 (2007): 1113–1132; Daekwan Kim, Choton Basu, GM Naidu, and Erin Cavusgil, "The Innovativeness of Born-Globals and Customer Orientation: Learning from Indian Born-Globals," *Journal of Business Research* 64, no. 8 (2011): 879–886; G. Knight and S. T. Cavusgil, "Innovation, Organizational Capabilities, and the Born-Global Firm," *Journal of International Business Studies* 35, no. 2 (2004): 124–141; B. Oviatt and P. McDougall, "Toward a Theory of International New Ventures," *Journal of International Business Studies* 25, no. 1 (1994): 45–64.

Geo Search in the chapter opener illustrates the evolution of international business—more and more organizations are active in commerce around the world. Despite being a small, young firm, Geo Search found a ready market for its products well beyond its home country. Once the domain of large multinational firms, today, SMEs also benefit from active participation in global commerce. Global business is undertaken by a wide range of people and organizations, including manufacturers, suppliers, distributors, consultants, and financial institutions, as well as governments and international agencies.

In this chapter, we discuss the people and organizations that make globalization happen and their role in company value chains. We describe how major participants fit in the value chains of international firms. We also summarize the entry strategies common to global business. We begin by describing the major categories of organizations that participate in international business today.

Focal firm
The initiator of an international business transaction, which conceives, designs, and produces offerings intended for consumption by customers worldwide. Focal firms are primarily MNEs and SMEs.

Distribution channel intermediary
A specialist firm that provides various logistics and marketing services for focal firms as part of international supply chains, both in the home country and abroad.

Facilitator
A firm or an individual with special expertise in banking, legal advice, customs clearance, or related support services that assists focal firms in the performance of international business transactions.

 ## Four Types of Participants in International Business

International business requires numerous organizations, with varying motives, to work together as a coordinated team, contributing different types of expertise and inputs.

There are four major categories of participants:

1. A **focal firm** is the initiator of an international business transaction. It conceives, designs, and produces offerings intended for consumption by customers worldwide. Focal firms take center stage in international business. They are primarily large multinational enterprises (MNEs; also known as multinational corporations or MNCs) and small and medium-sized enterprises (SMEs). Some are privately owned companies, others are public, stock-held firms, and still others are state enterprises owned by governments. Some focal firms are manufacturing businesses, while others are in the service sector.

2. A **distribution channel intermediary** is a specialist firm that provides various logistics and marketing services for focal firms as part of international supply chains, both in the focal firm's home country and abroad. Typical intermediaries include independent distributors and sales representatives, usually located in foreign markets where they provide distribution and marketing services to focal firms on a contractual basis.

3. A **facilitator** is a firm or an individual with special expertise in banking, legal advice, customs clearance, or related support services that helps focal firms perform international business transactions. Facilitators include logistics service providers, freight forwarders, banks,

and other support firms that assist focal firms in performing specific functions. A **freight forwarder** is a specialized logistics service provider that arranges international shipping on behalf of exporting firms, much like a travel agent for cargo. Facilitators are found in both the home country and abroad.

4. *Governments* or the public sector are also active in international business as suppliers, buyers, and regulators. State-owned enterprises account for a substantial portion of economic value added in many countries, even rapidly liberalizing emerging markets such as Russia, China, and Brazil. Governments in advanced economies like France, Australia, and Sweden have significant ownership of companies in telecommunications, banking, and natural resources. The recent global financial crisis led governments to step up their involvement in business, especially as regulators.

Freight forwarder
A specialized logistics service provider that arranges international shipping on behalf of exporting firms.

The activities of firms, intermediaries, and facilitators in international business overlap to some degree. The focal firm performs certain activities internally and delegates other functions to intermediaries and facilitators when their special expertise is needed. In other words, the focal firm becomes a client of intermediaries and facilitators who provide services on a contractual basis.

While focal firms, intermediaries, and facilitators represent the supply side of international business transactions, customers or buyers make up the demand side. Customers consist of:

- Individual *consumers and households*,
- *Retailers*—businesses that purchase finished goods for the purpose of resale, and
- *Organizational buyers*—businesses, institutions, and governments that purchase goods and services as inputs to a production process, or as supplies needed to run a business or organization. Governments and nonprofit organizations such as CARE (www.care.org) and UNICEF (www.unicef.org) also often constitute important customers around the world.

 ## Participants Arranged by Value-Chain Activity

It is useful to think of the four categories of participants in terms of the firm's value chain. Focal firms, intermediaries, and facilitators in particular all are engaged in one or more critical value-adding activities such as procurement, manufacturing, marketing, transportation, distribution, and support—configured across several countries. The value chain is thus the complete business system of the focal firm, comprising all the activities that the focal firm performs.

In international business, the focal firm may retain core activities such as production and marketing within its own organization and delegate distribution and customer service responsibilities to independent contractors, such as foreign-based distributors. In this way, the resulting business system is subject to internationalization. Individual value-adding activities can be configured in multiple countries. Exhibit 3.1 shows the stages in the value chain where channel intermediaries and facilitators usually operate. It also identifies typical intermediaries and facilitators critical to the functioning of international business transactions.

In exporting firms, much of the value chain is concentrated within one nation—the home country. In highly international firms, management may perform a variety of value-chain activities—production, marketing, distribution—within several countries. Such firms configure their value chains in numerous countries and may source from multiple foreign suppliers. MNEs strive to rationalize each of their value chains by locating each activity in a country with the most favorable combination of cost, quality, logistical considerations, and other criteria.

As an example, Exhibit 3.2 shows the national and geographic diversity of typical suppliers that provide content for the Apple iPhone. Apple sources components for the iPhone from several dozen primary suppliers. The suppliers are headquartered in Germany, Japan, and numerous other countries, in addition to the United States. The suppliers usually manufacture the components in low-cost countries, and then ship them to iPhone factories, such as those owned by Foxconn in China. As you can see, manufacturing products such as cell phones involves a truly international value chain.

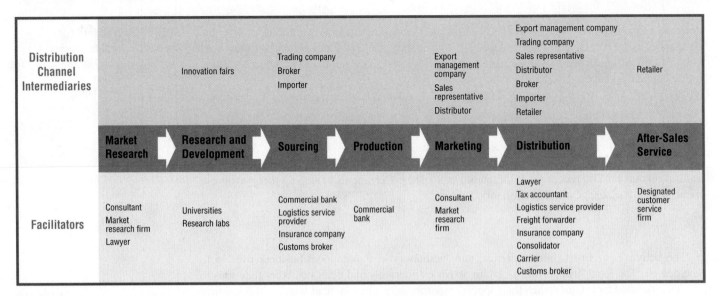

Distribution Channel Intermediaries		Innovation fairs		Trading company Broker Importer				Export management company Sales representative Distributor		Export management company Trading company Sales representative Distributor Broker Importer Retailer		Retailer

Market Research	→	Research and Development	→	Sourcing	→	Production	→	Marketing	→	Distribution	→	After-Sales Service

Facilitators		Consultant Market research firm Lawyer		Universities Research labs		Commercial bank Logistics service provider Insurance company Customs broker		Commercial bank		Consultant Market research firm		Lawyer Tax accountant Logistics service provider Freight forwarder Insurance company Consolidator Carrier Customs broker		Designated customer service firm

EXHIBIT 3.1

Typical Positions of Intermediaries and Facilitators in the International Value Chain

EXHIBIT 3.2

Typical Suppliers of Components for the Apple iPhone

Sources: Based on Gregg Keizer, "iPhone 4 Parts Cost Apple Just $171," *Computerworld*, June 28, 2010, accessed at www.computerworld.com; Arik Hesseldahl, "Apple IPhone 4 Parts Cost About $188," *Bloomberg Businessweek*, June 28, 2010, accessed at www.businessweek.com; Arik Hesseldahl, "Apple's iPhone 3GS: What It Costs to Make," *Bloomberg Businessweek*, June 23, 2009, accessed at www.businessweek.com; *The Times of India*, "Look Who Makes A5 Chip for Apple iPhone 4S, iPad2," December 16, 2011, accessed at timesofindia.indiatimes.com.

Illustrating the International Value Chain Using Dell Inc.

Depending on the number of products offered and the complexity of operations, companies may develop and manage numerous value chains. Dell makes a variety of products, each with its own value chain. Exhibit 3.3 illustrates the value chain for the production and marketing of Dell notebook computers. Let's take the example of Tom, a Dell customer who placed an order for a notebook. Such orders can be placed online at www.Dell.com or by telephone with a Dell sales representative. After Tom placed his order, the representative entered the specifications into Dell's order management system; verified his credit card through Dell's workflow

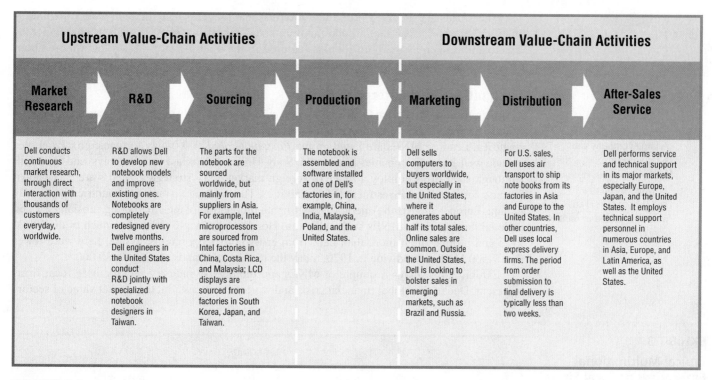

Upstream Value-Chain Activities				Downstream Value-Chain Activities			
Market Research	**R&D**	**Sourcing**	**Production**	**Marketing**	**Distribution**	**After-Sales Service**	
Dell conducts continuous market research, through direct interaction with thousands of customers everyday, worldwide.	R&D allows Dell to develop new notebook models and improve existing ones. Notebooks are completely redesigned every twelve months. Dell engineers in the United States conduct R&D jointly with specialized notebook designers in Taiwan.	The parts for the notebook are sourced worldwide, but mainly from suppliers in Asia. For example, Intel microprocessors are sourced from Intel factories in China, Costa Rica, and Malaysia; LCD displays are sourced from factories in South Korea, Japan, and Taiwan.	The notebook is assembled and software installed at one of Dell's factories in, for example, China, India, Malaysia, Poland, and the United States.	Dell sells computers to buyers worldwide, but especially in the United States, where it generates about half its total sales. Online sales are common. Outside the United States, Dell is looking to bolster sales in emerging markets, such as Brazil and Russia.	For U.S. sales, Dell uses air transport to ship note books from its factories in Asia and Europe to the United States. In other countries, Dell uses local express delivery firms. The period from order submission to final delivery is typically less than two weeks.	Dell performs service and technical support in its major markets, especially Europe, Japan, and the United States. It employs technical support personnel in numerous countries in Asia, Europe, and Latin America, as well as the United States.	

EXHIBIT 3.3

Dell's International Value Chain

Sources: Based on Annual Report 2011, Dell, www.dell.com; Thomas Friedman, *The World Is Flat* (New York: Farrar, Straus, & Giroux, 2005); D. Hofman, K. O'Marah, and C. Elvy, *The Gartner Supply Chain Top 25 for 2011* (Gartner, Inc., June 1, 2011), accessed at www.gartner.com.

connection with Visa, a global financial services facilitator; and released the order into Dell's production system. Tom's order was processed at the Dell notebook factory in Malaysia, where employees access the parts that comprise the 30 key components of Dell notebooks from nearby suppliers. The total supply chain for Tom's computer, including multiple tiers of suppliers, encompasses about 400 companies, primarily in Asia, but also in Europe and the Americas.

On a typical day, Dell processes orders for more than 120,000 computers, which are sold and distributed to customers worldwide. Although Dell is based in Texas, non-U.S. orders account for roughly half its total sales (about $61 billion in 2011). As growth in U.S. sales flattens over time, the proportion of non-U.S. sales will grow. Shipping is handled via air transport. For example, from the Dell Malaysia factory to the United States, Dell might charter a China Airlines 747 that makes the flight six days a week. Each jet carries 25,000 Dell notebooks that together weigh more than 100,000 kilograms, or 220,000 pounds. A hallmark of Dell's value chain is collaboration. Founder Michael Dell and senior managers constantly work with their suppliers to make process improvements in Dell's value chain.

 Focal Firms in International Business

Imagine a typical theatrical production. There are script writers, stage managers, lighting technicians, musicians, set directors, business managers, and publicity staff, in addition to performing actors. Each participant contributes in different ways, and much coordination among them is required. Advance planning, preparation, timeliness, and synchronization are critical to ultimate success. In the same way, international business transactions require the participation of many specialist organizations, exact timing, and precision.

Source: MANAN VATSYAYANA/AFP/Getty Images/Newscom

Coca-Cola derives about 80 percent of its revenues outside the United States. U.S. market importance has declined due to changing consumer preferences that favor healthier options like water and juices. Pictured is company CEO Muhtar Kent.

Focal firms are the most prominent international players. They include well-known multinational enterprises and small and medium-sized exporting firms, as well as contemporary organizations such as the born globals featured in the opening story. Let's learn more about each of these key actors in international business.

The Multinational Enterprise (MNE)

Multinational enterprise (MNE)
A large company with substantial resources that performs various business activities through a network of subsidiaries and affiliates located in multiple countries.

A **multinational enterprise (MNE)** is a large company with substantial resources that performs various business activities through a network of subsidiaries and affiliates located in multiple countries. Leading MNEs are listed on the *Fortune Global 500* (www.fortune.com). Examples include well-known companies like Nestlé, Sony, Unilever, Nokia, Ford, Barclays, and Shell Oil. Although such firms employ a range of foreign market entry strategies, MNEs are best known for their foreign direct investment (FDI) activities. They operate in multiple countries, especially in Asia, Europe, and North America, by setting up production plants, marketing subsidiaries, and regional headquarters. MNEs such as Exxon, Honda, and Coca-Cola derive much of their total sales and profits, often more than half, from cross-border operations. While there were fewer than 7,500 MNEs worldwide in 1970, today the total count stands at roughly 80,000.[1]

Exhibit 3.4 displays a sample of MNEs and the diverse industry sectors these focal firms represent. Due to the global financial crisis and worldwide recession, the market value of sectors

EXHIBIT 3.4

Typical Multinational Enterprises as Focal Firms (Ranked by Industry Sector Size)

Sources: Based on *Fortune,* "Fortune Global 500," Industries, 2011, accessed at http://money.cnn.com/magazines/fortune/; FTSE, "FTSE Global Sector Index Series," accessed at http://www.ftse.com; MSCI, "MSCI Global Sector Indices," accessed at http://www.msci.com; S&P Global 1200, 2012, accessed at www.standardandpoors.com.

Sector	2012 *Market Value (US $ billions)*	*Percentage of World Total*	*Representative Firms*
Financial Services	$3,940	18.0%	Capital One, Danske Bank, Mitsui Sumitomo Bank
Technology	2,820	13.0	Microsoft, Oracle, Hoya, Taiwan Semiconductor Manufacturing
Energy	2,645	12.0	Mobil, Total, China Oilfield Services
Consumer Staples	2,476	11.0	Procter & Gamble, Unilever, China Mengniu Dairy, Honda
Industrials	2,356	11.0	Landstar Systems, Shenzhen Expressway, Haldex
Health Care	2,233	10.0	GlaxoSmithKline, Novartis, Baxter International
Consumer Discretionary	2,165	10.0	Coach, Adidas, Salomon, Matsushita Electric
Materials	1,650	7.0	Dow Chemical, Alcan, Vitro SA
Communication Services	1,127	5.0	AT&T, China Mobile, Royal KPN
Utilities	890	4.0	Duke Energy, Empresa Nacional de Electricidad SA, Hong Kong and China Gas, Ltd.
TOTAL	**22,302**	**100.0**	

in the exhibit declined substantially in recent years. The largest changes occurred in the financial and consumer discretionary sectors, which declined in value by 50 percent or more between 2007 and 2012.

Some focal firms operate in the services sector, including airlines, retailers, and construction companies. Examples include HSBC in banking, CIGNA in insurance, Bouygues in construction, Accor in hospitality, Disney in entertainment, Nextel in telecommunications, and Best Buy in retailing. Although retailers are usually classified as intermediaries, some large ones such as IKEA, Walmart, and Gap are considered focal firms themselves. In addition, nontraditional Internet-mediated businesses that deliver knowledge-based offerings such as music, movies, and software online have joined the ranks of global focal firms. Amazon and Netflix are examples.

Not all focal firms are private businesses. In developing countries and centrally planned economies, some focal firms are partly or wholly owned by the government. Lenovo Group is China's leading computer maker. It owns the former PC business of IBM and is about 25 percent government-owned. CNOOC is a huge oil company that tried to buy Unocal in the United States in 2005. It is 70 percent owned by the Chinese government. Numerous other leading Chinese MNEs—China Mobile and China Netcom in telephony, Dongfeng Motor Corporation and Shanghai Automotive in cars, and China Life in insurance—are wholly or partly owned by the Chinese government.

MNEs have played a major role in the current phase of globalization. In the years following World War II, most multinationals, typically from the United States and the United Kingdom, went abroad seeking raw materials, production efficiencies, and foreign-based customers. Today, these firms undertake sourcing, manufacturing, servicing, and marketing activities that span all areas of the world.

A notable transition in the first decade of the twenty-first century is the rise of emerging market MNEs. This trend is illustrated in Exhibit 3.5, which shows the number of MNEs listed in *Fortune* magazine's "Global 500," the 500 largest multinational firms worldwide. The exhibit reveals that just as the number of MNEs based in the United States and Japan has declined steadily during the 2000s, the number of MNEs based in Brazil, China, India, and Russia has risen. The increase of Global 500 MNEs in China, from nine firms in 2001 to 61 today, is particularly significant. We should note that, during the 2000s, the number of Global 500 MNEs based in each of France and Germany has remained relatively stable at about 36 firms each. The number of MNEs based in the United Kingdom has held steady at about 33, and South Korea has remained at about 13 firms. The trend reflected in Exhibit 3.5 suggests a sort of "balancing" of MNE power—where the United States and Japan once dominated the Global 500, today emerging market MNEs are on the rise.

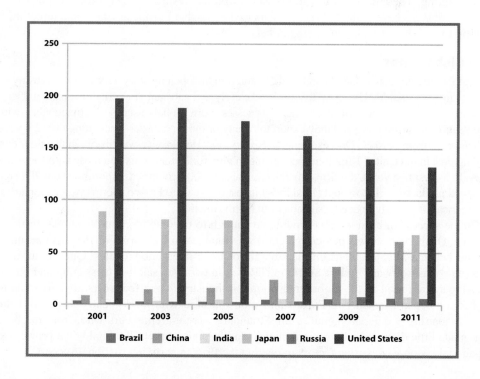

EXHIBIT 3.5

Largest MNEs in the Fortune Global 500, During the 2000s

Sources: Based on *Fortune*, "The World's Largest Corporations," July 22, 2002, pp. F-1–F-13; "Global 500," *CNNMoney*, for 2005, 2007, and 2011, accessed at http://money.cnn.com; Paola Hjelt, "The Fortune Global 500," *Fortune*, July 26, 2004, pp. 159–186.

A typical MNE, and one whose products you may have sampled, is Sodexo (www.sodexo.com), the world's second-largest contract food service provider. One of the largest employers in Europe, Sodexo's 380,000 employees provide cafeteria-style food to universities, hospitals, corporations, and public institutions at 33,900 sites in more than 80 countries. Sodexo serves more than 40 million consumers per day and earns revenues topping $20 billion annually. Typical customers include the British-Dutch firm Unilever, Germany's Ministry of Foreign Affairs, and the U.S. Marine Corps. Sodexo is the food source for numerous college cafeterias in Australia, Canada, and the United States. Chances are, if you eat in a university cafeteria, it's a Sodexo operation.

Small and Medium-Sized Enterprises

Small and medium-sized enterprise (SME)
A company with 500 or fewer employees (as defined in Canada and the United States).

Another type of focal firm that initiates cross-border business transactions is the SME. As defined in Canada and the United States, **small and medium-sized enterprises (SMEs)** are manufacturers or service providers with fewer than 500 employees (in the European Union and numerous other countries, they are defined as having fewer than 250 employees). SMEs now make up the majority of companies active in international business. Nearly all firms, including large MNEs, started out small. Compared to large multinationals, SMEs can be more flexible and quicker to respond to global business opportunities. They are usually less bureaucratic, more adaptable, and more entrepreneurial, and often sustain entrepreneurship and innovation in national economies.

Being smaller organizations, SMEs are constrained by limited financial and human resources. This explains why they usually choose exporting as their main strategy for entering foreign markets. Their limited resources prevent them from undertaking FDI, an expensive entry mode. As their operations grow, some gradually establish company-owned sales offices or subsidiaries in key target markets.

Due to their smaller size, SMEs often target specialized products to market niches too small to interest large MNEs. SMEs owe much of their international success to support provided by intermediaries and facilitators in foreign markets, and to globe-spanning logistics specialists such as FedEx and DHL. Smaller firms also rely on information and communications technologies that allow them to identify global market niches and efficiently serve specialized buyer needs. SMEs are gaining equal footing with large multinationals in marketing sophisticated products around the world.

In Eastern Europe, the development of emerging market countries is driven increasingly by the rise of fast-growing SMEs. Examples include the Latvian coffee shop chain Double Coffee and the Hungarian employment recruiter CVO Group. Many of Eastern Europe's small firms operate not in manufacturing but in intellectual, knowledge-intensive industries such as software and consulting. The rise of Eastern European SMEs has resulted largely from two trends: the access these firms have gained in recent years to the massive European Union and direct investment by foreign investors in emerging markets.[2]

Born Global Firms

Born global firm
A young entrepreneurial company that initiates international business activity early in its evolution, moving rapidly into foreign markets.

Born global firms, such as Geo Search Ltd., featured in the opening story, represent a relatively new breed of international SME—those that undertake early and substantial internationalization. Despite the scarce resources typical of most small businesses, born globals usually internationalize within three years of their founding and may export to twenty or more countries, generating over 25 percent of their sales from abroad. One example is History and Heraldry (www.historyandheraldry.com), a born global in the United Kingdom specializing in gifts for history buffs and those with English ancestry. In its first five years, the firm expanded its sales to sixty countries, exporting about 70 percent of its total production. History and Heraldry's biggest markets are France, Germany, Italy, Spain, and the Americas. It recently opened a subsidiary in North America.[3]

Some successful born globals grow large enough to become large multinational firms. For example, QualComm (www.qualcomm.com) was founded in California in 1985 and eventually grew to become a major MNE on the strength of huge international sales. QualComm developed the e-mail software Eudora and OmniTRACS, a two-way satellite messaging and position reporting system used in the global transportation industry. Just a few years after its founding, QualComm began exporting to Europe and soon followed with market entry in Brazil, China, India, Indonesia, and Japan. QualComm's founders were entrepreneurs who, from the beginning, made little distinction between domestic and foreign markets. Technological prowess and managerial vision were strong factors in making the firm an early international success.

The born global phenomenon represents a new reality in international business. In countries like Australia, Denmark, Ireland, and the United States, born globals account for a substantial proportion of national exports. In many cases, born globals offer leading-edge products with strong potential to generate international sales. They leverage the Internet and communications technologies to facilitate early and efficient international operations.

The emergence of born globals is associated with *international entrepreneurship*, in which innovative, smaller firms pursue business opportunities everywhere, regardless of national borders. Communications and transportation technologies, falling trade barriers, and the emergence of niche markets worldwide have increased the ability of contemporary firms to view the whole world as their marketplace. Entrepreneurial managers are creative, proactive, and comfortable dealing with risk. They are usually quick to adapt company strategies as circumstances evolve. The widespread emergence of born globals implies that any firm, regardless of size or experience, can succeed in international business.[4]

Source: gyn9037/Shutterstock

Born global firms are international from their founding. Vix Technology is an Australian born global that makes fare management equipment for public transit systems worldwide.

 ## International Entry Strategies of Focal Firms

One way to analyze focal firms in international business is in terms of the entry strategies they use to expand abroad. Earlier, we noted that the larger MNEs tend to expand abroad through FDI. By contrast, smaller firms tend to be exporters. Both MNEs and SMEs often rely on contractual relationships such as franchising and licensing.

A Framework for Classifying International Entry Strategies

Exhibit 3.6 shows the variety of foreign market entry modes that focal firms use and the foreign partners they seek. The first column lists three categories of international business transactions: (i) transactions that involve the trade of products; (ii) transactions that involve contractual exchange of services or intangibles; and (iii) transactions based on investing equity ownership in foreign-based enterprises.

The second column in Exhibit 3.6 identifies the types of focal firms engaged in international business. Some focal firms are manufacturing businesses such as Sharp, John Deere, and Land Rover. They use manufacturing processes to produce tangible products that they sell in foreign markets. Trading companies are brokers of goods and services. Service providers are firms in the services sector, such as insurance companies and hotel chains. Some services firms supply their clients with expertise, purely intangible offerings such as advice and training. Examples include lawyers and consulting firms.

The second column also identifies **licensors** of various types of intellectual property, including patents and know-how. A licensor is a firm that enters a contractual agreement with a foreign partner to allow the partner the right to use certain intellectual property for a specified period of time in exchange for royalties or other compensation. A **franchisor** is a firm that grants another the right to use an entire business system in exchange for fees, royalties, or other forms of compensation. Franchisors are essentially sophisticated licensors and include companies like McDonald's and Hertz Car Rental. Other firms, particularly in the construction, engineering, design, or architectural industries, provide their offerings via turnkey contracting. **Turnkey contractors** are focal firms or a consortium of firms that plan, finance, organize, manage, and implement all phases of a project and then hand it over to a foreign customer after training local personnel.

The third column in Exhibit 3.6 identifies the foreign market entry strategy, or the mode of internationalization, that the above-mentioned companies employ. A foreign market entry strategy refers to the manner in which the focal firm internationalizes, whether through exporting,

Licensor
A firm that enters a contractual agreement with a foreign partner to allow the partner the right to use certain intellectual property for a specified period of time in exchange for royalties or other compensation.

Franchisor
A firm that grants another the right to use an entire business system in exchange for fees, royalties, or other forms of compensation.

Turnkey contractors
Focal firms or a consortium of firms that plan, finance, organize, manage, and implement all phases of a project and then hand it over to a foreign customer after training local personnel.

Nature of International Transaction	Types of Focal Firm	Foreign Market Entry Strategy	Location of Major Activities	Typical Foreign Partners
Trade of products	Small manufacturer	Exporting	Home country	Distributor, agent, or other independent representative
	Large manufacturer	Exporting	Mainly abroad	Company-owned office or subsidiary
	Manufacturer	Importing (e.g., sourcing)	Home	Independent supplier
	Importer	Importing	Home	Trader or manufacturer
	Trading company	Exporting and Importing	Home	Trader or manufacturer
Contractual exchange of services or intangibles	Service provider	Exporting	Usually abroad	Agent, branch, or subsidiary
	Supplier of expertise or technical assistance	Consulting services	Abroad (temporarily)	Client
	Licensor with patent	Licensing	Home	Licensee
	Licensor with know-how	Licensing (technology transfer)	Home	Licensee
	Franchisor	Franchising	Home	Franchisee
	Service contractor	Management/Marketing service contracting	Abroad	Business owner or sponsor
	Construction/Engineering/ Design/ Architectural Firm	Turnkey contracting or build-own-transfer	Abroad (temporarily)	Project owner
	Manufacturer	Non-equity, project-based, partnerships	Home or abroad	Manufacturer
Equity ownership in foreign-based enterprises	MNE	FDI via greenfield investment	Abroad	None
	MNE	FDI via acquisition	Abroad	Acquired company
	MNE	Equity joint venture	Abroad	Local business partner(s)

EXHIBIT 3.6

International Business Transactions, Types of Focal Firms, and Foreign Market Entry Strategies

importing, licensing, or FDI. The type of entry mode depends on the nature of the business as well as the nature of the focal firm, its products, and its goals. When the nature of business is dealing in intangibles, such as professional services, the focal firm may enter into agency relationships with a foreign partner. This is common among banks, advertising agencies, and market research firms. Licensing and franchising are common in the international transfer of intangibles. A franchisor makes a contract with a foreign franchisee; a supplier of expertise makes a contract with a foreign client, and so forth.

In undertaking international business, the focal firm has the option of serving customers either through foreign investment or by relying on the support of independent intermediaries located abroad. In the former case, the firm will set up company-owned manufacturing and distribution facilities abroad.

The fourth column in Exhibit 3.6 identifies the location of major activities. For example, most exporters carry out major activities—manufacturing, marketing, and sales—in their home country; they produce goods at home and ship them to customers abroad. MNEs and other large firms, however, tend to carry out major activities in multiple countries; they produce goods and sell them to customers primarily located abroad.

The last column in Exhibit 3.6 identifies the nature of the foreign partner. In almost all cases, the focal firm relies on intermediaries as well as support firms located in foreign markets. Significant activities are typically delegated to these foreign partners, including marketing, distribution, sales, and customer service. MNEs have seen a strong trend in recent years away from fully integrated operations toward the delegation of certain noncore functions to outside vendors, a practice known as outsourcing. Outsourcing involves the firm in a variety of foreign partnerships. For example, Nike maintains its own design and marketing operations, but outsources production of its footwear to independent suppliers located abroad.

Other Types of International Entry Strategies

Let's develop a fuller understanding of focal firms other than the MNEs and SMEs that are highlighted in Exhibit 3.6. Some focal firms expand into foreign markets by entering into contractual relationships with foreign partners. Licensing and franchising are examples of contractual relationships. Occasionally, the licensor sells essential components or services to the licensee as part of their ongoing relationship. Licensing allows companies to internationalize rapidly while remaining in their home market. For example, Anheuser-Busch signed a licensing agreement with the Japanese beer brewer Kirin, under which Kirin produces and distributes Budweiser beer in Japan. The agreement has substantial potential, given Japan's $30 billion-a-year beer market.[5] In another example, Canadian toymaker Mega Bloks signed an agreement with Disney that gives the SME the right to produce toys that feature Disney characters such as Winnie the Pooh and the Power Rangers.[6]

Like licensors, the franchisor remains in its home market and permits its foreign partners to carry out activities in their markets. The franchisor assists the franchisee in setting up its operation and then maintains ongoing control over aspects of the franchisee's business, such as operations, procurement, quality control, and marketing. The franchisee benefits by gaining access to a proven business system. Major international franchisors include Subway, Curves, Pizza Hut, KFC, RE/MAX, and McDonald's.

Turnkey contractors specialize in international construction, engineering, design, and architectural projects, usually for airports, hospitals, factories, power plants, oil refineries, campuses, and upgrades to public transportation such as bridges, roadways, and rail systems. In a typical turnkey contract, the contractor plans, finances, organizes, manages, and implements all phases of a construction project, providing hardware and know-how to produce what the project sponsor requires. Hardware includes buildings, equipment, and inventory that comprise the tangible aspects of the system. Know-how is the knowledge about technologies, operational expertise, and managerial skills that the contractor transfers to the customer during and after completing the project.[7]

Turnkey projects are typically awarded on the basis of open bidding, in which many potential contractors participate. Some are highly publicized megaprojects, such as the European Channel Tunnel, the Hong Kong Airport, and the Three Gorges Dam in China. Typical examples of turnkey projects include upgrades to public transportation networks such as bridges, roadways, and rail systems. Most metro projects are financed largely by public funding. They are typically in Asia and Western Europe, where demand is driven by intensifying urbanization and worsening congestion. One of the world's largest publicly funded heavy-rail projects is underway in Delhi, India. Delhi Metro Rail Ltd. (www.delhimetrorail.com) commissioned the estimated $2.3 billion turnkey project to build roads and tunnels that run through the city's central business district. The turnkey consortium includes numerous local firms as well as Sweden's Skanska AB, one of the world's largest construction companies.[8]

An increasingly popular type of turnkey contract in the developing economies is the *build-own-transfer* venture. In this arrangement, the contractors acquire an ownership stake in the facility for a period of time until it is turned over to the client. The contractors also provide ongoing advice, training, and assistance in navigating regulatory requirements and obtaining needed approvals from government authorities. At some point after a successful period of operation, the contractors divest their interest in the project.

Exhibit 3.7 identifies the top construction contractors in the world based on revenues from projects outside their home countries. Large-scale construction is an intensely global industry. Top firms are based in Europe and the United States and derive much of their total revenues from international projects. Many have established reputations in specialized project areas such as airports, steel plants, refineries, high-speed rail, and environmental projects.[9]

An *international collaborative venture* is a cross-border business alliance in which partnering firms pool their resources to create a new venture, sharing the associated costs and risks. Collaborative ventures represent a middle ground between exporting and FDI. Collaborative arrangements help the focal firm increase international business, compete more effectively with

Source: simon gurney/Shutterstock

Turnkey contractors develop construction projects and then transfer ownership to local customers. Numerous turnkey contractors helped renovate the Macau Airport in southeast Asia.

EXHIBIT 3.7 Top International Construction Contractors

Rank	Contractor (Home Country)	Approximate Revenues (in millions of US$)		Example of Recently Completed Mega-Project
		International	Total	
1	*Hochtief AG* (Germany)	$24,582	$26,720	New airport, Berlin
2	*Vinci* (France)	16,558	$45,060	Channel tunnel, Britain-France
3	*Bechtel* (United States)	12,500	27,900	Hong Kong Airport, China
4	*Bouygues* (France)	12,432	41,380	Groene Hart Tunnel, Netherlands
5	*Skanska AB* (Sweden)	11,632	18,020	Oresund Bridge, Denmark
6	*Saipem* (Italy)	11,605	14,790	Blue Stream gas pipeline, Russia-Turkey
7	*Fluor* (United States)	11,566	20,850	Shell Rayong Refinery, Thailand
8	*Strabag SE* (Austria)	10,870	16,410	Xiaolangdi Dam, China

Sources: Based on *Engineering News-Record*, "The Top 225 International Contractors 2011," accessed at www.enr.com, January 3, 2012; *Fortune* "Global 500" at money.cnn.com/magazines/fortune/global500, accessed April 26, 2012; company profiles from Hoovers.com; and corporate Web sites.

rivals, take advantage of complementary technologies and expertise, overcome trade barriers, connect with customers abroad, configure value chains more effectively, and generate economies of scale in production and marketing.

Joint ventures (JVs) and project-based, nonequity ventures are both examples of international collaborative ventures. A **joint venture partner** is a focal firm that creates and jointly owns a new legal entity through equity investment or pooling of assets. Partners form JVs to share costs and risks, gain access to needed resources, gain economies of scale, and pursue long-term strategic goals. For example, in 2011, China's Lenovo and Japan's NEC Corporation (NEC) entered a joint venture to produce personal computers and target sales to Japan, the world's third largest PC market. The venture combined NEC's market reputation, product development capabilities, and knowledge of customer needs in Japan with Lenovo's strong capital position, technological expertise, and global supplier network. The Chinese computer giant invested $175 million to take a 51 percent stake in the JV.[10]

Partners in a **project-based, nonequity venture** are focal firms that collaborate to undertake a given project with a relatively narrow scope and well-defined timetable, but without creating a new legal entity. In contrast to JVs, which involve equity investment by the parent companies, project-based partnerships are less formal, short-term, nonequity ventures. The partners pool their resources and expertise for a limited time to perform some mutually beneficial task, such as joint R&D or marketing, but do not form a new enterprise.[11]

One example is Cisco Systems (www.cisco.com), the worldwide leader in Internet networking technology, which expanded its operations by partnering with key foreign players. Cisco formed an alliance with Japan's Fujitsu to jointly develop routers and switches that enable clients to build Internet protocol networks for advanced telecommunications. In Italy, Cisco teamed with Italtel to jointly develop network solutions for the convergence of voice, data, and video to meet growing global demands. Cisco also formed an alliance with the Chinese telecom ZTE to tap Asian markets. The two companies are collaborating to provide equipment and services to telecommunications operators in the Asia-Pacific region.[12]

Joint venture partner
A focal firm that creates and jointly owns a new legal entity through equity investment or pooling of assets.

Project-based, nonequity venture partners
A collaboration in which the partners create a project with a relatively narrow scope and a well-defined timetable, without creating a new legal entity.

 ## Distribution Channel Intermediaries in International Business

A second category of international business participant is the distribution channel intermediary. They are physical distribution and marketing service providers in the value chain for focal firms. Distribution channel intermediaries:

- deliver products and services in the home country and abroad;

- may undertake advertising, sales, customer service, and other key functions in the target market on behalf of focal firms;
- may offer warehousing, customer support, and other logistics services on behalf of focal firms.

A worldwide survey by McKinsey Quarterly found that MNE executives are particularly concerned about the capabilities needed to manage global supply chains and distribution channels, as well as the recruitment and retention of skilled personnel in individual foreign markets.[13] These findings emphasize the importance of intermediaries in international business.

Intermediaries are of many different types, ranging from large international companies to small, highly specialized operations. Techdata (www.techdata.com) is a large distributor of laptops, peripherals, and other information technology products. Like typical wholesalers, the firm buys such goods from manufacturers and then resells them to retail stores. In 2012, for example, Techdata distributed such products to thousands of retailers in 100 countries worldwide.

For most exporters, relying on an independent foreign distributor is a low-cost way to enter foreign markets. The intermediary's intimate knowledge, contacts, and services in the local market can provide a strong support system for exporters inexperienced in international business or too small to undertake market-based activities themselves. There are three major categories of intermediaries: those based in the foreign target market, those based in the home country, and those that operate via the Internet.

Intermediaries Based in the Foreign Market

In most cases, intermediaries are based in the exporter's target market. They provide a multitude of services, including conducting market research, appointing local agents or commission representatives, exhibiting products at trade shows, arranging local transportation for cargo, and clearing products through customs. Intermediaries also orchestrate local marketing activities, including product adaptation, advertising, selling, and after-sales service. Many finance sales and extend credit, facilitating prompt payment to the exporter. In short, intermediaries based in the foreign market can function like the exporter's local partner, handling all needed local business functions.

A **foreign distributor** is a foreign market-based intermediary that works under contract for an exporter and takes title to and distributes the exporter's products in a national market or territory, often performing marketing functions such as sales, promotion, and after-sales service. Foreign distributors are essentially independent wholesalers that purchase merchandise from exporters (at a discount) and resell it after adding a profit margin. Because they take title to the goods, foreign distributors are often called *merchant distributors*. They promote, sell, and maintain an inventory of the exporter's products in the foreign market. They also typically maintain substantial physical resources and provide financing, technical support, and after-sales service for the product, relieving the exporter of these functions abroad. Distributors may carry a variety of noncompeting complementary products, such as home appliances and consumer electronics. For consumer goods, the distributor usually sells to retailers. For industrial goods, the distributor sells to other businesses and/or directly to end users. Distributors are a good choice for firms that seek a stable, committed presence in the target market. They typically have substantial knowledge of the exporter's products and of the local market.

An **agent** is an intermediary (often an individual or a small firm) that handles orders to buy and sell commodities, products, and services in international business transactions for a commission. Also known as a broker, an agent may act for either the buyer or seller but does not assume title or ownership of the goods. The typical agent is compensated by commission, expressed as a percentage of the price of the product sold. In economic terms, the agent brings buyers and sellers together. Agents operate under contract for a definite period of time (often as little as one year), renewable by mutual agreement. The contract defines territory, terms of sale, compensation, and grounds and procedures for terminating the agreement.[14]

The function of the agent is especially important in markets made up of many small, widely dispersed buyers and sellers. For example, brokers on the London Metal Exchange (LME; www.lme.co.uk) deal in copper, silver, nickel, and other metals sourced from mining operations worldwide. The volume of metal buying and selling is huge—around $5 billion per year—and the suppliers are widely dispersed worldwide. The LME greatly increases the efficiency with which manufacturing firms access the metal ingredients they need to conduct manufacturing

Foreign distributor
A foreign market-based intermediary that works under contract for an exporter, takes title to, and distributes the exporter's products in a national market or territory, often performing marketing functions such as sales, promotion, and after-sales service.

Agent
An intermediary (often an individual or a small firm) that handles orders to buy and sell commodities, products, and services in international business transactions for a commission.

Source: Tristar Photos/Alamy

Logistics service providers move product shipments on behalf of manufacturers and intermediaries to destinations worldwide. Here cargo is offloaded from an aircraft owned by DHL, one of the largest transport providers in Europe and the Middle East.

operations. Agents are common in the international trade of commodities, especially agricultural goods and base minerals. In the services sector, agents often transact sales of insurance and securities.

A **manufacturer's representative** is an intermediary contracted by the exporter to represent and sell its merchandise or services in a designated country or territory. Manufacturer's representatives go by various names, depending on the industry in which they work—agents, sales representatives, or service representatives. In essence, they act as contracted sales personnel in a designated target market on behalf of the exporter, but usually with broad powers and autonomy. Manufacturer's representatives may handle various noncompetitive, complementary lines of products or services. They do not take title to the goods they represent and are most often compensated by commission. With this type of representation, the exporter usually ships merchandise directly to the foreign customer or end user. Manufacturer's representatives do not maintain physical facilities, marketing, or customer support capabilities, so these functions must be handled primarily by the exporter.

Manufacturer's representative
An intermediary contracted by the exporter to represent and sell its merchandise or services in a designated country or territory.

In consumer markets, firms convey their products to end users through *retailers*. A retailer represents the last link between distributors and end users. Some national retail chains have expanded abroad and are now providing retail services in multiple countries. For example, Seibu, Carrefour, Royal Ahold, and Tesco are major retail store chains based in Japan, France, the Netherlands, and the United Kingdom, respectively. Some firms, for example Rolex and Ralph Lauren, sell their products directly to major retailers. Often, a traveling sales representative facilitates such transactions. Large international retailers such as Carrefour and Walmart maintain purchasing offices abroad. Walmart and Toys "R" Us have opened hundreds of stores worldwide, especially in Mexico, Canada, Japan, China, and Europe. IKEA, a Swedish company, is one of the world's largest furniture retailers. Dealing directly with foreign-based retailers is efficient because it shortens distribution channels and reduces distribution costs.

Ethical Connections

Recently, many more MNEs are investing in developing economies. MNE business activities can affect age-old customs and practices, threatening local traditions. Large-scale merchants such as Carrefour and Walmart have changed retailing in many developing economies, putting *tiendas* and other small shops out of business. Fast-food restaurants such as Dunkin' Donuts and McDonald's have altered traditional eating habits, shifting preferences in some countries toward less healthy choices.

Intermediaries Based in the Home Country

Some intermediaries are domestically based. Wholesaler importers bring in products or commodities from foreign countries for sale in the home market, re-export, or use in the manufacture of finished products. Manufacturers also import a range of raw materials, parts, and components used in the production of higher value-added products. They may also import a complementary collection of products and services to supplement or augment their own product range. Retailers such as department stores, specialized stores, mail-order houses, and catalogue firms import many of the products they sell. A trip to retailers such as Best Buy, Canadian Tire, or Marks & Spencer reveals that most of their offerings are sourced from abroad, especially from low labor-cost countries.

Wholesalers import input goods that they in turn sell to manufacturers and retailers. A typical importer in this category is Capacitor Industries Inc. (www.capacitorindustries.com), an SME that imports low-cost electronic components from China and sells them to motor makers and other manufacturers in the United States and other countries. Capacitors are tiny devices that store electrical charges, keep motors running, and protect computers from surges. Capacitor Industries' strategy is simple—buy from a low-cost country and sell in an advanced economy at a profit. Importing from China and other low-cost suppliers means it can undercut the prices of domestic suppliers by up to 30 percent.

For exporting firms that prefer to minimize the complexity of selling internationally, a **trading company** serves as an intermediary that engages in import and export of various commodities, products, and services. A trading company assumes the international marketing function on behalf of producers, especially those with limited international business experience. Large trading companies operate much like agents, coordinating sales of countless products in markets worldwide. Typically, they are high-volume, low-margin resellers compensated by adding profit margins to what they sell.

Trading companies are very common in commodities and agricultural goods such as grain. Companies such as Cargill (www.cargill.com) provide a useful service as international resellers of agricultural goods. With 138,000 employees in about seventy countries and annual sales of roughly $120 billion, Cargill is one of the largest private firms in the United States. It buys, sorts, ships, and sells a wide range of commodities, including coffee, sugar, cotton, oil, hemp, rubber, and livestock, controlling about 25 percent of U.S. grain exports and one-fifth of the U.S. meat market. Most of its profits come from turning commodities into value-added products, including oils, syrups, and flour. The company also processes the ingredients that many food companies use to produce cereal, frozen dinners, and cake mixes.

Exhibit 3.8 provides a list of the largest trading companies in the world. What strikes you about these firms? First, they tend to be high-volume, low-margin resellers dealing largely in commodities such as minerals, metals, and basic consumer products. Second, note that seven of the ten are based in Japan, where trading companies long have played a critical role in external trade. Being an island country with few natural resources, over time Japan became very good at importing parts and materials needed in manufacturing. Trading companies are also common in South Korea, India, and Europe.

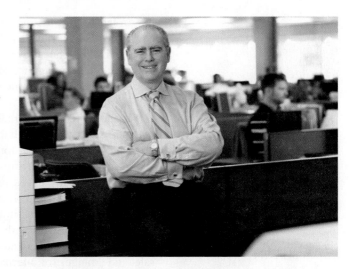

AJC International, based in Atlanta, Georgia, is a trading company founded by Eric Joiner (shown here) and Gerald Allison. A world leader in marketing frozen and refrigerated food products, AJC brings together suppliers and customers in more than 140 countries on six continents. Its multicultural workforce represents 34 nationalities speaking 27 languages.

Trading company
An intermediary that engages in import and export of a variety of commodities, products, and services.

EXHIBIT 3.8 World's Largest Trading Companies

Rank based on annual Revenues	Company (Home Country)	Revenues ($ millions)	Profits ($ millions)	Profits as percentage of total revenues
1	Toyota Tsusho (Japan)	$69,310	$ 569	0.82
2	Mitsubishi (Japan)	60,793	5,408	8.90
3	Noble Group (China)	56,696	606	1.07
4	Mitsui (Japan)	54,635	4,295	7.86
5	Sinochem (China)	49,537	798	1.61
6	Sojitz (Japan)	48,440	193	0.40
7	Marubeni (Japan)	43,011	1,594	3.71
8	Itochu (Japan)	42,612	1,880	4.41
9	Sumitomo (Japan)	36,218	2,367	6.54
10	COFCO (China)	26,469	800	3.02

Sources: Based on Forbes Global 2000, at www.forbes.com; Fortune Global 500, at money.cnn.com/magazines/fortune; corporate profiles at Hoovers.com.

In Japan, large trading companies are known as *sogo shosha*. In Japan and China alike, trading companies usually engage in both exporting and importing and are specialists in low-margin, high-volume trading. They may also supply a range of manufacturing, financial, and logistical services. To stay close to foreign markets, trading company managers travel widely, employ extensive networks of local offices, participate in trade shows, and establish business relationships with agents and distributors worldwide.

In the United States, trading companies have had a relatively negligible impact on the volume of export activity. Although the U.S. Congress passed the Export Trading Company (ETC) Act in 1982, providing incentives for the formation of trading companies, few were formed. One deterrent is the preference of U.S. firms to pursue international expansion independently of other firms.[15]

Export management company (EMC)
A domestically based intermediary that acts as an export agent on behalf of a client company.

A domestically based intermediary is the **export management company (EMC)**, which acts as an export agent on behalf of a (usually inexperienced) client company. For example, Sharco is an EMC based in Chicago that assists manufacturers in the heating, ventilation, and refrigeration industries with exporting their products to Asia and the Middle East. In return for a commission, an EMC finds export customers on behalf of the client firm, negotiates terms of sale, and arranges for international shipping. While typically much smaller than a trading company, some EMCs have well-established networks of foreign distributors in place that allow exported products immediate access to foreign markets. EMCs are often supply-driven, visiting the manufacturer's facilities regularly to learn about new products and even to develop foreign-market strategies. But because of the indirect nature of the export sale, the manufacturer runs the risk of losing control over how its products are marketed abroad, with possible negative consequences for its international image.

Online Intermediaries

Some focal firms use the Internet to sell products directly to customers rather than going through traditional wholesale and retail channels. By eliminating traditional intermediaries, companies can sell their products more cheaply and faster. This benefits SMEs in particular because they usually lack the often substantial resources needed to undertake conventional international operations.

Online intermediaries broker transactions between buyers and sellers worldwide. Traditional retailers establish Web sites or link with online service providers to create an electronic presence. The electronic sites of retailers like Tesco (www.tesco.com) and Walmart (www.walmart.com) complement existing physical distribution infrastructure and bring more customers into physical outlets. Read more about Internet-based international intermediaries in the Global Trend feature.

Facilitators in International Business

The third category of participant in international business is facilitators, independent individuals or firms that assist the internationalization and foreign operations of focal firms and make it possible for transactions to occur efficiently, smoothly, and on time. Facilitators include banks, international trade lawyers, freight forwarders, customs brokers, and consultants. Their number and role have grown due to the complexity of international business operations, intense competition, and technological advances. Facilitators provide many useful services, from conducting market research to identifying potential business partners and providing legal advice. They rely heavily on information technology and the Internet to carry out their facilitating activities.

Logistics service provider
A transportation specialist that arranges for physical distribution and storage of products on behalf of focal firms, as well as controlling information between the point of origin and the point of consumption.

An important facilitator of international trade is the **logistics service provider**, a transportation specialist that arranges for physical distribution and storage of products on behalf of focal firms, as well as controlling information between the point of origin and the point of consumption. Companies such as DHL, FedEx, UPS, and TNT provide cost-effective means for delivering cargo anywhere in the world. They also offer traditional distributor functions such as warehousing, inventory management, and order tracking. FedEx, a leading express shipping company, delivers approximately 3.5 million packages of freight per day and offers supply-chain management services. It delivers to some 220 countries and territories, covering virtually the entire planet with its fleet of more than 690 aircraft and more than 50,000 cars, trucks, and trailers. FedEx's business in China, India, Mexico, and the Middle East has grown rapidly.

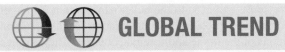

GLOBAL TREND

Online Retailers Surge Ahead

During the recent recession, online sales were one of the few bright spots in retailing, surging by 25 percent or more for many firms. In a poor economy, buyers view the Internet as a cheaper and easier way to find bargains. EBay sells 50,000 categories of merchandise, with some 100 million registered users in about forty countries worldwide. Amazon .com is the leading online retailer with millions of visitors every week. In addition to selling books, Amazon generates almost half its revenue from merchandise sales. Both eBay and Amazon obtain about half their sales outside the United States.

Conventional retailers also develop Web sites. Walmart's site is second only to Amazon in number of annual visitors. Walmart has increased its online presence and is pursuing sales in Brazil, China, Japan, and numerous other countries. In the United Kingdom, popular e-retailers include Argos, a catalogue merchant, and Tesco, Britain's biggest supermarket chain. The hottest online products include toys, books, computer games, clothing, and jewelry.

Launching an Internet-based sales operation offering thousands of products is complex, and the challenge is even greater in international markets. Localizing a Web site may require major modifications to accommodate differences in language, culture, customs, and technical sophistication of the target locale. The online retailer must adapt its merchandise and product packaging to suit local needs. In much of the world, electronic payment systems remain a mystery. Many people are reluctant to buy used goods, which affects sales of retailers like eBay.

Many firms use social networking to market their offerings. Facebook is the leading example, with more than one billion users worldwide. The global audience of social networkers is growing rapidly, with Europe's rising by more than 30 percent annually and those in the Middle East/Africa region and Latin America growing at well-above-average rates. Social networking is extremely popular in China because most media are heavily regulated and the Internet is the only medium where people can express themselves freely.

China now has the most Internet users, an astonishing 400 million. The success of international online retailing depends on the availability of information technology. When ranked by the proportion of citizens who use the Internet (the "penetration rate"), small European countries such as Monaco, Iceland, and Norway rank highest, with penetration rates above 90 percent. The highest penetration rate in Asia is in South Korea (81%). Other notable countries include the Netherlands (penetration rate of 88%), New Zealand (84%), the United Kingdom (82%), Canada (79%), Australia (78%), and the United States (78%). By contrast, in countries like Iran, Indonesia, Nigeria, Russia, and Colombia, online retailers can target only a small portion of the local population. In Africa and parts of South Asia, few people own computers and Internet penetration is even lower.

Sources: V. Furness, "When Bricks Meet Clicks," *Revolution*, March 2009, pp. 56–58; K. Hille, "Increased Marketing Lifts Baidu Traffic," *Financial Times*, February 20, 2009, p. 17; Hoovers.com corporate profiles of Walmart, Amazon.com, and eBay; *Internet World Stats*, "Internet Usage Statistics," at www.internetworldstats.com; International Telecommunications Union, *Measuring the Information Society 2011*, Geneva, Switzerland: International Telecommunications Union; S. Murphy, "A Touch of Local Flavor," *Chain Store Age*, May 2008, p. 144; "Shopping Folly," *New Media Age*, February 5, 2009, p. 25; L. Wu, Y. Cai, and D. Liu, "Online Shopping Among Chinese Consumers: An Exploratory Investigation of Demographics and Value Orientation," *International Journal of Consumer Studies*, 35 no. 4, (2011): 458–469.

Following the recent global recession, footwear manufacturers took steps to streamline global supply chains. China is the source of about 85 percent of footwear imports into the United States. Various U.S. shoe companies take advantage of supply chain services provided by FedEx, UPS, and other logistics service providers to ensure timely, cost-effective shipment to retail stores in North America. For example, shoe firms that have their manufacturing done in China sort and repackage footwear at UPS facilities in southern China. Shoes are then delivered directly to U.S. retail stores. By using outside express delivery firms, footwear companies get their products to market faster and at lower cost. To serve the international distribution needs of U.S. firms, UPS has built more than fifty warehouses in China. For example, Bakers Footwear Group, which has 230 shoe stores in the United States, streamlined its supply chain to reduce transit times and transportation costs from producers in Asia.[16]

International manufacturers use common carriers, companies that own the ships, trucks, airplanes, and other transportation equipment they use to transport goods around the world. Common carriers play a vital role in international business and global trade. Maersk (www .maerskline.com) is a leading carrier, based in Denmark and operating some 500 ships that move containerized cargo around the world. You may have seen Maersk containers traveling down the highway, on the backs of trucks and lorries, on their way to being loaded on ocean-going ships. A consolidator is a type of shipping company that combines the cargo of more than one exporter into international shipping containers for shipment abroad.

Most exporters use the services of freight forwarders because they are a critical facilitator in international business. Usually based in major port cities, freight forwarders arrange international shipments for the focal firm to a foreign entry port, and even to the buyer's location in the target foreign market. They are experts on transportation methods and documentation for international trade, as well as the export rules and regulations of the home and foreign countries. They arrange for clearance of shipments through customs on the importing side of the transaction. Freight forwarders are an excellent source of advice on shipping requirements such as packing, containerization, and labeling.

Customs brokers
Specialist enterprises that arrange clearance of products through customs on behalf of importing firms.

Governments typically charge tariffs and taxes, and devise complex rules for the import of products into the countries they govern. **Customs brokers** (or *customs house brokers*) are specialist enterprises that arrange clearance of products through customs on behalf of importing firms. They are to importing what freight forwarders are to exporting. They prepare and process required documentation and ensure goods are cleared through customs in destination countries. They understand the regulations of the national customs service and other government agencies that affect the import of products. Usually the freight forwarder, based in the home country, works with a customs house broker based in the destination country in handling importing operations.

Various players facilitate the financial operations of international business. *Commercial banks* make possible the exchange of foreign currencies and provide financing to buyers and sellers who usually require credit to finance transactions. The process of getting paid often takes longer in international than in domestic transactions, so a focal firm may need a loan from a commercial bank. Commercial banks can also transfer funds to individuals or banks abroad; provide introduction letters and letters of credit to travelers; supply credit information on potential representatives or foreign buyers; and collect foreign invoices, drafts, and other foreign receivables. Within each country, large banks in major cities maintain correspondent relationships with smaller banks spread around the nation or the world or operate their own foreign branches, thus providing a direct channel to foreign customers.

Banking is one of the most multinational business sectors. Barclays, Citicorp, and Fuji Bank have as many international branches as any of the largest manufacturing MNEs. These banks frequently provide consultation and guidance free of charge to their clients, since they derive income from loans to the exporter and from fees for special services.

Many banks are reluctant to extend credit to SMEs, as these smaller firms usually lack substantial collateral and they have a higher failure rate than large MNEs. In the United States, smaller firms often turn to the *Export Import Bank* (Ex-IM Bank; www.exim.gov), a federal agency that assists exporters in financing sales of their products and services in foreign markets. The Ex-IM Bank provides direct loans, working capital loans, loan guarantees, and other financial products aimed at supporting the exporting activities of smaller firms.

In other countries, particularly in the developing world, governments provide financing at favorable rates even to foreign firms, often through public development banks and agencies. Such loans are used to finance construction of infrastructure projects such as dams and power plants. Incoming investment usually results in new jobs, technology transfer, and/or substantial foreign exchange. Australia, Canada, Ireland, France, and numerous other countries similarly provide financing to MNEs to build factories and other large-scale operations in their countries. In the United States, several state development agencies have provided loans to automakers like BMW, Honda, Mercedes, and Toyota to establish plants in individual states.

Focal firms and other participants also use the services of *international trade lawyers* to help navigate international legal environments. The best trade lawyers are knowledgeable about their client's industry, the laws and regulations of target nations, and appropriate business methods in the legal/regulatory context. Firms need international trade lawyers to negotiate contracts for the

Source: G P Bowater/Alamy

Commercial banks such as this one at the Mall of the Emirates in Dubai are key facilitators in international commercial transactions, providing financing, transferring funds, and exchanging foreign currencies. It is no wonder that banking is one of the most multinational of all business sectors.

sale and distribution of goods and services to customers, intermediaries, or facilitators. Lawyers support negotiations on joint venture and strategic alliance agreements or for reaching agreement on international franchising and licensing. International trade lawyers also assist in resolving disputes with foreign business partners. If the firm wants to protect its intellectual property by applying for patents or trademarks abroad, international patent attorneys play a supportive role.

Insurance companies provide coverage against commercial and political risks. Internationally, losses occur often because of the wide range of natural and human-made circumstances to which the firm's products are exposed as they make their way through the value chain. For example, goods shipped across the ocean are occasionally damaged in transit. Insurance helps defray the losses resulting from such damage.

International business consultants advise internationalizing firms on various aspects of doing business abroad and alert them to foreign market opportunities. *Consultants* help companies improve their performance by analyzing existing business problems and helping management develop future plans. Particularly helpful are *tax accountants*, who can advise companies on minimizing tax obligations resulting from multicountry operations. *Market research firms* are a potential key resource for identifying and targeting foreign buyers. They possess or can gain access to information on markets, competitors, and the methods of international business.

 ## Governments in International Business

Governments operate at the local, provincial, national, and supranational levels to make and enforce laws and regulations, and to provide basic economic security by devising fiscal and monetary policies. Recently, many governments have developed new legislation aimed at protecting the natural environment. For example, the U.S. and European governments are cooperating to develop policies to cut carbon dioxide emissions. Multilateral regulations are deemed necessary to address pollution and other challenges in the natural environment.[17]

Governments also regulate markets. During the recent global financial crisis, governments moved to stimulate national economies, through such programs as the Economic Stimulus Act in the United States, the European Union stimulus plan, and the Economic Stimulus Plan in China.[18] In some cases, important companies were nationalized. For example, the governments of Belgium, Luxembourg, and the Netherlands took control of Fortis, a large bank services company that faced financial ruin. In the United States, the U.S. Treasury took partial ownership of General Motors.

National finance ministers and central bank directors coordinated efforts aimed at restoring order following the global financial crisis. *Central banks* are the monetary authorities in each country that issue currency and regulate national money supplies. Australia, Canada, China, Indonesia, the United States, and numerous European countries cut bank interest rates and injected billions into national money supplies. The European Central Bank (www.ecb.int) devised new banking regulations with the goal of averting future crises.[19]

At the G-20 Summit in 2009, heads of state announced a range of synchronized policy initiatives intended to revive the global economy, stimulate employment, reform national financial systems, and improve global institutions like the International Monetary Fund. At the G-20 Summit in 2011, officials announced a new round of regulations on certain categories of international portfolio investments.[20] Officials from various countries coordinated efforts to restore international growth by providing more credit and liquidity in world banking systems. Some governments advocated creating a new, global currency to replace the U.S. dollar as the favored currency in international business. Efforts at reform were revived in 2012 during the sovereign debt crisis in Europe.[21]

Governments also participate in international business by investing in other economies. The trend is best exemplified by the **sovereign wealth funds (SWFs)**, state-owned investment funds that undertake systematic, global investment activities to generate income or to achieve policy objectives, such as reviving a collapsed economy. In 2008, the governments of Singapore, Kuwait, and South Korea provided much of a $21 billion lifeline to Citigroup and Merrill Lynch, two banks that lost fortunes in the global financial crisis. In 2012, China's SWFs dramatically increased investments in Europe, to acquire debt-ridden European firms.

Sovereign wealth fund (SWF)
A state-owned investment fund that undertakes systematic, global investment activities.

While SWFs have been around for decades, their numbers increased dramatically in the 2000s. Many are based in oil-producing countries and originate from massive commodity sales. For example, Kuwait's SWF derives from oil revenues and amounts to several hundred billion dollars. Some funds represent other types of assets, such as the SWF in Quebec, Canada, based on provincial pension funds. Holdings of some SWFs exceed the GDPs of the national economies of countries into which they invest. For example, the Abu Dhabi Investment Authority, the Government Pension Fund of Norway, and the China Investment Corporation each have several hundred billion dollars under management. Collectively, SWFs now amount to several trillion dollars.

Given their size, critics charge that SWFs substantially affect their investment targets, even to the point of endangering national interests. To address the potential harm of SWFs, some governments have passed legislation to restrict inward SWF investments. In 2008, for example, Germany passed a law that requires parliamentary approval for foreign investments that acquire more than 25 percent of a German company. The United States has a similar law.[22]

Some experts believe governments' role in the world economy should be curtailed and advocate capitalism and free trade as the best means for global economic success.[23] We discuss the role of government in international business in later chapters.

CLOSING CASE — DHL, FedEx, and UPS: Shifting Fortunes in the Global Logistics Services Industry

DHL is focused on international delivery. The firm ended its domestic air express service in France, the United Kingdom, and the United States in 2009. In the United States, DHL's troubles resulted from a declining market for express packages and inability to compete with rivals FedEx and UPS. Although DHL still offers U.S. customers international package services, its status as the world's largest logistics facilitator remains in doubt.

When Adrian Dalsey, Larry Hillbolm, and Robert Lynn founded DHL as a door-to-door delivery service between San Francisco and Honolulu in 1969, no one imagined the business would evolve into an international express delivery group linking 120,000 destinations in more than 200 countries. Now owned by the German company Deutsche Post World Net, DHL offers express services, international air and ocean freight, contract logistics, and various value-added services. Despite failing to maintain its solid U.S. presence, the firm remains the market leader for courier express delivery in Europe and Asia.

Global Supply-Chain and Logistics Industry

The supply-chain and logistics industry includes companies that move raw materials, finished goods, packages, and documents across the globe. Four major trends have changed it dramatically since the 1970s—globalization, deregulation, digitization, and outsourcing. The massive increase in international trade has increased the complexity of corporate supply chains. MNEs and other internationalizing firms require speed and efficiency in moving goods through supply chains around the world. To address this need, specialized logistics service providers like DHL, UPS, and FedEx organize, coordinate, and control supply chains through a global presence and skillful use of leading-edge technologies. These facilitating firms control thousands of trucks and aircraft, sophisticated information tracking systems, and global networks of offices and warehouses. Collectively, logistics service providers represent an industry unto themselves.

Global Competitors

Founded in 1907, United Parcel Service (UPS) is one of the oldest competitors. Its primary business is delivering packages and documents worldwide. UPS also provides global supply chain services. FedEx oversees a vast empire, providing transportation, e-commerce, and business services in the United States and abroad. Although a relatively young firm, FedEx experienced rapid growth and is now one of the top three logistics providers worldwide. Founded in Australia, TNT began acquiring interests in other companies, which helped it grow into a large multinational firm. TNT has acquired dozens of companies over time.

Global Positioning

In the courier, express, and parcel market, DHL International is the leader in Europe, thanks to its efficient national express networks, served by company-owned vehicles. DHL is also the leader in China and Japan and holds 35 percent market share of the international express segment in the Asia Pacific region. It acquired a controlling interest in the Indian express company, Blue Dart, strengthening its ability to serve customers in India and China. DHL is now the global leader in airfreight, offering those services in regions not covered by competitors via its extensive air and freight network. DHL is the leading provider of ocean freight and contract logistics.

Express delivery is a low-margin business. Logistics service providers attempt to increase profits by adding higher-value services such as door-to-door logistics management across networks of corporate value chains. DHL targets its services to industries with enormous global logistical needs, like the automotive, pharmaceutical, electronics, consumer goods, and fashion industries. When such contracts are signed, they are long term, on average three years in length. Recent investments have allowed DHL to provide warehousing and warehouse transportation services to clients as diverse as BMW, PepsiCo, Unisys, Electrolux, and Deutsche Telekom.

DHL's Experience in the United States

The United States represents 35 percent of the global logistics market. Over one-third of all global Fortune 500 companies are headquartered in the United States, and countless key decisions about global logistics and transport orders are made there. The market is intensely competitive and concentrated, with the top five competitors controlling nearly half of it. The largest sector is ground courier service, worth about $30 billion annually and dominated by the U.S. Postal Service.

Despite performing well in Canada and Mexico, DHL won only a number-three position in the United States, following FedEx and UPS. Its strategy was to focus on small and medium-sized firms. To this end, the firm spent $1.1 billion to acquire Airborne Express, once the number-three U.S. express service. DHL next sought to restructure itself, cutting operations and many services by one-third. But this move alienated customers and many switched to FedEx or UPS. DHL's problems were further aggravated by the economic downturn that began in 2008. Squeezed by mounting losses, management decided to terminate DHL's U.S. operations but maintain its U.S. Global Mail Division.

Case Questions

1. Describe the various services provided by logistics service providers. What is the role of these services in focal firms' value-chain activities?
2. Supply-chain management has evolved over time, largely due to globalization and technological advances. What does the future hold? Can you anticipate changes to the supply chain that would further alter the express and logistics industry?
3. What factors do focal firms consider when choosing one logistics service provider over another? In what ways do the global logistical and transportation needs of focal firms vary from one industry to another? Give some examples.
4. Given the importance of the U.S. market in the global express industry, should DHL reconsider its decision to withdraw from this segment? Lacking a significant presence in the United States, what should DHL management do to grow the firm and improve earnings?
5. What strategies should facilitator companies such as DHL, UPS, and FedEx implement during an economic recession? What steps can they take to ensure their survival, while remaining prepared for the upsurge of new business once the economy

Challenges in the Global Economy

When the economy slows, profits suffer at many firms. Already operating on slim margins, facilitators are vulnerable. Retailers reduce inventories and pressure facilitators to cut the cost of delivering goods. Numerous retailers have gone out of business—for example, Borders book stores, Circuit City, and Woolworths. Business failures hurt logistics firms' revenues. Economic challenges compel delivery and logistics firms to rethink internal processes, cut costs, and seek alternative revenue sources. Some cut services to certain geographic areas, lay off workers, and refocus on value-added portions of the business. Global logistics providers are struggling to find the right balance between running lean operations during hard times and gearing up for new business in good times.

improves? Have they overlooked the fast-growing emerging markets?

Sources: Bruce Barnard, "Deutsche Post DHL Raises Profit Outlook," *Journal of Commerce*, November 9, 2011, pp. 1–2; Corporate profile of Deutsche Post AG and DHL at Hoovers.com; Deutsche Post DHL, *Annual Report 2011*, retrieved from http://www.dp-dhl.com/reports; T. Mucha, "Pouring It on to Compete with UPS and FedEx," *Business 2.0* 6, no. 2 (2005): 60; B. Barnard, "Deutsche Post Unveils New Strategy, New Name," *Journal of Commerce*, March 11, 2009, p. 6; *Datamonitor*, "Deutsche Post AG SWOT Analysis," August 2011, pp. 1–9; D. Hannon, "DHL's Move Leaves Package Market Share Up For Grabs," *Purchasing*, January 15, 2009, p. 11; D. Hannon, "DHL to Exit US Express Shipping Market," *Purchasing*, March 26, 2008, p. 24; J. Ott, "Cargo Casualty," *Aviation Week and Space Technology*, February 2, 2009, p. 13; A. Roth, "UPS Woes Reflect Wide Economic Slump," *Wall Street Journal*, February 4, 2009, p. B6; A. Roth, "DHL Beats a Retreat from the US," *Wall Street Journal*, November 11, 2008, p. B1.

This case was written by Tracy González-Padron, University of Colorado at Colorado Springs, and updated by Professor Carol Sánchez and Ashley Stickney, Grand Valley State University, Grand Rapids, MI.

CHAPTER ESSENTIALS

MyManagementLab

Go to **mymanagementlab.com** to complete the problem marked with this icon ⭐.

Key Terms

agent   67
born global firm   62
customs brokers   72
distribution channel intermediary   56

export management company
   (EMC)   70
facilitator   56
focal firm   56

foreign distributor   67
franchisor   63
freight forwarder   57
joint venture partner   66

Summary

In this chapter, you learned about:

1. Four types of participants in international business

International business transactions require the participation of numerous focal firms, intermediaries, facilitators, and governments. A **focal firm** is the initiator of an international business transaction that conceives, designs, and produces the offerings for customers worldwide. A **distribution channel intermediary** is a specialist firm that provides a variety of logistics and marketing services for focal firms as part of the international supply chain, both in the home country and abroad. A **facilitator** is a firm or individual with special expertise such as legal advice, banking, and customs clearance that assists focal firms in the performance of international business transactions. *Governments* are increasingly important participants in international business.

2. Participants arranged by value-chain activity

Focal firms, intermediaries, and facilitators all make up participants in global value chains. The value chain is the complete business system of the focal firm, comprising all the focal firm's activities, including R&D, sourcing, production, marketing, and distribution. Channel intermediaries and facilitators support the focal firm by performing value-adding functions. In focal firms that export, most of the value chain is concentrated in the home country. In highly international firms, value-chain activities may be performed in various countries.

3. Focal firms in international business

Focal firms include **multinational enterprises (MNEs)**, large global corporations such as Sony and Ford. MNEs operate in multiple countries by setting up factories, marketing subsidiaries, and regional headquarters. **Small and medium-sized enterprises (SMEs)** now make up the majority of internationally active firms. They are flexible firms that emphasize exporting and leverage the help of intermediaries and facilitators to succeed in international business. Born globals are a category of international SMEs that internationalize at or near their founding.

4. International entry strategies of focal firms

Focal firms include a **licensor**, a firm that enters a contractual agreement with a foreign partner that allows the latter the right to use certain intellectual property for a specified period of time in exchange for royalties or other compensation. A **franchisor** is a firm that grants another the right to use an entire business system in exchange for fees, royalties, or other forms of compensation. A **turnkey contractor** is a focal firm or a consortium of firms that plans, finances, organizes, manages, and implements all phases of a project and then hands it over to a foreign customer. A **joint venture partner** is a focal firm that creates and jointly owns a new legal entity through equity investment or pooling of assets. **Project-based, nonequity venture partners** are focal firms that collaborate through a project with a relatively narrow scope and a well-defined timetable, without creating a new legal entity.

5. Distribution channel intermediaries in international business

Distribution channel intermediaries move products and services across national borders and eventually to end users. They perform key downstream functions in the target market on behalf of focal firms, including marketing. A **foreign distributor** is a foreign market-based intermediary that works under contract for an exporter and takes title to and distributes the exporter's products in a market abroad, often performing marketing functions such as sales and after-sales service. An **agent** is an intermediary that handles orders to buy and sell commodities, products, and services in international transactions for a commission. A **manufacturer's representative** is an intermediary contracted by the exporter to represent and sell its offerings in a designated country or territory. A **trading company** is an intermediary that imports and exports various commodities, products, and services. An **export management company (EMC)** is an intermediary that acts as an export agent on behalf of client companies.

6. Facilitators in international business

Facilitators assist with international business transactions. A **logistics service provider** is a transportation specialist that arranges physical distribution and storage of products on behalf of focal firms, as well as controlling information between the point of origin and the point of consumption. A **freight forwarder** arranges international shipping on behalf of exporting firms, much like a travel agent for cargo. A **customs broker** is a specialist that arranges clearance of products through customs on behalf of importing firms. Other facilitators include banks, lawyers, insurance companies, consultants, and market research firms.

7. **Governments in international business**

    Governments are increasingly active in international business. They make and enforce laws and regulations, and provide numerous other functions. Numerous national governments collaborated to address challenges that emerged in the global recession. Governments also invest in other economies, often through **sovereign wealth funds (SWFs)**, state-owned investment funds that undertake systematic global investment activities.

Test Your Comprehension

1. Identify and briefly define the four major categories of participants in international business.

2. In the stages of a typical international value chain, what role does each of the four categories of participants typically play?

3. What are the specific characteristics of focal firms? Distinguish the characteristics of international MNEs, SMEs, and born global firms.

4. What are major distribution channel intermediaries based in the home country and those based abroad?

5. What are online intermediaries? How do focal firms use the Internet to carry out international activities?

6. What are the characteristics of facilitators? List and define the major types of facilitators.

7. What role do governments play in international business? What are the characteristics of sovereign wealth funds?

Apply Your Understanding AACSB: Reflective Thinking Skills, Communication Abilities, Ethical Understanding and Reasoning Abilities

1. Focal firms, distribution channel intermediaries, and facilitators each assume a different and critical role in the performance of international business transactions. Think about the degree of interdependency that exists among these groups. What would happen if distribution channel intermediaries could not provide competent services to the focal firm? What if adequate facilitators were not available to the focal firm? To what degree would the focal firm's international business performance be hampered? Under what circumstances would the focal firm choose to internalize its value-chain activities in international business rather than delegate them to channel intermediaries and facilitators? What would be the consequences of retaining distribution and support activities within the firm?

2. Assume that after graduation you get a job at Kokanee Corporation, an SME that manufactures Italian tile, granite countertops, and other high-quality building materials for residential construction projects. Your boss, Eugenia Kimball, wants to begin exporting Kokanee's products to foreign markets. Prepare a memo for her in which you briefly describe the kinds of intermediaries and facilitators with whom Kokanee should work to develop and maintain successful export operations.

3. *Ethical Dilemma*: You are Vice President of Manufacturing at MicroKey Company, a major producer of computer keyboards with factories in various countries that provide jobs to thousands of local residents. The firm imports many of the raw materials used to manufacture its keyboards abroad. At one of its factories in Russia, MicroKey has begun to experience problems getting parts and components processed through customs, resulting in delays that are hurting profits. Upon conferring with colleagues at the plant, you are advised the problem can be solved if MicroKey makes a payment to local officials, a common practice in the area. The bribe would expedite passage through customs. However, you believe bribery is unethical. Moreover, it is illegal in much of the world. For example, under laws of Canada, the United States, and most European countries, a manager can be prosecuted for offering bribes, even in countries where the practice is accepted. What should you do? Do you make the payment, realizing it will help your firm and it reflects the way business is normally carried out in that part of the world?

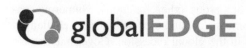

AACSB: Reflective Thinking Skills, Use of Information Technology

Refer to Chapter 1, page 24, for instructions on how to access and use globalEDGE™.

1. Visit the government agency or ministry in your country responsible for supporting international business. For example, in the United States, visit the Department of Commerce (www.doc.gov). In Canada, visit Industry Canada (www.ic.gc.ca). In Denmark, visit the Ministry of Economic and Business Affairs (www.oem.dk). Identify and describe the most important support functions that the agency provides to companies that do international business. One approach is to sketch out a typical value chain and then systematically identify the support services the agency offers. For example, for the distribution link in the value chain, numerous governments provide "matchmaker" services, trade missions, and commercial services that link manufacturing firms with appropriate distributors located abroad.

2. Visit the Toyota Motor Corporation (www.toyota-global.com) and click on "Company." Toyota has a complex value chain.

Based on the information provided at the Web site, address the following questions: What types of upstream (for example, R&D, sourcing, manufacturing) value-chain activities does Toyota perform? What types of downstream value-chain activities (for example, marketing, distribution, after-sales service) does Toyota perform? Identify the types of participants (mainly intermediaries and facilitators) that Toyota is likely to use at each stage of the value chain.

3. Your company is about to initiate export activities in a country of your choice. You will need to identify distribution channel intermediaries and freight forwarders to facilitate the distribution and delivery of your products to end users in this country. Visit the Reference Desk and Global Resource Directory of globalEDGE™. What sources of information are especially helpful to you in identifying suitable foreign distributors and freight forwarders? What do you learn from these sources?

MyManagementLab

Go to **mymanagementlab.com** for Auto-graded writing questions as well as the following Assisted-graded writing questions:

3-1. What is unique about such focal firms as franchisors, licensors, and turnkey contractors?

3-2. What role do distribution channel intermediaries fulfill?

3-3. Mymanagementlab Only – comprehensive writing assignment for this chapter.

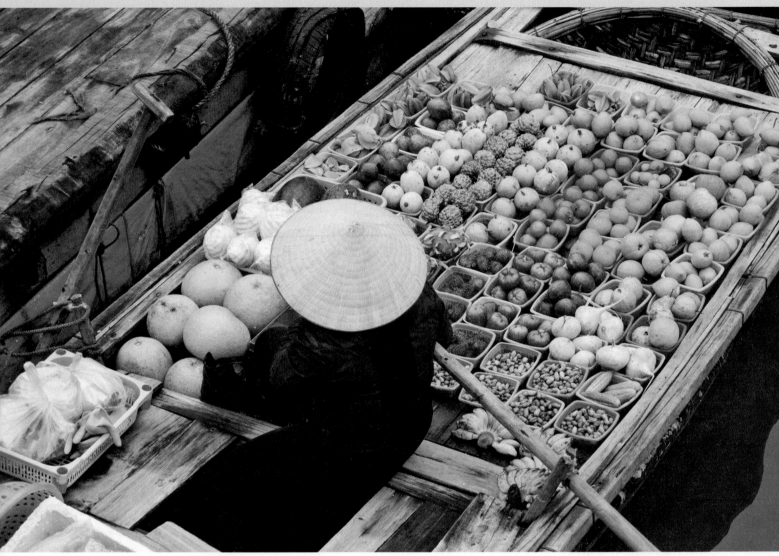

Source: © mkmakingphotos/Fotolia

Culture and Management: Google in China

Google has enjoyed spectacular success since its founding in 1998. The search engine firm operates in more than 50 countries and established operations in China in 2006. Google brought its laid-back Silicon Valley culture to sprawling headquarters in Beijing, which was outfitted with a fully equipped gym, foosball tables, videogames, and other frills.

Google clashed with the Chinese government, which closely monitors business in China, especially firms from abroad. As a condition for entering China, Google agreed to censor certain types of search results, especially those that criticize the Chinese government. Google pushed the limits by complying as little as possible with government orders to block search engine content.

Google's Chinese employees experienced difficulties adjusting to the firm's freewheeling style. Many were uncomfortable with company policy that requires employees to devote 20 percent of their work time to developing independent projects. Google blocked its Chinese engineers from accessing the firm's software code. The policy emerged in response to China's loose approach to private property rights, which encourages access to foreign technology and know-how.

CHAPTER 4

The Cultural Environment of International Business

 LEARNING OBJECTIVES *In this chapter, you will learn about the following:*

1. The nature of cross-cultural risk
2. Characteristics of culture
3. Lenses to understand culture
4. Subjective and objective dimensions of culture

5. Language: A key dimension of culture
6. Cultural change
7. Context of international business
8. Overcoming cross-cultural risk: Managerial guidelines

MyManagementLab®

⭐ **Improve Your Grade!**

Over 10 million students improved their results using the Pearson MyLabs. Visit **mymanagementlab.com** for simulations, tutorials, and end-of-chapter problems.

Google hired a Chinese executive to manage the firm's government relations. However, communication gaps arose partly because she could not speak English. She criticized Google corporate management for not working hard enough to understand Chinese customs. Later, she was fired after giving free iPods to government officials. Giving expensive gifts to public officials is often viewed as a form of bribery in Western cultures, but is more accepted in parts of Asia.

Management grew alarmed when Chinese hackers accessed sensitive information in Google's private files. In some cases, Chinese government officials hacked the Gmail accounts of Chinese dissidents and human rights activists. A government official launched a personal campaign against the firm when he Googled himself and found an abundance of critical material. Eventually, Google senior management grew weary of China and decided to stop complying with government censorship rules.

In 2010, Google withdrew from mainland China. Google's China personnel were shocked by this decision, which was reached without gaining their input or support. Many had begun to think of themselves as members of the "Google family."

Google's experience in China demonstrates the importance of culture in international business. China has a *collectivist* mind-set, which emphasizes conformity, duty, prescribed roles, and sacrifice for the greater good. Family-style management emphasizes personal relations and leaders concerned for employee happiness. Families are at the center of Chinese culture. In society, family members "know their place" and maintain the family name. Younger generations respect and obey their elders. At one time, a father could legally kill his children if they displeased him. Such is the cultural context in which Google confronted the Chinese government.

The Chinese are *long-term oriented* and invest much time in planning business ventures. They emphasize patience, respect for tradition, and hard work. They avoid conflict and favor societal harmony. The focus on harmony derives from teachings of the ancient philosopher Confucius, who urged a nonassertive approach to resolving differences. China is a *high-context, relationship-oriented* culture. Maintaining strong, long-term relationships is essential to developing trust. Major decisions are rarely taken without informing employees first.

Guanxi refers to informal personal relationships that emphasize reciprocal obligations and the exchange of favors. In China, guanxi profoundly influences commercial activities and organizational behaviors. An individual or firm that receives favors from another has a moral obligation to reciprocate and maintain the relationship. In China, government officials did many favors for Google, starting with allowing it to launch its business there. Skillful guanxi can open dialogue, build trust, and facilitate the exchange of favors that augment business performance.

In 2012, Google renewed efforts to enter China, acknowledging that it cannot afford to miss out on the world's biggest Internet market. Top management has softened its position, and is seeking to introduce new services in China, especially those not subject to censorship.

SOURCES: H. Chen, A. Ellinger, and Y. Tian, "Manufacturer–Supplier Guanxi Strategy," *Industrial Marketing Management* 40, no. 4 (2011): 550–560; W. Chunxia, "The Influence of Confucian Culture on Business Management," *International Journal of Business Anthropology* 1, no. 2 (2010): 117–134; A. Efrati, L. Chao, and K. Zhang, "Google Softens China Stance," *Wall Street Journal*, January 12, 2012, pp. B1–B2; E. Fyrwald, "Five Keys to Profiting in China," *Bloomberg BusinessWeek*, March 16, 2011, accessed from www.Businessweek.com; P. Gwynne, "Google's Experience Raises Doubts about High-Tech Business in China," *Research Technology Management*, May/June, 2010, pp. 2–3; S. Levy, "Google and Its Ordeal in Ordeal in China," *Fortune*, May 2, 2011, accessed at http://money.cnn.com/magazines/fortune; S. Levy, *In the Plex: How Google Thinks, Works, and Shapes Our Lives* (New York: Simon & Schuster, 2011); *New York Times*, "China and Intellectual Property," Dec. 23, 2010, accessed at www.nytimes.com; A. Rabkin, "The Social(ist) Networks," *Fast Company*, February 2011, pp. 68–75.

Culture
The learned, shared, and enduring orientation patterns in a society. People demonstrate their culture through values, ideas, attitudes, behaviors, and symbols.

The opening story on Google's entry into China highlights the challenges of operating in diverse national cultures. In international business, success requires sensitivity to national interests and cultural expectations. By contrast, Google corporate management displayed an ethnocentric orientation, viewing China through the lens of American values and business customs. As reflected in the story, **culture** refers to the learned, shared, and lasting orientation patterns in a society. In China and around the world, people demonstrate their culture through values, ideas, attitudes, behaviors, and symbols. In international business, firms such as Google step into cultural environments characterized by unfamiliar languages and unique value systems, beliefs, behaviors, and norms. These differences influence all dimensions of international business.

Exhibit 4.1 summarizes the culture-related essentials addressed in this chapter. Scholars have offered various models and explanations on culture. Culture influences the various social environments that managers encounter. Religion and language are particularly relevant expressions of culture. Culture is difficult to identify and analyze, but its effects on international business are profound. Culture is evolving constantly and is affected by globalization and numerous other contemporary trends. In this chapter, we focus on the business dimensions of culture and implications for managers.[1]

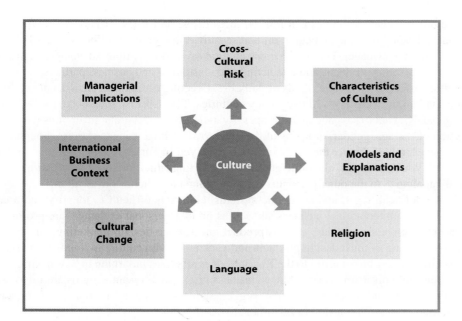

EXHIBIT 4.1

Essentials for Understanding Culture in International Business

 ## The Nature of Cross-Cultural Risk

Culture represents one of the four risks of international business that we introduced in Chapter 1. We highlight these risks in Exhibit 4.2. **Cross-cultural risk** is a situation or event in which a cultural misunderstanding puts some human value at stake. Misunderstanding and miscommunication arise because people have differing values and expectations. They do not always communicate (verbally or nonverbally) what the other party is anticipating, or may have different ways of communicating. For example, a head nod has different meanings in India and the United Kingdom.

Cross-cultural risk
A situation or event in which a cultural misunderstanding puts some human value at stake.

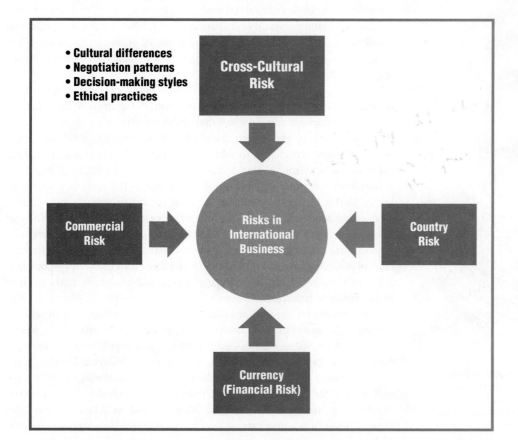

EXHIBIT 4.2

The Four Major Risks in International Business

Cross-cultural misunderstandings can ruin business deals, hurt sales, or harm the corporate image. Today, developing an appreciation of, and sensitivity for, cultural differences has become an imperative for any manager. Those with cross-cultural savvy hold various advantages in managing employees, marketing products, and interacting with customers and business partners.

Culture affects even simple rituals of daily life. Greeting ceremonies are a deeply embedded cultural marker and have evolved over many centuries. They specify such behaviors as whether to shake hands, what to say, and how far apart to stand. These cultural conventions may vary as a function of the age, gender, or status of the greeters. In China, friends express thoughtfulness by asking each other whether they have had their meal yet. In Turkey, a typical greeting is "What is new with you?" In Japan, elaborate greeting and parting rituals are the norm, and individuals routinely apologize to the other party just before ending a telephone conversation.

Unlike political, legal, and economic systems, culture is difficult to identify and analyze, but its effects on international business, as well as on interpersonal exchange, are profound. Its effects on value-chain activities, such as product and service design, marketing, and sales, are substantial. Managers must design products and packaging with culture in mind, even regarding color. While red may be beautiful to the Russians, it symbolizes mourning in South Africa. Items such as pens are universally acceptable as business gifts, but chrysanthemums are often associated with funerals and handkerchiefs may suggest sadness. In some cultures, knives or scissors imply cutting off the relationship or other negative sentiments.

Some firms train their employees about foreign cultures, helping them become cross-culturally proficient. In California's Silicon Valley, Intel offers a seminar called "Working with India" to enhance work effectiveness with the estimated 400,000 Indian nationals in the valley. Computer firm AMD flies IT workers from India to its facilities in Texas for a month of cultural training with U.S. managers. Workers role-play and study subjects such as Indian movies, political history, and Hinduism. Training includes lessons on assigning work (Indian workers may agree to unattainable deadlines), preparing food (many Indians eat vegetarian food), and socializing (since it is polite to initially decline an invitation to a colleague's home, managers should offer more than once).[2]

Cross-cultural risk can be triggered by an **ethnocentric orientation**— using our own culture as the standard for judging other cultures. Most of us are raised in a single culture; we have a tendency to view the world primarily from our own perspective. Ethnocentric tendencies are widespread and entail the belief that one's own race, religion, or ethnic group is somehow superior to others. In this way, having an ethnocentric orientation is an obstacle to cultural understanding.[3]

International business scholar Howard Perlmutter described ethnocentric views as "home-country orientation."[4] He argued that international managers should give up their ethnocentric orientations in favor of a polycentric or geocentric orientation. **Polycentric orientation** refers to a host-country mind-set in which the manager develops a strong affinity with the country in which she or he conducts business. **Geocentric orientation** refers to a global mind-set in which the manager is able to understand a business or market without regard to country boundaries. Geocentric tendencies are like a cognitive orientation that combines an openness to, and awareness of, diversity across cultures.[5] Managers with a geocentric orientation make a deliberate effort to develop skills for successful social behavior with members of other cultures.[6] They adopt new ways of thinking, learn to analyze cultures, and avoid the temptation to judge different behavior as inferior.[7]

We encounter unfamiliar cultures at home as well as in international dealings. Buyers visit from abroad to make deals, domestic firms source from suppliers located in distant countries, and employees increasingly have diverse cultural backgrounds. For example, Maurice Dancer is the head concierge at The Pierre, a luxury hotel in New York City. When the Indian firm Taj Hotels Resorts and Palaces (www.tajhotels.com) acquired the Pierre's management contract, Maurice had to adapt his management style to fit the new owners' corporate culture. He adapted to aspects

Ethnocentric orientation
Using our own culture as the standard for judging other cultures.

Polycentric orientation
A host-country mind-set in which the manager develops a strong affinity with the country in which she or he conducts business.

Geocentric orientation
A global mind-set in which the manager is able to understand a business or market without regard to country boundaries.

Source: iStock

Limited interaction among societies, such as between Kenyans, Mexicans, and Russians, tends to magnify differences in values, behaviors, and symbols. Such differences decrease, however, with growing cross-cultural interaction.

of Indian culture, demonstrated in Taj's administrative style. Maurice also manages employees from Asia, Europe, and Latin America who bring cultural traits to their jobs typical of their home countries. For example, Asians may be reserved when dealing with customers. In the past, Maurice had to encourage Asian subordinates to be more outgoing. Finally, much of The Pierre's clientele is foreign-born. Without even leaving the United States, Maurice interacts with a wide variety of foreign cultures every day.

The cross-cultural integration of firms like The Pierre is yet another manifestation of globalization. Globalization is leading to convergence of cultural values as well. While people worldwide maintain traditional cultural values, common norms and expectations of behavior are gradually emerging, and many universal values apply to cross-cultural encounters.

Cross-cultural encounters are increasingly common. Maurice Dancer (far right), head concierge at The Pierre hotel in New York, interacts with a wide variety of international cultures every day, without even leaving the United States.

 ## Characteristics of Culture

Anthropologists study culture perhaps more than any other scholars. Anthropologists view culture as people's shared experiences and the schemas they acquire on the basis of those experiences.[8] Gary Ferraro sees culture as all the things that people have, think, and do as members of their society.[9] Ann Jordan views culture as an integrated system of shared thoughts, actions, and material artifacts that characterize a group or society.[10] In a typical greeting scenario, for example, an executive holds the *thought* that he wants to meet a prospective client. Upon meeting, the executive performs the appropriate *action*, a handshake in some societies and a bow in others. The executive may then exchange business cards or gifts, which constitute *artifacts*. Anthropologists view culture as an umbrella concept, within which various *systems* are incorporated, such as economic, political, technological, and educational systems.

Geert Hofstede, a well-known Dutch organizational anthropologist, views culture as a "collective mental programming" of people.[11] The "software of the mind," or how we think and reason, differentiates us from other groups. Such intangible orientations shape our behavior. Another scholar, Harry Triandis, views culture as an interplay of sameness and differences; all cultures are simultaneously very similar and very different.[12] While as human beings we share many commonalities and universals, as groups of people or societies we exhibit many differences. For example, some cultures are more complex than others. Some are more individualistic, while others are more collectivist. Some impose many norms, rules, and constraints on social behavior, while others impose very few.

Culture captures how the members of the society live—for instance, how they feed, clothe, and shelter themselves. It also explains how they behave toward each other and with other groups. Finally, it defines their beliefs and values and the way they perceive the meaning of life.

What Culture Is *Not*

Now that you have an idea of what culture is, let's also define what it is not.

Culture is:

- **Not right or wrong.** Culture is relative; there is no cultural absolute. People of different nationalities simply perceive the world differently. Each culture has its own notions of acceptable and unacceptable behavior. In some Islamic cultures, for example, a wife cannot divorce her husband. In many countries, nudity is acceptable on TV. In Japan and Turkey, wearing shoes in the home is taboo.

- **Not about individual behavior.** Culture is about groups. It refers to a collective phenomenon of shared values and meanings. Thus, while culture defines the collective behavior of each society, individuals often behave differently. In most countries, for example, men wear their hair short. But a few mavericks have very long hair and stand out among their peers. In other countries, men may wear makeup. But such behavior does not represent the cultural values of the larger population.
- **Not inherited.** Culture is derived from the social environment. People are not born with a shared set of values and attitudes. Children gradually acquire specific ways of thinking and behaving as they are raised in a society. In the United States, for example, children usually acquire values of individualism and Christianity. But in China, children learn to depend on family members and acquire values based on Confucianism. Culture is passed from generation to generation by parents, teachers, mentors, peers, and leaders. Transnational media, such as movies and the Internet, play a large role in transmitting culture.

Socialization and Acculturation

Socialization

The process of learning the rules and behavioral patterns appropriate to one's given society.

This process of learning the rules and behavioral patterns appropriate to one's society is called **socialization**. Each society has rules—do's, don'ts, expectations, and preferences that guide behavior, particularly of children as they mature.[13] Such rules may be explicitly stated—for example, "we don't do things that way around here." Or they may be implicit, that is, everyone is expected to know how to function at work, at school, with friends, and so forth. Breaking a rule amounts to a failure to conform. As each of us matures, failing to follow society's rules provides opportunities for learning what the rules are. Socialization is cultural learning and provides the means to acquire cultural understandings and orientations shared by a particular society. It is a subtle process; we often adapt our behavior unconsciously and unwittingly.

Acculturation

The process of adjusting and adapting to a culture other than one's own.

Acculturation is the process of adjusting and adapting to a culture other than one's own. It is commonly experienced by people who live in other countries for extended periods, such as expatriate workers. In many ways, acculturation is challenging because adults are often less flexible than children.

The Many Dimensions of Culture

More than any other feature of human civilization, culture signals the differences among societies on the basis of language, habits, customs, and modes of thought. Yet most of us are not completely aware of how culture affects our behavior until we come into contact with people from other cultures.

Exhibit 4.3 illustrates the iceberg concept of culture using three layers of awareness: high culture, folk culture, and deep culture. Anthropologists use the iceberg metaphor to understand culture's many dimensions, some subtle and some not so subtle. Above the surface certain characteristics are visible, but below, unseen to the observer, is a massive base of assumptions, attitudes, and values that strongly influence decision making, relationships, conflict, and other dimensions of international business. While conditioned by our own cultural traits, we are usually unaware of the nine-tenths of our cultural makeup that exists below the surface. Often we are not aware of our own culture unless we encounter another one.

Lenses to Understand Culture

When they study culture, anthropologists distinguish between "emic" and "etic" perspectives. An "emic" analysis of culture describes behavior in terms meaningful to a person functioning within the culture. Scholars examine the culture from the perspective of those who dwell there, gaining their viewpoints and seeing the world as they do.[14] By contrast, an "etic" analysis is from the perspective of an outside observer. It aims to be scientific and "culturally neutral."[15] An etic observer compares the culture to others and explains it in unbiased, objective terms.

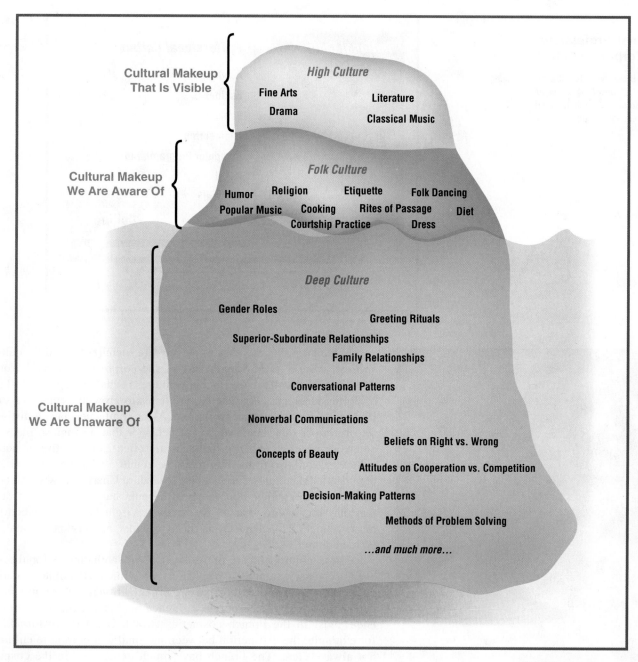

EXHIBIT 4.3

Culture as an Iceberg

Culture is linked with particular groups based on various factors, including:

- **Geography.** Unique cultural perspectives arise within distinct analytical levels—the world, the nation, the region, individual cities, and the neighborhoods where we live.
- **Ethnicity.** Nations consist of distinct ethnic groups. In England, for example, people of African, Indian, and Middle Eastern heritage tend to perceive reality in their own way.
- **Gender.** Men and women often experience the world differently.
- **Age.** Imagine how each of seniors, baby boomers, teenagers, and children perceive their communities and the world.
- **Language.** As we will see later in this chapter, language is a vital dimension that both reflects, and is reflected by, cultural differences.
- **Occupation.** Depending on your field, you may view matters uniquely, whether from the perspective of a blue-collar worker, a day laborer, a licensed professional, or an artist.[16]

EXHIBIT 4.4

National, Professional, and Corporate Culture

Source: Based on V. Terpstra and K. David, *Cultural Environment of International Business*, 3rd ed. (Cincinnati, OH: South-Western, 1991).

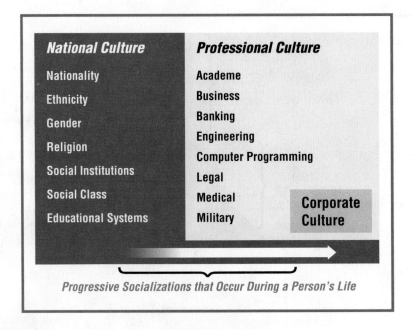

National Culture	Professional Culture
Nationality	Academe
Ethnicity	Business
Gender	Banking
Religion	Engineering
Social Institutions	Computer Programming
Social Class	Legal
Educational Systems	Medical
	Military

Corporate Culture

Progressive Socializations that Occur During a Person's Life

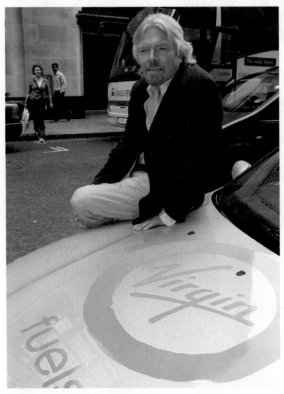

Source: © Daily Mail/Rex/Alamy

The edgy, risk-taking culture of companies under the Virgin brand owes much to the independent and flamboyant spirit of company founder Richard Branson and contrasts sharply with the conservative cultures of other British firms, despite sharing the same national culture.

Low-context culture
A culture that relies on elaborate verbal explanations, putting much emphasis on spoken words.

Exhibit 4.4 suggests that employees are socialized into three cultures: *national culture, professional culture*, and *corporate culture*.[17] Working effectively within these overlapping cultures is challenging. The influence of professional and corporate culture tends to grow as people are socialized into a profession and workplace. Most companies have a distinctive set of norms, values, and modes of behavior that distinguish them from other organizations. Such differences are often as distinctive as national culture, so that two firms from the same country can have vastly different organizational cultures. For example, Standard Chartered (www.standardchartered.com), a time-honored British bank, has a conservative culture that may be slow to change. By contrast, Virgin (www.virgin.com), the much younger British music and travel provider, has an experimental, risk-taking culture.

These cultural layers present yet another challenge for the manager: To what extent is a particular behavior attributable to national culture? In companies with a strong organizational culture, it is hard to determine where the corporate influence begins and the national influence ends. In the French cosmetics firm L'Oreal (www.loreal.com), for example, the distinction between national and corporate cultures is not always clear. The French have much experience in the cosmetics and fashion industries, but L'Oreal is a global firm staffed by managers from around the world. Their influence has shaped L'Oreal into a unique organization distinctive within French culture. Thus, in international business, the tendency to attribute all differences to national culture is simplistic.

High- and Low-Context Cultures

Context, or "the information surrounding an event," strongly influences culture, especially communication behavior. Anthropologist Edward T. Hall made a distinction between cultures he characterized as "low context" and "high context."[18] **Low-context cultures** rely on elaborate verbal explanations, putting great emphasis on spoken words. As Exhibit 4.5 shows, the low-context countries tend to be in northern Europe and North America, which have long traditions of rhetoric, placing central importance on delivering verbal messages. The primary function of speech in such cultures is to express ideas and thoughts clearly, logically, and convincingly. Communication is direct and explicit, and meaning is

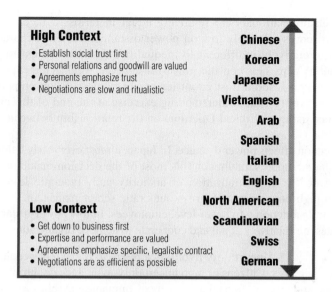

EXHIBIT 4.5

Hall's High- and Low-Context Typology of Cultures

Source: Based on *Beyond Culture* by Edward T. Hall, copyright © 1976, 1981 by Edward T. Hall. Used by permission of Doubleday, a division of Random House, Inc. For online information about other Random House, Inc. books and authors, see the Internet Web Site at http://www.randomhouse.com.

straightforward. For example, in negotiations Americans typically come to the point and do not beat around the bush. Low-context cultures tend to value expertise and performance and conduct negotiations as efficiently as possible. These cultures use specific, legalistic contracts to conclude agreements.

By contrast, **high-context cultures** such as Japan and China emphasize nonverbal messages and view communication as a means to promote smooth, harmonious relationships. They prefer an indirect and polite face-saving style that emphasizes a mutual sense of care and respect for others. They are on guard not to embarrass or offend others. This helps explain why Japanese people hesitate to say "no" when expressing disagreement. They are more likely to say "it is different," an ambiguous response. In East Asian cultures, showing impatience, frustration, irritation, or anger disrupts harmony and is considered rude and offensive. Asians tend to be soft-spoken, and people typically are sensitive to context and nonverbal cues (body language). At a business luncheon in Tokyo, for example, the boss is almost always the senior-looking individual seated farthest from the entrance to the room. This arises because reverence for superiors is the norm in Japan. To succeed in Asian cultures, it is critical to have a keen eye for nonverbal signs and body language. Negotiations tend to be slow and ritualistic, and agreement is founded on trust.

High-context culture
A culture that emphasizes nonverbal messages and views communication as a means to promote smooth, harmonious relationships.

Hofstede's Research on National Culture

Dutch anthropologist Geert Hofstede conducted one of the early empirical studies of national cultural traits. He collected data on the values and attitudes of 116,000 employees at IBM Corporation representing diverse nationality, age, and gender. Hofstede identified four independent dimensions of national culture, which we describe next.[19]

INDIVIDUALISM VERSUS COLLECTIVISM **Individualism versus collectivism** refers to whether a person functions primarily as an individual or as part of a group. In individualistic societies, ties among people are relatively loose, and each person tends to focus on his or her own self-interest. These societies prefer individualism over group conformity. Competition for resources is the norm, and those who compete best are rewarded financially. Australia, Canada, the United Kingdom, and the United States tend to be strongly individualistic societies. In collectivist societies, by contrast, ties among individuals are more important than individualism. Business is conducted in the context of a group in which others' views are strongly considered. The group is all-important, as life is fundamentally a cooperative experience. Conformity and compromise help maintain group harmony. China, Panama, and South Korea are examples of strongly collectivist societies.

Individualism versus collectivism
Describes whether a person functions primarily as an individual or as part of a group.

POWER DISTANCE **Power distance** describes how a society deals with the inequalities in power that exist among people. In societies with low power distance, the gaps between the powerful and weak are minimal. In Denmark and Sweden, for example, tax and social

Power distance
Describes how a society deals with the inequalities in power that exist among people.

welfare systems ensure nationals are relatively equal in terms of income and power. The United States also scores relatively low on power distance. Societies characterized by high power distance are relatively indifferent to inequalities and allow them to grow over time. There are substantial gaps between the powerful and the weak. Guatemala, Malaysia, the Philippines, and several Middle East countries are examples of countries that exhibit high power distance. The Apply Your Understanding exercise at the end of this chapter illustrates high power distance using an Ethical Dilemma on the relationship between an executive and a maid in Colombia.

Social stratification affects power distance. In Japan, almost everybody belongs to the middle class, while in India the upper stratum controls most of the decision making and buying power. In companies, the degree of centralization of authority and autocratic leadership determines power distance. In high power-distance firms, autocratic senior managements focuses power at the top and grants little autonomy to lower-level employees. In low power-distance firms, managers and subordinates are relatively equal and cooperate to achieve organizational goals.

Uncertainty avoidance
The extent to which people can tolerate risk and uncertainty in their lives.

UNCERTAINTY AVOIDANCE **Uncertainty avoidance** refers to the extent people can tolerate risk and uncertainty in their lives. Citizens of high uncertainty-avoidance countries create institutions that minimize risk and ensure financial security. Companies emphasize stable careers and produce many rules to regulate worker actions and minimize ambiguity. Managers may be slow to make decisions as they investigate the nature and potential outcomes of several options. Belgium, France, and Japan are countries that score high on uncertainty avoidance.

Societies that score low on uncertainty avoidance socialize their members to accept and become accustomed to uncertainty. Managers are entrepreneurial and relatively comfortable taking risks, and they make decisions relatively quickly. People accept each day as it comes and take their jobs in stride because they are less concerned about ensuring their future. They tend to tolerate behavior and opinions different from their own because they do not feel threatened by them. India, Ireland, Jamaica, and the United States are leading examples of countries with low uncertainty avoidance.

Masculinity versus femininity
Refers to a society's orientation based on traditional male and female values. Masculine cultures tend to value competitiveness, assertiveness, ambition, and the accumulation of wealth. Feminine cultures emphasize nurturing roles, interdependence among people, and taking care of less fortunate people.

MASCULINITY VERSUS FEMININITY **Masculinity versus femininity** refers to a society's orientation based on traditional male and female values. Masculine cultures tend to value competitiveness, assertiveness, ambition, and the accumulation of wealth. They are characterized by men and women who are assertive and focused on career and earning money, and may care little for others. Typical examples include Australia and Japan. The United States is a moderately masculine society. Hispanic cultures are relatively masculine and display a zest for action, daring, and competitiveness. In business, the masculinity dimension manifests as self-confidence, proactiveness, and leadership. Conversely, in feminine cultures, such as the Scandinavian countries, both men and women emphasize nurturing roles, interdependence among people, and caring for less fortunate people. Welfare systems are highly developed and education is subsidized.

Source: SVLuma/Shutterstock

Mexico emphasizes collectivism and loyalty to the group. Business is characterized by long-term, easy-going relationships. Substantial power distance is the norm in larger companies, where the dress code is typically conservative.

THE FIFTH DIMENSION: LONG-TERM VERSUS SHORT-TERM ORIENTATION Hofstede's four dimensions of cultural orientation are widely accepted. They provide a tool to interpret cultural differences and a foundation for classifying countries. Yet, the Hofstede framework suffers from some limitations. First, his study was based on data collected from 1968 to 1972. Much has changed since then, including successive phases of globalization, widespread exposure to transnational media, technological advances, and changes in the role of women in the workforce. The framework fails to account for convergence of cultural values that has occurred during the last several decades. Second, Hofstede's findings are based on the employees of a single firm—IBM—in a single industry, making it difficult to generalize. Third, the data were collected using questionnaires, which are inferior for probing deep cultural issues. Finally, Hofstede did not capture all potential dimensions of culture.

Later, Hofstede added a fifth dimension to his framework: **long-term versus short-term orientation**.[20] It refers to the degree to which people and organizations defer gratification to achieve long-term success. Firms and people in cultures with a long-term orientation tend to take the long view to planning and living. They focus on years and decades. The long-term dimension is best illustrated by the so-called Asian values—cultural orientations of several Asian societies, including China, Japan, and Singapore. These values are partly based on the teachings of the Chinese philosopher Confucius (K'ung-fu-tzu), who lived about 2,500 years ago. In addition to long-term orientation, Confucius advocated other values that are still the basis for much of Asian culture today. These include discipline, loyalty, hard work, regard for education, esteem for family, focus on group harmony, and control over one's desires. Scholars credit these values for the *East Asian miracle*, the remarkable economic growth and modernization of East Asian nations during the last several decades.[21] By contrast, the United States and most other Western countries emphasize a short-term orientation.

The Hofstede framework should be viewed as only a general guide, useful for a deeper understanding in cross-national interactions with business partners, customers, and value-chain members.

Cultural Metaphors

A metaphor is a figure of speech that uses the attributes of one thing to describe a different thing. Metaphors are useful because they provide models that help simplify explanations of complex phenomena, such as culture.[22] Martin Gannon offered a particularly insightful analysis of cultural orientations.[23] In his view, a **cultural metaphor** refers to a distinctive tradition or institution strongly associated with a particular society. It is a guide to deciphering people's attitudes, values, and behavior.

For example, American football is a cultural metaphor for traditions in the United States, such as being a team player and having a strong leader who moves an organization aggressively toward a desired goal. The Swedish *stuga* (cottage or summer home) is a cultural metaphor for Swedes' love of nature and desire for individualism through self-development. Other examples of cultural metaphors include the Japanese garden (tranquility), the Turkish coffeehouse (social interaction), the Israeli kibbutz (community), and the Spanish bullfight (ritual). The Brazilian concept of *jeito* or *jeitinho Brasileiro* refers to an ability to cope with the challenges of daily life through creative problem solving or manipulating the arduous bureaucracy of the country. In the Brazilian context, manipulation, smooth talking, and patronage are not necessarily viewed negatively, because individuals often use these methods to conduct business.

Idioms

An **idiom** is an expression whose symbolic meaning is different from its literal meaning. It is a phrase you cannot understand by knowing only what the individual words in the phrase mean. For example, "to roll out the red carpet" is to extravagantly welcome a guest—no red carpet is actually used. The phrase is misunderstood when interpreted in a literal way. In Spanish, the idiom *"no está el horno para bolos"* literally means "the oven isn't ready for bread rolls." But the phrase is understood as "the time isn't right." In Japanese, the phrase *"uma ga au"* literally means "our horses meet," but the everyday meaning is "we get along with each other." Idioms exist in virtually every culture, and people often use them as a short way to express a larger concept. Managers can study national idioms to gain a better understanding of cultural values. Exhibit 4.6 offers several expressions that reveal cultural traits of different societies.

Subjective and Objective Dimensions of Culture

We saw in Exhibit 4.3 that there are numerous dimensions of national culture. We can group them into two broad dimensions: subjective and objective. The *subjective dimension* includes values and attitudes, deal versus relationship orientation, manners and customs, perceptions of

Long-term versus short-term orientation
Refers to the degree to which people and organizations defer gratification to achieve long-term success.

Cultural metaphor
A distinctive tradition or institution strongly associated with a particular society.

Country Realities

China is home to Mandarin Chinese, the language with the world's largest number of speakers. Although Hindi and English are widely spoken in India, the country is home to roughly 440 separate languages. Italy is home to the largest number of major languages in Europe, including Italian, Catalan, French, German, Greek, and English. In Latin America, Spanish and Portuguese are the most common languages. On the African continent, English and French are widely spoken.

Idiom
An expression whose symbolic meaning is different from its literal meaning.

EXHIBIT 4.6 Idioms that Symbolize Cultural Values

Country	Expression	Underlying Value
Japan	"The nail that sticks out gets hammered down."	Group conformity
Australia and New Zealand	"The tall poppy gets cut down." (Criticism of a person who is perceived as presumptuous, attention-seeking, or without merit.)	Egalitarianism
Sweden and other Scandinavian countries	"*Janteloven*" or "Jante Law." "Don't think you're anyone special or that you're better than us."	Modesty
Korea	"A tiger dies leaving its leather, a man dies leaving his name."	Honor
Turkey	"Steel that works, does not rust."	Hard work
United States	"Necessity is the mother of invention."	Resourcefulness
Thailand	"If you follow older people, dogs won't bite you."	Wisdom

time, perceptions of space, and religion. The *objective dimension* includes symbolic, material, and creative productions, such as the tools, architecture, and infrastructure unique to a society. In this section, we examine key examples of each dimension.

Values and Attitudes

Values represent a person's judgments about what is good or bad, acceptable or unacceptable, important or unimportant, and normal or abnormal.[24] Our values guide the development of our attitudes and preferences. *Attitudes* are similar to opinions but are often unconsciously held and may not have a rational basis. *Prejudices* are rigidly held attitudes, usually unfavorable and usually aimed at particular groups of people.[25] For example, typical values in North America, northern Europe, and Japan include hard work, punctuality, and the acquisition of wealth. People from such countries may misjudge those from developing economies who may not embrace such values.

Deal versus Relationship Orientation

In deal-oriented cultures, managers focus on the task at hand and prefer getting down to business. At the extreme, such managers may even avoid small talk and other preliminaries. They prefer to seal agreements with a legalistic contract, and take an impersonal approach to settling disputes. Australia, northern Europe, and North America are deal-oriented cultures. By contrast, relationship-oriented cultures emphasize affiliations with people. Managers seek to build trust and rapport and get to know the other party in business interactions. For example, it took nine years for Volkswagen to negotiate the opening of a car factory in China, a strongly relationship-oriented society. For the Chinese, Japanese, and many in Latin America, relationships are often more important than the deal.[26] Trust is valued in business agreements.

Example: Contrasting Mexico and the United States

Culture can differ sharply, even between neighboring countries. Exhibit 4.7 examines cultural differences between Mexico and the United States.

Manners and Customs

Source: Erico Sugita/Reuters/Corbis

In Japan and South Korea, bowing is common in business and personal settings.

Manners and customs are ways of behaving and conducting oneself in public and business situations. Some countries are characterized by egalitarian, informal cultures,

EXHIBIT 4.7 Perceived Cultural Attributes of Mexico and the United States

Dimension	Mexico	United States
Role of context	High-context culture that values social trust, personal goodwill, and ritualized business	Low-context culture that emphasizes efficiency, explicit communications, and "getting down to business"
Individualism versus collectivism	Relatively group oriented. Extended families, teamwork, and group loyalty are valued.	Relatively individualistic. Emphasis on personal freedom and working alone. Group loyalty is less valued.
Time orientation	Fluid and polychronic. Long-term relationships are valued. Mexicans emphasize the past and believe they have little control over the future.	Rigid and monochronic. Business is short-term oriented and values profit above all else. Americans believe they can control the future.
Space perceptions	Conversational distance is close. Personal space is less valued.	Conversational distance is ample. Personal space is highly valued.
Religion	Christianity is very influential in daily life, and often in business.	Americans' religious orientation is diverse and declining.
Language	Spanish dominates, with little linguistic diversity.	While English dominates, there is much linguistic diversity.
Negotiations	Tend to progress slowly. Decisions take time. Legalism is avoided in agreements.	Emphasis on efficiency and quick decision making. Agreements are often legalistic.
Business relations	Relationship-oriented. Mexicans are easy-going, valuing personal bonds.	Deal-oriented. Business performance takes precedence over relationships.
Business meetings	Arriving late is acceptable. Meetings are informal and usually don't follow a strict agenda.	Americans are time-oriented, arriving promptly to meetings, which often follow a formal agenda.
Superior-subordinate relations	Firms are hierarchical, with much power distance. Senior managers are relatively authoritarian.	Lower power distance. Firms are "flatter," with less hierarchy. Relations with superiors are informal and easy-going.
Style of dress in business	Conservative, emphasizing dark suits. High-status personnel are expected to dress the part.	Business casual is widely accepted. "Dressing the part" is less important.

Sources: Based on Geert Hofstede, *Culture's Consequences* (Beverly Hills, CA: Sage, 1980); Boye De Mente, *The Mexican Mind* (Beverly Hills, CA: Phoenix Books, 2011); Lucila Ortiz, *A Primer for Spanish Language, Culture and Economics* (Bloomington, IN: Xlibris, 2011).

in which people are equal and work together cooperatively. In other countries, people are more formal, and status, hierarchy, power, and respect are important. Customs that vary most worldwide are those related to eating habits and mealtimes, work hours and holidays, drinking and toasting, appropriate behavior at social gatherings, gift giving, and the role of women. Handshaking varies across the world: limp handshakes, firm handshakes, elbow-grasping handshakes, and no handshake at all. In much of the world, people greet by kissing each other on both cheeks. In some countries it is appropriate to kiss the other's hand. In Southeast Asia, greeting involves placing the palms together in front of the chest, as in praying. In Japan, bowing is the norm.[27] Gift giving is a complex ritual in much of the world. It is ingrained in Japanese culture, where it is usually a blunder to not offer a gift in initial meetings. The Middle East is characterized by generous gift giving.

Perceptions of Time

In business, time dictates expectations about planning, scheduling, profit streams, and promptness, or what constitutes lateness in arriving for work and meetings. Japanese managers tend to prepare strategic plans for extended periods, such as a decade. The planning horizon for Western companies is much shorter, typically a few years. Some societies are more oriented to the past, others to the present, and still others to the future. People in past-oriented cultures believe plans should be evaluated in terms of their fit with established traditions, customs, and wisdom. Innovation and change are infrequent and are justified to the extent they fit with past experience. Europeans are relatively past-oriented, aiming to conserve traditions and historical precedents.

By contrast, young countries like Australia, Canada, and the United States are relatively focused on the present. They have a **monochronic** view of time—a rigid orientation in which the individual is focused on schedules, punctuality, and time as a resource. People in these cultures view time as *linear*, like a river flowing into the future, carrying workers from one activity to the

Monochronic
A rigid orientation to time, in which the individual is focused on schedules, punctuality, and time as a resource.

next. In such cultures, managers make commitments, set deadlines, and adhere to a strict schedule of meetings and activities. Punctuality is a virtue and time is money. Throughout the day, workers glance at their watches, their computer's clock, or the clock on the wall. Managers and investors are impatient and want quick returns. Company performance is measured quarterly. In this way, people in the United States have acquired a reputation for being hurried and impatient. Indeed, the word *business* was originally spelled *busyness*.

Polychronic
A flexible, nonlinear orientation to time, whereby the individual takes a long-term perspective and emphasizes human relationships.

Some cultures have a **polychronic** perspective on time. In such societies, instead of performing single tasks serially, people are inclined to do many things at once. In this way, members of polychronic cultures are easily distracted. They can change plans often and easily, and long delays are sometimes needed before taking action. Punctuality per se is relatively unimportant, and managers consider time commitments flexible. They do not adhere strictly to the clock and schedules. They put more value on relationships and spending time with people.

Chinese and Japanese firms are future-oriented, focusing not on how the firm will perform next quarter, but on how it will perform a decade from now. Large Japanese firms offer lifetime employment and invest heavily in employee training, expecting workers to remain with the firm for 30 or 40 years. Latin Americans similarly have a flexible perception of time and are more inclined to arrive late for appointments than people from other cultures. In the Middle East, strict Muslims view destiny as the will of God ("Inshallah" or "God willing" is a frequently used phrase) and downplay the importance of future planning. They perceive appointments as relatively vague future obligations.

Perceptions of Space

Cultures also differ in their perceptions of physical space; we have our own sense of personal space and feel uncomfortable if others violate it. Conversational distance is closer in Latin America than in northern Europe or the United States. When a North American national interacts with a Latin American, he or she may unconsciously back up to maintain personal space. Those who live in crowded Japan or Belgium have smaller personal space requirements than those who live in land-rich Russia or the United States. In Japan, it is common for employee workspaces to be crowded together in the same room, desks pushed against each other. One large office space might accommodate fifty employees. North American firms partition individual workspaces and provide private offices for more important employees. In Islamic countries, close proximity may be discouraged between a man and a woman who are not married.

Religion

Religion is a system of common beliefs or attitudes concerning a higher being or a system of thought that people consider to be sacred, divine, or the highest truth. Religion includes the moral codes, values, institutions, traditions, and rituals associated with this system. Religious conceptions of right and wrong have played a major role in the development of ethics and social responsibility. Almost every culture is underpinned by religious beliefs. Because religion influences culture, it also affects managerial and customer behavior in various ways. Exhibit 4.8 shows the dominant religions worldwide.

Although this exhibit displays the most common religion in each location, most countries are home to people of various beliefs. Religion appears to have a positive effect on economic activity.[28] Religious affiliations help create bonds of trust and shared commitment, which facilitate lending and trade. Religion can boost GDP in a country by reducing corruption, and by increasing respect for law and order. Conversely, a lack of ethical values tends to coincide with economic decay.

Christianity substantially affects culture and business. For example, Sunday is still regarded a day of rest when most people do not work. Scholars suggest a relationship between Protestantism and capitalism.[29] Protestantism emphasizes the necessity of hard work to achieve worldly success and as a duty that benefits both the individual and society. Protestantism has long emphasized religious freedom and independent thinking. Such views are consistent with the political and economic freedoms that encouraged the rise of capitalism, especially in Europe and North America.

Islam is based on the *Qur'an*, the religion's holy book. In most Middle East countries, Islam is the basis for government and legal systems. Islam strongly influences culture and society. Most Muslims adhere to Islamic law, known as *Sharia*, which covers aspects of daily life, economic activity, and public governance. Islam disapproves of economic activity that might harm others or that is not in the public interest. Islam encourages free trade by prohibiting restraints such as monopolies and price fixing. The *Qur'an* condemns charging interest for money loaned. Thus, banks in Islamic countries have devised methods for financing debt without violating Sharia law. Many multinational firms are reaching out to Muslim communities. Nokia launched a mobile phone that shows Muslims the direction toward Mecca, Islam's holiest site, when they pray. Heineken, the Dutch brewing giant, rolled out the nonalcoholic malt drink *Fayrouz* for the Islamic market. Experienced MNEs operating in Islamic countries respect Sharia law and avoid business activities that exploit people.[30]

Hinduism is the dominant indigenous religion of South Asia, especially India. Hindus believe in reincarnation, a cycle of birth, life, death, and rebirth. The nature of actions taken during one's lifetime, *karma*, determines future destiny. *Karma* implies that people are born into a social level, or *caste*, because of their good or bad deeds in earlier lives.[31] Such thinking can influence superior-subordinate relations in organizations. Some scholars view Hinduism's quest for spiritual enlightenment as potentially at odds with the profit orientation of business and entrepreneurship.[32] However, others argue that business management can be enhanced by embracing Hinduism's teachings in areas such as self-control, discipline, and devotion to duty.[33]

Ethical Connections

Ethical values vary by culture. Consider two scenarios given to students. In scenario one, a car salesman failed to inform his superiors about a serious engine problem of a car he had received as trade-in on a new car sale. In scenario two, a dealership neglected to fully repair a car transmission under warranty in the hope of securing lucrative repair work after the warranty expired. Students from China and Russia felt relatively little harm had been done in these scenarios, while students from Finland and South Korea judged the scenarios to be unethical.

Source: M. Ahmed, Y. Kung; J. Eichenseher, "Business Students' Perception of Ethics and Moral Judgment," *Journal of Business Ethics*, 43 (2003): 89–102.

Buddhism is both a religion and philosophy that encompasses various traditions and practices. It is common to Asia, especially China and Japan. Buddhism promotes harmony and peaceful relations with others. In this way, it supports harmony and stability in commercial relations. Buddhism also encourages tolerance for others and mutual cooperation, which are good for business. Followers are comfortable with acquiring wealth, as long as it is done with harmony and patience. Buddhism promotes a life centered on spiritual rather than worldly matters. Accordingly, it is seen to support ethical and responsible behavior in business. However, Buddhism's focus on spirituality and moderation can restrain entrepreneurial action.

Now that we have reviewed the subjective dimensions of culture, we turn to its objective dimensions—symbolic and material productions.

Symbolic Productions

A *symbol* can be letters, figures, colors, or other characters that communicate a meaning. For example, the cross is the main symbol of Christianity. The red star was the symbol of the former Soviet Union. National symbols include flags, anthems, seals, monuments, and historical myths. These symbols represent nations and national values and help to unite people. Mathematicians and scientists use symbols as types of language. Businesses have many types of symbols, in the form of trademarks, logos, and brands. Can you easily identify popular company logos such as Apple's apple, Cadbury's unique lettering, and the three diamonds of Mitsubishi?

Material Productions and Creative Expressions of Culture

Material productions are artifacts, objects, and technological systems that people construct to cope with their environments. They are integral to human life and provide the means to accomplish objectives, as well as to communicate and conduct exchanges within and between societies. The most important technology-based material productions are the infrastructures that supply energy, transportation, and communications. Others include social infrastructure (systems that provide housing, education, and health care), financial infrastructure (systems for managing means of exchange in

EXHIBIT 4.8

World Religions

Sources: Based on http://www.godweb.org/religionsofworld.htm and http://www.mapsofworld.com/religion-map.htm.

ARCTIC OCEAN

NORWAY
SWEDEN
FINLAND
ESTONIA
LATVIA
LITHUANIA

RUSSIA

UNITED
KINGDOM
BELGIUM
IRELAND
NETHER-
LANDS
DENMARK
RUSSIA
BELARUS
GERMANY
POLAND
LUXEMBOURG
CZECH
REP.
UKRAINE
FRANCE
LIECH.
AUSTRIA
SLOVAKIA
SWITZ.
SLOVENIA
HUNGARY
MOLDOVA
CROATIA
ROMANIA
MONACO
BOSNIA
HERZEGOVINA
SERBIA AND
MONTENEGRO
BULGARIA
ITALY
MACEDONIA
GEORGIA
ANDORRA
ALBANIA
SPAIN
GREECE
TURKEY
PORTUGAL
CYPRUS
ARMENIA
AZERBAIJAN
TUNISIA

KAZAKHSTAN

MONGOLIA

UZBEKISTAN
KYRGYZSTAN
TURKMENISTAN
TAJIKISTAN

NORTH
KOREA
SOUTH
KOREA
JAPAN

CHINA

SYRIA
LEBANON
ISRAEL
JORDAN
IRAQ
IRAN
AFGHANISTAN
MOROCCO
KUWAIT
PAKISTAN
WESTERN
SAHARA
ALGERIA
LIBYA
EGYPT
QATAR
UNITED ARAB
EMIRATES
SAUDI
ARABIA
OMAN
NEPAL
BHUTAN
BANGLADESH
TAIWAN
MAURITANIA
MALI
NIGER
CHAD
INDIA
MYANMAR
(BURMA)
LAOS
SENEGAL
GAMBIA
GUINEA-BISSAU
BURKINA
FASO
ERITREA
YEMEN
THAILAND
VIETNAM
GUINEA
NIGERIA
SUDAN
CAMBODIA
SIERRA LEONE
IVORY
COAST
GHANA
TOGO
BENIN
DJIBOUTI
SOMALIA
PHILIPPINES
LIBERIA
CENTRAL
AFRICAN
REPUBLIC
ETHIOPIA
CAMEROON
SRI
LANKA
BRUNEI
MALAYSIA
EQUATORIAL
GUINEA
GABON
CONGO
REPUBLIC
UGANDA
SINGAPORE
CONGO
DEMOCRATIC
REPUBLIC
(ZAIRE)
RWANDA
BURUNDI
KENYA
INDONESIA
PAPUA
NEW
GUINEA
SOLOMON
ISLANDS
TANZANIA

PACIFIC
OCEAN

INDIAN
OCEAN

SOUTH
ATLANTIC
OCEAN

ANGOLA
ZAMBIA
MALAWI
MOZAMBIQUE
NAMIBIA
ZIMBABWE
MADAGASCAR
MAURITIUS
RÉUNION
BOTSWANA
SWAZILAND
SOUTH
AFRICA
LESOTHO

VANUATU
FIJI

NEW
CALEDONIA

AUSTRALIA

NEW
ZEALAND

Christianity
Judaism
Hinduism
Islam

Buddhism
Nature religion
Chinese religion
Other groups

97

banks and other financial institutions), and marketing infrastructure (systems that support marketing-related activities, such as ad agencies).

Creative expressions of culture include arts, folklore, music, dance, theater, and high cuisine. Food is among the most interesting cultural markers. In Japan, pizza is often topped with fish and seaweed. In the United States, pizza can be piled high with meat. In France, it often comes with various cheeses. McDonald's aims for a standardized menu worldwide, but often must vary offerings to suit individual countries. In India, for example, McDonald's offers items such as "paneer salsa wrap," and various chicken and vegetarian burgers, to comply with Indians distaste for red meat, which is rooted in religious beliefs. McDonald's experienced much difficulty adapting its menu to the tastes of consumers in Bolivia.[34]

Language: A Key Dimension of Culture

Often described as the expression or mirror of culture, language is not only essential for communications, it also provides insights into culture. The world has nearly 7,000 active languages, including more than 2,000 each in Africa and Asia. But most of these languages have only a few thousand speakers.[35] Exhibit 4.9 highlights the world's major languages. Arabic comprises fifteen major and often highly distinct language variants across forty-six countries. In much of the world, English tends to dominate cross-national commerce. MNEs whose first language is English typically perform better in international business.[36] However, buyers always prefer appeals offered in their native tongue. Subordinates usually respond more eagerly when they receive instructions in their mother language. Linguistic proficiency is a great asset in international business because it facilitates cross-cultural communications and understanding. Learning one or more common languages can greatly enhance an international business career.

EXHIBIT 4.9

The Most Common Primary Languages in the World

Sources: Based on R. Gordon (ed.), *Ethnologue: Languages of the World*, 16th ed. (Dallas, TX: SIL International, 2009 at http://www.ethnologue.com), and CIA World Factbook, 2011, at http://www.cia.gov.

World Rank	Language	Approximate Number of Native Speakers (Millions)	Countries with Substantial Number of Native Speakers
1	Chinese	1,213	China, Singapore
2	Spanish	329	Argentina, Mexico, Spain
3	English	328	Australia, Canada, United States
4	Arabic	221	Algeria, Egypt, Saudi Arabia
5	Hindi	182	India
6	Bengali	181	Bangladesh, India
7	Portuguese	178	Brazil, Portugal
8	Russian	144	Russia, Kazakhstan, Ukraine
9	Japanese	122	Japan
10	German	90	Austria, Germany
11	Javanese	85	Indonesia, Malaysia
16	French	68	Canada, France, Mali
17	Korean	66	South Korea, North Korea
18	Tamil	66	India, Sri Lanka
19	Italian	62	Italy, Malta, San Marino
20	Turkish	51	Turkey, Turkmenistan

Company and Location	Intended Ad Slogan	Literal Translation
Parker Pen Company in Latin America	"Use Parker Pen, avoid embarrassment!"	"Use Parker Pen, avoid pregnancy!"
Pepsi in Germany	"Come Alive with Pepsi"	"Come out of the grave with Pepsi."
Pepsi in Taiwan	"Come Alive with Pepsi"	"Pepsi brings your ancestors back from the dead."
Fisher Body (car exteriors) in Belgium	"Body by Fisher"	"Corpse by Fisher"
Salem cigarettes in Japan	"Salem—Feeling Free"	"Smoking Salem makes your mind feel free and empty."

EXHIBIT 4.10

Blunders in International Advertising

Language has both verbal and nonverbal characteristics. Much language is unspoken and entails facial expressions and gestures.[37] In fact, most verbal messages are accompanied by nonverbal ones. In this and other ways, language is extremely subtle.

Sometimes it is difficult to find words to convey the same meaning in a different language. For example, a one-word equivalent to "aftertaste" does not exist in many languages. Even when a word can be translated well into other languages, its concept and meaning may not be universal. The Japanese word *muzukashii* can be variously translated as "difficult," "delicate," or "I don't want to discuss it," but in business negotiations it usually means "out of the question."

National languages, dialects, and translation have a tendency to complicate straightforward communication. Ignorance can be embarrassing. Advertising themes often lose their original meaning in translation or convey unfavorable interpretations. Even people from different countries who speak the same language may experience communication problems because of unique colloquial words. The same word can convey different meanings in the two countries. Exhibit 4.10 shows how the popular slogans of some languages translate into offensive phrases in other languages. Exhibit 4.11 shows how two English-speaking countries interpret the same word in very different ways. These exhibits demonstrate how easy it is for misinterpretations to get in the way of intended meaning.

Business jargon unique to a culture can also impede communication. For example, many expressions in United States English are based on sports or military terms and pose problems for non-U.S. businesspeople. Examples of English jargon that puzzle nonnative speakers include: "the bottom line," "to beat around the bush," "shooting from the hip," and "feather in your cap." Imagine the difficulty professional interpreters encounter in translating such phrases!

EXHIBIT 4.11

Examples of Differences in Meaning between the United Kingdom and the United States

Word	Meaning in U.S. English	Meaning in British English
Scheme	A somewhat devious plan	A plan
Redundant	Repetitive	Fired or laid off
Sharp	Smart	Conniving, unethical
To table	To put as issue on hold	To take up an issue
To bomb	To fail miserably	To succeed grandly
Windscreen	A screen that protects against wind	Automobile windshield

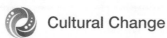 Cultural Change

We have seen that culture is relatively stable. However, the globalization of markets, transnational media, technological advances, and government regulations substantially influence culture, and culture is so powerful and pervasive that it influences these factors in turn. In this section, we explore the link between culture and factors that can transform it over time.

Technology, the Internet, and Culture

Technological advances are a key determinant of culture and cultural change. They have freed up leisure time and led to the proliferation of computers, multimedia, and communications systems that bring geographically separated cultures in closer contact than ever before. Communications, information, and transportation technologies have increased people's ability to learn about and connect with unfamiliar cultures. Just as distinctive societies developed in the distant past because regions had limited contact with each other, today cultures are homogenizing due to increased contact among peoples of the world.

The Internet and other technologies help promote foreign cultures. Artistic traditions from Africa, Asia, and Latin America have received a big boost from the rise of world cinema and television. We can also choose our information sources. People usually prefer information in their native language that represents familiar culture. Thus, Spanish speakers in the United States prefer Spanish mass media, limiting the culturally homogenizing effect of English-speaking media. Global communications allow widely dispersed ethnic groups to remain in touch with each other.[38] The number of Internet users is growing rapidly worldwide, and the potential for cultural blunders arising from international e-mail use is higher than ever. To help reduce such problems, managers can use software that instantly converts messages into any of dozens of languages.[39]

Globalization's Effect on Culture: Are Cultures Converging?

There is little consensus about globalization's effects on culture. On the one hand, critics charge that globalization harms local cultures and their artistic expressions and sensibilities, replacing them with a homogeneous, often "Americanized" culture. Others argue that increased global communications is positive because it permits the free flow of cultural ideas, beliefs, and values. Clearly, globalization is a major factor in the emergence of a common worldwide culture.

People in many parts of the world consume the same Big Macs and Coca-Colas, watch the same movies, listen to the same music, drive the same cars, and stay in the same hotels. Although food often represents a distinct culture, hamburgers, tacos, and pizza are increasingly popular worldwide.[40] Movies and TV shows promote the convergence of customs, fashions, and other manifestations of culture. Today, college students listen to much the same music and wear similar clothing worldwide. In Trinidad, the U.S. television series *The Young and the Restless* is so popular that in many places work effectively stops when it airs, and it has inspired calypso songs of the same name. *CSI Miami* and *Desperate Housewives* have ranked among the most popular TV series worldwide. The iconic Barbie doll has become a global phenomenon, even as the values it represents do not fit conservative cultures.[41]

In reality, however, the larger trend is more complex than these examples imply. As international business integrates the world's economies, it also increases the choices available to local people by making their countries culturally richer. Cultural homogeneity and heterogeneity are not mutually exclusive alternatives or substitutes; they may exist simultaneously. Cross-cultural exchange promotes innovation and creativity. Globalization brings a wider menu of choices to consumers and increases diversity within society.[42] Cultural flows originate in many places. Just as McDonald's hamburgers are popular in Japan, so is Vietnamese food in the United States and Japanese sushi in Europe. Integration and the spread of ideas and images tend to provoke reactions and resistance to cultural homogenization, thereby spurring individual peoples to insist on their differences. While some past customs will disappear due to globalization, the process is also liberating people culturally by undermining the ideological conformity of nationalism.

Context of International Business

Effective handling of the cross-cultural interface is a critical source of firms' competitive advantage. Managers not only need to develop empathy and tolerance toward cultural differences but also must acquire a sufficient degree of factual knowledge about the beliefs and values of foreign counterparts. Cross-cultural proficiency is paramount in many managerial tasks, including:

- Developing products and services
- Preparing advertising and promotional materials
- Preparing for international trade fairs and exhibitions
- Screening and selecting foreign distributors and other partners
- Communicating and interacting with foreign business partners
- Negotiating and structuring international business ventures
- Interacting with current and potential customers from abroad[43]

Let's consider specific examples of how cross-cultural differences may complicate company activities.[44]

Developing products and services   Cultural differences necessitate adapting marketing activities to suit the specific needs of target markets. In China, Burger King (www.burgerking.com/bkglobal) had to introduce the concept of all-beef hamburgers to local consumers. The Chinese prefer chicken, so the firm also added several chicken dishes to its menu. In addition, KFC offers "pumpkin porridge" and "Beijing chicken rolls" to accommodate local tastes.

Organizational structure   Some companies prefer to delegate authority to country managers, which results in a *decentralized* organizational structure. Other firms have *centralized* structures, in which power is concentrated at regional or corporate headquarters. Firms may be bureaucratic or entrepreneurial. How do you deal with a bureaucratic partner or manage distantly located, decentralized subsidiaries?

Teamwork   Cooperating with partners and host-country nationals to achieve common organizational goals is critical to business success. But what should managers do if foreign and domestic nationals don't get along? The Chinese home appliance manufacturer Haier (www.haier.com) delayed acquiring overseas firms because management felt it lacked the ability to manage foreign nationals and integrate differing cultural systems.

Pay-for-performance system   In some countries, merit is not the main basis for promoting employees. In China and Japan, a person's age is the most important determinant. But how do such workers perform when Western firms evaluate them using performance-based measures?

Lifetime employment   In some Asian countries, firms are very protective of their employees who may work for the same company all their lives. The expectations that arise from such devoted relationships can complicate dealings with outside firms. Western managers may struggle to motivate employees who expect they will always have the same job.

Union–management relationships   In Germany, union bosses hold the same status as top-level managers and are allowed to sit on corporate boards. Many European firms have a business culture in which workers are relatively equal to managers. This approach can reduce the flexibility of company operations because it makes it harder to lay off workers.

Attitudes toward ambiguity   In some countries, people have a hard time tolerating *ambiguity*, which refers to situations in which information can be understood in more than one way. For example, some bosses give exact and detailed instructions, while others give vague and incomplete instructions. If you're not comfortable working with minimum guidance or taking independent action, then you may not fit well into some cultures.

Negotiations   Negotiations arise in virtually all aspects of business, as when the firm takes on a partner or a supplier–buyer relationship. Goals, interests, ethics, and cultural assumptions vary cross-culturally, which may complicate forming and maintaining business relationships. In most of Northern Europe, negotiations are relatively efficient, impersonal, and unsociable; negotiators "get down to business" quickly.

Culture and the Services Sector

In the advanced economies, firms that engage in services such as lodging and retailing account for a greater share of FDI than firms that manufacture products.[45] Contact-based services such as architecture, consulting, and legal services bring providers into direct contact with foreign customers. Asset-based services include banks, restaurants, and retail stores.[46]

Cultural differences can create problems for service firms and lead to mishaps in the exchange process. The greater the cultural distance between the service provider and its customers, the more likely there will be cognitive and communication gaps. Imagine a Western lawyer who tries to establish a law office in China. Without a thorough knowledge of Chinese culture and language, the lawyer's efforts can be futile. Imagine how much success a Western restaurant chain would have in Russia if it knew nothing of Russian food culture or the work habits of Russian workers!

Differences in language and national character have the same effect as trade barriers. Service firms that internationalize through FDI are vulnerable because each firm is shaped by both a national and an organizational culture.[47] A Chinese bank that establishes a branch in New York or London remains distinctly Chinese because its business approach is based on Chinese culture.[48]

To overcome these challenges, service firms seek to understand the cultures and languages of the countries where they do business. For example, at the global express company FedEx, management constantly seeks to hire, train, and motivate hundreds of sales representatives who speak different languages, represent different cultures, and serve different markets.[49] Without such efforts, service firms would not likely succeed at international business.

The *Recent Grad in IB* feature highlights the cross-cultural experiences of Chinese-born Lawrence Yu, who lived, studied, and worked in the United States. Having an inquiring mind and being open to new experiences helped Lawrence bridge cultural gaps.

 Overcoming Cross-Cultural Risk: Managerial Guidelines

Seasoned managers attest to the importance of a deep knowledge of culture and language in international business. Managers can achieve effective cross-cultural interaction by keeping an open mind, being inquisitive, and not rushing to conclusions about others' behaviors.

Even experienced managers undergo cultural training that emphasizes observational skills and human relations techniques. Skills are more important than pure information because skills can be transferred across countries, while information is often country-specific. Planning that combines informal mentoring from experienced managers and formal training through seminars, courses, and simulations abroad and at home can go far in helping managers meet cross-cultural challenges.

Although every culture is unique, certain basic guidelines are appropriate for consistent cross-cultural success. Let's review three guidelines managers can follow in preparing for successful cross-cultural encounters.

Guideline 1: Acquire factual and interpretive knowledge about the other culture, and try to speak the language. Successful managers acquire a base of knowledge about the values, attitudes, and lifestyles of the cultures with which they interact. Managers study the political and economic background of target countries—their history, current national affairs, and perceptions about other cultures. Such knowledge facilitates understanding the partner's mind-set, organization, and objectives. Decisions and events become substantially easier to interpret. Sincere interest in the target culture helps establish trust and respect, laying the foundation for open and productive relationships. Even modest

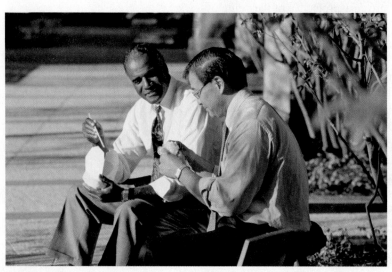

Source: Getty Images-Photodisc

Cross-cultural proficiency increases the effectiveness of meetings and other encounters in international business.

ZHIBO (LAWRENCE) YU

Lawrence's major: Supply-Chain Management
Objectives: Make a difference in the world. Exciting career in international business.
Jobs held since graduating:

- Global Supply Manager, Logistics Program Manager, Dell Inc., Austin, Texas
- Senior Manager, Lenovo, Beijing, China

Since opening to foreign investors, China's economy has grown rapidly. Lawrence Yu lived in China and witnessed amazing changes there as a teenager in the 1990s. He ate at McDonald's, wore Nike shoes, and watched NBA games. At 16, Lawrence came to the United States and eventually earned a bachelor's degree in supply-chain management.

While in college, Lawrence went on a study-abroad program in Mexico where he studied Spanish, lived with a Mexican family, and toured manufacturing firms. He got an internship at Whirlpool Corporation, where he created an asset-tracking system for the global procurement group and conducted market research in China. After Whirlpool, he completed another internship with Unilever North America.

After graduation, Lawrence worked at Dell Inc. as a master scheduler for notebook computers. He was primarily responsible for forecasting, planning, lead-time setting, and product transition management. One of Dell's key suppliers is located in Malaysia. Since Chinese was the first language of most of the Malaysian team members, Lawrence helped to increase communication quality and work efficiency. Management next sent Lawrence to Dell China to work with the procurement group in Shanghai.

After working as a master scheduler, Lawrence was recruited to Dell Global Logistics as a program manager, where his responsibilities included business reviews, financial analysis, contract negotiations, and process-improvement projects. With responsibility for overseeing eight U.S. logistics centers and a 100-truck fleet, Lawrence learned people-management skills and the ability to make decisions under pressure.

Lawrence was then promoted to Global Supply Manager, helping administer Dell's annual spending in semiconductor products. In this role, he negotiated prices with suppliers such as Samsung, Siemens, and Kingston. Most recently, Lawrence accepted a position as a senior manager at Lenovo headquarters in Beijing.

Lawrence's Advice for an International Business Career

"While it was risky, I'm glad I did it. Language barriers, cultural differences, and being apart from family were all difficult. Language can be improved over time, and culture can be learned while you live in that culture. I got used to living alone pretty fast. In addition to going to class, by living, studying, and working in another country, I was naturally learning every day. The knowledge you gain from being in another country cannot be learned any other way. I now have greater confidence in whatever I pursue than I ever had before, thanks to my international experience!"

attempts to speak the local language are welcome. Higher levels of language proficiency pave the way for acquiring competitive advantages. In the long run, managers who can converse in multiple languages are more likely to negotiate successfully and have positive business interactions.

Guideline 2: Avoid cultural bias. Problems arise when managers make ethnocentric assumptions that foreigners think and behave just like the folks back home. Ethnocentric assumptions lead to poor business strategies in both planning and execution. Managers new to international business can find the behavior of a foreigner odd and perhaps improper. For example, it is easy to be offended when a foreign counterpart does not appreciate our food, history, entertainment, or everyday traditions. In this way, cultural bias can be a significant barrier to successful interpersonal communication.

A person's own culture conditions how he or she reacts to different values, behavior, or systems. Most people unconsciously assume those in other countries experience the world as they do. They view their own culture as the norm; everything else may seem strange. This

GLOBAL TREND

Minimizing Cross-Cultural Bias with Critical Incident Analysis

To compete effectively, companies must continually improve ways to communicate with and manage customers and partners around the world. Global teams with members from various cultural backgrounds enable firms to profit from knowledge amassed across the organization's worldwide operations. Such teams function best when the members engage in high-quality communications, minimizing miscommunications caused by differences in language and culture.

Nevertheless, inexperienced managers often misunderstand the behavior of foreign counterparts, which hinders the effectiveness of cross-cultural meetings. One way to minimize such problems is *critical incident analysis (CIA)*.

Consider the following scenario: Working on a joint product design, engineers from Ford (United States) and Mazda (Japan) interact intensively with each other. Ford wants to share its engineering studies and critical materials with its Japanese counterpart. After a week of interaction, the Ford team has grown uncomfortable because the Japanese appear strangely indifferent and do not exhibit much reaction. When the teams meet, the Japanese appear to keep conversation among themselves and offer little feedback. Eventually, the Ford team's surprise turns to frustration and anger. They now believe the Japanese

are arrogant, indifferent about Ford's designs, and uninterested in collaboration.

In reality, the Ford team has jumped to conclusions and judged the Japanese with its own culturally bound expectations. An expert on Japanese business culture could have provided alternative explanations. For one, the Japanese engineers may not be proficient in English. They are unable to explain themselves easily or to understand the Ford team's briefings, which all occur in English. Japanese are generally thoughtful and typically show respect for counterparts by listening intently while remaining quiet. Furthermore, before their team meets in private and reaches consensus, Japanese usually refrain from speaking out. These and other explanations are all plausible in the context of Japanese culture.

What should you do when confronted with an awkward or uncomfortable situation in a cross-cultural interaction? CIA involves the following steps:

1. Identify the situations where you need to be culturally aware to interact effectively with people from another culture. These may include socializing, working in groups, negotiating, and reaching agreement.
2. When confronted with seemingly strange behavior, discipline yourself

to avoid making hasty judgments. Instead, try to view the situation or the problem in terms of the unfamiliar culture. Make observations and gather objective information from native citizens or secondary sources. In this way, you can isolate the self-reference criterion that led to your possibly inaccurate conclusion.
3. Learn to make a variety of interpretations of others' behavior, to select the most likely one in the cultural context, and only then to formulate your own response. In this way, you can avoid the self-reference criterion and likely make a better decision.
4. Learn from this process and continuously improve.

Sources: Elizabeth K. Briody, Robert T. Trotter, and Tracy L. Meerwarth, *Transforming Culture: Creating and Sustaining a Better Manufacturing Organization* (New York: Palgrave Macmillan, 2010); Robert Keller, Christoph Senn, and Axel Thoma, "Worldly Wise: Attracting and Managing Customers Isn't the Same When Business Goes Global," *Wall Street Journal*, March 3, 2007, p. R5; "Cross-Functional Project Groups in Research and New Product Development," *Academy of Management Journal* 44, no. 3 (2001): 547–555; David Armstrong, "Building Teams Across Borders," *Executive Excellence* 17, no. 3 (2000): 10.

Self-reference criterion
The tendency to view other cultures through the lens of your own culture.

Critical incident analysis (CIA)
A method for analyzing awkward situations in cross-cultural encounters by developing objectivity and empathy for other points of view.

is known as the **self-reference criterion**—the tendency to view other cultures through the lens of your own culture. Understanding the self-reference criterion is a critical first step to avoiding cultural bias and ethnocentric reactions.

Critical incident analysis (CIA) is a method that managers use to analyze awkward situations in cross-cultural encounters. CIA encourages a more effective approach to cultural differences by helping managers develop objectivity and empathy for other points of view. The *Global Trend* feature details how managers can avoid the self-reference criterion by using CIA.

Guideline 3: Develop cross-cultural skills. Working effectively with counterparts from other cultures requires you to make an investment in your professional development. Each culture has its own ways of conducting business transactions, negotiations, and dispute resolution. You are exposed to high levels of *ambiguity* regarding concepts and relationships that can be understood in a variety of ways.[50] Success in international business requires you to strive for cross-cultural proficiency. It is can be obtained from various sources, including reading books, cross-cultural training, learning from expatriates, and befriending natives in one's own country. Direct experience with the culture is generally best. There is no substitute for direct experience with cross-cultural groups and situations.[51]

Ultimately, cross-cultural proficiency is characterized by four key personality traits:

1. **Tolerance for ambiguity:** The ability to tolerate uncertainty and apparent of clarity in the thinking and actions of others.
2. **Perceptiveness:** The ability to closely observe and appreciate hard-to-see information in the speech and behavior of others.
3. **Valuing personal relationships:** The ability to recognize the importance of interpersonal relationships, which is often much more important than achieving one-time goals or winning arguments.
4. **Flexibility and adaptability:** The ability to be creative in finding innovative solutions, to be open-minded about outcomes, and to show grace and kindness under pressure.

Managers with a geocentric view of the world are generally better at understanding and accommodating similarities and differences among cultures. Successful multinational firms seek to instill a geocentric cultural mind-set in their employees and use a geocentric staffing policy to hire the best people for each position, regardless of national origin. Over time, such firms develop a core group of managers who are comfortable in any cultural context.

One way for managers to determine the skills they need to approach cultural issues is to measure their cultural intelligence.[52] *Cultural intelligence (CQ)* is a person's ability to function effectively in situations characterized by cultural diversity. It focuses on specific capabilities important for high-quality personal relationships and effectiveness in culturally diverse settings and work groups.

CLOSING CASE   Hollywood's Influence on Global Culture

The most commercially successful filmmaker of all time, Steven Spielberg, is synonymous with U.S. cinema. He has directed and produced international blockbusters like *Jurassic Park, War of the Worlds*, and the Indiana Jones movies. As U.S. dominance of the international film industry grows, Spielberg also has been the target of complaints about how Hollywood is changing world cultures. The values represented in his films are often viewed as part of the larger trend of the homogenization or, worse, Americanization of global values and beliefs.

Jurassic Park ignited a storm of protest. Film critics and cultural ministries around the globe found it to be a brainless film, lacking plot and succeeding wholly through special effects and big-budget bells and whistles. French officials labeled the film a threat to their national identity. Three leading filmmakers—Pedro Almodóvar, Bernardo Bertolucci, and Wim Wenders—wrote Spielberg to reprimand him for the poor quality of the film, calling him personally responsible for undermining their efforts to keep culturally rich European cinema afloat.

Another popular U.S. movie, *Lost in Translation*, came under fire from Los Angeles to Tokyo. Set in Japan's capital and starring Bill Murray, the film was nominated for four Academy Awards and won for best screenplay. It also won three Golden Globes. But it was criticized for its portrayal of Japanese people as robotic caricatures who mix up their Ls and Rs. The image-conscious Japanese were disappointed by their depiction as comic relief. In a scene where Bill Murray's character is taking a shower in what is meant to be a five-star hotel, he has to bend and contort to get his head under the shower head. In reality, there isn't a five-star hotel in Tokyo that hasn't accounted for the

varying heights of its potential guests. Another scene, in which Murray is shown towering at least a foot above an elevator full of local businessmen, mocks the smaller physique of the Japanese. The film was seen to reinforce negative stereotypes about the Japanese.

Is the U.S. film industry overwhelming the cultures of the world? And if so, can the world really blame Hollywood? American studios produce two-thirds or more of the films viewed internationally. The European film industry is now about one-ninth the size it was in 1945. After aerospace, Hollywood is often the United States' largest net export. The copyright-based industries, which also include software, books, music, and TV, contributed more to the U.S. economy in the 2000s than any single manufacturing sector. While the United States imports few foreign films, Hollywood's output remains in high demand worldwide. Today, foreign films hold less than 1 percent of the U.S. market.

Distorting History and Religious Values

Under attack since their origin, Hollywood war films are widely accused of presenting biased accounts of history. War movies portray U.S. soldiers as patriotic heroes, protecting all that is good from all that is evil. *Apocalypse Now* painted an ethnocentric view of the Vietnam War, focusing on the U.S. tragedy while ignoring that of the Vietnamese.

Mel Gibson's controversial film *The Passion of the Christ* enraged religious groups and governments in various countries. The government of Malaysia found it inappropriate for its largely Muslim population and banned its initial release in the country. (Christians were later allowed to view it.) International organizations and individuals also attacked *The*

Passion of the Christ as anti-Semitic. Other nations with deep religious values were offended by *Brokeback Mountain*, which portrayed a homosexual relationship between two cowboys in the United States.

Crucial to U.S. dominance of world cinema is widespread acceptance of the cultural associations inherent in Hollywood films, an obstacle competitors must overcome. U.S. stars and Hollywood directors are well established in the international movie scene, and their drawing power transcends national boundaries. Hollywood's global success is partly based on the association of the American lifestyle, seen as attractive to many around the world.

Movies and Comparative Advantage

According to the theory of comparative advantage, countries should specialize in producing what they do best and import the rest. Economists argue this theory applies to films as much as to any industry. Movies are like any other commodity, they say, and the United States has advantages in producing entertainment and exporting it to the rest of the world. However, critics suggest such an assertion ignores the fact that movies influence national culture and social development. The motion picture industry is a venue for enhancing cultural identity. As a former Canadian Prime Minister noted, the culture inherent in movies is not a commodity; it is usually intrinsic to the nations that create them.

This view highlights why governments often engage in *cultural protectionism*—a systematic effort to prevent local film industries from being swamped by U.S. imports. This effort includes erecting legal and bureaucratic trade barriers to prevent the import of foreign films, especially from the United States. Governments may also subsidize domestic filmmakers to ensure the survival and growth of the home-country film industry. *Quotas* restrict the number of foreign films that can be imported or require that a minimum number of movies be produced domestically.

However, subsidies can weaken film industries by insulating them from competitive pressures and reducing their ability to create globally viable films. Quotas may prevent movie-goers from seeing the films they want to see. Cultural protectionism can result in the local production of films simply to fulfill government mandates. At one time France had its own booming film industry. But a complex system of quotas and subsidies has done little to slow its gradual demise. Meanwhile, the proportion of Hollywood revenues generated from abroad continues to grow.

A Cultural Dilemma

Despite plenty of arguments on both sides of this ongoing debate, many big-budget Hollywood movies these days are in fact multinational creations. The James Bond thriller *Quantum of Solace*, with its German-Swiss director and stars hailing from Ukraine, France, and the United Kingdom, was filmed in Austria, Chile, Italy, Panama, and the United Kingdom. Russell Crowe, Charlize Theron, Penelope Cruz, Nicole Kidman, and Daniel Craig are just a few of the many global stars not from the United States. Two of the seven major film companies collectively known as Hollywood aren't even U.S. firms. Hollywood is not as "American" as it once was.

In recent years, movies from various regions—Africa, Eastern Europe, Southeast Asia, and Latin America—are enjoying increasing popularity. This has resulted thanks to the Internet, more movie channels on TV, innovative distribution systems, and technologies that help expose audiences to a far greater range of films.

As the lines connecting Hollywood with the United States are increasingly blurred, protectionists should not abandon their quest to salvage the intellectual and artistic quality of films. In an interview with *The New York Times*, French director Eric Rohmer stated that his countrymen should fight back with high-quality movies, not protectionism.

AACSB: Reflective Thinking Skills

Case Questions

1. Most aspects of foreign culture, like language, religion, gender roles, and problem-solving strategies, are hard for the casual observer to understand. In what ways do Hollywood movies affect national culture outside the United States? What aspects of U.S. culture do Hollywood films promote around the world? Can you observe any positive effects of Hollywood movies on world cultures?

2. Culture plays a key role in business. In what ways have movies influenced managerial tasks, company activities, and other ways of doing business around the world? Can watching foreign films be an effective way of learning how to do business abroad? Justify your answer.

3. Hollywood movies are very popular abroad, but foreign films are little viewed in the United States. What factors determine the high demand for Hollywood films? Why are they so popular in Europe, Japan, Latin America, and elsewhere? Why are foreign films so little demanded in the United States? What can foreign filmmakers do to increase demand for their movies in the United States?

4. Worldwide, protectionism of most goods is declining. Do movies constitute a separate category, or should they be treated like any other good? Given the nature of movies, should a country shield and support its own film industry via protectionism? Are there better ways to maintain and enhance a home-grown film industry? Justify your answer.

Sources: K. Lee, "'The Little State Department': Hollywood and the MPAA's Influence." *Northwestern Journal of International Law & Business* 28, no. 2 (2008): 371–383; K. Day, "Totally Lost in Translation," *The Guardian*, January 24, 2004; J. Delacroix and J. Bornon, "Can Protectionism Ever Be Respectable?" *The Independent Review* 9, no. 3 (2005): 353–365; A. Marvasti and E. Canterbery, "Cultural and Other Barriers to Motion Picture Trade," *Economic Inquiry*, January 2005, pp. 39–55; A. Scott, "A Golden Age of Foreign Films, Mostly Unseen," *New York Times*, January 26, 2011, at www.nytimes.com; T. Teachout, "Cultural Protectionism," *Wall Street Journal*, July 10, 1998, p. W11.

Note: This case was written by Sonia Prusaitis, under the supervision of Dr. Gary Knight.

CHAPTER ESSENTIALS

MyManagementLab
Go to **mymanagementlab.com** to complete the problems marked with this icon ⭐.

Key Terms

acculturation 86	high-context culture 89	monochronic 93
critical incident analysis (CIA) 104	idiom 91	polycentric orientation 84
cross-cultural risk 83	individualism versus collectivism 89	polychronic 94
cultural metaphor 91	long-term versus short-term	power distance 89
culture 82	orientation 91	self-reference criterion 104
ethnocentric orientation 84	low-context culture 88	socialization 86
geocentric orientation 84	masculinity versus femininity 90	uncertainty avoidance 90

Summary

In this chapter, you learned about:

1. The nature of cross-cultural risk

In international business, we step into different cultural environments characterized by unfamiliar languages, distinctive motivations, and different values. **Culture** is the learned, shared, and enduring orientations of a society, expressed in values, ideas, attitudes, behaviors, and other meaningful symbols and artifacts. **Cross-cultural** risk arises from a situation or event in which a cultural misunderstanding puts some human value at stake. **Ethnocentric orientation** refers to using our own culture as the standard for judging other cultures. **Polycentric orientation** refers to a host country mind-set that gives the manager greater affinity with the country in which she or he conducts business. **Geocentric orientation** refers to a global mind-set with which the manager is able to understand a business or market without regard to country boundaries.

2. Characteristics of culture

National culture influences consumer behavior, managerial effectiveness, and the range of value-chain operations, such as product and service design, marketing, and sales. The influence of professional and corporate cultures grows as people are socialized into a profession and their workplace. Most corporations exhibit a distinctive set of norms, values, and beliefs that distinguish them from other organizations. Managers can misinterpret the extent to which a counterpart's behavior is attributable to national, professional, or corporate culture.

3. Lenses to understand culture

Low-context cultures rely on elaborated verbal explanations, putting much emphasis on spoken words. **High-context cultures** emphasize nonverbal communications and a more holistic approach to communication that promotes harmonious relationships. Hofstede's typology of cultural dimensions consists of **individualism versus collectivism**, **power distance**, **uncertainty avoidance**, **masculinity versus femininity**, and **long-term versus short-term orientation**. Culture can be interpreted through **cultural metaphors**, distinctive traditions or institutions that serve as a guide or map for deciphering attitudes, values, and behavior. An **idiom** is an expression whose symbolic meaning is different from its literal meaning.

4. Subjective and objective dimensions of culture

Values and attitudes are shared beliefs or norms that individuals have internalized. **Monochronic** cultures exhibit a rigid orientation to time in which the individual is focused on schedules, punctuality, and time as a resource. **Polychronic** cultures have a flexible, nonlinear orientation to time in which the individual takes a long-term perspective. Religion provides meaning and motivation that define people's ideals and values. Symbolic and material productions refer to the intangible and tangible meanings, institutions, and structures that cultures construct for themselves.

5. Language: A key dimension of culture

There are nearly 7,000 active languages in the world, but most have only a few thousand speakers. The major languages include Mandarin Chinese, Hindi, English, Spanish, and Arabic. Language has both verbal and non-verbal characteristics and is conditioned by our environment. Sometimes it is hard to find words to convey the same meaning in two different languages.

6. Cultural change

While culture is relatively stable, it is influenced by contemporary issues. In contact-based services, providers interact directly with foreign nationals in culture-laden transactions. Cultural differences may lead to mishaps in the exchange process. Technological advances are a key determinant of culture and cultural change. Improved transportation and communications technologies have removed the boundaries that once separated nations. Technology also promotes culture. The Internet emphasizes the role of language in communications. Globalization promotes common culture and the consumption of similar products and services worldwide.

7. Context of international business

Culture matters in international business in areas such as developing products and services, interacting with foreign business partners, selecting foreign distributors, negotiating, dealing with customers, preparing for trade fairs, and preparing promotional materials. Cross-cultural differences complicate workplace issues such as teamwork, employment, pay-for-performance systems, organizational structures, union–management relationships, and attitudes toward ambiguity. Managers need to develop understanding and skills in dealing with other cultures.

8. Overcoming cross-cultural risk: Managerial guidelines

Managerial guidelines include the need to acquire factual and interpretive knowledge about the other culture, and to try to speak the language. Managers should avoid cultural bias and engage in **critical incident analysis** to avoid the **self-reference criterion**. Critical incident analysis requires being culturally aware, not making value judgments, and selecting the most likely interpretation of foreign behaviors. Experienced managers develop cross-cultural skills, including tolerating ambiguity, developing perceptiveness, valuing personal relationships, and being flexible and adaptable. Cultural intelligence is the ability to function effectively in culturally diverse situations.

Test Your Comprehension

1. Describe culture and cross-cultural risk.

⭐ 2. Distinguish between socialization and acculturation.

3. Distinguish the three layers of culture. What are the major elements of country-level and professional culture?

4. How does a manager with a deal orientation differ from a manager with a relationship orientation?

5. What are the two major perceptions of time, and how does each affect international business?

6. What are the five dimensions that make up Hofstede's model of culture?

⭐ 7. Distinguish between cultural metaphors and idioms.

Apply Your Understanding AACSB: Communication Abilities, Reflective Thinking Skills, Ethical Understanding and Reasoning Abilities, Multicultural and Diversity Understanding

1. Suppose you get a job at Kismet Indemnity, a life insurance company. In its 45-year history, Kismet has never done any international business. Now its president, Randall Fraser, wants to expand abroad. You have noted in meetings that he seems to lack much awareness of the role of culture. Write a memo to him in which you explain why culture matters in international business. Be sure to speculate on the effects of various dimensions of culture on sales of life insurance.

2. People tend to see other cultures from their own point of view. They accept their own culture and its ways as the norm—everything else seems foreign, or even mysterious. This chapter described a technique called critical incident analysis (CIA) that encourages an objective reaction to cultural differences by helping managers develop empathy for other points of view. Using the CIA approach, define a situation that you or someone else has experienced that led to a cross-cultural misunderstanding—perhaps an interaction with a fellow student, a visit to a store in your town, or an experience you had while traveling abroad. Explain what actually happened and how a more culturally sensitive

response might have been possible if you or your fellow student had used CIA.

3. *Ethical Dilemma*: Suppose you work for a multinational firm and are posted to Bogota, Colombia. After renting a house in a posh neighborhood, you hire a full-time maid to perform household chores, a common practice among wealthy Colombians. A colleague at work tells you local maids are typically poor women who live in Bogota's slums and earn about $200 a month. As an executive, you feel guilty about paying such a cheap wage when you can afford much more. But for cultural and socioeconomic reasons, your colleague insists you cannot pay more than the going rate. Doing so might embarrass your maid and risk upsetting the economic balance in her community. Analyze this dilemma. Do you pay your maid the customary local rate or a higher wage? Justify your decision. Can you think of any creative solutions to this dilemma?

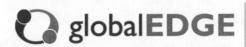

globalEDGE INTERNET EXERCISES
(http://www.globalEDGE.msu.edu)

AACSB: Reflective Thinking Skills

Refer to Chapter 1, page 24, for instructions on how to access and use globalEDGE™.

1. Ethnologue (www.ethnologue.com/web.asp) is a site that lists the world's known languages. It is an excellent resource for scholars and others with language interests and contains statistical summaries of the number of language speakers by language size, family, and country. Using Ethnologue, try the following:
   a. Visit the "Languages of China" site by clicking on the Country link, and then China. What is the population of China? Of the country's more than 200 languages, which has the largest number of speakers? Which has the second-most speakers? How do these figures compare to the total number of English speakers in the English-speaking countries of Australia, Canada, New Zealand, the United Kingdom, and the United States?
   b. Visit the "Languages of Spain" site. How many people live in Spain? How many native Spanish speakers are in Spain? How many languages altogether are spoken in Spain? If you decided to learn Spanish in Spain, what part of Spain would you stay in?
   c. Switzerland is one of the smallest European countries. What are the major languages of Switzerland, and how many speakers does each have?
   d. Find the table "Linguistic Diversity of Countries," which shows the population for each language as a proportion of the total population for most countries. What are the most linguistically diversified countries in the world? What are the least diversified countries?

2. Cultural intelligence is a person's ability to function effectively in situations characterized by cultural diversity. Various online resources feature cultural intelligence scales, which you can find by entering "cultural intelligence" using Google or some other search engine. What are the components of cultural intelligence? Answer the questions on the scale and calculate your score on cultural intelligence. Compare your score to those of your classmates.

3. Various Web sites list cultural blunders or *faux pas* (false steps) that people make in their international interactions. Neglecting to develop relationships (as in "Just sign the contract, I'm in a hurry!") and making too-casual use of first names (as in "Just call me Bill!") are examples of such blunders. Research online sources such as International Education Systems (www.marybosrock.com), or simply by entering "cultural blunders" in an Internet search engine, to identify examples of improper cultural behaviors. How can managers avoid these errors?

MyManagementLab

Go to **mymanagementlab.com** for Auto-graded writing questions as well as the following Assisted-graded writing questions:

4-1. Explain why culture matters in international business. In what types of contexts can cross-cultural differences cause concerns for managers.

4-2. Summarize the three major guidelines for success in cross-cultural settings.

4-3. Mymanagementlab Only – comprehensive writing assignment for this chapter.

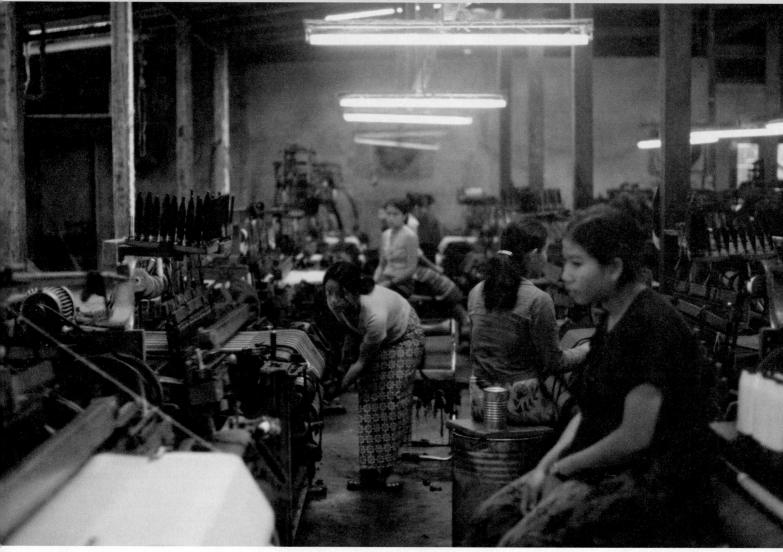

Source: © Eye Ubiquitous/Alamy

Corporate Social Responsibility at Coca-Cola

As one of the largest beverage companies, Coca-Cola ("Coke") has a major impact on human and natural environments. Coke has 93,000 employees and more than 900 bottling and manufacturing facilities worldwide. The firm generates about 75 percent of its more than $30 billion in sales from international markets.

In the past, critics have charged that Coke generates pollution, endangers scarce water supplies, markets soft drinks to teenagers, and tolerates inferior workplace conditions in developing economies.

In the meantime, Coca-Cola management has adopted responsible and sustainable approaches in its global operations. Coke has invested millions to develop superior wastewater treatment facilities. In arid areas, it implemented programs to replace all the water it extracts from local aquifers. From China to the Americas, the firm runs water-conservation programs.

Management makes continual efforts to reduce energy consumption throughout its bottling and manufacturing facilities. In Uruguay, Coke uses hybrid electric trucks to deliver product in congested areas to reduce pollution. In North America,

Ethics, Sustainability, and Corporate Social Responsibility in International Business

 LEARNING OBJECTIVES *In this chapter, you will learn about the following:*

1. Ethical challenges in international business
2. Key aspects of international ethics
3. Corporate social responsibility
4. The role of sustainability in international operations
5. Corporate governance and its implications for managers
6. A framework for making ethical decisions

MyManagementLab®

⭐ **Improve Your Grade!**

Over 10 million students improved their results using the Pearson MyLabs. Visit **mymanagementlab.com** for simulations, tutorials, and end-of-chapter problems.

Coke operates hundreds of hybrid delivery trucks, which are 30 percent more fuel efficient than diesel counterparts. Coke management is expanding the hybrid program to Europe. The firm switched to 100 percent renewable energy in numerous operating facilities. One plant in Belgium uses 100 percent geothermal energy. Coke is also improving the technology used in vending machines to reduce harmful greenhouse gases.

Coke manages the entire life cycle of product packaging. For example, used bottles are converted into plastic chips, which are then made into new bottles. Many bottles are made from 30 percent plant-based materials, making them more biodegradable. One facility recycles 100 million pounds of plastic bottles annually, equivalent to nearly 2 billion Coca-Cola bottles a year. Management aims to recycle 100 percent of Coke's bottles and cans by 2020. Coke's "Live Positively" pledge is a code of conduct for the firm's sustainability goals. For example, the firm is committed to responsible marketing practices, and avoids advertising aimed at children. Coke established a Workplace Rights Policy that confirms management's commitment to avoiding child labor and discrimination;

offering fair wages and work hours; and ensuring occupational health and safety. Coke's Anti-Bribery Policy provides guidance on how to conduct business in an ethical and legal manner.

The firm's Manual Distribution Center (MDC) program promotes economic development in poor countries. Numerous micro-distribution centers in Africa employ entrepreneurs who distribute product to local retailers in hard-to-reach areas. The MDCs account for over 80 percent of company sales in East Africa while providing small-business ownership and jobs to more than 12,000 people. The MDCs meet customer needs while supporting the sustainability of countless African communities. Coke is seeking to apply similar models in India, China, Indonesia, and Latin America.

SOURCES: "Return To Sender," *BrandPackaging*, Apr/May 2010, pp. 40–42; "The Coca-Cola Company," *Economics Week*, June 5, 2009, p. 7; Andrew Batson, "Coke Aims to Improve Water Recycling," *Wall Street Journal*, June 6, 2007, p. A10; Paul Barrett, "Coke's Got An America Problem," *Bloomberg Businessweek*, October 4–10, 2010, pp. 94–95; Carol Birkland, "Clean Air Initiatives," *Fleet Equipment*, May 2010, p. 2; Coca-Cola Company, *2010/2011 Sustainability Report*, retrieved from http://www.thecoca-colacompany.com; Elizabeth Fuhrman, "Recycling Shows Packaging's Sustainable Value," *Beverage Industry*, November 2009, pp. 42–44; Betsy McKay, "Coke Makes Cleanup Gains," *Wall Street Journal*, January 16, 2008, p. B3A; "The New Face of Africa," *Fortune*, November 21, 2011, Special Advertising Section.

Ethical behavior is an essential component for successful business in today's global environment.[1] Global business leaders define ethical behavior in terms of four key components: (1) ethics, (2) corporate social responsibility, (3) sustainability, and (4) governance. The opening story describes Coca-Cola's ethical approach to international business. **Ethics** are moral principles and values that govern the behavior of people, firms, and governments, regarding right and wrong.[2] By contrast, **corruption** is the abuse of power to achieve illegitimate personal gain. More than 30 percent of MNEs believe corruption is a major concern in their activities worldwide.[3]

As examples of unethical behavior, firms may:

- Falsify or misrepresent contracts or financial statements;
- Pay or accept bribes, kickbacks, or inappropriate gifts;
- Tolerate sweatshop conditions or otherwise abuse employees;
- Undertake false advertising and other deceptive marketing practices;
- Engage in pricing that is deceptive, discriminatory, or predatory;
- Deceive or abuse intermediaries in international channels; and
- Engage in activities that harm the natural environment.[4]

Coca-Cola demonstrates social responsibility by ensuring safe working conditions, treating customers and intermediaries fairly, and preventing illicit business activities abroad. **Corporate social responsibility (CSR)** refers to operating a business in a manner that meets or exceeds the ethical, legal, and commercial expectations of customers, shareholders, employees, and the communities where the firm does business. Coke also undertakes programs to conserve energy and water, reduce harmful greenhouse gases, and recycle cans and bottles.

Sustainability means meeting humanity's needs without harming future generations. The sustainable firm aims to carry out value chain activities in ways that protect and preserve economic, social, and natural environments. For example, sustainable firms pay fair wages, ensure worker safety, and avoid emitting toxic waste.

Exhibit 5.1 summarizes key managerial approaches addressed in this chapter. Firms operate in a global environment characterized by both ethical and unethical participants and myriad opportunities to engage in corruption. Management can overcome such challenges by developing a system of corporate governance that emphasizes ethics, corporate social responsibility, and sustainability in all value-chain activities.

Corporate governance is the system of procedures and processes by which corporations are managed, directed, and controlled. It provides the means through which firms undertake ethical behaviors, CSR, and sustainability. Ethics and appropriate behavior are essential in international business. Because standards of ethical behavior vary around the world, simply obeying the law is usually insufficient to ensure against violating such standards. Worldwide variance in ethical standards makes ethics a complex issue in international business.

Ethics
Moral principles and values that govern the behavior of people, firms, and governments, regarding right and wrong.

Corruption
The abuse of power to achieve illegitimate personal gain.

Corporate social responsibility (CSR)
A manner of operating a business that meets or exceeds the ethical, legal, commercial, and public expectations of customers, shareholders, employees, and communities.

Sustainability
Meeting humanity's needs without harming future generations.

Corporate governance
The system of procedures and processes by which corporations are managed, directed, and controlled.

CHAPTER 5 • ETHICS, SUSTAINABILITY, AND CORPORATE SOCIAL RESPONSIBILITY IN INTERNATIONAL BUSINESS **113**

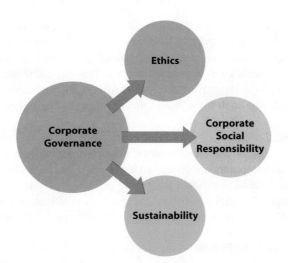

EXHIBIT 5.1

Organizing Framework for Ethical Behavior in International Business

Ethics and appropriate behavior transcend all international business activities and figure prominently in management decisions about financial performance and competitive advantage. However, corruption is commonplace in many countries, especially those lacking transparent business systems. Most companies seek to ensure ethical practices in their international operations. The most advanced firms proactively emphasize not just ethical behavior, but also corporate social responsibility and sustainability. An integrated, strategic approach to ethical, sustainable, and socially-responsible behavior provides firms with competitive advantages, including stronger relationships with customers, employees, shareholders, suppliers, and the communities where they do business. Let us examine the critical role of ethical conduct in international business.

 Ethical Challenges in International Business

Companies around the world now regard ethics as a strategic component in business decisions. Increasingly ethical behavior is seen to play a vital role in determining competitive advantage and long-term company performance. Firms encounter ethical challenges in a range of international activities:

- *Unethical management practices* are especially common in countries that lack appropriate regulation and professional standards. A corporate culture that advocates profit over sustainability and human welfare can lead to employee abuse, harmful procedures, and other unsustainable practices. The global financial crisis that began in 2008 resulted in part because senior managers in banks and financial firms neglected to devise safeguards against making bad loans or offering high-risk securities. Lax management standards also give rise to dishonest accounting practices, in which companies provide deceptive information to investors, customers, and government authorities.
- *Global sourcing* is the procurement of products or services from suppliers located abroad. In a typical scenario, the focal firm buys parts and components from foreign companies that manufacture such goods. In some cases, firms establish their own supply factories abroad. Global sourcing raises concerns about ensuring human rights and protecting the environment. Some companies operate sweatshop factories in which employees are children or work long hours for very low wages, often in harsh conditions.[5] Many factories generate substantial pollution. The use of third-party suppliers is challenging for firms like Nike and Philips, with thousands of partners that operate in a range of cultures and belief systems worldwide.
- *Deceptive marketing, advertising, and selling* to induce people to buy products. Marketers may make false claims about the quality or effectiveness of a product. Advances in communications technologies allow fraudulent marketers to easily target victims in foreign countries. The transnational nature of such scams makes it difficult for law enforcers to catch and prosecute perpetrators. Easy accessibility of the Internet has led shady online

marketers to harm unsuspecting consumers. In developing economies, for example, most online drug stores operate illegally.[6] The drugs offered by such outlets are often fake and may harm users. Phony Viagra made in Thailand was found to contain vodka; bogus Tamiflu has been manufactured with vitamin C and lactose, and some fake medications contain lethal amounts of dangerous chemicals. Although the pharmaceutical industry and governments pursue such firms, violators are often elusive and beyond the reach of authorities.

- *Defective or harmful products or packaging* can lead to disastrous outcomes for public health and safety or for natural environments. For example, millions of electronic products from cell phones to computers are discarded every year. Products that could be recycled end up in landfills. Excessive product packaging generates pollution, and consumes energy and natural resources. Excessive use of plastic packaging is wasteful. Because plastic does not easily decompose, plastic waste is steadily increasing on land and in the oceans.

Intellectual Property Violations

Illicit use of intellectual property represents yet another ethical violation, especially common in international business. **Intellectual property** refers to ideas or works created by individuals or firms and includes a variety of proprietary, intangible assets: discoveries and inventions; artistic, musical, and literary works; and words, phrases, symbols, and designs. Intellectual property may be stolen or copied illicitly. In Russia, for example, software and movies produced by such firms as Microsoft and Disney often fall prey to *counterfeiting*; the assets are reproduced without compensating those who originally created them. Widely recognized global brands—Rolex, Louis Vuitton, and Tommy Hilfiger, among others—are often counterfeited, eroding firms' brand equity and competitive advantages.

Intellectual property
Ideas or works created by individuals or firms, including discoveries and inventions; artistic, musical, and literary works; and words, phrases, symbols, and designs.

Trademarks, copyrights, and patents are examples of **intellectual property rights**, the legal claim through which proprietary assets are protected from unauthorized use by other parties. *Trademarks* are distinctive signs and indicators that firms use to identify their products and services. *Copyrights* grant protections to the creators of art, music, books, software, movies, and TV shows. *Patents* confer the exclusive right to manufacture, use, and sell products or processes. Intellectual property rights are not guaranteed in much of the world. Laws enacted in one country are enforceable only in that country and confer no protection abroad.[7]

Intellectual property rights
The legal claim through which the proprietary assets of firms and individuals are protected from unauthorized use by other parties.

Firms' intellectual property often fall victim to counterfeiting. "Piracy" is equivalent to counterfeiting; it is the unauthorized production and selling of previously copyrighted works. The total value of internationally traded counterfeit and pirated products was expected to reach nearly $1 trillion annually by 2015. The total value of domestically produced and consumed counterfeit and pirated products was expected to reach nearly $600 billion annually by 2015.[8] Counterfeiting and piracy hurt the world economy in various ways, especially regarding trade, foreign investment, employment, innovation, criminal activity, and the environment. Counterfeiting and piracy harm company sales and pricing, and increase business costs. The brand value of heavily counterfeited goods can decline over time. Counterfeiting and piracy also reduce government tax revenues and the moral integrity of nations.

For consumers, counterfeit and pirated products are usually of inferior quality. Counterfeit goods can unknowingly be used in manufacturing, military, critical infrastructure, and consumer products, all of which threaten health and safety.[9] For example, the consumer products company Johnson & Johnson discovered that counterfeiters were selling fake versions of its OneTouch test strips, used by diabetes patients in Canada and the United States. Criminals were promoting bogus versions of OneTouch, which diabetes sufferers use to

Source: © epa european pressphoto agency b.v./Alamy

Workers at a Foxconn factory in China, a leading supplier to Apple. Following charges about poor working conditions at Foxconn plants, Apple and Foxconn took steps to improve the work environment.

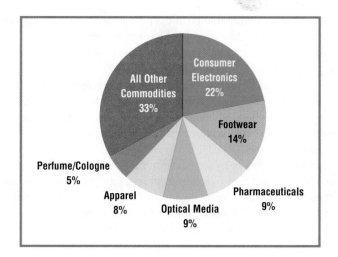

EXHIBIT 5.2

Top Counterfeit Commodities Seized, United States, 2011

Source: Based on CBP Office of International Trade (2012), *Intellectual Property Rights: Fiscal Year 2011 Seizure Statistics*, Washington, DC: U.S. Immigration and Customs Enforcement, at http://www.ice.gov/doclib/iprcenter/pdf/ipr-fy-2011-seizure-report.pdf.

monitor blood-sugar levels. Fake strips give false readings, which can be life-threatening if they cause patients to take too much or too little insulin, the drug used to treat diabetes.[10]

The United States is the top market for counterfeit and pirated goods. In 2011, U.S. Department of Homeland Security agents seized counterfeit and pirated products at U.S. borders with an estimated retail value of more than $1.1 billion. Exhibit 5.2 highlights the categories of illicit commodities seized. Among the most counterfeited goods are consumer electronics, footwear, and pharmaceuticals. In 2011, by far the largest single source of counterfeit products was China, which accounted for 62 percent of Homeland Security seizures. This was followed by Hong Kong, an administrative region of China, amounting to 18 percent of seizures. India represented just 3 percent of seizures, and all other countries accounted for the remaining 17 percent.[11]

MNEs seeking to do business within China may become victims of domestic counterfeiting activities. For example, Disney has struggled to launch its DVD movie business in China, due to rampant local piracy. Legitimate Disney DVDs of films like *Finding Nemo* and *The Lion King* cost up to ten times as much as knockoffs, restricting sales to a trickle.[12]

In Russia, illicit Web sites sell popular music downloads for as little as 5 cents apiece, or less than one U.S. dollar for an entire CD. Russia's laws regarding counterfeiting are often insufficient to thwart such crimes, and enforcement is weak.[13] Suppose you work for a small online retailer that decides to offer pirated music via the company Web site to potential buyers in Russia and other emerging markets with weak intellectual property laws. How should you respond to this dilemma? Later in this chapter, we present a framework that you can use to analyze this and countless other ethical problems that managers encounter in international business.

Bribery

Bribery refers to offering, giving, receiving, or soliciting anything of value to influence the actions of a government official or a corporate manager. Bribery is acceptable in much of the world. It is estimated that more than $1 trillion in bribes are paid worldwide every year to gain access to important markets and achieve other business goals. One study found that 40 percent of business executives have been asked to pay a bribe when dealing with public institutions. Twenty percent claimed to have lost business because of bribes paid by competitors.[14] Bribery often takes the form of *grease payments*, small inducements intended to expedite transactions and gain other favors. In many countries, such facilitating payments are both legal and acceptable.

Bribery is especially common in developing economies, such as Egypt, Indonesia, Nigeria, and Pakistan. In such places, it can be nearly impossible to achieve important business objectives without paying bribes to public officials and other individuals. The problem is especially common in the global energy, mining, and telecommunications industries. Firms from these industries—such as Halliburton and Siemens—have been implicated in major bribery scandals.

Bribery has produced harmful consequences, such as illegal logging in Indonesia, terrible work conditions in China, and poorly constructed buildings that collapsed in Turkey. Paying bribes increases the risks and costs of doing business. It promotes a culture of dishonesty and immorality that opens the door to other types of wrongdoing. It threatens fair competition, merit-based selection, and other equitable business practices. In this way, bribery poses a fundamental threat to confidence in and functioning of market economies.[15]

Corruption

Corruption is an extreme form of unethical behavior. It may appear as political corruption, in which officials abuse public power or profit improperly from government resources. It may arise as police corruption, in which law enforcement officials obtain financial or other benefits in exchange for granting favors, such as not pursuing crimes. In firms, corruption occurs across the range of value chain activities.

Various organizations assess corruption around the world. The most well-known organization is Transparency International (www.transparency.org) and its *Corruption Perceptions Index*, which measures managers' perceptions of bribery, embezzlement, and other illicit behavior worldwide.[16] Exhibit 5.3 lists a sample of countries and their perceived levels of corruption, on a scale of 1 to 100. Countries with the lowest scores have the least corruption, such as Canada and Denmark.

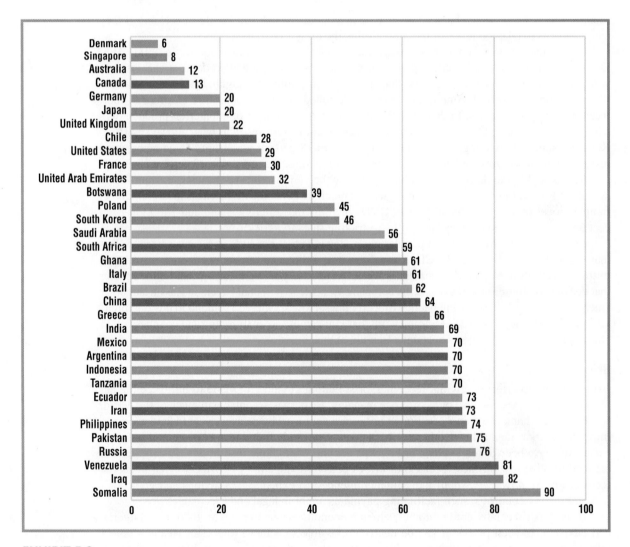

EXHIBIT 5.3

Corruption Perceptions Index 2011

Note: Countries with the highest scores have the most corruption.

Source: Based on *Corruption Perceptions Index.* Copyright © 2011 Transparency International: The Global Coalition Against Corruption, www.transparency.org.

Countries with minimal corruption attract much direct investment because managers know business in such nations is conducted fairly. Commercial laws are fair and adequately enforced. Financial and accounting information is transparent, reliable, and easily accessed. By contrast, foreign firms are reluctant to invest in countries such as Somalia and Venezuela, due to rampant corruption. In Russia, entrepreneurs typically must pay thousands of dollars in bribes to officials to gain the right to launch their businesses and run them efficiently.

Corruption harms the poorest in societies. For example, many are forced to pay bribes to gain access to needed products and services, such as water, electricity, and phone utilities. Widespread corruption hinders economic development. This relationship points to an important dilemma—trade and investment help reduce poverty, but MNEs avoid doing business with corrupt countries.

Various bodies have issued international conventions against corruption. Numerous countries have signed the antibribery convention developed by the Organisation for Economic Co-operation and Development (OECD). The United Nations issued a declaration against corruption in international transactions. The U.S. Foreign Corrupt Practices Act (FCPA) makes it illegal for U.S. firms to offer bribes to foreign parties to secure or retain business. Under the FCPA, firms may be fined $2 million and managers can be imprisoned for up to five years.

 ## Key Aspects of International Ethics

Business plays an enormous role worldwide, affecting people and nations by creating jobs, wealth, and societal value. The goal of business is to make money. But experienced managers understand due consideration also must be given to business ethics. Just as reputation affects the success of individuals, it is critical to companies as well. Failure to protect and nurture the corporate image translates into poor performance and potential ruin. Ethical behavior is critical to business success. Let's examine ethics in terms of value to firms, how ethics vary worldwide, and the role of the MNE.

The Value of Behaving Ethically

Ethical behavior is important for several reasons:

- It is simply the right thing to do.
- It is often prescribed within laws and regulations. Violating laws and regulations has obvious legal consequences.
- It is demanded by customers and governments.
- Firms that commit ethical blunders attract unwanted attention from opinion leaders and the news media.
- Ethical behavior is good business, leading to enhanced corporate image and selling prospects.

The firm with a reputation for high ethical standards gains advantages in hiring, motivating employees, partnering, and dealing with foreign governments. Firms that behave unethically run the risk of criminal or civil prosecution, hurting their own reputations, harming employee morale and recruitment efforts, and exposing themselves to blackmailers or other unscrupulous parties.[17] For all these reasons, companies incorporate ethical considerations in their international activities.

In host countries, firms with iconic global brands, such as Coca-Cola and Volkswagen, are especially conspicuous to consumers and can become targets of public protest. Increasingly, governments insist that firms behave in ways that serve the public interest. For example, the European Union restricts the use of lead, mercury, and other harmful substances in manufacturing, and requires firms to collect and recycle unwanted electronic products. Canada has well-developed complaint procedures for dealing with bribery, including liaison officers in 25 countries and a Web site (www.recol.ca) for filing complaints about possible corruption.[18] However, a major challenge is that ethical standards vary worldwide.

Variation in Ethical Standards among Countries

Appropriate behavior in one culture may be viewed as unethical elsewhere.[19] Let's review some examples:

- In China, counterfeiters frequently publish translated versions of imported books without compensating the original publisher or authors, an illegal practice in most of the world.
- In parts of Africa, accepting expensive gifts from suppliers is acceptable, even if considered improper elsewhere.
- In the United States, CEOs receive compensation often a hundred times greater than that of low-ranking subordinates, a practice considered inappropriate elsewhere.
- Finland and Sweden ban advertising directed at children, but the practice is well accepted in other parts of Europe.

Standards vary by level of economic development. Africa is beset by widespread hunger and some restaurant workers "steal" food on the job to take home to their families. Is this equivalent to restaurant workers stealing food in rich countries? Standards change over time. Although slavery is no longer tolerated, some multinational firms today tolerate working conditions that are akin to it. In China, many MNEs operate factories that pollute local water supplies.

Relativism

Belief that ethical truths are not absolute but differ from group to group.

Normativism

Belief that ethical behavioral standards are universal, and firms and individuals should seek to uphold them around the world.

Scholars and managers examine ethics from two distinct perspectives: relativism and normativism.[20]

Relativism The belief that ethical truths are not absolute but differ from group to group; according to this perspective, a good rule is "When in Rome, do as the Romans do." Thus, a Japanese firm that believes bribery is wrong might nevertheless pay bribes in countries where the practice is customary and culturally acceptable. Relativists opt for passive acceptance of the values, behaviors, and practices that prevail in each of the countries where they do business.

Normativism The belief that ethical behavioral standards are universal, and firms and individuals should seek to uphold them consistently around the world. According to this view, the Japanese firm that believes bribery is wrong will enforce this standard everywhere in the world. The United Nations and other agencies encourage firms to follow a normative approach. Sophisticated firms attempt to correct unethical practices that arise in their ongoing business dealings around the world.[21]

Most firms apply a combination of relativism and normativism abroad. Rightly or wrongly, they strike a balance between corporate values developed in the home country and local standards. However, this approach puts them at risk of violating norms that are increasingly universal. In countries with questionable ethical norms, it is usually best to maintain ethical standards *superior* to what is required by local laws and values. This strategy helps garner goodwill and averts potentially damaging publicity.

An Ethical Dilemma

Deciding what is right and wrong is not always clear. Firms with extensive international operations may face multiple and sometimes conflicting laws and regulations. Requirements may be ambiguous or inconsistent. Occasionally laws in foreign countries conflict with, or fall short of, home-country laws. In the United States, for example, the Occupational Safety and Health Administration (OSHA) specifies numerous regulations regarding labor and employment conditions. However, in most countries, such regulations are relatively underdeveloped, or don't exist at all. National legal systems are often weak and laws are poorly enforced. Many multinational firms struggle to find the right balance between acceptable practices at home and abroad. What should management do? Should it follow weak local laws or follow the laws of the home country? Even when a country has a sound legal system, or even when the firm has a strong code of ethics, managers regularly face the challenge of determining appropriate behavior.

An *ethical dilemma* is a predicament with major conflicts among different interests in which determining the most appropriate course of action is confounded by a set of solutions that are equally justifiable, and often equally imperfect. Possible actions may be mutually exclusive—the choice of one automatically negates the other(s).[22]

Imagine you are a manager and visit a factory owned by an affiliate in Colombia, only to discover the use of child labor in the plant. Upon studying the problem, you learn that child labor is accepted in many developing economies. There are more than 50 million children working in India alone. Girls are vulnerable, and may be abused or exploited. Work prevents children from attending school, which would improve their prospects for a better life. But you also learn that without their children's income, families often go hungry. If the kids are dismissed from the plant, many will turn to other income sources, including prostitution and street crime. The age at which children are deemed adults varies worldwide, sometimes as low as 15 years. What should you do? Do you make a fuss about the immorality of child labor, or do you look the other way?

This example is typical of the type of ethical dilemmas that employees encounter in international business. Managers working internationally may be most exposed because they can be caught between home country ethical norms and those encountered abroad.

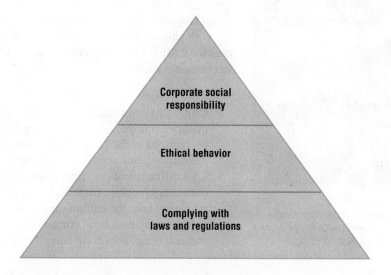

Source: © B. O'Kane/Alamy

Global companies with well-known brands like McDonald's are especially conspicuous to consumers and need strong ethical values to thrive under public scrutiny. This airport restaurant is in Madrid, Spain.

Linking Ethics, Corruption, and Responsible Behavior

In a world of seemingly endless ethical challenges, how should managers and companies respond? Consider the framework in Exhibit 5.4. After complying with local law (the bottom of the pyramid), management should ensure that company activities follow high ethical standards (the middle). As they expand abroad, most firms believe it is sufficient to comply with laws, regulations, and basic ethical standards. However, in addition, sophisticated MNEs now emphasize socially responsible behavior (the top of the pyramid). Let's examine this notion in more detail.

Corporate Social Responsibility

Adhering to CSR implies a proactive approach to ethical behavior in which firms not only seek to maximize profits, but also to benefit society and the environment. Typical CSR values include:

- Avoiding human rights abuses,
- Upholding the right to join or form labor unions,

EXHIBIT 5.4

The Pyramid of Ethical Behavior

Corporate social responsibility

Ethical behavior

Complying with laws and regulations

- Eliminating compulsory and child labor,
- Avoiding workplace discrimination,
- Protecting the natural environment,
- Guarding against corruption, and
- Engaging in philanthropy, such as donating money, products, or volunteer labor to good causes.[23]

CSR is about business giving back to society. However, many firms have been slow to adopt CSR. Failure to adopt CSR behaviors can have adverse, even ruinous, consequences. Efforts by the China National Petroleum Company (CNPC) to raise money on the New York Stock Exchange were harmed by the firm's activities in Sudan, which human rights groups had criticized. The Shell Oil Company has experienced protests and lost revenues due to opposition to its oil-drilling activities in Nigeria, which are seen as harming community interests and generating toxic waste. In India, Walmart experienced lost sales and massive protests because of concerns the firm's market entry would hurt small retailers in the region.[24]

Many companies have improved their performance by adopting CSR. Petrobras (www .petrobras.com) is a Brazilian oil company that developed CSR programs aimed at reducing poverty and child labor, as well as promoting youth education and rights for people with disabilities. In Africa, Petrobras has built hospitals, schools, and day-care centers. In Colombia, it developed a program to train community health agents. In Nigeria, Petrobras cooperates with a local non-governmental organization to provide HIV/AIDS prevention education.[25]

Motorola (www.motorola.com) has delivered more than 16 million low-cost mobile phones to people in fifty developing countries. It developed a mobile phone system for disease management in Africa, through which field health workers file patient reports and check drug supplies. Cellular connectivity helps professionals in poor areas deal more effectively with disease outbreaks, medicine shortages, and health maintenance. Efficient telecommunications promote productivity and raise GDP levels.[26]

Exhibit 5.5 summarizes additional CSR initiatives undertaken by firms worldwide. For example, Africa accounts for most deaths from AIDS. However, few Africans can afford medications used to treat the disease. GlaxoSmithKline (GSK) is a large pharmaceutical firm that offers its AIDS medications to Africans at or below its production costs. In volume terms, GSK sells about 90 percent of its vaccines at not-for-profit prices to customers in developing economies.[27] In Scotland, the large utility firm Scottish and Southern Energy (SSE) emphasizes sustainability in providing energy to its customers. The firm provides electricity through numerous wind farms. Only two of SSE's power plants are fueled by coal, which is more polluting than other energy sources.[28]

Source: © Bob Daemmrich/Alamy

Environmentally friendly policies are an important part of most corporate social responsibility programs. Accepting computers and parts for recycling is an example of CSR initiatives at companies such as Acer and Apple.

The Value of CSR

Customers, partners, shareholders, and the media increasingly believe firms have an obligation to be socially responsible to the societies where they operate. As with ethical behavior, there is a strong business case for CSR.[29] Let's examine the rationale for CSR in international business.

- CSR is simply the right thing to do.
- CSR helps companies recruit and retain high-quality employees. It also improves employee perceptions of the firm, which in turn enhances their loyalty and focus on company goals.
- CSR differentiates the firm in the marketplace and enhances branding, particularly useful in foreign markets where the entrant may be unknown or struggling against local competitors. Consumers prefer buying from companies they trust.

EXHIBIT 5.5 Corporate Social Responsibility: A Sampling of MNE Accomplishments

Company	Industry	Sample Accomplishments
ABN AMRO (Netherlands)	Financial Services	Finances various socially responsible projects, including biomass fuels and micro enterprises.
Dell (United States)	Computers	Accepts old computers from customers for recycling, free of charge.
GlaxoSmithKline (United Kingdom)	Pharmaceuticals	Devotes substantial R&D to poor-country ailments, such as malaria and tuberculosis. Was first to offer AIDS medication at cost.
HSBC (United Kingdom)	Banking	Emphasizes development of financing products for firms in the green energy and battery technology industries.
Nokia (Finland)	Telecommunications	Makes telephones for low-income consumers. Has been a leader in environmental practices, such as phasing out toxic materials.
Norsk Hydro (Norway)	Oil and gas	Cut greenhouse gas emissions by 32 percent. Consistently measures the social and environmental impact of its projects.
Unilever (Netherlands and United Kingdom)	Consumer products	Emphasizes the use of ingredients that minimize the threat of deforestation. Strives to use only energy efficient computers and other information technologies in its global operations.
Duke Energy (United States)	Power utility	Undertakes energy production through various green initiatives, such as wind and solar power. Operates energy efficiency programs for customers.
Toyota (Japan)	Automobiles	The world leader in developing efficient gas-electric vehicles, such as the top-selling Prius.

Sources: Based on Pete Engardio, "Beyond the Green Corporation," *Business Week*, January 29, 2007, pp. 50–64; MIT Sloan Management Review and Boston Consulting Group, *Sustainability: The 'Embracers' Seize Advantage*, research report (Cambridge, MA: Massachusetts Institute of Technology, 2011).

- CSR enhances the quality and effectiveness of intermediary relationships and collaborative ventures. Suppliers, intermediaries, and potential joint venture partners prefer collaborating with reliable firms with strong reputations.
- CSR helps reduce business costs. For example, firms save money when they minimize packaging, recycle materials, trim energy use, and reduce operational waste.
- CSR helps avoid increased taxation, regulation, or legal action by government authorities. In 2009, for example, Denmark enacted laws that require firms to incorporate CSR activities and describe them in their financial reports.

Consumers, other stakeholders, and the media increasingly look to companies to be socially and environmentally responsible. Communications technology allows them to learn quickly about the misdeeds of any firm with which they do business. Over time many consumers prefer products made by firms with strong CSR. The *Global Trend* examines the role of CSR in the multinational firm.

In addition to profit-seeking focal firms, more nongovernmental organizations (NGOs) are undertaking international CSR initiatives, often in conjunction with multinational firms. For example, NGOs such as CARE, Médecins Sans Frontières, and the Bangladesh Rural Advancement Committee work to reduce global poverty and frequently partner with private companies to provide vital products and services.[30]

 ## The Role of Sustainability in International Operations

In a world of increasing population and finite resources, ever-expanding trade and investment have important implications for Earth and the future of humankind. Sustainability is an ideal endorsed by economic development experts, environmentalists, and human rights activists. Companies also increasingly embrace sustainability issues.

GLOBAL TREND

Global Corporate Social Responsibility Rises to the Top of the MNE Agenda

As companies internationalize, they increasingly confront the question of how to be good global citizens. Global corporate social responsibility addresses issues such as workers' rights, workers' pay compared to a reasonable living standard, company activities that disrupt traditional communities and lifestyles, and environmental damage. A study by McKinsey & Co. found executives worldwide overwhelmingly embrace the idea that firms have societal and environmental obligations in addition to ensuring profitability.

IKEA (www.ikea.com) proactively promotes social and environmental responsibility. The firm employs its own specially trained auditors and environmental coordinators. Its products must be manufactured under acceptable working conditions by suppliers who take responsibility for the environment. All must meet the standards of the Forest Stewardship Council. IKEA and its suppliers

work closely with UNICEF, Save the Children, and the World Wildlife Fund to prevent child labor and support responsible forestry. All work is in conjunction with the UN Convention on the Rights of the Child. The IKEA Foundation supports various charitable causes through generous contributions.

Governments and stakeholders have expectations of how multinational firms should fulfill their global social responsibilities. Appropriate actions include contributing to a region's employment opportunities, protecting workers and communities from physical harm, providing good working conditions, avoiding discriminatory hiring and work practices, maintaining transparency and avoiding corruption, reducing poverty and injustice, and improving access to quality health care and education.

Accepting social and environmental accountability is increasingly part of how

international business gets done. The task is complex, because when companies step onto the global stage, they encounter a wide variety of stakeholders whose expectations often appear overwhelming or even contradictory. Social and environmental problems can appear baffling to headquarters managers, who may lack international experience. Thus, country managers often decide what issues are important and how to address them.

Sources: McKinsey & Co., "From Risk to Opportunity: How Global Executives View Sociopolitical Issues: The McKinsey Quarterly Survey on the Role of Business in Society," 2006, *The McKinsey Quarterly*, retrieved from www .mckinseyquarterly.com; MIT Sloan Management Review and Boston Consulting Group, *Sustainability: The 'Embracers' Seize Advantage*, research report (Cambridge, MA: Massachusetts Institute of Technology, 2011).

A sustainable business simultaneously pursues three types of interests:

1. Economic interests refer to the firm's economic impact on the localities where it does business. Management considers the effect of the firm's activities on such local concerns as job creation, wages, tax flows, disadvantaged communities, public works, and other areas where the firm can contribute positively to local economic interests.

2. Social interests refer to how the firm performs relative to societies and social justice, often termed *social impact*. The firm with a strong social interest aims to optimize work conditions and diversity in hiring. It avoids using sweatshops, child labor, and other practices that harm workers. Instead, the sustainable firm provides safe work environments, health insurance, retirement benefits, and educational opportunities for employees.

3. Environmental interests refer to the extent of the firm's contribution to preserving environmental quality, commonly known as *environmental impact*. This concept refers to reducing the effect of the firm's value-chain activities on the natural environment. The sustainable firm maximizes its use of recycled or renewable raw materials and environmentally friendly energy. It minimizes pollutants, designs production lines to use water and energy efficiently, and constantly seeks ways to reduce waste. Many firms establish a green purchasing policy, through which they source inputs that support environmental interests.[31]

Exhibit 5.6 shows the level of air pollution in selected cities worldwide. Industrialization and other economic activity generate pollutants, which can affect human health, often causing heart and respiratory diseases. In the developing world, air pollution also results from burning dung, wood, and coal, which people use to meet basic energy needs. As indicated in the exhibit, poor industrializing countries tend to produce more air pollution. As nations advance economically, however, they usually develop regulations and technologies that reduce pollutants.

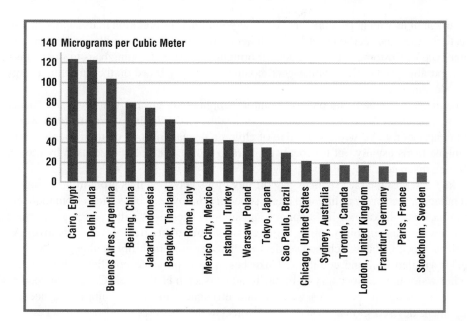

EXHIBIT 5.6

Air Pollution in Selected Cities (particulate matter concentration in micrograms per cubic meter)

Source: Based on World Bank, *World Development Indicators 2011*, Washington DC: World Bank.

MNEs hold much responsibility to ensure they follow sustainable practices. Businesses function by utilizing resources and raw materials derived from the natural environment. Industrial activities produce smog, acid rain, and other toxins. Many industrial firms use or produce synthetic chemicals and materials that contain hazardous substances. Consumer and industrial products are themselves a major source of toxic waste.[32]

Firms employ vast quantities of water resources, contributing to the creation or expansion of deserts ("desertification"), and loss of important ecosystems around the world. Many countries endure chronic water shortages and industrial activity pollutes clean water supplies. Residential and industrial activity results in land loss and the destruction of ecosystems needed for healthy natural environments. Long-term, successful business performance necessitates healthy ecosystems.

Businesses are major consumers of all the natural environment offers, and hence must take pains to ensure ecological sustainability. Reversing environmental damage requires industrialized countries to substantially reduce their emissions of pollutants. The pace with which resources and raw materials are depleted should not exceed their rate of regeneration. The rate of waste production should not exceed the environment's ability

Source: © Tim Gainey/Alamy

As water grows scarce in much the world, some multinational firms are conserving their use of this critical resource. Coca-Cola, a major water consumer, conducts a water sustainability program to address shortages in India.

to absorb it. Firms increasingly seek ways to employ renewable resources and to minimize pollutants in their operations.[33] MNEs are among the most important stewards of the environment through skillful use of innovative technologies, improved water productivity, addressing shortages in vulnerable areas, and planning that incorporates sustainability practices.

The Canadian aluminum giant Alcan (www.alcan.com) has invested huge sums to develop clean, fuel-efficient manufacturing technologies. By emphasizing sustainability, Alcan reduced its greenhouse gas output by one-quarter, while increasing production by 40 percent. Alcan is installing additional technology that will further reduce toxic emissions, while increasing energy efficiency in its smelting plants.[34]

The British supermarket chain Tesco (www.tesco.com) uses wind power to provide electricity for many of its U.K. stores and has installed massive solar panels on its U.S. facilities. The firm cut

Country Realities

More than 5 million people die annually from lung cancer and other smoking-related ailments. Smoking also harms national GDP because it incurs billions in tax-funded health care costs. The average price of a pack of cigarettes is high in many countries, relative to local incomes. As cigarette sales have declined in the advanced economies, British American Tobacco, Philip Morris International, and other cigarette companies have targeted emerging markets. In China a pack sells for the equivalent of $2, but smokers earn only a few thousand dollars per year. About 60 percent of Chinese men smoke, making China home to the largest number of smokers. In Ukraine, the average smoker consumes 2,500 cigarettes per year. Russia has the highest density of smokers, where 70 percent of men smoke, and the average lifespan is less than 60 years, partly due to high cigarette consumption.

Sources: N. Byrnes and F. Balfour, "Philip Morris Unbound," *Business Week,* May 4, 2009, pp. 39–42; B. McKay, "Where There's Smoke: Emerging World," *Wall Street Journal,* February 7, 2008, pp. B1–B2.

energy usage in its warehouses and operates low-pollution transportation in its supply chains. It attempts to measure the "carbon costs" of each item it sells to reduce the pollution burden of serving customer needs. Customers are rewarded for bringing reusable shopping bags to stores, instead of using disposable plastic. Senior managers' bonuses are partly based on their meeting energy- and waste-reduction targets.[35]

The most advanced companies monitor suppliers to ensure that they use sustainable practices. For example, following charges that some of its Indian subcontractors were using forced child labor, GAP withdrew a line of children's wear from its clothing stores worldwide. Sustainable firms usually opt for local suppliers to reduce the pollution caused by transporting goods long distances.[36]

Like CSR, sustainable practices pay off in various ways, such as promoting a strong corporate reputation, the ability to hire and retain superior employees, cost savings from more efficient production, better linkages with suppliers, and smoother relations with foreign governments.

Achieving sustainability often requires the firm to be flexible and creative. A good example is Coca-Cola, which had to deal with water sustainability challenges. As water resources dwindled in some countries, Coke began to experience conflicts with communities and other water users, especially in India. To address such challenges, Coke developed a water sustainability program that goes well beyond efficiency and legal compliance needs alone. Management devised global projects that protect water resources and ensure access to clean drinking water. Coke mobilized the international community to anticipate and deal with ever-severe water crises worldwide.[37]

 ## Corporate Governance and Its Implications for Managers

The challenge for management is to increase awareness of ethical, CSR, and sustainability throughout the firm and to view them as opportunities to improve society, the environment, and company performance. Corporate governance provides the means through which firms undertake ethical behaviors, CSR, and sustainability.[38] Employees must learn to recognize and manage the ethical problems that confront the firm. Let's explore this issue in detail. As shown in the box below, scholars have devised five standards that managers can use to examine ethical problems.[39]

Ethical Standards for Corporate Governance

Utilitarian Approach	Rights Approach	Fairness Approach	Common Good Approach	Virtue Approach
The best ethical action is the one that provides the most good or the least harm. It produces the greatest balance of good over harm to customers, employees, shareholders, the community, and the natural environment.	The best action protects and respects the moral rights of everyone involved. It is based on the belief that, regardless of how you deal with an ethical dilemma, human dignity must be preserved.	The best action treats everyone equally and fairly. Workers should be paid a fair wage that provides a decent standard of living, and colleagues and customers should be treated as we would like to be treated.	The best action emphasizes the welfare of the entire community or nation. It asks what action contributes most to the quality of life of all affected people. Respect and compassion for all, especially the vulnerable, is the basis for decision making.	The best action emphasizes virtues that provide for the full development of our humanity. The most important virtues are truth, courage, compassion, generosity, tolerance, love, integrity, and prudence.

Using these five approaches to analyze ethical problems can be challenging because they occasionally conflict with each other, and not everyone agrees on which standard to use in all situations. Different cultures adhere to differing norms of morality and human rights and basic standards of right and wrong. Moreover, ethical dilemmas are complex and proposed approaches may not provide adequate guidance in determining the best course of action. Nevertheless, each standard is useful because it helps guide ethical behavior in almost any predicament. More often than not, they lead to similar solutions.

Code of Conduct

A code of conduct outlines the responsibilities and practices expected of an organization and the individuals who work there. Corporate codes of conduct emphasize standards related to ethics and social responsibilities. A good code of conduct defines the values and principles that are intended to guide the decisions, procedures, and systems of the firm. It aims to ensure respect for the rights of all constituents affected by company operations. The code should serve as a tool to encourage employee discussion on how to deal with the ethical dilemmas that confront the firm. In helping identify ethical problems, the firm's code of conduct should be designed to function like a moral compass for company operations worldwide.[40] Like a mission statement, it should guide employee behavior in all situations, so the firm avoids behaviors that compromise ethical standards wherever it does business.

Deciding What Constitutes Ethical Behavior

When it comes to ensuring ethical behavior, experienced managers follow a systematic process. First, they are sensitive to ethical problems. Before entering a country and throughout operations there, managers remain alert to the various ethical challenges the firm may encounter. They scan operations in each country and potential partners for the possibility of ethical abuses. Such scanning is an ongoing process, because company operations and environments evolve continuously. With enough practice, management creates a systematic approach to scanning and a culture within the firm that supports alertness and ongoing analysis of potential ethical concerns.

Managers should focus not only on specific national environments but also on proposed and existing value-chain activities, which often take place in multiple countries. In each country and venture, areas that merit particular attention encompass commercial environments, labor conditions, partners, customers, accounting practices, and conditions regarding the natural environment, as well as the range of the firm's potential or existing value-chain activities, including sourcing, production, marketing, and distribution.

A study in the *Harvard Business Review* found that improper ethical behavior results when:

- **Top management sets goals and incentives aimed at promoting good outcomes (e.g., profits) that instead encourage bad behaviors.** For example, law and accounting firms often encourage employees to maximize the hours they bill for their services. Under pressure, some employees "pad" their hours or charge clients for work they didn't do.
- **Employees overlook unethical behavior in others because of peer pressure or self-interest.** A manager may fail to complain about toxic waste discharged by a subsidiary because he doesn't want to "rock the boat."
- **Managers tolerate lower ethical standards in value-chain activities performed by suppliers or third-party firms.** Coffee producers sometimes ignore the poor working conditions of supplier farmers in Africa and Latin America.
- **Unethical practices are allowed to accumulate in the firm slowly over time.** When bad behavior is widespread throughout the firm, smaller infractions seem less noticeable. A corrupt environment usually fosters ongoing corruption.
- **Bad means are justified by good ends.** Pharmaceutical firms sometimes use unethical testing procedures in poor countries in order to validate of the effectiveness of new medications for disorders such as cancer and AIDS. The drugs help people, but may be developed through bad practice.[41]

Once managers develop an ongoing awareness of potential ethical abuses, the next step is to systematically explore the ethical aspects of each decision the firm may make regarding its current and potential activities. To further clarify the process of scanning for and analyzing potential ethical problems, we next provide a framework for making ethical decisions.

 A Framework for Making Ethical Decisions

Scholars suggest that managers follow a systematic approach to resolving ethical problems. Exhibit 5.7 presents a five-step framework for arriving at ethical decisions. The framework will help you arrive at appropriate solutions.[42] With practice, it can become second nature. The steps in the framework are explained below.

EXHIBIT 5.7

Framework for Arriving at Ethical Decisions

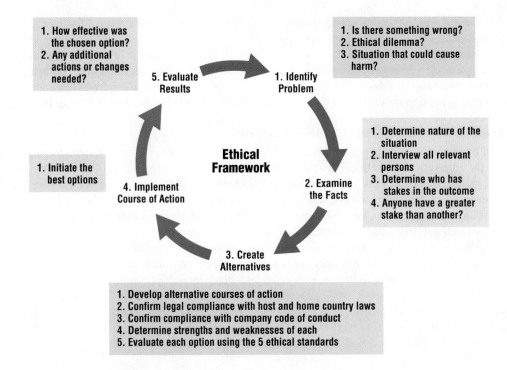

1. **Identify the problem.** The first step is to acknowledge the presence of an ethical problem. Ask questions such as: Is there something wrong? Is an ethical dilemma present? Is there a situation that might harm personnel, customers, the community, or the nation? In international business, recognizing the issue can be tricky because subtleties of the situation may be outside your knowledge or experience. Often, it is best to rely on your instincts—if some activity or action feels wrong, it probably is.

2. **Examine the facts.** Determine the nature and dimensions of the situation. Have all the relevant persons and groups been consulted? What individuals or groups have a stake in the outcome? How much weight should be given to the interests of each? Do some parties have a greater stake because they are disadvantaged or have a special need? This stage is often challenging because determining specific details and distinguishing facts from irrelevant information can be tricky. The process often involves interviewing personnel and stakeholders who may offer differing versions or opinions on the issue at hand. The manager's task is to identify and validate the most useful, valid information that makes clear the true nature of the problem.

3. **Create alternatives.** Identify potential courses of action and evaluate each. Initially, consistent with the pyramid of ethical behavior, review any proposed action to ensure it is legal. If it violates host or home country laws or international treaties, it should be rejected. Next, review any proposed action to ensure it is acceptable according to company policy and the firm's code of conduct. If discrepancies are found, the action should be rejected. Finally, evaluate each proposed action to assess its consistency with accepted ethical standards, using the approaches described earlier:

- Utilitarian—which action results in the most good and least harm?

- Rights—which action respects the rights of everyone involved?

- Fairness—which action treats people most fairly?

- Common good—which action contributes most to the overall quality of life of the people affected?

- Virtue—which action embodies the character strengths you value?

The goal is to arrive at the best decision or most appropriate course of action. Consider consulting local colleagues familiar with the situation, to provide insights and generate options. Assess the consequences of each action from the perspective of all parties it will affect.

Any decision should be tested by asking if you would feel comfortable explaining it to your mother, a colleague you respect, or a valued mentor. If you had to defend the decision on television, would you be comfortable doing so?

4. Implement course of action. Put the chosen plan into action. This implies creating new rules, processes, or procedures, and putting these into effect. Implementation is critical because it determines the success or failure of the chosen action. Managers need to be particularly diligent at this stage, to ensure the action is carried out per plan.

5. Evaluate results. Once the decision is implemented, you will need to assess how effective it was. How did it turn out? If you had it to do again, would you do anything differently? Results evaluation may require collecting, analyzing, and using information to answer questions about the chosen course of action. The goal is to ensure the action achieves its intended effect, and find out if the firm should modify the approach or pursue a different one.

The steps in this framework will help you arrive at appropriate solutions to ethical problems. To briefly illustrate, let's revisit the example of you as a manager visiting a company factory in Colombia, where you discover child labor. Without the children's income, their families may go hungry, or the children may turn to illicit activity, such as street crime. Having identified the problem, you examine facts by consulting colleagues both at the plant and headquarters. You seek information on the status of the employed children, as well as local law and customs on child labor. You then create alternative possible solutions, ensuring they are legal and consistent with company policy. Keeping the five ethical standards in mind, you evaluate each proposed action. Finally, you choose and implement the best course of action, and evaluate its effectiveness.

Embracing CSR and Sustainability

In a world ever sensitive to social and environmental issues, more firms are undertaking the following types of activities:

- Develop closer relations with foreign stakeholders to better understand their needs and work jointly toward solutions
- Build internal and external capabilities to enhance the firm's contribution to the local community and global environment
- Ensure diverse voices are heard by creating organizational structures that employ managers and workers from around the world
- Develop global CSR standards and objectives that are communicated and implemented across the firm worldwide
- Train managers in global CSR principles and integrate these into managerial responsibilities

Managers must make ethical behavior, CSR and sustainability a part of company activities and operations. MNE pursuits generate environmental harm and bring firms into contact with various activities—from R&D to manufacturing to marketing—that can pose various ethical dilemmas. Business executives should balance their obligation to shareholders with explicit contributions to the broader public good. Most executives agree that generating high returns for investors should be accompanied by a focus on providing good jobs, supporting social causes in local communities, and going beyond legal requirements to minimize pollution and other negative effects of business.

A Global Consensus

Incorporating ethics, CSR, and sustainability into global operations is a path to long-term company success. Various resources are available to assist managers. International organizations such as the United Nations, the World Bank, and the International Monetary Fund have launched programs to combat international corruption.

The International Chamber of Commerce has adopted "Rules of Conduct to Combat Extortion and Bribery," and the United Nations issued a "Declaration against Corruption and Bribery in International Commercial Transactions." The Organisation for Economic Co-operation and Development (OECD) has developed an antibribery agreement, which was signed by its thirty member nations (essentially, all the advanced economies) plus several Latin American countries.[43]

The *United Nations Global Compact* (see www.unglobalcompact.org) is a policy platform and practical framework for companies committed to sustainability and responsible business practices. It seeks to align business operations and strategies with universally accepted principles in the areas of human rights, labor, corruption, and the natural environment. It is the world's largest voluntary corporate citizenship initiative, representing thousands of businesses in more than 135 countries.

The *Global Reporting Initiative* (www.globalreporting.org) pioneered the development of the most widely used sustainability reporting framework. The framework sets out the principles and indicators that organizations can use to measure and report their economic, environmental, and social performance. Today, most large MNEs produce sustainability reports, many following the GRI guidelines.

Ultimately, CSR and sustainability require the firm to go "deep, wide, and local." *Going deep* means institutionalizing appropriate behavior into the organization's culture so it becomes part and parcel of strategy. *Going wide* implies a continuous effort to understand how CSR and sustainability affect every aspect of the firm's operations worldwide. *Going local* goes hand-in-hand with globalization. It requires the firm to examine its global operations to identify and improve specific local issues that affect customers, competitive position, reputation, and any other dimension that affects the firm's operations worldwide.[44]

To make ethical practices, CSR, and sustainability succeed in the firm, it is important to undertake a systematic and ongoing process of education for employees, suppliers, and intermediaries alike. As the firm builds a track record of changes and successes, it will begin to build a culture of appropriate behavior in its operations worldwide.

CLOSING CASE   Corruption at Siemens

One day in 2004, a senior executive at Siemens Company said he received a disturbing phone call from a Saudi Arabian businessman. The caller said he represented a Saudi consulting firm that had been a business partner of Siemens. He wanted $910 million in U.S. currency in payments and if Siemens didn't pay up, he would forward documents to government authorities detailing bribes paid on Siemens' behalf to win telecommunications contracts in Saudi Arabia. The incident was the beginning of a series of events—police raids, forensic investigations, and arrests of top executives—that became one of the biggest corruption cases in corporate history.

Based in Germany, Siemens is one of the world's largest electronics and industrial engineering firms. It produces industrial controls, lighting products, power generation equipment, and transportation systems. Siemens operates in 190 countries, with recent annual revenues exceeding $100 billion.

A Culture of Corruption?

Since the 1970s, Siemens has been stung by a series of scandals, many of them including accusations of bribery brought by governments in numerous countries, the European Union, and the United Nations. One former executive was accused of handling $77 million in bribes. Another admitted to bribing a labor union. A court found that Siemens had paid millions in 2007 to bribe government officials in Libya, Nigeria, and Russia.

Investigators alleged there was a culture at Siemens, endorsed by senior managers, to use bribes and slush funds to win contracts, especially in its communications and power-generation divisions. Millions of dollars were regularly dispensed, the money carted off to foreign destinations in suitcases by managers who often felt confident they were doing "business as usual."

Reckoning and Deliverance

In the end, bribery caught up with Siemens. In a ruling under the Foreign Corrupt Practices Act, U.S. authorities ordered the company to pay $800 million in fines. The United States found that, in order to win infrastructure contracts, Siemens allegedly spent more than $1 billion bribing government officials around the world, including the former President of Argentina. The U.S. Securities and Exchange Commission (SEC) claimed that Siemens made more than 4,000 bribe payments over seven years. Payments were intended to obtain contracts to supply medical devices in Russia, transmission lines in China, transit systems in Venezuela, medical equipment in Vietnam, power equipment in Iraq, and telecommunications equipment in Bangladesh. In 2006, a U.S. grand jury indicted Siemens and two of its employees in a fraud scheme to pay $500,000 to win a $49 million contract. In 2007, two former Siemens officials were convicted of bribery for their involvement in multimillion-dollar payments to officials of a power utility in Italy.

In response to the scandals, some Siemens customers indicated they would delay ordering telecommunications equipment from the firm, and Nokia Corporation announced it would postpone a planned joint venture. In 2008, Siemens' profits declined, partly due to the creation of a fund for expenses related to bribery investigations. In 2009, the World Bank required Siemens to pay $100 million to help global anticorruption efforts and to forego bidding on World Bank development projects for two years. In the end, Siemens' two top executives, the chairman and the CEO, were forced to resign.

In Germany, Siemens executives indicted in the scandal received only suspended prison sentences. A German court ordered Siemens to pay $284 million, a modest fine for a firm that usually generates billions in annual net profits. Germany is the world's leading exporter, and bribery cases often include efforts to generate foreign business, especially in developing economies. Until 1999, German firms were permitted to write off such bribes as business expenses. Many European countries did not outlaw paying bribes overseas until the late 1990s.

Remedial Actions

In the wake of the scandal, Siemens management took steps to prevent further bribery. The company appointed a law firm to conduct an independent review of its compliance system and uncover possible improprieties. Sixty-five countries were flagged for scrutiny. Siemens' own internal investigation identified more than $1.5 billion in suspicious transactions worldwide between 2000 and 2006. Management remarked on the difficulty of closely monitoring activities of the firm's 430,000 employees in 190 countries and bank accounts that once numbered 5,000 and handled up to 50 million transactions a day. International subsidiaries were free to act with substantial autonomy.

Siemens hired an independent ombudsman, strengthened its business-conduct code, and established a task force to improve internal controls over international funds transfers, reduce the number of bank accounts, and supervise the opening and maintaining of bank accounts. Subsidiaries were required to provide comprehensive details of all transactions. The German government tightened standards for managers, seeking to ensure that those at all large firms report regularly to supervisory boards regarding compliance with ethics codes.

Conclusion

In the United States, the number of companies reporting foreign corruption investigations into their activities abroad is up sharply. Foreign companies that do business in the United States are attracting greater scrutiny as well. In most countries, however, antibribery laws are weak or poorly enforced. Bribery is difficult to detect when funds are channeled through consultants and other intermediaries, or when company operations are widely dispersed and decentralized.

Why should firms care about bribery? For one thing, it is bad business. Bribery distorts legitimate efforts to sustain and enhance company performance. Where corruption becomes a pattern, eventually the firm is caught and its reputation tarnished. Corruption also inhibits development in poor countries and is at the root of persistent poverty in many. It sustains repressive governments and can lead to the failure of societies and national economies.

The best firms create a culture in which ethical conduct is valued as highly as efforts to maximize sales and profits. It is insufficient to merely publicize the need for integrity; managers must lead through ongoing actions that demonstrate adherence to ethical standards. They should establish transparency and compliance processes that ensure senior executives know what is going on throughout the firm.

AACSB: Reflective Thinking Skills, Multicultural and Diversity Understanding, Ethical Understanding and Reasoning Abilities

Case Questions

1. What does the case suggest is the value of ethical behavior? What did Siemens gain by introducing controls to minimize the likelihood of corruption?

2. Most countries lack adequate laws or enforcement to deal with bribery and other forms of corruption. Why is this? How do countries benefit from a strong rule of law that minimizes corruption?

3. Do you think Siemens was penalized enough for its corruption? Why or why not? What can governments or other organizations do to discourage firms and others from engaging in corrupt behavior?

4. Some argue that because ethical standards are lax in many countries, Siemens and other firms must pay bribes to obtain new business. Do you agree with this view? Stated differently, when doing business around the world, is it generally better to emphasize normativism or relativism? Justify your answer.

Sources: C. Bray, J. Palazzolo, S. Romig, and P. Grontzki, "Former Siemens Executives Facing U.S. Bribery Charges," *Wall Street Journal,* December 14, 2011, p. B3; M. Esterl and D. Crawford, "Siemens to Pay Huge Fine in Bribery Inquiry," *Wall Street Journal,* December 15, 2008, p. B1; "Siemens to Tighten Controls on Money," *Financial Times,* April 18, 2007, p. 16; "Action against Bribery Requires Political Will," *Financial Times,* April 10, 2007, p. 14; V. Fuhrmans, "Siemens Settles with World Bank on Bribes," *Wall Street Journal,* July 3, 2009, p. B1; M. Hamblen, "Selloff Plans, Fraud Probe Put Spotlight on Siemens," *Computerworld,* December 18, 2006, p. 12; R. Minder, "Siemens Bows to Pressure for Transparency," *Financial Times,* December 12, 2006, p. 24; A. Preuschat, "Siemens Posts Loss Due to Charges But Says Its Orders Remain Strong," *Wall Street Journal,* November 14, 2008, p. B3; C. Verschoor, "Siemens AG Is Latest Fallen Ethics Idol," *Strategic Finance* 89, no. 5 (2007): 11–13; "Two Siemens Ex-Officials Convicted in Bribery Case," *Wall Street Journal,* May 15, 2007, p. C6; D. Crawford and M. Esterl, "Siemens Fine Ends a Bribery Probe," *Wall Street Journal,* October 5, 2007, p. A2; D. Crawford and M. Esterl, "Siemens Probe Spotlights Murky Role of Consultants," *Wall Street Journal,* April 20, 2007, p. A1; D. Crawford and M. Esterl, "Widening Scandal: At Siemens, Witnesses Cite Pattern of Bribery," *Wall Street Journal,* January 31, 2007, p. A1; M. Esterl, "Ethics Hurdle: Corruption Scandal at Siemens May Derail Restructuring Drive," *Wall Street Journal,* December 18, 2006, p. A1; M. Esterl, "Siemens CEO Hopes New Audit Cuts Scope of Suspected Fraud," *Wall Street Journal,* December 22, 2006, p. B.4; R. Milne, "Siemens 'Had a System for Paying Bribes,'" *Financial Times,* March 14, 2007, p. 27; R. Milne and M. Scheele, "Probe Finds 'General Practice' of Alleged Bribery at Siemens," *Financial Times,* May 7, 2007, p. 1; D. Crawford and M. Esterl, "Siemens Ruling Details Bribery Across the Globe," *Wall Street Journal,* November 16, 2007, p. A1; D. Crawford and M. Esterl, "Inside Bribery Probe of Siemens," *Wall Street Journal,* December 28, 2007, p. A4; M. Esterl and D. Crawford, "Ex-Siemens Manager Sentenced," *Wall Street Journal,* November 25, 2008, p. B2; M. Esterl and D. Crawford, "At Siemens, A Conviction Could Trigger More Cases," *Wall Street Journal,* July 29, 2008, p. B1; "Stopping the Rot; Face Value," *The Economist,* March 8, 2008, p. 89; "Bavarian Baksheesh; The Siemens Scandal," *The Economist,* December 20, 2008, p. 112.

CHAPTER ESSENTIALS

MyManagementLab

Go to **mymanagementlab.com** to complete the problems marked with this icon ⭐.

Key Terms

corporate governance   112
corporate social responsibility
   (CSR)   112
corruption   112

ethics   112
intellectual property   114
intellectual property rights   114
normativism   118

relativism   118
sustainability   112

Summary

In this chapter, you learned about:

1. Ethical challenges in international business

Ethics are the moral principles and values that govern the behavior of people, firms, and governments. **Corporate social responsibility (CSR)** refers to operating a business in a manner that meets or exceeds the ethical, legal, and commercial expectations of customers, shareholders, employees, and communities. **Sustainability** means meeting humanity's needs without harming future generations. **Corporate governance** is the system of procedures and processes by which corporations are managed, directed, and controlled. Unethical behavior is revealed in international business in management, global sourcing, and marketing, often as piracy, bribery, and **corruption** Governments aim to protect **intellectual property**. However, protection is not guaranteed in much of the world.

2. Key aspects of international ethics

Behaving ethically adds value to the firm in various ways. But ethical standards vary around the world. **Relativism** is the belief that ethical truths are not absolute but differ from group to group. **Normativism** holds that ethical standards are universal, and firms and individuals should seek to uphold them consistently around the world. An *ethical dilemma* is a predicament with major conflicts among different interests. Determining the best course of action is confounded by several possible solutions that may be equally justifiable.

3. Corporate social responsibility

In addition to complying with laws, regulations, and basic ethical standards, prudent MNEs emphasize corporate social responsibility in their activities. A strong business rationale for CSR includes the firm's ability to motivate employees and develop superior strategy. Failure to develop a CSR has important negative consequences for the firm.

4. The role of sustainability in international operations

Sustainable businesses simultaneously pursue three types of interests: economic, social, and environmental. They maximize the use of recycled or renewable materials and environmentally friendly energy. They reduce waste in manufacturing and minimize harmful air and water pollution. They provide health insurance and training and care for employees in various other ways. They are active in the local community with initiatives in education, health care, and environmental protection. Sustainable firms choose and work with suppliers that adhere to high social and environmental standards.

5. Corporate governance and its implications for managers

A focus on ethics, CSR, and sustainability is in the firm's best interests, in terms of business strategy and organizational performance. Scholars have devised five standards managers can use to examine ethical dilemmas, based on utilitarianism, rights, fairness, common good, and virtue.

Senior managers should develop a *code of ethics* that describes what the firm expects of its employees when facing ethical dilemmas.

6. A framework for making ethical decisions

Scholars have devised a five-step framework for making ethical decisions. Initially, the manager should recognize the existence of an ethical problem. The next steps are to get the facts, evaluate alternative courses of action, and then implement and evaluate the decision made. Ethical behavior and CSR must be part of managers' day-to-day pursuits. Various resources are available to assist managers, such as the United Nations and the World Bank.

Test Your Comprehension

1. Distinguish between ethics and corruption in international business.

2. What is the Corruption Perceptions Index, and how can a manager use it to assess international risk?

3. Describe typical ethical problems that firms encounter in international business.

4. What is intellectual property? What industries are most affected by threats to intellectual property?

5. Distinguish relativism and normativism. Which one should the firm apply in its activities?

6. What is an ethical dilemma? Give an example of an ethical dilemma that MNEs encounter abroad.

7. What is corporate social responsibility (CSR)? How does it differ from general ethical behavior?

⭐ 8. What is sustainability? How might the firm undertake sustainability in its value-chain activities?

9. Describe the five standards managers can use to examine ethical dilemmas.

10. Describe the steps in the framework for ethical conduct.

⭐ 11. What steps can the firm take to develop its orientation to CSR and sustainability in international operations?

Apply Your Understanding AACSB: Reflective Thinking Skills, Analytic Skills, Communication Abilities, Ethical Understanding and Reasoning Abilities

1. Ethical Dilemma: You were recently hired by ThunderCat Corporation, a major aircraft producer with a manufacturing presence in numerous countries. ThunderCat's sales personnel constantly travel the world, selling fighter jets and commercial aircraft to airlines and foreign governments. You are keenly aware that countries vary enormously in terms of culture, laws, and political systems. Top management has asked you to develop a code of ethics to guide ThunderCat employees in their interactions anywhere in the world. Given the diversity of countries where ThunderCat operates, what sort of code will you develop? What issues should you consider? Given the diversity of countries around the world, is it possible to develop a code that guides ethical behavior everywhere?

2. Ethical Dilemma: Royal Dutch Shell has been doing business in Nigeria since the 1920s and has announced new plans to develop oil and gas projects there. However, over the years Shell has experienced a series of complex issues. Its operations are centered in Nigeria's Ogoni region, where the local citizens have protested Shell's drilling and refining activities, which harm the natural environment and reduce the amount of available farmland. Protestors also accuse Shell of extracting wealth from the region without adequately compensating local residents. Following sabotage of its facilities, the firm suspended some of its Nigerian operations. It then came under pressure to divest its Nigerian operations and pay reparations to the local people. Despite these problems, Shell has persisted in Nigeria. Management instituted various community development programs in the region, budgeted at $50 million per year. Using the ethical framework in this chapter, identify steps Shell can take to be a better corporate citizen in Nigeria.

3. Ethical Dilemma: Suppose you are president of Orwell Corporation, a firm that makes high-tech surveillance equipment. You have received an offer from the government of North Korea to bid on a huge contract to install a network of 4,000 surveillance cameras

throughout the country. The North Koreans say the system will be used to prevent crime and monitor traffic jams. But you know the repressive regime will use the technology to target dissent and repress human rights, resulting in jail time and even torture for citizens who engage in free speech and other legitimate activities. Moreover, your nation's government has laws prohibiting the export of crime-control products to North Korea, although the restrictions don't apply to surveillance cameras. What should you do? Do you bid on the project? Or do you abstain, not wishing to support repression in a tyrannical regime? (Note: This dilemma is similar to real dilemmas faced by Cisco and other firms that have marketed surveillance equipment to repressive governments.)

globalEDGE INTERNET EXERCISES
(http://www.globalEDGE.msu.edu)

AACSB: Analytic Skills, Use of Information Technology, Ethical Understanding and Reasoning Abilities

Refer to Chapter 1, page 24, for instructions on how to access and use globalEDGE™.

1. Various organizations have devised international standards for ethical corporate behavior. These include the United Nations "Universal Declaration for Human Rights" (available at www.un.org), the OECD's "Guidelines for Multinational Enterprise" (www.oecd.org), the International Labour Organization's "Minimum Labor Standards" (www.ilo.org), and the U.S. Department of Commerce's "Model Business Principles" (www.commerce.gov). Visit these online portals and prepare a set of guidelines firms can follow in pursuing acceptable ethical standards in international business.

2. Transparency International (www.transparency.org) publishes information about the nature of corruption around the world. Suppose you worked at a firm that makes computer software and wanted to begin doing business in Brazil and Russia. Your task is to examine reports and indices on these countries at the Transparency International site and write a brief report explaining how your firm should conduct business in these countries, with a view to avoiding problems associated with corruption. Key issues to consider include bribery and threats to intellectual property.

3. The Web sites for Lenovo (China; www.lenovo.com), Nokia (Finland; www.nokia.com), and Banco do Brasil (Brazil; www.bb.com.br, click on "English") contain information about how these firms undertake corporate social responsibility (CSR). Visit each Web site and write a report in which you compare and contrast each firm's CSR. Which firm appears most effective in CSR? How does the CSR of a bank differ from that of manufacturing firms such as Lenovo and Nokia? Lenovo and Banco do Brasil are based in emerging markets, while Nokia is in an advanced economy. What differences in the firms' CSR orientations can you detect based on this distinction? Justify your answer.

MyManagementLab

Go to **mymanagementlab.com** for Auto-graded writing questions as well as the following Assisted-graded writing questions:

5-1. What advantages do firms gain from behaving according to high ethical standards?

5-2. Why is CSR important to the internationalizing firm?

5-3. Mymanagementlab Only – comprehensive writing assignment for this chapter.

Source: © Giles Robberts/Alamy

Apple's Comparative and Competitive Advantages

Apple products were once made in the United States. Today, however, almost all of the 70 million iPhones, 30 million iPads, and 60 million other products that Apple sells globally each year are manufactured outside the United States. How did that happen?

Apple (annual revenues: $110 billion) has expanded internationally from its humble roots in the United States to more than 70 markets worldwide. In terms of total sales, North and South America account for about one-third, and Europe and Asia generate about one-quarter each. After the United States, Japan

is Apple's best country market, producing about 5 percent of total sales.

Apple orchestrates its value chains via contractual relations with suppliers around the world—some 700,000 people engineer, build, and assemble its products under contract. One of Apple's goals is to obtain comparative advantages from specific countries. *Comparative advantage* refers to superior features of a country that provide distinctive benefits, typically derived from either natural endowments or deliberate policies. Comparative advantage includes inherited resources, such as

CHAPTER 6

Theories of International Trade and Investment

 LEARNING OBJECTIVES *In this chapter, you will learn about the following:*

1. Why do nations trade?
2. How can nations enhance their competitive advantage?
3. Why and how do firms internationalize?
4. How can internationalizing firms gain and sustain competitive advantage?

MyManagementLab®

⭐ **Improve Your Grade!**

Over 10 million students improved their results using the Pearson MyLabs.
Visit **mymanagementlab.com** for simulations, tutorials, and end-of-chapter problems.

labor and land, and acquired resources, like entrepreneurial orientation and innovative capacity.

An iPhone contains hundreds of parts, about 90 percent of which are manufactured in countries outside the United States. Apple sources semiconductors from Germany, memory chips from Korea, display panels from Taiwan, and rare metals from Africa. All these components are assembled in China, which offers comparative advantages for manufacturing. Much of China's success is explained by its superior *factor proportions*. According to factor proportions theory, each country should specialize in making products that intensively use production factors (such as labor, land, capital) that it has in abundance and import goods that intensively use relatively scarce production factors. Because China has abundant low-cost labor, its firms specialize in producing labor-intensive products.

Apple exemplifies superior *innovation*. Apple suppliers excel at developing new product designs, innovative production processes, and new ways of organizing. Innovation promotes *productivity*, the value of output produced by a unit of labor or capital. The more productive a firm is, the more efficiently it uses its resources. Productivity is vital to the success of firms and nations alike. Over time, improving productivity is raising living standards in emerging markets such as China, India, Mexico, and Poland.

Configuring its value chains on a global scale enables Apple to produce the best possible products and maximize its competitive advantages. *Competitive advantage* refers to assets and competencies that are difficult for competitors to imitate and thus help firms succeed. Apple management believes the economies of scale of overseas factories as well as the diligence, flexibility, and industrial skills of foreign workers have outpaced counterparts in the United States.

Apple enjoys a *monopolistic advantage* by controlling cutting-edge knowledge in the development of smartphones, computers, and other products. The firm does most of its own R&D and product development in company-owned facilities in California.

Another key to Apple's success is its ability to engage in global *free trade*. Free trade produces the following outcomes: (i) consumers and firms can obtain the products they desire at lower cost; (ii) parts and other inputs obtained in this way reduce company expenses, which translates into higher profits; and (iii) consumers pay less for the products and services they need, which increases their living standards.

Apple has struggled to ensure sustainable conditions at its Chinese contract factories. Apple's biggest supplier is Foxconn, a leading electronics manufacturer. Workers in Foxconn's China factories have complained about long hours, low wages, and living in overcrowded dormitories. Some have even committed suicide. In response, more than 250,000 protesters signed a petition demanding better labor conditions for Apple contract workers abroad. Foxconn raised wages and moved some production to India, in search of cheaper labor. Foxconn also installed robots in several factories, laying off thousands of workers. Apple is struggling to strike the right balance between low-cost manufacturing and ensuring the safety and happiness of the thousands of workers who build the Iphones, Ipads, and other products that consumers love around the world.

SOURCES: Apple Inc., *Form 10-K (Annual Report)* 2011, accessed at http://investor.apple.com; Colin Campbell, "Foxconn's Robot Empire," *Maclean's*, November 21, 2011, p. 41; Charles Duhigg and Keith Bradsher, "How the U.S. Lost Out on iPhone Work," *New York Times*, January 21, 2012, accessed at www.nytimes.com; Hoovers.com, profile of Apple, Inc.; Adam Lashinsky, *Inside Apple: How America's Most Admired—and Secretive—Company Really Works* (New York: Business Plus, 2012); Adam Satariano, "Protesters to Target Apple Supplier Conditions," *Bloomberg*, February 8, 2012, accessed at www.bloomberg.com; Paul Theroux, "How Apple Revolutionized Our World," *Newsweek*, September 5, 2011, pp. 36–37; Jessica Vascellaro and Owen Fletcher, "Apple Navigates China Maze," *Wall Street Journal*, January 14, 2012, pp. B1–B2.

The opening story explains the trade, investment, and performance achievements of Apple, Inc. The technology giant benefits enormously from international business. The advantages provided by suppliers and nations in Asia, Europe, and elsewhere have propelled the firm to global success. China, Japan, Germany, South Korea, and numerous other countries have taken proactive steps to enhance their standing in the world economy. Emerging markets are reaping the rewards of various comparative and competitive advantages.

In this chapter, we review theories and explanations of why nations and firms undertake international activities.[1] We explain comparative and competitive advantages, and how such resources support nations and firms in global commerce. We address the underlying economic rationale for international business activity and explain why global trade and investment take place.

We address such questions as:

- What is the underlying economic rationale for international business activity?
- Why does trade take place?
- What are the gains from trade and investment?

Comparative advantage describes superior features of a country that provide unique benefits in global competition, typically derived from either natural endowments or

Comparative advantage
Superior features of a country that provide unique benefits in global competition, typically derived from either natural endowments or deliberate national policies.

deliberate national policies. Also known as *country-specific advantage*, comparative advantage includes inherited resources, such as labor, climate, arable land, and petroleum reserves, such as those enjoyed by the Gulf nations. Other types of comparative advantages are acquired over time, such as entrepreneurial orientation, availability of venture capital, and innovative capacity.

Competitive advantage describes organizational assets and competencies that are difficult for competitors to imitate and thus help firms enter and succeed in foreign markets. These competencies take various forms, such as specific knowledge, capabilities, innovativeness, superior strategies, or close relationships with suppliers. Competitive advantage is also known as firm-specific advantage.

In recent years business executives and scholars have used *competitive advantage* to refer to the advantages possessed by nations *and* individual firms in international trade and investment. To be consistent with the recent literature, we adopt this convention as well.

Exhibit 6.1 categorizes leading theories of international trade and investment into two broad groups. The first group includes nation-level theories. These are classical theories, widely accepted since the sixteenth century. They address two questions: (1) *Why* do nations trade? (2) *How* can nations enhance their competitive advantage?

The second group includes firm-level theories. These are more contemporary theories of how firms can create and sustain superior organizational performance. Firm-level explanations address two additional questions: (3) *Why* and *how* do firms internationalize? and (4) *How* can internationalizing firms gain and sustain competitive advantage?

We organize the remainder of our discussion according to the four fundamental questions.

Competitive advantage
Distinctive assets or competencies of a firm that are difficult for competitors to imitate and are typically derived from specific knowledge, capabilities, skills, or superior strategies.

EXHIBIT 6.1

Theories of International Trade and Investment

Why Do Nations Trade?

Why do nations trade with one another? The short answer is that trade enables countries to use their national resources more efficiently through specialization. Trade allows industries and workers to be more productive. These outcomes help keep the cost of many everyday products low, translating into higher living standards. Without international trade, most nations would be unable to feed, clothe, and house their citizens at current levels. Even resource-rich countries like the United States would suffer immensely without trade. Some types of food would become unavailable or very expensive. Coffee and sugar would be luxury items. Petroleum-based energy sources would dwindle. Vehicles would stop running, freight would go undelivered, and people would not be able to heat their homes in winter. In short, not only do nations, companies, and citizens benefit from international trade, modern life is virtually impossible without it.

Classical Theories

Six classical perspectives explain the underlying rationale for trade among nations: the mercantilist view, absolute advantage principle, comparative advantage principle, factor proportions theory, international product life cycle theory, and new trade theory.

Mercantilism

The belief that national prosperity is the result of a positive balance of trade, achieved by maximizing exports and minimizing imports.

MERCANTILISM The earliest explanations of international business emerged with the rise of European nation-states in the 1500s, when gold and silver were the most important sources of wealth, and nations sought to amass as much of these treasures as possible. Nations received payment for exports in gold, so exports increased their gold stock, while imports reduced it because they paid for imports with their gold. Exports were seen as good and imports as bad. Because the nation's power and strength increase as its wealth increases, **mercantilism** argues that national prosperity results from a positive balance of trade achieved by maximizing exports and minimizing or even impeding imports.

Mercantilism explains why nations attempt to run a *trade surplus*—that is, to export more goods than they import. Today many people believe that running a trade surplus is beneficial. They subscribe to a view known as *neo-mercantilism*. Labor unions (which seek to protect home-country jobs), farmers (who want to keep crop prices high), and certain manufacturers (those that rely heavily on exports) all tend to support neo-mercantilism.

However, mercantilism tends to harm firms that import, especially those that import raw materials and parts used in the manufacture of finished products. Mercantilism also harms consumers, because restricting imports reduces the choice of products they can buy. Product shortages that result from import restrictions may lead to higher prices—that is, inflation. When taken to an extreme, mercantilism may invite "beggar thy neighbor" policies, promoting the benefits of one country at the expense of others. By contrast, free trade is a generally superior approach.

Free trade

Relative absence of restrictions to the flow of goods and services between nations.

Free trade refers to the relative absence of restrictions to the flow of goods and services between nations. It typically produces the following outcomes:

- Consumers and firms can more readily buy the products they want.
- Imported products tend to be cheaper than domestically produced products (because access to world-scale supplies forces prices down, mainly from increased competition, or because the goods are produced in lower-cost countries).
- Lower-cost imports help reduce company expenses, thereby raising their profits (which may be passed on to workers in the form of higher wages).
- Lower-cost imports help consumers save money, thereby increasing their living standards.
- Unrestricted international trade generally increases the overall prosperity of poor countries.

ABSOLUTE ADVANTAGE PRINCIPLE In *An Inquiry into the Nature and Causes of the Wealth of Nations*, a landmark book published in 1776, Scottish political economist Adam Smith attacked the mercantilist view by suggesting that nations benefit most from free trade. Smith argued that mercantilism deprives individuals of the ability to trade freely and to benefit from voluntary exchange. By trying to minimize imports, a country wastes much of its national resources in the production of goods it is not suited to produce efficiently. The inefficiencies of mercantilism end up reducing the wealth of the nation as a whole while enriching a limited number of individuals and interest groups. Relative to others, each country is more efficient in the production of some products and less efficient in the production of other products. Smith's **absolute advantage principle** states that a country benefits by producing primarily those products in which it has an absolute advantage, meaning goods it can produce using fewer resources than another country. Each country thus increases its welfare by specializing in the production of certain products, exporting them, and importing others. This approach allows the nation to consume more than it otherwise could, generally at lower cost.

Exhibit 6.2 illustrates how the absolute advantage principle works in practice. Consider two nations, France and Germany, engaged in a trading relationship. Panel (a) of the exhibit shows a hypothetical example in which France has an absolute advantage in the production of cloth, and Germany has an absolute advantage in the production of wheat. Assume labor is the only factor of production used in making both goods. (Firms employ *factors of production*—for example, labor, capital, entrepreneurship, and technology—to produce products and services.) It takes an average worker in France 6 days to produce one ton of cloth and 8 days to produce one ton of wheat. It takes an average worker in Germany 10 days to produce one ton of cloth and 4 days to produce one ton of wheat.

France has an absolute advantage in the production of cloth, since it takes only 6 days of labor to produce one ton compared to 10 days for Germany. Germany has an absolute advantage in the production of wheat, since it takes only 4 days to produce one ton compared to 8 days for France. If both France and Germany were to specialize, exchanging cloth and wheat at a ratio of one-to-one, France could employ more of its resources to produce cloth and Germany could employ more of its resources to produce wheat. France would be able to import one ton of wheat in exchange for one ton of cloth, thereby "paying" only 6 labor days for one ton of wheat. If France had produced the wheat itself, it would have used 8 labor days, so it gains 2 labor days from the trade. In a similar way, Germany gains from trade with France.

The point is further illustrated by the graph in panel (b) of Exhibit 6.2. Here, the different combinations of cloth and wheat that France can produce

Source: © Georgios Kollidas/Fotolia

Scottish political economist Adam Smith was among the first to articulate the advantages of international trade.

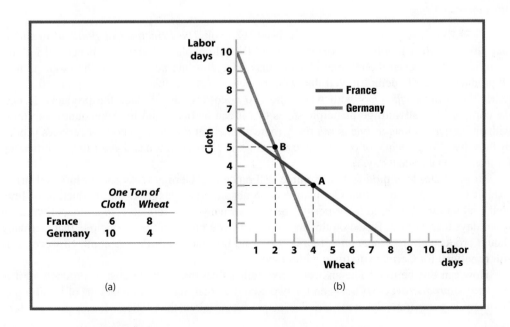

(a)

(b)

EXHIBIT 6.2

Example of Absolute Advantage (Labor Cost in Days of Production for One Ton)

	One Ton of	
	Cloth	*Wheat*
France	6	8
Germany	10	4

are represented by the blue line, France's *production possibilities frontier*. The different combinations of cloth and wheat that Germany can produce are indicated by the red line, Germany's production possibilities frontier. As shown, France is more efficient at producing cloth, and Germany is more efficient at producing wheat. Suppose the countries do not trade with each other and each devotes half its labor days to producing each of cloth and wheat. France (point A in the graph) spends 3 labor days to produce ½ ton of cloth and 4 labor days to produce ½ ton of wheat. Germany (point B in the graph) spends 5 labor days to produce ½ ton of cloth and 2 labor days to produce ½ ton of wheat. Without trade, it costs the two countries a combined total of 14 labor days to produce one ton of cloth and one ton of wheat. By contrast, if each country were to specialize and trade with the other, France would invest 6 days to produce one ton of cloth and Germany would invest 4 days to produce one ton of wheat, for a total of just 10 labor days. Thus, by specializing and trading, each country has saved an average of 2 labor days ((14–10)/2).

Trading means France and Germany obtain the goods they need for less labor. In this way, each country employs its labor and other resources more efficiently, thereby increasing its standard of living. To employ a more contemporary example, Japan has no natural holdings of oil, but it manufactures some of the world's best automobiles. Saudi Arabia produces much oil, but lacks a substantial car industry. Given this state of resources, it is wasteful for each country to attempt to produce both oil and cars. By trading with each other, Japan and Saudi Arabia employ their respective resources more efficiently in a mutually beneficial relationship. Japan gets oil that it refines to power cars, and Saudi Arabia gets the cars its citizens need. By extending this example we see that freely trading countries achieve substantial gains from trade. Brazil can produce coffee more cheaply than Germany; Australia can produce wool more cheaply than Switzerland; Britain can provide financial services more cheaply than Zimbabwe; and so forth.

Ethical Connections

A *market failure* is an interruption in free trade, resulting in inefficient allocation of goods and services. In many developing economies, corruption is a common source of market failure. For example, goods and services are often unfairly granted to those who pay bribes. Since free trade reduces poverty by promoting efficient allocation of goods and services, governments should act to restrict bribery and other forms of corruption.

Historically, the concept of absolute advantage provided perhaps the earliest sound rationale for international trade. However, it failed to consider more subtle advantages that trading nations enjoy. Later analysis revealed that a country benefits from international trade even when it lacks an absolute advantage. Such thinking led to the principle of *comparative advantage*.

COMPARATIVE ADVANTAGE PRINCIPLE In his 1817 book *The Principles of Political Economy and Taxation*, British political economist David Ricardo explained why it is beneficial for two countries to trade even though one of them may have absolute advantage in the production of all products. Ricardo demonstrated that what matters is not the absolute cost of production, but rather the *relative efficiency* with which the two countries can produce the products. Hence, the **comparative advantage principle** states that it can be beneficial for two countries to trade without barriers as long as one is *relatively* more efficient at producing goods or services needed by the other. The principle of comparative advantage is the foundation and overriding justification for international trade today.

To illustrate, let's modify the example of France and Germany. As shown in panel (a) of Exhibit 6.3, suppose now that Germany has an absolute advantage in the production of both cloth and wheat. That is, in labor-per-day terms, Germany can produce *both* cloth and wheat in fewer days than France. Based on this new scenario, you might initially conclude that Germany should produce all the wheat and cloth it needs and not trade with France at all. However, it is still beneficial for Germany to trade with France.

How can this be true? The answer is that rather than the absolute cost of production, it is the *ratio of production costs* between the two countries that matters. In panel (a) of Exhibit 6.3, Germany is comparatively more efficient at producing cloth than wheat: It can produce four

Comparative advantage principle
It can be beneficial for two countries to trade without barriers as long as one is relatively more efficient at producing goods or services needed by the other. What matters is not the absolute cost of production but rather the relative efficiency with which a country can produce the product.

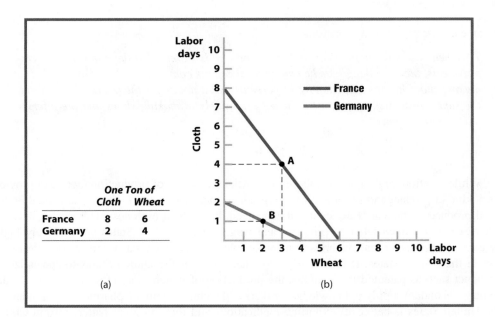

EXHIBIT 6.3

Example of Comparative Advantage (Labor Cost in Days of Production for One Ton)

times as much cloth as France (8/2), but only 1.5 times as much wheat (6/4). Thus, Germany should devote all its resources to producing cloth and import all the wheat it needs from France. France should specialize in producing wheat and import all its cloth from Germany. Both countries then can each produce and consume relatively more of the goods they desire for a given level of labor cost.

This is further illustrated in panel (b) of Exhibit 6.3. In Germany, it takes only 2 labor days to produce one ton of cloth and 4 labor days to produce one ton of wheat. Given 4 labor days, Germany can produce 2 tons of cloth or 1 ton of wheat, or any combination in between on its production possibilities frontier (the red line). In France, using 8 labor days will produce 1 ton of cloth or 1.33 tons of wheat (8/6), or any combination in between on its production possibilities frontier (the blue line). Again, suppose the countries do not trade with each other, and each devotes half its labor days to producing each of cloth and wheat. In this case, it takes France (point A in the graph) a total of 7 labor days to produce ½ ton of cloth and ½ ton of wheat. However, it takes Germany (point B in the graph) just 3 labor days to produce the same quantity of these commodities. Without trade, it would take the two countries a total of 10 labor days to produce 1 ton of cloth and 1 ton of wheat. By contrast, if the two countries began trading, and if Germany specialized in producing cloth and France specialized in wheat, it would take only 8 days to produce the same volume of these commodities. Thus, even when Germany holds an absolute advantage in producing both cloth and wheat, the two countries can reduce their combined resource costs by specializing and trading.

Another way to understand comparative advantage is to consider opportunity cost, the value of a foregone alternative activity. In panel (a) of Exhibit 6.3, if Germany produces 1 ton of wheat, it forgoes 2 tons of cloth. However, if France produces 1 ton of wheat, it forgoes only 0.75 tons of cloth. Thus, France should specialize in wheat. Similarly, if France produces 1 ton of cloth, it forgoes 1.33 tons of wheat. But if Germany produces 1 ton of cloth, it forgoes only 0.5 ton of wheat. Thus, Germany should specialize in cloth. The opportunity cost of producing wheat is lower in France, and the opportunity cost of producing cloth is lower in Germany.

Source: leungchopan/Shutterstock

It would be wasteful for Saudi Arabia to produce both oil and cars. Instead, it can focus on extracting and refining petroleum while procuring cars from Japan, which has no natural holdings of oil but manufactures some of the best automobiles in the world.

In an example provided by Ricardo:

Two men can make both shoes and hats, and one is superior to the other in both employments, but in making hats he can only exceed his competitor by 20 percent, and in making shoes he can excel him by 33 percent; will it not be for the interest of both that the superior man should employ himself exclusively in making shoes and the inferior man in making hats?[2]

While a nation might conceivably have a sufficient variety of production factors to provide every kind of product and service, it cannot produce each with equal facility. The United States could produce all the car batteries its citizens need, but only at high cost. This occurs because batteries require much labor to produce, and wages in the United States are relatively high. By contrast, producing car batteries is a reasonable activity in China, where wages are lower than in the United States. It is advantageous, therefore, for the United States to specialize in a product such as patented medications, the production of which more efficiently employs the country's abundant supply of knowledge workers and technology in the pharmaceutical industry. The United States is better off exporting medications and importing car batteries from China. The comparative advantage view is optimistic because it implies that a nation need not be the first-, second-, or even third-best producer of particular products to benefit from international trade. Indeed, it is generally advantageous for all countries to participate in international trade.

Source: Joe Belanger/Shutterstock

The United States could produce all the car batteries its citizens need, but only at a high cost. China is more efficient at producing car batteries, and the United States is relatively more efficient at producing pharmaceutical medications. Thus, the United States is better off exporting pharmaceuticals and importing car batteries from China.

Initially, comparative advantage scholars focused on the importance of *inherited* or *natural resource advantages*, such as fertile land, abundant minerals, and favorable climate. Because South Africa has extensive mineral deposits, it produces and exports diamonds. Because Argentina has much agricultural land and a suitable climate, it grows and exports wheat.

It has become clear that countries can also *create* or *acquire* comparative advantage. Consider the case of Japan. In the years following World War II, Japan systematically acquired a collection of advantages that benefited its consumer electronics industry. The investments made by Japan's government, banks, and manufacturing firms paid off enormously. Companies such as Hitachi, Panasonic, and Sony invested massive resources to acquire the knowledge and skills needed to become the world leaders in consumer electronics. Today Japan accounts for nearly half the industry's total world production, including digital cameras, flat panel TVs, and personal computers. More recently, South Korea has made similar investments, giving rise to leading-edge firms like LG and Samsung. We elaborate on the acquired advantages of countries later in the chapter.

Limitations of Early Trade Theories

While the concepts of absolute advantage and comparative advantage provide the rationale for international trade, they fail to account for factors that make contemporary trade complex, including:

- Traded products are not just commodities anymore, such as wheat and cloth. Today, many traded goods are characterized by strong branding and differentiated features.
- International transportation, critical for cross-border trade to take place, adds to the cost of importing.

- Government restrictions such as tariffs (taxes on imports), import barriers, and regulations can hamper international trade.
- Large-scale production in certain industries may bring about scale economies, and therefore lower prices, that help offset weak national comparative advantage.
- Just as Japan did after World War II, governments may target and invest in certain industries, build infrastructure, or provide subsidies, all to boost the competitive advantages of home-country firms.
- Many services, such as banking and retailing, cannot be traded in the usual sense and must be internationalized via foreign direct investment. Thus, classical theories have limited applicability to international commerce in services.
- Modern telecommunications and the Internet facilitate global trade in many services at very low cost.
- The primary participants in international trade are individual firms that differ in significant ways. Far from being homogenous enterprises, many are highly entrepreneurial and innovative or have access to exceptional human talent, all of which support international business success. In other cases, some firms may need to trade internationally if their home markets are too small to support their growth or sales objectives.

In the following sections, we discuss additional theories that scholars introduced in view of the limitations of early trade theories.

FACTOR PROPORTIONS THEORY A significant contribution to explaining international trade came in the 1920s, when two Swedish economists, Eli Heckscher and his student, Bertil Ohlin, proposed the *factor proportions theory*, sometimes called the factor endowments theory.[3] This view rests on two premises: (1) products differ in the types and quantities of factors (labor, natural resources, and capital) required for their production; and (2) countries differ in the type and quantity of production factors they possess. Each country should export products that intensively use relatively abundant factors of production and import goods that intensively use relatively scarce factors of production. For example, the United States produces and exports capital-intensive products, such as pharmaceuticals and commercial aircraft, while Argentina produces land-intensive products, such as wine and sunflower seeds.

Factor proportions theory differs somewhat from earlier theories by emphasizing the importance of each nation's factors of production. The theory states that, in addition to differences in the *efficiency* of production, differences in the *quantity* of factors of production held by countries also determine international trade patterns. This leads to a *per-unit-cost advantage* due to the abundance of a given factor of production, say labor, over another, say land, which is not in as much supply. Originally, labor was the most important factor of production. This explains why, for example, countries like China and India have become popular manufacturing bases; they have huge bases of workers.

In the 1950s, Russian-born economist Wassily Leontief pointed to empirical findings that seemed to contradict the factor proportions theory. The theory suggests that because the United States has abundant capital, it should be an exporter of capital-intensive products. However, Leontief's analysis, termed the *Leontief paradox*, revealed that the United States often exported labor-intensive goods and imported more capital-intensive goods than the theory would ordinarily predict. What accounts for the inconsistency? One explanation is that numerous factors determine the composition of a country's exports and imports. Another is that, in Leontief's time, U.S. labor was relatively more productive than labor elsewhere in the world.

Perhaps the main contribution of the Leontief paradox is its suggestion that international trade is complex and cannot be fully explained by a single theory. Subsequent refinements of factor proportions theory suggested that other country-level assets—knowledge, technology, and capital—are instrumental in explaining each nation's international trade prowess. Taiwan, for example, is very strong in information technology and is home to a sizable population of knowledge workers in the IT sector. These factors helped make Taiwan a leader in the global computer industry.

Factor proportions theory describes how abundant production factors give rise to national advantages. Russia, for example, has a very large workforce in numerous industries.

INTERNATIONAL PRODUCT LIFE CYCLE THEORY In a 1966 article, Harvard Professor Raymond Vernon sought to explain international trade based on the evolutionary process that occurs in the development and diffusion of products to markets around the world.[4] In his *International Product Life Cycle (IPLC) Theory,* Vernon observed that each product and its manufacturing technologies go through three stages of evolution: introduction, maturity, and standardization. This is illustrated in Exhibit 6.4.

In the introduction stage, a new product typically originates in an advanced economy, such as the United States. Such countries possess abundant capital and R&D capabilities, providing key advantages in the invention of new goods. Advanced economies also have abundant, high-income consumers who are willing to try new products, which are often expensive. During the introduction stage, the new product is produced in the inventing country, which enjoys a temporary monopoly.

As the product enters the maturity phase, the product's inventors mass-produce it and seek to export it to other advanced economies. Gradually, however, the product's manufacturing becomes more routine and foreign firms begin producing alternative versions, ending the inventor's monopoly power. At this stage, as competition intensifies and export orders begin to come from lower-income countries, the inventor may earn only a narrow profit margin.

In the standardization phase, knowledge about how to produce the product is widespread and manufacturing has become straightforward. Early in the product's evolution, production required specialized workers skilled in R&D and manufacturing. Once standardized, however, mass production is the dominant activity and can be accomplished using cheaper inputs

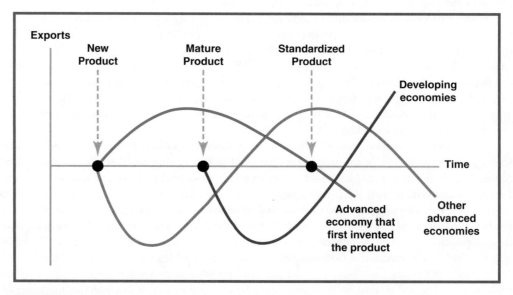

EXHIBIT 6.4

Illustration of Vernon's International Product Life Cycle

Source: Adapted from Raymond Vernon, "International Investment and International Trade in the Product Cycle," *Quarterly Journal of Economics* 80 (May 1966): 190–207 and http://www.provenmodels.com/583/international-product-life-cycle/raymond-vernon.

and low-cost labor. Production shifts to low-income countries where competitors enjoy low-cost advantages and can economically serve export markets worldwide. The country that invented the product eventually becomes a net importer. It and other advanced economies become saturated with imports of the good from developing economies. In effect, exporting the product has caused its underlying technology to become widely known and standardized around the world.

As an example, consider the evolution of television sets. The base technology was invented in the United States, and U.S. firms began domestic production of TV sets in the 1940s. U.S. sales grew rapidly for many years. However, once TVs became a standardized product, production shifted to China, Mexico, and other countries that offered lower-cost production. Today the United States imports nearly all its TVs from such countries.

The IPLC illustrates that national advantages do not last forever. Firms worldwide are continuously creating new products, and others are constantly imitating them. The product cycle is continually beginning and ending. Vernon assumed the product diffusion process occurs slowly enough to generate temporary differences between countries in their access and use of new technologies. This assumption is no longer valid today—the IPLC has become much shorter as new products diffuse much more quickly around the world. Buyers in emerging markets are particularly eager to adopt new technologies as soon as they become available. This trend explains the rapid spread of new consumer electronics such as digital assistants and mobile phones around the world.

NEW TRADE THEORY Beginning in the 1970s, economists observed that trade was growing fastest among industrialized countries with similar factors of production. In some new industries, there appeared to be no clear comparative advantage. The solution to this puzzle became known as *new trade theory*. It argues that increasing returns to scale, especially *economies of scale*, are important for superior international performance in industries that succeed best as their production volume increases. For example, the commercial aircraft industry has high fixed costs that necessitate high-volume sales to achieve profitability. As a nation specializes in the production of such goods, productivity increases and unit costs fall, providing significant benefits to the local economy.

Many national markets are small, and the domestic producer may not achieve economies of scale because it cannot sell products in large volume. New trade theory implies that firms can solve this problem by exporting, thereby gaining access to the much larger global marketplace. Several industries achieve minimally profitable economies of scale by selling their output in multiple markets worldwide. The effect of increasing returns to scale allows the nation to specialize in a smaller number of industries in which it may not necessarily hold factor or comparative advantages. According to new trade theory, trade is thus beneficial even for countries that produce only a limited variety of products.

How Can Nations Enhance Their Competitive Advantage?

The globalization of markets has fostered a new type of competition—a race among nations to reposition themselves as attractive for business and investment. The most advantaged nations today possess national competitive advantage, maximized when numerous industries collectively possess firm-level competitive advantages and the nation itself has comparative advantages that benefit those particular industries. This notion is illustrated in Exhibit 6.5.

Many governments create policies designed to encourage competitive advantage, often by developing world-class economic sectors and prosperous geographic regions. These policies aim to assist firms to develop acquired advantages.

Contemporary Theories

Three key modern perspectives that help explain the development of national competitive advantage are the competitive advantage of nations, the determinants of national competitive advantage, and national industrial policy.

THE COMPETITIVE ADVANTAGE OF NATIONS Just as scholars recognized that international business is good for individual nations, they increasingly sought to explain how nations can

EXHIBIT 6.5

Comparative Advantage and Competitive Advantage

position themselves for international business success. An important contribution came from Professor Michael Porter in his 1990 book, *The Competitive Advantage of Nations.*[5] According to Porter, the competitive advantage of a nation depends on the collective competitive advantages of the nation's firms. Over time, this relationship is reciprocal: The competitive advantages held by the nation tend to drive the development of new firms and industries with these same competitive advantages.

For example, Britain achieved a substantial national competitive advantage in the prescription drug industry due to its first-rate pharmaceutical firms, including GlaxoSmithKline and AstraZeneca. The United States has a national competitive advantage in service industries because of many leading firms, such as Goldman Sachs (investment banking), Marsh & McLennan (insurance), and Booz & Company (consulting). The presence of these and numerous other strong services firms, in turn, has engendered overall national competencies in the global services sector.

At both the firm and national levels, competitive advantage and technological advances grow out of *innovation.*[6] Companies innovate in various ways: They develop new product designs, new production processes, new approaches to marketing, new ways of organizing or training, and so forth. Firms sustain innovation (and by extension, competitive advantage) by continually finding better products, services, and ways of doing things.[7] For example, Australia's Vix (www.vix-erg.com) is a world leader in fare collection equipment and software systems for the transit industry. The firm has installed systems in subways, bus networks, and other mass transit systems in major cities like Melbourne, Rome, San Francisco, Stockholm, and Singapore. It has won numerous awards for its innovative products, which have allowed the firm to internationalize quickly. Vix's investment in R&D has been significant, running as high as 23 percent of the firm's revenue.

Innovation results primarily from research and development. Worldwide, more scientists and engineers are engaged in R&D than ever before. Among the industries most dependent on technological innovation are biotechnology, information technology, new materials, pharmaceuticals, robotics, medical equipment, fiber optics, and various electronics-based industries.

The management consultancy Booz & Company (www.booz.com) annually reports on MNEs that spend the most on R&D, the *Global Innovation 1000*. Most top European, Japanese, and U.S. firms spend half or more of their total R&D in countries other than where they are headquartered. The firms do this for several reasons:

- Gain access to talent—gifted engineers and scientists reside around the world in countries like China and India.
- Cut costs by hiring lower-paid engineers and scientists abroad to replace higher-paid personnel in the home country.
- Get closer to key markets, where they gain insights on specific characteristics of target markets during the product development process.[8] This explains why, in addition to low-cost emerging markets, Europe and the United States are popular sites for R&D by foreign companies, as firms seek to understand and create new products for the world's most lucrative markets.

The more innovative firms in a nation, the stronger the nation's competitive advantage. Innovation also promotes *productivity*, the value of the output produced by a unit of labor or capital. The more productive a firm is, the more efficiently it uses its resources. The more productive the firms in a nation are, the more efficiently the nation uses its resources.[9] At the national level, productivity is a key determinant of the nation's long-run standard of living and a basic source of national per-capita income growth. Exhibit 6.6 depicts productivity levels in various nations over time, measured as output per hour of workers in manufacturing. In the early 1990s, South Korea was the least productive of the nations shown. Over time, however, South Korea increased its productivity and now outshines the other nations. Since productivity is measured as output per unit of labor or capital, a nation can increase its productivity either by increasing its relative output or by reducing its input for a given level of output.

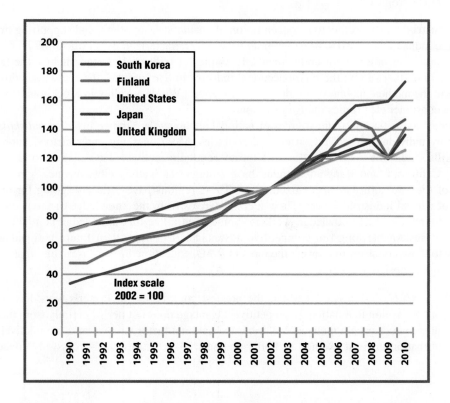

EXHIBIT 6.6

Productivity Levels in Selected Countries: Output per Hour in Manufacturing, 1990–2010, Index Scale, 2002 = 100

Source: Based on U.S. Department of Labor, Bureau of Labor Statistics, 2011, www.bls.gov.

DETERMINANTS OF NATIONAL COMPETITIVE ADVANTAGE As part of his explanation in *The Competitive Advantage of Nations*, Michael Porter argued that competitive advantage at both the company and national levels originates from the presence and quality in the country of four major elements, which we review next.

1. *Demand conditions* refer to the nature of home-market demand for specific products and services. The strength and sophistication of buyer demand facilitates the development of competitive advantages in particular industries. The presence of highly demanding customers pressures firms to innovate faster and produce better products. For example, an affluent, aging population in the United States inspired the development of world-class healthcare companies such as Pfizer and Eli Lilly in pharmaceuticals and Boston Scientific and Medtronic in medical equipment.

2. *Factor conditions* describe the nation's position in factors of production, such as labor, natural resources, capital, technology, entrepreneurship, and know-how. Consistent with factor proportions theory, each nation has a relative abundance of certain factor endowments, a situation that helps determine the nature of its national competitive advantage. For example, Germany's abundance of workers with strong engineering skills has propelled the country to commanding heights in the global engineering and design industries.

3. *Related and supporting industries* refer to the presence of clusters of suppliers, competitors, and complementary firms that excel in particular industries. The resulting business environment is highly supportive for the founding of particular types of firms. Operating within a mass of related and supporting industries provides advantages through information and knowledge synergies, economies of scale and scope, and access to appropriate or superior inputs.

4. *Firm strategy, structure, and rivalry* refer to the nature of domestic rivalry and conditions in a nation that determine how firms are created, organized, and managed. The presence of strong competitors in a nation helps create and maintain national competitive advantage. Japan has one of the world's most competitive consumer electronics industries, with major players like Nintendo, NEC, Sharp, and Sony producing semiconductors, computers, video games, and liquid crystal displays. Vigorous competitive rivalry puts these firms under continual pressure to innovate and improve. They compete not only for market share, but also for human talent, technical leadership, and superior product quality. Intense rivalry has pushed firms like Sony to a leading position in the industry worldwide and allowed Japan to emerge as the top country in consumer electronics.[10]

Industrial cluster refers to a concentration of businesses, suppliers, and supporting firms in the same industry at a particular geographic location, characterized by a critical mass of human talent, capital, or other factor endowments. Examples of industrial clusters include the fashion industry in northern Italy; the pharmaceutical industry in Switzerland; the footwear industry in Vietnam; the medical technology industry in Singapore; Wireless Valley in Stockholm, Sweden; and the consumer electronics industry in Japan.

Today, the most important sources of national advantage are the *knowledge and skills* possessed by individual firms, industries, and countries. More than any other factors, knowledge and skills determine where MNEs will locate economic activity around the world. Silicon Valley, California, and Bangalore, India, have emerged as leading-edge business clusters because of the availability of specialized talent. These regions have little else going for them in terms of natural industrial power. Their success derives from the knowledge of the people employed there, so-called knowledge workers. Some even argue that knowledge is now the only source of sustainable long-run competitive advantage. If correct, then future national wealth will go to those countries that invest the most in R&D, education, and infrastructure that support knowledge-intensive industries.

NATIONAL INDUSTRIAL POLICY Perhaps the greatest contribution of Porter's work has been to underscore the notion that national competitive advantage does not derive entirely from the store of natural resources each country holds. Inherited national factor endowments are relatively less important than in the past. Rather, as Porter emphasized, countries can successfully create new

---

Country Realities

All else being equal, a nation's productivity rises with an increase in worker output, or through a decrease in the number of workers producing a given level of output. One way to improve productivity is to leverage technology. For example, productivity rises by employing information technology (IT) to improve worker efficiency. This helps explain why many countries are investing huge sums in IT education and to improve national infrastructure in computer systems and applications.

Industrial cluster
A concentration of businesses, suppliers, and supporting firms in the same industry at a particular location, characterized by a critical mass of human talent, capital, or other factor endowments.

advantages and develop factor conditions they deem important for their success. The government can devote resources to improve national infrastructure, education systems, and capital formation. In short, any country, regardless of its initial circumstances, can attain economic prosperity by systematically cultivating new and superior factor endowments.

Nations can develop these endowments through proactive **national industrial policy**. Such a policy encourages economic development, often in collaboration with the private sector, to develop or support high value-adding industries that generate superior corporate profits, higher worker wages, and tax revenues. Dubai pursued a national industrial policy to become an international commercial center in the information and communications technology (ICT) sector. Historically, nations have favored more traditional industries, including automobiles, shipbuilding, and heavy machinery—all with long value chains that generate substantial added value. As the Dubai example illustrates, successful nations increasingly favor high value-adding, knowledge-intensive industries such as IT, biotechnology, medical technology, and financial services. Not only do these industries provide substantial revenues to the nation, they also lead to the development of supplier and support companies that further enhance national prosperity. Singapore's *Innovation Manifesto* has propelled the city-state to becoming one of the most technologically sophisticated countries in the world.

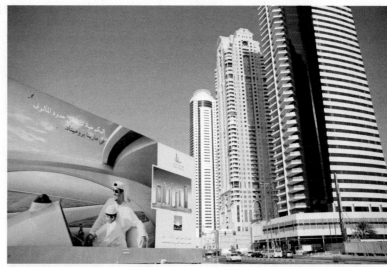

Source: Gavin Thomas/Dorling Kindersley Ltd.

Visionary national industrial policy is transforming Dubai into a high value-adding economy based on IT, biotechnology, financial services, and other knowledge-intensive industries.

National industrial policy
A proactive economic development plan initiated by the government, often in collaboration with the private sector, that aims to develop or support particular industries within the nation.

National industrial policies designed to build new capabilities and encourage the emergence of new industries typically include these specifics:

- Tax incentives to encourage citizens to save and invest, which provides capital for public and private investment in R&D, plant, equipment, and worker skills
- Monetary and fiscal policies, such as low-interest loans, that provide a stable supply of capital for company investment needs
- Rigorous educational systems at the precollege and university levels that ensure a steady stream of competent workers who support high technology or high value-adding industries in the sciences, engineering, and business administration
- Development and maintenance of strong national infrastructure in areas such as IT, communication systems, and transportation
- Creation of strong legal and regulatory systems to ensure that citizens are confident about the soundness and stability of the national economy[11]

NATIONAL INDUSTRIAL POLICY IN PRACTICE How well does national industrial policy work in practice? Let's examine New Zealand and the outcomes of its repositioning, implemented through collaboration between the nation's public and private sectors. For much of the early twentieth century, government policies had limited New Zealand's ability to flourish and trade with the rest of the world. Living standards were low and many wondered whether New Zealand had a future. Then, in the 1980s, the New Zealand government undertook pro-trade policies in cooperation with the private sector that resulted in national advantages, helping New Zealand's economy grow rapidly and achieve high living standards. The accomplishments are summarized in Exhibit 6.7. Between 1992 and 2012, New Zealand raised its per-capita GDP from 51 percent to 89 percent of the average of the G7 countries, the world's seven largest advanced economies. This represents an improvement of about 75 percent in real terms of personal income. During the

EXHIBIT 6.7 Transformation of New Zealand's Economy, 1992 to 2012

Statistic	New Zealand in 1992	New Zealand in 2012
GDP per capita	51% of the G7 average	89% of the G7 average
Unemployment rate	9.8%	5.6%
National debt	89% of the nation's GDP	30% of the nation's GDP

Source: adam.golabek

Following many years of poor economic performance, the government of New Zealand implemented various national industrial policies that succeeded in elevating several key economic indicators, thus raising living standards for the New Zealand people.

period, New Zealand's unemployment rate declined by almost half, to 5.6 percent. The government reduced its national debt as a proportion of GDP from 89 to 30 percent, giving the nation a solid financial foundation. New Zealand's per-capita GDP dipped during the global recession but stabilized in 2012 to more than $40,000, among the highest in the world.

Beginning in the 1980s, New Zealand's government systematically transformed the country from an agrarian, protectionist, regulated economy to an industrialized, free-market economy that competes globally. New Zealand's success resulted from a combination of factors:

- Government-controlled wages, prices, and interest rates were freed and allowed to fluctuate according to market forces.
- The banking sector was liberalized, foreign exchange controls were eliminated, and the New Zealand dollar was allowed to float according to market forces.
- Most trade barriers were removed and New Zealand joined several free-trade agreements.
- Subsidies formerly granted to agriculture and other sectors were eliminated.
- The government worked earnestly with labor unions to reduce wage inflation, helping to ensure that jobs remained in New Zealand and not outsourced to lower-wage countries.
- The government initiated programs to encourage development of a knowledge economy. New Zealanders continuously upgraded skills and knowledge, providing a supply of scientists, engineers, and trained managers.[12]
- Personal and corporate income tax rates were reduced, and the tax base was diversified to stabilize government revenues. The move helped to foster entrepreneurship, boosted consumer spending, and increased the nation's attractiveness for investment from abroad.
- The government cut spending and borrowing, leading to lower interest rates and stimulating the economy.
- State-owned enterprises—such as the national airline, post office, telecom, and other utilities—were sold off to the private sector.[13]

Dynamic growth boosted real incomes and greatly improved living standards in New Zealand. Recently, *Forbes* magazine and the World Bank ranked New Zealand as the second most business friendly country in the world.[14] Market-oriented policies helped make New Zealand an important economy and a major player in world trade, dramatically raising living standards for its citizens.

Read the *Global Trend* feature for more examples of proactive nation repositioning to create new comparative advantages.

GLOBAL TREND

Moving from Comparative to National Competitive Advantages

The principle of comparative advantage and factor endowment theory imply that nations should nurture industries that use inputs inherent or abundant in their environment. Today, however, numerous countries with few natural or other resources have created their own competitive advantages through skillful application of national industrial policies. In most cases, these acquired advantages have become more critical than natural endowments. Here are some examples:

Singapore is a free-market economy with high per-capita GDP. Beginning in the 1960s, the government adopted pro-business, pro-investment, export-oriented policies, combined with state-directed investments in strategic corporations. The approach stimulated economic growth that averaged 8 percent from 1960 to 1999. Singapore cut taxes and government spending and encouraged massive inward investment in high-value industries such as electronics, engineering, and chemicals. The country boasts a highly educated labor force, state-of-the-art telecommunications facilities, and excellent infrastructure—its airport and seaport are among the best in the world.

In the past two decades, *Ireland* lowered the basic corporate tax rate to zero, initiated earnest dialogue with labor unions, and emphasized high value-adding industries such as pharmaceuticals, biochemistry, and information technology. The country invested heavily in education, providing a steady supply of skilled workers, including scientists, engineers, and business school graduates. Attracted by these developments, foreign MNEs began investing in the country. Ireland became a major player in world trade and now hosts some 1,000 foreign firms. International trade, inward FDI, and economic development dramatically raised living standards for its citizens.

Bangalore is India's third largest city and a center of information technology and business support services. Cooperating with private interests, India reduced restrictions on trade and investment, resulting in a big influx of foreign FDI. The public-private partnership also emphasized high-value industries such as biotechnology and business consulting and capitalized on Bangalore's large, well-educated, English-speaking workforce.

In the *Czech Republic*, economic reforms and exports to the European Union (EU) led to economic prosperity. The Czech government harmonized its laws and regulations with those of the EU by reforming its judicial system, financial markets regulation, intellectual property rights protection, and other areas important to investors. It also privatized state-owned companies. Government FDI incentives attracted firms like Toyota, ING, Siemens, Daewoo, DHL, and South African Breweries.

Vietnam's government privatized state enterprises and modernized the economy, emphasizing competitive, export-driven industries. It ramped up the country's exports of everything from shoes to ships, modernized its intellectual property regime, entered several free-trade agreements, and revamped its educational system to provide a constant stream of skilled workers. The government also built infrastructure, including roads, railways, and power stations. Reforms have attracted much inward FDI from firms like Intel. The national savings rate increased severalfold. Economic repositioning dramatically reduced Vietnam's poverty rate.

 ## Why and How Do Firms Internationalize?

Company Internationalization

Earlier theories of international trade focused on why and how cross-national business occurs. However, in the 1960s scholars began to develop theories about the managerial and organizational aspects of firm internationalization.

INTERNATIONALIZATION PROCESS OF THE FIRM Scholars developed the *internationalization process model* in the 1970s to describe how companies expand abroad. According to this model, internationalization takes place in incremental stages over a long time.[15] Typically, firms start without much analysis or planning and begin to export, the simplest form of international activity, and progress to FDI, the most complex. The gradual and incremental nature of internationalization often results from managers' uncertainty and uneasiness about how to proceed, because they lack information about foreign markets and experience with cross-border transactions.

The model is illustrated in Exhibit 6.8. A firm starts out in a *domestic focus* phase and is preoccupied with business in its home market. Management may be unable or unwilling to get

EXHIBIT 6.8

Stages in the Internationalization Process of the Firm

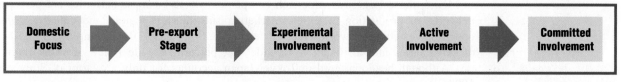

started in international business because of concerns over its readiness or perceived obstacles in foreign markets. Eventually, the firm advances to the *pre-export stage*, often because it receives unsolicited product orders from abroad. In this stage, management investigates the feasibility of undertaking international business. Subsequently, the firm advances to the *experimental involvement stage* by initiating limited international activity, typically in the form of basic exporting. As managers begin to view foreign expansion more favorably, they undertake *active involvement* in international business through systematic exploration of international options and the commitment of managerial time and resources to achieving international success. Ultimately management may advance to the *committed involvement stage*, characterized by genuine interest and commitment of resources to making international business a key part of the firm's profit-making and value-chain activities. In this stage, the firm targets numerous foreign markets via various entry modes, especially FDI.[16]

To illustrate, let's examine of the consumer electronics firm Sony Corporation, founded in Japan in 1946 (www.sony.com). In the 1950s, Sony began exporting transistor radios and other products to Australia, Europe, and North America. In the 1960s, it entered joint ventures with various partners abroad, including CBS and Texas Instruments. Around the same time, Sony used FDI to establish sales offices in Hong Kong, Switzerland, and the United States. Later, the firm set up factories in numerous countries to manufacture consumer electronics. Sony established its first television factory in the United States in San Diego in 1972. Today it has joint ventures and wholly owned operations in hundreds of locations worldwide, including five R&D centers and nine plants in Europe that produce computers, game consoles, personal navigation devices, and portable audio players. Sony's experience illustrates the internationalization process well.[17]

BORN GLOBALS AND INTERNATIONAL ENTREPRENEURSHIP Because international business has long been the domain of large, resource-rich MNEs, earlier theories tended to focus on them. Today scholars question the slow and gradual process proposed by the internationalization process model.[18] Despite the scarcity of financial, human, and tangible resources that characterize most new businesses, *born global firms* are young companies that internationalize early in their evolution. Among the reasons are the growing intensity of international competition, the integration of world economies under globalization, and advances in communication and transportation technologies that reduce the cost of venturing abroad and make it easier to internationalize earlier and faster than ever before. The born global phenomenon has given rise to a new field of scholarly inquiry, *international entrepreneurship*.[19] Current trends suggest that early internationalizing firms will gradually become the norm in international business.

How Can Internationalizing Firms Gain and Sustain Competitive Advantage?

So far we have focused on the internationalization processes of individual firms, including smaller firms or those new to international business. Since the 1950s, MNEs such as Nestlé, Unilever, Sony, Coca-Cola, and Caterpillar have expanded abroad on a massive scale, shaping international patterns of trade, investment, and technology flows. Over time, the aggregate activities of these firms became a key driving force of globalization and ongoing integration of world economies. So important is the rise of the MNE that it ranks with the development of electric power or the invention of the aircraft as one of the major events of modern history. Let's examine MNEs and their internationalization processes in more detail.

FDI-Based Explanations

Most explanations of international business have emphasized FDI, the preferred entry strategy of MNEs, those large, resource-rich companies whose business activities are performed via networks of production facilities, marketing subsidiaries, regional headquarters, and other operations established worldwide. For example, Sony has 170,000 employees and hundreds of subsidiaries and affiliates worldwide that perform a wide range of value-chain activities. Although headquartered in Tokyo, Japan accounts for only a quarter of Sony's roughly $90 billion in global sales.

Sony exemplifies the borderless MNE that locates its activities wherever it can maximize competitive advantages. One way to illustrate the huge volume of FDI is to examine *FDI stock*, which describes the total value of assets that MNEs own abroad via their investment activities. Exhibit 6.9 shows the stock and growth of inward FDI from 2000 to 2010, for a group of leading FDI destination countries. The exhibit highlights three interesting points. First, even smaller economies such as Belgium and Ireland are popular destinations for firms' FDI. Second, both advanced economies and emerging markets are major recipients of FDI. Third, the stock of FDI in emerging markets such as India, Russia, and Saudi Arabia grew very rapidly in the decade through 2010, reflecting their growing importance as target markets and production centers. Historically, most of the world's FDI was invested both by and in Western Europe, the United States, and Japan. But emerging markets now account for a huge proportion of global FDI. Unfortunately, Africa receives relatively little, which hinders the ability to raise living standards in the region.[20]

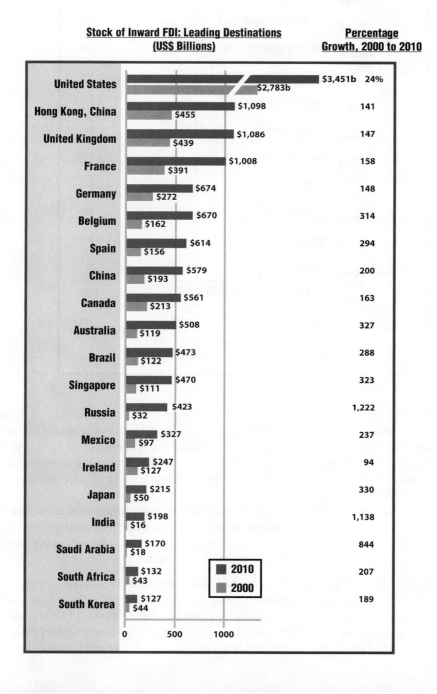

Stock of Inward FDI: Leading Destinations (US$ Billions) — Percentage Growth, 2000 to 2010

Country	2010	2000	Percentage Growth, 2000 to 2010
United States	$3,451b	$2,783b	24%
Hong Kong, China	$1,098	$455	141
United Kingdom	$1,086	$439	147
France	$1,008	$391	158
Germany	$674	$272	148
Belgium	$670	$162	314
Spain	$614	$156	294
China	$579	$193	200
Canada	$561	$213	163
Australia	$508	$119	327
Brazil	$473	$122	288
Singapore	$470	$111	323
Russia	$423	$32	1,222
Mexico	$327	$97	237
Ireland	$247	$127	94
Japan	$215	$50	330
India	$198	$16	1,138
Saudi Arabia	$170	$18	844
South Africa	$132	$43	207
South Korea	$127	$44	189

EXHIBIT 6.9

Stock of Inward FDI: Leading FDI Destinations (Billions of U.S. dollars) and Percentage Growth, 2000 to 2010

Sources: Based on UNCTAD, *World Investment Report* 2011 (New York: United Nations, 2011, p. 191, "Annex table I.2. FDI stock, by region and economy, 1990, 2000, 2010"), accessed January 29, 2012 at http://www.unctad.org/templates/WebFlyer.asp?intItemID=6018&lang=1.

EXHIBIT 6.10

Stock of Outward FDI: Top Sources of Outward FDI (Billions of U.S. dollars) and Percentage Growth, 2000 to 2010

Sources: Based on UNCTAD, *World Investment Report* 2011 (New York: United Nations, 2011, p. 191, "Annex table I.2. FDI stock, by region and economy, 1990, 2000, 2010"), accessed January 29, 2012 at http://www.unctad.org/templates/WebFlyer.asp?intItemID=6018&lang=1.

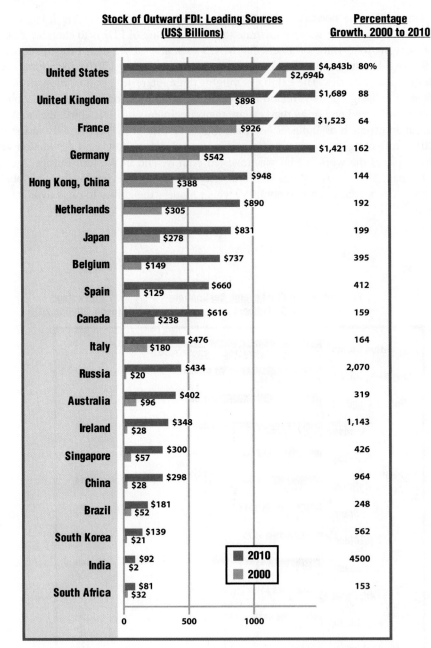

Exhibit 6.10 shows the stock and growth of outward FDI for a collection of the leading FDI-providing countries. MNEs invest billions abroad every year to establish and expand factories and other facilities. Note that firms from both advanced economies and emerging markets invest substantial FDI abroad. Emerging markets such as China, India, and Russia have greatly increased their FDI investments in recent years. Total outward FDI stock now constitutes nearly one-third of global GDP, a huge amount.[21]

FDI is such an important entry strategy that scholars have developed three alternative theories of how firms can use it to gain and sustain competitive advantage: the monopolistic advantage theory, internalization theory, and Dunning's eclectic paradigm. These theoretical perspectives are summarized in Exhibit 6.11 and described in the following sections.

MONOPOLISTIC ADVANTAGE THEORY A monopolistic advantage is a valuable resource that a company holds and leverages to generate profits, and which few other firms have. According to monopolistic advantage theory, companies that internationalize through FDI are more likely to succeed if they own or control certain advantages that foreign competitors do not generally possess. When this occurs, the advantaged firm has a degree of monopoly power that helps it

Theory	Key Characteristics	Benefits	Examples
Monopolistic Advantage Theory	The firm controls one or more resources, or offers relatively unique products and services that provide it a degree of monopoly power relative to foreign markets and competitors.	The firm can operate foreign subsidiaries more profitably than the local firms that compete in their own markets.	The European pharmaceutical Novartis earns substantial profits by marketing various patent medications through its subsidiaries worldwide.
Internalization Theory	The firm acquires and retains one or more value-chain activities within the firm.	• Minimizes the disadvantages of relying on intermediaries, collaborators, or other external partners. • Ensures greater control over foreign operations, helping to maximize product quality, reliable manufacturing processes, and sound marketing practices. • Reduces the risk that knowledge and proprietary assets will be lost to competitors.	The Japanese MNE Toshiba: • Owns and operates factories in dozens of countries to manufacture laptop computers. • Controls its own manufacturing processes, ensuring quality output. • Ensures its marketing activities are carried out per headquarters' plan. • Retains key assets within the firm, such as leading-edge knowledge for producing the next generation of laptops.
Dunning's Eclectic Paradigm	• *Ownership-specific advantages*: The firm owns knowledge, skills, capabilities, processes, or physical assets. • *Location-specific advantages*: Factors in individual countries provide specific benefits, such as natural resources, skilled labor, low-cost labor, and inexpensive capital. • *Internalization advantages*: The firm benefits from internalizing foreign manufacturing, distribution, or other value-chain activities.	Provides various advantages relative to competitors, including the ability to own, control, and optimize value-chain activities—R&D, production, marketing, sales distribution, after-sales service, as well as relationships with customers and key contacts—performed at the most beneficial locations worldwide.	The German MNE Siemens: • Owns factories at locations worldwide that provide optimal access to natural resources, as well as skilled and low-cost labor. • Leverages the knowledge base of its employees in 190 countries. • Internalizes a wide range of manufacturing activities in categories such as lighting, medical equipment, and transportation machinery.

EXHIBIT 6.11

Theoretical Perspectives on Why Firms Choose FDI

compete more effectively abroad. This monopolistic advantage should be specific to the MNE itself, such as a proprietary technology or a brand name, rather than to the locations where it does business. This theory argues that at least two conditions should be present for a firm to prefer targeting a foreign market rather than its home market. First, returns obtainable in the foreign market should be superior to those available in the home market. This would provide the firm with incentives to expand abroad to take advantage of its monopoly power. Second, returns obtainable in the foreign market should be superior to those earned by its domestic competitors in its industry in the foreign market. This would give the firm an opportunity to make monopoly profits that domestic companies in the foreign market cannot imitate.

To illustrate, let's revisit Sony Corporation. By being on the leading edge of innovation, Sony established numerous pioneering standards in the consumer electronics industry.

Over the course of several decades, Sony's superior R&D and internal control mechanisms allowed the firm to acquire and maintain a large body of relatively unique knowledge. This unique knowledge provided the firm with various monopolistic advantages. Sony invented numerous popular products that were, for a time at least, relatively unique. Continuous innovation within the firm allowed Sony to maintain this uniqueness for many years. Sony used its superior innovativeness to develop monopoly power and dominate world markets in such products as the PlayStation and Blu-ray disc format. As the Sony example implies, the most important monopolistic advantages are superior knowledge and intangible skills. Superior, proprietary knowledge has allowed Sony to create differentiated products that provide unique value to customers.[22]

INTERNALIZATION THEORY Numerous scholars have investigated the specific benefits that MNEs derive from FDI-based entry. For example, when Procter & Gamble entered Japan, management initially considered exporting and FDI. With exporting, P&G would have had to contract with an independent Japanese distributor to handle warehousing and marketing of its soap, diapers, and other products. However, because of trade barriers imposed by the Japanese government, the strong market power of local Japanese firms, and the risk of losing control over its proprietary knowledge, P&G chose instead to enter Japan via FDI. It established its own marketing subsidiary and, eventually, national headquarters in Tokyo. This arrangement provided various benefits P&G would not have received had it entered Japan by contracting with Japanese distributors it did not own.

Internalization theory
An explanation of the process by which firms acquire and retain one or more value-chain activities inside the firm, minimizing the disadvantages of dealing with external partners and allowing for greater control over foreign operations.

Internalization theory explains the process by which firms acquire and retain one or more value-chain activities inside the firm, as P&G did in Japan. Internalizing value-chain activities helps minimize the disadvantages of dealing with external partners for performing arms-length activities such as exporting and licensing. Internalization also gives the firm greater control over its foreign operations.

For example, the MNE might internalize the supplier function by acquiring or establishing its own plant in the foreign market to produce needed inputs itself instead of buying them from a foreign, independent supplier. Or it might internalize the marketing function by establishing its own distribution subsidiary abroad, instead of contracting with an independent foreign distributor to handle its marketing in the foreign market. The MNE is ultimately a vehicle for bypassing the bottlenecks and costs of the international, inter-firm exchange of goods, materials, and workers. In this way, the firm *replaces* business activities performed by independent suppliers in external markets with business activities it performs itself.

In the 1950s, for example, Sony followed a policy of exporting its products to Europe and North America. However, management soon realized it could accelerate and improve the performance of international operations by creating its own sales and production facilities in strategic markets abroad. Thus, in the 1960s, Sony internalized much of its global production and distribution channels by establishing company-owned subsidiaries in Europe, the United States, and other key markets. To ensure product quality, Sony internalized production of semiconductors and circuit boards for use in making cell phones and PlayStations. Recently, Sony transferred production of camcorders from a plant run by a joint venture partner in China to a wholly owned Sony plant in Japan. The move allowed Sony to improve supply-chain management and manufacturing of camcorders.

In addition to consumer electronics, Sony has long been a major player in the movie industry, through its subsidiary Sony Pictures Entertainment (SPE). Acquiring the Loews chain of movie theaters in the United States allowed SPE to internalize a substantial portion of the distribution channel for its film business, ensuring its movies would be supplied to thousands of movie screens. Since its founding, Sony has consistently internalized key units to maintain control over the most important links in its global value chains.

Another key reason companies internalize certain value-chain functions is to control proprietary knowledge critical to the development, production, and sale of their products and services. Because independent foreign companies are outside the MNE's direct control, they can acquire and use the knowledge to their own advantage, perhaps becoming competitors in the process. FDI allows the MNE to control and optimally use its knowledge in foreign markets.[23]

DUNNING'S ECLECTIC PARADIGM Professor John Dunning proposed the *eclectic paradigm* as a framework for determining the extent and pattern of the value-chain operations that companies own abroad. He drew from various theoretical perspectives, including comparative advantage, factor proportions, monopolistic advantage, and internalization advantage. Thus, the eclectic paradigm is often viewed as the most comprehensive of FDI theories. The eclectic paradigm specifies three conditions that determine whether a company will internationalize via FDI: ownership-specific advantages, location-specific advantages, and internalization advantages.

To successfully enter and conduct business in a foreign market, the MNE must possess *ownership-specific advantages* relative to other firms already doing business in the market. That is, it should hold knowledge, skills, capabilities, key relationships, and other assets that allow it to compete effectively in foreign markets. These assets amount to the firm's competitive advantages. To ensure international success, the advantages must be substantial enough to offset the costs the firm incurs in establishing and operating foreign operations. The advantages should also be specific to the MNE that possesses them and not readily transferable to other firms, such as proprietary technology, managerial skills, trademarks or brand names, economies of scale, and access to substantial financial resources. The more valuable the firm's ownership-specific advantages, the more likely it is to internationalize via FDI.[24]

Let's use Alcoa, the Aluminum Corporation of America (www.alcoa.com), to illustrate. Alcoa has 60,000 employees in thirty-five countries. The company's integrated operations include bauxite mining and aluminum refining. Its products include primary aluminum (which it refines from bauxite), automotive components, and sheet aluminum for beverage cans and Reynolds Wrap®.

One of Alcoa's most important ownership-specific advantages is the proprietary technology it has acquired through its R&D activities. It has also acquired special managerial and marketing skills in the production and marketing of refined aluminum. The firm has a well-known brand name that helps increase sales. As a large firm, Alcoa also profits from economies of scale and the ability to finance expensive projects. These advantages have allowed Alcoa to generate maximal profits from its international operations.

The second condition that determines whether a firm will internationalize via FDI is the presence of *location-specific advantages*, the comparative advantages available in individual foreign countries, such as natural resources, skilled labor, low-cost labor, and inexpensive capital. For example, Alcoa located refineries in Brazil because of that country's huge deposits of bauxite, a mineral found in relatively few other locations worldwide. The Amazon and other major rivers in Brazil generate huge amounts of hydroelectric power, a critical ingredient in electricity-intensive aluminum refining. Alcoa also benefits from Brazil's low-cost, relatively well-educated laborers who work in the firm's refineries. The presence of these location-specific advantages helped persuade Alcoa to locate in Brazil through FDI.

The third condition that determines FDI-based internationalization is the presence of *internalization advantages*, benefits that the firm derives from internalizing foreign-based manufacturing, distribution, or other stages in its value chain. When profitable, the firm will transfer its ownership-specific advantages across national borders within its own organization rather than dissipating them to independent, foreign entities. The FDI decision depends on which is the best option—internalization versus utilizing external partners, whether they are licensees, distributors, or suppliers. Internalization advantages include the ability to control how the firm's products are produced or marketed, the ability to prevent unintended dissemination of the firm's proprietary knowledge, and the ability to reduce buyer uncertainty about the value of products the firm offers.[25]

Alcoa had five reasons to internalize many of its operations instead of letting external suppliers handle them. First, its management wants to minimize dissemination of knowledge about its aluminum-refining operations—knowledge the firm acquired at great expense. Second, internalization provides the best net return, allowing Alcoa to minimize the cost of operations. Third, Alcoa needs to control sales of its aluminum products to avoid depressing world aluminum prices through oversupply. Fourth, the firm wants to be able to apply a differential pricing strategy, charging different prices to different customers, a strategy it could not follow very effectively without the control over distribution that internalization provides. Finally, aluminum refining is a complex business, and Alcoa wants to control it to maintain the quality of its products.

Non-FDI-Based Explanations

FDI became a popular entry mode with the rise of the MNE in the 1960s and 1970s. In the 1980s, firms began to recognize the importance of collaborative ventures and other flexible entry strategies.

INTERNATIONAL COLLABORATIVE VENTURES A collaborative venture is a form of cooperation between two or more firms. There are two major types: (1) equity-based *joint ventures* that result in the formation of a new legal entity; and (2) non-equity-based strategic alliances in which firms partner temporarily to work on projects related to R&D, design, manufacturing, or any other value-adding activity. In both cases, collaborating firms pool resources and capabilities and generate synergy. In other words, collaboration allows the partners to carry out activities that each might be unable to perform on its own. Collaborating firms share the risk of their joint efforts, which reduces vulnerability for any one partner.

Collaboration is a critical activity in international business. A firm sometimes has no choice but to partner with other companies in order to use resources and capabilities unavailable within its own organization. In addition, occasionally a government will restrict companies from entering its national market via wholly owned FDI. For example, the Mexican government prohibits foreign firms from attaining full ownership of ventures in its domestic oil industry because oil is critical to Mexico's economy. Where such restrictions exist, the firm may have no choice but to collaborate with a foreign partner to enter the market.[26]

A collaborative venture can give a company access to foreign partners' know-how, capital, distribution channels, marketing assets, or the ability to overcome government-imposed obstacles. By collaborating, the firm can position itself better to create new products and enter new markets. For example, Starbucks now boasts more than 900 coffee shops in Japan, thanks to a joint venture with its local partner, Sazaby League, Ltd. The venture allowed Starbucks to internationalize and to navigate the marketplace with the help of a knowledgeable local partner.[27]

NETWORKS AND RELATIONAL ASSETS Networks and relational assets represent the economically beneficial long-term *relationships* the firm undertakes with other business entities, such as manufacturers, distributors, suppliers, retailers, consultants, banks, transportation suppliers, governments, and any other organization that can provide needed capabilities. Firm-level relational assets represent a distinct competitive advantage in international business. Japanese keiretsu, complex groupings of firms with interlinked ownership and trading relationships that foster inter-firm organizational learning, are their predecessors.[28] Like the keiretsu, networks are neither formal organizations with clearly defined hierarchical structures nor impersonal, decentralized markets.

The International Marketing and Purchasing (IMP) research consortium in Europe (www .impgroup.org) has driven much of the theory development on networks.[29] Network theory was proposed to compensate for the inability of traditional organizational theories to account for much that goes on in business markets.[30] In networks, buyers and sellers become bound to one another through ongoing exchanges and linkages of products, services, finance, technology, and know-how. Continued interaction among the partners results in stable relationships based on cooperation and creates value and competitive advantage even among competitors. Network linkages represent a key route by which many companies expand their business abroad, develop new markets, and develop new products. In international business, mutually beneficial and enduring strategic relationships provide real advantages to partners and reduce uncertainty and transaction costs.

Sony Corporation has countless network connections that provide substantial benefits. It has done extensive joint R&D with the Dutch electronics giant Philips and is well connected in the Japanese financial sector, where it launched Sony Bank, Sony Life Insurance, and Sony Bank Securities. These allied companies provide Sony with much of the financing it needs to conduct R&D and perform other key value-chain activities. In short, Sony's network and relational assets have been critical to its success.

As we'll see later in this book, in the contemporary global economy, firms have increasingly shied away from making permanent, direct investments in host countries. Instead, many firms now opt for more flexible collaborative ventures or other relationships with independent business partners abroad.

CLOSING CASE   Hyundai: Leading the Way in the Global Auto Industry

The global automotive industry is one of the largest and most internationalized business sectors. There are seventeen major global automotive companies producing more than one million cars a year. Hyundai Motor Company is South Korea's number one carmaker and the tenth largest in the world, generating about $100 billion in annual sales. It sells vehicles in over 190 countries, producing about a dozen car and minivan models, plus trucks, buses, and other commercial vehicles. Popular models in the United States are the Accent and Sonata, while exports to Europe and Asia include the GRD and Equus.

The Industry

During the recent global financial crisis, global automotive sales declined to near-record lows. Automotive industry profits suffered due to significant excess production capacity. Although there is capacity to produce 80 million cars worldwide, total global demand fell to only about 60 million a year. This led to consolidations and divestitures, including those between Ford and Land Rover; Jaguar and Volvo; Fiat and Chrysler; and General Motors and Opel, among others. Consistent with new trade theory, the required scale compels automakers to target world markets, where they can achieve economies of scale and maximize sales.

The Industry in South Korea

Despite its large size, the car market in South Korea (Korea) is insufficient to sustain indigenous automakers like Hyundai and Kia. Korea holds numerous competitive advantages in the car industry. The country is a world center of new technology development. Korea has abundant, cost-effective knowledge workers who drive innovations in design, features, production, and product quality. The country also has a high savings rate, with massive inward FDI, which ensures a ready supply of capital for carmakers to fund R&D and other ventures. Collectively, Korea's abundance of production factors in cost-effective labor, knowledge workers, high technology, and capital represent key location-specific advantages.

Korean consumers are demanding, so carmakers take great pains to produce high-quality automobiles. Intense rivalry in the domestic auto industry ensures that carmakers and auto parts producers improve products continuously.

The Korean economy is dominated by several conglomerates, called *chaebols*. They include Hyundai, Samsung, LG, and SK and account for about 40 percent of Korea's GDP and exports.

The Korean government has imposed stringent accounting controls on many of these firms. The government cooperates closely with the business sector, protecting some industries, ensuring funds for others, and sponsoring still others. The government promoted imports of raw materials and technology at the expense of consumer goods and encouraged savings and investment over consumption. Partly due to these efforts, Korea is home to a substantial industrial cluster for the production of cars and car parts. The nation benefits from the presence of numerous suppliers and manufacturers in the global automotive industry.

In past years, Hyundai also benefited from a weak Korean won (Korea's currency), making prices for Hyundai cars cheaper for customers in Europe and the United States who buy imported cars in their local currencies. Hyundai owes much of its success to favorable international exchange rates.

Background on Hyundai

Hyundai was founded in 1947 by Chung Ju-yung, a visionary entrepreneur from a peasant background. By the 1970s, the firm had begun an aggressive effort to develop engineering capabilities and new designs in the auto industry. In the 1980s, Hyundai began exporting the Excel, an economy car priced at $4,995, to the United States. An instant success, Excel exports grew to 250,000 units per year. But the Excel suffered from quality issues and a weak dealer network. Buyer confidence waned in the late 1990s and Hyundai's brand equity weakened. In response to complaints, Hyundai initiated major quality improvement programs and introduced a 10-year power train warranty program, unprecedented in the auto industry. The strategy was a major turning point for the firm.

Geographic Diversification

In 1997, Hyundai built a car factory in Turkey, giving the firm convenient access to key markets in the Middle East and Europe. Next, Hyundai opened a plant in India and within a few years became the country's best-selling brand of imported car. In 2002, Hyundai launched a factory in China, doubling production, and is aiming for 20 percent share of the Chinese car market. The firm also partnered with Guangzhou Motor Group, winning entry to China's huge commercial-vehicle market. In addition to gaining access to low-cost, high-quality labor in emerging markets, Hyundai hopes its presence in local showrooms will improve consumer awareness and drive new sales. Most recently, Hyundai has been ramping up sales in Europe.

Hyundai uses FDI to develop key operations around the world. Management chooses locations based on the advantages they bring to the firm. The firm established plants in Iran, Sudan, Taiwan, Vietnam, Venezuela, and numerous other countries. Recently, the firm opened plants in Europe and the United States. Hyundai has R&D centers in Europe, Japan, and North America. It has distribution centers and marketing subsidiaries at various locations that deliver parts to its expanding base of car dealers worldwide. Hyundai also has regional headquarters in Asia, Europe, and North America. To guarantee control over production and marketing, the firm has internalized many of its operations.

To remain competitive, Hyundai employs inexpensive, high-quality labor. Engines, tires, and other key inputs are sourced from low-cost suppliers. The firm has entered various collaborative ventures to cooperate in R&D, design, manufacturing, and other value-adding activities. These allow Hyundai access to foreign partners' know-how, capital, distribution channels, marketing assets, and the ability to overcome government-imposed obstacles. For example, Hyundai partnered with DaimlerChrysler to develop new technologies and improve supply-chain management. Compared to Japanese or Western rivals, Hyundai has superior cost advantages in the acquisition of high-quality inputs.

While Japanese auto giants such as Toyota and Honda rely heavily on U.S. sales for their profits, Hyundai is more diversified. North America accounts for only 22 percent of Hyundai's total sales, while Europe and Asia (excluding Korea) represent about 30 percent.

Hyundai recently launched its first luxury model, the Genesis. The Elantra was named the North American Car of the Year at the 2012 Detroit Auto Show, trumping industry favorites like the Ford Focus and Volkswagen Passat.

A recent marketing innovation is the "Assurance Program" under which buyers can return recently purchased cars if they lose their job within one year of purchase. The program even pays the customer's lease payments for up to 90 days while the customer searches for a new job. Owners who elect to keep their cars are not required to reimburse Hyundai.

Recent Events

Hyundai continues to launch new marketing campaigns and replaced General Motors as the official automotive sponsor of the Academy Awards. Hyundai has pursued internationalization aggressively. While many global firms struggle to stay afloat during a crisis, Hyundai is seeking to expand. Hyundai sees the crisis as an opportunity, with plans to emerge even stronger. Hyundai has improved quality and increased sales against all odds. Given its focus on quality, energy efficiency, cost control, and customer satisfaction, perhaps Hyundai is the new standard bearer in the global auto industry.

AACSB: Reflective Thinking Skills, Analytic Skills, Multiculturalism, and Diversity

Case Questions

1. What are the roles of comparative and competitive advantages in Hyundai's success? Illustrate your answers by providing specific examples of natural and acquired advantages that Hyundai employs to succeed in the global car industry.

2. In terms of factor proportions theory, what abundant factors does Hyundai leverage in its worldwide operations? Provide examples and explain how Hyundai exemplifies the theory. In what ways does Hyundai's success contradict the theory? Justify your answer.

3. Discuss Hyundai and its position in the global car industry in terms of the determinants of national competitive advantage. What is the role of demand conditions; factor conditions; related and supporting industries; and firm strategy, structure, and rivalry to Hyundai's international success?

4. The Korean government has been instrumental to Hyundai's success. In terms of national industrial policy, what has the government done to support Hyundai? What can the government do to encourage future success at Hyundai? What can the government in your country do to support development or maintenance of a strong auto industry?

5. Consistent with Dunning's Eclectic Paradigm, describe the ownership-specific advantages, location-specific advantages,

and internalization advantages held by Hyundai. Which of these advantages do you believe has been most instrumental to the firm's success? Justify your answer.

Sources: "2012 Hyundai Elantra: Why It Won Car of the Year Award," *International Business Times*, January 9, 2012, retrieved from www.ibtimes .com; "Hyundai Floors It in the US," *BusinessWeek*, February 23, 2009, p. 30; "Business: Sui Genesis; Hyundai's Surprising Success," *Economist*, March 7, 2009, retrieved from http://www.economist.com; "Hyundai Motor Company," *Hoover's Company Records*, February 17, 2012, retrieved from http://www .hoovers.com; T. Murphy, "Hyundai Ratchets Up Momentum," *Ward's Auto World*, March 2010, p. 28; "2009 Production Statistics," *OICA*, 2010, retrieved from http://www.oica.net; "Survey: Driving Change," *Economist*, September 2, 2004, pp. 15–24; "The Quick and the Dead," *Economist*, January 27, 2005, retrieved from http://www.economist.com; R. Steers, *Made in Korea* (New York: Routledge, 1999); Chris Reiter, "The Contender," *Bloomberg Businessweek*, January 30, 2012, pp. 21–22; M. Schuman, "Hyundai Revs Up," *Time*, April 25, 2005, pp. 27–30; "Special Report: The Car Company in Front—Toyota," *Economist*, January 29, 2005, pp. 73–77.

Note: This case was written by Nukhet Vardar, Yeditepe University, Turkey, and updated by Carol Sánchez and Claire Liang, Grand Valley State University, Michigan.

CHAPTER ESSENTIALS

MyManagementLab

Go to **mymanagementlab.com** to complete the problems marked with this icon ⭐.

Key Terms

absolute advantage principle 139	competitive advantage 137	internalization theory 156
comparative advantage 136	free trade 138	mercantilism 138
comparative advantage principle 140	industrial cluster 148	national industrial policy 149

Summary

In this chapter, you learned about:

1. Why do nations trade?

Each nation specializes in producing certain goods and services and then trades with other nations to acquire those goods and services in which it is not specialized. Classical explanations of international trade began with **mercantilism,** which argued that nations should seek to maximize their wealth by exporting more than they import. The **absolute advantage principle** argues that a country benefits by producing only those products in which it has absolute advantage or can produce using fewer resources than another country. The principle of **comparative advantage** contends that countries should specialize and export those goods in which they have a relative advantage compared to other countries. Comparative advantage is based on *natural advantages* and *acquired advantages*. **Competitive advantage** derives from distinctive assets or competencies of a firm, such as cost, size, or innovation strengths, which are difficult for competitors to replicate or imitate. *Factor proportions theory* holds that nations specialize in the production of goods and services whose factors of production they hold in abundance. *International product life cycle theory* describes how a product may be invented in one country and eventually mass-produced in other countries, with the innovating country losing its initial competitive advantage.

2. How can nations enhance their competitive advantage?

A major recent contribution to trade theory is Porter's determinants of national competitive advantage, which specify the four conditions in each nation that give rise to national competitive advantages: *demand conditions*; *factor conditions*; *related and supporting industries*; and *firm strategy, structure, and rivalry*. An **industrial cluster** is a concentration of companies in the same industry in a given location that interact closely with one another, gaining mutual competitive advantage. Competitive advantage of nations describes how nations acquire international trade advantages by developing specific skills, technologies, and industries. **National industrial policy** refers to efforts by governments to direct national resources to developing expertise in specific industries.

3. Why and how do firms internationalize?

The *internationalization process model* describes how companies expand into international business gradually, usually going from simple exporting to the most committed stage, FDI. Born global firms internationalize at or near their founding and are part of the emergent field of international entrepreneurship.

4. How can internationalizing firms gain and sustain competitive advantage?

MNEs have value chains that span geographic locations worldwide. Foreign direct investment means that firms invest at various locations to establish factories, marketing subsidiaries, or regional headquarters. *Monopolistic advantage theory* describes how companies succeed internationally by developing resources and capabilities that few other firms possess. Internalization is the process of acquiring and maintaining one or more value-chain activities inside the firm to minimize the disadvantages of subcontracting these activities to external firms. **Internalization theory** explains the tendency of MNEs to internalize value-chain stages when it is to their advantage. The *eclectic paradigm* specifies that the international firm should possess certain internal competitive advantages, called *ownership-specific advantages*, *location-specific advantages*, and *internalization advantages*. Many companies engage in international *collaborative ventures*, interfirm partnerships that give them access to assets and other advantages held by foreign partners.

Test Your Comprehension AACSB: Reflective Thinking Skills, Analytic Skills

1. Describe the classical theories of international trade. Which theories do you believe are relevant today?

2. What is the difference between the concepts of absolute advantage and comparative advantage?

3. Summarize factor proportions theory. What factors are most abundant in the following countries: China, Japan, Germany, Saudi Arabia, and the United States? Visit globalEDGE™ for helpful information.

⭐4. What are the main sources of national competitive advantage? Think about a successful product in your country; what are the sources of competitive advantage that explain its success?

⭐5. Do you believe your country should adopt a national industrial policy? Why or why not?

6. Describe the internationalization process of the firm. Review the background of major MNEs by visiting their

Web sites. What is the nature of internationalization in these firms? What is the nature of internationalization in born global firms?

7. FDI-based explanations of international business evolved over time. Describe the evolution of these explanations from monopolistic advantage theory, through internalization theory, to the eclectic paradigm.

8. What are ownership-specific advantages, location-specific advantages, and internalization advantages?

Apply Your Understanding   AACSB: Reflective Thinking Skills, Analytic Skills, Communication Abilities, Ethical Understanding and Reasoning Abilities

1. South Africa is home to huge reserves of coal, gold, diamonds, and natural gas. In addition to their intrinsic value, gold and diamonds have many industrial uses. Precious mineral mining has transformed South Africa into a major emerging market economy. To handle international shipping, the government developed major ports that connect South Africa to markets worldwide. South Africa is also home to a large pool of low-wage workers in mining and related industries. The government has devised a collection of plans that support specific industries, especially mining. These developments support a cluster of highly specialized firms in the mining and extractive industries. Some of the world's most knowledgeable firms in these industries are concentrated in South Africa, especially De Beers SA (www.debeers.com). De Beers has substantial capabilities in marketing and international strategy and a near-monopoly in the global diamond industry. The firm partners with MNEs that hold major financial resources. Use the theories discussed in this chapter to explain the advantages held by South Africa and De Beers. What insights emerge from these theories that shed light on South Africa and De Beers?

2. Economist Lester Thurow once posed the question "If you were the president of your own country and could specialize in one of two industries, computer chips or potato chips, which would you choose?" When faced with this question, many people choose potato chips, because "everybody can use potato chips, but not everybody can use computer chips." But the answer is much more complex. Whether to choose computer chips or potato chips depends on such factors as the relationship between national wealth and the amount of value added in manufacturing products, the possibility that the country can benefit from monopoly power (few countries can make computer chips), and the likelihood of spin-off industries (computer chip technology gives rise to other technologies, such as computers). In light of these and other possible considerations, which would you choose: computer chips or potato chips? Justify your answer.

3. *Ethical Dilemma:* To reduce poverty in Africa, government officials want to increase African exports to Europe. Africa's top exports include agricultural products, such as meat, coffee, peanuts, and fruit, and many Africans depend on food exports for their livelihood. However, the European Union (EU) imposes high trade barriers on the import of agricultural products. Among various reasons, Europeans are concerned about food quality and the EU has adopted rigorous agricultural safety standards. But the tough regulations hurt African countries, which have experienced problems with food toxins and bovine diseases in the past. In addition, the agricultural lobby in Europe is powerful and farmers are heavily subsidized by the EU. Many European politicians do not want to risk angering Europe's farm lobby by supporting free international trade in agricultural products. Suppose you are part of an EU government task force investigating trade barriers on African agricultural imports. Using the ethical framework in Chapter 5, analyze the arguments for and against agricultural trade with Africa. What should the EU do? Justify your answer.

globalEDGE INTERNET EXERCISES
(http://www.globalEDGE.msu.edu)

AACSB: Analytic Skills, Use of Information Technology

Refer to Chapter 1, page 24, for instructions on how to access and use globalEDGE™.

1. Your company is interested in importing wines from Argentina. In analyzing this opportunity, you want to identify the strengths and weaknesses of the Argentine wine industry. What are the conditions that make Argentina a favorable location for wine cultivation? Provide a short description of the current status of Argentina's wine exports and a list of the top importing countries of Argentine wines. In addition to globalEDGE™, some useful Web sites for this research include www.winesofargentina.org and www.ita.doc.gov.

2. Volvo (www.volvo.com) and Pilkington (www.pilkington .com) are major multinational firms with operations that span the globe. Investigate these firms by visiting their Web sites, as well as www.hoovers.com (a site that provides specific company information) and globalEDGE™. For each company,

describe its ownership-specific advantages, location-specific advantages, and internalization advantages.

3. The World Bank works to alleviate world poverty. The Bank provides information about conditions in developing countries, which it uses to measure progress in economic and social development. World Development Indicators (www.worldbank.org/ data) is the Bank's premier source for data on international development. The Bank measures more than 800 indicators of national conditions regarding people, environment, and economy. Consult the Web site, click on World Development Indicators, and answer the following questions: (a) In countries with developing economies, what indicators are most associated with poverty? (b) What types of industries are most typically found in poor countries? (c) Based on comparing development indicators in poor and affluent countries, speculate on what types of actions governments in developing countries can take to help spur economic development and alleviate poverty.

MyManagementLab

Go to **mymanagementlab.com** for Auto-graded writing questions as well as the following Assisted-graded writing questions:

6-1. Why do nations engage in international business? That is, what are the benefits of international trade and investment?

6-2. Summarize the international product life cycle theory. Use the theory to explain the international evolution of automobiles and laptop computers.

6-3. Mymanagementlab Only – comprehensive writing assignment for this chapter.

The Political and Legal Realities of Doing Business in Russia

Paying bribes to gain favors, whether small or large amounts, is commonplace in many countries. In Russia, it is not unusual for business people to make payments to facilitate business, and some bribes exceed U.S. $100,000, enough to buy a small flat in Moscow. Survey data suggest that most Russians consider paying bribes a normal cost of doing business.

Counterfeiting is also a problem. Take a walk through the open-air markets in Moscow, and you will likely find vendors selling pirated software, music, and movies. Russian police are aware of these products but usually do not issue fines or arrest the sellers. Some corrupt officers even get a cut of the vendors' total sales.

In the corruption index compiled by Transparency International, Russia ranks high among countries where bribery and questionable business practices exist. President Vladimir Putin even remarked that anyone who successfully registers a business in Russia deserves a medal. Vague and overlapping regulations enrich a host of public officials. Any new venture may necessitate dozens of government licenses, and each license may require paying a bribe.

CHAPTER 7

Political and Legal Systems in National Environments

LEARNING OBJECTIVES *In this chapter, you will learn about the following:*

1. The nature of country risk
2. Political and legal environments in international business
3. Political systems
4. Legal systems
5. Participants in political and legal systems
6. Types of country risk produced by political systems
7. Types of country risk produced by legal systems
8. Managing country risk

There are also countless incidents of strong-handed government interference in the private sector. Criminal raiders, sometimes in collaboration with government officials, have seized independently operating businesses. One example is Yukos, an oil company once controlled by the Russian industrialist Mikhail Khodorkovsky, who was imprisoned by the government for alleged tax evasion. Claiming that Yukos owed back taxes, Russia's government sold part of the firm and kept the $9.3 billion in proceeds.

Organized crime is also part of the difficult landscape. The deputy chairman of Russia's central bank was shot dead in Moscow. He was trying to reform a corrupt banking system and had closed dozens of banks linked to organized crime. Other contract killings have occurred, as criminal organizations have attempted to maintain their stronghold on much of Russia's economy. Criminal groups are believed to control some large Russian firms. Foreign MNEs routinely perform background checks on employees and contractors to identify people linked to organized crime. Foreign companies provide for the security of staff and facilities.

Many direct investors hesitate to do business in Russia. Corruption and crime have raised doubts about Russia's evolving legal system and its commitment to market economics. Ambiguous regulations, inadequate laws, and capricious enforcement pose important challenges. Numerous firms, from Boeing to IKEA, have invested billions in Russia. Potential rewards are promising for firms that plan ahead and protect their assets.

SOURCES: "Russia Economy: Grease My Palm," *EIU ViewsWire*, November 28, 2008, p. 1; Luminiţa Ionescu, "Contemporary Economic Crime and Corruption in Russia," *Economics, Management & Financial Markets 6*, no. 2 (2011): 137–142; "RUSSIA: Corporate Raiding Challenges Investors," *Oxford Analytica Daily Brief Service*, August 21, 2008, p. 1; "Business: The Reluctant Briber," *Economist*, November 4, 2006, p. 79; A. Kouznetsov and M. Dass, "Areas of Corruption in the Distribution of Foreign-Made Goods Where a Firm's Size and Origin Play a Role: The Russian Experience," *Journal of East-West Business 16*, no. 1 (2010): 24–44; C. Matlack and M. Elder, "The Peril and Promise of Investing in Russia," *BusinessWeek*, October 5, 2009, pp. 48–52.

Most of us expect a familiar business landscape when we conduct business at home. But foreign markets differ in terms of political and legal systems, as well as business norms. As illustrated by the opening story, foreign markets often pose major challenges and create vulnerabilities for the firm. Managers must be able to navigate difficult regulations and practices and avoid unethical or questionable conduct.

At the same time, the political and legal context may also present opportunities for companies. Preferential subsidies, government incentives, and protection from competition reduce business costs and influence strategic decision making. Many governments encourage domestic investment from foreign MNEs by offering tax holidays and cash incentives to employ local workers.

 ## The Nature of Country Risk

Country risk

Exposure to potential loss or adverse effects on company operations and profitability caused by developments in a country's political and/or legal environments.

Country risk is defined as exposure to potential loss or adverse effects on company operations and profitability caused by developments in a country's political and/or legal environments. Sometimes termed *political risk*, it is one of four major types of international business risks introduced in Chapter 1. While the immediate cause of country risk is a political or legal factor, underlying such factors may be economic, social, or technological developments. Exhibit 7.1 identifies dimensions of country risk prevalent in international business. We address them in this chapter. Government intervention, protectionism, and barriers to trade and investment are particularly notable in international business. Mismanagement or failure of the national economy can lead to financial crises, recessions, market downturns, currency crises, and inflation. Such events usually arise from business cycles, poor monetary or fiscal policies, a defective regulatory environment, or imbalances in the underlying economic fundamentals of the host country.

Political or legislative actions can harm business interests, such as laws that are unexpectedly strict or result in unintended consequences. Many laws favor host-country interests—that is, interests in foreign countries where the firm has direct operations. For example, Coca-Cola's business suffered in Germany after the German government enacted a recycling plan that required consumers to return nonreusable soda containers to stores for a refund of 0.25 euros. Rather than coping with unwanted returns, big supermarket chains responded by yanking Coke from their shelves and pushing their own store brands instead.[1] In China, the government censors material that is critical of its actions and policies. Yahoo must monitor the information that appears on its Web sites to prevent the Chinese government from closing its China operations. In 2010, Google took a censorship stand against the Chinese government when it moved its search engine business to Hong Kong.

How Prevalent Is Country Risk?

Exhibit 7.2 presents the level of country risk in selected countries, measured as political stability, legal environment, economic indicators, and tax policy. Iraq is risky in the wake of war and efforts to establish political stability. Venezuela is dominated by an unpredictable, dictatorial government. Libya has experienced popular unrest. Such countries suffer from unstable governments,

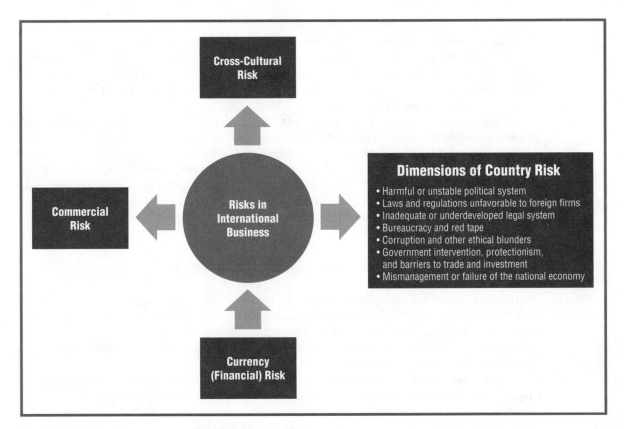

EXHIBIT 7.1

Country Risk as One of Four Major Risks in International Business

underdeveloped legal systems, or biased law enforcement. Conversely, countries such as Canada, Japan, and Singapore are characterized by stable, transparent, and well-founded political and legal systems. Exhibit 7.2 implies that risk tends to be lower in countries with a favorable legal climate and political stability and higher in countries with political instability and substantial government intervention. Many of the riskiest states are poor countries that would benefit enormously from

EXHIBIT 7.2

Country Risk in Selected Countries, 2011 (ranked 0 to 10; a high number indicates greater risk)

Source: Based on Economist Intelligence Unit (2011), "Risk Briefing," www.viewswire.eiu.com, accessed January 28, 2012.

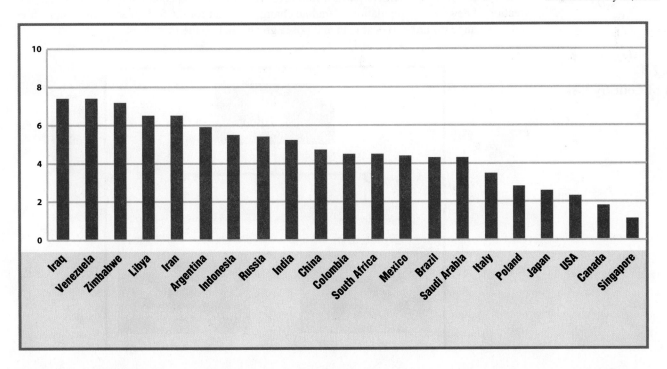

direct investment and integration into the world economy.[2] For the complete list of countries ranked by risk, visit the Risk Briefing site at the Economist Intelligence Unit (www.viewswire.eiu.com).

Country risk may affect all firms in a country equally or only a subset. Unrest in Egypt in 2011 tended to affect all firms. By contrast, the Russian government targeted only Yukos with politically motivated persecution, despite the presence of several competitors in Russia like ConocoPhillips and Royal Dutch Shell.[3]

Country risk occasionally occurs in India. When they held power in India's government, Hindu nationalists openly opposed foreign investment and influence on Indian society and enacted laws that targeted foreign firms for harassment. The KFC restaurant chain stepped up security after local political groups threatened to destroy the firm's fast-food outlets. About one hundred farmers ransacked a KFC restaurant in Bangalore. ArcelorMittal, Nissan, and numerous other firms have faced delays in establishing operations in India due to government bureaucracy and Indian activist groups, which often oppose industrial development.[4]

 ## Political and Legal Environments in International Business

Political system

A set of formal institutions that constitute a government.

A **political system** is a set of formal institutions that constitute a government. It includes legislative bodies, political parties, lobbying groups, and trade unions. The principal functions of a political system are to provide protection from external threats, establish stability based on laws, and govern the allocation of valued resources among the members of a society. A political system also defines how these groups interact with each other.

Each country's political system is unique, having evolved within a particular historical, economic, and cultural context. Political systems are also constantly evolving in response to constituent demands and the evolution of the national and international environment. *Constituents* are the people and organizations that support the political system and receive government resources.

Legal system

A system for interpreting and enforcing laws.

A **legal system** is a system for interpreting and enforcing laws. Laws, regulations, and rules establish norms for conduct. A legal system incorporates institutions and procedures for ensuring order and resolving disputes in commercial activities, as well as taxing economic output and protecting intellectual property and other company assets.

Exhibit 7.3 identifies the aspects of political and legal systems that contribute to country risk. Political and legal systems are dynamic and constantly changing. The two systems are interdependent—changes in one affect the other. Adverse developments in political and legal systems give rise to country risk. They can result from installation of a new government, shifting values or priorities in political parties, initiatives developed by special interest groups, and the creation of new laws or regulations. Gradual change is easier for the firm to accommodate, while sudden change is harder to deal with and poses greater risk to the firm.

EXHIBIT 7.3

Sources of Country Risk

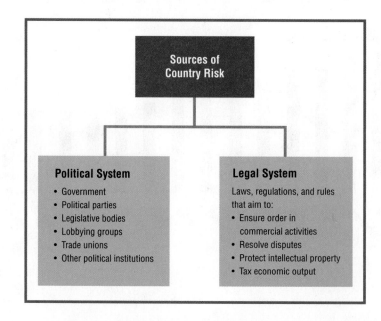

Unfavorable developments give rise to new conditions that may threaten the firm's products, services, or business activities. For example, a new import tariff may increase the cost of a key component used to manufacture a product. A modification in labor law may alter the hours the firm's employees are allowed to work. The installation of a new political leader may lead to government takeover of corporate assets.

Country risk is *always* present, but its nature and intensity vary over time and from country to country. In China, for example, the government is currently overhauling the national legal system, making it more consistent with Western systems. Some new regulations have been poorly formulated or are confusing or contradictory. For example, at one point, the Beijing government announced that foreign investments in China's Internet industry were illegal. By this time Western firms had already invested millions in the Chinese dot.com sector, without notice that the investments were inappropriate. In disputes between local and foreign firms, governments are often inclined to protect local interests. Even where Western firms obtain favorable judgments in the courts, they may not be enforced. Let's delve into political and legal systems in more detail.

Political Systems

The world is characterized by three major types of political systems: totalitarianism, socialism, and democracy. Exhibit 7.4 highlights countries that exemplify these systems. These categories are not mutually exclusive. Most democracies also include some elements of socialism. Most former totalitarian regimes now embrace a mix of socialism and democracy. To resolve the recent global financial crisis, governments in Europe and the United States implemented relatively socialistic policies, such as nationalizing firms in the banking and automotive industries. China applied some democratic approaches, such as land reforms and open markets, to stimulate commercial activity.

Totalitarianism

Well-known totalitarian states from the past include Nazi Germany (1933–1945), Spain (1939–1975), China (1949–1980s), and the Soviet Union (1918–1991). Under totalitarianism, the state attempts to regulate most aspects of public and private behavior. A totalitarian government seeks to control not only all economic and political matters but also the attitudes, values, and beliefs of the citizenry. Often, the entire population is mobilized in support of the state and a political or religious ideology. Totalitarian states are generally either theocratic (religion-based) or secular (non-religion-based). Usually there is a state party led by a dictator, such as Kim Jong-un in North Korea. Party membership is mandatory for those seeking to advance within the social and economic hierarchy. Power is maintained by means of secret police, propaganda disseminated through state-controlled mass media, regulation of free discussion and criticism, and the use of terror tactics. Totalitarian states usually do not tolerate activities by individuals or groups such as churches, labor unions, or political parties that are not directed toward the state's goals.[5]

Over time, many of the world's totalitarian states have either disappeared or evolved toward democracy and capitalism. China initiated major reforms in the 1980s, and the Soviet Union collapsed in 1991. Agricultural land and state enterprises were sold to private interests and entrepreneurs gained the right to establish their own businesses. The transition has not been

Elements of Totalitarianism Found in	Elements of Socialism Found in	Largely Democratic
Cuba	Bolivia	Australia
North Korea	China	Canada
Several countries in Africa (such as Eritrea, Sudan, Equatorial Guinea, Zimbabwe)	Egypt	Japan
	India	New Zealand
	Romania	United States
	Russia	Most European countries
	Venezuela	Most Latin American countries

EXHIBIT 7.4

Examples of Countries under Various Political Systems

easy, and former totalitarian states continue to maintain political control, including government intervention in business (as in Russia in the opening story). Former Soviet Union states and China are still characterized by substantial red tape and bureaucracy that hinder economic activity (for examples, see the World Bank's www.doingbusiness.org). Today, numerous states exhibit elements of totalitarianism, particularly in Africa, Asia, and the Middle East. Several countries are controlled by individuals with substantial dictatorial powers.

Socialism

Socialism's fundamental tenet is that capital and wealth should be vested in the state and used primarily as a means of production rather than for profit. Socialism is based on a collectivist ideology in which the collective welfare of people is seen to outweigh the welfare of the individual. Socialists argue that capitalists receive a disproportionate amount of society's wealth relative to workers. They believe that in a capitalist society, the pay of workers does not represent the full value of their labor, and thus government should control the basic means of production, distribution, and commercial activity.

Socialism has manifested itself in much of the world as *social democracy* and has been most successful in Western Europe. It has also played a major role in the political systems of large countries such as Brazil and India, and today it remains a viable system in much of the world. In social democratic regimes, such as Italy and Norway, government frequently intervenes in the private sector and in business activities. Corporate income tax rates are often relatively high, as in France and Sweden. Even robust economies like Germany have experienced net outflows of FDI as businesses seek to escape extensive regulation.

Democracy

Democracy is characterized by two major features:

Source: Dhoxax/Shutterstock

By protecting private property rights, democracies promote entrepreneurship. The proprietors of these shops in Denmark enjoy the profits of their ownership.

- *Private property rights*, or the ability to own property and assets and to increase one's asset base by accumulating private wealth. Property includes tangibles, such as land and buildings, as well as intangibles, such as stocks, contracts, patent rights, and intellectual assets. Democratic governments devise laws that protect property rights. People and firms can acquire property, use it, buy or sell it, and bequeath it to whomever they want. These rights are important because they encourage individual initiative, ambition, and innovation, as well as thrift and the desire to accumulate wealth. People are less likely to have these qualities if there is uncertainty about whether they can control their property or profit from it.
- *Limited government*. The government performs only essential functions that serve all citizens, such as conducting national defense, maintaining law and order and diplomatic relations, and constructing and maintaining infrastructure such as roads, schools, and public works. State control and intervention in the economic activities of private individuals or firms is minimal. By allowing market forces to determine economic activity, the government ensures resources are allocated with maximal efficiency.[6]

Under democracy, the individual pursuits of people and firms are sometimes at odds with equality and justice. Because people have differing levels of personal and financial resources, each performs with varying degrees of success, leading to inequalities. Critics of pure democracy argue that when these inequalities become excessive, government should step in to correct them. Each society balances individual freedom with broader social goals. In democracies such as Japan and Sweden, the democracy's rights and freedoms are construed in larger societal terms rather than on behalf of individuals.

Most democracies include elements of socialism, such as government intervention in the affairs of individuals and firms. Socialism emerges because of abuses or negative externalities that occur in purely democratic or capitalistic systems. Japan has been striving to achieve the right balance between democracy and socialism. Poor management practices and an economic recession led to the bankruptcy of thousands of Japanese firms. To maintain jobs and economic stability, the Japanese government intervened to support numerous large firms and banks that, under pure capitalism, would have failed. But such policies have led to inflexibility in the Japanese economy and a delay of needed structural improvements.

Many countries, including Australia, Canada, the United States, and those in Europe, are best described as having a mixed political system—characterized by a strong private sector and a strong public sector, with considerable government regulation and control.

Democracy's Link to Economic Freedom and Openness

Compared to totalitarianism and socialism, democracy is associated with greater economic freedom and higher living standards. Economic freedom flourishes when governments support the institutions necessary for that freedom, such as freely operating markets and the rule of law.[7] Exhibit 7.5 reveals that the greater the political freedom in a nation, the more economic freedom its citizens enjoy. As countries develop economic ties with foreign trading partners and integrate themselves with the global economy, they tend to liberalize their markets and reduce restrictions on foreign business. This happened, for example, with the introduction of economic reforms and open markets in India in the 1990s.

Political freedom is characterized by free and fair elections; the right to form political parties; fair electoral laws; existence of a parliament or other legislative body; freedom from

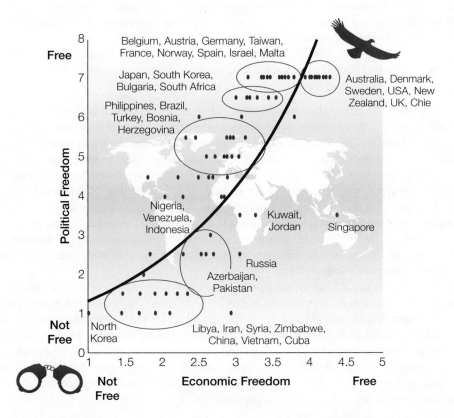

EXHIBIT 7.5

Relationship between Political Freedom and Economic Freedom for a Sample of Countries

Source: Based on data at Freedom House, 2012. Accessed at http://www.freedomhouse.org.

domination by the military, foreign powers, or religious hierarchies; and self-determination for cultural, ethnic, and religious minorities. Economic freedom is related to the extent of government interference in business, the strictness of the regulatory environment, and the ease with which commercial activity is carried out according to market forces. Visit Freedom House (www.freedomhouse.org) to view the latest information on political and economic freedom around the world.

Democracy is closely associated with *openness*, or lack of regulation or barriers to the entry of firms in foreign markets. The greater the openness, the fewer the constraints placed on foreign firms. Absence of excessive regulations also benefits buyers because openness increases the quantity and variety of products available. Competition pressures firms to continuously improve product quality. Increased efficiency and lower prices may follow. After India's government lowered entry barriers in the Indian automobile market, foreign automakers steadily entered the market. Their presence increased the number of models available for sale, raised the quality of available cars, and lowered prices. A similar phenomenon occurred in the mobile telephone market in China.[8]

The Relationship between Political Systems and Economic Systems

Each political system tends to be associated with a particular type of economic system. Generally speaking, totalitarianism is associated with command economies, democracy with market economies, and socialism with mixed economies. Let's review these economic systems.

COMMAND ECONOMY Also known as a centrally planned economy, a command economy makes the state a dominant force in the production and distribution of goods and services. Central planners make resource allocation decisions, and the state owns major sectors of the economy. In command economies, sizable bureaucracy thrives, and central planning tends to be less efficient than market forces in synchronizing supply and demand. For example, goods shortages were so common in the Soviet Union that people often waited in lines for hours to buy basic necessities like sugar and bread. Today, countries such as China and Russia still exhibit some characteristics of command economies. However, the system is gradually dying out in favor of market economies and mixed economies.

MARKET ECONOMY In a market economy, market forces—the interaction of supply and demand—determine prices. Government intervention in the marketplace is limited, and economic decisions are left to individuals and firms. Market economies are closely associated with capitalism, in which the means of production are privately owned and operated. Participants typically exhibit a market-oriented mentality and entrepreneurial spirit. The task of the state is to establish a legal system that protects private property and contractual agreements. However, the government may also intervene to address the inequalities that market economies sometimes produce.

MIXED ECONOMY A mixed economy exhibits the features of both a market economy and a command economy. It combines state intervention and market mechanisms for organizing production and distribution. Most industries are under private ownership, and entrepreneurs freely establish, own, and operate corporations. But the government also controls certain functions, such as pension programs, labor regulation, minimum wage levels, and environmental regulation. State-owned enterprises operate in key sectors such as transportation, telecommunications, and energy. In France, for example, the government owns key banks and some key industries, such as aluminum refining. One car company, Renault, is partially state owned, but another, Peugeot, is not. In Germany, Japan, Norway, Singapore, and Sweden, the government often works closely with business and labor groups to determine industrial policy, regulate wage rates, and/or provide subsidies to support specific industries.

The last century saw a large increase in the number of mixed economies and a concurrent rise in government involvement in economic matters. For example, in the United States, combined government spending increased from about 27 percent of GDP in 1960 to roughly 40 percent today, and is expected to attain 50 percent by 2038. In Belgium, Denmark, France, Sweden, and several other countries in Europe, annual government spending now exceeds 50 percent of GDP. In recent years, governments in Europe, Japan, and North America have imposed many new regulations on private firms.[9] Regulations were adopted that covered workplace safety, minimum wages, pension benefits, and environmental protection.

Country Realities

Home to a huge base of oil reserves, Libya is one of Africa's wealthiest countries. But Libya's economy is state-dominated, which hinders investment from abroad. Recent political unrest and civil war interrupted the country's huge oil output, which may remain volatile for some time. Fortunately, Libya has an educated workforce and little government debt. The country has much potential to prosper by leveraging the oil and tourism industries. Progress can come through wise public policies that foster investment and economic development.

Legal Systems

Legal systems provide a framework of rules and norms of conduct that mandate, limit, or permit specified relationships among people and organizations and provide punishments for those who violate these rules and norms. Laws require or limit specific actions while empowering citizens to engage in others, such as entering into contracts and seeking remedies for contract violations. Legal systems are dynamic—they evolve over time to represent each nation's changing social values and the evolution of their social, political, economic, and technological environments.

Prevailing political systems—totalitarianism, socialism, and democracy—tend to influence their respective legal systems. Democracies tend to encourage market forces and free trade. In countries with well-developed legal systems, such as Australia, Canada, Japan, the United States, and most European countries, laws are widely known and understood. They are effective and legitimate because they are applied to all citizens equally, issued by means of formal procedures by recognized government authorities, and enforced systematically and fairly by police forces and formally organized judicial bodies.

In these countries, a culture of law exists in which citizens consistently respect and follow the rule of law. **Rule of law** refers to a legal system in which rules are clear, publicly disclosed, fairly enforced, and widely respected by individuals, organizations, and the government. International business flourishes in societies where the rule of law prevails. In the United States, for example, the Securities and Exchange Act encourages confidence in business transactions by requiring public companies to frequently disclose their financial indicators to investors. Legal systems can be eroded by declining respect for the law, weak government authority, or burdensome restrictions that attempt to forbid behavior prevalent in the society. In the absence of the rule of law, firms must contend with great uncertainty and economic activity may be impeded.

Nations are primarily governed by one of four basic legal systems: common law, civil law, religious law, or mixed. These legal systems are the foundation for laws and regulations. Exhibit 7.6 provides examples of countries where these legal systems are dominant.

Common Law

Also known as case law, common law is a legal system that originated in England and spread to Australia, Canada, the United States, and former members of the British Commonwealth. The basis of common law is tradition, previous cases, and legal precedents set by the nation's courts through interpretation of statutes, legislation, and past rulings. The national legislature in common-law countries (such as Parliament in Britain and Congress in the United States) holds ultimate power to pass or amend laws. In the United States, because the constitution is difficult to amend, the Supreme Court and even lower courts have much flexibility to interpret the law. Because common law is more open to interpretation by courts, it is more flexible than other legal systems. Judges in a common-law system have substantial power to interpret laws based on the unique circumstances of individual cases, including commercial disputes and other business situations.

Rule of law
A legal system in which rules are clear, publicly disclosed, fairly enforced, and widely respected by individuals, organizations, and the government.

EXHIBIT 7.6

Dominant Legal Systems in Selected Countries

Source: Based on World Legal Systems at www.juriglobe.ca.

Primarily Common Law	Primarily Civil Law	Primarily Religious Law	Mixed Systems
Australia	Much of western	Much of the	Bangladesh
Canada	Europe and Latin	Middle East and	India
Ireland	America	North Africa	Indonesia
New Zealand	Japan	Afghanistan	Israel
United Kingdom	Russia	Mauritania	Kenya
United States	South Korea	Pakistan	Malaysia
		Sudan	Philippines

Civil Law

Also known as code law, civil law is found in France, Germany, Italy, Japan, Turkey, and Latin America. Its origins go back to Roman law and the Napoleonic Code. Civil law is based on an all-inclusive system of laws that have been "codified"; the laws are clearly written and accessible. It is divided into three separate codes: commercial, civil, and criminal. Civil law is considered complete as a result of catchall provisions found within the law. Rules and principles form the starting point for legal reasoning and administering justice. The codified rules emerge as specific laws and codes of conduct produced by a legislative body or some other supreme authority.

Both common law and civil law systems originated in western Europe and represent the common values of western Europeans. A key difference between the two systems is that common law is primarily judicial in origin and based on court decisions, whereas civil law is primarily legislative in origin and based on laws passed by national and local legislatures. Differences in common and civil law give rise to differing business approaches in different countries. These are highlighted in Exhibit 7.7. In reality, common-law systems generally contain elements of civil law and vice versa. The two systems complement each other, and countries that employ one also tend to employ some elements of the other.

Religious Law

This legal system is strongly influenced by religious beliefs, ethical codes, and moral values viewed as mandated by a supreme being. The most important religious legal systems are based on Hindu, Jewish, and Islamic law. Among these, the most widespread is Islamic law, found mainly in the Middle East and North Africa. In addition to these areas, other countries with substantial populations of Muslims (followers of Islam) include India (about 175 million Muslims), Indonesia (205 million), Nigeria (75 million), and Pakistan (178 million). Islamic law, also known as the *shariah*, is based on the Qur'an, the holy book of Muslims, and the teachings of the Prophet Mohammed. Adherents generally do not differentiate between religious and secular life. Islamic law governs relationships among people, between people and the state, and between people and a supreme being. It spells out norms of behavior regarding politics, economics, banking, contracts, marriage, and many other social issues. Thus, Islamic law might be said to encompass all possible human relationships. Because it is seen as divinely ordained, it is relatively static and absolute. Unlike other legal systems, it evolves very little over time.

Most Muslim countries currently maintain a dual system, in which both religious and secular courts coexist. Other countries with large Muslim populations, such as Indonesia, Bangladesh, and Pakistan, have secular constitutions and laws. Turkey, another country with a majority Muslim population, has a strongly secular constitution. Saudi Arabia and Iran are unusual in that religious courts have authority over all aspects of jurisprudence.

EXHIBIT 7.7

Examples of Differences between Common Law and Civil Law

Legal Issues	Civil Law	Common Law
Ownership of intellectual property	Determined by registration.	Determined by prior use.
Enforcing agreements	Commercial agreements become enforceable only if properly notarized or registered.	Proof of agreement is sufficient for enforcing contracts.
Specificity of contracts	Contracts tend to be brief because many potential problems are already covered in the civil code.	Contracts tend to be very detailed, with all possible contingencies spelled out. Usually more costly to draft a contract.
Compliance with contracts	Noncompliance is extended to include unforeseeable human acts such as labor strikes and riots.	Acts of God (floods, lightning, hurricanes, etc.) are the only justifiable excuses for noncompliance with the provisions of contracts.

Modern liberal movements within Islam oppose traditional views of religious law. For example, strict interpretation of Islamic law prohibits the giving and receiving of interest on loans or investments. To comply with Islamic law, financial institutions employ a variant of international banking known as "Islamic finance," based on the principles of shariah law. Many Western banks—for example, JP Morgan and Deutsche Bank—have subsidiaries in Muslim countries that comply with shariah laws. Instead of requiring interest payments, they charge administrative fees or take equity positions in the projects they finance. Many issue *sukuks*, Islamic-compliant bonds that offer revenue from an asset, such as a rental property, rather than interest. The global market for shariah-compliant financial instruments now exceeds $1 trillion.[10]

Mixed Systems

Mixed systems consist of two or more legal systems operating together. In most countries, legal systems evolve over time, adopting elements of one system or another that reflect their unique needs. The contrast between civil law and common law has become blurred as many countries combine them. For example, legal systems in South Africa and the Philippines mix elements of civil law and common law. Legal systems in Indonesia and most Middle Eastern countries share elements of civil law and Islamic law.

Source: Mark Shenley/Alamy

Iranian women with Iran's flag attend a football match in Tehran after the Iranian government rescinded a quarter-century ban that had prohibited women from going to stadiums for sports events.

Historically, socialist law was a legal system found in the former Soviet Union, China, and a few states in Africa. It was based on civil law, with elements of socialist principles that emphasized state ownership of property. The rights of the state dominated those of the individual. When the Soviet Union collapsed and China began transitioning to capitalism, socialist law gave way to other legal systems, especially civil law.

 ## Participants in Political and Legal Systems

Political and legal systems evolve from the interplay among various societal institutions, at both the national and international levels. Five types of participants are active in transforming political and legal systems.

Government

The government, or the public sector, is the most important participant, operating at national, state, and local levels. Governments have the power to enact and enforce laws. They strongly influence how firms enter host countries and how they conduct business there. Governments regulate international business activity through a complex system of institutions, agencies, and public officials. Agencies that possess such powers in the United States include the U.S. Trade Representative and the International Trade Administration (www.ita.doc.gov). In Canada, such functions are handled by the Ministry of Foreign Affairs (www.international.gc.ca), the Ministry of Finance, and the Export and Import Controls Bureau. Similar agencies operate in Australia, Britain, and virtually all other countries.

International Organizations

Supranational agencies such as the World Trade Organization (www.wto.org), the United Nations (www.un.org), and the World Bank (www.worldbank.org) strongly influence international business. For example, the United Nations Conference on Trade and Development (UNCTAD, www.unctad.org) helps oversee international trade and development in the areas of investment, finance, technology, and enterprise development. Such organizations facilitate free and fair trade by providing administrative guidance, governing frameworks, and, occasionally, financial support.

Regional Economic Blocs

Regional trade organizations, such as the European Union (EU), the North American Free Trade Agreement (NAFTA), and the Association of Southeast Asian Nations (ASEAN), aim to advance the economic and political interests of their members. The EU is especially well developed, with its own executive, legislative, and bureaucratic bodies. It enacts and enforces laws and regulations that directly affect business. For example, following new regulations forced by Lithuania's entry into the EU, the supermarket chain IKI had to spend millions to build separate entrances for fresh meat delivery in each of its 136 stores.[11]

Special Interest Groups

Special interest groups serve the interests of particular countries, industries, or causes. For example, the Organisation for Economic Co-operation and Development (OECD, www.oecd.org) supports the economic developmental and business goals of advanced economies. The Organization of Petroleum Exporting Countries (OPEC, www.opec.org) is a powerful cartel that controls global oil prices, which, in turn, affect consumer prices and everyone's cost of doing business. OPEC emerged as a powerful voice for oil-producing countries, including Saudi Arabia, Iran, Venezuela, Nigeria, and Indonesia. Other groups exercise similar control over the production and allocation of commodities such as sugar, coffee, and iron ore.

Special interest groups engage in political activity to advance specific causes, ranging from labor rights to environmental protection. They often influence national political processes and produce outcomes with far-reaching consequences for business. Many target particular industries and affect individual firms accordingly. Special interest groups operate not only in host countries but also in the home country. For example, well-orchestrated U.S. interest groups forced U.S.-owned firms to reduce their investments in South Africa when its apartheid policies were in force.[12] Greenpeace, Friends of the Earth, and other environmentalist groups opposed construction of the Keystone pipeline system, intended to transport synthetic crude oil from Canada to the United States. Protesters argued the pipeline would produce oil spills, polluting ground water and killing wildlife. Environmentalist groups were instrumental in halting construction of the pipeline in 2012.[13] Greenpeace also has been successful in pressuring appliance manufacturers to produce environmentally friendly refrigerators in Germany and the United States.[14] Exhibit 7.8 provides a sample of interest groups and their likely stance toward various business issues.

Competing Firms

Rival domestic firms with a strong presence in the host country naturally have an interest in opposing the entry of foreign firms into the local market and may lobby their government for protection. For example, host-country competitors often complain when foreign firms receive financial support from the parent or host-country governments. Asterix, a French theme park, opposed French government support for the U.S.-based Disney when the latter established Disneyland Paris. Similarly, U.S. automakers in Detroit opposed BMW's construction of a factory in South Carolina. However, the state government of South Carolina supported the BMW facility on the grounds that it would generate jobs and increase tax revenues.

EXHIBIT 7.8 Issues of Concern to Special Interest Groups

Group	Typical Issue	Example
Labor unions	Oppose imported goods and global sourcing	U.S. united steelworkers union opposed imports of steel from China
Competing businesses	Dislike competition from foreign firms	Japanese rice producers opposed imports of rice from the United States
Customers	May avoid foreign-made products. Dislike improper marketing practices.	Motorists in Australia accused BP of unfair pricing of petroleum products
Conservationists	Fight against wildlife loss and destruction of the natural environment	Environmentalists oppose lumber imports from countries with tropical rain forests

Types of Country Risk Produced by Political Systems

How do political systems create challenges for firms engaged in international business? Let's examine the specific risks produced by political systems.

Government Takeover of Corporate Assets

Governments occasionally seize the assets of corporations. The industry sectors most often targeted by government seizure are natural resources (for example, mining and petroleum), utilities, and manufacturing. Fortunately, aggressive seizure is less common these days as governments in many developing countries have adopted institutional reforms that aim to attract FDI from abroad and foster economic growth.

Government seizure takes on various forms:

- *Confiscation* is the seizure of corporate assets without compensation. Beginning in the 1980s, for example, Zimbabwe's dictator Robert Mugabe systematically seized more than 5,000 farms owned by farmers of mostly European descent, and redistributed the land to native Zimbabweans. Recently, Mugabe announced plans to confiscate mines owned by foreign mining companies.[15]

- *Expropriation* is seizure with compensation. In Venezuela, ExxonMobil and ConocoPhillips were forced to abandon multi-billion-dollar investments in the local oil industry. Recently, Venezuela President Hugo Chavez ordered troops to seize two plants owned by Mexico's Cemex, the country's largest cement producer. In 2008, gradual yet persistent pressure from the Russian government led TNK-BP, a Russian subsidiary of British energy giant BP, to sell a major stake in its oil business to the national gas monopoly Gazprom.[16]

- *Nationalization* describes government seizure of an entire industry, with or without compensation. For example, the government of Bolivia nationalized much of the oil and gas industry in that country. In 2008, President Hugo Chavez nationalized the cement industry in Venezuela.[17] Nationalization occurs in advanced economies as well. Following the global financial crisis, the federal government of Iceland nationalized most of the country's banking industry.[18]

"Creeping expropriation" is a subtle form of country risk in which governments modify laws and regulations after foreign MNEs have made substantial local investments in property and plants.[19] Examples include abrupt termination of contracts and the creation of new laws that favor local firms. As reported in the opening story, corporate raiders and government officials in Russia occasionally raid the offices of competitors and subject them to questionable criminal investigations. Such tactics occasionally force foreign MNEs to cede control of their operations to local interests.[20] Governments in Bolivia, Kazakhstan, Russia, and Venezuela have modified tax regimes to extract revenues from foreign coal, oil, and gas companies. Troops stormed the Kazakhstan offices of U.S. mining company AES to enforce an alleged tax fine amounting to some $200 million. One of the country's largest providers of electricity, AES reduced its operations in Kazakhstan in the wake of persistent abuse by the Kazakh government.[21] Subtle or devious approaches to government takeover make country risk harder to predict.

Embargoes and Sanctions

Most countries are signatories to international treaties and agreements that specify rules, principles, and standards of behavior in international business. Nevertheless, governments may unilaterally resort to sanctions and embargoes to respond to offensive activities of foreign countries. A *sanction* is a type of trade penalty imposed on one or more countries by one or more other countries. Sanctions typically take the form of tariffs, trade barriers, import duties, and import or export quotas. They generally arise in the context of an unresolved trade or policy dispute, such as a disagreement about the fairness of some international trade practice. There is

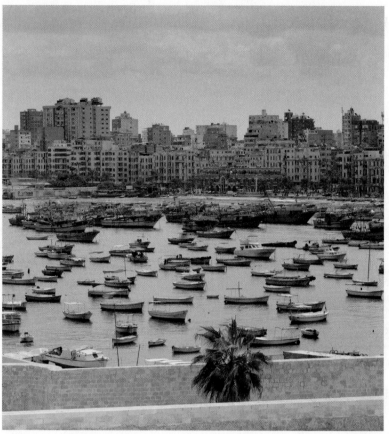

Source: javarman/Shutterstock

Exports of natural gas and other commodities were threatened in the wake of revolution in Egypt in 2011. Shown here is the harbor at Alexandria, Egypt's chief port.

much evidence suggesting that sanctions often do not achieve desired outcomes. For example, the United States has imposed trade sanctions on Iran and Syria. However, goods continue to flow in and out of both countries from China, Germany, Japan, and numerous other trading partners.[22]

An *embargo* is an official ban on exports to or imports from a particular country, in order to isolate it and punish its government. It is generally more serious than a sanction and is used as a political punishment for some disapproved policies or acts. For example, the United States has enforced embargoes against Iran and North Korea, at times labeled as state sponsors of terrorism. The European Union has enacted embargoes against Belarus, Sudan, and China in certain areas, such as foreign travel, to protest human rights and weapon-trading violations.

Boycotts against Firms or Nations

Consumers and special interest groups occasionally target particular firms perceived to have harmed local interests. Consumers may refuse to patronize firms that behave inappropriately. A *boycott* is a voluntary refusal to engage in commercial dealings with a nation or a company. Boycotts and public protests result in lost sales and increased costs (for public relations activities needed to restore the firm's image). Disneyland Paris and McDonald's have been the targets of boycotts by French farmers, who believe these firms represent U.S. agricultural policies and globalization, which many French citizens despise. Activists in numerous countries organized a boycott of petroleum company BP following its oil spill in the Gulf of Mexico in 2010.[23]

Terrorism

Terrorism is the threat or actual use of force or violence to attain a political goal through fear, coercion, or intimidation.[24] It is sometimes sponsored by national governments. Terrorism has escalated in much of the world, as exemplified by the September 11, 2001, attacks in the United States and the 2011 terrorist bombing of Moscow's Domodedovo Airport. In India, more than 30,000 people have died in terrorist attacks since 1993.[25] In addition to causing loss of life, terrorism can severely damage commercial infrastructure and disrupt business activities. It induces fear in consumers, who reduce their purchasing, potentially leading to economic recession. The hospitality, aviation, entertainment, and retailing industries can be particularly affected. Terrorism also affects financial markets. In the days following the 9/11 attacks, the value of the U.S. stock market dropped some 14 percent.[26]

War, Insurrection, and Violence

War, insurrection, and other forms of violence pose significant problems for business operations. While such events usually do not affect companies directly, their indirect effects can be disastrous. Violent conflict among drug cartels and security services along the U.S.-Mexico border has led some firms and financiers to withdraw investments from Mexico because of perceived heightened risks and political instability. In India, Tata Motors (www.tatamotors.com) shifted the location of a major new factory due to violent protests by local farmers who feared the loss of their livelihood.[27] To minimize losses from violent acts, firms can purchase risk insurance.

Example: Country Risk in the Middle East

Arab countries of the Middle East experience various risks, which can hinder entrepreneurial activity and inward investment. In 2011 and 2012, Egypt, Libya, Syria, and other Arab states were affected by citizen revolts protesting authoritarian regimes and political corruption.[28]

The 2011 uprising in Egypt overthrew the country's long-standing ruler. The rebellion halted industrial production, closed banks, and triggered capital flight. Tourism, a key source of revenue for Egypt, declined by one-third. Consumer and investor confidence fell and affected the value-chain activities of countless firms.[29] Many worried the crisis would disrupt cargo transportation through the Suez Canal, a key world shipping route.[30] A sharp decline in Egypt's currency added to the nation's already substantial price inflation.[31]

A survey of business leaders by the World Economic Forum ranked Middle Eastern countries on factors that hinder business. In the Middle East, the survey found that restrictive labor regulations and poorly educated workers hinder labor-intensive ventures, such as factories. Bureaucracy and corruption deter launching new firms and running existing ones. By contrast, crime and theft are relatively minor concerns in the Middle East. The World Economic Forum advocates policies in the region that spur job creation via private sector development of high value-adding businesses.[32]

 ## Types of Country Risk Produced by Legal Systems

In addition to political concerns, country risk also arises due to peculiarities of national legal systems. Especially relevant to international business are *commercial law*, which specifically covers business transactions, and *private law*, which regulates relationships between persons and organizations, including contracts, and liabilities that may arise due to negligent behavior. In many countries, the legal system favors home-country nationals. Laws are designed to promote the interests of local businesses and the local economy.

Legal systems in both the host country and the home country pose various challenges to firms, which we review next.

Country Risk Arising from the Host-Country Legal Environment

Governments in host countries impose various laws and regulations on foreign companies doing business there.

FOREIGN INVESTMENT LAWS These laws affect the type of entry strategy firms choose, as well as their operations and performance. Many nations impose restrictions on inward FDI. For example, Japan's *daitenhoo* (large retail store law) restricted foreigners from opening warehouse-style stores such as Walmart or Toys "R" Us. The law protected smaller shops by requiring large-scale retailers to obtain the approval of local retailers, a painstaking and time-consuming process. In Malaysia, firms seeking to invest in local businesses must obtain permission from the Malaysian Industrial Development Authority. The United States restricts foreign investments that might affect national security. Proposed investments can be reviewed by the U.S. Committee on Investments. In 2006, the U.S. Congress opposed a management contract that would have granted control of several U.S. ports to Dubai Ports World, a firm based in the United Arab Emirates. Under opposition from the U.S. public and Congress, the firm abandoned its investment plans.

Source: Peter Wilson © Dorling Kindersley

In Japan, foreign-owned large stores such as Carrefour and Walmart have faced restrictive laws designed to protect local retailers.

CONTROLS ON OPERATING FORMS AND PRACTICES Governments impose laws and regulations on how firms can conduct production, marketing, and distribution activities within their borders. Such restrictions can hinder company performance abroad. For example, host countries may require companies to obtain permits to import or export. They may devise complex regulations that complicate transportation and logistical activities or limit the options for entry strategies. In China's huge telecommunications market, the government requires foreign investors to seek joint ventures with local firms; local operations cannot be wholly owned by foreigners. The government's goal is to ensure that China maintains control of its telecommunications industry and obtains inward transfer of technology, knowledge, and capital.[33]

MARKETING AND DISTRIBUTION LAWS These laws determine which practices are allowed in advertising, promotion, and distribution. For example, Finland, France, and Norway prohibit cigarette advertising on television. Germany largely prohibits comparative advertising, in which a product is promoted as superior to a competing brand. Many countries cap the prices of critical goods and services, such as food and health care. Such constraints affect firms' marketing and profitability. Product safety and liability laws hold manufacturers and sellers responsible for damage, injury, or death caused by defective products. In the case of violations, firms and company executives are subject to legal penalties such as fines or imprisonment, as well as civil lawsuits. Product liability laws in developing countries are generally weak. Some firms take advantage of these weaknesses. For example, as litigants pursued tobacco companies in Europe and the United States, these companies shifted much of their marketing of cigarettes to developing countries.

LAWS ON INCOME REPATRIATION MNEs earn profits in various countries and typically seek ways to transfer these funds back to their home country. However, in some countries, governments devise laws that restrict such transfers. The action is often taken to preserve hard currencies, such as euros, U.S. dollars, or Japanese yen. Repatriation restrictions limit the amount of net income or dividends that firms can remit to their home-country headquarters. While such constraints often discourage inward FDI, they are common in countries experiencing a shortage of hard currencies.

ENVIRONMENTAL LAWS Governments enact laws to preserve natural resources; to combat pollution and the abuse of air, earth, and water resources; and to ensure health and safety. In Germany, for example, companies must follow strict recycling regulations. Manufacturers and distributors bear the burden of recycling product packaging. Governments usually try to balance environmental laws against the impact such regulations may have on employment, entrepreneurship, and economic development. For example, environmental standards in Mexico are looser or less well enforced than in some other countries, but the Mexican government is reluctant to strengthen them for fear that foreign MNEs may reduce their investments there.

CONTRACT LAWS International contracts attach rights, duties, and obligations to the contracting parties. Contracts are used in five main types of business transactions: (1) sale of goods or services, especially large sales; (2) distribution of the firm's products through foreign distributors; (3) licensing and franchising—that is, a contractual relationship that allows a firm to use another company's intellectual property, marketing tools, or other assets for a fee; (4) FDI, especially in collaboration with a foreign entity, in order to create and operate a foreign subsidiary; and (5) joint ventures and other types of cross-border collaborations.

Numerous countries are attempting to develop an international standard for international sales contracts. The United Nations Convention on Contracts for the International Sale of Goods (CISG) is a uniform text of law for international sales contracts. More than 75 countries are now party to the CISG, covering about three-quarters of all world trade. Unless excluded by the express terms of a contract, the CISG is deemed to supersede any otherwise applicable domestic law(s) regarding an international sales transaction.

INTERNET AND E-COMMERCE REGULATIONS Internet and e-commerce regulations are the new frontier in legal systems. As highlighted in the *Global Trend*, these laws are still evolving. Firms that undertake e-commerce in countries with weak laws face considerable risk. In China, for example, the government has developed legislation to ensure security and privacy due to the rapid spread of the Internet and e-commerce. Many consumer-privacy laws have yet to be enacted, and progress has been delayed on the development of methods to protect private data from criminal or competitive eyes. Protections for online contracting methods have been implemented with the recent adoption of e-signature laws. Emergent e-signature laws offer protections for online contracting.

INADEQUATE OR UNDERDEVELOPED LEGAL SYSTEMS Just as laws and regulations can lead to country risk, an underdeveloped regulatory environment or poor enforcement of existing laws can also pose challenges for the firm. Worldwide, safeguards for intellectual property are often inadequate. Regulations to protect intellectual property may exist on paper but not be adequately enforced. When an innovator invents a new product, develops new computer software, or produces some other type of intellectual property, another party may copy and sell the innovation without paying the inventor. As reported in the opening story, Russia's legal framework is relatively weak and inconsistent. Russian courts lack substantial experience ruling on business matters. Due to the unpredictable and potentially harmful legal environment, Western firms frequently abandon joint ventures and other business initiatives in Russia.[34]

Inadequate legal protection is most common in developing economies, but can be a factor in developed economies as well. The most recent global financial crisis was precipitated, in part, by insufficient regulation in the financial and banking sectors of the United States, Europe, and other regions. Government authorities have been considering how regulatory structures can be revamped to provide a sounder footing for connecting global savers and investors, as well as reliable methods

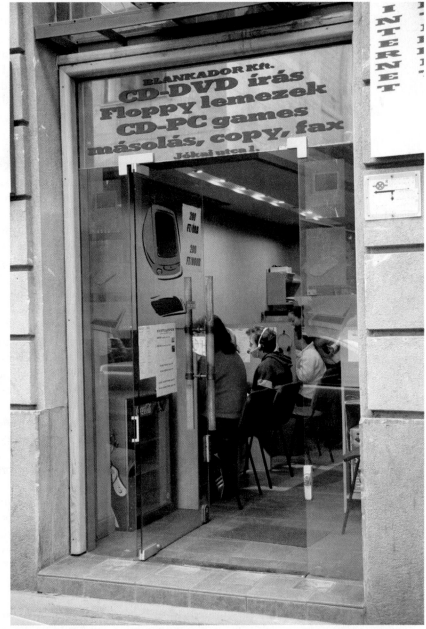

Source: Demetrio Carrasco © Dorling Kindersley

Governments around the world are contemplating ways to tax and regulate e-commerce and the Internet. Pictured is an Internet café in Budapest, Hungary.

for managing financial instability. Governments seek to expand regulation, provide new means to increase transparency and information flows, and find ways to harmonize regulatory policies and legal frameworks across national borders. Banks and other financial institutions are revising disclosure rules to make information more specific and consistent. Some experts believe the financial crisis does not imply that more regulation is needed. Rather, they argue for more intelligent regulation, better enforcement of existing regulation, and better supervision of financial institutions.[35]

Country Risk Arising from the Home-Country Legal Environment

Does country risk arise only due to the host country's legal environment? Home-country legal systems are just as relevant. **Extraterritoriality** refers to the application of home-country laws to persons or conduct outside national borders. In most cases, such laws are intended to prosecute individuals or firms located abroad for some type of wrongdoing.

Extraterritoriality
Application of home-country laws to persons or conduct outside national borders.

Examples of extraterritoriality in international business abound. A French court ordered Yahoo! to bar access to Nazi-related items on its Web site in France and to remove related messages and images from its sites accessible in the United States.[36] In 2001, the United States enacted the Patriot Act, authorizing the U.S. government to seize funds held by non-U.S. banks in the United States. The European Union pursued the U.S. firm Microsoft for perceived monopolistic practices in the marketing of its operating system software. Monopolies are considered harmful because they can unfairly restrain trade. Businesses generally oppose extraterritoriality because it tends to increase the costs and uncertainty of operating abroad.

THE FOREIGN CORRUPT PRACTICES ACT (FCPA) Passed by the U.S. government in 1977, the Foreign Corrupt Practices Act (FCPA) banned firms from offering bribes to foreign parties in order to secure or retain business. The FCPA was enacted after more than 400 U.S. companies admitted paying bribes to foreign government officials and politicians. The Act was strengthened in 1998 to cover foreign firms and managers who act in furtherance of corrupt payments while in the United States. The FCPA also requires companies with securities listed in the United States to meet U.S. accounting provisions. Such firms must devise and maintain accounting systems that control and record all company expenditures.[37] One problem with the FCPA is that a "bribe" is not clearly defined. For example, the Act draws a distinction between bribery and "facilitation" payments; the latter may be permissible if making such payments does not violate local laws.[38]

Some U.S. managers argue the FCPA harms their interests because foreign competitors often are not constrained by such laws. FCPA criminal and civil penalties are increasingly harsh. Firms can be fined up to $2 million, while individuals can be fined up to $100,000 and face imprisonment. Recently, the U.S. Justice Department stepped up FCPA prosecutions against smaller companies and non-U.S. firms that do business in the United States. In 2010, the United States settled allegations against Panalpina, a Switzerland-based logistics company, regarding claims it had violated the FCPA in Nigeria to secure energy contracts.[39]

ANTIBOYCOTT REGULATIONS Such rules prevent companies from participating in restrictive trade practices or boycotts imposed by foreign countries against other countries. Firms are not allowed to participate in boycotts to the extent they discriminate against others on the basis of race, religion, gender, or national origin. For example, some Arab nations have long boycotted Israel because of political disagreements and made it a requirement for any foreign company that wishes to do business with the Arab countries to also observe this boycott. The antiboycott regulations passed by the U.S. Congress in 1977 effectively prohibit U.S. firms from participating in the boycott of Israel when operating in these Arab nations.

ACCOUNTING AND REPORTING LAWS Accounting practices and standards differ greatly around the world, posing difficulties for firms. For example, when assigning value to stocks and other securities, most countries use the lower of cost or market value. Brazil, however, encourages firms to adjust portfolio valuations because of historically high inflation. When valuing physical assets such as plant and equipment, Canada uses historical costs. Some Latin American countries use inflation-adjusted market value. While firms can write off uncollectible accounts in the United States, the allowance is not permitted in France, Spain, and South Africa. Research and development costs are expensed as incurred in most of the world but capitalized in South Korea and Spain. Belgium, Malaysia, and Italy use both conventions.

Transparency
The degree to which companies regularly reveal substantial information about their financial condition and accounting practices.

TRANSPARENCY IN FINANCIAL REPORTING The timing and transparency of financial reporting vary widely around the world. **Transparency** is the degree to which firms regularly reveal substantial information about their financial condition and accounting practices. In the United States, public firms are required to report financial results to stockholders and to the Securities and Exchange Commission each quarter. In much of the world, however, financial statements are prepared annually or less often, and they often lack transparency. Transparency improves business decision making and the ability of citizens to hold companies accountable.

GLOBAL TREND

Evolving Legal Aspects of E-Commerce

While still a fraction of world trade, international e-commerce is growing fast. E-commerce reduces traditional barriers of distance from markets.

However, most countries lack adequate legal protections, leaving e-commerce fraught with thorny issues. For example, individuals or firms that place information, photographs, or music online may be violating the intellectual property laws of some countries but not others. Although electronic contracts are in digital format, existing contract law typically covers only paper documents. Consumers who use the Internet to make purchases with credit cards may risk identity theft and fraud.

Taxation of international e-commerce is complex because of the difficulty of defining merchandise sold online. Do software, books, and music constitute products— or services? For tax purposes, the two categories are usually treated differently. E-commerce can also circumvent tariffs and other trade barriers. Most e-commerce is free of customs duties because it is too difficult to apply them. A related problem is identifying the location of a sale. When a customer in Japan buys software from Microsoft's Web site, which is based in the United States, does the sale originate in Japan or the United States? Such questions affect not only taxation but also legal jurisdiction in the event of disputes between buyers and sellers.

E-commerce laws are evolving differently in different countries and represent the distinct values, culture, and approaches of each locale. The resulting inconsistency can create conflicts between national jurisdictions. When creating e-commerce law, some governments favor strong control and regulation. Others opt for a liberal, hands-off approach. The European Union aims to accelerate integration of the EU single market through increased e-commerce in Europe, to create a "single digital market."

Strong legal frameworks are needed to ensure trust between buyers and sellers. Experts argue that evolving regulatory frameworks should be governed by consistent principles that lead to predictable results, regardless of where buyers and sellers reside. Law enforcement authorities need to cooperate cross-nationally to reduce online crime. Governments must devise frameworks that ensure the security of electronic payment systems and the privacy of online data but are not so restrictive as to hinder the promise of international e-commerce.

Several international organizations are driving efforts to devise internationally appropriate laws. For example, the *United Nations Commission on International Trade Law (UNCITRAL)* developed the Model Law on Electronic Commerce to ensure that online transactions and legal documents are legally recognized and that a course of action is available to enforce them. The UNCITRAL model is only a guide, and national governments are not bound by it.

Sources: C. Primo Braga, "E-Commerce Regulation: New Game, New Rules?," *Quarterly Review of Economics and Finance* 45, no. 2/3 (2005): 541–558; *Economist*, "The Coming Retail Boom," February 4, 2012, p. 72; George Takach, "E-Procurement E-Performance," *Summit*, May/June 2008, pp. 16–17; UNCITRAL Model Law on Electronic Commerce Guide to Enactment, retrieved from United Nations Web site at http://www.un.org; Ling Zhu and Sherry Thatcher, "National Information Ecology: A New Institutional Economics Perspective on Global E-Commerce Adoption," *Journal of Electronic Commerce Research* 11, no. 1 (2010): 53–72.

In 2010, the U.S. Congress passed the Dodd–Frank Wall Street Reform and Consumer Protection Act, which aims to increase transparency in the United States financial sector. Passed in response to the late-2000s recession, the Act created an oversight board that monitors banking activities. It aims to reduce financial risk-taking by restricting certain banking activities and requiring bank executives to be responsible for compliance. Running to more than 2,000 pages of new regulations, banks have condemned the Act for imposing too many regulatory costs. U.S. affiliates of foreign multinational banks must comply with the Act's provisions. In an effort to avoid rigid financial requirements, some European banks are reducing their banking activities in the United States. In 2011, the European Union introduced the Basel III global regulatory standard, which aims to increase the quality and transparency of the capital base of European banks. U.S. banks will be required to comply with the new Basel III rules.[40]

Ethical Connections

Many countries lack antibribery laws for international transactions. The *Organisation for Economic Cooperation and Development* recently called for a ban on "grease payments," small-scale bribes intended to speed up telephone hookups, government paperwork, and other everyday matters in international commerce. A culture of grease payments and other corruption is corrosive, harming the rule of law and sustainable economic development.

Managing Country Risk

How should managers respond to country risk? In the discussion that follows, we highlight several specific strategies managers can employ to manage country risk.

Proactive Environmental Scanning

Anticipating country risk requires advance research. Initially, managers develop a comprehensive understanding of the political and legal environment in target countries. They then engage in *scanning* to assess potential risks and threats to the firm. Scanning allows the firm to improve practices in ways that conform with local laws and political realities and to create a positive environment for business success.[41]

One of the best sources of intelligence in the scanning process is employees working in the host country. They are knowledgeable about evolving events and can evaluate them in the context of local history, culture, and politics. Embassy and trade association officials regularly develop and analyze intelligence on the local political scene. Some consulting firms, such as PRS Group (www.prsgroup.com) and Business Entrepreneurial Risk Intelligence (www.beri.com), specialize in country-risk assessment and provide guidelines for appropriate strategic responses. Once the firm has researched the political climate and contingencies of the target environment, it develops and implements strategies to facilitate effective management of relations with policymakers and other helpful contacts in the host country. The firm then takes steps to minimize its exposure to country risks that threaten its performance.

Strict Adherence to Ethical Standards

Ethical behavior is important not only for its own sake but also because it helps insulate the firm from some country risks that less-conscientious firms encounter. Those companies that engage in questionable practices or operate outside the law naturally invite redress from the governments of the host countries where they do business.

Alliances with Qualified Local Partners

A practical approach to reducing country risk is to enter target markets in collaboration with a knowledgeable and reliable local partner. Qualified local partners are better informed about local conditions and better situated to establish stable relations with the local government. Western firms often enter China and Russia by partnering with local firms that assist in navigating complex legal and political landscapes.

Protection through Legal Contracts

A legal contract spells out the rights and obligations of each party. Contract law varies widely from country to country, and firms must adhere to local standards. For example, a Canadian firm doing business in Belgium generally must comply with the laws of both Belgium and Canada, as well as with the evolving laws of the European Union.

Firms generally employ any of three approaches for resolving international disputes:

1. *Conciliation* is the least adversarial method. It is a formal process of negotiation with the objective to resolve differences in a friendly manner. The parties in a dispute employ a conciliator, who meets separately with each in an attempt to resolve their differences. Parties can also employ mediation committees—groups of informed citizens—to resolve civil disputes.
2. *Arbitration* is a process in which a neutral third party hears both sides of a case and decides in favor of one party or the other, based on an objective assessment of the facts. Compared to litigation, arbitration saves time and expense, while maintaining the confidentiality of proceedings. Arbitration is often handled by supranational organizations, such as the International Chamber of Commerce in Paris or the Stockholm Chamber of Commerce.
3. *Litigation* is the most adversarial approach and occurs when one party files a lawsuit against another in order to achieve desired ends. Litigation is most common in the United States; most other countries favor arbitration or conciliation.

CLOSING CASE Political, Legal, and Ethical Dilemmas in the Global Pharmaceutical Industry

The $900 billion global pharmaceutical industry is dominated by about ten firms; five are headquartered in the United States, two in the United Kingdom, two in Switzerland, and one in Israel. Examples include GlaxoSmithKline (United Kingdom, www.gsk.com), Novartis AG (Switzerland, www.novartis.com), Teva (Israel, www.tevapharm.com), Merck (United States, www.merck.com), and Pfizer (United States, www.pfizer.com). Europe and the United States account for roughly 25 percent and 50 percent of worldwide pharmaceutical sales, respectively. The industry is confronted with several challenges.

High Cost of Research and Development

Pharmaceutical firms engage in large-scale, intensive R&D to create and market drugs meant to treat everything from cancer to hair loss. Thousands of pharmaceutical drugs allow people to live longer and healthier lives. Europe and the United States are home to the major pharmaceutical firms and to industry R&D. They benefit from strong patent protection laws and abundant investment capital. According to industry statistics, it takes 12 to 15 years, and more than $800 million in R&D expense, to successfully bring a new pharmaceutical compound to market. Only 1 in 10,000 investigated and tested compounds is approved for patient use. Only three out of every ten new, approved compounds are successful enough to recover their R&D costs. For their successful products, pharmaceutical firms must charge prices high enough to recover not only the high costs of product development, but also to recover the cost of products that never achieve profitability.

Limited Protection for Intellectual Property

Governments grant patents and provide other types of protections for intellectual property. In practice, such protection is frequently inadequate, especially in developing countries. India has a history of weak intellectual property protection, which has discouraged R&D and innovation. It is one of the world's poorest countries, and very few of its citizens can afford health care or medications. In 1972, a major revision to the Indian Patent Act revoked all patents for medicines. Following this dramatic shift, foreign-branded pharmaceutical manufacturers abandoned India, and numerous pharmaceutical "chop shops" emerged. The new firms freely infringed on drug patents and engaged in a selling "free-for-all" in the huge Indian pharmaceutical market. They reverse-engineered patented compounds developed by European and U.S. companies and began selling the pirated generics at drastically lower prices. The foreign pharmaceuticals launched legal actions against these violations but, in the absence of strict patent protection and with little local competition, India's generic drug manufacturers flourished.

The Challenge from Generic Brands

Under World Trade Organization (WTO) rules, a patent protects a drug inventor from competition for up to 20 years. In reality, when the lengthy testing and approval phase is factored in, the effective life of a drug patent is often less than 12 years. The manufacturer typically has only 5 to 8 years of patent protection in which to recover its investment before generic manufacturers can legally enter the market. Once a patent expires, generic manufacturers have the right to produce medications originally invented by major pharmaceuticals. Generic manufacturers typically sell the medications that they produce at very low prices. Patent protections are important because they encourage innovation by allowing inventors a limited opportunity to recover their

R&D investments. However, patent protection laws governing pharmaceuticals differ substantially around the world.

A *branded compound* is produced under patent protection by a pharmaceutical manufacturer that has undertaken expensive R&D to invent the drug. Each year, pharmaceutical firms typically invest some 20 percent of revenues into R&D to invent new compounds. "Approved generic compounds," manufactured in countries with strict bio-equivalency regulations, are comparable to branded compounds in safety, efficacy, and intended use. The main reason that generic manufacturers can charge lower prices is that they do not incur the high costs of R&D to develop new drugs. Because the medications are already established in the marketplace, generic manufacturers also incur substantially lower marketing and sales expenses.

In the world of generic drugs, Israel-based Teva is the largest manufacturer with global sales of more than $16 billion. Teva and other generic producers have greatly increased their world market share in recent years due to the patent expiration of leading medications and rising demand for medications in developing economies and countries with weak patent protection. In the United States alone, generic medications now account for over half of all dispensed prescriptions. Once a branded compound's patent expires, generic manufacturers, after receiving government approval, begin producing generic versions almost immediately. Retail prices for the compound can fall by as much as 90 percent within 12 to 18 months.

Counterfeit Drugs

Many governments fail to ensure the quality of imported medicines. As a result, a growing industry of counterfeit and bio-inequivalent medications has emerged worldwide. A counterfeit ring from China supplied 1 million fake OneTouch Test Strips (used to treat diabetes) to hundreds of pharmacies in Canada, India, the United States, and numerous other countries. A healthy 22-year-old woman in Argentina died from liver failure after receiving iron injections to treat mild anemia. The medicine she received was a highly toxic counterfeit. In Niger, some 2,500 people died after receiving fake vaccines for meningitis. Recently, European Union officials seized more than 35 million fake pills at ports around Europe, including drugs intended to treat malaria, cancer, cholesterol, and pain.

The United Nations estimates that sales of counterfeit pharmaceuticals exceeds $500 billion annually. Counterfeiting is greatest in countries where regulatory oversight is weakest. The WHO estimates that up to 30 percent of medicines sold in developing countries may be counterfeit. It is estimated that between 200,000 and 300,000 people die each year in China due to counterfeit or substandard medicine.

Internet-based pharmacies are especially dubious. A woman in Canada died of metal poisoning after taking a tainted prescription medicine obtained from an Internet pharmacy. MarkMonitor, an industry watchdog, found that only a fraction of several thousand online pharmacies it examined were legitimate. Many of the pharmacies claiming to be based in Canada and the United States were in fact traced to China, Russia, and India. It is estimated that over 50 percent of medicines sold through the Internet are fake—often containing no or too little of the active ingredient.

Because of the threats posed by counterfeit manufacturers, branded pharmaceutical firms spend significant resources to protect their patents and intellectual property around the world. Branded pharmaceutical manufacturers have pursued legal actions at the WTO and against individual nations. In 1995, the WTO's agreement on Trade-Related Aspects of Intellectual Property Rights (TRIPS) was approved by approximately 150 WTO member countries.

Neglected Therapeutic Areas

A large portion of pharmaceutical research is focused on developing treatments for diseases that can return the cost of capital and generate profits. For these reasons, pharmaceutical firms tend to target the most attractive markets. For example, these firms are much more likely to develop a drug for cancer and central nervous system diseases (such as psychiatric ailments) than for ailments common to poor countries (such as tuberculosis). Some in the pharmaceutical industry believe that R&D is too costly and risky to invest in diseases common to poor countries.

At the same time, governmental and private initiatives have begun to address these market realities by providing incentive packages and public-private partnerships. For example, the Bill and Melinda Gates Foundation (www.gatesfoundation.org) is investing billions of dollars to fight AIDS, tuberculosis, and various infectious diseases that affect developing countries.

Public Scrutiny

The pharmaceutical industry's actions are often subject to public scrutiny. For example, the government of South Africa got into a tussle with several manufacturers of branded AIDS drugs. Because of high prices,

the government sanctioned the importation of nonapproved generics. The reaction from branded pharmaceutical manufacturers was to sue South Africa, which created an international backlash against the firms. Not only did the episode generate much negative publicity for the branded pharmaceutical firms, it made people more aware of the generic drug industry and its potential for helping those affected by the AIDS pandemic. In the wake of the South African debacle, Brazil and several other countries threatened to break patents if pharmaceutical firms did not make their drugs more affordable. In the interest of good public relations, several branded pharmaceutical firms began to offer their AIDS drugs at lower prices in Africa. In all, the pharmaceutical firms have developed at least eighty-eight medicines to treat AIDS and related conditions. The United States and various European governments have provided billions of dollars in subsidies to support AIDS treatment in Africa.

The Future

Without adequate intellectual property protection, the pharmaceutical industry has fewer incentives to invent new drugs. At the same time, consumers in poor countries need access to drugs but can't afford them. Lax intellectual property laws facilitate the production of cheap generic drugs, but without these protections, major pharmaceutical firms have fewer incentives to fund the R&D that results in new treatments for the diseases that plague the world.

Case Questions

1. Specify the types of country risks that pharmaceutical firms face in international business. How do the political and legal systems of countries affect the global pharmaceutical industry?
2. People need medications, but the poor often cannot afford them. Governments may not provide subsidies for health care and medications. Meanwhile, pharmaceutical firms focus their R&D on compounds likely to provide the best returns. What is the proper role of the following groups in addressing these dilemmas: national governments, branded pharmaceutical firms, and generic manufacturers?
3. Consult www.phrma.org, The Pharmaceutical Research and Manufacturers of America. What steps is the branded industry taking to address the various ethical issues it faces, such as providing affordable drugs to poor countries?
4. Consult the TRIPS agreement at the WTO portal (www.wto.org). What are the latest developments regarding this treaty? What types of protection does this treaty provide to pharmaceutical firms? What enforcement mechanisms does TRIPS provide for ensuring that these protections will be carried out?
5. Recommend a strategy that management at a large pharmaceutical firm should employ to reduce the likelihood of political and legal risks that such firms face. What steps should management take to minimize its exposure to such risks?

Sources: "Competitive Landscape," *U.S. Pharma & Healthcare Report*, no. 4 (2011): 63–69; Robert Coopman, "The Road Ahead for Research-Based Drug Companies," *Chain Drug Review*, January 2, 2012, p. 71; Chris Enyinda, Chris Mbah, and Alphonso Ogbuehi, "An Empirical Analysis of Risk Mitigation in the Pharmaceutical Industry Supply Chain: A Developing-Country Perspective," *Thunderbird International Business Review* 52, no. 1 (2010): 54–69; Sarah Houlton, "Cracking Down on Counterfeit Drugs," *Pharmaceutical Executive*, February 2009, p. 18; Nancy Shute, "Fake Medications Are a Growing Threat," *US News and World Report*, August 21, 2007, retrieved from http://www.health.usnews.com; P. Trouiller et al., "Drug Development for Neglected Diseases," *Lancet* 359 (June 2002): 2188–2194; G. Glass, "Patent Attack," *Pharmaceutical Executive* 25, no. 4 (2005): 76–81; "Survey: Prescription for Change," *Economist*, June 18, 2005; "Business: Big Generic Pharma; Pharmaceuticals," *Economist*, July 30, 2005; "Business: Corrupted; Medications and Intellectual Property," *Economist*, July 23, 2005; IMAP, *Pharmaceuticals & Biotech Industry Global Report—2011*, retrieved from http://www.imap.com; Pharmaceutical Research and Manufacturers Association of America, "What Goes Into the Cost of Prescription Drugs?," June 2005, retrieved from http://www.phrma.org; World Health Organization, "Counterfeit Medicines," Fact Sheet No. 275, November 14, 2006, retrieved from http://www.wto.int; Peter Pitts, "Counterfeit Drugs and China," 2009, retrieved from the Center for Medicine in the Public Interest Web site http://www.cmpi.org; U.S. Food and Drug Administration, "Counterfeit Drugs," 2009, retrieved from http://www.fda.gov/counterfeit/.

Note: Kevin McGarry assisted in the development of this case.

CHAPTER ESSENTIALS

MyManagementLab

Go to **mymanagementlab.com** to complete the problems marked with this icon ⭐.

Key Terms

country risk   166
extraterritoriality   181

legal system   168
political system   168

rule of law   173
transparency   182

Summary

In this chapter, you learned about:

1. The nature of country risk

International business is influenced by political and legal systems. **Country risk** refers to exposure to potential loss or to adverse effects on company operations and profitability caused by developments in national political and legal environments.

2. Political and legal environments in international business

A **political system** is a set of formal institutions that constitute a government. A **legal system** is a system for interpreting and enforcing laws. Adverse developments in political and legal systems increase country risk. These can result from events such as a change in government or the creation of new laws or regulations.

3. Political systems

The three major political systems are totalitarianism, socialism, and democracy. They provide frameworks within which laws are established and nations are governed. Democracy is characterized by private property rights and limited government. Socialism occurs mainly as social democracy. Today, most governments combine elements of socialism and democracy. Totalitarianism is associated with command economies, socialism with mixed economies, and democracy with market economies.

4. Legal systems

There are four major legal systems: common law, civil law, religious law, and mixed systems. The **rule of law** implies a legal system in which laws are clear, understood, respected, and fairly enforced.

5. Participants in political and legal systems

Actors include government, which exists at the national, state, and municipal levels. The World Trade Organization and the United Nations are typical of international organizations that influence international business. Special interest groups serve specific industries or country groupings and include labor unions, environmental organizations, and consumers that promote particular viewpoints. Companies deal with competing firms in foreign markets, which may undertake political activities aimed at influencing market entry and firm performance.

6. Types of country risk produced by political systems

Governments impose constraints on corporate operating methods in areas such as production, marketing, and distribution. Governments may expropriate or confiscate the assets of foreign firms. Governments or groups of countries also impose embargoes and sanctions that restrict trade with certain countries. Boycotts are an attempt to halt trade or prevent business activities and are usually pursued for political reasons. War and revolution have serious consequences for international firms. Terrorism has become more salient recently.

7. Types of country risk produced by legal systems

Foreign investment laws restrict FDI in various ways. Such laws include controls on operating forms and practices, regulations affecting marketing and distribution, restrictions on income repatriation, environmental laws, and Internet and e-commerce regulations. **Extraterritoriality** is the application of home-country laws to conduct outside of national borders. Antiboycott regulations prevent companies from participating in restrictive trade practices. Accounting and reporting laws vary around the world. **Transparency** is the degree to which firms reveal substantial and regular information about their financial condition and accounting practices.

8. **Managing country risk**

Successful management requires developing an understanding of the political and legal context abroad. The firm should scan the environment proactively. It should strictly adhere to ethical standards. Country risk is also managed by allying with qualified local partners abroad. The firm should seek protection through legal contracts.

Test Your Comprehension AACSB: Reflective Thinking Skills

1. What are the components of political systems? What are the components of legal systems? How do these systems lead to country risk?

2. Distinguish between totalitarianism, socialism, and democracy. What are the implications of each for internationalizing firms?

3. What are the specific characteristics of democracy? How do these characteristics facilitate international business?

4. Describe the major types of legal systems. Which systems are most widely encountered?

⭐ 5. Who are the major actors in political and legal systems? Which participant do you believe is most influential in international business?

⭐ 6. Describe proactive actions that firms can take to minimize country risk.

Apply Your Understanding AACSB: Reflective Thinking Skills, Communication Abilities, Ethical Understanding and Reasoning Abilities

1. Country risk refers to the ways governments restrict, or fail to restrict, business activities. The nature of such restrictions varies around the world. In each country, national economic success substantially depends on the quality of laws and regulations. Government must strike the right balance—too little regulation promotes uncertainty; too much causes hardship. Country risk is revealed in various ways:

   • Foreign investment laws
   • Controls on operating forms and practices
   • Environmental laws
   • Contract laws
   • E-commerce laws
   • Underdeveloped legal systems
   • Accounting and reporting laws

   Conduct research online and give specific examples of each type of country risk. Describe how each might help or hinder company activities.

2. Suppose you get a job at Aoki Corporation, a firm that manufactures glass for industrial and consumer markets. Aoki is a large firm but has little international experience. Senior managers are considering a plan to move Aoki's manufacturing to China, Mexico, or Eastern Europe, and to begin selling its glass in Latin America and Europe. However, they know little about the country risks that Aoki may encounter. Describe how each of the following factors might contribute to country risk as Aoki ventures abroad: foreign investment laws, controls on operating forms and practices, and laws regarding repatriation of income, environment, and contracts.

3. *Ethical Dilemma*: The United States imposed a trade and investment embargo on Iran. U.S. citizens were barred from doing business with Iran. Proponents argue the embargo is justified because Iran has supported terrorism and is developing nuclear weapons. However, critics condemn the trade sanctions for several reasons. First, they argue the sanctions represent a "double standard," as the United States supports other countries that have engaged in terrorism and other bad behaviors. Second, the best way to nurture healthy dissent and civil society in Iran may be to engage the country, rather than restrict economic relationships. Third, the sanctions harm the Iranian people, who are deprived of the benefits of trade with the United States. Fourth, the sanctions are largely ineffective since other countries supply Iran with products it needs. Finally, the sanctions harm U.S. companies, especially oil and gas firms, which cannot do business with Iran. What is your view? Using the Ethical Framework in Chapter 5, analyze the arguments for and against trade with Iran. Can the United States, acting alone, compel desired changes in Iran by imposing sanctions? Justify your answer.

INTERNET EXERCISES
(http://www.globalEDGE.msu.edu)

AACSB: Reflective Thinking Skills, Communication Abilities, Use of Information Technology, Ethical Understanding and Reasoning Abilities

Refer to Chapter 1, page 24, for instructions on how to access and use globalEDGE™.

1. Supranational organizations such as the World Bank (www .worldbank.org) and the World Trade Organization (www .wto.org) oversee much of the legal framework within which the world trading system operates. Political frameworks for industries or country groupings are influenced by organizations such as the Organization of Petroleum Exporting Countries (www.opec.org) and the Organisation for Economic Co-operation and Development (www.oecd.org). Using globalEDGE™ and the online portals cited here, address the following question: What is the goal of each organization, and how does it go about achieving its goal? By viewing the news and press releases at each Web site, summarize the latest initiatives of each organization.

2. When companies venture abroad, managers seek information on the legal and political environments in each country. This information is available from various Web sources, as illustrated in the following exercises. (I) Suppose you want to sign up distributors in the European Union and want to learn about EU contract law. What should you do? Consult the globalEDGE™ portal to learn about EU trade and contract laws. Try the following: At globalEDGE™, click Reference Desk, then Global Resource Directory, then Trade Law. Describe the resources there for learning about contract law in Europe. (II) The Central Intelligence Agency's portal provides up-to-date information about national governments and political environments. Go to www.cia.gov, click on World Factbook, and summarize the political environment in each of China, Colombia, France, and Russia.

3. Freedom House is a nonprofit organization that monitors the state of freedom worldwide. It conducts an annual "Freedom in the World Survey," which you can view at www.freedomhouse.org. The survey compares the state of political rights and civil liberties in nearly 200 countries over time. Visit the site and answer the following questions: (a) What is the role of political rights and civil liberties in the Freedom House rankings? (b) What can governments in these countries do to facilitate more rapid social and political development? (c) What are the implications of the rankings for companies doing international business?

MyManagementLab

Go to **mymanagementlab.com** for Auto-graded writing questions as well as the following Assisted-graded writing questions:

7-1. What is the relationship between political freedom and economic freedom?

7-2. Summarize how political and legal systems affect international business.

7-3. Mymanagementlab Only – comprehensive writing assignment for this chapter.

Source: Luciano Mortula/Shutterstock

India's Transition to a Liberal Economy

India is a study in contrasts. It is the world's leading emerging economy in information technology and e-business. However, India is awash in trade barriers, business regulations, and a powerful bureaucracy. Not only does the Indian federal government impose countless regulations, standards, and administrative hurdles on businesses, each of India's twenty-eight states also imposes its own local bureaucracy and red tape. Import taxes and controls on foreign investment are substantial, with tariffs averaging over 15 percent on many products, compared to less than 4 percent in Europe, Japan,

and the United States. Hundreds of commodities, from cement to household appliances, can be imported only after receiving government approval. Licensing fees, testing procedures, and other hurdles can be costly to importers.

Since the early 1980s, however, India's government has been liberalizing the nation's regulatory regime. The government has abolished many import licenses and reduced tariffs substantially. It is freeing the economy from state control by selling many state enterprises to the private sector and to foreign investors.

CHAPTER 8

Government Intervention in International Business

LEARNING OBJECTIVES *In this chapter, you will learn about the following:*

1. The nature of government intervention
2. Rationale for government intervention
3. Instruments of government intervention
4. Consequences of government intervention
5. Evolution of government intervention
6. How firms can respond to government intervention

MyManagementLab®

⭐ **Improve Your Grade!**

Over 10 million students improved their results using the Pearson MyLabs.
Visit **mymanagementlab.com** for simulations, tutorials, and end-of-chapter problems.

India has always had a huge sector of small retailers. The country is home to 10 million "mom-and-pop" shops scattered across 500,000 cities and villages. The arrival of big-box retailers triggered a storm of controversy, sparking widespread protests from small merchants. Although Walmart (www.walmart.com) opened its first Indian branch in 2009, the store cannot sell directly to consumers and is restricted to wholesaling. In 2012, the Indian government yielded to political pressure and denied Walmart, Carrefour, and other foreign retailers the opportunity to participate in the country's huge retailing sector. In a joint venture with the Indian firm Bharti Enterprises, Walmart had planned to open numerous stores nationwide.

India's economic revolution is unleashing the country's entrepreneurial potential. The government is establishing Special Economic Zones (SEZs), virtual foreign territories that offer foreign firms the benefits of India's low-cost, high-skilled labor. In a typical SEZ, firms are exempt from trade barriers, sales and income taxes, licensing requirements, FDI restrictions, and customs clearance procedures. Mahindra City is home to an 840-acre SEZ that boasts a $277 million software development center built by Infosys Technologies, India's leading IT firm.

In Europe and North America, the outsourcing of jobs to India has generated calls for protectionism—trade barriers and defensive measures intended to minimize the export of jobs abroad. U.S. and European trade unions host numerous Web sites that denounce outsourcing and offshoring. Trade barriers and government bureaucracy in India, as well as calls for protectionism in Europe and North America, exemplify the complex world of government intervention.

SOURCES: Sy Banerjee, Thomas Hemphill, and Mark Perry, "India Doors To Wal-Mart Shut By Crony Capitalism," *Investors Business Daily*, December 28, 2011, p. A13; E. Bellman, "Wal-Mart Exports Big-Box Concept to India," *Wall Street Journal*, May 29, 2009, p. A4; J. Lamont, "Strike-hit India Eyes Fuel Price Cuts," *Financial Times*, January 8, 2009, retrieved from http://www.ft.com; Central Intelligence Agency, *World Factbook*, 2012, retrieved from http://www.cia.gov/cia/publications/factbook; "Survey: A World of Opportunity," *Economist*, November 13, 2004, p. 15; Oxford Analytica Daily Brief Service, "India: Civil Service Flaws Obstruct Development," January 28, 2010, p. 1; United States Trade Representative, *National Trade Estimate Report on Foreign Trade Barriers: India*, 2012, retrieved from http://www.ustr.gov.

Governments intervene in trade and investment to achieve political, social, or economic objectives. They often create trade barriers that benefit specific interest groups, such as domestic firms, industries, and labor unions. A key rationale is to create jobs by protecting industries from foreign competition. Governments also intervene to support home-grown industries or firms.

Government intervention is at odds with *free trade*, the unrestricted flow of products, services, and capital across national borders. Market liberalization and free trade are best for supporting economic growth and national living standards.[1] One study of more than one hundred countries in the 50 years after 1945 found a strong association between market openness—that is, unimpeded free trade—and economic growth. Countries with an open economy enjoyed average annual per-capita GDP growth of 4.49 percent, while relatively closed countries—those with less free trade—grew at only 0.69 percent per year.[2]

Exhibit 8.1 shows how increasing free trade translates into an expanded production possibilities frontier, moving from PPF1 to PPF2. Let's use Poland as an example. Over time, Poland lowered trade barriers and participated more freely in international trade, adopting the principle of comparative advantage.[3] As Poland expanded its free trade, the country focused on producing and exporting goods it was best suited to produce, and importing those goods that other nations produce more efficiently. The end result was that Poland's production possibilities frontier for products and services shifted outward (Exhibit 8.1). Due to growing free trade, Poland began

EXHIBIT 8.1

Benefits of Free Trade: Outward Shift of Production Possibilities Frontier for Products and Services

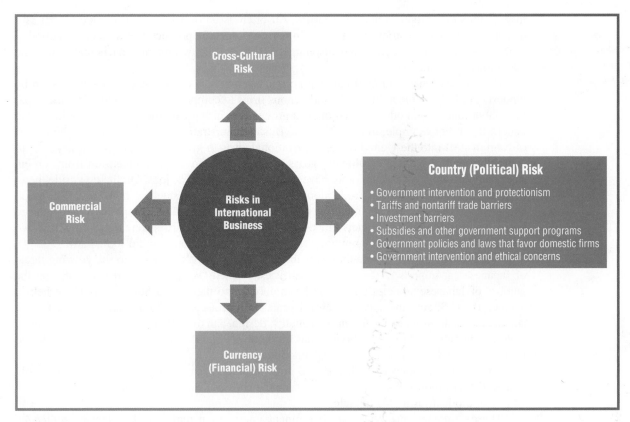

EXHIBIT 8.2

Government Intervention as a Component of Country Risk

to use its resources more efficiently, generating more overall profits for firms and workers, and, in turn, acquiring more resources with which to import the goods that Polish consumers desire.

As it gradually embraced free trade, Poland's average annual income rose, from about $1,625 in 1990 to more than $14,000 in 2012. These gains did not occur without some turmoil—unemployment in Poland increased in some industries as jobs producing certain goods shifted to other countries better suited to make those goods. However, free trade's positive effects substantially outweighed the negative ones.[4] Free trade provides enormous benefits for economic growth and the welfare of nations worldwide.

In reality, however, governments intervene in business and the international marketplace in ways that obstruct the free flow of trade and investment. Intervention alters the competitive position of companies and industries and the status of citizens. As highlighted in Exhibit 8.2, intervention is an important dimension of country risk. In this chapter, we examine the nature, rationale, and consequences of government intervention. We also describe what companies can do to enhance international performance in the face of government intervention worldwide.

 ## The Nature of Government Intervention

Government intervention is often motivated by **protectionism**, which refers to national economic policies designed to restrict free trade and protect domestic industries from foreign competition. Protectionism is typically manifested by tariffs, nontariff barriers such as quotas, and arbitrary administrative rules designed to discourage imports. A **tariff** (also known as a *duty*) is a tax imposed by a government on imported products, effectively increasing the cost of acquisition for the customer. A **nontariff trade barrier** is a government policy, regulation, or procedure that impedes trade through means other than explicit tariffs. Trade barriers are enforced as products pass through **customs**, the checkpoints at the ports of entry in each country where government officials

Protectionism
National economic policies designed to restrict free trade and protect domestic industries from foreign competition.

Tariff
A tax imposed on imported products, effectively increasing the cost of acquisition for the customer.

Nontariff trade barrier
A government policy, regulation, or procedure that impedes trade through means other than explicit tariffs.

Customs
Checkpoints at the ports of entry in each country where government officials inspect imported products and levy tariffs.

Quota
A quantitative restriction placed on imports of a specific product over a specified period of time.

inspect imported products and levy tariffs. An often-used form of nontariff trade barrier is a **quota**, a quantitative restriction placed on imports of a specific product over a specified period of time. Government intervention may also target FDI flows via investment barriers that restrict the operations of foreign firms.

Government intervention affects the normal operation of economic activity in a nation by hindering or helping the ability of its indigenous firms to compete internationally. Often companies, labor unions, and other special interest groups convince governments to adopt policies that benefit them. For example, in the 2000s, the Bush administration imposed tariffs on the import of foreign steel into the United States. The rationale was to give the U.S. steel industry time to restructure and revive itself following years of decline due to tough competition from foreign steel manufacturers. The action may have saved hundreds of U.S. jobs. On the downside, however, the tariffs also increased production costs for firms that use steel, such as Ford, Whirlpool, and General Electric. Higher material costs made these firms less competitive and reduced prospects for selling their products in world markets.[5] The steel tariffs were removed within two years, but in the process of attempting to do good, the government also did some harm.

Another example of intervention was the U.S. government's response to the growing threat of Japanese car imports in the 1980s, when it established "voluntary export restraints" on the number of Japanese vehicles that could be imported into the United States. This move helped insulate the U.S. auto industry for several years. In a protected environment, however, Detroit automakers had less incentive to improve quality, design, and overall product appeal. Government intervention motivated by protectionism has been one of several factors that, over time, weakened Detroit's ability to compete in the global auto industry.

Protectionist policies may also lead to price inflation because tariffs can restrict the supply of a particular product. Tariffs may also reduce the choices available to buyers by restricting the variety of products available for sale.

These examples illustrate that government intervention may lead to adverse *unintended consequences*—unfavorable outcomes of policies or laws. In a complex world, legislators and policymakers cannot foresee all possible outcomes. The problem of unintended consequences suggests that government intervention should be planned and implemented with great care.

 ## Rationale for Government Intervention

Why does a government intervene in trade and investment activities? There are four main motives.

Tariffs and other forms of intervention allow governments to:

1. **Generate revenue.** For example, the "Hamilton Tariff," enacted July 4, 1789, was the second statute passed by the newly founded United States, providing revenue for the federal government. Today, Ghana and Sierra Leone generate more than 25 percent of their total government revenue from tariffs.
2. **Ensure citizen safety, security, and welfare.** For example, governments pass laws to prevent importation of harmful products such as contaminated food.
3. **Pursue economic, political, or social objectives.** In most cases, tariffs and similar forms of intervention are intended to promote job growth and economic development.
4. **Serve company and industrial interests.** Governments may devise regulations to stimulate development of home-grown industries.

Special interest groups often advocate *trade and investment barriers* that protect their interests. Consider the recent trade dispute between Mexico and the United States over Mexican cement. The U.S. government imposed duties of about $50 per ton on the import of Mexican cement after U.S. cement makers lobbied Congress. The stakes were huge, as Mexican imports can reach 10 percent of U.S. domestic cement consumption. Mexico proposed substituting import quotas in place of the tariffs. The two governments have negotiated for years to resolve the dispute.[6]

Trade and investment barriers can be considered either defensive or offensive. Governments impose defensive barriers to safeguard industries, workers, and special interest groups and to promote national security. Governments impose offensive barriers to pursue strategic or public policy objectives, such as increasing employment or generating tax revenues. Let's review the specific rationale for government intervention.

Defensive Rationale

Four major defensive motives are particularly relevant: protection of the nation's economy, protection of an infant industry, national security, and national culture and identity.

PROTECTION OF THE NATIONAL ECONOMY Proponents argue that firms in advanced economies cannot compete with those in developing countries that employ low-cost labor. In the opening story, labor activists called for government intervention to prevent the outsourcing of jobs from Europe and North America to India. Protectionists demand trade barriers to curtail the import of low-priced products, fearing that advanced-economy manufacturers will be undersold, wages will fall, and home-country jobs will be lost.

In response, critics counter that protectionism is at odds with the theory of comparative advantage, according to which nations should engage in more international trade, not less. Trade barriers interfere with country-specific specialization of labor. When countries specialize in the products they can produce best and then trade for the rest, they perform better in the long run, delivering superior living standards to their citizens. Critics also charge that blocking imports reduces the availability and increases the cost of products sold in the home market. Industries cannot access all the input products they need. Finally, protectionism can trigger retaliation, resulting in foreign governments imposing their own trade barriers, which reduces sales prospects for exporters.

PROTECTION OF AN INFANT INDUSTRY In an emerging industry, companies are often inexperienced and lack the latest technologies and know-how. They may also lack the scale typical of larger competitors in established industries abroad. An infant industry may need temporary protection from foreign competitors. Governments can impose temporary trade barriers on foreign imports to ensure that young firms gain a large share of the domestic market. Protecting infant industries has allowed some countries to develop a modern industrial sector. For example, government intervention allowed Japan and South Korea to become dominant players in the global automobile and consumer electronics industries.

Once in place, such protection may be hard to remove. Industry owners and workers tend to lobby to preserve government protection. Infant industries in many countries (especially in Latin America, South Asia, and Eastern Europe) have shown a tendency to remain dependent on government protection for many years. Protected companies may become inefficient, costing the nation's citizens higher taxes and higher prices for the products produced by the protected industry.[7]

NATIONAL SECURITY Countries impose trade restrictions on products viewed as critical to national defense and security, such as military technology and computers that help maintain domestic production in security-related products. For example, Russia blocked a bid by German engineering giant Siemens to purchase the Russian turbine manufacturer OAO Power Machines, on grounds of national security. The Russian government has strict legislation that limits foreign investment in sectors considered vital to Russia's national interests.[8] Countries may also impose **export controls**, government measures intended to manage or prevent the export of certain products or trade with certain countries. For example, many countries prohibit exports of plutonium to North Korea because it can be used to make nuclear weapons. The United States generally blocks exports of nuclear and military technology to countries it deems state sponsors of terrorism, such as Iran, Libya, and Syria.

Export control
A government measure intended to manage or prevent the export of certain products or trade with certain countries.

Ethical Connections

North Korea is a dictatorship with a poor record of human rights and one of the world's lowest living standards. Australia, Canada, the European Union, and the United States have long imposed trade embargos against North Korea, due to national security concerns. International trade is known to improve economic conditions in poor countries, and foreign government sanctions are making North Korea's terrible poverty even worse.

Source: © Guillaume Tunzini/Fotolia

To safeguard its national culture, the French government prevents foreign companies from owning television and movie companies in France. Shown here is Cannes, the site of France's popular film festival.

NATIONAL CULTURE AND IDENTITY Should foreign entities, say the Japanese or the Saudis, be allowed to purchase national landmarks such as the Eiffel Tower or Rockefeller Center? In most countries, certain occupations, industries, and public assets are seen as central to national culture and identity. Governments may impose trade barriers to restrict imports of products or services seen to threaten such national assets. Switzerland has imposed trade barriers to preserve its long-established tradition in watchmaking. In the United States, authorities opposed Japanese investors' purchase of the Seattle Mariners baseball team, because it is viewed as part of the national heritage. France does not allow significant foreign ownership of its TV stations because of concerns about foreign influence on French culture.

Offensive Rationale

Offensive rationales for government intervention fall into two categories: national strategic priorities and increasing employment.

NATIONAL STRATEGIC PRIORITIES Government intervention sometimes aims to encourage the development of industries that bolster the nation's economy. It is a *proactive* variation of the infant industry rationale and related to national industrial policy. Countries with many high-tech or high value-adding industries, such as information technology, pharmaceuticals, car manufacturing, or financial services, create better jobs and higher tax revenues than economies based on low value-adding industries, such as agriculture, textile manufacturing, or discount retailing. Accordingly, governments in Germany, South Korea, and numerous other countries have devised policies that promote the development of relatively desirable industries. The government may provide financing for investment in high-tech or high value-adding industries, encourage citizens to save money to ensure a steady supply of loanable funds for industrial investment, and fund public education to provide citizens the skills and flexibility they need to perform in key industries.[9]

INCREASING EMPLOYMENT Governments often impose import barriers to protect employment in designated industries. Insulating domestic firms from foreign competition stimulates national output, leading to more jobs in the protected industries. The effect is usually strongest in import-intensive industries that employ much labor. For example, the Chinese government has traditionally required foreign companies to enter its huge markets through joint ventures with local Chinese firms. This policy creates jobs for Chinese workers. A joint venture between Shanghai Automotive Industry Corporation (SAIC) and Volkswagen created jobs in China.

 Instruments of Government Intervention

Principal instruments of trade intervention and the traditional forms of protectionism are tariffs and nontariff trade barriers. Individual countries or groups of countries, such as the European Union (http://www.europa.eu), can impose these barriers. In aggregate, barriers constitute a serious impediment to cross-border business. The United Nations estimated that trade barriers alone cost developing countries more than $500 billion in lost trading opportunities with developed countries every year.[10] Exhibit 8.3 highlights the most common forms of government intervention and their effects.

Tariffs

Some countries impose *export tariffs*, taxes on products exported by their own companies. For example, Russia charges a duty on its oil exports with the intention of generating government revenue and maintaining high oil stocks within Russia. The most common type of tariff, however, is the *import tariff*, a tax levied on imported products.

EXHIBIT 8.3 Types and Effects of Government Intervention

Intervention Type	Definition	Practical Effect on Customers, Firms, or Government	Contemporary Examples
Tariff	Tax imposed on imported products.	Increases cost to the importer, exporter, and usually the buyer of the product. Discourages product imports. Generates government revenue.	Switzerland charges a 37% tariff on imported agricultural products. Bolivia charges a 35% tariff on most apparel and textiles.
Quota	Quantitative restriction on imports of a product during a specified period of time.	Gives early importers monopoly power and the ability to charge higher prices. Harms late importers. Usually results in higher prices to the buyer.	Japan maintains strict quotas on the import of leather shoes and various types of seafood.
Local content requirements	Requirement that firms include a minimum percentage of locally-sourced inputs in the production of given products or services.	Discourages imports of raw materials, parts, and supplies, which harms manufacturers' sourcing options. May result in higher costs and lower product quality for buyers.	At least 50% of the value of all cars assembled in Venezuela must be from parts or other inputs produced in Venezuela.
Regulations and technical standards	Safety, health, or technical regulations; labeling requirements.	May hinder the entry of imported products; and reduce the quantity of available products, resulting in higher costs to importers and buyers.	Saudi Arabia bans imports of firearms and used clothing. The EU requires extensive testing on thousands of imported chemicals.
Administrative and bureaucratic procedures	Complex procedures or requirements imposed on importers or foreign investors that hinder trade and investment.	Slows the import of products or services. Hinders or delays firms' investment activities.	Russia imposes extensive inspections and bureaucratic procedures on the import of alcoholic beverages.
FDI and ownership restrictions	Rules that limit the ability of foreign firms to invest in certain industries or acquire local firms.	Limits how much foreigners can invest in a country, and/or the proportion of ownership that foreigners can hold in firms in the country.	In Switzerland, foreign-owned insurance companies must by managed by a Swiss national, and most board members must be European citizens.
Subsidy	Financing or other resources that a government grants to a firm or group of firms, to ensure their survival or success.	Increases the competitive advantage of the grantee, while diminishing the competitive advantages of those that do not receive the subsidy.	Turkey gives export subsidies of up to 20% to local, Turkish producers of wheat and sugar.
Countervailing duty	Duties imposed on products imported into a country to offset subsidies given to producers in the exporting country.	Reduces or eliminates the competitive advantages provided by subsidies.	India imposes countervailing duties on the import of numerous products.
Anti-dumping duty	Tax charged on an imported product whose price is below usual prices in the local market or below the cost to manufacture the product.	Reduces or eliminates the competitive advantage of imported products priced at abnormally low levels.	The United States has imposed anti-dumping duties on imports of low-cost steel, to support U.S.-based steel manufacturers.

Source: Based on the Office of the United States Trade Representative, retrieved from http://www.ustr.gov.

Import tariffs are usually *ad valorem*—that is, they are assessed as a percentage of the value of the imported product. Or a government may impose a *specific tariff*—a flat fee or fixed amount per unit of the imported product—based on weight, volume, or surface area, such as barrels of oil or square meters of fabric. A *revenue tariff* is intended to raise money for the government. A tariff on cigarette imports, for example, produces a steady flow of revenue. A *protective tariff* aims to protect domestic industries from foreign competition. A *prohibitive tariff* is one so high that no one can import any of the items.

The amount of a tariff is determined by examining a product's harmonized code. Products are classified under about 8,000 different unique codes in the *harmonized tariff* or *harmonized code* schedule, a standardized system used worldwide. Without this system, firms and governments might have differing opinions on product definitions and the tariffs charged.

EXHIBIT 8.4 A Sampling of Import Tariffs, Percentages

Country	Average Import Tariff	
	Agricultural Products	Non-agricultural Products
Australia	1.3%	3.0%
Canada	11.3	2.6
China	15.6	8.7
European Union	12.8	4.0
India	31.8	10.1
Japan	17.3	2.5
Mexico	21.5	7.1
United States	4.9	3.3

Note: Exhibit shows the average, most favored nation applied tariff.

Source: Based on *World Tariff Profiles 2011*, World Trade Organization, retrieved from www.wto.org.

Import tariffs can generate substantial revenue for national governments. This helps explain why they are common in developing economies. Even in advanced economies, tariffs provide a significant source of revenue for the government. The United States charges tariffs on many consumer, agricultural, and labor-intensive products. The U.S. typically collects high tariffs (often 48 percent) on imports of basic, low-quality shoes, and low tariffs (just 9 percent) on luxury shoes. Low-income shoe buyers end up paying the highest tariffs. The European Union applies tariffs of up to 191 percent on meat, 118 percent on cereals, and 106 percent on sugar and confectionary products.[11]

Exhibit 8.4 provides a sample of import tariffs in selected countries. Despite its reputation as a challenging market to enter, Japan maintains average tariffs for nonagricultural products at low levels. Under the North American Free Trade Agreement (NAFTA), Canada, Mexico, and the United States have eliminated nearly all tariffs on product imports from each other. However, Mexico maintains significant tariffs with the rest of the world—21.5 percent for agricultural products and 7.1 percent for nonagricultural goods. India's tariffs are relatively high, especially in agriculture, where the average rate is 31.8 percent. India's tariff system lacks transparency, and officially published tariff information is sometimes hard to find. China has reduced its tariffs since joining the World Trade Organization (WTO, www.wto.org) in 2001, but trade barriers remain high in some areas.

In Africa, over half of all workers are employed in agriculture. Significant tariffs and other trade barriers in the advanced economies hinder imports of agricultural goods from Africa, which worsens already-severe poverty in many African countries.

Because high tariffs inhibit free trade and economic growth, governments have tended to reduce them over time. This was the primary goal of the General Agreement on Tariffs and Trade (GATT; now the WTO). Countries as diverse as Chile, Hungary, Turkey, and South Korea have liberalized their previously protected markets, lowering trade barriers and subjecting themselves to greater competition from abroad. Exhibit 8.5 illustrates trends in average world tariff rates over time. Notice that developing economies have been lowering their tariff rates since the early 1980s. Continued reductions represent a major driver of market globalization.

Nontariff Trade Barriers

Nontariff trade barriers are government policies or measures that restrict trade without imposing a direct tax or duty. They include quotas, import licenses, local content requirements, government regulations, and administrative or bureaucratic procedures. The use of nontariff barriers has grown substantially in recent decades. Governments sometimes prefer them because they are easier to conceal from the WTO and other organizations that monitor international trade.

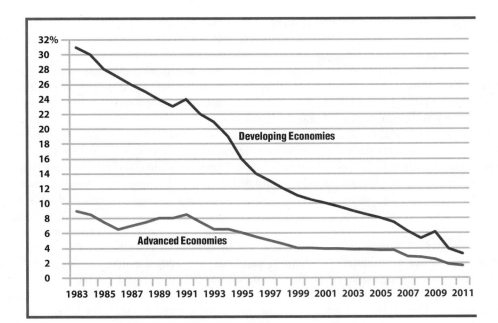

EXHIBIT 8.5

Trends in Average Tariff Rates, Percentages

Source: Based on The World Bank, http://www.data.worldbank.org.

Quotas restrict the physical volume or value of products that firms can import into a country. In a classic type of quota, the U.S. government imposed an upper limit of roughly 2 million pounds on the total amount of sugar that can be imported into the United States each year. Sugar imports that exceed this level face a tariff of several cents per pound. The upside is that U.S. sugar producers are protected from cheaper imports, giving them a competitive edge over foreign sugar producers. The downside is that U.S. consumers and producers of certain types of products, such as Hershey's and Coca-Cola, pay more for sugar. It also means companies that manufacture products containing sugar may save money by moving production to countries that do not impose quotas or tariffs on sugar.

Governments can impose voluntary quotas, under which firms agree to limit exports of certain products. These are also known as *voluntary export restraints*, or VERs. For example, import quotas in the European Union led to an impasse in which millions of Chinese-made garments piled up at ports and borders in Europe. The EU impounded the clothing because China had exceeded the voluntary import quotas it had negotiated with the EU. The action created hardship for European retailers, who had ordered their clothing stocks several months in advance.[12]

Governments occasionally require importing firms to obtain an **import license**, a formal permission to import, which restricts imports in a way that is similar to quotas. (Do not confuse import licenses with "licensing," a strategy for entering foreign markets in which one firm allows another the right to use its intellectual property in return for a fee.) Governments sell import licenses to companies on a competitive basis or grant the licenses on a first-come, first-served basis. This tends to discriminate against smaller firms, which typically lack the resources to purchase them. Obtaining a license can be costly and complicated. In some countries, importers must pay hefty fees to government authorities. In other countries, they must deal with bureaucratic red tape. In Russia a complex web of licensing requirements limits imports of alcoholic beverages. Until the 1990s, the government of India imposed the "license raj," an especially elaborate system of licenses that regulated establishing and running businesses in the country.

Local content requirements require manufacturers to include a minimum of local value added—that is, production that takes place locally. Local content requirements are usually imposed in countries that are members of an economic bloc, such as the EU and NAFTA. The so-called *rules of origin requirement* specifies that a certain proportion of products and supplies, or of intermediate goods used in local manufacturing, must be produced within the bloc. For a car manufacturer, the tires or windshields it purchases from another firm are intermediate goods. When the firm does not meet this requirement, the products become subject to trade barriers that member governments normally impose on nonmember countries. Thus, producers within the NAFTA zone of Canada, Mexico, and the United States pay no tariffs on the products and supplies they obtain from each other, unlike countries such as China or the United Kingdom that

Import license
Government authorization granted to a firm for importing a product.

are not part of NAFTA. Roughly 60 percent of the value of a car manufactured within NAFTA must originate within the NAFTA member countries. If this condition were not met, the product became subject to the tariffs charged to non-NAFTA countries.

Government regulations and technical standards are another type of nontariff trade barrier. Examples include safety regulations for motor vehicles and electrical equipment, health regulations for hygienic food preparation, labeling requirements that indicate a product's country of origin, technical standards for computers, and bureaucratic procedures for customs clearance, including excessive red tape and slow approval processes. The European Union strictly regulates food that has been genetically modified (GM), a policy that blocks some food imports into Europe from the United States. In China, the government requires foreign firms to obtain special permits to import GM foods. Chinese government censorship of material it considers subversive has hindered Google's attempts to enter China's huge Internet market.[13]

Governments may impose *administrative or bureaucratic procedures* that hinder the activities of importers or foreign firms. For example, the opening story revealed how India's business sector is burdened by countless regulations, standards, and administrative hurdles at the state and federal levels. In Mexico, government-imposed bureaucratic procedures led United Parcel Service to temporarily suspend its ground delivery service across the U.S.-Mexican border. Similarly, the United States barred Mexican trucks from entering the United States on the grounds that they were unsafe. Business regulations vary worldwide. Many countries in Africa and Latin America impose countless bureaucratic procedures that hinder commercial activities and business start-ups. By contrast, Australia, Canada, Ireland, New Zealand, Singapore, and the United Kingdom impose relatively few such procedures.[14]

Saudi Arabia is home to various restrictive practices that hinder international trade. Every foreign business traveler to the Arab kingdom must hold an entry visa that can be obtained only by securing the support of a sponsor—a Saudi citizen or organization who vouches for the visitor's actions. Because few Saudis are willing to assume such responsibility, foreigners who want to do business in Saudi Arabia face great difficulty.[15]

Convoluted administrative procedures are widespread in national customs agencies. The revenue generated by tariffs depends on how customs authorities classify imported products. Products often appear to fit two or more tariff categories. For example, a sport utility vehicle could be classified as a truck, a car, or a van. Each of these categories can entail a different tariff. Depending on the judgment of the customs agent, the applicable tariff might end up being high or low. Because thousands of categories exist for customs classification, a product and its corresponding tariff can be easily misclassified, by accident or intent.

Investment Barriers

As we saw in the opening story on India, countries also impose restrictions on FDI and ownership that restrict the ability of foreign firms to invest in some industry sectors or acquire local firms. Excessive restrictions in India prevent the approval of countless investment proposals that could produce billions of dollars in revenue to the local economy and government. Worldwide, FDI and ownership restrictions are particularly common in such industries as broadcasting, utilities, air transportation, military technology, and financial services, as well as industries in which the government has major holdings, such as oil and key minerals. The Mexican government restricts FDI by foreign investors to protect its oil industry, which is deemed critical to the nation's security. The Canadian government restricts foreign ownership of local movie studios and TV networks to protect its indigenous film and TV industries from excessive foreign influence. FDI and ownership restrictions are particularly burdensome in the services sector because services usually cannot be exported and providers must establish a physical presence in target markets to conduct business there. Occasionally, governments impose investment barriers aimed at protecting home-country industries and jobs.

Currency control
Restrictions on the outflow of hard currency from a country or on the inflow of foreign currencies.

Currency controls restrict the outflow of widely used currencies, such as the dollar, euro, and yen, and occasionally the inflow of foreign currencies. Controls can help conserve especially valuable currency or reduce the risk of capital flight. They are particularly common in developing economies. Some countries employ a system of dual official exchange rates, offering exporters a relatively favorable rate to encourage exports, while importers receive a relatively unfavorable rate to discourage imports.

Currency controls both help and harm firms that establish foreign subsidiaries through FDI. They favor companies when they export their products from the host country but harm those that rely heavily on imported parts and components. Controls also restrict the ability of MNEs to *repatriate* their profits—that is, transfer revenues from profitable operations back to the home country.

As an example, in Venezuela, currency controls have led to a shortage of dollars and other hard currencies. Multinational firms avoid doing business in Venezuela because strict currency rules limit the amount of profits they can take out of the country or limit their ability to receive payment for imports at reasonable prices. Venezuela imposed the controls to keep imports inexpensive and maintain a base of hard currencies in the country.[16]

Source: © Keith Dannemiller/Alamy

State-owned oil company PEMEX (Petroleos de Mexico) benefits from investment barriers in Mexico that prevent foreign firms from gaining control of Mexican oil companies.

Subsidies and Other Government Support Programs

Subsidies are monetary or other resources that a government grants to a firm or group of firms, intended either to encourage exports or simply to facilitate the production and marketing of products at reduced prices, to help ensure the involved companies prosper. Subsidies come in the form of outright cash disbursements, material inputs, services, tax breaks, the construction of infrastructure, and government contracts at inflated prices. For example, the French government has provided large subsidies to Air France, the national airline.

The *Closing Case* focuses on European government support of Airbus, the leading European manufacturer of commercial aircraft. Perhaps the ultimate examples of subsidized firms are in China. Several leading corporations, such as China Minmetals ($39 billion annual sales) and Shanghai Automotive ($34 billion annual sales), are in fact state enterprises wholly or partly owned by the Chinese government, which provides them with huge financial resources. Indeed, state-owned enterprises account for more than 40 percent of China's economic output.[17]

Critics argue that subsidies confer unfair advantages on recipients by reducing their cost of doing business. In India, the government provides massive subsidies to state-owned oil companies, which allow them to offer gasoline at very low prices. Foreign MNEs such as Royal Dutch Shell cannot compete profitably against rivals that offer such prices and consequently avoid doing business in the market.[18] The WTO prohibits subsidies when it can be proven that they hinder free trade. Subsidies, however, are hard to define. For example, when a government provides land, infrastructure, telecommunications systems, or utilities to the firms in a corporate park, this is technically a subsidy. Yet many view this type of support as an appropriate public function.

In Europe and the United States, governments frequently provide agricultural subsidies to supplement the income of farmers and help manage the supply of agricultural commodities. The U.S. government grants subsidies for more than two dozen commodities, including corn, soybeans, wheat, cotton, and rice.[19] In Europe, the Common Agricultural Policy (CAP) is a system of subsidies that represents about 40 percent of the EU's budget, amounting to tens of billions of euros annually. The CAP and U.S. subsidies have been criticized for promoting unfair competition and high prices because they tend to prevent developing economies from exporting their agricultural goods to Europe and the United States. Subsidies encourage overproduction and therefore lower food prices at home, making agricultural imports from developing countries less competitive.[20]

Governments sometimes retaliate against subsidies by imposing **countervailing duties**, tariffs on products imported into a country to offset subsidies given to producers or exporters in the exporting country. In this way, the duty serves to cancel out the effect of the subsidy, eliminating the price advantage the exporters would otherwise obtain.

Subsidies may allow a manufacturer to practice **dumping**—that is, to charge an unusually low price for exported products, typically lower than that for domestic or third-country customers,

Subsidy
Monetary or other resources that a government grants to a firm or group of firms, usually intended to encourage exports or to facilitate the production and marketing of products at reduced prices, to ensure the favored firms prosper.

Countervailing duty
Tariff imposed on products imported into a country to offset subsidies given to producers or exporters in the exporting country.

Dumping
Pricing exported products at less than their normal value, generally less than their price in the domestic or third-country markets, or at less than production cost.

The Ministry of Economy, Trade, and Industry in Japan is typical of national federal agencies that promote international trade and investment.

or even lower than the cost to manufacture the good.[21] The European Union has provided billions of euros in subsidies every year to EU sugar producers, which allowed Europe to become one of the world's largest sugar exporters at artificially low prices. Without the subsidies Europe would be one of the world's biggest sugar importers.

Dumping violates WTO rules because it amounts to unfair competition. But dumping is hard to prove because firms usually do not reveal data on their cost structures. A large MNE that charges very low prices could conceivably drive competitors out of a foreign market, achieve a monopoly, and then raise prices later. Governments in the importing country often respond to dumping by imposing an **antidumping duty**—a tax imposed on products deemed to be dumped and thereby causing injury to producers of competing products in the importing country. The WTO allows this practice.[22] The duties are generally equal to the difference between the product's export price and their normal value.

Antidumping duty

A tax imposed on products deemed to be dumped and causing injury to producers of competing products in the importing country.

Investment incentive

Transfer payment or tax concession made directly to foreign firms to entice them to invest in the country.

Government subsidies are not always direct or overt. For example, governments may support home-country businesses by funding R&D, granting tax exemptions, and offering business development services such as market information, trade missions, and privileged access to key foreign contacts. Most countries have agencies and ministries that provide such services to facilitate the international activities of their own firms. Examples include the Department of Foreign Affairs and International Trade in Canada (www.dfait-maeci.gc.ca), U.K. Trade & Investment in the United Kingdom (www.uktradeinvest.gov.uk), and the International Trade Administration of the U.S. Department of Commerce (www.doc.gov).

Related to subsidies are governmental **investment incentives**, transfer payments or tax concessions made directly to individual foreign firms to entice them to invest in the country. Hong Kong's government put up most of the cash to build the Hong Kong Disney park (www.park .hongkongdisneyland.com). While the park and facilities cost about $1.81 billion, the government provided Disney an investment of $1.74 billion to develop the site.

Recently, Austin, Texas, and Albany, New York, competed for the chance to have the Korean manufacturer Samsung Electronics (www.samsung.com) build a semiconductor plant in their regions. Austin offered $225 million worth of tax relief and other concessions in its successful bid to attract Samsung's $300 million plant, estimated to create nearly 1,000 new jobs locally. To entice MNEs to establish local production facilities, the country of Macedonia offers such incentives as low corporate taxes, immediate access to utilities and transportation, and financial support for training workers (see www.investinmacedonia.com).

Such incentives often help the economic development in a particular region or community. In the 1990s, Germany encouraged foreign companies to invest in the economically disadvantaged East German states by providing tax and investment incentives. The government of Ireland has undertaken various initiatives aimed at promoting Ireland as a place to do business. It targeted foreign companies in the high-tech sector—including medical instruments, pharmaceuticals, and computer software—and offered preferential corporate tax rates of 12 percent. These targeted efforts paid dividends by creating substantial new employment and helping diversify the Irish economy away from agricultural activities.

Governments also support domestic industries by adopting *procurement policies* that restrict purchases to home-country suppliers. Several governments require that air travel purchased with government funds be booked with home-country carriers. Such policies are especially common in countries with large public sectors, such as China and Russia. In the United States, government agencies favor domestic suppliers unless their prices are high compared to foreign suppliers. In Japan, government agencies often do not even consider foreign bids, regardless of pricing. Public procurement agencies often impose requirements that effectively exclude foreign suppliers.

Consequences of Government Intervention

As illustrated in Exhibit 8.5, average tariffs have declined over time. Simultaneously, as shown in Exhibit 8.6, world trade and GDP have flourished. Decreasing trade barriers are a major factor in the growth of global commerce and consequently in rising incomes around the world. Firms that participate actively in international trade and investment not only improve their performance but also contribute to reducing global poverty.[23]

One way of evaluating the effects of government intervention is to examine each nation's level of *economic freedom*, defined as the "absence of government coercion or constraint on the production, distribution, or consumption of goods and services beyond the extent necessary for citizens to protect and maintain liberty itself. In other words, people are free to work, produce, consume, and invest in the ways they feel are most productive."[24] The *Index of Economic Freedom* measures economic freedom in 179 countries.

Exhibit 8.7 shows the degree of economic freedom for each country in the Index for 2012, based on criteria such as the level of trade barriers, rule of law, level of business regulation, and protection of intellectual property rights.[25] The Index classifies virtually all the advanced economies as "free," all the emerging markets as either "free" or "mostly free," and all the developing economies as "mostly unfree" or "repressed," underscoring the close relationship between limited government intervention and economic freedom.

Economic freedom flourishes when government supports the institutions necessary for that freedom and provides an appropriate level of intervention and regulation. In 2010 for the first time, the United States fell into the second highest category, due to increased U.S. federal government intervention in that nation's economy, following the recent global financial crisis. The United Kingdom scores especially well on business freedom and property rights. Canada has been a strong proponent of the Anti-Counterfeiting Trade Agreement (ACTA), which established an international framework for combating infringement of intellectual property rights.[26]

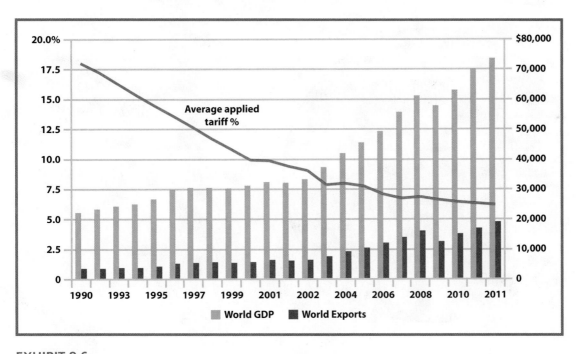

EXHIBIT 8.6

Relationship between Tariffs, World GDP, and the Volume of World Trade

Note: Tariffs given as average percent (red line), World GDP given in billions of U.S.$ (blue column), and Volume of World Trade given in billions of U.S.$ (purple column). Left axis measures Tariffs. Right axis measures World GDP and Volume of World Trade.

Sources: Based on International Monetary Fund World Economic Outlook Database, at www.imf.org; UNCTAD, at http://www .unctadstat.unctad.org; World Bank, http://www.data.worldbank.org.

EXHIBIT 8.7

Countries Ranked by Level of Economic Freedom, 2012

Sources: Based on *2012 Index of Economic Freedom*, The Heritage Foundation, Washington, DC, and the *Wall Street Journal*, New York, accessed at http://www.heritage.org.

ARCTIC OCEAN

United Kingdom

Ireland

Norway
Sweden
Finland

Estonia
Latvia
Lithuania
Russia
Belarus

R u s s i a

Denmark

Netherlands
Germany
Belgium
Luxembourg
France
Switz.

Poland

Czech
Rep.
Austria
Slovenia
Croatia
Hungary
Slovakia

Ukraine

Moldova
Romania
Bosnia
Herzegovina
Serbia
Bulgaria
Montenegro
Macedonia
Albania

Kazakhstan

Mongolia

North
Korea

Liech.

Monaco
Andorra

Italy

Portugal

Spain

Greece

Malta

Turkey

Georgia
Azerbaijan
Armenia

Uzbekistan

Kyrgyzstan

South
Korea

Japan

Tunisia

Cyprus

Syria
Lebanon
Israel
Jordan

Iraq

Iran

Turkmenistan

Tajikistan

C h i n a

Afghanistan

PACIFIC
OCEAN

Morocco

Algeria

Libya

Egypt

Kuwait
Bahrain
Qatar

United
Arab
Emirates

Pakistan

Nepal

Bhutan

Macau

Taiwan

Western
Sahara

Saudi
Arabia

Oman

I n d i a

Bangladesh

Hong
Kong

Mauritania

Mali

Niger

Chad

Eritrea

Yemen

Myanmar
(Burma)

Laos

Senegal
Gambia
Guinea-bissau
Sierra Leone

Burkina
Faso

Nigeria

Sudan

Djibouti

Somalia

Thailand

Vietnam

Liberia

Ivory
Coast

Ghana
Togo
Benin

Central
African
Republic

Ethiopia

Cambodia

Philippines

Cameroon

Uganda

Sri
Lanka

Brunei

Micronesia

Equatorial
Guinea
Gabon

Congo
Republic

Congo
Democratic
Republic
(Zaire)

Rwanda
Burundi

Kenya

Maldives

Malaysia

Singapore

Tanzania

Seychelles

INDIAN

I n d o n e s i a

Papua
New
Guinea

Solomon
Islands

SOUTH

OCEAN

Timor-leste

Samoa

ATLANTIC

Angola

Zambia

Malawi

Comoros

Vanuatu

Fiji

OCEAN

Namibia

Botswana

Zimbabwe

Mozambique

Madagascar

Mauritius
Réunion

New
Caledonia

Tonga

Australia

Swaziland

South
Africa

Lesotho

New
Zealand

Level of economic freedom

- 80-100% free
- 70-79.9% free
- 60-69.9% free
- 50-59.9% free
- 0-49.9% free
- Not ranked
- Others

Government intervention and trade barriers raise ethical concerns for developing economies. For example, United States import tariffs on clothing and shoes often exceed 20 percent. The tariffs hurt poor countries like Bangladesh, Pakistan, India, and several nations in Africa, where clothing and shoe exporters are concentrated. United States' tariffs on imports from Cambodia are far higher than on imports from the United Kingdom. The tariffs that confront less-developed economies are often several times those faced by the richest countries.[27]

Government intervention can also offset harmful effects. For example, trade barriers can create or protect jobs. Subsidies can help counterbalance harmful consequences that disproportionately affect the poor. In Denmark, for example, globalization has affected thousands of workers whose jobs have been shifted to other countries with lower labor costs. The Danish government provides generous subsidies to the unemployed, aimed at retraining workers to upgrade their job skills or find work in other fields.[28]

 ## Evolution of Government Intervention

A century ago, trade barriers worldwide were relatively high. The trading environment worsened through two world wars and the Great Depression. In 1938, the United States passed the Smoot-Hawley Tariff Act, which raised U.S. tariffs to near-record highs of more than 50 percent, compared to only about 4 percent today. Tariffs that other countries imposed to retaliate against Smoot-Hawley choked off foreign markets for U.S. agricultural products, leading to plummeting farm prices and many bank failures. In an effort to revive trade, governments began to reduce restrictive tariffs. By the late 1940s, prudent policymaking had begun to substantially reduce tariffs worldwide.

In the 1950s, Latin America and other developing nations adopted protectionist policies aimed at industrialization and economic development. Governments imposed high tariffs and quotas on imports from the developed world, established government-supported enterprises to make the products they formerly imported, and sought to substitute local production for imports. Known as *import substitution*, the approach did not succeed. Companies enjoyed big government subsidies and the protection of high tariffs and quotas. However, these enterprises never became competitive in world markets or raised living standards to the levels of free-trading countries. Meanwhile, the protected industries required ongoing subsidies. Most countries that experimented with import substitution eventually rejected it.

By contrast, from the 1970s onward, Singapore, Hong Kong, Taiwan, and South Korea achieved rapid economic growth by encouraging the development of export-intensive industries. Their model, known as *export-led development*, proved much more successful than import substitution. These countries, along with others in East Asia, such as Malaysia, Thailand, and Indonesia, substantially increased living standards and gained strong international trading links. A rising middle class helped transform these countries into competitive economies.

Elsewhere in Asia, Japan had launched an ambitious program of industrialization and export-led development. The country's rise from poverty in the 1940s to one of the world's wealthiest countries by the 1980s has been called the *Japanese miracle*. The feat was achieved with the help of national strategic policies, including tariffs that fostered and protected Japan's infant industries such as automobiles, shipbuilding, and consumer electronics.

India once embraced a model of high trade and investment barriers, state intervention in labor and financial markets, a large public sector, heavy business regulation, and central planning. The model contributed to the nation's poor economic performance over several decades. Beginning in the early 1990s, however, India began to open its markets to foreign trade and investment. Trade liberalization and privatization of state enterprises have progressed slowly, but reforms have fueled much progress. Between 1992 and 2012, India's average annual income rose from about $330 in real terms to more than $1,400 in 2012, an impressive achievement.

After adopting communism in 1949, China relied on centralized economic planning, in which agriculture and manufacturing were controlled by state-run industries. The country remained relatively closed to international trade until the 1980s, when it began to liberalize its economy. In 2001, China joined the WTO and committed to reducing trade barriers. Trade has stimulated the Chinese economy. By 2012, its GDP was more than ten times the 1995 level, and the value of exports had reached nearly $1.9 trillion. China has become a leading exporter of manufactured products and home to numerous large MNEs that compete with Western firms.

General Agreement on Tariffs and Trade

In 1947, twenty-three nations signed the General Agreement on Tariffs and Trade (GATT), the first major effort to systematically reduce trade barriers worldwide. The GATT created: (1) a process to reduce tariffs through continuous negotiations among member nations; (2) an agency to serve as watchdog over world trade; and (3) a forum for resolving trade disputes.

The GATT introduced the concept of *most favored nation* (renamed *normal trade relations* in 1998), according to which each signatory nation agreed to extend the tariff reductions covered in a trade agreement with a trading partner to all other countries. Thus, a concession to one country became a concession to all. Eventually, the GATT was superseded by the WTO in 1995 and grew to include about 150 member nations. The organization proved extremely effective and resulted in the greatest global decline in trade barriers in history. The *Global Trend* feature highlights the founding and current progress of the WTO.

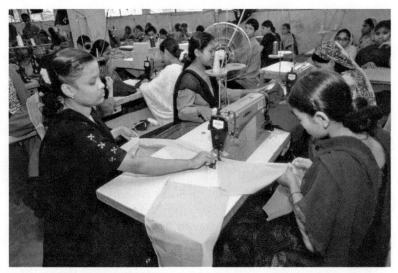

Source: Liba Taylor/Alamy

Bangladesh is a major clothing exporter that faces high tariffs. Here, women work at Dhaka, the Bangladesh capital and a center of garment manufacturing.

 GLOBAL TREND

The World Trade Organization and Collapse of the Doha Round

Based in Geneva, Switzerland, the World Trade Organization (www.wto.org) is the main watchdog for world trade and counts some 150 countries as its members. The WTO works to ensure world trade operates smoothly, fairly, and with as few restrictions as possible. Since joining the WTO in 2001, for example, China has gradually reduced import tariffs and quotas. Most recently, the WTO has been working to reduce trade barriers in the agricultural and services sectors.

Services like the expertise of a lawyer or an accountant are intangible. Consequently, as they do not pass through ports or customs stations, governments usually cannot impose tariffs on them. Thus, services are subject to various *nontariff* trade barriers. For example, some countries in Europe refuse to license foreign insurance companies. In transportation, the United States and numerous other nations require their own merchandise fleets to carry their country's cargo, creating a barrier to foreign-based cargo handlers.

Governments also restrict services by setting licensing and professional standards that may be difficult for foreigners to meet. Regulations usually ensure that law, medicine, accounting, and other professions are undertaken by people who are educated locally, speak the national language, and are socialized according to local standards and norms. Standards in one country are usually not recognized by other countries. Thus, lawyers, doctors, accountants, and many other professionals face restrictions when attempting to do business abroad.

The Doha Development Agenda was a round of WTO negotiations launched in Qatar in 2001 that sought to reduce barriers in the services sector. The WTO wants to ensure that banks, hotel chains, insurance firms, tour operators, transport companies, and other service firms enjoy the same trade and investment freedoms that apply to goods producers. The Doha Agenda also sought freer trade in agricultural goods, where restraints are particularly burdensome to developing countries. Free global trade in agricultural products is the best way to ensure widespread access and lower prices for food. Doha was the first round of WTO negotiations in which big emerging markets, especially Brazil, China, and India, played a strong role. The unique circumstances of such countries have increased the complexity of negotiations.

Unfortunately, the talks collapsed in 2008 when trade negotiators were unable to reach agreement. The main reason was that, under WTO rules, all nations were required to agree to all parts of the final deal. This proved impossible for various reasons. For example, China and India insisted on protecting the agricultural sectors in their countries. India alone has more than 200 million farmers, and the Indian government is reluctant to expose them to international competition. In the wake of Doha's collapse, many nations are choosing to concentrate on negotiating bilateral (two-country) and regional trade deals instead. As of mid-2012, the Doha round of talks had not yet restarted.

Sources: P. Coy, "Free Trade: After the Impasse," *BusinessWeek*, August 11, 2008, p. 29; "Beyond Doha," *Economist*, October 11, 2008, pp. 30–33; Carolyn Evans, "Bilateralism, Multilateralism, and Trade Rules," *FRBSF Economic Letter*, January 9, 2012, pp. 1–5; Oxford Analytica Daily Brief Service, "International: Stalled Doha Spurs Trade Discrimination," February 12, 2010, p. 1; United States Trade Representative, "National Trade Estimate Report," 2011, retrieved from http://www.ustr.gov; World Trade Organization, 2007, retrieved from http://www.wto.org.

Intervention and the Global Financial Crisis

The recent global recession and financial crisis have raised new questions about government's role in business and the world economy. The crisis arose largely from inadequate regulation and insufficient enforcement of current regulations in the banking and finance sectors. In response, governments worldwide increased regulation and examined ways to improve enforcement. For example, the U.S. government has increased the power of its Treasury Department, Federal Reserve System, and Federal Deposit Insurance Corporation (FDIC). The European Central Bank is creating a new agency that aims to take aggressive action in needed areas. The European Union has increased oversight of multinational banks and supervision of financial institutions. The United Nations has called for greater transparency in financial activities and closure of loopholes that allow excessive speculation in global finance.[29]

Some governments increased protectionism in an effort to safeguard jobs and wage levels. Argentina and Brazil, for example, increased import tariffs on numerous products. Russia raised tariffs on dozens of goods, including cars and combine harvesters.[30] Hoping to jump-start economic growth, governments also increased subsidies to their own industries. The EU granted more than $50 billion in aid to Daimler (Germany), Skoda (Czech Republic), and other struggling carmakers in Europe. The government of the United Kingdom provided substantial subsidies to U.K. banks and financial institutions. China has pumped hundreds of billions of dollars into its own economy.[31]

In addition to the harmful fallout of the recession and financial crisis, rising protectionism impacted international commerce. Ripple effects of government reforms are extending beyond the banking and financial areas.[32]

 ## How Firms Can Respond to Government Intervention

Although managers' initial tendency might be to avoid markets with high trade and investment barriers or excessive government intervention, this course is not usually practical. Depending on the industry and country, firms generally must cope with protectionism and other forms of intervention. In extractive industries such as aluminum and petroleum, for example, companies may have little choice but to operate in nations that impose formidable barriers. The food-processing, biotechnology, and pharmaceutical industries also encounter countless laws and regulations abroad.

Strategies for Managers

We've seen that China, India, and numerous other countries in Africa, Asia, Latin America, and Eastern and Central Europe feature extensive trade barriers and government involvement. Yet many firms seek to target emerging markets and developing economies because of the huge long-term potential they offer.[33] Firms devise various strategies to manage harmful government intervention.

RESEARCH TO GATHER KNOWLEDGE AND INTELLIGENCE Experienced managers continually scan the business environment to identify the nature of government intervention and to plan market-entry strategies and host-country operations. They review their return-on-investment criteria to account for the increased cost and risk of trade and investment barriers. For example, the EU is devising new guidelines that affect company operations in areas ranging from product liability laws to standards for investment in European industries.

CHOOSE THE MOST APPROPRIATE ENTRY STRATEGIES Tariffs and most nontariff trade barriers apply to exporting, whereas investment barriers apply to FDI. Most firms choose exporting as their initial entry strategy. However, if high tariffs are present, managers should consider other strategies, such as FDI, licensing, and joint ventures that allow the firm to operate directly in the target market, avoiding import barriers. For example, Taiwan's Foxconn, a contract manufacturer for Apple and other electronics firms, built a factory in Brazil partly to avoid the country's high tariffs on imported goods.

However, even investment-based entry is affected by tariffs if it requires importing raw materials and parts to manufacture finished products in the host country. Tariffs usually vary with the *form* of an imported product. To minimize tariff costs, many companies ship manufactured products "knocked-down" and assemble them in the target market. In countries with relatively high tariffs on imported personal computers, importers often bring in the parts and assemble the computers locally. Eastman Kodak (www.kodak.com) imports parts and components into the United States, which it then uses to manufacture photographic equipment. Kodak could produce the finished equipment abroad, but the tariff on parts and components is lower. By manufacturing in the United States, Kodak avoids paying higher tariffs.[34]

Source: © Bernd Kröger/Fotolia

Many firms lobby national governments, such as Germany's parliament in Berlin, for lower barriers to trade and investment.

TAKE ADVANTAGE OF FOREIGN TRADE ZONES In an effort to create jobs and stimulate local economic development, governments establish foreign trade zones (also known as *free trade zones* or *free ports*). A **foreign trade zone (FTZ)** is an area within a country that receives imported goods for assembly or other processing and subsequent re-export.[35] Products brought into an FTZ are not subject to duties, taxes, or quotas until they, or the products made from them, enter into the non-FTZ commercial territory of the country where the FTZ is located. Firms use FTZs to assemble foreign dutiable materials and components into finished products, which are then re-exported. Alternatively, firms may use FTZs to manage inventory of parts, components, or finished products that the firm will eventually need at some other location. In the United States, for example, Japanese carmakers store vehicles at the port of Jacksonville, Florida, without having to pay duties until the cars are shipped to U.S. dealerships.

FTZs exist in more than seventy-five countries, usually near seaports or airports. They can be as small as a factory or as large as an entire country. The United States is home to several hundred FTZs used by thousands of firms. The Colon Free Zone (www.colonfreezone.com), located on the Atlantic side of the Panama Canal, is an enormous FTZ where products are imported, stored, modified, repacked, and re-exported without being subject to tariffs or customs regulations. The many private firms and wholesalers that set up shop inside the huge zone transship their merchandise from Panama to other parts of the Western Hemisphere and Europe. Some firms obtain FTZ status within their own physical facilities.

A successful experiment with FTZs has been **maquiladoras**—export-assembly plants in northern Mexico along the U.S. border that produce components and finished products, usually destined for the United States. Since the 1960s, "maquilas" have imported materials and equipment on a tariff-free basis for assembly or manufacturing and then re-exported the assembled products. Today under NAFTA, maquiladoras employ millions of Mexicans who assemble clothing, furniture, car parts, electronics, and other goods. The arrangement enables firms from the United States, Asia, and Europe to tap low-cost labor, favorable duties, and government incentives while serving the U.S. market. Maquilas account for about half of Mexico's exports.

SEEK FAVORABLE CUSTOMS CLASSIFICATIONS FOR EXPORTED PRODUCTS One approach for reducing exposure to trade barriers is to have exported products classified in the appropriate harmonized product code. As noted earlier in this chapter, many products can be classified within two or more categories, each of which may imply a different tariff. For example, some telecommunications equipment can be classified as electric machinery, electronics, or measuring devices. The manufacturer should analyze the trade barriers on differing categories to ensure exported products are classified under the lowest tariff code. Or the manufacturer may be able to modify the exported product in a way that helps minimize trade barriers. South Korea faced a quota on the export of nonrubber footwear to the United States. By shifting manufacturing to rubber-soled shoes, Korean firms greatly increased their footwear exports.

TAKE ADVANTAGE OF INVESTMENT INCENTIVES AND OTHER GOVERNMENT SUPPORT PROGRAMS Obtaining economic development incentives from host- or home-country governments is another strategy to reduce the cost of trade and investment barriers. When Mercedes built a factory

Foreign trade zone (FTZ)

An area within a country that receives imported goods for assembly or other processing and re-export. For customs purposes the FTZ is treated as if it is outside the country's borders.

Maquiladoras

Export-assembly plants in northern Mexico along the U.S. border that produce components and typically finished products destined for the United States on a tariff-free basis.

in Alabama, it benefitted from reduced taxes and direct subsidies provided by the Alabama state government. When Siemens built a semiconductor plant in Portugal, it received subsidies from the Portuguese government and the EU. Incentives cover nearly 40 percent of Siemens's investment and training costs. In Europe, Japan, and the United States, governments increasingly provide incentives to entice firms to set up shop within their borders. In addition to cash outlays, incentives also include reduced utility rates, employee training programs, tax holidays, and construction of new roads and other infrastructure.

LOBBY FOR FREER TRADE AND INVESTMENT More nations are liberalizing markets to create jobs and increase tax revenues. The trend results partly from the efforts of firms to lobby domestic and foreign governments to lower their trade and investment barriers. The Japanese have achieved much success in reducing trade barriers by lobbying U.S. and European governments. In China, domestic and foreign firms lobby the government to relax protectionist policies and regulations that make China a difficult place to do business. Foreign firms often hire former Chinese government officials to help lobby their former colleagues.[36] European automakers have obtained various concessions by lobbying individual state governments in the United States. BMW leased its 1,039-acre factory site in South Carolina at an annual rent of one dollar. The private sector lobbies federal authorities to undertake government-to-government trade negotiations, aimed at lowering barriers. Private firms bring complaints to world bodies, especially the WTO, to address unfair trading practices of key international markets.

CLOSING CASE — Government Intervention at Airbus and Boeing

In the 1960s, United States companies such as Boeing (www.boeing.com) and McDonnell Douglas were the dominant players in global aircraft manufacturing. Boeing was founded in 1916 in Seattle, and had many years to develop the critical mass necessary to become the world's leading aerospace manufacturer. During World War II and the subsequent Cold War years, Boeing was the recipient of many lucrative contracts from the U.S. Department of Defense.

In Europe, no single country possessed the means to launch an aerospace company capable of challenging Boeing. Manufacturing commercial aircraft is complex and capital-intensive and requires a highly skilled workforce. In the 1970s, the governments of France, Germany, Spain, and the United Kingdom formed an alliance, supported with massive government subsidies, to create Airbus S.A.S. (www.airbus.com). By 1981, the four-country alliance succeeded in becoming the world's number-two civil aircraft manufacturer. Airbus launched the A300, among the best-selling commercial aircraft of all time. Airbus also created the A320, receiving more than 400 orders before its first flight and becoming the fastest-selling large passenger jet in aviation history. By 1992, Airbus had captured roughly one-third of the global commercial aircraft market.

Government Support for Airbus

Since the 1940s, European governments have pursued public policies based on democratic socialism. Under this system, the government plays a strong role in the national economy and provides key services such as health care, mass transit, and sometimes banking and housing. Most Europeans are accustomed to government playing a significant role in guiding the national economy.

In this context, Airbus has benefitted enormously from government support. The firm has received tens of billions of euros of subsidies and soft loans from the four founding country governments and the EU. Airbus must repay the loans only if it achieves profitability. Government

aid has financed, in whole or part, every major Airbus aircraft model. European governments have forgiven Airbus's debt, provided huge equity infusions, dedicated infrastructure support, and financed R&D for civil aircraft projects.

Airbus is currently a stock-held company jointly owned by the British, Germans, French, and Spanish. It is based in Toulouse, France, but has R&D and production operations scattered throughout Europe. European governments justify their financial aid to Airbus on several grounds. First, Airbus R&D activities result in the development of valuable new technologies. Second, Airbus provides jobs to some 53,000 skilled and semiskilled Europeans. Third, its value-chain activities attract massive amounts of capital into Europe. Finally, Airbus generates enormous tax revenues.

Complaints about Unfair Government Intervention

Boeing and the U.S. government have long complained about the massive subsidies and soft loans that were responsible not only for Airbus's birth, but also for its ongoing success. The outcry became louder in the 2000s, when Airbus surpassed Boeing in annual sales, becoming the world's leading commercial aircraft manufacturer. Boeing has argued that Airbus never would have gotten this far without government support.

In 2005, the U.S. Trade Representative brought its case to the WTO. The case arose because EU member states approved $3.7 billion in new subsidies and soft loans to Airbus. The case alleged that financial aid for the A350, A380, and earlier Airbus aircraft qualified as subsidies under the WTO's Agreement on Subsidies and Countervailing Measures (ASCM) and that the subsidies were actionable because they adversely affected international trade. Under the ASCM, subsidies to specific firms or industries from a government or other public bodies are prohibited. Airbus had applied to the governments of France, Germany, Spain, and the United Kingdom for aid to launch its model A350.

In 2011, the WTO ruled that EU aid to Airbus had caused Boeing to lose market share in Asia and other markets. EU officials argued that government subsidies to Airbus were permissible and that it was up to individual EU countries to decide whether to provide them. However, the WTO also ruled that Boeing received more than $5 billion in U.S. government subsidies in the development of the 787 Dreamliner.

Government Support for Boeing

The EU argues the United States government has indirectly subsidized Boeing through massive defense contracts paid via tax dollars. The U.S. government gave Boeing more than $23 billion in indirect government subsidies by means of R&D funding and other indirect support from the Pentagon and NASA, the nation's space agency. Boeing is at liberty to use the knowledge acquired from such projects to produce civilian aircraft. The state of Washington, Boeing's primary manufacturing and assembly location, has provided the firm with tax breaks, infrastructure support, and other incentives totaling billions of dollars.

The EU also has a case at the WTO regarding Boeing's relations with Japanese business partners. Boeing entered an alliance with Japan's Mitsubishi, Kawasaki, and Fuji to build the 787 Dreamliner. The Japanese firms provided billions in soft loans, repayable only if the aircraft is commercially successful.

New Aircraft from Airbus and Boeing

In 2007, Airbus launched the A380, an innovative airplane with an upper deck extending the entire length of the fuselage and a cabin that provides 50 percent more floor space than Boeing's largest aircraft. The A380 can seat between 555 and 853 passengers, depending on the seating configuration. It has a maximum range of 15,000 kilometers (8,000 nautical miles). The total cost to develop and launch the A380 reached 15 billion euros (U.S. $21 billion), partly supported by funding from European governments.

Boeing successfully launched the 787 Dreamliner in 2007 and is ahead of Airbus in launching innovative and fuel-efficient aircraft. Airbus is developing a mid-sized A350 model to compete with Boeing's 787.

In 2008, the government of China established a company to make passenger jumbo jets, part of its quest to challenge Boeing and Airbus in the global aircraft industry. China Commercial Aircraft Co. was established in Shanghai amid forecasts that China's domestic market for commercial aircraft will increase fivefold by 2026.

Global Financial Crisis

The recent global financial crisis adversely impacted Airbus and Boeing. Both companies had to reduce output and lay off thousands of workers. Following sharp drops in passenger traffic, airlines grounded planes and cut routes. Longer term, Airbus aims to reorganize its global operations, outsource more manufacturing, and sell all or part of six factories. It has begun to produce aircraft in the United States. Airbus and Boeing are generating much new business from emerging markets, and ramped up production substantially to meet anticipated demand. In 2012, however, an industry expert warned that both Airbus and Boeing were producing too many commercial aircraft, risking a potential global glut.

AACSB: Reflective Thinking Skills, Ethical Understanding and Reasoning Abilities

Case Questions

1. Where do you stand? Do you think EU subsidies and soft loans to Airbus are fair? Why or why not? What advantages does Airbus gain from free financial support from the EU governments? Are complaints about EU subsidies fair in light of Europe's history of democratic socialism?

2. Do you believe U.S. military contracts with Boeing amount to subsidies? Have these types of payments provided Boeing with unfair advantages? Justify your answer.

3. Assuming that Airbus cannot compete without subsidies and loans, is it likely that the EU will discontinue its financial support of Airbus? Is it in the EU's interests to continue supporting Airbus? Justify your answer.

4. In the event the WTO rules against Airbus and tells it to stop accepting subsidies and soft loans, how should Airbus management respond? What new approaches can management pursue to maintain Airbus's lead in the global commercial aircraft industry?

Sources: Doug Cameron and David Kesmodel, "Warning is Issued about Plane Glut," *Wall Street Journal*, February 23, 2012, pp. B6–B6; Corporate profiles of Airbus and Boeing at http://www.hoovers.com; K. Epstein & J. Crown, "Globalization Bites Boeing," *BusinessWeek*, March 24, 2008, p. 32; D. Gauthier-Villars & D. Michaels, "Airbus Buyers Get French Aid," *Wall Street Journal*, January 27, 2009, p. B4; Max Kingsley-Jones, "Throwing Down the Gauntlet," *Airline Business*, October 2011, pp. 28–30; N. Luthra, "Boeing to Sell India $2.1 Billion in Planes," *Wall Street Journal*, January 6, 2009, p. B4; D. Michaels, "Airbus Trims Jumbo Output as Carriers Defer Orders," *Wall Street Journal*, May 7, 2009, p. B1; Pilita Clark, Joshua Chaffin, and James Politi, "WTO Rules that Boeing Received $5.3bn in Aid," *Financial Times*, April 1, 2011, p. 19; "China to Make Jumbo Jetliners, Trim Roles of Boeing, Airbus," *Wall Street Journal*, May 12, 2008, p. B4; "How Airbus Flew Past Its American Rival," *Financial Times*, March 17, 2005, p. 6; J. Lunsford and D. Michaels, "Bet on Huge Plane Trips Up Airbus," *Wall Street Journal*, June 15, 2006, p. A1; Stephan Wittig, "The WTO Panel Report on Boeing subsidies: A Critical Assessment," *Intereconomics*, May 2011, pp. 148–153.

Note: The authors acknowledge the assistance of Stephanie Regales with this case.

CHAPTER ESSENTIALS

MyManagementLab

Go to **mymanagementlab.com** to complete the problems marked with this icon ⭐.

Key Terms

antidumping duty 202	export control 195	nontariff trade barrier 193
countervailing duty 201	foreign trade zone (FTZ) 209	protectionism 193
currency control 200	import license 199	quota 194
customs 193	investment incentive 202	subsidy 201
dumping 201	maquiladoras 209	tariff 193

Summary

In this chapter, you learned about:

1. **The nature of government intervention**

   Despite the value of free trade, governments often intervene in international business. **Protectionism** refers to national economic policies designed to restrict free trade and protect domestic industries from foreign competition. Government intervention arises typically in the form of tariffs, nontariff trade barriers, and investment barriers. **Tariffs** are taxes on imported products, imposed mainly to collect government revenue and protect domestic industries from foreign competition. **Nontariff trade barriers** consist of policies that restrict trade without directly imposing a tax. An example of a nontariff trade barrier is a quota, a quantitative restriction on imports. Managers find out what tariffs apply to their products by consulting harmonized code schedules, available from government agencies.

2. **Rationale for government intervention**

   Governments impose trade and investment barriers to achieve political, social, or economic objectives. Such barriers are either defensive or offensive. A key rationale is the protection of the nation's economy, its industries, and its workers. **Export controls** limit trade in sensitive products deemed critical to national security. Governments also impose barriers to protect infant industries.

3. **Instruments of government intervention**

   Governments also impose regulations and technical standards, as well as administrative and bureaucratic procedures. Countries may also impose **currency controls** to

minimize international withdrawal of national currency. FDI and ownership restrictions ensure that the nation maintains partial or full ownership of firms within its national borders. Governments also provide **subsidies**, a form of payment or other material support. Foreign governments may offset foreign subsidies by imposing **countervailing duties**. With **dumping**, a firm charges abnormally low prices abroad. A government may respond to dumping by imposing an **antidumping duty**. Governments support home-grown firms by providing investment incentives and biased government procurement policies.

4. **Consequences of government intervention**

   Economic freedom refers to the extent of government intervention in the national economy. Government intervention and trade barriers can raise ethical concerns that affect developing economies and low-income consumers. However, government intervention also can be used to offset such harmful effects.

5. **Evolution of government intervention**

   Intervention has a long history. In the late 1800s, many countries imposed substantial protectionism. From the 1930s onward, countries reduced trade barriers worldwide. The nature and outcomes of government intervention have varied across Latin America, Japan, India, and China. The most important development for reducing trade barriers was the General Agreement on Tariffs and Trade (GATT), replaced by the World Trade Organization (WTO). The 150 members of the WTO account for nearly all world trade.

The recent global financial crisis arose from inadequate regulation in the banking and finance sectors. In response, governments implemented new regulations and some protectionism. Government reforms have had ripple effects extending beyond the financial sector.

6. How firms can respond to government intervention

Firms should conduct research to understand the extent and nature of trade and investment barriers abroad. When trade barriers are substantial, FDI or joint ventures are often the most appropriate entry strategies. Where importing is essential, the firm can take advantage of **foreign trade zones**, areas where imports receive preferential tariff treatment. Government assistance in the form of subsidies and incentives helps reduce the impact of protectionism. Firms sometimes lobby the home and foreign governments for freer trade and investment.

Test Your Comprehension AACSB: Reflective Thinking Skills

1. Distinguish among tariffs, nontariff trade barriers, investment barriers, and government subsidies.

2. What are the major types of nontariff trade barriers? Suggest business strategies for minimizing the effect of nontariff trade barriers.

3. Distinguish between countervailing duties and antidumping duties.

⭐ 4. In what ways do government subsidies and procurement policies amount to protectionism?

5. What is the rationale for intervention? Why do governments engage in protectionism?

⭐ 6. How has government intervention evolved during the global financial crisis?

⭐ 7. Describe various company strategies to manage government intervention.

8. What is the role of FDI, licensing, and joint ventures in reducing the impact of import tariffs?

Apply Your Understanding AACSB: Ethical Understanding and Reasoning Abilities, Reflective Thinking Skills, Communication Abilities

1. TelComm Corporation is a manufacturer of components for the cell phone industry. TelComm founder Alex Bell heard that China has the world's largest number of cell phone users and wants to begin exporting the firm's products there. But TelComm has little international experience. Mr. Bell is unaware of the various types of nontariff trade barriers that TelComm might face in China and other foreign markets. Please summarize major nontariff trade barriers to Mr. Bell. What types of investment barriers might TelComm face in the event management decides to establish a factory in China to manufacture cell phone components? What can TelComm management do to minimize the threat of these nontariff trade and investment barriers?

2. *Ethical Dilemma*: The United States steel industry, once the world leader, now produces less steel than China, Japan, or the European Union. American steel producers are threatened by price-competitive suppliers in India, Russia, and other emerging markets. The U.S. steel industry dealt with this threat by launching a lobbying campaign to persuade the U.S. government to impose barriers on the import of foreign steel. The following advertisement is an example of this effort:

> In recent years, the United States has lost millions of manufacturing jobs because domestic factories have shifted their operations to low-wage countries. Manufacturing assures our national defense, our global leadership, and the living standards of more than 17 million workers. Other nations subsidize their domestic steel industries. Longer-term, subsidized imports will destroy a vital American industry and U.S. jobs. In an uncertain and dangerous world, does America really want to become dependent on China, India, Russia, and developing countries for something so basic as steel?

Evaluate this statement. How valid is the argument? Using the Ethical Framework in Chapter 5, analyze the arguments for and against imposing trade barriers on the import of steel from abroad. Should the U.S. government impose trade barriers? What is the effect of barriers on (a) U.S. steel producers, (b) U.S. firms that use a lot of steel to manufacture finished products, and (c) consumers of products made with U.S. steel. Recall that China, India, and Russia are emerging markets with substantial poverty. What is the effect of the barriers on these countries?

3. *Ethical Dilemma*: You are Vice President for International Sales at FoodTrade, a large trading company that exports processed foods to Africa. You are often frustrated that African countries impose high tariffs (typically 75 percent) on processed food imports. These barriers raise FoodTrade's cost of doing business and make your prices less competitive in African markets. But Africa suffers from widespread poverty and African governments use tariffs to raise needed revenues and achieve policy objectives. Using the concepts in this chapter and the Ethical Framework in Chapter 5, analyze the arguments for and against high agricultural tariffs in Africa. How do the tariffs harm or benefit Africa? Do you perceive any ethical concerns in Africa's use of high tariffs on agricultural goods? What ethical concerns do you perceive in FoodTrade's efforts to avoid the tariffs? How should FoodTrade respond to the tariffs?

globalEDGE INTERNET EXERCISES
(http://www.globalEDGE.msu.edu)

AACSB: Reflective Thinking Skills, Analytic Skills, Ethical Understanding and Reasoning Abilities

Refer to Chapter 1, page 24, for instructions on how to access and use globalEDGE™.

1. Your firm is considering exporting to two countries: Kenya and Vietnam. However, management's knowledge about the trade policies of these countries is limited. Conduct a search at globalEDGE™ to identify the current import policies, tariffs, and restrictions in these countries. Prepare a brief report on your findings. In addition to globalEDGE™, other useful sites include the World Trade Organization (www.wto.org; enter country name in the search engine) and the U.S. Commercial Service (www.buyusa.gov).

2. The United States Trade Representative (USTR) develops international trade and investment policies for the U.S. government. Visit the USTR Web site from globalEDGE™ or directly (www.ustr.gov). Search for "National Trade Estimate Report" for the latest year. This document summarizes trade barriers around the world. See the reports for the country of your choice. What are the country's import policies and practices? What are its nontariff trade barriers? What about barriers in the services sector? Are there any sectors that seem to be particularly protected (for example, energy, telecommunications)? What is the nature of government restrictions on e-commerce? If you worked at a firm that exported its products to the country, how would you use the USTR report to develop international business strategies?

3. Visit the following Web portals and review their perspectives on the debate about free trade and government policies on trade barriers. Given the inherent conflict between national interests, special interests, asymmetries in world wage rates, and other economic conditions, what is the best path forward for national governments? That is, should governments generally favor free trade, or should they intervene to protect national interests? Justify your answer.

http://www.aflcio.org/globaleconomy
http://www.citizen.org/trade
http://www.heritage.org/issues
http://www.sierraclub.org/trade
http://www.wto.org.

MyManagementLab

Go to **mymanagementlab.com** for Auto-graded writing questions as well as the following Assisted-graded writing questions:

8-1. Discuss the relationship between government intervention and protectionism.

8-2. How did government intervention evolve between the first and second halves of the twentieth century?

8-3. Mymanagementlab Only – comprehensive writing assignment for this chapter.

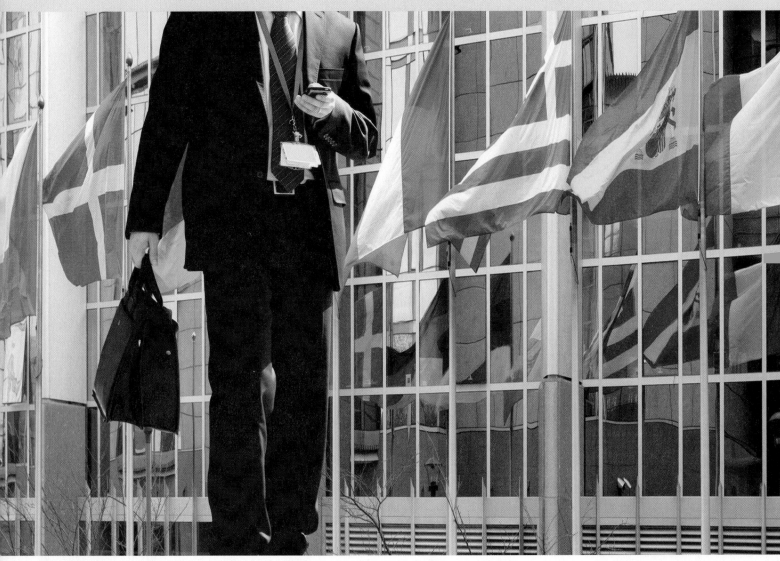

Evolution of the European Union

In 1957, six countries—Belgium, France, Italy, Luxembourg, the Netherlands, and West Germany—formed an alliance called the European Economic Community (EEC). Its successor is today's European Union (EU), which was established in 1992 and now includes twenty-eight countries from both Eastern and Western Europe with a total of twenty-three official languages among them. The EU is the world's most advanced and largest regional economic bloc, with a half-billion people and about $18 trillion in annual GDP. A regional economic bloc (or economic bloc) is an alliance of two or more countries that agree to eliminate tariffs and other restrictions to the cross-border flow of products, services, capital, and, occasionally, labor.

Trade and investment within Europe have become much easier since the 1950s. The member states allow investors from other member countries to freely establish and conduct business and transfer capital. Gradual elimination of bureaucracy at Europe's national borders cut delivery times and reduced transportation costs. The EU eliminated the need to use most customs clearance documents. Seventeen EU countries have adopted the euro as their common currency, helping to lower

CHAPTER 9

Regional Economic Integration

LEARNING OBJECTIVES *In this chapter, you will learn about the following:*

1. Regional integration and economic blocs
2. Levels of regional integration
3. The leading economic blocs
4. Advantages of regional integration
5. Success factors for regional integration
6. Ethical dilemmas and drawbacks of regional integration
7. Management implications of regional integration

MyManagementLab®

⭐ **Improve Your Grade!**

Over 10 million students improved their results using the Pearson MyLabs. Visit **mymanagementlab.com** for simulations, tutorials, and end-of-chapter problems.

business transaction costs and increase the transparency of pricing throughout the continent.

The EU is home to the headquarters of some of the world's most important firms. Allianz, an insurance company founded in Germany, offers a variety of life, health, and casualty insurance. While previously its management viewed Europe as a collection of disparate countries, Allianz treats Europe increasingly as one large marketplace. In strategy-making, management emphasizes a pan-European approach, which cuts costs and increases the efficiency of Allianz's operations throughout Europe.

Development of the EU has allowed Allianz to internationalize faster than other insurers. The firm is present in all the new EU countries, such as Poland, Hungary, and the Czech Republic, which are proving to be among Allianz's most profitable markets. Allianz changed its legal status from a German company to a *Societas Europaea* (SE), a European company based in and regulated by the EU as a whole. SE status allows such firms to operate seamlessly across all twenty-eight EU countries.

The EU is at a crossroads today. Member countries aim to develop a European constitution to clarify distribution of powers and legitimize the EU's federal authority, in much the same way the U.S. Constitution does for the United States. However, the EU economy has been sluggish for more than a decade; GDP growth and productivity stagnated and unemployment has hovered between 8 percent and 12 percent. The situation worsened during the recent global recession. In 2012, the EU sought to rescue member countries fiscally weakened during the global economic crisis. Greece's economy faced collapse due to massive government debt. Greece's financial travails forced the euro-zone countries further along a path to greater economic coordination.

Economic blocs are a fixture of the emerging landscape of international trade and investment. The challenges facing the EU today may be typical of those faced by economic blocs in the most advanced stages of development. Such alliances represent a long-term trend and may be a stepping-stone to the emergence of worldwide free trade.

SOURCES: Elizabeth Bomberg, John Peterson, and Richard Corbett, *The European Union: How Does it Work?* 3rd ed. (New York: Oxford University Press, 2012); Matthew Dalton, "Europe Struggles Over Greek Details," *Wall Street Journal*, February 14, 2012, p. A8; "Retake the Reins: The European Union Must Harmonise Financial Regulation," *Financial Times*, January 23, 2009, p. 8; "How the EU Works," retrieved from http://www.europa.eu; Corporate profile of Allianz at http://www.hoovers.com; U.S. Commercial Service, *Doing Business in the European Union* (Washington, DC: U.S. and Foreign Commercial Service and U.S. Department of State, 2011).

Regional economic integration
The growing economic interdependence that results when two or more countries within a geographic region form an alliance aimed at reducing barriers to trade and investment.

Free trade agreement
A formal arrangement between two or more countries to reduce or eliminate tariffs, quotas, and barriers to trade in products and services.

The opening story highlights one of the most remarkable features of contemporary international business: the worldwide trend toward **regional economic integration**. Also known as *regional integration*, regional economic integration refers to the growing economic interdependence that results when two or more countries within a geographic region form an alliance aimed at reducing barriers to trade and investment. As happened following formation of the European Union (EU), regional integration increases economic activity and makes doing business easier among nations within the alliance. At a minimum, the countries in an economic bloc become parties to a **free trade agreement**, a formal arrangement between two or more countries to reduce or eliminate tariffs, quotas, and other barriers to trade in products and services. The member nations also undertake cross-border investments within the bloc.

In the last half-century, most countries have sought to cooperate with others, aiming for some degree of regional integration. Today, more than 50 percent of world trade occurs as part of a preferential trade agreement signed by groups of countries. The trend is based on the premise that, by cooperating, nations within a common geographic region connected by historical, cultural, linguistic, economic, or political factors can gain mutual advantages.[1] Economic integration may be particularly important in the face of economic crises and other trends that can reduce national enthusiasm for free trade and incite countries to become more isolated from one another. As occurred in the EU, the free trade that results from regional integration fosters the internationalization of countless firms. Living standards usually rise due to increased specialization, lower prices, greater choices, increased productivity, and more efficient use of resources.

To better understand regional integration, think of international business as existing along a continuum where, at one extreme, the world operates as one large free-trade area in which there are no tariffs or quotas, all countries use the same currency, and products, services, capital, and workers can move freely among nations without restriction. At the other extreme of this continuum is a world of prohibitive barriers to trade and investment in which countries have separate currencies and very little commercial interaction with each other. Regional integration represents a compromise, a middle-ground within this continuum. Two of the best-known examples are the European Union (EU) and the North American Free Trade Agreement (NAFTA). NAFTA consists of Canada, Mexico, and the United States.

This chapter explains the nature and advantages of regional integration. We distinguish the levels of regional integration and describe the leading economic blocs. Because regional integration holds important implications for international business, we highlight key strategies that firms undertake to address the resultant opportunities and challenges.

Regional Integration and Economic Blocs

Regional integration results from the formation of a *regional economic integration bloc* or, simply, an economic bloc. This refers to a geographic area that consists of two or more countries that agree to pursue economic integration by reducing tariffs and other restrictions to the cross-border flow of products, services, capital, and, in more advanced stages, labor. (In this text, following convention, we use the French term *bloc* instead of *block*.)

More advanced economic blocs, such as the EU, permit the free flow of capital, labor, and technology among their member countries. The EU is also harmonizing monetary policy (to manage the money supply and currency values) and fiscal policy (to manage government finances, especially tax revenues) and gradually integrating the economies of its member nations. Simultaneously, recent crises in Greece, Italy, Spain, and Portugal, and general discord among EU members, are challenging the progress of regional integration in Europe.

Why would a nation opt to be a member of an economic bloc instead of working toward a system of worldwide free trade? The main reason is that reaching agreement on free trade is much easier in negotiations among a handful of countries than among all the nations in the world. This helps explain why there are hundreds of regional trade integration blocs around the world today. They present both opportunities and challenges to internationalizing firms.

Since 1947, the General Agreement on Tariffs and Trade (GATT) and later the World Trade Organization (WTO) have achieved much success in fostering economic integration on a *global* scale. The WTO recognizes regional integration can play an important role in liberalizing trade and fostering economic development. However, regional economic blocs are powerful and the WTO has encountered various challenges in dealing with them. Slow progress in liberalizing trade, especially for agricultural products, has prompted many developing countries to seek alternatives to the global trading system favored by the WTO. The WTO is continuing negotiations with economic blocs, with the aim of exercising better control over their evolution and of minimizing risks associated with regional economic integration.[2]

 ## Levels of Regional Integration

Regional integration allows distinct national economies to become economically linked and interdependent through greater cross-national movement of products, services, and factors of production. It allows member states to use resources more productively. The total output of the integrated bloc is generally greater than the summated output of the individual states.

Exhibit 9.1 identifies five possible levels of regional integration. We can think of these levels as a continuum, with economic interconnectedness progressing from a low level of integration—the free trade area—through higher levels to the most advanced form of integration—the *political union*. The political union represents the ultimate degree of integration among countries, which no countries have yet achieved.

The **free trade area** is the simplest and most common arrangement, in which member countries agree to gradually eliminate formal barriers to trade in products and services within the bloc, while each member country maintains an independent international trade policy with countries outside the bloc. NAFTA is an example. The free trade area emphasizes the pursuit of comparative advantage for a group of countries rather than for individual states. Governments may impose local content requirements, which specify that producers located within the member countries provide a certain proportion of products and supplies used in local manufacturing. If the content requirement is not met, the product becomes subject to the tariffs that member governments normally impose on nonmember countries.

The **customs union** is the second level of regional integration, similar to a free trade area except that member states harmonize their external trade policies and adopt *common* tariff and nontariff barriers on imports from nonmember countries. MERCOSUR, an economic bloc in Latin America, is an example of this type of arrangement. The adoption of a common tariff system means that an exporter outside MERCOSUR faces the *same* tariffs and nontariff barriers when trading with *any* MERCOSUR member country. Determining the most appropriate common external tariff is challenging, because member countries must agree on

Free trade area
A stage of regional integration in which member countries agree to eliminate tariffs and other barriers to trade in products and services within the bloc.

Customs union
A stage of regional integration in which the member countries agree to adopt common tariff and nontariff barriers on imports from nonmember countries.

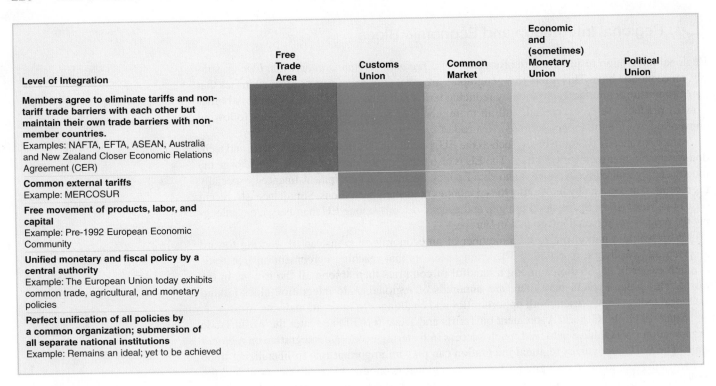

Level of Integration	Free Trade Area	Customs Union	Common Market	Economic and (sometimes) Monetary Union	Political Union
Members agree to eliminate tariffs and non-tariff trade barriers with each other but maintain their own trade barriers with non-member countries. Examples: NAFTA, EFTA, ASEAN, Australia and New Zealand Closer Economic Relations Agreement (CER)					
Common external tariffs Example: MERCOSUR					
Free movement of products, labor, and capital Example: Pre-1992 European Economic Community					
Unified monetary and fiscal policy by a central authority Example: The European Union today exhibits common trade, agricultural, and monetary policies					
Perfect unification of all policies by a common organization; submersion of all separate national institutions Example: Remains an ideal; yet to be achieved					

EXHIBIT 9.1

Five Potential Levels of Regional Integration among Nations

(For example, a *customs union* has the features of a free trade area, plus common external tariffs.)

Source: Based on Bela Balassa, *The Theory of Economic Integration* (Santa Barbara, CA: Greenwood Press Reprint, 1982).

Common market

A stage of regional integration in which trade barriers are reduced or removed, common external barriers are established, and products, services, and factors of production are allowed to move freely among the member countries.

Economic union

A stage of regional integration in which member countries enjoy all the advantages of early stages, but also strive to have common fiscal and monetary policies.

the percentage level of the tariff and on how to distribute proceeds from the tariff among the member countries.

In the third stage of regional integration, member countries establish a **common market** (also known as a single market), in which trade barriers are reduced or removed, common external barriers are established, and products, services, and *factors of production* such as capital, labor, and technology are allowed to move freely among the member countries. Like a customs union, a common market also establishes a common trade policy with nonmember countries. The EU is a common market. It has gradually reduced or eliminated restrictions on immigration and the cross-border flow of capital. A worker from an EU country has the right to work in other EU countries, and EU firms can freely transfer funds among their subsidiaries within the bloc.

Common markets are hard to create because they require substantial cooperation on labor and economic policies. Since labor and capital can flow freely inside the bloc, benefits to individual members vary; skilled labor may move to countries where wages are higher, and investment capital may flow to countries where returns are greater. In the EU, for example, Germany has seen an influx of workers from Poland and the Czech Republic, because these workers can earn much higher wages in Germany than they can in their home countries.

An **economic union** is the fourth stage of regional integration, in which member countries enjoy all the advantages of early stages but also strive to have common fiscal and monetary policies. At the extreme, each member country adopts identical tax rates. The bloc aims for standardized monetary policy, which requires establishing fixed exchange rates and free convertibility of currencies among the member states, in addition to allowing the free movement of capital. This standardization helps eliminate discriminatory practices that might favor one member state over another. Through greater mobility of products, services, and production factors, an economic union enables firms within the bloc to locate productive activities in member states with the most favorable economic policies.

The EU has made great strides toward achieving an economic union. For example, seventeen EU countries have established a *monetary union* in which a single currency, the euro, is now in circulation. Monetary union and the euro have greatly increased the ease with which European financial institutions establish branches across the EU and offer banking services, insurance, and savings products. The single currency also makes trading and investment easier for European firms doing business within the union.

To achieve greater economic integration, economic union member countries strive to eliminate border controls, harmonize product and labeling standards, and establish region-wide policies for energy, agriculture, and social services. An economic union also requires its members to standardize laws and regulations regarding competition, mergers, and other corporate behaviors. To facilitate free trade in services, member countries harmonize procedures for licensing of professionals so that a doctor or lawyer qualified in one country can practice in any other country.

The United States provides a good analogy for an economic union. Imagine each state is like an individual country, but all are joined together in a union. The members have a common currency and a single central bank with a uniform monetary policy. Trade among the members takes place unobstructed, and both labor and capital move freely among them. The federal government applies a uniform tax and fiscal policy. Just as would occur in an economic union, the individual U.S. states also govern themselves in such areas as education, police protection, and local taxes. This analogy only goes so far, of course. The United States is a country and, unlike members of a real economic union, the states cannot withdraw.

 ## The Leading Economic Blocs

Examples of regional integration can be found on all continents. In this section, we discuss notable blocs in Europe, the Americas, Asia, the Middle East, and Africa. The leading economic blocs are illustrated in Exhibit 9.2.

Europe has the longest experience with regional integration and is home to several economic blocs. The most important of these are the EU and the European Free Trade Association. Exhibit 9.3 shows these two blocs in detail.

The European Union (EU)

Exhibit 9.4 highlights notable features of the member countries in the EU, the world's most integrated economic bloc. "PPP terms" in the exhibit refers to purchasing power parity (PPP), which means per-capita GDP figures have been adjusted for price differences. The PPP concept suggests that, in the long run, exchange rates should move toward levels that would equalize the prices of an identical basket of goods and services in any two countries. Since prices vary greatly among countries, economists adjust ordinary GDP figures for differences in purchasing power. Adjusted per-capita GDP more accurately represents the amount of products that consumers in a given country can buy, using their own currency and remaining consistent with their standard of living.

The European Union has taken the specific steps to become an economic union:

Market access. Tariffs and most nontariff barriers have been eliminated for trade in products and services. Rules of origin favor manufacturing using inputs produced in the EU.

Common market. Barriers to the cross-national movement of production factors—labor, capital, and technology—have been removed. For example, an Italian worker now has the right to get a job in Ireland, and a French company can invest freely in Spain.

Trade rules. Customs procedures and regulations have been eliminated, streamlining transportation and logistics within Europe.

Standards harmonization. Technical standards, regulations, and enforcement procedures related to products, services, and commercial activities are being harmonized. For example, where British firms once used imperial measures (pounds, ounces, and inches), they have converted to the metric system used by all EU countries. German food merchants that once had their own standard for handling meat and produce now follow procedures prescribed by the EU.

EXHIBIT 9.2
The Most Active Economic Blocs

ARCTIC OCEAN

NORWAY
SWEDEN
FINLAND

RUSSIA

ESTONIA
UNITED
KINGDOM
DENMARK
LATVIA
LITHUANIA
RUSSIA
BELARUS
IRELAND
NETHERLANDS
POLAND
GERMANY
BELGIUM
CZECH
LUXEMBOURG
REP. SLOVAKIA
UKRAINE
FRANCE
LIECH. AUSTRIA
HUNGARY
MOLDOVA
SWITZ.
SLOVENIA
ROMANIA
CROATIA
MONACO
BOSNIA-
HERZEGOVINA
SERBIA AND
MONTENEGRO
BULGARIA
ANDORRA
ITALY
ALBANIA
MACEDONIA
GEORGIA
SPAIN
GREECE
TURKEY
PORTUGAL
TUNISIA
CYPRUS
SYRIA
ARMENIA
AZERBAIJAN
KAZAKHSTAN
UZBEKISTAN
KYRGYZSTAN
TURKMENISTAN
TAJIKISTAN
MONGOLIA

LEBANON
ISRAEL
IRAQ
JORDAN
KUWAIT
IRAN
AFGHANISTAN
QATAR
UNITED ARAB
EMIRATES
PAKISTAN
NEPAL
BHUTAN
CHINA
NORTH
KOREA
SOUTH
KOREA
JAPAN

MOROCCO
WESTERN
SAHARA
ALGERIA
LIBYA
EGYPT
SAUDI
ARABIA
OMAN
INDIA
BANGLADESH
MYANMAR
(BURMA)
LAOS
TAIWAN

PACIFIC
OCEAN

MAURITANIA
MALI
NIGER
CHAD
SUDAN
ERITREA
YEMEN
THAILAND
VIETNAM
SENEGAL
AMBIA
UINEA-BISSAU
GUINEA
BURKINA
FASO
NIGERIA
DJIBOUTI
CAMBODIA
PHILIPPINES
ERRA LEONE
GHANA
TOGO
BENIN
IVORY
COAST
CENTRAL AFRICAN
REPUBLIC
ETHIOPIA
SOMALIA
SRI
LANKA
LIBERIA
CAMEROON
BRUNEI
MALAYSIA
SINGAPORE
EQUATORIAL
GUINEA
CONGO
REPUBLIC
GABON
UGANDA
CONGO
DEMOCRATIC
REPUBLIC
(ZAIRE)
KENYA
RWANDA
BURUNDI
INDONESIA
PAPUA
NEW
GUINEA
SOLOMON
ISLANDS

INDIAN
OCEAN

TANZANIA

SOUTH
ATLANTIC
OCEAN

ANGOLA
ZAMBIA
MALAWI
MOZAMBIQUE
NAMIBIA
ZIMBABWE
BOTSWANA
MADAGASCAR
MAURITIUS
RÉUNION
VANUATU
FIJI

NEW
CALEDONIA
AUSTRALIA

SWAZILAND
SOUTH
AFRICA
LESOTHO

NEW
ZEALAND

The most active economic blocs

EU   MERCOSUR   ASEAN
EFTA   CARICOM   APEC
NAFTA   CAN   CER

EXHIBIT 9.3

Economic Integration in Europe

In the long run, the EU is seeking to adopt common fiscal, monetary, taxation, and social welfare policies. Introduction of the euro—the EU's common currency and now one of the world's leading currencies—simplified cross-border trade and enhanced Europe's international competitiveness. However, national governments had to cede monetary power to the *European Central Bank*, which is based in Luxembourg and oversees EU monetary functions.

The EU has four additional institutions. The *Council of the European Union* comprises representatives from each member country, and makes decisions regarding economic policy, budgets, foreign policy, and admission of new member countries. The *European Commission* is also composed of delegates from each member state. It proposes legislation and policies and is responsible for implementing the decisions of the European Parliament and the Council of the EU. The *European Parliament* consists of elected representatives that hold joint sessions each month. The Parliament develops EU legislation, supervises EU institutions, and makes decisions

EXHIBIT 9.4 Key Features of the European Union Member Countries, 2012

Members	Population (millions)	GDP (U.S.$ billions)	GDP per capita (U.S.$; PPP terms)	Exports as a percentage of GDP
Austria	8	$441	$42,774	46%
Belgium	11	549	38,387	104
Bulgaria	7	58	14,188	21
Croatia	4	67	18,860	18
Cyprus	1	26	29,234	6
Czech Republic	11	233	26,626	51
Denmark	6	363	38,605	48
Estonia	1	24	21,228	47
Finland	5	285	37,762	37
France	64	2,889	35,751	24
Germany	82	3,708	38,902	43
Greece	11	306	37,333	7
Hungary	10	148	20,201	51
Ireland	5	227	40,650	66
Italy	61	2,287	30,451	25
Latvia	2	29	16,124	29
Lithuania	3	46	19,725	37
Luxembourg	0.5	67	86,645	48
Malta	0.4	10	26,426	24
Netherlands	17	882	45,160	84
Poland	38	557	20,954	22
Portugal	11	241	22,979	20
Romania	21	203	12,952	19
Slovak Republic	5	101	24,387	54
Slovenia	2	54	30,063	52
Spain	46	1,575	31,216	18
Sweden	9	630	42,495	44
United Kingdom	61	2,604	36,681	19
	Total: 503	Total: $18,610		

Sources: Based on International Monetary Fund at http://www.imf.org and European Union at http://www.europa.eu.

about the EU budget. The *European Court of Justice* interprets and enforces EU laws and settles legal disputes between member states.[3]

The *Global Trend* feature discusses the specific challenges of integrating new member states into the EU. Since 2004, fourteen new states have joined. The new members, mainly in Eastern Europe, are important, low-cost manufacturing sites for EU firms.[4] Peugeot and Citroën now produce cars at a plant in the Czech Republic that, at full capacity, can turn out 320,000 vehicles per year. South Korea's Hyundai now produces the Kia brand of cars at a plant in Slovakia, while Japan's Suzuki makes cars in Hungary. Output of automobiles in the eastern region is growing rapidly.[5] Most of the newest EU entrants are one-time satellites of the former Soviet Union and have economic growth rates higher than their Western European counterparts. They are poised to achieve per-capita income levels similar to those of the EU's wealthier countries within several years. However, their ascension poses special challenges. Less-developed economies such as Romania, Bulgaria, and Lithuania will require years of developmental aid to catch up.[6] Crises afflict even long-standing EU members such as Greece and Spain.

The EU faces other challenges as well, including the tension between the forces for regional integration and the forces for retaining national identity. EU countries recognize that relinquishing autonomy in certain key areas and combining resources across national borders are necessary steps to achieve regional integration. However, some, particularly the United Kingdom, are reluctant to surrender certain sovereign rights. They insist on maintaining their ability to set their own monetary and fiscal policies and to undertake their own national military defense. In many ways, the EU is still a work in progress. In light of recent economic and financial crises that have beset EU countries, the UK's insistence on maintaining its autonomy may prove the wise choice.

The Common Agricultural Policy (CAP) has long been a fixture of the European bloc. The CAP is a system of agricultural subsidies and programs that guarantees a minimum price to EU farmers and ranchers. Its original goals were to provide a fair living standard for agricultural producers and food at reasonable prices. In reality, however, the CAP has increased food prices in Europe and consumes almost half the EU's annual budget. It complicates negotiations with the WTO for reducing global trade barriers. The CAP's high import tariffs also affect exporters in developing economies, such as Africa, that rely heavily on agricultural production. The EU is working to reform the CAP, but progress has been slow.

European Free Trade Association (EFTA)

The second-largest free trade area in Europe is the EFTA (www.efta.int), established in 1960 by Austria, Britain, Denmark, Norway, Portugal, Sweden, and Switzerland. Most of these countries eventually left the EFTA to join the EU; current EFTA members are Iceland, Liechtenstein, Norway, and Switzerland. The bloc promotes free trade and strengthens economic relations with other European countries and the world. The EFTA Secretariat, headquartered in Geneva, has negotiated trade agreements with several non-European countries. EFTA members cooperate with the EU via bilateral free trade agreements and, since 1994, through the European Economic Area arrangement, which allows for free movement of people, products, services, and capital throughout the combined area of the EFTA and the EU.

North American Free Trade Agreement (NAFTA)

Consisting of Canada, Mexico, and the United States, the NAFTA launched in 1994. It is the most significant economic bloc in the Americas and comparable to the EU in size (see www.nafta-sec-alena.org). Exhibit 9.5 highlights key features of the NAFTA countries. Its passage was smoothed by the existence, since the 1960s, of the *maquiladora* program. Under this program, U.S. firms were allowed to locate manufacturing facilities in an area just south of the U.S. border and access low-cost labor and other advantages in Mexico without having to pay significant tariffs.

What has NAFTA accomplished for its members? Initially, the accord increased market access between Canada, Mexico, and the United States. It eliminated tariffs and most nontariff

EXHIBIT 9.5 North American Free Trade Agreement (NAFTA), 2012

Member	Population (millions)	GDP (U.S.$ billions)	GDP per capita (U.S.$; PPP terms)	Exports as a percentage of GDP
Canada	35	1,826	41,326	21
Mexico	111	1,242	15,675	24
United States	316	15,495	49,055	8
	Total: 462	Total: 18,563		

Source: Based on International Monetary Fund at http://www.imf.org.

GLOBAL TREND

Troubles in the European Union

Southern European countries—especially Greece, Italy, and Portugal—are burdened with high government debt, the result of large-scale overspending. Such countries have been unable to refinance their government debt without financial support from other EU countries and international agencies such as the IMF. Capital flight has led to higher interest rates, which harms efforts to pay down debt. In the EU, the need to coordinate economic policies across diverse countries, each with distinctive goals and problems, has proven challenging.

Since the EU's founding, Northern Europe has had to subsidize poorer southern European countries. European finance ministers have approved rescue packages aimed at increasing financial stability in heavily indebted countries. EU leaders also sought to create a common fiscal union, aimed at further financial stabilization. Banks throughout Europe have been deeply affected because many loaned huge sums to EU countries at risk of defaulting on their sovereign debt.

The EU debt crisis arose from various causes. Longer life spans have led to more seniors drawing government pensions.

Simultaneously, falling birth rates mean there are fewer working-age people paying government taxes that support pension programs. Southern European countries have spent massive sums on pensions and social programs. When they join the EU, countries pledge to limit their deficit spending and debt levels. However, several countries circumvented these rules and masked their deficit and debt levels, partly by using complex financial instruments.

The "eurozone" is the group of EU countries that use a single currency, the euro. Such countries follow a uniform monetary policy set by the European Central Bank. Sharing a common currency across the eurozone countries limits options for dealing with fiscal and monetary crises at the national level. When a debt crisis or some other fiscal or monetary problem arises in one eurozone country, it usually cannot be isolated locally. In other parts of the world, when a nation faces a debt crisis, it can increase its money supply, which cheapens the value of its currency and helps increase export and tax revenues. Such an option is not available, however, to countries like Italy and Spain that use the euro as their national currency.

The debt crisis has provoked protests in Greece and other countries, as pensioners and others affected by austerity measures have seen their incomes fall. The crisis also affects the likelihood of admitting new countries to the EU. As managing the EU has proven increasingly difficult, officials in existing member countries are reluctant to allow new countries join the EU bloc.

The EU debt crisis emphasizes the importance of economic compatibility and sound fiscal and monetary management of the members of economic blocs. It reveals how problems in one bloc country can harm other member countries.

Sources: Maneet Ahuja, "Greenspan: Why European Union Is Doomed to Fail," *CNBC,* October 25, 2011, retrieved from www.cnbc.com; Stephen Bernard and Katy Burne, "S&P Declares Greece in Default," *Wall Street Journal,* February 28, 2012, p. C3; Leslie Norton, "A World of Risk in 2012," *Barron's,* December 26, 2011, pp. 32–33; Shawn Tully, "Will Europe Come Tumbling Down?," *Fortune,* September 5, 2011, pp. 64–69; "The Chaos of Greece," *Wall Street Journal,* February 14, 2012, p. A18; S. Wagstyl, "Fifth Anniversary Fails to Assuage Public Concerns," *Financial Times,* May 5, 2009, p. 6.

---

barriers for products and services traded in the bloc and made it possible for member-country firms to bid for government contracts in all three countries. NAFTA also established trade rules and uniform customs procedures and regulations, while prohibiting the use of standards and technical regulations as trade barriers. The members agreed to rules for investment and intellectual property rights. NAFTA also provides for dispute settlement in such areas as investment, unfair pricing, labor issues, and the environment.

Since the bloc's inception, Canada and Mexico have become the most important export markets of the United States, accounting for about one-third of U.S. exports. In the three-year period through 2012, the largest increase in U.S. export growth stemmed from exports to Canada and Mexico. In the 1980s, Mexico's tariffs averaged 100 percent and gradually decreased over time, eventually disappearing under NAFTA. Annual NAFTA foreign investment in Mexico rose dramatically as U.S. and Canadian firms invested in their southern neighbor. Following NAFTA's passage, Mexico's per-capita income has risen substantially, making Mexico into Latin America's wealthiest country in per-capita income terms.[7]

NAFTA stimulated restructuring of the labor market in North America. Falling trade barriers triggered job losses in the North as factories were "exported" to Mexico to profit from its low-cost labor. Increased purchasing power of Mexican consumers meant they could afford to buy U.S. and Canadian imports. NAFTA also required member countries to strengthen their labor standards, which helped improve working conditions and compliance with labor laws. NAFTA included provisions that promote sustainable development and environmental protection. In a recent development, Quebec is easing commerce and labor barriers with France, and Canada is in negotiations to join the EU. Canada and the United States are taking steps to streamline regulations and bureaucratic hassles, which have tended to hinder trade between NAFTA's two northern members.[8]

Compared to the EU or NAFTA, some economic blocs are less stable and have been less successful. These blocs, which we examine next, are located in Latin America, Asia, the Middle East, and Africa.

El Mercado Comun del Sur (MERCOSUR)

Established in 1991, MERCOSUR, or the *El Mercado Comun del Sur* (the Southern Common Market), is the strongest economic bloc in South America (see www.mercosur.int). Exhibit 9.6 lists its membership and key features. Within its borders, MERCOSUR established the free movement of products and services, a common external tariff and trade policy, and coordinated monetary and fiscal policies. An additional priority is the construction of reliable infrastructure—roads, electricity grids, and gas pipelines—across a landmass larger than Mexico and the United States combined. MERCOSUR eventually aims to become an economic union.

MERCOSUR's early progress was impressive. It attracted much investment from nonmember countries, especially in the auto industry. During its first six years, trade among the member countries increased substantially. MERCOSUR has increased regional interdependence and political cooperation.[9] In addition to its regular members, MERCOSUR also has five associate members, which have access to preferential trade but not to the tariff benefits of full members. MERCOSUR also has trade agreements with nations outside the bloc. In the future, it may become integrated with NAFTA and the Dominican Republic–Central American Free Trade Agreement (DR-CAFTA) as part of a proposed Free Trade Area of the Americas (FTAA), bringing free trade to the entire western hemisphere.

The Caribbean Community (CARICOM)

Composed of roughly twenty-five member and associate member states around the Caribbean Sea, CARICOM was established in 1973 to lower trade barriers and institute a common external tariff (see www.caricom.org). The bloc has met with little success in stimulating economic development, however, due to economic difficulties of the individual members and their inability to agree on basic issues. The bloc is progressing toward establishing the Caribbean Single Market, a common market that allows for a greater degree of free movement for products, services, capital, and labor and gives citizens of all CARICOM countries the right to establish businesses throughout the region.

Comunidad Andina de Naciones (CAN)

Long called the Andean Pact, the Comunidad Andina de Naciones (CAN) was established in 1969. Its main members are Bolivia, Colombia, Ecuador, and Peru (see www.comunidadandina.org). CAN is expected to merge with MERCOSUR to form a new economic bloc that encompasses

EXHIBIT 9.6 El Mercado Comun del Sur (MERCOSUR), 2012

Member	Population (millions)	GDP (U.S.$ billions)	GDP per capita (U.S.$; PPP terms)	Exports as a percentage of GDP
Argentina	41	$469	$18,202	11%
Brazil	197	2,617	12,304	9
Paraguay	7	27	5,772	15
Uruguay	3	53	16,232	15
Venezuela	30	312	12,734	19
Bolivia*	11	26	5,017	13
Chile*	18	247	16,913	27
Colombia*	47	340	10,595	9
Ecuador*	15	72	8,617	15
Peru*	30	179	10,507	13
	Total: 399	Total: 4,342		

Source: Based on International Monetary Fund at http://www.imf.org.

all of South America. The pact achieved little progress in its first twenty years, with intrabloc trade reaching only 5 percent of the bloc members' total trade.[10] This low trade rate is partially due to geography: The Andes mountain range makes cross-border land transportation costly and cumbersome.

Association of Southeast Asian Nations (ASEAN)

ASEAN, the Association of Southeast Asian Nations, was created in 1967 with the goal of maintaining political stability and promoting regional economic and social development among its members, shown in Exhibit 9.7 (see www.aseansec.org). ASEAN created a free trade area in which many tariffs were reduced to less than 5 percent. Further regional integration has been slowed by large economic differences among the member countries. For example, oil-rich Brunei has a per-capita income of nearly $50,000, while Vietnam's is only about $3,000. Were ASEAN to become a common market or economic union, millions of job seekers from poor member countries would likely migrate to wealthier member countries, potentially disrupting the economies of these latter nations. Consequently, ASEAN is unlikely to advance beyond its free trade area status for decades to come. In the long run, ASEAN aims to incorporate international trading powerhouses like Japan and China, whose membership would accelerate the development of extensive trade relationships.

Asia Pacific Economic Cooperation (APEC)

APEC, or Asia Pacific Economic Cooperation, aims for greater free trade and economic integration of the Pacific Rim countries. It incorporates twenty-one nations on both sides of the Pacific, including Australia, Canada, Chile, China, Japan, Mexico, Russia, and the United States (see www.apec.org). Its members account for 85 percent of total regional trade, as well as one-third of the world's population and over half its GDP. APEC aspires to remove trade and investment barriers by 2020. Progress has been slowed by economic and political turmoil in some member countries, as well as failure to agree on foundational issues. Members also have varying national economic priorities, and the inclusion of less-affluent Asian countries alongside strong international traders like Australia, Japan, and the United States complicates agreement on a range of issues.

Australia and New Zealand Closer Economic Relations Agreement (CER)

Founded in 1983, the Closer Economic Relations Agreement (CER) sought to accelerate growing free trade between Australia and New Zealand, deepening economic integration of the two nations. The CER gained importance when Australia and New Zealand lost their privileged status in the British market as Britain joined the EU. Many believe the CER has been one of the

EXHIBIT 9.7 Association of Southeast Asian Nations (ASEAN), 2012

Member	Population (millions)	GDP (U.S.$ billions)	GDP per capita (U.S.$; PPP terms)	Exports as a percentage of GDP
Brunei	0.4	$16	$49,925	46%
Cambodia	15	15	2,435	17
Indonesia	243	936	4,955	15
Laos	7	9	2,860	10
Malaysia	29	267	16,270	48
Myanmar	64	52	1,387	11
Philippines	98	232	4,275	14
Singapore	5	284	62,095	120
Thailand	65	379	10,204	33
Vietnam	90	137	3,560	26
	Total: 616.4	Total: 2,327		

Source: Based on International Monetary Fund at http://www.imf.org.

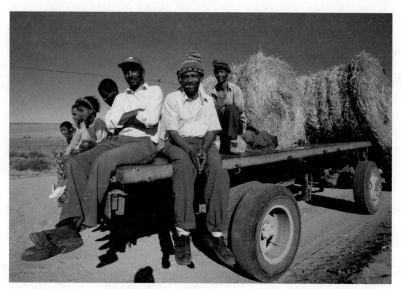

Source: Shaen Adey © Dorling Kindersley

These workers harvest wheat in Africa, used to make bread. External tariffs of NAFTA and the EU hinder African agricultural exports to Europe and North America.

world's most successful economic blocs. In 2009, its members concluded important negotiations on creating a free trade agreement with the ASEAN countries.

Economic Integration in the Middle East and Africa

The Middle East and North Africa are home to primarily Islamic countries in which oil is often the driving economic force. The Middle East's main regional organization is the Gulf Cooperation Council (GCC; see www.gcc-sg.org.htm). Established in 1981 to coordinate economic, social, and cultural affairs, the GCC consists of Bahrain, Kuwait, Oman, Qatar, Saudi Arabia, and the United Arab Emirates. Specific GCC initiatives include coordination of the petroleum industry, abolition of certain tariffs, and liberalization of investment, as well as harmonization of banking, financial, and monetary policies. In 2008, the GCC established a common market among all its member countries.

Elsewhere in the Middle East, efforts toward regional economic integration include the Arab Maghreb Union (composed of Algeria, Libya, Mauritania, Morocco, and Tunisia), which is still struggling to become a viable economic bloc. The Economic Cooperation Organization (ECO) is an international organization that now includes ten Middle Eastern and Asian countries seeking to promote trade and investment opportunities in the region. Such groups are very early attempts at regional integration that may foster the development of inter-Arab trade and investment. Another grouping, the Arab League, is a long-standing political organization with twenty-two member states that promotes unity and nationalism in the Middle East. It has been relatively unsuccessful in fostering regional economic development.

African countries want better access to Europe and North America for sales of their farm and textile products. To increase their bargaining power, they have established at least nine economic blocs. Most notable are the Southern African Development Community, the Economic Community of West African States, and the Economic Community of Central African States. However, these groups have had little impact on regional trade, due in part to political turmoil and misunderstandings about free trade as well as underdeveloped economic and transportation systems, political instability, civil unrest, and war, in the region.

 ## Advantages of Regional Integration

Since the 1990s, regional integration has become, by far, the most popular form of reciprocal trade liberalization.[11] Nations seek at least four objectives in pursuing regional integration, which we review next.[12]

EXPAND MARKET SIZE Regional integration greatly increases the scale of the marketplace for firms inside the economic bloc. For example, while Belgium has a population of just 10 million, membership in the EU gives Belgian firms free access to a total market of nearly 500 million EU buyers. In a similar way, management at Allianz, the German insurance firm featured in the opening story, has come to view Europe as one large marketplace. When NAFTA was formed, Canadian firms gained access to the much larger markets of Mexico and the United States, and consumers in all three countries access a wider selection of products and services.

ACHIEVE SCALE ECONOMIES AND ENHANCED PRODUCTIVITY Expansion of market size within an economic bloc gives member country firms the opportunity to increase the scale of operations in both production and marketing, gaining greater concentration and increased efficiency. While a German firm may be only moderately efficient when producing 10,000 units of product for Germany, it greatly increases its efficiency by producing 50,000 units for the much larger EU market. Internationalization inside the bloc helps firms learn to compete outside the bloc as well. Companies enjoy additional benefits through increased access to factors of production that now flow freely across national borders within the bloc. Labor and other inputs are allocated more efficiently among the member countries. More efficient resource usage leads to lower prices for consumers.

ATTRACT DIRECT INVESTMENT FROM OUTSIDE THE BLOC Foreign firms prefer to invest in countries that are part of an economic bloc because factories they build there receive preferential treatment for exports to all member countries within the bloc. Many non-European firms—for example, General Mills, Samsung, and Tata—invested heavily in the EU to take advantage of Europe's economic integration. By establishing operations in a single EU country, these firms gain free trade access to the entire EU market.

ACQUIRE STRONGER DEFENSIVE AND POLITICAL POSTURE Regional integration helps strengthen member countries relative to other nations and world regions. This was one of the motives for creating the European

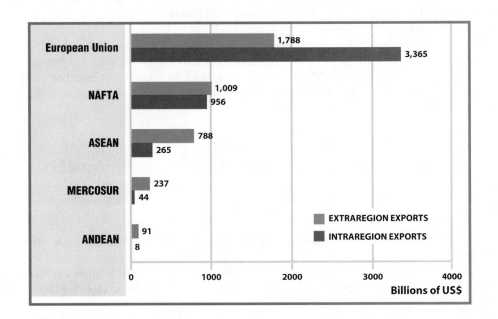

Source: kycstudio/iStock

MERCOSUR includes Argentina, Brazil, Paraguay, and Uruguay. The bloc aims to expand market size, achieve scale economies, attract foreign direct investment, and build defensive and political posture. Shown is the MERCOSUR headquarters in Montevideo, Uruguay.

Community (the precursor to the EU), whose members sought to fortify their mutual defense against the former Soviet Union. Today, the EU is one way Europe counterbalances the power and international influence of the United States. Forming an economic bloc also helps countries gain bargaining and political power in world affairs. For example, the EU enjoys greater influence with the WTO in trade negotiations than any individual member country. Broadly speaking, countries are more powerful when they cooperate than when they operate alone.

 ## Success Factors for Regional Integration

Regional economic blocs have attained varying degrees of success. Exhibit 9.8 shows the value of exports within economic blocs and from blocs to the rest of the world. For example, trade among the EU member countries amounts to about $3.4 trillion of exports. By contrast, exports from the

EXHIBIT 9.8

Exports within and from Regional Economic Blocs (billions of US$)

Source: Based on World Trade Organization, *International Trade Statistics 2011*, retrieved from www.wto.org.

Bloc	Extraregion Exports	Intraregion Exports
European Union	1,788	3,365
NAFTA	1,009	956
ASEAN	788	265
MERCOSUR	237	44
ANDEAN	91	8

Billions of US$

EU countries to the rest of the world amount to some $1.7 trillion. In the EU, within-bloc exports account for about 65 percent of the bloc's total exports. On the other hand, within-bloc exports account for only 16 percent of total exports in the MERCOSUR bloc, and only 8 percent in the Andean bloc. The MERCOSUR and Andean blocs have not succeeded in generating much trade among their member countries.

Experience with regional economic integration suggests that the most successful economic blocs tend to possess the following characteristics.

CROSS-NATIONAL ECONOMIC DYNAMISM Before nations can succeed as an economic bloc, there must be strong potential for trade and development among the member countries. *Economic dynamism* is the propensity for entrepreneurial activity and the existence of business systems that can support it, in a given business environment. Nations typically form economic blocs in the hope of spurring economic activity across national borders. If the basis for such activity is lacking among the member countries, forming a bloc may have little effect. Economic dynamism is often deficient in developing economies that lack a substantial base of companies and entrepreneurs.

ECONOMIC SIMILARITY The more similar the economies of the member countries, the more likely the economic bloc will succeed. Large wage rate differences mean workers in lower-wage countries will migrate to higher-wage countries. Economic instability in one member country can spread quickly and harm the economies of the other members. Compatibility of economic characteristics is so important that the EU requires its current and prospective members to meet strict membership conditions, ideally low inflation, low unemployment, reasonable wages, and stable economic conditions.

POLITICAL SIMILARITY Similarity in political systems enhances prospects for a successful bloc. Countries that seek to integrate regionally should share similar aspirations and a willingness to surrender national autonomy for the larger goals of the proposed union. For example, most of the existing EU members are characterized by a long history of stable, socially democratic forms of government. By contrast, many Europeans have been reluctant to allow Ukraine to enter the EU, partly due to the country's history of socialism and political turmoil.[13]

SIMILARITY OF CULTURE AND LANGUAGE Cultural and linguistic similarity among the countries in an economic bloc provides the basis for mutual understanding and cooperation. The MERCOSUR bloc enjoys advantages because its members share many cultural and linguistic similarities. Under NAFTA, it was easier for Canadian firms to establish trade and investment relationships in the United States than in Mexico because of similarities between the two northern countries.

GEOGRAPHIC PROXIMITY Most economic blocs are formed by countries within the same geographic region. Close geographic proximity facilitates transportation of products, labor, and other factors of production. Neighboring countries also tend to share culture and language.

While all four types of similarities enhance the potential for successful regional integration, economic interests are often most important. Dissimilarity in one area can be overcome by similarity in the other areas. This was demonstrated in the EU, whose member countries, despite strong cultural and linguistic differences, achieved common goals based on pure economic interests.

 ## Ethical Dilemmas and Drawbacks of Regional Integration

Regional integration is not a uniformly positive trend; it can give rise to ethical and moral concerns. These include:

TRADE DIVERSION Regional integration gives rise to both trade creation and trade diversion. Trade creation means trade is generated among the countries inside the economic bloc because, as barriers fall, each member country tends to begin trading more with members than with nonmembers. As this occurs, members trade less with countries outside the bloc, leading to trade diversion. In this way, national trade patterns are altered: More trade takes place inside the bloc, and less with countries outside the bloc.

Suppose that before the formation of NAFTA, Canada's government had imposed a tariff of 100 percent on imports of wine from the United States and a tariff of 50 percent on wine imports from France. Further assume Canada had always imported its wine from France because the lower tariff made French wine cheaper than U.S. wine. Then, after NAFTA was launched, the U.S. tariff was eliminated and U.S. wine became cheaper than French wine. At this point, Canada reduced its wine imports from France and began importing wine from the United States. This exemplifies trade diversion (stopping wine imports from France) and trade creation (starting wine imports from the United States). Such outcomes suggest the EU, NAFTA, and other economic blocs may become "economic fortresses," resulting in a decline in trade between blocs that exceeds the gains from trade within the blocs. However, the historical record indicates there has been relatively little trade diversion among the world's leading economic integration blocs.[14]

REDUCED GLOBAL FREE TRADE In more advanced stages, regional integration can give rise to two opposing tendencies. On the one hand, a country that reduces trade barriers is moving toward free trade. On the other hand, an economic bloc that imposes external trade barriers is moving away from worldwide free trade.

For example, countries that form a customs union impose common external trade barriers, and some member countries' external tariffs may actually rise. Suppose Germany, the largest EU member, once had a 10 percent tariff on imported footwear. Assume that in the process of developing a common market, the EU countries collectively imposed a 20 percent tariff on footwear imports. In effect, Germany's external tariff on footwear has increased. In this way, regional integration can result in higher tariffs, making buyers inside the bloc worse off because they must pay higher prices for the products they want to consume. Tariffs also counteract comparative advantages and interfere with trade flows that should be dictated by national endowments. All told, external trade barriers imposed by economic blocs result in a net loss in well-being to all members in the bloc.

Finally, because foreign firms sell less into a bloc that imposes restrictions, they are harmed as well. When external suppliers are based in developing economies, the consequences are significant. By limiting imports from such countries, trade barriers imposed by economic blocs threaten the ability of producers in these countries to improve their living conditions. Agricultural tariffs imposed by the EU and NAFTA blocs, for instance, do the most harm to farmers in Africa, South America, and other areas characterized by substantial poverty. Suppose you were a government trade official in Europe or North America. Use the Ethical Framework in Chapter 5 to analyze the pros and cons of advanced-economy nations imposing high trade barriers on imports of agricultural goods from Africa and other poor regions.

The empirical evidence on whether regional integration reduces global free trade is inconclusive. So far, the record suggests that regional integration has done little to hinder the development of broad-based trade. It may well be that regional free trade is a stepping-stone on the path to the liberalization of trade among nations generally.[15]

Sustainability of Firms and National Assets

LOSS OF NATIONAL IDENTITY When nations join in an economic bloc, increased cross-border contact has a homogenizing effect in which national cultural identity is diluted as the members become more similar to each other. Sustaining national identity becomes increasing challenging. For this reason, member countries typically retain the right to protect certain industries vital to national heritage or security. For example, because Canada fears its indigenous culture will be diluted by an invasion of U.S. movie and television programming, it

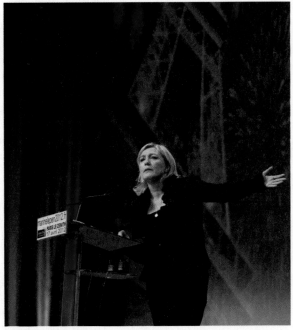

Source: © epa european pressphoto agency b.v./Alamy

Some nations fear regional integration triggers cross-border assimilation, diminishing the distinctiveness of individual countries. Pictured here is Marine Le Pen, leader of the Front National political party in France, which opposes large-scale immigration.

restricts U.S. movie and TV producers from investing in its film market. In this way, Canadian TV and movie interests remain largely in the hands of Canadians.

SACRIFICE OF AUTONOMY Later stages of regional integration require member countries to establish a central authority to manage the bloc's affairs. Each participating country must sacrifice some of its autonomy, such as control over its own economy. In this way, nations that join an economic bloc risk losing some of their national sovereignty. Concerns about national sovereignty have been a stumbling block in the development of the EU. In the United Kingdom, critics see the passage of many new laws and regulations by centralized EU authorities as a direct threat to British self-governance.[16] The British have resisted joining the European Monetary Union because such a move would reduce the power they currently hold over their own currency, economy, and monetary regime.

TRANSFER OF POWER TO ADVANTAGED FIRMS Regional integration can concentrate economic power in the hands of a few, relatively advantaged firms. Development of the regional marketplace attracts new competitors from other bloc countries or from outside the bloc into formerly protected national markets. Foreign invaders that are larger, have stronger brands, or enjoy other advantages can overwhelm local firms in their home markets. Regional integration also encourages mergers and acquisitions within the bloc, creating large companies that can dominate smaller firms. For example, as the DR-CAFTA accord eliminated trade barriers that once protected Central American economies, numerous U.S. firms entered these countries to manufacture and sell products. Large U.S. firms with substantial resources can dominate markets in Central America.

FAILURE OF SMALL OR WEAK FIRMS As trade and investment barriers decline, protections are eliminated that previously shielded smaller or weaker firms from foreign competition. Many local firms find themselves battling new, often better-resourced rivals. New competitive pressures particularly threaten the sustainability of smaller firms. The risk can be substantial for companies in smaller bloc countries or in industries that lack comparative advantages. Under NAFTA, many U.S. companies in industries covered by the accord relocated their production to Mexico, which has low wage rates. As a result, numerous firms in the U.S. tomato-growing industry went out of business as that industry shifted south to Mexico.

CORPORATE RESTRUCTURING AND JOB LOSS Many firms must restructure to meet the competitive challenges posed in the new, enlarged marketplace of regional integration. Increased competitive pressures and corporate restructuring may lead to worker layoffs or reassignments to distant locations. MERCOSUR was a factor in the layoff of thousands of workers in Argentina's auto parts manufacturing sector. When they negotiate regional integration agreements, national governments sometimes include provisions intended to minimize job losses and the failure of smaller firms. NAFTA included various clauses aimed at softening the effects of economic restructuring, maintaining, or improving labor conditions for workers in the member countries, and retraining workers who lost their jobs due to NAFTA.

Regional integration is often controversial because of potential negative consequences. Critics suggest NAFTA has disproportionately helped some and harmed others. Industrialization has increased pollution in Mexico. Thousands of Canadian firms faced bankruptcy or were taken over by foreigners. In Europe, EU-imposed standards have forced firms to substantially revise manufacturing practices, packaging, and other value-chain activities. Mass migration of workers into high-income countries has triggered increased social problems.

However, there is evidence that job losses, pollution, and other problems are the result of broader forces associated with rising productivity, economic development, and growing world demand for goods and services. Dynamism in world economies has been increasing for decades, well before regional integration. Manufacturing's contribution to employment in Europe and the United States has fallen steadily since the 1950s, due to globalization, automation, and other factors. Jobs transfer to low-cost-labor countries is facilitated by inexpensive international transportation and communications, and by falling trade barriers. Developing economies endure much pollution, mainly from unregulated industrial development not related to regional integration.[17] Most governments regard regional integration as advantageous. Thus, nations worldwide continue to pursue free trade and economic interdependence within their regions.

Management Implications of Regional Integration

Many firms confront new opportunities and threats that arise from regional economic integration. Economic integration suggests at least five implications for firms.

INTERNATIONALIZATION BY FIRMS INSIDE THE ECONOMIC BLOC Initially, regional integration pressures or encourages companies to internationalize into neighboring countries within the bloc. The elimination of trade and investment barriers presents new opportunities to source input goods from foreign suppliers within the bloc. Internationalizing into neighboring, familiar countries provides many firm with the confidence and skills to further internationalize to markets outside the bloc. For example, following NAFTA's launch, many U.S. companies entered Canada and gained valuable international experience that inspired them to expand onward to Europe and Asia.

RATIONALIZATION OF OPERATIONS The creation of an economic bloc decreases the importance of national boundaries. Instead of viewing the bloc as a collection of disparate countries, firms begin to view the bloc as a unified whole. Managers develop strategies and value-chain activities suited to the region as a whole, rather than to individual countries. *Rationalization* is the process of restructuring and consolidating company operations following regional integration to reduce redundancy and costs and increase the efficiency of operations. Management may combine two or more factories into a single factory, eliminating duplication and increasing economies of scale. In this way, the firm that formerly operated factories in each of several countries benefits by consolidating the factories into a single, central location inside the economic bloc.

Caterpillar, the U.S. manufacturer of earth-moving equipment, was one of many firms that shifted its focus from serving individual European countries to serving the EU region. Caterpillar undertook a massive program of rationalization and modernization at its EU plants to streamline production, reduce inventories, increase economies of scale, and lower operating costs.

Companies can apply rationalization to other value-chain functions such as distribution, logistics, purchasing, and R&D. Formation of the EU and subsequent elimination of trade barriers, customs checkpoints, and country-specific transportation regulations allowed U.S. firms to restructure their EU distribution channels to make them better suited to the greatly enlarged EU marketplace. Creation of the economic bloc eliminated the need for separate distribution strategies in individual countries. Instead, the firms developed a *global* approach for the larger marketplace, generating economies of scale in distribution.

MERGERS AND ACQUISITIONS The formation of economic blocs also leads to mergers and acquisitions (M&A), sometimes due to rationalization. Two giant engineering firms, Asea AB of Sweden and Brown, Boveri & Co. of Switzerland, merged to form Asea Brown Boveri (ABB), facilitated by development of the EU. The merger allowed the new firm to increase its R&D activities and pool greater capital funding for major projects, such as construction of power plants and large-scale industrial equipment.

REGIONAL PRODUCTS AND MARKETING STRATEGY In advanced stages of regional integration, member countries tend to harmonize product standards and commercial regulations. This allows companies to standardize products and streamline marketing activities. In the enlarged marketplace, firms begin to sell a few product models rather than dozens, which provides economies of scale and enormous cost savings.[18] For example, J. I. Case Company once produced seventeen versions of its Magnum model of farm tractors to comply with widely

Source: Henry Nowick/Shutterstock

Regional integration arrangements have induced countless firms to rationalize their international operations. Caterpillar, the manufacturer of earthmoving equipment, shifted its focus from serving individual European countries to serving the EU bloc as a whole.

varying national regulations on lights, brakes, and other product specifications. Harmonization of EU product standards allowed the firm to standardize its tractor and produce only a handful of models appropriate for serving the whole EU market.[19]

INTERNATIONALIZATION BY FIRMS FROM OUTSIDE THE BLOC The most effective way for a foreign firm to enter an economic bloc is to establish a physical presence there via foreign direct investment (FDI). By building a production facility, marketing subsidiary, or regional headquarters anywhere inside a bloc, the outsider gains access to the entire bloc and to advantages enjoyed by local firms based inside the bloc. Since formation of the EU, Britain has become the largest recipient of FDI from the United States. Many U.S. firms choose Britain as the beachhead to gain access to the massive EU market. Many European firms likewise have established factories in Mexico to access countries in the NAFTA bloc.

In 1990, there were approximately fifty regional economic integration agreements worldwide. Today, some 400 are in various stages of development, and many nations belong to more than one. Since the Doha round of global trade negotiations collapsed in 2008, countries have been putting more emphasis on developing regional trade agreements.[20] Economic blocs are joining with other blocs around the world. Several countries, including Canada and India, are negotiating free trade agreements with the EU.[21] Other intercontinental blocs are underway. Meanwhile, evidence suggests that regional economic integration is not slowing the progress of global free trade. Rather, global free trade will tend to emerge as economic blocs link up with each other over time. The evidence suggests regional economic integration is gradually giving way to a system of free trade worldwide.

CLOSING CASE

Russell Brands: Choosing between Global and Regional Free Trade

Russell Brands is a leading manufacturer of sportswear, including sweatshirts, sweatpants, and T-shirts. Owned by Berkshire Hathaway, Russell is based in Bowling Green, Kentucky. Its main competitors include Adidas, Nike, Benetton, and Zara. Russell controls every step of the manufacturing process, from weaving raw yarn into fabric, to dyeing, cutting, and sewing, to selling garments through retailers. Russell's brands include JERZEES, American Athletic, Brooks, Cross Creek, Huffy Sports, Russell Athletic, and Spalding. The firm sells through mass merchandisers, department stores such as Walmart, and golf pro shops. Russell sells its apparel in about one hundred countries. Recently, the firm contracted with Kangwei, one of China's largest sports brands, to manufacture and market athletic apparel there. Kangwei runs more than 1,000 retail stores in China and plans to open several hundred more to offer Spalding apparel.

Unlike Nike and Adidas, Russell does not enjoy much brand loyalty, which prevents the firm from charging premium prices. To cut costs, Russell needs to manufacture its products in low-cost countries. Management was pleased with passage of the Dominican Republic–Central American Free Trade Agreement (DR-CAFTA) in 2005. The pact eliminated trade barriers between the United States and six Latin American countries: Guatemala, Honduras, El Salvador, Nicaragua, Costa Rica, and the Dominican Republic. Following DR-CAFTA's passage, Central American countries experienced a significant rise in FDI from abroad. The apparel and clothing sector, consisting of firms like Russell, were among the biggest beneficiaries.

Prior to DR-CAFTA, many North American apparel companies sourced from China and other Asian nations, where production costs are low. DR-CAFTA virtually eliminated tariffs on trade between the United States, Central America, and the Dominican Republic. Now Russell can cost-effectively source raw materials in Central America, manufacture fabric in the United States, then send the fabric to its factories in Honduras for assembly. Once the garments are completed, they are re-exported to the United States for distribution. Without DR-CAFTA, it would not have been cost effective to make fabric in the United States, export it to Asia, and have the products manufactured there and then re-exported back. Under that scenario, Russell would have shifted all its manufacturing to China.

Background on DR-CAFTA

In the past, Latin American countries were shielded from international competition in the textiles sector by the protectionist Multi-Fibre Agreement (MFA), which imposed strict import quotas. When the MFA expired in 2005, many countries began importing cheap apparel from low-cost producers in Asia. China dramatically increased its apparel exports to the United States, impacting U.S. and Central American producers that long had supplied Western markets. For example, Alabama was once the world center of sock manufacturing. When the MFA expired, the sock capital shifted to Datang, China. Alabama sock workers were paid $10 an hour on average, compared to 75 cents an hour in Datang.

Following expiration of the MFA, China began flooding the United States with apparel. China's share of finished clothing exports to the U.S., once less than 20 percent, leaped past 50 percent in some segments. To protect its home-grown apparel industry, the United States reimposed some trade barriers against Chinese imports. The U.S. government justified this action in part because China's currency, the yuan, is considered undervalued, making Chinese exports artificially cheap. Such protection of the U.S. apparel industry is only temporary. WTO rules require the U.S. government to remove the trade barriers, at which time Chinese exports to the United States will increase.

Many in the U.S. apparel industry see DR-CAFTA as perhaps the only way to compete with China. DR-CAFTA helps maintain much apparel production in the Western hemisphere by creating a bigger apparel market in the region and granting favorable trade status to apparel producers who manufacture their products using raw material from the DR-CAFTA region.

The United States is the biggest apparel market, importing more than $9 billion worth of apparel from the DR-CAFTA countries annually in recent years. As the biggest shipper in dollar value, Honduras exports cotton blouses, shirts, and underwear, among other goods. Meanwhile, DR-CAFTA gave U.S. producers an equal footing to sell their products to Central America. The region is the second largest market for U.S. textiles and yarn, which Central American manufacturers use to produce finished apparel.

The Situation in Honduras

Russell manufactures much of its garments in Honduras, a poor Central American country with 7 million people, one-quarter of whom are illiterate. Honduras has an annual per-capita GDP of about $4,500, with 65 percent of the population living below the poverty line. Growth remains dependent on the U.S. economy, its largest trading partner. Honduras sends more than two-thirds of its exported goods to the United States and receives about 50 percent of its imports from that country. The Honduran government is counting on the DR-CAFTA agreement to increase trade with the United States and the Central American region.

Honduras's apparel sector employs more than 110,000 people, or 30 percent of the country's total industrial employment. The Honduran government used incentives to create a large cluster of apparel firms. In addition to low-cost labor, Honduras offers a generous tax package: Firms pay no income tax, value-added tax, or duties. Honduran apparel

manufacturers can truck their merchandise to Puerto Cortes, Central America's biggest port, in just 30 minutes. From there, it takes only 22 hours to reach Miami by container ship. By comparison, it takes up to a month to make similar shipments from China. Honduras is investing to improve Puerto Cortes and create a "Textiles and Apparel University" to train future managers and supervisors. To counter Chinese competition, the apparel industry in Honduras has begun to offer the "total package"— buying fabric, designing garments, and doing final assembly.

Russell's Dilemmas

Russell management must decide whether to keep its manufacturing in Honduras or move everything to China. Another possibility is to establish production in Eastern Europe to gain access to the huge EU market. Adidas and Nike are pursuing markets in China and other Asian countries. Labor costs for manufacturing apparel are similar in Central America and China. In both locations, workers earn around a dollar per hour and can produce more than one hundred garments per day from precut cloth. Labor costs are roughly $2 an hour in Eastern Europe, but producers are advantaged by being so close to the 500 million consumers in the EU.

Management at Russell is monitoring the proposed FTAA, which would widen access to the Latin American marketplace with its 500 million consumers. Maintaining a presence in Latin America gives Russell a favorable position for targeting new markets there. Recently, growth prospects in several Central American countries declined, partly due to their heavy dependence on trade with the United States and other advanced economies, which reduced their imports from the region during the global recession.

AACSB: Reflective Thinking Skills, Ethical Understanding and Reasoning Abilities

Case Questions

1. China has the most comparative advantages in producing apparel. Free trade theory implies that retailers should import clothing from the most efficient country. Given this, and potential drawbacks of regional integration, would it be better to allow free trade to take its natural course? That is, should DR-CAFTA be rescinded and apparel retailers allowed to import from the most cost-effective suppliers, wherever they are located worldwide?

2. What are the advantages and disadvantages of DR-CAFTA to Honduran firms? To Honduras as a nation? Should free trade be extended throughout Latin America via the proposed Free Trade Area of the Americas (FTAA)?

3. Honduras is a poor country that faces job losses in its apparel sector from growing foreign competition. What can the Honduran government do to help keep jobs in Honduras? Should the government try to attract more foreign investment into Honduras? What steps could the government take to attract more FDI?

4. Russell Brands is smaller than Adidas and Nike. What should Russell do to counter these firms? What should Russell do to

counter the flood of low-cost athletic apparel now entering the United States from China? What can Russell do to ensure its future survival and success?

Sources: D. Clark, "Adjustment Problems in Developing Countries and the U.S.-Central America-Dominican Republic Free Trade Agreement," *The International Trade Journal*, January 2009, pp. 31–37; R. Knee and S. Nall, "The CAFTA Effect," *Journal of Commerce*, September 15, 2008, p. 3; J. Authers, "Employment Shrinks in the Textile Sector," *Financial Times*, March 10, 2006, p. 5; J. Borneman, "Regional Support in a Global Fight," *Textile World*, May/June 2006, pp. 26–32; Central Intelligence Agency, *CIA World Factbook*, entry on Honduras, 2009; G. Colvin, "Saving America's Socks," *Fortune*, August 22, 2005, p. 38; "Textiles: Losing Their Shirts," October 16, 2004, pp. 59–60; Corporate profiles of Russell, Nike, and Adidas, retrieved from http://www.hoovers.com; Mateusz Filipski, J. Taylor, and Siwa Msangi, "Effects of Free Trade on Women and Immigrants: CAFTA and the Rural Dominican Republic," *World Development* 39, no. 10 (2011): 1862–1877; E. Morphy, "Trade Watch: CAFTA—The Rocky Path to Regional Free Trade," *Foreign Direct Investment*, October 1, 2005, p. 1.

CHAPTER ESSENTIALS

MyManagementLab
Go to **mymanagementlab.com** to complete the problems marked with this icon ⭐.

Key Terms

common market   220

customs union   219

economic union   220

free trade agreement   218

free trade area   219

regional economic integration   218

Summary

In this chapter, you learned about:

1. Regional integration and economic blocs

Under regional economic integration, groups of countries form alliances to promote free trade, cross-national investment, and other mutual goals. This integration results from *regional economic integration blocs* (or economic blocs), in which member countries agree to eliminate tariffs and other restrictions on the cross-national flow of products, services, capital, and, in more advanced stages, labor within the bloc. At minimum, the countries in an economic bloc become parties to a **free trade agreement**, which eliminates tariffs, quotas, and other trade barriers.

2. Levels of regional integration

For countries that become members of an economic bloc, there are various stages of regional integration. First is the **free trade area**, which eliminates tariffs and other trade barriers. Second is the **customs union**, a free trade area in which common trade barriers are imposed on nonmember countries. Third is the **common market**, a customs union in which factors of production move freely among the members. Fourth is the economic union, a common market in which some important economic policies are harmonized among the member states. A true *political union* does not yet exist.

3. The leading economic blocs

There are hundreds of economic integration agreements in the world. The European Union (EU) is the most advanced, comprising twenty-eight countries in Europe. It has increased market access, improved trade rules, and harmonized standards among its members. Europe is also home to the European Free Trade Association. In the Americas, the most notable bloc is the North American Free Trade Agreement (NAFTA), consisting of Canada, Mexico, and the United States. NAFTA has reached only the free trade–area stage of regional integration. Other economic blocs in the Americas include MERCOSUR, CARICOM, and CAN. In the Asia/Pacific region, ASEAN, APEC, and the Australia and New Zealand Closer Economic Relations Agreement (CER) are the leading blocs. Economic blocs in Africa and the Middle East have experienced only limited success.

4. Advantages of regional integration

Regional integration contributes to corporate and industrial growth and hence to economic growth, better living standards, and higher tax revenues for the member countries. It increases market size by integrating the economies within a region. It increases economies of scale and factor productivity among firms in the member countries and attracts foreign investors to the bloc. Regional integration also increases competition and economic dynamism within the bloc and increases the bloc's political power.

5. Success factors for regional integration

The most successful blocs consist of countries that are relatively similar in terms of culture, language, and economic and political structures. Members also are usually close to each other geographically. They can overcome major differences in any one of these factors if there are strong similarities in all the other factors.

6. Ethical dilemmas and drawbacks of regional integration

Regional integration simultaneously leads to trade creation, whereby new trade is generated among the countries inside the bloc, and trade diversion, in which member countries reduce trade with countries outside the bloc. Regional integration entails specific disadvantages. It can reduce global free trade, particularly when member countries form a customs union that results in substantial trade barriers to countries outside the bloc. When economic blocs involve many countries of various sizes, regional integration can concentrate power into large firms and large nations inside the bloc. Regional integration results in economic restructuring, which may harm particular industries and firms. When a country joins an economic bloc, it must relinquish some of its autonomy and national power to the bloc's central authority. Individual countries risk losing some of their national identity.

7. **Management implications of regional integration**

Regional integration leads to increased internationalization by firms inside their economic bloc. Firms reconfigure and rationalize their operations in line with the larger internal market. Management reconfigures value-chain activities on a pan-regional basis. The formation of economic blocs also leads to mergers and acquisitions because the emergence of a new, larger market favors the creation of larger firms. Managers revise marketing strategies by standardizing products and developing regional brands. Regional integration also leads firms from outside the bloc to expand into the bloc, often via direct investment. However, regional integration leads to competitive pressures and other challenges to firms inside the bloc, some of which may lay off workers or go out of business.

Test Your Comprehension AACSB: Ethical Understanding and Reasoning Abilities, Reflective Thinking Skills

1. What is a regional economic integration bloc (also called an economic bloc)?

2. Differentiate between a free trade area and a customs union. Differentiate between a customs union and a common market.

3. What are the world's leading economic blocs? Which blocs are most advanced in terms of regional integration?

4. Describe the major characteristics of the EU and NAFTA.

⭐ 5. Why do nations seek to join or form economic blocs? What are the advantages of such arrangements?

6. What national conditions contribute to the success of economic integration?

7. Explain the drawbacks and ethical dilemmas of regional integration for nations. Explain the drawbacks and ethical dilemmas for firms.

8. Distinguish between trade creation and trade diversion.

⭐ 9. What strategies should companies employ to maximize the benefits of regional integration?

Apply Your Understanding AACSB: Ethical Understanding and Reasoning Abilities, Reflective Thinking Skills, Communication Abilities

1. There are hundreds of economic integration agreements in effect around the world. Virtually every country is party to one or more free trade agreements. Supporters argue that free trade is good for nations. What is the basis for their support? That is, what are the specific benefits that countries seek by joining an economic bloc? What is the main economic bloc for your country? From your perspective, what advantages has bloc membership brought to your country? What disadvantages has bloc membership produced?

2. Levi Strauss & Co. makes and sells blue jeans, Dockers, and Slates brand name apparel in over 60 countries. With the onset of regional integration in the EU and Latin America, Levis management revised the firm's production and marketing strategies, to make them more appropriate for regional, as opposed to national, operations. Based on the regional integration changes underway in these areas, and on your understanding of the business implications of regional integration, what should Levis do? In answering, think in terms of Levis' major value chain activities, especially production and marketing. What are the pros and cons to Levis of producing and marketing its apparel on a regional basis, as opposed to a national or global basis? Justify your answer.

3. *Ethical Dilemma*: Suppose you are a member of a government task force evaluating the future of NAFTA between Canada, Mexico, and the United States. Proponents want to transform NAFTA into a common market by removing barriers to the movement of labor. The goal is to reduce poverty in Mexico by allowing Mexican citizens to work freely in Canada and the United States. Per-capita income in Mexico is less than $10,000, compared to more than $40,000 in Canada and the United States. Critics oppose the common market because of the huge

income difference. They argue that an open border would induce millions of Mexicans to migrate northward seeking work and threaten the jobs and wages of millions of Americans and Canadians. Proponents argue that, as economic integration progressed under a common market, average wages in the three countries would equalize and eliminate pressures on northern job markets. Analyze this situation using the Ethical Framework in Chapter 5. Should the task force recommend the common market? Or is the potential harm too great for Canada and the United States? If NAFTA became a common market, what could U.S. and Canadian firms do to maintain their competitiveness relative to Mexican firms, given Mexico's advantage in low wages?

 globalEDGE **INTERNET EXERCISES**
(http://www.globalEDGE.msu.edu)

AACSB: Reflective Thinking Skills, Analytic Skills, Ethical Understanding and Reasoning Abilities

Refer to Chapter 1, page 24, for instructions on how to access and use globalEDGE™.

1. There has been much opposition to the Free Trade Area of the Americas (FTAA). For a sampling of arguments against this proposed pact, visit www.globalexchange.org, www.citizenstrade.org, and www.corpwatch.org. Also visit the official site of the FTAA at www.ftaa-alca.org, or obtain information on the proposed pact from globalEDGE™. Based on your reading of this chapter, evaluate the arguments against the FTAA. Do you agree with arguments made by the critics? Why or why not? Would the proposed FTAA harm small Latin American countries? Would it be a boon only to large countries such as Brazil, Canada, and the United States? Justify your answers.

2. Visit the Web sites of three major economic blocs. One way to do this is to enter the acronyms for each bloc into a globalEDGE™ search. Using the "Success Factors for Regional Integration" framework highlighted in this chapter, discuss the likely long-term prospects for success in each of these blocs. For each bloc, which of the success factors are strongest, and which are weakest? Which bloc seems to have the best chances for long-term success? Why?

3. NAFTA is a free trade area, and the EU is a common market. Visit the Web sites of these two economic blocs, www.nafta-sec-alena.org and www.europa.eu, and explain the business strategy implications of each type of economic bloc. Small and medium-sized enterprises (SMEs) tend to be disadvantaged when it comes to competing against large corporations in regional economic blocs. What steps can SMEs, in particular, take to maximize prospects for success when doing business in a free trade area? What steps can SMEs take when doing business in a common market?

MyManagementLab

Go to **mymanagementlab.com** for Auto-graded writing questions as well as the following Assisted-graded writing questions:

9-1. What is the role of free trade agreements in the formation of economic blocs?

9-2. Distinguish the different levels of economic integration.

9-3. Mymanagementlab Only – comprehensive writing assignment for this chapter.

The New Global Challengers: MNEs from Emerging Markets

Emerging markets are countries such as Brazil, China, India, Russia, and Turkey that, in contrast to already advanced economies, are now experiencing rapid industrialization, modernization, and economic growth. They represent attractive markets and low-cost manufacturing bases, but they have high-risk business environments with evolving commercial infrastructure and legal systems. Despite their drawbacks, emerging markets have begun to produce *new global challengers*, top firms that are fast becoming key contenders in world markets.

The Boston Consulting Group has identified the top 100 new global challengers. Many of these firms are from China and India. Mexico's Cemex is one of the world's largest cement producers and Russia's Lukoil has big ambitions in global energy. In Turkey, diversified conglomerate Koc Holding owns Arcelik, a giant home appliance producer.

The Brazilian food processor Brasil Foods exemplifies the challengers' international entrepreneurial savvy. The firm has annual revenues of more than $15 billion, operates farms, and markets processed foods and ready-to-eat meals. Brasil

CHAPTER 10

Understanding Emerging Markets

 LEARNING OBJECTIVES *In this chapter, you will learn about the following:*

1. Advanced economies, developing economies, and emerging markets
2. What makes emerging markets attractive for international business
3. Assessing the true potential of emerging markets
4. Risks and challenges of emerging markets
5. Success strategies for emerging markets
6. Corporate social responsibility, sustainability, and the crisis of global poverty
7. The special case of Africa

MyManagementLab®

⭐ **Improve Your Grade!**

Over 10 million students improved their results using the Pearson MyLabs. Visit **mymanagementlab.com** for simulations, tutorials, and end-of-chapter problems.

Foods has built world-class distribution and supply-chain management systems, and exports about half its annual production.

In their home countries, new global challengers leverage low-cost labor, as well as engineering and managerial talent often superior to that of competitors in advanced economies. Many new global challengers are family-owned or family-run businesses (family conglomerates), and enjoy numerous advantages. They often access low-interest loans from home-country, government-owned banks.

Many are expanding internationally by taking their established brands to global markets. China's Hisense sells its branded televisions and air conditioners in more than 40 countries, including the best-selling brand of flat-panel TV in France. Hisense also makes stylish consumer electronics at low prices.

Some new global challengers leverage superior engineering capability. Hong Kong's Johnson Electric is the world leader in small electric motors for automotive and consumer applications. Brazil's Embraer taps the large pool of experienced but low-cost engineers in that country to build innovative small jets. It has become the world's leading producer of regional jet aircraft.

Many global challengers benefit from local bases of natural resources. Russia's Rusal is extracting the country's rich reserves of bauxite to produce aluminum for international markets. Most the world's natural resources are located in developing economies, and a growing number of new global challengers use these to their advantage. China's CNOOC, for example, has been acquiring oil and gas reserves in Asia and Africa.

The new global challengers pose a growing competitive challenge to companies from advanced economies such as Europe, Japan, and North America. The challengers represent an important trend in international business.

SOURCES: G. Adolph and J. Pettit, "The Rise of the New Blue Chips," *Strategy and Business*, Autumn 2008, pp. 8–10; Boston Consulting Group, *The New Global Challengers* (Boston: Boston Consulting Group, 2006); Boston Consulting Group, *The 2009 BCG 100 New Global Challengers* (Boston: Boston Consulting Group, 2009); "'Multilatinas' on the Move," *Business Latin America*, January 9, 2012, pp. 4–5; "Emerging-Market Multinationals: The Challengers," *Economist*, January 12, 2008, pp. 62–63; Juichuan Chang, "The Early and Rapid Internationalization of Asian Emerging MNEs," *Competitiveness Review*, March 1, 2011, pp. 171–187; N. Kumar, "India Unleashed," *Business Strategy Review* 20, no. 1 (2009): 4.

The opening story describes how emerging market countries such as Brazil, China, Russia, and India are giving birth to companies that are challenging traditional MNEs from the advanced economies. These *new global challenger* firms leverage local advantages such as low-cost labor and superior skills to compete successfully around the world. Historically, most trade and investment were conducted among the advanced economies, the world's wealthiest countries. Today, however, developing economies and especially emerging markets play important and growing roles in international business.

In this chapter we discuss emerging market economies and contrast them with advanced and developing economies. Each country group poses distinctive opportunities and risks. By analyzing a country in terms of its stage of economic development, the manager can gain insights into the purchasing power of its citizens, the sophistication of its business sector, the adequacy of its commercial infrastructure, and numerous other areas. Let's explore the country groups in detail.

 ## Advanced Economies, Developing Economies, and Emerging Markets

The map in Exhibit 10.1 highlights the country groups differentiated by degree of economic development and per-capita income. Let's define them:

Advanced economies
Post-industrial countries characterized by high per-capita income, highly competitive industries, and well-developed commercial infrastructure.

Developing economies
Low-income countries characterized by limited industrialization and stagnant economies.

Emerging markets
Former developing economies that have achieved substantial industrialization, modernization, and rapid economic growth since the 1980s.

> **Advanced Economies** Post-industrial countries characterized by high per-capita income, highly competitive industries, and well-developed commercial infrastructures. They are the world's richest nations and include Australia, Canada, Japan, New Zealand, the United States, and most European countries.
>
> **Developing Economies** Low-income countries characterized by limited industrialization and stagnant economies. They make up the largest group of countries and include Bangladesh, Nicaragua, and Zaire.
>
> **Emerging Markets** Also called emerging market economies, they are former developing economies that have achieved considerable industrialization, modernization, and rapid economic growth since the 1980s. Some forty countries are considered emerging markets and are found mainly in Asia, Latin America, and Eastern Europe. The largest are Brazil, Russia, India, and China (sometimes abbreviated "BRIC").

Exhibit 10.2 provides an overview of key differences among the three country groups. The group with the largest number of countries by far is the developing economies. However, they contribute least to world GDP and their citizens have very low incomes. Their *disposable income*, the proportion of personal income they spend on purchases other than food, clothing, and housing is very limited. More than one-third of all developing economy residents live on less than $2 per day.[1] The combination of low income and often high birth rates promotes poverty in these countries.

Exhibit 10.2 also reveals countries' technological development. The developing economies are at a very early stage, while the emerging markets are quickly catching up to the advanced economies. *Technology* is the knowledge and application of tools, techniques, systems and methods of organization to serve industry, science, and the arts. Technology is vital to economic development and includes not just hardware computers, telephones, and industrial machinery; it also includes the associated software—knowledge management, educational systems, worker skill levels, banking infrastructure, and so forth. In the advanced economies and emerging markets, information and communications technologies have had an enormous impact on knowledge acquisition and on worker and personal productivity. A lack of such technologies in the developing economies helps explain why they are well behind the other countries in education, economic output, and future prospects.

Another way to visualize the three groups of countries is to examine a map of the world at night, shown in Exhibit 10.3. The advanced economies are the most visible areas because, with the highest levels of industrialization, they are generally the most brightly lit. The map also suggests significant economic activity in the emerging market countries. However, it reveals very low levels of industrialization across large stretches of Africa, central Asia, eastern Russia, and major parts of Latin America. These represent developing economies and other areas with little or no industrialization and limited economic development. Note how areas of advanced industrialization tend to consume the most energy. Increasingly, nations must consider how economic development can be achieved without excessive ecological harm. Let's discuss the three country categories in detail.

Advanced Economies

Having reached a mature state of industrial development, advanced economies have largely evolved from manufacturing economies into service-based economies. Home to only about 14 percent of the world's population, they have long dominated international business. They account for nearly two-thirds of world GDP, more than half of world trade in products, and three-quarters of world trade in services.

Advanced economies have democratic, multiparty systems of government. Their economic systems are usually based on capitalism. They have tremendous purchasing power, with few restrictions on international trade and investment. They host the world's largest MNEs. A leading example is Australia, which has one of the world's best-performing economies and one of the highest per-capita income levels worldwide. Australia emphasizes responsible fiscal and monetary policies, including low government debt. The government has wisely invested in education and infrastructure, with a focus on innovation and productivity. Robust economic reforms has spurred rapid growth of the Australian economy. Australia benefits from close economic ties with China, and other emerging markets in Asia. Australia is home to some of the world's leading MNEs, including BHP Billiton, Westfield, and AXA Asia Pacific.[2]

Developing Economies

Developing economies are sometimes called *underdeveloped countries* or *third-world countries*. These terms are imprecise and often offensive because, despite poor economic conditions, developing economies tend to be highly developed in historical and cultural terms.

Developing economies are hindered by high infant mortality, malnutrition, short life expectancy, illiteracy, and poor education systems. For example, the proportion of children who finish primary school in most African countries is less than 50 percent.[3] Because education is strongly correlated with economic development, poverty tends to persist. Lack of adequate health care is a major concern. Some 95 percent of the world's AIDS victims are found in developing economies, an additional hardship that hampers their development. Many adults cannot work or care for their children and require significant medical care. As a result, productivity is stagnant in many areas, leading to a vicious cycle of persistent poverty.

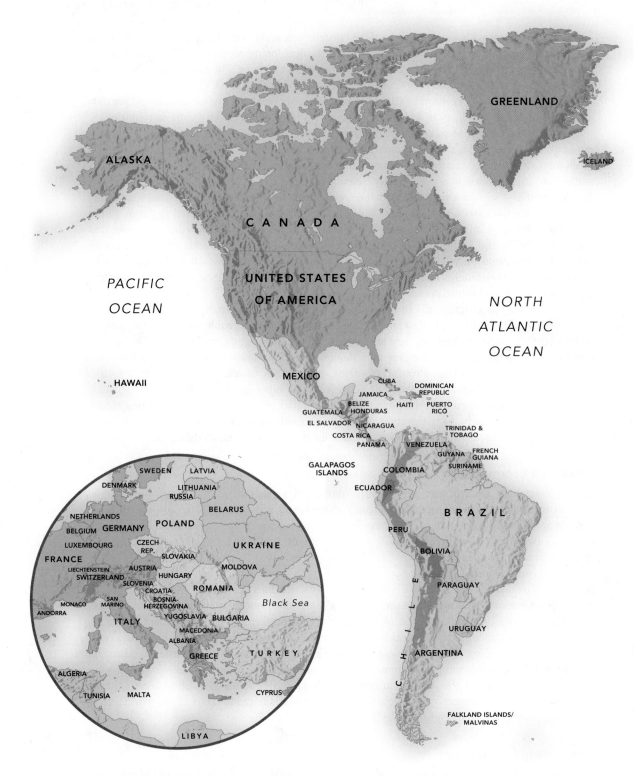

EXHIBIT 10.1

Advanced Economies, Developing Economies, and Emerging Markets

ARCTIC OCEAN

NORWAY

SWEDEN

FINLAND

ESTONIA

NETHERLANDS

IRELAND
UNITED
KINGDOM

DENMARK

BELGIUM

LATVIA

LITHUANIA

RUSSIA

BELARUS

GERMANY

POLAND

LUXEMBOURG

CZECH
REP.

SLOVAKIA

UKRAINE

FRANCE

LIECH.

AUSTRIA

HUNGARY

MOLDOVA

SWITZ.

SLOVENIA

ROMANIA

CROATIA

BOSNIA

MONACO

HERZEGOVINA

ANDORRA

ITALY

YUGOSLAVIA

BULGARIA

GEORGIA

ALBANIA

MACEDONIA

SPAIN

ARMENIA

AZERBAIJAN

UZBEKISTAN

KYRGYZSTAN

PORTUGAL

GREECE

TURKEY

TURKMENISTAN

TAJIKISTAN

TUNISIA

CYPRUS

SYRIA

LEBANON

IRAQ

AFGHANISTAN

ISRAEL

JORDAN

IRAN

PAKISTAN

MOROCCO

KUWAIT

NEPAL

BHUTAN

ALGERIA

LIBYA

EGYPT

QATAR

UNITED ARAB
EMIRATES

SAUDI
ARABIA

OMAN

INDIA

BANGLADESH

MYANMAR
(BURMA)

LAOS

WESTERN
SAHARA

MAURITANIA

MALI

NIGER

CHAD

ERITREA

YEMEN

THAILAND

VIETNAM

NEGAL

AMBIA

SUDAN

DJIBOUTI

CAMBODIA

IINEA-BISSAU

BURKINA
FASO

GUINEA

NIGERIA

BENIN

SOMALIA

ERRA LEONE

IVORY
COAST

GHANA

TOGO

CENTRAL AFRICAN
REPUBLIC

ETHIOPIA

LIBERIA

CAMEROON

SRI
LANKA

BRUNEI

EQUATORIAL
GUINEA

CONGO
REPUBLIC

UGANDA

MALAYSIA

SINGAPORE

GABON

CONGO
DEMOCRATIC
REPUBLIC
(ZAIRE)

RWANDA

KENYA

BURUNDI

INDONESIA

PAPUA
NEW
GUINEA

TANZANIA

SOLOMON
ISLANDS

ANGOLA

ZAMBIA

MALAWI

MOZAMBIQUE

NAMIBIA

ZIMBABWE

MADAGASCAR

MAURITIUS

BOTSWANA

RÉUNION

SWAZILAND

SOUTH
AFRICA

LESOTHO

RUSSIA

KAZAKHSTAN

MONGOLIA

CHINA

NORTH
KOREA

SOUTH
KOREA

JAPAN

TAIWAN

PHILIPPINES

INDIAN
OCEAN

PACIFIC
OCEAN

SOUTH
ATLANTIC
OCEAN

AUSTRALIA

VANUATU

FIJI

NEW
CALEDONIA

NEW
ZEALAND

Advanced Economies - Post-industrial countries characterized by high per-capita income, highly competitive industries, and well-developed commercial infrastructure.

Emerging Markets - Former developing economies that have achieved substantial industrialization, modernization, and rapid economic growth since the 1980s.

Developing Economies - Low-income countries characterized by limited industrialization and stagnant economies.

EXHIBIT 10.2 Key Differences among the Three Major Country Groups

Dimension	Advanced Economies	Developing Economies	Emerging Markets
Representative Countries	Canada, France, Japan, United Kingdom, United States	Angola, Bolivia, Nigeria, Bangladesh	Brazil, China, India, Indonesia, Turkey
Approximate Number of Countries	35	120	40
Population (% of world)	14%	25%	61%
Approximate Average Per-Capita Income (U.S. dollars; PPP basis)	$44,155	$3,618	$11,050
Approximate Share of World GDP (PPP basis)	65%	4%	31%
Population (millions)	979	1,706	4,155
Telephone Lines per 1,000 People (fixed and mobile)	803	442	694
Personal Computers per 1,000 People	517	39	191
Internet Users per 1,000 People	751	165	422
Motor vehicles per 1,000 people	537	65	236

Sources: Based on World Bank at http://www.worldbank.org and International Monetary Fund at http://www.imf.org.

EXHIBIT 10.3

The World at Night, Showing Varying Areas of Industrialization

Source: C. Mayhew and R. Simmon (NASA/GSFC), NOAA/NGDC, DMSP Digital Archive.

Governments in developing economies are often severely indebted. Some countries in Africa, Latin America, and South Asia have debt levels that approach or exceed their annual gross domestic product. This means it would cost a year's worth of national productive output just to pay off the national debt. Much of Africa's poverty is the result of government policies that discourage entrepreneurship, trade, and investment. For example, starting a new business in sub-Saharan countries in Africa can require a dozen different approvals and take two or more months to complete. In the advanced economies, by contrast, starting a new business requires only half as many approvals and two weeks to complete.[4] Bureaucracy and red tape in developing economies deter firms from these countries from participating in the global economy.

As Exhibit 10.4 illustrates, there are substantial differences in critical economic conditions across the three country groups. In particular, the exhibit reveals that developing economies lack numerous conditions needed for successful economic development, including low trade barriers and substantial international trade and investment. Advanced economies rank well in these areas, and emerging markets are showing consistent improvement.

EXHIBIT 10.4 **Trade Conditions with Major Country Groups**

Trade Condition	Advanced Economies	Developing Economies	Emerging Markets
Industry	Highly developed	Poor	Rapidly improving
Competition	Substantial	Limited	Moderate, but increasing
Trade Barriers	Minimal	Moderate to high	Rapidly liberalizing
Trade Volume	High	Low	High
Inward FDI	High	Low	Moderate to High

Sources: Based on International Monetary Fund at http://www.imf.org, World Bank, 2012 at http://www.worldbank.org, and Central Intelligence Agency, *CIA World Factbook 2012* at http://www.cia.gov/cia/publications/factbook.

Emerging Market Economies

Emerging markets are found in East and South Asia, Eastern Europe, Southern Africa, Latin America, and the Middle East. Perhaps their most distinguishing characteristic is rapidly improving living standards and a growing middle class with rising economic aspirations.[5] As a result, they have become very attractive destinations for exports, FDI, and global sourcing.

Because their economies are changing so dynamically, Hong Kong, Israel, Singapore, South Korea, and Taiwan have likely developed beyond the emerging market stage. Several emerging markets will join the group of wealthy nations in the not-too-distant future. Bulgaria and Romania received a boost when they joined the European Union and adopted stable monetary and trade policies. They leverage their low-cost labor to attract investment from Western Europe, thereby boosting their economies.

Similarly, some countries currently classified as developing economies have the potential to become emerging markets in the near future. These "frontier economies" include the European countries of Estonia, Latvia, Lithuania, Slovakia; the Latin American countries of Costa Rica, Panama, and Uruguay; and Kazakhstan, Nigeria, and the United Arab Emirates.

Finally, economic prosperity often varies within emerging markets. There are usually two parallel economies—those in urban areas and those in rural areas. Compared to rural areas, urban areas tend to have more developed economic infrastructure and consumers with greater discretionary income.

Certain emerging markets that have evolved from centrally planned economies to liberalized markets—specifically China, Russia, and several countries in Eastern Europe—are called **transition economies**. These countries were once socialist states but have been largely transformed into capitalism-based systems, partly through a process of **privatization**—the transfer of state-owned industries to private concerns. Privatization and the promotion of new, privately owned businesses have allowed the transition economies to attract substantial direct investment from abroad. Long burdened by excessive regulation and entrenched government bureaucracy, they are gradually introducing legal frameworks to protect business and consumer interests and ensure intellectual property rights. They hold much potential.[6]

Privatization has provided many opportunities for foreign firms to enter transition economies by purchasing former state enterprises. In Eastern Europe, Western companies are leveraging inexpensive labor and other regional advantages to manufacture products bound for export markets. Poland, the Czech Republic, Hungary, and other former East Bloc countries have made great strides in political and economic restructuring. These countries are well on their way to more advanced stages of economic development.

Exhibit 10.5 contrasts the national characteristics of emerging markets with the other two country groups. Of particular note, the least economically developed countries tend to be rooted in the agriculture and commodities sectors, which provide little foundation for wealth creation. By contrast, emerging markets and advanced economies specialize in the manufacturing and services sectors, in which ample added value promotes superior living standards.

Exhibit 10.6 shows that emerging markets account for a substantial proportion of world GDP. Similarly, they represent more than 30 percent of exports and receive more than one-third of world FDI. As Exhibit 10.7 shows, emerging markets have been growing much faster than

Transition economies
A subset of emerging markets that evolved from centrally planned economies into liberalized markets.

Privatization
Transfer of state-owned industries to private concerns.

EXHIBIT 10.5 National Characteristics of Major Country Groups

Characteristic	Advanced Economies	Developing Economies	Emerging Markets
Median Age of Citizens	39 years	24 years	32 years
Major Sector Focus	Services, branded products	Agriculture, commodities	Manufacturing, some services
Economic and Political Freedom	Free or mostly free	Mostly repressed	Moderately free or mostly not free
Economic/Political System	Market	Command or Mixed	Mixed
Regulatory Environment	Minimal regulations	Highly regulated, burdensome	Achieved much economic liberalization
Country Risk	Low	moderate to high	Variable
Intellectual Property Protection	Strong	Weak	Moderate and improving
Infrastructure	Well-developed	Inadequate	Moderate but improving

Sources: Based on International Monetary Fund at http://www.imf.org, World Bank at http://www.worldbank.org, and Central Intelligence Agency, *CIA World Factbook 2012* at http://www.cia.gov/cia/publications/factbook.

EXHIBIT 10.6

Why They Matter: Emerging Markets as a Percent of World Total

Sources: Based on "The New Titans," *Economist*, September 14, 2006, survey section; International Monetary Fund at http://www.imf.org; Central Intelligence Agency, *CIA World Factbook 2012*, at http://www.cia.gov/cia/publications/factbook; World Bank at http://www.worldbank.org.

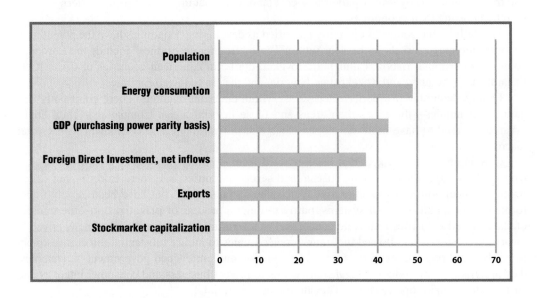

advanced economies. The emerging markets collectively enjoy an average annual GDP growth rate of around 7 percent, a remarkable feat.

Emerging markets possess numerous advantages that have fostered their rise. The presence of low-cost labor, knowledge workers, government support, low-cost capital, and powerful, highly networked conglomerates have helped make these countries formidable challengers in the global marketplace. As highlighted in the opening story, **new global challengers** are leading firms from emerging markets that are fast becoming key contenders in world markets. One is Orascom Telecom (www.orascomtelecom.com), an Egyptian mobile telecommunications provider that has become an industry leader in Africa and the Middle East. Orascom has strung together a telecom empire of more than 100 million subscribers, stretching from North Africa to Bangladesh. Operating expenses in Egypt are much lower than in Europe, because engineers and salespeople work for less. In Europe, Chinese and Russian companies have been acquiring major European firms, such as Saab and Volvo. Chinese and Russian firms are

New global challengers
Leading firms from emerging markets that are fast becoming key contenders in world markets.

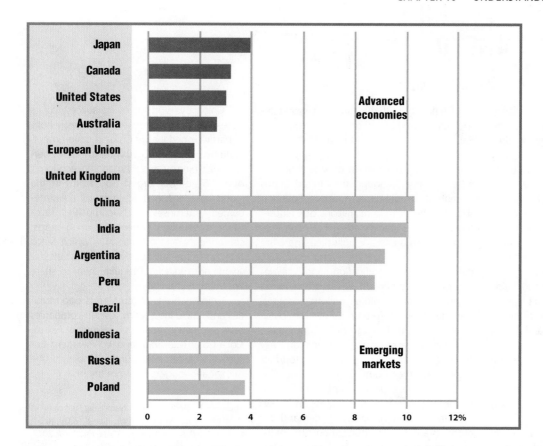

EXHIBIT 10.7

GDP Growth Rates in Advanced Economies and Emerging Markets

Source: Based on International Monetary Fund (2012), World Economic Outlook Database, at http://www.imf.org.

investing huge sums in a range of sectors in Europe, including engineering, high-tech, energy, finance, and utilities.[7]

Each year, *Forbes* magazine catalogs the leading 2,000 global firms. Analysis reveals that between 2005 and 2011, a total of 158 MNEs entered the list from just four emerging market countries: China, India, Brazil, and Russia. During the same period, 295 firms from the United States, Japan, and the United Kingdom *fell off* the Forbes list. In 1990, only nineteen companies from low-income countries were among the *Fortune* Global 500 listing of the world's largest MNEs. By 2012, China alone had 73 companies in the Global 500. These statistics reveal how many new global challengers are displacing traditional MNEs from the advanced economies and becoming key competitors in world markets. Managers need to devise innovative strategies to skillfully compete with them.[8]

China is the largest emerging market, with a population of 1.3 billion people, one-fifth of the world's total. Its economy continues to grow at an impressive rate, and its role in international business is expanding rapidly. The country already has produced numerous new global challengers, such as Shanghai Automotive (China's top automaker), Sinopec (a large oil company), and Shanghai Baosteel (a steel manufacturer). Since 1993, the share of world merchandise exports from Japan, the United States, and most European countries has declined. In the same period, the proportion of goods produced and shipped from China has risen sharply; it now accounts for more than 10 percent of total world merchandise exports. The figure is impressive given that most of the world's 200 or so countries engage in product exporting.[9] The *Global Trend* highlights China's growing role in international business.

What Makes Emerging Markets Attractive for International Business

Emerging markets are attractive to internationalizing firms as target markets, manufacturing bases, and sourcing destinations.

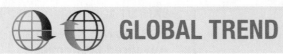

GLOBAL TREND

China's Evolving Opportunities and Challenges

In the past two decades, China has achieved explosive economic growth, often 10 percent or more per year. Although income per person is still modest, China is now the world's second-largest economy (after the United States). After joining the WTO, China expanded its role as a global manufacturing site, and intensified its massive exports to countries worldwide. Investment poured in from MNEs that perceive a bright future for China as both a manufacturing platform and a huge buyer market. The country now attracts more than $100 billion annually in FDI. China is the world's leading consumer of automobiles, bicycles, motorcycles, shoes, mobile phones, and luxury goods. Worldwide, every year China consumes more than 20 percent of numerous categories of commodities.

Success in China has come slowly for most foreign firms. A big challenge is low per-capita income. About one-third of China's population (roughly 400 million people) lives on less than $3 per day. Of a total population of 1.3 billion, the realistic target consumer segment is the 250 million residents of urban areas, largely in the developed eastern region. Other challenges include regional differences in language, autonomous local governments, and inadequate infrastructure. Local Chinese companies—new global challengers—are coming on strong, and competing fiercely with foreign companies in the huge Chinese market.

China's growth has strained world resources, leading to higher commodity prices. Rapid, underregulated industrialization has produced much environmental degradation. China emits more carbon dioxide than any other country (although the United States is highest in per-capita terms). Pollution shortens the lifespan of millions of Chinese. Most power is generated in low-tech coal plants, which are major polluters. There are also serious problems of water pollution, deforestation, desertification, and soil deterioration. Factories in China are required to follow only minimal pollution control standards, which further harms the natural environment. Firms from Europe, Japan, the United States, and other economically advanced areas must follow much tougher standards in their home countries.

The Chinese government is beginning to develop clean technologies and new industries based on growing demand for products and services that support the natural environment. China is investing hundreds of billions of dollars in wastewater treatment infrastructure and energy-saving power production. China is already a world leader in developing green industries and renewable energy. It has become a major manufacturer of solar photovoltaic technology and wind turbines, much of it for export. Due to an extensive system of rivers, China has massive potential to install hydroelectric power.

China owes much of its success to its state-owned enterprises—companies wholly or partly owned by the Chinese government. State-owned firms account for about 45 percent of China's rapidly expanding economy. About 61 of the largest 500 MNEs in the world are Chinese, and almost all are state-owned enterprises. Such companies favor Chinese suppliers when procuring parts, components, and other inputs, which tends to exclude foreign firms from important development projects or require them to share important technology.

China is home to numerous opportunities and challenges. Many foreign companies have succeeded in China, including Airbus, Coca-Cola, Motorola, and Volkswagen. But success requires a deep understanding of the market and long-term commitment.

Sources: F. Balfour, "The Surprising Strength of Southeast Asia," *BusinessWeek*, June 8, 2009, p. 34; Central Intelligence Agency, *World Factbook 2012*, at http://www.cia.gov/cia/publications/factbook; Bob Davis and Jason Dean, "State-Run Firms are the Giants of China's Economy," *Wall Street Journal*, February 23, 2012, p. A12; Y. Ma, "China's View of Climate Change," *Policy Review*, June/July 2010, pp. 27–44; George Stalk and David Michael, "What the West Doesn't Get About China," *Harvard Business Review*, June 2011, pp. 25–27; A. Wahl, "Clean and Green China," *Canadian Business*, Summer 2009, pp. 103–104; J. Warren, "China's Green Future," *Far Eastern Economic Review*, December 2008, pp. 53–57.

Emerging Markets as Target Markets

Emerging markets have become important target markets for a wide variety of products and services. The largest emerging markets have doubled their share of world imports in the last few years. The growing middle class in emerging markets implies rising demand for various consumer products, such as electronics and automobiles, and services such as health care.[10] Roughly one-quarter of Mexico's 112 million people enjoy affluence equivalent to that of the middle class in the advanced economies. In some product categories, demand is growing fastest in emerging markets. For example, the fastest-growing markets for power tool companies such as Black & Decker and Robert Bosch are in Asia, Latin America, Africa, and the Middle East.[11] Even during the recent global recession, technology firms such as Cisco, Hewlett-Packard, and Intel generated a large and growing proportion of their revenues from sales to such countries.[12]

Firms in the global pharmaceutical companies such as Pfizer and GlaxoSmithKline increased their emphasis on developing and marketing drugs in emerging markets. Industry insiders forecast that medication sales in the biggest emerging markets will hit $300 billion by 2017, equal to today's sales in the top five European markets and the United States combined. Already Merck and Pfizer have launched popular drugs in India, using innovative pricing strategies that make once-expensive medications affordable for millions of low-income consumers.[13]

Businesses in emerging markets are important targets for machinery and equipment sales. In this category, markets are huge for textile machinery in India, for agricultural equipment in China, and for oil and gas exploration technology in Russia. In a similar way, governments and state enterprises in emerging markets are major targets for sales of infrastructure-related products and services such as machinery, power transmission equipment, transportation equipment, high-technology products, and other products that countries in the middle stage of development typically need.

Emerging Markets as Manufacturing Bases

Firms from Japan, Europe, the United States, and other advanced economies have invested vast sums to develop manufacturing facilities in emerging markets. These markets are home to low-wage, high-quality labor for manufacturing and assembly operations. In addition, some emerging markets have large reserves of raw materials and natural resources. Mexico and China are important production platforms for manufacturing cars and consumer electronics. South Africa is a key source for industrial diamonds. Brazil is a center for mining bauxite, the main ingredient in aluminum. Thailand has become an important manufacturing location for Japanese MNEs such as Sony and Sharp. Motorola, Intel, and Philips manufacture semiconductors in Malaysia and Taiwan.

Emerging markets enjoy considerable success in certain industries, such as Brazil in iron ore and processed foods, Taiwan and Malaysia in personal computers, and South Africa in mining. Individual firms, including those highlighted in the opening story, have also become world-class companies. Two of the world's top-selling beer brands are new global challengers based in China (Snow, made by China Resources Snow Breweries) and Brazil (Skol, made by InBev). Together, these firms produce more than 50 million barrels of beer annually.[14] South Korea's Samsung is the world's largest electronics company and the leading producer of semiconductors and flat screen TVs. It has displaced Sony (Japan) and Motorola (USA) in these industries.

Source: © Keith Dannemiller/Alamy

Emerging markets are excellent locations for global sourcing. These workers in Mexico are making aircraft parts for export to the United States.

Emerging Markets as Sourcing Destinations

Increasingly, companies sub-contract their non-core business activities to specialized contractors. This trend is known as **outsourcing**—the procurement of selected value-chain activities, including production of intermediate goods or finished products, from independent suppliers or company-owned subsidiaries. Outsourcing helps firms become more efficient, concentrate on their core competencies, and obtain competitive advantages. When sourcing relies on foreign suppliers or production bases, it is known as **global sourcing** or *offshoring*.

Emerging markets serve as excellent platforms for sourcing. Numerous MNEs have established call centers in Eastern Europe, India, and the Philippines. Firms in the IT industry such as Dell and IBM reap big benefits from the ability to outsource certain technological functions to knowledge workers in India. Intel and Microsoft have many of their programming activities performed in Bangalore, India. Investments from abroad benefit emerging markets as they lead to new jobs and production capacity, transfer of technology and know-how, and linkages to the global marketplace.

Outsourcing
The procurement of selected value-chain activities, including production of intermediate goods or finished products, from independent suppliers.

Global sourcing
The procurement of products or services from independent suppliers or company-owned subsidiaries located abroad for consumption in the home country or a third country.

 ## Assessing the True Potential of Emerging Markets

When targeting emerging markets for sales, for manufacturing, or as sourcing bases, MNEs must obtain reliable information to support managerial decision-making. However, emerging markets are characterized by unique circumstances that usually hinder managers' ability to acquire needed facts and figures. Limited data, unreliable information, or the high cost of conducting market research pose formidable challenges for estimating the true potential of emerging markets. In such cases, MNEs may need to improvise and use creative methods to generate needed findings.[15]

In the early stages of market research, managers examine three important statistics to estimate market potential: per-capita income, size of the middle class, and market potential indicators. Let's examine each in turn.

Per-Capita Income as an Indicator of Market Potential

When evaluating the potential of individual markets, managers often start by examining aggregate country data, such as gross national income (GNI) or per-capita GDP, expressed in terms of a reference currency such as the U.S. dollar. The second column in Exhibit 10.8 provides per-capita GDP for a sample of emerging markets, and for the United States for comparison. For example, China's per-capita GDP converted at market exchange rates is $5,715, while that of the United States is $49,055.

However, per-capita GDP converted at market exchange rates paints an inaccurate picture of market potential because it overlooks the substantial price differences between advanced economies and emerging markets. Prices are usually lower for most products and services in emerging markets. For example, a U.S. dollar exchanged and spent in China will buy much more than a dollar spent in the United States.

Purchasing power parity (PPP)
An adjustment for prices that reflects the amount of goods that consumers can buy in their home country, using their own currency and consistent with their own standard of living.

What should managers do to accurately estimate market potential? The answer lies in using per-capita GDP figures adjusted for price differences. Economists estimate real buying power by calculating GDP statistics based on **purchasing power parity (PPP)**. The PPP concept suggests that, in the long run, exchange rates should move toward levels that would equalize the prices of an identical basket of goods and services in any two countries. Since prices vary greatly among countries, economists adjust ordinary GDP figures for differences in purchasing power. Adjusted per-capita GDP more accurately represents the amount of products consumers can buy in a given country, using *their own currency* and consistent with *their own standard of living.*

Now examine per-capita GDP, adjusted for purchasing power parity, for the same sample of countries in the third column in Exhibit 10.8. Note that a more accurate estimate of China's per-capita GDP is $9,204—about 60 percent more than the per-capita GDP at market exchange rates. Compare the two figures for other countries as well. These adjusted estimates help explain

EXHIBIT 10.8 Difference in Per Capita GDP, in Conventional and Purchasing Power Parity (PPP) Terms, 2012

Country	Per-Capita GDP, Converted using Market Exchange Rates (U.S.$)	Per-Capita GDP, Converted using PPP Exchange Rates (U.S.$)
Argentina	$11,358	$18,202
Brazil	13,316	12,304
Bulgaria	7,742	14,188
China	5,715	9,204
Hungary	14,861	20,201
South Korea	25,949	33,397
Mexico	11,210	15,675
Russia	14,918	17,613
Turkey	10,988	14,931
United States	49,055	49,055

Source: Based on International Monetary Fund, *World Economic Outlook Database 2012,* at http://www.imf.org.

why firms target emerging markets despite the seemingly low income levels in conventional income statistics.

Another way to illustrate the PPP concept is to examine the Big Mac Index developed by *The Economist* newsmagazine (www.economist.com). The Index first gathers information about the price of hamburgers at McDonald's restaurants worldwide. It then compares the prices based on actual exchange rates to those based on the PPP price of Big Macs to assess whether a nation's currency is under- or over-valued. Exhibit 10.9 presents the Big Mac Index for the most recent year. It reveals that the currencies of most European countries (mainly the euro) are overvalued, while those of most developing economies or emerging markets are undervalued. The Big Mac Index also implies the Chinese yuan is undervalued. It suggests the yuan is 42 percent below its fair-value benchmark with the dollar.[16]

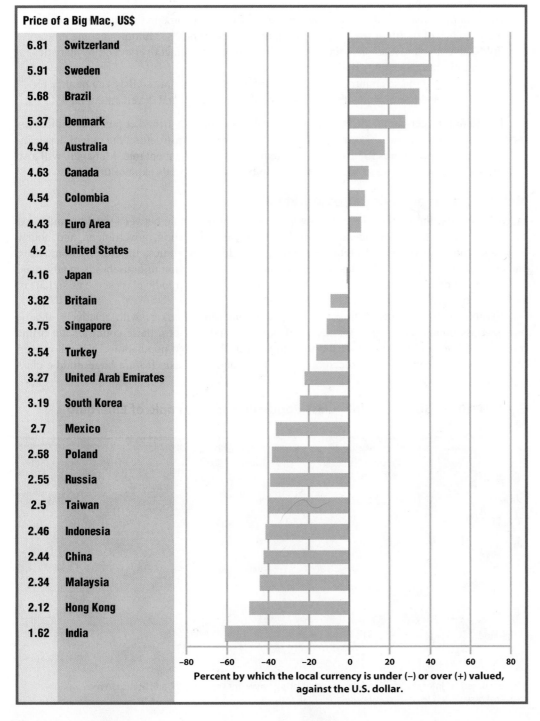

Price of a Big Mac, US$

6.81	Switzerland
5.91	Sweden
5.68	Brazil
5.37	Denmark
4.94	Australia
4.63	Canada
4.54	Colombia
4.43	Euro Area
4.2	United States
4.16	Japan
3.82	Britain
3.75	Singapore
3.54	Turkey
3.27	United Arab Emirates
3.19	South Korea
2.7	Mexico
2.58	Poland
2.55	Russia
2.5	Taiwan
2.46	Indonesia
2.44	China
2.34	Malaysia
2.12	Hong Kong
1.62	India

Percent by which the local currency is under (–) or over (+) valued, against the U.S. dollar.

EXHIBIT 10.9

The Big Mac Index

Source: Re-created from "Burgernomics Shows Switzerland Has the Most Overvalued Currency," January 12, 2012. From *The Economist* online.

Even when per-capita income is adjusted for purchasing power parity, managers should exercise care in relying on it as an indicator of market potential in an emerging or developing economy. There are four reasons for this caution:

1. Official data do not account for the informal economy, where economic transactions are not officially recorded and are therefore left out of national GDP calculations. In developing economies, the informal economy is often as large as the formal economy. Countries usually lack sophisticated taxation systems, and individuals and businesses often under-report income to minimize tax obligations. Also not normally captured by national GDP estimates are barter exchanges in which no money changes hands.

2. Most people in emerging markets and developing economies are on the low end of the income scale. As you may recall from your statistics training, "mean" or "average" does not accurately represent a nonnormal distribution; often, median income more accurately depicts purchasing power.

3. *Household income* is substantially larger than per-capita income in these countries due to the presence of multiple wage earners in individual households. Multiple-income house-holds have much greater spending power than individuals, a fact overlooked by statistics that emphasize per-capita GDP.

4. Governments in these countries may underreport national income so they can qualify for low-interest loans and grants from international aid agencies and development banks.

In addition to per-capita GDP, managers should examine other market potential indicators, including GDP growth rate, income distribution, commercial infrastructure, the rate of urbanization, consumer expenditures for discretionary items, and unemployment rate. Managers will also find the size and growth rate of the middle class to be revealing. Let's explore this next.

Middle Class as an Indicator of Market Potential

In every country, the middle class represents the segment of people between wealthy and poor. They have economic independence; work in businesses, education, government, and hourly jobs; and consume various discretionary items, including electronics, furniture, automobiles, and entertainment. The middle class makes up the largest proportion of households in advanced economies. In emerging markets, the size and growth rate of the middle class serve as signals of a dynamic market economy.

Exhibit 10.10 provides data for a sample of emerging markets with relatively sizable middle-class populations.[17] For marketers of products and services, these countries are prime prospects. China and India rank at the very top, given their large populations. Note, however, the trade-off between various indicators. While India and Indonesia feature large middle-class

EXHIBIT 10.10 Size of Middle-Class Population for a Sample of Emerging Markets, 2012

Country	Middle Class Population (millions)	Percent of Income Held by Middle Class	Per-Capita GDP (PPP, U.S.$)
Brazil	70	39%	$11,273
China	589	46	7,544
India	397	47	3,408
Indonesia	95	47	4,347
Mexico	40	55	14,406
Russia	71	40	15,612
Thailand	31	45	9,221
Turkey	35	46	13,577

Sources: Based on International Monetary Fund at http://www.imf.org, World Bank at http://www.worldbank .org, and globalEDGE™ at http://www.globalEDGE.msu.edu.

populations in absolute terms, per-capita GDP in these countries is rather modest, especially when compared to South Korea, Russia, and Mexico. However, the percentage of income held by the middle class in India and Indonesia is relatively high, at 47 percent each.

Demographic trends indicate that, in the coming two decades, the proportion of middle-class households in emerging markets will become much bigger, acquiring enormous spending power. The most growth by far will occur in Asia, especially China. In population terms, Asia is expected to account for about half the world's middle class by the year 2020.[18] As incomes increase, spending patterns will evolve, fueling growth across various product and service categories.

 Risks and Challenges of Emerging Markets

Country risk takes on growing importance in an increasingly interdependent world. More MNEs are doing business in emerging markets, which are beset by various challenges.[19] National and regional crises have global implications, even for firms very remote from crisis locations.

Political Instability

The absence of reliable or consistent governance from recognized government authorities adds to business costs, increases risks, and reduces managers' ability to forecast business conditions. Political instability is associated with corruption and weak legal frameworks that discourage inward investment and the development of a reliable business environment. In Russia, for example, evolving political conditions threaten the business activities of foreign firms. Bureaucratic practices favor well-connected, home-grown firms. Western oil companies have been denied access to Russia's energy resources. In the 2012, *Ease of Doing Business* rankings of the World Bank, the Russian Federation received an overall ranking of 120 out of 183 countries (with first being the best). It ranked 111th in starting a business; 178th in dealing with construction permits; and 160th in trading across borders procedures (www.doingbusiness.org). These conditions discourage firms from entering the Russian market.[20]

Weak Intellectual Property Protection

Even when they exist, laws that safeguard intellectual property rights may not be enforced, or the judicial process may be painfully slow. In Argentina, for example, enforcement of copyrights on recorded music, videos, books, and computer software is inconsistent. Authorities attempt to stop shipments of pirated merchandise, but inadequate resources and slow court procedures hamper enforcement. Laws against Internet piracy are weak and ineffective.[21] Counterfeiting—unauthorized copying and production of a product—is common in China, Indonesia, and Russia, especially of software, DVDs, and CDs. In India, weak patent laws often discourage investment by foreign firms. In China, counterfeiting extends even to creating fake retail stores, imitating trademark retail outlets of top brands like Apple and Ikea.[22]

Bureaucracy, Red Tape, and Lack of Transparency

Burdensome administrative rules and excessive requirements for licenses, approvals, and paperwork all delay business activities. Canamo is a Venezuelan company that was eager to export its products. However, it first had to obtain numerous certificates and licenses from various government authorities in Venezuela, a jumble of paperwork that can take two to six months to complete. Faced with this long and unpredictable process, Canamo all but abandoned hope of entering the U.S. market.[23] In India, poor Internet infrastructure is a drag on the nation's economy. Officials want to increase access to broadband technology, but massive bureaucracy is delaying progress. Internet providers must obtain permission from upwards of a dozen government agencies just to lay Internet cable. The process is prohibitively expensive, which deters providers from entering the market.[24]

Excessive bureaucracy is usually associated with lack of transparency, suggesting that legal and political systems may not be open and accountable to the public. Bribery, kickbacks, and extortion, especially in the public sector, cause difficulty for managers. Where anti-corruption laws are weak, managers may be tempted to offer bribes to ensure the success of business deals. In *Transparency International's* ranking of the most corrupt countries (www.transparency.org), emerging markets such as Russia, Venezuela, and the Philippines are among those with substantial corruption.[25]

Country Realities

The quality of infrastructure in emerging markets presents both challenges and opportunities. In rural India, only about 20 percent of households have telephones. In total, just 60 percent of Indians have access to a phone. Less than 10 percent of all Indians use the Internet. Broadband technology is very limited. Telephoning and using the Internet can be challenging in India. But such conditions also offer huge opportunities for firms in the telecommunications and computer networking industries.

Poor Physical Infrastructure

In advanced economies, high-quality roads, drainage systems, sewers, and electrical utilities are taken for granted. However, in emerging markets, such basic infrastructure is often lacking. In India, many still do not have access to toilets and sewage treatment systems. Poor sanitation gives rise to illness, and thousands of Indian children die every week from diarrheal illness. India's ports, roads, railways, and airports are insufficient to handle the massive volumes of cargo that enter and leave the country every day. Industrial cities like Bangalore and Pune regularly experience power outages that can last 24 hours or more.[26] The government is working to improve infrastructure, but MNEs often must build their own systems and find creative solutions to support value-chain activities. In much of the world, firms find themselves building roads, installing localized energy sources, and developing other such systems in order to conduct business. A subsidiary of Tata Chemicals, part of India's giant Tata conglomerate, had to build its own road and railway infrastructure in Africa to support the firm's operations there.[27]

Partner Availability and Qualifications

Foreign firms should seek alliances with well-qualified local companies in countries characterized by inadequate legal and political frameworks. Through such partners, foreign firms can access local market knowledge, establish supplier and distributor networks, and develop key government contacts. However, partners that can provide these advantages are not always readily available in emerging markets, especially smaller ones.

Dominance of Family Conglomerates

Family conglomerate
A large, highly diversified company that is privately owned.

Many emerging market economies are dominated by family-owned rather than publicly owned businesses. A **family conglomerate** (FC) is a large, highly diversified company that is privately owned. FCs operate in industries ranging from banking to construction to manufacturing. They control the majority of economic activity and employment in emerging markets like South Korea, where they are called *chaebols*; in India, where they are called *business houses*; in Latin America, where they are called *grupos*; and in Turkey, where they are called *holding companies*. Exhibit 10.11 illustrates some of the world's leading FCs.

A typical FC may hold the largest market share in each of several industries in its home country. In South Korea, the top thirty FCs account for nearly half the economy's assets and industry revenues. Samsung is perhaps the most famous Korean FC. In Turkey, the Koc Group accounts for about 20 percent of trading on the Istanbul Stock Exchange, and Sabanci provides more than 5 percent of Turkey's national tax revenue. FCs enjoy various competitive advantages in their home countries, such as government protection and support, extensive networks in various industries, superior market knowledge, and access to capital. Hyundai Group was an early mover in South Korea's auto industry and now holds the largest share of that country's car market. When foreign automakers tried to enter the market, they found Hyundai's advantages overwhelming.

An FC's origins and growth often derive from a special relationship with the government, which protects it by providing subsidies, loans, and tax incentives and setting up market-entry barriers to competitors. In some cases, the government may even launch the FC, just as the Siam Cement Group was launched by the government of Thailand. One of the largest FCs in Indonesia, the Bimantara Citra Group, got its start by selling its foreign oil allocations to the state-owned oil monopoly. The Group has long enjoyed a close relationship with the Indonesian government and secured numerous lucrative contracts. When the Hyundai Group in South Korea experienced a financial crisis, the Korean government and Hyundai's major creditors provided more than $300 million in assistance, including credit extension and short-term loans.[28]

FCs provide huge tax revenues and facilitate national economic development, which helps explain why governments eagerly support them. The fact that they dominate the commercial landscape in many emerging markets suggests they will be either formidable competitors or capable partners, possibly with much bargaining power. We return to this issue in the next section.

EXHIBIT 10.11 A Sample of Leading Family Conglomerates

Family Conglomerate	Home Country	Primary sectors	Distinction
ALFA	Mexico	Petrochemicals, machinery, foods, electronics, telecommunications	One of the world's largest producers of engine blocks and petrochemicals
Astra	Indonesia	Motor vehicles, financial services, heavy equipment, agribusiness, information technology	Largest distributor of automobiles and motorcycles in Indonesia
Ayala	Philippines	Real estate, financial services, utilities, telecommunications, electronics	Oldest and largest conglomerate in the Philippines
Hyundai	South Korea	Automobiles, shipbuilding	Truly global car company, selling Sonatas, Elantras, and other models in nearly 200 countries
Reliance Industries	India	Petroleum products, retailing, chemicals, textiles, solar energy systems	Named by *Forbes* one of the "world's 100 most respected companies"
Russian Standard	Russia	Alcoholic beverages, banking, life insurance	The leading premium producer of vodka in Russia
Sabanci Holding	Turkey	Cars, cement, energy, retailing, insurance, telecom, tires, plastic, hotels, paper, tobacco	Controls about seventy companies, including Turkey's largest bank, Akbank
Tatung	Taiwan	Computers, liquid crystal display televisions, network devices, media players, home appliances	OEM manufacturer for HP, Acer and Dell. World's largest producer of flat panels for the TV industry
Votorantim Group	Brazil	Finance, energy, agribusiness, mining, steel, paper	One of the largest industrial conglomerates in Latin America

 ## Success Strategies for Emerging Markets

The "cookie-cutter" strategies that MNEs developed decades ago and refined in mature advanced-economy markets are often inappropriate for the unique circumstances in emerging markets. Foreign firms must devise creative strategies to succeed.[29] For example, Toyota developed a line of inexpensive cars, costing about $7,000, for low-income countries. In India, it built a large factory to boost its share of the Indian car market to 10 percent.[30] Renault and Volkswagen are building low-cost cars targeted to emerging markets such as China, India, and Russia.[31] In this section, we discuss strategies that firms employ to succeed in emerging markets.

Customize Offerings to Unique Emerging Market Needs

Successful firms develop a deep understanding of the distinctive characteristics of buyers, local suppliers, and distribution channels in emerging markets. They build constructive relationships with the communities where they operate, partly to better understand local conditions and partly to earn customer respect and loyalty. The ability to customize offerings and devise innovative business models depends largely on the firm's *flexibility* and entrepreneurial orientation. In emerging markets, many people are illiterate and fewer than one in four have regular access to the Internet and other computer-based systems.[32] Consequently, MNEs employ creative approaches to promote their offerings in local markets. Where suppliers and distribution channels are lacking, they develop their own infrastructure to obtain needed raw materials and components or move finished goods to local buyers.[33]

MNEs must set prices appropriate for local conditions. Incomes are relatively low and emerging market consumers cannot pay high prices. Many firms devise innovative products and packaging to keep prices low. In India, for example, General Electric developed a light-weight electrocardiograph machine that sells for just $1,500, far cheaper than similar machines in advanced economies. Low pricing means that doctors and clinics in poor areas can purchase the machine and offer healthcare for a fraction of the cost required by earlier technologies. In China, local Internet company Tencent developed a free messaging service that captured the local market for mobile phone communications. Chinese consumers prefer text messaging over voice communications because pricing is cheaper. In Brazil, local airliner *Gol Linhas Aereas Inteligentes* (www.voegol.com.br) dominates the market for air travel. Gol succeeded by emphasizing smaller, newer aircraft that have lower operating and maintenance costs and by leveraging information technology to issue e-tickets and promote Internet-based sales. In Brazil, Gol developed a deep understanding of the special needs of its customers, including lower income levels, simple travel requirements, and destinations in remote locations that hold limited appeal to larger airlines.[34]

Read the *Recent Grad in IB* feature on Andrew and Jamie Waskey, who learned to adapt themselves to life and work in various emerging markets.

Partner with Family Conglomerates

Family conglomerates are key players in their respective economies and have much capital to invest in new ventures. For example, most major FCs in Korea, as well as Koc and Sabanci in Turkey, Vitro in Mexico, and Astra in Indonesia, own their own financing operations in the form of insurance companies, banks, and securities brokers. Many FCs possess extensive distribution channels throughout their home countries. They have a deep understanding of local markets and customers.

For foreign firms wanting to do business in emerging markets, FCs can make valuable venture partners.[35] By collaborating with an FC, the foreign firm can:

Source: Andrey Bayda/Shutterstock

Emerging market governments are important potential customers for various products and services. Pictured here is a government ministry in Russia.

- Reduce the risks, time, and capital requirements of entering the market;
- Develop helpful relationships with governments and other key, local players;
- Target market opportunities more rapidly and effectively;
- Overcome infrastructure-related hurdles; and
- Leverage FC resources and local contacts.

There are many examples of successful FC partnering. Ford partnered with Kia to introduce the Sable line of cars in South Korea and benefitted from Kia's strong distribution and after-service network. Digital Equipment Corporation (DEC) designated Tatung, a Taiwanese FC, as the main distributor of its workstations and client-server products in Taiwan. DEC gained access to Tatung's local experience and distribution network. In Turkey, Danone, the French yogurt producer and owner of Evian brand of bottled water, entered a joint venture with Sabanci, a large local FC. Danone brought ample technical knowledge in packaging and bottling and a reputation for healthy friendly products, but it lacked information about the local market. As the Turkish market leader, Sabanci knew the market, retailers, and distributors. The collaboration helped make Danone the most popular bottled water in the first year after entry.

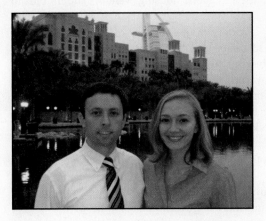

ANDREW & JAMIE WASKEY

Andrew's majors: Master of International Business (MIB), Bachelor's in Spanish
Jamie's majors: Master of International Business (MIB), Bachelor's in International Affairs and Modern Language
Andrew's jobs since graduation: Various positions in international logistics at DHL and other firms; Marketing Intern at U.S. Department of Commerce (Shanghai, China)
Jamie's jobs since graduation: Research Manager at YouGov (Dubai, United Arab Emirates); Market Research Analyst at Delta Air Lines (Atlanta, GA); Market Research Intern at U.S. Department of Commerce (Buenos Aires, Argentina)
Objectives: Leverage and grow our international expertise while accelerating the global positioning of our firms and creating a life filled with adventure.

Andrew and Jamie Waskey met during their Masters of International Business (MIB) Program at Georgia State University. As undergraduates, both majored in international studies and Spanish. They enjoy traveling and learning languages, especially in emerging markets in Latin America. After completing college, Andrew worked for DHL, the international logistics company. The MIB degree provided an internship with DHL and the U.S. Department of Commerce office in Shanghai, China.

After completing her undergrad degree, Jamie worked for a nonprofit organization. Desiring a career in international market research, she attended an MIB program. In her last semester, she completed an internship in Buenos Aires, Argentina, performing market research for the U.S. Department of Commerce there.

Andrew and Jamie got married after earning their MIB degrees and quickly secured international jobs in Atlanta with Delta Airlines and BlueLinx Corporation. Networking was key to obtaining these and later jobs. Both were committed to living and working abroad. Andrew next obtained a position with MKM Holdings/The Wafi Group in Dubai, in the firm's transportation division. In his job as a marketing and sales manager, he works with multicultural teams.

Jamie leveraged her contacts to secure a position with a UK-based market research consultancy in Dubai, YouGov. Jamie's favorite part of the job is the channel it provides for learning about and understanding the region's various cultures. She travels around the Middle East to places like Saudi Arabia.

Success Factors

- Set goals and be persistent in working toward them. If you want to work abroad, pursue your goal actively and remain fully committed.
- Know what you want to do. Develop a clear professional path.
- Leverage friends and other contacts to connect with key people in your field.

Build a personal network is key to securing an international position.

Advice for an International Career

- Adopt a patient, flexible, and light-hearted outlook. Maintaining a positive attitude and putting challenges in perspective will enrich your life abroad.
- Keep an open mind to differing conditions and attitudes in foreign environments.
- Be curious about everything. Immersing yourself in the local culture will allow you to adapt easily and acquire a different lens for viewing the world.

Challenges

- Mastering cross-cultural communication and differing management structures
- Adapting to different living situations
- Making friends
- Striking a healthy work–life balance

Target Governments in Emerging Markets

In emerging markets and developing economies, government agencies and state-owned enterprises are an important customer group for three reasons:

1. Governments buy enormous quantities of products (such as computers, furniture, office supplies, motor vehicles) and services (such as architectural, legal, and consulting services).
2. State enterprises in areas like railways, airlines, banking, oil, chemicals, and steel buy goods and services from foreign companies.
3. The public sector influences the procurement activities of various private or semi-private corporations. In India the government works directly in planning housing projects. Construction firms lobby the government to gain access to promising deals to build apartments and houses for local dwellers.

Tenders
Formal offers made by a
buyer to purchase certain
products or services.

Emerging market governments regularly announce **tenders**—formal offers made by a buyer to purchase certain products or services. A tender is also known as a request for proposals (RFPs). Government agencies seek bids from suppliers to procure bulk commodities, equipment, and technology or to build power plants, highways, dams, and public housing. Vendors submit bids to the government to work on these projects.

Governments in emerging markets as well as developing countries often formulate economic development plans and annual programs to build or improve national infrastructure. To find vendors, the government follows specific buying procedures that lead to large, lucrative sales to international vendors. Securing major government contracts usually requires substantial competencies and resources. Firms competing for such projects assemble a team of managers and technical experts, especially when pursuing large deals. Governments prefer dealing with vendors that offer complete sales and service packages. The most successful vendors also offer financing for major sales, in the form of low-interest loans or grants. Governments are attracted by deals that create local jobs, employ local resources, reduce import dependence, and provide other country-level advantages.

Bechtel, Siemens, General Electric, Hitachi, and other major vendors regularly participate in bidding for global tenders from emerging market governments. Some of the largest construction projects include the Panama Canal expansion and the Channel tunnel between Britain and France. Another mega project, the Three Gorges Dam (www.ctgpc.com) on the Yangtze River in China, is expected to cost about $25 billion when completed. It will be the largest hydroelectric dam in the world. Numerous global contractors worked on the project, including ABB, Kvaerner, Voith, Siemens, and General Electric. China is also spending nearly $250 billion through 2020 to lay 75,000 miles of new track for the country's crowded rail system. The project will increase China's existing rail network, which carries about one-quarter of the world's train cargo, by 150 percent. The mega-project is attracting interest from MNEs around the world.

Skillfully Challenge Emerging Market Competitors

As the opening story shows, the new global challengers have become formidable competitors thanks to various strengths, such as access to low-cost labor, skilled workforces, government support, and family conglomerates. For example, India's Mahindra & Mahindra (www.Mahindra .com) has been capturing market share in the global farm equipment industry that was long dominated by venerable names such as John Deere and Komatsu. Strong brands such as the Mahindra 5500, a powerful, high-quality tractor, sell for far less than competing models. One dealership in the U.S. state of Mississippi, a market long dominated by John Deere, sold more than 300 Mahindras in just four months.[36]

Advanced-economy firms can counter in various ways. Initially, managers must conduct research to develop an understanding of the new challengers. It is vital to analyze the advantages and strategies of the emergent firms, which often enjoy superior advantages in the industry in the target market. The next step is to acquire new capabilities that improve the firm's competitive advantages. For example, many incumbents are boosting their R&D to invent new, superior products. Others are partnering with competitors to pool resources against emerging market rivals. Incumbent firms can also match global challengers at their own game by leveraging low-cost labor and skilled workers in locations such as China, Mexico, and Eastern Europe. Many advanced economy firms partner with family conglomerates and others in emerging markets on critical value-chain activities such as R&D, manufacturing, and technical support.

Source: © Nightman/Fotolia

Investing in emerging markets helps foster economic development and modernize critical infrastructure, such as this aging port in Poland.

Corporate Social Responsibility, Sustainability, and The Crisis of Global Poverty

Most people in emerging markets and developing economies live in relative poverty. The World Economic Forum has identified poverty and economic disparity as critical challenges confronting the world.[37] Poverty is closely related to corruption and fragile states. It influences the likelihood of disease, food shortages, terrorism, illicit trade, and international migration. Despite robust growth in emerging markets, many nations are beset by cyclical poverty that reduces access to basic social infrastructure such as education, health care and sanitation, and increases the fragility of national governments.[38]

Companies engaged in international business can play an important role in facilitating economic development that helps alleviate poverty and raise living standards. When done in an environmentally sensitive manner, such efforts also help sustain natural environments. Businesses foster economic development via modernization projects and entrepreneurial activity in emerging markets and developing economies. Such efforts are a form of corporate social responsibility. In most cases they make good business sense, too. Let's examine how companies help address poverty around the world.

Foster Economic Development with Profitable Projects

Historically, few companies targeted poor countries because managers assumed there were few profitable opportunities. Today, however, firms that deploy suitable products and strategies earn substantial profits in emerging markets and developing economies. Unilever and P&G sell Sunsilk and Pantene shampoo for 2 cents per mini-sachet in India. Such pricing, while attractive to local Indians, is actually more profitable than pricing for Unilever and P&G shampoo in the advanced economies. Narayana Hrudayalaya is an insurance company that sells health insurance for less than 20 cents per person per month and has millions of customers. Amul, one of India's largest foodstuff firms, sells a wide range of food products to millions of poor people. Micromax, Qualcomm, and other technology companies are marketing low-cost cell phones in India. To succeed, such firms devise new business models in manufacturing, packaging, distribution, and market reach.[39]

Every day in India, some 20 million people travel long distances for work or pleasure. Hotel accommodations generally fall into two categories: cheap, low-quality lodgings for the poor and $350-per-night luxury hotels for the rich. To address the shortage of accommodations for middle-class travelers, Tata launched the Ginger chain of medium- priced hotels ($20–$40 per night; www.gingerhotels.com). To keep costs low, the hotels have minimal staff and few furnishings, but the rooms are clean and offer broadband Internet, flat-screen TV, and a work space. By devising an innovative business model, Tata captured a major, lucrative market in a poor country and simultaneously addressed an important need of lower-income travelers.[40]

The Swedish telecommunications company Ericsson (www.ericsson.com) helped modernize the telecom infrastructure in rural parts of Tanzania by installing phone lines and cellular systems that meet the communication needs of households, companies, and aid agencies.[41] The emergence of a significant cell phone market in Africa led to the development of related industries and the launch of local firms that produce accessories, such as devices for recharging cell phone batteries. Ericsson's experience suggests that market-based solutions not only contribute to social and economic transformation but can be profitable as well. In India, Ericsson produces optical fiber cables for local markets. In Vietnam, it leveraged financing from the World Bank to expand the country's telecommunications network.

Source: © morane/Fotolia

Africans are using cell phones to leapfrog landline-based telecom technologies. Newly installed cellular networks promote economic development by facilitating dramatic gains in productivity.

Advanced-economy firms that invest in developing economies and emerging markets support the development of infrastructure in transportation, communications, and energy systems. Firms create jobs and contribute to regional and sector development. Investment generates local tax revenues, which can be spent to improve living standards among the poor. Transferring technology and know-how promotes local innovation and enterprise. Many firms develop community-oriented social programs that foster economic and social development.

Microfinance to Facilitate Entrepreneurship

Microfinance provides small-scale financial services, such as "microcredit" and "microloans," that assist entrepreneurs to start businesses in poor countries. By taking small loans, frequently less than $100, small-scale entrepreneurs accumulate sufficient capital to launch successful businesses. This realization led economics professor Muhammad Yunus to found the Grameen Bank (www.grameen-info.org). Since then, millions of Grameen borrowers in South Asia have emerged from acute poverty. Aspiring entrepreneurs use the small loans to buy everything from cows that produce milk to sell in markets, to mobile phones that villagers can rent to make calls. Today, thousands of microfinance institutions provide loans to millions of poor people in developing economies worldwide.[42] The Grameen Bank now has more than 2,500 branches and has inspired similar poverty-reducing efforts, often sponsored by philanthropic organizations such as the Omidyar Network and the Bill and Melinda Gates Foundation. For his efforts, Yunus was awarded the 2006 Nobel Peace Prize.[43]

Recently, mainstream banks have begun to view microfinance as a source of future growth. Various institutions now offer small-scale insurance, mortgage lending, and other financial services in poor countries worldwide. In Mexico, Cemex's Patrimonio Hoy program (www.cemexmexico .com) has widened access to cement and other building materials by organizing low-income customers into groups of three families that monitor each other's progress in constructing their own homes and collectively paying off debts at regular intervals. Patrimonio Hoy and other Cemex programs have made home ownership a reality for tens of thousands of low-income Mexican families.

Ethical Connections

Africa bears the burden of about one-quarter of all disease worldwide, yet has only 3 percent of the world's healthcare workers. Most Africans cannot obtain adequate medical care. Every day, thousands die from treatable or preventable ailments such as malaria and AIDS. MNEs play a growing role to address such challenges. Private firms such as GlaxoSmithKline and General Electric employ innovative business approaches to provide needed medications and medical care to impoverished countries in Africa. Numerous firms have established clinics that provide low-cost health care.

Source: © David Dorey–The Philippines Collection/Alamy

Microfinance helps entrepreneurs in developing economies start businesses. Here a group of women attend a microfinance meeting in the Philippines.

 ## The Special Case of Africa

Much of Africa has stagnated and even regressed in terms of trade, investment, and per-capita income. Africa's GDP has improved little since the 1960s. Africa is afflicted by illiteracy, malnutrition, and inadequate sanitation and water supply. Unemployment is stubbornly high in many areas.[44]

However, several African countries have begun to experience economic success, with annual GDP growth now approaching 5 percent per year. Ghana is becoming a regional hub for financial and technological services. Nigeria is enjoying a boom in oil and banking. Zambia is developing strengths in mining and agriculture. Tanzania is investing in major power generation projects. Kenya has developed a large and diversified economy. Stock markets in Botswana, Nigeria, and Zambia are enjoying record levels of investment.[45] Botswana's diamond trade is experiencing a boom, thanks to investments from South Africa's De Beers company. De Beers is the world's largest diamond producer and recently entered a 50-50 joint venture with Botswana interests to develop the country's mining industry. In the course of this effort, De Beers built roads and schools, helped devise solutions for preventing and treating HIV/AIDS, and supported numerous programs to develop the economy in Botswana.[46]

For foreign MNEs, Africa looks increasingly attractive. In Africa, Coca-Cola sells over 100 brands and has more than 160 bottling and canning plants. The firm is one of the continent's largest private employers, with nearly 1 million permanent employees and retail partners. China's telecommunications giant Huawei has established production and sales operations throughout Africa, selling its mobile phones and network solutions. Huawei provides thousands of jobs for Africans. Chinese firms are also making huge investments in Africa installing green energy systems such as solar power. The giant food producer Nestlé expects nearly half its sales to come from Africa and other emerging markets by 2020. The firm's Africa sales have been growing faster than its combined global sales.[47]

Improving conditions in Africa are supported by two major trends. First, compared to earlier times, African governments are doing a better job of managing their national economies. Policy reforms in various countries, including Botswana, Ghana, Kenya, Mozambique, Nigeria, Tanzania, Uganda, and Zambia, emphasize economic and political freedom. In these countries, better governance is helping drive economic success.

Second, much of Africa has begun to receive a steady inflow of direct investment from abroad. China, India, and other emerging market firms are investing billions in Africa to manufacture and market various products and services. Inspired by such activity, more firms from Europe, Japan, and the United States are exploring Africa for business and investment opportunities. All told, annual flows of FDI and loans into Africa now exceed $60 billion per year. Much of this stems from the commodities boom, in which foreign firms are investing in Africa's oil industry.

Without reliable phone service, workers cannot find jobs and firms cannot operate efficiently. While Africa long lacked substantial landline telephony, cell phones are proving vital to the continent's development. Africans are using cell phones to leapfrog landline-based telecom technologies. Newly installed cellular networks promote economic development by facilitating dramatic gains in worker and company productivity. A study by the business consultancy McKinsey found that the economic impact of cellular telephony in poor countries is up to four times the value of the wireless operators alone.[48] Orascom, Millicom, and other telecom firms are establishing cell phone operations from Egypt to South Africa, applying business models that allow them to earn profits even in countries where people live on less than $2 per day.

Another factor in Africa's recent success is microfinance. Small African entrepreneurs can increasingly access small-scale loans to develop businesses ranging from cotton plantations to major construction projects. South Africa–based Blue Financial Services has more than 170 branches throughout Africa, offering small loans that local entrepreneurs use to develop new businesses.[49]

One promising investment target in Africa is the food processing sector. Firms are investing to profit from the region's abundant agricultural sector and food-producing potential. Companies are also beginning to address Africa's massive health care needs. Governments and international agencies cannot provide for all Africa's healthcare needs. In the meantime, MNEs are finding market opportunities. By employing innovative business models adapted to local conditions, they play a key role in addressing the continent's medical needs and generate profits. For example, establishing chains of low-cost clinics is helping address Africa's healthcare needs.[50]

The application of business models such as local entrepreneurship, microfinance, targeted marketing, and MNE direct investing holds enormous potential for addressing poverty in Africa.[51] In addition to telecommunications, agriculture, and health care, private firms have an important role to play in Africa by finding profitable ways to address needs in education, banking, electricity, and infrastructure development. As improvements are made in these areas, further investment to develop African economies will surely follow.

Critics charge that MNEs do much harm in Africa, such as exploiting local resources, operating sweatshops, and generating pollution. Where do you stand? Can MNEs successfully address poverty and other problems in Africa, or do such firms do more harm than good? Use the Ethical Framework in Chapter 5 to analyze this question.

CLOSING CASE	Tata Group: India's New Global Challenger

Tata, India's largest company, operates in seven distinct business sectors, including automobiles, chemicals, IT, consumer products, engineering, and consulting. Altogether, Tata comprises more than 90 separate firms. The chairman of Tata Group is Ratan Tata, the charismatic descendant of the company founder. Now in his seventies, he has emerged as a popular and respected corporate titan, known around the world. An avid aviator, he often flies his own Falcon 2000 jet to meetings around India.

As the group's chief visionary and dealmaker, Mr. Tata is aggressively expanding the Tata Group into world markets. One of the group subsidiaries, Tata Steel, recently purchased the Dutch-British steel giant Corus Group, for $13 billion. The move boosted Tata's steel-making capacity fivefold. Another group subsidiary, Tata Motors, became the focus of world attention when it acquired Jaguar and Land Rover from Ford for $2.3 billion. Tata Motors launched the Nano in 2009, which, at approximately $2,500, is the world's cheapest car. The Nano addresses a longtime dream of Ratan Tata to develop reliable but supercheap automobiles, revolutionize the global auto industry, and make India a major economic power. "Nano" means "small" in Gujarati, the language of Tata's founders.

Background on the Tata Group

Founded in 1868 in Bombay as a textile trading company, Tata gradually expanded into hotels, power plants, chemicals, steel production, and several other industries. The government of India long discouraged international trade by imposing high trade barriers and bureaucracy. As these restrictions loosened in the 1990s, Tata's international operations flourished. Tata Motors began producing cars in joint ventures with Fiat and Daimler-Benz. Tata bought 30 percent of the coal subsidiaries of an Indonesian mining company to supply coal for Tata's power plant in India. Altogether, the Tata Group has factories in numerous emerging markets, including Kenya, South Korea, Malaysia, Russia, and Thailand.

As India's biggest firm, Tata has many competitive advantages, including vast financial resources and access to capital on favorable terms; strong corporate image; connections with countless high-quality business partners; competitive cost structure, thanks to the huge, low-cost Indian labor pool; and long-standing relationships with national and state governments in India. In the auto industry, Tata Motors' reputation is growing. It counts on sister subsidiary Tata Steel to continuously provide steel to manufacture Nanos and other cars, a key advantage. The purchase of Corus Group, in addition to increasing steel capacity, also greatly expanded Tata's access to automakers across Europe and the United States.

Tata is arguably the most important of the new global challenger firms charging out of big emerging markets such as China, Brazil, India, and Russia. The emerging giants tap abundant low-cost labor, tech talent, and mineral resources to increasingly target the world's biggest growth markets. Brimming with cash and confidence, they export innovative business models honed in some of the world's most challenging markets. Governments and state-owned enterprises influence the procurement activities of corporations. Tata capitalizes on its family conglomerate networks to enhance its position as government supplier in numerous business sectors.

Tata Motors

Today, Tata Motors, or "Tamo," is one of India's largest motor vehicle companies. At present, Tamo's main market is India, but the firm also operates in other countries, especially in Asia. In 2009, Tamo unveiled the Nano, the world's cheapest car. Manufactured in India, the Nano seats up to five people and gets extremely good gas mileage. Initially, the car was targeted to India's middle class, the approximately 200 million people who earn $20,000 or more per year. Recently the country has experienced double-digit annual growth in car sales. India's population of 1.2 billion people, most of whom do not own cars, represents an enormous untapped market.

About one-quarter of all cars and trucks sold in India bear the Tamo brand. The firm's next logical target will be countries outside India, especially emerging markets that provide key growth opportunities. Tamo aims to transfer its vast experience in India to markets in Africa, Latin America, and the Middle East. In Asia, the countries of Indonesia, Thailand, and Vietnam appear ripe for sales of a cheap car. Millions of low-income consumers worldwide would love to own a car, but until the launch of the Nano, they have had few or no alternatives. The acquisition of Jaguar and Land Rover has increased Tamo's visibility through globally recognized brands and provided an entree to Europe and the United States.

Challenges

In India, 70 percent of the population still lives in the countryside, and the transition of land from agrarian to industrial use often meets with angry protest. Tamo was forced to abandon construction of a factory in West Bengal, India, intended to manufacture the Nano. Protesters surrounded the new Nano plant and blocked roads to prevent workers or deliveries from reaching the facility. Violence and threats to worker safety ensued for months during plant construction. West Bengal politicos encouraged labor unrest, leading to capital flight and making the region unfriendly to business. Ultimately, despite being 80 percent complete and costing $350 million, Tamo had to abandon the plant. Nano production was moved to another location in India.

Throughout India, Tamo works continuously to satisfy government authorities. India has a reputation for "suffocating bureaucracy" and its civil servants are among the least efficient in Asia. The country is awash in trade barriers, business regulations, and administrative hurdles. Many commodities can be imported only after receiving government approval. Import tariffs on parts and components can be substantial, often exceeding 25 percent. Licensing fees, testing procedures, and other hurdles are expensive and time-consuming. The commercial environment in India is still evolving and poses numerous hurdles for firms that do business there.

Perhaps the biggest challenge facing the Nano is generating sales in a tough market. Despite its low price tag, management needed to market the Nano as an aspirational status symbol. Tamo provided attractive financing packages for buyers. By 2012, however, Tamo had sold fewer than 200,000 Nanos. This is a low number, especially for a car whose profit model depends on high-volume sales. Production cost overruns forced Tamo to increase the Nano's starting price. Management admits the firm has not done enough to market the car.

Pollution and Overcrowding in India

Growing car ownership is severely straining India's already congested urban infrastructure. India's road network seems unable to absorb millions of new cars. Burgeoning car ownership in India and China are straining the world's already self-destructive carbon footprint. India suffers from severe pollution. Throughout southern Asia, a thick brown cloud of particulate blocks the sun, altering weather patterns and causing health problems. The cloud is a by-product of emissions from coal-fired power plants, cars and trucks, and wood-burning stoves. As India industrializes, the country's water, air, and soil are under increasing environmental pressure. Most Indians make their living from farming, and pollution has reduced growth yields of rice, wheat, maize, and sorghum.

Competitors

In addition to Tamo, several automakers have plans to enter the cheap car market in India. Renault, Nissan, and India's Bajaj Motors plan to jointly build a $2,500 car. Nissan CEO Carlos Ghosn aims to make emerging markets a cornerstone of his firm's plans for global growth. Ford, Hyundai, Toyota, and General Motors are all developing inexpensive, small cars for emerging markets. Several Chinese companies already manufacture various car models, both for export and domestic consumption, and a few firms are exploring ultra-cheap options. Japan's Suzuki sells the Maruti 800 in India, retailing for about $4,500.

Global Financial Crisis and Opportunities for Emerging Global Giants

Just as automotive sales declined in recent years, many automakers have launched new models, which boosted global competition. Tamo is well positioned to weather the recent global financial crisis. First, it enjoys low-cost production capacity, partly based on employing inexpensive labor in India. Second, the firm has significant experience in emerging markets, which are growing rapidly. By contrast, advanced-economy markets are largely saturated. Third, as the global financial crisis unfolded, many advanced-economy MNEs retrenched and focused more heavily on their home markets, especially in Europe and North America. For example, bankruptcy and restructuring led General Motors to refocus on the United States.

Corporate Social Responsibility and Sustainability

For decades Tata has promoted good works in India. Tata Steel spends millions every year on education, health, and agricultural development projects. It has developed irrigation systems that allow Indian farmers to grow cash crops. The firm has built schools, hospitals, and electrical plants and undertaken countless other socially responsible projects throughout India.

Similarly, Tamo undertakes various charitable activities in the communities where it operates. In 2008 Tamo acquired a major stake in Miljo Grenland/Innovasjon, a Norwegian electric car producer. Tamo is leveraging Miljo's know-how to launch a new electric vehicle, the Indica.

Another group company, Tata BP Solar, makes rooftop solar-electric systems for buildings. The firm offers low-cost, solar-powered water pumps, refrigerators, and lanterns for areas that normally lack electricity. It has fitted 50,000 homes with $300 systems that can power lights, hot plates, and TV sets.

Conclusion

In emerging markets and developing economies, family conglomerates are leveraging various advantages to dominate home-country markets. Today, the conglomerates are applying these same advantages to extend their reach to markets worldwide. Tata's numerous home country resources provide the firm with substantial competitive advantages and should allow it to perform well and capture market share from incumbent players in markets around the world.

AACSB: Reflective Thinking Skills, Ethical Understanding and Reasoning Abilities

Case Questions

1. Describe the various advantages that firms like Tata employ to become large industrial conglomerates. How can Tata use these same advantages to succeed in foreign markets?
2. What makes emerging markets attractive for international business? Discuss emerging markets as target markets, as platforms for manufacturing, and as sourcing destinations.
3. What is the relationship between trade barriers, bureaucracy, country risk, and the emergence of Tata as a major player in world trade? What is the role of declining government intervention in Tata's success in India and its ability to internationalize? What should Tata do to manage country risk in India and other emerging markets?
4. Given growth rates and other characteristics of emerging markets, what markets should Tamo target for sales of Nano cars? What country-level factors should Tamo consider as it evaluates the potential of various emerging markets?
5. As it prepares to expand abroad, how can Tamo improve its corporate social responsibility toward future customers in emerging markets? What can Tamo do to minimize the impact of its operations on the natural environment in Asia and elsewhere?

Sources: M. Aguiar et al., *The 2009 BCG 100 New Global Challengers*, Boston Consulting Group, retrieved from http://www.bcg.com; B. Coffin, "Cheap Cars, Costly Protests," *Risk Management*, December 2008, pp. 14–15; "Up to Their Necks in It," *Economist*, July 17, 2008, p. 42; "Emerging-Market Multinationals: Not So Nano," *Economist*, March 27, 2009, retrieved from http://www.economist.com; Corporate profiles on various Tata group companies from http://www.hoovers.com; A. Kazmin, "Tata Reroutes 'People's Car' to the Safety of Gujarat," *Financial Times*, October 8, 2008, p. 31; S. Sen, "Tata Group: Transforming the Sleeping Giant," *The ICFAI Journal of Business Strategy* 6, no. 1 (2009): 31–45; C. Squatriglia, "Does a $2,500 Tata Nano in India Mean Higher Gas Prices and More CO2 Everywhere Else?" *Autopia*, February 6, 2008, retrieved from http://www.wired.com/autopia/2008/02/2500-cars-in-in/; Alex Taylor, "Tata Takes on the World," *Fortune*, May 2, 2011, pp. 87–92; J. Thottam, "The Little Car that Couldn't," *Time*, October 24, 2011, pp. Business 1–4.

Note: This case was authored by Marta Szabo White, Ph.D., Georgia State University.

CHAPTER ESSENTIALS

Key Terms

advanced economies   244
developing economies   244
emerging markets   244
family conglomerate   258

global sourcing   253
new global challengers   250
outsourcing   253
privatization   249

purchasing power parity (PPP)   254
tenders   262
transition economies   249

Summary

In this chapter, you learned about:

1. **Advanced economies, developing economies, and emerging markets**

   Advanced economies are post-industrial countries characterized by high per-capita income, highly competitive industries, and well-developed commercial infrastructure. They consist mainly of post-industrial societies of Western Europe, Japan, the United States, Canada, Australia, and New Zealand. The **developing economies** are low-income countries that have not yet industrialized. Due to low buying power and limited resources, their participation in international business is limited. The **emerging markets** are former developing economies on their way to becoming advanced economies. Located mainly in Asia, Eastern Europe, and Latin America, emerging markets are transforming themselves into market-driven economies by liberalizing trade and investment policies, privatizing industries, and forming economic blocs. Brazil, Russia, India, and China are leading exemplars.

2. **What makes emerging markets attractive for international business**

   Emerging markets represent promising export markets for products and services. They are ideal bases for manufacturing activities. They are popular destinations for **global sourcing**—procurement of products and services from foreign locations.

3. **Assessing the true potential of emerging markets**

   In the early stages of market research, to reliably estimate demand in emerging markets, managers examine

three important statistics: per-capita income, size of the middle class, and market potential indicators. Income should be adjusted for **purchasing power parity**.

4. **Risks and challenges of emerging markets**

   Emerging markets pose various risks, including political instability, inadequate legal and institutional frameworks, lack of transparency, and inadequate intellectual property protection. **Family conglomerates** are large, diversified, family-owned businesses that dominate many emerging markets and represent formidable rivals and attractive choices for partnerships.

5. **Success strategies for emerging markets**

   Firms should adapt strategies and tactics to suit unique, local conditions. Some firms succeed by partnering with family conglomerates. Governments are often major buyers, but require specific strategies. Successful advanced-economy firms conduct research and acquire capabilities specific to target markets and leverage advantages available in emerging markets, such as low-cost labor.

6. **Corporate social responsibility, sustainability, and the crisis of global poverty**

   In emerging markets and developing economies, leading firms undertake activities that facilitate economic development. They can serve low-income countries with inexpensive, specifically designed products and services, and community involvement. Such efforts should aim to ensure environmental sustainability. Microfinance, availability of small-scale loans to emerging-market entrepreneurs, is promoting entrepreneurial initiatives.

7. The special case of Africa

Although Africa long stagnated in terms of income, trade, and investment, several African countries are beginning to experience economic success. Much of the continent has begun to receive substantial investment from abroad.

Africa is benefitting from microfinance and widespread diffusion of mobile telephones. For MNEs, agriculture, health care, and several other industries are promising investment targets. Firms can succeed by applying innovative business models.

Test Your Comprehension AACSB: Reflective Thinking Skills, Ethical Understanding and Reasoning Abilities

1. What are advanced economies, developing economies, and emerging markets? What are the major distinctions among these three country groups?

2. Explain why firms want to do business in emerging markets. What makes these markets attractive?

3. Describe the various risks and challenges encountered in emerging markets.

4. What is a family conglomerate (FC)? How do FCs differ from publicly owned companies? What role do FCs play in emerging markets?

5. Describe the process for selling to foreign governments and state enterprises.

6. Doing business in emerging markets involves strategies that are often distinct from those of other international venues. What types of business approaches can firms use when doing business in emerging markets?

7. How is Africa evolving? What can businesses do to support the development of Africa?

Apply Your Understanding AACSB: Communication Abilities, Reflective Thinking Skills

1. Suppose you work at Microsoft in their Xbox video game console division. Microsoft has long targeted Xbox to the advanced economies, especially in North America and Europe. Management would like to sell more Xbox 360s to emerging markets. What characteristics of emerging markets might make them attractive for sales of the Xbox? Identify the major risks and challenges that Microsoft might encounter in selling the Xbox 360 to emerging markets.

2. CBKing has been trying to export its products to various emerging markets and has enjoyed little success so far. You know a lot about emerging markets and have been anxious to share your views with CBKing's president, Mr. Roger Wilko. What strategies would you recommend Roger pursue in doing business with emerging markets? You conclude there is substantial demand among military and government agencies. Explain how your firm should go about selling to emerging market customers.

3. Ethical Dilemma: One mission of the International Monetary Fund (IMF) is to help poor countries overcome economic crises by providing loans and policy advice. During the global financial crisis, many countries suffered corporate bankruptcies, collapsing economies, and political turmoil. These effects particularly hurt Ukraine, which requested massive loans and other financial assistance from the IMF. Note, however, that taxpayers in advanced economies generally foot the bill for IMF activities, which often run to billions of dollars. Critics argue the IMF rescues countries that fail to put in place robust regulatory systems and responsible fiscal and monetary policies. The critics assert that economic prosperity is best determined by market forces and free enterprise. They claim that reviving poor countries is too costly and discourages responsible behavior because, if local officials know they can count on bailouts from wealthy countries, they are less likely to enact policies that ensure stable economic growth. Suppose you are a financial officer at the IMF. Where do you stand? Using the Ethical Framework in Chapter 5, decide if the IMF should bail out Ukraine.

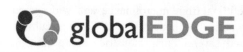

AACSB: Analytic Skills, Reflective Thinking Skills, Ethical Understanding and Reasoning Abilities

Refer to Chapter 1, page 24, for instructions on how to access and use globalEDGE™.

1. The World Bank sponsors the Doing Business database (www.doingbusiness.org), which provides measures of business regulations and their enforcement for countries worldwide. Firms can use these measures to analyze specific regulations that enhance or constrain investment, productivity, and growth. Visit the site and choose two emerging markets. Then answer the following questions: (a) How well does each country rank in terms of ease of starting a business, employing workers, and trading across borders? (b) How long does it take to start a business? (c) How much time does it take to pay taxes? (d) Review other statistics and identify which country is most friendly for doing business.

2. Using globalEDGE™, find the "country commercial guide" for two emerging markets of your choice. Compare the two countries on the following dimensions: "leading sectors for exports and investment" and "marketing products and services." (a) Which of the two countries is more promising for marketing laptop computers? (b) Which of the two countries is more promising for sales of portable electrical power generators?

(c) Which of the two countries is more promising for sales of telecommunications equipment? Justify your answers.

3. The three groups of countries described in this chapter can be contrasted in terms of degree of economic freedom. It refers to the extent to which economic activities in a nation can take place freely and without government restrictions. Various organizations have developed indexes of economic freedom, including the Cato Institute (www.cato.org), the Heritage Foundation (www.heritage.org), and the Fraser Institute (www.fraserinstitute.org). In measuring economic freedom, such indexes consider factors such as trade policies, extent of government intervention, monetary policies, inward foreign direct investment, property rights, and commercial infrastructure. Countries are classified into categories such as free, mostly free, mostly unfree, and repressed. Explore one of the economic freedom indexes by visiting one of the above sites, and entering "economic freedom" in the search engine. How are emerging market and developing economies classified? What is the relationship between market liberalization and economic development? How might market liberalization contribute to reducing poverty in developing economies?

MyManagementLab

Go to **mymanagementlab.com** for Auto-graded writing questions as well as the following Assisted-graded writing questions:

10-1. How can managers estimate the true market potential of emerging markets?

10-2. How can firms show corporate social responsibility in developing economies and emerging markets?

10-3. Mymanagementlab Only – comprehensive writing assignment for this chapter.

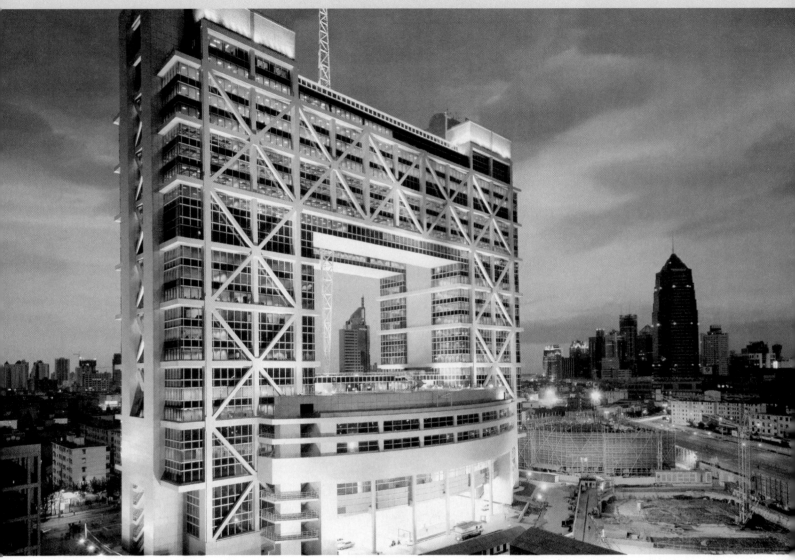

The European Union and the Euro

The European Union (EU) was established in 1993 and currently has twenty-seven member countries. The EU created the European Monetary Union (EMU) and the European Central Bank (ECB; www.ecb.int), with the goal of establishing a common currency, the euro. In 2002, euro banknotes and coins were issued, replacing older, national currencies. In 2012, the euro was the sole, official currency of seventeen EU member states: Austria, Belgium, Cyprus, Estonia, Finland, France, Germany, Greece, Ireland, Italy, Luxembourg, Malta, Netherlands, Portugal, Slovakia, Slovenia, and Spain. By establishing a common currency, the EMU seeks to knit these EU economies into a unified whole, eliminate risks arising from multiple exchange rates, and facilitate trade and price comparisons.

By using the single currency, MNEs operating in the "euro zone" have reduced business costs by simplifying their accounting and financial activities. The euro allows firms to coordinate prices across the EU.

The ECB treats the euro zone as one region rather than as separate countries with differing economic conditions.

CHAPTER 11

The International Monetary and Financial Environment

 LEARNING OBJECTIVES *In this chapter, you will learn about:*

1. Exchange rates and currencies in international business
2. How exchange rates are determined
3. Emergence of the modern exchange rate system
4. The monetary and financial systems
5. Key players in the monetary and financial systems
6. The global debt crisis

However, ECB monetary policy is complex because of the diverse economic and fiscal conditions that characterize each euro zone country. For example, the ECB aims to keep inflation low by carefully limiting the supply of euros. By contrast, the policy response for controlling deflation, which is just as harmful as inflation, is to increase the money supply. Thus, ECB policy that aims to fix deflation in one country might trigger inflation in another. The ECB struggles to formulate a one-size-fits-all monetary policy that suits economic conditions in all EMU countries.

ECB monetary policy is further complicated by the recent admission into the EU of lower-income Eastern European countries, such as Slovakia and Slovenia. As more countries join the EU, the risk of very diverse economic conditions across the union rises. Such pressures increased during the recent global financial crisis as ECB officials worried about weakening of the euro zone's banking system. Economic hardships struck Greece, Ireland, and Spain. The EU adopted a plan to assist Greece, including loans and surveillance from the ECB. The crisis renewed discussion about the risks of EU monetary integration.

As Greece's problems persisted into 2012, some skeptics began to predict the euro would ultimately fail. Such an outcome is unlikely since most "eurozone" countries have strong economies and are not likely to experience severe economic shocks. The more likely scenario is that one or two EU countries may withdraw from the eurozone.

A key goal of launching the euro was to shield EMU countries from currency volatility by creating a large, unified economy. For several years following its launch, the euro was relatively weak against the U.S. dollar, and then got stronger. A strong euro is problematic for European exporters because it makes their products more expensive to foreign importers. A strong euro also yields smaller earnings for European MNEs when they convert non-euro profits into euros. On the positive side, a stronger euro increases the buying power of European firms and consumers who purchase non-euro foreign goods.

The success of the euro as a unifying force in Europe has changed the international balance of power. The EU and EMU have empowered European governments to challenge U.S. policy initiatives in the wider global arena. The central banks of numerous countries—including Canada, China, and Russia—have given greater weight to the euro in their foreign currency reserves. Some governments are increasing their euro holdings, and Asia is now less dollar-centric than in the past.

SOURCES: T. Catan, "Spain's Struggles Illustrate Pitfalls of Europe's Common Currency," *Wall Street Journal*, September 14, 2009, p. A2; J. Perry, "ECB Expects No Recovery Before 2010," *Wall Street Journal*, June 10, 2009, p. A7; Carla Power, "Border Control," *Time International*, March 5, 2012, pp. 40–44; "Too Long an Illness," *Economist*, February 25, 2012, p. 66; S. Zwick, "World Rattles on Wobbly Euro/Dollar Axis," *Futures*, April 2010, pp. 22–26.

International business transactions take place within the global monetary and financial systems. Fluctuating exchange rates are an important challenge for international managers. The opening story explains how the European Union aimed to eliminate this problem in the EU by introducing a single currency, the euro. Before its launch, numerous national currencies—the French franc, the Spanish peso, the Italian Lira, among others—served as the means of exchange for conducting business in Europe.

As the barriers that once restricted global trade and investment have faded, the monetary and financial activities of firms and nations have intensified. When people think of international trade, they usually think of trade in products and services. However, the markets for foreign exchange and capital are much larger. Firms regularly trade the U.S. dollar, European euro, Japanese yen, and other leading currencies to meet their international business obligations. In this chapter, we explore the monetary and financial structure that makes trade and investment possible. We explain the nature, organization, and functions of the foreign exchange market and the monetary and financial issues that confront internationalizing firms.

Exchange Rates and Currencies in International Business

There are more than 150 currencies in use around the world today. Cross-border transactions occur through an exchange of these currencies between buyers and sellers. A currency is a form of money and a unit of exchange. The tendency of each country to prefer to use its own unique currency complicates international business transactions. When buying a product or service from a Mexican supplier, for example, you must convert your own currency into Mexican pesos to pay the supplier. The currency regime is being simplified in some locations, however. As we saw in the opening story, numerous countries in Europe use the euro. Other countries, such as Ecuador, Panama, and East Timor, have adopted the U.S. dollar as their currency, a process known as "dollarization."

The **exchange rate**—the price of one currency expressed in terms of another—varies over time. It links different national currencies so that buyers and sellers can make international price and cost comparisons. Exhibit 11.1 provides the exchange rates for the U.S. dollar and a sample of other currencies. The values of these national currencies, and thus their exchange rates, fluctuate constantly.

Exchange rate
The price of one currency expressed in terms of another; the number of units of one currency that can be exchanged for another.

EXHIBIT 11.1 U.S. Dollar Exchange Rates for a Sample of Currencies on March 8, 2012

Currency	Currency per One U.S. Dollar	U.S. Dollars per Unit of Currency
Australian dollar	0.940	1.064
Brazilian real	1.759	0.568
British pound	0.633	1.579
Canadian dollar	0.995	1.005
Chinese renminbi (yuan)	6.318	0.158
Euro	0.755	1.324
Indian rupee	50.405	0.020
Japanese yen	81.695	0.012
Mexican peso	12.801	0.078
New Zealand dollar	1.212	0.825
Norwegian kroner	5.604	0.178
Singapore dollar	1.253	0.798
Saudi Arabian riyal	3.750	0.267
South African rand	7.526	0.133
Turkish lira	1.776	0.563

Source: Adapted from www.x-rates.com.

Constantly fluctuating exchange rates require international managers to keep in mind three facts:

1. The prices the firm charges can be quoted in the firm's currency or in the currency of each foreign customer;
2. Because several months can pass between placement and delivery of an order, fluctuations in the exchange rate during that time can cost or earn the firm money;
3. The firm and its customers can use the exchange rate as it stands on the date of each transaction, or they can agree to use a specific exchange rate.

Exchange rate fluctuations and similar complications in international transactions create **currency risk**, the potential harm that can arise from changes in the price of one currency relative to another. It is one of the four types of international business risk that we introduced in Chapter 1. It is also referred to as *financial risk*. If you buy from a supplier whose currency is appreciating against yours, you may need to pay a larger amount of your currency to complete the purchase. If you expect payment from a customer whose currency is depreciating against your own, currency risk also arises, because you may receive a smaller amount of your currency if the sale price was expressed in the currency of the customer. Of course, if the foreign currency fluctuates in your favor, you may gain a windfall. Exporters or importers usually are not in the business of making money from currency speculation; rather, they worry about *losses* that arise from currency fluctuations.

Exporters and licensors also face risk because foreign buyers must either pay in a foreign currency or convert their currency into that of the vendor. Foreign direct investors face currency risk because they both receive payments and incur obligations in foreign currencies.

Currency risk
Potential harm that arises from changes in the price of one currency relative to another.

Convertible and Nonconvertible Currencies

A *convertible currency* can be readily exchanged for other currencies. The most readily convertible are called *hard currencies*. These are strong, stable currencies that are universally accepted and used most often for international transactions, such as the British pound, Canadian dollar,

Capital flight
The rapid sell-off by residents or foreigners of their holdings in a nation's currency or other assets, usually in response to a domestic crisis that causes investors to lose confidence in the country's economy.

European euro, Japanese yen, and U.S. dollar. Nations prefer to hold hard currencies as reserves because of their relative strength and stability in comparison to other currencies.

A currency is *nonconvertible* when it is not acceptable for international transactions. Some governments may not allow their currency to be converted into a foreign currency in order to preserve their supply of hard currencies, such as the euro or the U.S. dollar, or to avoid the problem of capital flight. **Capital flight** is the rapid sell-off by residents or foreigners of their holdings in a nation's currency or other assets, usually in response to a domestic crisis that causes them to lose confidence in the country's economy. The investors exchange their holdings in the weakening currency for those of another, often a hard currency. Capital flight from a country diminishes its ability to service debt and pay for imports.

As national economies have become more integrated in recent years, capital flight has become a relatively common occurrence. For example, at least $40 billion in roubles were reportedly withdrawn from Russia as foreign investors lost confidence in the Russian economy in the mid-2000s. After coming to power in Venezuela, President Hugo Chavez confiscated foreign company assets and engaged in questionable financial deals. Dubious governance, depreciating currency, and other economic problems panicked foreign investors and Venezuela's wealthier citizens, and they withdrew their liquid assets from the country's economy.[1] In some developing economies, currency convertibility is so strict that firms may avoid using currencies altogether and receive payments in goods; in other words, they engage in barter.

Foreign Exchange Markets

A critical function of money is to facilitate payment for the products and services the firm sells. Getting paid in your own country is straightforward: The U.S. dollar is accepted throughout the United States, the euro is widely used in Europe, and the Japanese need only yen when transacting with each other. But suppose a Canadian needs to pay a Japanese, or a Japanese needs to pay an Italian, or an Italian needs to pay a Canadian. What then? The Japanese wants to be paid in yen, the Italian wants to be paid in euros, and the Canadian wants to be paid in Canadian dollars. All these currencies are known as *foreign exchange*. **Foreign exchange** represents all forms of money that are traded internationally, including foreign currencies, bank deposits, checks, and electronic transfers. Foreign exchange resolves the problem of making international payments and facilitates international investment and borrowing among firms, banks, and governments.

Foreign exchange
All forms of money that are traded internationally, including foreign currencies, bank deposits, checks, and electronic transfers.

Foreign exchange market
The global marketplace for buying and selling national currencies.

Currencies such as the euro, yen, and U.S. dollar are traded on the **foreign exchange market**, the global marketplace for buying and selling national currencies. The market has no fixed location. Rather, trading occurs through continuous buying and selling among banks, currency traders, governments, and other exchange agents located worldwide. International business would be impossible without foreign exchange and the foreign exchange market.

Currency Risk

In 1999, eleven EU countries switched to the euro, eliminating the problem of exchange rate fluctuations in trade and investment with each other. By 2012, seventeen member states were participating in the euro zone. Other countries in Latin America, the Caribbean, and the Middle East have opted to use a regional or hard currency. The challenges posed by fluctuating exchange rates motivate countries to coordinate their monetary policies. Governments attempt to manage exchange rates by buying and selling hard currencies and by keeping inflation in check. However, the foreign exchange market has become so huge and its shifts so fluid that even major governments have difficulty controlling exchange rate movements.

As illustrated in Exhibit 11.2, exchange rate fluctuations between the euro, U.S. dollar, and other currencies are sometimes dramatic. In 2008, for example, the Indian rupee was trading at 41 rupees to the U.S. dollar. By 2009, the rate had fluctuated to 48 rupees, a depreciation of more than 20 percent. More rupees to the dollar means the rupee is worth less in terms of the dollar; hence, the rupee had depreciated in value. Implications for international business with India were substantial. In the span of only 18 months, Indian firms perceived a significant upturn in their exports, as Indian products became less expensive in dollar terms. Meanwhile, as rupee-buying power for dollars decreased, U.S. firms experienced a decline in their exports to India.[2] Exhibit 11.2 also shows that the French franc is one of the European currencies taken out of circulation and replaced by the euro.

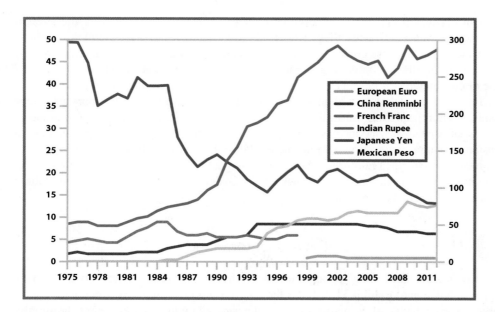

EXHIBIT 11.2

EXHIBIT 11.2

Selected Exchange Rates against the U.S. Dollar over Time

Note: Right-hand scale is for Japanese yen; left-hand scale is for all other currencies. For example, in 2008, the Mexican peso was trading at 11 pesos per one U.S. dollar. The euro became the common currency of various European Union countries in 1999, replacing the French franc and other European currencies.

Sources: Based on data from the International Monetary Fund and World Bank.

Fluctuating exchange rates affect both firms and customers. Suppose today the euro/dollar exchange rate is €1 = $1; that is, for a European to buy one U.S. dollar, she or he must pay one euro. Next, suppose that during the coming year the exchange rate goes to €1.50 = $1. Now the dollar is much more expensive to European firms and consumers than before—it costs 50 percent more to acquire a dollar. Let's examine the effect of this change on Europeans.

Effect on European Firms

- European firms must pay more for inputs from the United States, such as raw materials, components, and support services they use to produce finished products and services.
- Higher input costs reduce profitability and may force firms to raise prices to final customers; these higher prices reduce customer demand for goods and services.
- Because the euro has become less expensive for U.S. consumers, firms can increase their exports to the United States. Firms can even raise their export prices and remain competitive in the U.S. market.
- Increased exports to the United States generate higher revenues and higher profits.

Effect on European Consumers

- Because U.S. products and services now cost more, European consumers demand fewer of them.
- The cost of living rises for those Europeans who consume many dollar-denominated imports.
- Fewer European tourists can afford to visit the United States. Fewer European students study at U.S. universities.

Now, suppose the euro/dollar exchange rate goes to €0.50 = $1. What are the effects on European firms and consumers? They are essentially the opposite of those summarized above: European firms pay less for inputs from the United States, which means they can drop their prices on goods and services. Because U.S. products and services now cost less, consumers demand more of them.

A fluctuating exchange rate affects both sides of international transactions. Management must monitor exchange rates constantly and devise strategies to optimize firm performance in light of strong and weak currencies. We discuss these strategies in Chapter 20.

In 2010, profits at the Japanese company Nintendo (www.nintendo.com) plunged as sales of its Wii video game consoles collapsed in the United States and elsewhere. Like many firms in the export-dependent electronics industry, Nintendo suffered from the strength of the Japanese yen relative to other major trading currencies such as the dollar and the euro. Conversely, for Japanese consumers, the dollar is relatively cheaper, which encourages them to buy U.S. products. Nintendo generates nearly 90 percent of its sales outside Japan. The type of currency risk it faces is a natural outcome of its multi-country operations.[3]

In 2012, markets for Australian wines collapsed as the Australian dollar appreciated in value against the European Euro. Australian winemakers suffered a dual loss: Exports to Europe fell as the cost of Australian wine increased in Euro terms and domestic wine sales plunged as Aussie consumers embraced lower-priced Euro-based wines. Just as Australian wines became more expensive to cash-strapped Europeans, Australians bought up low-priced European wines. Prices for some imported wines dropped by as much as 30 percent. An appreciating Australian dollar triggered a recession in the Aussie wine industry.[4]

 How Exchange Rates Are Determined

In a free market, the "price" of any currency—that is, its exchange rate—is determined by supply and demand. Exhibit 11.3 shows the equilibrium price of euros, when purchased with dollars. The exchange of euros for dollars is determined by the intersection of the supply and demand curves. The intersection of R_1 and Q_1 represents the *equilibrium* point, where dollar buyers and euro sellers are satisfied with exchanging dollars for euros. R_1 represents the price in dollars that buyers are willing to pay, and Q_1 reflects the quantity of euros offered at that price. Since the global market for dollar/euro exchange is free and active, the price fluctuates constantly. Continuous shifts in the supply of and demand for euros result in continuous adjustments to new equilibrium positions. Note the exhibit reflects equilibrium in a free foreign exchange market, in which supply and demand adjust according to market forces. As we will see later in this chapter, some currencies are pegged to fixed exchange rates, and thus, may not respond to market forces.

As indicated in the exhibit, in a free market the levels of supply and demand for a currency vary inversely with its price. Thus, all else being equal:

- The greater the supply of a currency, the lower its price.
- The lower the supply of a currency, the higher its price.
- The greater the demand for a currency, the higher its price.
- The lower the demand for a currency, the lower its price.

Suppose a Canadian consumer wants to buy a BMW, sourced from Germany and priced at the nominal price of 25,000 euros. Assume further that the exchange rate of the euro to the Canadian dollar is €1 = $1.25. Now suppose the consumer delays six months, during

EXHIBIT 11.3

Equilibrium Price of Euros for Dollars

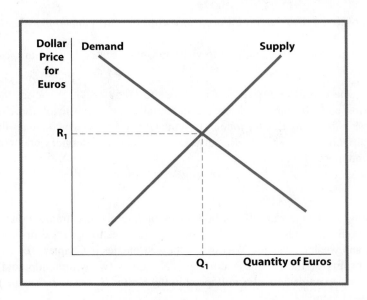

which the exchange rate shifts, becoming €1 = $1.50. That is, due to increased demand for and/or decreased supply of euros, the euro has become more expensive to Canadian customers. Assuming the euro price of the BMW remains unchanged, the car will now cost more in Canadian dollars, making the consumer less inclined to buy the BMW. By contrast, if, during the six-month period, the euro becomes cheaper (with, say, an exchange rate of €1 = $1), the Canadian consumer will be more inclined to buy the BMW. As this example implies, the greater the demand for a country's products and services, the greater the demand for its currency.

Four main factors influence the supply and demand for a currency: economic growth, interest rates and inflation, market psychology, and government action. Let's examine these in turn.

Economic Growth

Economic growth is the increase in value of the goods and services produced by an economy. To ensure accuracy, we usually measure economic growth of a nation as the annual increase in real GDP in which the inflation rate is subtracted from the growth rate. Economic growth results from continual economic activities, especially innovation and entrepreneurship. It implies a continued increase in business activities and a corresponding increase in consumer need for money to facilitate more economic transactions.

To accommodate economic growth, the **central bank** increases the nation's money supply. The central bank is the monetary authority in each country that regulates the money supply, issues currency, and manages the exchange rate of the nation's currency relative to other currencies. Economic growth is associated with an increase in the supply and demand of the nation's money supply and, by extension, the nation's currency. Thus, it has a strong influence on the supply and demand for national currencies. For example, recent rapid economic growth in East Asian countries has stimulated increased demand for their currencies by firms and individuals, both domestic and foreign.[5]

Central bank
The monetary authority in each nation that regulates the money supply and credit, issues currency, and manages the exchange rate of the nation's currency.

Inflation and Interest Rates

Inflation is an increase in the price of goods and services, so that money buys less than in preceding years. Exhibit 11.4 shows that inflation rates can reach high levels. Argentina, Zimbabwe, and some other countries have had prolonged periods of *hyperinflation*—persistent annual double-digit and sometimes triple-digit rates of price increases. A practical effect of hyperinflation is the need, say, for a restaurant owner to change the menu every few days in order to list the most recent prices. In a high-inflation environment, the purchasing power of the nation's currency is constantly falling. Interest rates and inflation are closely related. In countries with high inflation, interest rates tend to be high because investors expect to be compensated for the inflation-induced

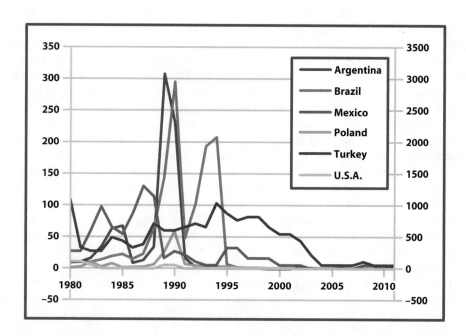

EXHIBIT 11.4

Inflation in Selected Countries, 1980–2011

Note: Chart shows annual percentage rate of inflation. Left-hand scale is for Mexico, Turkey, and the United States; right-hand scale is for Argentina, Brazil, and Poland.

Sources: Based on International Monetary Fund, World Economic Outlook Database, 2012, at http://www.imf.org and *CIA World Factbook*, at http://www.cia.gov.

decline in the value of their money. If inflation is running at 10 percent, for example, banks must pay more than 10 percent interest to attract customers to open savings accounts.

Inflation occurs when (1) demand for money grows more rapidly than supply, or (2) the central bank increases the nation's money supply faster than the rise in national productive output. Inflation is a common challenge for developing economies and emerging markets. It directly affects the value of the nation's currency. When inflation occurs, the value of the nation's currency will fall relative to foreign currencies. Triggered by big increases in the national money supply, for example, annual inflation in Brazil ran to more than 400 percent in the mid-1990s. Imagine the difficulty to both buyers and sellers of adjusting to a constant decline of the currency's value and ever-rising prices!

The link between interest rates and inflation, and between inflation and the value of currency, implies there is a relationship between real interest rates and the value of currency. For example, when interest rates in Japan are high, foreigners seek profits by buying Japan's interest-bearing investment opportunities, such as bonds and deposit certificates. Investment from abroad will have the effect of increasing demand for the Japanese yen.

Market Psychology

Exchange rates are often affected by *market psychology*, the unpredictable behavior of investors. *Herding* is the tendency of investors to mimic each others' actions. *Momentum trading* occurs when investors buy stocks whose prices have been rising and sell stocks whose prices have been falling. It is usually carried out with computers set to do massive buying or selling when asset prices reach certain levels. Herding and momentum trading tend to occur in the wake of financial crises. A case in point is Pakistan, which recently experienced a massive flight of portfolio investment amid concerns about its homeland security, untenable budgetary deficits, and high inflation (above 12 percent in 2012). Foreign investors panicked and many deserted the country.[6]

Government Action

The pricing of currencies affects company performance. When a nation's currency is expensive to foreigners, its exports are likely to fall.[7] When a nation's currency is cheap to foreigners, exports increase. When the value of a nation's currency depreciates over a prolonged period, consumer and investor confidence can be undermined. A steep currency depreciation weakens the nation's ability to pay foreign lenders, possibly leading to economic and political crisis.

To minimize these effects, governments often act to influence the value of their own currencies. The Chinese government regularly intervenes in the foreign exchange market to keep the renminbi undervalued, helping to ensure that Chinese exports remain strong.

Trade surplus
A condition in which a nation's exports exceed its imports for a specific period of time.

Trade deficit
A condition in which a nation's imports exceed its exports for a specific period of time.

An undervalued national currency can result in a **trade surplus**, which arises when a nation's exports exceed its imports for a specific period of time, causing a net inflow of foreign exchange. By contrast, a **trade deficit** results when a nation's imports exceed its exports for a specific period of time, causing a net outflow of foreign exchange. The *balance of trade* is the difference between the monetary value of a nation's exports and its imports over the course of a year. For example, if Germany exports cars to Kenya, money flows out of Kenya and into Germany, because the car importer in Kenya pays the exporter in Germany. This results in a surplus item in Germany's balance of trade and a deficit item in Kenya's balance of trade. If the total value of Kenya's imports from Germany becomes greater than the total value of Kenya's exports to Germany, Kenya will have a trade deficit with Germany. Factors that affect the balance of trade include the prices of goods manufactured at home, exchange rates, trade barriers, and the method the government uses to measure the trade balance.

Devaluation
Government action to reduce the official value of its currency, relative to other currencies.

Many economists believe a persistent trade deficit is harmful to the national economy. When a trade deficit becomes severe or persists for a long time, the nation's central bank may devalue its currency. A **devaluation** is a government action to reduce the official value of its currency relative to other currencies. It is usually accomplished by the buying and selling of currencies in the foreign exchange market. Devaluation aims to deter the nation's residents from importing from other countries, potentially reducing the trade deficit.[8]

Balance of payments
The annual accounting of all economic transactions of a nation with all other nations.

At a broader level, governments must manage their **balance of payments**, the annual accounting of all economic transactions of a nation with all other nations. The balance of payments is the nation's balance sheet of trade, investment, and transfer payments with the rest of the world. It represents the difference between the total amount of money coming into and going out of a country. Consider an American MNE that builds a factory in China. In the process, money flows from the United States to China, generating a deficit item for the United States and a surplus item for China in their respective balance of payments. The balance of payments is affected by other transactions as well, as when citizens donate money to a foreign charity, when governments provide foreign aid, or when tourists spend money abroad.

 ## Emergence of the Modern Exchange Rate System

During much of the period from the late 1800s through the 1920s, global trade grew significantly. Then the Great Depression (1929–1939) and World War II (1939–1945) coincided with a collapse of the international trading system and relationships among nations. Following the war, several countries came together to energize international commerce and devise a framework for stability in the international monetary and financial systems. In 1944, the governments of forty-four countries negotiated and signed the Bretton Woods Agreement.

The Bretton Woods Agreement

This agreement pegged the value of the U.S. dollar to an established value of gold, at a rate of $35 per ounce. The U.S. government agreed to buy and sell unlimited amounts of gold in order to maintain this fixed rate. Each of Bretton Woods' other signatory countries agreed to establish a par value of its currency in terms of the U.S. dollar and to maintain this pegged value through central bank intervention. In this way, the Bretton Woods system kept exchange rates of major currencies fixed at a prescribed level relative to the U.S. dollar and, therefore, to each other.

The demise of the Bretton Woods agreement began in the late 1960s when the U.S. government used deficit spending to finance both the Vietnam War and expensive government programs. Rising government spending stimulated the economy and U.S. citizens began buying more imported goods. This aggravated the U.S. balance of payments, and the United States began to experience trade deficits with Japan, Germany, and other European countries. Over time, demand for U.S. dollars so exceeded supply that the U.S. government could no longer maintain an adequate stock of gold. This situation put pressure on governments in Europe, Japan, and the United States to revalue their currencies. As a result, the link between the U.S. dollar and gold was suspended in 1971, and the promise to exchange gold for U.S. dollars was withdrawn. This action brought an end to the Bretton Woods system.

The Bretton Woods agreement left a legacy of principles and institutions that remain in use today. Specifically, Bretton Woods established:

- The concept of international monetary cooperation, especially among the central banks of leading nations.
- The importance of currency convertibility, in which countries agree not to impose restrictions on currency trading and to avoid discriminatory currency arrangements.
- The notion of fixing exchange rates within an international regime to minimize currency risk.
- The **International Monetary Fund (IMF**; www.imf.org) and the **World Bank** (www.worldbank.org). The IMF is an international agency that attempts to stabilize currencies by monitoring the foreign exchange systems of member countries and lending money to developing economies. The World Bank is an international agency that provides loans and technical assistance to low- and middle-income countries, with the goal of reducing poverty.

International Monetary Fund (IMF)
An international agency that aims to stabilize currencies by monitoring the foreign exchange systems of member countries and lending money to developing economies.

World Bank
An international agency that provides loans and technical assistance to low- and middle-income countries with the goal of reducing poverty.

Following the 1997 Asian financial crisis, finance ministers and central bank heads from twenty advanced and emerging market economies established the Group of Twenty (G-20), an international organization that aims to bring greater stability to the global financial system. Representing about 90 percent of the world economy, the members have met annually to develop

Source: Alan Briere/Dorling Kindersley Limited

The Bretton Woods Agreement, which set the course for contemporary global financial relations, was conceived by 44 nations at the Mount Washington Hotel in Bretton Woods, New Hampshire, United States, in 1944.

measures that promote economic growth and strong financial systems. They have held meetings in Canada, South Korea, the United Kingdom, and the United States. The members were instrumental in devising new policies to address the financial and economic crisis that began in 2008, which included increasing financial resources, coordinating expansionary macroeconomic policies, and enhancing national financial regulations. The G-20 cooperates closely with the IMF and World Bank.

The Modern Exchange Rate System

Today most major currencies are traded freely, with their value floating according to the forces of supply and demand. The official price of gold was formally abolished, and governments became free to choose the type of exchange rate system that best suited their individual needs. Fixed exchange rate systems were given equal status with floating exchange rate systems, and countries were no longer compelled to maintain specific pegged values for their currency. Instead, they were urged to pursue domestic economic policies that would support the stability of their currency relative to others. The exchange rate system today consists of two main types of foreign exchange management: the floating system and the fixed system.

THE FLOATING EXCHANGE RATE SYSTEM Most advanced economies use the floating exchange rate system, in which governments refrain from systematic intervention, and each nation's currency floats independently, according to market forces. Major world currencies—including the British pound, Canadian dollar, euro, U.S. dollar, and Japanese yen—float independently on world exchange markets, their exchange rates determined daily by supply and demand. The floating system gives governments the latitude to modify monetary policy to fit the circumstances they face at any time. If a country is running a trade deficit, the floating rate system allows it to be corrected more naturally than if the country uses a fixed exchange rate regime.

THE FIXED EXCHANGE RATE SYSTEM This approach is similar to the system used under the Bretton Woods agreement and is sometimes called a *pegged exchange* rate system. Using this system, the value of a currency is set relative to the value of another (or to the value of a basket of currencies) at a specified rate. As this "reference value" rises and falls, so does the currency pegged to it. In the past, some currencies were also fixed to some set value of gold.

Many developing economies and some emerging markets use the fixed system today. China pegs its currency to the value of a basket of currencies. Belize pegs its currency to the U.S. dollar. To maintain the peg, the governments of China and Belize, for instance, will intervene in currency markets to buy and sell dollars and other currencies to maintain the exchange rate at a fixed, preset level. A fixed regime promotes greater stability and predictability of exchange rate movements and helps stabilize a nation's economy. The central bank must stand ready to fill any gaps between supply and demand for its currency.

Many economists believe floating exchange rates are preferable to fixed because floating rates respond more naturally to the supply and demand for currencies in the foreign exchange market. In some situations, however, fixed exchange rates may be preferable for their greater stability. For example, the recent global financial crisis was contained in part because some countries use fixed exchange regimes. A fixed regime provided much stability to world currencies under the Bretton Woods system in the years following World War II.

At times, countries adhere to neither a purely fixed nor a floating exchange rate system. Rather, they try to hold the value of their currency within some *range* against the U.S. dollar or other important reference currency, in a system often referred to as *dirty float.* That is, the value of the currency is determined by market forces, but the central bank intervenes occasionally in the foreign exchange market to maintain the value of its currency within acceptable limits relative to a major reference currency. Many Western countries resort to this type of intervention from time to time.

The Monetary and Financial Systems

We have seen how currencies facilitate international transactions and how exchange rates affect the amount of international trade. Let's now examine the two systems that determine exchange rates: the international monetary system and the global financial system.

International Monetary System

Firms seek to get paid for the products and services they sell abroad. Portfolio investors seek to invest in stocks and other liquid assets around the world. The resulting monetary flows take the form of various currencies traded among nations. Accordingly, the **international monetary system** consists of the institutional frameworks, rules, and procedures that govern how national currencies are exchanged for one another. By providing a framework for the monetary and foreign exchange activities of firms and governments worldwide, the system facilitates international trade and investment. To function well, national governments and international agencies have focused on creating a system that inspires confidence and ensures liquidity in monetary and financial holdings.

Global Financial System

The **global financial system** consists of the collective financial institutions that facilitate and regulate flows of investment and capital funds worldwide. Key players in the system include finance ministries, national stock exchanges, commercial banks, central banks, the Bank for International Settlements, the World Bank, and the International Monetary Fund. Thus, the system incorporates the national and international banking systems, the international bond market, the collective of national stock markets, and the market for bank deposits denominated in foreign currencies.

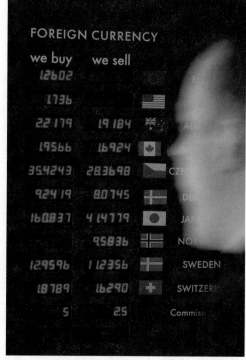

Source: Doomits/Shutterstock

The international monetary system provides the framework within which national currencies, including the U.S. dollar, British pound, and European Euro, are exchanged for one another.

International monetary system
Institutional framework, rules, and procedures by which national currencies are exchanged for one another.

Global financial system
The collective of financial institutions that facilitate and regulate investment and capital flows worldwide, such as central banks, commercial banks, and national stock exchanges.

The global financial system is built on the activities of firms, banks, and financial institutions engaged in ongoing international financial activity. It also has many linkages with national financial markets. Since the 1960s, the global financial system has grown substantially in volume and structure, becoming increasingly more efficient, competitive, and stable.

Today, the global financial system can accommodate massive cross-national flows of money and the huge foreign exchange markets these transactions have engendered. Initially triggered by the rapid growth in world trade and investment, the globalization of finance accelerated in the 1990s with the opening of the former Soviet Union and China to international business. More recently, very large flows of capital—mostly in the form of pension funds, mutual funds, and life insurance investments—have been pouring into stock markets worldwide. Firms can increasingly access a range of capital markets and financial instruments around the world.[9]

Money flowing abroad as portfolio investments is a relatively new trend. The volume of these flows is enormous. For example, more than 20 percent of total outstanding U.S. long-term securities are typically held by people outside the United States.[10] In developing economies, inward investment increases foreign exchange reserves, reduces the cost of capital, and stimulates local development of financial markets.

The growing integration of financial and monetary activity worldwide has several causes, including:

- The evolution of monetary and financial regulations worldwide;
- The development of new technologies and payment systems and the use of the Internet in global financial activities;
- Increased global and regional interdependence of financial markets; and
- The growing role of single-currency systems, such as the euro.

Capital flows are much more volatile than FDI-type investments, because it is much easier for investors to withdraw and reallocate liquid capital funds than FDI funds, which are directly tied to factories and other permanent operations that firms establish abroad.[11]

The globalization of financial flows has yielded many benefits, but it is also associated with increased risk. Economic difficulties in one country can quickly spread to other countries, like a contagion. Financial instability is worsened when governments fail to adequately regulate and monitor their banking and financial sectors.[12] The *Global Trend* feature explains the global financial crisis that began in 2008. Let's discuss various organizations that attempt to reduce capital flight and manage other challenges in the global monetary and financial systems.

Ethical Connections

The recent global financial crisis raised various ethical issues. Globalization of the financial sector allowed the crisis to spread quickly, harming people worldwide. However, financial globalization has contributed greatly to economic development in poor countries. Critics point to self-interest in the banking sector as a basic cause of the crisis. But self-interest is a natural human condition. Pensioners and other investors happily accept rapid gains in stocks and bonds, often ignorant of how the gains are made. Some argue the real cause of the crisis was a failure of governments to adequately regulate the financial sector.

 GLOBAL TREND

Global Financial Crisis

The recent crisis in the global financial and monetary systems was triggered in the United States, where investors lost confidence in the value of home mortgages. Beginning in 2008, commercial banks, mortgage lenders, and insurance companies entered a period of high volatility. Stock markets crashed around the world, and many national economies sank into a deep recession. In the ensuing months, much of the world experienced sharp declines in consumer wealth, economic activity, and international trade.

A key factor in the crisis was the widespread availability of "easy money." For several years, the U.S. central bank, the Federal Reserve Bank (www.federalreserve.gov), had pursued a policy of low interest rates, generating surplus capital in the United States and abroad. Simultaneously, China and other emerging markets had been investing enormous sums in treasury bonds and other securities in the United States. These trends led to the build-up of a vast global money supply—easy money that facilitated the excessive demand for housing and commodities such as oil and food and led to soaring price inflation in these goods.

Much of the money was used to finance the huge U.S. trade deficit, which had arisen from massive imports of consumer and industrial goods into the United States. In addition, U.S. banks and mortgage companies had granted billions of dollars in loans to individuals who spent excessively on homes and other consumer goods. Many of the loans were "securitized," or bundled into investment assets that were sold in financial markets worldwide. Over time, however, investors realized that many of the loans were high risk and unlikely to be repaid. As the overheated U.S. mortgage market cooled, the value of homes and securitized mortgages crashed, and the U.S. financial system fell into crisis.

Like a contagion, the crisis spread quickly to Europe and beyond. Countries not directly affected were caught up in a global recession triggered by the financial crisis. As the global economy slowed, demand for exports shrank, and export-dependent countries such as Japan and Mexico floundered. In some countries, central banks devalued their currencies. In several emerging markets, a currency crisis arose as foreign financiers quickly sold the investments they had made in local markets, which they perceived as too risky. Eastern Europe and Russia suffered capital flight as investors withdrew billions from local economies. Ireland, Spain, and several other advanced economies experienced negative GDP growth. Huge declines in industrial output occurred in many nations.

In Iceland, all three of the country's major banks collapsed, the national currency fell sharply, and the total value of shares in the Icelandic stock exchange fell by more than 90 percent.

Over time, governments took corrective measures, such as injecting massive sums into their national economies and launching aid packages. Numerous emerging markets obtained loans from the International Monetary Fund and World Bank. Others imposed trade and investment barriers. Gradually, governments began to cooperate in financial matters. Several have sought to create new regulations appropriate for the globalization of finance and a host of new investment approaches and opportunities. The crisis highlights the importance of strong regulation, transparency, and supervision of institutions in the global financial system.

Sources: "When Fortune Frowned," *Economist*, October 11, 2008, pp. 3–5; International Monetary Fund, *Note on the Group of Twenty Meeting of the Deputies*, January 31–February 1, 2009, London; Bethany McLean and Joe Nocera, *All the Devils Are Here: The Hidden History of the Financial Crisis* (New York: Portfolio, 2011); Gideon Rachman, "When Globalisation Goes into Reverse," *Financial Times*, February 2, 2009, p. 12; UNCTAD, *World Investment Report*, United Nations, New York, 2011; UNCTAD, *The Global Economic Crisis* (New York: United Nations, 2009).

Key Players in the Monetary and Financial Systems

A variety of national, international, private, and government players make up the international monetary system and the global financial system. Exhibit 11.5 highlights the major players and the relationships among them. These players operate at the levels of the firm, the nation, and the world.

The Firm

As companies engage in international trade and are paid by their customers abroad, they typically acquire large quantities of foreign exchange and must convert them into the currency of the home country. Firms also engage in investment, franchising, and licensing activities abroad that generate revenues they must exchange into their home currency. For example, Jim Moran Enterprises in Florida, the largest importer of Toyota cars in the United States, imports thousands of cars every year and must ultimately pay for them in Japanese yen. Moran deals with the foreign exchange market to convert U.S. dollars to yen.

Some MNEs with spare cash acquire foreign currencies for speculative purposes. Effectively, they invest in currencies with the intention of profiting from exchange rate fluctuations. Other firms may acquire foreign currency to invest in foreign stock markets and other foreign investment vehicles for short-term gains. Other private-sector players in the international monetary and financial systems include life insurance companies, savings and loan associations, and stockbrokers that manage pensions and mutual funds. Some large MNEs have in-house finance departments that manage their foreign exchange and financial transactions.

Nontraditional financial institutions play a key role in international funds transfers. Foreign residents in Australia, Canada, the United States, and countless other countries use wire-transfer technology to wire billions of dollars to family members in India, Mexico, and numerous other

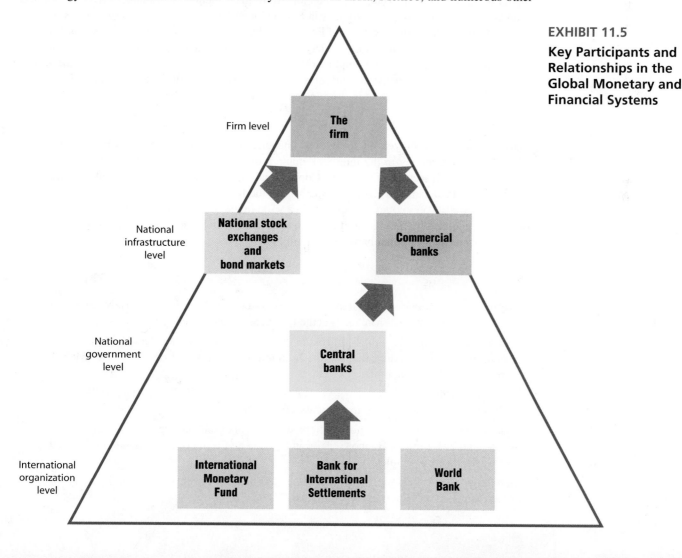

EXHIBIT 11.5

Key Participants and Relationships in the Global Monetary and Financial Systems

less-developed economies, where the funds are converted into local currencies. Such remittances by Africans living abroad constitute a major source of funds flowing into Africa, helping sustain the continent's poorest countries. Indeed, some nations receive more foreign income from remittances than from either foreign aid or inward FDI.[13] Read this chapter's *Recent Grad in IB* feature, which highlights Maria Keeley, who works in finance for a major multinational firm.

National Stock Exchanges and Bond Markets

Selling stock (shares of ownership) is an important way for firms to raise the funds they need to engage in international business. A *stock exchange* is a facility for trading securities and other financial instruments, including shares issued by companies, trust funds, pension funds, and corporate and government bonds. Information technology has revolutionized the functioning of stock markets, greatly reducing the speed and cost of transactions. Today, many exchanges are electronic networks not necessarily tied to a fixed location. Each country sets its own rules for issuing and redeeming stock.

Trade on a stock exchange is by members only. For example, the Tokyo Stock Exchange (TSE; www.tse.or.jp/english/) is the home stock market to such firms as Toyota, Sony, and Canon and the major vehicle through which some 2,000 Japanese firms raise capital to fund their business activities. Several foreign companies, such as BP and Chrysler, are also listed on the TSE. Today, MNEs often list themselves on a number of exchanges worldwide to maximize their ability to raise capital.

The character of markets varies worldwide. For example, the majority of shares in the Japanese market are held by corporations, while in Britain and the United States more shares are held by individuals. Despite these differences, stock exchanges are increasingly integrated into the global securities market.

Bonds are another type of security sold through banks and stockbrokers. They are a form of debt that corporations and governments incur by issuing interest-bearing certificates to raise capital. Bonds enable the issuer to finance long-term investments. For example, SK Telekom, the main wireless communications provider in South Korea, financed much of its operations by selling bonds in the global market. Several European telecommunications providers, such as Telecom Italia, Deutsche Telecom, and France Telecom, issued international bonds to fund their activities.[14]

In many national stock and bond markets, the most important players today are *institutional investors*—managers of pensions and mutual funds, as well as insurance companies. They have now assumed an enormous role in driving capital markets around the world.

Commercial Banks

Banks are important players in the global financial sector. They raise funds by attracting deposits, borrowing money in the interbank market, or issuing financial instruments in the global money market or securities markets. Commercial banks— for example, Bank of America, Mizuho Bank in Japan, and BBVA in Spain—are the foot soldiers of the international monetary system. They circulate money and engage in a wide range of international financial transactions. Banks are regulated by national and local governments, which have a strong interest in ensuring the solvency of their national banking system.

The many types of banks and their primary activities include the following:

Investment banks underwrite (guarantee the sale of) stock and bond issues and advise on mergers, such as the merger of Goldman Sachs in the United States and Nomura Securities in Japan.

Merchant banks provide capital to firms in the form of shares rather than loans. They are essentially investment banks that specialize in international operations. The Arab-Malaysian Merchant Bank is an example.

Private banks manage the assets of the very rich. Union Bank in Switzerland (UBS) and ABN AMRO Private Banking in Luxembourg are examples.

Offshore banks are located in jurisdictions with low taxation and regulation, such as Switzerland or Bermuda. Banco General in Panama and Bank of Nova Scotia in the British Virgin Islands are examples.

Commercial banks deal mainly with corporations or large businesses. Credit Lyonnais in France and Bank of America are examples.

MARIA KEELEY

International Financial Specialist
Maria's majors: Finance, International Business, and Spanish
Objectives: Move into the executive suite at Motorola or other multinational firm
Maria's jobs since graduation: Various jobs at Motorola—Credit Analyst (U.S.); Finance Manager (U.K.); Financial Controller (Dubai, United Arab Emirates)

In college, Maria Keeley spent a year in Spain and served as the president of the international business club. She majored in Finance, International Business, and Spanish. After graduation, she took a job as a credit analyst with Motorola (www.motorola.com), a leading producer of cell phones and other wireless handsets. Maria used analytical, problem-solving, and communication skills acquired in college to serve Motorola clients and subsidiaries throughout Latin America.

At Motorola, Maria analyzed risk levels of various customers and countries. She managed accounts receivables and conducted audits in Motorola's international operations. These duties required her to travel often to Latin America. Within her first year on the job, she became the primary contact for financial analysis support to northern Latin America, the Caribbean, and Central America. Her tasks included the analysis, tracking, and reconciliation of Motorola's funds for regional marketing activities.

Eager to gain experience in Europe, Maria volunteered to transfer to Motorola's London office, where she served as a finance manager in the firm's $160 million mobile phone business for the Middle East, North Africa, and Turkey. She also sought her CIMA certification, the British equivalent of certified public accountant (CPA). After two years in London, Maria transferred to Dubai, the United Arab Emirates, as Financial Controller in Motorola's Middle East region. In this role, she coordinated the management of Motorola's financial activities in the Islamic world.

Lessons Learned

Maria commented on her experience in the world of international financial management. "One of my big challenges was increased regulations that required stricter auditing of financial records in the wake of accounting scandals. It's critical to ensure that all of Motorola's legal entities are compliant worldwide. Local regulations also must be assimilated and integrated. The time I allocated to compliance activities greatly increased. Simultaneously, competition in the mobile devices industry grew, and I had to increase support to our sales and marketing operations as well."

"When based in England, I supported a big region with multiple time zones and work schedules. The work week in the Middle East varies from Saturday to Thursday, or from Sunday to Friday. Due to time differences, the region starts the day at least three hours before Britain. I was often on the phone with colleagues in the Middle East at 6 a.m. London time."

"The languages in my region are French (North Africa), Arabic (Middle East), and Turkish (Turkey). Although I studied Arabic, I still cannot carry a business conversation in Arabic and only manage to use my Spanish while visiting a particular distributor in Morocco that is partially owned by Telefonica (www.telefonica.com), Spain's telecom provider. Luckily, most of our business partners spoke English. There is definitely a disadvantage to not speaking the local language. In Turkey, for instance, some of our business partners do not speak English and so I relied on the sales team to translate conversations. Even when colleagues speak fluent English, particularly in North Africa, they often revert to their most comfortable language, in this case French."

"Much of the Islamic world has specific norms for women, who usually do not participate in professional business activities. But people generally treat me with respect. I have found that if I establish myself as a knowledgeable professional, people in the Middle East generally treat me as well as they do their male colleagues. There is one last cultural difference that puts me at a disadvantage: being a non-smoker in countries where people still smoke a lot. Most of the debriefing after a challenging meeting happens during cigarette breaks. Given the relaxed atmosphere, the parties are more likely to discuss issues in a candid manner. But I'm not willing to take up smoking to be more effective in my job. It is a cultural difference that I accept."

Maria's Advice

The qualities that contributed most to Maria's success include "hard work, having a deliberate career strategy, and cultivating relationships with helpful people both when I was in college and in the professional world. You really have to plan. Set goals for yourself and work hard to meet them." As for the future, Maria hopes to move into the executive suite at a multinational firm. But having a career, especially an international one, is still challenging these days for women who also want to start a family. Maria looks forward to fulfilling both her career and personal goals.

For firms, the most important functions of banks are to lend money to finance business activity, exchange foreign currencies, and facilitate adjustments in national money supplies. The major world banking centers are London, New York, Tokyo, Frankfurt, and Singapore, with London having the world's greatest concentration of international banks. Many banks are MNEs themselves, such as Citibank, Britain's HSBC, and Spain's BBVA. Smaller banks participate in international business by interacting with larger, correspondent banks abroad. A correspondent bank is a large bank that maintains relationships with other banks worldwide to facilitate international banking transactions.

Banking practices vary widely. In some countries, banks are owned by the state and are extensions of government. In other countries, they face little regulation and may lack safety nets that might prevent their failure. In developing economies, private banks are usually subject to substantial government regulation.

The density of banks varies cross-nationally. Consider Canada, Sweden, and the Netherlands. Just five banks in each country control more than 80 percent of all banking assets. In Germany, Italy, and the United States, by contrast, the top five banks control less than 30 percent of all banking assets. Banks also charge different rates for their services. For a typical customer, the annual price of core banking services in Italy is over $300, in the United States it is $150, and in China and the Netherlands it is only $50.[15]

Monetary intervention
The buying and selling of currencies by a central bank to maintain the exchange rate of a country's currency at some acceptable level.

In Africa, banking has long been problematic. Egypt and South Africa are among the few African countries that possess a thriving, home-grown banking sector. In the rest of Africa, industry and governments have tended to rely on international banks because local banks are often unstable and corrupt. In the past, heavy restrictions on foreign banks reduced competition, which delayed the development of a strong indigenous banking sector. Recently, however, globalization of the financial industry has contributed substantially to the development of efficient markets and financial institutions. Foreign banks have brought technology, managerial expertise, and new product ideas to Africa. Tough foreign competition has put pressure on indigenous banks to be more innovative. In addition, some innovative banks are using widespread mobile telephone technology to offer various banking services in Africa.[16]

Central Banks

As the official national bank of each country, the central bank regulates the money supply and credit, issues currency, and manages the rate of exchange. The central bank also seeks to ensure the safety and soundness of the national financial system, by supervising and regulating the nation's banking system. A key goal is to keep price inflation low. The central bank regulates the nation's money supply and credit by (1) buying and selling money in the banking system, (2) increasing or decreasing interest rates on funds loaned to commercial banks, or (3) buying and selling government securities, such as treasury bills and bonds. Many central banks also buy and sell government securities to finance government programs and activities.

Monetary intervention describes how central banks manipulate currency rates, usually with the aim of maintaining stable or orderly exchange rates. Such intervention is achieved by buying or selling currencies in the foreign exchange market. For example, if the central bank of the United States (called the Federal Reserve Bank) wants to support the value of the U.S. dollar, it might buy dollars in the foreign exchange market. By so doing, the supply of dollars is reduced, which increases the value of dollars still in circulation.

Other central banks include the Reserve Bank of India, the Bank of England, the Banque de France, and the Bank of Japan. They work with the

Source: Cupertino/Shutterstock

Chinese banks play a growing role in global finance. China is home to four of the world's largest banks: Bank of China, ICBC, Agricultural Bank of China, and China Construction Bank. Pictured here is the Chinese central bank headquarters in Beijing.

International Monetary Fund, the Bank for International Settlements, the Organisation for Economic Co-operation and Development (OECD), and other international agencies to ensure sound international monetary and financial policies in global markets.

The Bank for International Settlements

Based in Basel, Switzerland, the Bank for International Settlements (www.bis.org) is an international organization that fosters cooperation among central banks and other governmental agencies. It provides banking services to central banks and assists them in devising sound monetary policy. It seeks to support stability in the global monetary and financial systems and help governments avoid becoming too indebted. It also attempts to ensure that central banks maintain reserve assets and capital/asset ratios above prescribed international minimums. Maintaining adequate capital is prescribed by the Basel Capital Accord, a set of recommendations on how central banks should structure their banking laws and regulations.[17]

Source: Perfect Illusion/Shutterstock

Banks, stock exchanges, and other participants in the global monetary and financial systems make international business possible. Shown here is the central business district in Singapore.

International Monetary Fund

Headquartered in Washington, D.C., the IMF provides the framework of and determines the code of behavior for the international monetary system. The agency promotes international monetary cooperation, exchange rate stability, and orderly exchange arrangements and encourages countries to adopt sound economic policies. These functions are critical because economic crises can destroy jobs, slash incomes, and cause human suffering.

Governed today by 187 countries, the IMF stands ready to provide financial assistance in the form of loans and grants to support policy programs intended to correct macroeconomic problems. During the recent global financial crisis, the IMF pledged several billion dollars to assist Romania, Hungary, Ukraine, Turkey, and Pakistan, whose economies were impacted in the event.[18]

To help manage currency valuation worldwide, the IMF established a type of international reserve known as the **Special Drawing Right (SDR)**. The SDR is a unit of account or a reserve asset, a type of currency used by central banks to supplement their existing reserves in transactions with the IMF and to manage international exchange rates. For example, a central bank might use SDRs to purchase foreign currencies to manage the value of its currency on world markets. The value of the SDR is very stable because it is based on a basket of currencies: the euro, the Japanese yen, the U.K. pound, and the U.S. dollar.

The IMF plays an important role in addressing financial and monetary crises faced by nations around the world. Typical crises fall into three major categories.

A *currency crisis* results when the value of a nation's currency depreciates sharply or when its central bank must expend substantial reserves to defend the value of its currency, thereby pushing up interest rates. Currency crises occur more commonly in smaller countries and are sometimes the result of a sudden loss of confidence in the national economy or speculative buying and selling of the nation's currency.

A *banking crisis* results when domestic and foreign investors lose confidence in a nation's banking system, leading to widespread withdrawals of funds from banks and other financial

Special Drawing Right (SDR)
A unit of account or a reserve asset, a type of currency used by central banks to supplement their existing reserves in transactions with the IMF.

institutions. This situation arose in the United States in the 1930s when, during the Great Depression, millions of people panicked about their savings and rushed to withdraw funds from their bank accounts. The crisis led to the failure of numerous banks. Banking crises tend to occur in developing economies with inadequate regulatory and institutional frameworks. These crises can lead to other problems, such as exchange rate fluctuations, inflation, abrupt withdrawal of FDI funds, and general economic instability.

A *foreign debt crisis* arises when a national government borrows an excessive amount of money, either from banks or from the sale of government bonds. For example, China's total foreign debt now exceeds $200 billion. However, the debt is manageable because China has a huge reserve of foreign exchange. By contrast, Argentina's foreign debt reached roughly 150 percent of the country's GDP. In an effort to pay its debt, Argentina had to use financial resources that it might have invested instead in important national priorities. Indebted governments draw huge sums out of their national money supply, reducing the availability of these funds to consumers and to firms attempting to finance business activities.

The IMF assists countries in resolving crises by offering technical assistance and training. It provides assistance by setting fiscal policy, devising monetary and exchange rate policies, and supervising and regulating banking and financial systems. It also provides loans to help distressed countries in recovery. However, the agency has been criticized because its prescriptions often require national governments to undertake painful reforms. For example, the IMF may recommend that a government downsize state-owned enterprises or give up subsidies or price supports for basic commodities. Some critics charge the IMF harms countries by imposing too much austerity in times of financial distress. The IMF argues that any country in an economic crisis usually must undergo substantial restructuring, such as the deregulation of national industries or privatization of state enterprises. However, it is sometimes difficult to pinpoint whether IMF prescriptions cause more harm than good. At the 2009 G-20 summit, responding to the global financial crisis, the G-20 members pledged to increase the IMF's financial resources and increase its lending capacity.

The World Bank

Originally known as the International Bank for Reconstruction and Development, the World Bank (www.worldbank.org) was founded to fund reconstruction of Japan and Europe after World War II. Today it aims to reduce world poverty and is active in various development projects to bring water, electricity, and transportation infrastructure to poor countries. Headquartered in Washington, D.C., the bank is a specialized agency of the United Nations, with more than one hundred offices worldwide. It is supported by some 187 member countries that are jointly responsible for how the institution is financed and how its money is spent.

The World Bank's collection of subagencies oversees various international development activities. The International Development Association loans billions of dollars each year to the world's poorest countries. The International Finance Corporation works with the private sector to promote economic development. It invests in sustainable private enterprises in developing countries and provides equity, loans, loan guarantees, risk management products, and advisory services to clients in need. The Multilateral Investment Guarantee Agency aims to encourage FDI to developing countries by providing guarantees to foreign investors against losses caused by noncommercial risks.

The IMF and the World Bank often work together. While the IMF focuses on countries' economic performance, the World Bank emphasizes longer-term development and the reduction of poverty. The IMF makes short-term loans to help stabilize foreign exchange, and the World Bank makes long-term loans to promote economic development.

 The Global Debt Crisis

Growing imbalances in the finances of numerous national governments is an important emergent crisis affecting the international monetary and financial environment.[19] Exhibit 11.6 shows the amount of gross government debt as a percentage of GDP for selected countries. Debt is especially high in Japan and Greece. In these countries, as well as in Italy, Portugal, and the United States, the amount of government debt exceeds 100 percent of each nation's GDP. National debt

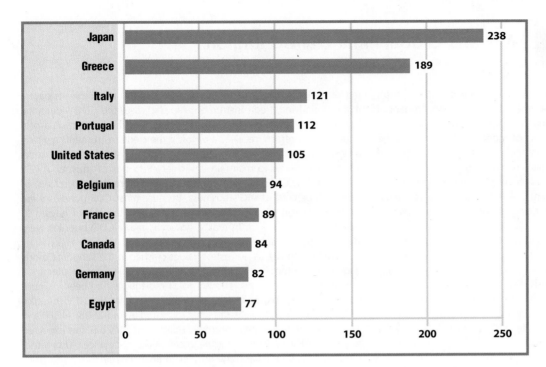

EXHIBIT 11.6

Gross Government Debt as a Percentage of GDP

Source: Based on International Monetary Fund, World Economic Outlook Database, 2012.

in total dollar terms is highest in the United States, but the measure is a less useful indicator than debt as a percentage of GDP. The reason is that countries can pay down their debt fairly easily if it is a relatively small percentage of their annual GDP. For example, the national debt of Mexico was about $500 billion in 2012. But because it represented only 44 percent of Mexico's GDP, its debt is not an immediate concern—it would take just five months (44 percent of a year) of national productive output for Mexico to pay off its national debt. By contrast, Japan's debt is approaching 250 percent of its GDP. Japan would need to give up roughly 250 percent of its annual GDP to pay its national debt.

Fiscal imbalances represent an important source of risk and uncertainty in the global business environment. Recently, debt has substantially increased in major advanced economies, due mainly to excessive government spending and insufficient revenues. Governments spent huge sums in the wake of the global financial crisis to bail out financial systems and reduce recessionary pressures. Governments are also faced with financing unfunded liabilities of pension and healthcare programs. Japan, the United States, numerous countries in Europe, and others are suffering under the weight of excessive government debt.[20] In 2012, credit rating agencies Moody's and Standard & Poor's downgraded the sovereign debt ratings of several European countries to reflect their susceptibility to growing financial and monetary risks.[21]

Research shows that national debt that exceeds 90 percent of a nation's GDP tends to diminish GDP growth, which exacerbates government debt.[22] As the government tries to pay down its debt, money is drawn out of the national money supply, which hinders economic activity and reduces tax revenues. In the past few years, numerous countries have surpassed the 90 percent threshold, including Japan, the United States, and several countries in Europe. The International Monetary Fund and other agencies have stated that, without significant adjustments, most advanced economies face serious threats to fiscal solvency in the long-run.[23]

The largest proportion of government debt results from national pension and healthcare programs. In the advanced economies, pension shortfalls have emerged because birth rates have declined in the past several decades, resulting in less workforce participation. Combined with the tendency for people to live longer, advanced economies face severe challenges in generating tax revenues sufficient to fund pensions and healthcare programs for seniors and others. MNEs should proceed with caution when entering countries with substantial government debt, as such nations tend to experience economic instability, reduced buyer purchasing power, and other challenges.

Country Realities

Greece's economic crisis has heightened tensions in Europe. Banks that loaned money to Greece expect big losses, as the nation defaults on many loans. Greek government public debt is the largest among member nations of the European Union. The EU and International Monetary Fund have imposed austerity measures on Greece, but these have been spurned by many in the nation. The crisis is rooted in excessive spending by the Greek government, which misrepresented official statistics to maintain Greece's status in the EU.

CLOSING CASE   AIG and Global Financial Contagion

Growing integration of financial and monetary sectors of the world's economies is yet another facet of globalization. National financial markets are increasingly interdependent. Globalization of finance is typified by massive cross-national flows of money and capital and the development of a giant foreign exchange market. Every day around the world, firms access global capital markets. Banks and brokers move huge sums across national borders via pensions, mutual funds, life insurance, and other investments. Among numerous benefits, financial globalization increases savings and reduces capital costs in developing economies.

The globalization of finance is driven mainly by falling investment barriers and the emergence of information and communications technologies. But capital flows are volatile: Investors can quickly withdraw and reallocate capital funds. Economic problems that arise in one country can spread quickly to other countries like a rampaging virus—thus, the term *contagion*. Financial instability is worsened when governments fail to adequately regulate and monitor their banking and financial sectors.

American International Group

When the financial crisis began in the United States in late 2008, many hoped other economies would escape its harmful effects. Analysts argued that rapid GDP growth in such emerging markets as Brazil, China, and India would continue, helping to lift sinking finances worldwide. But many nations could not avoid contagion and its pernicious effects.

In the United States, a notable casualty was American International Group (AIG; www.aig.com), the giant insurance company. AIG was founded in China and today is headquartered in New York City. Through its many subsidiaries, AIG offers insurance, pension plans, asset management, and financial services in more than 130 countries.

In 2008, the U.S. government provided AIG a bailout of $85 billion in exchange for an 80 percent ownership stake in the firm. AIG's near collapse was symptomatic of contagion that spread throughout the global financial system. In an effort to prevent the crisis from spreading worldwide, the U.S. government provided an additional $170 billion in bailout funds, with $44 billion going to U.S. financial institutions and other domestic interests and $58 billion going to non-U.S. financial institutions.

The Collapse of AIG

In its prime, AIG was the world's biggest insurer, trusted for stability and for the financial protection it offered. AIG exemplified how a financial services firm could multiply its success through global expansion. AIG Financial Products (AIGFP), one of numerous subsidiaries, was the source of AIG's collapse. In 2008, AIGFP reported assets of $860 billion, 116,000 employees, and average sales of more than $7 million per employee. Under pressure to increase revenues and profits in the late 1990s, AIGFP's London office began insuring bundles of debt, known as collateralized debt obligations (CDOs). A CDO is a type of security that derives its value from a portfolio of fixed-income assets. CDOs lump various types of debt—from the very safe to the very risky—into one bundle. Interest and principal payments are made based on the level of risk, with riskier vehicles offering higher coupon payments, higher interest rates, or lower prices to compensate the risk.

From there, AIGFP created an instrument to insure CDOs, called a credit default swap (CDS). A CDS is a contract in which the buyer makes periodic payments to the seller and in return receives a payoff if the underlying credit instrument—in this case, the CDO—defaults. CDS contracts are similar to insurance, because the buyer pays a premium and, in return, receives a payoff if the credit instrument, typically a bond or loan, fails to pay. However, unlike insurance, CDS sellers were not required to maintain any reserves to pay off buyers. AIGFP sold countless CDSs, generating revenues of more than $3 billion, or nearly 18 percent of AIG's business. Because most CDS bundles were relatively diversified, AIG management believed the risk of having to make payouts was low. In reality, however, many CDO bundles were stuffed with risky subprime mortgage loans.

Simultaneously, as real estate values crashed in the subprime mortgage crisis, homeowners were left with mortgage debt greater than the value of their homes. Thousands of mortgages had been "securitized"—that is, sold as investment vehicles such as the CDO bundles sold by AIG. When foreclosure rates escalated in mid-2008, AIGFP and its parent company faced enormous obligations they had not expected to pay. As AIGFP incurred massive losses, AIG's stock price plummeted. AIG's credit rating fell and the firm faced financial ruin.

Global Connections

AIG was at the forefront of the globalization of finance. The firm's network of operations involved investments—mutual funds, pension funds, and other financial instruments—with banks and financial institutions worldwide. The effects of AIG's failure were felt in such banking institutions as Societe Generale in France, Deutsche Bank in Germany, and Barclay's in England, which were heavily invested in AIG or insured by it. As the insurance giant fell into ruin, the fortunes of many non-U.S. financial institutions declined as well.

AIG's bailout occurred just as individual homeowners found themselves unable to repay debt and national economies fell into recession. At the same time, many Americans resented how their tax dollars were used on a massive scale to rescue AIG. Further controversy arose when AIG used nearly $60 billion of the bailout to pay off banks in Europe, much of it representing obligations that AIG incurred in its global transactions. In comparison, U.S. institutions received roughly $44 billion. The furor intensified when AIG tried to renegotiate loans with some of its American creditors, implying they were less important than European banks.

In the wake of the crisis, governments in various countries increased efforts to regulate the banking and finance sector. But regulation varies by nation, and multinational firms often prefer doing business in countries with minimal regulatory constraints. Overseas locations provide Wall Street banks with opportunities for "regulatory arbitrage"—that is, finding the most beneficial legal environments in which to do business. For example, before going bankrupt, Lehman Brothers established a subsidiary in the Netherlands that sold complex bonds valued at $35 billion. Resolving investor claims against Lehman's Dutch subsidiary was complicated because the notes were governed by a hodgepodge of laws in Britain and the Netherlands, as well as at the state and federal levels in the United States.

The Crisis in Emerging Markets

Eastern Europe is often characterized by a dangerous combination of devalued local currencies and mounting foreign currency debt. This occurs because, as they participate in the global economy, such countries as Hungary, Poland, and the Czech Republic must use "hard currencies," or widely recognized foreign exchange. Many homeowners in Poland pay their monthly mortgages in zlotys (Poland's national currency), but because the loans often originate in Britain, Germany, or the United States, they ultimately must be paid in pounds, euros, or dollars. As currencies in Eastern Europe lose value, nations in the region struggle to pay their foreign debt.

Part of the problem stems from an earlier time when Eastern European currencies appreciated in value, making loans denominated in British pounds and Swiss francs more attractive. For example, most home mortgages in Hungary were originally negotiated in Swiss francs. Meanwhile, the value of Eastern European currencies declined as much as 30 percent. In addition, the region depends heavily on exports to advanced economies, especially in Western Europe. As these latter countries fell into recession, exports from Eastern Europe fell, reducing their foreign exchange revenues. Countries also experienced sharp declines in foreign direct investment, further reducing national income levels.

At the same time, however, emerging markets have remained relatively strong. While financial crisis and recession afflicted the advanced economies, most emerging markets continued to grow their GDPs at rates often exceeding 6 percent. Emerging markets will not fully compensate for slow growth in Europe, Japan, and the United States. But it is ironic that countries once considered "less developed" may keep the world from reeling completely out of control.

The IMF and the World Bank

In the wake of the financial crisis, the International Monetary Fund stepped up efforts to foster cooperation, stability, and economic growth around the world. The IMF provided more than $100 billion in loans and credit to emerging countries hit by falling demand for their exports, collapsing financial markets, and wary consumers. For example, the IMF committed lending to Hungary, Iceland, Poland, and Ukraine. In 2009, Mexico was granted a credit line worth $47 billion. Similarly, the World Bank provided financial aid and technical assistance to numerous developing economies.

The Bank provides grants and low-interest loans to poor countries for investments in education, health, infrastructure, and private sector development. For example, the Bank loaned millions to El Salvador and other Latin American countries to buffer against the global financial crisis. In Africa, the Bank provided millions to finance highway construction and other infrastructure development. At the same time, however, while IMF and World Bank loans help struggling economies, they are yet another form of debt in a debt-fueled crisis and a debt-ridden world.

Note: For background on this case, see the *Global Trend* feature in this chapter.

Case Questions

1. Explain the advantages and disadvantages of the globalization of finance. How did it contribute to the global financial crisis?

2. Describe how the fall of AIG exemplifies contagion. How did the U.S. government bailout of AIG benefit foreign as well as U.S. firms and investors? Experts are advocating increased regulation to prevent contagion. At the national and international levels, what types of regulation might prevent future crises?

3. Several European countries have adopted a single currency, the euro. Describe how adopting the euro might benefit countries in Eastern Europe. What are the advantages and disadvantages of a single currency regime in international financial transactions?

4. As the world emerges from the global financial crisis, what is the potential role of each of the following: firms, banks, central banks, national governments, the International Monetary Fund, and the World Bank? What is the role of national governments in stimulating national economic growth?

Sources: D. Dickson, "IMF Role Grows with Crisis," *The Washington Times*, April 27, 2009; G. Gethard, "Falling Giant: A Case Study of AIG," 2009, *Investopedia.com*; Hoovers, Inc., Company Profile: American International Group Inc., 2012, retrieved from http://www.hoovers.com; P. Gumbel, "Global Breakdown," *Fortune*, October 13, 2008, p. 26; M. Mandel, "German and French Banks got $36 Billion from AIG Bailout," Unstructured Finance, *Business Week's* Wall Street News Blog, March 15, 2009, retrieved from http://www.businessweek.com/investing/wall_street_news_blog/; R. Samuelson, "A Global Free-For-All?" *Newsweek*, April 13, 2009; Jody Shenn and Saijel Kishan, "Why Toxic Debt Looks A Lot Less Toxic," *Bloomberg Businessweek*, February 20, 2012, p. 48; Trading Economics, Russia, Argentina, Brazil, China, India, 2009, retrieved from http://www.tradingeconomics.com/default.aspx; C. Whittall, "History Repeating," Risk, April 2009, p. 70.

This case was written by Professor Carol Sánchez and Jeffrey Sayers, of Grand Valley State University, Grand Rapids, Michigan.

CHAPTER ESSENTIALS

Key Terms

balance of payments   280
capital flight   276
central bank   279
currency risk   275
devaluation   280
exchange rate   274

foreign exchange   276
foreign exchange market   276
global financial system   283
International Monetary Fund
(IMF)   281
international monetary system   283

monetary intervention   288
Special Drawing Right (SDR)   289
trade deficit   280
trade surplus   280
World Bank   281

Summary

In this chapter, you learned about:

1. **Exchange rates and currencies in international business**

   Much of international trade requires the exchange of currencies, such as the dollar, euro, and yen. An **exchange rate** is the price of one currency expressed in terms of another. **Currency risk** arises from changes in exchange rates, and affects firms' international business prospects. A convertible currency is one that can be readily exchanged for other currencies. Some currencies are nonconvertible and not readily exchangeable. **Foreign exchange** refers to all forms of money that are traded internationally, including foreign currencies, bank deposits, checks, and electronic transfers. **Capital flight** refers to the tendency of international investors to drastically reduce their investments in a troubled currency or other assets. Currencies are exchanged in the **foreign exchange market**—the global marketplace for buying and selling currencies—mainly by banks and governments.

2. **How exchange rates are determined**

   Currency values are determined by various factors, including *economic growth, inflation, market psychology*, and *government action*. As inflation rises, so do interest rates, usually accompanied by a decrease in currency value. **Trade deficit** refers to the amount by which a nation's imports exceed its exports for a specific time period. **Trade surplus** is the amount by which a

nation's exports exceed its imports for a specific time period. Government action to influence exchange rates is broadly termed **monetary intervention**. When the goal is **devaluation**, the government acts to reduce the official value of its currency, relative to other currencies. The **balance of payments** is the annual accounting of *all* economic transactions of a nation with all other nations.

3. **Emergence of the modern exchange rate system**

   The Bretton Woods agreement of 1944 aimed to stabilize exchange rates worldwide. But the system collapsed in 1971 as currency values began floating according to market forces. Today, currency values are determined in some countries by a *floating exchange rate system*, according to market forces, and in developing economies by a *fixed exchange rate system*, controlled via government intervention. The **International Monetary Fund (IMF)** is a key international agency that aims to stabilize currencies by monitoring the foreign exchange systems of member countries and lending money to developing economies. The **World Bank** is an international agency that provides loans and technical assistance to low- and middle-income countries with the goal of reducing poverty.

4. **The monetary and financial systems**

   The **international monetary system** is the institutional framework, rules, and procedures by which national currencies are exchanged for each other. It includes institutional arrangements that countries put in place to govern exchange rates. The **global financial system** is the collective of financial institutions that facilitate and regulate investment and capital flows, and make possible massive trading of currencies and financial assets. It reflects the activities of companies, banks, and financial institutions, all engaged in ongoing financial activity.

5. Key players in the monetary and financial systems

Key participants include firms that generate revenues and acquire foreign exchange in the course of international business, invest abroad, and inject money into the financial system. Trading of securities and bonds takes place in *national stock exchanges* and *bond markets*. Each country has a **central bank**, the monetary authority that regulates the money supply and credit, issues currency, manages the rate of exchange, and acts as lender of last resort. The IMF employs **Special Drawing Rights**, a type of international reserve, to help manage currency valuation worldwide.

A *currency crisis* results when the value of the nation's currency depreciates sharply. A *banking crisis* results when investors lose confidence in a nation's banking system and massively withdraw funds. Excessive *foreign debt* can harm the stability of national financial systems.

6. The global debt crisis

Growing imbalance in the finances of numerous national governments is an important emergent global risk. Governments spent huge sums to bail out financial systems in the global financial crisis, and are faced with financing long-term liabilities of pension and healthcare programs. National debt that exceeds 90 percent of a nation's GDP diminishes GDP growth; numerous countries have surpassed this threshold. Firms doing international business must proceed with caution as massive government debt can indicate economic instability, reduced buyer purchasing power, and other challenges in national markets.

Test Your Comprehension AACSB: Reflective Thinking Skills

1. Distinguish between *exchange rate* and *foreign exchange*. What does each term mean?

2. Distinguish between convertible and nonconvertible currencies.

⭐ 3. Exchange rates fluctuate constantly. What is the effect of this fluctuation on firms engaged in international business?

4. What was the Bretton Woods agreement, and what is its legacy today?

5. Distinguish the two systems that make up the exchange rate system today.

6. What is the difference between the international monetary system and the global financial system?

7. What are the key players in the international monetary and financial systems?

8. What are the aims of the World Bank and the International Monetary Fund?

⭐ 9. What are the major causes of the global debt crisis?

10. What countries are most affected by the global debt crisis?

Apply Your Understanding AACSB: Reflective Thinking Skills, Analytic Skills and Ethical Understanding and Reasoning Abilities

1. Everest Company has been exporting its line of mountain-climbing equipment to buyers worldwide for 30 years. Top markets include France, Norway, Switzerland, India, and Japan. Customers in these countries always pay in their local currency. Everest's vice president for international sales often states that the firm's biggest day-to-day challenge is dealing with foreign currencies. Why does he say this? What are the consequences of fluctuating exchange rates for Everest's sales revenue and other performance indicators?

2. The European Union (EU) was established in 1993 and the European Central Bank (ECB) was established in 1998. Euro banknotes and coins were issued in 2002,

replacing traditional currencies such as the French franc and the German mark. More than a dozen EU countries have adopted the euro as their national currency, and are termed the "eurozone." Sharing a single currency eliminates exchange fluctuations and simplifies trade. Eurozone firms had to make various operational changes, especially regarding finance and accounting, but generally prefer dealing in the euro. The ECB views the eurozone as one region and must apply the same monetary policy to all EU members, but this is problematic at times. The United Kingdom opted not to join the monetary union, keeping the British pound as its currency. What types of competitive advantages and disadvantages are associated with the implementation of the euro from the perspective of the firm? What types of changes did firms make once the euro became the new currency? Was adopting the euro worth it? Why or why not?

3. *Ethical Dilemma:* You are an adviser to a legislator who oversees the banking industry. During the global financial crisis that began in 2008, several banks collapsed and private citizens lost much money. Problems arose largely due to inadequate or inappropriate regulation of the banking industry. In recent decades, however, an unrestricted global banking sector has produced numerous benefits. The relative absence of restrictions on international financial flows gave firms access to low-cost capital. The free flow of capital also provided much-needed funding to governments and entrepreneurs in poor countries. A liberated world currency market greatly facilitated international trade. Nations benefit enormously from inward capital flows as portfolio investments. Given the pros and cons of a relatively unregulated global banking system, how would you advise the legislator? Are new regulations needed in the banking sector? If so, what types of regulations? Use the Ethical Framework in Chapter 5 to help formulate your answer.

 INTERNET EXERCISES
(http://www.globalEDGE.msu.edu)

AACSB: Communication Abilities, Reflective Thinking Skills

Refer to Chapter 1, page 24, for instructions on how to access and use globalEDGE™.

1. There are numerous foreign exchange calculators on the Internet, such as www.x-rates.com. You can find them via globalEDGE™ or by entering the keywords "exchange rate" into a Google search. Visit one of these calculators and compare the exchange rates of various currencies, including the dollar, euro, yen, and renminbi. What is the rate for these currencies today? What was the euro–dollar exchange rate one year ago? What factors might have caused the fluctuation in this rate during the year? Does this Web site provide a way to trade foreign currencies? What is the amount of commission or other fees charged?

2. Assume you are a manager at a firm interested in doing business in Russia. As part of your initial analysis, top management would like to know about the level of currency and financial risks associated with the Russian market. Using resources at globalEDGE™, write a short report on the current status of these risks, as well as the state of the Russian financial system and historical exchange rate stability. Based on these findings, what is your recommendation?

3. The International Monetary Fund (IMF) lists its purposes as follows: (1) to promote international monetary cooperation via consultation and collaboration on international monetary problems; (2) to facilitate the expansion and balanced growth of international trade; and (3) to promote exchange stability, to maintain orderly exchange arrangements among members, and to avoid competitive exchange depreciation. Visit the IMF Web site (www.imf.org) and list several examples of how the IMF undertakes and accomplishes these goals. What kinds of specific actions has the IMF taken over the past year to address economic or financial crises of various nations?

MyManagementLab

Go to **mymanagementlab.com** for Auto-graded writing questions as well as the following Assisted-graded writing questions:

11-1. Summarize the four major factors that determine exchange rates.

11-2. What is the relationship between inflation, interest rates, and currency values?

11-3. Mymanagementlab Only – comprehensive writing assignment for this chapter.

Source: ITAR-TASS/Alamy

IKEA's Global Strategy

IKEA evolved from a small, Swedish company to become the leading global retailer of specialty furniture. Ingvar Kamprad founded the firm in Sweden in 1943. IKEA originally sold pens, picture frames, jewelry, and nylon stockings—anything Kamprad could sell at a low price. In 1950, IKEA began selling furniture and housewares. In the 1970s, the firm expanded into Europe and North America and began to grow rapidly. Total sales in 2011 exceeded $36 billion, making IKEA the world's largest furniture retailer. Usually located in major cities, IKEA stores are huge warehouse-style outlets that stock some 9,500 items, including everything for the home—from sofas to plants to kitchen utensils.

IKEA's philosophy is to offer high-quality, well-designed furnishings at low prices. Its functional, utilitarian, and space-saving pieces have a distinctive Scandinavian style and are "knock-down" furniture, which the customer assembles at home.

IKEA is owned by the Kamprad family, with corporate offices in the Netherlands, Sweden, and Belgium. Product development, purchasing, and warehousing are concentrated

CHAPTER 12

Strategy and Organization in the International Firm

LEARNING OBJECTIVES *In this chapter, you will learn about:*

1. Strategy in international business
2. Building the global firm
3. The integration-responsiveness framework
4. Strategies based on the integration-responsiveness framework
5. Organizational structure
6. Organizational structures for international operations

MyManagementLab®

⭐ **Improve Your Grade!**

Over 10 million students improved their results using the Pearson MyLabs. Visit **mymanagementlab.com** for simulations, tutorials, and end-of-chapter problems.

---

in Sweden. Its headquarters designs and develops IKEA's global branding and product line, often collaborating closely with external suppliers. About 30 percent of the merchandise is made in Asia and two-thirds in Europe. A few items are sourced in North America to address the specific needs of that market, but 90 percent of the product line is identical worldwide. Store managers constantly report market research to headquarters on sales and customer preferences.

IKEA targets moderate-income households with limited living space. The preferred market segment is progressive, well-educated people, who care little about status. Targeting a global customer segment allows IKEA to offer standardized products at uniform prices, a strategy that minimizes the costs of international operations. IKEA seeks scale economies by consolidating worldwide design, purchasing, and manufacturing.

Each IKEA store follows a centrally developed advertising strategy in which the catalogue is the most important marketing tool. In 2011, about 210 million copies were printed in twenty-seven languages, representing the largest circulation of a free publication in the world. Also available online (www.ikea.com), the catalogue is prepared in Sweden to ensure conformity with IKEA's cosmopolitan style. Each product has a unique proper name. IKEA uses Scandinavian rivers or cities for sofas (Henriksberg, Falkenberg), women's names for fabric (Linne, Mimmi, Adel), and men's names for wall units (Billy, Niklas, Ivar).

IKEA employees ("coworkers") worldwide are widely acknowledged as the basis for the firm's success. Corporate culture is informal. There are few titles, no executive parking spaces, and no corporate dining rooms. Managers fly economy class and stay in inexpensive hotels. Most initiatives are developed at headquarters in Sweden and communicated to all stores worldwide. This speeds decision making and ensures the IKEA culture is easily globalized. Management in each store is required to speak either English or Swedish to ensure efficient communications with headquarters.

IKEA organizes an "anti-bureaucratic week" each year in which managers wear sales clerks' uniforms and do everything from operating cash registers to driving forklifts. The system keeps managers in touch with all IKEA operations and close to suppliers, customers, and sales staff. The firm's culture, emphasizing consensus-based decision making, lets managers share their knowledge and skills with coworkers and helps employees and suppliers feel they are important members of a global organization. The strong appeal of global culture supports IKEA's continued growth.

IKEA manages 290 stores, twenty franchises, 130,000 employees, twenty-seven distribution centers, and 1,400 suppliers in fifty-four countries. IKEA chooses its markets strategically. The firm suspended investment in Russia because of burdensome government intervention. It has established several stores in key cities in China. Management is pondering expansion in India, but must deal with substantial government red tape. Elsewhere, IKEA faces much complexity in adapting to national markets regarding employment, operations, supplier relationships, and customer preferences. Among other challenges, IKEA must figure out how to:

- Incorporate customer feedback and design preferences from diverse markets into decision making at headquarters
- Reward employees and motivate suppliers despite varying business customs and expectations from country to country
- Achieve the real benefits of international operations—efficiency on a global scale and learning—while remaining responsive to local needs
- Keep designs standardized across markets yet respond to local preferences and trends
- Delegate adequate autonomy to local store managers while retaining central control

IKEA fared well during the recent global recession. Its value-oriented furniture and housewares appealed to customers during tough economic times.

SOURCES: "IKEA's Russian Saga," *Business Eastern Europe,* January 17, 2011, p. 2; "IKEA: How the Swedish Retailer Became a Global Cult Brand," *Business Week,* November 14, 2005, retrieved from http://www.businessweek.com; "Online Extra: IKEA's Design for Growth," *Business Week,* June 6, 2005, retrieved from http://www.businessweek.com; M. Lloyd, "IKEA Sees Opportunity During Hard Times," *Wall Street Journal,* February 18, 2009, p. B1; IKEA corporate Web site at http://www.IKEA-group.IKEA.com; IKEA company profile at http://www.hoovers.com; Amol Sharma, "IKEA Wary of Entering India," *Wall Street Journal,* January 24, 2012, p. B4.

As the IKEA opening story shows, multinational managers strive to coordinate sourcing, manufacturing, marketing, and other value-adding activities on a worldwide basis. They often adopt organization-wide standards and common processes. They also frequently seek to develop products that appeal to the broadest base of customers worldwide. Organizing the firm on a global scale is challenging. It requires skillfully configuring activities across diverse settings, integrating and coordinating these activities, and implementing common processes to ensure the activities are performed optimally. In addition, the firm must simultaneously respond to the specific needs and conditions that characterize the individual locations where it does business. In this chapter, we discuss the role of strategy and organization, and the various company attributes that support them, in building the successful international firm.

 ## Strategy in International Business

Strategy is a planned set of actions that managers employ to make best use of the firm's resources and core competencies to gain competitive advantage. When developing strategies, managers start by examining the firm's specific strengths and weaknesses. They then analyze the particular opportunities and challenges that confront the firm. Once they understand the firm's strengths, weaknesses, opportunities, and challenges, they decide which customers to target, what product lines to offer, how best to contend with competitors, and how generally to configure and coordinate the firm's activities around the world.

International strategy is strategy carried out in two or more countries. MNE managers develop international strategies to allocate scarce company resources and configure value-adding activities on a worldwide scale, participate in major markets, implement valuable partnerships abroad, and engage in competitive moves in response to foreign rivals.[1]

Managers devise strategies that develop and ensure the firm's competitive advantages. The most widely accepted prescription for building sustainable, competitive advantage in international business is that of Bartlett and Ghoshal.[2] These scholars argued the firm should strive to develop: "global-scale efficiency in its existing activities; multinational flexibility to manage diverse country-specific risks and opportunities; and learn from international exposure and exploit that learning on a worldwide basis."[3] Thus, firms that want to become globally competitive must seek simultaneously three strategic objectives—efficiency, flexibility, and learning.[4] Let's review these next.

EFFICIENCY *The firm must build efficient international value chains.* Efficiency refers to lowering the cost of the firm's operations and activities on a global scale. MNEs with multiple value chains must pay special attention to how they organize their R&D, manufacturing, product sourcing, marketing, and customer service activities. For example, automotive companies strive for scale economies by concentrating manufacturing and sourcing activities in a limited number of locations. For Toyota (www.toyota.com), this means manufacturing in low-cost countries such as China and in major markets like the United States. Toyota works with its suppliers to ensure they provide low-cost parts and components while maintaining quality. Its logistical operations for shipping its cars around the world are efficient and cost effective.

FLEXIBILITY *The firm must develop worldwide flexibility to accommodate diverse country-specific risks and opportunities.* The diversity and volatility of international environments are especially challenging for managers. Successful firms are skillful at tapping local resources and exploiting local opportunities in the markets where they do business. Managers may opt for contractual relationships with independent suppliers and distributors in one country, while engaging in direct investment in another. They may adapt their marketing and human resource practices to suit unique country conditions. Exchange rate fluctuations may prompt managers to switch to local sourcing or to adjust prices. The firm structures its operations to ensure it can respond to specific customer needs in individual markets, especially those critical to company performance.[5]

LEARNING *The firm must create the ability to learn from operating in international environments and exploit this learning on a worldwide basis.* The diversity of the international environment presents the internationalizing firm with unique learning opportunities. By operating in various countries, the MNE can acquire new technical and managerial know-how, new product ideas, improved R&D capabilities, partnering skills, and survival capabilities in unfamiliar environments. The firm's partners or subsidiaries capture and disseminate this learning throughout their corporate network. Take Procter & Gamble (www.pg.com) as an example. Although headquartered in the United States, P&G's research center in Belgium developed a special water-softening technology to deal with Europe's hard water. The firm's subsidiary in Japan formulated a laundry detergent that works well in cold water, to serve Japanese customers' preference for cold-water washing. After assimilating these innovations into its global knowledge base, P&G applied the knowledge to the development of products for other markets around the world.

Strategy

A planned set of actions that managers employ to make best use of the firm's resources and core competencies to gain competitive advantage.

International business success is ultimately determined by the degree to which the firm masters all three skills—efficiency, flexibility, and learning. It is often difficult to excel in all three simultaneously. One firm may be highly efficient, while another excels at flexibility and a third at learning. Many Japanese firms achieved international success by developing highly efficient manufacturing systems. Numerous European firms succeeded internationally by being locally responsive, despite sometimes failing to achieve optimal efficiency or technological leadership. Many MNEs from the United States have struggled to adapt their activities to the cultural and political diversity of national environments and instead have proven adept at achieving efficiency via economies of scale. During the recent global financial crisis, efficiency and flexibility became particularly important to the success of multinational firms.[6]

Building the Global Firm

Exhibit 12.1 illustrates the dimensions of the successful international firm. Truly global firms are characterized by visionary leadership, strong organizational culture, and superior organizational processes, as well as an appropriate organizational structure and strategies that optimize international operations.[7] We examine these dimensions next.

Visionary Leadership

Visionary leadership
A quality of executive management that provides inspirational guidance and motivation to personnel, leading the firm to a better future.

Visionary leadership is a quality of executive management that provides inspirational guidance and motivation to personnel, leading the firm to a better future. Visionary leaders exhibit superior creativity, discipline, and passion in the course of leading others to realization of their vision.[8] Leadership becomes more complex in firms as they increase the international component of their business activities because valuable organizational assets, such as productive capabilities, brands, and human resources, may be employed in many different countries and diverse business environments. Visionary leadership is vital in firms with complex international operations.

How do leaders differ from managers? The main difference is that managers are relatively focused on directing the firm's day-to-day operations. They are responsible for administering or controlling specific activities in the firm. Alternatively, leaders are visionary and hold a long-term perspective on the challenges and opportunities that confront the firm. Leaders are exceptionally skilled at motivating people and at setting the tone for how the firm will pursue its goals and objectives.

EXHIBIT 12.1

Key Dimensions of Successful International Firms

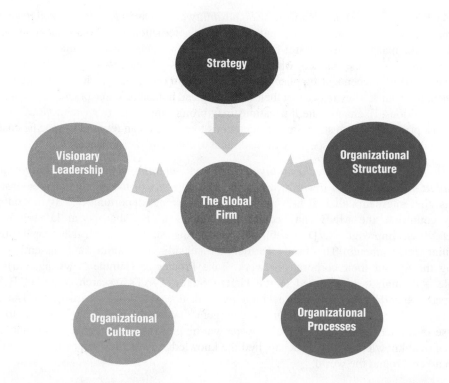

Consider Peter Brabeck, Chairman of Nestlé (www.nestle.com). From headquarters in Switzerland, Brabeck led Nestlé into the worldwide market for products that meet consumers' growing interest in health and nutrition. To pursue this market, Nestlé purchased Jenny Craig, the U.S. weight management and food-products company. In Germany, Nestlé launched an institute to advise consumers on dietary issues, dispensing nutritional advice to more than 300,000 customers per month. In France, Brabeck created a nutritional home-care service, providing for patients with special dietary needs. These initiatives position Nestlé in a growing global market and generate global brand loyalty for the firm's line of healthy food products.[9]

In international business, visionary leaders are characterized by four major traits:

- *International mind-set and cosmopolitan values.* Visionary leadership requires managers to acquire an international mind-set—an openness to, and awareness of, diversity across cultures.[10] Dogmatic, close-minded managers who lack vision and have difficulty adapting to other cultures are likely to fail. Those who are open minded, committed to internationalization, and ready to adapt to other cultures are likely to succeed.[11]
- *Willingness to commit resources.* The complexities of foreign markets imply that international ventures take more time than domestic ones to become profitable. Visionary leaders commit to them and unswervingly believe the firm will eventually succeed. Commitment drives them to develop the financial, human, and other resources their firms need to achieve their international goals. Highly committed firms engage in systematic international market expansion, allocate necessary resources, and empower structures and processes that ensure ultimate success.
- *Strategic vision.* Visionary leaders articulate a strategic vision—what the firm wants to be in the future and how it will get there. As they develop strategic vision, senior managers focus on the ideal picture of what the firm should become. The picture is a central rallying point for all plans, employees, and employee actions.[12]
- *Willingness to invest in human assets.* Visionary leaders must nurture the most critical asset of any organization—human capital. In global firms, senior leaders adopt such human resource practices as hiring foreign nationals, promoting multicountry careers, and providing cross-cultural and language training to develop international supermanagers.[13]

Synclayer is a Japanese SME that exemplifies strategic vision. By 2015, one in four Japanese—about 30 million people—will be over age 65. Top management at Synclayer (www.synclayer.com) anticipate a large and growing market for new products for the elderly. Their vision of achieving worldwide leadership in this market led Synclayer to develop, among other products, a system that allows homebound seniors to measure their blood pressure, temperature, and other vital signs, and send them to a healthcare service that can dispatch an ambulance if problems are detected. Synclayer's vision is to develop the products in Japan and then launch them in other countries with sizable elderly populations.[14]

Ratan Tata is chairperson of the Tata Group in India and oversees a $67 billion family conglomerate whose companies market a range of products from cars to watches. His group has made numerous international acquisitions (from Tetley Tea to the Anglo-Dutch steel firm Corus), reflecting a change in strategic vision from local to global. In its latest venture, Tata developed a $2,500 car, the Nano,

Source: Fluger Rene/Alamy

Ratan Tata is chairman of India's Tata group. Tata transformed the giant Indian conglomerate into a transnational organization, with operations throughout the world.

targeted to emerging markets worldwide. Another visionary leader is Fujio Cho, who led Toyota to record sales in the intensely competitive global car industry. His leadership style emphasized innovation, continuous improvement, and an ability to spot future-oriented opportunities, including the Prius hybrid and the youth-oriented Scion brands of Toyota cars. Toyota's main sales focus now is emerging markets, especially China and India.[15]

Organizational Culture

Organizational culture
The pattern of shared values, behavioral norms, systems, policies, and procedures that employees learn and adopt.

Organizational culture is the pattern of shared values, behavioral norms, systems, policies, and procedures that employees learn and adopt. It spells out the correct way for employees to perceive, think, and behave in relation to new problems and opportunities that confront the firm.[16] As the opening story about IKEA showed, organizational culture usually derives from the influence of founders and visionary leaders or some unique history of the firm.

At the Japanese electronics giant Canon (www.canon.com), CEO Fujio Mitarai has developed an organizational culture that emphasizes science and technology. Canon invests billions in R&D and is the world's second-largest recipient of new U.S. patents. Its technology focus extends from product development to the way goods are made on the factory floor; this focus has allowed Canon to become the world leader in digital cameras, copiers, printers, and flat-screen TVs.[17] Recent innovations have slashed production time and costs.

Similarly, focus on product quality is a pillar of the organizational culture at the South Korean firm Hyundai. The firm's leaders have set a goal of becoming the world-quality leader in the auto industry. A stringent quality approval system is enforced at each value-chain stage, including sourcing, procurement, manufacturing, marketing, and sales. Top managers hold quality oversight meetings every two weeks. A survey of 60,000 new car buyers ranked Hyundai third in overall quality, behind only Porsche and Lexus.[18]

Today, management at firms such as Canon and Hyundai seek to build a *global* organizational culture—an organizational environment that plays a key role in the development and execution of corporate global strategy.

Companies that proactively build a global organizational culture:[19]

- Value and promote a global perspective in all major initiatives
- Value global competence and cross-cultural skills among their employees
- Adopt a single corporate language for business communications
- Promote interdependency between headquarters and subsidiaries
- Subscribe to globally accepted ethical standards

Firms aspiring to become truly global seek to maintain strong ethical standards in all the markets where they do business. Ultimately, management should cultivate a culture that welcomes social responsibility and is deliberate about fulfilling its role.

Ethical Connections

The annual revenue of the five largest corporations exceeds the combined GDP of the world's poorest 100 countries. MNEs can do much to help reduce poverty. Global pharmaceuticals provide AIDS medications at cost to the poor in Africa. Global retailers develop distribution systems that increase access to needed goods at lower costs. MNEs engage in large-scale charity work. Critics argue that a company's duty is to its shareholders, not society at large. Many firms, however, defy such thinking. Bimbo, Pfizer, and Unilever are among many firms that support the world's poor while earning substantial profits.

Visionary leadership with organizational culture needs to be supplemented with processes that define how managers will carry out day-to-day activities to achieve company goals. Let's examine these organizational processes next.

Organizational Processes

Organizational processes are the managerial routines, behaviors, and mechanisms that allow the firm to function as intended. Typical processes include mechanisms for collecting strategic information, ensuring quality control in manufacturing, and maintaining efficient payment systems for international sales. General Electric has gained much competitive advantage by developing and continuously improving the many processes that comprise its value chains. For example, GE digitizes all key documents and uses intranets and the Internet to automate many activities and reduce operating costs.

Managers attempt to achieve global coordination and integration not just by subscribing to a particular organizational design, but also by implementing common processes or *globalizing mechanisms*. These common processes provide substantial interconnectedness within the MNE network and allow for meaningful cross-fertilization and knowledge. Globalizing mechanisms include *global teams* and *global information systems*.

Global teams are charged with problem solving and best-practice development within the firm.[20] A **global team** is an internationally distributed group of employees charged with a specific problem-solving or best-practice mandate that affects company operations, or a major aspect of company operations, worldwide.[21] Team members are drawn from geographically diverse units of the MNE and may interact via in-person meetings, corporate intranets, and video conferencing. In this way, a global team brings together employees with the experience, knowledge, and skills to resolve common challenges.

Tasks of global teams vary. *Strategic global teams* identify or implement initiatives that enhance the long-term direction of the firm in its global industry. *Operational global teams* focus on the efficient and effective operation of the business across the whole network.[22] The most successful teams are flexible, responsive, and innovative. To develop global strategies, the team should include culturally diverse managers whose business activities span the globe. Culturally diverse teams have three valuable roles: create a global view inside the firm while remaining in touch with local realities, generate creative ideas and make fully informed decisions about the firm's global operations, and ensure team decisions are implemented throughout the firm's global operations.

Top managers' desire to create a globally coordinated company is motivated by the need for world-scale efficiency and minimal redundancy. In the past, geographic distance and cross-cultural differences were impediments. Today, *global information systems*—global IT infrastructure and tools such as intranets, the Internet, and electronic data interchange—ensure that distant parts of the global network share knowledge and learn from each other.

When General Motors developed the Equinox, a sport utility vehicle to compete with Toyota's RAV4 and Honda's CR-V, it leveraged global information systems to tap GM capabilities around the world. The Equinox's V6 engine was built in China, with cooperation from engineers in Canada, China, Japan, and the United States. From a room in Toronto, engineers teleconferenced almost daily with their counterparts from Shanghai, Tokyo, and the United States. They exchanged virtual-reality renderings of the vehicle and collaborated on styling of exteriors and component design.

In later sections, we explain two especially critical dimensions of internationalizing firms: strategy and organizational structure. First, however, let's lay the foundation for these key concepts by distinguishing between multidomestic and global industries and by introducing the global integration–local responsiveness framework.

The Distinction between Multidomestic and Global Industries

Companies that specialize in particular industries, such as processed food, consumer products, fashion, retailing, and publishing, have long approached international business by catering to the specific needs and tastes of each of the countries where they do business. For example, the British publisher Bloomsbury translates each volume of its Harry Potter series into the local language in every country where the book is sold. Coca-Cola varies the formula of its beverages to suit differing conditions abroad. Industries such as this, in which the firm must adapt its offerings to suit the culture, laws, income level, and other specific characteristics of each country, are known as multidomestic industries. In such industries,

Organizational processes
Managerial routines, behaviors, and mechanisms that allow the firm to function as intended.

Global team
An internationally distributed group of employees charged with a specific problem-solving or best-practice mandate that affects company operations, or a major aspect of company operations, worldwide.

Country Realities

After adopting free-market policies, Chile emerged from military dictatorship to become one of the world's leading economies. The country signed trade agreements with nations worldwide. The government cooperated with the private sector to foster foreign investment and ensure a friendly business environment. Chile has experienced remarkable economic growth, far above the rest of Latin America. As conditions improved, poverty and infant mortality fell dramatically, and life expectancy grew. MNEs find Chile an attractive place to do business.

Multidomestic industry
An industry in which competition takes place on a country-by-country basis.

each country tends to have a unique set of competitors. Accordingly, a **multidomestic industry** is one in which competition takes place on a *country-by-country* basis.

By contrast, in other types of industries, such as aerospace, automobiles, metals, computers, chemicals, and industrial equipment, firms generally approach international business by catering to the needs and tastes of customers on a regional or global scale. For example, Dupont sells essentially the same chemicals around the world. Subaru markets very similar cars in most of the countries where it does business. Industries such as this, in which competition takes place on a *regional or worldwide* basis, are known as **global industries**. Most global industries are characterized by a handful of major players that compete head-on in multiple markets. Kodak must contend with the same rivals—Japan's Fuji and Europe's Agfa-Gevaert—around the world. In the earth-moving equipment industry, Caterpillar and Komatsu compete head-on in all major world markets.

Global industry
An industry in which competition is on a regional or worldwide scale.

 ## The Integration-Responsiveness Framework

Global integration
Coordination of the firm's value-chain activities across countries to achieve worldwide efficiency, synergy, and cross-fertilization in order to take maximum advantage of similarities between countries.

Global integration is the *coordination* of the firm's value-chain activities across multiple countries to achieve worldwide efficiency, synergy, and cross-fertilization in order to take advantage of similarities between countries. Firms that emphasize global integration are typically found in global industries. They make and sell products and services that are relatively standardized—that is, uniform or with minimal adaptation—to capitalize on converging customer needs and tastes worldwide. Such firms compete on a *regional or worldwide* basis. They seek to minimize operating costs by centralizing value-chain activities and emphasizing economies of scale.[23]

In contrast to global integration, many companies seek to respond to specific conditions in individual countries. They are typically found in multidomestic industries. They embrace **local responsiveness,** managing the firm's value-chain activities and addressing diverse opportunities and risks, on a *country-by-country* basis. Local responsiveness emphasizes meeting the specific needs of customers in individual markets.

Local responsiveness
Management of the firm's value-chain activities on a country-by-country basis to address diverse opportunities and risks.

When they operate internationally, firms try to strike the right balance between the objectives of global integration and local responsiveness. Exhibit 12.2 presents the *integration-responsiveness* (IR) *framework*, which illustrates the pressures companies face in attempting to achieve these often-conflicting objectives.[24] It was developed to help managers better understand the trade-offs common in international business.

The primary goal of firms that emphasize global integration is to maximize the efficiency of their value-chain activities on a worldwide scale. They seek to reduce redundancy in their

EXHIBIT 12.2

Integration-Responsiveness Framework: Competing Pressures on the Internationalizing Firm

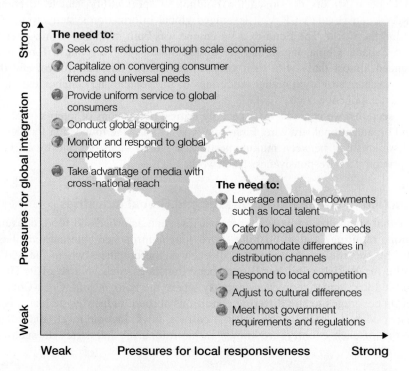

The need to:
- Seek cost reduction through scale economies
- Capitalize on converging consumer trends and universal needs
- Provide uniform service to global consumers
- Conduct global sourcing
- Monitor and respond to global competitors
- Take advantage of media with cross-national reach

The need to:
- Leverage national endowments such as local talent
- Cater to local customer needs
- Accommodate differences in distribution channels
- Respond to local competition
- Adjust to cultural differences
- Meet host government requirements and regulations

Pressures for global integration — Weak / Strong

Pressures for local responsiveness — Weak / Strong

operations. They acknowledge that designing numerous variations of the same product for individual markets is costly, and they minimize it. They also promote learning and cross-fertilization of knowledge within their global network in order to enhance innovation and gain competitive advantages. Senior management justifies global integration by citing converging buyer demand, spread of global brands, diffusion of uniform technology, availability of pan-regional media, and the need to monitor competitors on a global basis.

By contrast, companies that emphasize local responsiveness adjust the firm's practices to suit distinctive needs and conditions in each country. They adapt to local customer requirements, language, culture, regulation, the competitive environment, and the local distribution structure. For example, in Mexico, Walmart adjusts its store hours, employee training, compensation, product line, and promotional tools to suit local conditions.

Pressures for Global Integration

Let's examine the specific factors in Exhibit 12.2 that compel companies to globally integrate their activities:[25]

- *Seek cost reduction through scale economies.* Some industries profit from manufacturing in a few select locations, where firms can take advantage of economies of scale in production. Concentrating production also makes it easier to control the quality, speed, and cost of manufacturing.
- *Capitalize on converging consumer trends and universal needs.* Making and selling products that are standardized is more cost effective than adapting products for each market. For example, firms that make computer chips and electronic components can generally sell similar offerings worldwide. Standardization has become possible as buyer needs and tastes are increasingly similar worldwide.
- *Provide uniform service to global customers.* Services are easiest to standardize when firms can centralize their creation and delivery. MNEs with operations in numerous countries particularly value service inputs that are consistent worldwide.
- *Conduct global sourcing of raw materials, components, energy, and labor.* Firms face ongoing pressure to procure high-quality input goods cost effectively. Sourcing inputs from large-scale, centralized suppliers allows firms to obtain economies of scale, more consistent quality, lower costs, and generally more efficient operations.
- *Monitor and respond to global competitors.* Foreign rivals that compete on a global basis are usually more threatening than those that compete only locally. Thus, it is generally best to formulate strategies that challenge competitors on an integrated, global basis.
- *Take advantage of media that reaches buyers in multiple markets.* The availability of cost-effective, global media makes it possible for firms to design advertising and other promotional activities that target multiple countries simultaneously.

Pressures for Local Responsiveness

On the other hand, as portrayed in Exhibit 12.2, the following pressures compel companies to be locally responsive in individual countries:

- *Leverage natural endowments available to the firm.* Each country has distinctive resources such as raw materials and skilled knowledge workers that provide foreign firms with competitive advantages.
- *Cater to local customer needs.* Particularly in multidomestic industries, buyer needs vary from country to country. The internationalizing firm must adapt its products to meet diverse cross-national needs.
- *Accommodate differences in distribution channels.* Channels can vary from market to market and may increase the need for local responsiveness. In Latin America, small stores are the most common type of retailer. Foreign firms that ordinarily distribute their goods via large stores must adapt their approach when doing business there.
- *Respond to local competition.* Foreign firms are disadvantaged in markets that have numerous local competitors. To outdo local rivals, successful MNEs must devise offerings that best meet local demand.
- *Adjust to cultural differences.* Culture's influence on business activities can be substantial, depending on the market and the product. Where cultural differences are important, such

as in sales of food and clothing, the firm must adapt its products and marketing activities accordingly.

● *Meet host government requirements and regulations.* To protect local firms, governments sometimes impose trade barriers or other restrictions that hinder foreign firms. The MNE can overcome such obstacles by establishing local operations to attain the status of a local firm.

Strategies Based on the Integration-Responsiveness Framework

The integration-responsiveness framework is associated with four distinct strategies, summarized in Exhibit 12.3. Internationalizing firms pursue one or a combination of these.

In the **home replication strategy**, the firm views international business as separate from, and secondary to, its domestic business. Expanding abroad is viewed as an opportunity to generate additional sales for domestic product lines. Thus, the firm designs products with domestic customers in mind and pursues international business in order to extend product life cycles and replicate home-market success. Such a firm expects little useful knowledge to flow from its foreign operations.[26] Firms that make and sell commodities (such as raw materials and basic parts) sometimes use the home replication strategy because such products often do not require a sophisticated internationalization approach. The strategy can also succeed when the firm targets only markets that are similar to the home market.

Home replication strategy is typically employed by the smaller firm with products it wants to sell abroad to generate additional sales. It contracts with an intermediary in each of several foreign markets to import and distribute the product and generally does not adapt it for foreign customers. Because management knows little about international business and has limited human and financial resources, the firm relies heavily on its foreign intermediaries. A key consequence is that it maintains little control over how its products are marketed abroad. Replicating abroad what the firm normally does at home provides few competitive advantages in foreign markets. Consequently, for most internationalizing firms, home replication is usually an initial, temporary approach rather than a long-term strategy. It is often followed by inexperienced firms or those with limited international goals.

A second, more advanced approach is **multidomestic strategy** (sometimes called *multilocal strategy*), in which the internationalizing firm develops subsidiaries or affiliates in each of numerous foreign markets. The firm delegates autonomy to managers in each foreign unit,

Home replication strategy
An approach in which the firm views international business as separate from, and secondary to, its domestic business.

Multidomestic strategy
An approach to internationalization in which headquarters delegates considerable autonomy to each country manager, allowing him or her to operate independently and pursue local responsiveness.

EXHIBIT 12.3

Four Distinct Strategies Emerging from the Integration-Responsiveness Framework

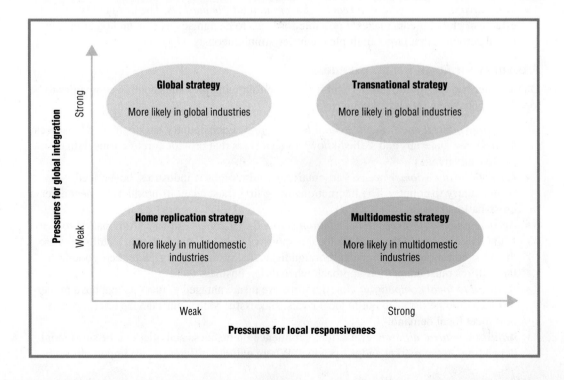

allowing them to operate independently and pursue local responsiveness. Using this strategy, headquarters recognizes and emphasizes differences between national markets. As a result, the firm allows subsidiaries to vary product and management practices by country. Country managers are often nationals of the host country and tend to function independently, with little incentive to share knowledge and experience with managers in other countries. Products and services are carefully adapted to suit the unique needs of each country.[27]

The food and beverage giant Nestlé (www.nestle.com) applies a multidomestic strategy. In each of its country subsidiaries, the firm employs highly autonomous nationals who adapt corporate strategic guidelines to meet specific local needs and conditions. Because of this approach, Nestlé is often perceived as a local firm in each of its markets. For example, the firm varies the taste of its Nescafé brand instant coffees. In Spain, the coffee has an intense, full-bodied flavor. In Northern Europe, it is mild and aromatic. Depending on the country, Nestlé sells its products through various channels, including supermarkets, small shops, market stalls, vending machines, mobile vendors, and even door-to-door. In Nigeria, it built a network of small warehouses and ships goods via pickup trucks. In China, the firm created a system of simple distribution links among villages that facilitate direct delivery by local vendors, often by bicycle. Nestlé also adapts its marketing. In patriotic Russia, advertising emphasizes Russian history and literature. In Africa, the firm hired local singers to visit villages and offer a mix of entertainment and product demonstrations. Nestlé also charges lower prices for its products in markets such as Brazil and China, to suit lower local buying power.[28]

The multidomestic approach has several advantages. If the foreign subsidiary includes a factory, locally produced products can be better adapted to the local market. There is minimal pressure on headquarters staff because local operations are managed by individual managers in each country. Firms with limited international experience find multidomestic strategy an easy option, as they can delegate many tasks to their country managers (or to foreign distributors, franchisees, or licensees, where they are used).

Multidomestic strategy has some disadvantages. Each foreign subsidiary manager tends to develop a local strategic plan, organizational culture, and business processes that can differ substantially from those of headquarters. Subsidiaries have little incentive to share their knowledge and experience with managers in the firm's other country markets. This may lead to reduced economies of scale. Limited information sharing also reduces the possibility of developing a knowledge-based competitive advantage.[29] While multidomestic strategy is more responsive to individual markets, it may lead to inefficient manufacturing, redundant operations, a proliferation of over-adapted products, and higher operating costs.[30]

These disadvantages may eventually lead management to abandon a multidomestic strategy in favor of a third approach—**global strategy**. With global strategy, headquarters seeks substantial control over its country operations in order to minimize redundancy and achieve maximum efficiency, learning, and integration worldwide. In the extreme, global strategy asks, "Why not make the same thing, the same way, everywhere?" Thus, global strategy emphasizes central coordination and control of international operations. Headquarters managers are often largely responsible for the firm's operations worldwide. Activities such as R&D and manufacturing are centralized at headquarters, and management tends to view the world as one large marketplace.[31]

An example of global strategy is Samsung Electronics (www.samsung.com). Once a manufacturer of home appliances in South Korea, the firm now manages a wide collection of global activities from company headquarters. Its integrated value chains mean Samsung's most advanced expertise in consumer electronics, technology, production, and distribution are continuously shared among the firm's business units worldwide. Its engineers continuously seek the most cost-effective ways to produce leading-edge products based on common parts and components. Samsung R&D personnel from Asia, Europe, and the Americas work in global teams to develop semiconductors, flat-screen TVs, smartphones, and other electronics based on standardized platforms, with little cross-national variation. For example, the firm developed the Galaxy smartphone, selling several hundred million units worldwide. In a typical Samsung smartphone, the internal electronics are identical wherever the product is sold. Internal software is varied to suit differing national preferences. The company intranet allows R&D teams to access ideas and specifications on how to create inputs that can be integrated into Samsung products, wherever they are made.

Parts and components are sourced from a limited number of top suppliers worldwide, who operate globally to deliver to as many of Samsung's factories as possible. Samsung does

Global strategy
An approach in which headquarters seeks substantial control over its country operations in order to minimize redundancy and maximize efficiency, learning, and integration worldwide.

Source: Carabay/Fotolia LLC

Samsung is a leading manufacturer of consumer electronics, responsible for about one-fifth of South Korea's total exports. The firm's global strategy relies on first-rate suppliers worldwide and manufacturing in low-cost countries.

Transnational strategy
A coordinated approach to internationalization in which the firm strives to be relatively responsive to local needs while retaining sufficient central control of operations to ensure efficiency and learning.

much of its manufacturing in China, Brazil, and other emerging markets to keep costs low. In total, Samsung sells its smartphones in more than 120 countries. Marketing activities are standardized and focus on making Samsung a globally recognized brand. By emphasizing global strategy, Samsung optimizes its value chains and enjoys superior performance around the world.[32]

Global strategy offers many advantages. It provides a substantial ability to respond to worldwide opportunities. It increases opportunities for cross-national learning and cross-fertilization of the firm's knowledge among all its subsidiaries. It creates economies of scale, which result in lower operational costs. Global strategy can also improve the quality of products and processes, primarily by simplifying manufacturing and other processes. High-quality products give rise to global brand recognition, increased consumer preference, and efficient international marketing programs.

Many factors make it easier to pursue global strategy, including converging buyer characteristics worldwide, growing acceptance of global brands, increased diffusion of uniform technology (especially in industrial markets), the spread of international collaborative ventures, and the integrating effects of globalization and advanced communications technologies.

Like other approaches, global strategy has limitations. It is challenging for management to closely coordinate the activities of widely dispersed international operations. The firm must maintain ongoing communications between headquarters and its subsidiaries, as well as between the subsidiaries. When carried to an extreme, global strategy results in a loss of responsiveness and flexibility in local markets.

A final alternative is **transnational strategy**, a coordinated approach to internationalization in which the firm strives to be relatively responsive to local needs while retaining sufficient central control of operations to ensure efficiency and learning. Transnational strategy combines the major advantages of multidomestic and global strategies while minimizing their disadvantages.[33] It is a flexible approach: *standardize where feasible; adapt where appropriate.*

To implement a transnational strategy, the firm should:

• Exploit scale economies by sourcing from a reduced set of global suppliers and concentrate manufacturing in relatively few locations where competitive advantages can be maximized
• Organize production, marketing, and other value-chain activities on a global scale
• Optimize local responsiveness and flexibility
• Facilitate global learning and knowledge transfer
• Coordinate global competitive moves—that is, rather than following a country-by-country approach, deal with competitors on a global, integrated basis[34]

One example of transnational strategy is Lenovo (www.lenovo.com), the Chinese producer of personal computers featured in the Closing Case. Lenovo went global when it bought the PC arm of IBM, gaining a global sales force and strong global brands, such as the Thinkpad line. The firm rotates its headquarters between China and the United States; its official language is English. Planning and design are done in the United States, while manufacturing is done in China (for Asian markets), Mexico (for the Americas), and Poland (for Europe). Lenovo concentrates production in these low-cost countries to maximize cost–efficiencies and economies of scale.

Lenovo's basic computers are the same, but the keyboards and internal software are adapted for each market to accommodate language differences. The firm's retailing Web sites look identical worldwide, but are adapted for language. Marketing operations, centralized to Bangalore, India, include global campaigns designed to sell computers in more than sixty countries with ads that can air in multiple regions. In short, Lenovo strikes a balance between pursuing global strategy and adapting its offerings and approaches, as needed, to suit individual markets.[35]

Given the difficulty of balancing central control and local responsiveness, most MNEs find it difficult to implement transnational strategy. In the long run, almost all need to include some elements of localized decision making, because each country has unique characteristics.

Having discussed distinct strategies that firms pursue in international expansion, let's now explore the related topic of organizational structure. While a strategy is the blueprint for action, a firm needs a structure with people, resources, and processes to implement it.

Source: Arkadiusz Komski/Fotolia LLC

China's Lenovo follows a transnational strategy. The firm's computers are similar worldwide except the keyboards and internal software, which are adapted for individual markets to suit language differences. Lenovo's retailing Web sites, which look identical across the world, are also adapted for language.

 ## Organizational Structure

Organizational structure describes the reporting relationships inside the firm or the "boxes and lines" that specify the links between people, functions, and processes that allow the firm to carry out its operations. Organizational structure dictates the reporting relationships through which the firm's vision and strategies are implemented. In the large, experienced MNE, these linkages are extensive and include the firm's subsidiaries and affiliates. A fundamental issue in organizational structure is how much decision-making responsibility the firm should retain at headquarters and how much it should delegate to foreign subsidiaries and affiliates. This is the choice between *centralization* and *decentralization*. Let's examine these options in more detail.

Organizational structure
Reporting relationships inside the firm that specify the links between people, functions, and processes.

Centralized or Decentralized Structure?

A *centralized approach* gives headquarters considerable authority and control over the firm's activities worldwide. A *decentralized approach* means substantial autonomy and decision-making authority are delegated to the firm's subsidiaries around the world. In every company, management tends to devise a structure consistent with its vision and strategies. Thus, MNEs that emphasize global integration tend to have a centralized structure. Those that emphasize local responsiveness tend to be decentralized.

Exhibit 12.4 identifies the typical contributions of headquarters and subsidiaries. Whether headquarters or the subsidiary will make decisions about the firm's value-chain activities

A subsidiary is the primary contributor to these activities:	Headquarters is the primary contributor to these activities:	Shared responsibility of subsidiary and headquarters:
• Sales • Marketing • Local market research • Human resource management • Compliance with local laws and regulations	• Capital planning • Transfer pricing • Global profitability	**With the subsidiary's lead:** • Geographic strategy • Local product and service development • Technical support and customer service • Local procurement **With the headquarters' lead:** • Broad corporate strategy • Global product development • Basic research and development • Global product sourcing • Development of global managers

EXHIBIT 12.4

Subsidiary and Headquarters Contributions

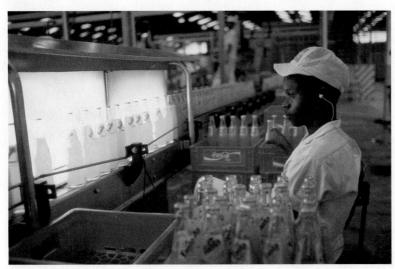

Source: Jenny Matthews/Alamy Images

A worker inspects production of Coca-Cola beverages in a plant in Africa. While Coca-Cola headquarters provides global brand support and broad marketing guidance to its bottlers in individual countries, the local bottler assumes responsibility for local customer research, local sales promotion, retailer support, and meeting local government requirements.

depends on the firm's products, the size of its markets, the nature of competitor operations, and the size and strategic importance of each foreign venture. Generally, the larger the financial outlay or the riskier the anticipated result, the more headquarters will contribute to decision making. For example, decisions about developing new products or building factories abroad tend to be centralized to headquarters. Decisions that affect two or more countries are best left to headquarters managers who have a regional or global perspective.[36] Decisions about local products that will be sold in only one country, however, are typically the joint responsibility of corporate and country-level managers, with the latter taking the lead role. Decisions on day-to-day human resource issues in individual subsidiaries are generally left to local managers.

Generally, it is neither beneficial nor feasible for the firm to centralize all its operations. Retaining some local autonomy is both desirable and necessary. Companies must strike the right balance between centralization and local autonomy. The challenge for managers is to achieve these goals simultaneously.[37] The phrase "Think globally, act locally" oversimplifies the true complexities of today's global competition; "Think globally and locally and act appropriately" better describes the reality faced by MNEs today.[38]

Planning shared by managers at headquarters and at subsidiaries, with negotiation and give-and-take on both sides, is vital to the design of effective strategies. Highly centralized, top-down decision making ignores subsidiary managers' intimate knowledge of host countries. Highly decentralized, bottom-up decision making by autonomous subsidiary managers ignores the big-picture knowledge of headquarters managers and fails to integrate strategies across countries and regions. Ultimately, however, most decisions are subject to headquarters approval. Headquarters management should promote positive, open-minded, collaborative relationships with country managers. Specifically, they should:

- Encourage local managers to identify with broad, corporate objectives
- Visit subsidiaries periodically to instill corporate values and priorities
- Rotate employees within the corporate network to promote development of a global perspective
- Encourage country managers to interact and share experiences with each other through regional and global meetings
- Provide incentives and penalties to promote compliance with headquarters' goals

 ## Organizational Structures for International Operations

As a general rule, "structure follows strategy." That is, we can think of organizational structure as a *tool* that facilitates the implementation of strategy and ultimately the firm's strategic vision.[39] Moreover, the organizational structure senior managers choose is largely the result of how important they consider international business and whether they prefer centralized or decentralized decision making. Organizational structures tend to evolve over time: As the firm's involvement in international business increases, it adopts increasingly complex organizational structures.

Exhibit 12.5 describes the advantages and disadvantages of each structure. Let's explore the major types of organizational structures.

EXHIBIT 12.5 Advantages and Disadvantages of International Organizational Structures

Structure	Advantages	Disadvantages
Export Department A unit within the firm charged with managing the firm's export operations	• Export activities unified under one department • Efficiencies in selling, distribution, and shipping • Small resource commitment	• Focus on the domestic market • Minimal learning about foreign markets • Minimal control of international operations. Potential to rely excessively on foreign intermediaries
International Division All international activities are centralized within one division in the firm, separate from domestic units	• Greater focus on internationalization • Concentration and development of international expertise • Increased commitment to, and coordination and management of, international operations	• Potential for fierce competition between domestic and international units for company resources • Limited knowledge sharing among the foreign units and with headquarters • R&D and future-oriented planning activities are separate for foreign operations and headquarters • Possibility that corporate management may favor domestic over international operations because most will have advanced through the domestic organization
Geographic Area Structure Management and control are decentralized to individual geographic regions, whose managers are responsible for operations within their region	• Greater responsiveness to customer needs and wants in each regional/local market • Better balance between global integration and local adaptation • Improved communications and coordination among the subsidiaries within each geographic region	• Geographic area managers' lack of *global* orientation for developing and managing products • Limited communications, coordination, and knowledge sharing with other geographic units and with headquarters • Limited economies of scale among the far-flung geographic regional units
Product Structure Management of international operations is organized by major product line	• Development of expertise with specific products, on a global basis • Individual product lines are coordinated and managed globally • Scale economies and sharing of product knowledge among units worldwide	• Duplication of corporate support functions for each product division • Possibility that headquarters may favor subsidiaries offering fastest returns • Potential for excessive focus on products and too little on developments in the firm's markets
Functional Structure Management of international operations is organized by functional activity	• Small central staff that provides strong central control and coordination • United, focused global strategy with a high degree of functional expertise	• Headquarters may lack expertise in coordinating functions in diverse geographic locations • Coordination becomes unwieldy when the firm has numerous product lines • May not respond well to specific customer needs in individual markets
Global Matrix Structure Blends product, geographic area, and functional structures to leverage the benefits of global strategy and local responsiveness	• Leverages the benefits of global strategy while responding to local needs • Aims to combine the best elements of the geographic area, product, and functional structures • Emphasizes interorganizational learning and knowledge sharing among the firm's units worldwide	• Dual reporting chain of command with risk of employees receiving contradictory instructions from multiple managers • Can result in conflicts • Difficulties managing many subsidiaries or products, or operations in many foreign markets

Export Department

For manufacturing firms, exporting is usually the first foreign market entry strategy. It rarely requires much organizational structure until export sales reach a critical point. Initially, the firm will channel exports through an outside intermediary, such as a foreign distributor. When export sales reach a substantial proportion of total sales, the firm will usually establish a

EXHIBIT 12.6

The Export Department Structure

Export department
A unit within the firm charged with managing the firm's export operations.

separate **export department** charged with managing export operations. The approach is most closely associated with home replication strategy. Exhibit 12.6 illustrates the export department structure.

International Division Structure

International division structure
An organizational design in which all international activities are centralized within one division in the firm, separate from domestic units.

Over time, as the firm undertakes more advanced activities abroad, management will typically create an **international division structure**, making a separate unit within the firm dedicated to managing its international operations. Exhibit 12.7 illustrates this structure. The decision to create a separate division is usually accompanied by a significant shift in resource allocation and an increased focus on international business.[40] Typically, a vice president of international operations is appointed, who reports directly to the corporate CEO. Division managers oversee the development and maintenance of relationships with foreign suppliers, distributors, and other value-chain partners. Over time, the division typically undertakes more advanced internationalization options, such as licensing and small-scale foreign direct investment. In the early stages, the structure is most closely associated with home replication strategy. However, with time, management may advance toward multidomestic or global strategies.

The international division structure offers several advantages. It centralizes management and coordination of international operations. It is staffed with international experts who focus on developing new business opportunities abroad and offering assistance and training for foreign operations. Its creation signals that management is committed to international operations.

However, this structure can lead to a domestic versus international power struggle over, for example, control of financial and human resources. There is likely to be little sharing of knowledge between the foreign units and domestic operations or among the foreign units themselves. R&D and future-oriented planning activities tend to remain separate and may be domestically focused. Products continue to be developed for the domestic market, with international needs considered only after domestic needs have been addressed. Given these problems, many companies eventually evolve out of the international division structure.[41]

EXHIBIT 12.7

The International Division Structure

Firms at advanced stages of internationalization establish more complex organizational structures. A major rationale is to reap the benefits of economies of scale and scope—that is, high-volume manufacturing and more efficient use of marketing and other strategic resources over a wider range of products and markets. There is greater emphasis on innovative potential through learning effects, pooling of resources, and know-how.

More advanced organizational structures emphasize a decentralized structure, typically organized around geographic areas, or a centralized structure, organized around product or functional lines. We describe these structures next.

Geographic Area Structure (Decentralized Structure)

Geographic area structure is an organizational arrangement in which management and control are highly decentralized to the level of individual geographic regions, where local managers are responsible for operations within their own regions. Exhibit 12.8 illustrates this type of organizational design. Firms that organize their operations geographically tend to market products that are relatively standardized across entire regions or groupings of countries. The structure is decentralized because headquarters management delegates operations for each locality to the respective regional managers. The structure is typically associated with multidomestic strategy.

Firms that use the geographic area approach are often in mature industries with narrow product lines, such as the pharmaceutical, food, automotive, cosmetics, and beverage industries. For example, Nestlé organizes itself into a South America division, a North America division, an Asia division, and so forth. Nestlé treats all geographic locations, including the domestic market, as equals. All areas work in unison toward a common global strategic vision. Assets, including capital, are distributed to ensure optimal return on corporate goals, not area goals. Geographic area units usually manufacture and market locally appropriate goods within their own areas.

The main advantage of the geographic area structure is the ability to strike a balance between global integration and local adaptation on a regional basis. The area managers have the authority to modify products and strategy. Improved communications and coordination between subsidiaries are possible within each region but are often lacking with other area units and corporate headquarters. Geographic area managers typically lack a *global* orientation when it comes to developing and managing products and other issues.[42]

> **Geographic area structure**
> An organizational design in which management and control are decentralized to the level of individual geographic regions.

Product Structure (Centralized Structure)

Under the **product structure**, the firm organizes its international operations by major product line. Each product division is responsible for producing and marketing a specific group of products worldwide. For example, product categories for Motorola's international operations include mobile phones and network solutions. Apple's product categories include the iPad, iPod, iPhone, and personal computers.

Exhibit 12.9 illustrates such an organization. Each international product division operates as a stand-alone profit center with substantial autonomy. The goal is to achieve a high degree of worldwide coordination within each product category. Increased coordination facilitates economies of scale and sharing of technology and product knowledge among the firm's operations worldwide. Thus, the product division structure is highly centralized and typically associated with global strategy.

> **Product structure**
> An arrangement in which management of international operations is organized by major product line.

EXHIBIT 12.8

The Geographic Area Structure

EXHIBIT 12.9

The Product Structure

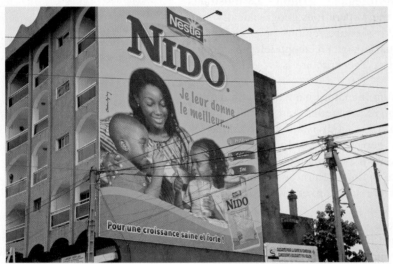

Source: Martin Barlow/Alamy Images

Nestlé uses a geographic area structure for organizing its international operations. In Africa, Nestlé conducts advertising in local languages. Pictured is a large ad for Nido milk powder in Cameroon.

The advantage of the product division structure is that all support functions, such as R&D, marketing, and manufacturing, are focused on the product. At the same time, products are easier to tailor for individual markets to meet specific buyer needs. The product division structure may lead to duplication of corporate support functions for each product division and a tendency for managers to focus their efforts on subsidiaries with the greatest potential for quick returns.[43]

Functional Structure (Centralized Structure)

In the **functional structure**, management of the firm's international operations is organized by functional activities, such as production and marketing. Exhibit 12.10 illustrates such an arrangement. For example, oil companies tend to organize their worldwide operations along two major functional lines—*production* and *marketing* of petroleum products. Some cruise ship lines engage in both shipbuilding and cruise marketing, two distinctive functions that require separate departments. The advantages of functional division are a small cen-

Functional structure
An arrangement in which management of the firm's international operations is organized by functional activity, such as production and marketing.

tral staff, which provides strong centralized control and coordination, and a united, focused global strategy with a high degree of functional expertise. However, the functional approach may falter if headquarters lacks expertise in coordinating manufacturing, marketing, and other functions in diverse geographic locations. In addition, when the firm deals with numerous product lines, coordination can become unwieldy.[44]

Global Matrix Structure

The experience of MNEs in the 1970s and 1980s highlighted the strengths and weaknesses of the organizational structures described above. The geographic area structure proved effective for responding to local needs but did little to enhance worldwide economies of scale and knowledge sharing among far-flung geographic units. The product structure overcame these shortcomings but was weak in responding to local needs. In the 1980s, conditions began to evolve quickly toward a global world economy. At the same time, in some markets, customers showed a renewed preference for local brands. Gradually, MNE managers realized that such trends required them to address global and local needs simultaneously.

Global matrix structure
An arrangement that blends the geographic area, product, and functional structures to leverage the benefits of a purely global strategy while keeping the firm responsive to local needs.

This new understanding led to the creation of the **global matrix structure**, an arrangement that seeks to leverage the benefits of global strategy and responsiveness to local needs. Specifically, the global matrix structure is a combination of the geographic area, product, and functional structures. It aims to reap the advantages of each while minimizing their disadvantages. Exhibit 12.11 shows such a structure. To make it work, headquarters management should simultaneously: (1) coordinate and control international operations, (2) respond to needs in individual countries, and (3) maximize interorganizational learning and knowledge sharing among the firm's units worldwide.[45]

EXHIBIT 12.10

The Functional Structure

The global matrix structure is closely associated with transnational strategy. Managerial responsibility for each product is shared by each product unit and the particular geographic areas of the firm. Thus, firms develop a dual reporting system in which, for example, an employee in a foreign subsidiary reports to two managers—the local subsidiary general manager and the corporate product division manager. Often the country manager is superior in authority. Global matrix structure recognizes the importance of flexible and responsive country-level operations and shows firms how to link those operations to optimize operational efficiency and competitive effectiveness. The manager working in this structure shares decision making with other managers, wherever they may be, to achieve best practice for the firm's operations worldwide.

Unilever, the $62 billion European producer of food, beverage, household, and personal care products, successfully applied the global matrix structure. Originally a merger between British and Dutch firms, Unilever (www.unilever.com) long pursued a multidomestic approach to international business. In the 1990s, for example, in order to manufacture ice cream, it regularly sourced more than thirty different types of vanilla. Its Rexona deodorant had thirty different packages and forty-eight distinctive formulations. Advertising and branding were handled locally and often amateurishly. Competitors with more centralized operations were able to respond faster to changing consumer tastes. They were better at coordinating their international units and had captured efficiencies by developing supplier channels that served many countries simultaneously. Despite a sales volume similar to P&G's, Unilever had twice as many employees. The decentralized structure of its international organization had produced needless duplication and countless obstacles to a more efficient global approach.

To address such problems, Unilever implemented a massive reorganization plan to centralize authority, reduce the autonomy of local subsidiaries, and create a global employee culture. The firm divested hundreds of businesses, cut 55,000 jobs, closed 145 factories, and discontinued 1,200 brands,

EXHIBIT 12.11

The Global Matrix Structure

Source: Chris Jenner/Shutterstock

The multinational firm Unilever, jointly headquartered in the United Kingdom and the Netherlands, offers many global brands such as Lipton tea, Hellman's spreads, Slimfast, and Dove personal care products. Management must balance global integration with local adaptation in product development, pricing, distribution, and marketing communications. Shown here is Unilever's British headquarters in London.

retaining about 400. Today, the firm develops new products using global teams that emphasize the *commonalities* among major-country markets. Local managers are not allowed to tinker with packaging, formulation, or advertising of global brands such as Dove soap. Unilever is well on the road to implementing a more balanced matrix approach to its global operations.[46]

Philips, the Dutch producer of electronics products, has long sought to apply a global matrix structure. Philips operates in more than one hundred countries worldwide. Management has structured the firm so that its product groups are integrated across all its major country markets, and, in turn, its organizational functions are integrated and coordinated across all areas and product groups. To streamline its matrix organization, Philips reorganized itself around three product core units: consumer electronics, health care, and lighting products. The matrix structure assigns various roles to regional executives: They hold responsibility for their respective regions, for the firm's core product units, and for the functions associated with the product units.[47]

Like the other organizational structures, the global matrix structure has limitations. The chain of command from superiors to subordinates can become muddled. Employees may receive contradictory instructions from multiple managers who may be located far apart and come from different cultural and business backgrounds. The matrix structure can waste managerial time and result in conflicts and organizational chaos. Potential limitations tend to emerge as the firm's international operations become more complex over time. For this reason, many firms that experimented with the global matrix structure eventually returned to simpler organizational arrangements.[48]

CLOSING CASE — Lenovo—The Global Challenger from an Emerging Market

The world's top personal computer (PC) producers are HP, Lenovo, Dell, and Acer. In 2011, Lenovo became the world's second-largest PC vendor, after HP. A Chinese firm, Lenovo generates more than $21 billion in total sales and holds about 33 percent of the PC market in China and 15 percent in other countries. In recent years, Lenovo has experienced rapid growth, even during periods of soft global demand. When Lenovo was founded in modest circumstances in 1984, no one imagined it would evolve into a *Fortune* Global 500 company with a presence in 160 countries. Today, from regional headquarters in each of Beijing, China, and Raleigh, North Carolina, Lenovo offers desktops, laptops, tablets, workstations, servers, and mobile phones to customers across the globe.

Company Strategy

The PC industry has reached maturity, especially in the advanced economies. Computers are commodities and profit margins are thin. The industry is global, which means firms compete with each other, and cater to customer needs, on a global scale. PC firms are under pressure to ensure company survival and success.

Key to Lenovo's success is ensuring organizational learning to continuously optimize the firm's value-chain activities. Lenovo uses

mergers and acquisitions (M&As) to acquire needed knowledge and other assets from partner firms, and to expand into markets worldwide. In 2005, Lenovo acquired the PC business of IBM. The deal instantly established Lenovo as the number-three PC maker worldwide. In 2011, Lenovo formed a merger with NEC, the largest PC vendor in Japan, to better access the huge Japanese PC market. The merger increased Lenovo's scale economies in manufacturing and marketing. Most recently, Lenovo acquired a half interest in Medion AG, a German PC and consumer-electronics firm, with the goal of expanding marketing and distribution in Europe.

Since 2010, Lenovo has followed a "Protect & Attack" strategy. While protecting its core business, especially the Chinese market, Lenovo is aggressively growing its market share in emerging markets and advanced economies, as well as in new product categories such as tablets and smartphones. The push into emerging markets benefits from Lenovo's deep knowledge of doing business in China. Lenovo now obtains about 20 percent of its revenues from emerging markets outside China.

Top management emphasizes global innovation, global products and branding, global human resources, and creating a corporate culture conducive to global success. Let's examine these strategies in detail.

Global Innovation

The acquisition of IBM's PC business allowed Lenovo to tap world-class technological know-how. Leveraging top-notch innovative capabilities from R&D facilities in Beijing, Raleigh, and Yokohama, Japan, Lenovo is a leading PC developer. Each facility has its own distinctive talent capability. Altogether, Lenovo owns more than 6,500 international patents. In 2011, *BusinessWeek* ranked Lenovo one of the "Top 50 Most Innovative Companies." Lenovo constantly invests in R&D for breakthrough technologies and innovative products. If needed, Lenovo can count on capital infusions from China's government, which maintains partial ownership in the firm.

At the Consumer Electronics Show in 2012, Lenovo unveiled 20 products, including a Windows-based smartphone, a half-tablet, a half-notebook, a smart TV, and a thin and lightweight "ultrabook" PC. Lenovo has the ability to foresee what consumers desire in information technology products, even before consumers know themselves. For example, Lenovo's "Yoga" is an ultrathin PC that doubles as a tablet.

Lenovo is increasingly on the leading edge of green technologies. ThinkPad PCs are built from up to 30 percent post-consumer content, using recycled material such as old water jugs. PCs meet the latest high-energy efficiency standards and rank high on eco-friendliness. PCs are shipped in 100-percent recycled packaging that can be tossed into a recycling bin.

Global Products and Branding

In developing its products, Lenovo emphasizes modular architecture—suppliers manufacture interchangeable components and modules, which are then snapped into PC cases rolling down assembly lines. The same parts—power supply units, processors, graphics cards, hard drives, and others—can be used to produce various PC models. Interfaces are standardized to facilitate production of PCs that are simultaneously differentiated but use standard parts and components, which minimize the cost of manufacturing computers and of designing new ones. Products are standardized worldwide, but elements such as keyboards and software are customized to respond to local language needs.

Marketing also responds to local conditions. For example, Lenovo is the most popular PC brand in rural China where the firm established a complex distribution network extending to small cities and towns. Prices are adapted to fit buying power of low-income consumers. Lenovo adjusts marketing to fit local traditions. In rural China, the firm markets "wedding computers," which come in red, the luckiest color to Chinese. Rural families often pool their money to buy a bride and groom their first PC as a wedding gift.

By purchasing IBM's PC business, Lenovo acquired the IBM brand name and the "ThinkPad" product brand. Lenovo leveraged the IBM name to build brand awareness on a global scale. Branding was supported through Lenovo's sponsorship of the Beijing Olympics in 2008. In 2010, Lenovo launched its first global branding campaign with the slogan "For Those Who Do" to engage consumers around the world. The firm is leveraging the power of global social media to target marketing campaigns to youth 18 to 25 years old. Its retailing Web sites look identical worldwide, but are adapted for language differences.

Global Human Resources

Lenovo worked hard to integrate Chinese business methods with an international workforce of 27,000 employees. Blending the distinctive national and organizational culture of IBM required hiring managers with a global mind-set and strong international background. Lenovo recruits globally savvy executives from other hi-tech firms and hires talented graduates of top universities to incubate them as future company leaders.

Lenovo developed a global training program that provides accelerated development opportunities for employees. The firm's human resources group works with managers to construct career maps and pipelines for every high-potential employee. All employees are asked to examine their career aspirations and the training they need to attain their goals. The career maps are linked to job slots around the world and employees have much latitude to achieve their dreams. Lenovo employees are ambitious and top management is serious about helping them develop their careers.

Global Culture

In 1994, Lenovo's founder Liu Chuanzhi forecast the firm would become a great, global company—an impressive leap of faith in the early 1990s. At the time, there were very few global Chinese firms, so Chuanzhi's vision stood out. It is Lenovo's vision that draws so many talented managers to work for the firm. Aiming to foster a global spirit, Lenovo's top-team meetings rotate among Beijing, Hong Kong, Singapore, Paris, and North Carolina. The firm's official language is English.

Senior management has instituted processes aimed at socializing young managers into the Lenovo organizational culture. Nationality doesn't matter; if an employee demonstrates capability and vision, there are no limits. Socialization creates broad, tacitly understood rules for appropriate action by managers at all levels in global operations. Lenovo managers become well acquainted with the firm's culture and goals. Wherever they operate, managers feel a strong connection to the firm, which guides decisions on company activities and facilitates global knowledge exchange. Connectedness builds trust and cooperation, and encourages communication and interaction, thereby facilitating the integration and assimilation of new knowledge and capabilities. Simultaneously, Lenovo management values the diversity of global cultures and the learning that accrues from foreign business environments. Key employees need to function with a global mind-set and cosmopolitan values.

Manufacturing and Value-Chain Management

Lenovo concentrates manufacturing at sites in China, as well as each of Argentina, India, Mexico, and Poland. Production in these low-cost countries generates cost efficiencies and economies of scale. Regional headquarters in the United States and operations in low-cost countries helps diversify sales across advanced economies and emerging markets. While investing huge sums in R&D and innovative product features, top management maintains a sharp focus on keeping manufacturing costs low. Sourcing of parts and components is done on a global scale. Sourcing from hundreds of high-quality suppliers ensures flexibility in logistics and production.

The diversity of partners and international environments helps Lenovo acquire new technical and managerial know-how, new product ideas, improved R&D, and partnering skills. Lenovo leverages the power of global information systems to share important knowledge among the firm's subsidiaries worldwide.

Lenovo aims for a leadership position in which it attains double-digit share in each of the markets where it does business. Management also aims to maintain a sharp focus on its customers, providing them with the most innovative products worldwide.

AACSB: Reflective Thinking Skills

Case Questions

1. What is strategy? How does Lenovo use strategy to succeed in the global marketplace? What strategies does Lenovo employ to maximize company efficiency and flexibility? What does Lenovo management do to foster organizational learning?

2. Describe Lenovo's organizational culture. What are the characteristics of Lenovo's culture? How does the culture help Lenovo achieve its international goals?

3. What is the nature of Lenovo's international strategy? Is the firm's strategy primarily multidomestic or global? Justify your answer. What advantages does Lenovo derive from the particular international strategy(s) that it pursues?

4. Examine Lenovo in terms of the integration-responsiveness framework. What are the pressures that Lenovo faces for local responsiveness? What are the pressures that Lenovo faces for global integration? What advantages do local responsiveness and global integration each bring to Lenovo?

Sources: Douglas Ready, Linda Hill, and Jay Conger, "Winning the Race for Talent in Emerging Markets," *Harvard Business Review*, November 2008, pp. 62–70; Lucy Handley, "Lenovo Plots Global Push to Vie with Dell and Apple," *Marketing Week*, March 31, 2011, p. 4; "Lenovo Overtakes Dell in Worldwide PC Shipments," *Channel Insider*, October 13, 2011, p. 1; Leslie Norton, "Protect and Attack," *Barron's*, February 6, 2012, p. 17; Deng Ping, "What Determines Performance of Cross-Border M&As by Chinese Companies? An Absorptive Capacity Perspective," *Thunderbird International Business Review* 52, no. 6 (2010): 509–524; Chuck Salter, "Protect and Attack: Lenovo's New Strategy," *Fast Company*, November 22, 2011, retrieved from www.factcompany.com; Rob Spiegel, "ThinkPad Laptop Goes Green," *Design News*, June, 2010, p. 24; Elizabeth Woyke, "Lenovo CEO Keeps Focus on Hardware, Eyes PC Market Crown," *Forbes*, January 10, 2012, p. 34; Liu Xiaohui and Trevor Buck, "The Internationalisation Strategies of Chinese Firms: Lenovo and BOE," *Journal of Chinese Economic & Business Studies* 7, no. 2 (2009): 167–181.

The case was written by Betty Feng and Lawrence Yu, under the supervision of S. Tamer Cavusgil.

CHAPTER ESSENTIALS

MyManagementLab

Go to **mymanagementlab.com** to complete the problems marked with this icon ⭐.

Key Terms

export department 314	global team 305	organizational processes 305
functional structure 316	home replication strategy 308	organizational structure 311
geographic area structure 315	international division structure 314	product structure 315
global integration 306	local responsiveness 306	strategy 301
global industry 306	multidomestic industry 306	transnational strategy 310
global matrix structure 316	multidomestic strategy 308	visionary leadership 302
global strategy 309	organizational culture 304	

Summary

In this chapter, you learned about:

1. Strategy in international business

Strategy is a planned set of actions that managers employ to make best use of the firm's resources and core competencies, in order to gain a competitive advantage. The firm that aspires to become globally competitive must simultaneously seek three key strategic objectives—efficiency, flexibility, and learning.

2. Building the global firm

Managers who exhibit **visionary leadership** possess an international mind-set, cosmopolitan values, and a globally strategic vision. They motivate and lead company personnel toward important organizational goals. They engage in strategic thinking, committing resources and human assets to realizing a global approach to business. Advanced international firms value global competence and cross-cultural skills, adopt a single language, and promote interdependency among headquarters and the firm's subsidiaries. They adopt an international **organizational culture**. They subscribe to globally accepted ethical standards and responsible citizenship. International **organizational processes** include **global teams** and global information systems.

3. The integration-responsiveness framework

The integration-responsiveness (IR) framework describes how internationalizing firms simultaneously seek global integration and local responsiveness. **Local responsiveness** refers to managing the firm's value-chain activities, and addressing diverse opportunities and risks, on a country-by-country basis. **Global integration** describes efforts to coordinate the firm's value-chain activities cross-nationally to achieve worldwide efficiency, synergy, and cross-fertilization to take maximum advantage of similarities across countries.

4. Strategies based on the integration-responsiveness framework

The IR framework presents four alternative strategies. Using **home replication strategy**, the firm views international business as separate from, and secondary to, its domestic business. Products are designed with domestic consumers in mind, and the firm is essentially a domestic company, with some foreign activities. **Multidomestic strategy** is a more committed approach, in which managers recognize and emphasize differences among national markets. They treat individual markets on a stand-alone basis, with little cross-national integration of company efforts. **Global strategy** aims to integrate the firm's major objectives, policies, and activities into a cohesive whole, targeted primarily to the global marketplace. Top management performs sourcing, resource allocation, market participation, and competitive moves on a global scale. Using **transnational strategy**, the firm strives to be more responsive to local needs while simultaneously retaining maximum global efficiency and emphasizing global learning and knowledge transfer. The strategy aims to combine the major benefits of both multidomestic and global strategies while minimizing their disadvantages.

5. Organizational structure

Organizational structure consists of the reporting relationships in the firm between people, functions, and processes that facilitate carrying out international operations. It determines where key decisions are made, the relationship between headquarters and subsidiaries, and the nature of international staffing. It also determines the degree of *centralization* and *decentralization* in decision making and value-chain activities in the firm's operations worldwide. The main role for headquarters managers is to provide broad leadership, while subsidiary managers are best at dealing with customers, handling employee issues, and initiating action in the field.

6. Organizational structures for international operations

The **export department** is the simplest organizational structure, in which a unit within the firm manages all export operations. Slightly more advanced is the **international division structure**, in which all international activities are centralized within one organizational unit, separate from the firm's domestic units. The **geographic area structure** features control and decision making that are decentralized to the level of individual geographic regions. Using the **product structure**, decision making and management of international operations are centralized and organized by major product line. The **functional structure** organizes decision making by functional activity, such as production and marketing. The **global matrix structure** blends the geographic area, product, and functional structures in an attempt to leverage the benefits of a purely global strategy and maximize global organizational learning while keeping the firm responsive to local needs.

Test Your Comprehension AACSB: Reflective Thinking Skills

1. Define visionary leadership. What are the traits of a manager who has visionary leadership?

2. Describe the distinction between multidomestic and global industries.

3. Describe the integration-responsiveness framework. What are the specific pressures for local responsiveness and for global integration?

4. What is the difference between global strategy and multidomestic strategy? Visit the Web site of Dell Computer (www.dell.com). Does Dell generally apply a global strategy or a multidomestic strategy? How can you tell?

5. Define transnational strategy. Give examples of firms that apply a transnational strategy.

⭐ 6. What is the difference between a centralized and a decentralized organizational structure? Why do firms often prefer to have a centralized structure?

7. What are the different organizational structures for international operations? Which structure(s) is most associated with global strategy?

⭐ 8. What is the global matrix structure? What are the advantages and disadvantages of this approach?

Apply Your Understanding AACSB: Communication Abilities, Reflective Thinking Skills, Ethical Understanding and Reasoning Abilities

1. AlumCo is a large producer of aluminum products. AlumCo now handles international operations through its export department. However, management believes this arrangement is no longer suited to the firm's growing international activities and wants to adopt a more sophisticated approach. What alternative organizational structures (international division, geographic area structure, etc.) should the firm consider? Make a recommendation to management regarding the most appropriate international structure that AlumCo should employ. For reference, check out the Web site of Alcan, the well-known Canadian aluminum firm, at www.alcan.com.

2. Barbie is the best-selling doll produced by Mattel, a U.S. company. Mattel is targeting Barbie to foreign markets but struggles to find the right strategy because of cultural differences. In Muslim countries, Barbie faces competition from doll producers that offer Islamic alternatives that feature conservative styling. In Latin America, competitors offer dolls with tanned skin and dark hair. In Asia, many girls prefer dolls with Asian features. The fun-loving image that Barbie projects in the U.S. market is often inappropriate abroad. In marketing Barbie abroad, should Mattel management apply a strategy that is global or multidomestic? What are the advantages and disadvantages of each approach? Is it possible to reach a compromise? Elaborate and justify your answer.

3. *Ethical Dilemma:* You were recently hired as a manager for international operations of Despoyle Chemical Corporation, a major manufacturer of dyes, fertilizers, and other industrial chemicals. Despoyle has chemical production plants in twenty-eight countries, including many developing economies. Despoyle has a decentralized organizational structure, and managers in individual countries operate their plants independently of headquarters. After visiting various Despoyle plants, you find the firm follows local environmental protection standards in different countries. In India, Despoyle allows pollutants to flow freely into local rivers. In Mexico, Despoyle generates pollution in local landfills and production sites. In Nigeria, Despoyle's factory emits air pollution that exceeds levels acceptable in more advanced countries. As a new manager, you are surprised by the firm's lax environmental practices around the world. What should you do? Do you complain to top management and risk angering your superiors? Do you try to modify Despoyle's environmental standards in different countries? What solution, if any, do you propose to address Despoyle's practices? Use the Ethical Framework in Chapter 5 to formulate your answer.

globalEDGE INTERNET EXERCISES
(http://www.globalEDGE.msu.edu)

Refer to Chapter 1, page 24, for instructions on how to access and use globalEDGE™.

1. Visit the Web sites for Toyota (www.toyota.com) and Procter & Gamble (www.pg.com). From what you can gather, how do these two firms organize their international activities? Do they seem to be applying multidomestic strategy or global strategy in their sourcing, manufacturing, product development, and marketing activities? How and why might an internationalizing firm evolve its approaches to internationalization over time?

2. Multinational firms play a key role in globalization. Various news organizations prepare classifications and rankings of MNEs (e.g., *Financial Times, Business Week, Forbes, Fortune*). Find two such rankings and identify the criteria used to rank the "top global firms". What countries are home to the great majority of MNEs on these lists? For each list, how "global" are the top three firms? That is, in what countries do they operate? Conduct a search for "rankings."

3. You work for an MNE that makes and markets cellular telephones. Senior managers want to begin selling the phones in Latin America. To pursue a transnational strategy, management wants to minimize adaptation of the phones. They have asked you for a briefing. Focusing on three Latin American countries, prepare a brief report that identifies the common features of Latin American markets that management should consider when developing the cell phones the firm will sell there. For example, what language should be used in the cell phones? What pricing should management use? You may wish to consult the country commercial guides, Country Insights, and market research reports available through globalEDGE™. In addition, the U.S. Department of Commerce (www.export.gov) is a useful resource.

MyManagementLab

Go to **mymanagementlab.com** for Auto-graded writing questions as well as the following Assisted-graded writing questions:

12-1. What are the primary strategic objectives in international business?

12-2. Describe the requisite dimensions that characterize truly successful, contemporary international firms.

12-3. Mymanagementlab Only – comprehensive writing assignment for this chapter.

Estimating Demand in Emerging Markets

Estimating the demand for products or services in emerging markets and developing economies is a challenging task for managers. These countries have unique commercial environments and may be limited in terms of reliable data, market research firms, and trained interviewers. Consumers in some of these countries may consider surveys an invasion of privacy. Survey respondents may try to please researchers by telling them what they want to hear rather than providing honest answers to their questions.

Three of the largest emerging markets—China, India, and Brazil—have a combined GDP of more than $19 trillion, surpassing that of the United States. Africa is among the biggest markets for mobile phone sales, growing to more than 100 million users in just a few years. Automakers are doing substantial business selling economy cars throughout Latin America, South Asia, and Eastern Europe. In short, emerging markets and developing economies are huge markets for products and services.

CHAPTER 13

Global Market Opportunity Assessment

LEARNING OBJECTIVES *In this chapter, you will learn about the following:*

1. Analyzing organizational readiness to internationalize

2. Assessing the suitability of products and services for foreign markets

3. Screening countries to identify target markets

4. Assessing industry market potential

5. Choosing foreign business partners

6. Estimating company sales potential

MyManagementLab®

⭐ **Improve Your Grade!**

Over 10 million students improved their results using the Pearson MyLabs.
Visit **mymanagementlab.com** for simulations, tutorials, and end-of-chapter problems.

Estimating demand in such countries requires managers to use innovative research methods for gaining insights or data. Let's consider two firms trying to estimate the demand for wallpaper and adhesive bandages in Morocco.

In Morocco, wealthy people tend to live in villas and condominiums, and are a target market for wallpaper sales. The government usually measures wallpaper imports by weight and value. Such information is little use for estimating wallpaper sales because firms sell wallpaper by the roll and different designs have different weights.

One wallpaper company examined data from various sources to estimate demand. First, managers reviewed a recent study of the number of water heaters purchased in Morocco. From past experience, they knew that if households purchased this "modern" convenience, they would likely buy wallpaper too. Second, managers reviewed government statistics on the level of domestic wallpaper sales, discretionary income by type of household, and home construction data. Third, they studied the lifestyle of a sample of local consumers and found that Moroccans typically shop for wallpaper to complement wall-to-wall carpets. Among married couples, the wife usually decides on decorations for the home. Customers are usually well-off; they include professionals, merchants, and high-ranking administrators. By triangulating data from these sources and using their own judgment, the wallpaper company made a reasonable estimate of demand for wallpaper.

In the case of adhesive bandages, available data revealed that 70 percent of demand for pharmaceutical items, including bandages, was met by wholesalers concentrated in Casablanca, Morocco's capital city. The country imported all its adhesive bandages. Demand was growing quickly, due to rapid population growth, free medication for the needy, and reimbursement programs for medical expenses. Although the government published import statistics, the information was confusing, because data on bandage imports was mixed together with data on other types of adhesives. The bandage data was superficial and incomplete, and widespread smuggling and gray marketing through unofficial distribution channels complicated demand estimates.

To gather more information, researchers interviewed bandage salespeople from Curad, Johnson & Johnson, and other firms. They visited retail stores to ask about sales, prevailing prices, competitive brands, and consumer attitudes. They found that consumers tend to be price-sensitive and rely on doctors and pharmacists to recommend bandage brands. Researchers also tallied statistics from the United Nations Development Program and other aid agencies that donate medical supplies to developing countries. They eventually arrived at a reasonable estimate of bandage sales by assimilating data from these various sources.

SOURCES: Nicolas Hamelin, Meriam Ellouzi, and Andrew Canterbury, "Consumer Ethnocentrism and Country-of-Origin Effects in the Moroccan Market," *Journal of Global Marketing* 24, no. 3 (2011): 228–244; Lyn Amine and S. Tamer Cavusgil, "Demand Estimation in a Developing Country Environment: Difficulties, Techniques, and Examples," *Journal of the Market Research Society* 28, no. 1 (1986): 43–65; Ashish Karamchandani, Mike Kubzansky, and Nishant Lalwani, "Is the Bottom Of the Pyramid Really for You?," *Harvard Business Review* 89, no. 3 (2011): 107–111; U.S. Commercial Service and the U.S. Department of State, *Country Commercial Guide Morocco Fiscal Year 2011*, retrieved from http://www.buyusainfo.net.

Managers' choices determine the future of the firm. Making good choices depends on having objective evidence and hard data about how best to configure value-chain activities, and about what products and services to offer and where to offer them. The more managers know about an opportunity, the better equipped they will be to exploit it. This is particularly true in international business, which usually entails more uncertainty than domestic business.[1] To skillfully navigate foreign markets, managers require substantial information on potential threats and opportunities and how to conduct business abroad.[2] Managers devise strategies as part of planned actions to optimize the firm's competitive advantages. Planning involves estimating, forecasting, and problem solving and therefore requires substantial information inputs.

Central to a firm's research is identifying and defining the best business opportunities in the global marketplace. A **global market opportunity** is a favorable combination of circumstances, locations, and timing that offers prospects for exporting, investing, sourcing, or partnering in foreign markets. In such locations, the firm may perceive opportunities to sell its products and services; establish factories or other production facilities to produce its offerings cheaper or more competently; procure raw materials, components, or services of lower cost or superior quality; or enter beneficial collaborations with foreign partners. Global market opportunities can enhance company performance, often far beyond what the firm can achieve in its home market.

For example, vendors of automatic dishwashers and dishwasher soap, such as Sweden's Electrolux and Britain's Reckitt Benckiser, aim to expand sales. Markets for such products are largely saturated in Germany and the United States. More promising are affluent countries where few households own dishwashers. In the United Kingdom, only 40 percent of households have a dishwasher. The numbers are similar in France (52 percent), Spain (49 percent), and Turkey (25 percent). Dishwashers are convenient and save time. Vendors assert that manual

Global market opportunity
Favorable combination of circumstances, locations, and timing that offers prospects for exporting, investing, sourcing, or partnering in foreign markets.

dish-cleaning amounts to spending one week a year at the kitchen sink. However, generating sales poses numerous challenges. First, space is limited in many European kitchens. Second, many Europeans believe automatic dishwashers waste water, which is generally not true, especially with the latest energy-saving models. Finally, old habits die hard—many homeowners see no reason to buy a dishwasher. Market research is helping firms overcome such challenges and generating dishwasher sales across Europe.[3]

In this chapter, we discuss six key tasks that managers should perform to define and pursue global market opportunities. Exhibit 13.1 illustrates the tasks, objectives, and procedures associated

Task	Objective	Procedure
1. Analyze organizational readiness to internationalize	To provide an objective assessment of the company's preparedness to engage in international business activity.	● Examine company strengths and weaknesses, relative to international business, by evaluating the availability in the firm of key factors, such as: — appropriate financial and tangible resources — relevant skills and competencies — commitment by senior management to international expansion ● Take action to eliminate deficiencies in the firm that hinder achieving company goals.
2. Assess the suitability of the firm's products and services for foreign markets	To conduct a systematic assessment of the suitability of the firm's products and services for international customers; to evaluate the degree of fit between the product or service and foreign customer needs.	● For each possible target market, identify those factors that may hinder market potential. Determine how the product or service may need to be adapted for each market. Specifically, for each potential market, assess the firm's products and services with regard to such factors as: — foreign customer characteristics and preferences — relevant laws and regulations — requirements of channel intermediaries — characteristics of competitors' offerings
3. Screen countries to identify target markets	To reduce the number of countries that warrant in-depth investigation as potential target markets to a manageable few.	● Identify the five or six country markets that hold the best potential for the firm by assessing each candidate country market with regard to such criteria as: — size and growth rate — 'market intensity' (customers' buying power) — 'consumption capacity' (size and growth rate of the middle class) — receptivity to imports — infrastructure for doing business — degree of economic freedom — country risk
4. Assess industry market potential	To estimate the most likely share of industry sales within each target country; to investigate and evaluate any potential barriers to market entry.	● Develop 3- to 5-year forecast of industry sales for each target market. Specifically, assess industry market potential in each market by examining such criteria as: — market size and growth rate — relevant trends in the industry — degree of competitive intensity — tariff and nontariff trade barriers — relevant standards and regulations — availability and sophistication of local distribution intermediaries — specific customer requirements and preferences — industry-specific market potential indicators — industry-specific market entry barriers

(continues)

EXHIBIT 13.1

Key Tasks in Global Market Opportunity Assessment

5. Choose foreign business partners	To decide on the type of foreign business partner, clarify ideal partner qualifications, and determine appropriate market entry strategy.	● Determine what value-adding activities must be performed by foreign business partners.
		● Based on needed value-adding activities, determine the most desirable attributes in foreign business partners.
		● Assess and select foreign business partners. That is, evaluate each potential business partner based on criteria such as:
		  — specific industry expertise
		  — commitment to the international venture
		  — access to local distribution channels
		  — financial strength
		  — technical expertise
		  — quality of staff
		  — appropriate facilities and infrastructure

6. Estimate company sales potential	To estimate the most likely share of industry sales the company can achieve, over a period of time, for each target market.	● Develop 3- to 5-year forecast of company sales in each target market. Estimate the potential to sell the firm's product or service, based on criteria such as:
		  — capabilities of partners
		  — access to distribution
		  — competitive intensity
		  — pricing and financing
		  — market penetration timetable of the firm
		  — risk tolerance of senior managers
		● Determine the factors that will influence company sales potential

EXHIBIT 13.1
(continued)

with each task. The process is especially appropriate for pursuing marketing or collaborative venture opportunities abroad. The six tasks are:

1. Analyze organizational readiness to internationalize.
2. Assess the suitability of the firm's products and services for foreign markets.
3. Screen countries to identify attractive target markets.
4. Assess the industry market potential, or the market demand, for the product(s) or service(s) in selected target markets.
5. Choose qualified business partners, such as distributors or suppliers.
6. Estimate company sales potential for each target market.

In carrying out this systematic process, the manager will need to employ objective *selection criteria* by which to make choices, as listed in the final column of Exhibit 13.1. Let's examine each task in detail.

 Task One: Analyze Organizational Readiness to Internationalize

Before undertaking an international venture, whether launching a product abroad or sourcing from a foreign supplier, the firm should conduct a formal assessment of its readiness to internationalize. An evaluation of organizational capabilities is useful both for companies new to international business and those with considerable experience. Such a self-audit is similar to a SWOT analysis—that is, an evaluation of the firm's strengths, weaknesses, opportunities, and threats.

When assessing the firm's readiness to internationalize, managers peer into their organization to determine the degree to which it has the motivation, resources, and skills necessary to successfully engage in international business. They measure the firm's degree of international experience; the goals and objectives it envisions for internationalization; the quantity and quality of skills, capabilities, and resources available for internationalization; and the actual and potential support provided by the firm's network of relationships. If one or more key resources is lacking, management must acquire or develop them *before* allowing the contemplated venture to go forward. Organizational culture plays an important role, because key employees should possess the motivation and commitment to expand the firm's activities into foreign markets.

Managers also examine conditions in the external business environment by studying opportunities and threats in target markets. They research the specific needs and preferences of buyers, as well as the nature of competing products and the risks inherent in such markets.

Consider Home Instead, Inc. (www.homeinstead.com), a small U.S. firm that provides services for the elderly who choose to live independently at home but require companionship, assistance with meal preparation, and help with shopping and housekeeping. After assessing its readiness to internationalize, management perceived numerous international opportunities, especially in Japan, but also recognized deficiencies in key capabilities. The firm hired Yoshino Nakajima, who is fluent in Japanese and an expert on the Japanese market, as vice president for international development. She launched the franchise in Japan, which captured substantial market share. Next, management tapped into the global network of 1,700 trade specialists of the United States Commercial Service, a government agency that provided the firm with leads and contacts in countries it had identified as the best target markets. Today, Home Instead has numerous franchises in Asia and Europe. Its international operations are thriving.[4]

A formal analysis of organizational readiness to internationalize requires managers to address the following questions:

- *What do we hope to gain from international business?* Objectives might include increasing sales or profits, following key customers who locate abroad, challenging competitors in their home markets, or pursuing a global strategy of establishing production and marketing operations at various locations worldwide.
- *Is international expansion consistent with other firm goals, now or in the future?* The firm should evaluate and manage internationalization in the context of its mission and business plan to ensure it represents the best use of company resources.
- *What demands will internationalization place on firm resources,* such as management, human resources, and finance, as well as production and marketing capacity? How will the firm meet such demands? Management must ensure it has sufficient production and marketing capacity to serve foreign markets. Channel members become frustrated when inadequate capacity prevents the firm from fulfilling customer orders abroad.
- *What is the basis of the firm's competitive advantage?* Companies seek competitive advantages by doing things better than their competitors. Competitive advantages can be based on strong R&D, superior input goods, cost-effective or innovative manufacturing capacity, skillful marketing, highly effective distribution channels, or other capabilities.

Diagnostic tools help managers audit the firm's readiness to internationalize. One of the best known is CORE (COmpany Readiness to Export, developed by Tamer Cavusgil in the 1990s; see www.globalEDGE.msu.edu). CORE has been widely adopted by individual firms, consultants, and the U.S. Department of Commerce. Because it was developed from extensive research on factors that contribute to successful exporting, it is also an ideal tutorial for self-learning and training.

CORE asks managers questions about their organizational resources, skills, and motivation to objectively assess the firm's readiness to successfully engage in exporting. It generates assessments of both organizational and product readiness to identify the useful assets managers have and the additional ones they need to make internationalization succeed. The assessment emphasizes exporting, since it is the typical entry mode for most newly internationalizing firms.

Assessing organizational readiness to internationalize is an ongoing process. Managers should continuously verify the firm's ability to modify its products to suit conditions, needs, and tastes

Source: David Pearson/Alamy Images

Levi makes tight-fit jeans to accommodate the Japanese physique and loose-fitting jeans to accommodate tastes in Islamic countries.

in foreign markets. In marketing its denim jeans, for example, Levi Strauss (www.levi.com; click on "global sites") assessed its ability to adapt its products for various markets. In evaluating entry into Islamic countries, Levi discovered that women avoid wearing tight-fitting attire, so the firm made a line of loose-fitting jeans. When Levi entered Japan, management assessed the firm's ability to make its famous blue jeans tighter and slimmer, to fit the smaller physique of many Japanese. When targeting consumers in hot climates, Levi evaluated its ability to produce shorts and thinner denim in bright colors.[5]

Task Two: Assess the Suitability of Products and Services for Foreign Markets

Once management has confirmed the firm's readiness to internationalize, it next determines the suitability of its products and services for foreign markets. Most companies produce a portfolio of offerings, some or all of which may be suitable for selling abroad.

Products or services with the best international prospects tend to have one or more of the following characteristics:

1. *Sell well in the domestic market.* Offerings received well at home are likely to succeed abroad, especially where similar needs and conditions exist.
2. *Cater to universal needs.* For example, buyers worldwide demand personal-care products, medical devices, and banking services. International sales may be promising if the product or service is unique or has important features that are appealing to foreign customers and are hard for foreign firms to duplicate.
3. *Address a need not well served in particular foreign markets.* Potential may exist in countries where the product or service does not currently exist, or where demand is just starting to emerge.
4. *Address a new or emergent need abroad.* Demand for some products and services may arise suddenly from a disaster or emergent trend. In Haiti, for example, an earthquake created an urgent need for easy-to-build housing. In emerging markets, growing affluence is spurring demand for restaurants and hospitality services.

One of the simplest ways to find out if a product or service will sell abroad is to ask intermediaries in the target market about likely local demand for it. Managers also might attend an industry trade fair in the target market and interview prospective customers or distributors. Since trade fairs often draw participants from entire regions, such as Asia or Europe, this approach is efficient for learning about the market potential of several countries at once.

To deepen knowledge about the international market potential of a product or service, managers should obtain answers to the following questions:

• *Who initiates purchasing?* Homemakers are usually the chief decision makers for household products. Professional buyers make purchases on behalf of firms.
• *Who uses the product or service?* Children consume various products, but their parents may be the actual buyers. Employees consume products bought by the firms where they work.

- *Why do people buy the product or service?* What specific needs does it fulfill? Such needs vary worldwide. In advanced economies, for example, consumers use Honda's gas-powered generators for recreational purposes; in developing economies households buy them for everyday heating and lighting.
- *Where do people purchase the product or service?* Once the researcher understands where the offering is typically purchased, it is useful to visit likely vendors to assess sales potential, whether the good should be adapted for the market, and how best to price, promote, and distribute it.
- *What economic, cultural, geographic, and other factors in the target market may limit sales?* Countries vary substantially in terms of buyer income levels, preferences, climate, and other factors that can inhibit or facilitate purchasing behavior.

Task Three: Screen Countries to Identify Target Markets

Screening to identify the best countries is an essential task, especially in the early stages of internationalization. For most firms, it is also the most time-consuming part of opportunity assessment. Failure to choose the right countries not only results in financial loss; it also incurs opportunity costs, tying up resources the firm might have used more profitably elsewhere. Exporting, foreign direct investment (FDI), and sourcing each require a different set of screening criteria. Let's see why.

Screening Countries for Exporting

Exporters first examine such criteria as population, income, demographic characteristics, government stability, and nature of the general business environment in individual countries. Statistics that span several years help determine which markets are growing and which are shrinking. The exporter can buy research reports

Source: Chen Chao/Dorling Kindersley Limited

Products that already sell well at home are among those most likely to succeed abroad. As a manager, given Starbuck's positioning, would you have supported opening this store in China?

from market research firms that provide assessments and key statistics on specific markets. National governments provide much useful information, typically free of charge. In the United States, for example, the Department of Commerce (www.export.gov) conducts and publishes numerous market surveys, such as *The Water Supply and Wastewater Treatment Market in China, Automotive Parts and Equipment Industry Guide in France*, and *Country Commercial Guide for Brazil*.

Some firms target countries that are psychically near—that is, countries similar to the home country in culture, legal environment, and other factors. Such countries fit management's comfort zone. Australian firms often choose Britain, New Zealand, or the United States as their first foreign market. As managerial experience, knowledge, and confidence grow, firms expand into more complex and culturally distant markets, such as China or Japan.

Other firms are more venturesome and target nontraditional, higher-risk countries. The born-global companies exemplify this trend. Ongoing globalization, as well as advances in communication and transportation technologies, have reduced the foreignness of most countries, and hence the cost and risk of entering them. Even small firms now routinely reach out to culturally distant countries, including emerging markets and developing economies.

Information needed for country screening varies by product type or industry. In marketing consumer electronics, for example, the researcher emphasizes countries with large populations, discretionary income, and ample electricity. For farming equipment, the best targets are

Source: Jon Arnold Images Ltd/Alamy Images

When deciding on target markets, internationalizing firms often choose regional hubs, which serve as critical entry points for important national or regional markets. Pictured here is Hong Kong, an important entry hub for China.

countries with substantial agricultural land and farmers. Health insurance companies target countries with many doctors and hospitals.

Read the *Global Trend* feature to learn about current trends that are producing international market opportunities.

Often, the firm may target a geographical region or a group of countries rather than individual countries. This approach is usually more cost effective, particularly in markets with similar characteristics. The European Union includes twenty-seven countries that are relatively similar in income levels, regulations, and infrastructure. When entering Europe, firms often devise a pan-European strategy that considers many EU member countries simultaneously, rather than planning separate efforts in individual countries.

In other cases, the firm may target so-called *gateway countries*, or regional hubs, that serve as entry points to nearby or affiliated markets. Singapore is the gateway to southeast Asian countries, Hong Kong is an important gateway to China, Turkey is a good platform for the central Asian republics, Panama is a friendly entry to Latin America, and Finland is a portal to Russia. Firms base their operations in a gateway country so they can serve the larger adjacent region.

Growing national GDP is among the most important indicators of capacity to purchase products and services. Exhibit 13.2 portrays the world's most promising export markets, based on aggregate GDP growth. The exhibit highlights the countries most expected to grow their GDPs through 2016, and their expected incremental contribution to world GDP. China leads by far, and is expected to contribute nearly 30 percent ($8,547 billion) to increased global GDP by 2016. Note that most countries in the exhibit are emerging markets. Clearly, Brazil, Russia, India, and China, known collectively as the "BRIC" countries, show remarkable potential as target markets in coming years.

EXHIBIT 13.2

Most Promising Export Markets in Incremental Contribution to World GDP, 2010 through 2016, Percent and Dollar Volume in US$ Billions

Source: Based on World Economic Outlook Databases, International Monetary Fund, at www.imf.org.

GLOBAL TREND

Global Macro Trends That Affect International Business

Within each industry, managers should regularly assess long-term trends in product markets, in technology, and globalization. Firms succeed when they ride these currents; those that swim against them usually struggle. In sectors such as banking, telecommunications, and technology, almost two-thirds of Western firms' recent sales growth has come from targeting the right customer markets and geographic regions.

What trends are managers tracking that signal future market opportunities? A study by McKinsey consultants (www.mckinsey .com) identified the following.

Centers of economic activity are shifting

Economic liberalization, technological advances, capital market developments, and demographic changes are shifting the centers of economic activity. Today, Asia accounts for more than 35 percent of world GDP, exceeding that of Europe and the United States. Some functions in Asia—manufacturing and IT services, for example—are major beneficiaries. China is now home to some of the world's largest banks. Emerging markets elsewhere are becoming centers of activity as well.

Need to increase organizational productivity

Populations are aging across the developed countries, leaving fewer young people to work and pay taxes. With fewer workers to draw on, governments and firms must become more productive and creative to maintain economic output. Governments must provide services more efficiently and at lower cost. Firms must use natural resources more efficiently than ever before.

More consumers, especially in emerging markets

Almost a billion new consumers are entering the global marketplace, as economic growth in emerging markets pushes them beyond the threshold level of $5,000 in annual household income, a point when people begin to spend on discretionary goods. In 2013, consumers' spending power in emerging economies reached $10 trillion, near the spending power of the Eurozone countries in Europe.

The shifting talent battlefield

The shift to knowledge-intensive industries highlights a growing scarcity of knowledge workers. Increasing integration of labor markets such as China, India, and Eastern Europe is opening vast new talent sources. Emerging markets now have tens of millions of university-educated young professionals, more than double the number in the advanced economies.

Growing demand for natural resources

As economic growth accelerates, especially in emerging markets, use of natural resources will grow at unprecedented rates. Demand for oil is rising fast, opening opportunities for global energy firms. In China, demand for copper, steel, and aluminum has tripled, offering opportunities for mining companies. Water shortages are increasingly common. Thriving with higher and more volatile resource prices means companies must enhance the efficiency with which they use resources.

Widespread access to information

Individuals and firms access knowledge with growing ease around the world. Google and other search engines instantly provide nearly limitless information, and knowledge production is growing. Worldwide patent applications have been rising 20 percent a year as companies devise new models of knowledge production, access, and distribution.

Sources: Ian Davis, "The New Normal," *McKinsey Quarterly*, March 2009, retrieved from http://www.mckinseyquarterly.com; Ian Davis and E. Stephenson, "Ten Trends to Watch in 2006," *McKinsey Quarterly*, January 2006, retrieved from www.mckinsey.com; Richard Dobbs, Jeremy Oppenheim, and Fraser Thompson, "Mobilizing for a Resource Revolution," *McKinsey Quarterly*, January 2012, accessed at www.mckinseyquarterly.com.

Country Realities

Brazil is one of the top new markets for medications and other health products. Average income has reached a level at which Brazil's 70 million middle-class consumers now spend substantially on health care. Global pharmaceutical firms are targeting medications to Brazilian consumers, especially senior citizens, who are prone to diabetes, heart disease, and respiratory ailments. Brazilians increasingly buy health insurance, which enables them to invest in personal health care.

Source: S. Agarwal, J. d'Almeida, and T. Francis, "Capturing the Brazilian Pharma Opportunity, April 2012, *McKinsey Quarterly*, retrieved from www.mckinseyquarterly.com.

SCREENING METHODOLOGY FOR POTENTIAL COUNTRY MARKETS It is expensive and impractical to target all the nearly 200 countries worldwide. Management must choose markets that offer the best prospects. Two basic methods for doing this are: (i) gradual elimination and (ii) indexing and ranking.

Gradual elimination. The researcher that applies *gradual elimination* starts with a large number of prospective target countries and gradually narrows the choices by examining increasingly specific information. As indicated in Exhibit 13.1, the researcher aims to reduce the number of countries that warrant in-depth investigation as potential target markets to a manageable five or six. Because research is expensive, it is essential to eliminate unattractive markets quickly. Targeting a less-crowded economy with a product that is not yet widely available may be more profitable than targeting saturated and more competitive markets in Europe, Japan, and North America.

In the early stages, the researcher first obtains general information on macro-level indicators such as population, income, and economic growth before delving into specific information. GlobalEDGE™ (www.globalEDGE.msu.edu) and numerous other sources provide broad screening data. The researcher then employs more specific indicators, such as import statistics, to narrow the choices. Import statistics help reveal the size of the market, the presence of competitors, and the market's viability for new sales. The research also should examine the level of the country's exports, because some countries, such as Panama and Singapore, function as major transit points for international shipments and may not be actual product users. By analyzing research data and gradually narrowing the choices, the researcher identifies the most promising markets for further exploration.

Indexing and ranking. A second method for choosing the most promising foreign markets is *indexing and ranking*, in which the researcher assigns scores to countries based on their overall market attractiveness. For each country, the researcher first identifies a comprehensive set of market-potential indicators and then uses one or more of them to represent a variable. Weights are assigned to each variable to establish its relative importance. The more important a variable, the greater its weight. The researcher uses the resulting weighted scores to rank the countries.

ASSESSING THE EXPORT POTENTIAL OF EMERGING MARKETS China, India, and numerous other emerging markets offer huge potential. For example, John Deere & Company saw an opportunity to sell small tractors to India's 300 million small farmers. After conducting extensive research, the firm developed four small tractor models for the market and is now doing big business there.[6]

The indexing and ranking method for identifying promising markets is illustrated by the Market Potential Index for Emerging Markets, developed by Tamer Cavusgil[7] and featured at globalEDGE™ (www.globalEDGE.msu.edu).[8] Presented in Exhibit 13.3, the index ranks countries on a collection of variables for emerging markets. From it, a manager would conclude that Hong Kong, Singapore, and China are attractive markets. China has steadily risen in the index in recent years, as have Hungary, Poland, and the Czech Republic. The data are also helpful for decisions on entry via FDI and for sourcing.

Exhibit 13.4 defines the variables and relative weights in the index. The assigned weights can be adjusted up or down to fit the unique characteristics of any industry. For example, in evaluating market size, food industry firms attach more weight to market size, while firms in the telecommunications equipment industry emphasize infrastructure and country risk. The researcher can add variables or countries to refine the tool for greater precision.

The size and growth rate of the middle class are often critical indicators of promising targets. The *middle class* is measured by the share of national income available to middle-income households. These consumers are good prospects for most firms because the wealthier class in most emerging markets is relatively small and the poorest segment has little disposable income. Exhibit 13.5 shows how the size of the middle class as a percentage of world population has consistently increased over time, thanks to rising affluence in emerging markets and developing economies. Recent research indicates the global middle class will continue to expand over time. Most of this increase will arise in the Asia Pacific region, especially China.[9] Note, however, that measures of per-capita income may underestimate the true potential of emerging markets due to imprecise measurement methods and the existence in many countries of a large, informal economy.

The relative size of the middle class, and the pace of its growth, also indicate how national income is distributed in a country. If income distribution is very unequal, the size of the middle class will be limited and the market will be less attractive.

In Exhibit 13.3, an analysis of the rankings for each of the dimensions reveals some interesting patterns. China ranks first in market size but thirteenth in economic freedom. It also ranks low in market intensity and commercial infrastructure, revealing there are always *trade-offs* in selecting target countries. No single country is attractive on all dimensions. Along with desirable features,

EXHIBIT 13.3 Market Potential Index for Emerging Markets, 2011

Country	Market Size		Market Growth Rate		Market Intensity		Market Consumption Capacity		Commercial Infrastructure		Economic Freedom		Market Receptivity		Country Risk		Overall Score	
	Rank	Index	Rank	Index	Rank	Index	Rank	Index	Rank	Index	Rank	Index	Rank	Index	Rank	Index	Rank	Index
Singapore	10	1	1	100	2	72	7	65	4	83	6	80	1	100	1	100	1	63
Hong Kong	10	1	9	29	1	100	9	59	1	100	2	93	2	86	2	95	2	58
China	1	100	2	93	14	1	6	67	13	36	13	7	11	4	8	55	3	55
South Korea	4	10	7	41	6	59	2	92	3	88	4	83	7	16	5	71	4	49
Czech Republic	10	1	11	18	10	45	1	100	2	92	3	89	8	14	3	76	5	45
India	2	38	3	83	12	35	6	67	14	17	12	50	13	2	14	42	6	41
Israel	10	1	12	17	5	63	5	76	6	73	5	81	4	20	7	61	7	40
Poland	7	4	10	21	7	60	4	79	6	73	6	80	10	5	6	69	7	40
Hungary	10	1	13	4	4	65	3	83	5	81	4	83	6	17	11	47	7	40
Turkey	5	6	4	70	3	66	7	65	11	49	8	60	11	4	13	43	8	38
Brazil	3	20	6	57	9	47	12	42	10	51	9	58	14	1	10	54	9	36
Mexico	4	10	8	40	8	59	10	47	12	46	7	65	5	18	12	45	10	35
Argentina	7	4	5	65	6	62	8	64	8	59	11	51	12	3	15	18	10	35
Malaysia	8	3	7	41	13	29	9	59	7	61	10	53	3	22	9	57	11	34
Chile	9	2	10	21	11	44	11	43	9	53	1	100	9	11	4	74	11	34

Note: Only the top 15 countries are provided here; consult www.globalEDGE.msu.edu for the complete list.

Source: Market Potential Index for Emerging Markets—2012, globalEDGE™ (www.globalEDGE.msu.edu/resourcedesk/mpi).

EXHIBIT 13.4 **Variables Used in the Market Potential Index for Emerging Markets**

Dimension	Definition	Weight	Measures Used
Market Size	Proportion of country's population concentrated in cities	10/50	• Urban population (million) • Electricity consumption (billion kwh)
Market Growth Rate	Pace of industrialization and economic development	6/50	• Average annual growth rate of primary energy use (%) • Real GDP growth rate (%)
Market Intensity	Buying power of the country's residents	7/50	• GNI per-capita estimates using PPP (U.S. dollars) • Private consumption as a percentage of GDP (%)
Market Consumption Capacity	Size and growth rate of the country's middle class	5/50	• Percentage share of middle class in consumption/income
Commercial Infrastructure	Ease of access to marketing, distribution, and communication channels	7/50	• Main telephone lines (per 100 habitants) • Cellular mobile subscribers (per 100 habitants) • Number of PCs (per 1000 habitants) • Paved road density (km per million people) • Internet users (per 100 habitants) • Population per retail outlet • Percentage of households with TV
Economic Freedom	Degree to which the country has liberalized its economy	5/50	• Economic Freedom Index • Political Freedom Index
Market Receptivity	Extent of country's openness to imports	6/50	• Per-capita imports from the United States (U.S. dollars) • Trade as a percentage of GDP (%)
Country Risk	Level of political risk	4/50	• Country risk rating

Source: Market Potential Index for Emerging Markets—2012, globalEDGE™ (www.globalEDGE.msu.edu/resourcedesk/mpi).

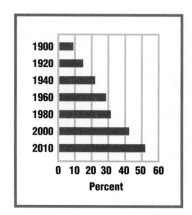

EXHIBIT 13.5

Middle Class Population in All Countries as a Percent of Total World Population

Sources: Based on Surjit S. Bhalla, *Imagine There's No Country: Poverty Inequality and Growth in the Era of Globalization,* (Washington DC: Institute for International Economics, 2002); *Economist,* "Burgeoning Bourgeoisie," February 14, 2009, Special Section, pp. 3–7; Homi Kharas, *The Emerging Middle Class In Developing Countries,* (Paris: OECD Development Centre, 2010).

the researcher also must contend with less desirable ones. For example, both Singapore and Hong Kong are favorable in terms of market receptivity, but they are city-states with small populations.

The top four countries in the index in Exhibit 13.3 are all East Asian emerging economies. In recent years, they have made tremendous strides in market liberalization, industrialization, and modernization. In South Korea, annual per-capita GDP growth often exceeds 5 percent and has grown tenfold in the last 40 years. South Korean firms have become world leaders in many industries, such as shipbuilding, telecommunications, and consumer electronics. They use pioneering technologies years ahead of their competitors and are overtaking other countries in broadband and mobile technologies. Asia's rapid economic development is one of the remarkable features of contemporary globalization.[10]

Country rankings like those in Exhibit 13.3 are not static; they evolve in the wake of macroeconomic events or country-specific developments. While India ranks relatively high, it may dramatically fall if a future government reverses market liberalization. The recent accession of Bulgaria and Romania into the European Union will likely improve the economic prospects of these countries. The introduction of modern banking systems and legal infrastructure should increase Russia's attractiveness as an export market. Chile has achieved substantial progress in economic reforms and higher living standards, while economic stagnation has reduced Argentina's attractiveness.

The variables suggested by ranking indicators are only a general guide for identifying promising countries in the early stages of research. After identifying a few high potential markets, the researcher must do more detailed analyses. Eventually, the researcher will supplement the indicators for specific industries. For medical equipment, for example, the researcher must gather specific data on healthcare expenditures and the number of physicians and hospital beds per capita. Firms in the financial services sector require specific data on commercial risk, interest rates, and density of banks. Depending on the industry, researchers may also apply different weights to each market-potential indicator. Population size is relatively less important for a firm that markets yachts than for one that sells footwear.

Country Screening for Foreign Direct Investment

FDI investments in plant, equipment, and other productive assets are costly and usually undertaken for the long term. Choosing the right targets is critical, and different variables apply than for exporting. For example, with FDI the availability of skilled labor and managerial talent in the target market is often very important.

Researchers identifying the best locations for FDI usually consider the following variables:

- Long-term prospects for growth and substantial returns
- Cost of doing business, based on the price and availability of commercial infrastructure, tax rates and wages, and high-level skills and capital markets
- Country risk, including regulatory, financial, political, and cultural barriers, and the legal environment for intellectual property protection
- Competitive environment and intensity of competition from other firms
- Government incentives such as tax holidays, subsidized training, grants, or low-interest loans

When screening countries for FDI, numerous sources provide useful information, such as the United Nations Conference on Trade and Development (UNCTAD; www.unctad.org) and the World Bank (www.worldbank.org). The consulting firm A. T. Kearney prepares the *Foreign Direct Investment Confidence Index* (www.atkearney.com), which tracks how political, economic, and regulatory changes affect the FDI preferences of the world's top 1,000 firms. By surveying executives, the index captures the most important variables for the sixty-five countries that receive more than 90 percent of global FDI investment.

Exhibit 13.6 displays the Foreign Direct Investment Confidence Index. It reveals that investors favor traditional investment destinations such as Germany and the United States. Advanced economies tend to invest huge sums in each other's markets. For example, Europe and the United

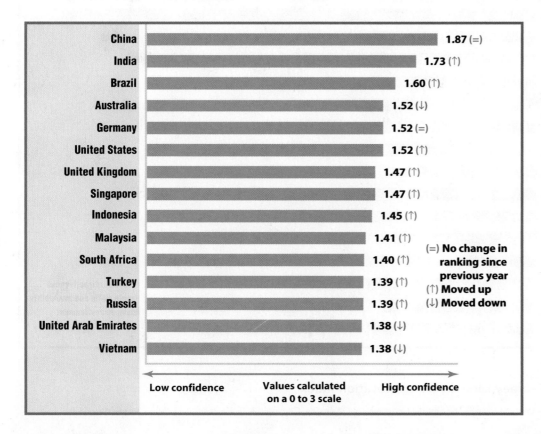

EXHIBIT 13.6

A. T. Kearney 2012 Foreign Direct Investment Confidence Index

Source: Foreign Direct Investment Confidence Index®, New Concerns in an Uncertain World, Copyright A. T. Kearney, 2012. All rights reserved.

States are each other's most important partners for FDI. Their transatlantic economy represents more than $2.5 trillion in total foreign affiliate sales and mutually supports nearly a quarter of the world's entire foreign affiliate workforce. Of particular interest in the FDI Confidence Index are China, India, and Brazil, which top the list.

Most of the top ten destinations are emerging markets. Investors prefer China because of its huge size, fast-growing consumer market, and position as an excellent, low-cost manufacturing site. China enjoys favorable government incentives and a stable macroeconomic climate. However, executives see India as the world's leader for business process and outsourcing IT services. India has a well-educated workforce, strong managerial talent, established rule of law, and relatively transparent transactions and rules.

Country Screening for Sourcing

Global sourcing and offshoring describe the practice of procuring finished products, intermediate goods, and services from suppliers located abroad. When seeking foreign sources of supply, managers examine such factors as cost and quality of inputs, stability of exchange rates, reliability of suppliers, and the presence of a workforce with superior technical skills.

Firms increasingly source services from abroad to obtain various advantages. A. T. Kearney prepares a *Global Services Location Index* (www.atkearney.com), presented in Exhibit 13.7. It compares the factors that make countries attractive as potential locations for offshoring service activities such as IT, business processes, and call centers. The index evaluates countries across forty-three criteria in three dimensions:

- *Financial attractiveness* accounts for compensation costs (average wages), infrastructure costs (for electricity and telecom systems), and tax and regulatory costs (tax burden, corruption, and fluctuating exchange rates).
- *People skills and availability* account for suppliers' experience and skills, labor-force availability, education and language proficiency, and employee-attrition rates.
- *Business environment* assesses economic and political aspects of the country, commercial infrastructure, cultural adaptability, and security of intellectual property.

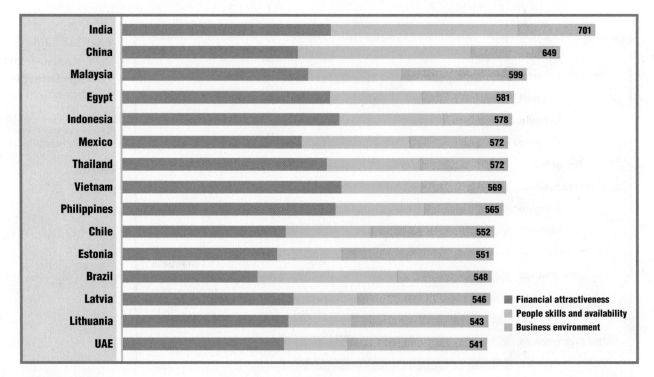

EXHIBIT 13.7

The 2011 A. T. Kearney Global Services Location Index

Source: Global Services Location Index®, The Shifting Geography of Offshoring, Copyright A. T. Kearney, 2011. All rights reserved.

Note that virtually all the top ten countries in Exhibit 13.7 are emerging markets, such as India, China, and Malaysia. Although the cost of labor is important, managers also cite productivity level, technical skills, and customer service skills as important factors. The Index credits India and China (and to a lesser extent, Brazil, Mexico, and Indonesia) with superior people skills.

 ## Task Four: Assess Industry Market Potential

The methods for screening countries discussed so far provide insights on individual markets and reduce the complexity of choosing appropriate foreign locations. Once the number of potential countries has been reduced to a manageable few, the next step is to conduct an in-depth analysis of each. In earlier stages, the researcher examined macro-level indicators. Now, because market potential is industry-specific, the researcher narrows the focus to industry-level indicators.

Industry market potential is an estimate of the likely sales for all firms in a specific industry during a particular period. It is different from *company sales potential*, the share of industry sales the focal firm itself can expect during a given year. Most firms forecast both industry market potential and company sales potential at least three years into the future.

Estimating industry market potential enables the researcher to refine the analysis and identify the most attractive countries for the firm's product or service, as well as gain industry-specific insights and understand how the firm needs to adapt its product and marketing approaches.

Industry market potential
An estimate of the likely sales for all firms in a specific industry during a particular period.

To estimate industry market potential, managers obtain data and insights on the following variables for each country:

- Size and growth rate of the market and trends in the specific industry
- Tariff and nontariff trade barriers to market entry
- Standards and regulations that affect the industry
- Availability and sophistication of distribution for the firm's offerings in the market
- Unique customer requirements and preferences
- Industry-specific market potential indicators

In addition to generic determinants of demand, each industry sector—from air conditioners to zippers—has its own *industry-specific potential indicators* or *distinctive drivers of demand.* Marketers of cameras, for example, examine climate-related factors such as the average number of sunny days in a typical year, given that most pictures are taken outdoors. A manufacturer of heavy machinery might examine the rate of industrialization and dependence on hydroelectricity. A marketer of cooling equipment and industrial filters will consider the number of institutional buyers, such as restaurants and hotels. These are all industry-specific market potential indicators.

The researcher also evaluates factors that affect marketing and use of the product, such as consumer characteristics, culture, distribution channels, and business practices. Because intellectual property rights vary worldwide, it is important to protect the firm's critical assets by examining regulations, trademark rules, and product liability. The researcher should also investigate subsidy and incentive programs from home and foreign governments that reduce the cost of foreign market entry.

Growth rates tend to be relatively high in new or rapidly innovating industries. The researcher should bear

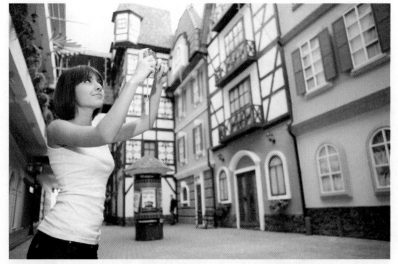

Source: snaptitude/Fotolia LLC

Camera makers account for climate in their estimates of demand, since most pictures are taken outdoors. What other industry-specific variables might they consider?

in mind that the product is likely to be in a different phase of its life cycle in each country. Countries in which the product is not currently available or in which competitors have only recently entered are often promising targets.

Managers use various methods to estimate industry market potential:

- *Simple trend analysis.* This method quantifies the total likely amount of industry market potential by examining aggregate production for the industry as a whole, adding imports from abroad and deducting exports. Trend analysis provides a rough estimate of the size of current industry sales in the country.
- *Monitoring key industry-specific indicators.* The manager examines unique industry drivers of market demand by collecting data from various sources. The earth-moving equipment company Caterpillar examines the volume of announced construction projects, number of issued building permits, growth rate of households, and infrastructure development to anticipate sales of its construction equipment.
- *Monitoring key competitors.* Here, the manager investigates the degree of major competitor activity in the countries of interest. If Caterpillar is considering Chile as a potential market, its managers investigate the current involvement of its main competitor, the Japanese firm Komatsu, in Chile and gather competitive intelligence to anticipate Komatsu's likely future moves in Chile.
- *Following key customers around the world.* Automotive suppliers can anticipate their future markets by monitoring the international expansion of their customers such as Honda or Mercedes-Benz. Caterpillar follows its current customers such as Bechtel and Fluor as they bid for contracts or establish operations in specific markets.
- *Tapping into supplier networks.* Many suppliers serve multiple clients and can be a major source of information about competitors. Firms gain valuable leads from current suppliers by asking them about the activities of competitors, as long as the questions are ethical and don't expose competitors' trade secrets and other proprietary information.
- *Attending international trade fairs.* By attending a trade fair in the target country, the manager can learn much about market characteristics and other factors that indicate industry sales potential. Trade fairs also help identify potential distributors and other business partners.

Source: atm2003/Fotolia LLC

Demand is growing in Europe for environmental technologies and green products. These workers are installing solar panels on a house in Italy.

Data Sources for Estimating Industry Market Potential

For each target country, the manager seeks data that directly or indirectly report levels of industry sales and production, as well as the intensity of exports and imports in the product category of interest. Exhibit 13.8 summarizes sites useful for estimating industry market potential, as well as accessing various statistics for conducting market opportunity assessment and other research.

One useful source in the United States is the market research section at export.gov (www.export.gov/mrktresearch). Specific reports available at this site include:

- *Best Market and Market Update* reports that provide extensive industry, country, and market research to pinpoint top export markets and entry strategies.

EXHIBIT 13.8 A Sampling of Sites for Conducting International Business Research

SITE	ADDRESS	DESCRIPTION
globalEDGE™	globalEDGE.msu.edu	Data, information, search engines, and diagnostic tools on a full range of international business topics
Export.gov	www.export.gov	Country commercial guides and other United States government resources to support exporting and other international business activities
UK Trade and Investment	www.uktradeinvest.gov.uk	United Kingdom data and resources to support international business
Industry Canada	www.ic.gc.ca	Canada data and resources to support international business
United Nations Conference on Trade and Development (UNCTAD)	www.unctad.org	Country fact sheets and statistics for analysis of international trade, FDI, and economic trends
World Trade Organization (WTO)	www.wto.org	Statistics on tariffs, government intervention, and economic conditions worldwide
World Bank	www.worldbank.org	National and international statistics, financial and technical information, sectoral data, trends in the world economy
World Bank Doing Business	www.doingbusiness.org	Reports on doing business in various countries
International Monetary Fund (IMF)	www.imf.org	Data and statistics on countries, and economic and financial indicators
A.T. Kearney	www.atkearney.com	Various indices, including the Foreign Direct Investment Confidence Index

- *Country Commercial Guides*, which comprehensively profile the political, economic, and commercial environment of some 150 countries.
- *Industry Overviews* and *Industry/Regional Reports* that describe conditions in specific industries.

Managers often must be creative in finding and consulting resources that shed light on the task at hand. Data and resources in international research are rarely complete or precise. Consider Teltone Inc. The firm wished to enter Mexico with its inexpensive brand of cellular telephones and needed to estimate industry-wide demand. It consulted numerous sources, including reports by the International Telecommunications Union (in Geneva, Switzerland), Export.gov, and several United Nations publications. Managers researched the size of the Mexican upper class and its average income, the nature of support infrastructure for cellular systems in Mexico, and the nature and number of retail stores that could handle cell phones. They also accessed statistics from the National Telecommunications Trade Association on the number of competitors active in Mexico and their sales volumes. From these sources, Teltone was able to make a rough estimate of market size for telephones and prices in Mexico.

The *Recent Grad in IB* feature profiles Javier Estrada, who found exciting opportunities in his young career in international market research and working in emerging markets.

 ## Task Five: Choosing Foreign Business Partners

Business partners are critical to international business success. Key partners include distribution-channel intermediaries, facilitators, suppliers, and collaborative venture partners such as joint venture partners, licensees, and franchisees. Once the firm has selected a target market, it must identify the types of partners it needs for its foreign market venture, negotiate terms with them, and support and monitor their conduct.

JAVIER ESTRADA

Javier's major: Business
Objectives: Integrating business skills with social planning in a public agency and pursuing a career in politics
Jobs held since graduating:
- United Nations World Food Programme in Guatemala and Honduras
- Director of Research, Bates Advertising, Dominican Republic
- Director of a major charity in Mexico

Javier Estrada graduated from a state university several years ago with a bachelor's degree in business. He moved to the Dominican Republic, where he took a research position in the local office of Bates Advertising, a global ad agency that handled accounts such as Wendy's, Purina, and Bell South. In this position, Javier investigated the local target market—how the market responded to key brands, the level of market share, and the most effective ways to reach target markets with advertising and other marketing communications tools. According to Javier, "The real challenge in international advertising is not in the large, established brands, but in the small, poorly positioned one."

A typical day for Javier included meeting with colleagues to discuss the progress of research projects and assessing the next steps on behalf of his clients. Javier implemented consumer surveys to learn what specific benefits Latin American consumers were seeking. He used the information from this research to craft advertising campaigns tailored to customer needs and attitudes. In creating surveys, Javier researched various secondary data sources on the Internet and in Bates's private library.

He visited Santo Domingo to meet with local experts and gain an authentic feel for the market. He used a comprehensive report prepared by the United States Department of Commerce International Trade Administration on the target market. Javier developed Spanish-language questionnaires to gain an even deeper understanding of the market. He sent questionnaires to random samples of typical consumers throughout the Dominican Republic. He then analyzed the completed questionnaires and presented the results to his superiors. Findings from these studies helped Javier prepare reports with recommendations on the most appropriate advertising strategies for the Dominican Republic.

Success Factors

"My parents felt strongly that our lives should be influenced not only by the quality of our education, but also by our travels....In school we were among the most traveled kids." Javier was lucky enough to visit several countries during his teens and twenties. He comments: "You get to know yourself when you're completely alone in a new culture and establishing a network of friends and work contacts." International experience contributed to Javier's independent spirit and his ability to function successfully around the world.

In his market research position, Javier enjoyed going to other countries and meeting different people. "My job provided the chance to help companies develop marketing programs appropriate for their customers. I would not have gotten the job if I had not worked hard in school. Management training provided me with the skills to perform effectively. Sensitivity is important, since you need to be able to communicate with people who are culturally different from you. You need a strong empathy for your customers. You need to identify which research questions are best."

What's Ahead?

Javier has ever-higher goals for his career. He has been long concerned about poverty issues in Latin America, and his experiences with the United Nations affected him profoundly. Javier earned a master's degree in social policy and planning from the London School of Economics. Having worked in both business and development, Javier found his passion in integrating his business skills with social planning at the governmental level. Recently, Javier worked for a major charity organization in Mexico. He says, "I need to dream big."

Licensing
Arrangement in which the owner of intellectual property grants a firm the right to use that property for a specified period of time in exchange for royalties or other compensation.

Exporters tend to collaborate with foreign market intermediaries such as distributors and agents. Firms that choose to sell their intellectual property, such as know-how, trademarks, and copyrights, may work through foreign licensees. These **licensing** partners are independent businesses that apply intellectual property to produce products in their own country. In **franchising**, the foreign partner is a franchisee, an independent business abroad that acquires rights and skills from the focal firm to conduct operations in its own market (such as in the fast-food or car-rental industries). The focal firm can also internationalize by initiating an **international collaborative venture**, a business activity undertaken jointly with other firms. Such collaborations may be project-based or require equity investments. Other types of international partnerships include global sourcing, contract manufacturing, and supplier partnerships. We describe these in detail in later chapters.

Criteria for Choosing a Partner

The focal firm must identify the ideal qualifications of potential foreign partners. The firm should seek a good fit in terms of both strategy (common goals and objectives) and resources (complementary core competencies and value-chain activities). It is helpful to anticipate the likely synergy with the prospective partner for the intermediate-term, three to six years into the future.

Take the case of Brunswick Corporation (www.brunswick.com), a manufacturer of recreational goods such as boats and bowling equipment. When screening for potential foreign distributors, this firm looks for:

- Financial soundness and resourcefulness, to ensure the venture receives the appropriate level of support initially and in the long run
- Competent and professional management, with qualified technical and sales staff
- Solid knowledge of the industry, with access to distribution channels and end users in the marketplace
- Reputation in the marketplace and good connections with local government (political clout is often helpful, especially in emerging markets)
- Commitment, loyalty, and willingness to invest in the venture and grow it over time

Firms also seek partners with complementary expertise. For example, while the focal firm may bring engineering and manufacturing expertise to the partnership, the local distributor may bring knowledge of local customers and distribution channels.

Desirable characteristics are not always available in prospective partners. If a company enters a foreign market late, it may have to pick the second-best or even less-qualified partner. The firm should then be ready and able to strengthen the partner's capabilities by transferring appropriate managerial skills, technical know-how, and other resources.

Searching for Prospective Partners

The process of screening and evaluating business partners can be overwhelming. Commercial banks, consulting firms, and trade journals, as well as country and regional business directories such as *Kompass* and *Dun and Bradstreet*, are helpful in developing a list of partner candidates. National governments offer inexpensive services that assist firms in finding partners in specific markets. The knowledge portal globalEDGE™ (www.globalEDGE.msu.edu) provides additional resources, including diagnostic tools, to help managers systematically choose partner candidates.

Onsite visits and research from independent sources and trade fairs are crucial in the early stages of assessing a partner. Many firms ask prospective partners to prepare a formal business plan before entering an agreement. The quality of the plan illuminates the prospective partner's capabilities and level of commitment.

 ## Task Six: Estimate Company Sales Potential

Once managers have identified several promising country markets, verified industry market potential, and assessed the availability of qualified business partners, the next step is to determine **company sales potential** in each country. Company sales potential is an estimate of the share of annual industry sales the firm expects to generate in a particular target market. Estimating it can be especially challenging because of the need to obtain detailed information from the market and make fundamental assumptions to project the firm's revenues and expenses three to five years into the future. Estimates of company sale potential are rarely precise. They usually require the researcher to make judgment calls and think creatively.

In Vietnam, for example, research suggests that few people have a banking relationship. However, demand for banking is growing by as

Franchising
Arrangement in which the firm allows another the right to use an entire business system in exchange for fees, royalties, or other forms of compensation.

International collaborative venture
Cross-border business alliance whereby partnering firms pool their resources and share costs and risks to undertake a new business venture; also referred to as an "international partnership" or an "international strategic alliance."

Company sales potential
An estimate of the share of annual industry sales that the firm expects to generate in a particular target market.

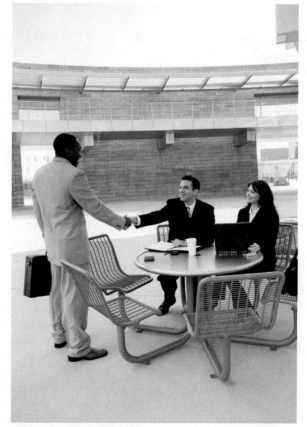
Source: Stephen Coburn/Shutterstock

Firms seeking a foreign business partner emphasize qualifications, including common goals and competent management.

much as 25 percent per year. Vietnamese 21 to 29 year olds are attractive targets because they are less wary of banking and more open to foreign banks than their elders. Vietnam's economy is growing rapidly, with rising household income and few competitors.[11] Suppose a bank from your country is considering entering the market in Vietnam. How would it estimate its sales potential? We address such issues next.

When estimating company sales potential in a foreign market, managers collect and review various research findings and assess the following:

- *Intensity of the competitive environment.* Local or third-country competitors are likely to intensify their own marketing efforts when confronted by new entrants. Their actions are often unpredictable and not easily observed.
- *Pricing and financing of sales.* The degree to which pricing and financing are attractive to both customers and channel members is critical to initial entry and ultimate success.
- *Financial resources.* Sufficient capital is a prerequisite for any project. International ventures are often costly.
- *Human resources.* Management must ensure it has personnel with sufficient capabilities in language, culture, and other areas to do business in target markets.
- *Partner capabilities.* The competencies and resources of foreign partners, including channel intermediaries and facilitators, influence how quickly the firm can enter and generate sales in the market.
- *Access to distribution channels.* The ability to establish and make best use of channel intermediaries and distribution infrastructure in the target market determines sales.
- *Market penetration timetable.* A key decision is whether managers opt for gradual or rapid market entry. Gradual entry gives the firm time to develop and leverage resources and strategies but may cede market share to competitors. Rapid entry can ensure first-mover advantages but also tax the firm's resources and capabilities.
- *Risk tolerance of senior managers.* Results depend on the level of resources top management is willing to commit, which in turn depends on management's tolerance for risk.
- *Special links, contacts, and capabilities of the firm.* The extent of the focal firm's network in the market—its existing relationships with customers, channel members, and suppliers—can strongly affect venture success.
- *Reputation.* The firm can succeed faster in the market if target customers are already familiar with its brand name and reputation.

Such a comprehensive assessment should lead to general estimates of potential sales, which managers can compare to actual sales of incumbent firms in the market, when such data are available.

Estimating company sales typically starts from multiple angles and converges on an ultimate estimate that relies heavily on judgment. Exhibit 13.9 provides a framework to estimate company sales. After combining information about customers, intermediaries, and competition, the researcher decides whether the result points to a reasonable estimate. Managers may make multiple estimates based on best-case, worst-case, and most-likely case scenarios. They will usually make assumptions about the degree of firm effort, price aggressiveness, possible competitive reactions, degree of intermediary effort, and so on. The firm's sales prospects also hinge on factors both controllable by management (such as prices charged to intermediaries and customers) and uncontrollable (such as the intensity of competition). Ultimately, estimating company sales potential is more art than science.

Practical Approaches to Estimating Company Sales Potential

When estimating sales potential, it is best to begin with the factors suggested in Exhibit 13.9.

Customer characteristics
- Demographics
- Growth of demand
- Size of customer segment
- Intensity
- Purchasing power

Customer receptivity
- Perceived benefits of product
- Promotional effort directed to customers

Competitive positioning of focal brand
- Unique selling proposition of product
- What are its superior features compared to competitive offerings

Company Sales Potential

Channel effort and productivity
- Margins and incentives offered to distribution intermediaries

Competition
- Intensity
- Relative strength
- Potential reactions to market entrants

Pricing
- The cost of product landed in the foreign market (a function of international shipping costs, tariffs, etc.)
- Customary margins for distributors
- Whether the firm pursues a penetration versus skimming pricing

EXHIBIT 13.9

A Framework for Estimating Company Sales Potential in the Foreign Market

The following activities are especially helpful for estimating company sales potential:

- *Survey of end users and intermediaries.* The firm can survey a sample of customers and distributors to determine the level of potential sales.
- *Trade audits.* Managers may visit retail outlets and question channel members to assess competitors' strengths and price levels. In this approach, managers estimate market potential through the eyes of intermediaries (distributors) responsible for handling the product in the market. The trade audit can also indicate opportunities for alternative distribution approaches and clarify the firm's standing relative to competitors.
- *Competitor assessment.* The firm should benchmark itself against principal competitor(s) in the market and estimate how much sales it can attract away from them. If top competitors are large and powerful, competing head-on might prove too costly. Even in countries dominated by large firms, however, research may reveal untapped or underserved market segments that can be attractive, particularly for smaller firms.
- *Estimates from local partners.* Collaborators such as distributors, franchisees, or licensees already experienced in the market are often best positioned to develop estimates of market share and sales potential.
- *Limited marketing efforts to test the waters.* Some companies may choose to engage in a limited entry in the foreign market—a sort of test market—to gauge sales potential or better understand the market. From these early results, it is possible to forecast longer-term sales.

In developing economies and emerging markets, where information sources are often lacking, two other techniques are useful for estimating company sales potential. These are *analogy* and *proxy indicators*. We illustrated these approaches in the opening story.

- *Analogy*. Using this method, the researcher draws on known statistics from one country to gain insights into the same phenomenon for another, similar country. For example, if the researcher knows the total consumption of citrus drinks in Hungary, then—assuming citrus drink consumption patterns do not vary much in neighboring Romania—a rough estimate of Romania's consumption can be made, adjusting, of course, for the difference in population. If a firm knows X number of bottles of antibiotics are sold in a country with Y number of physicians per thousand people, it can assume the same ratio (of bottles per 1,000 physicians) will apply in a similar country.

- *Proxy indicators*. With proxy indicators, the researcher uses known information about one product category to infer potential about another product category, especially if the two are complementary. A proxy indicator of demand for professional hand tools might be the level of construction activity in the country; for a particular piece of surgical equipment, it might be the total number of surgeries performed.

A firm contemplating a major market entry via FDI should make its market research especially comprehensive. When Britain's huge retailer Tesco assessed its entry into the United States, researchers investigated every detail of the country's in-store offerings and grocery buyer behavior. The firm set up a mock store in Los Angeles and invited groups of 250 customers in to watch how they shopped, then asked for feedback. The researchers moved into sixty California families' homes for two weeks, sifting through their cupboards and refrigerators, shopping and cooking with them, and keeping diaries of their every movement, from how they got their kids to school to what they did at night. Such research has helped make Tesco a top food retailer worldwide.[12]

Ethical Connections

Market research has revealed substantial demand for "green products," especially in the advanced economies. However, international marketers often make false claims about the origins or effectiveness of the products they market. For example, packaging often states a product is made from recycled waste, but such claims are hard to prove. Some merchandise is labeled "all natural," but some natural ingredients are actually harmful. Many labels claim a product is "organic," but the term is ill-defined and may not actually support human health or the natural environment.

In Conclusion

Some firms are attracted to foreign markets by the promise of revenues and profits, others by the prospect of increasing production efficiency. Still others internationalize to subdue competitive pressures or keep pace with rivals. Whatever the rationale, when companies fail in international ventures, it is often because they neglect to conduct a systematic and comprehensive assessment of global market opportunity.[13]

Although we have presented the six tasks of global market opportunity assessment in a sequence, firms do not necessarily pursue them that way. They may pursue two or more simultaneously. The process is dynamic—market conditions change, partner performance fluctuates, and competitive intensity may increase. These events require managers to constantly evaluate their decisions and commitments, remaining open to course changes as circumstances dictate.

Some choices that managers make are interrelated. For example, the choice of business partner is a function of the country. The type of distributor to use varies from market to market—say, for example, between the Netherlands and Nigeria. The degree of country risk may imply a need for a politically well-connected business partner. In nontraditional markets, such as Vietnam, the firm may need a partner that can serve as both distributor and cultural adviser.

Even the most attractive country cannot compensate for a poor partner. Despite growing availability of information on individual countries, many firms struggle to identify qualified and interested business partners, especially in emerging markets. The most qualified partners may already represent other foreign firms. This necessitates recruiting second- or even third-best candidates and then committing adequate resources to ensure their success.

| CLOSING CASE | Advanced Biomedical Devices: Assessing Readiness to Export |

Dr. Richard Bentley, a well-known British surgeon who developed a medical device that helps the wound-healing process, was so committed to the ground-breaking technology that he left his surgical practice to found Advanced Biomedical Devices, Inc. (ABD), headquartered in the eastern United States. ABD plans to initiate exporting activities and just completed the process of assessing its readiness, using CORE (COmpany Readiness to Export).

ABD's product line includes several innovative devices called Speedheal that promote healing and also reduce postsurgical pain by keeping the wound area from swelling. Speedheal oxygenates the wound area by pulsing electrons through the bandage covering the wound. The devices are very small and portable. Versions exist for different types of surgeries: hand surgery, face lifts, abdominal procedures, and so on.

Dr. Bentley launched ABD with a skillful management team whose members have worked extensively in the European market, the Pacific Rim, and Latin America. ABD's manufacturing director is from Germany, and another manager lived in France and Malaysia for several years.

Thanks to high demand, Speedheal sales increased rapidly, primarily through medical product distributors that sold to hospitals and clinics throughout the United States. Growth approached 20 percent in some years, and the staff grew to 85 people. The firm's success stimulated the entry of competitors offering similar products, but rivals never achieved the degree of miniaturization in ABD's products. Miniaturization thus remains one of Speedheal's competitive advantages. Management's projections for ABD's future growth remain positive.

Dreams of International Expansion

ABD had received unsolicited orders from abroad and learned a great deal about handling international transactions, including foreign exchange, letters of credit, and logistics. Though ABD's plan to internationalize was in its early stages, management intended to expand beyond occasional export sales to target key world markets. Its managers preferred dealing with psychically close markets—those with familiar culture, business customs, and legal and banking systems. But they were willing to consider others, especially large and fast-growing markets and those promising superior profitability.

One expected benefit was the opportunity for ABD to learn from global competitors and markets. Many trends that start in foreign markets eventually reach the home country, and often the best way to track them is to do business internationally. Management also believed it could reduce ABD's overall risks by diversifying sales to various foreign markets. Finally, internationalization would help preempt competitors in particular foreign markets.

International Strategic Intent

Dr. Bentley and his management team formulated some questions to clarify ABD's internationalization goals. They knew that answering the questions would help clarify ABD's strategic intent for going international. Management also wanted to develop a comprehensive strategic plan that would lay the foundation for international success. Following a series of meetings, the team reached consensus on the following key elements of ABD's initial strategic direction:

- Top management will strongly commit to internationalization, and ABD will pursue foreign markets aggressively. The firm will hire a vice president for international sales in the coming year.
- ABD will invest up to 20 percent of company earnings in export opportunities.

- ABD will begin building distributor relationships in a number of countries.
- ABD will establish a marketing subsidiary in at least one foreign location within three to five years and hire salespeople who select and manage the distributors in their market area.
- Management will seek to ensure that all international ventures reach profitability within two years of their launch.
- Management will develop international marketing plans for each target market, each with its own budget.
- Plans call for international sales to reach 35 percent of total sales within four years.
- ABD will establish an annual budget of $220,000 to finance international activities for each of the first three years. Of that, about $60,000 will be devoted to market research to determine the best target markets and to understand competitors.

Product Readiness for Export

Following approval of ABD's strategic intent, Dr. Bentley and his management team addressed questions about the challenges of internationalization. The first dealt with training sales representatives in foreign markets to sell medical devices to hospitals and clinics, the primary end markets for ABD products. Sales reps require training because they deal with doctors, nurses, and other professionals who are deeply involved in decision making about purchases of hospital supplies. Because training costs can be high in foreign markets, Dr. Bentley wanted to ensure ABD was prepared to make this investment.

Dr. Bentley also raised the issue of after-sales service, which can be challenging in foreign markets. Because ABD's products were seldom defective, the solution for a defective product was to replace it rather than trying to make a repair. U.S. customers counted on a ready backup stock in the event of product defects. ABD planned to employ the same solution for its foreign operations, and management assumed there would be no need for a separate staff to deal with after-sales service. Because Speedheal devices are small and lightweight (though valuable), per-unit transportation costs are very low. In fact, in urgent situations abroad, ABD already made it a practice to ship a replacement device by air.

While management well understood pricing in the United States, there was much it did not know about foreign pricing. Dr. Bentley and several managers had attended trade fairs in Europe and concluded that ABD's prices were not too high, particularly since no other firms offered similar products. In fact, ABD had filled unsolicited orders from Europe and found that customers never challenged its pricing. In the end, however, management decided research was needed to refine ABD's pricing approach.

Next, the team discussed foreign inventory management. Because the devices were cheap to transport by air freight, distributors could replenish inventories quickly and economically, a significant benefit because they would not have to maintain much inventory to support sales. On the other hand, Speedheal devices were sensitive to changes in temperature and humidity and functioned best when warehoused in climate-controlled facilities. Such warehousing was increasingly common, so ABD should have no problem locating the right warehousing in Europe and elsewhere.

ABD's management realized the firm's flexible packaging put them in a good position to enter foreign markets, and they were also prepared to modify the product in various ways to meet worldwide standards and regulations. Two in particular were the CE mark, a mandatory safety mark required on toys, machinery, and low-voltage equipment, and ISO standards, which aim to make development and manufacturing of products efficient, safe, and clean.

Knowledge, Skills, and Resources

In a subsequent meeting, the ABD team considered less tangible aspects of the firm's readiness to internationalize. Management knew critical self-assessment was vital to long-term success, and internationalization would require additional working capital for foreign warehousing, longer shipping times, and larger inventories abroad. Other costs included legal help, freight forwarding, international transportation, customs duties, bank charges, rent for foreign offices, and approval for certain regulatory issues. ABD's management was not completely clear on the amount of these costs, but they were willing to learn. While it would use letters of credit when first opening new markets, ABD would opt for open-account payment systems (payable in 30 or 60 days, depending on the market).

Dr. Bentley also considered the appropriate growth rate for the firm. A company's business could increase rapidly, demanding more product than the firm could reasonably supply. Or domestic sales could drop sharply, requiring management to divert all efforts to rescuing domestic operations, thus disrupting the export program.

Competitive intelligence was another concern. A key incentive for venturing abroad was to learn more about foreign competitors. Some major medical device manufacturers marketed their products in the United States, while others were based strictly abroad. ABD

would have to research and understand the strategies and marketing practices of the important competitors. Dr. Bentley recognized the importance of getting patent coverage on his inventions around the world and of protecting the intellectual property rights of his firm. He planned to retain legal counsel, at home and abroad, to protect ABD's critical assets from patent infringements; to develop suitable distribution and agent agreements, sales agreements, and licensing; and to ensure compliance with local employment laws.

Management believed ABD's initial foreign markets would be Australia, Canada, Western Europe, and Japan, because of their large proportion of affluent consumers with the ability to pay for sophisticated medical care. Thus, ABD had gathered information about the markets and competition in those countries but recognized that it needed to do much more.

Managerial Capabilities for Long-Term Internationalization

One concern was whether management would be able to cope with deepening internationalization. In the end, the ABD team recognized that they were right to take painstaking efforts to determine the firm's readiness to export. Extensive meetings and preliminary research provided the basis for developing initial strategies and action programs, as well as for identifying improvements to make the company stronger in the coming years.

AACSB: Reflective Thinking Skills, Analytic Skills

Case Questions

1. Do you believe ABD's products are in a state of readiness to begin exporting to Europe? Why or why not? Are the products ready for exporting to emerging markets (e.g., China, Mexico, Russia)? Why or why not? What factors suggest Speedheal products might enjoy demand in all types of foreign markets?
2. Does management at ABD possess the appropriate knowledge, skills, and capabilities for internationalization? Justify your answer. What steps should management take to better prepare the firm, managers, and employees to internationalize?
3. How well did ABD complete the key tasks in global market opportunity assessment? Evaluate whether it accomplished each task well or poorly. Did ABD achieve each of the objectives set out for the tasks?

4. If you were a member of ABD's management team, what countries would you recommend targeting first? As a manager, you would need to justify your recommendation. A good approach is to investigate key characteristics of specific countries via globalEDGE™ (www.globalEDGE.msu.edu) or similar Web sites.
5. What approaches could ABD employ to estimate the firm's sales potential for markets in Europe and other affluent economies? Justify your answer.

Note: This case was written by Myron M. Miller, Michigan State University (retired), in association with Professor S. Tamer Cavusgil.

CHAPTER ESSENTIALS

MyManagementLab

Go to **mymanagementlab.com** to complete the problems marked with this icon ⭐.

Key Terms

Summary

In this chapter, you learned about:

1. Analyzing organizational readiness to internationalize

A **global market opportunity** is a favorable combination of circumstances, locations, or timing that offer prospects for exporting, investing, sourcing, or partnering in foreign markets. The firm may perceive opportunities to sell, establish factories, obtain inputs of lower cost or superior quality, or enter collaborative arrangements with foreign partners that support the focal firm's goals. There are six key tasks that managers perform in defining and pursuing global market opportunities. As the first task, management assesses the firm's readiness to internationalize. Management assesses the strengths and weaknesses in the firm's ability to do international business. It assesses the external business environment by conducting formal research on the opportunities and threats that face the firm. The firm must develop resources it lacks. Diagnostic tools, such as CORE (**CO**mpany **R**eadiness to **E**xport), facilitate a self-audit of readiness to internationalize.

2. Assessing the suitability of products and services for foreign markets

Products and services that are good candidates for selling abroad sell well in the domestic market, cater to universal needs, address a need not well served in the target market, or address a new or emergent need abroad. Management should ask the following questions: Who initiates purchasing in the market? Who uses the offering? Why do people buy it? Where is the product or service purchased? What economic, cultural, geographic, and other factors can limit sales?

3. Screening countries to identify target markets

Whether the firm is engaged in importing (sourcing from abroad), investing, or exporting, the choice of country is critical, particularly in the early stages of internationalization. The best markets are large and fast-growing. The nature of information necessary for country screening varies by product type and industry. There are two basic screening methods: gradual elimination and ranking and indexing.

4. Assessing industry market potential

Once a firm reduces the number of potential country targets to five or six, the next step is to conduct in-depth analyses of each. **Industry market potential** is an estimate of the likely sales for all firms in the specific industry for a particular period. Each industry sector also has its own *industry-specific potential indicators*. Among the methods for assessing industry market potential are performing simple trend analysis, monitoring key industry-specific indicators, monitoring key competitors, following key customers around the world, tapping into supplier networks, and attending international trade fairs.

5. Choosing foreign business partners

International business partners include distribution channel intermediaries, facilitators, suppliers, joint venture partners, licensees, and franchisees. Some partners undertake **licensing, franchising**, and **international collaborative ventures**. Management in the focal firm must decide the types of partners it needs, identify suitable partner candidates, negotiate the terms of relationships with chosen partners, support the partners, and monitor their performance.

6. Estimating company sales potential

Company sales potential is the share of annual industry sales the firm can realistically achieve in the target country. Estimating company sales potential requires the researcher to obtain highly refined market information. Among the most influential determinants of company sales potential are: partner capabilities, access to distribution channels in the market, intensity of the competitive environment, pricing and financing of sales, quality of human and financial resources, timetable for market entry, risk tolerance of senior managers, the firm's contacts and capabilities, and its reputation in the market.

Test Your Comprehension AACSB: Reflective Thinking Skills

1. What is a global market opportunity? What types of opportunities do firms seek abroad?

2. Identify and explain the six major tasks in global market opportunity assessment.

3. Identify the issues managers consider when they analyze organizational readiness to internationalize.

⭐ 4. Describe the characteristics of products or services most likely to sell well in foreign markets.

5. What are the typical variables used in indexing and ranking?

6. What types of variables should the researcher consider when screening for each of the following: export markets, foreign direct investment, and global sourcing?

7. What tasks does assessing industry market potential entail?

⭐ 8. What are the major issues to consider when selecting foreign business partners?

Apply Your Understanding AACSB: Communication Abilities, Reflective Thinking Skills, Ethical Understanding and Reasoning Abilities

1. Target® is a large retailer with about 1,800 stores in the United States, but very few in other countries. It has a reputation for merchandising thousands of trendy yet inexpensive products for the home, including apparel, furniture, electronics, toys, and sporting goods. Management wants to open stores in major European cities but will have limited floor space there. Target hires you as a consultant to decide which products to offer in Europe. Write a brief report in which you describe the selection criteria you will use and offer some examples to back up your ideas. Be sure to justify your answer using the advice and other information included in this chapter.

2. Upon graduation, you are hired by Pullman Corporation, a manufacturer of accessories for luxury cars. Management wants you to conduct research to locate foreign markets with the best sales potential. You discover that markets are fairly saturated in advanced economies, but you are aware of numerous *emerging markets* that the industry has overlooked. Using your knowledge of Exhibit 13.3, Emerging Market Potential Indicators, develop a list of the top five emerging markets Pullman should target. Be sure to justify your choice, based on indicators from this chapter such as market size, market growth rate, market intensity, and market consumption capacity.

3. *Ethical Dilemma:* Ryan Staton is the Export Manager at Juneau Industries, a manufacturer of office furnishings. He has identified Russia as a promising market and decides to attend a furniture trade fair in Moscow. As he prepares for the fair, a consultant suggests hiring two female models in revealing clothing to work the company's booth. The consultant says the models will "create buzz" and increase Juneau's visibility at the crowded fair. Staton is skeptical and seeks advice from two colleagues. One colleague says the idea "amounts to exploiting women and could invite sexual harassment charges.... It is sex discrimination. The booth workers' gender and good looks are a condition for their employment." Another colleague tells Staton that hiring the models is no problem. He says those who oppose such a practice "perpetuate stereotypes of women as delicate creatures who cannot decide what's best for themselves." Besides, he continues, "Russia is a male-dominated society and people are not offended by such practices." What do you think? Using the Ethical Framework in Chapter 5, analyze the issue and make a recommendation.

 INTERNET EXERCISES
(http://www.globalEDGE.msu.edu)

AACSB: Reflective Thinking Skills, Use of Information Technology

Refer to Chapter 1, page 24, for instructions on how to access and use globalEDGE™.

1. China is a huge attractive market, with growing affluence. Before exporting to China, most firms conduct market research to better understand the Chinese market. Two useful research sites are the China Business Information Center (CBIC; www.export.gov/china) and UK Trade and Investment (www.uktradeinvest.gov.uk). At the CBIC, for example, firms can find out if they are "China Ready." They can access trade leads and read current news about business in China. Suppose you are hired by a firm that wants to begin exporting to China three products: (a) breakfast cereal, (b) popular music on CDs, and (c) laptop computers. For each of these product categories, using the above Web sites and globalEDGE™, prepare a list of the information that the firm should gather prior to making a decision to export to China.

2. Walmart is a huge retailer, but gets only about a quarter of its sales from outside the United States. Coles is one of the largest retailers in Australia and gets very little of its sales outside Australia. Assess the international retailing sector using online resources, such as globalEDGE™ and A. T. Kearney (www.atkearney.com). Based on your research: (a) What factors should these top retailers consider in choosing countries for internationalizing their operations? (b) What are the best markets for these firms to target for foreign expansion? (c) What types of questions should management at each firm ask in assessing their readiness to internationalize?

3. The United States Census Bureau tracks foreign trade statistics. Visit the site at www.census.gov/foreign-trade and find the most recent versions of the report "Profile of U.S. Exporting Companies" by entering this title in the search engine. Peruse the report and address the following questions: (a) What types of firms export from the United States? That is, what is the breakdown by company type of U.S. exporters? For example, are the exporters mainly large or small firms? Do they operate mainly in the manufacturing, agricultural, or services sectors? (b) What is the role of small and medium-sized exporters in U.S. trade? What percent of U.S. exporters are these types of firms, and for what proportion of total exports do they account? (c) What countries are the three favorite targets of U.S. exporters? According to the report, what factors make these countries the top markets for U.S. firms?

MyManagementLab

Go to **mymanagementlab.com** for Auto-graded writing questions as well as the following Assisted-graded writing questions:

13-1. Summarize the screening methodology for potential country markets.

13-2. How can firms estimate company sales potential?

13-3. Mymanagementlab Only – comprehensive writing assignment for this chapter.

Source: soleg/Fotolia LLC

Exporter's Dogged Pursuit of International Customers

Is your pet having a bad hair day? Is your horse's mane looking dull? Sharon Doherty, president of Vellus Products, Inc., can help. Vellus is a small U.S. firm that makes shampoos, conditioners, brushes, and other grooming products for pets. According to Doherty, shampoos for people don't work well on pets because animals' skin is sensitive and easily irritated.

Vellus's first export sale was to a Taiwanese importer who purchased $25,000 worth of products to sell at dog shows. The word was out. "I started receiving calls from people around the world who heard of our products and asked how they could buy them," Doherty recalls. "But I needed to do market research and learn more about ways of doing business in these countries." Vellus had to adapt some of its marketing for foreign markets to meet local conditions.

Vellus has become very familiar with the cultural aspects of pet care. In England, dog exhibitors prefer less poofed-out

CHAPTER 14

Exporting and Countertrade

 LEARNING OBJECTIVES *In this chapter, you will learn about:*

1. An overview of foreign market entry strategies

2. Characteristics of internationalization

3. Exporting as a foreign market entry strategy

4. Managing export-import transactions

5. Payment methods in exporting and importing

6. Export-import financing

7. Identifying and working with foreign intermediaries

8. Countertrade: A popular approach for emerging markets and developing economies

---

MyManagementLab®

⭐ **Improve Your Grade!**

Over 10 million students improved their results using the Pearson MyLabs.
Visit **mymanagementlab.com** for simulations, tutorials, and end-of-chapter problems.

---

topknots than those in show dogs in the United States, where owners prefer more exotic topknots. In England, dog exhibitors prefer Shih-Tzus with a big head, long back, and stature somewhat lower to the ground, while U.S. exhibitors prefer Shih-Tzus with more leg and a shorter back. These preferences determine the types of shampoos and brushes that each country needs.

For Vellus and countless other firms, exporting increases sales and profits and diversifies the customer base. As an entry strategy, exporting is low cost, low risk, and uncomplicated. These are big advantages for smaller firms like Vellus that typically lack substantial financial and human resources. Exporting also helps stabilize fluctuations in sales volume. For example, because dog shows take place abroad during different parts of the year, exporting helps stabilize Vellus's sales levels.

Firms like Vellus take advantage of support provided by intermediaries located abroad. Doherty often gives advice and guidance to her foreign-based distributors, sharing her knowledge and understanding of importing along with marketing in the dog-show network. She says the advice is much appreciated and goes far in building long-term relationships. Doherty also makes sure to do her homework on potential distributors. "Gather as much information as you can," she advises. "Don't make any assumptions—the wrong choice can cost your business valuable time and money."

Exporters such as Vellus locate foreign distributors using various methods. One approach is to attend a trade fair in the target country. Vellus's management discovered potential distributors by attending foreign dog shows. Other companies consult country and regional business directories, foreign yellow pages, industry trade associations, and government sources.

Vellus received guidance from government agencies that support small-firm exporting. "They provided lots of help and excellent information," Doherty said. Because she's done her homework, it's no wonder Vellus continues to flourish. The firm has a wide range of clients, from the rich and famous to breeders and individual pet owners around the world. The president of the United Arab Emirates is a regular customer; his stables buy Vellus products for his horses twice a year.

To date, Vellus has sold its products in more than thirty countries, including Australia, Canada, China, England, Finland, New Zealand, Norway, Singapore, South Africa, and Sweden. Roughly half the firm's revenues come from exports. All told, more than 300 breeds of pampered pooches are strutting their stuff with the help of Vellus Products. Management has registered the firm's trademark in fifteen countries and looks to expand export sales.

SOURCES: Sharon Doherty, "Greetings from Vellus U.S.A," *Sharon Kay's Notes*, Winter 2011–2012, retrieved from www.vellus.com; J. Judy, "Worldwise Women," *Small Business News*, July 1, 1998, p. 21; S. Pavilkey, "Pet Product Maker Gives International Clients Royal Treatment," *Business First*, January 19, 2001, p. A20; C. Cultice, "Best in Show: Vellus Products," *World Trade*, January 2007, p. 70; company Web site at http://www.vellus.com; H. Shoemack and P. Rath, *Essentials of Exporting and Importing* (New York: Fairchild Publications, 2009).

The vast majority of economic activity takes place outside the home country, and thus it makes sense for firms to engage in international business. Internationalization helps companies grow and become more competitive. The opening story on Vellus Products, paints a picture of a typical young firm that wants to expand abroad. When management at Vellus and other firms decides to internationalize, it must choose the most appropriate entry strategy. Such strategies range from global sourcing, exporting, and licensing, to joint ventures and foreign direct investment. Young companies like Vellus prefer exporting because it is generally the simplest approach, and provides many advantages.

This chapter has two major goals: to summarize foreign entry strategies and to provide a detailed overview on exporting. We examine the advantages and disadvantages of exporting, and the steps that experienced firms follow to ensure success. We explore the nature of export intermediaries and examine the various methods that buyers use to pay for imported goods. Initially, we summarize the various entry strategies and the characteristics of internationalization.

 ## An Overview of Foreign Market Entry Strategies

Importing or global sourcing
The procurement of products or services from independent suppliers or company-owned subsidiaries located abroad for consumption in the home country or a third country.

The choice of entry strategy is one of the key decisions that management makes in international business. Let's review the options. Recall Chapter 3, where we discussed three categories of internationalization strategies for the focal firm:

1. *Trade of products and services* are generally *home-based* international exchange activities, such as *global sourcing, exporting,* and *countertrade*. **Importing** or **global sourcing**, also known as *global procurement*, or global purchasing, is the strategy of buying products and services from foreign sources and bringing them into the home country or a third country.

While sourcing and importing represent an inbound flow, exporting represents *outbound* international business. Thus, **exporting** refers to the strategy of producing products or services in one country (often the producer's home country) and selling and distributing them to customers located in other countries. In both global sourcing and exporting, the firm manages its international operations largely from the home country. We address global sourcing in Chapter 17. **Countertrade** refers to an international business transaction in which full or partial payments are made in kind rather than cash. That is, instead of receiving money as payment for exported products, the firm receives other products or commodities.

2. *Equity or ownership-based international business activities* typically are *foreign direct investment (FDI)* and equity-based *collaborative ventures.* In contrast to home-based international operations, here the firm establishes a presence in the foreign market by investing capital in and securing ownership of a factory, subsidiary, or other facility there. Collaborative ventures include joint ventures in which the firm makes similar equity investments abroad, but in partnership with another company. We discuss FDI and collaborative ventures in Chapter 15.

3. *Contractual relationships* usually take the form of *licensing* and *franchising*, in which the firm allows a foreign partner to use its intellectual property in return for royalties or other compensation. Firms such as McDonalds, Dunkin Donuts, and Century 21 Real Estate use franchising to serve customers abroad. We discuss contractual strategies for foreign market entry in Chapter 16.

Each foreign market entry strategy has advantages and disadvantages, and each places specific demands on the firm's managerial and financial resources. Exporting, licensing, and franchising require a relatively low level of managerial commitment and dedicated resources. By contrast, FDI and equity-based collaborative ventures necessitate a high level of commitment and resources.

Exporting
The strategy of producing products or services in one country (often the producer's home country), and selling and distributing them to customers located in other countries.

Countertrade
An international business transaction where all or partial payments are made in kind rather than cash.

When contemplating international expansion, firms often struggle to decide which entry strategy is best. Experienced managers consider the following factors:

- *Goals* and *objectives* of the firm, such as desired profitability, market share, or competitive positioning
- The degree of *control* the firm desires over the decisions, operations, and strategic assets involved in the venture
- The specific financial, organizational, and technological *resources* and *capabilities* available to the firm (for example, capital, managers, technology)
- The degree of *risk* that management can tolerate in each proposed foreign venture, relative to the firm's goals
- The *characteristics of the product or service* to be offered
- *Conditions in the target country*, such as legal, cultural, and economic circumstances, and the nature of business infrastructure, such as distribution and transportation systems
- The nature and extent of *competition* from existing rivals and from firms that may enter the market later
- The availability and capabilities of *partners* in the market
- The *value-adding activities* the firm is willing to perform itself in the market and what activities it will leave to partners
- The long-term *strategic importance* of the market

While all these factors are relevant, perhaps none is more critical than the degree of control the firm wants to maintain over the venture. *Control* is the ability to influence the decisions, operations, and strategic resources involved in the foreign venture. Without control, the focal firm tends to experience difficulty in carrying out strategy, coordinating actions, and resolving disputes that often arise when two pursue their own interests.[1]

EXHIBIT 14.1

A Classification of Foreign Market Entry Strategies Based on Levels of Control, Resource Commitment, Flexibility, and Risk

Exhibit 14.1 illustrates another useful way to organize foreign market entry strategies based on the degree of control each strategy affords the focal firm over foreign operations.

On the continuum of control in Exhibit 14.1, the arm's-length buyer-seller relationships of exporting represent little or no control at one extreme, while FDI, through a wholly owned subsidiary, represents maximum control at the other extreme.

- *Low-control strategies* are exporting, countertrade, and global sourcing. They provide the least control over foreign operations, because the focal firm delegates considerable responsibility to foreign partners, such as distributors or suppliers.
- *Moderate-control strategies* are contractual relationships such as licensing and franchising and project-based collaborative ventures.
- *High-control strategies* are equity joint ventures and FDI. The focal firm attains maximum control by establishing a physical presence, and ownership of key assets, in the foreign market.

The arrangement of entry strategies in Exhibit 14.1 also highlights trade-offs that the focal firm faces when entering foreign markets. In particular, high-control strategies such as FDI imply the firm must:

- Make substantial *resource commitments*; FDI is costly.
- Establish a relatively permanent base in the market, which limits *flexibility* to reconfigure operations there as market and company conditions evolve over time.
- Endure increased *risk* due to uncertainty in the political and customer environments. Especially important are political risk, cultural risk, and currency risk, which we discussed earlier.

In addition to control, the specific characteristics of the product or service, such as fragility, perishability, and ratio of value to weight, can strongly influence the choice of entry strategy. For example, products with a low value/weight ratio (such as tires and beverages) are expensive to ship long distances, suggesting the firm should internationalize through a strategy other than exporting. Similarly, fragile or perishable goods (such as glass and fresh fruit) may be expensive or impractical to ship long distances because they require special handling or refrigeration. Complex products (such as copy machines and industrial machinery) require significant technical support and after-sales service, which necessitate a substantial presence in the foreign market, often via FDI.

Characteristics of Internationalization

Let's consider the nature and characteristics of firm internationalization.

Diverse Motives for Pursuing Internationalization

When selecting an entry mode, management must identify the firm's underlying motivation for venturing abroad.[2] Some motivations are *reactive* and others *proactive*. For example, following major customers abroad is a reactive move. When large automakers such as Ford or Toyota set up manufacturing in foreign countries, their suppliers, such as Denso and Lear, generally follow them abroad. In contrast, seeking high-growth markets abroad or preempting a competitor in its home market are proactive moves. Companies such as Vellus, discussed in the opening story, are pulled into international markets because of the unique appeal of their products. MNEs such as HP, Nestlé, IKEA, and Union Bank of Switzerland may venture abroad to enhance various competitive advantages, learn from foreign rivals, or acquire ideas about new products.

The motives of companies that undertake exporting, licensing, or franchising are usually straightforward. In most cases, management aims to maximize profits from investments the firm has made in products, services, and know-how by seeking greater unit sales and increasing market share in foreign markets. When such firms as Intel (computer technology) and Subway (restaurants) internationalize, they are essentially exploiting their competitive assets in a broader geographic space.

In contrast, FDI and collaborative ventures usually involve more complex motivations. They pose greater risks and require careful consideration of the likely costs and benefits of internationalization. For example, the Swedish appliance maker Electrolux (www.electrolux.com) has built assembly operations in such diverse markets as Hungary, Mexico, and Thailand. Home appliances represent a complex global industry in which profit margins are tight and competition is intense. By undertaking product development, manufacturing, supply-chain coordination, and workforce management in relatively risky markets, Electrolux has assumed formidable challenges.[3]

The Nature of Internationalization

We can identify certain patterns and characteristics associated with the process of international expansion:[4]

1. *Push and pull factors serve as initial triggers.* Typically a combination of triggers, internal to the firm and in its external environment, is responsible for initial international expansion. *Push factors* include unfavorable trends in the domestic market that compel firms to explore opportunities beyond national borders, such as declining demand, growing competition at home, and arrival at the mature phase in a product's life cycle. *Pull factors* are favorable conditions in foreign markets that make international expansion attractive, such as the potential for faster growth and higher profits, foreign government incentives, or increased opportunities to learn from competitors.

2. *Initial international expansion can be accidental or unplanned.* DLP, Inc., a manufacturer of medical devices for open-heart surgery, made its first major sale to foreign customers that its managers met at a trade fair. Without any deliberate plans, DLP got started in international business from its founding. Vellus Products, the firm in the opening story, started exporting because a foreign distributor decided to showcase the firm's products at a dog show in Taiwan.

3. *Risk and return must be balanced.* Managers weigh the potential profits, revenues, and goal achievement of internationalization against the investment of money, time, and other company resources. Because of higher costs and greater complexity, international ventures often take much time to become profitable. Managers' risk-taking preferences determine the firm's initial investments and its tolerance for delayed returns. Risk-averse managers prefer entering safe markets using conservative entry strategies. They usually

Source: Tracy Morgan/Dorling Kindersley

Vellus Products Inc. is a U.S.-based producer of grooming products for dogs, and exports to countries worldwide. It is one of many small and medium-sized enterprises that find success by internationalizing their unique products.

target markets with a culture and language similar to the home country. For example, a risk-averse U.S. firm would favor Canada over China. A risk-averse British firm would prefer Australia over Saudi Arabia.

4. *Internationalization is an ongoing learning experience.* By interacting in various national environments, the firm encounters numerous opportunities to learn and improve its business methods. Internationalization exposes managers to new ideas and valuable lessons that they can apply to the home market and to other foreign markets.[5] For example, when developing fuel-efficient automobiles for the United States, General Motors (GM) turned to its European operations, where it had been marketing smaller cars for some years. GM leveraged ideas it had acquired in Europe to develop fuel-saving cars for the U.S. market.

5. *Firms may evolve through stages of internationalization.* Historically, most companies opted for a gradual, incremental approach to international expansion. Even today, most firms internationalize in stages, employing relatively simple and low-risk strategies early on and progressing to more complex strategies as they gain experience and knowledge. Exhibit 14.2 illustrates the typical firm's internationalization stages and the justifications for each. Initially, management focuses on only the home market. As it begins to internationalize, the firm targets low-risk, culturally close markets, using simple entry strategies such as exporting or licensing. With growing experience and competence, the firm targets increasingly complex markets, using more challenging entry strategies such as FDI and collaborative ventures.

While companies generally follow the pattern described in Exhibit 14.2 when expanding abroad, today *born global* firms internationalize much earlier than companies did in the past. Born globals reach a stage of active engagement in international business within the first few years of their founding.

Stages of internationalization	Critical management activity or orientation	How the firm behaves
Domestic market focus	Exploit home market opportunities	Firm operates only in its home market due to limited resources or lack of motivation
Pre-internationalization stage	Research and evaluate the feasibility of undertaking international business activity	*Typical triggers from outside the firm:* • The firm receives unsolicited orders from foreign customers. • The firm is contacted by change agents (such as distributors), who want to represent it abroad. *Typical triggers from inside the firm:* • Managers seek to increase the firm's profits or other advantages. • Managers are proactive about international expansion.
Experimental involvement	Initiate limited international business activity, typically through exporting	• Managers consider foreign market opportunities attractive.
Active involvement	Explore international expansion, including entry strategies other than exporting	• Managers' accumulated experience reinforces expectations about the benefits of international business. • Managers commit further resources to international expansion. • Managers dedicate more resources to expand into new foreign markets.
Committed involvement	Allocate resources based on international opportunities	• The firm performs well in various international ventures. • The firm overcomes barriers to doing international business.

EXHIBIT 14.2

Typical Stages in Firm Internationalization

Source: Based on S. Tamer Cavusgil (1980) "On the Internationalization Process of Firms," *European Research* 8 (6): 273–281.

Exporting as a Foreign Market Entry Strategy

Because it entails limited risk, expense, and knowledge of foreign markets and transactions, most companies prefer exporting as their primary foreign market entry strategy. Typically, the focal firm retains its manufacturing activities in its home market but conducts marketing, distribution, and customer service activities in the export market, either itself or through an independent distributor or agent.

Source: Andrew Gentry/ Fotolia

Exporting is the entry strategy responsible for global trade and generates enormous earnings. Airbus is Europe's leading exporter of commercial aircraft. This Airbus jet is parked at the airport in Las Vegas, United States.

Exporting and the Global Economy

Exporting is the entry strategy responsible for the massive inflows and outflows that constitute global trade. Exporting generates enormous foreign-exchange earnings for nations. Japan has benefited from export earnings for years. China has become the leading exporter in various sectors, providing huge revenues to its economy. Smaller economies such as Belgium and Finland also add much to their foreign-exchange reserves from exporting and use them to pay for their sizable imports of foreign goods.

When government agencies cite statistics on trade deficits, trade surpluses, and the volume of merchandise trade for individual countries, these data generally refer to firms' collective exporting and importing activities. For example, the United States is the primary export market for Canadian goods and accounts for some three-quarters of Canadian exports each year. Two-way trade between Canada and the United States represents the world's largest bilateral trading relationship. China recently surpassed Europe, Japan, and the United States to become the world's top exporter of information technology (IT) products. The speed of China's ascent has been startling. Nearly all major Western IT firms have located substantial hardware production in China, mainly because of its low-cost manufacturing and capable factory workers. China's success has occurred largely at the expense of the United States, from which direct IT exports have declined substantially in recent years.[6]

Exporting: A Popular Entry Strategy

Exporting is a common entry strategy even among firms that have extensive international operations. Some of the largest exporters in the United States include aircraft manufacturers Boeing and Lockheed Martin Aero. Big trading companies that deal in commodities, such as Cargill and Marubeni, are also large-scale exporters. Large manufacturing firms typically account for the largest overall value of exports and make up about three-quarters of the total value of exports from the United States. However, the vast majority of exporting firms—more than 90 percent in most countries—are small and medium-sized enterprises (SMEs) with fewer than 500 employees.

As an entry strategy, exporting is very flexible. The exporter can both enter and withdraw from markets fairly easily, with minimal risk and expense. Firms employ exporting repeatedly during the internationalization process, generally at the early stages and again from production facilities that the firm eventually establishes at various foreign locations, destined for markets in other countries. Experienced international firms usually export in combination with other strategies, such as joint ventures and FDI. Toyota has used FDI to build factories in key locations in Asia, Europe, and North America from which it exports cars to neighboring countries and regions.

The volume of world exports has grown enormously.[7] As revealed in Exhibit 14.3, various manufacturing industries, and firms in those industries, depend heavily on international trade. The analysis is limited to large, publicly traded manufacturing companies in the United States. The data represent international sales from both the headquarters country and the firm's foreign subsidiaries. The exhibit suggests that firms in industries such as computers, chemicals, and medical equipment are more dependent on international sales than firms in electrical equipment, publishing, and autos. What are the common features of the most geographically diversified industries? Many are high value-added, high-technology industries subject to the forces of globalization.

EXHIBIT 14.3 **Typical International Sales Intensity of Various United States–Based Industries**

Industry	Average International Sales in the Industry (as percentage of total sales)	Example of a Leading Firm in the Industry	Example Firm's International Sales (as percentage of total sales)
Computers & other electronic products	60%	Fairchild Semiconductor International Inc.	92%
Chemicals	44	OM Group Inc.	84
Medical instruments & equipment	42	Bio-Rad Laboratories Inc.	66
Motor vehicle parts	42	TRW Automotive Holdings Corp.	70
Communications equipment	40	3Com Corp.	90
Pharmaceuticals	37	Merck & Co.	70
Aerospace & defense	36	Boeing Corp.	39
Food	32	Chiquita Brands International Inc.	41
Plastics	32	Tupperware Corp.	73
Apparel	31	Nike Inc.	66
Beverages	30	Coca-Cola Co.	75
Electrical equipment & appliances	28	Exide Technologies	61
Publishing & printing (including software)	27	Oracle Corp.	56
Motor vehicles	26	Paccar Inc.	68

Sources: Based on *Industry Week*, http://www.industryweek.com, Industry Week 500; Hoovers corporate profiles at http://www.hoovers.com.

Service Sector Exports

In most advanced economies, services are the largest component of economic activity. Services marketed abroad include travel, construction, engineering, education, banking, insurance, and entertainment. Hollywood film studios earn billions by exporting their movies and videos. Construction firms send their employees abroad to work on major construction projects. Accountants and engineers often provide their services via the Internet, by telephone and mail, and by visiting customers directly in their home countries. Insurance packages can be created in a central location, such as London, and then exported via mail and the Internet to customers in other countries. The U.S. firm PMI Mortgage Insurance Co. exports mortgage insurance packages to various foreign markets and enjoys considerable success in Asia and various European countries.[8]

However, many *pure* services cannot be exported because they cannot be transported. You cannot box up a haircut and ship it overseas. Most retailing firms, such as Carrefour and Marks & Spencer, offer their services by establishing retail stores in their target markets—that is, they internationalize via FDI because retailing requires direct contact with customers. Many services firms can export *some* of what they produce but rely on other entry strategies to provide other offerings abroad. For example, while Ernst & Young (www.ey.com) can export *some* accounting services by sending its employees abroad, in other cases it will establish a physical presence abroad by setting up an office and hiring local personnel to perform local accounting services.

International travel usually counts as a service export. For example, when a Chinese tourist visits the United States or when a foreign student pays tuition at your university, it is considered a services "export" in official statistics. When patients visit India to undergo surgery—a trend known as "medical tourism"—it is counted as exporting in India's national accounts. In France and the United States, tourism generates more foreign exchange than exports of most categories of merchandise.[9] Such exports imply the customer travels internationally to consume some service located abroad.

However, most services are delivered to foreign customers either through local representatives or agents or in conjunction with other entry strategies such as FDI, franchising, or licensing. The Internet provides the means to export some types of services, from airline tickets to architectural services, helping to make the service sector one of the fastest-growing areas of exports in international business.[10]

Services can also promote and maintain product exports, many of which would not take place without their support. Few people would buy a car if there were no repair services available to maintain it. Thus, firms that export cars must also provide a means for the vehicles to be repaired in the recipient countries. They establish customer service facilities in target markets through FDI, or they contract with local shops to provide such services.

Advantages and Disadvantages of Exporting

The low-cost, low-risk nature of exporting, combined with the ability to leverage foreign partners, makes it especially suitable for SMEs. In the $1 billion U.S. wine export industry, small California wineries sell nearly 20 percent of their total output abroad. They also face the challenge at home of imports from cost-effective wine-producing countries such as Chile and South Africa.[11] The *Global Trend* feature describes how SMEs are increasingly active in exporting.

Advantages of Exporting

- Increase overall sales volume, improve market share, and generate profit margins that are often more favorable than in the domestic market
- Increase economies of scale, reducing per-unit costs of manufacturing
- Diversify customer base, reducing dependence on home markets
- Stabilize fluctuations in sales associated with economic cycles or seasonality of demand
- Minimize the cost of foreign market entry; the firm can use exporting to test new markets before committing greater resources through FDI
- Minimize risk and maximize flexibility, compared to other entry strategies
- Leverage the capabilities of foreign distributors and other business partners located abroad

 GLOBAL TREND

The Emergence of SME Exporters

The role of small and medium-sized enterprises (SMEs) in exporting continues to grow. SME exporters tend to grow faster, increase employment faster, and pay higher wages than nonexporting SMEs. Not only do SMEs export directly, many also export indirectly through wholesalers, and as producers of intermediate goods and services inputs to other exporting firms. Direct and indirect exports by SMEs support many millions of jobs. In the United States, SMEs account for more than 40 percent of the total value-added of U.S. exports of goods and services. Many SMEs are wholesalers, distributors, and other nonmanufacturing firms.

Australia, Canada, China, New Zealand, the United Kingdom, and the United States have undertaken aggressive campaigns to help more SMEs become exporters. Governments sponsor trade fairs and trade missions that connect SMEs with distributors and other facilitators in promising foreign markets. The World Bank assists SME exporters from emerging markets by increasing access to capital and developing their

international business skills. While most SMEs export to advanced economies, an increasing number also target emerging markets. These firms do not necessarily require large markets since they tend to cater to smaller niches.

E.J. Ajax is a small manufacturer of complex metal stampings (three-dimensional metal parts for assembling cars, appliances, and machinery). Looking to expand its export sales, the firm established relationships with distributors in Mexico, China, and Saudi Arabia. Another SME, Optical Xport, exports optical lenses and frames to customers in West and Central Africa from its low-cost manufacturing base in Senegal. These efforts increase the flow of medical supplies and eyeglasses to the poor in Africa and Latin America.

Certain advantages differentiate SMEs from larger and more experienced firms:

- *Flexibility*—the ability to rapidly adapt to foreign market opportunities.
- *Quick response*—faster decision making and implementation of new operating methods.

- *Customization*—the ability to customize products to foreign buyers, with greater ease and smaller production runs.
- *Risk taking*—an entrepreneurial spirit, high-growth aspirations, and a strong determination to succeed.

SMEs leverage such advantages in markets worldwide. They benefit numerous emerging markets, which typically lack access to numerous products and services.

Sources: Igor Filatotchev, Xiaohui Liu, Trevor Buck, and Mike Wright, "The Export Orientation and Export Performance of High-Technology SMEs in Emerging Markets," *Journal of International Business Studies* 40, no. 6 (2009): 1005–1022; Kent Neupert, C. Christopher Baughn, and T. Dao, "SME Exporting Challenges in Transitional and Developed Economies," *Journal of Small Business and Enterprise Development* 13, no. 4 (2006): 535–544; Wagner Kamakura, Julio Ramón-Jerónimo, and Julio Gravel, "A Dynamic Perspective to the Internationalization of Small-Medium Enterprises," *Journal of the Academy of Marketing Science* 40, no. 2 (2012): 236–251; K. Thuermer, "Small Business Takes to Export," *World Trade* 21, no. 12 (2008): 40–43.

Disadvantages of Exporting

- Exporting offers fewer opportunities to learn about customers, competitors, and other unique aspects of the foreign market because the firm does not establish a physical presence there (in contrast to FDI).
- With exporting, the firm must acquire and dedicate capabilities to conduct complex transactions, which can strain organizational resources. Exporters must become proficient in international sales contracts and transactions, new financing methods, and logistics and documentation.
- Exporting exposes the firm to tariffs and other trade barriers, as well as fluctuations in exchange rates. Exporters can be priced out of foreign markets if shifting exchange rates make their products too costly to foreign buyers. For example, the U.S. dollar lost 10 percent in value against the Japanese yen in 2010–2011. As the yen became more expensive in dollar terms, U.S. buyers reduced their imports of Japanese goods.

A Systematic Approach to Exporting

Experienced managers use a systematic approach to successful exporting by assessing potential markets, organizing the firm to undertake exporting, acquiring appropriate skills and competencies, and implementing export operations. Exhibit 14.4 highlights the steps in this process. Let's examine each in detail.

STEP ONE: ASSESS GLOBAL MARKET OPPORTUNITY As a first step, management assesses the various global market opportunities available to the firm. It analyzes the readiness of the firm and its products to carry out exporting, screens for the most attractive export markets, identifies qualified intermediaries and other foreign business partners, and estimates industry market potential and company sales potential. Managers often visit the most promising countries to deepen their understanding of them. Participating in foreign trade shows and trade missions is useful for identifying market potential and foreign intermediaries. We explained Global Market Opportunity Assessment (GMOA) in detail in Chapter 13.

STEP TWO: ORGANIZE FOR EXPORTING Next, managers ask: What types of managerial, financial, and productive resources should the firm commit to the export venture? What timetable should the firm follow to achieve exporting goals? To what degree should the firm rely on domestic and foreign intermediaries to implement exporting?

Exhibit 14.5 illustrates alternative organizational arrangements in exporting. **Indirect exporting** is accomplished by contracting with intermediaries located in the firm's home market. Smaller exporters, or those new to international business, typically hire an export management company

Indirect exporting
Exporting that is accomplished by contracting with intermediaries located in the firm's home market.

EXHIBIT 14.4

A Systematic Approach to Exporting

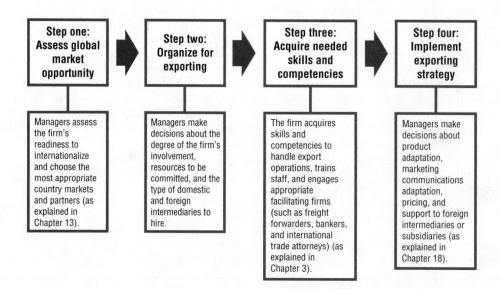

Step one: Assess global market opportunity	Step two: Organize for exporting	Step three: Acquire needed skills and competencies	Step four: Implement exporting strategy
Managers assess the firm's readiness to internationalize and choose the most appropriate country markets and partners (as explained in Chapter 13).	Managers make decisions about the degree of the firm's involvement, resources to be committed, and the type of domestic and foreign intermediaries to hire.	The firm acquires skills and competencies to handle export operations, trains staff, and engages appropriate facilitating firms (such as freight forwarders, bankers, and international trade attorneys) (as explained in Chapter 3).	Managers make decisions about product adaptation, marketing communications adaptation, pricing, and support to foreign intermediaries or subsidiaries (as explained in Chapter 18).

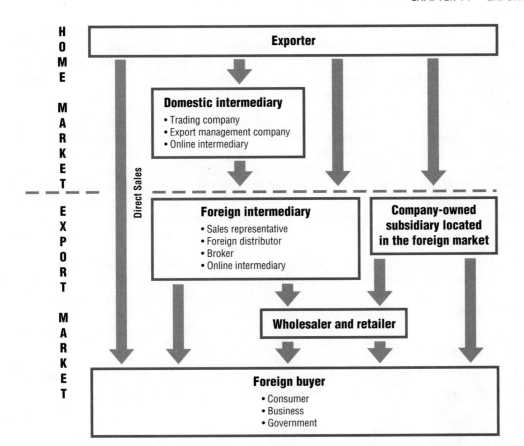

EXHIBIT 14.5

Alternative Organizational Arrangements for Exporting

or a trading company based in their home country. These intermediaries assume responsibility for finding foreign buyers, shipping products, and getting paid. For most firms, indirect exporting's main advantage is the ability to internationalize while avoiding the risks and complexity of direct exporting. The novice firm can start exporting with low startup costs, few risks, and no fixed capital requirements, but with prospects for increasing sales.

In contrast, **direct exporting** is typically achieved by contracting with intermediaries located in the foreign market. The foreign intermediaries serve as an extension of the exporter, negotiating on behalf of the exporter and assuming such responsibilities as local supply-chain management, pricing, and customer service. The main advantage of direct exporting is that it gives the exporter greater control over the export process and potential for higher profits, as well as a closer relationship with foreign buyers and the marketplace. However, the exporter also must dedicate substantial time, personnel, and corporate resources to developing and managing export operations.

Direct and indirect exporting are not mutually exclusive. Many firms use both, but for different markets. Key considerations for choosing between direct or indirect exporting are: (1) the time, capital, and expertise that management is willing to commit; (2) the strategic importance of the foreign market; (3) the nature of the firm's products, including the need for after-sales support; and (4) the availability of capable foreign intermediaries in the target market.

At a more advanced stage, the firm may establish a sales office or a **company-owned subsidiary** in the foreign market to handle marketing, physical distribution, promotion, and customer service activities. Such a subsidiary allows the firm to directly manage major tasks in the market such as attending trade fairs, doing market research, engaging distributors, and finding and serving customers. Companies tend to establish subsidiaries in markets that are large or strategically important. At the extreme, the firm may establish distribution centers and warehouses or a full-function marketing subsidiary staffed with a local sales force. For example, exports of Australia-based Webspy company's (www.webspy.com) Internet software make up 80 percent of the firm's annual revenue. Initially Webspy exported exclusively through independent foreign distributors. Eventually, however, the firm established sales subsidiaries in London and Seattle to serve its two most important regional markets, Europe and North America (www.austrade.gov.au).

Direct exporting
Exporting that is accomplished by contracting with intermediaries located in the foreign market.

Company-owned subsidiary
A representative office of the focal firm that handles marketing, physical distribution, promotion, and customer service activities in the foreign market.

STEP THREE: ACQUIRE NEEDED SKILLS AND COMPETENCIES Export transactions require specialized skills and competencies in areas such as product development, distribution, logistics, finance, contract law, and currency management. Also useful are foreign language skills and the ability to interact well in foreign cultures. Fortunately, numerous facilitators, such as those described in Chapter 3, are available to assist firms that lack specific competencies.

STEP FOUR: EXPORT MANAGEMENT In the final stage, the firm implements and manages its exporting strategy, often requiring management to refine approaches to suit market conditions. *Product adaptation* means modifying a product to make it fit the needs and tastes of the buyers in the target market. When Microsoft markets computer software in Japan, the software must be written in Japanese. Even Vellus, the firm discussed in the opening story, must vary the dog-grooming products it sells abroad due to differing conditions. The dog brushes and shampoos that Vellus sells in the United States may not sell in the United Kingdom, and vice versa. In export markets with many competitors, the exporter needs to adapt its products to gain competitive advantage.

Marketing communications adaptation refers to modifying advertising, selling style, public relations, and promotional activities to suit individual markets. *Price competitiveness* keeps foreign pricing in line with that of competitors. SMEs often lack the resources to compete with larger rivals on pricing. In order to succeed, they compete not by charging low prices, but by emphasizing their products' nonprice benefits, such as quality, reliability, and brand leadership. *Distribution strategy* often hinges on developing strong and mutually beneficial relations with foreign intermediaries.[12] We address details of export marketing strategy in Chapter 18.

Importing

The counterpart of exporting is *importing*, in which the firm chooses to buy products and services from foreign sources and bring them into the home market. The sourcing may be from independent suppliers abroad or from company-owned subsidiaries or affiliates.

Manufacturing firms typically import raw materials and parts, and use them to assemble finished products. Retailers usually obtain a substantial portion of their merchandise from foreign suppliers. In the United States, retailers such as Walmart, Home Depot, Best Buy, and Target are among the largest importers. By itself, Walmart accounts for more than 10 percent of U.S. imports from China, over $30 billion per year. Other large importers include electronics firms such as Philips and food wholesalers including Chiquita.

The fundamentals of exporting, payments, and financing also apply to importing. Exporting and importing collectively refer to *international trade*. Exhibit 14.6 summarizes the top trading partners of selected countries and the European Union (EU), counting their combined imports and exports. The exhibit reveals some interesting patterns. As single countries, Canada and the United States are each others' top trading partners, suggesting that much international trade is regional, rather than global. The chart for Canada reveals its heavy dependence on trade with the United States. China is a top trading partner with the United States, mostly due to its massive merchandise exports. The EU trades most with China and the United States. Overall, the exhibit reveals that most international trade occurs among the advanced economies and increasingly between the advanced economies and emerging markets.

Source: Chris Christoforou/Rough Guides/Dorling Kindersley

China is a major exporter of machinery, furniture, and other goods. El Corte Ingles and other department stores worldwide source much of their apparel and footwear from exporting manufacturers in China.

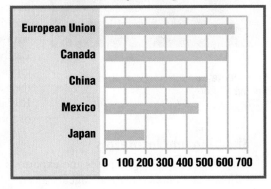

EXHIBIT 14.6

Top Trading Partners of Selected Countries

Note: Values shown represent the sum of merchandise exports and imports in billions of U.S. dollars, in 2011.

Sources: Based on *CIA World Factbook*, at http://www.cia.gov; European Commission, Trade, at http://ec.europa.eu; Industry Canada, at http://www.ic.gc.ca; U.S.–China Business Council, at http://www.uschina.org.

 ## Managing Export-Import Transactions

When comparing domestic and international business transactions, key differences arise in documentation and shipping.

Documentation

Documentation refers to the official forms and other paperwork required in export transactions for shipping and customs procedures. The exporter usually first issues a *quotation* or *pro forma invoice* upon request by potential customers. It informs them about the price and description of the exporter's product or service. The *commercial invoice* is the actual demand for payment issued by the exporter when a sale is made.

Firms typically distribute exported goods by ocean transport, although some use air transport. The *bill of lading* is the basic contract between exporter and shipper. It authorizes a shipping company to transport the goods to the buyer's destination and also serves as the importer's receipt and proof of title for purchase of the goods. The shipper's *export declaration* lists the contact information of the exporter and the buyer (or importer), as well as a full description of the products being shipped. Government authorities use the export declaration to ascertain the content of shipments, control exports, and compile statistics on the goods entering and leaving the country. The *certificate of origin* is the "birth certificate" of the goods being shipped and indicates the country where they originate. Exporters usually purchase an *insurance certificate* to protect the exported goods against damage, loss, pilferage (theft), and, in some cases, delay.

Documentation
Official forms and other paperwork required in export transactions for shipping and customs procedures.

Source: Rolf Richardson/Alamy Images

Export transactions generally ship products through seaports and other maritime facilities, such as the Panama Canal.

The exporter typically entrusts the preparation of documents to an international freight forwarder. As we saw in Chapter 3, freight forwarders are among the key facilitators in international business, functioning like travel agents for cargo. They assist exporters with tactical and procedural aspects of exporting such as logistics, packing, and labeling. They arrange to have exported products cleared through customs and shipped to the buyer.

Another important document is the *license*, a permission to export. National governments sometimes require exporters to obtain a license for reasons of national security and foreign policy. Governments usually don't allow firms to export nuclear materials or harmful biological agents that can be used to create weapons. In addition, some governments impose sanctions on trade with certain countries as part of their foreign policy. Lastly, governments may forbid the export of certain types of essential goods, such as petroleum products, if they are in short supply in the home country. In 2010, Russia halted exports of certain grains, due to a shortage of foodstuffs in the country.

Shipping and Incoterms

International shipping exposes the exporter's products to adverse conditions and handling by various facilitators. Logistics agents ensure the goods arrive in good condition. Most export transactions involve shipping products from the exporter's factory to a nearby seaport or airport, and from there by ship or airplane to a foreign port, to be transferred to land-based transportation and conveyed to the customer. Some shipments to bordering countries are transported entirely overland by rail or truck. Throughout the delivery process the exporter incurs transportation costs and carries insurance against damage or loss during transit.

In the past, disputes sometimes arose over who should pay the cost of freight and insurance in international transactions: the foreign buyer or the seller (that is, the exporter). To eliminate such disputes, a system of universal, standard terms of sale and delivery, known as **Incoterms** (short for "International Commerce Terms"), was developed by the International Chamber of Commerce (www.iccwbo.org). Commonly used in international sales contracts, Incoterms specify how the buyer and the seller share the cost of freight and insurance, and at which point the buyer takes title to the goods. Exhibit 14.7 illustrates the implications of the three most commonly used Incoterms.

Incoterms

Universally accepted terms of sale that specify how the buyer and the seller share the cost of freight and insurance in an international transaction and at which point the buyer takes title to the goods.

 Payment Methods in Exporting and Importing

In the course of business transactions, receiving payment is relatively complicated in international business. Foreign currencies may be unstable, and governments may be reluctant to allow funds to leave the country. In the event of disputes, local laws and enforcement systems may favor local companies over foreign firms. Customers in developing economies often lack payment mechanisms such as credit cards and checking accounts.

In advanced economies and many emerging markets, firms may extend credit to buyers with the assurance they will be paid. It is typical for exporters to allow these customers several months to make payments or to structure payment on *open account*. If payment is not forthcoming, a legal system is usually in place to compel creditors to meet their obligations. In trading with some developing economies, however, exporters extend credit cautiously. They evaluate new customers carefully and may decline a request for credit if the risk is too great.

There are several methods for getting paid in international business. Listed roughly in order from most to least secure, they are: *cash in advance, letter of credit, open account*, and *countertrade*. While the last method, countertrade, can serve as a method of payment in international

EXHIBIT 14.7 Incoterms: Examples of How Transport Obligations, Costs, and Risks Are Shared between the Buyer and the Seller

Incoterms	Definition	Key Points	Arrangement of Shipping
EXW Ex works (named place)	Delivery takes place at the seller's premises or another named place (i.e., works, factory, or warehouse).	EXW represents minimal obligation for the seller; the buyer bears all costs and risks involved in claiming the goods from the seller's premises.	Buyer arranges shipping.
FOB Free on board (named port of shipment)	Delivery takes place when the goods pass the ship's rail at the named port of shipment, the port of origin in the seller's home country.	The buyer bears all the costs and risks of loss or damage upon delivery. The seller clears the goods for export.	Buyer arranges shipping.
CIF Cost, insurance, and freight (named port of destination)	Seller pays the cargo insurance and delivery of goods to the named port of destination. From the destination port, buyer is responsible for customs clearance and other costs and risks.	The seller pays for freight and insurance to transport the goods to the named port of destination. At that point, responsibility for the goods transfers from the seller to the buyer.	Seller arranges shipping and insurance.

Source: Based on International Chamber of Commerce, http://www.iccwbo.org.

transactions, it is also a distinct form of foreign market entry that deserves extensive treatment. We discuss it separately in this chapter. We explain each of the other three payment methods next.

Cash in Advance

When the exporter receives cash in advance, payment is collected before the goods are shipped to the customer. The main advantage is the exporter need not worry about collection problems and can access the funds almost immediately upon concluding the sale. From the buyer's standpoint, however, cash in advance is risky and may cause cash-flow problems. The buyer may hesitate for fear the exporter will not follow through with shipment, particularly if the buyer does not know the exporter well. For these reasons, cash in advance is unpopular with buyers and tends to discourage sales. Exporters who insist on it tend to lose out to competitors who offer more favorable payment terms.

Letter of Credit

A documentary letter of credit, or simply a letter of credit, resolves most of the problems associated with cash in advance. Because it protects the interests of both seller and buyer, it has become the most popular method for getting paid in export transactions. Essentially, a **letter of credit** is a contract between the banks of the buyer and seller that ensures payment from the buyer to the seller upon receipt of an export shipment. It amounts to a substitution of each bank's name and credit for the name and credit of the buyer and seller. The system works because virtually all banks have established relationships with correspondent banks around the world.

Once established, an *irrevocable letter of credit* cannot be canceled without agreement of both buyer and seller. The selling firm will be paid as long as it fulfills its part of the agreement. The letter of credit immediately establishes trust between buyer and seller. Among the countless firms that use it is Pinewood Healthcare (www.pinewood.ie), a pharmaceutical firm. Exports account for 70 percent of Pinewood's sales. When the firm first started exporting to Africa, it sometimes experienced difficulties getting paid. The situation improved greatly when it began contracting sales via letter of credit.[13]

The letter of credit also specifies the documents the exporter is required to present, such as a bill of lading, commercial invoice, and certificate of insurance. Before making a payment, the buyer's bank verifies that all documents meet the requirements the buyer and seller agreed to in the letter of credit. If not, the discrepancy must be resolved before the bank makes the payment.

Letter of credit
Contract between the banks of a buyer and a seller that ensures payment from the buyer to the seller upon receipt of an export shipment.

EXHIBIT 14.8

Letter of Credit Cycle

Exhibit 14.8 presents the typical cycle of an international sale through a letter of credit. As shown in the exhibit:

1. An "Exporter" signs a contract for sale of goods to a foreign buyer, the "Importer."
2. The Importer asks its bank (the "Importer's Bank") to open a letter of credit in favor of the Exporter, the beneficiary of the credit.
3. The Importer's Bank notifies the "Exporter's Bank" that a letter of credit has been issued.
4. The Exporter's Bank confirms the validity of the letter of credit.
5. The Exporter prepares and ships the products to the Importer as specified in the letter of credit.
6. The Exporter presents the shipment documents to its bank, the Exporter's Bank, which examines them to ensure they fully comply with the terms of the letter of credit. The documents typically include an invoice, bill of lading, and insurance certificate, as specified in the letter of credit.
7. The Exporter's Bank sends the documents to the Importer's Bank, which similarly examines them to ensure they comply fully with the letter of credit.
8. Upon confirmation that everything is in order, the Importer's Bank makes full payment for the goods to the Exporter, via the Exporter's Bank.
9. The Importer makes full payment to its bank within the time period granted, which, in many countries, can extend to several months.

A related payment method is the *draft*. Similar to a check, the draft is a financial instrument that instructs a bank to pay a precise amount of a specific currency to the bearer on demand or at a future date. For both letters of credit and drafts, the buyer must make payment upon presentation of documents that convey title to the purchased goods and confirm that specific steps have been taken to prepare the goods and their shipment to the buyer. Letters of credit and drafts can be paid immediately or at a later date. In addition, the exporter can sell any drafts and letters of credit in its possession, to avoid having to wait weeks or months to be paid for its exports.

Open Account

When the exporter uses an *open account*, the buyer pays the exporter at some future time following receipt of the goods, in much the same way a retail customer pays a department store on account for products he or she has purchased. Because of the risk involved, exporters use this approach only with customers of long-standing or excellent credit, or with a subsidiary owned by the exporter. The exporter simply bills the customer, who is expected to pay under agreed terms at some future time. However, in international transactions, open account is risky, and the firm should structure such payment methods with care.

Export-Import Financing

Financing implies the buyer or seller obtains a short-term loan to fulfill an export sale. The ability to finance sales often differentiates successful exporters from other firms. If an SME receives a large order from a foreign buyer, access to the working capital provided from financing can determine the firm's ability to fill the order. The ability to offer attractive payment terms is often necessary to generate sales. If a competitor offers better terms for a similar product, the exporter may lose sales.

The ability of an exporter or importer to obtain financing for export sales is influenced by four key factors:

1. *Creditworthiness of the exporter.* Firms with little collateral or minimal international experience, or large export orders that exceed their manufacturing capacity, may encounter difficulty in obtaining financing from banks and other lenders at reasonable interest rates, or they may not receive financing at all.
2. *Creditworthiness of the importer.* An export sales transaction often hinges on the ability of the buyer to obtain sufficient funds to purchase the goods. Some buyers, particularly from developing economies or countries with currency controls, may be unable to secure financing.
3. *Riskiness of the sale.* Banks are reluctant to loan funds for risky transactions, and international sales are usually more risky than domestic ones. Riskiness is a function of the value and marketability of the good being sold, the extent of uncertainty surrounding the sale, the degree of political and economic stability in the buyer's country, and the likelihood the loan will be repaid. In addition, resource-poor SMEs are considered high risk and often cannot obtain financing.
4. *Timing of the sale.* influences the cost of financing. In international trade, the exporter usually wants to be paid as soon as possible, while the buyer prefers to delay payment, especially until it has received or resold the goods. Banks and other financial institutions may hesitate to finance a sale if the time to complete it is considerable.

Creditworthiness, risk, and timing also affect the cost of financing, which in turn affects the pricing and profitability of sales and the payment terms the exporter can offer. Fortunately, there are various sources for financing international sales, which we discuss next.

Commercial Banks

The same commercial banks that finance domestic activities can often finance export sales. A logical first step for the exporter is to approach the local commercial bank with which it already does business, or a commercial bank with an international department that is familiar with exporting and may also provide international banking services such as letters of credit. Another option is to have the bank make a loan directly to the foreign buyer to finance the sale.

Factoring, Forfaiting, and Confirming

Factoring is the discounting of a foreign account receivable by transferring title of the sold item and its account receivable to a factoring house (an organization that specializes in purchasing accounts receivable) for cash at a discount from the face value. *Forfaiting* is the selling, at a discount, of long-term accounts receivable of the seller or promissory notes of the foreign buyer. Numerous forfaiting houses specialize in this practice. *Confirming* is a financial service in which an independent company confirms an export order in the seller's country and makes payment for the goods in that country's currency.

Distribution Channel Intermediaries

In addition to acting as export representatives, many intermediaries such as trading and export management companies provide short-term financing or simply purchase exported goods directly from the manufacturer, eliminating the need for financing and any risks associated with the export transaction.

Buyers and Suppliers

Foreign buyers of expensive products often make down payments that reduce the need for financing from other sources. In addition, buyers may make incremental payments as production of the goods or project is completed. Some industries use letters of credit that allow for progress payments upon inspection by the buyer's agent or receipt of a statement by the exporter that a certain percentage of the product has been completed. In addition, vendors from whom the exporter buys input goods or supplies may be willing to offer more favorable payment terms to the exporter if they are confident they will receive payment.

Intracorporate Financing

Large multinational enterprises with foreign subsidiaries have many more options for financing exports. The MNE may allow its subsidiary to retain a higher-than-usual level of its own profits in order to finance export sales. The parent firm may provide loans, equity investments, and trade credit (such as extensions on accounts payable) as funding for the international selling activities of its subsidiaries. The parent can also guarantee loans obtained from foreign banks by its subsidiaries. Finally, large MNEs can often access equity financing by selling corporate bonds or shares in stock markets.

Government Assistance Programs

Numerous government agencies offer programs to assist exporters with their financing needs. Some provide loans or grants to the exporter, while others offer guarantee programs that require the participation of a bank or other approved lender. Under such arrangements, the government pledges to repay a loan made by a commercial bank in the event the importer is unable to repay.

In the United States, the *Export-Import Bank* (Ex-Im Bank; www.exim.gov) is a government agency that issues credit insurance to protect firms against default on exports sold under short-term credit. Canada's Export Development Corporation (www.edc.ca), India's Export Credit & Guarantee Corporation (www.ecgc.in), and Argentina's Compania Argentina de Seguros de Credito (www.casce.com.ar) provide services similar to those of the Ex-Im Bank. Government assistance programs are especially useful to SMEs, which often cannot obtain financing from other sources. For example, the U.S. Small Business Administration (www.sba.gov) helps small exporters obtain trade financing.

Multilateral Development Banks (MDBs)

Multilateral development banks (MDBs)
International financial institutions owned by multiple governments within world regions or other groups.

Multilateral development banks (MDBs) are international financial institutions owned by multiple governments within world regions or other groups. Their individual and collective objective is to promote economic and social progress in their member countries, many of which are developing countries. MDBs include the African Development Bank (www.afdb.org), the Asian Development Bank (www.adb.org), the European Bank for Reconstruction and Development (www.ebrd.com), the Inter-American Development Bank (www.iadb.org), and the World Bank Group (www.worldbank.org). These institutions fulfill their missions by providing loans, technical cooperation, grants, capital investment, and other types of assistance to governments and agencies in the member countries.

 Identifying and Working with Foreign Intermediaries

As the opening story emphasizes, success in exporting usually depends on establishing strong relationships with distributors, sales representatives, and other foreign market intermediaries. Direct exporters often struggle to find appropriate intermediaries in target countries. Various sources are available for finding intermediaries abroad, including:

- Country and regional business directories, such as Kompass (Europe), Bottin International (worldwide), Nordisk Handelskelander (Scandinavia), and the Japanese Trade Directory. Other directories include: Dun and Bradstreet, Reuben H. Donnelly, Kelly's Directory, and Johnson Publishing, as well as foreign Yellow Pages (often available online).
- Trade associations that support specific industries, such as the National Furniture Manufacturers Association or the National Association of Automotive Parts Manufacturers.

- Government departments, ministries, and agencies charged with assisting economic and trade development, such as Austrade in Australia (www.austrade.gov.au), Export Development Canada (www.edc.ca), and the International Trade Administration of the U.S. Department of Commerce (www.trade.gov).
- Commercial attachés in embassies and consulates abroad.
- Branch offices of certain foreign government agencies located in the exporter's country, such as JETRO, the Japan External Trade Organization (www.jetro.org).
- Freight forwarders and trade consultants with specific knowledge about the exporter's target markets.

The exporter should consider attending a trade fair in the target country. Trade fairs are not only excellent sites to meet potential intermediaries, they also provide the means to become familiar with key players in the local industry and to generally learn about the target market. Visiting the target market is often the best way to identify and qualify intermediaries. On-site visits afford managers direct exposure to the market and opportunities to meet prospective intermediaries. Managers can also inspect the facilities as well as gauge the capabilities, technical personnel, and sales capabilities of prospective intermediaries. Once they have narrowed the choices, experienced exporters often request prospective intermediaries to prepare a business plan for the proposed venture. Its quality and sophistication provide a basis for judging the candidate's true capabilities.

Working with Foreign Intermediaries

In exporting, the most typical intermediary is the foreign-based independent distributor. The exporter relies on the distributor for much of the marketing, physical distribution, and customer service activities in the export market and greatly depends on his or her capabilities. Experienced exporters go to great lengths to build relational assets—that is, high-quality, enduring business and social relationships – with key intermediaries and facilitators abroad. Sharon Doherty (in the opening story) succeeded in exporting by developing close relationships with qualified foreign distributors. While competitors can usually replicate the exporter's other competitive attributes, such as product features or marketing skills, strong ties with competent foreign intermediaries are built over time and provide the exporter with an enduring competitive advantage.

Firms develop relationships with their intermediaries in various ways. They can cultivate mutually beneficial, bonding relationships; genuinely respond to intermediary needs; and build solidarity by demonstrating solid commitment, remaining reliable, and building trust.[14] Capstone Turbine Corporation (www.capstoneturbine.com) is a manufacturer of clean-technology microturbine energy systems. When exporting to a particular country, Capstone initially develops a close working relationship with the country's top importer, which then becomes Capstone's conduit to other companies in the country. The recipe is a success: Capstone now receives two-thirds of its revenues from abroad, much of it from developing economies.[15]

To create a positive working relationship, the exporter should be sensitive to the intermediary's objectives and aspirations. This requires developing a good understanding of the intermediary's needs and working earnestly to address them. In general, foreign intermediaries expect exporters to provide:

- Good, reliable products for which there is a ready market
- Products that provide significant profits
- Opportunities to handle other product lines
- Support for marketing communications, advertising, and product warranties
- A payment method that does not unduly burden the intermediary
- Training for intermediary staff and the opportunity to visit the exporter's facilities (at the exporter's expense) to gain firsthand knowledge of the exporter's operations

Source: LovelaceMedia/Shutterstock

Working closely with foreign intermediaries helps green energy manufacturer Capstone Turbine Corporation earn two-thirds of its revenues from abroad. Using Capstone microturbine technology, hybrid sports cars are fuel efficient and produce almost no exhaust.

- Help establishing after-sales service facilities, including training of local technical representatives and the means to replace defective parts, as well as a ready supply of spare parts, to maintain or repair the products

The exporter in turn has expectations its intermediaries should meet. Exhibit 14.9 summarizes the selection criteria that experienced exporters use to qualify prospective intermediaries.

When Intermediary Relations Go Bad

Despite good intentions, disputes can arise between the exporter and its intermediaries on issues such as:

- Compensation arrangements (e.g., the intermediary may wish to be compensated even if not directly responsible for a sale in its territory)
- Pricing practices
- Advertising and promotion practices and the extent of advertising support
- After-sales service
- Return policies
- Adequate inventory levels
- Incentives for promoting new products
- Adapting the product for local customers

In anticipation of such disagreements, exporters generally establish a contract-based, legal relationship with the partner. Some firms require candidate intermediaries to undergo a probationary period during which they evaluate performance. If it is suboptimal or if disputes appear likely to emerge, the exporter may impose special requirements or even terminate the relationship.

In a typical contract, the exporter binds the intermediary to achieve certain performance objectives and handle the product in a specified manner. The contract clarifies the tasks and

EXHIBIT 14.9 Criteria for Evaluating Export Intermediaries

Intermediary Dimension	Evaluation Criteria
Organizational Strengths	• Ability to finance sales and growth in the market • Ability to provide financing to customers • Management team quality • Reputation with customers • Connections with influential people or government agencies in the market
Product-Related Factors	• Knowledge about the exporter's product • Quality and superiority of all product lines handled by the intermediary • Ability to ensure security for patents and other intellectual property rights • Extent to which intermediary handles competing product lines
Marketing Capabilities	• Experience with the product line and target customers • Extent of geographic coverage provided in the target market • Quality and quantity of sales force • Ability to formulate and implement marketing plans
Managerial Commitment	• Percent of intermediary's business consisting of a single supplier • Willingness to maintain inventory sufficient to fully serve the market • Commitment to achieving exporter's sales targets

Sources: Based on *Business International*, "How to Evaluate Foreign Distributors," pp. 145–149 (May 10, 1985); S. Tamer Cavusgil, Poh-Lin Yeoh, and Michel Mitri, "Selecting Foreign Distributors: An Expert Systems Approach," *Industrial Marketing Management* 24, no. 4(1995): 297–304; International Trade Administration, *Basic Guide to Exporting: The Official Government Resource for Small and Medium-Sized Businesses* (Washington, DC: International Trade Administration, 2011); Franklin Root, *Entry Strategies for International Markets* (Hoboken, NJ: Jossey-Bass, 1983/1998).

responsibilities of both parties, specifies the duration of the relationship, defines the intermediary's sales territory, and explains the dispute resolution and termination processes if, for instance, the intermediary falls short of performance requirements such as sales targets.

Exporters need to ascertain the legal requirements for termination in advance and specify the intermediary's rights for compensation. In many countries, commercial regulations favor local intermediaries and may require the exporter to indemnify—that is, compensate—the intermediary even if there is just cause for termination. In some countries, legal contracts may prove insufficient to protect the exporter's interests. Many countries in Africa and Latin America lack strong legal frameworks, which can make contracts hard to enforce.

Just as in their domestic operations, exporters occasionally encounter problems with buyers or intermediaries who default on payment. As a rule, problems with bad debt are easier to avoid than to correct after they occur. Before entering an agreement, the exporter should perform a credit and other background checks on potential intermediaries and large-scale buyers. In terms of payment mechanisms, cash in advance or a letter of credit is usually best. In addition to ensuring payment, the letter of credit encourages a high degree of trust between buyer and seller. The exporter can also buy insurance from insurance companies specialized in international transactions to cover commercial credit risks.

Some buyers may default on payment. When this happens, the exporter's best recourse is to negotiate with the offending party. With patience, understanding, and flexibility, conflicts often can be resolved to the satisfaction of both sides. If negotiations fail and the cost of termination is substantial, the exporter may need to seek assistance from its bank or attorney. At the extreme, the exporter may pursue litigation, arbitration, or other legal means for enforcing payment on a sale.

Countertrade: A Popular Approach for Emerging Markets and Developing Economies

Countertrade refers to paying for goods or services using other goods or services when conventional means of payment are difficult or unavailable. Similar to barter, countertrade is especially common when dealing with governments is developing economies and emerging markets. Consider Caterpillar, which exported earth-moving equipment to Venezuela. In exchange, the Venezuelan government gave Caterpillar 350,000 tons of iron ore. Middle Eastern countries occasionally pay for imported goods with crude oil, as when Saudi Arabia purchased jets from Boeing.

Exhibit 14.10 illustrates the multiple transactions in countertrade deals. Typically, the focal firm is a Western company, say General Electric (GE), that wishes to sell its products or technology—for example, jet engines—to a developing-country government. When Indonesia's

EXHIBIT 14.10

A Countertrade Transaction Where Products Are Received from the Customer as Partial or Full Payment

government fell short of hard currency, for example, it was unable to pay in cash and asked GE to accept some local products as partial payment.

Typically the products that developing countries offer are commodities (for example, agricultural grains, minerals, or manufactured goods with limited international sales potential). If a firm agrees to take these products, it must arrange to sell them to convert the goods to cash. Compared to conventional transactions in which buyers pay with cash, countertrade is complicated. Multiple transactions can take years to complete.

Philip Morris exported cigarettes to Russia for which it received industrial chemicals as payment. It shipped the chemicals to China and received glassware in exchange that it then sold for cash in North America. As payment for its exports, Coca-Cola at one point received tomato paste from buyers in Turkey and beer from buyers in Poland.

Magnitude and Drivers of Countertrade

Many MNEs have pursued nontraditional trade deals since the 1960s, not only in developing economies but also in the advanced economies. While the full extent of countertrade is unknown, some observers estimate it accounts for as much as one-third of all world trade. Countertrade deals are common in large-scale government procurement projects. In South Korea, for example, countertrade is mandated for government telecommunications and defense procurement exceeding $1 million. In Asia, Indonesia led the way early by requiring countertrade for large-scale public sector purchases. Eastern European nations and Russia have practiced barter and countertrade transactions for many years. Countertrade arises in developing economies mainly because such countries often experience a shortage of hard currencies – for example, U.S. dollars, European euros, or Japanese yen. Firms based in developing economies that want to do international business often need to develop countertrade capabilities.

Types of Countertrade

There are four main types of countertrade: barter, compensation deals, counterpurchase, and buy-back agreements.

Barter—the oldest form of trade—is the direct exchange of goods without any money. Though less common today, barter is still used (even in domestic trade) in straightforward, one-shot deals. It requires a single contract (rather than two or more contracts typical of other forms), has a short time span (other countertrade deals may stretch over several years), and is less complicated (other forms usually require managerial commitment and additional resources).

Compensation deals include payment in both goods and cash. For example, a company may sell its equipment to the government of Brazil and receive half the payment in hard currency and the other half in merchandise.

Counterpurchase, also known as a back-to-back transaction or offset agreement, requires two distinct contracts. In the first, the seller agrees to a set price for goods and receives cash from the buyer. However, this first deal is contingent on a second contract in which the seller also agrees to purchase goods from the buyer (or produce and assemble a certain proportion of goods in the buyer's country) for the same cash amount as the first transaction or a set percentage of it. If the two exchanges are not of equal value, the difference can be paid in cash. Counterpurchase is common in the defense industry, in which a government that buys military hardware might require a foreign defense contractor to purchase some local products or contribute to local employment.

Finally, in a product **buy-back agreement**, the seller agrees to supply technology or equipment to construct a facility and receives payment in the form of goods produced by the facility. For example, the seller might design and build a factory in the buyer's country to manufacture tractors. The seller is compensated by receiving finished tractors from the factory it built, which it then sells in world markets. In essence, the original transaction trades goods and services that produce other goods and services, which are then received in payment. Product buy-back agreements may require several years to complete and therefore entail substantial risk.

Barter
A type of countertrade in which goods are directly exchanged without the transfer of any money.

Compensation deals
A type of countertrade in which payment is in both goods and cash.

Counterpurchase
A type of countertrade with two distinct contracts. In the first, the seller agrees to a set price for goods and receives cash from the buyer. This first deal is contingent on a second in which the seller agrees to purchase goods from the buyer for the same amount as in the first contract or a set percentage of same.

Buy-back agreement
A type of countertrade in which the seller agrees to supply technology or equipment to construct a facility and receives payment in the form of goods produced by the facility.

Risks of Countertrade

Firms can encounter five problems in countertrade.

1. The goods the customer offers may be inferior in quality, with limited sales potential in international markets.
2. Putting a market value on the goods the customer offers may prove difficult, especially if they are commodities or of low quality. In addition, the buyer may not have the opportunity to inspect the goods or analyze their marketability before the sale.
3. The parties to countertrade transactions tend to pad their prices. As a result, the cash the seller receives upon selling received goods may prove less than expected. In a typical scenario, General Electric (GE) will place the products it receives as payment in countertrade (furniture, tomato paste) with a broker who sells them in world markets for a commission. GE builds the cost of disposing of the goods into the price it quotes to the buyer. The buyer, anticipating that GE will quote a price on the high end, will pass the extra cost on to its customers. Thus, the resulting transaction between GE and the buyer is inefficient.
4. Countertrade is usually complex, cumbersome, and time-consuming. Deals are often difficult to bring to conclusion.
5. Government rules can make countertrade highly bureaucratic and often prove frustrating for the exporting firm.

Ethical Connections

The global diamond trade is linked to violence and crime. Profits from the export of "blood diamonds" are often used to finance war and terrorism. In Africa and various countries worldwide, the diamond trade attracts organized crime, corruption, and global terrorist groups. International organizations work to prevent illicit diamond trade, and firms such as De Beers have established guidelines to reduce the bloodshed associated with global trade in the valuable mineral. In some areas, however, the diamond trade continues to fund genocide, slavery, and war.

Why Consider Countertrade?

Although most firms avoid countertrade, there are five reasons to consider it.

1. The alternative may be no trade at all, as in the case of countertrade mandated by national governments.
2. Countertrade can help the firm get a foothold in new markets, leading to new customer relationships. For example, in the mining industry, certain types of minerals are available only in developing economies. Mining rights may be available only to firms willing to countertrade.
3. Many firms use countertrade creatively to develop new sources of supply. The firm can develop new suppliers in the process.
4. Firms have used countertrade as a way to repatriate profits frozen in a foreign subsidiary's blocked accounts. Otherwise unable to access its funds, the firm will scout the local market for products it can successfully export. General Motors' former Motors Trading subsidiary was created to generate trade credits—that is, sell its vehicles in return for contributing to exports of merchandise originating from that country.
5. Some companies seek to develop managers with a trading mentality. Multinational firms such as GM, GE, Siemens, and Toshiba have set up separate divisions to develop global managers who are entrepreneurial, innovative, politically connected, and highly knowledgeable about a range of commodities and tradable goods. These firms recognize the value of such attributes for pursuing international deals and attempt to foster them by engaging their managers in countertrade. Acquired skills contribute to international performance, not only in countertrade deals, but in various other cross-border transactions.

CLOSING CASE Barrett Farm Foods: A Small Firm's International Launch

Philip Austin, general manager of Barrett Farm Foods, was thrilled after returning from the food industry trade fair in Cologne, Germany—the largest food and beverage fair in the world. Barrett Farm Foods, based in Melbourne, Victoria, is Australia's sixth-largest food company. It distributes both bulk agricultural commodities and processed food products. Among others, it sells macadamia nuts, cereal bars, garlic, ginger, dried fruits, and honey throughout Australia. Barrett has had a healthy rate of growth over the past decade, and its sales reached USD $215 million last year. While Barrett is well known in the domestic market, its international experience has been limited to responding to occasional, unsolicited orders from foreign customers. In completing these export orders, Barrett has relied on intermediaries in Australia that provided assistance for international logistics and payments. Yet Austin is enthusiastic about substantially expanding the export business over the next few years.

Recognizing an Opportunity

What prompted Austin to attend the Cologne fair was a report from Austrade, the Australian government's trade promotion agency, which highlighted the potential of Australian foodstuffs exports. According to Austrade, Australian food exports exceeded AU $30 billion last year. Austrade believes processed foodstuffs are the coming trend and wants to boost exports.

But this raises a dilemma: Much of current exports are primarily raw foods, not processed foods. If just 10 percent of processed food value-adding were done in Australia, the country's balance of trade would improve. For example, instead of exporting raw grains to Europe, Austrade wants Australian producers to process the grains into bread and other bakery products, thereby creating jobs for Australians. Austrade believes meat, cereal, sugar, dairy commodities, and marine products have the most potential for food processing.

Meeting with Potential Export Customers at the Cologne Fair

At the Cologne fair, Barrett's nut-and-honey cereal bars and butter-like spread were a hit. Luigi Cairati, a senior executive with the Italian supermarket chain Standa, was keen on doing business with Barrett. He pointed out that, over the past decade, there has been an explosion of interest among European supermarkets for exotic foods and vegetables, with each group competing to display produce from around the world. Standa was seeking new products from other countries, partly to meet off-season demand for fruit and vegetables. Gabrielle Martin, purchasing manager for French food group Fauchon, also confirmed her interest in showcasing exotic and high-quality food in Fauchon stores. She added that Europeans view Australia as exotic and pollution-free and as a producer of quality products. In addition, the market for canned fruit is opening up as the fruit crop from trees in Europe declines over time.

Austin also met Peter Telford, an agent from the United Kingdom who showed interest in representing Barrett in the European Union

(EU). Telford emphasized his knowledge of the market, extensive contacts, and prior business experience. He noted that other Australian firms, such as Burns Philip, Elders-IXL, and Southern Farmers, are already doing business in Europe. He pointed to several success stories, including Sydney-based pastry manufacturer, C & M Antoniou, which established a small plant in Britain to avoid the wall of agricultural duties in the EU market. The company now supplies several British supermarket chains, including Marks & Spencer, Tesco, and Sainsbury's. Another Australian group, Buderim Ginger, expanded its operations from Britain into continental Europe by opening an office in Germany.

Creating a Task Force

After the fair, Austin created a three-person task force among his senior managers and charged them with implementing an export drive. He felt an export volume of USD $30 million for the first year was reasonable. To identify the most promising exports, Barrett would examine its current product offerings. It would appoint an agent, such as Peter Telford, to facilitate EU sales. The people Austin met at the Cologne fair were potential customers to contact for immediate sales. Barrett could also forward some product and company literature to European importers, identify and appoint one or more distributors in Europe that have access to supermarkets and other large-scale buyers, and revamp its Web site to attract export business.

While Barrett senior managers shared Austin's enthusiasm about exporting to Europe, they did not share his optimism. Barrett had little internal expertise to deal with the complexities of international shipping, export documentation, and receiving payments from export customers. In addition, they knew export transactions take time to complete, and the firm would have to arrange for financing of export sales. Most importantly, senior managers felt they would have to invest in creating a small export team and hire or train employees in export operations.

Food is a complex business, in part because it is perishable, often requiring special equipment for distribution. Europe also has many differences in national tastes, regulations, and market structures. While Australians love Vegemite—a brown, salty breakfast spread made from yeast—the product enjoys little popularity outside Australia. With no name recognition in Europe, Barrett may have to resort to store branding, which will generate lower profit margins.

Barrett would have to rely on foreign intermediaries with access to well-known supermarket chains to distribute its products. Is Peter Telford the right choice? What is the appropriate commission structure for compensating intermediaries? With many larger, more experienced competitors in the EU, Barrett must keep its pricing competitive, although the complexity of pricing can overwhelm inexperienced managers. Barrett's senior managers also realize that prices strongly affect sales and profits. The euro, Europe's common currency, simplified pricing strategy, but numerous challenges remain. Prices are affected by transportation costs, buyer demand, exchange rates, tariffs, competitors' pricing, regulatory compliance, and the costs of marketing and physical distribution.

AACSB: Reflective Thinking Skills, Analytic Skills

Case Questions

1. Do you see any problems with Philip Austin's plan for European expansion? Do you support his entrepreneurial approach to exporting? What should be the features of a more systematic approach to exporting?

2. Why did Barrett choose exporting as its entry strategy for Europe, as opposed to foreign direct investment or licensing? What advantages does exporting provide to Barrett? What are the potential drawbacks of exporting for Barrett?

3. What challenges can Barrett expect in its export drive? What types of new capabilities does the firm need to acquire to manage its export transactions?

4. How should Barrett choose between direct and indirect exporting? What are the ideal characteristics of European intermediaries for Barrett? Where can Barrett turn for financing its export sales?

5. There are already numerous companies selling processed foods in Europe. What can Barrett do to compete successfully against these firms?

6. Why does Austrade want Australian firms to focus on exporting processed foods? Why is exporting high value-added products good for Australia?

CHAPTER ESSENTIALS

MyManagementLab

Go to **mymanagementlab.com** to complete the problems marked with this icon ⭐.

Key Terms

barter   374
buy-back agreement   374
company-owned subsidiary   363
compensation deals   374
counterpurchase   374
countertrade   355

direct exporting   363
documentation   365
exporting   355
global sourcing   354
importing   354
Incoterms   366

indirect exporting   362
letter of credit   367
multilateral development banks
    (MDBs)   370

Summary

In this chapter, you learned about:

1. An overview of foreign market entry strategies

Market entry strategies consist of *exporting, sourcing*, and *foreign direct investment*, as well as *licensing, franchising*, and *nonequity alliances*. Each strategy has advantages and disadvantages. To select a strategy, managers must consider the firm's resources and capabilities, conditions in the target country, risks inherent in each venture, competition from existing and potential rivals, and the characteristics of the product or service to be offered in the market. **Importing** is buying products and services from sources located abroad for use at home. It is also called **global sourcing**, global purchasing, or global procurement.

2. Characteristics of internationalization

Firms internationalize due to *push factors* and *pull factors*. Initial internationalization may be unplanned. Management must balance risk against return. Each international venture

provides learning experiences that encourage further internationalization. Firms generally pass through stages of internationalization, going from relatively simple to more complex entry strategies.

3. Exporting as a foreign market entry strategy

Exporting is producing at home and then shipping products abroad, to be sold and delivered to foreign customers via intermediaries. It is the strategy most firms favor when they first internationalize. It is also a relatively flexible entry strategy, allowing the firm to readily withdraw in case of problems in the target market. A systematic approach to exporting requires managers to perform a global market opportunity assessment, make organizational arrangements for exporting, acquire needed skills and competencies, and design and implement the export strategy. Among the organizational arrangements for exporting are **indirect exporting**, **direct exporting**, and establishing a **company-owned subsidiary**.

4. Managing export-import transactions

Management must become familiar with customs clearance, international goods transportation, and **documentation**, the required forms and other paperwork used to conclude international sales. The exporter typically entrusts preparation of documents to a freight forwarder. **Incoterms** are universally accepted terms of sale that effectively specify what is and is not included in the price of a product sold internationally.

5. Payment methods in exporting and importing

Exporting also requires knowledge of payment methods, such as cash in advance, letter of credit, open account, and countertrade. For most firms, **letter of credit** is best because it establishes immediate trust and protects both buyer and seller.

6. Export-import financing

Intense competition in export markets mandates that exporters offer attractive payment terms to their customers. Sources of finance for export transactions include commercial banks; *factoring, forfaiting*, and *confirming*; distribution channel intermediaries; intercompany financing; government assistance programs; and **multilateral development banks**.

7. Identifying and working with foreign intermediaries

Managers can identify intermediaries, such as sales representatives and distributors, from a variety of public and private information sources. It is best to develop long-term relationships with these business partners, who perform a variety of functions abroad on behalf of the exporter, by cultivating mutually beneficial bonds, genuinely responding to distributor needs, and encouraging loyalty.

8. Countertrade: A popular approach for emerging markets and developing economies

Countertrade is an international business transaction in which full or partial payment is made in kind (goods or services) rather than in cash. There are four types of countertrade. **Barter** is the direct exchange of goods without any money. **Compensation deals** include payment in both goods and cash. With **counterpurchase**, the seller agrees to sell its product at a set price and receive cash payment from the buyer. The deal is contingent on a second transaction in which the seller agrees to purchase goods from the buyer for the same amount as the first sale or a set percentage of it. **Buy-back agreements** commit the seller to supply technology or equipment to construct a facility and receive payment in the form of goods produced by the facility.

Test Your Comprehension AACSB: Reflective Thinking Skills

1. What are the major foreign market entry strategies? What are the characteristics of each?

2. What is exporting? What are its advantages and disadvantages?

3. Describe the organizing framework for exporting. What steps should the firm follow to ensure exporting success?

⭐ 4. What are the major tasks involved in managing export transactions?

5. Explain the payment methods that exporters typically use. What is the most reliable payment method, and how do exporters carry it out?

6. What are Incoterms, and why do firms follow them?

⭐ 7. What steps should the exporter take to ensure success in working with intermediaries?

8. Explain the nature, role, and risks involved in countertrade.

Apply Your Understanding AACSB: Communication Abilities, Reflective Thinking Skills, Ethical Understanding and Reasoning Abilities

1. Moose & Walrus (M&W) is a manufacturer of a popular line of clothing for young people. M&W is firmly established in its home market, which is relatively saturated and has little prospects for future sales growth. Top management has decided to export M&W's clothing line to Japan, Turkey, and various European countries. Suppose you are hired by M&W to assist with internationalization. Prepare a briefing for senior managers that describes:
   - The advantages and disadvantages of exporting
   - A systematic approach to exporting
   - A systematic approach to managing export-import transactions
   - Export payment methods

   What factors should M&W consider regarding the possible need to adapt its clothing styles for its target markets?

2. Antenna Communications Technologies, Inc. (ACT) is a small satellite technology communications firm. Its product is a multibeam antenna that allows customers in the broadcast industry to receive signals from up to thirty-five satellites simultaneously. The firm has little international business experience. ACT recently hired you as its export manager and, based on extensive research, you find substantial demand for the product in Africa, China, Russia, and Saudi Arabia. Having followed most of the steps in the organizing framework for exporting, you decide direct exporting is the best entry strategy for ACT. Your next task is to find distributors in the target markets. How will you approach this task? What resources should you access to find distributors in these markets? Once established, what is the best way to maintain solid relations with foreign distributors? Finally, what payment method should ACT use for most of its prospective markets?

3. *Ethical Dilemma:* You are hired by EcoPure Industries, a manufacturer of components for hybrid motor vehicles. EcoPure emphasizes social responsibility in its business dealings and uses three foreign market entry strategies: exporting, joint ventures, and FDI. Exporting implies the sale of products to customers located abroad, usually under contract with foreign intermediaries that organize marketing and distribution activities in local markets. Using joint ventures, EcoPure partners with foreign firms to access their technology, expertise, production factors, or other assets. Using FDI, EcoPure invests funds to establish factories or other subsidiaries overseas. Each of the strategies—exporting, joint venture, and FDI—is vulnerable to particular types of ethical dilemmas, and top management has directed you to identify and describe the most typical ones. Using the Ethical Framework and other material in Chapter 5 as a guide, what types of ethical problems might arise in each type of entry strategy? Which entry strategy most likely gives rise to ethical problems? Be sure to justify your answer.

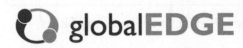

AACSB: Communication Abilities, Reflective Thinking Skills

Refer to Chapter 1, page 24, for instructions on how to access and use globalEDGE™.

1. You work for a firm that manufactures children's toys. Despite little international experience, management wants to start exporting. Your boss understands the importance of using strong distributors abroad but knows little about how to find them. You are aware that many national governments offer programs that help new exporters find intermediaries in foreign countries. Examples include trade missions, trade shows, and matchmaker programs (in which the exporter is matched with foreign intermediaries). In the United States, the International Trade Administration (ITA) provides various services to help exporters find foreign distributors. Visit the ITA Web site (www .ita.doc.gov), or the main trade support agency of your country (via globalEDGE™), and see what programs are available. Then prepare a memo to your boss in which you describe specific programs to help your firm get started in exporting.

2. Suppose you work for a major trading company exporting timber from Canada, petroleum from Britain, and processed food products from the United States. To enhance your career prospects, you want to learn more about the export of these goods from their respective countries. Visit globalEDGE™ and research current international news about these industries in the countries indicated. Based on your findings, prepare a brief report on the current status of each in the context of your firm's exporting efforts.

3. Suppose your employer wants to export its products and get paid through letter of credit (LC). You have volunteered to become the company's LC expert. One way to accomplish this is to visit globalEDGE™ and do a search on the keywords "letter of credit." Another is to visit the Web sites of major banks to learn about procedures and instructions for getting paid via LC. Visit the Web sites of CIBC (www.cibc.com), the National Australia Bank (www.national.com.au), and HSBC (www.hsbc .com) to see what you can learn about LCs. For each bank, what are the requirements for getting an LC? What services does the bank offer in regard to LCs? Can you get training in LCs from these banks?

MyManagementLab

Go to **mymanagementlab.com** for Auto-graded writing questions as well as the following Assisted-graded writing questions:

14-1. Describe the typical internationalization process a firm may use in expanding abroad.

14-2. How would you go about identifying suitable foreign intermediaries?

14-3. Mymanagementlab Only – comprehensive writing assignment for this chapter.

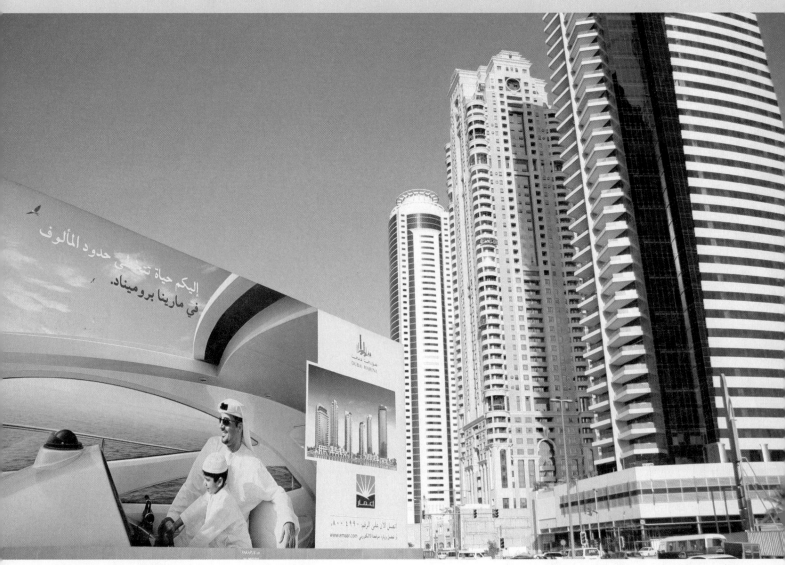

Source: Gavin Thomas/Dorling Kindersley

Huawei's Investments in Africa

Africa is the world's second most populous continent, with a population just over one billion. Africa is plagued by unstable governments and poor economic conditions. Most people in sub-Saharan Africa live on less than two dollars per day. Recently, however, Africa has been growing economically in part due to increased investment from abroad. Some 30 percent of all Chinese FDI between 2005 and 2010 was made in Africa and the Middle East.

Chinese investment in Africa is targeted to extractive industries, mainly petroleum and mining, as well as higher-value industries, such as textiles and telecommunications. African demand for mobile communications is growing rapidly, surpassing many advanced economies. In Ethiopia, for example, the number of cell phone users increased from 700,000 to more than 12 million in the five years through 2012.

A key player in African development is Huawei Technologies, China's largest telecommunications equipment manufacturer, with annual revenues of $28 billion. Huawei (pronounced who-ah-way) employs more than 140,000 people, including 4000 in Africa. Since establishing a presence

CHAPTER 15

Foreign Direct Investment and Collaborative Ventures

LEARNING OBJECTIVES *In this chapter, you will learn about:*

1. International investment and collaboration
2. Motives for FDI and collaborative ventures
3. Characteristics of foreign direct investment
4. Types of foreign direct investment
5. International collaborative ventures
6. Managing collaborative ventures
7. The experience of retailers in foreign markets

MyManagementLab®

⭐ **Improve Your Grade!**

Over 10 million students improved their results using the Pearson MyLabs.
Visit **mymanagementlab.com** for simulations, tutorials, and end-of-chapter problems.

---

there in the 1990s, Huawei has developed cell phone networks throughout the continent. In the past decade, Huawei has invested more than $1.5 billion in Africa, which now accounts for about 12 percent of its annual revenue.

Huawei leveraged FDI and collaborative ventures in Africa to establish two R&D facilities, four regional headquarters, six training centers, and 20 representative offices. Despite various challenges, Huawei's operations there have proven very profitable. The firm leverages economies of scale, inexpensive labor, and numerous other advantages to keep costs low. Efficient

operations allow Huawei to price its cell phones lower than Ericson, Nokia, or other competitors. The ability of Chinese firms to operate profitably in poor countries is perhaps the main reason China's companies are outpacing firms from Europe, Japan, and North America in expanding their presence in Africa.

Recently, Huawei entered a partnership with Bharti Airtel, an Indian mobile communications firm, to develop mobile networks across Africa. In Uganda, Huawei developed a government data center and several large-scale projects connecting agencies to a central network. In Ghana, Huawei invested more than $100 million to develop telecom facilities. In Northern Africa, Huawei entered a joint venture with ZTE Corporation to expand mobile networks in nine cities and build 800,000 phone lines. In Algeria, Huawei established a 3G mobile network to complement a cell network completed by ZTE.

Chinese investment in African telecommunications has fostered entrepreneurship and created thousands of jobs. In many ways, telecom infrastructure is the backbone of national economic activity. Infrastructure investments contribute directly to economic development, and indirectly by allowing businesses to interact in ways that foster synergies and commercial activity. The expansion of cell networks allows Africans, many of whom live in isolated areas, to find jobs and interact with important contacts. Connecting to the Internet further enhances commercial growth. China's Africa investments benefit not only Africans, but also European and U.S. firms. These companies benefit from the roads, railways, telephony, energy systems, and other infrastructure that Chinese firms have helped to develop.

As manufacturing costs in China rise and the African middle class expands, Chinese firms will likely invest much more in Africa. China is playing a key role by financing and providing needed development expertise. Various African countries are streamlining regulations and creating business-friendly environments, increasing their attractiveness for more FDI.

SOURCES: Africa Monitor: Southern Africa, "China: Future Partnership," January 2012, p. 12; *Africa Research Bulletin*, "Telecommunications: Africa," February 2011, pp. 18957C–18958C; Huawei; Economist, "Trying to Pull Together," April 23, 2011, pp. 73–75; Howard French, "The Next Empire," *The Atlantic*, May 2010, retrieved from www.theatlantic.com; Paulin Houanye and Sibao Shen, "Foreign Direct Investment in Africa: Securing Chinese's Investment for a Lasting Development in Africa," *Global Conference on Business & Finance Proceedings* 7, no. 1 (2012): 143–156; Huawei Technologies Company, "Africa Fact Sheet," December 10, 2011, retrieved from www.huawei.com; Andrea Marshall, "China's Mighty Telecom Footprint in Africa," *eLearning Africa News Portal*, February 21, 2011, retrieved from www.elearning-africa.com; Hejuan Zhao and Zhang Yuzhe, "China's Telecoms and Wireless Drums for Africa," *Caixin Online*, February 22, 2012, retrieved from english.caixin.com.

The opening story highlights the benefits of foreign direct investment (FDI) and collaborative ventures, to both to firms and nations. The worldwide spread of capital and ownership via FDI is one of the remarkable facets of globalization. Consider Tata Motors (www.tatamotors.com), India's largest automaker that obtains much of its sales from abroad. Tata recently paid $2.3 billion to purchase Jaguar and Land Rover from Ford Motor Company. Tata owns numerous Jaguar and Land Rover car factories around Asia and Europe. Recently, Renault and Nissan partnered with Tata to distribute the Nano in Europe, which Tata unveiled as the world's cheapest car. Tata also acquired 70 percent of Miljo, a Norwegian electric vehicle maker. In South Korea, Tata purchased Daewoo Commercial Vehicle Company, a leading manufacturer of trucks and tractors.[1]

In this chapter, we examine the nature of FDI and collaborative ventures. We explain the motives that drive companies to use these entry strategies. We highlight numerous companies engaged in FDI as well as best practices for investment and partnering success. We also examine retailers, a distinctive category of foreign investors in the services sector.

 ## International Investment and Collaboration

Foreign direct investment (FDI) is an internationalization strategy in which the firm establishes a physical presence abroad through direct ownership of productive assets such as capital, technology, labor, land, plant, and equipment.

An **international collaborative** venture is a cross-border business partnership in which collaborating firms pool their resources and share costs and risks of a new venture. Here the focal firm partners with one or more companies to pursue a joint project or initiative. International collaborative ventures are also sometimes called "international partnerships" or "international strategic alliances."

Consider the following example from the beer industry. In 2002, South African Breweries (www.sabmiller.com) established a major presence in the U.S. beer market by buying Miller

---

Foreign direct investment (FDI)
An internationalization strategy in which the firm establishes a physical presence abroad through acquisition of productive assets such as capital, technology, labor, land, plant, and equipment.

International collaborative venture
A cross-border business alliance in which partnering firms pool their resources and share costs and risks to undertake a new business venture; also referred to as an "international partnership" or an "international strategic alliance."

Brewing. After changing its name to SABMiller plc., the firm next acquired 97 percent of Bavaria S.A., South America's second-largest brewer. In 2006, SABMiller acquired Foster's India for $120 million, gaining control of nearly 50 percent of the Indian beer market. In 2011, the firm acquired Foster's, Australia's largest brewer. In China, SABMiller entered a joint venture with CR Snow Breweries, helping to make SABMiller the largest brewer in China. A **joint venture** is a form of collaboration between two or more firms to create a new, jointly owned enterprise. Unlike collaborative arrangements where no new entity is created, the partners in a joint venture typically invest money to create a new enterprise, which may endure for many years. A partner in a joint venture may enjoy minority, equal, or majority ownership. Through numerous FDI and collaborative ventures in the 2000s, SABMiller has become the world's third-largest brewer, with operations in more than sixty countries.[2] Both FDI and international collaborative ventures are fundamental strategies that focal firms use to expand abroad.

Joint venture
A form of collaboration between two or more firms to create a new, jointly owned enterprise.

Trends in Foreign Direct Investment and Collaborative Ventures

FDI is the most advanced and complex foreign market entry strategy. Firms use FDI to establish manufacturing plants, marketing subsidiaries, or other facilities in target countries. Because this involves investing substantial resources to establish a physical presence abroad, FDI is riskier than other entry strategies.

More than sixty cross-border acquisitions valued at over $3 billion each were consummated in 2011. The top three recipients of FDI were Belgium, China, and the United States.[3] Recent examples of cross-border investments include:

- General Motors invested more than $3 billion in Mexico to build manufacturing capacity, including a new factory in San Luis Potosi.
- Japan's Daiichi Sankyo pharmaceutical paid $4.6 billion to acquire Ranbaxy Laboratories, India's largest producer of generic medications.
- The Dutch manufacturer AkzoNobel spent $338 million to build a chemical factory in China.
- SABIC Corporation, a Saudi Arabia firm, paid $11.6 billion to acquire GE Plastics from General Electric.
- Yildiz, a Turkish holding company that owns the confectionary company Ulker, acquired chocolatier Godiva from Campbell Soup Company.
- China Film Group formed a partnership with Japan's Sony Pictures to make movies in California.

These and other examples illustrate several trends:

1. Companies from both advanced economies and emerging markets are active in FDI.
2. Destination or recipient countries for such investments are both advanced economies and emerging markets.
3. Firms use various strategies to enter foreign markets, including acquisitions and collaborative ventures.
4. Firms from all types of industries, including services, are active in FDI and collaborative ventures. Major retailers began expanding abroad in the 1970s, including Metro AG (Germany), Royal Ahold (Netherlands), Tesco (United Kingdom), and Walmart (United States).
5. Direct investment by foreign firms occasionally inflames citizens' patriotic passions. In the United States, for example, Chinese oil company CNOOC's attempt to buy Unocal Corporation raised concerns about a Chinese state enterprise gaining control of a key U.S. firm in the energy sector. Strong opposition drove the U.S. Congress to ban the deal.

 ## Motives for FDI and Collaborative Ventures

While the ultimate goal of FDI and international collaborative ventures is to enhance company competitiveness in the global marketplace, managers pursue these strategies for complex reasons. As shown in Exhibit 15.1, we classify the reasons into three categories: market-seeking motives, resource- or asset-seeking motives, and efficiency-seeking motives.[4] In many cases, the firm aims to satisfy several motives simultaneously, within a single venture. Let's examine these motives in more detail.

EXHIBIT 15.1

Firm Motives for Foreign Direct Investment and Collaborative Ventures

Market-Seeking Motives

Managers may seek new market opportunities as a result of either unfavorable developments in their home market (that is, they may be pushed into international markets) or attractive opportunities abroad (they may be pulled into international markets). There are three primary market-seeking motivations:

1. *Gain access to new markets or opportunities.* The existence of a substantial mark motivates many firms to produce offerings at or near customer locations. Local production improves customer service and reduces the cost of transporting goods to buyer locations. Coca-Cola, Samsung, and Siemens all generate more sales abroad than in their home markets. The opening story highlights Huawei Technologies, a Chinese firm that has invested billions in Africa to gain access to fast-growing mobile phone markets there.
2. *Follow key customers.* Firms often follow their key customers abroad to preempt other vendors from serving them. Establishing local operations also positions the firm to better serve customer needs. Tradegar Industries supplies the plastic that its customer Procter & Gamble uses to manufacture disposable diapers. When P&G built a plant in China, Tradegar followed P&G there, establishing production in China as well.
3. *Compete with key rivals in their own markets.* Some MNEs may choose to confront current or potential competitors directly, in the competitors' home market. The strategic purpose is to weaken the competitor by forcing it to expend resources to defend its market. In the earth-moving equipment industry, Caterpillar entered a joint venture with Mitsubishi to put pressure on the market share and profitability of their common rival, Japan's Komatsu. The need to spend substantial resources to defend its home market reduced Komatsu's ability to expand abroad.[5]

Resource- or Asset-Seeking Motives

Firms frequently want to acquire production factors that are more abundant or less costly in a foreign market. They may also seek complementary resources and capabilities of partner companies headquartered abroad. Specifically, FDI or collaborative ventures may be motivated by the firm's desire to attain the following assets:

1. *Raw materials needed in extractive and agricultural industries.* Firms in the mining, oil, and crop-growing industries have little choice but to go where the raw materials are located. In the wine industry, companies establish wineries in countries suited for growing grapes, such as France and Chile. Oil companies establish refineries in countries with abundant petroleum reserves such as Kuwait.
2. *Knowledge or other assets.*[6] By establishing a local presence through FDI, the firm is better positioned to deepen its understanding of target markets. FDI provides the foreign firm better access to market knowledge, customers, distribution systems, and control over local operations. By collaborating in R&D, production, and marketing, the

focal firm can benefit from the partner's know-how. When Whirlpool entered Europe, it partnered with Philips to benefit from the latter's well-known brand name and distribution network. Royal Dutch Shell and PetroChina established a $1.3 billion joint venture to extract gas and oil from the Changbei gas field in China. Through this venture, PetroChina is acquiring knowledge about Shell's advanced technologies for extracting fossil fuels from deep shale deposits. In turn, Shell gained access to the gas field and is learning from PetroChina how to navigate the complex Chinese energy market, gradually becoming the world's biggest.[7]

3. *Technological and managerial know-how.*[8] The firm may benefit by establishing a presence in a key industrial cluster, such as the robotics industry in Japan, chemicals in Germany, fashion in Italy, or software in the United States. Companies can obtain many advantages from locating at the hub of knowledge development and innovation in a given industry. Denmark, Finland, Israel, New Zealand, Sweden, and the United States are considered ideal for R&D in the biotechnology industry because they have abundant biotech knowledge workers.[9] Many firms enter a collaborative venture abroad as a prelude to wholly owned FDI. Collaboration with a local partner reduces the risks of entry and provides the entrant local expertise before launching operations of its own in the market.

Efficiency-Seeking Motives

Through international expansion, the firm increases its *economies of scale*. As indicated in Exhibit 15.2, international expansion allows the firm to increase sales and employ company assets across a larger number of products and markets. As the quantity of productive output is increased from Q_1 to Q_2, the per-unit cost of production tends to decline, for example, from C_1 to C_2. In turn, profits rise as the firm's average cost of operations declines. Similarly, with increasing output, the per-unit cost of other productive activities—R&D, marketing, distribution, customer support—declines as well.

The economies of scale phenomenon occurs for various reasons:

1. *Falling fixed costs.* Many industries and productive tasks have high per-unit fixed costs that decline the more the task is performed. For example, imagine the per-unit cost of the first car that rolls off an assembly line—production cannot occur unless the firm builds a factory. As more cars are produced, the cost to build the factory is amortized across many cars and the average cost per car declines.
2. *Managerial resource efficiencies.* International expansion implies the firm employs a relatively fixed number of headquarters staff across more subsidiaries and affiliates. In this way, managerial talent is utilized more efficiently.
3. *Specialization of labor.* When productive output increases, the firm hires more workers, who become more specialized in their tasks. As they specialize, workers become more proficient, producing more output per hour worked.
4. *Volume discounts.* Suppliers usually offer discounts for large-quantity purchases. Per-unit sourcing costs fall as the firm buys more parts, components, and other inputs.
5. *Financial economies.* Compared to small firms, large companies usually can access capital at lower cost. This arises because large firms are relatively powerful and tend to borrow large sums.

Internationalization also increases *economies of scope*, which refers to the cost-savings that arise from using a relatively fixed base of managerial talent, facilities, and other company assets across a larger marketplace. For example, Unilever uses the same base of managers and marketing experts at its Netherlands headquarters to develop advertising for numerous product lines for many countries in Europe. This is more efficient than delegating the task to individual managers in each European country. The cost-reducing benefits of doing business in numerous countries simultaneously are substantial. In fact, the drive to achieve economies of scale and scope is a key

EXHIBIT 15.2

**Economies of Scale
Long-Run Average Cost**

rationale for undertaking international business. MNEs usually concentrate production in only a few locations to increase the efficiency of manufacturing.[10] Many firms develop global brands to increase the efficiency of marketing activities.

In addition to attaining economies of scale and scope, firms engage in international business to achieve four major efficiency-seeking goals:

1. *Reduce sourcing and production costs by accessing inexpensive labor and other cheap inputs to the production process.*[11] This motive accounts for the massive investment by foreign firms in factories and service-producing facilities in China, Mexico, Eastern Europe, and India. MNEs establish factories in such locations to reduce production costs.

2. *Locate production near customers.* In industries that need to be especially sensitive to customer needs or in which tastes change rapidly, managers often locate factories or assembly operations near important customers. Zara and Forever 21 locate much of their garment production in key fashion markets such as Europe. Production is more expensive, but the clothing gets into shops faster and more closely represents the latest fashion trends.[12]

3. *Take advantage of government incentives.*[13] In addition to restricting imports, governments frequently offer subsidies and tax concessions to foreign firms to encourage them to invest locally. Governments encourage inward FDI because it provides local jobs and capital, increases tax revenue, and transfers skills and technologies.

4. *Avoid trade barriers.* Companies often enter markets via FDI to avoid tariffs and other trade barriers, as these usually apply only to exporting. By establishing a physical presence inside a country or an economic bloc, the foreign company obtains the same advantages as local firms. Partnering with a local firm also helps overcome regulations or trade barriers and satisfy local content rules. The desire to avoid trade barriers helps explain why numerous Japanese automakers established factories in the United States. However, this motive is declining in importance because trade barriers have fallen substantially in many countries.

Source: Peter Bush/Dorling Kindersley

Firms in the wine industry engage in foreign direct investment and collaborative ventures to access raw materials; in this case, farm land suitable for cultivating wine grapes. Pictured is a vineyard in New Zealand.

Characteristics of Foreign Direct Investment

Internationalizing through FDI enables the firm to maintain a physical presence in key markets, secure direct access to customers and partners, and perform critical value-chain activities in the market. FDI is an equity or ownership form of foreign market entry. It is the entry strategy most associated with large MNEs—such as Bombardier, Ford, and Unilever—that have extensive physical operations around the world. As they venture abroad, firms that specialize in products usually establish manufacturing plants. Firms that offer services, such as banks, cruise lines, and restaurant chains, usually establish agency relationships and retail facilities.

KONE is a major manufacturer based in Finland. You may have used KONE's products without knowing it, because KONE is a leading producer of elevators and escalators. Read the *Recent Grad in IB* profile featuring Jennifer Knippen, who went to work for KONE after college. Her case illustrates how you can acquire valuable international business experience by working for a foreign-owned company in your home country.

Samsung (www.samsung.com), the South Korean electronics giant, first entered the United States through FDI in the 1980s and also used FDI to establish low-cost factories in Mexico, Southeast Asia, and Eastern Europe. In the 1990s, Samsung acquired capabilities, via acquisition, for developing and producing semiconductors. The firm then used FDI to establish numerous R&D centers—in China, India, Israel, Japan, the United Kingdom, and the United States—that drive the development of leading technologies in digital media, appliances, telecommunications, and semiconductors. Most of Samsung's sales are from international operations—in Asia (49 percent), Europe (23 percent), and the United States (28 percent)—which are facilitated through the firm's roughly sixty-four foreign sales affiliates. Samsung also has thirty-eight manufacturing plants and three logistics centers located abroad, all established via FDI. Samsung has surpassed Motorola to become the biggest-selling brand of mobile phone in the United States.[14]

Do not confuse FDI with **international portfolio investment**, which refers to passive ownership of foreign securities, such as stocks and bonds, for the purpose of generating financial returns. International portfolio investment is a form of international investment, but it is not FDI, which seeks ownership control of a business abroad and represents a long-term commitment. The United Nations uses the benchmark of at least 10 percent ownership in the enterprise to differentiate FDI from portfolio investment. However, this percentage may be misleading, because control is not usually achieved unless the investor owns at least 50 percent of a foreign venture.

International portfolio investment
Passive ownership of foreign securities such as stocks and bonds for the purpose of generating financial returns.

Key features of foreign direct investment include:

- *Substantial resource commitment*. As the ultimate internationalization strategy, it is far more taxing on the firm's resources and capabilities than any other entry strategy. For example, the U.S. firm General Electric owns more than $400 billion in factories, subsidiaries, and other operations outside the United States.[15]
- *Local presence and operations*. With FDI, the firm establishes itself directly in the market, leading to direct contact with customers, intermediaries, facilitators, and governments. Some firms concentrate operations in one or a few locations; others disperse their FDI among many countries. The MNE network may become so extensive that the firm effectively loses its nationality. Nestlé, for example, is based in Switzerland but generates more than 90 percent of its sales from abroad. The Indian MNE Tata Consultancy Services generates most of its revenues in North America, while rival IBM, a U.S. company, obtains nearly two-thirds of its sales from abroad.[16]
- *Firms invest in countries that provide specific comparative advantages*. Managers invest in countries based on the advantages these locations offer. Thus, firms tend to perform R&D in countries with leading-edge knowledge for their industry, source from countries home to suppliers that provide superior goods, build factories in locations with low labor costs, and establish marketing subsidiaries in countries with excellent sales potential.
- *Substantial risk and uncertainty*. Establishing a permanent, fixed presence abroad makes the firm vulnerable to country risk and intervention by local governments. In addition to

You Can Do It | RECENT GRAD IN IB

JENNIFER KNIPPEN

Jennifer's majors: Economics and International Business
Jobs held since graduating:
- Sales Engineer, KONE, Inc.

Jennifer Knippen was inspired to pursue an international career after participating in a study-abroad program in Valencia, Spain. After graduating with dual majors in economics and international business, she returned to Spain for five months of intensive training in Spanish and traveled through various regions to broaden her education.

When she returned home, Jennifer attended a career fair, which led to a sales engineer position with the U.S. subsidiary of KONE, Inc., a leading manufacturer of elevators and escalators based in Finland. Her experience at KONE was both challenging and inspiring. Jennifer had to learn a technical product in the demanding construction industry.

As a sales engineer, she consulted architects in the design stages of a project—cost analysis, equipment specifications, building integration, and code compliance. She next generated a proposal to the general contractor working on the project. She managed the project through completion (more than a year). Jennifer managed multiple projects at a time while still meeting annual and quarterly sales budgets.

Managers at KONE praised Jennifer's strong presentations and relationship-building skills. She began working on high-rise projects with some of the top architectural and construction firms. Through pre-selling, with KONE's global support and resources, Jennifer stimulated substantial demand. Eventually she was awarded "Best in Class" for the highest-volume sales in her region.

Jennifer experienced the benefits and challenges that come with working for a local subsidiary of an international parent company. KONE has enjoyed big success in Europe and other parts of the world and has applied a similar approach in the United States. One of the challenges Jennifer faced was strict U.S. building code regulations. She also had to monitor fluctuations in the euro–dollar exchange rate, because these greatly affect the sales price of imported equipment.

What's Ahead?

Jennifer returned to school to complete an MBA in international business. She thought her experience, coupled with an advanced degree in international management, would position her well for an exciting international career. Jennifer is excited about what lies ahead.

Success Factors for a Career in International Business

Foreign travel and a study-abroad program in college inspired Jennifer to pursue an international career. Learning Spanish enhanced her credentials to secure an international business job. Jennifer set career goals and worked hard to achieve them.

---

local labor practices, direct investors also must contend with local economic conditions, such as inflation and recessions. French automaker Renault recently acquired a 25 percent stake in Russian automaker AvtoVAZ to produce Lada brand cars in Russia. However, the 40-year-old AvtoVAZ plant is plagued by inefficient operations, a slow workforce, and a history of organized crime.[17] Business in Russia often requires paying bribes, and the country has a history of high inflation and other macroeconomic concerns. The Russian government often intervenes in the private sector.

- *Intense dealings in the host market.* Firms that enter via FDI necessarily deal more intensely with culture and other aspects of the host country. MNEs with high-profile, conspicuous operations are especially vulnerable to close public scrutiny of their actions. To minimize potential problems, managers often favor investing in countries that are culturally and linguistically familiar. When setting up shop in continental Europe, for example, U.S. firms frequently choose the Netherlands because English is widely spoken there.[18]

Challenges of FDI

FDI poses formidable challenges for the firm. Even a large, well-established company like Disney (www.disney.com) experienced several failures in its foreign investing.[19] When Disney established Tokyo Disneyland, its management incorrectly assumed the Disneyland experience could not be successfully transferred to Japan. So instead of investing, Disney opted to license rights in Japan for nominal profits. Tokyo Disneyland proved to be a huge success. Not wanting to repeat the same mistake, management opted to retain an FDI stake in its next theme park—Disneyland Paris. But it proved to be a financial sinkhole. Having learned from these experiences, Disney has made the latest theme park, Hong Kong Disneyland, more successful. Disney owns just 47 percent of the venture, making the Hong Kong government the major partner. Management wants to expand the park, but negotiations with the Hong Kong government were tense and complicated. After receiving permission from the Chinese government, Disney broke ground to build the new Shanghai Disneyland, with completion expected in 2016. Management is worried about intellectual property violations in China, which may reduce profits from licensing Disney movies, animated characters, and other valuable properties.[20]

Source: Karen Trist/Dorling Kindersley

Vodafone is one of the most international firms due to its very extensive FDI activities. This mobile phone service provider invests to establish retail outlets in Africa, Asia-Pacific, Europe, the Middle East, and the Americas.

Corporate Social Responsibility, Sustainability, and FDI

Multinational firms increasingly strive to behave in *socially responsible* ways in host countries. Many are investing in local communities and seeking to establish global standards of fair treatment for workers. Unilever (www.unilever.com), the giant Dutch-British producer of consumer products, operates a free community laundry in a São Paulo slum, provides financing to assist tomato growers to convert to environmentally friendly irrigation, and recycles 17 million pounds of waste annually at one of its toothpaste factories. In Bangladesh, where there are relatively few doctors, Unilever funds a hospital that offers free medical care to the needy. In Ghana, the company teaches palm oil producers to reuse plant waste while providing drinkable water to deprived communities. In India, Unilever provides small loans to help women in remote villages start small-scale enterprises. In all the countries where it operates, Unilever discloses how much carbon dioxide and hazardous waste it produces.[21]

Many other MNEs are responding to such global agendas as *sustainability*, or meeting humanity's needs without harming future generations. For example, automakers such as Toyota, Renault, and Volkswagen are investing in fuel-efficient and clean technologies. Nokia is a leader in phasing out toxic materials. Dell was among the first to accept old PC hardware from consumers and recycle it for free. GlaxoSmithKline and Merck offer AIDS drugs at cost in numerous impoverished countries. Suncor Energy assists Native Americans to deal with social and ecological issues in Canada's far north.

Ethical Connections

FDI offers numerous benefits to recipient countries. However, FDI may produce side effects that harm the natural environment, especially in countries with weak environmental laws. Pollution and ecological destruction may emerge alongside rapid economic growth. One MNE, a manufacturer of food additives, allowed untreated wastewater to flow into the ThiVai river in Vietnam. Resulting pollution nearly destroyed the livelihood of thousands of downstream farmers. Firms must behave responsibly in their international dealings. Governments must not allow development goals to compromise citizen well-being.

Source: H. Nguyen and H. Pham, "The Dark Side of Development in Vietnam," *Journal of Macromarketing* 32, no. 1 (2012): 74–86.

Most Active Firms in FDI

Exhibit 15.3 provides a sample of leading MNEs engaged in FDI. General Electric, Toyota, and other firms in the exhibit are listed based on the volume of factories, subsidiaries, and other assets they own in foreign countries. For example, Toyota is a car manufacturer with various subsidiaries around the world. Individual Toyota subsidiaries engage in the range of value-chain activities, including R&D, manufacturing, marketing, sales, and customer service. The most internationally active MNEs are in the automotive, oil, and telecommunications industries.

Service Firms and FDI

Companies in the services sector, such as retailing, construction, and personal care, must offer their services where they are consumed. This usually requires establishing either a permanent presence through FDI (as in retailing) or a temporary relocation of the service company personnel (as in the construction industry).[22] Management consulting is a service usually embodied in experts who interact directly with clients to dispense advice. To reach their customers, firms such as McKinsey and Cap Gemini have established numerous offices in foreign markets. Many support services, such as advertising, insurance, accounting, legal work, and overnight package delivery, are also best provided at the customer's location. FDI is vital for internationalizing services.[23]

Intrawest, Inc., which is building several ski resorts in China, has offices at various locations in China. Banks establish branches around the world because banking services are usually provided directly to customers wherever they do business. Exhibit 15.4 portrays the world's most international financial institutions and the breadth of their operations abroad. The firms are ranked based on the number of foreign subsidiaries and affiliates, and the number of countries where they do business. For example, Citigroup has representative offices in seventy-five countries.

Leading Destinations for FDI

Advanced economies such as Australia, Canada, Japan, Netherlands, the United Kingdom, and the United States long have been popular destinations for FDI because of their strong per-capita GDP, GDP growth rate, density of knowledge workers, and superior business infrastructure, such as telephone systems and energy sources.[24] In recent years, however, developing

EXHIBIT 15.3 World's Most International Non-Financial MNEs, Based on Volume of Foreign Assets

Company	Home Country	Industry	Approximate Sales (billions of U.S. dollars)		Approximate Number of Subsidiaries and Affiliates	
			Foreign	Total	Foreign	Total
General Electric	United States	Electrical & electronic equipment	$78	$147	785	1,117
Royal Dutch Shell	United Kingdom & Netherlands	Petroleum	310	484	518	926
Total	France	Petroleum	172	224	429	598
Toyota Motor	Japan	Motor vehicles	142	229	169	419
E.ON	Germany	Electricity, gas, and water	57	123	279	590
BP	United Kingdom	Petroleum	255	386	337	529
Exxon Mobil	United States	Petroleum	330	486	278	346
Electricite de France	France	Electricity, gas, and water	43	88	199	249
Ford Motor	United States	Motor vehicles	64	136	162	247
Vodafone	United Kingdom	Telecommunications	61	74	30	130

Sources: Based on Hoovers company database at www.hoovers.com, 2012; UNCTAD, *World Investment Report 2009* (New York: United Nations, 2009, p. 225, "Annex table A.1.9. The World's Top 100 Non-Financial TNCs, Ranked by Foreign Assets"), accessed March 31, 2012 at www.unctad.org.

EXHIBIT 15.4 World's Most International Financial MNEs, Based on Breadth of Worldwide Operations

Company	Home Country	Approximate Sales (billions of U.S. dollars)		Approximate Number of Subsidiaries and Affiliates		Approximate Number of Host Countries
		Foreign	Total	Foreign	Total	
Citigroup	United States	$73	$103	723	1,020	75
HSBC Bank	United Kingdom	69	106	683	1,048	54
Société Générale	France	56	86	345	526	53
Allianz SE	Germany	97	130	612	823	52
ABN AMRO	Netherlands	16	22	703	945	48
BNP Paribas	France	79	124	425	664	48
UBS	Switzerland	40	43	432	465	35
Unicredito Italiano	Italy	37	43	1,052	1,111	34
Zurich Financial Services	Switzerland	55	68	383	393	34

Sources: Based on Hoovers company database at www.hoovers.com, 2012; UNCTAD, *World Investment Report 2009* (New York: United Nations, 2009, p. 225, "Annex table A.1.12. The Top 50 Financial TNCs Ranked by Geographical Spread Index (GSI), 2008"), accessed April 1, 2012 at www.unctad.org.

economies and emerging markets have gained much appeal as FDI destinations. This is illustrated by the Inward FDI Performance Index, developed by the United Nations Conference on Trade and Development. It suggests that, between 2007 and 2010, the volume of FDI flowing into advanced economies fell, while the amount flowing into developing economies and emerging markets increased. This continuing trend bodes well for less-developed economies since FDI is a key determinant of economic development and living standards.[25]

According to A. T. Kearney's Global Location Index, the top destinations for foreign investment today are China and India (www.atkearney.com). China is popular because of its size, rapid growth rate, and low labor costs. It is an important platform where MNEs manufacture products for export to key markets in Asia and elsewhere. India is popular because of its managerial talent, well-educated workforce, and relatively fewer cultural barriers.[26] China and India are also attractive for strategic reasons: They have a great amount of long-term potential as target markets and new sources of competitive advantage.

Factors to Consider in Choosing FDI Locations

Exhibit 15.5 lists the criteria firms use to evaluate countries as potential targets for FDI projects. Suppose Taiwan-based Acer (www.acer.com) wants to build a new computer factory. Its managers will research the best country in which to build it, looking at country and regional factors, infrastructural factors, political factors, profit retention factors, and human resource factors.

As an example, consider the attractiveness of Eastern European nations as FDI destinations. Several of the selection criteria noted in Exhibit 15.5 have attracted foreign firms to these countries. In the Czech Republic, giant Chinese electronics manufacturer Sichuan Changhong (www.changhong.com) built a $30 million factory that produces up to 1 million flat-screen televisions per year. Numerous automakers, from Ford to Nissan, have built factories in the region. Wages in Eastern Europe are relatively low; engineers in Slovakia earn half of what

Source: spectrumblue/Fotolia

Business-friendly Ireland is one of the world's top FDI destinations. Shown is the North Wall Quay complex in Dublin, which houses key European operations of Citigroup and numerous other international banks.

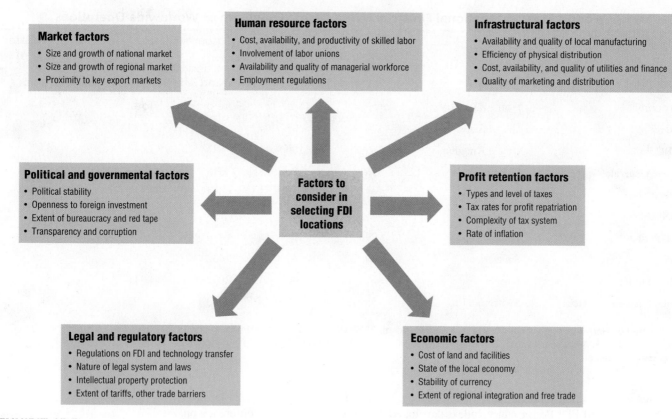

EXHIBIT 15.5

Factors to Consider in Selecting Foreign Direct Investment Locations

Source: Entry Strategies for International Markets by Franklin R. Root. Copyright © 1994 by John Wiley & Sons, Inc. Reprinted by permission of John Wiley & Sons, Inc.

Western engineers make, and assembly-line workers one-third to one-fifth. In addition, East European governments offer incentives, from financing to low taxes, as in Slovakia where all taxes are a simple 19 percent. By comparison, personal income tax rates often exceed 30 percent in Germany. Eastern Europe also provides ready access to the huge EU market.[27]

Just as Eastern Europe has become a popular FDI destination, production of cars and other products has fallen in the United States, France, and Canada, due to higher business costs, uncertainty, and government intervention.[28] Managers examine a combination of criteria when making decisions about where in the world to establish operations via FDI.

 ## Types of Foreign Direct Investment

We can classify FDI activities by form (greenfield versus mergers and acquisitions), nature of ownership (wholly owned versus joint venture), and level of integration (horizontal versus vertical).

Greenfield Investment versus Mergers and Acquisitions

Greenfield investment
Direct investment to build a new manufacturing, marketing, or administrative facility, as opposed to acquiring existing facilities.

Acquisition
Direct investment to purchase an existing company or facility.

Greenfield investment occurs when a firm invests to build a new manufacturing, marketing, or administrative facility, as opposed to acquiring existing facilities. As the name *greenfield* implies, the investing firm typically buys an empty plot of land and builds a production plant, marketing subsidiary, or other facility there for its own use. This is exactly what Ford did when it established its large factory in Rayong, Thailand, to manufacture small cars for emerging markets.

An **acquisition** is the purchase of an existing company or facility. When Home Depot entered Mexico, it acquired the stores and assets of an existing retailer of building products, Home Mart.[29] The Chinese personal computer manufacturer Lenovo made an ambitious acquisition of IBM's PC business, which now accounts for some two-thirds of its annual revenue. The deal provided Lenovo with valuable strategic assets such as brands and distribution networks and helped it rapidly extend its market reach and become a global player.[30]

A **merger** is a special type of acquisition in which two companies join to form a new, larger firm. Like joint ventures, mergers can generate many positive outcomes, including interpartner learning and resource sharing, increased scale economies, cost savings from eliminating duplicative activities, a broader range of products and services for sale, and greater market power. Cross-border mergers confront many challenges due to national differences in culture, competition policy, corporate values, and operating methods. Success requires substantial advance research, planning, and commitment. *Merger and acquisition* (M&A) activity is substantial in international business. The largest international M&As in recent years include the Kraft Foods (United States) merger with Cadbury (United Kingdom), Telefonica's (Spain) purchase of Brasilcel (Brazil), and Sinopec's (China) acquisition of Repsol Brasil (Brazil).[31]

Multinational enterprises may favor acquisition over greenfield FDI because, by acquiring an existing company, they gain ownership of existing assets such as plant, equipment, and human resources, as well as access to existing suppliers and customers. Unlike greenfield FDI, acquisition provides an immediate stream of revenue and accelerates the MNE's return on investment. However, host-country governments often pressure MNEs to undertake greenfield FDI because it creates new jobs and production capacity, facilitates technology and know-how transfer to locals, and improves linkages to the global marketplace. Many governments offer incentives to encourage greenfield investments, which may be sufficient to offset the advantages of acquisition-based entry.

Source: Christopher and Sally Gable/Dorling Kindersley

More companies are investing in Africa to develop dams and power plants. In addition to providing capital for local economies, such investments supply needed infrastructure. Pictured here is a power plant in South Africa.

Merger
A special type of acquisition in which two firms join to form a new, larger firm.

The Nature of Ownership in FDI

Foreign direct investors also choose their degree of control in the venture. This is accomplished through full or partial ownership, resulting in a commensurate degree of control over decision making on such issues as product development, expansion, and profit distribution. Firms can choose between a wholly owned or joint venture to secure control, which also determines the extent of their financial commitment. If the focal firm is pursuing partial ownership in an existing firm, this is known as **equity participation**.

Wholly owned direct investment is FDI in which the investor assumes 100 percent ownership of the business and secures complete managerial control over its operations. Numerous global car companies, for example, established fully owned manufacturing plants in the United States to serve the large U.S. market from within.[32] Exhibit 15.6 maps the location of Toyota's U.S. plants and the year of establishment. In contrast to wholly owned direct investment, an **equity joint venture** is a type of partnership in which a separate firm is created through the investment or pooling of assets by two or more parent firms that gain joint ownership of the new legal entity.[33] A partner in a joint venture may hold majority, equal (50–50), or minority ownership. Minority ownership provides little control over the operation.

A joint venture is an attractive entry strategy because many foreign markets are complex. Collaborating with a local partner enhances the foreign entrant's ability to navigate the local market. Collaborative ventures benefit small and medium-sized enterprises by providing them with needed capital and other assets. For example, Shanghai-based Tri Star International acquired a majority stake in Illinois-based Adams Pressed Metals, a manufacturer of parts for tractors and other earth-moving equipment. The cash infusion saved forty jobs at Adams and gave Tri Star access to the U.S. market and marketing know-how.[34]

A joint venture with a local partner may sometimes be the only entry strategy available to the focal firm, as when the government of a target country seeks to protect its important industries by prohibiting 100 percent foreign ownership in local enterprises. Mexico's government, for example, requires foreign MNEs to form joint ventures with local Mexican firms

Equity participation
Acquisition of partial ownership in an existing firm.

Wholly owned direct investment
A foreign direct investment in which the investor fully owns the foreign assets.

Equity joint venture
A type of partnership in which a separate firm is created through the investment or pooling of assets by two or more parent firms that gain joint ownership of the new legal entity.

EXHIBIT 15.6

Toyota's Direct Investments in Manufacturing Plants in the United States

Sources: Based on Alex Taylor, "America's Best Car Company," *Fortune*, March 19, 2007, pp. 98–101; Toyota Operations 2012, retrieved from www.toyota.com; Peter Valdes-Dapena, "Toyota Tells U.S. Plants 'Prepare to Shut Down'," *CNNMoney*, March 24, 2011, retrieved from www.money.cnn.com.

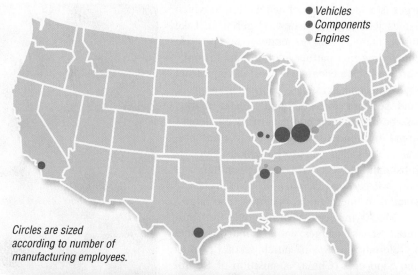

● Vehicles
● Components
● Engines

Circles are sized according to number of manufacturing employees.

Vehicle plants currently operating	Start of production	Models produced	Manufacturing employees
1. Long Beach, California	1972	Hino trucks, various parts	470
2. Georgetown, Kentucky	1986	Avalon, Camry, Solara	6,327
3. Princeton, Indiana	1996	Sequoia, Sienna, Highlander	3,933
4. San Antonio, Texas	2003	Tundra, Tacoma	2,299
5. Blue Springs, Mississippi	2010	Prius	2,000

when entering the country's oil industry, which is considered vital to Mexico's economic security. However, governments are relaxing such regulations in most industries and most are receptive to FDI.

Vertical versus Horizontal Integration

Vertical integration
An arrangement whereby the firm owns, or seeks to own, multiple stages of a value chain for producing, selling, and delivering a product or service.

Horizontal integration
An arrangement whereby the firm owns, or seeks to own, the activities performed in a single stage of its value chain.

A third way of classifying FDI is by whether integration takes place vertically or horizontally. **Vertical integration** is an arrangement whereby the firm owns, or seeks to own, multiple stages of a value chain for producing, selling, and delivering a product or service. Vertical FDI takes two forms. In forward vertical integration, the firm develops the capacity to sell its outputs by investing in downstream value-chain facilities—that is, in marketing and selling operations. In backward vertical integration, the firm acquires the capacity to provide inputs for its foreign or domestic production processes by investing in upstream facilities, such as factories or assembly plants. Firms can undertake both backward and forward vertical integration. In various countries, Honda owns both suppliers of car parts and dealerships that sell and distribute cars.

Horizontal integration is an arrangement in which the firm owns, or seeks to own, the activities performed in a single stage of its value chain. Microsoft's primary business is developing computer software. In addition to producing operating systems, word processing, and spreadsheet software, it has developed subsidiaries abroad that make other types of software, such as a Montreal-based firm that produces software for creating movie animations. Horizontal integration implies the firm invests in its own industry to expand its capacity and activities. A firm may acquire another firm engaged in an identical value-chain activity to achieve economies of scale, expand its product line, increase its profitability, or, in some cases, eliminate a competitor. The *Global Trend* feature describes the progress of FDI under turbulent global economic conditions.

GLOBAL TREND

FDI in the Global Economy

More than 82,000 multinational enterprises operate worldwide. Collectively, they control some 800,000 foreign subsidiaries and affiliates critical to the world economy. Foreign affiliates of MNEs account for about one-third of world exports of goods and services and employ more than 75 million people. These firms produce the FDI flows vital to the world economy. However, FDI flows declined during the recent recession and global financial crisis.

The crisis cost millions of jobs, reduced profits, and delayed internationalization projects for countless firms. The decline in FDI harmed poorer countries in Africa, Asia, and Latin America, which depend heavily on inward investment for financing. Global FDI flows fell below $1.2 trillion in 2009, down substantially from their historic high of $2 trillion in 2007. FDI returned to its earlier highs in 2013. Recently, the United States, China, and Belgium have been the biggest recipients of global FDI.

However, the recent recession hurt company profits and increased managers' perceptions of country risk, both of which translated into reduced investments in foreign ventures. The recession triggered sharp declines in cross-national merger and acquisition (M&A) activity. Global portfolio investments in the form of private equity funds were hit especially hard, because equity capital (money invested in stock markets) is very fluid. Thus, international investors were able to withdraw their investments quickly from countries. As lenders and investors became more risk-conscious, capital flows in global portfolio investments shrank.

Developing economies and emerging markets account for half of global FDI; their inflows continue to rise and represent primarily greenfield investments. In Africa, investment inflows have grown in the past several years. Much of the inflows have been for prospecting projects in search of

oil and base metals. Other investments were made in infrastructure development, such as the construction of dams and plants for generating power. As revealed in the opening story, Chinese firms have undertaken substantial investment activities in Africa. Increased political and economic stability in African governments has been a key factor encouraging FDI in Africa in recent years.

Sources: J. Espinoza, "Investment Outlook Is Mixed for Europe," *Wall Street Journal*, March 11, 2010, retrieved from http://www.wsj.com; "Global Outlook: FDI Trends—Emerging from Crisis," *Foreign Direct Investment*, February/March 2010, retrieved from http://www.fdimagazine.com; Paul Hannon, "Foreign Investment Climbs Slowly," *Wall Street Journal*, July 27, 2011, p. A11; A. Hawser, "Africa Leads the Way to a New Era," *Global Finance*, December 2009, pp. 47–49; UNCTAD, *Global Investment Trends Monitor*, January 24, 2012, retrieved from www.unctad.org; UNCTAD, *World Investment Report 2011* (New York: United Nations, 2011).

 ## International Collaborative Ventures

Collaborative ventures, sometimes called *international partnerships* or *international strategic alliances*, are essentially partnerships between two or more firms.[35] They help companies overcome together the often substantial risks and costs involved in achieving international projects that might exceed the capabilities of any one firm operating alone. Groups of firms sometimes form partnerships to accomplish large-scale goals such as developing new technologies or completing major projects such as power plants. By collaborating, the focal firm can draw on a range of complementary technologies, accessible only from other companies, to innovate and develop new products. Advantages such as these help explain why such partnerships have become enormously popular in recent decades.[36]

While collaboration can take place at similar or different levels of the value chain, it is typically focused on R&D, manufacturing, or marketing. International collaborative ventures greatly increase R&D productivity in high-technology sectors such as robotics, semiconductors, aircraft manufacturing, medical instruments, and pharmaceuticals.

Two basic types of collaborative ventures are equity joint ventures and project-based, non-equity ventures. *Equity joint ventures* are traditional collaborations of a type that has existed for decades. Recent years have seen a proliferation of *project-based collaborations*. Let's examine these ventures in detail.

Equity Joint Ventures

Joint ventures are normally formed when no one party possesses all the assets needed to exploit an available opportunity. In a typical international deal, the foreign partner contributes capital, technology, management expertise, training, or some type of product. The local partner contributes the use of its factory or other facilities, knowledge of the local language and culture, market navigation know-how, useful connections to the host-country government, or lower-cost production factors such as labor or raw materials. Western firms often seek joint ventures to gain access to markets in Asia.

The partnership allows the foreign firm to access key market knowledge, gain immediate access to a distribution system and customers, and attain greater control over local operations.

Procter & Gamble (P&G) is in a joint venture with Dolce & Gabbana, an Italian fashion house. Under the deal, P&G produces perfumes, while the Italian firm markets them in Europe, leveraging the local strength of its brand name.[37] The partnership provides both firms superior access to each other's strategic assets in R&D, production, branding, distribution, and market knowledge.

Samsung, the Korean electronics firm, began internationalizing in the 1970s through joint ventures with foreign-technology suppliers such as NEC, Sanyo, and Corning Glass Works. The partnerships allowed Samsung to acquire product designs and marketing outlets and gave management increasing confidence in foreign operations. As its capabilities grew, Samsung ventured into international production. Its earliest foreign manufacturing effort was a joint venture in Portugal, launched in 1982. In the 1990s, Samsung formed a joint venture with British supermarket chain Tesco to establish a chain of hypermarkets in South Korea. Aiming to enter the biopharmaceutical market, Samsung launched a joint venture in 2012 with U.S. biotechnology company Biogen Idec.[38]

Project-Based, Nonequity Ventures

Project-based, nonequity venture
A collaboration in which the partners create a project with a relatively narrow scope and a well-defined timetable, without creating a new legal entity.

Increasingly common in cross-border business, the **project-based, nonequity venture** is a collaboration in which the partners create a project with a relatively narrow scope and a well-defined timetable, without creating a new legal entity. Combining staff, resources, and capabilities, the partners collaborate on new technologies or products until the venture bears fruit or they no longer consider collaboration valuable. Such partnering reduces the enormous fixed costs of R&D, especially in technology and knowledge-intensive industries, and helps firms catch up with rivals. Russia's Rusnano and U.S. firm Crocus Technology entered a venture to research and produce advanced versions of MRAM chips, which can function as memory chips in iPhones, iPods, and similar products.[39]

IBM entered a strategic partnership for a limited period in which it provided outsourcing services to NTT, the Japanese telecommunications carrier, and NTT in turn provided outsourcing services and contacts for IBM to offer computer services sales to customers in Japan.[40] Germany's Siemens teamed with Motorola to develop the next generation of 300-mm 12-inch wafers, an important innovation in the global semiconductor industry. Motorola provided its expertise in advanced logic products and leading-edge manufacturing; Siemens contributed superior knowledge of random-access memory.

Differences Between Equity and Project-Based, Nonequity Ventures

In contrast to traditional equity joint ventures, project-based collaborations share the following distinctive characteristics:

1. No new legal entity is created. Partners carry on their activity within the guidelines of a contract.
2. Parent companies do not necessarily seek ownership of an ongoing enterprise. Instead, they contribute their knowledge, expertise, staff, and monetary resources to derive knowledge or other benefits.
3. Collaboration tends to have a well-defined timetable and end date; partners go their separate ways once they have accomplished their objectives or have no further reason for continuation.
4. Collaboration is narrower in scope than in equity joint venturing, typically emphasizing a single project, such as development, manufacturing, marketing, or distribution of a new product.

Exhibit 15.7 highlights advantages and disadvantages of the two types of international collaborative ventures.

Consortium

Consortium
A project-based, nonequity venture initiated by multiple partners to fulfill a large-scale project.

A **consortium** is a project-based, usually nonequity venture initiated by multiple partners to fulfill a large-scale project. It is typically formed with a contract that delineates the rights and obligations of each member. Work is allocated to the members on the same basis as profits. In a three-partner consortium, for example, if each party performs one-third of the work, then each earns one-third of the profits. Consortia are popular for innovation in industries such as commercial aircraft, computers, pharmaceuticals, and telecommunications, where the costs of developing and marketing a new product often reach hundreds of millions of dollars and require wide expertise. Boeing, Fuji, Kawasaki, and Mitsubishi joined forces to design and manufacture major components of the Boeing 767 aircraft. In China, South Korea's Doosan Group and the

EXHIBIT 15.7 Advantages and Disadvantages of International Collaborative Ventures

	Advantages	Disadvantages
Equity joint ventures	• Afford greater control over future directions • Facilitate transfer of knowledge between the partners • Common goals drive the joint venture	• Complex management structure • Coordination between the partners may be a concern • Difficult to terminate • Greater exposure to political risk
Project-based, nonequity ventures	• Easy to set up • Simple management structure; can be adjusted easily • Takes advantage of partners' respective strengths • Can respond quickly to changing technology and market conditions • Easy to terminate	• Knowledge transfer may be less straightforward between the partners • No equity commitment; thus, puts greater emphasis on trust, good communications, and developing relationships • Conflicts may be harder to resolve • Division of costs and benefits may strain relationship

U.S. firm Westinghouse partnered with China's State Nuclear Power Technology Corporation to build nuclear power plants. Westinghouse is majority owned by Japan's Toshiba Corporation.[41]

Often, several firms pool their resources to bid on a major project, such as building a power plant or a high-tech manufacturing facility. Each brings a unique specialty to the project but would be unable to win the bid on its own. No formal legal entity is created; each firm retains its individual identity. In this way, if one party withdraws, the consortium can continue with the remaining participants. iNavSat is a consortium formed among several European firms to develop and manage Europe's global satellite navigation system.

Cross-Licensing Agreements

A **cross-licensing agreement** is a project-based, nonequity venture in which the partners agree to allow access to licensed intellectual property developed by the other on preferential terms. Microsoft entered such an agreement with Japan's JVC to share patented knowledge on software and other products. Two firms also might enter a cross-distribution agreement, in which each partner has the right to distribute products or services produced by the other on preferential terms. The Star Alliance is an agreement among over twenty-five airlines—including Air Canada, United, Lufthansa, SAS, Singapore Airlines, and Air New Zealand—to market each others' airline flights (www.staralliance.com).

Cross-licensing agreement
A type of project-based, nonequity venture where partners agree to access licensed technology developed by the other on preferential terms.

 ## Managing Collaborative Ventures

In FDI and exporting, the focal firm emphasizes competing skillfully against rival companies. In collaborative ventures, however, the focal firm must cooperate with one or more other firms that, in different circumstances or other countries, may actually be its competitors. This requires managers to acquire skills in developing and consummating partnerships with other firms around the world.[42] Let's review the key managerial tasks in successful collaboration.

Understand Potential Risks in Collaboration

Firms that collaborate have decided partnering is preferred to going it alone. In short, the potential benefits outweigh potential risks. In analyzing a possible collaboration, management should address the following questions:

- Are we likely to grow dependent on, or become dominated by, the partner firm?
- By partnering, will we stifle growth and innovation in our own organization?
- Will we share our competencies excessively, to the point where corporate interests are threatened? How can we safeguard our core competencies?
- Will we be exposed to significant commercial, political, cultural, or currency risks?
- How effectively can we integrate the cultures and operations of the partner firms?
- Will we close off any growth opportunities by participating in this venture?
- Will managing the venture place an excessive burden on our corporate resources, such as managerial, financial, or technological resources?

The potential partner may be a current or potential competitor, is likely to have its own agenda, and will likely gain important competitive advantages from the relationship.[43] Management must protect its hard-won capabilities and other organizational assets to preserve its bargaining power and ability to compete. The firm does not want to become too dependent on its partner. Harmony is not necessarily the most important goal, and accepting some conflict and tension between the partners may be preferable to surrendering core skills. For example, Westinghouse shared thousands of technical documents and other intellectual property during its partnership with Chinese firms to build nuclear reactors in China. Intellectual property rights in China are weaker than in some other countries and the Chinese aim to become major developers of nuclear energy. Western industrial knowledge is certain to seep out to potential competitors, which will hurt future prospects of Westinghouse and other non-Chinese firms in the market.[44]

Pursue a Systematic Process for Partnering

The initial decision in internationalization is to choose the most appropriate target market, because the market determines the characteristics needed in a business partner. If the firm plans to enter an emerging market, for example, it may need a partner with political clout or connections. In this way, country targeting and partner selection are interdependent choices.

Exhibit 15.8 outlines the process for identifying and working with a suitable business partner.[45] It reveals that managers need to draw on their cross-cultural competence, legal expertise, and financial planning skills.

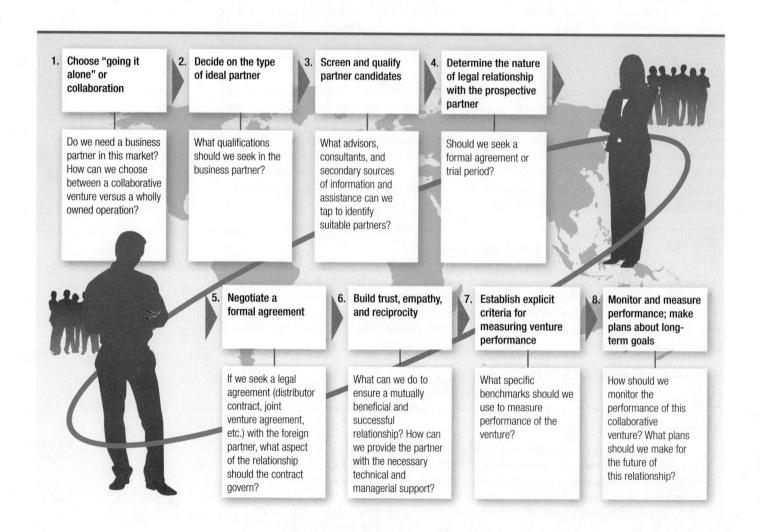

EXHIBIT 15.8

A Systematic Process for International Business Partnering

When managers first contemplate internationalization via FDI, they usually think in terms of a wholly owned operation. Many are accustomed to retaining the control and sole access to profits that come with 100 percent ownership. While the nature of the industry or product can make partnering less desirable, management should consider collaboration an option. Typically, the firm enters a collaborative venture when it discovers a weak or missing link in its value chain and chooses a partner that can remedy the deficiency. China is an increasingly popular venue for collaboration in the Internet service-provider industry. Both Microsoft and Google entered this huge market via joint ventures with local partners. But eBay and Yahoo entered China primarily via wholly owned FDI. Each firm chose the entry strategy most appropriate for its situation.[46]

Ensure Success with Collaborative Ventures

About half of all collaborative ventures fail within the first five years of operation because of unresolved disagreements, confusion about venture goals, and other problems. International ventures are particularly challenging because, in addition to complex business issues, managers must contend with differences in culture and language, as well as in political, legal, and economic systems. The failure rate of collaborative ventures is higher in developing economies than in advanced economies.[47] Companies as diverse as Avis, Daewoo, General Mills, and General Motors have experienced such failures.

French food giant Danone (www.danone.com) terminated its joint venture with a local Chinese partner after years of contentious relations. Danone had formed the partnership in 1996 at a time when the Chinese government often required such ventures from foreign firms.[48] In later years, however, the Chinese partner established a mirror business in which it sold, on the side, the same products the joint venture was marketing. The partner claimed that contract terms were unfair and accused Danone of trying to gain control of its other businesses.

Success in collaborative ventures is attained by following several guidelines:

- *Be cognizant of cultural differences*. International collaborations require that both parties learn and appreciate each other's corporate and national cultures. Cultural incompatibility can cause anger, frustration, and inefficiency. The partners may never arrive at a common set of values and organizational routines, especially if they are from very distinct cultures—say, Norway and Nigeria. Establishing cultural compatibility is a must.
- *Pursue common goals*. When partners have differing goals for the venture, or their goals change over time, they can find themselves operating at cross-purposes. Japanese firms tend to value market share over profitability, while U.S. firms value profitability over market share. Because different strategies are required to maximize each of these performance goals, a joint venture between Japanese and U.S. firms may fail. To overcome such challenges, partners need to regularly interact and communicate at three levels of the organization: senior management, operational management, and the workforce.
- *Give due attention to planning and management of the venture*. Without agreement on questions of management, decision making, and control, each partner may seek to control all the venture's operations, which can strain the managerial, financial, and technological resources of both. In some cases, equal governance and a sense of shared enterprise are best because they help partners view themselves as equals and reach consensus. In other cases, having a dominant partner in the relationship helps ensure success. When one of the partners is clearly the driver or the leader in the relationship, there is less likelihood of a stalemate or prolonged negotiations.
- *Safeguard core competencies*. Collaboration takes place between current or potential competitors that must walk a fine line between cooperation and competition. Volkswagen and General Motors succeeded in China by partnering with the Chinese firm, Shanghai Automotive Industry Corporation (SAIC; www.saicmotor.com). The Western firms transferred much technology and know-how to their Chinese partner. Having learned much

from them, SAIC is now becoming a significant player in the global automobile industry and even a competitor to its earlier partners.[49]

- *Adjust to shifting environmental circumstances.* When environmental conditions change, the rationale for a collaborative venture may weaken or disappear. An industry or economic downturn may shift priorities in one or both firms. Cost overruns can make the venture untenable. New government policies or regulations can increase costs or eliminate anticipated benefits. Flexibility is key for adjusting to changing conditions.

The Experience of Retailers in Foreign Markets

Retailers represent a special case of international service firms that internationalize substantially through FDI and collaborative ventures. Retailing takes various forms and includes department stores (Marks & Spencer, Macy's), specialty retailers (Body Shop, Gap), supermarkets (Sainsbury, Safeway), convenience stores (7-Eleven, Tom Thumb), discount stores (Zellers, Target), and big-box stores (Home Depot, IKEA). Walmart has more than 240 stores and tens of thousands of employees in China. It sources almost all its merchandise locally, providing jobs for thousands more Chinese.[50]

The major drivers of retailer internationalization include saturation of home-country markets, deregulation of international investment, and opportunities to benefit from lower costs abroad. Home Depot expanded abroad because the home improvement market in Canada and the United States is becoming saturated.[51] Most emerging markets exhibit pent-up demand, fast economic growth, a growing middle class, and increasingly sophisticated consumers. In densely populated developing countries, consumers are flocking to discount retailers that sell a wide selection of merchandise at low prices.

Retailers usually choose between FDI and franchising as a foreign market entry strategy. The larger, more experienced firms, such as Carrefour, Royal Ahold, and Walmart, tend to internationalize via FDI; that is, they typically own their stores and maintain direct control over operations and proprietary assets. Smaller and less internationally experienced firms such as Borders bookstores tend to rely on networks of independent franchisees. In franchising, the retailer adopts a business system from, and pays an ongoing fee to, a franchise operator. Other firms may employ a dual strategy—using FDI in some markets and franchising in others. While franchising facilitates rapid internationalization, compared to FDI, it affords the firm less control over its foreign operations, which can be risky in countries with unstable political or economic situations or weak intellectual property laws.

Source: Pavel Losevsky/Fotolia LLC

Retailers are a distinctive category of international service firms that usually internationalize through FDI and collaborative ventures. Pictured is a department store in Russia.

Many retailers have floundered in foreign markets.[52] When the French department store Galleries Lafayette opened in New York City, it could not compete with the city's numerous posh competitors. In its home market in the United Kingdom, Marks & Spencer succeeds with store layouts that blend food and clothing offerings in relatively small spaces, a formula that translated poorly in Canada and the United States. IKEA experienced problems in Japan where consumers value high-quality furnishings, not the low-cost products IKEA offers.

Walmart (www.walmart.com) is the world's largest retailer but failed in Germany because it could not compete with local competitors and eventually exited the market. In Mexico, Walmart constructed massive U.S.-style parking lots for its new super centers. But most Mexicans don't have cars and city bus stops were too far away, so shoppers could not haul their goods home. In Brazil, most families do their big shopping once a month on payday. Walmart built aisles too narrow and crowded to accommodate the rush and stocked shelves in urban São Paulo with unneeded leaf blowers. In Argentina, Walmart's red, white, and blue banners, reminiscent of the U.S. flag, offended local tastes. Sam's Club, Walmart's food discounting operation, flopped in Latin America partly because its huge multipack items were too big for local shoppers with low incomes and small apartments. Today Walmart is one of Latin America's most successful retailers, but required some years to perfect its operations there.[53]

Challenges of International Retailing

As these examples reveal, foreign markets pose big challenges for retailers. Retailing depends for much of its success on the store environment and the shopping experience and is strongly affected by factors in each national environment. Four barriers stand in the way of successfully transplanting home-market success to international markets:

1. *Culture and language* are a significant obstacle. Compared to most businesses, retailers are close to customers. They must respond to local market requirements by customizing their product and service portfolio, adapting store hours, modifying store size and layout, training local workers, and meeting labor union demands.
2. Consumers tend to develop strong *loyalty to indigenous retailers*. As Galleries Lafayette in New York and Walmart in Germany discovered, local firms usually enjoy great allegiance from local consumers.
3. Managers must address *legal and regulatory barriers* that can be idiosyncratic. Germany limits store hours, and most retailers are closed on Sundays. Japan's Large-Scale Store Law required foreign warehouse and discount retailers to get permission from existing small retailers before setting up shop. Although it has been relaxed in recent years, the law was a major obstacle to the entry of stores like Toys "R" Us. IKEA has been wary of entering India, due to excessive restrictions placed on foreign retailers.[54]
4. When entering a new market, retailers must develop *local sources* for thousands of products, including some that local suppliers may be unwilling or unable to provide. When Toys "R" Us entered Japan, local toy manufacturers were reluctant to work with the U.S. firm. Some retailers end up importing many of their offerings, which requires establishing complex and costly international supply chains.

International Retailing Success Factors

The most successful retailers pursue a systematic approach to international expansion. Initially, *advanced research and planning is essential*. A thorough understanding of the target market, combined with a sophisticated business plan, allows the firm to anticipate potential problems and prepare for success. In the run-up to launching stores in China, management at the giant French retailer Carrefour spent 12 years building up its business in Taiwan, where it developed a deep understanding of Chinese culture. It also learned how to forge alliances with local governments. These preparations helped Carrefour become China's biggest foreign retailer, rapidly developing a network of hypermarkets in twenty-five cities.[55]

In addition, international retailers need to *establish efficient logistics and purchasing networks* in each market where they operate. Scale economies in procurement are especially critical. Retailers need to organize sourcing and logistical operations to ensure they always maintain adequate inventory while minimizing the cost of operations.

International retailers should *assume an entrepreneurial, creative approach to foreign markets*. Virgin Megastore is a good example. Starting from one London location in 1975, founder Richard Branson expanded Virgin to numerous markets throughout Europe, North America, and Asia. The stores were big, well lit, and stocked music albums in a logical order, all innovations at the time. Consequently, sales turnover was much faster than that of smaller music retailers.

Retailers also must be willing to *adjust business model to suit local conditions*. Home Depot offers merchandise in Mexico that suits the small budgets of do-it-yourself builders. It has introduced payment plans and promotes the do-it-yourself mind-set in a country where most cannot afford to hire professional builders.[56] The major dimensions along which retailers differentiate themselves abroad include selection, price, marketing, store design, and the ways in which goods are displayed. They must proceed cautiously while adapting to local conditions, to avoid diluting or destroying the unique features that first made them successful.

IKEA, the world's largest furniture retailer, has enjoyed great success, launching over 200 furniture megastores in dozens of countries. Superior performance derives from strong leadership and skillful management of human resources, and from the careful balancing of global integration of operations with responsiveness to local tastes. In each store, IKEA (www.ikea. com) offers as many standardized products as possible while maintaining sufficient flexibility to accommodate specific local conditions. It tests the waters first and learns in smaller markets before entering big markets. For example, IKEA perfected its retailing model in German-speaking Switzerland before entering Germany.

CLOSING CASE   DaimlerChrysler: A Failed Global Merger

Daimler AG is Germany's well-known manufacturer of premium automobiles, especially Mercedes-Benz. Chrysler Corporation was long one of the "Big Three" U.S. automakers, known for cars, vans, and sport utility vehicles. When these two firms merged in 1998, the deal was announced at a press conference attended by more than 300 journalists. Excitement was so great that share prices of both companies rose by 10 percent.

At the time of the merger, Daimler and Chrysler were automotive giants, and critics questioned why two successful firms would combine forces. The main reason was that global automotive production had outstripped demand for cars, global competition had intensified, and automakers were scrambling to survive. Top management at Daimler believed the solution was to expand its product offerings and extend sales to more markets worldwide. Daimler sought to acquire Chrysler, to access the latter's complementary product line and customer base in the United States.

Daimler believed a hostile takeover would alienate customers, employees, and other constituents in Chrysler's home market. Thus, a friendly merger was arranged and portrayed as a "merger of equals." The resulting marriage of two titans led to the biggest merger in automotive history. Financed by a swap of stock shares, "DaimlerChrysler" was launched in 1998.

A Merger of Equals

The $37 billion deal created a company with 442,000 employees, market capitalization approaching $100 billion, daily production of 11,000 cars, and annual revenues of nearly $150 billion. DaimlerChrysler became the new top player in global automaking and sent shock waves through the industry worldwide. Since each company's strengths were seen to complement the other's weaknesses, the merger was viewed as a near-perfect union. It was contrasted with traditional takeovers in which a large firm swallowed a smaller firm, such as BMW's acquisition of Rover and Ford's purchase of Jaguar.

Goals of DaimlerChrysler were to grow globally and take advantage of scale economies resulting from combining operations for R&D, sourcing, distribution, and sales. Management expected cost savings of $3 billion annually. The merger brought strong financial power and a range of top-selling models under one roof. The venture would combine the image of Mercedes-Benz, representing speed, luxury, and engineering excellence with that of Chrysler, representing mainstream American values and a reliable name in minivans and sport utility vehicles. DaimlerChrysler would manufacture vehicles in thirty-four countries and sell in nearly 200. There was almost no overlap in products. Chrysler's main market was North America (93 percent of sales), while Mercedes dominated Europe (63 percent of sales). Each firm aimed to generate synergies in international sales and other value-chain activities.

Specifically, Daimler's goals in the merger were to:

- Broaden its market base. Until the merger, Daimler competed mainly for 20 percent of the world market, never reaching the remaining 80 percent.
- Reach more middle-class buyers, beyond those historically targeted by Mercedes.
- Build an image of a global multi-brand firm with a culture of innovation and sustainable cost structure.
- Jump ahead of competitors such as Toyota's Lexus and Volkswagen's Audi, through a balanced portfolio of vehicles in categories and price ranges worldwide.
- Generate cost saving by accessing Chrysler's supply chains for parts and components.

Chrysler's goals in the merger were to:

- Overcome the challenges of excess capacity and overproduction by consolidating operations with a strong partner.
- Become the premier auto company in the world.
- Increase sales through Daimler's extensive distribution network, especially in Europe.
- Improve quality with help from Daimler engineers.

Conflict

Shortly after the merger, however, problems began. The seeds of discontent were sown in the two years after the union when Chrysler lost $1.2 billion, closed six plants, and laid off 26,000 employees. Most top U.S. executives retired, quit or were fired, and were replaced with German executives. The resulting "brain drain" hindered achieving some of Daimler's goals. Declining fortunes at Chrysler were attributed to several factors, including intense competition, declining economic conditions, rising fuel costs, and challenges in the merger with Daimler.

Over time, numerous issues arose:

1. *Merger of equals.* From the beginning, Daimler sent mixed signals about equality of the merger. While insisting the two partners were equal, Daimler positioned itself as Chrysler's superior. The merger lacked sufficient clarity and direction regarding decision making, control, and operations management. The absence of equal governance hindered reaching consensus. Daimler ruled over Chrysler, fostering resentment and confusion.

2. *Venture identity.* The German and the U.S. organizations had distinct histories and personalities. Confusion arose about the identity of the new firm. Would it be American, German, or global? Would it be headquartered in Germany or the United States? Should the name be ChryslerDaimler, DaimlerChrysler, or something else? In the end, the venture assumed a German

identity. Identity issues sowed confusion among employees, customers, and others, affecting the quality of management and the venture's ability to raise capital.

3. *Culture clash*. Daimler was a relatively hierarchical, conservative organization, with centralized decision making. Chrysler was a flatter organization, with diffused authority and Midwest U.S. egalitarian values. Daimler overshadowed Chrysler, and refused most of Chrysler's demands. Approaches to employee compensation differed sharply, which stirred resentment. Cultural issues extended even to everyday operations. For example, shareholder meetings in Detroit featured German cuisine.

4. *Integration problems*. The two firms' product lines and marketing approaches proved difficult to integrate. Mercedes could not be produced on Chrysler production lines, and Chrysler minivans were a poor fit at Mercedes plants. Critics questioned whether customers would accept Daimler cars built by Chrysler employees in the U.S. Midwest, and Chrysler minivans and cars were difficult to market through Mercedes dealers. Both firms were reluctant to use the other's distribution channels.

5. *Absence of synergies*. Once seen as an asset, the lack of overlap between Chrysler and Daimler product lines proved problematic. The gulf between Mercedes' premium position and Chrysler's mainstream one hampered natural synergies in R&D, production, and other value-chain activities. The two firms failed to consolidate their supply bases and dealerships. Ultimately, Daimler and Chrysler goals differed sharply. Insufficient synergies strained the merger's managerial and financial resources.

6. *Growth ambitions*. Top management envisioned becoming the world's biggest automaker. The new firm aimed to expand into developing markets in Asia and Latin America. But DaimlerChrysler lacked a line-up of small cars suited to such markets. The venture evolved too quickly, unable to absorb massive change across a huge organization.

The Divorce

From the beginning, problems in the merger were real and visible. German dominance fostered an atmosphere of mistrust and resentment. Early enthusiasts were disappointed by the loss of Chrysler's identity. Managers in Germany and the United States could not reach sufficient accommodation on numerous issues. Trust was never fully established and turmoil became a dominant theme. As the venture faltered, relations soured and constituents grew pessimistic.

The "merger of equals" tagline, intended to foster goodwill, was a facade. Managers throughout Chrysler resented the venture's false premise. Daimler's domination filtered down through rank and file, creating a gloomy atmosphere. Many at Daimler viewed the relationship as temporary, and treated it as such. A lack of commitment and strategic vision hindered the development of a joint mission and strategies needed to ensure a successful venture. Following early Chrysler losses, German executives saw Chrysler as a drain on Daimler resources and viewed the merger with skepticism. Cultural differences hampered communications.

In 2007, following nine disappointing years, Daimler sold Chrysler to Cerberus Capital Management for about $8 billion, a major loss. In 2009, Chrysler filed for bankruptcy and took out billions in government loans to finance its restructuring. By 2012, skillful restructuring had revived Chrysler, regaining its status as one of the "Big Three". Daimler returned to its roots, and remains a successful global firm.

AACSB: Reflective Thinking Skills

Case Questions

1. In broad terms, what were each of Chrysler's and Daimler's motives for entering the merger? Evaluate the extent to which each firm accomplished these motives.

2. Explain how the DaimlerChrysler merger enhanced economies of scale and scope in the respective firms. How successful was the venture in attaining such economies?

3. What advantages did each of Chrysler and Daimler seek from their merger? What disadvantages did these firms bring to the venture? Elaborate.

4. The chapter identifies a collection of questions that managers should address before forming international collaborative ventures. In terms of potential risks in collaboration, what issues did top management at DaimlerChrysler fail to adequately understand? Elaborate.

5. Suggest a systematic process that Daimler could have followed to increase the likelihood of merger success. Provide examples on how Daimler might have made such a process succeed.

Sources: J. Badrtalei, and D. Bates, "Effect of Organizational Cultures on Mergers and Acquisitions", *International Journal of Management*, 24 (no. 2, 2007): 300–317; M. Blaško, J. M. Netter, and J. F. Sinkey, "Value Creation and Challenges of an International Transaction: The DaimlerChrysler Merger", *International Review of Financial Analysis*, 9 (no. 1, 2000): 77–102; *CNN Money*, DaimlerChrysler dawns, May 7, 1998, retrieved from http://money.cnn.com; "Divorced: What the Sale of Chrysler to a Private-Equity Firm Means for America's Car Industry," *The Economist*, May 19, 2007, PP. 67–68; S. Finkelstein, "The DaimlerChrysler Merger", Tuck School of Business, Dartmouth, no. 1-0071, 2002; Harald Hamprecht, "Clash of the Titans," *Automotive News*, September 12, 2011, pp. 3–17; L. Iacocca, "Iacocca: 'Daimler Screwed Chrysler'", *Business Week Online*, May 18, 2007, p. 14; J. Mateja, "DaimlerChrysler Talks Shop," *Chicago Tribune*, March 12, 2001; J. Snyder, and B. Wernle, "Chrysler Shriveled Under Schrempp", *Automotive News*, February 16, 2009, p. 23; B. Vlasic, K. Kerwin, D. Woodruff, T. Peterson, and L. Nathans, "The First Global Car Colossus", *Business Week*, May 18, 1998, p. 40–43; B. Vlasic and B. Stertz, *Taken for a Ride: How Daimler-Benz Drove Off with Chrysler*, New York: William Morrow, 2000; D. Waller, *Wheels on Fire: The Amazing Inside Story of the Daimler Chrysler Merger*, London: Hodder & Stoughton, 2001.

This case was written by Ayse Ozturk, Georgia State University, under the direction of Dr. Gary Knight.

CHAPTER ESSENTIALS

MyManagementLab

Go to **mymanagementlab.com** to complete the problems marked with this icon ★.

Key Terms

Summary

In this chapter, you learned about:

1. International investment and collaboration

Foreign direct investment (FDI) is an internationalization strategy where the firm establishes a physical presence abroad through ownership of productive assets such as capital, technology, labor, land, plant, and equipment. An **international collaborative venture** is a cross-border business alliance where partnering firms pool their resources and share costs and risks of the venture. A **joint venture** is a form of collaboration between two or more firms that leads to minority, equal, or majority ownership.

2. Motives for FDI and collaborative ventures

Firms employ FDI for various reasons, including *market-seeking motives*, to enter new markets and gain new customers; *resource/asset-seeking motives*, to acquire production factors that may be cheaper or more abundant in foreign markets; and *efficiency-seeking motives*, to enhance the efficiency of the firm's value-adding activities. These motives often occur in combination. Motivations for international collaborative ventures include the ability to gain access to new markets, opportunities, or knowledge; to undertake international activities too costly or risky for one firm alone; to reduce costs; to meet government requirements; and to prevent or reduce competition.

3. Characteristics of foreign direct investment

FDI is the most advanced and complex entry strategy and involves establishing manufacturing plants, marketing subsidiaries, or other facilities abroad. For the firm,

FDI requires substantial resource commitment, local presence and operations in target countries, and the ability to access comparative advantages. It also entails greater risk as compared to other entry modes. FDI is most commonly used by MNEs—large firms with extensive international operations. Services are intangible and typically cannot be exported. Services are usually location-bound and require firms to establish a foreign presence, generally via FDI. **International portfolio-investment** is passive ownership of foreign securities such as stocks and bonds.

4. Types of foreign direct investment

FDI can be **wholly owned direct investment**, in which the firm owns 100 percent of foreign operations, or an equity joint venture with one or more partners. Firms may engage in **greenfield investment** by building a facility from scratch or by acquiring an existing facility from another firm through **acquisition**. With **vertical integration**, the firm seeks to own multiple stages of its value chain. With **horizontal integration**, the firm seeks to own activities involved in a single stage of its value chain. A **merger** is a special type of acquisition in which two companies join together to form a new, larger firm.

5. International collaborative ventures

Joint ventures (JVs) are normally formed when no one party possesses all the assets needed to exploit an opportunity. Joint ventures are an example of ownership-based collaborations. The **project-based, nonequity venture** emphasizes a contractual relationship between the partners and is formed to pursue certain goals or meet an important business need while the partners remain independent. A **consortium** is a project-based, nonequity venture initiated by multiple firms to undertake a large-scale activity that is beyond the capabilities of the individual members.

6. Managing collaborative ventures

Collaboration requires management to clearly define its goals and strategies. It requires much research and analysis up-front, as well as strong negotiation skills. Decisions are made regarding allocation of responsibilities in management, production, finance, and marketing, as well as how to handle day-to-day operations and plans for the future. At least half of all collaborative ventures fail prematurely. Firms should choose their partners carefully and follow a systematic process for managing ventures.

7. The experience of retailers in foreign markets

Because retailing requires intensive customer interaction, it is particularly susceptible to culture, income levels, and other conditions abroad. Success depends on adapting to local conditions while maintaining the retailer's unique features and value proposition. International retailers face cultural and language barriers, strong customer loyalty to local retailers, legal and regulatory barriers, and the need to develop local supply sources. Retailer success also depends on advanced research and planning, establishing efficient logistics and purchasing networks, using an entrepreneurial and creative approach to foreign markets, and adjusting the business model to suit local needs.

Test Your Comprehension AACSB: Reflective Thinking Skills, Analytic Skills

1. What are the various types of FDI? Distinguish between acquisition and greenfield.

⭐ 2. What are the major motivations for undertaking FDI?

3. Delineate the types of firms involved in FDI. Are there any types of companies that can internationalize only via FDI? Elaborate.

4. Identify the different types of collaborative ventures. What type of venture is best for entering a culturally distant market like Malaysia? For the next generation of products in its industry? For undertaking a short-term project, such as building infrastructure (e.g., highway, dam) abroad?

5. What are the major motives for undertaking FDI for a small firm whose sales are dwindling in its home market?

For a firm that wants to enter a country with high trade barriers? For a firm with high manufacturing costs in its home market? For a hotel chain? For a large, diversified firm seeking to enter various markets worldwide for a variety of reasons?

6. What factors should management consider when deciding where in the world to establish a factory? A marketing subsidiary? A regional headquarters?

7. What steps should the firm take to ensure the success of its international collaborative ventures?

⭐ 8. What are the risks of international retailing? What can a retailer—such as a department store or a restaurant—do to maximize its chances of succeeding in foreign markets?

Apply Your Understanding AACSB: Communication Abilities, Reflective Thinking Skills, Ethical Understanding and Reasoning Abilities

1. Suppose you get a job at MobileTV, a small manufacturer of TV sets installed in cars and boats. Business has declined recently, foreign rivals from emerging markets are increasing competition, and management is worried. Because MobileTV does all its manufacturing in Canada and the United Kingdom, it lacks cost advantages and its prices are relatively high. After studying the problem, you conclude MobileTV should move much of its production to Mexico. But top management knows little about FDI. Prepare a report to management detailing the advantages of establishing a production base in Mexico. Why should the firm be interested in foreign manufacturing? Recommend which type of FDI MobileTV should use

in Mexico. Finally, what advantages and disadvantages should the venture expect from manufacturing in Mexico?

2. Suppose you work for Aoki Corporation, a producer of processed foods. Your boss, Hiroshi Aoki, heard there is a big market for processed foods in Europe but does not know how to enter or do business there. You recommend entering Europe through a joint venture with a local European firm. Prepare a memo to Aoki explaining the objectives and risks of internationalizing via collaborative ventures. Explain why a collaborative venture might be a better entry strategy than wholly owned FDI. Keep in mind that processed food is a culturally

sensitive product that entails various complexities in marketing and distribution. What type of European partner should Aoki seek?

3. **Ethical Dilemma:** Censorship standards vary worldwide. What is acceptable in some countries, such as nudity on television, criticizing authority, or revealing government secrets that affect national security, is unacceptable in others. Google is an Internet service multinational that used FDI to establish operations in China. Google enjoyed growing market success for several years. Eventually, however, Chinese government officials blocked Google from the market because Google refused to censor links to Web sites on sensitive topics, such as independence for Taiwan and criticism of the Chinese government. Government censorship requirements eventually forced Google to withdraw from mainland China, a move that ceded market share to Chinese competitors and hurt Google's profits. Suppose you are an international manager at Google. Should Google have exited China, or should it reestablish its presence there and comply with Chinese censorship rules? Using the Ethical Framework in Chapter 5, analyze the arguments for and against Google's withdrawal from China. What can Google do to address the problem effectively?

INTERNET EXERCISES
(http://www.globalEDGE.msu.edu)

AACSB: Communication Abilities, Reflective Thinking Skills, Use of Information Technology

Refer to Chapter 1, page 24, for instructions on how to access and use globalEDGE™.

1. Suppose your company wants to establish a factory in Latin America to make and sell products in the region. It has narrowed the pool of candidate countries to Argentina, Brazil, and Chile. Your task is to write a report that compares the FDI environments of these countries. One approach is to obtain the Country Fact Sheet for each nation from UNCTAD (www.unctad.org), a United Nations agency that gathers FDI data. You can access this data either through globalEDGE™ or the UNCTAD site. By examining the fact sheets, answer each of the following questions individually for Argentina, Brazil, and Chile:
   a. What nations are the major trading partners of each country in the region? (This indicates the size and stability of existing trading relationships with key partners.)
   b. Which companies are the leading firms now doing FDI in each country? (This helps identify key competitors.)
   c. What is each country's rating on the FDI Performance Index? (This rating indicates the performance that typical firms have experienced when investing in each country.)
   d. What is the level of merger and acquisition activity in each country? (This shows the maturity of each country for acquisition-based FDI.) Elaborate and justify your findings.

2. Suppose your firm aims to identify prospective countries for direct investment. Your boss has requested a report on the attractiveness of alternative locations based on their potential FDI return. A colleague mentions a tool called the "FDI Confidence Index." Consult this resource and write a report in which you identify the top FDI destinations, as well as the criteria used to construct the index. The Confidence Index is published by the consulting firm A. T. Kearney, based on an annual survey of CEOs at the world's top MNEs. Access the index by entering "FDI Confidence Index" at globalEDGE™ or directly at www.atkearney.com. Download the PDF file to do your research.

3. Assume you own a company that manufactures medical products in the biotechnology industry. You want to establish a foreign plant to manufacture your products and are seeking countries with a high concentration of knowledge workers. Thus, you decide to collect information about the "knowledge economy" abroad. The World Bank highlights the state of the knowledge economy in various countries. The data are accessible by visiting the World Bank site (www.worldbank.org) and entering the keywords "Knowledge Economy Index" in the search engine. You will be able to find several articles and retrieve information about these countries. Visit the site and prepare a report on the knowledge economy for each of the following: Singapore, South Korea, and Spain.

MyManagementLab

Go to **mymanagementlab.com** for Auto-graded writing questions as well as the following Assisted-graded writing questions:

15-1. Governments often provide incentives to encourage foreign firms to invest within their national borders. Why do governments encourage inward FDI?

15-2. Explain what steps a firm should take to successfully launch a collaborative venture with a foreign partner.

15-3. Mymanagementlab Only – comprehensive writing assignment for this chapter.

Harry Potter: The Magic of Licensing

One of the hottest properties in merchandise licensing is Harry Potter (www.harrypotter.warnerbros.com), the literary phenomenon that has grossed billions of dollars in retail sales globally to date. Not bad for a bespectacled 11-year-old boy. The fictional Harry has come a long way since he appeared in a 1997 children's book, the first of eight, by then-unknown author J. K. Rowling. In novels that appeal to both children and adults, Harry has evolved from an unhappy orphan to a confident young wizard. Young people love Harry because he's a fantastic combination of cool kid and good kid. Adults like

the series' classic theme of good versus evil. Globally, Potter books have sold more than 400 million copies in sixty-seven languages in nearly 200 countries.

Warner Brothers, which purchased exclusive licensing rights to the series, produced and released eight Harry Potter movies, all of which rank among the thirty top-grossing films of all time. The final film, *Harry Potter and the Deathly Hallows— Part 2*, was the highest grossing movie of 2011.

Warner allows companies worldwide to use Potter-related images on manufactured products such as game software,

CHAPTER 16

Licensing, Franchising, and Other Contractual Strategies

 LEARNING OBJECTIVES *In this chapter, you will learn about:*

1. Contractual entry strategies
2. Licensing as an entry strategy
3. Advantages and disadvantages of licensing
4. Franchising as an entry strategy
5. Advantages and disadvantages of franchising
6. Other contractual entry strategies
7. Infringement of intellectual property: A global problem
8. Guidelines for protecting intellectual property

MyManagementLab®

⭐ **Improve Your Grade!**

Over 10 million students improved their results using the Pearson MyLabs. Visit **mymanagementlab.com** for simulations, tutorials, and end-of-chapter problems.

---

children's furniture, school supplies, toys, and clothing in exchange for a *royalty*, a percentage of the sale generated by the licensed product that the manufacturer pays to the licensor. The ability to associate these images with manufactured products greatly increases the products' sales potential, allowing them to command high prices. Licensing deals (and book sales) have made Rowling one of the wealthiest women in the United Kingdom.

Warner licenses Harry Potter to a number of companies. Some produce *artifacts*, products seen in the films that do not have Harry's name on them. California's Jelly Belly Candy Company created Harry's favorite candy, Bertie Bott's Every Flavour Beans, in flavors such as earwax and sardine. LEGO makes construction kits for kids to build their own Hogwarts castle, and Mattel makes Harry Potter toys, including card games, play sets, chess sets, and action figures.

Electronic Arts (EA), the popular software game producer, paid Warner for a license to develop and market video games played on the Internet, video game consoles such as Sony's PlayStation, and cell phones. Fans can play a virtual version of Quidditch, which is like aerial polo with contestants flying on broomsticks. In 2009, EA released the video game version of Harry Potter and the Half-Blood Prince, selling millions of copies worldwide.

Goodwin Weavers, a home furnishings company, also has a Harry Potter license and produces Potter tapestry throws, wall hangings, decorative pillows, "pillow buddies," and fleece. P.J. Kids made a line of Potter beds that sold extremely well despite a price tag of nearly $2,000, demonstrating the magic of licensing a popular brand. Warner also sells licenses to service firms. For example, the theme park attraction, The Wizarding World of Harry Potter, opened at Universal Orlando Resort in Florida.

The licensing process has been self-generating—each new Harry Potter book yielded a movie, which boosted book sales, which promoted sales of Potter-licensed products and services. Warner reports the top markets for Potter-licensed products are the United States, United Kingdom, Germany, Japan, France, South Korea, Russia, and China.

Rowling and Warner have exercised restraint: They don't want to license Potter to just anyone, though experts estimate the hot property may have generated 300 product licenses in the United States alone. Warner wants to ensure overexposure doesn't kill the golden goose.

One risk that Warner face is intellectual property violations. These occur when a firm or individual uses the licensed item to generate profits without permission of the property's owner. For example, some 80 percent of recorded music and business software sold in China is counterfeit. Pirated DVD versions of Potter movies are sold on the streets of Chinese cities for as little as one dollar, often before the films have their official premieres there. Unauthorized foreign translations of the books posted on the Internet diminish future book sales. To combat book counterfeiting, the series' official Chinese publisher printed the Potter books on green paper and advised the local media—newspapers, magazines, television—how to recognize the real version.

SOURCES: Brian Bethune, "The Afterlife of Harry Potter," *Maclean's*, July 18, 2011, pp. 52–54; Ben Charny, "EA Bets on Harry Potter to Help Sell More Games," *Wall Street Journal*, May 13, 2009, p. B1; Stuart Derrick, "Brands Cash in on Literary Scene," *Promotions & Incentives*, July/August 2005, pp. 13–14; "Harry Potter and the Publishing Goldmine," *Economist.com/Global Agenda*, June 23, 2003, p. 1; Sheila O'Mara, "Harry— Licensing's Golden Child," *Home Textiles Today*, January/February 2002, p. 10; Tony Lisanti, "Warner Bros. and the Magic World of Harry Potter," *License! Global*, June 2009, pp. 66–70; Lauren Schuker, "Second 'Harry Potter' Park Planned," *Wall Street Journal*, December 1, 2011, p. B6.

Contractual entry strategies in international business
Cross-border exchanges where the relationship between the focal firm and its foreign partner is governed by an explicit contract.

Intellectual property
Ideas or works created by individuals or firms, including discoveries and inventions; artistic, musical, and literary works; and words, phrases, symbols, and designs.

Intellectual property rights
The legal claim through which the proprietary assets of firms and individuals are protected from unauthorized use by other parties.

Licensing
Arrangement in which the owner of intellectual property grants a firm the right to use that property for a specific time period in exchange for royalties or other compensation.

Licensing—granting a right to use property to others—has grown enormously in international business. In the opening story, J. K. Rowling, creator of Harry Potter, has earned millions of dollars by allowing manufacturers of various products and services to use the Potter image as part of their offerings. Such transactions imply a contractual relationship between those who own the property and those given permission to use it. For companies that own licensable properties such as technology, artistic works, logos, and business systems, licensing can be a very lucrative business around the world.

In this chapter, we address licensing, franchising, and other types of cross-border contractual relationships. **Contractual entry strategies in international business** are cross-border exchanges in which the relationship between the focal firm and its foreign partner is governed by an explicit contract. **Intellectual property** describes ideas or works created by individuals or firms, including discoveries and inventions; artistic, musical, and literary works; and words, phrases, symbols, and designs. Harry Potter is a leading example. As explained in Chapter 5, intellectual property is safeguarded through **intellectual property rights,** the legal claim through which proprietary assets are protected from unauthorized use by other parties.[1]

 Contractual Entry Strategies

Two common types of contractual entry strategies are licensing and franchising. **Licensing** is an arrangement in which the owner of intellectual property grants another firm the right to use that property for a specific time period in exchange for *royalties* or other compensation. As described in the opening story, a **royalty** is a fee paid periodically to compensate a licensor for the temporary use of its intellectual property, often based on a percentage of gross sales generated from the use of the licensed asset. As an entry strategy, licensing requires neither substantial capital investment nor involvement of the licensor in the foreign market. Licensing is a relatively inexpensive way for the firm to establish a presence in the market without having to resort to expensive foreign direct investment (FDI).

Franchising is an advanced form of licensing in which the firm allows another the right to use an entire business system in exchange for fees, royalties, or other forms of compensation.

The above types of contractual relationships are common in international business and allow companies to routinely transfer their knowledge assets to foreign partners. Professional service firms such as those in architecture, engineering, advertising, and consulting extend their international reach through contracts with foreign partners. Similarly, retailing, fast food, car rental, television programming, and animation firms rely on licensing and franchising agreements. 7-Eleven (www.7-eleven.com) runs the world's largest chain of convenience stores, with about 45,000 locations in eighteen countries. While the parent firm in Japan owns most of them, several thousand in Canada, Japan, Mexico, and the United States are operated by entrepreneurs through franchising arrangements.

Unique Aspects of Contractual Relationships

Cross-border contractual relationships share several common characteristics:

- *They are governed by a contract that provides the focal firm with a moderate level of control over the foreign partner.* A formal agreement specifies the rights and obligations of both partners. Control refers to the ability of the focal firm to influence the decisions, operations, and strategic resources of the foreign venture and ensure the partner undertakes assigned activities and procedures. The focal firm also maintains ownership and jurisdiction over its intellectual property. However, contractual agreements do not afford the same level of control as foreign direct investment, since they require the focal firm to rely on independent businesses abroad.
- *They typically include the exchange of intangibles and services.* Intangibles that firms exchange include various intellectual property, technical assistance, and know-how. Firms also may exchange products or equipment to support the foreign partner.
- *Firms can pursue them independently or in conjunction with other entry strategies.* In pursuing international opportunities, firms may employ contractual agreements alone, or they may combine them with FDI and exporting.[2] The use of such agreements is context specific; that is, the firm may use a contractual relationship with certain customers, countries, or products, but not others. For example, while licensing is common for certain types of products, it is not appropriate for others.
- *They provide dynamic, flexible choice.* Some focal firms use contractual agreements to make their initial entry in foreign markets. Then, as conditions evolve, they switch to another, often more advanced entry strategy. For example, franchisors such as McDonald's or Coca-Cola occasionally acquire some of their franchisees and bottlers. In doing so, they switch from a contractual approach to a direct investment strategy.
- *They often reduce local perceptions of the focal firm as a foreign enterprise.* A contractual relationship with a local firm allows the focal firm to blend into the local market, attracting less attention and less of the criticism often directed at firms that enter through more visible strategies such as FDI.
- *They generate a consistent level of earnings from foreign operations.* In comparison to FDI, contractual relationships are less susceptible to volatility and risk, and tend to bring both parties a predictable stream of revenue.[3]

Contractual relationships emphasize the exchange of intellectual property, which includes various types:

- A *patent* provides an inventor the right to prevent others from using or selling an invention for a fixed period—typically, up to 20 years.[4] It is granted to those who invent or discover a new and useful process, device, manufactured product, or an improvement on these.

Royalty
A fee paid periodically to compensate a licensor for the temporary use of its intellectual property, often based on a percentage of gross sales generated from the use of the licensed asset.

Franchising
Arrangement in which the firm allows another the right to use an entire business system in exchange for fees, royalties, or other forms of compensation.

- A *trademark* is a distinctive design, symbol, logo, word, or series of words placed on a product label. It identifies a product or service as coming from a common source and having a certain level of quality. Examples include Honda's H-shaped symbol, McDonald's golden arches, and Izod's alligator mark.
- A *copyright* protects original works of authorship, giving the creator the exclusive right to reproduce the work, display and perform it publicly, and authorize others to perform these activities. Copyrights cover music, art, literature, films, and computer software.
- An *industrial design* describes the appearance or features of a product. The design is intended to improve the product's aesthetics and usability as well as increase its production efficiency, performance, or marketability. The Apple iPod is a well-known industrial design. A *trade secret* is confidential know-how or information that has commercial value.[5] Trade secrets include production methods, business plans, and customer lists. The formula to produce Coca-Cola is a trade secret.
- A *collective mark* is a logo belonging to an organization whose members use it to identify themselves and associate their products with a level of quality or accuracy, geographical origin, or other positive characteristic. "DIN" is the collective mark for the German Institute for Standardization, typically found on home appliances in Europe.

Intellectual property rights derive from patents, trademarks, copyrights, and other protections associated with intellectual property. Such rights provide inventors with a monopoly advantage for a specified period of time, so they can exploit their inventions not only to recoup their investment costs and create commercial advantage, but also to acquire power and market dominance free of direct competition. The availability and enforcement of these rights vary from country to country. Without such legal protection and the assurance of commercial rewards, most firms and individuals would have little incentive to invent.

 ## Licensing as an Entry Strategy

A licensing agreement specifies the nature of the relationship between the owner of intellectual property, the *licensor*, and the user of the property, the *licensee*. High-technology firms routinely license their patents and know-how to foreign companies. For example, Intel has licensed the right to a new process for manufacturing computer chips to a chip manufacturer in Germany.

In the opening story, Warner licenses images from the Harry Potter books and movies to companies worldwide. Disney (www.disney.go.com) licenses the right to use its cartoon characters to shirt and hat manufacturers in China. It also licenses its trademark names and logos to manufacturers of apparel, toys, and watches for sale worldwide. Licensing allows Disney to create synergies with foreign partners, which can adapt materials, colors, and other design elements to suit local tastes and market a product similar to one Disney already may offer in the United States.

Exhibit 16.1 illustrates the nature of the licensing agreement.[6] Upon signing a licensing contract, the licensee pays the licensor a fixed amount up front *and* an ongoing royalty of typically 2 to 5 percent of gross sales generated from using the licensed asset. The fixed amount covers the licensor's initial costs of transferring the licensed asset to the licensee, including consultation, training in how to deploy the asset, engineering, or adaptation. Certain types of licensable assets, such as copyrights and trademarks, may have lower transfer costs. The royalty percentage may escalate with increasing sales.

A typical licensing contract runs five to seven years and is renewable at the option of the parties. Initially, the licensor provides technical information and assistance to the licensee. Once the relationship has been established and the licensee fully understands its role, the licensor usually plays an advisory role but usually has no direct involvement in the market and provides no ongoing managerial guidance. Most firms enter into *exclusive agreements*, in which the licensee is not permitted to share the licensed asset with any other company within a prescribed territory. In addition to operating in its domestic market, the licensee also may be permitted to export to other countries.

EXHIBIT 16.1

Licensing as a Foreign Market Entry Strategy

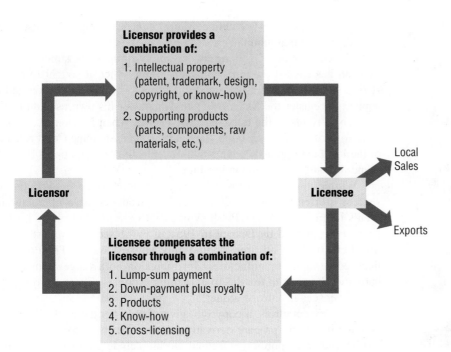

If the licensor is an MNE, it may enter a licensing arrangement with its own wholly or partly owned foreign affiliate. In this case, licensing is an efficient way to compensate the foreign affiliate, especially when it is a separate legal entity, and transfer intellectual property to it within a formal legal framework.

In the fashion industry, Hugo Boss, Pierre Cardin, and other strong brands generate substantial profits from licensing deals for jeans, fragrances, and watches. Saks Inc. entered China by licensing its Saks Fifth Avenue name for a flagship department store in Shanghai. Saks generates revenue from the agreement and controls which merchandise is sold in China but has no other involvement. Licensing brings greater awareness of Saks Fifth Avenue to Asia without requiring Saks itself to operate the store, thereby reducing its risk.[7]

The national origin of some popular brands might surprise you. Planters and Sunkist are brands owned by U.S. companies and sold in Singapore and the United Kingdom through licensing agreements with local companies. Evian bottled water is owned by the French company Danone and distributed in the United States under license by Coca-Cola. Game shows such as the *Price is Right* and *Family Feud* are owned by FremantleMedia, a United Kingdom company that licenses these programs for broadcast around the world. A review of annual reports from 120 of the largest multinational food companies revealed that at least half engage in some form of international product licensing.[8]

There are two major types of licensing agreements: (1) trademark and copyright licensing and (2) know-how licensing. Let's review each.

Trademark and Copyright Licensing

Trademark licensing grants a firm permission to use another firm's proprietary names, characters, or logos for a specified period of time in exchange for a royalty. Trademarks appear on such merchandise as clothing, games, food, beverages, gifts, novelties, toys, and home furnishings. Organizations and individuals with name-brand appeal benefit from trademark licensing, such as BBC Worldwide, Disney, Harley-Davidson, David Beckham, and even your favorite university. A famous trademark like Harry Potter can generate millions of dollars to the owner. In general, worldwide retail sales of licensed merchandise exceed $175 billion annually.[9]

In Canada, the United States, and numerous other countries, firms acquire rights to trademarks through first use and continuous usage. In other countries, however, rights to trademarks are acquired through registration with government authorities. Many firms register their trademarks in the countries where they do business to protect the asset. When a firm registers its trademark, it formally notifies government authorities that it owns the trademark and is entitled

Source: © Malcolm Fairman/Alamy

The Japanese firm Sanrio licenses its trademark characters to apparel and accessory manufacturers worldwide, generating substantial revenue. Shown here is the Hello Kitty store in Osaka, Japan.

Know-how agreement
Contract in which the focal firm provides technological or management knowledge about how to design, manufacture, or deliver a product or a service.

to intellectual property protection. Many countries require local use of the registered mark to maintain the registration.

The convention of gaining ownership to a trademark simply through registration has caused concerns for many firms. When it sought to enter South Africa, McDonald's was frustrated to learn a local businessperson had already applied to register the McDonald's trademark for his own use and to have the company's rights to the trademark withdrawn. When McDonald's protested in court to establish its ownership, the South African Supreme Court ruled in favor of the local entrepreneur. McDonald's eventually won on appeal but only after spending a significant sum in legal fees.[10]

Winnie the Pooh (www.disney.go.com/pooh) is one of the biggest success stories of trademark licensing. Introduced as a character in children's literature in 1926, Pooh evolved into a multi-billion-dollar licensing property. Acquired by Disney in 1961, it is the second-highest earning fictional character of all time, behind only Mickey Mouse. The Pooh image is licensed to many manufacturers for inclusion on a range of products from baby merchandise to textiles to gardening products. There are roughly 1,000 Pooh licensees in Europe alone.[11]

In many countries, a copyright gives the owner the exclusive right to reproduce the work, prepare derivative works, distribute copies, or perform or display the work publicly. Original works include art, music, and literature, as well as computer software. The term of protection varies by country, but the creator's life plus 50 years is typical. Because many countries offer little or no copyright protection, it is wise to investigate local copyright laws before publishing a work abroad.[12]

Know-How Licensing

Gaining access to technology is an important rationale for licensing. A **know-how agreement** is a contract in which the focal firm provides technological or management knowledge about how to design, manufacture, or deliver a product or a service to a licensee in exchange for a royalty. The royalty may be a lump sum, a *running royalty* based on the volume of products produced from the know-how, or a combination of both.

In some industries, such as pharmaceuticals and semiconductors, inventions and other intellectual property are acquired in reciprocal licensing arrangements between firms in the same or similar industries. Known as *cross-licensing*, the practice is common in industries with rapid technological advances that often build on each other. Technology licensing from competitors reduces the cost of innovation by avoiding duplication of research, while reducing the risk of excluding any one firm from access to new developments.

AT&T (www.att.com) once held most of the key patents in the semiconductor industry. As more firms entered the industry and the pace of research and development (R&D) quickened, AT&T risked being surpassed by competitors in Europe, Japan, and the United States, where thousands of semiconductor patents were being awarded. In such a complex network of patents, few firms would have succeeded without obtaining licenses from competitors. AT&T, Intel, Siemens, and numerous other competitors began licensing their patents to each other, creating synergies that greatly accelerated innovation in semiconductors.

In the pharmaceutical industry, the R&D expense to develop new drugs can reach billions of dollars. Pharmaceutical firms want to launch new drugs quickly in order to recoup these costs and expedite product development. Thus, the firms frequently cross-license technologies to each other, exchanging scientific knowledge about producing specific products, as well as the right to distribute them in certain geographic regions.[13] In other industries, firms may license technology and know-how from competitors to compensate for insufficient knowledge, fill gaps in their product lineups, enter new businesses, or save time and money.

The World's Top Licensing Firms

Exhibit 16.2 lists the world's leading licensing firms by annual revenues. All but one (Sanrio) are based in the United States. The greatest amount of licensing occurs in the apparel, games, and toy industries. Disney recently acquired Marvel Entertainment for $4 billion, greatly expanding

EXHIBIT 16.2 Leading Licensors Ranked by Licensing Revenues (Total Retail Sales of Licensed Products)

Rank	Firm Name	Annual Licensing Revenues (U.S. $ billions)	Typical Deals
1	Disney Consumer Products	$28.6	Toy and apparel licensing for Disney movies such as *Little Mermaid* and *Hannah Montana: The Movie*, and characters such as Winnie the Pooh and Mickey Mouse
2	ICONIX	12.0	Apparel licensing for such brands as OP, Starter, and Danskin
3	Phillips-Van Heusen	8.7	Apparel and accessories licensing for such brands as Arrow, Izod, and Van Heusen
4	Mattel	7.0	Toy manufacturer and licensor of iconic toy and game brands such as Barbie, Hot Wheels, and UNO
5	Warner Bros. Consumer Products	6.0	Toy and apparel licensing from movies such as *Batman*, *Scooby-Doo*, and *Harry Potter*
6	Marvel Entertainment	5.6	Toy, game, and apparel licensing for Marvel comic characters such as *Iron Man*, *Fantastic Four*, and *X-Men*
7	Nickelodeon & Viacomm Consumer Products	5.5	Toy and apparel licensing for TV programs such as *SpongeBob SquarePants* and *Dora the Explorer*
8	Sanrio (Japan)	5.0	Toys and apparel tied to the Hello Kitty character
9	Major League Baseball	5.0	Baseball-related video games, apparel, toys
10	The Collegiate Licensing Company	4.3	Licensed merchandise for universities and collegiate sports teams

Sources: Based on Annual reports of the individual firms; Company profiles at www.hoovers.com; International Licensing Industry Merchandisers' Association, at www.licensing.org; *License! Global,* "Top 100 Global Licensors," May 2011, pp.19–41.

Disney's inventory of licensed assets. Licensing sales have benefited immensely from the emergence of large-scale retailers, such as Carrefour, Walmart, and Amazon.com.

 ## Advantages and Disadvantages of Licensing

Exhibit 16.3 summarizes the advantages and disadvantages of licensing from the perspective of the licensor. Let's highlight some key points.

Advantages of Licensing

Licensing requires neither substantial capital investment nor direct involvement of the licensor in the foreign market. Unlike other entry strategies, the licensor need not establish a physical presence in the market or maintain inventory there. Simultaneously, the licensee benefits by gaining access to a key technology at a much lower cost and in less time than if it had developed the technology itself.[14] Licensing makes entry possible in countries that restrict foreign ownership in security-sensitive industries, such as defense and energy. Licensing also facilitates entry in markets that are difficult to enter because of trade barriers, tariffs, and bureaucratic requirements, which usually apply only to exporting or FDI.

Licensing can be used as a low-cost strategy to test the viability of foreign markets. By establishing a relationship with a local licensee, the foreign firm can learn about the target market and devise the best future strategy for establishing a more durable presence there. For example, Swiss pharmaceutical manufacturer Roche entered a licensing agreement with Chugai Pharmaceuticals in Japan, where success requires substantial knowledge of the local market and the drug approval process. The relationship accelerated Roche's penetration of the huge Japanese market.[15] Licensing can also help the firm develop its brand name in a target market and preempt the later entry of competitors.

EXHIBIT 16.3 Advantages and Disadvantages of Licensing to the Licensor

Advantages	Disadvantages
• Does not require capital investment or presence of the licensor in the foreign market	• Revenues are usually more modest than with other entry strategies
• Ability to generate royalty income from existing intellectual property	• Difficult to maintain control over how the licensed asset is used
• Appropriate for entering markets that pose substantial country risk	• Risk of losing control of important intellectual property, or dissipating it to competitors
• Useful when trade barriers reduce the viability of exporting or when governments restrict ownership of local operations by foreign firms	• The licensee may infringe the licensor's intellectual property and become a competitor
• Useful for testing a foreign market prior to entry via FDI	• Does not guarantee a basis for future expansion in the market
• Useful as a strategy to preemptively enter a market before rivals	• Not ideal for products, services, or knowledge that are highly complex
	• Dispute resolution is complex and may not produce satisfactory results

Disadvantages of Licensing

From the licensor's standpoint, licensing is a relatively passive entry strategy. Profits tend to be lower than those from exporting or FDI, and licensing does not guarantee a basis for future expansion. To earn royalties, the licensor must rely on the licensee's sales and marketing prowess. A weak partner will provide only meager royalties. Also, licensing provides limited control over how the licensor's asset is used. If the licensee produces a substandard product, the licensor's reputation can be harmed. To avoid such problems, experienced firms require foreign licensees to meet minimum quality and performance standards. For example, Budweiser beer is made and distributed in Japan through a licensing arrangement with Kirin (www.kirin.co.jp/english). Kirin is one of Japan's most reputable brewers and produces the beer according to Budweiser's strict standards.

If the licensee is very successful, the licensor may regret not entering the market through a more lucrative entry strategy. This happened to Disney, which developed Disneyland Tokyo through a licensing arrangement with a Japanese partner. When the theme park proved more successful than originally forecast, Disney management wished it had used FDI to develop Disneyland Tokyo itself. In Mexico, Televisa (www.televisa.com), the largest producer of Spanish-language TV programming, opted for a licensing arrangement with California-based Univision to enter the U.S. market. Although there are more than 35 million native Spanish speakers in the United States, Televisa receives only 9 percent of Univision's Spanish market advertising revenue.

Because licensing requires sharing intellectual property with other firms, the risk of creating a future competitor is substantial.[16] The rival may exploit the licensor's intellectual property by entering third countries or creating products based on knowledge gained in the relationship. This scenario has played out in the auto, computer chip, and consumer electronics industries in Asia as Western firms have transferred process technologies to firms in China, Japan, and South Korea. Japan's Sony (www.sony.com) originally licensed transistor technology from U.S. inventor Bell Laboratories to make hearing aids. But instead Sony used the technology to create small, battery-powered transistor radios and soon grew to become a global leader in this product.[17]

Source: © Eddie Gerald/Alamy

Licensors run the risk of creating competitors, as Mattel discovered when it granted a license to a Brazilian firm to market Barbie dolls. The latter firm went on to create a competitor to Barbie, the Susi doll.

The U.S. toymaker Mattel licensed rights to distribute the Barbie doll to the Brazilian toymaker Estrela (www.estrela.com.br). Once the agreement expired, Estrela developed its own Barbie look-alike—"Susi"—which surpassed sales of Barbie dolls in Brazil. Estrela then launched the Susi doll throughout South America to great success. In Japan, Mattel entered a licensing agreement with local toymaker Takara (www.takaratomy.co.jp), which adapted the Barbie doll for Japanese girls. When the agreement expired, Takara continued to sell the doll under the name "Jenny," becoming a competitor to Mattel in the world's second-biggest toy market.[18]

 ## Franchising as an Entry Strategy

Franchising is an advanced form of licensing in which the focal firm, the *franchisor*, allows an entrepreneur, the *franchisee*, the right to use an entire business system in exchange for compensation. As with licensing, an explicit contract defines the terms of the relationship. McDonald's, Subway, Hertz, and FedEx are well-established international franchisors. Others that use franchising to expand abroad include Benetton, Body Shop, Yves Rocher, and Marks & Spencer. Franchising is common in international retailing. However, some retailers such as IKEA and Starbucks favor direct investment and internationalize via company-owned outlets. Ownership provides these firms with greater control over foreign operations but also typically restricts their ability to expand more rapidly abroad.

Exhibit 16.4 reveals characteristics of franchising worldwide. The exhibit shows that franchises generate the biggest volume of sales in advanced economies such as the United States, Europe, and Japan. However, the largest number of franchises is found in less-economically

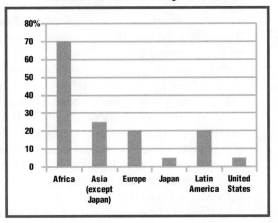

EXHIBIT 16.4

Characteristics of Franchising Around the World

Source: Based on UNCTAD, *World Investment Report 2011* (New York: United Nations, 2011).

EXHIBIT 16.5

Franchising as a Foreign Market Entry Strategy

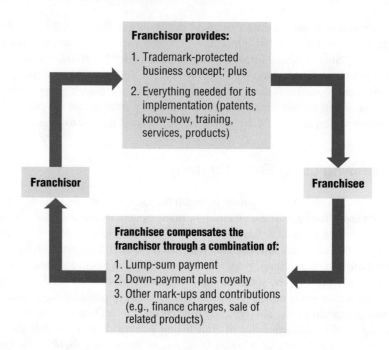

developed countries of Asia. Many of these are *microfranchises*, operated by one or two people. Franchising is a big job creator in developing economies in Asia and Latin America, helping to raise living standards. As many franchise firms were first established in the United States, it has attracted few franchises from abroad. By contrast, a large proportion of franchises in Africa and less-developed Asia are international.

Exhibit 16.5 shows the nature of the franchising agreement. Most firms undertake *business format franchising* (sometimes called *system franchising*).[19] The franchisor transfers to the franchisee a total business method, including production and marketing methods, sales systems, procedures, and management know-how, as well as the use of its name and usage rights for products, patents, and trademarks.[20] The franchisor also provides the franchisee with training, ongoing support, incentive programs, and the right to participate in cooperative marketing programs.

In return, the franchisee pays some type of compensation to the franchisor, usually a royalty representing a percentage of the franchisee's revenues. The franchisee may be required to purchase certain equipment and supplies from the franchisor to ensure standardized products and consistent quality. Burger King and Subway require franchisees to buy food preparation equipment from specified suppliers.

While licensing relationships are often short-lived, franchising parties normally establish an ongoing relationship that may last many years, making for a more stable long-term entry strategy. In addition, franchisors often combine franchising with other entry strategies. For example, about 70 percent of the more than 2,400 Body Shop stores worldwide are operated by franchisees, while the rest are owned by Body Shop headquarters (www.thebodyshop.com). Large retailers such as Carrefour often employ both franchising and FDI when expanding abroad.

Franchising is more comprehensive than licensing because the franchisor prescribes virtually all of the business activities of the franchisee. The franchisor tightly controls the business system to ensure consistent standards. International franchisors employ globally recognized trademarks and attempt to guarantee the customer a uniform retail experience and consistent product quality.

Completely standardized business activities, however, are difficult to replicate across diverse markets. Differences in local tastes, available ingredients, and physical space may necessitate changes to the franchise formula. McDonald's offers teriyaki burgers in Japan, wine in France, and a McPork sandwich in Spain. In China, KFC offers shredded carrots, fungus, and bamboo shoots instead of the coleslaw it sells in Western countries.[21] Limited land in Japan forced KFC to reconfigure its cooking equipment from a wide horizontal design to a narrower, more vertical design that saves space. Japanese KFCs are often multistoried restaurants to save on the high cost of land. The challenge is to strike the right balance, adapting the format to respond to local markets without affecting the overall image and service of the franchise.[22]

Country Realities

China and India are home to more than 2.5 billion people and are promising markets for fast-food franchising. However, most residents of developing economies and emerging markets lack sufficient income to patronize restaurants. Most do not live in the major urbanized areas where international franchisors are concentrated. Laws in such countries vary substantially and often evolve quickly. Food and eating habits are deeply rooted in national culture. Successful franchisors carefully investigate the economic, demographic, legal, and cultural dimensions of foreign countries before targeting them with franchised operations.

Some focal firms may choose to work with a single, coordinating franchisee in a particular country or region. In this **master franchise** arrangement, an independent company is licensed to establish, develop, and manage the entire franchising network in its market. The master franchisee has the right to subfranchise to other independent businesses and thus assume the role of the local franchisor. McDonald's is organized this way in Japan. By delegating the responsibilities of identifying and working with its franchisees directly, the focal firm gives up considerable control over its foreign market operations. From the focal firm's perspective, however, the arrangement is the least capital- and time-intensive.

Master franchisees prefer this arrangement because it provides them with an exclusive, large, predefined territory (often an entire country) and substantial scale economies from operating numerous sales outlets simultaneously. They gain access to a proven retailing and marketing concept and partnership with a corporate headquarters and master franchisees in other territories, which typically provide support, know-how, and the latest innovations in the field. Master franchising accounts for as much as 80 percent of international franchising deals. Sbarro, Inc., the pizza chain, operates via master franchises in Belgium, Canada, Guatemala, Kuwait, the Philippines, and the United Kingdom.[23]

Franchisors are internationalizing rapidly. The *Global Trend* feature discusses the internationalization of franchisors, particularly in emerging markets.

Master franchise
Arrangement in which an independent company is licensed to establish, develop, and manage the entire franchising network in its market and has the right to subfranchise to other franchisees, assuming the role of local franchisor.

Who Are the Top Global Franchisors?

Franchising is a global phenomenon and accounts for a large proportion of international trade in services, especially fast-food outlets, professional business services, home improvement, and various types of retailers. Yum! Brands, Inc., owns the KFC, Pizza Hut, and Taco Bell brands of franchised restaurants. KFC now has more than 3,500 stores in China, and Pizza Hut has 560, making Yum! one of the largest retail developers in China.[24] Exhibit 16.6 profiles several other leading global franchisors.

The United States is home to the largest number of franchisors and dominates international franchising. U.S. franchisors and their franchisees account for about $2 trillion in annual U.S. retail sales—more than 40 percent of total U.S. retail sales. Approximately one in every twelve retail establishments in the United States is a franchised business. The United Kingdom is home to numerous home-grown franchisors, like Eden Delicious and Perfect Pizza. Annual franchised sales of fast food in the United Kingdom are said to account for 30 percent of all food eaten outside the home.[25]

The ability to exchange information instantaneously through the Internet enhances the franchisor's ability to control international operations and saves time and money. Some franchisees use electronic point-of-sale equipment that links their sales and inventory data to the franchisor's central warehouse and distribution network. Information technology also allows the franchisor to serve customers or franchisees with central accounting and other business process functions.

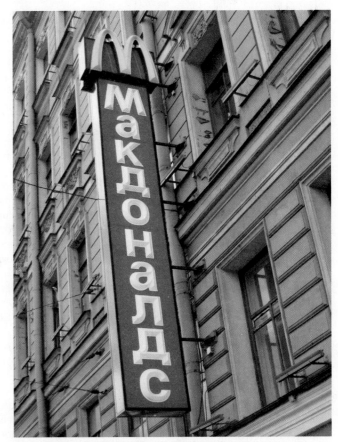

Source: Jonathan Smith/Rough Guides Dorling Kindersley

U.S. firms dominate international franchising, especially in the fast-food industry. This McDonald's restaurant is in St. Petersburg, Russia.

EXHIBIT 16.6 Leading International Franchisors

Franchisor	Type of Business	International Profile	Major Markets
Subway	Submarine sandwiches and salads	34,500 shops in 98 countries	Canada, Australia, United Kingdom, New Zealand, Germany
McDonald's	Fast-food restaurants	33,500 restaurants in 119 countries	Canada, France, United Kingdom, Australia, China
7-Eleven	Convenience stores	35,141 stores in 15 countries	Japan, Thailand, Mexico, United States
KFC	Chicken, sandwiches, pot pies	20,200 outlets in 100 countries	Brazil, China, Japan, France
Pizza Hut	Pizza, pasta, chicken wings	13,000 outlets in 90 countries	China, Brazil, Canada, Japan
Dunkin Donuts	Coffee and donuts	10,000 restaurants in 30 countries	China, Japan, Taiwan
Jani-King	Commercial cleaning	13,046 franchisees in 18 countries	Canada, Australia, Brazil, France, Malaysia
Kumon Math & Reading Centers	Supplemental education	26,311 franchises in 40 countries	Canada, Japan, United States
Curves	Women's fitness and weight-loss	10,000 centers in 60 countries	Brazil, France, Mexico, Australia, Ireland, United Kingdom
UPS Store/ Mail Boxes Etc.	Postal, business, and communications services	6,000 locations in 40 countries	Canada, Germany, China, India

Sources: Based on Entrepreneur.com; Hoovers.com; company Web sites and reports.

 GLOBAL TREND

Internationalization of Franchising: Emerging Markets

International franchising has a prosperous history going back to the 1970s, when U.S. brands such as McDonald's, Burger King, KFC, and Pizza Hut became familiar sights in cities worldwide. Australia, Canada, Japan, the United States, the United Kingdom, and other countries in Europe have long been popular franchise destinations. Historically, U.S. franchisors targeted Europe as their initial market abroad, and within Europe, the United Kingdom is often the first choice because of its linguistic and cultural familiarity.

Franchisors view international expansion as an important way to diversify their portfolios. Nearly two-thirds of franchisors currently operate in international locations. Top management at about three-quarters of franchisors indicate they plan to start or accelerate international ventures. When expanding abroad, franchisors must consider the economic health of a country or region, availability of qualified labor, and other factors that help ensure sustained growth.

Most firms, especially fast-food franchisors, prefer entering a new national market via a master franchising approach. The advantages are increased speed of market development, relatively small capital outlay, and access to knowledgeable local entrepreneurs to help navigate the often-complex conditions in foreign markets.

As markets in Europe and other advanced economies become saturated, franchisors are looking to emerging markets such as Brazil, China, India, Mexico, and Russia. Subway is doing big business in Eastern Europe. Avis car rental enjoys much success in Latin America. Ben & Jerry's doles out ice cream in Thailand and Turkey. About 70 percent of the countries where KFC does business are developing economies. Emerging markets account for half the world's population and present the most dynamic potential for long-term growth.

Estimates suggest international franchised companies provide more than 2.4 million jobs in developing economies. Franchises help provide needed modernization in business methods, distribution networks, and commercial infrastructure. They help build local capabilities and skills, both by bringing in expatriate staff and by training local personnel. Because franchising is less risky, it is often preferred over FDI for entering developing economies.

Sources: Stephen Choo, Tim Mazzarol, and Geoff Soutar, "The Selection of International Retail Franchisees in East Asia," *Asia Pacific Journal of Marketing and Logistics* 19, no. 4 (2007): 380–389; A. Kazmin, "Attention to Local Palates Pays Off," *Financial Times*, January 29, 2010, p. 3; G. Knack, "Strategies for International Development in Uncertain Times," *Franchising World*, November 2008, pp. 75–76; M. Shay, "Franchising Is Key to Global Economic Recovery," *Franchising World*, March 2009, p. 6; UNCTAD, *World Investment Report 2011* (New York: United Nations).

Advantages and Disadvantages of Franchising

In an ideal relationship, franchisor and franchisee complement each other. The franchisor possesses economies of scale, a wealth of intellectual property, and know-how about its industry, while the franchisee has entrepreneurial drive and substantial knowledge about the local market and how to run a business there. A large pool of well-chosen franchisees greatly enhances the speed and quality of the franchisor's performance abroad.[26] For example, KFC internationalized quickly and performed well worldwide by developing franchisees in 100 countries with some 20,000 restaurants serving more than 12 million customers per day.

The Franchisor Perspective

Exhibit 16.7 highlights the advantages and disadvantages of franchising to the franchisor. Firms prefer franchising when they lack the capital or international experience to establish themselves abroad through FDI, or when offering the product through exporting or basic licensing is ineffective as an internationalization strategy. Foreign markets often provide greater profitability than the home market. For example, the Beijing KFC store has generated more sales than any other KFC outlet worldwide partly due to the novelty and popularity of the offering and the lack of direct competition. Governments in host countries often encourage franchising by foreign entrants because most of the profits and investment remain in the local economy.

For the franchisor, franchising is a low-risk, low-cost entry strategy. It offers the ability to develop international markets relatively quickly and on a larger scale than possible for most non-franchise firms. The franchisor can generate profit with only incremental investments in capital, staff, production, and distribution.

The major disadvantages include the need to maintain control over potentially thousands of outlets worldwide and the risk of creating competitors. When the franchising agreement is terminated, some franchisees leverage their newly acquired knowledge to remain in business, often by slightly altering the franchisor's brand name or trademark. Franchisees may also jeopardize the franchisor's image by not upholding its standards. Dunkin' Donuts experienced problems in Russia when it discovered some franchisees were selling vodka along with donuts.

When the franchisor depends heavily on a foreign partner as master franchisee, it is critical to cultivate friendly, durable relationships. However, even experienced franchisors encounter big problems. In 2010, nearly 30 years after opening its first outlet in Japan, restaurant chain Wendy's could not reach a new agreement with its Japanese master franchisee, Zensho Company, and chose to close its restaurants there. The move disappointed countless Japanese fans, who formed long lines in front of Wendy's outlets in the days before the chain shut down. By 2013, however, Wendy's reestablished itself in Japan, via a joint venture with Higa Industries.[27]

Another major challenge is to become familiar with foreign laws and regulations. The European Union has strict laws that favor the franchisee, sometimes hampering the franchisor's ability to maintain control over operations. Laws and foreign exchange circumstances affect the payment of royalties.

EXHIBIT 16.7 Advantages and Disadvantages of Franchising to the Franchisor

Advantages	Disadvantages
• Entry into numerous foreign markets can be accomplished quickly and cost effectively	• Maintaining control over franchisee may be difficult
• No need to invest substantial capital	• Conflicts with franchisee are likely, including legal disputes
• Established brand name encourages early and ongoing sales potential abroad	• Preserving franchisor's image in the foreign market may be challenging
• The firm can leverage franchisees' knowledge to efficiently navigate and develop local markets	• Requires monitoring and evaluating performance of franchisees, and providing ongoing assistance
	• Franchisees may take advantage of acquired knowledge and become competitors in the future

The Franchisee Perspective

Exhibit 16.8 highlights the advantages and disadvantages of franchising from the franchisee's side. Entrepreneurs that open a franchised store benefit from the franchisor's established formula. Customers are more likely to patronize a well-known franchise, which helps the franchisee succeed more quickly. Franchising is especially beneficial to SMEs, many of which lack substantial resources and strong managerial skills. The big advantage is the ability to launch a business using a tested business model. In essence, franchising amounts to cloning best practices. It greatly increases the small firm's chances for success by duplicating a tried-and-true business format.[28]

However, starting a franchise is usually costly, and may require the franchisee to build a shop or invest in expensive equipment. Unlike independent store owners, franchisees must satisfy the franchisor's demands. This can be problematic for international franchisees when the franchisor knows little about foreign markets or how to do business there.

Managerial Guidelines for Licensing and Franchising

Licensing and franchising are complex undertakings and require skillful research, planning, and execution. The focal firm must conduct advance research on the host country's laws on intellectual property, repatriation of royalties, and contracting with local partners. Key challenges of the focal firm include establishing whose national law takes precedence for interpreting and enforcing the contract, deciding whether to grant an exclusive or nonexclusive arrangement, and determining the geographic scope of territory to be granted to the foreign partner.

As with other entry strategies, the key to success is often finding the right partner abroad. The focal firm should carefully identify, screen, and train potential partners who are unlikely to become competitors in the future. The most qualified franchisees tend to have entrepreneurial drive, access to capital and prime real estate, a successful business track record, good relationships with local and national government agencies, strong links to other firms (including facilitators), a pool of motivated employees, and a willingness to accept oversight and follow company procedures. In emerging markets, a knowledgeable, locally connected partner can help sort through various operational problems. In China and Russia, partnering with a state-owned enterprise may be necessary to gain access to key resources and navigate legal and political environments.

For franchisors, developing capable partners in local supply chains is also a prerequisite. Franchisees need a reliable supply chain to obtain input products and supplies. In developing economies and emerging markets, host-country suppliers may be inadequate for providing a sufficient quantity or quality of input goods. In Turkey, Little Caesars pizza franchisees found it difficult to locate dairy companies that could produce the cheese varieties they required. In other countries, KFC developed its own supply-chain network, ensuring dependable delivery of chicken and other critical inputs. In Russia and Thailand, McDonald's had to develop its own supply lines for potatoes to ensure the quality of its French fries. When McDonald's first entered India, it faced resistance from the government. Relations improved as the government recognized McDonald's would work with Indian farmers to improve the country's agricultural practices and was committed to being a good corporate citizen.

EXHIBIT 16.8 Advantages and Disadvantages of Franchising to the Franchisee

Advantages	Disadvantages
• Gain a well-known, recognizable brand name	• Initial investment or royalty payments may be substantial
• Acquire training and know-how; receive ongoing support from the franchisor	• Franchisee is required to purchase supplies, equipment, and products from the franchisor only
• Operate an independent business	• The franchisor holds much power, including superior bargaining power
• Increase likelihood of business success	• Franchisor's outlets may proliferate in the region, creating competition for the franchisee
• Become part of an established international network	• Franchisor may impose inappropriate technical or managerial systems on the Franchisee

Other Contractual Entry Strategies

Licensing and franchising are especially salient contractual entry strategies. In addition, firms employ other contract-based approaches to venture abroad. Global sourcing is a specific type of international contracting that we address in Chapter 17. Other types of contractual agreements deal with building major construction projects, manufacturing products under contract, providing management and marketing services, or leasing major assets. Here, we discuss turnkey contracting, build-operate-transfer arrangements, management contracts, and leasing.

Turnkey Contracting

Turnkey contracting is an arrangement in which the focal firm or a consortium of firms plans, finances, organizes, manages, and implements all phases of a project abroad and then hands it over to a foreign customer after training local workers. Contractors are typically firms in construction, engineering, design, and architectural services. In a typical turnkey project, a contractor builds a major facility (such as a nuclear power plant or a subway system), puts it into operation, and then hands it over to the project sponsor, often a national government. The contractor may provide follow-up services such as testing and operational support.

Among the most popular turnkey projects are extensions and upgrades to metro systems, such as bridges, roadways, and railways, and the construction of airports, harbors, refineries, and hospitals. Financed largely from public budgets, most large-scale infrastructure projects are in the Mideast and East Asia, where industrialization and growing affluence are driving demand. In Abu Dhabi, a collection of companies received a multi-billion-dollar contract to build an integrated processing plant for natural gas. The team included JGC of Japan, Tecnimont of Italy, and Hyundai Engineering & Construction (HDEC; www.en.hdec.kr) of South Korea. HDEC has built industrial, infrastructure, commercial, and multifamily residential projects in about fifty countries.[29]

Other examples are Hochtief AG of Germany and Skanska AB of Sweden. See Exhibit 3.7 in Chapter 3 for a list of top international construction companies. Such firms have undertaken some of the world's most important infrastructure projects, such as the Three Gorges Dam in China and the Chunnel linking England to France. California-based Bechtel participated in projects such as the renovation of London's 140-year-old subway, the cleanup of the Chernobyl nuclear plant in Russia, and construction of nuclear power plants in South Korea.[30] In Russia, a consortium of firms is building a huge power plant in the Arkhangelsk region to support the thriving mining industry there.[31]

Build-Operate-Transfer Arrangements (BOT)

Under a **build-operate-transfer (BOT)** arrangement, a firm or consortium of firms contracts to build a major facility abroad, such as a dam or water treatment plant; operates it for a specified period; and then transfers ownership to the project sponsor, typically the host-country government or public utility. Compared to turnkey contracting, a unique feature of turnkey contracting is that, instead of transferring control of the completed facility to the project sponsor, the builder first operates it for a number of years.

While the consortium operates the facility, it can charge user fees, tolls, and rentals to recover its investment and generate profits. Or the host-country government can pay the BOT partner for services provided by the facility, such as water from a treatment plant, at a price calculated over the life of the contract, to cover its construction and operating costs and provide a reasonable return.

Turnkey contracting
Arrangement in which the focal firm or a consortium of firms plans, finances, organizes, manages, and implements all phases of a project abroad and then hands it over to a foreign customer after training local workers.

Build-operate-transfer (BOT)
Arrangement in which the firm or a consortium of firms contracts to build a major facility abroad, operate it for a specified period, and then transfer control to the project sponsor, typically the host-country government or public utility.

Source: © Bethany Dawn

The spectacular Petronas Twin Towers complex in Kuala Lumpur, Malaysia, was a turnkey project built by Bovis Lend Lease, a leading project management and construction company. Among the firms with offices in the Towers are Accenture, Al Jazeera English, Huawei Technologies, Microsoft, and Reuters.

Governments often grant BOT concessions to get needed infrastructure built cost effectively. Typical projects include sewage treatment plants, highways, airports, mass transit systems, and telecommunications networks. In Vietnam, rapid growth in industry and tourism has greatly increased demand for electric power. The Vietnamese government commissioned the construction of the 720 megawatt *Phu My 3* power plant, the country's first privately owned major energy facility, as a BOT project by Siemens Power Generation (Germany). It is owned by a consortium that includes BP (United Kingdom) and Kyushu Electric Power (Japan).[32]

Management Contracts

Management contract
Arrangement in which a contractor supplies managerial know-how to operate a hotel, hospital, airport, or other facility in exchange for compensation.

Under a **management contract,** a contractor supplies managerial know-how to operate a hotel, hospital, airport, or other facility in exchange for compensation. The client organization receives assistance in managing local operations, while the management company generates revenues without having to make a capital outlay. Much of Disney's income from its theme parks in France and Japan comes from providing management services for the parks, which are largely owned by other interests. BAA Limited manages the retailing and catering operations of various airports in Europe and the United States. Both the Marriott and Four Seasons corporations run luxury hotels around the world through management contracts without owning them.

Management contracts can help foreign governments with infrastructure projects when the country lacks local people with the skills to run them. Occasionally the offering of a management contract is the critical element in winning a bid for other types of entry strategies, such as BOT deals and turnkey operations. A key disadvantage of management contracts is that they involve training foreign firms that may become future competitors.[33]

Leasing

In international leasing, another contractual strategy, a focal firm (the lessor) rents out machinery or equipment to corporate or government clients abroad (lessees), often for several years at a time. The lessor retains ownership of the property throughout the lease period and receives regular payments from the lessee. From the perspective of the lessee, leasing helps reduce the costs of using needed machinery and equipment. A major advantage for the lessor is the ability to gain quick access to target markets, while putting assets to use earning profits. In some countries, firms opt to lease rather than buy needed equipment due to tax benefits.[34] International leasing benefits developing economies that may lack the financial resources to purchase needed equipment.

Amsterdam-based ING Lease International Equipment Management owns and leases Boeing commercial aircraft to clients such as Brazil's Varig airlines. Dubai-based Oasis Leasing leases aircraft to Air New Zealand, Virgin Express, and Macedonian Airlines. One of the top leasing firms is Japan's ORIX (www.orix.co.jp), which leases everything from computers and measuring equipment to aircraft and ships. The firm operates 1,500 offices worldwide and generated more than $12 billion in sales in 2013.

The Special Case of Internationalization by Professional Service Firms

Professional services include such industries as accounting, advertising, market research, consulting, engineering, legal counsel, and IT services. Firms in these industries have internationalized rapidly during the past three decades. Some have simply followed their key clients abroad. The Internet supports the international spread of some business process services such as software engineering, which is increasingly centralized in cost-effective locations such as India and Eastern Europe.

When they internationalize, professional service firms encounter three unique challenges:

1. Professional qualifications that allow firms to practice law, dentistry, medicine, or accounting in the home country are rarely recognized by other countries. If you are a licensed accountant in your country and want to practice accounting in some other country, you usually must earn local certification there.
2. Professionals who work abroad for long periods generally must obtain employment visas in the countries where they are employed.
3. Professional services often require intensive interaction with the local public, which necessitates language and cultural skills.[35]

Professional service firms employ a mix of direct investment and contractual strategies to enter foreign markets. An advertising agency such as Publicis Groupe, headquartered in France, maintains a network of company-owned branches around the world while simultaneously entering contractual relationships with independent local firms. Focal firms in professional services are likely to serve their major markets with direct investment and operate company-owned offices there. In small markets, however, they will enter contractual relationships with independent partner firms in the same line of business, typically known as *agents*, *affiliates*, or *representatives*. PriceWaterhouseCoopers, a leading accounting firm, can contract with indigenous accounting firms in smaller markets where it chooses not to have its own offices. Focal firms with limited international experience often prefer to employ foreign partners that can provide international business know-how.

 ## Infringement of Intellectual Property: A Global Problem

We have seen that working with independent partners through contractual arrangements provides the focal firm with only moderate control over foreign partners. Thus, safeguarding intellectual property and foreign operations can pose challenges. Laws that govern contractual obligations are not always clear, conflicts arise due to cultural and language differences, and contract enforcement abroad is often costly or unattainable.

Infringement of intellectual property is the unauthorized use, publication, or reproduction of products and services protected by a patent, copyright, trademark, or other intellectual property right. Such a violation amounts to piracy and takes the form of production and distribution of counterfeit goods. Counterfeiting and piracy can be particularly troublesome in emerging markets and developing economies, where intellectual property laws are usually weak or poorly enforced.[36]

The total value of counterfeit and pirated goods crossing borders and traded online worldwide exceeds $600 billion annually.[37] The most commonly counterfeited goods include consumer electronics, footwear, pharmaceutical drugs, apparel, and optical media such as CDs and DVDs. For example, annual piracy losses in CDs and music exceed $100 million in Brazil, and losses in business software exceed $1 billion in Russia.[38] Counterfeiters may use a product name that differs only slightly from that of a well-known brand; it is similar enough that buyers associate it with the genuine product but just different enough so that prosecution is hampered. While firms such as Rolex and Tommy Hilfiger are well-known victims, counterfeiting is also common in such industrial products as medical devices and car parts. Counterfeiters even have faked entire motor vehicles. Authorities uncovered 23 unauthorized Apple stores in southeast China, selling fake iPads and counterfeit smartphones.[39]

Cisco Systems sued its Chinese joint venture partner, Huawei Technologies Co., for pirating its networking software and infringing patents. The lawsuit also cited Huawei, the largest telecommunications equipment manufacturer in China, for illegally using technical documentation that Cisco had copyrighted in its own product manuals.[40] Although Microsoft's Windows and Office products dominate the software market, the firm receives no payment when its software is copied and distributed by unauthorized parties. Up to 90 percent of computer software in Russia may be pirated. As a result, Microsoft sells its products only to corporate customers. The firm battles piracy even among the employees in its Russian subsidiary.[41]

Infringement of intellectual property
Unauthorized use, publication, or reproduction of products or services protected by a patent, copyright, trademark, or other intellectual property right.

Ethical Connections

Counterfeiting is not confined to lower-income countries. Raids of retail outlets in the United States net millions of dollars worth of counterfeit products every year. In 2012, for example, federal authorities in New York and New Jersey arrested dozens of people on charges of retailing $325 million worth of counterfeit fashions and footwear, including Burberry scarves, Gucci handbags, Lacoste shirts, Nike shoes, and much more.

Source: WWD: Women's Wear Daily, "$325M Counterfeit Bust," March 5, 2012, p. 1.

The Internet has added a new dimension to international counterfeiting. In Russia, Web sites sell popular music downloads for as little as 5 cents each, or less than $1 for an entire CD. The sites are easily accessed by shoppers in countries where they are outlawed under intellectual property laws and use low prices to attract music fans worldwide. Fake medications sold via the Internet account for a significant percentage of prescription drugs sold online. Consumers have died from consuming fake medications.[42]

When consumers buy counterfeit goods, payments accrue not to the firm that invented the product, but rather to illicit enterprises. Counterfeiting negatively affects consumer attitudes about the branding and quality of legitimate goods. The quality of counterfeit goods is almost always inferior to that of the original, proprietary goods that they duplicate. In these and other ways, counterfeiting and piracy erode the firm's brand equity and competitive advantage. Where counterfeiting and piracy are commonplace, companies are reluctant to invent, innovate, and market legitimate products, which reduces consumer choices and ultimately lowers living standards.

 ## Guidelines for Protecting Intellectual Property

In advanced economies, intellectual property is usually protected within established legal systems and methods of recourse. A firm can initiate legal action against someone who infringes on its intellectual assets and will usually achieve a satisfactory remedy. Advanced economies have taken the lead in signing treaties that support international protection of intellectual property, including the Paris Convention for the Protection of Industrial Property, the Berne Convention for the Protection of Literary and Artistic Works, and the Rome Convention for the Protection of Performers and Broadcasting Organizations. The World Intellectual Property Organization (WIPO; www.wipo.int) is an agency of the United Nations that administers these multilateral agreements.

Recently, the World Trade Organization (WTO; www.wto.org) created the Agreement on Trade-Related Aspects of Intellectual Property Rights (TRIPS), a comprehensive international treaty that lays out remedies, dispute-resolution procedures, and enforcements to protect intellectual property. The WTO is pressuring member countries to comply with the accord and can discipline violators through the dispute settlement mechanism. At the same time, TRIPS provides exceptions that benefit developing economies, such as the ability to access needed patent medication for ailments such as AIDS.

While most countries are signatories to WIPO, TRIPS, and various treaties, intellectual property infringements remain a huge problem. Rights granted by a patent, trademark registration, or copyright apply only in the country where they are obtained; they confer no protection abroad. Enforcement depends on the attitudes of local officials, substantive requirements of the law, and court procedures. As a result, former licensees and franchisees can launch illicit businesses using proprietary knowledge to which they are no longer entitled.

Experienced firms devise sophisticated approaches to reduce the likelihood of intellectual property violations and help avoid their adverse effects, especially in countries with weak property rights. Exhibit 16.9 illustrates such approaches, internal to the firm and in its external environment.[43]

Let's elaborate on key strategies. Before undertaking contractual entry strategies abroad, management needs to understand local intellectual property laws and enforcement procedures, particularly when exposed assets are valuable. The firm should register patents, trademarks, trade secrets, and copyrights with local governments, especially in countries with weak anti-piracy laws. Some companies lobby national governments and international organizations for stronger intellectual property laws and more vigilant enforcement, albeit with limited success.

Management must ensure that licensing and franchising agreements provide for oversight to ensure intellectual property is used as intended. Licensing contracts should include provisions that require the licensee to share improvements or technological developments on the licensed asset with the licensor.[44] Noncompete clauses in employee contracts help prevent employees from serving competitors for some years after leaving the firm.[45]

Monitoring franchisee, distribution, and marketing channels for asset infringements helps avoid problems. The firm should monitor the activities of local business partners for potential leaks of vital information and assets.[46] Trade secrets must be guarded closely. Using password-based security systems, surveillance, and firewalls limits access to intellectual property. Intel and Microsoft release only limited information about key technologies to partner firms. The firm can deter much potential piracy by aggressively pursuing criminal prosecution or litigation against those who pilfer its logos, proprietary processes, and other key assets. Mead Data Central, Inc.,

EXHIBIT 16.9 Protecting Intellectual Property (IP)

Internal: Strategic	Register IP in each target country	Segregate value-chain activities to maintain IP secrecy	Emphasize leading-edge, specialized, or hard-to-understand technologies	Collaborate with ethical partners	Emphasize IP protections in partner contracts
Internal: Operational	Employ strict processes and technologies to protect IP	Hire ethical employees	Educate employees and partners on the harm of violating IP rights	Develop trusting relations with partners	Perform audits to ensure partner compliance
External: Operating Environment	Research to understand IP laws and protections in target countries	Educate customers on the harm of IP violations	Pursue IP violators via prosecution and other legal means	Cultivate government contacts in IP laws and enforcement	Lobby governments for stronger IP protections

Sources: Based on Thomas Duening, Robert Hisrich, and Michael Lechter (2010), *Technology Entrepreneurship: Creating, Capturing, and Protecting Value* (Burlington, MA: Academic Press); Meagan Dietz, Sarena Shao-Tin Lin, and Lei Yang, "Protecting Intellectual Property in China," *McKinsey Quarterly* (2005), retrieved from www.mckinseyquarterly.com; Marcus Keupp, Angela Beckenbauer, and Oliver Gassmann, "Enforcing Intellectual Property Rights in Weak Appropriability Regimes," *Management International Review* 50, no. 1 (2010): 109–130.

owner of the Lexis-Nexis brand of computerized legal research services, sued Toyota when the Japanese firm began selling its new luxury automobiles under the name "Lexus." The suit failed, but it showed Mead's determination to protect its assets.[47]

The firm should leverage technological approaches to minimize counterfeiting. Many companies build biotech tags, electronic signatures, or holograms into their products to differentiate them from fakes. In the long run, the best way to cope with infringement is to continuously update technologies and products. The firm that regularly renews its technologies can stay ahead of counterfeiters by marketing products that counterfeiters cannot imitate fast enough. Even when licensing violations occur, the firm is protected because the stolen property rapidly becomes obsolete.

Ultimately, when contractual strategies prove undesirable or ineffective, management may opt to enter target markets via FDI, through which the firm acquires ownership, and thus greater control, over important assets.

CLOSING CASE   Subway and the Challenges of Franchising in China

Subway, the fast-food marketer of submarine sandwiches and salads, has more than 34,000 stores in ninety-eight countries and generates $15 billion in annual revenues. The franchising chain opened its first international restaurant in Bahrain in 1984. Since then, Subway (www .subway.com) has expanded worldwide and generates about one-fifth of its annual revenues abroad. The firm expects foreign markets to contribute much of its future growth.

Subway is one of the most successful fast-food chains in China. Fish and tuna salad sandwiches are the top sellers. By 2006, Subway had opened about forty stores in China. The franchise had its share of initial setbacks. Subway's master franchisee in Beijing, Jim Bryant, lost money to a scheming partner and had to teach the franchising concept to a country that had never heard of it. Until recently, there was no word in Chinese for "franchise."

Cultural problems are still an ongoing challenge. After Bryant opened his first Subway shop, customers stood outside and watched for a few days. When they finally tried to buy a sandwich, many were confused and Bryant printed signs explaining how to order. Some didn't believe the tuna salad was made from fish because they could

not see the head or tail. Others didn't like the idea of touching their food, so they would gradually peel off the paper wrapping and eat the sandwich like a banana. To make matters worse, few customers liked sandwiches. Subway has had to create menu items that suit local tastes, such as "Roasted Duck Sub."

Subway—or Sai Bei Wei (Mandarin for "tastes better than others")—has forged ahead. Bryant has recruited numerous committed franchisees that he monitors closely to maintain quality. He recruits local entrepreneurs, trains them to become franchisees, and acts as a liaison between them and Subway headquarters. For this work, he receives half of their $10,000 initial fee and one-third of their 8 percent royalty fees. Today, there are more than 300 Subway stores in China.

Other multinational franchisors still face significant challenges in China, particularly in dealing with the ambiguous legal environment, finding appropriate partners, and identifying the most suitable marketing, financing, and logistics strategies. Famous brands like A&W, Dunkin' Donuts, and Rainforest Cafe have all experienced these issues.

Why China for Franchising?

On the surface, franchising in China is attractive because of its huge market, long-term growth potential, and dramatic rise in disposable income among its rapidly expanding urban population. The market for fast food is estimated at $15 billion per year. China's urban population, the target market for casual dining, has expanded at a 5 percent compound annual growth rate over the past several years, a trend expected to continue. Increasingly hectic lifestyles have led to an increase in meals the Chinese eat outside the home. Surveys reveal that Chinese consumers are interested in sampling non-Chinese foods.

Market researchers have identified several major benefits to franchising in China:

- *A win-win proposition.* Restaurants were one of the first industries the government opened to private ownership in the early 1980s. Franchising in China combines the Western know-how of franchisors with the local market knowledge of franchisees. Many Chinese have strong entrepreneurial instincts and are eager to launch their own businesses.
- *Minimal entry costs.* Because much of the cost of launching a restaurant is borne by local entrepreneurs, franchising minimizes the costs to franchisors of entering the market.
- *Rapid expansion.* By leveraging the resources of numerous local entrepreneurs, the franchisor can get set up quickly. Franchising is superior to other entry strategies for rapidly establishing many outlets throughout any new market.
- *Brand consistency.* Because franchisors are required to strictly adhere to company operating procedures and policies, brand consistency is easier to maintain.
- *Circumvention of legal constraints.* Franchising allows the focal firm to avoid trade barriers associated with exporting and FDI, common in China.

Challenges of Franchising in China

China's market also poses many challenges for franchisors:

- *Knowledge gap.* Despite the likely pool of potential franchisees, realistically, few Chinese have significant knowledge about how to start and operate a business. There is still much confusion about franchising among lawmakers, entrepreneurs, and consumers. Focal firms must educate government officials, potential franchisees, and creditors on the basics of franchising, a process that consumes energy, time, and money.
- *Ambiguous legal environment.* Franchisors need to closely examine China's legal system regarding contracts and intellectual property rights. The Chinese government introduced regulations permitting franchising in 1997. The legal system is evolving and has numerous loopholes and ambiguities. Some critical elements are not covered. The situation has led to diverse interpretations of the legality of franchising in China. Franchisors must be vigilant about protecting trademarks. A local imitator can quickly dilute or damage a trademark a focal firm has built up through much expense and effort. Branding is important to franchising success, but consumers become confused if several similar brands are present. Chinese imitators have launched restaurants that use similar logos and menus, and even accept coupons from Subway when consumers mix up the two stores.
- *Escalating start-up costs.* Ordinarily, entry through franchising is cost effective. However, various challenges, combined with linguistic and cultural barriers, can increase the up-front investment and resource demands of new entrants in China and delay profitability. Given the shortage of restaurant equipment in China, the franchisor may have to invest in store equipment and lease it to the franchisee, at least until the franchisee can afford to buy it. Franchisors must be patient. McDonald's has been in China since the early 1990s and has devoted substantial resources to building its brand. But few firms have its resources.

Perhaps the biggest challenge of launching franchises in China is finding the right partners. It is paradoxical that entrepreneurs with the capital to start a restaurant often lack the business experience or entrepreneurial drive, while entrepreneurs with sufficient drive and expertise often lack the start-up capital. Subway's franchise fee of $10,000 is equivalent to two years' salary for the average Chinese. The banking system in China is still developing. Capital sources for small businesses are limited. Entrepreneurs often borrow funds from family members and friends to launch business ventures. Fortunately, Chinese banks are increasingly open to franchising. The Bank of China established a comprehensive credit line of $12 million for Kodak franchisees.

Availability and financing of suitable real estate are major considerations as well, particularly for initial showcase stores where location is critical. According to established Chinese law, local and foreign investors are allowed to develop, use, and administer real estate. But in many cases, the Chinese government owns real estate that is not available for individuals to purchase. Private property laws are underdeveloped, and franchisees occasionally risk eviction. Fortunately, a growing number of malls and shopping centers are good locations for franchised restaurants.

The Chinese authorities maintain restrictions on the repatriation of profits to the home country. Strict rules discourage repatriation of the initial investment, making this capital rather illiquid. To avoid this problem, firms make initial capital investments in stages to minimize the risk of not being able to withdraw overinvested funds. Fortunately, China is gradually relaxing its restrictions, and franchisors have been reinvesting their profits back into China to continue to fund the growth of their operations. Reinvesting profits also provides a natural hedge against exchange rate fluctuations.

Learning from the Success of Others

Experience has shown that new entrants to China often benefit from establishing a presence in Hong Kong and then moving inland to the southern provinces. Before it was absorbed by mainland China, Hong Kong was one of the world's leading capitalist economies. It is an excellent pro-business location to gain experience for doing business in China. In other cases, franchisors have launched stores in smaller Chinese cities, gaining experience there before expanding into more costly, competitive urban environments such as Beijing and Shanghai.

Adapting offerings to local tastes appears to be a prerequisite. Suppliers and business infrastructure in the country are often lacking. Franchisors spend much money to develop supplier and distribution networks. They may also need to build logistical infrastructure to move inputs from suppliers to individual stores. McDonald's has replicated its supply chain, bringing its key suppliers, such as potato supplier Simplot, to China. There is no one best approach in China. For instance, TGI Friday's imports roughly three-quarters of its food supplies, which helps maintain quality. But heavy importing is expensive and exposes profitability to exchange rate fluctuations.

AACSB: Reflective Thinking Skills, Multicultural and Diversity Understanding

Case Questions

1. Subway brings to China various intellectual property in the form of trademarks, patents, and an entire business system. What are the specific threats to Subway's intellectual property in China? What can Subway do to protect its intellectual property in China?
2. What do you think about Subway's method and level of compensating its master franchisee and regular franchisees in China? Is the method satisfactory? Is there room for improvement?
3. What are the advantages and disadvantages of franchising in China from Jim Bryant's perspective? What can Bryant do to overcome the disadvantages? From Subway's perspective, is franchising the best entry strategy for China?
4. Subway faces various cultural challenges in China. What are these challenges, and what can Subway and its master franchisee do to overcome them?

Sources: Carlye Adler, "How China Eats a Sandwich," *Fortune*, March 21, 2005, pp. F210B–F210D; Ilan Alon, "Interview: International Franchising in China with Kodak," *Thunderbird International Business Review* 43, no. 6 (2001): 737–746; Laurie Burkitt, Loretta Chao, Melissa Powers, and Yoli Zhang, "Made in China: Fake Stores," *Wall Street Journal*, August 3, 2011, pp. B1–B2; A. Dayal-Gulati and Angela Lee, *Kellogg on China: Strategies for Success* (Evanston, IL: Northwestern University Press, 2004); William Edwards, "The Pros and Consequences of Franchising in China," *Chinabusinessreview.com*, July–September, 2011, pp. 41–43; Richard Gibson, "Foreign Flavors: When Going Abroad, You Should Think of Franchising as a Cookie-Cutter Business; Unless, of Course, You Want to Succeed," *Wall Street Journal*, September 25, 2006, p. R8; Subway corporate Web site at http://www.subway.com.

CHAPTER ESSENTIALS

MyManagementLab

Go to **mymanagementlab.com** to complete the problems marked with this icon ⭐.

Key Terms

build-operate-transfer (BOT) 425	intellectual property 412	master franchise 421
contractual entry strategies in international business 412	intellectual property rights 412	royalty 413
franchising 413	know-how agreement 416	turnkey contracting 425
infringement of intellectual property 427	licensing 412	
	management contract 426	

Summary

In this chapter, you learned about:

1. Contractual entry strategies

Contractual entry strategies in international business grant foreign partners permission to use the focal firm's **intellectual property** in exchange for a continuous stream of payments. **Intellectual property rights** are the legal claims through which the proprietary assets of firms and individuals are protected from unauthorized use by other parties. Firms run the risk of disclosing their intellectual property to outside partners. **Licensing** grants a firm the right to use another firm's intellectual property for a specified period of time in exchange for royalties or other compensation. **Franchising** allows one firm the right to use another's entire business system in exchange for fees, royalties, or other forms of compensation. A

royalty is a fee paid to the licensor at regular intervals to compensate for the temporary use of intellectual property. Under a **know-how agreement,** the focal firm provides technological or managerial knowledge about how to design, manufacture, or deliver a product or service.

2. Licensing as an entry strategy

The agreement between the licensor and the licensee is for a specific time period in a specific country or region. The licensor may enter an exclusive agreement with the licensee to minimize competition with other licensees in the same territory. Once the relationship is established and the licensee fully understands its role, the licensor has little additional input. Licensing is widely used in the fashion and toy industries.

3. Advantages and disadvantages of licensing

Licensing's main advantage to the licensor is it does not require substantial capital investment or physical presence in the foreign market. The licensor can avoid political risk, government regulations, and other risks associated with FDI. However, licensing generates lower profits and limits the firm's ability to control its intellectual property. The licensee may become a competitor once the licensing agreement expires.

4. Franchising as an entry strategy

Franchisors employ widely identifiable trademarks and attempt to guarantee the customer a consistent retail experience and product quality. A **master franchise** is an arrangement whereby a franchisee obtains the rights to, and is responsible for, developing franchised outlets to serve a country or a region. Franchising is common in international retailing but difficult to replicate across diverse markets.

5. Advantages and disadvantages of franchising

Franchising allows franchisees to gain access to well-known, well-established brand names and business systems, allowing them to launch successful businesses with minimal risk. The franchisor can rapidly internationalize by leveraging the drive and knowledge of local franchisees but risks disseminating its intellectual property to unauthorized parties.

6. Other contractual entry strategies

Under **build-operate-transfer (BOT)** arrangements, the firm contracts to build a major facility, such as a power plant, which it operates for a period of years and then transfers to the host-country government or other public entity. In turnkey contracting, one or several firms plan, finance, organize, and manage all phases of a project which, once completed, they hand over to a host-country customer. **Management contracts** occur when a company contracts with another to supply management know-how in the operation of a factory or service facility, such as a hotel. With leasing, the firm rents machinery or equipment, usually for a long period, to clients located abroad.

7. Infringement of intellectual property: A global problem

Infringement of intellectual property rights takes place through counterfeiting and piracy, which cost companies billions of dollars per year. Several hundred billion dollars worth of counterfeit and pirated goods cross national borders every year. The Internet facilitates much piracy worldwide. Counterfeiting affects many of the most well-known multinational firms, hurting company performance by eroding competitive advantage and brand equity.

8. Guidelines for protecting intellectual property

Managers must proactively safeguard their proprietary assets by registering patents, trademarks, and other assets in each country and minimize operations in major counterfeiting countries and countries with weak intellectual property laws. Managers must also train employees and licensees in the proper legal use of intellectual property and vigilantly track down and prosecute violators.

Test Your Comprehension AACSB: Reflective Thinking Skills

1. Distinguish between the major types of intellectual property: trademarks, copyrights, patents, industrial designs, and trade secrets.

2. What are the major characteristics of licensing? What are the major characteristics of franchising?

⭐ 3. What are the advantages and disadvantages of franchising from the perspective of franchisors and franchisees?

4. Name the industry sectors that rely the most on franchising to tap foreign markets.

5. Define and distinguish the following contractual entry strategies: build-operate-transfer, turnkey projects, management contracts, and leasing.

⭐ 6. What are the best practices in managing international contractual relationships?

Apply Your Understanding AACSB: Communication Abilities, Reflective Thinking Skills

1. Warner Brothers is doing a thriving business by licensing images of Harry Potter characters. Firms that manufacture software, games, clothing, and other products enter into licensing agreements with Warner, paying the firm ongoing compensation to produce goods that feature Potter images. However, some illicit operators produce products that feature Potter images *without* entering a licensing agreement with Warner. What steps can Warner take to address this problem? Some nations lack substantial intellectual property protections, and are characterized by significant, ongoing counterfeiting of corporate assets. What can Warner do to protect Harry Potter from intellectual property infringement in such countries? Intellectual property violations are especially common in China. Should Warner avoid licensing Potter in China? Justify your answer.

2. Suppose upon graduation you get a job with Hitachi America, Ltd. (www.hitachi.us), the U.S. subsidiary of the giant Japanese firm. Hitachi uses various contractual entry strategies in its international operations. These include build-operate-transfer and turnkey projects in the infrastructure development sector, management contracts to run nuclear power plants, and leasing of heavy earthmoving equipment to foreign governments. Hitachi America wants to extend its reach into Latin America. Prepare a brief report for senior management in which you explain the various ways to implement its existing entry strategies in this region.

3. *Ethical Dilemma:* You are the president of Dynamic Publishing, a firm that publishes textbooks. During an overseas trip you assess the prospects for marketing Dynamic's textbooks abroad. Visiting a university in a developing country, you discover that many students use photocopied or locally reproduced versions of Dynamic's books. Upon investigation, you are advised that most students could not afford to attend college if they were required to pay full price for the books. You are dismayed by the clear violation of intellectual property rights. You believe Dynamic cannot maintain profitability if its intellectual property is infringed. You also feel obligated to protect the rights of the authors of Dynamic's textbooks. At the same time, however, you are sympathetic to the students' plight. Using the Ethical Framework in Chapter 5, analyze the dilemma presented here. Should you try to enforce Dynamic's intellectual property rights, or should you look the other way and allow the illicit photocopying to continue? Is there a creative solution to this problem?

globalEDGE | **INTERNET EXERCISES**
(http://www.globalEDGE.msu.edu)

AACSB: Reflective Thinking Skills

Refer to Chapter 1, page 24, for instructions on how to access and use globalEDGE™.

1. Suppose you get a job at the office of the International Intellectual Property Alliance (IIPA; www.iipa.com). You learn that worldwide piracy of products is rampant. Your boss assigns you to draft a brief policy memo in which you address the following questions:
   - What is the worldwide scope of piracy? What industries are most affected by piracy, and what is the financial loss from piracy in each of these industries?
   - What are the top five countries that are the greatest sources of piracy?
   - What strategies do you recommend for combating piracy? In addition to globalEDGE™ and the IIPA portal, other useful sites for this exercise are the Office of the United States Trade Representative (www.ustr.gov), United Nations (www.un.org), and the Business Software Alliance (www.bsa.org).

2. Suppose you are an international entrepreneur and want to open your own franchise somewhere in Europe. You decide to conduct research to identify the most promising franchise and learn how to become a franchisee. Entrepreneur.com publishes an annual list of the top 200 franchisors seeking international franchisees. Visit www.entrepreneur.com for the list or search for "franchising" at globalEDGE™. Choose the franchise that interests you most (for example, Subway, Spar, Century 21, Benetton), and visit its corporate Web site. Based on information from the Web site, as well as globalEDGE™ and Hoovers.com, address the following questions:

   - How many franchised operations does this firm have outside its home country?
   - What are the major countries in which the firm has franchises? Are there any patterns in terms of the countries where this firm is established?
   - According to the application information provided at the corporate site, what qualifications is the firm seeking in new franchisees?
   - What types of training and support does the firm provide for its franchisees?

3. The International Licensing Industry Merchandisers' Association (LIMA; www.licensing.org) is an organization with offices worldwide. It supports merchandise licensing through education, networking, and professional standards development. Suppose you work for an animation company that has developed several popular cartoon characters that have licensing potential, in the same way that Disney licenses its cartoon characters. Your company wants to learn more about how to license its cartoon characters. Visit the LIMA Web site and write a memo that addresses the following:
   - Who are the major members of LIMA?
   - What are the major trade shows that your firm can attend to exhibit its licensable products and learn more about licensing?
   - What types of seminars and training are available to learn more about becoming a licensor?
   - Based on the information provided at the site, what can you learn about anti-counterfeiting activities and challenges in licensing?

MyManagementLab

Go to **mymanagementlab.com** for Auto-graded writing questions as well as the following Assisted-graded writing questions:

16-1. What are the advantages and disadvantages of licensing?

16-2. Suppose you work for a firm that holds valuable intellectual property and is contemplating various international business projects. What strategies would you recommend to management for protecting the firm's intellectual property?

16-3. Mymanagementlab Only – comprehensive writing assignment for this chapter.

Source: 06photo/Shutterstock

Global Sourcing of Pharmaceutical Drug Trials

In India, about 2 million people per year participate in human clinical trials for new drugs. Pharmaceutical firms conduct some 40 percent of such human trials in emerging markets because such countries offer numerous advantages: (1) lower costs for recruitment of physicians and patients, (2) large potential patient populations, (3) diversity of patients and medical conditions, and (4) less likelihood of patients taking other medicines that could interact with the drug under study. Clinical trials also provide a means to enter and learn about emerging markets, which pharmaceutical firms consider promising for future growth of sales and profits.

It currently costs more than $1 billion to develop and bring a new drug to market in the United States. More than half the cost is incurred in confirming drug safety, tolerance, and effectiveness in human drug trials required by the U.S. Food and Drug Administration (FDA; www.fda.gov) and similar agencies worldwide. Because recruiting patients accounts for approximately 40 percent of the trial budget, testing in emerging

CHAPTER 17

Global Sourcing

LEARNING OBJECTIVES *In this chapter, you will learn about:*

1. Outsourcing, global sourcing, and offshoring
2. Benefits of global sourcing
3. Risks of global sourcing
4. Strategies for minimizing the risks of global sourcing
5. Implementing global sourcing through supply-chain management
6. Global sourcing, corporate social responsibility, and sustainability

MyManagementLab®

⭐ **Improve Your Grade!**

Over 10 million students improved their results using the Pearson MyLabs. Visit **mymanagementlab.com** for simulations, tutorials, and end-of-chapter problems.

markets greatly reduces recruitment costs. A drug trial costs about $30,000 per patient in the United States versus about $3,000 in Romania. Lowering costs has become especially important, due to the recent global recession and pressures from governments to reduce healthcare expenditures.

Pharmaceutical firms typically outsource human drug trials to contract research organizations (CROs), which in turn hire physicians in local communities and hospitals to recruit patients. For example, almost every major Western pharmaceutical firm conducts some clinical trials in hospitals in Russia. The country's centralized hospital system recruits patients for trials

quickly, saving millions of dollars and many months of effort in the drug development process.

Offshoring clinical trials raises questions about ethics and oversight. While most trials in emerging markets have been conducted without problems, and patients there often consider them a way to access advanced medical treatment, some breakdowns have occurred. One study found a quarter of all trials in developing economies did not receive adequate official oversight to ensure compliance and safety. The FDA inspects only a small proportion of these trial sites. In a recent year, more than 500 drug trials were conducted in

Russia at some 3,000 sites. In that same year, the FDA was able to inspect only about 100 sites worldwide. It criticized about one-third of the sites for failure to follow protocol and cited nearly 10 percent for failure to report adverse patient reactions to the trial drugs. The European Medicines Agency (EMA; www.ema.europa.eu), the EU's drugs regulator, inspects only a few dozen trial sites per year for good clinical practice.

Physicians in Russia can triple or quadruple their monthly incomes by operating as trial investigators and recruiting patients. This financial incentive raises potential conflicts for doctors, some of whom may induce patients to participate. Some trials have endangered patients or been conducted without proper ethical review. Pfizer was sued for testing a meningitis drug on Nigerian children without their parents' consent, resulting in five deaths. A Nigerian human clinical trial for an antiretroviral drug was shut down amid concerns that researchers did not store the drugs or handle the scientific data properly.

SOURCES: "Indian Pharma Trials," *Chemistry & Industry*, February 2012, p. 51; Dinesh Sharma, "Outsourcing Big Pharma," *Health Affairs*, March 2010, pp. 563–564; Geeta Anand and Shirley Wang, "New Concern for Drug Tests Abroad," *Wall Street Journal*, March 23, 2009, p. B2; A. T. Kearney, "Make Your Move: Taking Clinical Trials to the Best Location," 2010, retrieved from http://www.atkearney.com; Pete Engardio, Arlene Weintraub, and Nandini Lakshman, "Outsourcing the Drug Industry," *Business Week*, September 15, 2008, p. 48; Philip Fiscus, "Global Risks for Drug Manufacturers," *Risk Management*, May 2009, p. 55; Andrew Jack, "Drugs Company Ethics on Trial in Developing World," *Financial Times*, June 8, 2009, retrieved from http://www.ft.com; PhRMA, *Pharmaceutical Industry Profile* 2009, retrieved from http://www.phrma.org; D. Ramesh, "Cost Cutting Becomes the Pharma Industry's Mantra," *Chemical Week*, September 28–October 5, 2009, pp. 24–27; "Clinical Trials Market Will Exceed $30BN by 2015," *Worldwide Biotech*, August 2011, pp. 1–2.

As the opening story suggests, companies in the pharmaceutical industry outsource much of their human clinical trials to emerging markets, in order to reduce product development costs and increase speed to market. Global sourcing has changed the way companies do business in all kinds of industries. Focal firms shop the world for inputs or finished products to meet efficiency and strategic objectives and to remain competitive. The search for the best sources of products and services is an ongoing task for managers. Many of the products sold by general retailers such as Best Buy and Marks & Spencer are sourced from low-cost suppliers in emerging markets. Steinway procures parts and components from a dozen foreign countries to manufacture grand pianos. HP provides technical support to its customers from call centers based in India.

In many cases, firms move entire sections of their value chains abroad, such as R&D, manufacturing, or technical support. In the sports apparel industry, firms such as Nike and Reebok subcontract nearly all their athletic shoe production to lower-cost foreign manufacturers. Clothing retailer Gap sources more than 80 percent of its apparel from suppliers in Asia. The Gap, Nike, and Reebok function primarily as brand owners and marketers, not as manufacturers.[1] Apple sources some 70 percent of its production from abroad while focusing internal resources on continuously improving its software and product designs. This allows Apple management to optimize usage of the firm's finite capital resources and focus on its core competencies.

The total worldwide sourcing market for product manufacturing and services now exceeds $1 trillion. The IT industry alone in India now employs more than 2 million people and indirectly affects the lives of more than 8 million people. Global sourcing employs more than 500,000 people in the Philippines. Worldwide, the most frequently outsourced business processes include logistics and procurement, sales and marketing, and customer service, followed by finance and accounting.[2] Global sourcing by the private sector now accounts for more than half of all imports by major countries.[3]

Outsourcing
The procurement of selected value-adding activities, including production of intermediate goods or finished products, from independent suppliers.

 ## Outsourcing, Global Sourcing, and Offshoring

Outsourcing refers to the procurement of selected value-adding activities, including production of intermediate goods or finished products, from external independent suppliers. Firms outsource because they generally are not superior at performing *all* value-chain activities and it is more cost effective to outsource these activities. **Business process outsourcing (BPO)** occurs when firms procure, from an external supplier, services such as accounting, payroll, human resource functions, travel services, IT services, customer service, and technical support.[4] Companies contract with third-party service providers to reduce the cost of performing service tasks that are not part of the firm's core competencies or not critical to maintaining its competitive position in the marketplace. BPO can be divided into two categories: *back-office activities*, which include internal, upstream business functions such as payroll and billing, and *front-office activities*, which include downstream, customer-related services such as marketing or technical support.

In undertaking outsourcing, managers face two key decisions: (1) which, if any, value-chain activities should be outsourced, and (2) where in the world these activities should be performed. Let's consider these choices.

Decision 1: Outsource or Not?

Managers must decide between *internalization* and *externalization*—whether each value-adding activity should be conducted in house or by an external, independent supplier. In business, this is traditionally known as the *make* or *buy* decision: "Should we make a product or perform a value-chain activity ourselves, or should we source it from an outside contractor?"

Firms usually internalize those value-chain activities they consider part of their *core competencies*, those that they perform particularly well or that use proprietary knowledge they want to control. Canon uses its core competencies in precision mechanics, fine optics, and microelectronics to produce some of the world's best cameras, printers, and copiers. It usually performs R&D and product design itself to reduce the risk of divulging proprietary knowledge to competitors and to generate continuous improvement in these competencies. By contrast, firms will usually source from *external* suppliers when they can obtain non-core products, components, or services at lower cost or from suppliers specialized in providing them.

Decision 2: Where in the World Should Value-Adding Activities Be Located?

A second key decision that firms face is whether to keep each value-adding activity in the home country or locate it in a foreign country. **Configuration of value-adding activity** refers to the pattern or geographic arrangement of locations where the firm carries out value-chain activities.[5] Instead of concentrating value-adding activities in their home country, many firms configure them across the world to save money, reduce delivery time, access factors of production, or extract maximum advantages relative to competitors.

This helps explain the migration of manufacturing industries from Europe, Japan, and the United States to emerging markets in Asia, Latin America, and Eastern Europe. Depending on the firm and the industry, management may decide to concentrate certain value-adding activities in just one or a handful of locations, while dispersing others to numerous countries. External suppliers are typically located in countries characterized by low-cost labor, competent production processes, and specific knowledge about relevant engineering and development activities.[6]

To run its global network of package shipping, DHL established offices in countries and cities worldwide. It also set up high-tech tracking centers in Arizona, Malaysia, and the Czech Republic. DHL management chose these specific locations for shipment tracking because, in a world of twenty-four time zones, they are each about eight time zones distant from each other. This configuration allows DHL staffers to track the locations of shipments worldwide, 24 hours a day.

German automaker Bayerische Motoren Werke AG (BMW; www.bmw.com) employs more than 60,000 factory workers at seventeen sites in six countries to manufacture sedans, coupes, and convertibles. Workers at the Munich plant build the BMW 3 Series and supply engines and key body components to other BMW factories abroad. In the United States, BMW has a plant in South Carolina that makes about 300,000 vehicles annually for the world market. In northeast China, BMW makes cars in a joint venture with Brilliance China Automotive Holdings Ltd. In India, BMW has a manufacturing presence to serve the needs of the rapidly growing South Asia market. Management must configure BMW's sourcing at the best locations worldwide to minimize costs (for example, by producing in China), hire skilled people (by producing in Germany), remain close to key markets (by producing in China, India, and the United States), and succeed in the intensely competitive global car industry.[7]

Business process outsourcing (BPO) The outsourcing to independent suppliers of business service functions such as accounting, payroll, human resource functions, travel services, IT services, customer service, or technical support.

Configuration of value-adding activity The pattern or geographic arrangement of locations where the firm carries out value-chain activities.

Global Sourcing

Global sourcing
The procurement of products or services from independent suppliers or company-owned subsidiaries located abroad for consumption in the home country or a third country.

Global sourcing is the procurement of products or services from independent suppliers or company-owned subsidiaries located abroad for consumption in the home country or a third country. Also called *global procurement* or *global purchasing*, global sourcing amounts to importing—an inbound flow of goods and services. It is an entry strategy that relies on a contractual relationship between the buyer (the focal firm) and a foreign source of supply. Dell (www.dell.com) relies extensively on a manufacturing network, composed largely of independent suppliers located around the world. Exhibit 17.1 details how Dell assembles components from suppliers in numerous locations for its Dell Inspiron notebook computer.[8]

Global sourcing is a low-control strategy in which the focal firm sources from independent suppliers through contractual agreements, as opposed to the high-control strategy of buying from company-owned subsidiaries. Global sourcing frequently represents the firm's initial involvement in international business. For many firms, it increases management's awareness about other international opportunities. Based on experience it gains through such *inward internationalization*, the firm may progress to exporting, direct investment, or other forms of *outward internationalization*.

An established business practice, global sourcing has gained momentum in the current phase of globalization.[9] Contractors such as Softtek in Mexico help U.S. banks develop customized software, manage IT systems, and perform support and maintenance for commercial finance operations. Softtek (www.softtek.com) has 3,500 employees, mostly engineers. Its outsourcing facilities are located in Brazil, Colombia, Peru, and Venezuela. Argentina boasts one of the best-educated workforces in Latin America and is aggressively promoting its software development centers. The low salaries of software engineers (typically less than $12,000 a year) have persuaded such companies as Disney, Peugeot, and Repsol to have Web site design and software development performed in Argentina.

EXHIBIT 17.1

Sourcing for the Dell Inspiron Notebook Computer

Sources: Based on Thomas Friedman, *The World Is Flat 3.0* (New York: Picado, 2007); "Dell's Current Suppliers, Fiscal Year 2011" at www.dell.com.

LCD display from a factory in South Korea (LG Phillips LCD), Japan (Toshiba), or Taiwan (AU Optronics)

Battery from a Japanese-owned factory in Mexico or Malaysia or China (Sanyo), or a Taiwanese factory (Simplo)

Intel microprocessor from an Intel factory in China, Malaysia, the Philippines, or Costa Rica

Keyboard from a Japanese-owned factory (Alps) or a Taiwanese-owned factory (Darfon), all in China

Modem from a Chinese-owned company in China (Foxconn) or a Taiwanese-owned company in China (Lite-On)

Intel microprocessor from an Intel factory in China, Malaysia, the Philippines, or Costa Rica

Hard disk drive from a Japanese-owned company in Thailand (Hitachi or Fujitsu), or a Japanese-owned factory in the Philippines (Toshiba)

Motherboard from a Taiwanese-owned factory in China (Quanta), or a Taiwanese-owned factory in Taiwan (Compal)

Memory from a factory in Italy (ST), Taiwan (Nanya), or Germany (Infineon)

The growth of global sourcing has been driven by three key factors:

- *Technological advances in communications, especially the Internet and international telecommunications.* Access to vast online information means focal firms can quickly find suppliers that meet specific needs, anywhere in the world. Firms can communicate continuously with foreign suppliers at very low cost.
- *Falling costs of international business.* Tariffs and other trade barriers have declined substantially. Efficient communication and transportation systems have made international procurement cost effective and accessible to any firm.
- *Entrepreneurship and rapid economic transformation in emerging markets.* China, India, and other emerging markets have quickly developed as important suppliers of various products and services. Entrepreneurial suppliers aggressively pursue sourcing partnerships with foreign buyers.

The decisions about whether and where to outsource can be seen in the framework in Exhibit 17.2. The focal firm can source from independent suppliers (wherein the activity is externalized, or outsourced), from company-owned subsidiaries and affiliates (wherein the activity is internalized), or from both. In the exhibit, Cells C and D represent the global sourcing scenarios. While global sourcing implies procurement from foreign locations, in some cases the focal firm may source from its own wholly owned subsidiary or an affiliate jointly owned with another firm (Cell C). This is **captive sourcing**. Genpact was a captive sourcing unit of General Electric (GE), with annual revenues of more than $1 billion and more than 37,000 employees worldwide. Now an independent company based in India, Genpact (www.genpact.com) is one of the largest providers of business-process outsourcing services.[10]

> **Captive sourcing**
> Sourcing from the firm's own production facilities.

The relationship between the focal firm and its foreign supplier (Cell D in Exhibit 17.2) may take the form of **contract manufacturing**, an arrangement in which the focal firm contracts with an independent supplier to manufacture products according to well-defined specifications. Once it has manufactured the products or components, the supplier delivers them to the focal firm, which then markets, sells, and distributes them. In essence, the focal firm "rents" the manufacturing capacity of the foreign contractor. Contract manufacturing accounts for more than half of all manufacturing in the toy, sporting goods, consumer electronics, and automotive industries. It is also common in the pharmaceuticals, furniture, semiconductor, apparel, and footwear industries.[11]

> **Contract manufacturing**
> An arrangement in which the focal firm contracts with an independent supplier to manufacture products according to well-defined specifications.

Patheon is a leading global pharmaceutical contract manufacturer (www.patheon.com). It operates eleven production facilities in Europe and North America, producing over-the-counter drugs and several top-selling prescription medications on contract to many of the world's twenty largest pharmaceutical firms. Patheon generates about half its sales in North America and the other half in Europe.[12]

EXHIBIT 17.2 The Nature of Outsourcing and Global Sourcing

	Value-adding activity is internalized	Value-adding activity is externalized (outsourced)
Value-adding activity kept in home country	*A* Keep production in-house, in home country	*B* Outsource production to third-party provider at home
Value-adding activity conducted abroad (global sourcing)	*C* Delegate production to foreign subsidiary or affiliate (captive sourcing)	*D* Outsource production to a third-party provider abroad (contract manufacturing or global sourcing from independent suppliers)

Sources: Based on B. Kedia and D. Mukherjee, "Understanding Offshoring: A Research Framework Based on Disintegration, Location and Externalization Advantages," Journal of World Business 44, no. 3 (2009): 250–261; Information Economy Report 2009 (New York: United Nations, 2009); World Investment Report 2004 (New York: UNCTAD, 2004).

Have you ever heard of Taiwan's Hon Hai Precision Industry Company? Also known as Foxconn, Hon Hai is a leading contract manufacturer in the global electronics industry, with annual sales of more than $100 billion. Hon Hai (www.foxconn.com) works under contract for many well-known companies, churning out PlayStations for Sony; iPods, iPhones, and iPads for Apple; printers and PCs for Hewlett-Packard; and thousands of other products. The firm employs more than 1 million people in scores of contract factories worldwide, from Malaysia to Mexico.[13]

Ethical Connections

If you call customer service for your cell phone or computer, you may speak to someone on the other side of the world. Outsourcing to countries where labor is cheaper helps companies lower labor costs and improve profits. In a global economy, domestic workers compete with overseas workers for jobs whose output can be transmitted by telephone or the Internet. Jobs once performed by domestic workers are effectively shipped overseas. Working conditions in emerging markets occasionally amount to sweatshop conditions. At the same time, however, global sourcing from emerging markets creates jobs for those who may otherwise face poverty.

Offshoring

Offshoring

The relocation of a business process or entire manufacturing facility to a foreign country.

Offshoring is the relocation of a business process or entire manufacturing facility to a foreign country. It is common in the service sector, including banking, software code writing, legal services, and customer-service activities.[14] Large legal hubs have emerged in India that provide services such as drafting contracts and patent applications, conducting research and negotiations, and performing paralegal work, all on behalf of Western clients. With lawyers in Europe and North America costing $300 an hour or more, law firms in India can cut Western companies' legal bills by up to 75 percent.[15]

In each of the business functions—human resources, accounting, finance, marketing, and customer service—certain tasks are considered routine and discrete. Many are candidates for offshoring as long as their performance by independent suppliers does not threaten or diminish the focal firm's core competencies or strategic assets. Examples of functions successfully offshored to foreign providers include billing and credit card processing in finance, creating customer databases and recording sales transactions in marketing, and payroll maintenance and benefits administration in human resources.

India is the current leader in the processing of advanced economies' relocated business services. Its market share has grown dramatically in the 2000s and is expected to increase by several hundred percent between 2010 and 2020, thanks to India's huge pool of qualified labor working for as little as 25 percent of what comparable workers get in the advanced economies.[16] The recent economic turndown is expected to pressure advanced-economy firms to seek further ways to reduce costs, to the benefit of service suppliers in India. Firms in Eastern Europe perform support activities for architectural and engineering firms from Western Europe and the United States. Accountants in the Philippines perform support work for major accounting firms. Accenture has back-office operations and call centers in Costa Rica. Many IT support services for customers in Germany are actually based in the Czech Republic and Romania. South Africa is the base for technical and user-support services for English-, French-, and German-speaking customers throughout Europe.[17]

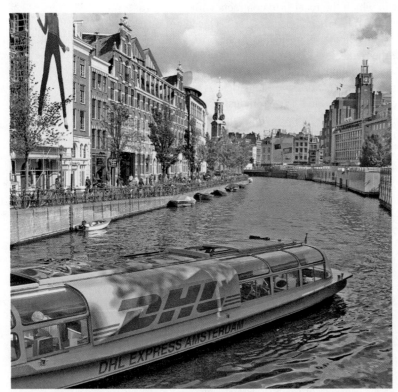

Source: Danita Delimont/Alamy

Running a business as far-flung as DHL's package delivery service requires support offices around the world. This delivery boat travels the Amstel River in Amsterdam. DHL has tracking centers in three time zones that are 8 hours apart, allowing it to offer 24-hour worldwide tracking service.

Scope of Global Sourcing

Not all business activities or processes lend themselves to global sourcing. Many jobs in the service sector cannot be separated from their place of consumption. People usually do not travel abroad to see a banker, doctor, dentist, or accountant.[18] Personal contact is vital at the downstream end of virtually all value chains. Fewer than 5 percent of jobs in the United States that require substantial customer interaction (such as in retailing) have been transferred to low-wage economies. Fewer than 15 percent of all service jobs have moved from advanced economies to emerging markets. Many firms employ global sourcing to build presence in foreign markets, which enhances company performance through increased sales. Job losses in advanced economies are relatively modest. Job losses tend to be compensated by the creation of new, usually higher-skill jobs.[19]

Many firms, such as Harley-Davidson (www.harley-davidson.com) in the United States, have their own reasons for keeping production at home. Harley-Davidson both assembles its motorcycles and procures key components such as the engine, transmission, gas tank, brake system, and headlight assembly in the United States.[20] Harley-Davidson customers view the product as a U.S. icon and highly value its "Made in the U.S.A." character.

Industries that benefit most from global sourcing are characterized by:

- Large-scale manufacturing whose primary competitive advantage is efficiency and low cost
- High labor intensity in product and service production, such as garment manufacturing and call centers
- Uniform customer needs and standardized technologies and processes in production and other value-chain activities, such as automobiles and machine parts
- Established products with a predictable pattern of sales, such as components for consumer electronics
- Information intensity whose functions and activities can be easily transmitted via the Internet, such as accounting, billing, and payroll
- Outputs that are easily codified and transmitted over the Internet or by telephone, such as software preparation, technical support, and customer service

Diversity of Countries That Initiate and Receive Outsourced Work

The *Global Trend* feature highlights the ongoing rivalry between China and India as they compete to be the world's leading destinations for global sourcing. For example, diamond processing is a labor-intensive industry that uses standardized processes to make diamond jewelry and equipment used for fine cutting. For five centuries the industry was concentrated in Antwerp, Belgium. Today, diamond cutting is increasingly outsourced to firms in India that perform the work more cost-effectively. China is also emerging as an important participant in diamond cutting. In addition to China and India, numerous other countries are active players. Global sourcing is practiced by firms around the world.[21]

Companies headquartered in the advanced economies outsource the most services by volume. More than 75 percent of major U.S. financial institutions send a portion of their IT work offshore. In Europe and Japan, the majority of large firms outsource some of their services, most often to China and India, followed by countries in Eastern Europe, Latin America, and the Middle East. In Asia, the Philippines is a successful recent entrant in global services sourcing. It draws on solid English skills and long-standing cultural ties with the West to attract call-center work.[22]

Exhibit 17.3 lists a sampling of key firms that offer global sourcing services, organized by geographic region. In Egypt, Xceed Contact Center (www.xceedcc.com) handles calls in Arabic and European languages on behalf of Carrefour, Microsoft, and Oracle. Safety and advanced legal systems in Singapore and Dubai give them an edge in handling high-security and business-continuity services. Central and South American countries seek call-center contracts for the Spanish-speaking Hispanic market in the United States.[23] With Europe as its largest export market, Vietnam dramatically increased outsourced production in the 2000s because it

GLOBAL TREND

China and India: Chief Rivals in the Global Sourcing Game

India is the world's leading offshoring destination for software development and back-office services such as telephone call centers and financial accounting activities. It is a world leader in the IT industry, thanks partly to indigenous MNEs such as Infosys (www.infosys.com) and Wipro (www.wipro.com). Infosys rivals Microsoft as one of the world's top software firms.

China has a long history as a center of manufacturing for countless Western companies. Typical is the case of the U.S. firm Keurig. Management found its single-serving coffeemakers were overpriced at $250 due to high manufacturing costs. It outsourced manufacturing to a partner in China at much lower cost. This decision enabled Keurig to offer new models for as little as $99, resulting in a significant increase in both unit and dollar sales.

China aims to surpass India in services outsourcing. The Chinese government is making huge investments to upgrade worker training and the quality of its universities.

China has several major advantages:

- *Large pool of highly skilled, low-cost labor.* China graduates 350,000 engineers every year, nearly four times as many as the United States.
- *Important site for global research and development.*
- *Large domestic market*, with rapid and sustainable economic growth.

- *Increasingly pro-business government*, with a range of policies favoring foreign firms that manufacture in China.

China also has several disadvantages:

- *Weak intellectual property protection*, frustrating firms with valuable intellectual assets and sophisticated technologies.
- *Complex culture and language*, often confounding foreign firms.
- *Suboptimal business infrastructure*, which hampers manufacturing, distribution, and other value-chain activities.
- *Government bureaucracy*, including infighting among various agencies. Resultant chaos hampers Chinese and foreign entrepreneurs.
- *Rising labor costs*, gradually reducing China's attractiveness as a sourcing destination. A Boston Consulting Group study found that rising Chinese wages will close the cost gap between China and numerous advanced economies, making China relatively unattractive as a sourcing destination for many goods by 2016.

Like China, India is characterized by a large pool of highly skilled, low-cost labor, global R&D capabilities, and a large

domestic market. In addition, India benefits from:

- *Superior intellectual property protection.*
- *Workforce with English language skills.*
- *Business infrastructure* that is often superior to that of China.

However, India also suffers from substantial government bureaucracy. Despite this, India has become an enabler of growth in various global industries through expansion of its own offshoring firms into other countries. It is likely to remain the global-sourcing leader in the services sector for some time to come.

Sources: "Buyers Turn to Cheaper Markets to Counter Yuan," *Global Sources*, January 2011, retrieved from www.globalsources.com; Harold Sirkin, Michael Zinser, and Douglas Hohner, *Made in America, Again* (Boston: Boston Consulting Group, August 2011); Bruce Einhorn and Evan Applegate, "China Boosts the Minimum Wage," *Bloomberg Businessweek*, March 12–18, 2012, p. 16; A. T. Kearney, "Geography of Offshoring Is Shifting, According to A.T. Kearney Study," May 18, 2009, retrieved from http://www.atkearney.com; Alan Beattie, "Ethical Rules Impose Perverse Incentives," *Financial Times*, January 30, 2009, retrieved from http://www.ft.com; Pete Engardio, "China's Eroding Advantage," *Business Week*, June 15, 2009, pp. 54–55; Rahul Sachitanand, "IT Morphs Yet Again," *Business Today*, December 27, 2009, retrieved from http://businesstoday.intoday.in/

EXHIBIT 17.3 Key Players in Global Sourcing by Region

	Central and Eastern Europe	Central and South Asia	Latin America and the Caribbean	Middle East and Africa
Top-Ranked Countries	Czech Republic, Bulgaria, Slovakia, Poland, Hungary	India, China, South Korea, Taiwan, Philippines, Singapore, Malaysia, Thailand	Chile, Brazil, Mexico, Costa Rica, Argentina	Egypt, Jordan, United Arab Emirates, Ghana, Tunisia, Dubai
Up-and-Comers	Romania, Russia, Ukraine, Belarus	Indonesia, Vietnam, Sri Lanka	Jamaica, Panama, Nicaragua, Colombia	South Africa, Israel, Turkey, Morocco
Typical Local Providers	*EPAM Systems* (Belarus, software development); *Softengi* (Ukraine, software engineering)	*NCS* (Singapore, business processes); *Bluem* (China, IT services); *BroadenGate* (China, software development)	*Sonda* (Chile, business processes); *Neoris* (Mexico, IT services); *Politec* (Brazil, IT services)	*Xceed* (Egypt, software development); *Ness Technologies* (Israel, IT services, *Jeraisy Group* (Saudi Arabia, IT services)

Sources: Based on Penny Crosman, "Worldsourcers," *Wall Street & Technology*, July 1980, p. 26; Pete Engardio, "The Future of Outsourcing: How It's Transforming Whole Industries and Changing the Way We Work," *Business Week*, January 30, 2006, p. 58; UNCTAD, *World Investment Report 2011* (New York: United Nations, 2011).

offers modern but low-cost operations, skilled but inexpensive labor, and access to local sources unburdened by trade restrictions.[24]

The most favored countries in A. T. Kearney's Global Services Location Index (www .atkearney.com) are emerging markets and developing economies: India, China, Malaysia, Thailand, Indonesia, Egypt, Chile, and the Philippines. Canada and the United States are the only advanced economies in the top 30 destinations. To help firms identify countries for outsourcing value-chain activities, the index emphasizes various criteria: the country's financial structure (compensation costs, infrastructure costs, tax and regulatory costs), the availability and skills of its people (cumulative business-process experience and skills; labor force availability, education, and language; and worker attrition rates), and the nature of the business environment (the country's political and economic environment, physical infrastructure, cultural adaptability, and security of intellectual property).[25]

Strategic Choices in Global Sourcing

Exhibit 17.4 explains the strategic implications of the two key sourcing and location choices that firms face: whether to perform specific value-adding activities themselves or to outsource them, and whether to concentrate each activity in the home country or disperse it abroad. The exhibit portrays a typical value chain, ranging from R&D and design to customer service. The first row indicates the degree to which management considers each value-adding activity a strategic asset to the firm. The second row indicates whether the activity tends to be internalized inside the focal firm or outsourced to a foreign supplier. The third row indicates where management typically locates an activity.

In addition to large firms, global sourcing provides big benefits for small and medium-sized enterprises (SMEs). Main Street businesses from car dealerships to real estate firms increasingly farm out accounting, support services, and design work to suppliers in Brazil, Hungary, India, and other top destinations. Outsourcing brokers and international online sites such as www. guru.com and www.vworker.com do big business serving the global sourcing needs of countless SMEs. Internet search engines allow small firms to find service vendors anywhere in the world. An auto dealership in New York hired an Internet developer in Brazil to design a multimedia Web site to sell cars online. A real estate agent in California uses suppliers in Hungary, India, and Portugal to design graphics, manage databases, and update online information.[26]

EXHIBIT 17.4

Typical Choices of Outsourcing and Geographic Dispersion of Value-Chain Activities among Firms

	R&D, Design	Manufacturing of Parts, Components	Manufacturing or Assembly of Finished Products	Marketing and Branding	Sales and Distribution	Customer Service
Importance of this activity to the firm as a strategic asset	High importance	Low importance	Low to medium importance	High importance	Medium importance	Medium importance
Likelihood of internalizing rather than outsourcing this activity	High	Low	Low to medium	High	Low to medium	Low to medium
Geographic configuration: Overall tendency to locate activity at home or abroad	Usually concentrated at home	Usually dispersed across various markets	Usually concentrated in a few markets	Branding concentrated at home; Marketing concentrated or dispersed to individual markets	Dispersed to individual markets	Dispersed to individual markets, except call centers, which are often concentrated

Benefits of Global Sourcing

Like other international entry strategies, global sourcing offers both benefits and risks. Exhibit 17.5 provides an overview. The exhibit lists two primary reasons to pursue global sourcing: cost efficiency and the ability to achieve strategic goals. Let's consider these in detail.

Cost Efficiency

Cost efficiency is the primary rationale for sourcing abroad. Exhibit 17.6 reveals typical labor cost per hour of workers in various locations. Labor costs in the emerging markets, such as Indonesia and Mexico, are far less expensive than in the advanced economies. A worker in business process outsourcing in Egypt or the Philippines earns less than $5,000 per year. A call-center worker in India earns roughly $500 per month, while the same worker in Europe or the United States earns $2,000 to $3,000 monthly. This wage discrepancy explains why firms like HP, Accenture, Citicorp, Dell, and HSBC grew their Indian operations 30 to 50 percent a year during the 2000s.[27]

Ability to Achieve Strategic Goals

The strategic view of global sourcing—called *transformational outsourcing*—suggests that just as the firm achieves gains in efficiency, productivity, quality, and revenues by leveraging offshore talent, it also obtains the means to turn around failing businesses, speed up innovation, restructure operations, and fund otherwise-unaffordable development projects.[28] Global sourcing allows the firm to free expensive analysts, engineers, and managers from routine tasks to spend more time researching, innovating, managing, and generally undertaking high-value-adding activities that contribute more productively to increasing company performance.[29] In this way, global sourcing becomes a catalyst to overhaul organizational processes and company operations and increase the firm's overall competitive advantages. It allows the firm to achieve large, longer-term strategic goals.

The clothing company Liz Claiborne sold its sourcing operations, which handle all aspects of production from finding materials to manufacturing garments, to Li & Fung Group, based in Hong Kong. Li & Fung (www.lifunggroup.com) specializes in managing the supply chains

EXHIBIT 17.5

Benefits and Risks of Global Sourcing

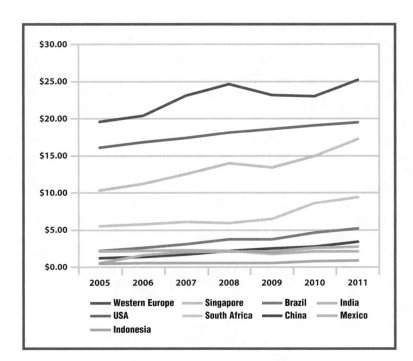

EXHIBIT 17.6

Labor Cost per Hour of Typical Workers in Various Locations, in U.S. Dollars

Source: Based on International Labour Organisation (ILO), Statistics and Databases, www.ilo.org.

of dozens of brands and retailers worldwide, including Walmart, Target, and Limited Brands. Claiborne management took the step to dramatically shift the firm's business model and focus on its core competencies, such as marketing and distribution.[30]

The twin objectives of cost efficiency and achieving strategic goals are often both present in a particular global sourcing activity. Global sourcing can provide other benefits as well, including:

- *Faster corporate growth.* Firms can focus their resources on performing more profitable activities such as R&D or building relationships with customers. For example, they can expand their staff of engineers and researchers while keeping constant their cost of product development as a percentage of sales.[31]
- *Access to qualified personnel abroad.* Countries such as China, India, the Philippines, and Ireland offer abundant pools of educated engineers, managers, and other specialists to help firms achieve their goals. Disney has much of its animation work done in Japan because some of the world's best animators are located there.
- *Improved productivity and service.* Manufacturing productivity and other value-chain activities can be improved by suppliers that specialize in these activities. Penske Truck Leasing improved its efficiency and customer service by outsourcing dozens of business processes to Mexico and India. Global sourcing also enables firms to provide 24/7 coverage of customer service.
- *Business process redesign.* By reconfiguring their value-chain systems or reengineering their business processes, companies can improve their production efficiency and resource utilization. Multinational firms see offshoring as a catalyst for a broader plan to overhaul outdated company operations.[32]
- *Increased speed to market.* By shifting software development and editorial work to India and the Philippines, the U.S.-Dutch publisher Wolters

Source: Vasily Smirnov/Shutterstock

Global automobile companies outsource much of their production to manufacturers in China. Global sourcing helps reduce costs, improves productivity, and facilitates the redesign of critical value-chain activities.

Kluwer was able to produce a greater variety of books and journals and publish them faster. As the opening story describes, big pharmaceutical firms get new medications to market faster with global sourcing of clinical drug trials.

- *Access to new markets.* Sourcing provides an entrée to the market, an understanding of local customers, and the means to initiate marketing activities there. Firms can also use global sourcing to serve countries that may be otherwise closed due to protectionism. By moving many of its R&D operations to Russia, the telecommunications firm Nortel gained an important foothold in a market that needs telephone switching equipment and other communications infrastructure. Indian conglomerate Tata Group (www.tata.com) established a call center in the United States to expand its growing presence in the U.S. market.[33]

- *Technological flexibility.* Leveraging independent suppliers abroad provides firms the flexibility to quickly change sources of supply, employing whichever suppliers offer the most advanced technologies. In this way, sourcing provides greater organizational flexibility and faster responsiveness to evolving buyer needs.

- *Improved agility by shedding unnecessary overhead.* Unburdened by a large bureaucracy and administrative overhead, companies can be more responsive to opportunities and adapt more easily to environmental changes, such as new competitors.

Combined, these benefits give firms the ability to continuously renew their strategic positions. Outsourcing specialists such as Accenture and Genpact meticulously dissect the workflow of other firms' human resources, finance, or IT departments. This helps the specialists build new IT platforms, redesign all processes, and administer programs, acting as virtual subsidiaries to their client firms. The specialists then disperse work among global networks of staff from Asia to Eastern Europe and elsewhere.[34]

 ## Risks of Global Sourcing

In addition to potential benefits, global sourcing also brings unexpected complications. Studies show that as many as half of all outsourcing arrangements are terminated earlier than planned. As summarized in Exhibit 17.5, global sourcing introduces the following major risks.[35]

- *Lower-than-expected cost savings.* International transactions are often more complex and costly than expected. Conflicts and misunderstandings may arise from differences in the national and organizational cultures between the focal firm and foreign supplier. Initial or ongoing costs can be substantial. Establishing an outsourcing facility can be surprisingly expensive, due to the need to upgrade poor infrastructure or locate it in a large city to attract sufficient skilled labor. The cost of labor is rising in many countries, which shrinks labor-cost savings over time.[36]

- *Environmental factors.* Environmental challenges include currency fluctuations, tariffs and other trade barriers, high energy and transportation costs, adverse macroeconomic events, labor strikes, and natural disasters. Firms that source from countries whose currencies are strengthening experience higher costs. Many countries suffer from poor public infrastructure, as exemplified by power outages and poor road and rail networks. In 2011, a massive earthquake in Japan interrupted exports of parts and components from Japanese suppliers for several months. Hapag-Lloyd, OOCL, and other large shipping companies banned their ships from docking in Tokyo Bay ports over concerns about radiation from Fukushima nuclear plants damaged in the quake. Many companies that normally source from Japan had to find alternative suppliers until operations there were restored.[37] In 2012, a massive power outage in India left several hundred million people without power and disrupted businesses and transport systems.

- *Weak legal environment.* Many popular locations for global sourcing (for example, China, India, and Russia) have weak intellectual property laws and poor enforcement, which can erode key strategic assets. Inadequate legal systems, red tape, convoluted tax systems, and complex business regulations complicate local operations in many countries.

- *Inadequate or low-skilled workers.* Some foreign suppliers may be staffed by employees who lack appropriate knowledge about the tasks with which they are charged. Other suppliers suffer rapid turnover of skilled employees. In India, typical operations in business processing may lose 20 percent or more of their workers each year, and good managers are often in short supply. In 2011, customer complaints about the quality of service led the U.K. subsidiary of Banco Santander to move its bank customer call centers from India back to the United Kingdom.[38]

- *Overreliance on suppliers.* Unreliable suppliers may put earlier work aside when they gain a more important client. Suppliers occasionally encounter financial difficulties or are acquired by other firms with different priorities and procedures. When such events occur, management at the focal firm may find itself scrambling to find alternate suppliers. Overreliance can shift control of key activities too much in favor of the supplier and reduce the focal firm's control of important value-chain tasks.

- *Risk of creating competitors.* As the focal firm shares its intellectual property and business-process knowledge with foreign suppliers, it also runs the risk of creating future rivals. Schwinn, long the leader in the global bicycle industry, transferred much of its production and core expertise to lower-cost foreign suppliers, which acquired sufficient knowledge to become competitors, eventually forcing Schwinn into bankruptcy (from which it later recovered).

- *Erosion of morale and commitment among home-country employees.* Global sourcing can leave employees caught in the middle between their employer and their employer's clients. At the extreme, workers find themselves in a psychological limbo, unclear who their employer really is. When outsourcing forces retained and outsourced staff to work side by side, tensions and uncertainty may evolve into an "us-versus-them" syndrome and diminish employee commitment and enthusiasm.

Strategies for Minimizing the Risks of Global Sourcing

Experience suggests several managerial guidelines for achieving success in global sourcing:

- *Go offshore for the right reasons.* The best rationale is strategic. Most companies cite cost cutting as the main reason for global sourcing. After the first year, however, the amount of money saved tends to decline. Global sourcing provides more beneficial, long-term goals such as enhancing the quality of offerings, improving overall productivity, and freeing knowledge workers and other core resources that can be redeployed to improve long-term performance. To maximize returns, management should analyze its value-chain activities and outsource those in which it is relatively weak, that offer relatively little value to the bottom line, or that can be performed more effectively by others, yet are not critical to the firm's core competencies.

- *Get employees on board.* Global sourcing can invite opposition from employees and other organizational stakeholders. Disaffected middle managers may undermine projects and other goals that offshoring seeks to achieve. Poorly planned sourcing projects create unnecessary tension and harm employee morale. Senior management should seek employee support by reaching a consensus of managers and labor, developing alternatives for redeploying laid-off workers, and soliciting employee help in choosing foreign partners. When Dutch bank ABN Amro (www.abnamro.com) decided to offshore accounting and finance functions, it set up a full-time communications department to explain the move to employees in advance. Executives held town hall–style meetings with employees and involved labor unions in managing the shift. These steps allowed offshoring to proceed more smoothly, enhancing company performance.[39]

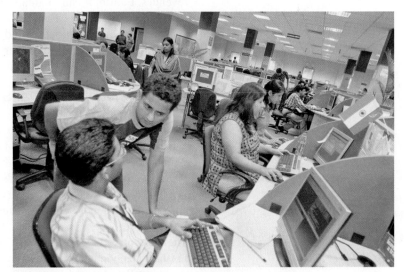

Source: Fredrik Renander/Alamy

Minimizing the risks of global sourcing entails several, critical strategies. Following a careful selection process, the focal firm should invest in collaborating and communicating with suppliers. Pictured is a call center in New Delhi, India.

- *Choose carefully between a captive operation and contracting with outside suppliers.* Managers should be vigilant about striking the right balance between the organizational activities they retain inside the firm and those they source from outside. Many firms establish their own sourcing operations abroad to maintain control of outsourced activities and technologies. When Boeing sought to outsource key value-chain tasks, management established a company-owned center in Moscow where it employs 1,100 low-cost aerospace engineers. The Russian team works on a range of projects, including the design of titanium parts for the new Boeing 787 Dreamliner jet.[40]
- *Choose suppliers carefully.* Finding and managing foreign suppliers is complex. The focal firm may have limited influence over suppliers' manufacturing and processes. Suppliers may engage in opportunistic behavior or act in bad faith. To ensure the success of sourcing ventures, the focal firm must exercise great care to identify and screen potential suppliers and then monitor the activities of those suppliers from which it sources.
- *Emphasize effective communications with suppliers.* Global sourcing may fail if buyers and suppliers spend too little time getting well acquainted. They rush into a deal before clarifying each other's expectations, giving rise to misunderstandings and inferior results. Because production quality in an emerging market may vary over time, managers at the focal firm may need to closely monitor manufacturing processes. To avoid mistakes and frustration, partners must share necessary information.[41] Where differing business philosophies and practices lead partners to approach the same issue differently, effective communication helps minimize misunderstandings that diminish buyer–supplier relationships.
- *Invest in supplier development and collaboration.* When a business function is delegated to a supplier, the parties need to exchange information, transfer knowledge, troubleshoot, coordinate, and monitor. Benefits emerge when the focal firm adjusts its processes and product requirements to match foreign supplier capabilities. Close collaboration with suppliers in codevelopment and codesign activities enables the focal firm to continuously tap ideas for new products, processes, technologies, and improvements. Efforts to build strong relationships foster a moral contract between the focal firm and the supplier, one that is often more effective than a formal legal contract.
- *Safeguard interests.* The focal firm should protect its interests in the supplier relationship. First, it can advise the supplier against engaging in activities that harm the firm's reputation. Second, it can escalate commitments by investing incrementally in the partner (such as sharing knowledge and providing training), allowing for ongoing review, learning, and adjustment. Third, it can share costs and revenues by building a stake for the supplier so that, in case of failure to meet expectations, the supplier also suffers costs or foregoes revenues. Fourth, it can maintain flexibility by keeping open its options for finding alternate partners if needed. Finally, the focal firm can keep the partner at bay by withholding access to intellectual property and key assets. If conflicts are unresolved by negotiations, one option is to acquire full or partial ownership of the supplier.

 ## Implementing Global Sourcing Through Supply-Chain Management

A key reason sourcing products from distant markets has become a major business phenomenon is the efficiency with which goods can be physically moved from one part of the globe to another.

Global supply chain
The firm's integrated network of sourcing, production, and distribution, organized on a worldwide scale and located in countries where competitive advantage can be maximized.

A **global supply chain** is the firm's integrated network of sourcing, production, and distribution, organized on a worldwide scale and located in countries where competitive advantage can be maximized. Global supply-chain management includes both upstream (supplier) and downstream (customer) flows.

The concepts of supply chain and value chain are related but distinct. Recall that the value chain is the collection of activities intended to design, produce, market, deliver, and support a product or service. By contrast, the supply chain is the collection of logistics specialists and activities that provides inputs to manufacturers or retailers.

Skillful supply-chain management serves to optimize value-chain activities. Sourcing from numerous suppliers scattered around the world is neither economical nor feasible without an efficient supply-chain system. Casual observers are impressed by the vast collection of products in a supermarket or department store that originated from dozens of different countries. The speed with which these products are delivered to end users is equally impressive.

Consider a customer in Canada who orders a Dell laptop computer. The order is typically routed to the Dell factory in Malaysia, where workers must access thirty distinct component parts that originate with Dell suppliers scattered around the world. Indeed, the total supply chain for a typical Dell computer, including multiple tiers of suppliers, typically includes some 400 companies in Asia, Europe, and the Americas. Dell is so skilled at managing all this complexity that customers typically receive their computers within two weeks of submitting an order.[42]

Boeing's new 787 Dreamliner is a fuel-saving, medium-sized passenger aircraft that uses carbon composite for the fuselage instead of aluminum. The lightweight jet has spacious interiors and extra cabin pressure, for a more comfortable journey. However, the most remarkable aspect of the Dreamliner is the extent of outsourcing. Boeing (www.boeing.com) is responsible for manufacturing only about 10 percent of the jet's value—the tail fin and final assembly. As indicated in Exhibit 17.7, some forty suppliers worldwide contribute the remaining 90 percent. The wings are built in Japan, the carbon composite fuselage in Italy, and the landing gear in France. The global dispersion of manufacturing responsibility has allowed Boeing to transform itself into a systems integrator and focus on its core capabilities—design, marketing, and branding.

Nevertheless, the execution of this global manufacturing network has been far from flawless. The 787's inaugural flight and deliveries were delayed more than two years. Production delays cost Boeing several billion dollars in lost earnings. Much of the difficulty is attributable to the complexity of coordinating a global supply-chain network.[43]

Networks of supply-chain hubs and providers of global delivery service are an integral part of global supply chains. Many focal firms delegate supply-chain activities to such independent

EXHIBIT 17.7

Where Boeing Sources the Components for Its New 787 Aircraft

Sources: Based on Boeing, "787 Dreamliner: International Team Facts," 2012, retrieved from www.boeing.com; Mark Tatge, "Global Gamble," *Forbes*, April 17, 2006, pp. 78–80. Image source: Mechanik/Shutterstock

Kansas and Oklahoma (U.S.)
Co: Spirit Aerosystems
Part: Leading edges

Japan
Co: Kawasaki Heavy Industries
Part: Fixed trailing edge

Australia
Co: Hawker de Havilland
Part: Movable trailing edges

Sweden
Co: Saab Aerostructures
Part: Cargo doors, access doors

Washington (U.S.), Canada, Australia
Co: Boeing Fredrickson
Part: Vertical tail assembly

Italy, Texas (U.S.)
Co: Alenia/Vought
Part: Horizontal stabilizer, center fuselage, aft fuselage

Japan
Co: Fuji Heavy Industries
Part: Center wing box

Japan
Co: Mitsubishi Heavy Industries
Part: Wing box

Japan
Co: Kawasaki Heavy Industries
Part: Fuselage, wheel well

France
Co: Latecoere
Part: Passenger doors

Kansas and Oklahoma (U.S.)
Co: Spirit Aerosystems
Part: Forward fuselage

France
Co: Messier-Dowty
Part: Landing gear

Washington (U.S.), Canada, Australia
Co: Boeing Winnipeg
Part: Wing-to-body fairing

Korea
Co: Korean Airlines-Aerospace Division
Part: Wingtips

Ohio (U.S.)
Co: General Electric
Part: Engines

United Kingdom
Co: Rolls-Royce
Part: Engines

North Carolina (U.S.)
Co: Goodrich
Part: Nacelles

Kansas and Oklahoma (U.S.)
Co: Spirit Aerosystems
Part: Engine pylons

logistics service providers as DHL, FedEx, and TNT. Consulting firms that manage the logistics of other firms are called *third-party logistics providers (3PLs)*. Using a 3PL is often the best solution for international logistics, especially for firms that produce at low volumes or lack the resources and expertise to create their own logistics network.

A good example of evolving supply-chain management is the integration of the European Union. The removal of border controls allowed supply-chain managers to redraw the maps of their sourcing and distribution activities throughout Europe. Warehousing and distribution centers were consolidated and centralized. In another instance, the computer chip company Intel significantly reduced shipping costs by consolidating its freight expenditures into four transportation suppliers. As a result, from its fourteen manufacturing sites around the world, Intel considerably improved on-time delivery and customer-service performance.[44]

Exhibit 17.8 illustrates the stages, functions, and activities in the supply chain. It reveals how suppliers interact with the focal firm and how these, in turn, interact with distributors and retailers.

Information and Communications Technology

Costs of physically delivering a product to an export market may account for as much as 40 percent of the good's total cost. Skillful supply-chain management reduces this cost while increasing customer satisfaction. Experienced firms use information and communications technologies (ICTs) to streamline supply chains, reducing costs and increasing distribution efficiency. For example, *electronic data interchange (EDI)* automatically passes orders directly from customers to suppliers through a sophisticated ICT platform. The U.K.'s Tesco supermarket chain (www.tesco.com) greatly reduced inventory costs by using an EDI system to link point-of-sale data to logistics managers. Tesco tracks product purchases down to the minute, and many canned foods that once sat in its warehouses for days or weeks now come directly from suppliers to Tesco stores.[45]

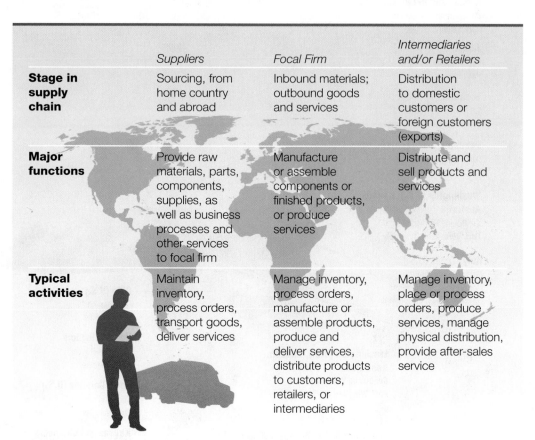

	Suppliers	Focal Firm	Intermediaries and/or Retailers
Stage in supply chain	Sourcing, from home country and abroad	Inbound materials; outbound goods and services	Distribution to domestic customers or foreign customers (exports)
Major functions	Provide raw materials, parts, components, supplies, as well as business processes and other services to focal firm	Manufacture or assemble components or finished products, or produce services	Distribute and sell products and services
Typical activities	Maintain inventory, process orders, transport goods, deliver services	Manage inventory, process orders, manufacture or assemble products, produce and deliver services, distribute products to customers, retailers, or intermediaries	Manage inventory, place or process orders, produce services, manage physical distribution, provide after-sales service

EXHIBIT 17.8

Stages, Functions, and Activities in the Global Supply Chain

Specialized software enhances information sharing and improves efficiency by allowing the firm to track international shipments and clear customs. Many firms digitize key documents such as customs declarations and invoices, which improves speed and reduces order processing costs and shipping procedures. The most sophisticated supply chains are characterized by reliable, capable partners connected through automated, real-time communications. In an efficient system, the focal firm and its supply-chain partners continuously communicate and share information to constantly meet the demands of the marketplace. The Spanish retailer Zara uses EDI technology to optimize supply-chain management, inventory management, and responsiveness to consumer demands. Store managers use wireless personal digital assistants and instantaneous communications to help headquarters conduct ongoing market research. Such technologies have allowed Zara to become the leader in rapid-response retailing.[46]

Logistics and Transportation

Logistics physically moves goods through the supply chain. It incorporates information, transportation, inventory, warehousing, materials handling, and similar activities associated with the delivery of raw materials, parts, components, and finished products. Managers seek to reduce moving and storage costs by using just-in-time inventory systems. Internationally, logistics are complex due to wide geographic distances, multiple legal environments, and the often inadequate and costly nature of distribution infrastructure in individual countries. The more diverse the firm's global supply chain, the greater the cost of logistics.

Competent logistics management is critical, especially for just-in-time inventory systems. The California ports of Los Angeles (www.portoflosangeles.org) and Long Beach (www.polb.com) handle more than 40 percent of imports into the United States, processing over 24,000 shipping containers per day. Infrastructure deficiencies and increasing demand can result in long delays, which translate into longer transit times and higher costs for U.S. importers. Because of delays, Toys "R" Us had to build 10 extra days into its supply chain. MGA Entertainment lost $40 million in revenues when it could not deliver its best-selling Bratz dolls to retailers on time.[47] As a result of poor supply-chain planning, Microsoft's Xbox 360 games console sold out soon after launch. Scarcity led to high prices in unofficial channels. On eBay, Xbox consoles sold for as much as $1,000, compared with the official price of about $400.[48]

Transportation Modes

International logistics usually make use of multiple *transportation modes*, including land, ocean, and air transport. Land transportation is conducted via highways and railroads, ocean transport is via container ships, and air transport is via commercial or cargo aircraft. Transportation modes involve several trade-offs. The three main considerations are *cost*, *transit time* to deliver the goods, and *predictability*, the match between anticipated and actual transit times.

Let's compare ocean, land, and air transport:

- Ocean transport accounts for about 90 percent of international shipments. It is slower than air, but far cheaper. It was revolutionized by the development of 20- and 40-foot shipping containers, the big boxes that sit atop seagoing vessels. A modern ship's ability to carry thousands of containers yields economies of scale, making ocean transport very cost effective, often accounting for only 1 percent of a product's final price.
- Land transport is usually more expensive than ocean transport but cheaper than air. Exporters often opt for ocean shipping even when land transport is available. For example, some Mexican firms send goods to Canada by ship.
- Air transport is fast and extremely predictable, but expensive. It is used mostly to transport perishable products (like food and flowers), products with a high value-to-weight ratio (like fine jewelry and laptop computers), and urgently needed goods (like medicines and emergency supplies). While the use of air freight has increased because of gradually declining cost, it still accounts for only 1 percent of international shipments.

Global Sourcing, Corporate Social Responsibility, and Sustainability

The business community sees global sourcing as a way to maintain or increase business competitiveness, and enhance long-term company sustainability. Others view it negatively, focusing on the loss of local jobs. After IBM workers in Europe went on strike against offshoring, shareholders at IBM's annual meeting argued for an anti-offshoring resolution. In the United States, 27,000 Boeing machinists went on strike to protest the aircraft company's decision to globally outsource jobs in the production of the 787 Dreamliner jet.[49]

The general public also criticizes offshoring. When the state of Indiana awarded a $15 million IT services contract to a supplier that planned to use technicians from India to do some of the work, the Indiana Senate intervened and cancelled the deal. However, the state recently leased management of the Indiana Toll Road to an Australian-Spanish partnership for 75 years for $3.8 billion. The city of New Orleans has outsourced management of its mass transit system to the French firm Veolia Environnement.[50]

Potential Harm to Local and National Economy from Global Sourcing

Critics of global sourcing point to three potential problems. Global sourcing can result in (1) job losses in the home country, (2) reduced national competitiveness, and (3) declining standards of living. Regarding the last two concerns, critics worry that, as more tasks are performed at lower cost with comparable quality in other countries, high-wage countries will lose their national competitiveness. Long-held knowledge and skills will eventually drain away to other countries, they fear, and the lower wages paid abroad will eventually pull down wages in the home country, leading to lower living standards.

A major concern is job losses. The number of jobs in the U.S. legal industry outsourced to foreign contractors now exceeds 25,000 per year.[51] During the first two years of the recent global recession (2009 and 2010), large American corporations cut U.S. payrolls by a net of 500,000 jobs. Simultaneously, the same firms created some 700,000 jobs overseas.[52] Projections are that more than 3 million jobs will be outsourced from the United States by 2015.[53] Critics say this amounts to exporting jobs.

Job losses also rise when companies increase their sourcing of input and finished goods from abroad. Walmart sources as much as 70 percent of its finished merchandise from abroad. This has led citizens to form a protest group called Walmartwatch.com, which claims millions of U.S. jobs have been lost due to Walmart's global sourcing.[54] Job losses are occurring in developing economies as well. For example, in the textile industry, El Salvador, Honduras, Indonesia, and Turkey have seen jobs gradually transferred to China, India, and Pakistan.[55]

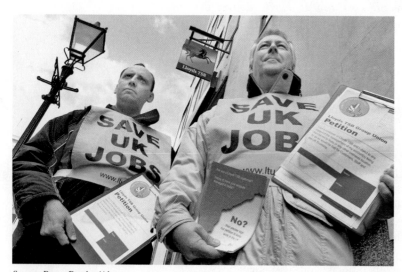

Source: Roger Bamber/Alamy

Global sourcing has sparked protests in many countries. Here, trade union members at Lloyds TSB bank in the United Kingdom protest the outsourcing of jobs to India.

Consider the potentially devastating effect of job losses on a small community. For nearly 40 years Electrolux (www.electrolux.com), the Swedish home-appliance company, manufactured refrigerators in Greenville, Michigan, providing 2,700 jobs. Once the world's largest refrigerator factory, the plant developed weak financial performance and high labor costs. Electrolux closed the factory and established a *maquiladora* plant in Juarez, Mexico, seeking to profit from lower wages and the El Paso Foreign Trade Zone just across the border in Texas. Management believed it was acting in the firm's best interest and strengthening its global competitiveness. From Greenville's standpoint, however, the decision was devastating. How could so many jobs be replaced in such a small community? What would happen to the town's social and economic landscape? Wage concessions by the labor union and over $100 million in grants and tax breaks in Michigan were insufficient to halt the closure.[56]

From such examples, it is easy to see the clash of interests between firms and local communities. It takes considerable time for laid-off workers to find new jobs. According to one estimate, as many as one-third of laid-off U.S. workers cannot find suitable employment within a year. Older workers in particular struggle to learn the skills needed for new positions. The rate of redeployment is likely to be even lower in Europe, where unemployment rates are already high, and in Japan, where employment practices are less flexible. In Germany, the percentage of workers who are not reemployed within a year of losing their jobs is as high as 60 percent. Under such circumstances, global sourcing may increase unemployment rates, reduce income levels, and harm the local community and national economy.[57]

Public Policy on Global Sourcing

The consequences of global sourcing for the national economy and workers are not fully known. A recent study argues that official statistics understate the impact of offshoring on national economies.[58] The study found that import growth, adjusted for inflation, is faster than the official numbers show. The study concluded that more of the gain in living standards in recent years has come from cheap imports and less from increased domestic productivity.

Offshoring is a process of *creative destruction*, a concept first proposed by the Austrian economist Joseph Schumpeter.[59] According to this view, firms' innovative activities tend to make mature products obsolete over time: The introduction of personal computers essentially eliminated the typewriter industry, the DVD player eliminated the VCR, and so on. Just as offshoring results in job losses and adverse effects for particular groups and economic sectors, it also creates new advantages and opportunities for firms and consumers alike. Sourcing usually enhances company sustainability for the long term. New industries created through creative destruction will create new jobs and innovative products.

Public policy should strive to mitigate the potential harm global sourcing can cause.[60] Governments can use economic and fiscal policies to encourage the development of new technologies by helping entrepreneurs reap the financial benefits of their work and keeping the cost of capital for financing R&D low. Another useful policy is to ensure the nation has a strong educational system, including technical schools and well-funded universities that supply engineers, scientists, managers, and knowledge workers. A strong educational system provides firms with pools of high-quality labor. As firms restructure through global sourcing efforts, flexibility acquired through education ensures that many who lose jobs can be redeployed in other positions.

CLOSING CASE   Wolverine World Wide

Wolverine World Wide, Inc., is a leading designer, producer, and marketer of quality casual, outdoor, and work footwear. Based in the U.S. state of Michigan, it sells millions of pairs of popular shoes and boots in 180 countries. The company markets well-known brands such as Hush Puppies, Merrell, and Wolverine. The firm also makes licensed footwear under the Caterpillar ("CAT"), Harley-Davidson, and Patagonia brands. Key competitors include Timberland, Sketchers, and Deckers. Wolverine's main competitive advantages are well-recognized brand names, wide range of distribution channels, and diversified manufacturing and sourcing. Products are supplied worldwide through retail stores, catalog sales, and the Internet.

Although Wolverine's annual sales regularly exceed $1 billion, they dipped recently, due to the global recession and unexpected exchange rate fluctuations. Wolverine generates most of its sales abroad. In Europe, the firm markets footwear through numerous company-owned subsidiaries. Long focused on the U.S. market, Wolverine internationalized quickly. For example, European sales rose from almost zero in 2000 to more than 8 million pairs by 2011. Wolverine conducts continuous R&D to design products appropriate for each foreign market, while remaining consistent with its global brand position. The

firm aims to expand sales in Europe and to emerging markets such as Brazil, Chile, India, and Russia.

The Footwear Industry

In 2011, global production of shoes and boots surpassed 16 billion pairs. Total industry revenues exceeded $200 billion. The United States is the largest national retail market, followed by China, India, and Japan. Europe is the largest regional market. In an industry characterized by many competitors and consumers who shop on price, profit margins are slim and firms must keep manufacturing costs low. Footwear companies are constantly seeking cost savings throughout their supply chains.

The great majority of footwear sold in Europe, Japan, and North America is imported, and most imports come from China, the leading manufacturer of footwear. Other important supplier countries include Mexico, India, and Vietnam. Western firms such as Nike, Clarks, and Wolverine typically contract with foreign manufacturers to produce footwear, which they then sell to markets worldwide.

China's strength as an export platform keeps costs, and thus prices, low for Western consumers. However, recent skilled-labor shortages in China are putting upward pressure on wages. Some global firms are looking to China's interior or to other countries for lower-cost contract manufacturers.

Wolverine Global Sourcing

Historically Wolverine produced most of its footwear itself in company-owned factories in the United States. Over time, however, the firm shifted the focus of its in-house activities from manufacturing to designing, marketing, and distributing its footwear brands. Today, Wolverine outsources production of more than 90 percent of its products to independent suppliers, with the remainder produced at company-operated facilities. Although Wolverine contracts with manufacturers throughout Asia and Latin America, most of its footwear is produced in China. Management wants to achieve sufficient flexibility to properly balance the need for timely shipments, high-quality products, and competitive pricing.

Managing wide-ranging value chains in many countries is challenging for Wolverine. Global sourcing exposes the firm to various risks, including possible shortages of qualified workers and production capacity, overreliance on independent suppliers, and strengthening foreign currency values, which affects the cost of imports. Wolverine frequently experiences inventory shortages in key markets, which upset the timing of customer shipments and hurt brand loyalty.

Transit time from China to Wolverine's warehouses in Europe and North America averages about one month. Sourcing from distant locations affects production schedules, transportation costs, insurance, and delivery timelines, leading to higher costs that must be absorbed in final product pricing.

The fixed exchange rate regime that China uses for its currency, the yuan, helps keep its exports cheap to the rest of the world. But Western countries and the World Trade Organization have regularly pressured China to rescind the regime. If the yuan strengthened, the cost of products imported from China would increase substantially.

Given its heavy reliance on global sourcing, Wolverine must maintain positive relationships with its suppliers. The firm has offices in Asia to facilitate and develop strategies for sourcing and importing quality footwear. Several Wolverine managers have worked in China, and headquarters managers fly to China regularly to meet with suppliers, inspect their facilities, and strengthen relationships.

In order to monitor product quality and labor conditions, Wolverine established guidelines for each of its independent manufacturers. The firm's "Engagement Criteria for Partners & Sources" aim to ensure suppliers comply with health and safety regulations, environmentally safe practices, fair employee treatment, and ethical business standards. Wolverine tries to reduce its ecological footprint by using biodegradable shoe forms and soy-based inks in footwear production and recycled cardboard and paper for its packaging.

Supply-Chain Management

Footwear manufacturing is complex. Many boots and shoes require more than 100 separate components, a jigsaw puzzle that demands superior capabilities in manufacturing. Suppliers also must have first-rate skills in planning, design, transportation, and logistics. Wolverine coordinates the firm's numerous global supply chains from company headquarters. It uses a custom Internet application to collect, exchange, and share sourcing information with suppliers, licensees, and buyers worldwide. All the relevant players in the supply chain are automatically linked. In this way, management instantly knows when a supplier accepts an order and when it ships the product.

Recent Events

Wolverine's brand portfolio has expanded over time, increasing the challenge of managing multiple, independent brands through a decentralized operational platform. Several Wolverine brands came from acquisitions, and brand groups cultivated relationships with suppliers that served the individual brand but hurt the firm's overall cost structure. Individualized relationships with numerous foreign suppliers led to production inefficiencies and higher costs.

Recently, to increase efficiency and control costs, management launched a corporate restructuring plan to reduce and standardize operations and supply-chain functions. The firm centralized value-chain management and reduced operational costs company-wide. Restructuring affected Wolverine's global supply chain through outsourcing more operations and pressuring suppliers to cut manufacturing costs. Other elements of the plan included consolidating distribution operations into fewer facilities, increasing outsourcing of raw materials, and reducing the workforce directly employed by the firm.

Management set several strategic priorities, including improving operational planning, streamlining the product development process, and building strategic partnerships with the firm's best suppliers, especially those that perform well regarding price, quality, delivery, and corporate responsibility. Management also sought to improve product distribution, logistics, and customer service to enhance service for each brand at the lowest possible cost. As supply-chain management was centralized to headquarters, however, brand managers and suppliers worried about losing control of design and production. As the restructuring process evolved, tensions occasionally arose with key suppliers and other value-chain members.

Following years of record profits, performance at Wolverine slowed during the recent global recession. Top management wondered how they could continue to balance cost reductions and competitive pricing with the need to deliver innovative, well-designed, high-quality footwear that appeals to customers in a variety of markets worldwide.

AACSB: Reflective Thinking Skills

Case Questions

1. In the highly competitive global footwear industry, what are the most important decisions faced by firms like Wolverine in their drive to obtain superior performance? What approaches did Wolverine follow to configure and coordinate its value-chain activities worldwide?

2. What are the three key drivers of the growth of global sourcing? Explain how these drivers affect the global footwear industry and Wolverine.

3. Referring to Exhibits 17.2 and 17.4, what is the nature of Wolverine's approach to global sourcing? In your view, what value-chain activities should Wolverine outsource and what activities should it internalize? Justify your answer.

4. What are the specific benefits that Wolverine obtains from global sourcing? What specific threats and risks does it face? What strategies can Wolverine employ to minimize the risks and threats it faces from global sourcing?

5. What steps is management taking to ensure Wolverine is a socially responsible firm? Using the Ethical Framework and other material from Chapter 5, what further actions can Wolverine take to ensure its operations are ethical and socially responsible?

Sources: AROQ Limited, "US: Wolverine to Cut 450 Jobs, Restructure Supply Chain," www.Just-style.com, January 10, 2009; M. Bertolinia, E. Bottania, A. Rizzia, and M. Bevilacquab, "Lead Time Reduction through ICT Application in the Footwear Industry: A Case Study," *International Journal of Production Economics* 110, no. 1–2 (2007), pp. 198–212; A. Field, "Apparel: Dressed for Success," *Journal of Commerce*, May 26, 2008, p. 1; Standard & Poor's, "Apparel & Footwear Industry Analysis: Retailers & Brands," Comparative Company Analysis, May 5, 2009; Michelle Tay, "Wolverine Hunts for Growth," *FN: Footwear News*, February 6, 2012,

p. 14; Wolverine World Wide, "Annual Reports" for 2009, 2010, and 2011, retrieved from http://www.wolverineworldwide.com; SATRA Technology Centre, "World Footwear Markets 2008: Global Statistics 2003–2008"; N. Zubko, "An Automatic Connection: Electronic Transaction Tools Help Manufacturers Connect with Suppliers to Streamline Sourcing Efforts," *Industry Week*, July 2008, pp. 26–27.

Note: An original version of this case was prepared by Professor Carol Sánchez, Todd Callis, and Raman Somal.

CHAPTER ESSENTIALS

MyManagementLab

Go to **mymanagementlab.com** to complete the problems marked with this icon ⭐.

Key Terms

business process outsourcing (BPO)   439
captive sourcing   441
configuration of value-adding
   activity   439

contract manufacturing   441
global sourcing   440
global supply chain   450

offshoring   442
outsourcing   438

Summary

In this chapter, you learned about:

1. Outsourcing, global sourcing, and offshoring

Global sourcing refers to the procurement of products or services from suppliers or company-owned subsidiaries located abroad for consumption in the home country or a third country. **Outsourcing** is the procurement of selected value-adding activities, including production of intermediate goods or finished products, from external independent suppliers. **Business process outsourcing** refers to the outsourcing of business functions such as finance, accounting, and human resources. Procurement can be from either independent suppliers or via company-owned subsidiaries or affiliates. **Offshoring** refers to the relocation of a business process or entire manufacturing facility to a foreign country. Managers make two strategic decisions regarding value-adding activities: whether to *make* or *buy* inputs and where to locate value-adding activity—that is, the geographic

configuration of value-adding activity. **Contract manufacturing** is an arrangement in which the focal firm contracts with an independent supplier to have the supplier manufacture products according to well-defined specifications.

2. Benefits of global sourcing

Global sourcing aims to reduce the cost of doing business or to achieve other strategic goals. For some entrepreneurs, global outsourcing has provided the means to turn around failing businesses, speed up the pace of innovation, or fund development projects that are otherwise unaffordable. Other benefits of global sourcing include faster corporate growth, the ability to access qualified personnel, improved productivity and service, redesigned business processes, faster foreign market entry, access to new markets, and technological flexibility. Global sourcing also allows firms to focus on their core activities and continuously renew their strategic assets.

3. **Risks of global sourcing**

Risks include failing to realize anticipated cost savings, dealing with environmental uncertainty, creating competitors, engaging suppliers with insufficient training, relying too much on suppliers, and eroding the morale of existing employees.

4. **Strategies for minimizing the risks of global sourcing**

Firms should develop a strategic perspective in making global sourcing decisions. Although cost cutting is usually the first rationale, global sourcing is also a means to create customer value and improve the firm's competitive advantages. It is a tool to enhance the quality of offerings, improve productivity, and free up resources that can be redeployed to improve long-term performance. To make global sourcing succeed, management should gain employee cooperation, emphasize strong supplier relations, safeguard its interests in the supplier relationship, and choose the right foreign suppliers.

5. **Implementing global sourcing through supply-chain management**

The efficiency with which goods can be physically moved from one part of the globe to another makes global sourcing feasible. **Global supply chain** refers to the firm's integrated network of sourcing, production, and distribution, organized on a world scale and located in countries where competitive advantage can be maximized.

6. **Global sourcing, corporate social responsibility, and sustainability**

Global sourcing is a means to sustain or enhance firm competitiveness but can also contribute to job losses and declining living standards. Some firms outsource to suppliers that employ low-cost labor. Attempts to prohibit global sourcing are impractical. Governments should enact policies in the home country that encourage job retention and growth by reducing the cost of doing business, by encouraging entrepreneurship and technological development, and by developing a strong educational system and upgrading the modern skills of the population.

Test Your Comprehension AACSB: Reflective Thinking Skills, Ethical Understanding and Reasoning Abilities

1. Distinguish between outsourcing, global sourcing, and offshoring.

2. What is business process outsourcing? What are its implications for company strategy and performance?

3. Identify the benefits that companies receive from global sourcing. Why do firms outsource to foreign suppliers?

4. What two countries are the most important global sourcing destinations today? What are the basic differences between these two countries, and what activities are typically outsourced to each?

5. In what service industries are jobs commonly outsourced to foreign suppliers?

⭐ 6. What are the risks that firms face in global sourcing?

⭐ 7. What steps can managers take to minimize the risks of global sourcing?

8. What are the major guidelines for strategic global sourcing? What actions can management take to make global sourcing succeed?

9. What are the advantages and disadvantages of global sourcing to the nation? What public policy initiatives are likely to reduce the disadvantages of global sourcing?

Apply Your Understanding   AACSB: Reflective Thinking Skills, Ethical Understanding and Reasoning Abilities

1. *Ethical Dilemma:* Revisit the opening story at the beginning of this chapter. Assume you have started a new job as a junior manager at a pharmaceutical firm. Management is considering having clinical trials of a new medication performed by a subcontractor in Russia. What are the benefits and specific strategic goals that your firm can achieve by undertaking global sourcing? According to the opening story, conducting clinical trials in Russia can be risky because quality control is sometimes lax. Testing is occasionally done without adequate oversight. Some breakdowns in ethical and scientific processes may compromise the reliability of findings from clinical trials. What should you do? Using the Ethical Framework in Chapter 5, analyze the ethical consequences of subcontracting clinical trials to the Russian firm.

2. Suppose your new job is at Intel, the world's largest semiconductor company and inventor of the microprocessors found in many personal computers. Intel combines advanced chip design capability with a leading-edge manufacturing capability. The firm is well known for innovative R&D and products. Intel does much of its manufacturing in China, to take advantage of low-cost labor and an educated workforce capable of producing knowledge-intensive products. Intel has stepped up R&D activity in China and collaborates with Chinese firms in new-technology development. Identify the risks that Intel faces in its operations in China. What strategies and proactive measures can Intel management take to safeguard its interests? What long-term strategic goals does Intel achieve by offshoring from China?

3. *Ethical Dilemma:* Suppose you work at your national legislature for a legislator who must decide how to vote on an upcoming bill. The bill is a new law that would restrict the ability of firms in your country to outsource work to countries that pay less than the average wage in your country. Proponents of the legislation note that outsourcing leads to job losses in your country. Foreign suppliers often employ factory workers who toil long hours for low wages in harsh conditions, sometimes using child labor. Many countries have poor environmental standards, with factories generating excess pollution. However, opponents of the new legislation point to the benefits of global sourcing. They argue that outsourced work provides needed jobs that decrease poverty in developing economies. By reconfiguring value chains to the most cost-efficient locations, companies in your country can reduce production costs, allowing them to hire more workers and reduce prices charged to customers. What recommendation will you make on how to vote on the proposed bill? Use the Ethical Framework in Chapter 5 to analyze the pros and cons of global sourcing.

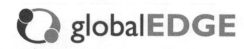

globalEDGE   INTERNET EXERCISES
(http://www.globalEDGE.msu.edu)

AACSB: Reflective Thinking Skills, Ethical Understanding and Reasoning Abilities, Use of Information Technology, Analytic Skills

Refer to Chapter 1, page 24, for instructions on how to access and use globalEDGE™.

1. You work for a software company that aims to outsource some of its software development to a foreign supplier. At present, you are considering three countries: Hungary, Mexico, and Russia. You need to learn more about the capabilities of these countries as sites for the outsourcing of software development. One approach is to visit the research section of the World Bank (www.worldbank.org), where you should click the link to "Countries". For each of the three countries, find and analyze variables that indicate the quality of the local software and IT environment. Based on your findings, which country appears strongest for meeting the needs of your firm?

2. International labor standards are complex and closely related to global sourcing. In particular, the use of sweatshops has attracted much attention. A sweatshop is a factory characterized by very low wages, long hours, and poor working conditions. Some sweatshops employ children in unsafe conditions. Pro-labor groups advocate for minimum labor standards in foreign factories. Suppose your future employer wants to outsource a portion of its production to certain developing countries, but is concerned about the possibility of employing sweatshop labor. Visit the Web sites of groups that encourage minimum standards in labor conditions (for example, www.workersrights.org, www.usas.org, www.corpwatch.org, or enter the keywords "labor conditions" at globalEDGE™) and prepare a memo to your employer that discusses the major concerns of those who advocate minimum labor standards.

3. Top management at the firm where you work just decided to outsource your company's *accounting* functions to India. Unclear on how to proceed, management has asked you to find candidate suppliers in India. Initial research reveals that Bangalore, Mumbai, and Delhi are the top locations in India for global sourcing of accounting and other services. Next, you decide to check the online Yellow Pages (such as indianyellowpages.com or yellowpages.co.in) and search for appropriate Indian firms. Find three firms in India that specialize in *accounting* and examine their Web sites. Describe and compare the services that each firm provides. What criteria should you use to choose the best supplier? Which firm seems most qualified and reputable for providing outsourcing of accounting services?

MyManagementLab

Go to **mymanagementlab.com** for Auto-graded writing questions as well as the following Assisted-graded writing questions:

17-1. What are the two strategic decisions that managers face regarding the firm's international value chain, and what are their implications for company performance?

17-2. What are the characteristics that make countries attractive as global sourcing destinations?

17-3. Mymanagementlab Only – comprehensive writing assignment for this chapter.

Source: Simon Bracken/Dorling Kindersley

MTV's Passage to India

MTV Networks (www.mtv.com) is broadcast in more than 160 countries in thirty-two languages, reaching 640 million viewers. About one in four people worldwide is between 15 and 34 years old, and MTV targets this huge market. Some 70 percent of MTV programming is developed locally or adapted for each of its markets. While MTV flourishes in Europe and Latin America, it competes against numerous local brands in India.

India is a huge market, with a half-billion people in the target youth segment. The number of households with TV sets has grown rapidly. There are roughly 100 distinctive cable channels in India, each vying for limited advertising dollars. Competition for cable subscribers is intense, and profit margins are often thin.

Initially, MTV developed a regional marketing strategy by delivering pan-Asian music. MTV India's chief competitor, Star TV, adapted its music channel, [V], to accommodate local Indian preferences. By 2010, eight music channels were competing in the Indian market. Newcomer Mastii was typical of these, offering a unique format that combined local music with humor. After launch, Mastii stunned the industry by

CHAPTER 18

Marketing in the Global Firm

LEARNING OBJECTIVES *In this chapter, you will learn about:*

1. Global market segmentation
2. Standardization and adaptation of international marketing
3. Global branding and product development
4. International pricing
5. International marketing communications
6. International distribution

MyManagementLab®

⭐ **Improve Your Grade!**

Over 10 million students improved their results using the Pearson MyLabs.
Visit **mymanagementlab.com** for simulations, tutorials, and end-of-chapter problems.

quickly rising to a top position in television ratings, demonstrating the fickleness of the market. By 2012, Mastii was competing neck-in-neck with MTV.

After surveying its audience, [V] reformulated itself, creating a new collection of youth-centric Indian shows, such as *Lovenet* and *Dare to Date*. The shows quickly climbed in the ratings. Management's insight was to transform [V] from a "music-only" format to a full-featured youth entertainment channel. Where [V] once offered music 95 percent of the time, today the figure is just 20 percent.

In response, MTV management adapted its programming. Ratings soared when Bollywood music was included and hosts began speaking more Hindi. MTV India also targeted Indian youth with cricket matches and fashion shows. The firm established innovative relationships with advertisers by developing local programming. Management worked with Honda to develop *Roadies*, a series that documented the experiences of young people traveling across India on Honda motorbikes. As the focus and sophistication of its strategy improved, MTV India increased its market share and surpassed [V].

Today MTV India obtains half its income from various branding, licensing, and distribution schemes. Licensing and merchandising of consumer products—toys, eyewear, apparel, smartphones, credit cards—are an important revenue source. MTV's Digital Music Store offers paid downloads of Hindi and international music from 15,000 songs. MTV India has become a youth brand that encompasses a variety of selling and marketing programs.

However, MTV Network's corporate management is concerned that the firm may not be reaping the full benefits of global marketing strategy. Programming is broadcast worldwide, but many channels are highly localized, reducing potential gains from economies of scale. MTV needed to balance local needs with cost-effective, uniform programming that sells in multiple countries. The network assembled a global planning team to develop ideas. MTV continues to seek international growth from emerging markets like China, India, and Mexico. The goal is to strike the right balance between local adaptation and global standardization.

SOURCES: Anumeha Chaturvedi, "[V]Can Do It," *Business Today*, November 28, 2010, p. 28; Anumeha Chaturvedi, "Song, Dance and Some Mastiii," *Business Today*, May 15, 2011, p. 16; Marc Gunther, "MTV's Passage to India," *Fortune*, August 9, 2004, pp.117–21; "MTV: Music Television," retrieved from http://www.viacom.com; "MTV Networks India," retrieved from http://www.mtvindia.com; Andre Paine, "Global Shakeup for MTV Programming," *Billboard*, February 21, 2009, pp. 14–15; Anusha Subramanian, "Beyond Music and TV," *Business Today*, February 21, 2010, pp. 78–80.

In international business, marketing is concerned with identifying, measuring, and pursuing customer needs and market opportunities abroad. In this chapter, we are concerned with the marketing activities that firms use to satisfy customers in the exchange of products and services worldwide. Internationally, marketing is a critical activity because it is the primary conduit through which the firm finds and interacts with customers abroad.

Exhibit 18.1 provides a framework for marketing activities and previews the topics of this chapter. The outer ring represents the cultural, social, political, legal, and regulatory environment of foreign markets. These environmental conditions influence the way the firm develops and adapts products. It affects product pricing, distribution, and promotional activities. In high-inflation countries, for example, management must review prices frequently. Across diverse cultures, the firm must adapt the positioning or selling propositions of its products to suit local customer expectations. It must ensure its products comply with local government regulations.

The middle ring in Exhibit 18.1 represents **global marketing strategy**—a plan of action the firm develops for foreign markets that guides its decision making on (1) how to position itself and its offerings, (2) which customer segments to target, and (3) to what degree it should standardize or adapt its marketing program elements.[1] We investigate the balance between marketing standardization and adaptation and the development of global brands, as well as the critical roles played by elements of the marketing mix. We begin by examining global market segmentation.

Global marketing strategy
A plan of action for foreign markets that guides the firm in deciding how to position itself and its offerings, which customer segments to target, and the degree to which it should standardize or adapt its marketing program elements.

Global Market Segmentation

Market segmentation is the process of dividing the firm's total customer base into homogeneous clusters in a way that allows management to formulate unique marketing strategies for each group. Within each market segment, customers exhibit similar characteristics, including income level, lifestyle, demographic profile, and desired product benefits. For example, in selling its earthmoving equipment, Caterpillar develops distinct marketing approaches for several major market segments—farmers, construction firms, the military, and others. In setting prices, Caterpillar creates value-priced tractors for farmers, moderately priced earthmoving equipment for construction firms, and high-priced, heavy-duty vehicles for the military.

In international business, firms frequently formulate market segments by grouping countries based on macro-level variables, such as level of economic development or cultural dimensions. Many MNEs group Latin American countries based on a common language (Spanish) or European countries based on similar economic conditions. This approach has proven most effective for

EXHIBIT 18.1

Organizing Framework for Marketing in the International Firm

The Environment of International Business

Diverse Cultural, Political, Legal, Monetary, and Financial Environment of the Firm

Global Marketing Strategy

Targeting Customer Segments and Positioning

International Marketing Program Standardization and Adaptation

Global Branding and Product Development	International Pricing
International Distribution	International Marketing Communications

Global market segment

A group of customers who share common characteristics across many national markets.

product categories in which governments play a key regulatory role (such as telecommunications, medical products, and processed foods) or where national characteristics prevail in determining product acceptance and usage.[2]

Today, firms increasingly target global market segments. A **global market segment** is a group of customers who share similar characteristics across many national markets. Firms target such buyers using a relatively uniform marketing strategy and programs. For example, MTV in the opening story targets a relatively homogenous youth market that exists in most of the world. This segment generally follows global media, is quick to embrace new fashions and trends, and has significant disposable income. Another global market segment is frequent business travelers. They are affluent, eager consumers of premium hotels, clothing, jewelry, and other products that represent luxury and style.

A key objective in pursuing global market segments is to uniquely position the firm's offerings in the minds of target customers. *Positioning* is a marketing strategy in which the firm develops both the product and its marketing to evoke a distinct impression in the customer's mind, emphasizing differences from competitors' offerings. In the theme park business, Disney positions itself

Source: Britta Jaschinski/Dorling Kindersley

Popular music stars such as Adele and Rihanna target the global market segment of young adults who love music. These fans are at a club in Berlin, Germany.

as standing for family values and "good, clean fun" to attract families around the world.[3] Starbucks positions its products at customers with sophisticated tastes who do not mind paying several dollars for a cup of coffee. BMW wants to compete in the premium car market segment.

Positioning may also evoke the specific *attributes* that consumers associate with a product. Diet Coke elicits an image of someone who wants to lose or maintain weight. When Coca-Cola first entered Japan, research revealed that Japanese women do not like products labeled "diet," nor is the population considered overweight. Thus, management altered the product's positioning in Japan by changing the name to Coke Light.

Internationalizing firms aim for a *global positioning strategy*, which positions the offering similarly in the minds of targeted buyers worldwide. Starbucks, Volvo, and Sony successfully use this approach. Consumers worldwide view these strong brands in the same way. Global positioning strategy reduces international marketing costs by addressing the shared expectations of a global customer market segment.[4]

 ## Standardization and Adaptation of International Marketing

Adaptation
The firm's efforts to modify one or more elements of its international marketing program to accommodate specific customer requirements in a particular market.

Standardization
The firm's efforts to make its marketing program elements uniform, with a view to targeting entire regions, or even the global marketplace, with the same product or service.

In addition to guiding targeting and positioning, global marketing strategy also articulates the degree to which the firm's marketing program should vary between different foreign markets. **Adaptation** refers to modifying one or more elements of the firm's international marketing program to accommodate specific customer requirements in a particular market. **Standardization** refers to making the marketing program elements uniform, with a view to targeting entire regions, or even the global marketplace, with the same product or service.

In the center of Exhibit 18.1, we identify the key elements of the marketing program (sometimes referred to as the *marketing mix*) affected by the standardization/adaptation decision. These are: global branding and product development, international pricing, international marketing communications, and international distribution. In the international context, marketing strategy tackles the complexity of having both global and local competitors, as well as cross-national differences in culture, language, living standards, economic conditions, regulations, and quality of business infrastructure. A key challenge is to resolve the trade-offs between standardization and adaptation.

When they enter international markets, managers undertake a broad corporate strategy in which they attempt to strike an ideal balance between *global integration* and *local responsiveness*. As discussed in Chapter 12, global integration seeks cross-national synergy in the firm's value-chain activities in order to take maximum advantage of similarities between countries, while local responsiveness aims to meet the specific needs of buyers in individual countries. How the firm resolves the balance between global integration and local responsiveness also affects how it makes standardization and adaptation decisions in its marketing program elements.

Exhibit 18.2 highlights the trade-offs between standardization and adaptation in international marketing. Let's examine the advantages of each approach.

Standardization

Standardization represents a tendency toward global integration. Standardization is more likely to be pursued in global industries such as aircraft manufacturing, pharmaceuticals, and credit cards. Airbus, Pfizer, and MasterCard use a standardized marketing strategy with great success. Their offerings are largely uniform across many markets worldwide.

A standardized marketing approach is most appropriate when:
- Similar market segments exist across countries.
- Customers seek similar features in the product or service.
- Products have universal specifications.
- Business customers have converging expectations or needs regarding specifications, quality, performance, and other product attributes.

The viability of standardization varies across industries and product categories. Commodities, industrial equipment, and technology products lend themselves to a high degree of standardization.

Standardization
Exemplifies global integration and is more appropriate in global industries.
Pursue when:
• Similar market segments exist across countries
• Customers seek similar features
• Products have universal specifications
• Business customers have converging expectations

Adaptation
Exemplifies local responsiveness and is more appropriate in multidomestic industries.
Pursue when there are distinct:
• National preferences
• Laws and regulations
• Living standards and economic conditions
• National infrastructure

Complete Standardization

Complete Adaptation

Advantages
• Cost reduction
• Improved planning and control
• Ability to portray a consistent image and build global brands

Advantages
• Meet needs of customers more precisely
• Enjoy unique appeal
• Comply with government regulations
• Achieve greater success in combating customer resistance

EXHIBIT 18.2

Trade-offs between Adaptation and Standardization of International Marketing Program

Popular consumer electronics such as Sony's PlayStation, Apple's iPod, and Canon digital cameras, as well as well-known fashion accessories like Rolex watches and Louis Vuitton handbags, are largely standardized around the world. Automotive parts, building materials, dinnerware, and basic food ingredients are other products that require little or no adaptation.

Advertising may be standardized too. One TV ad featured an attractive 25-year-old British woman eagerly anticipating a scoop of Haagen-Dazs ice cream. The same ad was broadcast worldwide, with voice-overs in French, Portuguese, Spanish, and Mandarin Chinese.[5] Gillette (www.gillette.com) sells shaving products using uniform marketing in all the countries where it does business and often introduces them with simultaneous global launches, under universal brand names such as Trak II, Sensor, and Fusion. Gillette's global approach has achieved an impressive 70 percent global market share, while minimizing marketing and distribution costs.[6]

When managers build on commonalities in customer preferences and attempt to standardize their international marketing program, they can expect at least three major benefits:

• *Cost reduction.* Standardization reduces costs by making possible economies of scale in design, sourcing, manufacturing, and marketing. Offering a similar marketing program to the global marketplace or across entire regions is more efficient than having to adapt products for each of the numerous individual markets. Electrolux (based in Sweden, www.electrolux.com) once made hundreds of refrigerator models to accommodate the diverse tastes and regulatory requirements of each country in Europe. As product standards and tastes gradually harmonized across the European Union, Electrolux was able to reduce the number of its refrigerator models to a few dozen, consolidate manufacturing facilities, and streamline its marketing activities across the EU. The resulting consolidation saved Electrolux millions of euros. Electrolux used the money to invest in R&D to develop advanced features and superior technology.

• *Improved planning and control.* Standardization reduces the complexity of planning and control of value-adding activities. The ability to offer fewer products allows Electrolux to simplify quality control and reduce the number of replacement parts it needs to stock. Marketing activities are also simplified. Instead of designing a unique marketing campaign

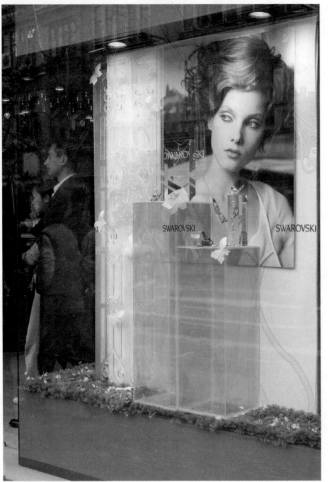

Source: Chen Chao/Dorling Kindersley

Luxury products such as Rolex watches and Swarovsky jewelry are largely standardized around the world. Here shoppers are pictured at a Swarovsky outlet in Shanghai, China.

for each country in Europe, the firm is able to simultaneously offer a relatively standardized campaign for numerous countries.

- *Ability to portray a consistent image and build global brands.* A brand is a name, sign, symbol, or design intended to identify the firm's product and to differentiate it from those of competitors. A **global brand** is one whose positioning, advertising strategy, look, and personality are standardized worldwide. Global branding increases customer interest and reduces the confusion that can arise when the firm offers numerous adapted products and marketing programs.[7]

Read the *Recent Grad in IB* story about John Dykhouse to learn how working in brand strategy and marketing can provide the basis for an exciting international business career.

Adaptation

Although firms usually prefer to standardize their products, adaptation is often necessitated due to differences across countries in language, culture, economic conditions, and other factors. Adaptation is useful in *multidomestic industries*, such as publishing and software, which tailor their offerings to suit individual markets. It may be as straightforward as translating labels, instructions, or books into a foreign language or as complex as completely modifying a product to fit unique market conditions. Local adaptation can provide the marketer with important advantages. Managers consider several different rationales when adapting marketing program elements, which we explore next.

- *Differences in national preferences.* Companies adapt their products to suit the specific, unique wants and needs of customers in individual markets. For example, Häagen-Dazs operates more than 900 ice cream shops in 50 countries. In Japan, customers favor green tea–flavored ice cream. In Latin America, *dulce de leche* flavor is preferred. Customers in France enjoy ice cream chocolate fondue. In China, shops feature ice cream and mooncakes to celebrate the lunar festival popular in Chinese culture.[8]

When *The Simpsons* cartoon series was broadcast in Saudi Arabia, it was adapted for language and local Islamic sensibilities. The show was renamed *Al Shamshoon*, Homer Simpson's name was changed to "Omar," and Bart Simpson became "Badr." In addition to translating the show into Arabic, producers had to address the way the Simpson daughter and mother dress. Producers removed references to potentially offensive practices, such as consuming pork and beer. They changed Homer Simpson's Duff beer to soda, hot dogs to Egyptian beef sausages, and donuts to the popular Arab cookies called *kahk*. Moe's Bar was edited out of the show. As one Arab viewer told ABC News, "We are a totally different culture, so you can't talk about the same subject in the same way."[9]

McDonald's has been able to standardize its hamburgers across most world markets, but not all. Some cultures and religions shun the consumption of beef. McDonald's substitutes lamb or chicken in its burgers in some markets such as India. It also adds additional items such as *Kofte* burgers (hamburger with special spices) in Turkey. In Hong Kong, burgers are sandwiched between buns made of glutinous rice. McDonald's outlets in Norway serve "McLaks," a grilled salmon sandwich with dill sauce. In Berlin, consumers can savor a beer with their double cheeseburgers and fries. In some Arab countries, the "McArabia," a spicy chicken filet on flatbread, has been a success. Customers in France can get a burger on a baguette bun.[10]

- *Differences in living standards and economic conditions.* Because income levels vary greatly worldwide, firms adjust both the pricing and the complexity of their product offerings for individual markets. In Asia, BlackBerry-maker Research In Motion reduced

JOHN DYKHOUSE

John's major: Bachelor of Business Administration (International Business, Marketing)
Objectives: Inspiration, business success, adventure, a global outlook on life, community involvement, and helping others achieve their goals
Internships during college: Non-profit marketing; business innovations for a large consumer packaged goods firm
Jobs held since graduating:
- Associate Brand Manager, Amway Corporate Marketing, Nutrition Brands
- Brand Manager, Amway Corporate Marketing, Nutrition Brands
- Trade Development Manager, Amway Global, Health Brands

A single decision made in the blink of an eye can shape your life. As an undergraduate, John Dykhouse decided to study abroad in Grenoble, France, for one year. John notes, "For the first time, I understood that learning a new culture and language doesn't open doors just to communication, but to a new way of thinking."

Upon graduation, the combination of international experience and several marketing-related internships helped John obtain a position at Amway Corporation. Over time, he became Associate Brand Manager with Nutrilite, a brand of vitamins, minerals, and dietary supplements sold in many countries worldwide. His job responsibilities included managing several product categories within the brand, managing a global product portfolio, marketing communications, and pricing, to name a few.

Within two years, John was offered the position of Brand Manager. With this new role came a shift into the world of athletic sponsorships. The position gave John the chance to work with professional athletes and their agencies to further develop their brands through awareness-generating sponsorships and events around the world. His work brought John back to Europe many times, as well as to Korea and Japan, to perform various functions in the corporate strategy he helped create. In his newest position, John is working in Trade Development to create training tools, product campaigns, and digital strategies.

John's Advice for Career Success

1. Be a good communicator. With international work, think about when to use simplified English, and be brief.
2. Be persistent. Many people give up on the first, second, or even third try. You will likely make a few blunders during an international career. Treat these as learning experiences, and move on—just don't make them again.
3. Find a great mentor, and learn from him or her.
4. Be a team player. You will likely work with people who come from cultures you don't completely understand. Make sure you explore what is behind their opinions, be respectful, and at times, be cautious.
5. Be curious. Take in the sights, sounds, people, and even some smells of the places you visit.
6. Don't skip lunch. While it's tempting to sit at a desk to work through lunch, it is better to lunch with mentors and colleagues—you will have very productive discussions, helping you navigate through challenges in your career.

In the coming years, John plans to complete an MBA, with an emphasis on Brand Management and International Business.

---

prices on some of its smartphone models to make them more affordable for lower-income segments.[11] Dell sells inexpensive simplified versions of its computers in developing economies. Inflation and economic recessions also influence pricing policy. A recession signals a drop in consumer confidence, and the firm may need to reduce prices to generate sales. High inflation can rapidly erode profits, even as prices rise. Exchange rate fluctuations also necessitate adjustments. When the importing country currency is weak, the purchasing power of its consumers is reduced.

- *Differences in laws and regulations.* Germany, Norway, and Switzerland are among the countries that restrict advertising directed at children. Packaged foods in Europe are often labeled in several different languages, including English, French, German, and Spanish. In Quebec, Canada's French-speaking province, local law requires product packaging to be in both English and French. In some markets, the use of certain sales promotion activities such as coupons and sales contests is restricted.
- *Differences in national infrastructure.* The quality and reach of transportation networks, marketing intermediaries, and overall business infrastructure influence the marketing communications and distribution systems that firms employ abroad. Infrastructure is especially

poor in the rural parts of developing economies, necessitating innovative approaches for getting products to customers. Road and rail networks in western China are underdeveloped, so firms use small trucks to reach retailers in outlying communities. Undeveloped media also require substantial adaptations to carry marketing communications. In rural Vietnam, most consumers cannot access television, magazines, or the Internet. Radio, billboards, and brochures are favored for targeting low-income buyers.

The advantages of adapting the international marketing program to the local market include the following:

- Meet the needs of local customers more precisely
- Create unique appeal for the product
- Comply with local or national government regulations
- Achieve greater success in challenging local and global competitors

Adaptation also provides managers an opportunity to explore alternate ways of marketing the product or service. What they learn in the process can guide R&D efforts, often leading to superior products for sale abroad and at home. Products developed or modified for foreign markets sometimes prove so successful that they are launched as new products in the firm's home market. After developing an inexpensive, battery-powered electrocardiograph machine for doctors in China and India, General Electric realized the device's potential for advanced economies and began marketing it to rural clinics and visiting nurses in the United States.[12]

Standardization and Adaptation: A Balancing Act

A managerial decision about standardization and adaptation is not an either/or decision but rather a balancing act. There are good arguments and outcomes that favor both options; it is up to senior marketing managers and the global new-product planning team to sort out the trade-offs given the distinctive environments where the firm operates.

Perhaps the most important distinction between standardization and adaptation is that standardization helps the firm cut costs, while local adaptation helps the firm more precisely cater to local needs and requirements. However, adaptation is costly and time-consuming, often requiring substantial modifications to product design, manufacturing, pricing, distribution, and communications. Thus, managers usually prefer standardization. Many firms adapt marketing program elements *only when necessary* to respond to local customer preferences and mandated regulations. Unilever (www.unilever.com) streamlined the number of its brands from more than 1,600 to about 400 and focused attention on a dozen or so global ones. However, the firm had to retain many local adaptations to suit individual markets.[13]

Typically, for a given product or service, managers both standardize and adapt in varying degrees. Some marketing mix elements are standardized, some are localized, and others require a compromise among corporate, regional, and local decision makers. For example, the firm might offer a standardized product worldwide but modify its pricing and advertising for different markets. Management decides not only *what* elements to adapt, but also *how much* to adapt them. IKEA offers uniform products across its markets while modifying, say, the size of beds or chests of drawers in individual countries. It emphasizes its catalog as the principal promotional tool worldwide but supplements it with TV advertising in some major markets.

Companies rarely find it feasible or practical to follow a "one offering–one world" strategy across *all* dimensions of the marketing program. Automakers tried for years to market a "world car" that meets customer preferences everywhere and complies with various

Source: Tom Craig/Alamy

Popular consumer electronics such as Apple's iPod can gain a worldwide following and require little adaptation from country to country. This fan is using his iPod at the Louvre Museum in Paris, France.

governments' safety specifications. Ambitious experiments such as the Ford Mondeo failed to meet the approval of customers and regulatory bodies around the world. Ford was forced to modify its design to accommodate climate and geography (which affected engine specifications), government emissions standards, gas prices, and customer preferences for frills such as cupholders.

As a compromise, some firms pursue standardization as part of a *regional* strategy, formulating international marketing elements to exploit commonalities across a geographic region instead of the whole world. General Motors (www.gm.com) markets distinctive car models for China (Buick, HRV), Europe (Opel, Vauxhall), and North America (Cadillac, Chevrolet). Convergence of regional preferences, regional economic integration, harmonization of product standards, and growth of regional media and distribution channels all make regional marketing more feasible than pursuing global marketing approaches.[14]

 ## Global Branding and Product Development

Global marketing strategy poses unique challenges and opportunities for managers, especially in branding and product development. Let's examine these topics.

Global Branding

A key outcome of global positioning strategy is the development of a global brand. Well-known global brands include Hollywood movies (*Spider-Man*), pop stars (Adele), sports figures (David Beckham), personal care products (Gillette Sensor), toys (Barbie), credit cards (Visa), food (Cadbury chocolate), beverages (Heineken), furniture (IKEA), and consumer electronics (iPod).[15] Consumers prefer globally branded products because branding provides a sense of trust and confidence in their purchasing.[16]

A strong global brand enhances the efficiency and effectiveness of marketing programs, stimulates brand loyalty, allows the firm to charge premium prices, increases its leverage with intermediaries and retailers, and generally enhances its competitive advantage in global markets.[17] The firm can reduce its marketing and advertising costs by concentrating on a single global brand instead of numerous national brands. The strength of a global brand is best measured by its *brand equity*—the market value of the brand. Exhibit 18.3 provides brand equity figures for selected global brands.

The most successful global brands tend to have several of the following characteristics:

- High, conspicuous visibility, such as consumer electronics and jeans.
- Status symbols, such as cars and jewelry.
- Widespread appeal, due to innovative features that seem to fit everyone's lifestyle, such as mobile phones, credit cards, and cosmetics.
- Close identification with a particular country, such as Levi's (U.S. style) and IKEA furniture (Scandinavian style).

Still, in other cases, global brands reap the benefits of first-mover advantages in offering new and novel products or services. In 1971, the first Starbucks opened in Seattle, Washington, and offered freshly brewed coffee in a comfortable setting that encouraged people to sit and relax. Distinctive Louis Vuitton handbags and accessories are favored by fashionable shoppers worldwide. Samsung propelled itself into consumer electronics with unique design and leading-edge technology.

Developing and maintaining a global brand name is one of the best ways for firms to build global recognition. The Eveready Battery Co. consolidated its various national brand names—such as Ucar, Wonder, and Mazda—into one global brand name, Energizer. The move greatly increased the efficiency of Eveready's marketing efforts worldwide. While most managers conceive brands for a national market and then internationalize them, the preferred approach is to build a global brand from the beginning with input from all major markets. Several firms have succeeded in this approach, including Japan's Sony Corporation. "Sony" was derived from the Latin for "sound." The Japanese car company Datsun switched its name to Nissan to create a unified global brand worldwide.[18]

EXHIBIT 18.3 Top Global Brands, by Region

Company	Brand Value (US$ billions)	Country of Origin	Main Product or Service
Asian Brands			
Toyota	27.7	Japan	Cars
Samsung	23.4	South Korea	Consumer electronics
Honda	19.4	Japan	Cars
Canon	11.7	Japan	Copiers, cameras
Sony	9.9	Japan	Consumer electronics
European Brands			
Mercedes-Benz	27.4	Germany	Cars
Nokia	25.1	Finland	Cell phones
BMW	24.6	Germany	Cars
Louis Vuitton	23.2	France	Fashion accessories
H&M	16.5	Sweden	Clothing retailing
U.S. Brands			
Coca-Cola	71.9	United States	Soft drinks
IBM	69.9	United States	IT services and consulting
Microsoft	59.1	United States	Software
Google	55.3	United States	Internet services, software
GE	42.8	United States	Appliances, jet engines

Sources: Based on Interbrand, "2011 Ranking of the Top 100 Brands," www.interbrand.com, and Hoovers.com company profiles, www.hoovers.com.

Global branding also helps the MNE compete more effectively with popular local brands that appeal to buyers' sense of local tradition, pride, and preference. In Peru, Inca Kola was long a successful local brand that established itself as "Peru's Drink." Its experience reveals how local brands can be vulnerable to the market power of strong global brands. Coca-Cola purchased 50 percent of the Inca Kola Corporation. Coke and Inca Cola each have about 30 percent of the Peruvian market, giving Coca-Cola an edge since it owns half the other brand.

Global Product Development

In developing products with multi-country potential, managers emphasize their commonalities across countries rather than the differences between them.[19] A basic product will incorporate only core features into which the firm can inexpensively implement variations for individual markets. For example, while the basic computers that Dell sells worldwide are essentially identical, the letters on its keyboards and the languages used in its software are unique to countries or major regions. Many firms design products using *modular architecture*, a collection of *standardized* components and subsystems that they can rapidly assemble in various configurations to suit the needs of individual markets. Honda and Toyota design models like the Accord and Corolla around a standardized platform to which modular components, parts, and features are added to suit specific needs and tastes.

Concerned about duplication of effort across its divisions, General Motors Corporation centralized engineering operations and created a *Global Product Development Council,* which oversees $8 billion in annual spending on the development of new car models. The council promotes company-wide use of GM's best car platforms, wherever they are developed worldwide. It adapted the Holden Monaro from GM's Australian subsidiary for North America as the GTO rather than creating a totally new model. As a result, development cost a modest $50 million instead of the $500 million typical for creating a new model.[20]

A *global new-product planning team* is a group of managers within a firm that determines which elements of the product will be standardized and which will be adapted locally. The team also decides how to launch products. Launch may be simultaneous across numerous countries or it may be handled on a sequential basis. Sequential release implies launching a product one country at a time and is often preferred for products that require local adaptation.

Global new-product planning teams formulate best practices that the firm implements in all its units worldwide. These teams assemble employees with specialized knowledge and expertise from various geographically diverse units of the MNE, who collaborate in a project to develop workable solutions to common problems. For example, the iXi Bike was designed by a team from France, the United Kingdom, and the United States for France's iXi Bicycle Company. The bike fits easily into the trunk of a small car. The Logiq & Vivid E9 is a mobile ultrasound system developed by a global team from France, Japan, and the United States. Used for medical examinations, the ergonomic equipment offers substantial efficiency with minimal environmental impact. A global new-product planning team from the Netherlands and the United States created the Nuance Syringe, an electronic needle used to repair teeth.[21]

Increasingly, managers understand the role marketing can play in targeting developing economies, where the firm can contribute to raising the living standards of local residents. Read the *Global Trend* box to learn more about this development.

 GLOBAL TREND

Growing Role for Marketing in Developing Economies

Some 4 billion people live in developing economies that suffer severe poverty. Bottom of the pyramid (BOP) countries represent the poorest segment of humanity, often living on less than $2,000 per year. BOP consumers lack the financial resources to buy products and services that raise their standard of living. Inadequate distribution and marketing infrastructure hamper their access. For daily necessities, BOP consumers typically pay high prices, contributing to their poverty.

In the private sector, companies have historically targeted advanced economies. Many firms are investing in emerging markets. Leading companies are revising their business models to target BOP markets as well. This is partly due to advances in information and communications technologies that facilitate a larger reach at lower costs, lower marketing transaction costs, lower pricing, and distribution channel management. When they do business in BOP countries, firms often hire local citizens to assist in developing products and services, distribution channels, and other infrastructure that improve economic conditions and the lives of consumers. In all these ways, firms can play a substantial role in addressing global poverty.

Let's examine how companies succeed in developing economies:

1. Recognize the long-term potential of BOP markets, which can be large and fast-growing. By developing a complete line of appropriate health and home care products, packaging, and pricing for BOP customers in India, Unilever created a $2.6 billion portfolio of products that generate a high return on investment.
2. Prior to entry, perform opportunity assessment and market research. Management must be careful to adapt products appropriately and ensure pricing is suited to local income levels. This often requires firms to get "embedded" in the local market to develop insights unique to BOP countries.
3. Do not underestimate the intensity of local competition. Local firms know and understand local consumers and often demonstrate a strong capability to develop and successfully implement well-thought-out marketing strategies. Moreover, firms native to BOP countries may enjoy financial and other support from local authorities and banks that are not available to foreign firms.
4. Establish appropriate partners and other connections at the national and local levels to develop effective business operations. Often, this means recruiting employees with the right connections.
5. Do not be seduced by the time-honored attractiveness of "middle-class" market segments where premium pricing, strong brands, and heavy promotion are perceived as the only path to success. Rather, today many firms target the lower-income segment, which is generally much larger in size. They need to devise creative strategies, including competitively priced products and innovative promotion and distribution methods.

Sources: Tarun Khanna, Krishna Palepu, and Giles Jackson, "Winning in Emerging Markets: A Roadmap for Strategy and Execution," *Journal of Business-to-Business Marketing* 19, no. 2 (2012): 174–180; Vijay Mahajan and Kamini Banga, *The 86% Solution: How to Succeed in the Biggest Market Opportunity of the 21st Century* (Upper Saddle River, NJ: Wharton School Publishing, 2006); C. K. Prahalad, *The Fortune at the Bottom of the Pyramid* (Upper Saddle River, NJ: Wharton School Publishing, 2006); Ravi Ramamurti, "Competing with emerging Market Multinationals," *Business Horizons* 55, no. 3 (2012): 241–249.

International Pricing

Pricing is complex. It is particularly challenging in international business, with multiple currencies, trade barriers, added costs, diverse regulations, and typically longer distribution channels.[22] Given lower incomes in much of the world, firms often feel pressure to lower prices. Conversely, prices tend to escalate because of tariffs, taxes, and higher markups by foreign intermediaries. Price variations among different markets can lead to **gray market activity**—legal importation of genuine products into a country by intermediaries other than authorized distributors (also known as parallel imports). We discuss gray markets later in this chapter.

Gray market activity
Legal importation of genuine products into a country by intermediaries other than authorized distributors (also known as parallel imports).

Prices influence customers' perception of value, determine the level of motivation of foreign intermediaries, affect promotional spending and strategy, and compensate for weaknesses in other elements of the marketing mix. Let's explore the unique aspects of international pricing.

Factors That Affect International Pricing

Factors that influence international pricing fall into four categories.

1. *Nature of the market.* Buyers' income level and demographic profile are major factors that influence their ability to pay for products and services. Most countries are emerging markets or developing economies where most consumers lack significant disposable income. Thus, prices must be set lower. By contrast, local regulation, climate, infrastructure, and other factors often drive the firm to modify products, communications, and other marketing elements. Such adjustments cost money. Food items shipped to hot climates require refrigeration, which drives up costs. In countries with many rural residents or those with poor distribution systems, delivering products to widely dispersed customers necessitates higher pricing because of steeper shipping costs. In addition, foreign governments impose tariffs, taxes, or other costs that lead to higher prices. They also enforce health rules, safety standards, and other regulations that increase the cost of doing business locally. In Canada, for example, the government imposes price limits on prescription drugs, which reduces pharmaceutical firms' pricing flexibility.

2. *Nature of the product or industry.* Products with substantial added value—such as cars or high-end computers—usually necessitate charging relatively high prices. A specialized product, or one with a technological edge, gives a company greater price flexibility. When the firm holds a relative monopoly in a product (such as Microsoft's operating system software), it can generally charge premium prices.

3. *Type of distribution system.* Firms that export rely on independent distributors based abroad. Distributors often modify pricing to suit their own goals. Some distributors mark up prices substantially—up to 200 percent in some countries—which can harm the exporter's image and pricing strategy in the market. By contrast, when the firm internationalizes via FDI by establishing company-owned marketing subsidiaries abroad, management maintains control over pricing strategy. Firms that make direct sales to end users also control their pricing and can quickly make adjustments to suit local conditions.

4. *Location of the production facility.* Locating manufacturing in those countries with low-cost labor enables a firm to charge lower prices. Locating factories in or near major markets cuts transportation costs and may reduce problems created by foreign exchange fluctuations. Daimler established a factory in Hungary to produce Mercedes-Benz cars. Wages are one-fifth those in Germany, Daimler's home country. Major markets in Western Europe are only a few hours away by truck and rail. Achieving lower manufacturing costs helps Daimler compete more effectively with rival BMW.[23]

Exhibit 18.4 lists internal and external factors that influence how firms set international prices. Internally, management accounts for its own objectives regarding profit and market share, the cost of goods sold, and the degree of control desired over international pricing. Externally, management must account for customer characteristics, competitor prices, exchange rates, tariffs, taxes, and costs related to generating international sales, as well as transporting and distributing the goods. Many countries in Europe and elsewhere charge value-added taxes (VATs) on imported products. Unlike a sales tax, which is calculated based on the retail sales price, the VAT is determined as a percentage of the gross margin—the difference between the

Internal to the Firm

- Management's profit and market share expectations
- Cost of manufacturing, marketing, and other value-chain activities
- The degree of control management desires over price setting in foreign markets

External Factors

- Customer expectations, purchasing power, and sensitivity to price increases
- Nature of competitors' offerings, prices, and strategy
- International customer costs
  - Product/package modification; labeling and market requirements
  - Documentation (certificate of origin, invoices, banking fees)
  - Financing costs
  - Packing and container charges
  - Shipping (inspection, warehousing, freight forwarder's fee)
  - Insurance
- Landed cost
  - Tariffs (customs duty, import tax, customs clearance fee)
  - Warehousing charges at the port of import; local transportation
- Importer's cost
  - Value-added tax and other applicable taxes paid by the importer
  - Local intermediary (distributor, wholesaler, retailer) margins
  - Cost of financing inventory
- Anticipated fluctuations in currency exchange rates

EXHIBIT 18.4

Internal and External Factors That Affect International Pricing

sales price and the cost to the seller of the item sold. In the EU, for example, VAT rates range between 15 and 25 percent, which adds substantially to local prices.

A Framework for Setting International Prices

Managers examine the suitability of prices at several levels in the international distribution channel—importers, wholesalers, retailers, and end users—and then set prices accordingly. Exhibit 18.5 presents a systematic approach for managers to use in setting international prices.[24]

Let's illustrate the international pricing framework with an example. Suppose a leading U.S. musical instrument manufacturer, Melody Corporation, wants to begin exporting electric guitars to Japan and needs to set prices. Melody decides to export its John Mayer brand of guitar, which retails for $2,000 in the United States. Initial research reveals that additional costs of shipping, insurance, and a 5 percent Japanese tariff will add a total of $300 to the price of each guitar, bringing the total landed price to $2,300. Melody has identified an importer in Japan, Aoki Wholesalers, which wants to add a 10 percent profit margin to the cost of each imported guitar. Thus, the total price once a guitar leaves Aoki's Japan warehouse is $2,530. This is the *floor price*, the lowest acceptable price to Melody, since management doesn't want Japanese earnings to dip below those in the United States.

Next, market research on income levels and competitor prices reveals that Japanese musicians are willing to pay prices about 30 percent above typical U.S. prices for high-quality instruments. Given this information, Melody management believes Japan can sustain a ceiling price for the Mayer guitar of $2,600. Additional research provides estimates for Melody's sales potential at the floor price and at the ceiling price. Managers eventually decide on a suggested price of $2,560. Research has revealed this is the most appropriate price in light of factors in Japan such as local purchasing power, size of the market, market growth, competitors' prices, and Japanese attitudes on the relationship of price to product quality. Management also feels the price is reasonable given Melody's pricing in other markets, such as Hawaii and Australia. Accordingly, the

Step 1. Estimate the "landed" price of the product in the foreign market by totaling all costs associated with shipping the product to the customer's location.

Step 2. Estimate the price the importer or distributor will charge when it adds its profit margin.

Step 3. Estimate the target price range for end users. Determine:
- Floor price (lowest acceptable price to the firm, based on cost considerations)
- Ceiling price (highest possible price, based on customer purchasing power, price sensitivity, and competitive considerations)

Step 4. Assess the company sales potential at the price the firm is most likely to charge (between the floor price and ceiling price).

Step 5. Select a suitable pricing strategy based on corporate goals and preferences from:
- Rigid cost-plus pricing
- Flexible cost-plus pricing
- Incremental pricing

Step 6. Check consistency with current prices across product lines, key customers, and foreign markets (in order to deter potential gray market activity).

Step 7. Implement pricing strategy and tactics, and set intermediary and end-user prices. Then, continuously monitor market performance and make pricing adjustments as necessary to accommodate evolving market conditions.

EXHIBIT 18.5

Key Steps in International Price Setting

firm implements the price level for end users and the corresponding price for Aoki, the importer. Melody begins shipping guitars to Japan and monitors the marketplace, tracking demand and the need to adjust prices in light of demand, economic conditions, and other emergent factors.

Step 5 in Exhibit 18.5 identifies three common pricing strategies in international business:

- *Rigid cost-plus pricing* refers to setting a fixed price for all export markets. It is an approach favored by less experienced exporters. In most cases, management simply adds a flat percentage to its domestic price to compensate for the added costs of doing business abroad. The export customer's final price includes a markup to cover transporting and marketing the product, as well as profit margins for both intermediaries and the manufacturer. A key disadvantage of this method is it may fail to account for local market conditions, such as buyer demand, income level, and competition.
- *Flexible cost-plus pricing* is used when management includes any added costs of doing business abroad in its final price. Management also accounts for local market and competitive conditions, such as customer purchasing power, demand, competitor prices, and other external variables, as identified in Exhibit 18.4. This approach is more sophisticated than rigid cost-plus pricing because it accounts for specific circumstances in the target market. For example, the fashion retailer Zara uses this approach, adapting prices to suit conditions in each of the countries where it does business.
- *Incremental pricing* refers to setting prices to cover only the firm's variable costs, but not its fixed costs. Here, management assumes fixed costs are already paid from sales of the product in the firm's home country or other markets. The approach enables the firm to offer competitive prices, but it may result in suboptimal profits. When carried to an extreme, incremental pricing may invite competitors to accuse a company of dumping—charging a lower price for exported products, sometimes below manufacturing cost, potentially driving local suppliers out of business. Dumping may be regarded as unfair or illegal, leading to sanctions from the World Trade Organization (www.wto.org).

Managing International Price Escalation

International price escalation refers to the problem of end-user prices reaching exorbitant levels in the export market, caused by multilayered distribution channels, intermediary margins, tariffs, and other international customer costs (identified in Exhibit 18.4). International price

International price escalation
The problem of end-user prices reaching exorbitant levels in the export market, caused by multilayered distribution channels, intermediary margins, tariffs, and other international customer costs.

escalation means the retail price in the export market can be much higher than the price in the firm's home market, creating a competitive disadvantage for the exporter. Corporations can use five key strategies to combat export price escalation abroad, which we review next.[25]

1. *Shorten the distribution channel* to establish a more direct route to reach the final customer by bypassing some intermediaries in the channel. With a shorter channel, there are fewer intermediaries to compensate, which reduces the product's final price.
2. *Redesign the product* to remove costly features. Whirlpool developed a no-frills, simplified washing machine that it manufactures inexpensively and sells for a lower price in developing economies.
3. *Ship products unassembled,* as parts and components, to qualify for lower import tariffs. Then perform final assembly in the foreign market, ideally by using low-cost labor. Some firms have their product assembled in Foreign Trade Zones, where import costs are lower and government incentives may be available.[26]
4. *Reclassify the exported product* to qualify for lower tariffs. Suppose Motorola faces a high tariff when exporting "telecommunications equipment" to Bolivia. By having the product reclassified as "computer equipment," Motorola might be able to export the product under a lower tariff. The practice is possible because imported products often fit more than one product category for determining tariffs.
5. *Move production or sourcing to another country* to take advantage of lower production costs or favorable currency rates.

Managing Pricing Under Varying Currency Conditions

In export markets, a strong domestic currency can reduce competitiveness, while a weakening domestic currency makes the firm's foreign pricing more competitive. Exhibit 18.6 presents various firm responses to a weakening or appreciating domestic currency.[27]

Transfer Pricing

Transfer pricing, or intracorporate pricing, refers to the practice of pricing intermediate or finished products exchanged among the subsidiaries and affiliates of the same corporate family located in different countries.[28] For example, when the Ford auto parts plant in South Africa sells parts to the Ford factory in Spain, it charges a transfer price for this intracorporate transaction. This price generally differs from the market prices Ford charges its usual customers.

Transfer pricing
The practice of pricing intermediate or finished products exchanged among the subsidiaries and affiliates of the same corporate family located in different countries.

EXHIBIT 18.6 Strategies for Dealing with Varying Currency Conditions

When the exporter gains a price advantage because its home-country currency is WEAKENING relative to the customer's currency, then it should:	When the exporter suffers from a price disadvantage because its home-country currency is APPRECIATING relative to the customer's currency, then it should:
Stress the benefits of the firm's low prices to foreign customers.	Accentuate competitive strengths in *nonprice* elements of exporter's marketing program, such as product quality, delivery, and services.
Maintain normal price levels, expand the product line, or add more costly features.	Consider lowering prices by improving productivity, reducing production costs, or eliminating costly product features.
Exploit greater export opportunities in markets where this favorable exchange rate exists.	Concentrate exporting to those countries whose currencies have not weakened in relation to the exporter.
Speed repatriation of foreign-earned income and collections.	Maintain foreign-earned income in the customer's currency and delay collection of foreign accounts receivable (assuming the customer's currency likely will regain strength over a reasonable time period).
Minimize expenditures in the customer's currency (for example, for advertising and local transportation).	Maximize expenditures in the customer's currency.

MNEs such as Ford manage their internal prices primarily for two reasons.[29] First, it gives them a way to repatriate—that is, bring back to the home country—the profits from a country that restricts MNEs from taking their earnings out, often due to a shortage of its own currency. High prices charged to its foreign affiliate serve as an alternative means of transferring money out of the affiliate's country. The strategy works because controls imposed on money transferred in this way are not normally as strict as controls imposed on straight repatriation of profits.

Second, transfer pricing can help MNEs shift profits out of a country that has high corporate income taxes into a country with low corporate income taxes to increase company-wide profitability. In this case, the MNE may opt to maximize the expenses (and therefore minimize the profits) of the foreign-country affiliate by charging high prices for goods sold to the affiliate. MNEs typically centralize transfer pricing under the direction of the chief financial officer at corporate headquarters.

Consider Exhibit 18.7 for a simple illustration of transfer pricing. A subsidiary may buy or sell a finished or intermediate product from another affiliate below cost, at cost, or above cost. Suppose the MNE treats Subsidiary A as a favored unit. That is, Subsidiary A is allowed to *source at or below cost* and *sell at a relatively high price* when transacting with other subsidiaries. Over time, Subsidiary A will achieve superior financial results at the expense of Subsidiaries B, C, and D. Why would the MNE headquarters allow this? In general, headquarters would do this to optimize profits of the firm as a whole. A subsidiary would receive such a favorable treatment if it is located in a country with:

- Lower corporate income-tax rates,
- High tariffs for the product in question,
- Favorable accounting rules for calculating corporate income,
- Political stability,
- Little or no restrictions on profit repatriation, or
- Strategic importance to the MNE.

While the subsidiary's financial performance has been boosted in an artificial way, the earnings of the MNE as a whole are optimized. However, this benefit frequently comes at a cost. First, there is the complication of internal control measures. Manipulating transfer prices may make it more difficult to determine the true profit contribution of a subsidiary. Second, morale problems typically surface at a subsidiary whose profit performance has been made to look worse than it really is. Third, some subsidiary managers may react negatively to price manipulation. Fourth, as local businesses, subsidiaries must abide by local accounting rules. Legal problems will arise if they follow accounting standards not accepted by the host government. Indeed, governments often scrutinize MNE transfer pricing practices to ensure foreign firms pay their fair share of taxes by reporting accurate earnings. Thus, transfer pricing must be managed with great care.

EXHIBIT 18.7

How Transfer Pricing Can Help Maximize Corporate-Wide Reported Earnings

Manufacturer ships the product to authorized distributors in the export market

Manufacturer in the source country: Country A

Product is available locally from authorized distributors/retailers at a higher price than export markets

A gray marketer in the importing country purchases the product, ships it to the exporting country or to a third country, and sells it through unauthorized distributors to customers

Importing country: Country B

Product is available at a lower price from authorized distributors/retailers than the original source country

EXHIBIT 18.8

Illustration of Gray Market Activity

Gray Market Activity (Parallel Imports)

Caterpillar, Duracell, Gucci, and Sony all have been the target of gray market activity. Exhibit 18.8 illustrates the nature of flows and relationships in gray market activity—the legal importation of genuine products into a country by intermediaries who are not authorized distributors.[30]

Consider a manufacturer that produces its products in one country and exports them to another, illustrated by the green arrow between countries A and B in Exhibit 18.8. If the going price of the product happens to be sufficiently lower in Country B, then gray market brokers can exploit arbitrage opportunities—buy the product at a low price in Country B, import it into the original source country, and sell it at a high price there, illustrated by the orange arrow.

In this scenario, the first transaction, illustrated by the green arrow, is carried out by authorized channel intermediaries. The second transaction, illustrated by the orange arrow, is carried out by unauthorized intermediaries. Often referred to as *gray marketers*, the unauthorized intermediaries are typically independent entrepreneurs. Because their transactions parallel those of authorized distributors, gray market activity is also called *parallel importation.*

In Canada, pharmaceutical drug prices are determined by the government, which essentially imposes price controls. Consequently, drug prices are often lower there than in the United States. Because of this difference, some U.S. consumers purchase their prescription drugs from online pharmacies in Canada with savings. Although Canadian pharmacies are not technically authorized to sell medications to people in the United States, many do so anyway. Worldwide, gray market activity is common in pharmaceuticals, cameras, watches, computers, perfumes, and even construction equipment.[31]

The root cause of gray market activity is a large enough difference in price of the same product between two countries. Such price differences arise due to: (i) the manufacturer's inability to coordinate prices across its markets; (ii) deliberate efforts by the firm to charge higher prices in some countries when competitive conditions permit; or (iii) exchange rate fluctuations that result in a price gap between products priced in two different currencies.

Manufacturers of branded products are concerned about gray market activity because it can lead to:

- A *tarnished brand image* when customers realize the product is available at a lower price through alternative channels, particularly less-prestigious outlets.
- *Strained manufacturer-distributor relations* that can arise when parallel imports result in lost sales to authorized distributors.
- *Disruptions in company planning* that occur in regional sales forecasting, pricing strategies, merchandising plans, and general marketing efforts.

Source: Demetrio Carrasco/Dorling Kindersley

Benetton is typical of many firms that apply a global, standardized approach to advertising and distribution. This Benetton store is in Venice, Italy.

Managers can pursue at least four strategies to cope with gray market imports:[32]

1. Aggressively cut prices in countries and regions targeted by gray market brokers.
2. Hinder the flow of products into markets where gray market brokers procure the product. For instance, in dealing with the pharmaceutical gray market between Canada and the United States, the U.S. firm Pfizer could reduce shipment of its cholesterol drug Lipitor to Canada to levels just sufficient for local use by Canadians.
3. Design products with exclusive features that strongly appeal to customers. Adding distinctive features unique to each market reduces the likelihood that products will be channeled elsewhere.
4. Publicize the limitations of gray market channels. Trademark owners publicize the disadvantages of buying gray market goods to potential buyers.

 International Marketing Communications

Companies use *marketing communications* (also known as *marketing promotion*) to provide information to, and communicate with, existing and potential customers, with the ultimate aim of stimulating demand. The various activities of marketing communications vary substantially around the world. Let's examine them in more detail.

International Advertising

Firms conduct advertising via *media*, which includes direct mail, radio, television, cinema, billboards, transit, print media, and the Internet. *Transit* refers to ads placed in buses, trains, and subways; they are particularly useful in large cities. *Print media* are newspapers, magazines, and trade journals. Managers assess the availability and viability of media by examining the amount and types of advertising spending already occurring in each market. In 2012, advertising expenditures on major media surpassed approximately $170 billion in North America, $100 billion in Western Europe, and $125 billion in the Asia-Pacific region. Total spending on advertising worldwide reached almost $500 billllion.[33] Five western firms—Yum Brands, Pernod Ricard, Avon Products, Colgate-Palmolive, and P&G—spend more than 10 percent of their ad budgets in just one country, China.[34]

The availability and quality of media closely determine the feasibility and nature of marketing communications. Exhibit 18.9 provides statistics on media for various countries. The literacy rate indicates the number of people who can read, which is necessary to understand much advertising. Other data reveal the diversity of communication media in selected countries. In developing economies, TV, radio, newspapers, and the Internet are often quite limited. The firm must use creative approaches to advertise in countries with low literacy rates and limited media infrastructure. Certain media selections make sense for some countries but not others. In Mexico and Peru, for example, marketers emphasize television advertising, in Kuwait and Norway they concentrate on print media, and in Bolivia firms use a lot of outdoor advertising on billboards and buildings. About half of all advertising funds in Italy are spent on television, more than double the figure for the United Kingdom, where newspapers attract the largest proportion of ad spending.[35]

International advertising expenditures vary depending on the size and extent of the firm's foreign operations. Smaller firms often lack the resources to advertise on TV or to develop a foreign sales force. Differences in culture, laws, and media availability mean it is seldom possible to duplicate in foreign markets the type and mix of advertising used in the home market. For example, the Italian government limits television advertising on state channels to 12 percent of airtime per hour and 4 percent per week. Mexico and Peru require that firms produce commercials for the local audience in their respective countries and use local actors.

Culture determines buyer attitudes toward the role and function of advertising, humor content, the depiction of characters (such as the roles of men and women), and decency standards. Advertising conveys a message encoded in language, symbols, colors, and other attributes, each of which may have distinctive meanings. Buyer receptiveness differs as a function of culture and language. In China, Nike ran an ad in which NBA basketball star LeBron James battles—and

EXHIBIT 18.9 Media Characteristics in Selected Countries

	Literacy Rate (percentage of population)	Households with Television (percentage of all households)	Radio Stations (per one million people)	Daily Newspapers (number of titles per one million people)	Internet Users (percentage of population)
Argentina	97%	97%	31.0	4.8	67%
Australia	99	99	29.0	2.4	90
China	92	97	0.5	0.7	38
Ethiopia	43	2	0.1	0.1	1
India	61	66	0.2	1.7	10
Japan	99	100	2.4	0.8	80
Mexico	86	95	12.6	2.9	37
Netherlands	99	99	34.2	2.3	90
Nigeria	68	44	0.8	0.3	29
Saudi Arabia	79	98	2.6	0.5	44
United Kingdom	99	99	14.8	1.8	84
United States	99	99	44.8	5.0	78

Note: Data are for the most recent year available.

Sources: Based on *CIA World Factbook* at http://www.cia.gov; World Bank at www.worldbank.org; Internet World Stats, "Internet Usage Statistics," www.internetworldstats.com.

defeats—a computer-generated Chinese Kung Fu master. Chinese consumers were offended and China's national government banned the ad.[36]

Many MNEs employ relatively standardized advertising around the world, an approach that simplifies the communications strategy and saves money. Benetton, the Italian clothing manufacturer, has enjoyed much success by using essentially the same "United Colors of Benetton" ad campaigns in markets worldwide. Levi Strauss's (www.levi.com) advertising approach is similar around the world, stressing the all-American image of its jeans. One TV ad in Indonesia showed teenagers cruising around a U.S. town in 1960s convertibles. In Japan, Levi Strauss frequently used James Dean, the 1950s U.S. film star, as the centerpiece of its advertising. The dialogue in Levi's ads is often in English worldwide.[37]

Most MNEs employ advertising agencies to create promotional content and select media for foreign markets. The choice is usually between a home-country-based agency with international expertise, a local agency based in the target market, or a *global advertising agency* that has offices in the target market. Exhibit 18.10 identifies leading global advertising agencies. These firms maintain networks of affiliates and local offices around the world. They can create advertising that is both global and sensitive to local conditions while offering a range of additional services such as market research, publicity, and package design.

International Promotional Activities

Promotional activities are short-term marketing activities intended to stimulate an initial purchase, immediate purchase, or increased purchases of the product and to improve intermediary effectiveness and cooperation. They include tools such as coupons, point-of-purchase displays, demonstrations, samples, contests, gifts, and Internet interfacing.

Greece, Portugal, and Spain permit virtually every type of promotion, and Germany, Norway, and Switzerland forbid or restrict some. Couponing is illegal or restricted in some countries. Other promotional activities, such as giveaways, may be considered unethical or distasteful. In much of the world, such activities are uncommon and may be misunderstood. Promotions usually require a high level of intermediary or retailer sophistication to succeed.

EXHIBIT 18.10 Large Global Advertising Agencies

Rank	Agency	Headquarters	Worldwide Revenue (billions of dollars)
1	Dentsu	Japan	$22.12
2	WPP	Ireland	15.88
3	Omnicom Group	United States	13.87
4	Publicis	France	7.81
5	Interpublic Group	United States	7.01
6	Hakuhodo	Japan	6.88
7	Havas	France	2.06
8	Aegis	United Kingdom	1.80
9	Media Planning Group	Spain	1.10
10	Young & Rubicam	United States	1.00

Sources: Based on Forbes, "The World's Biggest Public Companies, 2011," retrieved from www.forbes.com; Hoovers.com, company profiles, retrieved from www.hoovers.com.

 ## International Distribution

Distribution refers to the processes of getting the product or service from its place of origin to the customer. Distribution is the most inflexible of the marketing program elements—once a firm establishes a distribution channel, it may be difficult to change it. As discussed in Chapters 3 and 14, the most common approaches to international distribution include engaging independent intermediaries (for exporting firms), or establishing marketing and sales subsidiaries directly in target markets (an FDI-based approach). The exporting firm ships goods to its intermediary, which moves the product through customs and the foreign distribution channel to retail outlets or end users.

Ethical Connections

Walmart paid some $24 million in bribes to mayors, zoning officials, and other bureaucrats in Mexico to obtain building permits, clearances, and preferential treatment. The bribes were paid to expedite construction of the firm's huge network of stores in Mexico. Confronted with news of corruption at the firm's Mexican subsidiary, top executives focused on minimizing damage to Walmart's image, rather than on rooting out wrongdoing. When the scandal was revealed, Walmart's stock price fell, and the firm exposed itself to prosecution from government officials.

David Barstow, "Vast Mexico Bribery Case Hushed Up by Wal-Mart After Top-Level Struggle," *New York Times*, April 22, 2012, p. A1.

By contrast, the foreign direct investor establishes its own operations in the market, working directly with customers and retailers to move offerings through the channel into the local marketplace. Using this approach, the firm will lease, acquire, or set up a sales office, warehouse, or an entire distribution channel, directly in the target market. Direct investment provides various advantages. First, it helps ensure control over marketing and distribution activities in the target market. Second, it facilitates monitoring the performance of employees and other actors in the local market. Third, it allows the firm to get close to the market, which is especially helpful when the market is complex or rapidly changing. A key disadvantage of direct investment is its high cost.

Some firms bypass traditional distribution systems altogether by using *direct marketing*— selling directly to end users. It typically implies using the Internet to provide detailed product information and the means for foreigners to buy offerings. Some firms such as Amazon.com are entirely Internet based, with no retail stores. Others, such as Coles, Tesco, and Home Depot, combine direct marketing with traditional retailing.

Channel length refers to the number of distributors or other intermediaries that it takes to get the product from the manufacturer to the market. The longer the channel, the more intermediaries the firm must compensate, and the costlier the channel. For example, Japan is characterized by long distribution channels, with numerous intermediaries. High channel costs contribute to international price escalation, creating a competitive disadvantage for the firm.

Distribution is especially challenging in emerging markets and developing economies, where delivery infrastructure is often poor. Nestlé expects nearly half its sales to come from emerging markets by 2020. In South Africa, the firm employs 80 sales personnel to sell baby food, nondairy creamers, and other products in areas characterized by poverty and small-scale retailing. Nestlé has invested almost a billion dollars in Africa to build up supply chains and distribution channels. Delivery is often accomplished by taxi or bicycle, or on foot. Small-scale retailing accounts for about one-third of Nestlé's distribution in Africa.[38]

Global Account Management

In a gradually globalizing world, foreign customers increasingly seek uniform and consistent prices, quality, and customer service. **Global account management (GAM)** means serving a key global customer in a consistent and standardized manner, regardless of where in the world it operates. Walmart is a key global account for Procter & Gamble, purchasing a substantial amount of P&G products. Walmart expects consistent service, including uniform prices for the same P&G product regardless of where in the world it is delivered.

Key accounts such as Migros, Zellers, and Walmart typically purchase from a collection of preferred suppliers that meet their specifications. Suppliers target these key customers by shifting resources from national, regional, and function-based operations to GAM, whose programs feature dedicated cross-functional teams, specialized coordination activities for specific accounts, and formalized structures and processes. Private IT-based portals facilitate the implementation of such systems. Each global customer is assigned a global account manager, or team, who provides the customer with coordinated marketing support and service across various countries.[39]

Global account management (GAM)
Serving a key global customer in a consistent and standardized manner, regardless of where in the world it operates.

CLOSING CASE — H&M: International Marketing Success Story

H&M is a Swedish clothing retailer specializing in "fast fashion" and "cheap chic" styles for men, women, and children. The firm generates about $20 billion in global sales, making it one of the world's largest fashion retailers. The Gap and Zara are key competitors. When H&M opens a new store, it is accompanied by much attention and interest. From New York to Berlin to Tokyo, store openings typically receive massive media coverage. The Pasadena, California, store launch was covered from news helicopters, and numerous people slept outside the store the night before it opened. Such excitement is typical of H&M store launches worldwide.

The firm began as a women's clothing retailer, Hennes, and later merged with the Swedish men's store Mauritz. Management changed the name to H&M to simplify worldwide perception of the brand.

Initially, H&M was cautious with international expansion, restricting its reach to nearby European countries, where Germany, France, and the United Kingdom became top markets. In 2000, H&M opened its first U.S. store on Fifth Avenue in New York. The firm expanded into China, Japan, Russia, South Korea, and the Middle East. Today, H&M has more than 90,000 employees operating some 2,500 stores in about forty-five countries. The retailer's top markets are Europe, Canada, and the United States.

On the heels of the spacious Fifth Avenue store launch, H&M opened several more outlets in the United States. The success of its Manhattan store did not consistently translate to other locations. Some new stores were too big, forcing management to downsize them. In the United States, H&M quickly learned that styles vary between cities and suburban locales. Management focused trendy fashions in city stores and maintained more conservative items at suburban mall stores. A decision to launch a colorful apparel collection backfired, forcing retreat to traditional styles with subdued shades. Compared to Europe, top management noted that U.S. stores need to be more inviting, and U.S. salespeople prefer focusing on a single segment, like children's wear or men's clothing.

Rapid Response Retailing

H&M emphasizes fast turnaround, the ability to take a garment from design to store shelf in three weeks. Though this falls short of competitor Zara's two-week turnaround, H&M's prices are usually lower. Known for its flexibility, H&M constantly monitors sales, restocking stores daily to quickly replenish popular merchandise.

Another cost-saving measure comes from outsourcing apparel manufacturing to 700 independent suppliers via twenty production offices, primarily in Asia and Europe. Large quantities of materials are ordered from suppliers, allowing economies of scale that are passed on to consumers.

Rapid response retailing means that H&M ensures the right product gets to the right stores at the right time. It requires careful cost control and management of lead times with suppliers, factories, and distributors. The approach results in prices substantially lower than competitors.

Market Segments and Branding

The H&M brand symbolizes "fashion and quality at the best price." Men's and women's collections emphasize innovative styling for fashion-minded people of all ages. Strong branding increases marketing effectiveness, stimulates brand loyalty, and enhances customer confidence in purchase decisions. It helps customers know what H&M stands for—simple, stylish fashions offered at popular prices. The brand drives management decisions on how to design products and where and how to launch new stores.

Most H&M stores are located in Europe, where brand awareness is substantial. However, brand awareness is still limited in other parts of the world. In some markets, building a strong brand remains challenging. Weak brand image limits H&M's sales potential and its ability to recruit and retain employees, who are crucial to long-term success.

Marketing

H&M has more than 100 in-house designers who interpret apparel trends and create fashions accessible to everyone. H&M collaborates with well-known designers, offering limited edition clothing lines in some stores. For example, collaboration with Chanel design chief Karl Lagerfeld drew large crowds to H&M stores, selling out the exclusive line in only three days. Other design partners include Stella McCartney, Madonna, and Versace. At the Tokyo store opening, H&M introduced a collection with Comme des Garçons, one of Japan's most respected fashion houses. The initial response exceeded expectations, with customers waiting in line for three days before the launch.

H&M employs unique strategies to reach target markets and attract customers to new stores. Management is careful to choose the location of stores in each city, preferring exclusive shopping districts with high traffic. Stores are intended to be fun, inspiring, and inviting, with interior design and displays that communicate what H&M stands for. Together, the products, shop floors, displays, and staff make up the whole package that communicates the H&M brand.

The firm employs conventional promotional tactics such as print advertisements and catalogues, as well as more novel approaches. *H&M Magazine* offers readers a mix of fashion and the latest lifestyle trends. The firm has its own Facebook page and sends out "tweets" on Twitter, maintaining a social network with fans around the world. The H&M YouTube site offers Fashion TV and inspirational films.

Use of celebrities like Benicio Del Toro and Molly Sims helps maintain a trendy image. H&M experiments with nontraditional methods to communicate with customers. Partnering with marketing agencies Mobiento and Adiento, H&M launched a mobile marketing campaign targeted to 20- to 40-year-old women. The campaign included banner ads placed on carrier portals and media sites, and a Web site with click-through slideshows and animated images of the firm's latest designs. Beyond promoting new additions to its apparel collection, the campaign drove customers to the H&M Club and its loyalty rewards program. Consumers received alerts and mobile coupons redeemable at nearby stores.

Recently, the firm expanded beyond traditional apparel by venturing into the home textiles business. H&M Home's products, including pillows, towels, curtains, and other textile products, are sold online and by mail. With this addition, H&M now competes with Spanish retailer Zara in the home textile market.

Global Strategy and Localization

H&M management follows a global approach by emphasizing a uniform global brand and similar apparel in all its stores. Company designers at headquarters draw inspiration from key markets so that different regions' styles are incorporated into apparel designs. The product assortment is 80 percent the same in all markets, and local managers adjust the remaining 20 percent to fit local tastes. Apparel offered in the Tokyo stores is essentially the same as that offered in Europe, but the presentation is modified.

The head office provides substantial guidance on global strategy, while store managers localize tactics to their markets. At individual stores, local managers can adapt pricing, advertising, and product range to suit local conditions. The firm offers smaller sizes in Asia, conservative apparel in Islamic countries, and garments adjusted for seasonal differences between the northern and southern hemispheres. In a fickle industry, H&M has been a smashing success. The firm has applied skillful marketing to triumph in markets around the world.

AACSB: Reflective Thinking Skills

Case Questions

1. Visit H&M's Web site at www.hm.com. What are the characteristics of H&M's global market segment(s)? How does H&M position itself in the minds of target customers around the world?

2. How does management at H&M use global branding and global product development to create and offer its fashions? How does the firm use marketing mix elements to market its offerings around the world?

3. A key aspect of H&M's strategy is to provide value to customers by maximizing perceived product benefits, minimizing prices, or both. Given this, how can H&M further increase the value of its offerings to customers? That is, what steps can management take to increase the benefits and reduce the prices that its customers encounter when shopping for H&M products?

4. How does H&M strike a balance between standardization and adaptation of its marketing program? What advantages does H&M gain from standardization? From adaptation? What factors drive management to adapt offerings in particular markets?

5. Increasingly, H&M targets emerging markets like China, Russia, and Saudi Arabia, which are often characterized by distinctive cultures, lower incomes, and inexperience with leading-edge fashion. Thinking in terms of marketing program elements, what can management do to ensure H&M succeeds in these markets?

Sources: Dan Butcher, "Retail Giant H&M Runs Multifaceted Mobile Marketing Campaign," 2009, retrieved from http://www.mobilemarketer .com; Patricia Cheng, "H&M Customers, Lured by Madonna Line, Flock to Asia Store Debut," 2009, retrieved from http://www.bloomberg.com; H&M corporate Web site at http://www.hm.com; "Clothing Culture: International Designers Cut Their Cloth to Suit Local Tastes: Management Briefing: Japan," *Just-Style*, October 2009, pp. 13–16; Ingrid Giertz-Mårtenson, "H&M—Documenting the Story of One of the World's Largest Fashion Retailers," *Business History* 54, no. 1 (2012): 108–115; Ana Roncha, "Nordic Brands Towards a Design-Oriented Concept," *Journal of Brand Management* 16, no. 1–2 (2008): 21–29; Marina Strauss, "H&M's Next Move: Taking It to the Streets," *The Globe and Mail*, May 22, 2009, retrieved from http://www.theglobeandmail.com; Stephen Wigley and C. R. Chiang, "Retail Internationalisation in Practice: Per Una in the UK and Taiwan," *International Journal of Retail & Distribution Management* 37, no. 3 (2009): 250–270; Stephen Wigley and Christopher Moore, "The Operationalisation of International Fashion Retailer Success," *Journal of Fashion Marketing and Management* 11, no. 2 (2007): 281–296; *WWD: Women's Wear Daily*, "Versace's H&M Invasion," November 18, 2011, p. 4.

Note: This case was prepared by Professor Erin Cavusgil, University of Michigan Flint, for classroom discussion.

CHAPTER ESSENTIALS

Key Terms

adaptation   466
global account management
   (GAM)   483
global brand   468

global market segment   465
global marketing strategy   464
gray market activity   474
international price escalation   476

standardization   466
transfer pricing   477

Summary

In this chapter, you learned about:

1. Global market segmentation

Developing a marketing strategy requires managers to assess the unique foreign market environment and then make choices about market segments, targeting, and positioning. **Global marketing strategy** is a plan of action that guides the firm in how to position itself and its offerings in foreign markets, which customer segments to pursue, and to what degree its marketing program elements should be standardized and adapted. A **global market segment** is a group of customers who share common characteristics across many national markets.

2. Standardization and adaptation of international marketing

How management balances **adaptation** and **standardization** determines the extent to which the firm must modify a product and its marketing to suit foreign markets. On the whole, firms prefer to standardize their products to achieve scale economies and minimize complexity. A **global market segment** is a group of customers that shares common characteristics across many national markets. *Positioning* strategy involves using marketing to create a particular image of a product or service, especially relative to competitor offerings, among the firm's customers worldwide.

3. Global branding and product development

A **global brand** is perceived similarly in all the firm's markets and increases marketing strategy effectiveness, allowing the firm to charge higher prices and deal more effectively with channel members and competitors. In developing products with multicountry potential, managers

emphasize the commonalities across countries rather than the differences. The development of global products facilitates economies of scale in R&D, production, and marketing. Innovation and design in international product development are increasingly performed by *global teams*—internationally distributed groups of people with a specific mandate to make or implement decisions that are international in scope.

4. International pricing

International prices are determined by factors both internal and external to the firm that often cause prices to inflate abroad. A special challenge for exporters in pricing is **international price escalation**—the problem of end-user prices reaching exorbitant levels in the export market, caused by multilayered distribution channels, intermediary margins, tariffs, and other international customer costs. **Transfer pricing** is the practice of pricing intermediate or finished products exchanged among the subsidiaries and affiliates of the same corporate family located in different countries. **Gray market activity**, also known as parallel imports, refers to legal importation of genuine products into a country by intermediaries other than authorized distributors.

5. International marketing communications

International marketing communications involves the management of advertising and promotional activities across national borders. Managers are often compelled to adapt their international communications due to unique legal, cultural, and socioeconomic factors in foreign markets. Firms must also accommodate literacy levels, language, and available media.

6. **International distribution**

Firms usually engage foreign intermediaries or foreign-based subsidiaries to reach customers in international markets. Some firms bypass traditional distribution systems by using *direct marketing. Channel length* refers to the number of distributors or other intermediaries it takes to get the product from the manufacturer to the market. Long channels are relatively costly. In working with key business customers, firms may undertake **global account management (GAM)**—servicing key global customers in a consistent and standardized manner, regardless of where in the world they operate.

Test Your Comprehension AACSB: Reflective Thinking Skills, Ethical Understanding and Reasoning Abilities

1. Describe the marketing program elements and how each influences sales and performance in international business.

2. Audrey Corp. has historically adapted its offerings for all its foreign markets, leading to a proliferation of product variations. Explain why Audrey Corp. might want to consider a global marketing strategy. What are the benefits of a global marketing strategy?

3. Distinguish between adaptation and standardization in international marketing.

⭐ 4. Consider Toshiba's laptop computer division. In terms of the marketing program elements, what attributes of laptop computers does the firm need to adapt and which attributes can it standardize for international markets?

5. What is the role of market segmentation and positioning in international marketing? What is a global market segment?

6. What are the most important factors to consider when formulating international pricing strategies? What steps would you follow in arriving at international prices?

⭐ 7. Suppose export customers of a consumer product are highly sensitive to price. However, the firm is experiencing substantial price escalation in the market. What factors may be causing this situation? What can management do to reduce the harmful impact of international price escalation?

8. Describe the role of distribution in international business.

Apply Your Understanding AACSB: Reflective Thinking Skills, Analytic Skills, Ethical Understanding and Reasoning Abilities

1. Products must be adapted to accommodate national differences arising from customer preferences and each market's economic conditions, climate, culture, and language. Think about the following products: packaged flour, swimsuits, textbooks, and automobiles. Describe how a firm would need to adapt the marketing for each of these products to suit conditions in China, Germany, and Saudi Arabia. In particular, think about the nature of the product, its pricing and distribution, and the marketing communications associated with it. China is an emerging market with low per-capita income, Saudi Arabia is an emerging market with a conservative culture rooted in Islam, and Germany is an advanced economy with a liberal culture. You may wish to consult globalEDGE™ (www.globalEDGE.msu.edu) to learn more about these specific markets.

2. Office Depot (www.officedepot.com), the North American supplier of office equipment and supplies, has stores in Japan, Mexico, and Poland. Suppose the firm has decided to launch its own line of notebook computers and wants to know how to price them in each of these markets. What factors should Office Depot consider in setting prices in each market? Should the firm standardize its pricing, or should prices be adapted to each of Japan, Mexico, and Poland? Suppose Office Depot's final prices proved to be too high for Mexico; what steps could management take to lower the price and still generate profits from selling notebooks there? Suggest a step-by-step approach to international pricing.

3. *Ethical Dilemma:* You just assumed a senior management position with Philip Morris (PM), a major manufacturer of cigarettes. As cigarette sales have declined in the advanced economies, PM has increased its marketing efforts in developing economies and emerging markets, where demand for smoking tobacco remains strong. Because of the enormous population in such countries,

PM expects to generate huge sales. However, many of the countries have high illiteracy rates and people are not very aware of the harmful health effects of smoking cigarettes. Many people become addicted to smoking. Given these factors, is it ethical to target such countries with cigarettes? Using the Ethical Framework in Chapter 5, analyze the arguments for and against marketing cigarettes to developing economies and emerging markets. As a senior manager, what steps should you take, if any, to address the dilemma?

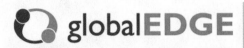 **INTERNET EXERCISES**
(http://www.globalEDGE.msu.edu)

AACSB: Reflective Thinking Skills

Refer to Chapter 1, page 24, for instructions on how to access and use globalEDGE™.

1. Global branding is key to international marketing success. Each year *Interbrand* (www.interbrand.com) publishes a ranking of the top 100 global brands. The ranking can be accessed by searching at the *Interbrand* site, or by entering "best global brands" in a Google search. For this exercise, locate and retrieve the most current ranking and answer the following questions:
   a. In your view, what are the strengths and weaknesses of the methodology *Interbrand* uses to estimate brand equity?
   b. What patterns do you detect in terms of the countries and industries most represented in the top 100 list?
   c. According to *Interbrand*, what managerial guidelines will help a company develop a strong global brand?
2. Procter and Gamble (P&G) and Unilever are the two leading firms in the consumer products industry for offerings such as soap, shampoo, and laundry detergent. P&G (www.pg.com)
is based in the United States, and Unilever (www.unilever.com) is based in Europe. What are the major regional markets of each firm? What products does each firm offer through a global marketing strategy? Structure your answer in terms of the marketing-mix elements. That is, what global strategy approaches does each firm use for the product, its pricing, communications, and distribution?
3. *A third-party logistics provider (3PL)* provides outsourced or "third-party" logistics services to companies for part or all of their distribution activities. Examples include C.H. Robinson Worldwide, Maersk Logistics, and FedEx. Your firm needs to find a 3PL to handle its distribution efforts abroad. Your task is to locate two 3PLs online and address the following questions:
   a. What logistical services does each firm provide?
   b. What types of customers does each 3PL serve?
   c. Where are their headquarters and branch offices located?
   d. Based on the information provided, which of the two 3PLs would you most likely choose? Why?

MyManagementLab

Go to **mymanagementlab.com** for Auto-graded writing questions as well as the following Assisted-graded writing questions:

18-1. William Corporation is a manufacturer of high-quality men's and women's fashions. What steps should you take to transform William into a well-recognized global brand?

18-2. What are the most important factors to consider when designing strategy for international marketing communications?

18-3. Mymanagementlab Only – comprehensive writing assignment for this chapter.

Source: View Stock/Alamy

Johnson & Johnson: A Leader in International Human Resource Management

Johnson & Johnson (J&J) is a leading global manufacturer of pharmaceutical and consumer healthcare products, with well-known brands such as Band-Aid, Tylenol, Neutrogena, and Listerine. Total sales exceed $65 billion, about half of which come from North America, one-quarter from Europe, 20 percent from the Asia-Pacific region and Africa, and the rest from Latin America and other regions. J&J's decentralized workforce includes more than 118,000 employees in over 250 business units operating in more than 60 countries worldwide.

J&J (www.jnj.com) pays special attention to the care and management of human resources. For more than six decades, J&J's Credo has articulated the firm's commitment to employees. A section of the Credo reads:

We are responsible to our employees worldwide. Everyone must be considered as an individual. We must respect their dignity and recognize their merit. They must have a sense of security in their jobs. Compensation

CHAPTER 19

Human Resource Management in the Global Firm

 LEARNING OBJECTIVES *In this chapter, you will learn about:*

1. The strategic role of human resources in international business
2. International staffing policy
3. Preparation and training of international employees
4. International performance appraisal
5. Compensation of employees
6. International labor relations
7. Diversity in the international workforce

MyManagementLab®

★ Improve Your Grade!

Over 10 million students improved their results using the Pearson MyLabs. Visit **mymanagementlab.com** for simulations, tutorials, and end-of-chapter problems.

---

must be fair and adequate, and working conditions clean, orderly and safe. We must be mindful of our employees' family responsibilities. Employees must feel free to make suggestions and complaints. There must be equal opportunity for employment, development and advancement. We must provide competent, ethical management.

Riddhi Parikh, Human Resources Manager at J&J in India, relies on the Credo when employee action is needed, such

as authorizing employee expenses, without having to consult her manager. Riddhi says the Credo gives her the freedom to make her own decisions and to learn and advance at J&J at her own pace. J&J has created a pleasant work environment; employee turnover is relatively small. J&J managers worldwide are empowered to make important decisions within their scope of operations.

Johnson & Johnson attempts to hire "the best and the brightest" to fill its leadership pipeline. Senior executives are responsible for developing managers for global operations.

The company chairman is evaluated in part on his ability to develop managers. The executive committee spends much of its time seeking and nurturing talent. The J&J Leadership Development Program drives company culture and superior business performance. As part of the development process, employees learn new skills to move across functional boundaries and take up new international assignments.

Many firms link merit increases and discretionary bonuses to the new skills their managers acquire. J&J's sophisticated evaluation system uses a "total rewards" compensation approach in which management considers all the rewards available. These include opportunities worldwide for learning and development such as attending the J&J Law School, an online curriculum, or the J&J Leadership Development Program, which rotates participants through classroom and on-the-job training on various parts of the business.

J&J also emphasizes diversity in hiring. Managers are rewarded for their efforts to hire minorities, women, and people from varied cultural backgrounds, which is crucial to expanding the firm's global markets. J&J developed a Women's Leadership Initiative in its international units, even in emerging markets such as India.

SOURCES: Cindy Crosby and Greg Zlevor, "Johnson & Johnson's Transformational Leadership Program Prepares Quality Leaders for Global Challenges," *Global Business and Organizational Excellence* 29, no. 2 (2010): 19–25; Debi O'Donovan, "Johnson and Johnson Takes World View on Compensation," *Employee Benefits*, June 2011, p. 7; Desda Moss, "The Value of Giving," *HRMagazine*, December 2009, pp. 22–26; Carolynn Cameron, "Johnson & Johnson Canada's Design, Development and Business Impact of a Local Leadership Development Program," *Organization Development Journal* 25, no. 2 (2007): 65–70; Johnson & Johnson company profile retrieved from http://www.hoovers.com; Shivani Lath, "Johnson & Johnson: Living by Its Credo," *Business Today*, November 5, 2006, p. 126; Daisy Maxey, "CEO Compensation Survey," *Wall Street Journal*, April 9, 2007, p. R.4; Johnson and Johnson, *Annual Report 2011*, retrieved from www.jnj.com.

Leading firms refer to their employees as "human talent," "human capital," or "intangible assets," emphasizing that they represent a strategic investment rather than a cost. This is especially apparent in knowledge-intensive industries such as management consulting, banking, advertising, engineering, and architecture. Without problem solvers, knowledge workers, and other creative personnel, firms such as McKinsey, Pixar, Gucci, Nokia, and many others would have great difficulty competing globally.

Managers at Johnson & Johnson recognize that their employees and the knowledge they possess are among their most important strategic assets. Recruiting, managing, and retaining human resources are especially challenging at firms with global operations. For example, consider Siemens (www.siemens.com), the German MNE. In 2010, Siemens employed more than 360,000 people in some 190 countries: 205,000 throughout Europe, 83,000 in North and South America, 61,000 in the Asia-Pacific region, and 11,000 in Africa, the Middle East, and Russia. Like Siemens, Hutchison Whampoa, IBM, ArcelorMittal, Nestlé, Matsushita, McDonald's, Unilever, Volkswagen, and Walmart each has more than 100,000 employees working outside their home countries.

In this chapter, we examine the critical role of human resources in the multinational enterprise. We describe the planning and training that firms undertake to recruit and prepare employees to work in international operations. We explain the complexities of compensating managers who work abroad, the complex nature of international labor relations, and the value of maintaining a diverse workforce, especially of managers with varied global experience. Initially, we begin by examining the strategic role that managers and the workforce play in company operations around the world.

International human resource management (IHRM)

The planning, selection, training, employment, and evaluation of employees for international operations.

 ## The Strategic Role of Human Resources in International Business

International human resource management (IHRM) refers to the planning, selection, training, employment, and evaluation of employees for international operations.[1] Management grapples with a wide range of challenges in hiring and managing workers within the distinctive cultural and legal frameworks that govern employee practices around the world. International human resource managers, usually located at corporate or regional headquarters, support subsidiary managers by providing IHRM guidelines and by hiring, training, and evaluating employees for international operations.

In the foreign subsidiaries of multinational firms, there are three types of managers:

1. **Parent-country nationals (PCNs).** These managers are citizens of the country where the MNE is headquartered. They are also called "home-country nationals".
2. **Host-country nationals (HCNs).** They are citizens of the country where the MNE's subsidiary is located. They are typically the largest proportion of workers hired abroad and usually work in manufacturing, assembly, basic service activities, clerical work, and other nonmanagerial functions.
3. **Third-country nationals (TCNs).** They are citizens of countries other than the home or host country. They typically work in management and are usually hired because of their special knowledge or skills.[2]

For example, a Canadian MNE may employ Italian citizens in its subsidiary in Italy (HCNs), send Canadian citizens to work in the Asia-Pacific region on assignment (PCNs), or assign Swiss employees to its subsidiary in Turkey (TCNs).

Employees in any of the three categories assigned to work and reside in a foreign country for an extended period, usually a year or longer, are called **expatriates** (sometimes shortened to "expat"). A U.S. firm might employ a German manager in its subsidiary in France or transfer a Japanese executive to its U.S. headquarters.[3] Both these managers are expatriates. While expatriates comprise only a small percentage of the workforce in most MNEs, they perform many critical functions.

For IHRM managers, the ultimate challenge is to ensure the right person is in the right position at the right location with the right pay scale. In some countries it is easier to get work visas for employees with specific specialized skills. For example, the financial services and information technology sectors in southern India have experienced a shortage of mid- and senior-level managerial talent. Consequently, managers from as far away as Eastern Europe can obtain work visas and gain posts in India, receiving compensation packages that are now competitive by advanced economy standards.[4]

Differences between Domestic and International HRM

International human resource management is usually more complex than domestic human resource management. Exhibit 19.1 illustrates six factors that drive this complexity.[5] Let's examine each in turn.

1. *New HR responsibilities.* IHRM managers encounter numerous factors not necessarily present at home, including foreign taxation issues for expatriates, international relocation and

Parent-country national (PCN)
An employee who is a citizen of the country where the MNE is headquartered.

Host-country national (HCN)
An employee who is a citizen of the country where the MNE subsidiary or affiliate is located.

Third-country national (TCN)
An employee who is a citizen of a country other than the home or host country.

Expatriate
An employee assigned to work and reside in a foreign country for an extended period, usually a year or longer.

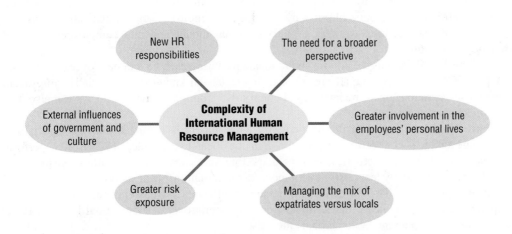

EXHIBIT 19.1

Factors That Increase the Complexity of Human Resource Management in International Business

orientation, expatriate support, host government relations, language translation services, and repatriation (returning the expatriate to his or her home country).

2. *Need for a broader, international perspective.* Management must account for all its PCNs, HCNs, and TCNs, who may be nationals of numerous countries. In an emerging market, such as Vietnam, compensation may need to include allowances for housing, education, and other facilities not readily available there. Large MNEs are often challenged by the need to establish a fair and comparable compensation scale for employees, regardless of nationality. For example, an Australian posted to Brazil can be subject to income tax from both countries. Tax equalization—ensuring there is no tax disincentive to take an international assignment—is complex.

3. *Greater involvement in employees' personal lives.* Human resource professionals help expatriates and their families with housing arrangements, health care, children's schooling, safety, and security, as well as appropriate compensation given higher living costs in some foreign locations.

4. *Managing the mix of expatriates versus locals.* Foreign subsidiaries may be staffed from the home country, the host country, and/or third countries. The mix of staff depends on several factors, including the firm's level of international experience, cost of living in the foreign location, and availability of qualified local staff.

5. *Greater risk exposure.* Employee productivity, labor union activism, employee turnover, and other human resource phenomena are often more pronounced abroad. Exposure to political risk and terrorism are major concerns for IHRM professionals and may require greater compensation and security arrangements for employees and their families.

6. *External influences of the government and national culture.* Employees must be hired, evaluated, and compensated in ways consistent with country and regional customs and regulations. Laws govern work hours, the firm's ability to dismiss or lay off employees, and severance pay. In many countries, labor unions are active in managing the firm. In France, Germany, and Spain, employees may work no more than a set number of hours per week, sometimes as few as 35. Italy's labor regulations are so complex that many companies delay hiring new workers.[6]

Key Tasks in International Human Resource Management

Exhibit 19.2 outlines six key tasks of international human resource managers. First is international staffing—activities related to recruiting, selecting, and placing employees. Second is preparing and training workers. Third is international performance appraisal, providing feedback necessary for employees' professional development. Fourth is formulating compensation and benefits packages that may vary greatly from country to country. Fifth is interacting with labor unions and collective bargaining. Sixth is achieving diversity in the international workforce. The remainder of this chapter is devoted to examining these tasks.

 ## International Staffing Policy

A critical task for MNEs is to determine the ideal mix of employees in the firm's foreign subsidiaries and affiliates.[7] The optimal mix varies by location, industry, stage in the value chain, and availability of qualified local workers. Country laws may dictate how many employees can come from nonlocal sources.

Exhibit 19.3 illustrates the criteria and rationale for hiring each type of employee.[8] Firms usually post PCNs abroad to take advantage of their specialized knowledge, especially in upstream value-chain operations, or to maintain local control over foreign operations. PCNs can also help develop local managers.

Firms prefer HCNs when the host-country environment is complex and their specialized knowledge or local connections are required in the local marketplace. HCNs often perform downstream value-chain activities, such as marketing and sales, which require extensive local knowledge.[9] It is usually less costly to compensate them than PCNs or TCNs.

Firms often prefer TCNs when senior management wants to transfer specific knowledge or corporate culture from third countries to host-country operations. Worldwide staffing with TCNs helps firms develop an integrated global enterprise.

EXHIBIT 19.2 Key Tasks and Challenges of International Human Resource Management

Task	Strategic Goals	Illustrative Challenges
International staffing policy	• Choose between home-country nationals, host-country nationals, and third-country nationals • Develop global managers • Recruit and select expatriates	• Avoid country bias, nepotism, and other local practices • Cultivate global mind-set
Preparation and training of international employees	• Increase effectiveness of international employees, leading to increased company performance • Train employees with an emphasis on area studies, practical information, and cross-cultural awareness	• Minimize culture shock and expatriate assignment failure
International performance appraisal	• Assess, over time, how effectively managers and other employees perform their jobs abroad	• Strike the right balance between standardized and localized employee performance benchmarks
Compensation of employees	• Develop guidelines and administer compensation (e.g., base salary, benefits, allowances, and incentives)	• Avoid double taxation of employees
International labor relations	• Manage and interact with labor unions, engage in collective bargaining, handle strikes and other labor disputes, wage rates, and possible workforce reduction	• Reduce absenteeism, workplace injuries due to negligence, and the occurrence of labor strikes
Diversity in the international workforce	• Recruit talent from diverse backgrounds to bring specific knowledge and experience to the firm's problems and opportunities	• Achieve gender diversity

EXHIBIT 19.3 Criteria for Selecting Employees for Foreign Operations

Staff with Parent-Country Nationals (PCNs) When...	Staff with Host-Country Nationals (HCNs) When...	Staff with Third-Country Nationals (TCNs) When...
Headquarters wants to maintain strong control over its foreign operations.	The country is distant in terms of culture or language (such as Japan), or when local operations emphasize downstream value-chain activities such as marketing and sales, as HCNs usually understand the local business environment best.	Top management wants to create a global culture among the firm's operations worldwide.
Headquarters wants to maintain control over valuable intellectual property that is easily dissipated when accessible by HCNs or TCNs.	Local connections and relations are critical to operational success (such as relations with the government in Russia).	Top management seeks unique perspectives for managing host-country operations.
Knowledge sharing is desirable among headquarters and the subsidiaries, particularly for developing local managers or the host-country organization.	The local government requires the MNE to employ a minimum proportion of local personnel, or tough immigration requirements prevent the long-term employment of expatriates.	Headquarters wants to transfer knowledge and technology from third countries to host-country operations.
Foreign operations emphasize R&D and manufacturing, because PCNs are usually more knowledgeable about such upstream value-chain activities.	Cost is an important consideration; salaries of PCNs, especially those with families, can be up to four times those of HCNs.	The firm cannot afford to pay the expensive compensation typical of PCNs.

Source: Eléonore H/Fotolia

Successful expatriates have family members who cope well in new environments. This family is touring Istanbul, Turkey.

Recruiting, Selecting, and Developing Talent

Recruitment is searching for and locating potential job candidates to fill the firm's needs. *Selection* is gathering information to evaluate and decide who should be employed in particular jobs. A big challenge for most MNEs is finding talented managers willing and qualified to work outside their home countries. Schlumberger Ltd. (www.slb.com) is a Texas oil company with operations worldwide. Schlumberger has turned its human resources department into a strategic asset for finding and developing talent, especially engineers, around the world. Among other initiatives, Schlumberger has assigned high-level executives as "ambassadors" to forty-four important engineering schools, such as Kazakhstan's Kazakh National Technical University, Beijing University, Massachusetts Institute of Technology, and Universidad Nacional Autónoma de México. IBM, Nokia, and Unilever are also proactive in finding and developing international talent.[10]

Developing talent is a multistep collaboration between human resource managers and executive management. Together, they need to:

- Analyze the firm's growth strategies and the mission-critical roles needed to achieve them;
- Define the desired skills, behaviors, and experiences for each role;
- Examine the firm's current supply of talent and create a plan to acquire needed talent;
- Develop talent internally and acquire existing or potential talent from outside the firm; and
- Assess current and potential talent according to each individual's performance over time, willingness to learn, learning skills, and commitment to career advancement.[11]

Cultivating Global Mind-Sets

Some firms are staffed by ethnocentric managers at headquarters who believe their ways of doing business are best and can be easily transferred to other countries.[12] More sophisticated MNEs have a *geocentric orientation*—they staff headquarters and subsidiaries with the most competent people, regardless of national origin. A geocentric orientation is synonymous with a *global mind-set*. Managers with a global mind-set are open to multiple cultural and strategic realities on both global and local levels.[13] They do not force headquarters business methods on foreign subsidiaries. However, most employees lack the skills, traits, or global mind-set needed for expatriate positions. Many managers prefer to remain at home.

Managers best suited to working in foreign environments typically have the following characteristics:[14]

- *Job knowledge.* In distant locations, managers need sufficient knowledge of the administrative and technical dimensions of their job and organization to fulfill company goals and objectives.
- *Self-reliance.* Having an entrepreneurial orientation, a proactive mind-set, and a strong sense of innovativeness are important because expatriate managers frequently function with increased independence abroad and limited support from headquarters.
- *Adaptability.* The manager should adjust well to foreign cultures. The most important traits are cultural empathy, flexibility, diplomacy, and a positive attitude for overcoming stressful situations.
- *Interpersonal skills.* The best candidates get along well with others. Building and maintaining relationships is key, particularly for managers who interact with numerous colleagues, employees, local partners, and government officials.[15]

- *Leadership ability.* The most successful managers view change positively. They skillfully manage threats and opportunities that confront the firm. They collaborate with employees to implement strategies and facilitate successful change.
- *Physical and emotional health.* Living abroad can be stressful. Expatriates must learn to adapt to the local culture. Medical care is often different and may be difficult to access.
- *Spouse and dependents prepared for living abroad.* The candidate's spouse and other family members need the desire and ability to cope with unfamiliar environments and cultures.

Employees with a global mindset strive to understand organizational and group dynamics to create consensus on a team.[16] Members of a *global team* require specialized training to work effectively with others from different cultures and life experiences.

Cultural Intelligence

Human resource managers need to prepare expatriates and their families to live and work effectively in new cultural environments. Employees should be trained to understand local government regulations, cultural norms, and language differences, and to adapt to local customs such as gift giving and business dining.

Cultural intelligence is an employee's ability to function effectively with those from different cultural backgrounds or in different cultural contexts.[17] It has four dimensions: (1) *strategy* describes how an employee makes sense of cross-cultural experiences through her or his judgments; (2) *knowledge* is the employee's understanding of cultural dimensions such as values, social norms, religious beliefs, and language; (3) *motivation* measures the employee's interest in interacting with people from different cultures and confidence in doing so effectively; and (4) *behavioral flexibility* is the employee's ability to adopt verbal and nonverbal behaviors appropriate in different cultures.[18]

Source: Terry Carter/Dorling Kindersley

Cultural intelligence implies the ability to function well in complex cultural environments.

Cultural intelligence
An employee's ability to function effectively in situations characterized by cultural diversity.

Expatriate Assignment Failure and Culture Shock

What happens when things go awry for the employee working abroad? **Expatriate assignment failure** describes the employee's premature return from an international assignment. It occurs when the employee is unable to perform well or because his or her family has difficulty adjusting. Such failure is costly to company productivity and goals, and adds to the costs of relocating. Failure can also affect expatriates themselves, leading to diminished careers or problems in their family lives. As many as one-third of foreign assignments end prematurely due to expatriate assignment failure. The rate is particularly high among employees assigned to countries with substantial culture and language differences.

A leading cause of expatriate assignment failure is **culture shock**—confusion and anxiety experienced by a person who lives in a foreign culture for an extended period.[19] It can affect the expatriate or family members and results from an inability to cope with the differences experienced in a foreign environment. Inadequate language and cross-cultural skills tend to worsen culture shock, as the expatriate is unable to function effectively in the foreign environment or fails to communicate well with locals.[20] Most expatriates and their families who experience culture shock overcome it, usually within a few months. But a few give up and return home early.

Expatriate assignment failure
An employee's premature return from an international assignment.

Culture shock
Confusion and anxiety experienced by a person who lives in a foreign culture for an extended period.

Preparation and Training of International Employees

Preparation is crucial to help employees better understand, adapt, and perform well in foreign environments?[21] International human resource managers must assist subsidiary management in assessing the needs of host-country workers and devise training programs that enable them to achieve their work objectives, whether in manufacturing, marketing, sales, after-sales services, or business processes such as accounting and records management.

Exhibit 19.4 highlights key features of preparation and training programs for international workers. Training consists of three components: (1) **area studies**—factual knowledge of the historical, political, and economic environment of the host country; (2) **practical information**—knowledge and skills necessary to function effectively in a country, including housing, health care, education, and daily living; and (3) **cross-cultural awareness**—the ability to interact effectively and appropriately with people from different language and cultural backgrounds.[22]

Employees benefit from training in the host-country language and learning to communicate more effectively with local colleagues and workers, suppliers, and customers. Language skills allow them to monitor competitors, recruit local talent, and improve relations with host-country officials and organizations. Language skills also increase employee insights and enjoyment of the local culture.[23]

Cross-cultural awareness training increases intercultural sensitivity and effectiveness. Managers need to be well versed in how best to supervise and communicate with local employees, negotiate with customers and suppliers, and adapt to the local culture. Training should help employees avoid the *self-reference criterion*—the tendency to view other cultures through the lens of your own culture.

Training methods vary. They include videos, lectures, assigned readings, case studies, books, Web-based instruction, critical incident analyses, simulations, role-playing, language training, field experience, and long-term immersion. In role-playing and simulations, the employee acts out typical encounters with foreigners. *Critical incident analysis* examines an episode in which tension arises between employee and foreign counterpart due to a cross-cultural misunderstanding. Field experience is a visit to the host country, usually for one or two weeks. Long-term immersion puts the employee in the country for several months or more, often for language and cultural training. In choosing training methods, the firm must strike a balance between rigor and the degree of interaction required abroad.[24]

Preparing Employees for Repatriation

Repatriation is the expatriate's return to his or her home country following completion of a foreign assignment. Like expatriation, it requires advance preparation, this time to help the employee avoid problems upon returning home. Some expatriates report financial difficulties upon returning, such as higher housing costs. Some find their international experience is not valued,

Area studies
Factual knowledge of the historical, political, and economic environment of the host country.

Practical information
Knowledge and skills necessary to function effectively in a country, including housing, health care, education, and daily living.

Cross-cultural awareness
Ability to interact effectively and appropriately with people from different language and cultural backgrounds.

Repatriation
The expatriate's return to his or her home country following the completion of a foreign assignment.

Goal	Desirable employee qualities	Training emphasizes	Training methods
Increase manager's effectiveness abroad; increase company performance	Technical competence, self-reliance, adaptability, interpersonal skills, leadership ability, physical and emotional health, spouse and dependents prepared for living abroad	• *Area studies*–host-country historical, political, economic, and cultural dimensions • *Practical information*–skills necessary to work effectively in host country • *Cultural awareness*–cross-cultural communication; negotiation techniques; reduction of ethnocentric orientation and self-reference criterion; language skills	Videos, lectures, assigned readings, case studies, critical incident analysis, simulations and role-playing, language training, field experience, long-term immersion

EXHIBIT 19.4

Key Features of Preparation and Training for International Employees

and they may be placed in lesser positions than they held abroad. Others experience "reverse culture shock," difficult readjustment to home-country culture. For those who have spent several years abroad, and for their families, adjustment to life back home may be stressful. As many as one-quarter of expatriates leave their firm within one year of returning home. Others refuse to undertake subsequent international assignments.[25]

International human resource managers can help reduce repatriation problems by providing counseling on the types of problems employees face upon returning home. While the expatriate is abroad, the firm can monitor his or her compensation and career path. After repatriation, the firm can provide bridge loans and other interim financial assistance, as well as counseling, to address both career and psychological needs. The firm needs to ensure the expatriate has a career position equal to, or better than, the one held before going abroad.[26]

Charting Global Careers for Employees

Like Johnson & Johnson in the opening story, many firms create career development programs that provide high-potential employees with opportunities to gain experience both at headquarters and in the firm's operations around the world. They do this because, as the firm generates an increasing proportion of sales and earnings from abroad, it needs globally experienced employees capable of managing company operations worldwide. This approach broadens the pool of global talent for managerial positions and visibly demonstrates top management's commitment to their global strategy.

For example, employees at Unilever (www.unilever.com) cannot advance far professionally without substantial international experience. This Anglo-Dutch firm has numerous programs to develop international leadership skills. Managers are rotated through various jobs and locations around the world, especially early in their careers. Unilever maintains a **global talent pool**—a searchable database of employees that profiles their international skills and potential for supporting the firm's global goals. Human resource managers search the database for the recruit with ideal qualifications, regardless of where he or she works in Unilever's global network. They identify the best global talent and present candidates to the appropriate business managers for final selection.[27]

Global talent pool
A searchable database of employees, profiling their international skill sets and potential for supporting the firm's global aspirations.

Performance appraisal
A formal process for assessing how effectively employees perform their jobs.

 ## International Performance Appraisal

Performance appraisal is a formal process for assessing how effectively employees perform their jobs. Appraisals help a manager identify problem areas where an employee needs to improve and where additional training is needed. Performance appraisals are typically conducted annually.

In appraising performance, managers compare mutually agreed-upon objectives with actual performance. MNEs typically devise diagnostic procedures to assess the performance of individual employees, see whether problems are attributable to inadequate skill levels, provide additional training and resources as needed, and terminate employees who consistently fail to achieve prescribed goals.

Firms assign employees duties or goals that vary from unit to unit. A new foreign subsidiary might be charged with establishing relationships with key customers and rapidly increasing sales. A manufacturing plant might be tasked with ensuring high productivity or maintaining high-quality output. When a subsidiary performs poorly, the local manager must resolve problems and get the unit back on track.

Source: Tony Souter/Dorling Kindersley

Learning about host-country culture, history, politics, and practical skills is critical to help expatriates succeed in international assignments and prepare their families for life abroad.

The following factors make performance evaluations more complex in the international context:[28]

- The problem of *noncomparable outcomes* arises because of differences in economic, political, legal, and cultural variables. For example, the firm should not punish a Mexican subsidiary manager because worker productivity is half that of home-country operations. Senior management must account for worker conditions, factory equipment, and other factors in Mexico that may cause lower productivity.[29] Different accounting rules may make financial results appear more favorable than under different accounting rules used in the home country.
- *Incomplete information* may result because headquarters is separated from foreign units by both time and distance. Headquarters staff often cannot directly observe employees working in foreign subsidiaries. To address this problem, subsidiary managers may be assessed by two evaluators—one from headquarters and one based abroad.
- Performance outcomes may be affected by the *maturity* of foreign operations. Relatively new subsidiaries may not achieve the same level of results as older subsidiaries staffed with more experienced personnel.

To avoid inaccurate or biased assessments, management needs to consider the presence of unique circumstances when appraising the performance of foreign subsidiaries, affiliates, and employees.[30]

 ## Compensation of Employees

Compensation packages vary across nations because of differences in legally mandated benefits, tax laws, cost of living, local tradition, and culture. Exhibit 19.5 presents the cost of living in selected cities. Some world business capitals are expensive. Employees posted at foreign sites often expect to be paid at a level that allows them to maintain their usual home-country standard of living. This can add substantially to company costs. Managers typically consider

EXHIBIT 19.5

Cost of Living Index in Various Cities, 2012 (Index scale; New York = 100)

Sources: Based on *Economist,* "Cost of Living Index," February 13, 2012, retrieved from www.economist.com; International Monetary Fund, "World Economic Outlook Database April 2012," retrieved from www.imf.org; *Numbeo,* "Cost of Living Index for 2012," retrieved from www.numbeo.com.

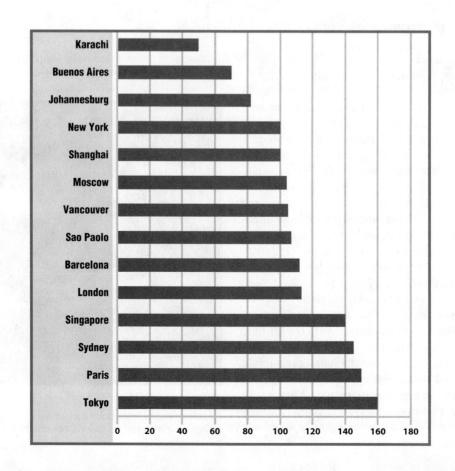

four elements when developing compensation packages for employees working abroad: (1) base remuneration or wages, (2) benefits, (3) allowances, and (4) incentives.

Base remuneration represents the salary or wages the employee typically receives in his or her home country. A local factory worker in Poland would receive wages equivalent to what average factory workers receive in the particular industry in Poland. A Japanese manager working in Singapore would receive a base salary comparable to that paid to managers at the same level in Japan. Expatriate salaries are usually paid in the home currency, the local currency, or some combination of both.

Benefits include healthcare plans, life insurance, unemployment insurance, and paid vacation days. They typically account for one-third of the total compensation package but vary as a function of local regulation, industry practice, and taxability. Expatriates usually receive the benefits normally accorded to home-country employees.

Allowance is an additional payment that allows the expatriate to maintain a standard of living similar to that at home. It is intended to pay for the added costs of housing, and sometimes food and clothing, in the relocation country. Additional support may be provided to cover relocation, children's education, travel, and business-related entertainment. Firms may provide additional hardship allowances to employees who work in countries with civil strife or other dangers, or in developing economies that lack essential housing, education, and other facilities.[31]

Given the potential hardships of working abroad, many MNEs also provide *incentives* to expatriate employees. The incentive is similar to a bonus. It is intended to motivate the employee to undertake extraordinary efforts to accomplish company goals abroad, particularly in new foreign markets. It is typically a one-time, lump-sum payment.[32]

In expatriate compensation, tax equalization is a special consideration. Expatriates may face two tax bills for the same pay, one from the host country and one from the home country. Most parent-country governments have devised regulations that allow the expatriate to minimize double taxation or pay income tax in only one country. When the employee incurs additional taxes, the employer will frequently reimburse her or him for this extra tax burden.

Country Realities

In Germany, decisions about the future career path of young people are made before they are twelve years old. Depending on academic records and career goals, students advance to one of several types of secondary schools. *Gymnasium* prepares advanced students for university education and professional or upper management careers. *Hauptschule* or *Realschule* schools provide vocational education. Upon graduation, many of these students work in factories or as government clerks. An apprenticeship system allows students to take vocational courses and work in companies doing in-service training or internships, a path to jobs in labor and technical fields.

International Labor Relations

Labor relations is the process through which management and workers identify and determine job relationships that will apply in the workplace. *Labor unions* (also called trade unions) provide a means for **collective bargaining**—joint negotiations between management and hourly labor and technical staff regarding wages and working conditions. When the firm and labor union negotiate a relationship, they formalize it with a contract. Labor regulations vary substantially, from minimal rules in some developing economies to detailed laws and regulations in many advanced economies.

Exhibit 19.6 illustrates the percentage of workers in each country that have formal union memberships. Note the recent gradual decline of union membership in many advanced economies. It has fallen to less than 12 percent of workers in the United States and less than 20 percent in Australia, Germany, Japan, and the Czech Republic. However, union membership is relatively high in Sweden, where more than 60 percent of workers, mostly government employees, are unionized.[33]

In many countries, labor laws have become less union-friendly than in the past. Employees are less likely to form a union if they feel they are treated fairly by company management. The trend toward outsourcing manufacturing and business processes to foreign suppliers also contributes to declining membership.[34] Germany has a strong tradition of unionized labor. It has seen a net outflow of FDI in recent years as German firms have established manufacturing facilities in Eastern Europe and Southeast Asia.

When management and labor fail to reach agreement, the union may declare a *strike*—an organized, collective refusal to work with the aim of pressuring management to grant union demands. The incidence of strikes has declined worldwide, but they remain a powerful weapon with important implications for business. In 2009 labor unions throughout France held strikes to protest job cuts and falling pay. The strikes by transportation workers, automakers, oil workers, and even supermarket cashiers shut down trains and air travel, halted work in key industries, and closed numerous schools nationwide. A strike by workers at a Wintek factory in China delayed production of products for Apple. Chinese workers participate increasingly in labor unions, and strike to protest issues ranging from low pay to poor working conditions.[35]

Collective bargaining
Joint negotiations between management and hourly labor and technical staff regarding wages and working conditions.

EXHIBIT 19.6

Percentage of Workers Who Belong to Labor Unions, 2000 and 2010

Source: Based on *Organisation for Economic Cooperation and Development,* "Trade Union Density," accessed at http://www.oecd.org.

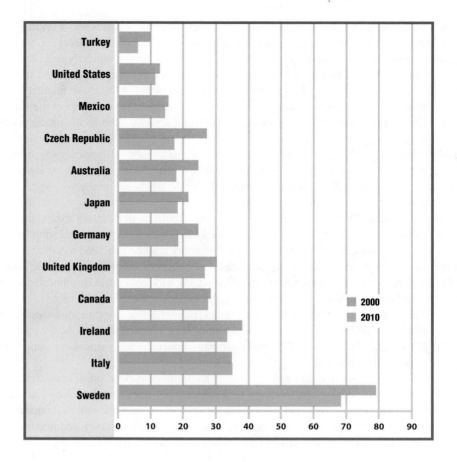

If a strike lasts more than a few days, a *mediator* or an *arbitrator* may be called in to negotiate between labor and management to end the dispute. A mediator is an expert in labor-management relations who brings both sides together and helps them reach a mutually acceptable settlement. An arbitrator is an expert third party who delivers a judgment in favor of one side or the other, after assessing arguments presented by both sides.

Ethical Connections

Executive compensation varies around the world. In China, the annual compensation of the president of a big bank is typically $300,000. In the United Kingdom, the pay may reach $3 million. In the United States, the compensation may exceed $10 million. Ethics experts argue that CEOs should not earn salaries hundreds of times greater than entry-level employees. Lopsided compensation can hurt employee morale. Others argue that pay should be tied to company profitability and firms cannot attract top talent unless they pay top salaries.

Distinctive Features of Labor around the World

Countries follow different approaches to labor, depending on their history, culture, tradition, and other local factors. In the United States, unionization is concentrated in such industries as automobiles and steel and among public-sector employees such as police and teachers. Union membership in the United States peaked in the 1950s, and the unionized labor force in various traditional industries has fallen in recent years. Globalization, capital mobility, and mass immigration from Mexico have affected the power of organized labor, leading to workforce restructuring. However, U.S. labor unions remain an important political force. Collective bargaining centers on wages, benefits, and workplace conditions and on representing members if management attempts to violate contract provisions.[36]

Labor activism and dispute resolution through unions have grown significantly in China in recent years. Given close ties between Chinese labor and government, Western managers usually deal extensively with China's national and local governments in managing labor relations.

Walmart had to officially recognize unions in China—something it does not normally do. China has a developing independent labor movement. Workers have staged thousands of strikes and protests there to demand better wages and working conditions.

Unions are a factor in reducing the occurrence of sweatshops and other poor working conditions in China.[37] The government has launched several initiatives to better protect workers' rights, including new legislation. A campaign by the All-China Federation of Trade Unions (ACFTU), the world's largest labor federation with over 130 million members, is seeking to unionize workers at all foreign firms operating in China. The ACFTU functions largely to bridge labor demands and the interests of the Chinese government.[38]

Unions in Europe often represent not only factory workers but white-collar workers such as physicians, engineers, and teachers. They hold considerable political power and may be allied with a particular political party, usually the Labor Party. A unique feature in Europe, especially in Germany and the Scandinavian countries, is labor union participation in determining wage rates, bonuses, profit sharing, holiday leaves, dismissals, and plant expansions and closings. The European Union requires even small enterprises to inform and consult employees about a range of business, employment, and work organization issues.[39] In Sweden, labor plays a significant role in shop-floor decisions and participates in such issues as product quality standards and how to organize the factory for greater efficiency and safety. In Sweden and Germany, labor participation in management may be mandated, and workers often sit on corporate boards, a practice known as **codetermination**.[40] By contrast, in South Korea, the United Kingdom, and the United States, relations between management and labor unions are often adversarial.

Codetermination
An industrial relations practice in which labor representatives sit on the corporate board and participate in company decision making.

Cost, Quality, and Productivity of Labor

Worker wages vary greatly worldwide. So do the quality and productivity of worker efforts. Advanced economies tend to pay relatively higher wages. Hourly wages are particularly high in Northern Europe. Lower wages in emerging markets and developing economies are commensurate with the lower costs of living in those countries; firms typically pay wages consistent with what local living standards and market conditions require.

Exhibit 19.7 displays the typical hourly wage rates of manufacturing workers in various countries. Firms from the advanced economies often prefer to manufacture their products in countries with lower wages. During the 2000s, U.S.-based multinational firms cut more than 850,000 jobs

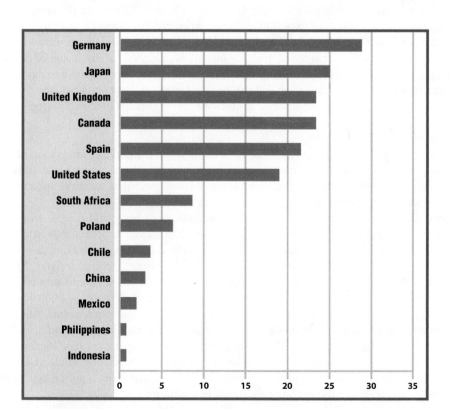

EXHIBIT 19.7

Wage Rate of Manufacturing Labor, in U.S. Dollars per Hour, 2012

Source: Based on Euromonitor International, "Wages per Hour in Manufacturing," retrieved from www.euromonitor.com; International Labour Organization, Labour Cost statistics, retrieved from www.ilo.org; World Bank, *Doing Business 2012,* retrieved from www.doingbusiness.org.

in the United States. Simultaneously they added about 1.5 million workers and 500,000 workers to their payrolls in Asia and Latin America, respectively. The most popular destinations for creating jobs included China, India, Brazil, and Mexico. In total, U.S. firms employ more than 1.5 million employees in Asia, and about 1 million in Mexico. More than 1 million people work for U.S. firms in the United Kingdom. France and Germany are also popular job sites—in each country, more than 500,000 locals work for U.S.-based firms.[41]

When firms hire workers abroad, they consider quality and trainability of labor as well as wage rates. Well-educated and skilled labor pools are scarce in some countries. Low productivity, poor work quality, and the cost of training offset some of the benefits of paying low wages. Firms must consider wages in the context of worker productivity. All else being equal, a worker in Romania who is paid half the wage of a comparable worker in Germany but is only half as productive provides no additional value. When outsourcing work to foreign suppliers, managers must ensure worker productivity in the host country meets acceptable levels. Firms may outsource or offshore work abroad only to discover the local level of productivity is less than expected.

Workforce Reduction and Employee Termination

When firms experience downturns or rising input costs, they may resort to workforce reduction to maintain profitability. In the recent global financial crisis, deteriorating economic conditions forced countless firms to lay off workers worldwide. General Motors closed its plant in Antwerp, Belgium, as part of a restructuring of global operations. The factory had employed more than 2,600 workers manufacturing the Opel for the European market. GM also announced plans to lay off 4,000 employees in Germany.[42] In the recent global financial crisis, several hundred thousand employees in the financial services industry lost work as banks, insurers, and money management firms shed jobs around the world.[43]

Laying off workers (or making them "redundant," as it is called in some countries) requires management to consider various factors, including local norms, regulations, and labor unions. Local custom obligates firms in Japan to avoid layoffs or find positions for dismissed workers in supplier organizations. Most European countries restrict firms' ability to lay off workers.

International human resource and legal managers need a full understanding of local laws and regulations on labor and worker dismissal. In the United States, declaring bankruptcy enables firms to shed labor during company reorganization. In this way auto parts manufacturer Delphi Corporation gained concessions from the United Auto Workers union on wages, benefits, and plant closings. Delphi reduced hourly wages from approximately $27 to $16 per hour.[44]

Many countries require "just cause" to terminate an employee. In most cases, just cause is satisfied if the employee becomes permanently disabled, is terminated within a probationary period (usually one to six months), or is found guilty of incompetence, theft, or disclosure of confidential information. If the firm cannot demonstrate just cause, local courts may require it to pay an indemnity, a sum of money upon termination that can be substantial. In most countries, the employee is considered the weaker party; thus, ambiguous cases are usually settled in the employee's favor.[45]

International Labor Trends

Labor is increasingly mobile across national borders thanks to the growing integration of national economies, the rapid expansion of multinational firms, and the rise of international collaborative ventures. As more countries liberalize their economies, many governments are eliminating protectionist policies that restrict work permits for foreigners.

Many countries are seeing an influx of immigrants, both legal and illegal, who compete with established workers by providing low-cost labor. Knowledge workers also flock to other nations, seeking work in specialized fields. Recent economic distress drove thousands of skilled professionals from Europe to Australia, Asia, and the Americas. Greece, Ireland, Spain, and Portugal saw thousands of their workers depart for such destinations. Thanks to a construction boom, Brazil lured engineers, architects, and other specialists to help carry out housing, energy, and infrastructure projects, much of it subsidized by the Brazilian government. Australia has proven an attractive destination to workers from Greece and other European countries.[46] Many nations, especially those with labor shortages or rapidly growing economies, loosen entry requirements to encourage immigration. Persian Gulf countries have long retained large labor pools from abroad. By contrast, Japan discourages worker immigration, a policy that, combined with a low birth rate, may produce labor shortages in the future.

Formation of global alliances by national labor unions is another recent trend. To help counter weakening union power, labor organizations have lobbied supranational organizations, such as the International Labour Office (a United Nations agency), to require MNEs to comply with labor standards and practices worldwide. Some national labor unions are joining forces with unions in other countries, forming global unions to equalize compensation and working conditions for workers in different geographical areas.[47] Subsidiaries of European firms in the United States have signed union-organizing agreements that compel their U.S. units to comply with European labor standards.[48] A few unions have succeeded in creating global agreements that affect all the subsidiaries of numerous MNEs. The UNI Global Union represents 900 unions with 20 million members around the world. Firms that have signed global agreements with the UNI include Carrefour (France), H&M (Sweden), Metro AG (Germany), and Telefonica (Spain).[49]

Firm Strategy in International Labor Relations

Labor relations differ markedly around the world. Many MNEs delegate the management of labor relations to their foreign subsidiaries. However, this can be a mistake because of the potential *global* impact of labor relations in any one country. Cross-border linkages give rise to complex interactions among differing national labor systems. Wage levels or labor unrest in one country affect the firm's activities in other countries. For example, a strike by 500 workers at an auto-parts factory in South Korea forced Hyundai to temporarily halt production of Santa Fe and Tucson sport utility vehicles, which the firm sells in North America. Yoosung Enterprise makes piston rings and other parts for Hyundai, General Motors, and Renault. A work stoppage threatened vehicle production and sales in various countries.[50] Because unions influence the cost of labor, productivity, worker morale, and firm performance, and because labor agreements made by foreign subsidiaries can create precedents for negotiations in other countries, managing labor relations on a global scale is often needed.

Skillful development and management of international human resource policies at headquarters helps ensure consistency. Many firms use a centralized information system on the company's intranet to provide continuous data on labor developments among subsidiaries. The approach helps managers anticipate employee concerns and resolve potential threats in cross-national labor relations. Firms also use intranets to communicate with employees worldwide and inform them of the firm's mission, objectives, ongoing challenges, and future threats. It is often easier to negotiate with labor unions when they understand the challenges that confront the firm.

IHRM assists global corporate and country executives in fulfilling their corporate social responsibility objectives. The *Global Trend* feature details how Nike is rising to this challenge.

 ## Diversity in the International Workforce

Highly developed MNEs embrace employees from diverse backgrounds and nationalities who bring vast knowledge and experience to the firm. Workers from various countries bring perspectives that management should leverage to perform better in markets worldwide. A multicultural workforce helps the firm develop a global mind-set, especially critical to companies with multinational ambitions.

Many internationally experienced personnel possess maturity and sophistication beyond that of employees who lack such experiences. International experience tends to enhance:

- Cross-cultural awareness and sensitivity;
- Confidence, initiative, and independence;
- Problem-solving and crisis management skills;
- Communication skills, including foreign language ability; and
- A greater ease in traveling on foreign assignments.

Obtaining substantial international experience, whether as an employee or a student, enhances prospects for an interesting career.

Women in International Business

Societies impose various roles on men and women. Some restrict women to a limited set of work roles and grant them fewer legal rights than men. In traditional societies, women are usually economically dependent on men. In Latin America, employers might consider a woman's

GLOBAL TREND

Corporate Social Responsibility and Sustainability in International Human Resource Management

Corporate actions affect employees, whether they work directly or indirectly for the firm. Heightened interest in this impact is compelling firms to become better corporate citizens abroad. Corporate social responsibility (CSR) means the firm should be responsive to all its stakeholders and operate in socially acceptable ways, including when hiring, contracting with, and managing employees.

Apparel and footwear is a low-tech industry, employing low-cost labor in emerging markets and developing economies. Firms like Nike and Reebok are primarily designers, marketers, and distributors of athletic footwear and apparel. They outsource nearly all their production to independent contractors located abroad. Nike (www.nike.com) relies on numerous suppliers that employ some 800,000 workers, mainly in China, Vietnam, Indonesia, and Thailand. These suppliers usually have limited bargaining power and often lack human resource policies to prevent labor exploitation.

Nike had long been accused of caring little for the welfare of its contract workers abroad. In the early 1990s, employees in some Nike factories in Asia were paid wages insufficient to sustain even basic nutritional needs. Many plants were operated like sweatshops, where workers labored for long hours in difficult conditions. Nike executives deflected the accusations by arguing that

because Nike did not own the factories, it was not responsible for conditions in them. Over time, however, negative publicity became a major public relations problem, and activist groups made Nike a major target for anti-globalization and anti-sweatshop movements.

To better understand the situation, Nike systematically assessed its suppliers' foreign factories. In the mid-2000s, it announced CSR goals to integrate corporate responsibility and sustainability into its business strategies and long-term growth. Nike demanded improved working conditions from its suppliers. It set benchmarks to improve labor conditions and eliminate long work hours. It developed auditing tools to measure compliance with new labor standards and approved supplier plans to invest in worker development and ensure its standards were followed.

Nike also developed a process to select suppliers based on their meeting minimal environmental, health, and safety standards and to monitor them for compliance. Today, Nike examines country-level factors such as quality of infrastructure, human rights, and economic and political conditions and aims to ensure that workers in its supply chains are paid fair wages. It is introducing collective bargaining training in all contract factories. Minimum wages are to be determined

through negotiations between labor and management.

Despite all these efforts, improvements are still needed. In some Nike contract factories, local managers are not yet fully complying with the firm's standards. Factory managers have sometimes denied inspectors access, and others have provided false information about work conditions. Some employees continue to work very long hours, some suppliers are still using child labor, and auditors have found evidence of physical abuse. Nike is working hard to meet its CSR and sustainability obligations.

Sources: David Doorey, "The Transparent Supply Chain: From Resistance to Implementation at Nike and Levi-Strauss," *Journal of Business Ethics* 103, no. 4 (2011): 587–603; Eugenia Levenson, "Citizen Nike," *Fortune*, November 24, 2008, p. 165; Richard Locke, *The Promise and Perils of Globalization: The Case of Nike* (Cambridge: Massachusetts Institute of Technology, 2007); Khalid Nadvi, "Global Standards, Global Governance and the Organization of Global Value Chains," *Journal of Economic Geography* 8 (2008): 323–343; Nike, "Nike CSR," 2007 press release retrieved from http://www.nike.com; Nike, "Workers in Contract Factories," 2007 company report retrieved from http://www.nike.com; Michael Skapinker, "Nike Ushers in a New Age of Corporate Responsibility," *Financial Times*, April 20, 2005, p. 11.

marital status in hiring. Some firms avoid hiring young married women with no children on the assumption they will soon leave to start families. In Asia and the Middle East, female managers are often mistaken for the wife or secretary of a male manager. In other countries, women have few opportunities to work outside the home and advance their own economic interests.

Female senior managers in international business are still more the exception than the norm.[51] Exhibit 19.8 presents the proportion of women working in senior management positions. The exhibit is based on findings of a survey of 3,000 senior executives in firms worldwide. Representation by women in senior management is highest in Russia and the Philippines. Among senior positions, women worldwide work most often as human resource directors and chief financial officers.[52]

Exhibit 19.8 suggests women still do not enjoy equal access to senior management positions in most countries. Even in the advanced economies, they are sometimes not afforded the same opportunities for education and training as their male colleagues. Although evidence suggests just as many women seek international positions as men, relatively few are asked to fill expatriate positions.[53]

There are several reasons for this. First, senior managers may assume women do not make suitable leaders abroad or that foreign men do not like reporting to female managers. Firms hesitate to send women to countries where traditional gender roles are the norm. Even obtaining a work visa can prove problematic in some male-dominated countries. In many countries, male

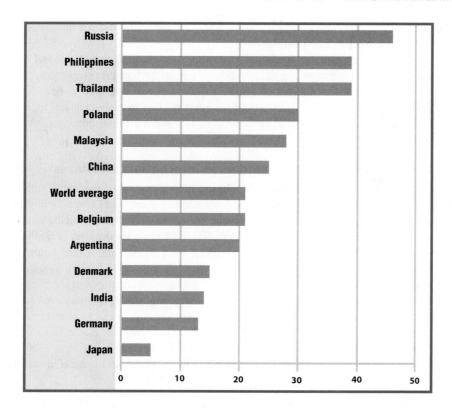

EXHIBIT 19.8

Average Percentage of Women in Senior Management Positions

Sources: Based on Grant Thornton International Ltd., "Women in Senior Management: Still Not Enough," *International Business Report 2012*, retrieved from www.gti.org.

managers drink together, go to sports events, or enjoy night life. Some women feel uncomfortable in such all-male settings.[54]

Having children and other family obligations can disrupt career paths. Although flexible and part-time work policies are often beneficial to women's progress up the corporate ladder, many firms do not provide such opportunities. Finally, because women currently occupy relatively few top management positions (in Europe, they hold only 15 percent of senior executive posts), there are fewer women with sufficient experience to send abroad for important positions.[55]

Yet the situation for working women is improving. In the advanced economies, more women are in the workforce than ever before. In the European Union, the majority of new jobs created since 2000 have been filled by women. In the United States, unemployment rates are lower for women than for men. Better-educated women are more likely to obtain jobs.[56]

Today, many more women are obtaining university degrees in business. Women account for about one-third of students in business masters programs in Europe and the United States. About one-half of recruits who join European firms are female university graduates.[57] In the United States, 140 women enroll in higher education each year for every 100 men; in Sweden, the rate is as high as 150.[58] Businesswomen increasingly form their own networks. In the United Kingdom, a group of women established *Women Directors on Boards*, which improves prospects for women to reach top management jobs. The *Association of Women in International Trade* is a U.S. organization that promotes the interests of women working in international business (www.wiit.org).

New legislation in Norway requires listed and state-owned companies to ensure that women hold at least 40 percent of seats on corporate boards. The legislation has been effective; female board representation now exceeds 45 percent in such companies. Since the

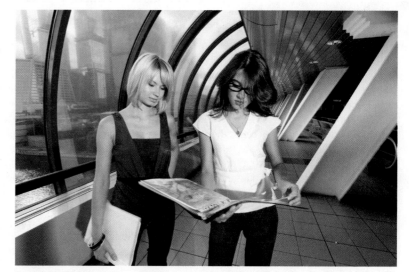

Source: Tan Kian Khoon/Shutterstock

Educated women increasingly succeed in international business in environments that were once the domain of men.

Norwegian legislation was introduced, Spain has followed suit with rules for female board representation and France has proposed similar laws.

A survey by Mercer Human Resource Consulting (www.mercer.com) found companies worldwide are substantially increasing the number of women on foreign assignments. About half the surveyed firms believe the number of female expatriates will continue to rise. At the same time, 15 percent of companies said they would not send women to male-oriented locations such as the Middle East. The survey included more than 100 multinational companies with nearly 17,000 male and female expatriates.[59]

Success Strategies for Women Managers in International Business

The chapter opener described how Johnson & Johnson links a portion of managers' compensation to efforts to hire minorities, women, and people from varied cultural backgrounds. In many countries, being a female expatriate can be an advantage for developing and leveraging strengths as a woman and as a manager. In the long run, managerial competence wins out over prejudice.[60]

Many women have found ways of overcoming senior management bias against sending females abroad. Obtaining foreign assignments is easier if you speak a foreign language or have other international skills. Substantial experience as a domestic manager or in short international assignments improves prospects for working abroad. Garnering strong support from senior management increases credibility. Once abroad in traditional societies, most women report the first reaction of surprise is often replaced by professionalism and respect. Some female graduates highlighted in the *Recent Grads in IB* feature in this book fit this trend.

Firms help ensure women achieve greater equality in international business in various ways:

- Provide training programs to develop female managerial talent
- Fill leadership roles in foreign assignments with qualified women
- Fill a minimal percentage of senior international executive posts with female employees
- Set targets for the number of women on executive boards
- Have female executives serve as mentors and role models for aspiring women

In addition, many firms have restructured promotion practices to accommodate workers raising children. Most firms in Germany and Sweden offer flexible work hours, allowing employees to arrange schedules around children's needs. Leading firms understand the need to forge a new paradigm of diverse and internationally successful female managers. Organizations like Accenture, Ernst & Young, and Vinson & Elkins all sponsor programs that assist women to advance in the global workplace.

CLOSING CASE   Evolving Human Resource Challenges at Sony

The Japanese electronics giant Sony employs 170,000 people worldwide, making and marketing PlayStation home video game systems, televisions, digital and video cameras, laptop computers, personal music players, and semiconductors. Europe, Japan, and North America each generate about a quarter of company sales; the remainder comes from the rest of the world. The firm has several entertainment divisions, including Epic and Sony Pictures Entertainment, and plants in China, Japan, Malaysia, Mexico, Spain, the United Kingdom, and the United States.

Sony has struggled in recent years because of the impact of the strong yen and the global recession. PlayStation faces serious competition from Nintendo's Wii system. The Sony Reader has been pressured by Amazon's Kindle and now iPad. The iPod and iPhone displaced Sony's music-player business .

The Manufacturing Workforce

Former Sony CEO Howard Stringer reorganized Sony, closing a dozen factories, cutting 18,000 jobs, and shifting component manufacturing to low-cost countries. In Indonesia, for example, the firm closed an audio equipment plant and laid off 1,000 workers.

Sony tries to avoid worker layoffs. Factories in the United Kingdom, where 4,000 people once made cathode-ray tubes, gradually lost their competitiveness after introduction of the flat-screen TV. Sony worked with unions to create enhanced severance packages and find new job opportunities in the region, and over time it restructured the plants to produce high-definition broadcast cameras. Sony built strong customer relationships, developed talent, created a new corporate culture, and aligned employees to the new strategy. The plants reinvented themselves by emphasizing best-in-class efforts to achieve preferred supplier status.

Sony's numerous plants and R&D centers in China employ scores of expatriates. China's attractions are its low-cost labor and superior worker skills, particularly for high-tech projects. Sony's R&D center in northern China employs over 20,000 software engineers. Nearby universities and technical institutes churn out thousands more engineering graduates each year. The high concentration of foreign firms in China (including Dell, Hitachi, IBM, and NEC) has created much competition for local talent.

Human Resource Philosophy

Sony has a highly developed approach to international human resource management. When recruiting new employees, executives seek candidates who have an entrepreneurial spirit, think creatively, and have strong communications skills. Sony's former chairman, Norio Ohga, was also an opera singer, an orchestral conductor, and a licensed jet pilot. His education in music and the arts, alongside science and engineering, strongly influenced the development of the firm's most successful products. In all areas, Sony encourages employees to structure their roles to make best use of their individual strengths.

In Sony's foreign subsidiaries, human resource managers spend time with executives and employees, linking the firm's objectives and strategies to employee capabilities. Senior managers identify key jobs for realizing the firm's objectives and analyze whether they have the best people in the most strategically important jobs and what talent they need to acquire.

When Sony Europe had to reinvent itself, the human resource group focused on identifying and leveraging the key strengths of managers to enhance corporate performance. The firm introduced mentoring projects that encouraged employees to focus on what they do best and maximize their contribution to increasing firm performance.

Training and Talent Development

Sony offers management trainee programs for its most promising recruits. Trainees are counseled to follow their passions and use their distinctive talents to advance the firm. They complete formal courses and training, tailored to individual demands and career aspirations. The firm established a mentoring and coaching network across all its talent pools. Executives coach their potential successors, who in turn act as mentors to younger upper-management candidates.

Sony develops global managers and does succession planning for top management jobs. Senior management grooms executives with strong analytical and intellectual qualities who are driven and not shy about taking risks. Programs stress visionary leadership, emotional intelligence, people skills, and the ability to influence others.

Sony implemented an extensive talent pipeline running vertically through the organization, developing and supporting high-potential employees from entry level all the way to senior levels of the firm. Management has a system of exhaustive interviews and assessments for identifying potential talent within Sony's own ranks. Executive candidates must be fluent in English and two other languages, have significant international experience, and possess the drive and ambition to take on international leadership roles.

Senior managers are required to continuously scan the employee pool to identify and groom potential talent. Recently the firm, long bound by its Japanese culture, launched initiatives to groom more English-speaking executives as a way to transform itself and remain on the cutting edge. Stringer appointed numerous non-Japanese leaders who are much younger than the traditional, seasoned Japanese management. Having a non-Japanese CEO helped shift the firm towards a geocentric staffing policy.

Sony hosts a closed-door conference in Tokyo, attended by more than 1,000 Sony managers from around the world. The conference aims to inspire leadership, convey the firm's strategic vision, and build cohesiveness for the global organization.

Corporate Social Responsibility

Sony pursues an "integrity approach" to foreign manufacturing operations and attempts to maintain workplace standards that exceed local requirements. As the firm expands internationally, management knows that actions today may be crucial for entry to new markets tomorrow. Exploiting low workplace standards in one country can ruin a reputation and jeopardize entry to new markets. Sony learned a lesson from its experiences in Mexico, where human rights groups accused it of violating worker rights.

Rather than simply following local standards in host countries, MNEs should strive to develop global standards for company operations. Sony has taken steps to standardize workplace norms so that management can benchmark internal performance, transfer expertise among countries, and apply holistic, cohesive planning and practices in operations worldwide. Sony is aiming for a universal employment standard, offering superior working conditions and locally relevant wages and benefits at all locations. Wages in foreign factories should provide a fair standard of living to all workers.

AACSB: Reflective Thinking Skills, Ethical Understanding and Reasoning Abilities, Multicultural and Diversity Understanding

Case Questions

1. Traditionally, Japanese MNEs followed an ethnocentric orientation in international staffing, in which managers from headquarters hold key subsidiary positions. Sony is shifting away from this model. What approach should Sony follow for staffing its subsidiaries? When recruiting expatriates for foreign operations, what characteristics should Sony emphasize to ensure its managers are adept at living and working abroad?

2. Sony faces challenges in finding suitable talent for its operations in China and Europe. What steps should it take to ensure it has an adequate pool of international managers and other talent for worldwide operations? What should Sony do to promote global mind-sets?

3. What is your view of Sony's training efforts? What steps could Sony take to improve its training in light of its multicountry operations?

4. Sony has experienced labor relations problems in Indonesia and elsewhere. What strategies should management follow to improve labor relations? What can it do to reduce the number and severity of labor difficulties the firm might face in the future?

5. What is your view of Sony's efforts at corporate social responsibility (CSR) in international operations? What steps can Sony take to improve CSR in organizing and managing its operations around the world, particularly in developing countries and emerging markets?

Sources: Richard Siklos, "Sony: Lost in Transformation," *Fortune,* July 6, 2009, p. 68; "Game On," *Economist,* March 7, 2009, p. 73; Hoover's profile of Sony retrieved from http://www.hoovers.com; Rebecca Johnson, "Can You Feel It?" *People Management* 13, no. 17 (2007): 1–4; Simon Kent, "Pooling Its Resources," *Personnel Today,* September 2005, pp. 23–24; David Turner, "Personality, Not University, Key to Job Hunting in Japan," *Financial Times,* September 22, 2005, p. 7; "Labor Department to Study Complaint Against Sony," *Wall Street Journal,* October 20, 1994, p. B2; Daisuke Wakabayashi and Yoshio Takahashi, "Sony's New CEO Vows to 'Revive' Company," *Wall Street Journal,* April 13, 2012, p. B4; Roy White, "Building on Employee Strengths at Sony Europe," *Strategic HR Review,* July/August 2006, pp. 28–31; *Works Management,* "Sony Workers Rally After Site is Torched in London Riots," September 2011, p. 7.

CHAPTER ESSENTIALS

MyManagementLab

Go to **mymanagementlab.com** to complete the problems marked with this icon ⭐.

Key Terms

area studies 496	expatriate 491	parent-country national
codetermination 501	expatriate assignment failure 495	(PCN) 491
collective bargaining 499	global talent pool 497	performance appraisal 497
cross-cultural awareness 496	host-country national (HCN) 491	practical information 496
cultural intelligence 495	international human resource	repatriation 496
culture shock 495	management (IHRM) 490	third-country national (TCN) 491

Summary

In this chapter, you learned about:

1. The strategic role of human resources in international business

International human resource management (IHRM) is the selection, training, employment, and motivation of employees for international operations. IHRM is more complex than its domestic counterpart. The firm must develop procedures, policies, and processes appropriate for each country where it does business. A **parent-country national (PCN)** is an employee who is a citizen of the country where the MNE is headquartered. A **host-country national (HCN)** is an employee who is a citizen of the country where the MNE subsidiary or affiliate is located. A **third-country national (TCN)** is an employee who is a citizen of a country other than the home or host country. An **expatriate** is an employee who is assigned to work and reside in a foreign country for an extended period, usually a year or longer. There are six key tasks in IHRM: international staffing policy; preparation and training of international employees; international **performance appraisal**; compensation, including formulation of benefit packages that vary from country to country; international labor relations; and managing diversity in the international workplace.

2. International staffing policy

IHRM managers determine the ideal mix of employees to work in the firm's subsidiaries and affiliates abroad. Managers best suited for working abroad typically have technical competence, self-reliance, adaptability, interpersonal skills, leadership ability, physical and emotional health, and, if present, a family prepared for living abroad. **Expatriate assignment failure** is the unplanned early return home of an employee or the failure of an expatriate to function effectively abroad. It is not unusual for expatriates to experience culture shock.

3. Preparation and training of international employees

Proper training and orientation of managers improves firm performance. Training for foreign assignments includes **area studies, practical information**, and **cross-cultural awareness**. Training includes methods such as videos, lectures, readings, simulations, and field experience. Acquiring language skills provides managers with numerous advantages. **Repatriation** is the return of the expatriate to the home country and requires advance preparation. Training is also important for the nonmanagerial workforce abroad.

4. International performance appraisal

International performance appraisals involve providing feedback on how well employees are doing their jobs, identifying problems and areas where more training is needed, and providing a basis to reward superior performance. Firms must develop systems for measuring the performance of foreign units. Various factors in the foreign environment can impede effective performance appraisal.

5. Compensation of employees

Compensation packages vary internationally because of differences in legally mandated benefits, tax laws, cost of living, local tradition, and culture. Expatriates expect to be compensated at a level that allows them to maintain their usual standard of living, which can be costly in some locations. Typical expatriate compensation includes four components: base salary, benefits, allowances, and incentives. Tax equalization must be considered because expatriates may face two tax bills for the same pay, from the host and home countries.

6. International labor relations

MNEs employ many nonmanagerial employees abroad, often represented by *labor unions*, to work in factories and perform other tasks. Management must ensure effective labor relations and take care when reducing the workforce. Along with the cost of labor, the quality and productivity of the workforce are important considerations. **Codetermination**, the participation of workers on boards of directors, is common in some countries. Labor unions are sometimes at odds with the realities of global competition and the influx of immigrants in many

countries. Leading MNEs establish an information system on labor developments, communicate with all employees, and formulate a standard policy on employment and working conditions worldwide.

7. Diversity in the international workforce

Experienced MNEs include people from diverse backgrounds, nationalities, and gender who bring a wealth of experience and knowledge to addressing the firm's problems and opportunities. Employee cultural diversity increases the complexity of interaction. Success comes from understanding and accepting differences, and then using them to enhance planning, strategy, and the firm's operations. In most countries, female managers in international business are still somewhat rare. Firms can take several steps to ensure women achieve more equality in international business.

Test Your Comprehension   AACSB: Reflective Thinking Skills, Ethical Understanding and Reasoning Abilities

⭐ **1.** What is international human resource management (IHRM)? Why is it important to internationalize firms? What is the role of IHRM in company strategy?

2. Under what circumstances would an MNE staff itself with (a) parent-country nationals, (b) host-country nationals, and (c) third-country nationals?

3. What are the characteristics of managers adept at working abroad?

4. What are the major components of training for foreign assignments?

5. What approaches can human resource managers follow to prepare expatriates for returning home?

6. What factors should human resource managers consider when appraising the performance of an employee working abroad?

7. Suppose you are working abroad as an expatriate for an MNE. What are typical components you would expect to have in your compensation package?

⭐ **8.** What are some key trends affecting international labor?

⭐ **9.** What measures can firms take to enhance the prospects of placing women in international business jobs?

Apply Your Understanding   AACSB: Communication Abilities, Reflective Thinking Skills, Ethical Understanding and Reasoning Abilities

1. Nissan Motor Co. is Japan's second-largest automotive company, with annual sales of more than USD $100 billion. The firm makes Maxima and Sentra cars, Altima and Infiniti upscale sedans, Frontier pickups, and the Xterra and Pathfinder SUVs. Some years ago, Nissan was on the verge of bankruptcy. Then Carlos Ghosn was installed as the firm's CEO. He closed inefficient factories, reduced purchasing costs, and introduced new products. Suppose Nissan asked you to advise them on IHRM issues. What specific human resource strategies would

you recommend to further enhance the firm's performance? In particular, how would you advise top management on development of global managers, preparation and training of employees, and how best to integrate the diversity of Japanese and Western managers who come from distinct cultural backgrounds?

2. Global Wannabe (GW), a manufacturer of musical instruments, is eager to internationalize. New to international business, within the coming four years, senior management wants GW to generate at least one-third of its sales from abroad by establishing foreign marketing subsidiaries and production bases in low-cost countries to cut manufacturing costs. GW's president, Larry Gerber, has appointed you to the task force charged with recruiting managers who can run GW's operations abroad. What guidelines would you offer to GW to recruit and select expatriates, while avoiding the problem of expatriate assignment failure, and evaluating the performance of employees posted abroad?

3. *Ethical Dilemma:* Many people in China toil in sweatshops, working long hours with low pay. Some factories lack heating or air-conditioning, and employees may work with hazardous materials. Workers may be fired if they complain. However, a growing labor union movement is taking hold in China. Despite management resistance, firms such as Tesco and Walmart are being forced to allow Chinese workers to unionize. Unions demand better working conditions and higher wages, and occasionally they go on strike. Management at some MNEs has prevented the workforce from unionizing. Other MNEs are establishing operations in Eastern Europe and Latin America, where labor unions are relatively weak. The Chinese government worries that unionization is hurting inward FDI by scaring foreign companies away from China. Suppose you work for Tesco or Walmart in China. Is it acceptable for your firm to prevent its workers from forming a union? What factors should management consider when determining the appropriateness and role of unions? To whom is your firm accountable—its employees or its shareholders? Can companies reach a fair compromise with workers? Analyze this dilemma by using the Ethical Framework in Chapter 5.

globalEDGE INTERNET EXERCISES
(http://www.globalEDGE.msu.edu)

AACSB: Communication Abilities, Reflective Thinking Skills, Use of Information Technology

Refer to Chapter 1, page 24, for instructions on how to access and use globalEDGE™.

1. Lifestyle factors such as the cost of living vary worldwide. One job of international human resource managers is to develop appropriate compensation packages for managers working abroad. The U.S. Department of State provides information firms can use to calculate compensation around the world. Prepare a report on the factors relevant to developing a compensation package for expatriates working in Prague and Tokyo, including "Living Costs Abroad," by accessing the State Department via globalEDGE™ (keywords "Travel/Living Abroad") or directly at aoprals.state.gov.

2. Stryker Inc. manufactures medical devices and wants to establish a factory in continental Europe. For the location, management must decide between France, Germany, and Poland. You have been assigned to research and recommend the best country from the three choices. Management prefers the country with the best overall profile of productive and low-cost workers. Good data sources for your research are the U.S. Bureau of Labor Statistics (www.bls.gov), the European Commission (www.epp .eurostat.ec.europa.eu), and the OECD (www.stats.oecd.org). Prepare a recommendation on which country—France, Germany, or Poland—would be the best choice to locate the factory. (Note: Such decisions are normally much more complex than implied here, but a preliminary analysis is a starting point for decision making.)

3. Executive Planet™ provides information for traveling managers and expatriates on how to live and do business in various countries. Suppose that you work for Virgin, the British airline, and are assigned to work in Virgin's office in an emerging market (choose an emerging market such as Argentina, India, Russia, Mexico, South Africa, or Turkey). You need to learn how to be effective in dealing with customers and colleagues in the chosen country. Select three topics (such as making appointments, business dress guidelines, or gift giving) and prepare an executive summary on how to behave regarding the topics you selected for your chosen country. You can find Executive Planet™ online via globalEDGE™ or by visiting the site directly at www.executiveplanet.com.

MyManagementLab

Go to **mymanagementlab.com** for Auto-graded writing questions as well as the following Assisted-graded writing questions:

19-1. What steps can senior managers take to develop global managers?

19-2. In what ways might an employee experience expatriate assignment failure?

19-3. Mymanagementlab Only – comprehensive writing assignment for this chapter.

A Small Firm Rides the Waves of Foreign Exchange

Markel Corporation is a Pennsylvania-based SME that makes wire and tubing for the automotive and fluid-handling industries. The firm exports to Germany, Spain, Japan, and numerous other countries, generating much of its annual sales from abroad. Markel faces the recurring challenges of fluctuating international currencies.

Every day, CEO Kim Reynolds scans the financial news to keep informed on how exchange rates are affecting sales and profits. An appreciating dollar makes Markel's products more expensive to European and Japanese customers, reducing demand from such sources. But the currency game works both ways—when the euro and yen strengthen, the buying power of European and Japanese customers increases, boosting Markel's sales.

Exchange-rate fluctuations in the $4 trillion-a-day world currency market impact small international firms. Markel experienced such a problem when it quoted prices in its customers' currencies. The firm lost more than $600,000 due to exchange-rate losses when the U.S. dollar weakened significantly against the Euro.

CHAPTER 20

Financial Management and Accounting in the Global Firm

LEARNING OBJECTIVES *In this chapter, you will learn about:*

1. Key tasks in international financial management
2. Decide on the capital structure
3. Raise funds for the firm
4. Manage working capital and cash flow
5. Perform capital budgeting
6. Manage currency risk
7. Manage the diversity of international accounting and tax practices

---

MyManagementLab®

⭐ **Improve Your Grade!**

Over 10 million students improved their results using the Pearson MyLabs. Visit **mymanagementlab.com** for simulations, tutorials, and end-of-chapter problems.

Let's illustrate with an example: suppose Markel sells merchandise to its Spanish importer for €50,000, payable in 90 days. The delay in getting paid exposes Markel to currency risk: If the euro depreciates during the 90-day period, Markel will receive fewer dollars.

To deal with fluctuating currency rates, Markel developed a three-part strategy:

- Quote prices in the customer's currency, which results in more consistent prices for the customer and generates more sales.

- Purchase forward contracts to stabilize future dollar-denominated revenues.

- Emphasize efficient company operations to make it through the times when exchange rates move in the wrong direction and hurt sales.

A forward contract is an agreement to buy or sell currency at an agreed-upon exchange rate for delivery at a specific future date. Firms like Markel buy *forward contracts* from banks to hedge exchange-rate exposure. For example, Markel might enter a forward agreement to sell €50,000, at a date 90 days in the future and an exchange rate agreed upon today, ensuring it receives a known dollar amount. The goal of such *hedging* is to balance purchases and sales of foreign currencies to minimize exposure to future currency risk.

When Markel's chief financial officer thinks the dollar is on its way up, he or she hedges the firm's expected euro revenue stream with a forward contract. But Markel's forecast isn't always correct. Suppose Markel buys a €50,000 contract at $1.05 per euro, or $52,500, but when the contract is exercised at the end of the 90-day period, the euro is actually trading at $1.08. Had Markel estimated correctly, it could have made an extra $1,500. Like most international firms, however, Markel does not try to make money on foreign-exchange trading. Its goal instead is to minimize its international currency risks.

SOURCES: Philip Alexander, "As Markets Deepen, Hedges Heighten," *Banker*, October 2011, Special Report, pp. 2–4; Barry Goss and Joost Pennings, "Reducing the Likelihood and Impact of Currency Crises," *The Banker*, January 2010, p. 8; Robert Wade, "The Perils of Cross-Border Payments," *World Trade*, June 2009, p. 8; Mark Landler and Simon Romero, "Diverging Fortunes, Tied to the Dollar," *New York Times*, December 11, 2004, retrieved from http://www.nytimes.com; Michael M. Phillips, "How a Small Firm Rides Foreign-Exchange Waves," *Wall Street Journal*, February 7, 2003, retrieved from http://www.wsj.com.

Markel, the firm in the opening story, pays close attention to *international financial management*—the acquisition and use of funds for cross-border trade, investment, R&D, manufacturing, marketing, outsourcing, and other commercial activities. It is a complex but critical business function. Firms face various international financial challenges: increasing globalization, integration of financial markets, rise of global e-commerce, expanding opportunities to profit from financial activities, and global financial crises.

Financial managers access funds from investors, foreign bond markets, local stock exchanges, foreign banks, venture capital firms, and intracorporate financing—wherever in the world capital is least costly. Their ability to minimize risk and seize opportunities depends on their financial management skills and their understanding of the laws and regulations that govern financial systems worldwide.

 ## Key Tasks in International Financial Management

International financial management is especially challenging for large MNEs. Motorola (www.motorola.com) has facilities in nearly fifty countries, and its network of subsidiaries and strategic business units raises funds in financial markets worldwide. International financial managers at firms like Markel and Motorola acquire and allocate financial resources for the firm's current and future activities to help maximize company value. In this chapter, we examine six financial management tasks that are key to MNE success, and highlighted in Exhibit 20.1:

1. *Decide on the capital structure.* Determine the ideal long-term mix of financing for the firm's international operations.
2. *Raise funds for the firm.* Obtain financing for funding value-adding activities and investment projects. Financing might come from selling stocks, borrowing money, or using internally generated funds.
3. *Manage working capital and cash flow.* Administer funds passing in and out of the firm's value-adding activities.
4. *Perform capital budgeting.* Assess the financial attractiveness of major investment projects, such as foreign expansion.
5. *Manage currency risk.* Oversee transactions in various foreign currencies and manage risk exposure resulting from exchange-rate fluctuations.
6. *Manage the diversity of international accounting and tax practices.* Learn to operate in a global environment with diverse accounting practices and international tax regimes.

The relevance of these tasks increases as the firm expands the scale of its international operations and must dedicate more attention to efficient cross-border acquisition and use of funds. Yet, it

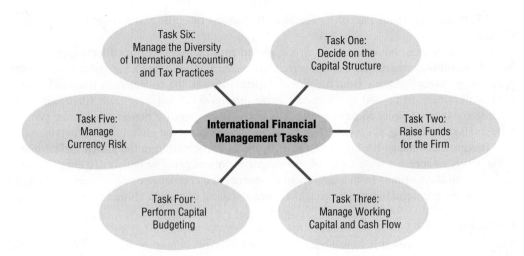

EXHIBIT 20.1

International Financial Management Tasks

is precisely this scale of global operations that gives the firm strategic flexibility thanks to increased opportunities to tap lower-cost capital, minimize taxes, achieve efficient scale of financial operations, and gain other advantages in the global financial marketplace. Let's delve into each of the six tasks.

 ## Task One: Decide on the Capital Structure

A *capital structure* is the mix of long-term equity financing and debt financing that firms use to support their international activities. Capital structure affects the profitability and stability of the firm and its international operations. Companies obtain capital in two basic ways: by borrowing it or by selling shares of ownership in the firm. **Equity financing** is selling shares of stock to investors, which provides them with an ownership interest—that is, *equity*—in the firm. The firm can also retain earnings—that is, reinvest profit rather than paying it out as dividends to investors. In new companies, founders often provide equity financing from their personal savings. **Debt financing** comes from either of two sources: (i) loans from banks and other financial intermediaries, or (ii) the sale of corporate bonds to individuals or institutions.

Debt service payments—the periodic principal and interest payments to pay off a loan—are a fixed cost. Using debt financing can add value to the firm because some governments allow firms to deduct interest payments from their taxes. To minimize the possibility of bankruptcy and maintain a good credit rating, most MNEs keep the debt proportion of their capital structure below a threshold they can service even in adverse conditions. Too much debt can force companies into financial distress and even bankruptcy.[1]

How much debt a firm should hold depends partly on the nature of its industry and its target markets. For example, an insurance company with relatively stable sales to affluent foreign markets can sustain a higher debt ratio than a consumer goods firm that sells to mostly poor countries with cyclical sales.

The riskiness of debt is perceived differently around the world. The average debt ratio in Germany, Italy, Japan, and numerous developing economies typically exceeds 50 percent. High reliance on debt financing can arise if a country lacks a well-developed stock market or other systems for obtaining capital from equity sources. Under such conditions, firms may have little choice but to borrow money from banks. In other nations, firms maintain close relationships with banks. In Japan, large MNEs are often part of a conglomerate or holding company that includes a bank. Sony Corporation has its own bank, Sony Bank.

Equity financing
The issuance of shares of stock to raise capital from investors and the use of retained earnings to reinvest in the firm.

Debt financing
The borrowing of money from banks or other financial intermediaries, or the sale of corporate bonds to individuals or institutions, to raise capital.

 ## Task Two: Raise Funds for the Firm

Lufthansa Airlines raised several hundred million euros by issuing stock shares to acquire A380 airplanes from Airbus. Grupo Mexico, a giant producer of copper and silver, issued millions of peso-denominated shares to pay expenses incurred by its foreign subsidiaries. Stanley Works,

Global money market
The collective financial markets where firms and governments raise short-term financing.

Global capital market
The collective financial markets where firms and governments raise intermediate and long-term financing.

the U.S. toolmaker, funds part of its Japanese operations by selling shares on the Tokyo Stock Exchange.

Companies can obtain financing in the **global money market**, the collective of financial markets worldwide where firms and governments raise *short-term* financing. Alternatively, companies may obtain financing from the **global capital market**, the collective of financial markets worldwide where firms and governments raise *intermediate* and *long-term* financing. Since funding for most projects comes from instruments whose maturity period is over one year, we refer to all such funding as *capital*. In this chapter, we focus on the global capital market.

The great advantage for international investors of participating in the global capital market is the ability to access a wide range of investment opportunities. The benefit for corporations is the ability to access funds from a large pool of sources at a competitive cost. Access to capital is one of the main criteria businesses consider when deciding to expand abroad.[2]

Financial Centers

The global capital market is concentrated in major *financial centers*, such as New York, London, and Tokyo, and increasingly Hong Kong, Singapore, and Shanghai. At these locations, firms can access the major suppliers of capital through banks, stock exchanges, and venture capitalists. Exhibit 20.2 lists the share of major financial activity in Japan, the United States, major European countries, and the rest of the world. The United Kingdom, France, and Germany are home to the largest proportion of foreign-exchange trading (42 percent), the United States has the largest share of private equity investment value (53 percent), and Japan has a sizeable portion of the world's bank deposits (20 percent). Within the "rest of world" category, China is emerging as an important center of global finance.

The global capital market is huge and growing rapidly, despite significant shrinkage during the recent global financial crisis. In 2011:

- International issues of equity in world securities markets amounted to about $500 billion, up from $83 billion in 1996.

EXHIBIT 20.2

Share of Financial Activity in Major World Regions, 2011 (percent)

Sources: Based on Bank for International Settlements, *BIS Quarterly Review*, March 2012, retrieved from www.bis.org; Charles Roxburgh, Susan Lund, and John Piotrowski, *Mapping Global Capital Markets 2011*, McKinsey Global Institute, August 2011, retrieved from www.mckinsey.com/mgi; TheCityUK, *Key Facts About UK Financial and Professional Services*, April 2012, retrieved from www.thecityuk.com.

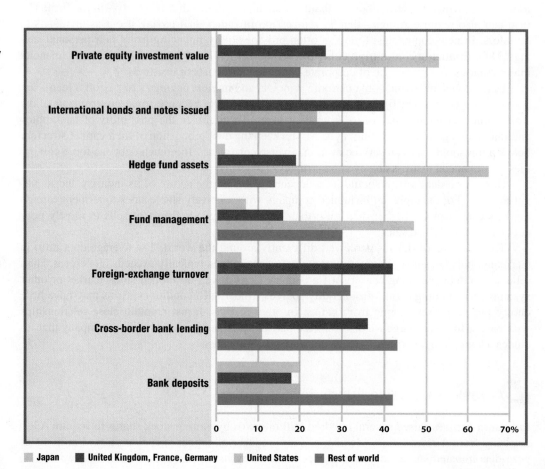

- The stock of cross-national bank loans and deposits exceeded $23,000 billion, up from $12,000 billion 10 years earlier.
- Outstanding international bonds and notes accounted for more than $27,000 billion, up from around $4,000 billion in 1998.[3]

The global capital market has grown rapidly due to:

- *Government deregulation*, which has made international movement of capital easier.
- *Innovation in information and communication technologies*, which have accelerated the ease and speed of global financial transactions.
- *Globalization* of business and global competition, which are compelling firms to seek cost-effective ways to finance international operations.
- Widespread *securitization* of financial instruments, which results in the conversion of illiquid financial instruments, such as bank loans, into tradable securities, such as bonds. Such instruments have a ready market worldwide.

Some of the above factors also contributed to the recent global financial crisis. Fueled by large-scale availability of credit and easy movement of capital across national borders, speculative ventures led to asset bubbles in commodities and real estate markets. As market participants realized that valuations in credit markets did not rest on solid fundamentals, asset prices quickly declined. The total world value of financial assets (stocks, bonds, and loans) declined from $194 trillion in 2007 to $178 trillion in 2008. Fortunately, robust growth returned 2010 and the total value of financial assets now exceeds $210 trillion.[4]

The global capital market provides three key advantages to the firm:

1. Broader base from which to draw funds to finance company operations.
2. Ability to obtain funds at lower, competitive costs due to increased access to a larger pool of funding sources from around the world.
3. Greater variety of investment opportunities for MNEs, professional investment firms, and individuals.

Sources of Funds for International Operations

Firms obtain funds for their activities from three primary sources: equity financing, debt financing, and intracorporate financing.

EQUITY FINANCING Using equity financing, the firm obtains capital by selling stock, which gives shareholders a percentage of ownership in the firm and, often, a stream of dividend payments. The main advantage is that the firm obtains capital without debt. However, whenever new equity is sold, the firm's ownership is diluted. Management also risks losing control in the event one or more shareholders acquire a controlling interest. Internationally, companies obtain equity financing in the **global equity market**—stock exchanges worldwide where investors and firms meet to buy and sell shares of stock. Exhibit 20.3 lists the world's largest stock exchanges. Note the dominance of exchanges in Europe, Japan, and the United States. NYSE Euronext (www.nyse.com) and NASDAQ OMX (www.nasdaq.com) are the largest in terms of volume of shares traded. Among the roughly 3,200 firms listed in NYSE Euronext, about 500 are foreign-owned firms from Europe, Canada, Asia, and Latin America.

As an investor, you are not limited to buying stock on the stock exchanges of your home country. Many investors today buy stocks on foreign exchanges, a trend driven by the large-scale activities of institutional investors.[5] Investing on foreign exchanges makes sense for two main reasons: (i) it provides new opportunities for lucrative investing, and (ii) it helps minimize losses during slumps in the home economy. For example, U.S. investors can buy stock from among

Global equity market
The worldwide market of funds for equity financing—stock exchanges around the world where investors and firms meet to buy and sell shares of stock.

EXHIBIT 20.3

Largest Stock Exchanges in the World

Source: Based on World Federation of Exchanges, *2011 WFE Market Highlights*, January 19, 2012, retrieved from www.world-exchanges.org.

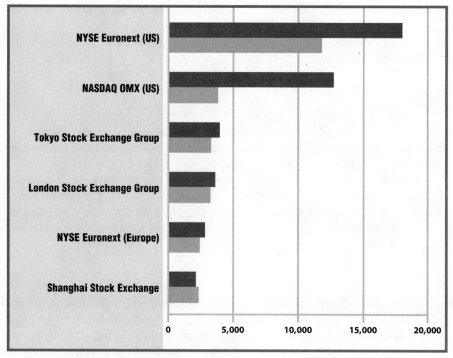

■ Total value of Share Trading (trillions of U.S. dollars)
▨ Domestic Equity Market Capitalization (trillions of U.S. dollars)

several hundred companies listed on the London exchange, including Kingfisher, Canon, and South African Breweries.[6]

Pension funds, which invest employee savings for retirement, represent the largest segment of international investing. The total value of private pension funds worldwide exceeds $19 trillion, substantially more than the GDP of the United States. Advanced economies account for more than 80 percent of pension investments. Pension funds in developing economies and emerging markets do not exist or remain substantially underdeveloped.[7] Japan is home to the world's largest public pension fund, amounting to more than $1 trillion. In 2012, the fund began investing in emerging market stocks and bonds, especially China, in order to generate higher returns.[8]

Mergers and collaborations between exchanges facilitate international trading. The merger of the NYSE (New York Stock Exchange) and the Euronext—a pan-European exchange with subsidiaries in Belgium, France, the Netherlands, Portugal, and the United Kingdom—contributed to increased transatlantic trading.[9] Thanks to the Internet, investors now trade on world stock markets at low cost. Even a small market like the Cayman Islands Stock Exchange (www.csx.com.ky) offers full online investing opportunities. Read the *Global Trend* feature to learn about the development of stock exchanges in emerging markets.

DEBT FINANCING In international business, debt financing consists primarily of international loans and the Eurocurrency market, as well as domestic and foreign bonds. We review these next.

International Loans Exhibit 20.4 shows the world's primary banking centers. In the past decade, China gained much momentum as a world banking center. In general, a firm can borrow from banks in its home market or in foreign markets. Borrowing internationally is complicated, however, by differences in national banking regulations, poor banking infrastructure, capital shortages, economic problems, and fluctuating currency values.[10] Banks are often reluctant to extend credit to small and medium-sized enterprises (SMEs), so these firms may turn to government agencies such as the Export Import (Ex-IM) Bank (www.exim.gov) in the United States, a federal agency for loans and loan guarantees. Governments in the developing world often provide loans to promote inward direct investment projects such as the construction of dams, power plants, and airports. Finally, many subsidiaries of large MNEs obtain loans from their parent firm or a sister subsidiary.

GLOBAL TREND

Emerging Markets as Investment Destinations

Many investors view stocks in emerging markets as a good investment opportunity because countries such as China, India, and Brazil are home to many fast-growth firms. During the past decade, economic growth in emerging markets has consistently exceeded growth in the advanced economies. Most emerging markets have enjoyed strong economic conditions, both during and after the recent global financial crisis. Compared to the advanced economies, emerging markets tend to have less public debt, higher domestic savings rates, and greater exports. High savings and exports are important because they provide nations with capital that their companies use to invest and build their businesses.

The majority of recent growth in global debt and equity has occurred in emerging markets, which are growing from a far smaller base than that of the advanced economies. China is now the world leader in initial public offerings (IPOs)—the first sale of stock of private firms to the public. The value of Chinese IPOs now exceeds $75 billion

annually. Chinese IPOs represented about 40 percent of the world total in 2011, a remarkable development. The rich world still commands about three-quarters of the world's financial assets. However, emerging markets' share of such assets is expected to double in the eight years from 2012, reaching as much as 36 percent of the world total by 2020. Thus, emerging markets are a promising opportunity for portfolio investment.

To accommodate demand to invest in emerging markets, local stock exchanges are becoming increasingly sophisticated. Those in Brazil and China have several hundred corporate listings, worth hundreds of billions of dollars. In smaller countries, the stock exchange may be a one-room operation with a blackboard and a telephone. Bhutan, Oman, and Kazakhstan have established small exchanges in the hope of becoming the next Chile or Singapore, which have very active exchanges.

However, investing in emerging market firms is often risky. Numerous Chinese IPOs

have failed. Some developing economies lack adequate transparency and sound legal frameworks needed to protect investors. In the recent financial crisis, industrial production and exports declined in numerous emerging markets, leading to currency devaluations. Investment flows declined significantly as banks reduced cross-border loans and many equity portfolio investors withdrew funds from the markets.

Sources: Bank for International Settlements, "81st Annual Report," June 26, 2011, retrieved from www.bis.org; *Emerging Markets Monitor,* "EM Equities Showing Increasing Value," April 2, 2012, pp. 1–3; Steve Johnson, "Pensions to Pour into EM Debt," *Financial Times,* January 25, 2010, p. 1; Richard Murphy, "New Global Hot Spots for Investors," *Fortune,* December 26, 2011, pp. 125–133; Charles Roxburgh, Susan Lund, Richard Dobbs, James Manyika, and Haihao Wu, "The Emerging Equity Gap: Growth and Stability in the New Investor Landscape," December 2011, McKinsey Global Institute, retrieved from www.mckinsey.com/mgi.

The Eurocurrency Market Another key source of loanable funds is money deposited in banks outside its country of origin. **Eurodollars** are U.S. dollars held in banks outside the United States, including foreign branches of U.S. banks. Thus, a U.S. dollar-denominated bank deposit in Barclays Bank in London or in Mizuho Bank in Tokyo is a Eurodollar deposit. More broadly, any currency deposited in a bank outside its origin country is called **Eurocurrency**. In addition to the U.S. dollar, the other main Eurocurrencies are the European euro, the British

Eurodollars
U.S. dollars held in banks outside the United States, including foreign branches of U.S. banks.

Eurocurrency
Any currency deposited in a bank outside its country of origin.

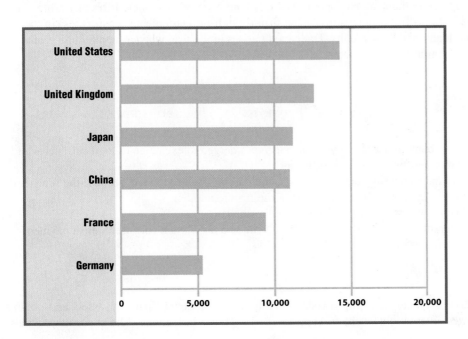

EXHIBIT 20.4

World's Primary Banking Centers, 2011 (total assets of commercial banks, in US$ billions)

Sources: Based on Bank for International Settlements, *Statistics,* 2012, retrieved from www.bis.org; International Monetary Fund, *Data and Statistics,* retrieved from www.imf.org; TheCityUK, *Banking,* May 2012, retrieved from www.thecityuk.com.

Source: Demetrio Carrasco/Dorling Kindersley

Eurodollars are deposited in banks outside the United States, such as this branch of BBVA in Peru. Generally, Eurocurrencies are funds banked outside their country of origin and represent a key source of capital for international business.

pound, and the Japanese yen. Eurodollars account for roughly two-thirds of all Eurocurrencies.[11] As much as two-thirds of U.S. banknotes are held outside the United States as a reserve currency.

Hitachi, Matsushita, and many other Japanese firms borrowed Eurodollars in Japan to help finance their operations worldwide. U.S. companies sometimes borrow euros or yen deposited in the United States to finance their activities. The Eurocurrency market is attractive to firms because these funds are not subject to the government regulations of their home-country banking systems. U.S. dollars in French banks and euros in U.S. banks are free of the reserve requirements of their home countries. Banks typically offer higher interest rates on Eurocurrency deposits and charge lower interest rates for Eurocurrency loans, contributing to the emergence of a huge Eurocurrency market.

Bonds A major source of debt financing is bonds. A **bond** is a debt instrument that enables the issuer (borrower) to raise capital by promising to repay the principal along with interest on a specified date (maturity). Firms, governments, states, and other institutions all sell bonds. Investors purchase bonds and redeem them at face value in the future. The **global bond market** is the international marketplace in which bonds are bought and sold, primarily through bond brokers.

Foreign bonds are sold outside the bond issuer's country in the currency of the country where issued. When Mexican cement giant Cemex sells dollar-denominated bonds in the United States, it is issuing foreign bonds. **Eurobonds** are sold outside the bond issuer's home country but denominated in its own currency. When Toyota sells yen-denominated bonds in the United States, it is issuing Eurobonds. The telecommunications giant AT&T has issued hundreds of millions of dollars in Eurobonds to support its international operations. Pharmaceutical firms Eli Lilly and Merck have funded much of their multinational operations with Eurobonds. Eurobonds are typically issued in denominations of $5,000 or $10,000, pay interest annually, and are sold in major financial centers, especially London.

INTRACORPORATE FINANCING Firms also obtain funding for international operations from within their network of subsidiaries and affiliates. At times, when some units of an MNE are cash-rich and others are cash-poor, they can lend each other money. **Intracorporate financing** refers to funds from sources inside the firm (both headquarters and subsidiaries) in the form of equity, loans, and trade credits. Trade credit arises in the firm when a supplier unit grants a buyer unit the option to pay at a later date.

Bond

A debt instrument that enables the issuer (borrower) to raise capital by promising to repay the principal along with interest on a specified date (maturity).

Global bond market

The international marketplace in which bonds are bought and sold, primarily through bond brokers.

Foreign bond

A bond sold outside the issuer's country and denominated in the currency of the country where issued.

Eurobond

A bond sold outside the issuer's home country but denominated in its own currency.

Intracorporate financing

Funds from sources inside the firm (both headquarters and subsidiaries) such as equity, loans, and trade credits.

Loaning funds to the firm's own foreign subsidiaries provides several advantages:

- Saves bank transaction costs, such as fees charged to exchange foreign currencies and to transfer funds between locations.
- Eliminates possible costly effects to the parent's balance sheet, because the funds are simply transferred from one area of the firm to another.
- Avoids the ownership dilution of equity financing.
- Can reduce the borrowing subsidiary's income tax burden because interest payments are often tax deductible.

IBM's global financing division invests in international financing assets and obtains and manages international debt to support IBM's global operations. The division provides loan financing to internal users for terms of two to five years. It provides inventory and accounts receivable financing to IBM's dealers and subsidiaries in various countries.[12]

Task Three: Manage Working Capital and Cash Flow

Working capital refers to the current assets of a company. *Net working capital* is the difference between current assets and current liabilities. As part of working capital management, firms manage all current accounts, such as cash, accounts receivable, inventory, and accounts payable. Cash comes from various sources, especially sales of goods and services. In the MNE, an important task of working capital management is ensuring cash is available where and when needed. Cash-flow needs arise from everyday company activities, such as paying for labor and materials, or paying taxes and interest on debt. To optimize global operations, international financial managers devise strategies for transferring funds among the firm's operations worldwide.

The volume and complexity of intracorporate transfers depends on the number of headquarters, subsidiaries, alliances, and business relationships the firm maintains worldwide. For companies with extensive international operations, the network of funds transfers can be vast. Roughly one-third of world trade results from collective trading activities within individual MNE networks.

Methods for Transferring Funds within the MNE

Financial managers employ various methods for transferring funds within the MNE. Funds must be moved efficiently, minimizing transaction costs and tax liabilities while maximizing returns the funds can earn. Exhibit 20.5 depicts a typical company with subsidiaries in Mexico and Taiwan. Within its network, this firm can transfer funds through trade credit, dividend remittances, royalty payments, fronting loans, transfer pricing, and multilateral netting. Here is how each works:

- Through *trade credit*, a subsidiary can defer payment for goods and services received from the parent firm. The 30-day credit is the U.S. norm, while 90-day credit is typical in Europe, with longer terms elsewhere.
- *Dividend remittances* are common for transferring funds from foreign subsidiaries to the parent but vary depending on tax levels and currency risks. Some host governments levy high taxes on dividend payments or limit how much MNEs can remit.
- *Royalty payments* are compensation paid to owners of intellectual property. Assuming the subsidiary has licensed technology, trademarks, or other assets from the parent or other subsidiaries, royalties can be an efficient way to transfer funds and are tax deductible in many countries. A parent MNE can collect royalties from its own subsidiaries as a way of generating funds.
- In a **fronting loan**, the parent deposits a large sum in a foreign bank, which transfers it to a subsidiary as a loan. Fronting allows the parent to circumvent restrictions that foreign governments impose on direct intracorporate loans. If the loan is made through a bank in a **tax haven**—a country hospitable to business and inward investment because of its low corporate income taxes—the parent can minimize taxes that might be due if the loan were made directly. While some countries restrict the amount of funds MNEs can transfer abroad, such restrictions usually do not apply to repayment of bank loans.

Fronting loan
A loan between the parent and its subsidiary, channeled through a large bank or other financial intermediary.

Tax haven
A country hospitable to business and inward investment because of its low corporate income taxes.

EXHIBIT 20.5

Typical Methods for Transferring Funds within the MNE

- *Transfer pricing* (also known as *intracorporate pricing*) is the means by which subsidiaries and affiliates charge each other as they exchange goods and services. Recall from Chapter 18 that firms can use transfer pricing to shift profits from high-tax to low-tax countries, optimizing internal cash flows.[13]

Multilateral Netting

In the past, cash was frequently held in each foreign subsidiary responsible for funding its own short-term needs. Today, MNE managers use a method known as *pooling* to bring surplus funds together in a regional or global *centralized depository*. They then direct these funds to needy subsidiaries or invest them to generate income.

A centralized depository lets managers reduce the size of highly liquid accounts and invest the funds, generally at the higher interest rates offered for large deposits, to generate maximal returns. If the depository is in a financial center (such as London, New York, or Sydney), management can also access various short-term investments that pay higher rates of return. Such depositories tend to centralize expertise and financial services, providing subsidiaries with more benefits at lower cost.

Large MNEs conduct numerous international transactions, each of which generates transaction costs. Suppose a firm's Japanese subsidiary owes the Spanish subsidiary $8 million and the Spanish subsidiary owes the Japanese subsidiary $5 million. While the firm could cancel these debts in separate transactions, a more intelligent solution that reduces transaction costs has the Japanese subsidiary pay the Spanish subsidiary $3 million. Transferring an amount considerably lower than either of the two original amounts greatly reduces transactions costs such as fees and delays in funds transfers.

Multilateral netting
Strategic reduction of cash transfers within the MNE family through the elimination of offsetting cash flows.

At a more sophisticated level, **multilateral netting** is the strategic reduction of cash transfers within the MNE family through the elimination of offsetting cash flows involving three or more subsidiaries that hold accounts payable or accounts receivable with another subsidiary. MNEs with numerous subsidiaries usually establish a netting center, a central exchange, that headquarters supervises. Philips, a leading Dutch consumer electronics firm (www.philips.com), has operating units in some sixty countries and a netting center to which subsidiaries regularly report all intracorporate balances on the same date. The center then advises each subsidiary of the amounts to pay and receive from other subsidiaries on a specified date, helping save Philips considerable money.

Ethical Connections

An imbalance between revenues and spending has pushed numerous national governments deep into debt. In Greece, Italy, Japan, and the United States, federal government debt now exceeds 100 percent of each nation's GDP. High government debt tends to reduce the amount of funds available for firms to invest in innovation and other key activities. In this way, government indebtedness can hurt economic growth, which reduces a country's attractiveness for investment from abroad. As less money flows into the country, its economy suffers further.

 Task Four: Perform Capital Budgeting

How do companies decide whether to launch a major exporting effort, acquire a distribution center, build a new factory, or refurbish industrial equipment? Firms have limited resources and cannot afford to invest in every project opportunity. The purpose of *capital budgeting* is to help managers decide which international projects provide the best financial return.

The decision depends on the project's initial investment requirement, its cost of capital, and the incremental cash flow or other advantages it can provide. Many variables affect the potential profitability of a venture. Investors in the fast-food industry consider the cost of alternate locations and the level of local competition, as well as the distance to highways, availability of public transportation, and amount of traffic at each location.[14]

Net Present Value Analysis of Capital Investment Projects

Managers typically perform net present value (NPV) analysis to evaluate domestic and international capital investment projects. NPV is the difference between the present value of a project's incremental cash flows and its initial investment requirement.[15]

Managers employing NPV address these in two ways. One is to estimate the incremental after-tax operating cash flows in the subsidiary's local currency and then discount them at the project's cost of capital, or required rate of return, appropriate for its risk characteristics. If the NPV is positive, the project is expected to earn its required return and add value to the subsidiary. This approach takes the *project's perspective* in capital budgeting, and managers can use it as a first screening method.[16]

The second approach, called the *parent's perspective*, estimates future cash flows from the project in the *functional currency* of the parent—that is, the currency of the primary economic environment in which it operates. Thus, U.S.-based firms' functional currency is the U.S. dollar; for Japan-based firms it is the yen. This conversion forecasts *spot exchange rates*, or forward rates, and calculates their present value using a discount rate in line with the required return on projects of similar risk. Managers then compute the NPV in the parent's functional currency by subtracting the initial investment cash flow from the present value of the project cash flows. To be acceptable, the project must add value to the parent company; thus, it must have positive NPV from the parent's perspective.

Source: Blacky/Fotolia

The Rheinauhafen district in Cologne, Germany houses German subsidiaries of numerous multinational firms, including Microsoft and Electronic Arts. Managers use capital budgeting to determine which foreign locations are best for establishing operations.

Estimating project cash flows is complex and requires forecasting a range of variables that contribute to anticipated revenues and costs over several years. The largest component of revenue is usually sales. Initial and ongoing costs typically include R&D, development of essential project resources, labor, factor inputs, and marketing.

Capital budgeting in the MNE is complicated by four factors:

1. Project cash flows are usually in a currency other than the reporting currency of the parent firm.
2. Tax rules in the project location and the parent's country usually differ.
3. Governments may restrict the transfer of funds from the project to the parent firm.
4. The project may be exposed to country risk, such as government intervention or adverse economic conditions.

 ## Task Five: Manage Currency Risk

Shifting currency values are among the biggest day-to-day challenges facing international firms, like Markel in the chapter opening story. Foreign direct investors face currency risk because they receive payments and incur obligations in foreign currencies. Managers of foreign investment portfolios also face currency risk. A Japanese stock might gain 15 percent in value, but if the yen falls 15 percent, the stock gain is zero.[17]

Currency crises affect other local asset prices, including debt, equipment, and real estate markets. Firms face currency risk when their cash flows and the value of their assets and liabilities change due to unexpected changes in foreign-exchange rates. Exporters and licensors face currency risk—from unexpected fluctuations in exchange rates—because foreign buyers typically pay in their own currency. If the firm could quote its prices and get paid in its home-country currency, it could eliminate its currency risk, but the risk would still exist for its foreign customers. To accommodate foreign buyers, companies frequently quote their prices in the buyer's currency. In international transactions, either the buyer or the seller incurs currency risk.

Three Types of Currency Exposure

Currency fluctuations result in three types of exposure for the firm: transaction exposure, translation exposure, and economic exposure.[18]

Transaction exposure is currency risk that firms face when outstanding accounts receivable or payable are denominated in foreign currencies. Suppose Gateway (www.gateway.com) imports 3 million Taiwan dollars' worth of computer keyboards and pays in the foreign currency. At the time of the purchase, suppose the exchange rate was US$1 = T$30, but Gateway pays on credit terms three months after the purchase. If during the three-month period the exchange rate shifts to US$1 = T$27, Gateway will have to pay an extra US$11,111 as a result of the rate change ([3,000,000/27] − [3,000,000/30]). From Gateway's standpoint, the Taiwan dollar has become more expensive. Such gains or losses are real. They affect the firm's value directly by affecting its cash flows and profit.

Translation exposure results when an MNE translates financial statements denominated in a foreign currency into the functional currency of the parent firm, as part of *consolidating* international financial results. **Consolidation** is the process of combining and integrating the financial results of foreign subsidiaries into the parent firm's financial records. Accounting practices usually require the firm to report consolidated financial results in the functional currency.

Translation exposure occurs because, as exchange rates fluctuate, so do the functional-currency values of exposed assets, liabilities, expenses, and revenues. Translating quarterly or annual foreign financial statements into the parent's functional currency results in gains or losses on the date financial statements are consolidated. When translated into dollars, the quarterly net income of the Japanese subsidiary of a U.S. MNE may drop if the Japanese yen depreciates against the dollar during the quarter. Note that gains or losses in translation exposure are "paper" or "virtual" changes and do not affect cash flows directly. This contrasts with transaction exposure, in which gains and losses are real.

Economic exposure (also known as *operating exposure*) results from exchange-rate fluctuations that affect the pricing of products and inputs, and the value of foreign investments. Exchange-rate fluctuations help or hurt sales by making the firm's products relatively more or less expensive for foreign buyers. If the yen appreciates against the euro, a European firm can expect to sell more goods in Japan because the Japanese have more buying power for buying euros. But if the yen weakens against the euro, the European firm's sales will likely drop in Japan unless management lowers its Japanese prices by an amount equivalent to the fall in the yen. Similarly, the firm may be harmed by currency shifts that raise the price of inputs sourced from abroad. The value of foreign investments can also fall, in home currency terms, with exchange-rate changes.

While transaction exposure is a factor in ongoing contractual transactions, economic exposure affects long-term profitability through changes in revenues and expenses and thus appears in the firm's financial statements. For example, weakening of the U.S. dollar against the euro gradually reduces the value of U.S. investments in Europe, increases the cost of Euro-denominated input goods, but improves the prospects for U.S. firms to sell their dollar-denominated products in the EU.

The three types of currency exposure can produce positive results when exchange rates fluctuate favorably for the firm. Managers are more concerned with fluctuations that harm the firm. Such problems help explain why many countries in Europe use a single currency, the euro. With a single medium of exchange, currency risk is eliminated in trade among the countries using the euro. For international firms operating outside the euro zone, however, currency risk is still a significant problem.

Foreign-Exchange Trading

A relatively limited number of currencies facilitate cross-border trade and investment. Around 62 percent of allocated foreign reserves are in U.S. dollars, 25 percent in euros, 4 percent in British pounds, 4 percent in Japanese yen, and 5 percent in the world's remaining national currencies.[19] The volume of currencies exchanged is huge. The daily volume of global trading in foreign exchange amounts to more than $4 trillion.[20] To put this in perspective, that is more than 100 times the daily value of global trade in products and services.

Information technology is critical to currency trading. For example, the Swiss investment bank UBS (www.ubs.com) offers a range of currency-related products. Customers transact nearly all their spot, forward, and currency-swap trades online using UBS's computer platforms in dozens of countries.[21] Citibank (www.citibank.com) leverages its comprehensive customer portal, CitiFX Interactive, to provide clients a wide range of services, including library research, currency trading, and analytical tools.[22]

Transaction exposure
The currency risk that firms face when outstanding accounts receivable or payable are denominated in foreign currencies.

Translation exposure
The currency risk that results when a firm translates financial statements denominated in a foreign currency into the functional currency of the parent firm, as part of consolidating international financial results.

Consolidation
The process of combining and integrating the financial results of foreign subsidiaries into the financial statements of the parent firm.

Economic exposure
The currency risk that results from exchange-rate fluctuations affecting the pricing of products, the cost of inputs, and the value of foreign investments.

Spot rate
The exchange rate applied when the current exchange rate is used for immediate receipt of a currency.

Large banks are the primary dealers in the currency markets. They quote the prices at which they will buy or sell currencies. If an importer wants to buy $100,000 in euros to finance a purchase from Austria, the currency exchange will typically be handled through the importer's bank. Large banks such as Citibank maintain reserves of major currencies and work with foreign *correspondent banks* to facilitate currency buying and selling. Currency transactions between banks occur in the *interbank market*.

Currency also can be bought and sold through brokers that specialize in matching up buyers and sellers. They are especially active in major financial centers such as London, New York, and Sydney. Trading can also be done through online brokers and dealers at sites like www.forex.com and www.everbank.com.

The foreign-exchange market uses specialized terminology to describe the functions that currency dealers perform. The **spot rate** is the exchange rate applied when the current exchange rate is used for immediate receipt of a currency. The rate applies to transactions between banks for delivery within two business days, or for immediate delivery for over-the-counter transactions involving nonbank customers—for example, when you buy currencies at airport kiosks.

The **forward rate** is the exchange rate applicable to the collection or delivery of foreign currencies at some future date. Dealers in the forward exchange market promise to receive or deliver foreign exchange at a specified time in the future, but at a rate determined at the time of the transaction. The primary function of the forward market is to provide protection against currency risk.

Dealers quote currency exchange rates in two ways. The **direct quote**, also known as the *normal quote*, is the number of units of domestic currency needed to acquire one unit of foreign currency. For example, on May 10, 2012, it cost $1.30 to acquire one euro (abbreviated as "€"). The **indirect quote** is the number of units of foreign currency obtained for one unit of domestic currency. For example, on May 10, 2012, it cost €0.77 to acquire $1.00. Please review the book's Appendix to learn more about currency trading.

You may have observed at airports that when foreign-exchange dealers quote prices, they always quote a *bid* (buy) rate and an *offer* (sell) rate at which they will buy or sell any particular currency. The difference between the bid and offer rates—*the spread*—is the margin on which the dealer earns a profit.

Source: Arto/Fotolia

Multinational firms must skillfully manage multiple-currency transactions and the risk associated with exchange rate fluctuations.

Forward rate
The exchange rate applicable to the collection or delivery of a foreign currency at some future date.

Direct quote
The number of units of domestic currency needed to acquire one unit of foreign currency; also known as the normal quote.

Indirect quote
The number of units of foreign currency obtained for one unit of domestic currency.

Hedgers
Currency traders who seek to minimize their risk of exchange-rate fluctuations, often by entering into forward contracts or similar financial instruments.

Speculators
Currency traders who seek profits by investing in currencies with the expectation their value will change in the future.

Country Realities

China is rapidly becoming the world's largest economy and a center of global banking. The country's big trade surplus and foreign investment inflows together have created massive reserves of foreign exchange. Now home to several of the world's largest banks, the Chinese government is positioning Shanghai as a global financial hub.

Types of Currency Traders

Hedgers, speculators, and arbitragers represent the three main types of currency traders. **Hedgers**, typically MNEs and other international trade or investment firms, seek to minimize their risk of exchange-rate fluctuations, often by entering into forward contracts or similar financial instruments. They are not necessarily interested in profiting from currency trading.

Speculators are currency traders who seek profits by investing in currencies with the expectation their value will rise in the future and then sell them later at the higher value. A speculator might purchase a certificate of deposit denominated in Mexican pesos or a money market account tied to the Chinese yuan, believing the value of these currencies will rise. The speculator can also bet on a currency's downturn by taking a *short position* in that currency. When investors take a short position, they sell a currency that they previously borrowed from a third party (usually a broker) with the intention of buying the identical currency back at a later date to return to the lender. In so doing, the short seller hopes to profit from a decline in the value of the currency between the sale and the repurchase, as the seller will pay less to buy the currency than the seller received on selling it. Exhibit 20.6 shows an example speculation in the foreign-exchange market through a forward contract.

EXHIBIT 20.6

An Example of Speculation in the Foreign-Exchange Market

Scenario: A speculator is offered a forward contract by a bank to be able to sell the bank €1 in exchange for $1.45 one year from now. Suppose that the speculator expects the spot exchange rate to be €1 = $1.40 a year from now. The speculator may try to profit from the difference between the expected spot exchange rate and the quoted forward exchange rate by entering into a forward contract with the offering bank. In this case, the speculator is taking a risk by attempting to make a profit based on an uncertain future spot exchange rate.

Outcome: If the spot exchange rate is actually €1 = $1.40 a year from now, the speculator earns a profit of $0.05. However, if the spot exchange rate turns out to be €1 = $1.50, the speculator will lose $0.05 as a result of having to sell the bank, through the forward contract, €1 for $1.45 instead of its actual spot value of $1.50.

Arbitragers

Currency traders who buy and sell the same currency in two or more foreign-exchange markets to profit from differences in the currency's exchange rate.

Arbitragers are currency traders who buy and sell the same currency in two or more foreign-exchange markets to profit from differences in the currency's exchange rate. But unlike the speculator who bets on the future price of a currency, the arbitrager attempts to profit from a current disequilibrium in currency markets based on known prices. If the euro-dollar exchange rate quoted in New York on Monday morning is €1 = $1.25, but the quoted exchange rate in London at that moment is €1 = $1.30, a trader could buy €1 million for $1.25 million in New York and simultaneously sell those euros in London for $1.3 million, yielding a riskless profit of $50,000 before commission and expenses. But don't get too excited! When such arbitrage opportunities exist, they quickly disappear because the very actions of the arbitragers force the exchange rates to adjust to the equilibrium level.

Exchange-Rate Forecasting

Losses due to exchange-rate risk are common in international business. European automakers such as Daimler, BMW, and Volkswagen have lost billions of dollars of sales to the United States, due to the euro's strong value relative to the dollar. Daimler reduced exports to the United States because the strong euro hurt U.S. sales. The euro-dollar exchange rate has forced European automakers to sell many models at higher dollar prices, which reduces their attractiveness to U.S. consumers. Analysts calculate the euro must trade at less than $1.50 to achieve profitable sales in the United States.[23]

Financial managers monitor currency trading daily, paying particular attention to the potential for momentum trading or herding behavior. *Momentum trading* is accomplished via computers programmed to conduct massive buying or selling when prices reach certain levels. *Herding* is the tendency of investors to mimic each others' actions. In 2012, companies withdraw approximately $80 billion from investments in Russia, due to concerns about political risk, economic woes, and corruption. As foreign investors liquidated holdings from the stock exchange and other markets in Russia, billions of dollars worth of Russian roubles were converted to foreign currencies, prompting depreciation of the rouble.[24] In most countries, exchange rates respond immediately to economic information, such as the election of a new government, labor disputes, and major supply shocks (for example, when oil-exporting countries suddenly announce a drop in supply). In addition to forecasting such events, managers must assess the likely actions of foreign-exchange traders.

Firms with extensive international operations develop sophisticated capabilities to forecast exchange rates that combine in-house forecasting with reports provided by major banks and professional forecasters. *Technical analysis* looks at recent movements in exchange rates and *fundamental analysis* studies involving macroeconomic data.

SMEs usually lack the resources to do substantial in-house forecasting and rely on forecasts provided by banks and from business news sources. A table in each issue of the *Economist* magazine describes recent exchange-rate trends. Other useful information sources include the Bank for International Settlements (www.bis.org), the World Bank (www.worldbank.org), and the European Central Bank (www.ecb.int).

Managing Exposure to Currency Risk Through Hedging

Suppose you want to buy a Toyota and the local car dealer insists you pay in Japanese yen. You probably wouldn't buy the car, partly because you'd need to acquire yen and partly because other dealers let you pay in your own currency. Customers around the world prefer to deal in their own currency. If firms insist on quoting prices and getting paid in their own currency, the burden is on foreign buyers to monitor and manage foreign exchange. Even small exporters learn to operate in foreign currencies to remain competitive. In so doing, they also learn to minimize their exposure to currency risk.

The most common method for managing exposure is **hedging**, using financial instruments and other measures to lock in guaranteed foreign-exchange positions. If the hedge is perfect, the firm is protected against the risk of adverse changes in the price of a currency. Banks offer forward contracts, options, and swap agreements to facilitate hedging and charge fees and interest payments on amounts borrowed to carry out the transactions. The firm must balance these costs against expected benefits.

In *passive hedging*, each exposure is hedged as it occurs and the hedge stays in place until maturity. In *active hedging*, the firm frequently reviews total exposure and hedges only a subset of its total exposures, usually those that pose the greatest risk. Hedges may be withdrawn before they reach maturity. Some active hedgers seek to profit from hedging, even maintaining active in-house trading desks. However, most firms are conservative and simply try to cover all exposures—or their most important ones—and leave hedges in place until maturity.

Hedging
Using financial instruments and other measures to reduce or eliminate exposure to currency risk by locking in guaranteed foreign-exchange positions.

Hedging Instruments

Having assessed its level of currency risk exposure, the firm attempts to balance exposed assets and exposed liabilities. The four most common hedging instruments are forward contracts, futures contracts, currency options, and currency swaps.

A **forward contract** is an agreement to exchange two currencies at a specified exchange rate on a set future date. No money changes hands until the delivery date of the contract. Banks quote forward prices in the same way as spot prices—with bid and ask prices at which they will buy or sell currencies. The bank's bid-ask spread is a cost for its customers.

Forward contracts are especially appropriate for hedging transaction exposure. Suppose Dow Chemical (www.dow.com) sells merchandise to a German importer for €100,000, payable in 90 days. During the 90 days, Dow has a transaction exposure to currency risk: It will receive fewer dollars if the euro depreciates during that time. To hedge against this risk, Dow executes a forward contract with a bank to sell €100,000 in 90 days at an exchange rate agreed upon today, ensuring it receives a known dollar amount in the future. Exhibit 20.7 illustrates the cash flows of Dow Chemical's forward market hedge.

Like a forward contract, a **futures contract** represents an agreement to buy or sell a currency in exchange for another at a specified price on a specified date. Unlike forward contracts, futures contracts are standardized to enable trading in organized exchanges, such as the Chicago Mercantile Exchange. While the terms of forward contracts are negotiated between a bank and its customer, futures contracts have standardized maturity periods and amounts. Futures contracts are especially useful for hedging transaction exposure.

A **currency option** differs from forward and futures contracts in that it gives the purchaser the right, but not the obligation, to buy a certain amount of foreign currency at a set exchange rate within a specified amount of time. The seller of the option must sell the currency at the buyer's discretion, at the price originally set. Currency options typically are traded on organized exchanges, such as the London Stock Exchange (www.londonstockexchange.com) and the Philadelphia Stock Exchange (PHLX; www.nasdaqtrader.com), and only for the major currencies.[25]

Forward contract
A contract to exchange two currencies at a specified exchange rate on a set future date.

Futures contract
An agreement to buy or sell a currency in exchange for another at a specified price on a specified date.

Currency option
A contract that gives the purchaser the right, but not the obligation, to buy a certain amount of foreign currency at a set exchange rate within a specified amount of time.

EXHIBIT 20.7

An Example of Hedging in the Foreign-Exchange Market

Scenario: Dow Chemical sells merchandise to a German importer for €100,000, payable in 90 days. Given that the U.S. dollar - euro spot exchange rate 90 days from now is not known today, Dow faces uncertainty regarding how much it will be receiving from its German customer in U.S. dollar terms. To hedge against this risk, Dow enters into a forward contract with a bank to sell €100,000 90 days from now at an exchange rate of €1 = $1.45 agreed upon today, ensuring that it receives a known dollar amount in future.

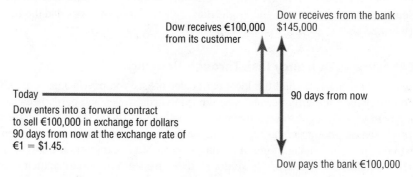

Dow receives €100,000 from its customer

Dow receives from the bank $145,000

Today

90 days from now

Dow enters into a forward contract to sell €100,000 in exchange for dollars 90 days from now at the exchange rate of €1 = $1.45.

Dow pays the bank €100,000

Outcome: Today, Dow is able to see that the €100,000 it will be receiving from its European customer will be worth $145,000 regardless of how much the actual spot price of the euro is 90 days from now.

There are two types of options. A *call option* is the right, but not the obligation, to buy a currency at a specified price within a specific period (called an *American option*) or on a specific date (called a *European option*).[26] A *put option* is the right to sell the currency at a specified price. Each option is for a specific amount of currency. On a recent date, Australian dollar option contracts were offered with a contract size of 50,000 Australian dollars on the NASDAQ OMX PHLX. Options are useful as an insurance policy or disaster hedge against adverse currency movements.

Currency swap

An agreement to exchange one currency for another, according to a specified schedule.

In a **currency swap**, two parties agree to exchange a given amount of one currency for another and, after a specified period of time, give back the original amounts. Thus, a swap is a simultaneous spot and forward transaction. When the agreement is activated, the parties exchange principals at the current spot rate. Usually each party must pay interest on the principal as well. If Party A loaned dollars and borrowed euros, it pays interest in euros and receives interest in dollars. Consider the following example: An MNE agrees to pay 4 percent compounded annually on a euro principal of €1,000,000 and receive 5 percent compounded annually on a U.S. dollar principal of $1,300,000 every year for two years. As a result, it will receive €1,000,000 and pay $1,300,000 today. It will then pay €40,000 annual interest and receive $65,000 annual interest for 2 years. At the end of the second year, the MNE will receive $1,300,000 and pay €1,000,000.

Best Practice in Minimizing Currency Exposure

Managing currency risk across many countries is challenging because management must keep abreast of the firm's evolving exposures, as well as shifting laws, regulations, and market conditions. Managers need to pursue a systematic approach to minimize currency risk.

Exhibit 20.8 presents guidelines that managers can use to minimize currency risk. The last recommendation, maintaining strategic flexibility in manufacturing and sourcing, is an ultimate solution. If the firm operates in numerous markets, each with varying degrees of currency, economic, and political stability, it will be well positioned to optimize its operations. For example, Dell outsources parts and components from various countries and can quickly shift sourcing from one country or supplier to another, depending on the favorability of exchange rates and other factors.

 ## Task Six: Manage the Diversity of International Accounting and Tax Practices

Accounting systems differ around the world, with dozens of approaches for determining company profits, R&D expenditures, and cost of goods sold.[27] Balance sheets and income statements vary internationally, not just in language, currency, and format, but also in their underlying

EXHIBIT 20.8 Managerial Guidelines for Minimizing Currency Risk

1. **Seek expert advice.** Initially, management should obtain expert help from banks and consultants to establish programs and strategies that minimize risk.

2. **Centralize currency management within the MNE.** While some currency management activities may be delegated to local managers, company headquarters should set basic guidelines for the subsidiaries to follow.

3. **Decide on the level of risk the firm can tolerate.** The level varies depending on the nature of the project, amount of capital at risk, and management's tolerance for risk.

4. **Devise a system to measure exchange-rate movements and currency risk.** The system should provide ongoing feedback to help management develop appropriate risk-minimizing strategies.

5. **Monitor changes in key currencies.** Exchange rates fluctuate constantly. Continuous monitoring can avert costly mistakes.

6. **Be wary of unstable currencies or those subject to exchange controls.** The manager should deal in stable, readily convertible currencies. Be wary of government restrictions that affect the ability to exchange currencies.

7. **Monitor long-term economic and regulatory trends.** Exchange-rate shifts usually follow evolving trends such as rising interest rates, inflation, labor unrest, and the coming to power of new governments.

8. **Distinguish economic exposure from transaction and translation exposures.** Managers often focus on reducing transaction and translation exposures. However, the long-run effects of economic exposure on company performance can produce even greater harm.

9. **Emphasize flexibility in international operations.** A flexible production and outsourcing strategy means the firm can shift production and outsourcing to various nations, to benefit from favorable exchange rates.

Transparency
The degree to which companies regularly reveal substantial information about their financial condition and accounting practices.

accounting principles. Financial statements prepared according to the rules of one country may be difficult to compare with those of another.

Transparency in Financial Reporting

Local accounting practices determine the degree of transparency in the reporting of financial information. **Transparency** is the degree to which companies regularly reveal substantial information about their financial condition and accounting practices. The more transparent a nation's accounting systems, the more regularly, comprehensively, and reliably the nation's public firms report their financial results to creditors, stockholders, and the government. Transparency facilitates better managerial decision making and lets investors accurately evaluate company performance. Chile, Costa Rica, and the Czech Republic have attracted greater FDI by increasing the transparency of their regulatory systems. By contrast, most developing economies are characterized by confusing accounting systems, delayed financial reporting, and published information that is unreliable or incomplete.

Transparency is an issue even in the advanced economies. The Sarbanes-Oxley Act of 2002 was enacted to improve U.S. accounting standards. It emerged in the wake of accounting scams at large corporations

Source: ImageState/Alamy

Transparency is the degree to which companies regularly reveal information about their financial condition and accounting practices. Pictured here is the stock exchange in Santiago, Chile, one of several countries attracting more inward investment by improving transparency in their business sectors.

like Enron and WorldCom. Sarbanes-Oxley makes corporate CEOs and CFOs personally responsible for the accuracy of annual reports and other financial data. Foreign affiliates of U.S. firms and foreign firms with significant U.S. operations are also required to comply with the act's provisions. A major challenge, however, is the cost of compliance.

Following the recent global financial crisis, governments and central banks in Asia, Europe, and the Americas increased the transparency and strictness of accounting standards and strengthened their supervision of banks and other financial institutions.[28]

Trends Toward Harmonization

The growth of international business has pressured multinational firms and international organizations such as the International Accounting Standards Board (IASB), the United Nations, the European Union, and the Asociación Interamericana de Contabilidad (Interamerican Association of Accounting) to harmonize world accounting systems, particularly regarding measurement, disclosure, and auditing standards. The IASB is attempting to develop a single set of high-quality, understandable, and enforceable global accounting standards that emphasize transparent and comparable information.

The IASB favors harmonization for several reasons:

- Enhances the reliability of financial reporting by increasing comparability and transparency of accounting practices.
- Helps reduce the cost of preparing financial statements.
- Increases the efficiency of consolidating financial information from various countries.
- Reduces risk for investors and help managers make better decisions by facilitating investment analysis.

Harmonization is particularly important to MNEs that seek foreign investors by listing on foreign stock exchanges. More than 120 countries require or allow the use of International Financial Reporting Standards (IFRS; www.ifrs.com) in public company accounting. In the United States, firms comply with Generally Accepted Accounting Practices (GAAP). However, many large U.S. firms, such as Procter & Gamble, use IFRS standards in their foreign subsidiaries. Europe's IASB and the U.S. Financial Accounting Standards Board have worked to harmonize GAAP and IFRS. However, the effort has been delayed in light of practical and political considerations in Europe and the United States.[29]

Consolidating the Financial Statements of Subsidiaries

A critical task in international accounting is *foreign currency translation*, or translating data denominated in foreign currencies into the firm's functional currency. Each of the firm's subsidiaries abroad normally maintains its financial records in the currency of the country where it is located. When subsidiary results are consolidated into headquarters' financial statements, they must be expressed in the parent's functional currency. Consolidation also facilitates headquarters' efforts to plan, evaluate, and control the firm's activities around the world.

When headquarters consolidates financial records, foreign currencies are translated into the functional currency using one of two methods: the **current rate method** or the temporal method. The current rate method translates foreign currency balance sheets and income statements at the current exchange rate—the spot exchange rate in effect on the day (in the case of balance sheets) or for the period (in the case of income statements) the statements are prepared. This method is typically used when translating records of foreign subsidiaries that are considered separate entities, rather than part of the parent firm's operations. Consider Computershare, an Australian firm that markets financial software through its network of subsidiaries worldwide. The company translates the financial statements of its subsidiaries using the current rate method because these subsidiaries are stand-alone legal entities. Amounts payable and receivable in foreign currencies are converted to Australian dollars at the exchange rate in effect on the day of consolidation.[30]

The current rate results in gains and losses, depending on the exchange rates in effect during the translation period. For example, the value of income received in a foreign currency six months earlier may differ substantially from its value on the day it is translated. For firms with extensive international operations, the accounting translation method can strongly influence company performance and valuation.

In the **temporal method**, the choice of exchange rate depends on the underlying method of valuation. If assets and liabilities are normally valued at historical cost, then they are translated at the historical rates—that is, the rates in effect when the assets were acquired. If assets and liabilities are normally valued at market cost, they are translated at the current rate of exchange. Thus, monetary items such as cash, receivables, and payables are translated at the current

Current rate method
Translation of foreign currency balance sheet and income statements at the current exchange rate—the spot exchange rate in effect on the day or for the period when the statements are prepared.

Temporal method
Translation of foreign currency balance sheet and income statements at an exchange rate that varies with the underlying method of valuation.

exchange rate. Nonmonetary items such as inventory and property, plant, and equipment are translated at historical rates.

According to U.S. accounting standards, if the functional currency of the subsidiary is that of the local operating environment (for example, if the yen is the main currency used by the Japanese subsidiary of a U.S. multinational firm), the company must use the current rate method. If the functional currency is the parent's currency, the MNE must use the temporal method. The choice of method can give rise to different profitability and other performance outcomes, and firms must adhere to accepted accounting practices and laws.

International Taxation

In the countries where they operate, companies pay direct taxes, indirect taxes, sales taxes, and value-added taxes, among others. *Direct taxes* are typically imposed on income from profits, capital gains, intracorporate transactions, royalties, interest, and dividends. *Indirect taxes* apply to firms that license or franchise products and services or that charge interest. In effect, the local government withholds some percentage of royalty payments or interest charges as tax. A *sales tax* is a flat percentage tax on the value of goods or services sold, paid by the ultimate user. A *value-added tax* (VAT) is payable at each stage of processing in the value chain of a product or service. VAT is calculated as a percentage of the difference between the sale and purchase price of a product and is common in Canada, Europe, and Latin America. Each business in a product's value chain is required to bill the VAT to its customers and pay the tax on its purchases, crediting the amounts it paid against the amounts due on its own activities. The net result is a tax on the added value of the good.

The most common form of direct tax is the *corporate income tax*. Exhibit 20.9 provides rates for a sample of countries. Called "corporation tax" in some localities, it affects international planning because it encourages managers to organize business operations in ways that minimize the tax, usually by deducting business expenses from revenues. In most countries, firms reduce their tax burden substantially by taking deductions and allowances provided within national laws. The *effective* rate of taxation for many MNEs is often considerably lower than that indicated in Exhibit 20.9.

Income tax influences the timing, magnitude, and composition of company investment in plant and equipment, R&D, inventories, and other assets. The exhibit reveals that many countries have reduced tax rates because they recognize high taxes can discourage investment.[31] In Russia, the corporate income tax was reduced from 35 percent in 2001 to 20 percent in 2011. In the Netherlands, the rate went from 35 to 25 percent. Ireland has the lowest income tax rate, 12.5 percent—a mainstay of its economic revitalization policy.

Almost since its founding in 1903, the U.S. automaker Ford sold cars in Canada, Japan, and other countries. At one time, whenever Ford sold cars in Canada, it was required to pay direct taxes on its income in both Canada and the United States.[32] Because of a lack of harmony in international tax rules, many MNEs were subject to double taxation, which reduced company earnings and discouraged firms from investing abroad. To resolve the problem, most countries signed tax treaties with their trading partners that help ensure firms pay an appropriate amount of tax. A typical tax treaty between country A and country B states that, if the firm pays income tax in A, it need not pay the tax in B (or vice versa) if the taxes are similar amounts. This result is accomplished with foreign tax credits—an automatic reduction in domestic tax liability when the firm can prove it has already paid income tax abroad. Or the firm may be liable to pay tax in each country, but the amount is prorated so the total is no more than the maximum tax in either country. Most tax treaties also obligate nations to assist each other in tax enforcement, ensuring that MNEs pay taxes in one country or the other to deter tax evasion.

Because tax systems vary around the world, MNEs have an incentive to structure their global activities in ways that minimize taxes. They take advantage of tax havens like the Bahamas, Luxembourg, Singapore, and Switzerland, either by establishing operations in them or by funneling business transactions through them. Nissan and Kraft Foods moved their European headquarters to Switzerland to take advantage of lower corporate tax rates. The Irish rock band U2 moved its music-publishing business to the Netherlands to shelter its songwriting royalties from taxation. Apple has subsidiaries in low-tax rate countries such as Ireland, the Netherlands, Luxembourg, and the British Virgin Islands.[33] The use of tax havens for tax reduction is generally legal but is restricted by some governments. The United States has limited firms' ability to

EXHIBIT 20.9

Corporate Income Tax Rates in Selected Countries (as a percent of corporate income, rounded to the nearest whole percent)

Source: Based on KPMG International, "Corporate & Indirect Tax Survey 2011," accessed at http://www.kpmg.com/global.

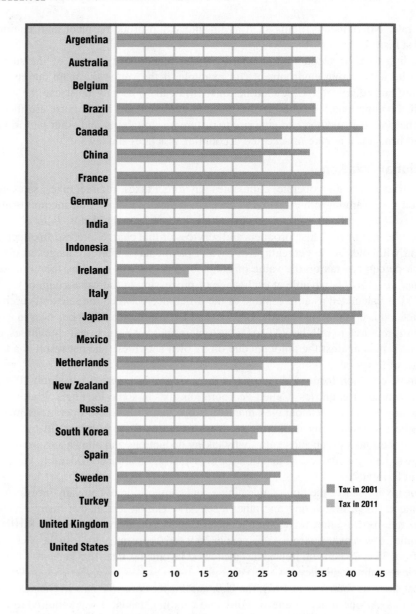

move major operations to such countries.[34] Corporations sometimes use tax havens to "park" revenues until needed elsewhere for trade or investment.

The OECD, World Bank, and other international organizations discourage the wrongful use of tax havens and lobby countries to develop transparent tax systems. The EU and OECD also pressure countries to reduce harmful tax competition. In Europe, foreign investors tend to establish operations in countries with low taxes and avoid countries with high taxes. Because this discourages European unity and economic development, EU governments are seeking to harmonize taxation throughout Europe.

Managing International Finance to Minimize Tax Burden

Taxation affects managerial decisions about the type of entry modes, the legal form of foreign operations, transfer pricing, methods for obtaining capital, and even the choice of target markets. Financial managers seek to legally minimize their tax obligations. In Japan, the government imposes a high tax on malt, a key beer ingredient. Partly to avoid the tax, firms that brew beer in Japan employ a distillation technology that eliminates the need for malt. The end product tastes like beer but is actually a type of liquor. Occasionally, governments may create tax breaks on income earned abroad.

Many techniques described in this chapter for transferring funds within the MNE and managing currency exposure are also useful for legally minimizing the firm's tax burdens.

Minimizing taxes is typically a key goal of transfer pricing strategies, for instance. MNEs also benefit from differences in tax rates and systems between countries. They establish holding companies or finance corporations in particular countries or operate in government-designated low-tax zones (Foreign Trade Zones), structuring production and selling activities to minimize tax obligations.

CLOSING CASE   International Financial Operations at Tektronix

An oscilloscope is a measuring device with a display screen that checks the condition of electronic equipment. In 1946, founders of U.S.-based Tektronix, Inc. (www.tek.com;) built their first oscilloscope from electronic parts purchased from government surplus sales. Its oscilloscopes and other measuring devices contributed immensely to the development of computers and communications equipment.

TEK, as the firm is known, because a public company in 1963. TEK employs several thousand employees in dozens of countries and earns roughly half its annual sales from North America, 25 percent from Europe, 15 percent from Japan, and the rest from other countries. TEK owes part of its original success to venture capital funding. However, the majority of its capital comes from equity financing and debt sources.

International Operations

TEK launched its first foreign distributor in Sweden in 1948. In later years, the firm set up many sales subsidiaries abroad. It developed joint ventures in Japan (Sony-TEK) and China to distribute TEK products in those countries. It also established manufacturing plants in Germany, Italy, and Malaysia. TEK still manufactures most of its products in the United States, while competitors HP, Kodak, and Xerox have manufacturing plants in numerous countries around the world. TEK management prefers to centralize manufacturing to synchronize production with R&D, ensure quality control, and exploit economies of scale.

Because TEK manufactures in the United States and sells abroad, it has substantial foreign-exchange exposure. Most of TEK's foreign sales are invoiced in local country currencies. If the U.S. dollar strengthens against those currencies, TEK's profits are reduced when it converts local country revenues into U.S. dollars. TEK also sources many inputs from abroad, which creates currency risks in its accounts payable.

For financial accounting, many of TEK's non-U.S. subsidiaries use their local country currencies as their functional currency. Thus, assets and liabilities are translated into U.S. dollars at end-of-period exchange rates. Income and expense items are translated at the average rate during the accounting period. To minimize currency risk, management deals proactively with transaction, translation, and economic exposures.

Tax-Related Decisions

While one goal of every MNE is to legally minimize domestic and foreign taxes, in recent years countries such as France and Germany have increased their tax audits of foreign firms' local country subsidiaries. To help address these and other tax challenges, TEK centralized all its European treasury functions, including cash management, inventory, and receivables, to the firm's subsidiary in England. In addition, the firm sets all the pricing for its markets worldwide at company headquarters. Such approaches provide efficiencies in company financial activities, simplify tax preparation, and enhance TEK's ability to use foreign tax credits. The goal is to legally minimize TEK's average tax rate across all its markets, which had been running at 32 percent.

Currency Risk Management

TEK has employed currency hedging selectively. Not all risks can be profitably hedged because of the high cost of banking fees and interest charges. As a result, TEK has experienced foreign-exchange losses in the past. To help minimize these losses, management established a unit at headquarters responsible for assessing and managing currency risk. TEK managers obtain intelligence from online sources and the forecasting departments of large banks and regularly monitor changes in key national currencies. Among the approaches that TEK applies are multilateral netting, offsetting cash flows, a centralized depository, forward contracts, and currency options.

Multilateral Netting

TEK has many ongoing transactions with and among its subsidiaries. Its financial managers can strategically reduce cash transfers, transaction costs, and bank fees by eliminating offsetting cash flows between headquarters and the local country subsidiaries. In TEK's multilateral netting process, all subsidiaries report to headquarters what is owed in foreign currencies to other subsidiaries, customers, suppliers, and headquarters. Financial managers then advise each subsidiary how much to pay to minimize the number and amount of inter-subsidiary cash transfers. Management also matches hedging instruments with the firm's most pressing currency exposures. The launch of the euro greatly simplified international transactions and reduced the need for some netting operations in Europe.

Offsetting Cash Flows

Whenever possible, management consolidates accounts receivable and accounts payable, matching them against one another. If TEK owes a French supplier 800,000 euros, it can grant a trade credit in the amount of 800,000 euros to a German customer, making the receivable and payable offset each other in the same currency. TEK also has some flexibility to change the invoicing currency of its subsidiaries and affiliates—for example, by denominating some invoices from its Japan subsidiary in yen instead of dollars. Cash flows are also offset with counterbalanced investments in Asia and Europe and skillful transfer pricing and other intracorporate financing activities. If headquarters wants to spend $1 million to establish a new subsidiary in Europe, it will direct existing European subsidiaries to retain a similar amount of their earnings in euros. Then, instead of converting the foreign earnings into U.S. dollars, TEK uses the retained euro earnings to build the new subsidiary.

Centralized Depository

While some currency management is delegated to local country managers, headquarters in the United States is in charge and sets guidelines for the subsidiaries to follow. Management pools funds into centralized depositories and directs them to subsidiaries where needed or invests them to generate income. Management also pools accounts receivable for some European subsidiaries into a regional depository, which makes receipt and dispersal of cash more manageable, creates economies of scale in the investment and other uses of excess cash, and reduces the need for local borrowing. The centralized approach also concentrates managerial expertise and financial services at one location. Finally, the firm employs an invoicing center that invoices foreign subsidiaries in the local currency but receives invoices in U.S. dollars.

Forward Contracts and Currency Options

TEK hedges against currency risk by taking positions in forward contracts. These instruments allow financial managers to buy or sell currency at a specific future date at an agreed-upon exchange rate. If there is much uncertainty about the value of a future receivable, management can guarantee a fixed exchange rate and minimize currency risk. The firm also employs currency options, contracts that grant the holder the right to buy or sell currency at a specified exchange rate

during a specified period of time. TEK uses currency futures contracts with maturities of one to three months to mitigate currency risk. At any time, the firm's currency contracts can exceed $100 million. The downside is that TEK must pay substantial trading fees and other costs for its currency hedging activities.

Other Financial Developments

Some years ago, TEK undertook a major restructuring of company operations. The sale of a major division generated proceeds of more than $900 million. Management used the funds partly to pay down the firm's corporate debt. In comparison to its equity holdings, the firm's debt is modest and manageable. Management favors a low debt-to-equity ratio.

While TEK regularly experiences fluctuations in sales and currency values, management has developed substantial expertise to weather difficult challenges. Careful planning and implementation of financial operations will help the firm continue to reign as the leader in oscilloscopes and other measuring equipment.

AACSB: Reflective Thinking Skills, Analytic Skills

Case Questions

1. What are the implications for currency risk of TEK focusing its manufacturing in the United States but generating most of its sales abroad? Competitors like HP and Kodak are more geographically diversified in their sourcing. What advantages does this create for them?

2. The case lists various approaches TEK follows to minimize its exposure to currency risk. If hired by TEK, what other strategies and tactics would you recommend to reduce the firm's exposure even further? Justify your answer.

3. TEK management attempts to maintain a reasonable ratio of debt to equity. Most firms prefer relatively low levels of debt in their capital structures. Why? What other approaches could TEK use to generate financing for its international operations? What approaches can TEK use to transfer funds within its operations worldwide?

4. The case describes approaches TEK follows to minimize its international tax liability. Based on your reading of the chapter, how would you advise TEK management to further reduce its taxes around the world?

Sources: "Tektronix Finds Surprising Results from Net Promoter Scores," *B to B*, June 9, 2008, p. 14; "Danaher to Acquire Tektronix," *Canadian Electronics*, November/December 2007, p. 1; Danaher, Inc., 2011 Annual Report, Washington, DC; Barton Eckert, "Tektronix Part of Strong Danaher Q2," *Portland Business Journal*, July 21, 2011, retrieved from www.bizjournals.com; Joseph Epstein, "Did Rip Van Winkle Really Lift Its Head?" *Financial World*, April 8, 2006, pp. 42–45; Lori Ioannou, "Taxing Issues," *International Business*, March 1995, pp. 42–45; Marshall Lee, *Winning with People: The First 40 Years of Tektronix* (Beaverton, OR: Tektronix, Inc., 1986); Tim McElligott, "This Way Out: Rick Wills, Tektronix," *Telephony*, June 4, 2001, pp. 190–191; Arthur Stonehill, Jerry Davies, Randahl Finnessy, and Michael Moffett, "Tektronix (C)," *Thunderbird International Business Review* 46, no. 4 (July/August 2004): 465–469; Tektronix, Inc., "Tektronix Named Finalist for 'Best in Test' 2010 Awards," press release retrieved from http://www.tek.com; Tektronix corporate profile retrieved from http://www.hoovers.com; Tektronix corporate Web site at www.tek.com.

CHAPTER ESSENTIALS

Key Terms

arbitragers   526
bond   520
consolidation   524
currency option   527
currency swap   528
current rate method   530
debt financing   515
direct quote   525
economic exposure   524
equity financing   515
Eurobond   520
Eurocurrency   519

Eurodollars   519
foreign bond   520
forward contract   527
forward rate   525
fronting loan   521
futures contract   527
global bond market   520
global capital market   516
global equity market   517
global money market   516
hedgers   525
hedging   527

indirect quote   525
intracorporate financing   520
multilateral netting   522
speculators   525
spot rate   525
tax haven   521
temporal method   530
transaction exposure   524
translation exposure   524
transparency   529

Summary

In this chapter, you learned about:

1. **Key tasks in international financial management**

   International financial management involves the acquisition and use of funds for cross-border trade and investment activities. Financial managers decide on the firm's capital structure, raise capital, manage working capital and cash flows, do capital budgeting, manage currency risk, and deal with diverse accounting and tax practices.

2. **Decide on the capital structure**

   The capital structure is the mix of long-term financing—**equity financing** and **debt financing**—that the firm uses to support its international activities. Equity financing is obtained by selling shares in stock markets and by retaining earnings. Debt financing is obtained by borrowing money from banks and other financial institutions or by selling bonds.

3. **Raise funds for the firm**

   Companies can raise money in the **global capital market**. Equity financing can be obtained in the **global equity market**—the stock exchanges throughout the world where investors and firms meet to buy and sell shares of stock. In terms of debt financing, firms may borrow in

the **Eurocurrency** market, which uses currency banked outside its country of origin. Firms also sell bonds—often **foreign bonds** or **Eurobonds**—in the global bond market. In addition, MNEs can support the operations of their subsidiaries through **intracorporate financing**.

4. **Manage working capital and cash flow**

   Net working capital is the difference between current assets and current liabilities. Firms often manage intracorporate funds by developing a *centralized depository*, into which funds are pooled from the firm's network of subsidiaries and affiliates to distribute to units that need funds. The various methods for transferring funds within the MNE include *dividend remittances, royalty payments, transfer pricing*, and *fronting loans*. A **fronting loan** is a loan from a parent firm to its subsidiary, channeled through a bank or other financial intermediary. **Multilateral netting** is the process of strategically reducing the number of cash transfers between the parent and subsidiaries by eliminating the offsetting cash flows between these entities.

5. **Perform capital budgeting**

   Capital budgeting rests on analyses that management undertakes to evaluate the viability of proposed international projects. Management calculates the *net present value* of a proposed project to decide whether it should be implemented.

6. Manage currency risk

There are three main types of currency exposure: transaction exposure, economic exposure, and translation exposure. A firm faces **transaction exposure** when outstanding accounts receivable or payable are denominated in foreign currencies. **Economic exposure** results from exchange-rate fluctuations affecting the pricing of products, the cost of inputs, and the value of foreign investments. **Translation exposure** arises as the firm combines the financial statements of foreign subsidiaries into the parent's financial statements, a process called **consolidation**. Currency trading takes place between banks and currency brokers, often on behalf of multinational firms. Currency traders include **hedgers, speculators**, and **arbitragers**. Managers attempt to forecast exchange rates to minimize their firm's exposure to currency risk. Approaches for minimizing exposure to currency risk include centralizing currency management, measuring currency risk, monitoring long-term trends, and emphasizing flexibility in international operations. Firms also employ **hedging**, the use of specialized financial instruments to balance positions in foreign currencies. Key hedging tools include **forward contracts, futures contracts, currency options**, and **currency swaps**.

7. Manage the diversity of international accounting and tax practices

Financial statements prepared in one country may be difficult to compare with those from other countries. Through **transparency**, firms regularly and comprehensively reveal reliable information about their financial condition and accounting practices. Various factors account for differences in national accounting systems. Several international organizations are aiming to harmonize cross-national accounting practices. Managers use the **current rate method** and the **temporal method** for currency translation. Internationally, firms seek to minimize taxes, which consist of direct taxes, indirect taxes, sales taxes, and value-added taxes. Governments use two major methods for eliminating multiple taxation: the foreign tax credit and tax treaties. **Tax havens** are countries with low taxes that are friendly to business and inward investment.

Test Your Comprehension AACSB: Reflective Thinking Skills

1. What are the components of the capital structure in the typical MNE? What about MNEs in Japan and Germany? What about a typical firm in your country?

⭐ 2. From a managerial perspective, what are the advantages and disadvantages of financing obtained from each of the following: equity, debt, and intracorporate sources?

⭐ 3. Suppose you had to raise capital to fund international value-adding activities and investment projects. From what types of sources (e.g., stock markets) would you most likely obtain each type of financing? What are financial centers and where are they located?

4. What are the major tasks in managing working capital and cash flow for international operations?

5. What are the major steps in capital budgeting? For what types of ventures do international managers typically engage in capital budgeting?

6. What are the types of currency exposure? Why is currency exposure potentially harmful to the firm's international operations? How can managers forecast currency exposure? What steps could you take to minimize currency exposure?

7. Who are the major players in foreign-exchange trading?

8. What are the major methods for translating foreign-currency denominated financial statements into the financial statements of the parent firm?

Apply Your Understanding AACSB: Reflective Thinking Skills, Analytic Skills, Ethical Understanding and Reasoning Abilities

1. Marite Perez is CEO of Havana, Inc., a large manufacturer of high-tech medical equipment based in North Miami Beach, Florida. The firm makes vital signs monitors, MRIs, X-ray machines, and other equipment for exploratory medical diagnostics. Marite wants to rapidly expand the firm into foreign markets. To accomplish this, she plans to invest much money in developing new products and establishing production and marketing subsidiaries abroad. What can Marite do to raise capital for these projects? What are the various methods that Marite might employ to raise capital for her firm? What are the advantages and disadvantages associated with each?

2. Michael Norton is the president of Liberty Enterprises, a large MNE based in Singapore that makes computers

and related peripherals. The firm has many subsidiaries around the world. Demand for Liberty's products has been growing in Asia and Europe, especially in Indonesia, Japan, France, and Spain. Michael has always used external sources to finance the firm's working capital needs. Currently, with rapidly expanding business, he needs to access more working capital. What is the feasibility of raising funds through intracorporate sources? What methods can Michael use to transfer funds within the firm? What should Michael know about multilateral netting?

3. *Ethical Dilemma:* Suppose you are president of West Turner Bank (WTB). WTB made loans for major construction projects in countries in Eastern Europe and North Africa. However, WTB's fortunes declined in recent years and the bank now faces financial ruin. WTB senior management decided to call in loans made to these countries, to shore up the bank's deteriorating finances. That is, management decided to force borrowers in the construction projects to immediately repay their loans. You know that calling the loans will cause thousands of workers in the affected countries to lose their jobs. What should you do? Use the Ethical Framework in Chapter 5 to analyze this situation. Can you find any "creative" solutions to the dilemma?

 INTERNET EXERCISES
(http://www.globalEDGE.msu.edu)

AACSB: Reflective Thinking Skills, Analytic Skills

Refer to Chapter 1, page 24, for instructions on how to access and use globalEDGE™.

1. The World Federation of Exchanges is the organization that represents major stock exchanges worldwide. Visit the online portal at www.world-exchanges.org and use the annual report of the Federation as well as detailed statistics available on individual exchanges to answer the following questions:
   a. What percentage of the world market capitalization is represented by the top 10 exchanges?
   b. For the most recent year, what exchanges accounted for the largest increases in market capitalization?
   c. Which exchanges have seen the greatest increase recently in the number of firms listed?
   d. Worldwide consolidation trends have also affected the stock exchanges. A good example is the merger of Paris-based Euronext with the NYSE. What are the underlying causes of these cross-border mergers?

2. Suppose your job is to ensure your firm has enough foreign exchange on hand to pay outstanding accounts payable. Assume your firm owes 1 million yen to a Japanese supplier, which is due exactly 60 days from now. Your task is to exchange dollars for the right amount of yen. To do this, you can enter a contract with a bank today to buy 1 million yen 60 days forward, or wait 60 days and buy 1 million yen at the then-prevailing spot exchange rate. Which alternative do you prefer, and why? If you expect the spot rate 60 days from now will be the same as it is today, what is the expected dollar cost of buying 1 million yen in the spot market 60 days from now? How many dollars will it cost you to obtain 1 million yen if you entered the forward contract? To obtain the spot exchange rates, go to www.ft.com and click on Markets, then Currencies; or go to globalEDGE™ and enter "exchange rates" in the search engine.

3. Many corporate Web sites provide financial information, including financial statements, as well as other information about companies' status and progress. As an institutional investor, you are thinking of investing in one of the following firms: Diageo (www.diageo.com), the premium drinks firm; Vivendi (www.vivendi.com), a French telecom; Grupo Carso (www.gcarso.com.mx), a major Mexican retailing conglomerate; and SK Telecom (www.sktelecom.com), the largest wireless communication services provider in South Korea. Look up each firm's corporate Web site. Based on the information provided, answer the following questions:
   a. How would you rate the transparency of each firm?
   b. How inclined are you to invest in each firm, based on the information provided? Justify your answer.
   c. In terms of transparency and investor-oriented information, which site is best?
   d. Based on the best site, what recommendations would you make to the firm that owns the weakest site to improve its transparency and attract investors?

MyManagementLab

Go to **mymanagementlab.com** for Auto-graded writing questions as well as the following Assisted-graded writing questions:

20-1. What are the major tasks in international financial management?

20-2. As an international tax consultant to an MNE, what steps would you take to minimize tax obligations around the world?

20-3. Mymanagementlab Only – comprehensive writing assignment for this chapter.

Appendix

The Math of Currency Trading

News outlets such as the *Financial Times* and the *Wall Street Journal*, as well as online sources, publish bilateral exchange-rate tables that list currency values in terms of other currencies. These tables report bid-ask midpoints and so do not represent prices that can actually be traded in the market. Here is an example:

	£	€	¥	$
U.K. pound (£)	1	0.9051	0.006865	0.6329
Euro (€)	1.1049	1	0.007585	0.6993
Japanese yen (¥)	145.68	131.85	1	92.20
U.S. dollar ($)	1.5800	1.4300	0.010846	1

The numeric cells contain the number of units of the currency in the left-most column that equal one unit of the currencies along the top row of the table (e.g., £0.9051/€1). Rather than trying to remember this convention, it is usually easier to infer the convention used in these tables from the values of your domestic currency. In the example above, Japanese and U.S. residents are likely to know that the dollar/yen price of 92.20 reflects a yen-per-dollar exchange rate of ¥92.20/$1, rather than a dollar-per-yen price. This is a direct price for a Japanese resident and an indirect price for a U.S. resident. The yen-per-dollar price is then simply the reciprocal of the dollar-per-yen price:

$$1/(¥92.20/\$) = \$0.010846/¥$$

Note that the values in this table are *internally consistent*. Thus, the yen-per-pound exchange rate must equal the yen-per-dollar rate times the dollar-per-pound rate:

$$¥145.68/£ = (¥92.20/\$) = (\$1.5800/£)$$

Alternatively, the yen-per-pound rate can be calculated by dividing the yen-per-dollar rate by the pound-per-dollar rate:

$$¥145.68/£ = (¥92.20/\$) / (£0.6329/\$)$$

Keeping track of the currency units ensures that the answer has the correct units.

Exchange rates that do not involve the domestic currency are called *cross rates*. Cross rates for infrequently traded currencies can be calculated by comparing them against an actively traded currency such as the dollar. For example, the cross rate between the Chilean Peso (CLP) and Japanese yen can be calculated by combining the CLP-per-dollar rate with the yen-per-dollar rate. If one U.S. dollar is worth 507.75 Chilean pesos, then the CLP-per-yen rate must be:

$$(CLP\ 507.15/\$) / (¥92.20/\$) = CLP\ 5.5005/¥$$

Again, it is important to keep track of the currency units to ensure the desired result.

> Glossary

Absolute advantage principle A country benefits by producing only those products in which it has an absolute advantage or that it can produce using fewer resources than another country.

Acculturation The process of adjusting and adapting to a culture other than one's own.

Acquisition Direct investment to purchase an existing company or facility.

Adaptation Firm's efforts to modify one or more elements of its international marketing program to accommodate specific customer requirements in a particular market.

Advanced economies Post-industrial countries characterized by high per-capita income, highly competitive industries, and well-developed commercial infrastructure.

Agent An intermediary (often an individual or a small firm) that handles orders to buy and sell commodities, products, and services in international business transactions for a commission.

Antidumping duty A tax imposed on products deemed to be dumped and causing injury to producers of competing products in the importing country.

Arbitragers Currency traders who buy and sell the same currency in two or more foreign-exchange markets to profit from differences in the currency's exchange rate.

Area studies Factual knowledge of the historical, political, and economic environment of the host country.

Balance of payments The annual accounting of all economic transactions of a nation with *all* other nations.

Barter A type of countertrade in which goods are directly exchanged without the transfer of any money.

Bond A debt instrument that enables the issuer (borrower) to raise capital by promising to repay the principal along with interest on a specified date (maturity).

Born global firm A young entrepreneurial company that initiates international business activity very early in its evolution, moving rapidly into foreign markets.

Build-operate-transfer (BOT) Arrangement in which the firm or a consortium of firms contracts to build a major facility abroad, operate it for a specified period, and then hand it over to the project sponsor, typically the host-country government or public utility.

Business process outsourcing (BPO) The outsourcing to independent suppliers of business service functions such as accounting, payroll, human resource functions, travel services, IT services, customer service, or technical support.

Buy-back agreement A type of countertrade in which the seller agrees to supply technology or equipment to construct a facility and receives payment in the form of goods produced by the facility.

Capital flight The rapid sell-off by residents or foreigners of their holdings in a nation's currency or other assets, usually in response to a domestic crisis that causes investors to lose confidence in the country's economy.

Captive sourcing Sourcing from the firm's own production facilities.

Central bank The monetary authority in each nation that regulates the money supply and credit, issues currency, and manages the exchange rate of the nation's currency.

Codetermination An industrial relations practice in which labor representatives sit on the corporate board and participate in company decision making.

Collective bargaining Joint negotiations between management and hourly labor and technical staff regarding wages and working conditions.

Commercial risk Firm's potential loss or failure from poorly developed or executed business strategies, tactics, or procedures.

Common market A stage of regional integration in which trade barriers are reduced or removed; common external barriers are established; and products, services, and *factors of production* are allowed to move freely among the member countries.

Company-owned subsidiary A representative office of the focal firm that handles marketing, physical distribution, promotion, and customer service activities in the foreign market.

Company sales potential An estimate of the share of annual industry sales that the firm expects to generate in a particular target market.

Comparative advantage Superior features of a country that provide unique benefits in global competition, typically derived from either natural endowments or deliberate national policies.

Comparative advantage principle It can be beneficial for two countries to trade without barriers as long as one is relatively more efficient at producing goods or services needed by the other. What matters is not the absolute cost of production but rather the relative efficiency with which a country can produce the product.

Compensation deals A type of countertrade in which payment is in both goods and cash.

Competitive advantage Distinctive assets or competencies of a firm that are difficult for competitors to imitate and are typically derived from specific knowledge, capabilities, skills, or superior strategies.

Configuration of value-adding activity The pattern or geographic arrangement of locations where the firm carries out value-chain activities.

Consolidation The process of combining and integrating the financial results of foreign subsidiaries into the financial statements of the parent firm.

Consortium A project-based, nonequity venture initiated by multiple partners to fulfill a large-scale project.

Contagion The tendency of a financial or monetary crisis in one country to spread rapidly to other countries, due to the ongoing integration of national economies.

Contract manufacturing An arrangement in which the focal firm contracts with an independent supplier to manufacture products according to well-defined specifications.

Contractual entry strategies in international business Cross-border exchanges where the relationship between the focal firm and its foreign partner is governed by an explicit contract.

Corporate governance The system of procedures and processes by which corporations are managed, directed, and controlled.

Corporate social responsibility (CSR) A manner of operating a business that meets or exceeds the ethical, legal, commercial, and public expectations of stakeholders, including customers, shareholders, employees, and communities.

Corruption The abuse of power to achieve illegitimate personal gain.

Counterpurchase A type of countertrade with two distinct contracts. In the first, the seller agrees to a set price for goods and receives cash from the buyer. This first deal is contingent on a second wherein the seller agrees to purchase goods from the buyer for the same amount as in the first contract or a set percentage of same.

Countertrade An international business transaction where all or partial payments are made in kind rather than cash.

Countervailing duty Tariff imposed on products imported into a country to offset subsidies given to producers or exporters in the exporting country.

Country risk Exposure to potential loss or adverse effects on company operations and profitability caused by developments in a country's political and/or legal environments.

Critical incident analysis (CIA) A method for analyzing awkward situations in cross-cultural encounters by developing objectivity and empathy for other points of view.

Cross-cultural awareness Ability to interact effectively and appropriately with people from different language and cultural backgrounds.

Cross-cultural risk A situation or event where a cultural misunderstanding puts some human value at stake.

Cross-licensing agreement A type of project-based, nonequity venture where partners agree to access licensed technology developed by the other on preferential terms.

Cultural intelligence An employee's ability to function effectively in situations characterized by cultural diversity.

Cultural metaphor A distinctive tradition or institution strongly associated with a particular society.

Culture The learned, shared, and enduring orientation patterns in a society. People demonstrate their culture through values, ideas, attitudes, behaviors, and symbols.

Culture shock Confusion and anxiety experienced by a person who lives in a foreign culture for an extended period.

Currency control Restrictions on the outflow of hard currency from a country or the inflow of foreign currencies.

Currency option A contract that gives the purchaser the right, but not the obligation, to buy a certain amount of foreign currency at a set exchange rate within a specified amount of time.

Currency risk Potential harm that arises from changes in the price of one currency relative to another.

Currency swap An agreement to exchange one currency for another, according to a specified schedule.

Current rate method Translation of foreign currency balance sheet and income statements at the current exchange rate—the spot exchange rate in effect on the day or for the period when the statements are prepared.

Customs Checkpoints at the ports of entry in each country where government officials inspect imported products and levy tariffs.

Customs brokers Specialist enterprises that arrange clearance of products through customs on behalf of importing firms.

Customs union A stage of regional integration in which the member countries agree to adopt common tariff and nontariff barriers on imports from nonmember countries.

Debt financing The borrowing of money from banks or other financial intermediaries, or the sale of corporate bonds to individuals or institutions, to raise capital.

Devaluation Government action to reduce the official value of its currency, relative to other currencies.

Developing economies Low-income countries characterized by limited industrialization and stagnant economies.

Direct exporting Exporting that is accomplished by contracting with intermediaries located in the foreign market.

Direct quote The number of units of domestic currency needed to acquire one unit of foreign currency; also known as the normal quote.

Distribution channel intermediary A specialist firm that provides various logistics and marketing services for focal firms as part of the international supply chain, both in the home country and abroad.

Documentation Official forms and other paperwork required in export transactions for shipping and customs procedures.

Dumping Pricing exported products at less than their normal value, generally less than their price in the domestic or third-country markets, or at less than production cost.

Economic exposure The currency risk that results from exchange-rate fluctuations affecting the pricing of products, the cost of inputs, and the value of foreign investments.

Economic union A stage of regional integration in which member countries enjoy all the advantages of early stages, but also strive to have common fiscal and monetary policies.

Emerging markets Former developing economies that have achieved substantial industrialization, modernization, and rapid economic growth since the 1980s.

Equity financing The issuance of shares of stock to raise capital from investors and the use of retained earnings to reinvest in the firm.

Equity joint venture A type of partnership in which a separate firm is created through the investment or pooling of assets by two or more parent firms that gain joint ownership of the new legal entity.

Equity participation Acquisition of partial ownership in an existing firm.

Ethics Moral principles and values that govern the behavior of people, firms, and governments, regarding right and wrong.

Ethnocentric orientation Using our own culture as the standard for judging other cultures.

Eurobond A bond sold outside the issuer's home country but denominated in its own currency.

Eurocurrency Any currency deposited in a bank outside its country of origin.

Eurodollars U.S. dollars held in banks outside the United States, including foreign branches of U.S. banks.

Exchange rate The price of one currency expressed in terms of another; the number of units of one currency that can be exchanged for another.

Expatriate An employee assigned to work and reside in a foreign country for an extended period, usually a year or longer.

Expatriate assignment failure An employee's premature return from an international assignment.

Export control A government measure intended to manage or prevent the export of certain products or trade with certain countries.

Export department A unit within the firm charged with managing the firm's export operations.

Export management company (EMC) A domestically based intermediary that acts as an export agent on behalf of a client company.

Exporting The strategy of producing products or services in one country (often the producer's home country), and selling and distributing them to customers located in other countries.

Extraterritoriality Application of home-country laws to persons or conduct outside national borders.

Facilitator A firm or an individual with special expertise in banking, legal advice, customs clearance, or related support services that assists focal firms in the performance of international business transactions.

Family conglomerate A large, highly diversified company that is privately owned.

Focal firm The initiator of an international business transaction, which conceives, designs, and produces offerings intended for consumption by customers worldwide. Focal firms are primarily MNEs and SMEs.

Foreign bond A bond sold outside the issuer's country and denominated in the currency of the country where issued.

Foreign direct investment (FDI) An internationalization strategy in which the firm establishes a physical presence abroad through acquisition of productive assets such as capital, technology, labor, land, plant, and equipment.

Foreign distributor A foreign market-based intermediary that works under contract for an exporter, takes title to, and distributes the exporter's products in a national market or territory, often performing marketing functions such as sales, promotion, and after-sales service.

Foreign exchange All forms of money that are traded internationally, including foreign currencies, bank deposits, checks, and electronic transfers.

Foreign-exchange market The global marketplace for buying and selling national currencies.

Foreign trade zone (FTZ) An area within a country that receives imported goods for assembly or other processing and re-export. For customs purposes, the FTZ is treated as if it is outside the country's borders.

Forward contract A contract to exchange two currencies at a specified exchange rate on a set future date.

Forward rate The exchange rate applicable to the collection or delivery of a foreign currency at some future date.

Franchising Arrangement in which the firm allows another the right to use an entire business system in exchange for fees, royalties, or other forms of compensation.

Franchisor A firm that grants another the right to use an entire business system in exchange for fees, royalties, or other forms of compensation.

Free trade Relative absence of restrictions to the flow of goods and services between nations.

Free trade agreement A formal arrangement between two or more countries to reduce or eliminate tariffs, quotas, and barriers to trade in products and services.

Free trade area A stage of regional integration in which member countries agree to eliminate tariffs and other barriers to trade in products and services within the bloc.

Freight forwarder A specialized logistics service provider that arranges international shipping on behalf of exporting firms.

Fronting loan A loan between the parent and its subsidiary, channeled through a large bank or other financial intermediary.

Functional structure An arrangement in which management of the firm's international operations is organized by functional activity, such as production and marketing.

Futures contract An agreement to buy or sell a currency in exchange for another at a specified price on a specified date.

Geocentric orientation A global mind-set in which the manager is able to understand a business or market without regard to country boundaries.

Geographic area structure An organizational design in which management and control are decentralized to the level of individual geographic regions.

Global account management (GAM) Serving a key global customer in a consistent and standardized manner, regardless of where in the world it operates.

Global bond market The international marketplace in which bonds are bought and sold, primarily through bond brokers.

Global brand A brand whose positioning, advertising strategy, look, and personality are standardized worldwide.

Global capital market The collective financial markets where firms and governments raise intermediate and long-term financing.

Global equity market The worldwide market of funds for equity financing—stock exchanges around the world where investors and firms meet to buy and sell shares of stock.

Global financial system The collective of financial institutions that facilitate and regulate investment and capital flows worldwide, such as central banks, commercial banks, and national stock exchanges.

Global industry An industry in which competition is on a regional or worldwide scale.

Global integration Coordination of the firm's value-chain activities across countries to achieve worldwide efficiency, synergy, and cross-fertilization in order to take maximum advantage of similarities between countries.

Global market opportunity Favorable combination of circumstances, locations, and timing that offers prospects for exporting, investing, sourcing, or partnering in foreign markets.

Global market segment A group of customers who share common characteristics across many national markets.

Global marketing strategy A plan of action for foreign markets that guides the firm in deciding how to position itself and its offerings, which customer segments to target, and the degree to which it should standardize or adapt its marketing program elements.

Global matrix structure An arrangement that blends the geographic area, product, and functional structures to leverage the benefits of a purely global strategy, while keeping the firm responsive to local needs.

Global money market The collective financial markets where firms and governments raise short-term financing.

Global sourcing The procurement of products or services from independent suppliers or company-owned subsidiaries located abroad for consumption in the home country or a third country.

Global strategy An approach where headquarters seeks substantial control over its country operations in order to minimize redundancy and maximize efficiency, learning, and integration worldwide.

Global supply chain The firm's integrated network of sourcing, production, and distribution, organized on a worldwide scale and located in countries where competitive advantage can be maximized.

Global talent pool A searchable database of employees, profiling their international skill sets and potential for supporting the firm's global aspirations.

Global team An internationally distributed group of employees charged with a specific problem-solving or best-practice mandate that affects the entire organization.

Globalization of markets Ongoing economic integration and growing interdependency of countries worldwide.

Gray market activity Legal importation of genuine products into a country by intermediaries other than authorized distributors (also known as parallel imports).

Greenfield investment Direct investment to build a new manufacturing, marketing, or administrative facility, as opposed to acquiring existing facilities.

Hedgers Currency traders who seek to minimize their risk of exchange-rate fluctuations, often by entering into forward contracts or similar financial instruments.

Hedging Using financial instruments and other measures to reduce or eliminate exposure to currency risk by locking in guaranteed foreign-exchange positions.

High-context culture A culture that emphasizes nonverbal messages and views communication as a means to promote smooth, harmonious relationships.

Home replication strategy An approach in which the firm views international business as separate from and secondary to its domestic business.

Horizontal integration An arrangement whereby the firm owns, or seeks to own, the activities performed in a single stage of its value chain.

Host-country national (HCN) An employee who is a citizen of the country where the MNE subsidiary or affiliate is located.

Idiom An expression whose symbolic meaning is different from its literal meaning.

Import license Government authorization granted to a firm for importing a product.

Importing or global sourcing Procurement of products or services from suppliers located abroad for consumption in the home country or a third country.

Incoterms Universally accepted terms of sale that specify how the buyer and the seller share the cost of freight and insurance in an international transaction and at which point the buyer takes title to the goods.

Indirect exporting Exporting that is accomplished by contracting with intermediaries located in the firm's home market.

Indirect quote The number of units of foreign currency obtained for one unit of domestic currency.

Individualism versus collectivism Describes whether a person functions primarily as an individual or as part of a group.

Industrial cluster A concentration of businesses, suppliers, and supporting firms in the same industry at a particular location, characterized by a critical mass of human talent, capital, or other factor endowments.

Industry market potential An estimate of the likely sales for all firms in a particular industry over a specific period.

Infringement of intellectual property Unauthorized use, publication, or reproduction of products or services protected by a patent, copyright, trademark, or other intellectual property right.

Intellectual property Ideas or works created by individuals or firms, including discoveries and inventions; artistic, musical, and literary works; and words, phrases, symbols, and designs.

Intellectual property rights The legal claim through which the proprietary assets of firms and individuals are protected from unauthorized use by other parties.

Internalization theory An explanation of the process by which firms acquire and retain one or more value-chain activities inside the firm, minimizing the disadvantages of dealing with external partners and allowing for greater control over foreign operations.

International business Performance of trade and investment activities by firms across national borders.

International collaborative venture Cross-border business alliance whereby partnering firms pool their resources and share costs and risks to undertake a new business venture; also referred to as an "international partnership" or an "international strategic alliance."

International division structure An organizational design in which all international activities are centralized within one division in the firm, separate from domestic units.

International human resource management (IHRM) The planning, selection, training, employment, and evaluation of employees for international operations.

International investment The transfer of assets to another country or the acquisition of assets in that country.

International Monetary Fund (IMF) An international agency that aims to stabilize currencies by monitoring the foreign-exchange systems of member countries and lending money to developing economies.

International monetary system Institutional framework, rules, and procedures by which national currencies are exchanged for one another.

International portfolio investment Passive ownership of foreign securities such as stocks and bonds for the purpose of generating financial returns.

International price escalation The problem of end-user prices reaching exorbitant levels in the export market caused by multilayered distribution channels, intermediary margins, tariffs, and other international customer costs.

International trade Exchange of products and services across national borders, typically through exporting and importing.

Intracorporate financing Funds from sources inside the firm (both headquarters and subsidiaries) such as equity, loans, and trade credits.

Investment incentive Transfer payment or tax concession made directly to foreign firms to entice them to invest in the country.

Joint venture A form of collaboration between two or more firms to create a new, jointly owned enterprise.

Joint venture partner A focal firm that creates and jointly owns a new legal entity through equity investment or pooling of assets.

Know-how agreement Contract in which the focal firm provides technological or management knowledge about how to design, manufacture, or deliver a product or a service.

Legal system A system for interpreting and enforcing laws.

Letter of credit Contract between the banks of a buyer and a seller that ensures payment from the buyer to the seller upon receipt of an export shipment.

Licensing Arrangement in which the owner of intellectual property grants a firm the right to use that property for a specified period of time in exchange for royalties or other compensation.

Licensor A firm that enters a contractual agreement with a foreign partner to allow the partner the right to use certain intellectual property for a specified period of time in exchange for royalties or other compensation.

Local responsiveness Management of the firm's value-chain activities on a country-by-country basis to address diverse opportunities and risks.

Logistics service provider A transportation specialist that arranges for physical distribution and storage of products on behalf of focal firms, and also controls information between the point of origin and the point of consumption.

Long-term versus short-term orientation Refers to the degree to which people and organizations defer gratification to achieve long-term success.

Low-context culture A culture that relies on elaborate verbal explanations, putting much emphasis on spoken words.

Management contract Arrangement in which a contractor supplies managerial know-how to operate a hotel, hospital, airport, or other facility in exchange for compensation.

Manufacturer's representative An intermediary contracted by the exporter to represent and sell its merchandise or services in a designated country or territory.

Maquiladoras Export-assembly plants in northern Mexico along the U.S. border that produce components and typically finished products destined for the United States on a tariff-free basis.

Masculinity versus femininity Refers to a society's orientation based on traditional male and female values. Masculine cultures tend to value competitiveness, assertiveness, ambition, and the accumulation of wealth. Feminine cultures emphasize nurturing roles, interdependence among people, and taking care of less fortunate people.

Master franchise Arrangement in which an independent company is licensed to establish, develop, and manage the entire franchising network in its market and has the right to subfranchise to other franchisees, assuming the role of local franchisor.

Mercantilism The belief that national prosperity is the result of a positive balance of trade, achieved by maximizing exports and minimizing imports.

Merger A special type of acquisition in which two firms join to form a new, larger firm.

Monetary intervention The buying and selling of currencies by a central bank to maintain the exchange rate of a country's currency at some acceptable level.

Monochronic A rigid orientation to time, in which the individual is focused on schedules, punctuality, and time as a resource.

Multidomestic industry An industry in which competition takes place on a country-by-country basis.

Multidomestic strategy An approach to firm internationalization in which headquarters delegates considerable autonomy to each country manager, allowing him or her to operate independently and pursue local responsiveness.

Multilateral development banks (MDB) International financial institutions owned by multiple governments within world regions or other groups.

Multilateral netting Strategic reduction of cash transfers within the MNE family through the elimination of offsetting cash flows.

Multinational enterprise (MNE) A large company with substantial resources that performs various business activities through a network of subsidiaries and affiliates located in multiple countries.

National industrial policy A proactive economic development plan initiated by the government, often in collaboration with the private sector, that aims to develop or support particular industries within the nation.

New global challengers Top firms from emerging markets that are fast becoming key contenders in world markets.

Nontariff trade barrier A government policy, regulation, or procedure that impedes trade through means other than explicit tariffs.

Normativism The belief that ethical behavioral standards are universal, and firms and individuals should seek to uphold them around the world.

Offshoring The relocation of a business process or entire manufacturing facility to a foreign country.

Organizational culture The pattern of shared values, behavioral norms, systems, policies, and procedures that employees learn and adopt.

Organizational processes Managerial routines, behaviors, and mechanisms that allow the firm to function as intended.

Organizational structure Reporting relationships inside the firm that specify the links between people, functions, and processes.

Outsourcing The procurement of selected value-adding activities, including production of intermediate goods or finished products, from independent suppliers.

Parent-country national (PCN) An employee who is a citizen of the country where the MNE is headquartered.

Performance appraisal A formal process for assessing how effectively employees perform their jobs.

Political system A set of formal institutions that constitute a government.

Polycentric orientation A host-country mind-set in which the manager develops a strong affinity with the country in which she or he conducts business.

Polychronic A flexible, nonlinear orientation to time, whereby the individual takes a long-term perspective and emphasizes human relationships.

Power distance Describes how a society deals with the inequalities in power that exist among people.

Practical information Knowledge and skills necessary to function effectively in a country, including housing, health care, education, and daily living.

Privatization Transfer of state-owned industries to private concerns.

Product structure An arrangement in which management of international operations is organized by major product line.

Project-based, nonequity venture A collaboration in which the partners create a project with a relatively narrow scope and a well-defined timetable, without creating a new legal entity.

Protectionism National economic policies designed to restrict free trade and protect domestic industries from foreign competition.

Purchasing Power Parity (PPP) An adjustment for prices that reflects the amount of goods that consumers can buy in their home country, using their own currency and consistent with their own standard of living.

Quota A quantitative restriction placed on imports of a specific product over a specified period of time.

Regional economic integration The growing economic interdependence that results when two or more countries within a geographic region form an alliance aimed at reducing barriers to trade and investment.

Relativism The belief that ethical truths are not absolute but differ from group to group.

Repatriation The expatriate's return to his or her home country following the completion of a foreign assignment.

Royalty A fee paid periodically to compensate a licensor for the temporary use of its intellectual property, often based on a percentage of gross sales generated from the use of the licensed asset.

Rule of law A legal system in which rules are clear, publicly disclosed, fairly enforced, and widely respected by individuals, organizations, and the government.

Self-reference criterion The tendency to view other cultures through the lens of our own culture.

Small and medium-sized enterprise (SME) A company with 500 or fewer employees (as defined in Canada and the United States).

Socialization The process of learning the rules and behavioral patterns appropriate to one's given society.

Sovereign wealth fund (SWF) A state-owned investment fund that undertakes systematic, global investment activities.

Special Drawing Right (SDR) A unit of account or a reserve asset, a type of currency used by central banks to supplement their existing reserves in transactions with the IMF.

Speculators Currency traders who seek profits by investing in currencies with the expectation their value will change in the future.

Spot rate The exchange rate applied when the current exchange rate is used for immediate receipt of a currency.

Standardization Firm's efforts to make its marketing program elements uniform, with a view to targeting entire regions, or even the global marketplace, with the same product or service.

Strategy A planned set of actions that managers employ to make best use of the firm's resources and core competencies to gain competitive advantage.

Subsidy Monetary or other resources that a government grants to a firm or group of firms, usually intended to encourage exports or to facilitate the production and marketing of products at reduced prices, to ensure the involved firms prosper.

Sustainability Meeting humanity's needs without harming future generations.

Tariff A tax imposed on imported products, effectively increasing the cost of acquisition for the customer.

Tax haven A country hospitable to business and inward investment because of its low corporate income taxes.

Temporal method Translation of foreign currency balance sheet and income statements at an exchange rate that varies with the underlying method of valuation.

Tenders Formal offers made by a buyer to purchase certain products or services.

Third-country national (TCN) An employee who is a citizen of a country other than the home or host country.

Trade deficit A condition in which a nation's imports exceed its exports for a specific period of time.

Trade surplus A condition in which a nation's exports exceed its imports for a specific period of time.

Trading company An intermediary that engages in import and export of a variety of commodities, products, and services.

Transaction exposure The currency risk firms face when outstanding accounts receivable or payable are denominated in foreign currencies.

Transfer pricing The practice of pricing intermediate or finished products exchanged among the subsidiaries and affiliates of the same corporate family located in different countries.

Transition economies A subset of emerging markets that evolved from centrally planned economies into liberalized markets.

Translation exposure The currency risk that results when a firm translates financial statements denominated in a foreign currency into the functional currency of the parent firm, as part of consolidating international financial results.

Transnational strategy A coordinated approach to internationalization in which the firm strives to be relatively responsive to local needs, while retaining sufficient central control of operations to ensure efficiency and learning.

Transparency The degree to which companies regularly reveal substantial information about their financial condition and accounting practices.

Turnkey contracting Arrangement in which the focal firm or a consortium of firms plans, finances, organizes, manages, and implements all phases of a project abroad and then hands it over to a foreign customer after training local workers.

Turnkey contractors Focal firms or a consortium of firms that plan, finance, organize, manage, and implement all phases of a project and then hand it over to a foreign customer after training local personnel.

Uncertainty avoidance The extent to which people can tolerate risk and uncertainty in their lives.

Value chain The sequence of value-adding activities performed by the firm in the course of developing, producing, marketing, and servicing a product.

Vertical integration An arrangement whereby the firm owns, or seeks to own, multiple stages of a value chain for producing, selling, and delivering a product or service.

Visionary leadership A quality of senior management that provides superior strategic guidance for managing efficiency, flexibility, and learning.

Wholly owned direct investment A foreign direct investment in which the investor fully owns the foreign assets.

World Bank An international agency that provides loans and technical assistance to low- and middle-income countries with the goal of reducing poverty.

World Trade Organization (WTO) A multilateral governing body empowered to regulate international trade and investment.

> Notes

Chapter 1

[1] We use the term *international business* to refer to the cross-border business activities of individual firms, while economists use *international trade* to refer to aggregate cross-border flows of products and services between nations. While international business describes an enterprise-level phenomenon, international trade describes the macrophenomenon of aggregate flows between nations.

[2] World Trade Organization, "Trade Growth to Ease in 2011 but Despite 2010 Record Surge, Crisis Hangover Persists" (Geneva: World Trade Organization, April 7, 2011, press release), at www.wto.org.

[3] "Numbers: International Trade Hits a Wall," *BusinessWeek*, January 26/February 2, 2009, p. 15; WTO, 2011.

[4] Dermot Doherty and Marthe Fourcade, "France's Unlikely Import: Weight Loss Centers," *Bloomberg Businessweek*, January 16–22, 2012, pp. 20–21.

[5] Danielle Kucera "EBay's Adventures in Brick and Mortar," *Bloomberg Businessweek*, November 11, 2011, pp. 46–48; Ebay corporate profile at http://www.hoovers.com; Nick Wingfield, "eBay Sets Sights on Indian Market with Acquisition," *Wall Street Journal*, June 23, 2004, p. A3.

[6] "Desert Song," The Economist, October 7, 2004, p. 88; "News: The Banker Country Awards 2007," *The Banker*, December 2007, p. 1.

[7] Steven Russolillo, "Financials Taking It on the Chin Again; More Layoffs Ahead for Industry," *Wall Street Journal*, December 12, 2011, at www.wsj.com

[8] Dave Shellock, "Signs of Deepening Recession Dent Confidence," *Financial Times*, February 14, 2009, p. 14; Gabriele Parussini, "World News: Euro-Zone Economic Outlook Darkens," *Wall Street Journal*, January 17, 2009, p. A7.

[9] Marc A. Miles et al., *2008 Index of Economic Freedom* (Washington, DC: The Heritage Foundation).

[10] Gabriele Parussini, "Euro-Zone Economic Outlook Darkens," *Wall Street Journal*, January 17, 2009, p. A7; M. Schuman, H. Hoff, L. Cendrowicz, and B. Crumley, "The Euro's Last Stand?" *Time International*, December 5, 2011, pp. 26–31.

[11] *Fortune*, "Global 500" (2011), accessed on March 22, 2012 at http://www.money.cnn.com/magazines/fortune/global500/2011/

[12] Bob Davis and Jason Dean, "State-Run Firms Are the Giants of China's Economy," *Wall Street Journal*, February 23, 2012, p. A12.

[13] Organisation for Economic Co-operation and Development, Globalization and Small and Medium Enterprises (SMEs), (Paris: OECD, 1997).

[14] Gary Knight and S. Tamer Cavusgil, "Innovation, Organizational Capabilities, and the Born-Global Firm," *Journal of International Business Studies* 35, no. 2 (2004): 124–141; Patricia McDougall, Scott Shane, and Benjamin Oviatt, "Explaining the Formation of International New Ventures: The Limits of Theories from International Business Research," *Journal of Business Venturing* 9, no. 6 (1994): 469–487; OECD (1997).

[15] UNCTAD, *World Investment Report 2010* (New York: United Nations, 2010).

[16] U.S. Department of Commerce (2009), http://www.commerce.gov.

[17] World Bank, *World Development Indicators* (Washington, DC: The World Bank, 2008).

[18] Sidney Weintraub, *NAFTA at Three: A Progress Report* (Washington, DC: Center for Strategic and International Studies, 1997).

[19] Christopher Bartlett and Sumantra Ghoshal, *Transnational Management: Text, Cases, and Readings in Cross-Border Management* (Homewood, IL: Irwin, 1992).

[20] Kerry Capell, "McDonald's Offers Ethics with Those Fries," *BusinessWeek*, January 9, 2007, retrieved from http://www.businessweek.com.

Chapter 2

[1] Thomas L. Friedman, "It's a Flat World, After All," *New York Times Magazine*, April 3, 2005, pp. 33–37.

[2] Ibid.

[3] Ibid.

[4] Hwy-Chang Moon, Joseph Cheng, Min-Young Kim, and Jin-Uk Kim, "FDI, Economic Decline and Recovery: Lessons from the Asian Financial Crisis," *Multinational Business Review*, 19 (no. 2, 2011): 120–132; Thomas Friedman, *The Lexis and the Olive Tree* (New York: Anchor Books, 2000).

[5] This discussion is based on Lawrence Beer, *Tracing the Roots of Globalization and Business Principles* (New York: Business Expert Press, 2011).

[6] The word *trade* comes from the Anglo-Saxon term *trada*, which means to walk in the footsteps of others. Ancient trade routes were the foundation for a high level of cross-cultural exchange of ideas that led to the development of religion, science, economic activity, and government. The phrase "all roads lead to Rome" is not so much a metaphorical reference to Rome's dominance of the world 2,000 years ago, but to the fact that Rome's territorial colonies were constructed as commercial resource centers to serve the needs of the Roman Empire and increase its wealth. In an empire that stretched from England to Israel and from Germany to Africa, the Romans created more than 300,000 kilometers of roads. Roman roads were the lifeblood of the state that allowed trade to flourish. The Roman Empire was so concerned with the interruption of its shipping lanes for imported goods that it dispatched army legions to protect those lanes.

In the Middle Ages, the Knights Templar acted as guardians for pilgrims making the hazardous journey to pay homage to the birthplace of the Christian religion. In addition to protecting

.s, this warrior order created the first international banking .em with the use of rudimentary traveler's checks, eliminating .ne need for travelers to carry valuables on their person.

In 1100, Genghis Kthan not only united the Mongols but created an empire beyond the Chinese border that included Korea and Japan in the East, Mesopotamia (modern-day Iraq and Syria), Russia, Poland, and Hungary. He instituted common laws and regulations over his domain, most notably the preservation of private property, to enhance and protect international trade.

Arab merchants traded in spices along land routes reaching from northern Arabia across modern-day Turkey, through Asia Minor, and finally reaching China. By concealing the origins of cinnamon, pepper, cloves, and nutmeg, traders gained a monopoly and controlled prices. Europeans came to believe that the spices came from Africa, when in fact they had merely changed hands in the region. Under the traditional trading system, spices, linen, silk, diamonds, pearls, and opium-based medicines reached Europe via indirect routes over land and sea. Representing one of the earliest systems of international distribution, the products passed through many hands on their long voyage. At every juncture, prices increased several fold. (This discussion is based on Lawrence Beer, 2011.)

[7] C. Chase-Dunn, Yukio Kawano, and Benjamin D. Brewer, "World Globalization Since 1795: Waves of Integration in the World-System," *American Sociological Review* 65, no. 1 (2000): 77–95.

[8] Lawrence Franko, *The European Multinationals* (Stamford, CN: Greylock Publishers, 1976).

[9] Louis Emmerij, "Globalization, Regionalization, and World Trade," *Columbia Journal of World Business* 27, no. 2 (1992): 6–13.

[10] Company profile of Vodafone, 2011, at http://www.hoovers .com/; "The Phenomenal Growth of Vodafone: Rapid Rise through an Aggressive Leader-ship Style," *Strategic Direction* 19, no. 7 (2003): 25–26; "Vodafone Agrees India Buy-Out for $5.46bn," *Global Telecoms Business*, July 2011, p. 7.

[11] "Operating Profit," *The Economist*, August 16, 2008: 74–76.

[12] Marcos Aguiar et al., *The New Global Challengers: How Top 100 Rapidly Developing Economies Are Changing the World*, Boston Consulting Group, May 25, 2006.

[13] GNI refers to the total value of goods and services produced within a country after taking into account payments made to, and income received from, other countries.

[14] Jeremy Siegel, *The Future for Investors* (New York: Crown Business, 2005).

[15] Michael E. Porter and Victor E. Millar, "How Information Gives You Competitive Advantage," *Harvard Business Review* 63 (July–August 1985): 149–160; S. Tamer Cavusgil, "Extending the Reach of E-Business," *Marketing Management* 11, no. 2 (2002): 24–29; Janice Burn and Karen Loch, "The Societal Impact of the World Wide Web—Key Challenges for the 21st Century," *Information Resources Management Journal* 14, no. 4 (2001): 4–12.

[16] International Telecommunications Union, *Measuring the Information Society 2011* (Geneva, Switzerland: International Telecommunications Union).

[17] "The Death of Distance: A Survey of Telecommunications," *The Economist*, September 30, 1995.

[18] United Nations, *Regional Shipping and Port Development*, (Bangkok, Thailand: Economic and Social Commission for Asia and the Pacific, 2011).

[19] F. Norris, "Crisis Is Over, but Where's the Fix?," *New York Times* (March 10, 2011), at www.nytimes.com; Gabriele Parussini, "World News: Euro-Zone Economic Out-look Darkens," *Wall Street Journal*, January 17, 2009, p. A7; Dave Shellock, "Signs of Deepening Recession Dent Confidence," *Financial Times*, February 14, 2009, p. 14; "When Fortune Frowned," *The Economist*, October 11, 2008, pp. 3–5.

[20] "A Monetary Malaise," *The Economist*, October 11, 2008, pp. 20–25.

[21] Shellock (2009); Norris (2011); Parussini (2009).

[22] Bin Jiang, Timothy Koller, and Zane Williams, "Mapping Decline and Recovery Across Sectors," *McKinsey on Finance*, (Winter 2009): 21–25.

[23] "When Fortune Frowned," pp. 3–5; International Monetary Fund, http://www.imf.org; Shellock (2009); Rich Miller and Simon Kennedy, "The U.S. Shops and the World Applauds," *Bloomberg Businessweek*, April 9–15, 2012, pp. 22–24.

[24] "A Very Short History of the Crisis," *The Economist*, November 12, 2011, Special Section, p. 5; D. Enrich and L. Stevens, "Old Debts Dog Europe's Banks," *Wall Street Journal*, November 7, 2011, pp. A1–A8; S. Fidler, "Options Dwindle For Euro Crisis," November 25, 2011, pp. A1–A8.

[25] Martin Wolf, *Why Globalization Works* (New Haven, CN: Yale University Press, 2004).

[26] "The Day the Factories Stopped," *The Economist*, October 23, 2004, p. 70.

[27] Pete Engrail et al., "The New Global Job Shift," *BusinessWeek*, February 3, 2003, p. 50.

[28] J. Newman, "Polaris Plant Closure to Begin in March; 484 Jobs to be Lost," *Wisconsin State Journal*, December 23, 2010, at http://www.host.madison.com/wsj

[29] David Wessel, "U.S. Firms Eager to Add Foreign Jobs," *Wall Street Journal*, November 22, 2011, p. B1.

[30] International Labour Organization, *Children in Hazardous Work* (Geneva: International Labour Organization, 2011).

[31] Tara Radon and Martin Calkins, "The Struggle Against Sweatshops: Moving Toward Responsible Global Business," *Journal of Business Ethics* 66, no. 2–3 (2006): 261–269.

[32] S. L. Bachman, "The Political Economy of Child Labor and its Impacts on International Business," *Business Economics* (July 2000): 30–41.

[33] D. Dollar (2004) "Globalization, Poverty and Inequality since 1980," *World Bank Policy Research Working Paper 3333*, June 2004, Washington, DC: World Bank.

[34] UNCTAD, *World Investment Report 2011* (New York: United Nations Conference on Trade And Development, 2012); World Bank, *World Bank Development Indicators 2012* (Washington DC: World Bank, 2012).

[35] Surjit Bhalla, *Imagine There's No Country: Poverty Inequality and Growth in the Era of Globalization*, (Washington DC: Peterson Institute, 2002).

[36] Wolf (2004).

[37] Michael Smith, "Trade and the Environment," *International Business* 5, no. 8 (1992): 74.

[38] "Main Street Masala," *Bloomberg BusinessWeek*, February 6–12, 2012, pp. 69–71.

[39] "A Glimmer of Light at Last? Africa's Economy," *The Economist*, June 24, 2006, p. 71; World Bank, 2012.

[40] Dambisa Moyo, *Dead Aid* (New York: Farrar, Straus and Giroux, 2009).

[41] Moyo (2009); Robert Farzad, "Can Greed Save Africa?" *BusinessWeek*, December 10, 2007, pp. 46–54; C. K. Prahalad, *The Fortune at the Bottom of the Pyramid* (Upper Saddle River, NJ: Wharton School Publishing, 2004); Robert Farzad (2007); Organisation for Economic Co-operation and Development and African Development Bank.

Chapter 3

[1] UNCTAD, *World Investment Report 2011* (New York: United Nations, 2011).

[2] A. Kobylanski and R. Szulc, "Development of Marketing Orientation in Small and Medium-Sized Enterprises Evidence from Eastern Europe," *International Journal of Management & Marketing Research*, 4, no. 1 (2011): 49–59; Carol Matlack, "Europe: Go East, Young Man," *BusinessWeek*, October 30, 2006, pp. 46–47.

[3] Alison Coleman, "How to Be an Expert at Export," *Financial Times*, October 26, 2005, p. 9.

[4] S. Tamer Cavusgil and Gary Knight, *Born Global Firms: The New International Enterprise*. (New York: Business Expert Press, 2009); D. De Clercq, R. Yavuz, and L. Zhou, "Learning and Knowledge in Early Internationalization Research: Past Accomplishments and Future Directions," *Journal of Business Venturing*, 27, no. 1 (2012): 143–165; Daekwan Kim, Choton Basu, GM Naidu, and Erin Cavusgil, "The Innovativeness of Born-Globals and Customer Orientation: Learning from Indian Born-Globals," *Journal of Business Research*, 64, no. 8 (2011): 879–886.

[5] Y. Ono, "Beer Venture of Anheuser, Kirin Goes Down Drain on Tepid Sales," *Wall Street Journal*, November 3, 1999, p. A23.

[6] C. Macdonald, "Toy Story," *Canadian Plastics* 61, no. 2 (2003): 17–18.

[7] W. Alsakini, K. Wikstrom, and J. Kiiras, "Proactive Schedule Management of Industrial Turnkey Projects in Developing Countries," *International Journal of Project Management* 22, no. 1 (2004): 75–82; Christian Hicks and Tom McGovern, "Product Life Cycle Management in Engineer-to-Order Industries," *International Journal of Technology Management*, 48, no. 2 (2009): 153–161.

[8] *Railway Gazette International*, "Turnkey in Taichung," April 2011, p. 18; Peter M. Reina, "Public Funds and Turnkey Contracts Fuel Growing Global Subway Work," *ENR*, October 25, 2004, p. 32.

[9] Peter Reina and Gary Tulacz, "The Top 225 International Contractors," *ENR: Engineering News-Record*, August 29, 2011: 45–66.

[10] "The Mighty, Fallen," *Economist*, March 5, 2011, p. 71.

[11] D. Kealey, D. Protheroe, D. MacDonald, and T. Vulpe, "International Projects: Some Lessons on Avoiding Failure and Maximizing Success," *Performance Improvement* 45, no. 3 (2006): 38–47; H. Ren, B. Gray, and K. Kim, "Performance of International Joint Ventures: What Factors Really Make a Difference and How?," *Journal of Management* 35, no. 3 (2009): 805–814.

[12] Charles Waltner, "Cisco Forms Strategic Alliance with Fujitsu," December 5, 2004, www.cisco.com; Cisco, "China's ZTE Forms Strategic Alliance with Cisco Systems," www.cisco.com; Italtel, "Italtel and Cisco Systems Alliance Mission," www.italtel.com

[13] "Managing Global Supply Chains," *McKinsey Quarterly*, July 2008, http://www.mckinseyquarterly.com

[14] Thomas Johnson and Donna Bade, *Export Import: Procedures and Documentation* (New York: AMACOM, 2010); U.S. Department of Commerce, *A Basic Guide to Exporting* (Washington, DC: U.S. Government Printing Office, 1992).

[15] S. Tamer Cavusgil, Lyn S. Amine, and Robert Weinstein, "Japanese Sogo Shosha in the U.S. Export Trading Companies," *Journal of the Academy of Marketing Science* 14, no. 3 (1986): 21–32.

[16] B. Mongelluzzo, "Footwear Imports Stepping Up," *Journal of Commerce*, May 30, 2011, p. 64A.

[17] Andrew Rettman, "EU Welcomes New U.S. CO2-Reduction Plan," *BusinessWeek*, April 2, 2009, http://www.businessweek.com

[18] *Economist*, "Staring into the Abyss," November 12, 2011, Special Section, pp. 3–4; Dave Shellock, "Signs of Deepening Recession Dent Confidence," *Financial Times*, February 14, 2009, p. 14; Gabriele Parussini, "World News: Euro-Zone Economic Outlook Darkens," *Wall Street Journal*, January 17, 2009, p. A7.

[19] Chris Giles, "Big Ideas Fail to Mop up Europe's Current Mess," *Financial Times*, February 26, 2009, p. 2.

[20] *Derivatives Week*, "G-20 Leaders Agree to Tougher Derivatives Regs," November 7, 2011, p. 15; Stanley Reed, "G-20 Summit: Thorny Issues, a Soothing Outcome?" *BusinessWeek*, 2009, http://www.businessweek.com

[21] Harvey Morris, "Dollar Reserve Reform Urged," *Financial Times*, March 27, 2009, p. 7.

[22] "Sovereign-Wealth Funds," *The Economist*, May 24, 2007, p. 54; "Capital Markets," *The Economist*, January 17, 2008, p. 62; Nuno Fernandes and Arturo Bris, "Sovereign Wealth Revalued," *Financial Times*, February 12, 2009, www.ft.com; E. Truman, "Are Asian Sovereign Wealth Funds Different?," *Asian Economic Policy Review* 6, no. 2 (2011): 249–268; Vivienne Walt, "Feasting On Europe," *Time International*, December 12, 2011, pp. 51–54.

[23] Bjorn Lomborg, "Help the Poor with Free Trade," *Forbes*, March 16, 2009, p. 12.

Chapter 4

[1] We thank anthropologist Elizabeth K. Briody for her helpful comments on this chapter.

[2] R. Rosmarin, "Mountain View Masala," *Business 2.0* (March 2005): 54–56.

[3] David Heenan and Howard Perlmutter, *Multinational Organization Development* (Reading, MA: Addison-Wesley, 1979).

[4] Howard Perlmutter, "The Tortuous Evolution of the Multinational Corporation," *Columbia Journal of World Business* 4, no. 1 (1969): 9–18.

[5] V. Govindarajan and A. Gupta, *The Quest for Global Dominance* (San Francisco: Jossey-Bass/Wiley, 2001).

[6] Robert Boyd and Peter Richerson, *Culture and Evolutionary Process* (Chicago: University of Chicago Press, 1985).

[7] Harry C. Triandis, *Culture and Social Behavior* (New York: McGraw-Hill, 1994).

[8] C. Strauss and N. Quinn, *A Cognitive Theory of Cultural Meaning* (Cambridge, UK: Cambridge University Press, 1997).

[9] Gary Ferraro, *Cultural Dimension of International Business,* 6th ed. (Upper Saddle River, NJ: Prentice Hall, 2009).

[10] Ann T. Jordan, *Business Anthropology* (Prospect Heights, Il: Waveland Press, 2003).

[11] Geert Hofstede, *Culture's Consequences* (Beverly Hills, CA: Sage, 1980).

[12] Harry C. Triandis, *Culture and Social Behavior* (New York: McGraw-Hill, 1994).

[13] Tracy Meerwarth, Elizabeth Briody, and Devadatta Kulkarni, "Discovering the Rules: Folk Knowledge for Improving GM Partnerships," *Human Organization*, 64 (no. 3, 2005): 286–302.

[14] Dell Hymes, *Language in Culture and Society* (New York: Harper and Row, 1964); Kenneth Pike (ed.), *Language in Relation to a Unified Theory of Structure of Human Behavior*, 2nd ed. (The Hague, Netherlands: Mouton, 1967).

[15] Ibid.

[16] Julian Steward, *Theory of Culture Change: The Methodology of Multilinear Evolution* (Champaign: University of Illinois Press, 1990).

[17] Vern Terpstra and Kenneth David, *The Cultural Environment of International Business,* 3rd ed. (Cincinnati, OH: Southwestern, 1991).

[18] Edward T. Hall, *Beyond Culture* (New York: Anchor, 1976); Edward Hall and Mildred Hall, *Understanding Cultural Differences* (Boston: Nicholas Brealey, 1990).

[19] Hofstede (1980).

[20] Ibid.

[21] Richard Priem, Leonard Love, and Margaret Shaffer, "Industrialization and Values Evolution: The Case of Hong Kong and Guangzhou, China," *Asia Pacific Journal of Management* 17, no. 3 (2000): 473–82.

[22] Elizabeth K. Briody and Robert T. Trotter, *Partnering for Organizational Performance: Collaboration and Culture in the Global Workplace* (Lanham, MD: Rowman & Littlefield, 2008); Andrew Ortony, "Why Metaphors Necessary and Not Just Nice," *Educational Theory*, 25, no. 1 (1975): 45–53.

[23] Martin Gannon and Associates, *Understanding Global Cultures: Metaphorical Journeys through 17 Countries* (Thousand Oaks, CA: Sage, 1994).

[24] F. Kluckhohn and F. Strodbeck, *Variations in Value Orientations* (Evanston, IL: Row Peterson, 1961).

[25] Alice Eagly and Shelly Chaiken, *The Psychology of Attitudes* (New York: Harcourt Brace Jovanovich, 1993).

[26] Joyce Osland, Silvio De Franco, and Asbjorn Osland, "Organizational Implications of Latin American Culture: Lessons for the Expatriate Manager," *Journal of Management Inquiry* 8, no. 2 (1999): 219–238.

[27] Roger Axtell, *The Do's and Taboos of International Trade* (New York: Wiley, 1994).

[28] Robert Grier, "The Effect of Religion on Economic Development," *Kyklos* 50, no. 1 (1997): 47–62; Rachel McCleary, "Religion and Economic Development," *Policy Review* (April/May 2008): 45–57; Rachel McCleary and Robert Barro, "Religion and Economy," *Journal of Economic Perspectives* 20, no. 2 (2006): 49–72.

[29] Adrian Furnham, *The Protestant Work Ethic* (London: Routledge, 1990); Max Weber, *The Protestant Ethic and the Spirit of Capitalism* (New York: Charles Scribner's Sons, 1959).

[30] Meg Carter, "Muslims Offer a New Mecca for Marketers," *Financial Times*, August 11, 2005, p. 1.

[31] *Economist*, "Untouchable and Unthinkable," October 6, 2007, pp. 15–16.

[32] Weber (1959); Furnham (1990).

[33] Charles Chow Hoi Hee, "A Holistic Approach to Business Management: Perspectives from the Bhagavad Gita," *Singapore Management Review* 29, no. 1 (2007): 73–84.

[34] Amy Kazmin, "Attention to Local Palates Pays Off," *Financial Times*, January 19, 2010, p. 3; Kristian Niemietz, "McDonald's Withdrawal from Bolivia: Capitalism in Action," November 22, 2011, Institute of Economic Affairs, retrieved from www.iea.org.uk.

[35] "Babel Runs Backwards," *The Economist*, January 1, 2005, pp. 58–60.

[36] Walid Hejazi and Juan Ma, "Gravity, the English Language and International Business," *The Multinational Business Review* 19, no. 2 (2011): 152–167.

[37] Edward T. Hall, *The Silent Language* (Garden City, NY: Anchor, 1981).

[38] J. M. Greig, "The End of Geography? Globalization, Communications, and Culture in the International System," *The Journal of Conflict Resolution* 46, no. 2 (2002): 225–44.

[39] R. Rosmarin, "Text Messaging Gets a Translator," *Business 2.0* (March 2005): 32; Nitish Singh, Vikas Kumar, and Daniel Baack, "Adaptation of Cultural Content: Evidence from B2C E-Commerce Firms," *European Journal of Marketing* 39, nos. 1/2 (2005): 71–86.

[40] Russell Belk, "Hyperreality and Globalization: Culture in the Age of Ronald McDonald," *Journal of International Consumer Marketing* 8, nos. 3/4 (1996): 23–37.

[41] Tyler Cowen, *Creative Destruction: How Globalization Is Changing the World's Cultures* (Princeton, NJ: Princeton University Press, 2002).

[42] Laszlo Tihanyi, David A. Griffith, and Craig J. Russell, "The Effect of Cultural Distance on Entry Mode Choice, International Diversification, and MNE Performance: A Meta-Analysis," *Journal of International Business Studies* 36, no. 3 (2005): 270–283.

[43] Sengun Yeniyurt and Janell Townsend, "Does Culture Explain Acceptance of New Products in a Country? An Empirical Investigation," *International Marketing Review* 20, no. 4 (2003): 377–396; Yong Zhang and James Neelankavil, "The Influence of Culture on Advertising Effectiveness in China and the USA: A Cross-Cultural Study," *European Journal of Marketing* 31, no. 2 (1997): 134–142.

[44] "Here Comes a Whopper," *The Economist*, October 25, 2008, p. 78; David A. Griffith, Michael Y. Hu, and John K. Ryans, Jr., "Process Standardization across Intra- and Intercultural Relationships," *Journal of International Business Studies* 31, no. 2 (2000): 303–324; Thomas Head, Clara Gong, Chunhui Ma et al., "Chinese Executives' Assessment of Organization Development Interventions," *Organization Development Journal* 24, no. 1 (2006): 28–40; K. Hille, "Haier Focuses on Marketing Instead of Takeovers," *Financial Times*, February 18, 2009, p. 7; Joel D. Nicholson and Yim-Yu Wong, "Culturally

Based Differences in Work Beliefs," *Management Research News* 24, no. 5 (2001): 1–10.

45 P. Dicken, *Global Shift: Transforming the World Economy* (New York: Guilford, 1998).

46 T. Clark and D. Rajaratnam, "International Services: Perspectives at Century's End," *Journal of Services Marketing* 13, nos. 4/5 (1999): 298–302.

47 B. Kogut, "Country Capabilities and the Permeability of Borders," *Strategic Management Journal* 12 (Summer 1991): 33–47.

48 T. Clark, D. Rajaratnam, and T. Smith, "Toward a Theory of International Services: Marketing Intangibles in a World of Nations," *Journal of International Marketing* 4, no. 2 (1996): 9–28.

49 S. Lorge, "Federal Express," *Sales and Marketing Management* 149, no. 11 (1997): 63.

50 Tomasz Lenartowicz and James P. Johnson, "A Cross-National Assessment of the Values of Latin America Managers: Contrasting Hues or Shades of Gray?" *Journal of International Business Studies* 34, no. 3 (2003): 266–268.

51 Elizabeth K. Briody, Robert T. Trotter, and Tracy L. Meerwarth, *Transforming Culture: Creating and Sustaining a Better Manufacturing Organization* (New York: Palgrave Macmillan, 2010).

52 James Johnson, Tomasz Lenartowicz, and Salvador Apud, "Cross-Cultural Competence in International Business: Toward a Definition and a Model," *Journal of International Business Studies* 37, no. 4 (2006): 525–535; Soon Ang, Linn Van Dyne, and Christine Koh, "Personality Correlates of the Four-Factor Model of Cultural Intelligence," *Group & Organization Management* 31, no. 1 (2006): 100–123.

Chapter 5

1 We are grateful to Professor Larry Beer, Arizona State University Emeritus, for his helpful comments regarding this chapter.

2 John Boatwright, *Ethics and the Conduct of Business*, 7th ed. (Upper Saddle River, NJ: Prentice-Hall, 2011); Naresh Malhotra and G. Miller, "An Integrated Model for Ethical Decisions," *Journal of Business Ethics* 17, no. 3 (1998): 263–280; D. McAlister, O. C. Ferrell, and L. Ferrell, *Business and Society* (Boston: Houghton Mifflin, 2003).

3 Marco Celentani, Juan-Jose Ganuza, and Jose-Luis Peydros, "Combating Corruption in International Business Transactions," *Economica* 71, no. 283 (2004): 417–449; William Olsen, *The Anti-Corruption Handbook*, (Hoboken, NJ: Wiley, 2010).

4 William Olsen, *The Anti-Corruption Handbook*, (Hoboken, NJ: Wiley, 2010); John Sullivan, *The Moral Compass of Companies: Business Ethics and Corporate Governance as Anti-Corruption Tools* (Washington, DC: International Finance Corporation, World Bank, 2009).

5 Tara Radin and Martin Calkins, "The Struggle against Sweatshops: Moving toward Responsible Global Business," *Journal of Business Ethics* 66 (2006): 261–268; Jeremy Snyder, "Exploitation and Sweatshop Labor: Perspectives and Issues," *Business Ethics Quarterly*, 20, no. 2 (2010): 187–213.

6 Brian Grow et al., "Bitter Pills," *Business Week*, December 18, 2006, p. 110.

7 Transparency International, *Progress Report: OECD Anti-Bribery Convention 2009*, retrieved from http://www.transparency.org

8 CBP Office of International Trade (2012), *Intellectual Property Rights: Fiscal Year 2011 Seizure Statistics*, Washington DC: U.S. Immigration and Customs Enforcement, at http://www.ice.gov/doclib/iprcenter/pdf/ipr-fy-2011-seizure-report.pdf

9 Frontier Economics (2011), *Estimating the Global Economic and Social Impacts of Counterfeiting and Piracy*, London: Frontier Economics, Ltd., accessed at The International Chamber of Commerce, www.iccwbo.org

10 P. Loftus, "U.S. Probes Alleged Seller of Fake J&J Diabetes Monitors," *Wall Street Journal*, April 8, 2010, p. B4.

11 CBP Office of International Trade (2012).

12 Sarah McBride and Loretta Chao, "Disney Fights Pirates at China Affiliate," *Wall Street Journal*, November 21, 2008, p. B1; Michael Schuman and Jeffrey Ressner, "Disney's Great Leap into China," *Time*, July 18, 2005: 52–54.

13 Vara Vauhini, "Russian Web Sites Offer Cheap Songs, But Piracy Is Issue," *Wall Street Journal*, January 26, 2005, p. D10.

14 Transparency International, *Global Corruption Report 2009* (Cambridge, UK: Cambridge University Press, 2009).

15 Ibid.

16 Transparency International, *Corruption Perceptions Index 2011* (Berlin: Transparency International, 2011), accessed at www.transparency.org

17 Larry Beer, *Business Ethics for the Global Business and the Global Manager: A Strategic Approach* (New York: Business Expert Press, 2010); *The McKinsey Quarterly*, "The Business of Sustainability," October 2011, retrieved from http://www.mckinsey-quarterly.com; Erin Cavusgil, "Merck and Vioxx: An Examination of an Ethical Decision-Making Model," *Journal of Business Ethics* 76, no. 4 (2007): 451–461; L. Kaufmann, F. Reimann, M. Ehrgott, and J. Rauer, "Sustainable Success," *Wall Street Journal*, June 22, 2009, retrieved from http://www.wsj.com; Malhotra and Miller (1998); McAlister, Ferrell, and Ferrell (2003); Michael Porter and Mark Kramer, "Strategy & Society: The Link Between Competitive Advantage and Corporate Social Responsibility," *Harvard Business Review*, December 2006, pp. 178–192.

18 Larry Beer (2010); Kaufmann, Reimann, Ehrgott, and Rauer (2009); Alan Muller and Ans Kolk, "Extrinsic and Intrinsic Drivers of Corporate Social Performance: Evidence from Foreign and Domestic Firms in Mexico," *Journal of Management Studies* 47, no. 1 (2010): 1–26.

19 Sullivan (2009); Muller and Kolk (2010); Transparency International, 2009.

20 Boatwright (2011); McAlister, Ferrell, and Ferrell (2003).

21 Transparency International (2009).

22 Larry Beer (2010); Kaufmann, Reimann, Ehrgott, and Rauer (2009); Alan Muller and Ans Kolk, "Extrinsic and Intrinsic Drivers of Corporate Social Performance: Evidence from Foreign and Domestic Firms in Mexico," *Journal of Management Studies* 47, no. 1 (2010): 1–26.

23 Alan Muller and Gail Whiteman, "Exploring the Geography of Corporate Philanthropic Disaster Response: A Study of Fortune Global 500 Firms," *Journal of Business* Ethics 84, no. 4 (2009): 589–603; UNCTAD, *World Investment Report 2009* (New York: United Nations Conference on Trade and Development, 2009); N. Isdell, *21st Century Capitalism*, speech to Council on Foreign Relations, New York, 2009, retrieved from http://fora.tv/2009/03/06/Neville_Isdell_ 21st_Century_Capitalism; K. Rehbein, S. Waddock, and S. Graves, "Understanding Shareholder

Activism: Which Corporations Are Targeted?" *Business and Society* 43, no. 3 (2004): 239–267.

24 V. Agarwal and Krishna Pokharel, "India's Populists Resist Big Retail; Fear of Chains Displacing Local Shops Stirs Backlash in Rapidly Growing Market," *Wall Street Journal*, October 9, 2007, p. A6; Chip Cummins, "Shell, Chevron to Cut Deliveries of Oil amid Protests in Nigeria," *Wall Street Journal*, December 23, 2004, p. A2; Stephen Fidler and John Labate, "Sudan Ties Jeopardise Chinese Oil Listing," *Financial Times*, October 6, 1999, p. 8; U. Idemudia, "Oil Extraction and Poverty Reduction in the Niger Delta: A Critical Examination of Partnership Initiatives," *Journal of Business Ethics* 90 (May 2009): 91–116; Sy Banerjee, Thomas Hemphill, and Mark Perry, "India Doors to Wal-Mart Shut by Crony Capitalism," *Investor's Business Daily*, December 28, 2011, p. A13.

25 UNCTAD, 2009.

26 Center for Corporate Citizenship, "In Good Company: Motorola," Boston College, Carroll School of Management, 2007, retrieved from http://www.bcccc.net

27 Andrew Witty, "New Strategies For Innovation In Global Health: A Pharmaceutical Industry Perspective," *Health Affairs* 30, no. 1 (2011): 118–126.

28 Ilana Polyak, "Greener Approach," *Financial Planning* 40, no. 8 (2010), accessed at www.financial-planning.com

29 C. Bhattacharya, Daniel Korschun, and Sankar Sen, "What Really Drives Value in Corporate Responsibility?," *McKinsey Quarterly*, December 2011, accessed at www.mckinseyquarterly.com; C. Bhattacharya, S. Sen, and D. Korschun, "Using Corporate Social Responsibility to Win the War for Talent," *MIT Sloan Management Review* 49, no. 2 (2008): 37–44; M. Orlitzky, F. Schmidt, and S. Rynes, "Corporate Social and Financial Performance: A Meta-analysis," *Organization Studies* 24, no. 3 (2003), pp. 403–441; Porter and Kramer (2006); Transparency International (2009); R. Trudel and J. Cotte, "Does Being Ethical Pay?" *Wall Street Journal*, May 12, 2008, p. R4; World Economic Forum, *More with Less: Scaling Sustainable Consumption and Resource Efficiency*, Geneva: World Economic Forum, accessed at www.weforum.org

30 Beer (2010); Philip Kotler and Nancy Lee, *Up and Out of Poverty: The Social Marketing Solution* (Upper Saddle River, NJ: Wharton School Publishing, 2009); Hildy Teegen, Jonathan Doh, and Sushil Vachani, "The Importance of Nongovernmental Organizations (NGOs) in Global Governance and Value Creation: An International Business Research Agenda," *Journal of International Business Studies* 35, no. 4 (2004): 463–483.

31 John Blewitt, *Understanding Sustainable Development* (London: Earthscan, 2008); Kaufmann, Reimann, Ehrgott, and Rauer (2009); Nancy Landrum and Sandra Edwards, *Sustainable Business: An Executive's Primer* (New York: Business Expert Press, 2009).

32 Transparency International (2009).

33 Jo Johnson and Aline van Duyn, "Forced Child Labour Claims Hit Clothes Retailers," *Financial Times*, October 29, 2007, p. 3; Kaufmann, Reimann, Ehrgott, and Rauer (2009); Nancy Landrum and Sandra Edwards, *Sustainable Business: An Executive's Primer* (New York: Business Expert Press, 2009).

34 Emmanuelle Bournay, *Vital Waste Graphics 2* (New York: United Nations, 2007); Transparency International, *Global Corruption Report: Climate Change*, (London: Earthscan, 2011).

35 Richard Dobbs, Jeremy Oppenheim, and Fraser Thompson, "Mobilizing for a Resource Revolution," *McKinsey Quarterly*, January 2012, accessed at www.mckinseyquarterly.com

36 Johnson and van Duyn (2007); Masha Zager, "Doing Well by Doing Good: Gap Inc.'s Social Responsibility Program," *Apparel*, August 2009, p. 10.

37 Andrew Batson, "Coke Aims to Improve Water Recycling," *Wall Street Journal*, June 6, 2007, p. A10; "The New Face of Africa," *Fortune*, November 21, 2011, Special Advertising Section; Daniel Vermeer and Robert Clemen, "Why Sustainability Is Still Going Strong," *Financial Times*, February 12, 2009, retrieved from http://www.ft.com

38 Bonini, Lendonca, and Oppenheim (2006); Muller and Kolk (2010).

39 Boatwright (2011); T. Low, L. Ferrell, and P. Mansfield, "A Review of Empirical Studies Assessing Ethical Decision Making in Business," *Journal of Business Ethics* 25, no. 3 (2000): 185–204; Malhotra and Miller (1998); McAlister, Ferrell, and Ferrell (2003).

40 Sullivan (2009).

41 Max Bazerman and Ann Tenbrunsel, "Ethical Breakdowns," *Harvard Business Review*, April 2011, pp. 58–65.

42 A version of this framework appeared originally in Issues in *Ethics* 1, no. 2(1988). It was developed at the Markkula Center for Applied Ethics at Santa Clara University, California. See also: Claire Andre and Manuel Velasquez (1988), "Thinking Ethically," *Issues in Ethics*, Vol. 1, No. 2, Markkula Center for Applied Ethics, Santa Clara University, accessed at http://www.scu.edu/ethics/publications/iie/v1n2/thinking.html.; Bonini, Lendonca, and Oppenheim (2006); Cavusgil (2007); Boatwright (2011); Low, Ferrell, and Mansfield (2000); Malhotra and Miller (1998); McAlister, Ferrell, and Ferrell (2003); UNCTAD, *World Investment Report 2006* (New York: UNCTAD, 2006); Sullivan (2009).

43 Transparency International (2009).

44 Vermeer and Clemen (2009).

Chapter 6

1 We thank Professors Attila Yaprak, Wayne State University, and Heechun Kim, Georgia State University, for their helpful comments on this chapter.

2 David Ricardo, *Principles of Political Economy and Taxation* (London: Everyman Edition, 1911; first published in 1817).

3 John Romalis, "Factor Proportions and the Structure of Commodity Trade," *The American Economic Review* 94, no. 1 (2004): 6–97.

4 Raymond Vernon, "International Investment and International Trade in the Product Cycle," *Quarterly Journal of Economics* 80 (May 1966): 190–207.

5 Michael Porter, *The Competitive Advantage of Nations* (New York: Free Press, 1990).

6 Mourad Dakhli and Dirk De Clercq, "Human Capital, Social Capital, and Innovation: A Multi-Country Study," *Entrepreneurship and Regional Development* 16, no. 2 (2004), 10–115.

7 Richard Nelson and Sidney Winter, *An Evolutionary Theory of Economic Change* (Cambridge, MA: Belknap Press, 1982).

8 Barry Jaruzelski and Kevin Dehoff, "Beyond Borders: The Global Innovation 1000," *Strategy_Business* 53 (2008): 52–67.

9 Richard Dobbs, Jeremy Oppenheim, and Fraser Thompson, "Mobilizing for a Resource Revolution," *Mckinsey Quarterly*, January 2012, accessed at www.mckinseyquarterly.com

[10] Chalmers Johnson, *MITI and the Japanese Miracle: The Growth of Industrial Policy, 1925–1975* (Stanford, CA: Stanford University Press, 1982).

[11] Clyde Prestowitz, *Trading Places* (New York: Basic Books, 1989); Lester Thurow, *Head to Head: The Coming Economic Battle Among Japan, Europe, and America* (New York: William Morrow, 1992).

[12] Dean Hyslop and Dave Mar, "Skill Upgrading in New Zealand, 1986–2001," *Australian Economic Review*, 42 (no. 4, 2009): 422–434.

[13] Graeme Wells, "Economic Reform and Macroeconomic Policy in New Zealand," *Australian Economic Review* (4th quarter, No. 92, 1990): 45–61.

[14] Kurt Badenhausen, "Best Countries for Business," *Forbes*, October 3, 2011, accessed at www.forbes.com

[15] Warren Bilkey, "An Attempted Integration of the Literature on the Export Behavior of Firms," *Journal of International Business Studies* 9 (Summer 1978): 3–46; S. Tamer Cavusgil, "On the Internationalization Process of Firms," *European Research* 8, no. 6 (1980): 27–81; Jan Johanson and Jan-Erik Vahlne, "The Internationalization Process of the Firm—A Model of Knowledge Development and Increasing Foreign Commitments," *Journal of International Business Studies* 8 (Spring/Summer 1977): 2–32.

[16] Warren Bilkey, "An Attempted Integration of the Literature on the Export Behavior of Firms," *Journal of International Business Studies* 9 (Summer 1978): 3–46; S. Tamer Cavusgil, "On the Internationalization Process of Firms," *European Research* 8, no. 6 (1980): 27–81; Jan Johanson and Jan-Erik Vahlne, "The Internationalization Process of the Firm—A Model of Knowledge Development and Increasing Foreign Commitments," *Journal of International Business Studies* 8 (Spring/Summer 1977): 2–32.

[17] *Sony History*, 2009, retrieved from http://www.sony.net/ Fun/SH

[18] G. Knight and S. T. Cavusgil, "The Born Global Firm: A Challenge to Traditional Internationalization Theory," in *Advances in International Marketing*, vol. 8, ed. S. T. Cavusgil and T. Madsen (Greenwich, CT: JAI Press, 1996), pp. 11–26.

[19] S. T. Cavusgil and Gary Knight, *Born Global Firms: A New International Enterprise* (New York: Business Expert Press, 2009); Gary Knight and S. T. Cavusgil, "Innovation, Organizational Capabilities, and the Born-Global Firm," *Journal of International Business Studies* 35, no. 2 (2004): 12–41; Benjamin Oviatt and Patricia McDougall, "Toward a Theory of International New Ventures," *Journal of International Business Studies* 25, no. 1 (1994): 4–64; Michael Rennie, "Born Global," *McKinsey Quarterly* no. 4 (1993): 4–52.

[20] UNCTAD, *World Investment Report 2011* (New York: United Nations, 2011), accessed January 29, 2012 at http://www.unctad .org/templates/WebFlyer.asp?intItemID=6018&lang=1

[21] Ibid.

[22] Stephen Hymer, *The International Operations of National Firms* (Cambridge, MA: MIT Press, 1976).

[23] Peter Buckley and Mark Casson, *The Future of the Multinational Enterprise* (London: MacMillan, 1976); John Dunning, "The Eclectic Paradigm of International Production: A Restatement and Some Possible Extensions," *Journal of International Business Studies*, 19 (1988): 1–31.

[24] Dunning (1988).

[25] Ibid.

[26] John Dunning, *International Production and the Multinational Enterprise* (London: Allen and Unwin, 1981); Bruce Kogut, "Joint Ventures: Theoretical and Empirical Perspectives," *Strategic Management Journal* 9 (1988): 319–332; P. Rajan Varadarajan and Margaret H. Cunningham, "Strategic Alliances: A Synthesis of Conceptual Foundations," *Journal of the Academy of Marketing Science* 23 (1995): 282–296.

[27] "For Starbucks, There's No Place Like Home," *Business-Week*, June 9, 2003, p. 48.

[28] James Lincoln, Christina Ahmadjian, and Eliot Mason, "Organizational Learning and Purchase-Supply Relations in Japan," *California Management Review* 40 no. 3 (1998): 244–264.

[29] Hakan Hakansson, *International Marketing and Purchasing of Industrial Goods: An Interaction Approach* (New York: Wiley, 1982).

[30] Ibid.

Chapter 7

[1] Jack Ewing, "Germany: A Cold Shoulder for Coca-Cola," *BusinessWeek,* May 2, 2005, p. 52.

[2] "Country Risk," *The Economist*, February 26, 2005, p. 102.

[3] "Getting Past Yukos," *BusinessWeek*, September 13, 2004, p. 52.

[4] S. Tamer Cavusgil, Pervez Ghauri, and Milind Agarwal, *Doing Business in Emerging Markets* (Thousand Oaks, CA: Sage, 2002); Mehul Srivastava, "What's Holding India Back," *Business Week*, October 19, 2009, pp. 38–44.

[5] Steven Soper, *Totalitarianism: A Conceptual Approach* (Lanham, MD: University Press of America, 1985); Carl J. Friedrich and Zbigniew Brzezinski, *Totalitarian Dictatorship and Autocracy,* 2nd ed. (Cambridge, MA: Harvard University Press, 1965).

[6] Milton Friedman and Rose Friedman, *Free to Choose* (New York: Harcourt Brace Jovanovich, 1980).

[7] Amartya Sen, *Development as Freedom* (New York: Alfred Knopf, 2001)

[8] Joseph Johnson and Gerald Tellis, "Drivers of Success for Market Entry into China and India," *Journal of Marketing* 72 (May 2008): 1–13.

[9] Arthur Brooks, "The Debt Ceiling and the Pursuit of Happiness," *Wall Street Journal*, July 25, 2011, accessed at www.wsj.com; Statistical Abstract of the United States, Economics and Statistics Administration (Washington, DC: U.S. Census Bureau, 2004).

[10] Ken Owens and Yvonne Thompson, "Sovereign Sukuk a Way to Revive the Celtic Tiger?," *Accountancy Ireland*, April (2011): 34–36; Maha Khan Phillips, "Doing God's Work; Islamic Finance Is Meant to Reconcile Both Commercial and Religious Ideals," *Wall Street Journal,* March 1, 2010, re-trieved from http://www.wsj.com; The Pew Forum, "Mapping the Global Muslim Population," 2009, retrieved from http:// www.pewforum.org.

[11] Phyllis Berman, "The Three Marketeers," *Forbes*, July 25, 2005, p. 78.

[12] Raman Kumar, William Lamb, and Richard Wokutch, "The End of the South African Sanctions, Institutional Ownership, and the Stock Price Performance of Boycotted Firms," *Business and Society* 41, no. 2 (2002): 133–165.

[13] Roger Bezdek, "Keystone Follies," *World Oil*, November 2011, p. 23.

[14] Kert Davies, "Greenfreeze F-Gas Victory! Greener Refrigerators Finally Legal in the U.S.," December 14, 2011, retrieved from www.greenpeace.org/usa

[15] *Economist*, "Your Mine is Mine," September 3, 2011, retrieved from www.economist.com

[16] *Economist*, "Strategic Move," April 12, 2008, p. 43.

[17] Ibid.

[18] Robert Wade and Silla Sigurgeirsdottir, "Iceland's Rise, Fall, Stabilisation and Beyond," *Cambridge Journal of Economics*, 36, no. 1 (2012): 127–144.

[19] David Wernick and Sumit Kundu, "Terrorism, Political Risk and International Business: Conceptual Considerations," in *Proceedings: 2008 Annual Conference, Academy of International Business* (East Lansing, MI: Academy of International Business, 2008).

[20] Ibid.

[21] Jason Bush, "Russia's Raiders," *BusinessWeek*, June 16, 2008, pp. 67–71; N. Vardi, "Power Putsch," *Forbes*, June 2, 2008, pp. 84–92.

[22] Matthew Philips, "What Trade Sanctions?," *Bloomberg BusinessWeek,* January 30–February 5, 2012, p. 16.

[23] Nicola Clark, "BP Hit by Boycott Threat Amid US Oil-Spill Crisis," *Marketing*, May 12, 2010, p. 1.

[24] Yonah Alexander, David Valton, and Paul Wilkinson, *Terrorism: Theory and Practice* (Boulder, CO: Westview, 1979).

[25] National Counterterrorism Center, *2010 Report on Terrorism*, April 30, 2011, retrieved from http://www.nctc.gov; M. Srivastava and N. Lakshman, "How Risky Is India?" *BusinessWeek*, December 4, 2008, retrieved from http://www.businessweek.com.

[26] Jonathan Laing, "Aftershock," *Barron's*, September 9, 2002, p. 23.

[27] V. Nair, "Tata Nano, World's Cheapest Car, Won't Help Pay Debt," *Bloomberg*, 2009, retrieved from http://www.bloomberg.com; Srivastava (2009).

[28] Guy Chazan, "Future of Libyan Oil is in Doubt," *Wall Street Journal*, March 22, 2011, p. C8; Guy Chazan, Carolyn Cui, Benoit Faucon, and Angel Gonzales, "West Shuns Libyan Crude," *Wall Street Journal*, March 8, 2011, pp. A1, A15.

[29] CBS News, "Egypt Crisis Stirs Concern for World Economy," January 31, 2011 accessed at www.cbsnews.com; Mariam Fam and Caroline Alexander, "Egypt's Economy Reels as Capital Flees," *Bloomberg Businessweek*, December 5–11, 2011, pp. 16–18.

[30] *WorldCargo News*, "Struggle for Power Threatens Egyptian Trade," February 4, 2011, accessed at www.worldcargonews.com.

[31] Jessica Mead and Katie Martin, "Egypt Intervenes on Currency Slide," *Wall Street Journal*, February 8, 2011, accessed at www.wsj.com

[32] World Economic Forum, *Arab World Competitiveness Report, 2011–2012* (Geneva: World Economic Forum, 2011), retrieved at www.weforum.org

[33] United States Trade Representative, *2011 National Trade Estimate Report on Foreign Trade Barriers*, Washington DC, March 2011, retrieved at http://www.ustr.gov

[34] Cavusgil, Ghauri, and Agarwal (2002).

[35] J. Fox, "New World Order," *Time*, February 16, 2009, p. 29; "Krise des Bankensystems: Zu viel Finanzinnovationen, zu wenig Regulierung?" *Ifo Schnelldienst*, November 14, 2008, pp. 3–15; Laura Kodres, "What Is to Be Done," *Finance & Development*, March 2009, pp. 23–27.

[36] International Chamber of Commerce, "Policy Statement: Extraterritoriality and Business," July 13, 2006.

[37] Kurt Stanberry, Barbara C. George, and Maria Ross, "Securities Fraud in the International Arena," *Business and Society* 30, no. 1 (1991): 27–36.

[38] Randall Hess and Edgar Kossack, "Bribery as an Organizational Response to Conflicting Environmental Expectations," *Academy of Marketing Science* 9, no. 3 (1981): 206–226; Judith Scott, Debora Gilliard, and Richard Scott, "Eliminating Bribery as a Transnational Marketing Strategy," *International Journal of Commerce & Management* 12, no. 1 (2002): 1–17.

[39] R. Edmonson, "Cracking Down on Corruption," *Journal of Commerce*, December 5, 2011, p. 17.

[40] Barry Gunderson, "How Recent Banking Regulations Affect Lenders," July/August 2011, pp. 28–31; Charles Wallace, "Foreign Banks More Worried about Volcker Rule," *Institutional Investor*, November 2011, p. 70.

[41] Joe Mullich, "Risk Management: Most Overlooked Risks," *Wall Street Journal,* January 17, 2012, p. B5.

Chapter 8

[1] David Dollar and Aart Kraay, "Trade, Growth, and Poverty," Policy Research Working Paper no. WPS 2615, June 2001, Washington, DC: World Bank, Development Research Group; Ailín González, "Impacto del Tratado de Libre Comercio de América Del Norte, La Unión Europea y El Tratado de Libre Comercio para República Dominicana y Centro América en las Exportaciones de Puerto Rico," *Revista Internacional Administración & Finanzas* 5, no. 4 (2012): 1–12; Romain Wacziarg and Karen Welch, "Trade Liberalization and Growth: New Evidence," *World Bank Economic Review*, 22, no. 2 (2008): 187–231; United Nations, *World Economic and Social Survey*, 2005, retrieved from http://www.un.org

[2] Jeffrey D. Sachs and Andrew Warner, "Economic Reform and the Process of Global Integration," *Brookings Papers on Economic Activity*, Issue no. 1 (Washington, DC: Brookings Institute, 1995); Heritage Foundation, retrieved from the Heritage Foundation Web site at http://www.heritage.org/research/features/index/

[3] David Ricardo, *Principles of Political Economy and Taxation* (London: Everyman Edition, 1911; first published in 1817).

[4] Andrzej Cieślik and Jan Hagemejer, "The Effectiveness of Preferential Trade Liberalization in Central and Eastern Europe," *International Trade Journal*, 25, no. 5 (2011): 516–538; International Monetary Fund, *World Economic Outlook Databases*, retrieved from www.imf.org; Delia Velculescu, "Poland: Bright Spot in Recession-Hit Europe," *IMF Survey Magazine*, August 13, 2009, International Monetary Fund, retrieved from www.imf.org

[5] "Bush Move Marks U.S. Trade Policy Turning Point," *Financial Times*, March 6, 2002, p. 6.

[6] Jim Carlton, "U.S. Nears Mexican Cement Pact," *Wall Street Journal*, August 29, 2005, p. A7.

[7] Stefanie Lenway, Kathleen Rehbein, and Laura Starks, "The Impact of Protectionism on Firm Wealth: The Experience of the Steel Industry," *Southern Economic Journal* 56, no. 4 (1990): 1079–1093.

[8] G. Chazan and G. White, "Kremlin Weighs on Growth," *Wall Street Journal*, October 17, 2005, p. A16.

[9] Robert Reich, *The Work of Nations: Preparing Ourselves for 21st Century Capitalism* (New York: Knopf, 1991); Lester Thurow, *Head to Head: The Coming Economic Battle among Japan, Europe, and America* (New York: William Morrow, 1992).

[10] World Trade Organization, "Trade Liberalization Statistics," retrieved from www.wto.org, February 27, 2012; United Nations, 2009, retrieved from the United Nations Web site on financial statistics at http://www.un.org/reports/financing/profile.htm

[11] Ed Gresser, "Shoe Tariffs: America's Worst Tax," *DLC Commentary,* December 13, 2010, retrieved from www.dlc.org; World Trade Organization, *Tariff Profile* on the European Union, 2012, retrieved from http://www.wto.org

[12] "Textiles: Knickers in a Twist," *The Economist*, August 27, 2005, p. 50.

[13] Amir Efrati, Loretta Chao, and Kersten Zhang, "Google Softens China Stance," *Wall Street Journal*, January 12, 2012, pp. B1–B2.

[14] World Bank, *Doing Business: Benchmarking Business Regulations*, 2009, retrieved from http://www.doingbusiness.org

[15] U.S. Trade Representative, "National Trade Estimate Report," 2009, retrieved from http://www.ustr.gov

[16] Corina Pons and Daniel Cancel, "Venezuela's Great Dollar Drought," *Bloomberg Businessweek*, February 28, 2011, pp. 15–16.

[17] Bob Davis and Jason Dean, "State-Run Firms Are the Giants of China's Economy," *Wall Street Journal*, February 23, 2012, p. A12.

[18] M. Kripalani, "India Takes a Bath on Oil Subsidies," *BusinessWeek*, June 16, 2008, p. 36.

[19] Michael Grunwald, "Down on The Farm," *Time International*, November 12, 2007, pp. 22–29.

[20] Ilze Upite and Irina Pilvere, "The EU Common Agricultural Policy for Agricultural and Rural Development," *Management Theory & Studies for Rural Business & Infrastructure Development* 27, no. 3 (2011): 183–190.

[21] World Trade Organization, Glossary, 2009, retrieved from http://www.wto.org

[22] Ibid.

[23] "World Trade: Barriers to Entry," *The Economist*, December 20, 2008, p. 121.

[24] Terry Miller, Kim Holmes, and Edwin Feulner, "Highlights of the 2012 Index of Economic Freedom" (Washington, DC: Heritage Foundation and Wall Street Journal), retrieved from http://www.heritage.org

[25] Heritage Foundation, *2012 Index of Economic Freedom* (Washington, DC: Heritage Foundation), retrieved from http://www.heritage.org

[26] Edwin Feulner, "A Step Backward for Economic Freedom in 2012," *Wall Street Journal*, January 12, 2012, retrieved from www.wsj.com

[27] Democratic Leadership Council, "Trade Fact of the Week: U.S. Tariffs Are 23 Times Higher on Cambodian Goods than on British Goods," retrieved from www.dlc.org; Smith (2002).

[28] C. Giles, "Big Ideas Fail to Mop Up Europe's Current Mess," *Financial Times*, February 26, 2009, p. 2.

[29] United Nations Conference on Trade and Development, *The Global Economic Crisis: Systemic Failures and Multilateral Remedies* (Geneva, Switzerland: United Nations, 2009).

[30] D. Brady, "Beware Politicians Bearing Election-Year Trade Deals," *Bloomberg Businessweek*, March 19–25, 2012, pp. 41–43; G. Rachman, "When Globalisation Goes into Reverse," *Financial Times*, February 2, 2009, retrieved from http://www.ft.com

[31] J. Miller, "Nations Rush to Establish New Barriers to Trade," *Wall Street Journal*, February 6, 2009, pp. A1, A6.

[32] R. Wright, "Financial Crises and Reform: Looking Back for Clues to the Future," *The McKinsey Quarterly*, December 2008.

[33] "In the Shadow of Prosperity," *The Economist*, January 20, 2007, pp. 32–34.

[34] Belay Seyoum and Juan Ramirez, "Foreign Trade Zones in the United States: A Study with Special Emphasis on the Proposal for Trade Agreement Parity," *Journal of Economic Studies*, 39, no. 1 (2012): 13–30.

[35] Militiades Chacholidades, *International Economics* (New York: McGraw-Hill, 1990); James Ingram, *International Economics* (New York: Wiley, 1983); William McDaniel and Edgar Kossack, "The Financial Benefits to Users of Foreign-Trade Zones," *Columbia Journal of World Business* 18, no. 3 (1983): 33–41.

[36] Eugene Salorio, Jean Boddewyn, and Nicolas Dahan, "Integrating Business Political Behavior with Economic and Organizational Strategies," *International Studies of Management & Organization* 35, no. 2 (2005): 28–35; Scott Kennedy, "The Barbarians Learn How to Lobby at the Gates of Industry," *Financial Times*, September 28, 2005, p. 5.

Chapter 9

[1] Bela Balassa, *The Theory of Economic Integration* (Homewood, IL: Irwin, 1961); Jacob Viner, *The Customs Union Issue* (New York: Carnegie Endowment for International Peace, 1950).

[2] J. Crawford and R. Fiorentino, *The Changing Landscape of Regional Trade Agreements*, Discussion Paper no. 8 (Geneva, Switzerland: World Trade Organization, 2005); Caroline Freund and Emanuel Ornelas, *Regional Trade Agreements*, Policy Research Working Paper 5314 (Washington DC: The World Bank Development Research Group Trade and Integration Team, May 2010).

[3] European Union, Web site at http://www.europa.eu

[4] "Transformed: EU Membership Has Worked Magic in Central Europe," *The Economist*, June 25, 2005, pp. 6–8.

[5] "European Carmakers: Driving Out of the East," *The Economist*, March 5, 2005, p. 60.

[6] R. Smyser, "The Core of the Global Economy," *The World & I*, April 2001, pp. 26–31.

[7] "Happy Birthday, NAFTA," *BusinessWeek*, December 22, 2003, p. 112; *Progressive Economy*, "A third of all U.S. export growth since 2009 has gone to Canada and Mexico," January 18, 2012, retrieved from www.globalworksfoundation.org

[8] P. Engardio, "This Would Be Bigger than NAFTA," *BusinessWeek*, October 27, 2008, p. 66; "Canada and the U.S. Try to Cuddle Up Again," *Bloomberg BusinessWeek*, September 19–25, 2011, pp. 19–20.

[9] Andre´s Malamud, "Mercosur Turns 15: Between Rising Rhetoric and Declining Achievement," *Cambridge Review of International Affairs* 18, no. 3 (2005): 421–436.

[10] George Garman and Debora Gilliard, "Economic Integration in the Americas: 1975–1992," *The Journal of Applied Business Research* 14, no. 3 (1998): 1–12.

[11] Freund and Ornelas (2010).

[12] Viner (1950); Franklin Root, *International Trade and Investment*, 5th ed. (Cincinnati, OH: South-Western Publishing, 1984); Emile Dreuil, James Anderson, Walter Block, and Michael Saliba, "The Trade Gap: The Fallacy of Anti World-Trade Sentiment," *Journal of Business Ethics* 45, no. 3 (2003): 269–278.

[13] EIU ViewsWire, "Ukraine Politics: The Viktor and Yulia Show, Continued," April 24, 2009, retrieved from http://www.viewswire.eiu.com; Oleg Riabokon, "Trade Liberalization for the Second Largest Country in Europe: Going West or East or Can It Be Both?" *Journal of World Trade* (February 2006): 69–112.

[14] Freund and Ornelas (2010).

[15] Ibid.

[16] "A Divided Union," *The Economist*, September 23, 2004, p. 64.

[17] Robert Lawrence and Lawrence Edwards, "Shattering the Myths about U.S. Trade Policy," *Harvard Business Review* (March 2012): 149–153.

[18] Subhash Jain and John K. Ryans, "A Normative Framework for Assessing Marketing Strategy Implications of Europe 1992," in *Euromarketing*, E. Kaynak and P. Ghauri, eds. (New York: International Business Press, 1994).

[19] "Transformed: EU Membership Has Worked Magic in Central Europe," *The Economist*, June 25, 2005, pp. 6–8.

[20] "Beyond Doha," *The Economist*, October 11, 2008, pp. 30–33.

[21] "The EU and India," *Financial Times*, September 23, 2008, p. 12; "Odd Man Out," *Forbes*, November 17, 2008, p. 20.

Chapter 10

[1] World Bank, *World Bank Development Indicators* (Washington, DC: World Bank, 2012).

[2] Australia Country Monitor, *Country Report: Australia*, March 2012, pp. 1–27; International Monetary Fund, *World Economic Outlook*, April 2012, retrieved from www.imf.org

[3] World Bank (2012).

[4] World Bank, *Doing Business: Economy Rankings*, 2012, retrieved from http://www.doingbusiness.org

[5] Fred Campano and Dominick Salvatore, *Income Distribution* (Oxford, UK: Oxford University Press, 2006); Mary Anastasia O'Grady, "The Rise of Mexico's Middle Class," *Wall Street Journal*, March 5, 2012, p. A13.

[6] Jack Behrman and Dennis Rondinelli, "The Transition to Market-Oriented Economies in Central and Eastern Europe," *European Business Journal* 12 (2000): 87–99.

[7] M. Bartiromo, "Power Player Naguib Sawiris," *BusinessWeek*, December 8, 2008, p. 23; Profile of Orascom at http://www.hoovers.com; Zoltan Simon, "The Russians Are Buying. And Buying," *Bloomberg BusinessWeek*, September 19–25, 2011, pp. 17–18; *Sydney Morning Herald*, "China Snubs Debt in European Spending Spree," February 6, 2012, retrieved from www.smh.com.au; Vivienne Walt, "Feasting On Europe," *Time International*, December 12, 2011, pp. 51–54.

[8] "Forbes Global 2000" for 2005 and 2011, retrieved from www.forbes.com; "Fortune Global 500" for 2005 and 2011, retrieved from http://www.money.cnn.com/magazines/fortune/global500

[9] "Britain's Lonely High-Flier," January 10, 2009, *The Economist*, pp. 60–61; UNCTAD, *UNCTAD Handbook of Statistics 2012* (New York: United Nations, 2012).

[10] "Two Billion More Bourgeois: The Middle Class in Emerging Markets," *The Economist*, February 14, 2009, p. 18.

[11] Michael Deneen and Andrew Gross, "The Global Market for Power Tools," *Business Economics*, July 2006, pp. 66–73; O'Grady (2012).

[12] L. Lee, "Thank Heaven for Emerging Markets," *BusinessWeek*, January 7, 2008, pp. 62–63.

[13] "Racing Down the Pyramid," *The Economist*, November 15, 2008, p. 76.

[14] Malcolm Moore, "SABMiller's Asia Chief Ari Mervis Raises a Glass to Snow Beer," *The Telegraph*, August 22, 2011, retrieved from www.telegraph.co.uk

[15] Ali Shah, "Business Strategies in the Emerging Markets," *Journal of Asia-Pacific Business* 13, no. 1 (2012): 4–15.

[16] *Economist*, "Burgernomics Shows Switzerland Has the Most Overvalued Currency," January 12, 2012, retrieved from www.economist.com

[17] The "percent of income held by middle class" refers to the percentile distribution of income in a nation. In particular, it represents the proportion of national income earned by the middle 60 percentile of the population when the top 20 percentile (the wealthiest) and the bottom 20 percentile (the poorest) are excluded. For example, the middle class—60 percent of the population sandwiched between the wealthiest and the poorest—in Brazil accounted for only 39 percent of national income, suggesting a relatively unequal distribution of national income.

[18] Surjit Bhalla, *Second among Equals: The Middle Class Kingdoms of India and China* (Washington, DC: Peterson Institute for International Economics, Washington, forthcoming); "Burgeoning Bourgeoisie: A Special Report on the New Middle Classes in Emerging Markets," *The Economist*, February 14, 2009, Special Section; Homi Kharas, *The Emerging Middle Class in Developing Countries*, Working Paper No. 285 (Paris: OECD Development Centre, 2010).

[19] Adel Al Khattab, "The Role of Corporate Risk Managers in Country Risk Management," *International Journal of Business and Management* 6, no. 1 (2011): 11–20.

[20] Ariel Cohen, "Putin's Crisis: Dealing with Russia's Political Upheaval," WebMemo #671, February 20, 2005, retrieved from http://www.doingbusiness.org; World Bank, *Doing Business 2010* (Washington, DC: The World Bank, 2010).

[21] United States Trade Representative, *National Trade Estimate Report on Foreign Trade Barriers*, 2012, retrieved from http://www.ustr.gov

[22] Laurie Burkitt and Loretta Chao, "Made in China: Fake Stores," *Wall Street Journal*, August 3, 2011, retrieved at www.wsj.com

[23] World Bank, *Doing Business 2009* (Washington, DC: The World Bank, 2009).

[24] Bruce Einhorn, "India Seeks Access to the Broadband Highway," *Bloomberg BusinessWeek*, November 21–27, 2011, pp. 19–20.

[25] Transparency International, *Corruption Perceptions Index 2011*, retrieved from http://www.transparency.org

[26] "Creaking, Groaning: Infrastructure Is India's Biggest Handicap," *The Economist*, December 13, 2008, pp. 11–13.

[27] M. Valente and A. Crane, "Private, but Public," *Wall Street Journal*, March 23, 2009, p. R6.

[28] Daekwan Kim, Destan Kandemir, and S. Tamer Cavusgil, "The Role of Family Conglomerates in Emerging Markets: What Western Companies Should Know," *Thunderbird International Business Review* 46 (2004): 13–20.

[29] A. Bhattacharya and D. Michael, "How Local Companies Keep Multinationals at Bay," *Harvard Business Review*, March 2008, pp. 85–95.

[30] Hans Greimel, "Tiny Etios for India Teaches Toyota to Simplify, Cut Costs," *Automotive News*, August 1, 2011, p. 46; Peter Marsh, "Toyota Gears Up for Production Drive in India," *Financial Times*, March 5, 2007, p. 21.

[31] G. Edmondson, "Renault's Race to Replace the Rickshaw," *BusinessWeek*, 2007, retrieved from http://www.businessweek .com

[32] "The World of the Internet," *Business 2.0*, August 2007, pp. 20–21.

[33] Ted London and Stuart Hart, "Reinventing Strategies for Emerging Markets: Beyond the Transnational Model," *Journal of International Business Studies* 35 (2004): 350–63; Valente & Crane (2009).

[34] A. Bhattacharya and D. Michael, "How Local Companies Keep Multinationals at Bay," *Harvard Business Review*, March 2008, pp. 85–95.

[35] Jeffrey Garten, *The Big Ten: The Big Emerging Markets and How They Will Change Our Lives* (New York: Basic Books, 1997); G. Kolodko, ed., *Emerging Market Economics: Globalization and Development* (Aldershot, Hants, England: Ashgate, 2003); Kim, Kandemir, and Cavusgil (2004).

[36] Pete Engardio, "Emerging Giants," *BusinessWeek*, July 31, 2006, pp. 40–49; Kushan Mitra, "Top Gun," *Business Today*, October 2, 2011, pp. 44–52.

[37] World Economic Forum, *Global Risks 2012*, 6th ed. (Geneva, Switzerland: World Economic Forum).

[38] Ibid.

[39] Bruce Einhorn, "Qualcomm Rewires for India," *Bloomberg BusinessWeek*, September 12–18, 2011, pp. 37–38; C. K. Prahalad, "Aid Is Not the Answer," *Wall Street Journal*, August 31, 2005, p. A8; C. K. Prahalad, *The Fortune at the Bottom of the Pyramid: Eradicating Poverty Through Profits* (Philadelphia: Wharton School Books, 2005); Jennifer Reingold, "Can P&G Make Money in Places Where People Earn $2 a Day?," *Fortune*, January 17, 2011, pp. 86–90.

[40] M. Bahree, "Cheaper Sleeper," *Forbes*, October 13, 2009, p. 100.

[41] International Telecommunications Union, "Africa Has 300 Million Mobile Phone Subscribers," 2009 press release retrieved from http://www.itu.int; "Mobile Phone Growth Biggest in Africa," *African Business*, April 2009, p. 8.

[42] Brigit Helms, *Access for All: Building Inclusive Financial Systems* (Washington, DC: The World Bank, 2006).

[43] "Grabbing Grameen," *Economist*, January 28, 2012, p. 67; Muhammad Yunus, *Creating a World Without Poverty* (New York: Public Affairs, 2009).

[44] Christopher Beshouri, "A Grassroots Approach to Emerging-Market Consumers," *The McKinsey Quarterly* 4 (2006), retrieved from http://www.mckinseyquarterly.com

[45] "Opportunity Knocks," *The Economist*, October 11, 2008, pp. 33–35.

[46] Farzad (2007); J. Nocera, "Diamonds Are Forever in Botswana," *New York Times*, August 9, 2008, p. C1.

[47] Randall Hackley, "Africa's Powerful New Friends in China," *Bloomberg BusinessWeek*, September 12–18, 2011, pp. 56–57; Devon Maylie, "By Foot, by Bike, by Taxi, Nestlé Expands in Africa," *Wall Street Journal*, December 1, 2011, p. B1; Tom Nevin, "Coca-Cola: 125 Years of Making Friends," *African Business*, December 1, 2011, pp. 44–45.

[48] L. Enriquez, S. Schmitgen, and G. Sun, "The True Value of Mobile Phones to Developing Markets," *McKinsey Quarterly*, February 2007, retrieved from http://www.mckinseyquarterly .com; J. Ewing, "Upwardly Mobile in Africa," *BusinessWeek*, September 24, 2007, pp. 64–71.

[49] Farzad (2007).

[50] M. Conway, S. Gupta, and K. Khajavi, "Addressing Africa's Health Workforce Crisis," *McKinsey Quarterly*, November 2007, retrieved from http://www.mckinseyquarterly.com

[51] *Economist*, "A Fall to Cheer," March 3, 2012, pp. 81–82; Dambisa Moyo, *When Help Does Harm* (New York: Farrar, Straus and Giroux, 2009); D. Zeng, ed., *Knowledge, Technology, and Cluster-Based Growth in Africa* (Washington, DC: The World Bank Group, 2008).

Chapter 11

[1] C. Belton, "Moscow Sees End to Capital Flight as Rouble Stabilises," *Financial Times*, February 27, 2007, p. 3; "Economic Structure and Context: Development and Strategy," Venezuela Country Monitor, January 2012, pp. 19–20; "The Weakening of the 'Strong Bolivar' Venezuela's Devaluation," *The Economist*, January 16, 2010, p. 39.

[2] *Federal Reserve Bulletin*, various years, at http://www.feder-alreserve.gov.

[3] Juro Osawa, "Yen Pulls Nintendo to a Loss," *Wall Street Journal*, July 30, 2010, p. B4

[4] David Fickling, "The Grapes of Currency Wrath," *Bloomberg BusinessWeek*, January 30–February 5, 2012, pp. 22–23.

[5] Peter Morgan, "The Role of Macroeconomic Policy in Rebalancing Growth," *Journal of Asian Economics* 23, no. 1 (2012): 13–25.

[6] Country Intelligence Report: Pakistan," *Pakistan Country Monitor*, March 2012, pp. 1–23; "Pakistan Economy: Crisis Averted?" *EIU ViewsWire*, July 10, 2009.

[7] Abdul-Hamid Sukar and Seid Hassan, "U.S. Exports and Time-Varying Volatility of Real Exchange Rate," *Global Finance Journal* 12 (2001): 109–114.

[8] Josef Brada, Ali Kutan, and Su Zhou, "The Exchange Rate and the Balance of Trade: The Turkish Experience," *The Journal of Development Studies* 33 (1997): 675–684.

[9] International Monetary Fund, *Global Financial Stability Report*, 2004, retrieved from http://www.imf.org.

[10] U.S. Department of the Treasury, *Preliminary Report on Foreign Holdings of U.S. Securities*, 2012, retrieved from http:// www.treas.gov.

[11] Alan Greenspan, "The Globalization of Finance," *The Cato Journal* 17 (1997), retrieved from http://www.cato.org.

[12] International Monetary Fund, "Effects of Financial Globalization on Developing Countries: Some Empirical Evidence," 2003, retrieved from http://www.imf.org.

[13] Meiling Pope et al, "Mobile Payments: The Reality on the Ground in Selected Asian Countries and the United States," *International Journal of Mobile Marketing* 6, no. 2 (2011): 88–104; Adam Thomson, "Families Struggle to Survive as Flow of Dollars Dries Up," *Financial Times*, August 19, 2009, p. 4.

[14] "Telcos Offer Incentives to Lure Bond Investors," *Corporate Finance*, July 2000, p. 4.

[15] "Open Wider: A Survey of International Banking," *The Economist*, May 21, 2005, special section.

[16] "AFRICA: Mobile Banking Prospects Remain Positive," *Oxford Analytica Daily Brief Service*, October 3, 2008, p. 1; Moin Siddiqi, "Banking in Africa," *African Business*, April 2000, pp. 25–27.

[17] Bank for International Settlements, *Consultative Document: The New Basel Capital Accord*, 2001, retrieved from http://www .bis.org.

[18] International Monetary Fund, *Financial Statements*, for the years ending April 30, 2010, and April 30, 2011, retrieved from http://www.imf.org.

[19] Mathias Dolls, Andreas Peichl, and Klaus Zimmermann, "A Challenge for the G20: Global Debt Brakes and Transnational Fiscal Supervisory Councils," *Intereconomics* 47, no. 1 (2012): 31–38; World Economic Forum, *Global Risks 2011*, 6th ed. (Geneva, Switzerland, 2011).

[20] Ibid.

[21] Liz Alderman and Rachel Donadio, "Debt Rating Cut for 9 Countries Amid Euro Woes," *New York Times*, January 14, 2012, pp. A1 and B6; Moody's, "Moody's Adjusts Ratings of 9 European Sovereigns to Capture Downside Risks," February 13, 2012, retrieved from www.moodys.com.

[22] World Economic Forum (2011).

[23] Gokhale, J. (2009); "Measuring the Unfunded Obligations of European Countries," National Centre for Policy Analysis (NCPA) Policy Report No. 319 (Washington, DC: National Center for Policy Analysis); International Monetary Fund, *United States: Selected Issues Paper, IMF Country Report No. 10/248*, July 12, 2010 (Washington, DC: International Monetary Fund); L. Kotlikoff, "A Hidden Fiscal Crisis?," *Finance and Development*, September 2010, (Washington, DC: International Monetary Fund).

Chapter 12

[1] S. Tamer Cavusgil, Sengun Yeniyurt, and Janell Townsend, "The Framework of a Global Company: A Conceptualization and Preliminary Validation," *Industrial Marketing Management* 33 (2004): 711–716; G. T. Hult, S. Deligonul, and S. Tamer Cavusgil, "The Hexagon of Market-Based Globalization: An Empirical Approach Towards Delineating the Extent of Globalization in Companies," in *New Perspectives in International Business Thought*, A. Lewin, ed. (London: Palgrave, 2006); George Yip, *Total Global Strategy II* (Upper Saddle River, NJ: Prentice Hall, 2003).

[2] Christopher A. Bartlett and Sumantra Ghoshal, *Managing Across Borders: The Transnational Solution* (Boston, MA: Harvard Business School Press, 1989).

[3] Christopher A. Bartlett and Sumantra Ghoshal, *Transnational Management: Text, Cases, and Readings in Cross-Border Management*, 3rd ed. (Boston, MA: Irwin/McGraw-Hill, 2000), p. 273.

[4] Ibid.

[5] Bruce Kogut, "Designing Global Strategies: Profiting from Operational Flexibility," *Strategic Management Journal* 27 (1985): 27–38.

[6] L. Bryan and D. Farrell, "Leading through Uncertainty," *The McKinsey Quarterly*, December 2008, retrieved from http://www .mckinseyquarterly.com

[7] Cavusgil, Yeniyurt, and Townsend (2004); Hult, Deligonul, and Cavusgil (2006); Yip (2003).

[8] Hult, Deligonul, and Cavusgil (2006); Ben L. Kedia and Akuro Mukherji, "Global Managers: Developing a Mindset for Global Competitiveness," *Journal of World Business* 34 (1999): 230–251; Robert Waterman, Tom Peters, and J. R. Philips, "Structure Is Not Organization," *Business Horizons* 23, no. 3 (1980): 14–26.

[9] Haig Simonian, "Climber Scales the Health Peak," *Financial Times*, August 21, 2006, p. 8.

[10] Stephen Rhinesmith, *A Manager's Guide to Globalization* (Homewood, IL: Business One Irwin, 1998).

[11] Gary A. Knight and S. Tamer Cavusgil, "Innovation, Organizational Capabilities, and the Born-Global Firm," *Journal of International Business Studies* 35 (2004): 124–141; Jeffrey Covin and Dennis Slevin, "Strategic Management of Small Firms in Hostile and Benign Environments," *Strategic Management Journal* 10 (January 1989): 75–87; G. T. Lumpkin and Gregory Dess, "Clarifying the Entrepreneurial Orientation Construct and Linking It to Performance," *Academy of Management Review* 21(1996): 135–172.

[12] Gary Hamel and C. K. Prahalad, "Strategic Intent," *Harvard Business Review*, May–June 1989, pp. 63–76.

[13] Cavusgil, Yeniyurt, and Townsend (2004).

[14] "The Grey Market: Hey, Big Spender," *The Economist*, December 3, 2005, pp. 59–60.

[15] "What You Can Learn from Toyota," *Business 2.0*, January/ February 2005, pp. 67–72; J. Soble, "Toyota Appoints Founder's Grandson as Next Chief Executive," *Financial Times*, January 21, 2009, p. 18; Alex Taylor, "Tata Takes on the World Building an Auto Empire in India," May 2, 2011, pp. 86–92.

[16] Joel Nicholson and Yim-Yu Wong, "Culturally Based Differences in Work Beliefs," *Management Research News* 24, no. 5 (2001): 1–10; Edgar H. Schein, *Organizational Culture and Leadership*, 2nd ed. (San Francisco: Jossey-Bass, 1997).

[17] Clay Chandler, "Canon's Big Gun," *Fortune,* February 6, 2006, pp. 92–98; Juro Osawa, "At Canon, Elder Gains Wider Leadership Role," *Wall Street Journal*, January 31, 2012, p. B5.

[18] David Aaker, "Remove Negatives to Remain Relevant," *Marketing News*, January 31, 2012, p. 14; Alex Taylor III, "Hyundai Smokes the Competition," *Fortune*, January 18, 2010, pp. 62–71.

[19] Cavusgil, Yeniyurt, and Townsend (2004); Rhinesmith (1998); George S. Yip, Johny K. Johansson, and J. Roos, "Effects of Nationality on Global Strategy," *Management International Review* 37 (1997): 365–385.

[20] Stephen Chen, Ronald Geluykens, and Chong Ju Choi, "The Importance of Language in Global Teams," *Management International Review* 46, no. 6 (2006): 679–696; Robert T. Keller, "Cross-Functional Project Groups in Research and New Product Development: Diversity, Communications, Job Stress, and Outcomes," *Academy of Management Journal* 44 (2001): 547– 555; Mary Maloney and Mary Zellmer-Bruhn, "Building Bridges, Windows and Cultures," *Management International Review* 46 (2006): 697–720.

[21] Martha L. Maznevski and Nicholas A. Athanassiou, "Guest Editors' Introduction to the Focused Issue: A New Direction for Global Teams Research," *Management International Review* 46 (2006): 631–646.

[22] Terence Brake, *Managing Globally* (New York: Dorling Kindersley, 2002).

[23] Bartlett and Ghoshal (1989); Gary Hamel and C. K. Prahalad, "Do You Really Have a Global Strategy?" *Harvard Business Review* 63 (July–August 1985): 139–149; T. Hout, Michael

Porter, and E. Rudden, "How Global Companies Win Out," *Harvard Business Review* 60 (September–October 1982): 98–105; Robert T. Moran and John R. Riesenberger, *The Global Challenge* (London: McGraw-Hill, 1994); Kenichi Ohmae, "Planning for a Global Harvest," *Harvard Business Review* 67 (July–August 1989): 136–145.

24 Bartlett and Ghoshal (1989); Timothy M. Devinney, David F. Midgley, and Sunil Venaik, "The Optimal Performance and the Global Firm: Formalizing and Extending the Integration-Responsiveness Framework," *Organization Science* 11 (2000): 674–695; Yves L. Doz, Christopher Bartlett, and C. K. Prahalad, "Global Competitive Pressures and Host Country Demands: Managing Tensions in MNCs," *California Management Review* 23 (1981): 63–74; Yadong Luo, "Determinants of Local Responsiveness: Perspectives from Foreign Subsidiaries in an Emerging Market," *Journal of Management* 26 (2001): 451–477; C. K. Prahalad, *The Strategic Process in a Multinational Corporation*, Unpublished doctoral dissertation (Graduate School of Business Administration, Harvard University, Cambridge, MA, 1975).

25 Bartlett and Ghoshal (1989); Moran and Riesenberger (1994).

26 Bartlett and Ghoshal (2000).

27 Bartlett and Ghoshal (2000); G. Ghislanzoni, R. Penttinen, and D. Turnbull, "The Multilocal Challenge: Managing Cross-Border Functions," *The McKinsey Quarterly*, 2008, retrieved from http://www.mckinseyquarterly.com

28 L. Chang, "Nestlé Stumbles in China's Evolving Market," *Wall Street Journal*, December 8, 2004, p. A10; G. Chazan, "Foreign Products Get Russian Makeovers," *Wall Street Journal*, January 16, 2001, p. A23; Nestlé Corporation, "Key Facts and History," 2009, retrieved from http://www.nestle.com; Greg Steinmetz and Tara Parker-Pope, "All Over the Map: At a Time When Companies Are Scrambling to Go Global, Nestlé Has Long Been There," *Wall Street Journal*, September 26, 1996, p. R4.

29 Moran and Riesenberger (1994).

30 Bartlett and Ghoshal (2000).

31 Bartlett and Ghoshal (1989); Hamel and Prahalad (1985); Hout, Porter, and Rudden (1982); Levitt (1983); Moran and Riesenberger (1994); Ohmae (1989).

32 Bong Choi, Jongweon Kim, Byung-hak Leem, Chang-Yeol Lee, and Han-kuk Hong, "Empirical Analysis of the Relationship Between Six Sigma Management Activities and Corporate Competitiveness: Focusing on Samsung Group in Korea," *International Journal of Operations & Production Management* 32, no. 5 (2012): 528–550; Evan Ramstad and Jung-Ah Lee, "Samsung's Profit Hits Fast Track," *Wall Street Journal*, April 9, 2012, p. B6.

33 Bartlett and Ghoshal (2000).

34 Shaoming Zou and S. Tamer Cavusgil, "The GMS: A Broad Conceptualization of Global Marketing Strategy and Its Effect on Firm Performance," *Journal of Marketing* 58 (January 2002): 1–21; Yip (2003).

35 Katrin Hille, "Back to the Future for Lenovo," *Financial Times*, February 12, 2009, p. 17; Chuan Zhi Liu, "Lenovo: An Example of Globalization of Chinese Enterprises," *Journal of International Business Studies* 38, no. 4 (2007): 573–577; Jane Spencer and Loretta Chao, "Lenovo Goes Global, But Not Without Strife," *Wall Street Journal*, November 4, 2008, p. B1; Elizabeth Woyke, "Lenovo CEO Keeps Focus on Hardware, Eyes PC Market Crown," Forbes, January 10, 2012, p. 34.

36 Pankaj Ghemawat, "Regional Strategies for Global Leadership," *Harvard Business Review* 83 (December 2005): 98–106.

37 Moran and Riesenberger (1994); Franklin Root, *Entry Strategies for International Markets* (San Francisco: Jossey-Bass, 1998).

38 Moran and Riesenberger (1994).

39 Alfred D. Chandler, *Strategy and Structure* (Cambridge, MA: MIT Press, 1962).

40 Moran and Riesenberger (1994).

41 Ibid.

42 Ibid.

43 Ibid.

44 Ibid.

45 Bartlett and Ghoshal (1989); Moran and Riesenberger (1994); G. T. Hult, Deligonul, and Cavusgil (2006).

46 Deborah Ball, "Despite Revamp, Unwieldy Unilever Falls behind Rivals," *Wall Street Journal*, January 3, 2005, pp. A1, A5; Unilever corporate profile at http://www.hoovers.com; "Unilever's Vital Shift in Direction," *Strategic Direction* 28, no. 2 (2012): 6–8.

47 Philip Atkinson, "Managing Chaos in a Matrix World," *Management Services*, November 2003, p. 8; Jennifer Pellet, "Fine-Tuning Philips," *Chief Executive*, March/April 2009, pp. 12–13.

48 Moran and Riesenberger (1994).

Chapter 13

1 Peter Liesch, Lawrence Welch, and Peter Buckley, "Risk and Uncertainty in Internationalisation and International Entrepreneurship Studies," *Management International Review* 51, no. 6 (2011): 851–873.

2 L. Bryan and D. Farrell, "Leading through Uncertainty," *The McKinsey Quarterly*, December 2008, retrieved from http://www.mckinseyquarterly.com

3 Matthew Boyle, "Persuading Brits to Give Up Their Dishrags," *Bloomberg Businessweek*, March 26–April 1, 2012, pp. 20–21.

4 F. Cunningham, "Commerce Department Helps Franchisors Go Global," *Franchising World*, December 2005, pp. 63–67.

5 D. Vrontis and P. Vronti, "Levi Strauss: An International Marketing Investigation," *Journal of Fashion Marketing and Management* 8 (2004): 389–398.

6 Shruti Singh and Ganesh Nagarajan, "Small Is Beautiful For John Deere," *Bloomberg Businessweek*, September 26, 2011, pp. 33–34.

7 S. Tamer Cavusgil, "Measuring the Potential of Emerging Markets: An Indexing Approach," *Business Horizons* 40 (January–February 1997): 87–91.

8 GlobalEDGE™, "Market Potential Index for Emerging Markets—2012," retrieved from www.globalEDGE.msu.edu/resourcedesk/mpi

9 "Burgeoning Bourgeoisie: A Special Report on the New Middle Classes in Emerging Markets," *The Economist*, February 14, 2009, Special Section; Homi Kharas, *The Emerging Middle Class In Developing Countries* (Paris: OECD Development Centre, 2010).

10 Lee Chi-Ho, "Korea's IT Industry in Transition," *SERI Quarterly*, January 2012, pp. 22–29.

11 N. Andrade, J. Lottner, and C. Roland, "How Young Consumers Could Shape Vietnam's Banks," *The McKinsey*

Quarterly, March 2008, retrieved from http://www.mckinsey-quarterly.com

[12] C. Miller and P. Olson, "Tesco's Landing," *Forbes*, June 4, 2007, pp. 116–118.

[13] Peter Enderwick, "The Imperative of Global Environmental Scanning," *Insights* 11, no. 1 (2011): 12–15.

Chapter 14

[1] Erin Anderson and Hubert Gatignon, "Modes of Foreign Entry: A Transaction Cost Analysis and Propositions," *Journal of International Business Studies* 17 (Fall 1986): 1–26; William H. Davidson, *Global Strategic Management* (New York: Wiley, 1982).

[2] Tao Gao, "The Contingency Framework of Foreign Entry Mode Decisions: Locating and Reinforcing the Weakest Link," *Multinational Business Review* 12 (2004): 37–68.

[3] "Escaping the Middle Market Trap: An Interview with the CEO of Electrolux," *McKinsey Quarterly* 4 (2006): 73–79.

[4] S. Tamer Cavusgil, "On the Internationalization Process of Firms," *European Research* 8 (1980): 273–281.

[5] Jan Johanson and J.-E. Vahlne, "The Internationalization Process of the Firm—A Model of Knowledge Development and Increasing Foreign Commitments," *Journal of International Business Studies* 8 (Spring–Summer 1977): 23–32; Robert Salomon and J. Myles Shaver, "Learning by Exporting: New Insights from Examining Firm Innovation," *Journal of Economics & Management Strategy* 14 (2005): 431–442.

[6] Lee Chi-Ho, "Korea's IT Industry in Transition," *SERI Quarterly*, January 2012, pp. 22–29; A. Porter, N. Newman, J. Roessner, D. Johnson, and X. Jin, "International High Tech Competitiveness: Does China Rank Number 1?" *Technology Analysis & Strategic Management* 21, no. 2 (2009): 173–183.

[7] UNCTAD, *Review of Maritime Transport 2011* (New York: United Nations).

[8] David Liu, "Exporting Mortgage Insurance Beyond the United States," *Housing Finance International* 14 (2000): 32–41.

[9] Austan Goolsbee, "Jeremy Lin and America's 'New Exports'," *Wall Street Journal*, February 22, 2012, p. A15; Anne Smith, "Health Care Bargains Abroad," *Kiplinger's Personal Finance*, January 2012, pp. 65–68.

[10] Javalgi Rajshekhar, Charles Martin, and Patricia Todd, "The Export of E-Services in the Age of Technology Transformation: Challenges and Implications for International Service Providers," *The Journal of Services Marketing* 18 (2004): 560–573.

[11] Institute for International Business, "The Global vs. Domestic Wine Industry," *Global Executive Forum*, Spring–Summer 2005, p. 12.

[12] S. Tamer Cavusgil and Shaoming Zou, "Marketing Strategy-Performance Relationship: An Investigation of the Empirical Link in Export Market Ventures," *Journal of Marketing* 58 (January 1994): 1–21.

[13] M. O'Flanagan, "Case Study: Exporting Gives Businesses a Healthy Outlook," *Sunday Business Post*, April 6, 2003.

[14] Chun Zhang, S. Tamer Cavusgil, and Anthony Roath, "Manufacturer Governance of Foreign Distributor Relationships: Do Relational Norms Enhance Competitiveness in the Export Market?" *Journal of International Business Studies* 34 (2003): 550–563.

[15] Capstone Turbine Corporation 2012 Annual Report, retrieved from http://www.capstoneturbine.com

Chapter 15

[1] Company profile of Tata at http://www.hoovers.com; P. Beckett, "Tata Chairman Doesn't Sweat the Timing on Global Expansion," *Wall Street Journal*, November 18, 2009, p. B1; Peter Harrop, "India Buys More of the UK Electric Vehicle Industry Cambridge, UK," *Automotive Industries*, January 2012, retrieved from www.dallasnews.com.

[2] Datamonitor, *Drinks MarketWatch Company Spotlight: SABMiller*, December 2011, pp. 18–24; company profile of SABMiller at http://www.hoovers.com

[3] UNCTAD, *Global Investment Trends Monitor* (New York: United Nations, January 24, 2012), retrieved from www.unctad.org

[4] John Dunning, *International Production and the Multinational Enterprise* (London: Allen and Unwin, 1981).

[5] Farok Contractor and Peter Lorange, eds., *Cooperative Strategies in International Markets* (Lexington, MA: Lexington Books, 1988); Gary Hamel, Yves Doz, and C. K. Prahalad, "Collaborate with Your Competitors—and Win," *Harvard Business Review* 67 (January–February 1989): 133–139; Katherine Harrigan, "Strategic Alliances: Their New Role in Global Competition," *Columbia Journal of World Business* 22 (Summer 1987): 67–69; Vern Terpstra and Bernard Simonin, "Strategic Alliances in the Triad," *Journal of International Marketing* 1 (1993): 4–25.

[6] Lilach Nachum and Srilata Zaheer, "The Persistence of Distance? The Impact of Technology on MNE Motivations for Foreign Investment," *Strategic Management Journal* 26 (2005): 747–767.

[7] Stanley Reed and Dexter Roberts, "What's Shell Doing in China," *Bloomberg Businessweek*, November 21–27, 2011, pp. 88–93.

[8] Wilbur Chung and Juan Alcacer, "Knowledge Seeking and Location Choice of Foreign Direct Investment in the United States," *Management Science* 48 (2002): 1534–1542.

[9] Anders Lotsson, "Tomorrow: A Sneak Preview," *Business 2.0* (August 2005): 77–84.

[10] Lilach Nachum and Cliff Wymbs, "Product Differentiation, External Economies and MNE Location Choices: M&As in Global Cities," *Journal of International Business Studies* 36 (2005): 415–423.

[11] Nachum and Zaheer (2005).

[12] "Retailing: Storm Clouds Over the Mall," *The Economist*, October 8, 2005, pp. 71–72.

[13] Barbara Katz and Joel Owen, "Should Governments Compete for Foreign Direct Investment?" *Journal of Economic Behavior & Organization* 59 (2006): 230–238.

[14] Samsung, *Step Forward: Samsung Profile 2009*, retrieved from http://www.samsung.com; Sheridan Prasso, "How Samsung Turned Up the Sizzle," *Fortune*, July 25, 2011, p. 28.

[15] "Biggest Transnational Companies," *The Economist*, October 3, 2009, p. 121.

[16] Steve Hamm, "IBM vs. Tata: Which Is More American?" *BusinessWeek*, May 5, 2008, p. 28.

[17] *Business Eastern Europe*, "Russia: The Joke Misfires," March 14, 2011, p. 9; Carol Matlack, "Carlos Ghosn's Russian Gambit," *BusinessWeek*, March 17, 2008, pp. 57–58.

[18] Thomas C. Head and P. Sorensen, "Attracting Foreign Direct Investment: The Potential Role of National Culture," *The Journal of American Academy of Business* 6 (2005): 305–309.

[19] Clay Chandler, "Mickey Mao," *Fortune,* April 18, 2005, pp. 170–178.

[20] Chandler (2005); Jane Leung and Kate Nicholson, "Disney Seeks to Consolidate Reputation in China," *Media,* November 19, 2009, p. 16; Kimburley Choi, "Disneyfication and Localisation: The Cultural Globalisation Process of Hong Kong Disneyland," *Urban Studies* 49, no. 2 (2012): 383–397.

[21] "Beyond the Green Corporation," *BusinessWeek,* January 29, 2007, pp. 50–64.

[22] M. K. Erramilli and C. P. Rao, "Service Firms' International Entry-Mode Choice: A Modified Transaction-Cost Analysis Approach," *Journal of Marketing* 57 (July 1993): 19–38; J. Li and S. Guisinger, "The Globalization of Service Multinationals in the 'Triad' Regions: Japan, Western Europe, and North America," *Journal of International Business Studies* 23 (1992): 675–696; United Nations, *The Transnationalization of Service Industries* (New York: Transnational Corporations and Management Division, Department of Economic and Social Development, 1993).

[23] Rajshekhar Javalgi, David A. Griffith, and D. Steven White, "An Empirical Examination of Factors Influencing the Internationalization of Service Firms," *Journal of Services Marketing* 17 (2003): 185–201.

[24] UNCTAD (2006).

[25] Hwy-Chang Moon, Joseph Cheng, Min-Young Kim and Jin-Uk Kim, "FDI, Economic Decline and Recovery: Lessons from the Asian Financial Crisis," *Multinational Business Review* 19, no. 2 (2011): 120–132; UNCTAD, *World Investment Report 2011* (New York: United Nations, 2011).

[26] A. T. Kearney, *FDI Confidence Index* (Alexandria, VA: Global Business Policy Council, 2004).

[27] Federation of European Employers, "Competitive Wage Costs" (London: Federation of European Employers, 2010), retrieved at www.fedee.com

[28] A.T. Kearney, "Cautious Investors Feed a Tentative Recovery: 2012 A.T. Kearney Foreign Direct Investment Confidence Index, retrieved at www.atkearney.com; David Rocks, "Made in China—Er, Veliko Turnovo," *BusinessWeek,* January 8, 2007, p. 43.

[29] Andrew Ward, "Home Depot in Mexico," *Financial Times,* April 6, 2006, p. 8.

[30] UNCTAD (2006).

[31] UNCTAD (2011).

[32] Alan Ohnsman, "Surprise! Carmakers Are a Recovery Bright Spot," *Bloomberg Businessweek,* November 7–13, 2011, pp. 19–20.

[33] In this book, we adopt the customary definition of "joint venture" where it is assumed to carry equity interest by the parent firms that founded it. That is, a joint venture is always an equity venture. Nevertheless, in the popular literature the term "equity venture" is incorrectly used to refer to all types of collaborative ventures, including project-based collaborations. Therefore, we will use the term "equity joint venture" rather than simply "joint venture" to avoid miscommunication.

[34] Paul Kaihla, "Why China Wants to Scoop Up Your Company," *Business 2.0,* June 2005, pp. 29–30.

[35] Farok Contractor and Peter Lorange, *Cooperative Strategies and Alliances* (Oxford, England: Elsevier Science, 2002); Janell Townsend, "Understanding Alliances: A Review of International Aspects in Strategic Marketing," *Marketing Intelligence & Planning* 21 (2003): 143–158.

[36] Donald Fites, "Make Your Dealers Your Partners," *Harvard Business Review* 74 (1996): 84–91; Masaaki Kotabe, Hildy Teegen, Preet Aulakh, Maria Cecilia Coutinho de Arruda, Roberto Santillan-Salgado, and Walter Greene, "Strategic Alliances in Emerging Latin America: A View from Brazilian, Chilean, and Mexican Companies," *Journal of World Business* 35 (2000): 114–132.

[37] Ellen Byron and Rachel Dodes, "P&G Flirts with Luxury Cosmetics," *Wall Street Journal,* March 9, 2009, p. B1.

[38] "Business Digest," *Chemistry & Industry,* January 2012, p. 14; Y. Kim and K. Ahn, "Samsung Tesco Homeplus and Corporate Social Responsibility," *Richard Ivey School of Business Case Collection,* July 29, 2009.

[39] Don Clark, "Chip Start-Up Joins With Russia In Memory Deal," *Wall Street Journal,* May 17, 2011, p. B7.

[40] Robert A. Guth, "IBM Announces Deal with Japan's NTT," *Wall Street Journal,* November 1, 2000, p. A23.

[41] Power Engineering, "Pressure Vessel for AP1000 Nuclear Reactor in China put in Place," November 2011, Special section p. 6.

[42] Contractor and Lorange (2002); Gary Hamel, "Competition for Competence and Inter-Partner Learning within International Strategic Alliances," *Strategic Management Journal* Special Issue: Global Strategy, 12 (Summer 1991): 83–103; Gary Hamel, Yves Doz, and C. K. Prahalad, "Collaborate with Your Competitors—and Win," *Harvard Business Review* 67 (January–February 1989): 133–139; S. Tamer Cavusgil, "International Partnering: A Systematic Framework for Collaborating with Foreign Business Partners," *Journal of International Marketing* 6 (1998): 91–107; Destan Kandemir, Attila Yaprak, and S. Tamer Cavusgil, "Alliance Orientation: Conceptualization, Measurement and Impact on Market Performance," *Journal of the Academy of Marketing Science* 34 (2006): 324–340.

[43] Ibid.

[44] Dexter Roberts and Stanley Reed, "China Wants Nuclear Reactors—Fast," *Bloomberg Businessweek,* December 6–12, 2010, pp. 15–17.

[45] S. Tamer Cavusgil, "International Partnering: A Systematic Framework for Collaborating with Foreign Business Partners," *Journal of International Marketing* 6 (1998): 91–107.

[46] "Asian Alliances: New Ties for VW, GM and Peugeot Citroen," *The Economist,* December 12, 2009, p. 72; "China: The Great Internet Race," *BusinessWeek,* June 13, 2005, pp. 54–55; Sing Keow Hoon-Halbauer, "Managing Relationships within Sino-Foreign Joint Ventures," *Journal of World Business* 34 (1999): 334–370.

[47] Cavusgil (1998); Kandemir, Yaprak, and Cavusgil (2006).

[48] James Areddy, "Danone Pulls Out of Disputed China Venture," *Wall Street Journal,* October 1, 2009, p. B1.

[49] "Asian Alliances" (2009).

[50] Dorinda Elliott and Bill Powell, "Wal-Mart Nation," *Time,* June 27, 2005, pp. 37–39; Mei Fong, "Retailers Still Expanding in China," *Wall Street Journal,* January 22, 2009, p. B1.

[51] Andrew Ward, "Home Depot in Mexico," *Financial Times,* April 6, 2006, p. 8.

[52] Andrew Roberts and Carol Matlack, "Once Wal-Mart's Equal, Carrefour Falls Behind," *Bloomberg Businessweek,* October 24–30, pp. 22–23.

[53] David Agren, Thierry Ogier, and Joachim Bamrud, "Walmart: Latin American Success," *Latin Trade,* July/August, 2011, pp. 24–27; Adrienne Sanders, "Yankee Imperialist," *Forbes,* December 13, 1999, p. 56.

[54] Amol Sharma, "IKEA Wary of Entering India," *Wall Street Journal*, January 24, 2012, p. B4.

[55] Clay Chandler, "The Great Wal-Mart of China," *Fortune*, July 25, 2005, pp. 104–116; Ming-Ling Chuang, James Donegan, Michele Ganon, and Kan Wei, "Walmart and Carrefour Experiences in China: Resolving the Structural Paradox," *Cross Cultural Management* 18, no. 4 (2011): 443–463.

[56] Andrew Ward, "Home Depot in Mexico," *Financial Times*, April 6, 2006, p. 8.

Chapter 16

[1] International Centre for Trade and Sustainable Development (ICTSD), *Property Rights: Implications for Development Policy, Policy Discussion Paper*, Intellectual Property Rights & Sustainable Development Series (Geneva, Switzerland: ICTSD and New York: UNCTAD, 2003).

[2] Farok J. Contractor, "Strategic Perspectives for International Licensing Managers: The Complementary Roles of Licensing, Investment and Trade in Global Operations," Working Paper no. 99.002 (Rutgers, NJ: Rutgers University, 1999).

[3] Ibid.

[4] ICTSD (2003).

[5] Kay Millonzi and William Passannante, "Beware of the Pirates: How to Protect Intellectual Property," *Risk Management* 43 (1996): 39–42.

[6] Robert W. Gomulkiewicz, Xuan-Thao Nguyen, and Danielle Conway-Jones, *Licensing Intellectual Property: Law & Application*, 2e (New York: Wolters Kluwer, 2011).

[7] Vanessa O'Connell and Mei Fong, "Saks to Follow Luxury Brands into China," *Wall Street Journal*, April 18, 2006, p. B1.

[8] Paige Albiniak, "A Really Long Running 'Feud'," *Broadcasting & Cable*, August 23, 2010, p. 32; Dennis Henderson, Ian Sheldon, and Kathleen Thomas, "International Licensing of Foods and Beverages Makes Markets Truly Global," *FoodReview* (September 1994): 7–12.

[9] Marc Lieberstein, Stephen Feingold, Christine James, and Paul Rosenblatt, "Current Developments and Best Practices in Trademark Licensing (Part I)," *Licensing Journal*, February 2011, pp. 20–28.

[10] "Management Brief: Johannesburgers and Fries," *The Economist*, September 27, 1997, pp. 113–114.

[11] "History of Merchandising," *The Licensing Journal*, April 2009, p. 23; U.S. Department of Commerce, *A Basic Guide to Exporting* (Washington, DC: U.S. Government Printing Office, 1992).

[12] Doug Desjardins, "Winnie the Pooh Out of Hibernation," *License! Global*, June 2010, p. 40.

[13] Piero Telesio, *Technology Licensing and Multinational Enterprises* (New York: Praeger, 1979).

[14] Ibid.

[15] "Roche Gains a Stronghold in Elusive Japanese Market," *Chemical Market Reporter*, December 17, 2001, p. 2.

[16] Telesio (1979).

[17] Akio Morita, Edwin Reingold, and Mitsuko Shimomura, *Made in Japan: Akio Morita and Sony* (New York: EP Dutton, 1986).

[18] Jan Golab, "King Barbie: How I Gussied Up America's Favorite Toy and Turned My Struggling Company into a Megatoyopoly," *Los Angeles Magazine*, August 1, 1994, p. 66; Mattel, Inc., annual reports (various years).

[19] F. Burton and A. Cross, "International Franchising: Market versus Hierarchy," in *Internationalisation Strategies*, G. Chryssochoidis, C. Millar, and J. Clegg, eds., pp. 135–152 (New York: St. Martin's Press, 2001).

[20] Hachemi Aliouche and Udo Schlentrich, "Towards a Strategic Model of Global Franchise Expansion," *Journal of Retailing* 87, no. 3 (2011): 345–365; Tendai Chikweche and Richard Fletcher, "Franchising at the Bottom of the Pyramid (BOP): an Alternative Distribution Approach," *International Review of Retail, Distribution & Consumer Research* 21, no. 4 (2011): 343–360.

[21] Adler, Carlye, "How China Eats a Sandwich," *Fortune*, March 21, 2005, pp. F210.

[22] K. Fladmoe-Lindquist, "International Franchising," in *Globalization of Services*, Y. Aharoni and L. Nachum, eds., pp. 197–216 (London: Routledge, 2000).

[23] Ibid.; C. Steinberg, "A Guide to Franchise Strategies," *World Trade* 7 (1994): 66–70.

[24] Lawrence Strauss "How Do You Say Yum in Chinese?," *Barron's*, January 28, 2012, pp. 36–37.

[25] David Kaufmann, "The Big Bang: How Franchising Became an Economic Powerhouse the World Over— Franchise 500®," *Entrepreneur*, January 2004, retrieved at http://www.entrepreneur.com; Melih Madanoglu, Kyuho Lee, and Gary Castrogiovanni, "Franchising and Firm Financial Performance among U.S. Restaurants," *Journal of Retailing* 87, no. 3 (2011): 406–417.

[26] Barry Quinn and Anne Marie Doherty, "Power and Control in International Retail Franchising," *International Marketing Review* 17 (2000): 354–363.

[27] Herng Shinn and Eleanor Warnock, "Wendy's Goes Beyond the Dollar Menu in Japan," *Bloomberg Businessweek*, January 9, 2012, pp. 25-26; "Wendy's Shuts Doors in Japan," *The New York Times*, January 2, 2010, p. B3.

[28] Stanworth (1991).

[29] "Public Funds and Turnkey Contracts Fuel Growing Global Subway Work," *ENR*, October 25, 2004, p. 32; "Abu Dhabi Awards $9 Billion in Gas Project Contracts," *Oil & Gas Journal*, July 27, 2009, pp. 32–33; Caroline Winter, "Who's Building the Big Projects," *Bloomberg Businessweek*, May 31–June 6, 2010, p. 12.

[30] "Full Steam Ahead with Nuclear Power," *Euromoney*, December 1980, p. 36.

[31] "MAN Power for a Diamond Project," *Modern Power Systems*, February, 2012, p. 24.

[32] Robert Peltier, "Phu My 3 Power Plant, Ho Chi Minh City, Vietnam," *Power*, August 2004, p. 42.

[33] Farok Contractor and Sumit Kundu, "Modal Choice in a World of Alliances: Analyzing Organizational Forms in the International Hotel Sector," *Journal of International Business Studies* 29 (1998): 325–356; V. Panvisavas and J. S. Taylor, "The Use of Management Contracts by International Hotel Firms in Thailand," *International Journal of Contemporary Hospitality Management* 18 (2006): 231–240.

[34] David A. Ricks and Saeed Samiee-Esfahani, "Leasing: It May Be Right Abroad Even When It Is Not at Home," *Journal of International Business Studies* 5 (1974): 87–90.

[35] Lloyd Downey, "Marketing Services: How TPOs Can Help," *International Trade Forum* 4 (2005): 7–8; Geoffrey Jones and Alexis Lefort, "McKinsey and the Globalization of Consultancy," Harvard Business School case study 9–806–035 (Cambridge, MA: Harvard Business School, 2006).

[36] Xiaobai Shen, "Developing Country Perspectives on Software," *International Journal of IT Standards & Standardization Research* 3 (2005): 21–43.

[37] International Chamber of Commerce, "OECD Study a Vital Step to Understanding the Global Scope of Counterfeiting," 2007, retrieved from http://www.iccwbo.org

[38] CBP Office of International Trade, *Intellectual Property Rights: Fiscal Year 2011 Seizure Statistics* (Washington, DC: U.S. Immigration and Customs Enforcement, 2012) at http://www.ice.gov/doclib/iprcenter/pdf/ipr-fy-2011-seizure-report.pdf

[39] Murray Hiebert, "Chinese Counterfeiters Turn Out Fake Car Parts," *Wall Street Journal*, March 3, 2004, p. A14; Joon Muller, "Stolen Cars," *Forbes*, February 16, 2004, p. 58; Brendan Murphy, Andy Sun, Philip Warden, Ana Damonte, and Raj Davoe, "IP Problems Don't Just Need IP Solutions," *Managing Intellectual Property*, March 2012, p. 17.

[40] Matthew Hamblen, "Cisco, Huawei Look to Settle Software-Copying Lawsuit," *Computer World*, October 6, 2003, p. 19.

[41] B. Cassell, "Microsoft Battles Piracy in Developing Markets," *Wall Street Journal*, December 23, 2004, p. B4.

[42] Jonathan Rockoff, "When Buying Drugs Online, First Consider the Source," *Wall Street Journal*, April 3, 2012, p. D2; Vauhini (2005), p. 59; Jack Goldsmith and Tim Wu, *Who Controls the Internet: Illusions of a Borderless World* (Oxford, England: Oxford University Press, 2006).

[43] Meagan Dietz, Sarena Shao-Tin Lin, and Lei Yang, "Protecting Intellectual Property in China," *The McKinsey Quarterly* 3 (2005): 6–10.

[44] A. Dayal-Gulati and Angela Lee, *Kellogg on China: Strategies for Success* (Evanston, IL: Northwestern University Press, 2004).

[45] Millonzi and Passannante (1996).

[46] Dietz, Shao-Tin Lin, and Yang (2005).

[47] Ibid.

Chapter 17

[1] UNCTAD, *World Investment Report 2011* (New York: United Nations, 2011).

[2] A.T. Kearney, *Offshoring Opportunities Amid Economic Turbulence*, 2011, retrieved from www.atkearney.com; Rupa Chanda, "India and Services Outsourcing in Asia," *The Singapore Economic Review* 53, no. 3 (2008), 419–447; Rahul Sachitanand, "IT Morphs Yet Again," *Business Today*, December 27, 2009, p. 7; UNCTAD, *World Investment Report 2011* (New York: United Nations, 2011).

[3] Duke University CIBER/Archstone Consulting, *Second Biannual Offshore Survey Results*, 2005; UNCTAD, *World Investment Report 2005* (New York: United Nations, 2005).

[4] "Outsourcing: Time to Bring It Back Home?" *The Economist*, March 5, 2005, p. 63.

[5] Michael E. Porter, *Competition in Global Industries* (Boston: Harvard Business School Press, 1986).

[6] Benito Arrunada and Xose H. Vazquez, "When Your Contract Manufacturer Becomes Your Competitor," *Harvard Business Review*, September 2006, pp. 135–145.

[7] Jamil Anderlini, "BMW Plans to Boost China Output after Demand Surge," *Financial Times*, November 13, 2009, p. 19; BMW Group, *Company Portrait: Locations*, retrieved from www.bmw.com, April 23, 2012; *Quality*, "BMW to Invest $900 Million, Add 300 Jobs at SC Plant," March 2012, p. 8.

[8] Thomas Friedman, *The World Is Flat 3.0: A Brief History of the Twenty-First Century* (New York: Picador, 2007).

[9] Geri Smith, "Can Latin America Challenge India?" *BusinessWeek*, January 30, 2006, Online Extra, retrieved from http://www.businessweek.com.

[10] Andrew Baxter, "GE Unit Plugs into the Outside World," *Financial Times*, September 28, 2005, p. 8; Corporate profile of Genpact at http://www.hoovers.com.

[11] UNCTAD (2011).

[12] "Patheon Inc.: Contract Drug Manufacturing and Development," *Shareowner*, November–December 2003, p. 36.

[13] Ruth Alexander, "Which Is the World's Biggest Employer?," *BBC News Magazine*, March 19, 2012, retrieved from www.bbc.co.uk; Bruce Einhorn, "A Juggernaut in Electronics," *BusinessWeek*, June 18, 2007, p. 46; Lorraine Luk, "Hon Hai Shifts Its Chinese Work Force," *Wall Street Journal*, August 19, 2010, p. B8.

[14] Masaaki Kotabe, Janet Murray, and Rajshekhar Javalgi, "Global Sourcing of Services and Market Performance: An Empirical Investigation," *Journal of International Marketing* 6 (1998): 10–31; Masaaki Kotabe and Janet Murray, "Outsourcing Service Activities," *Marketing Management* 10 (2001): 40–46.

[15] Joshua Freedman, "Distance Earning," *Lawyer*, November 21, 2011, pp. 14–16; Amy Kazmin, "Outsourcing: Law Firms Fuel the Demand for Offshore Services," *Financial Times*, January 30, 2009, retrieved from http://www.ft.com

[16] Institute for International Business, "Globalization of Work: Outsourcing and Offshoring," *Global Executive Forum*, Spring–Summer 2005, pp. 6–7; Niraj Sheth, "India Calls Are Now Taken at Home," *Wall Street Journal*, July 1, 2009, p. B6.

[17] A.T. Kearney, 2011; "Is Your Job Next?" *BusinessWeek*, February 3, 2003, retrieved from http://www.businessweek.com; Norihiko Shirouzu, "Engineering Jobs Become Car Makers New Export," *Wall Street Journal*, February 7, 2008, pp. B1–B2.

[18] Murray Weidenbaum, "Outsourcing: Pros and Cons," *Executive Speeches* 19 (2004): 31–35.

[19] Peter Marsh, "Foreign Threat to Service Jobs 'Overblown, says Study'," *Financial Times*, June 16, 2005, p. 12; Marcus Neureiter and Peter Nunnenkamp, "Outsourcing Motives, Location Choice and Labour Market Implications: An Empirical Analysis for European Countries," *Kyklos* 63, no. 2 (2010): 206–230.

[20] Kerry Capelli, "Zara Thrives by Breaking All the Rules," *BusinessWeek*, October 20, 2008, p. 66; "If You Can Make It Here…How Some Companies Manage to Keep Building Things in America," *New York Times*, September 4, 2005, section 3, p. 1.

[21] Chanda (2008); Kazmin (2009); Abdul Rasheed and K. Matthew Gilley, "Outsourcing: National- and Firm-Level Implications," *Thunderbird International Business Review* 47 (2005): 513–528.

[22] *Bloomberg Businessweek*, "So Long, Bangalore: Now Manila's on the Line," December 6–12, 2010, pp. 17–18; Penny Crosman, "Worldsourcers," *Wall Street & Technology*, July 2008, p. 26; Kazmin (2009); Everest Global, Inc., *Global Sourcing Market Vista*, Everest Research Institute, 2009, retrieved from http://www.everestresearchinstitute.com

[23] *BusinessWeek* (2003).

[24] Patrick Burnson, "Strained," *Logistics Management*, May 2009, p. 36.

[25] A. T. Kearney (2009).

[26] Pete Engardio, "Mom-and-Pop Multinationals," *BusinessWeek*, July 14 & 21, 2008, pp. 77–78.

[27] James Hookway and Josephine Cuneta, "World News: Philippine Call Centers Ring Up Business," *Wall Street Journal*, May 30, 2009, p. A14; Paulo Prada and Niraj Sheth, "Delta Air Ends Use of India Call Centers," *Wall Street Journal*, April 18, 2009, p. B1; Sheth (2009); *The Week*, "Where America's Jobs Went," March 25, 2011, p. 13.

[28] *BusinessWeek* (2003).

[29] Pete Engardio, "The Future of Outsourcing," *BusinessWeek*, January 30, 2006, pp. 50–64.

[30] Bruce Einhorn, "How Not to Sweat the Retail Details," *BusinessWeek*, May 25, 2009, pp. 52–54; Turloch Mooney, "Sourcing to Selling," *China Economic Review*, March 2011, p. 22.

[31] Duke University CIBER/Archstone Consulting (2005).

[32] *BusinessWeek* (2003).

[33] "Indian Call Center Lands in Ohio," *Fortune*, August 6, 2007, p. 23.

[34] Engardio (2006).

[35] Masaaki Kotabe and Janet Murray, "Global Sourcing Strategy and Sustainable Competitive Advantage," *Industrial Marketing Management* 33 (2004): 7–14.

[36] Harold Sirkin, Michael Zinser, and Douglas Hohner, *Made in America, Again* (Boston: Boston Consulting Group, August 2011).

[37] Keith Bradsher, "Global Supply Lines at Risk as Shipping Lines Shun Japan" *New York Times*, March 26, 2011, p. B1.

[38] BBC News, "Santander Brings Call Centres Back to UK," July 7, 2011, retrieved from www.bbc.co.uk; Jackie Range, "India Faces a Homegrown Staffing Issue: Not Enough Talent," *Wall Street Journal*, July 16, 2008, p. B8.

[39] Manjeet Kripalani, "Five Offshore Practices That Pay Off," *BusinessWeek*, January 30, 2006, pp. 60–61.

[40] *BusinessWeek* (2003).

[41] David Craig and Paul Willmott, "Outsourcing Grows Up," *The McKinsey Quarterly* (February 2005), Web exclusive, retrieved at http://www.mckinseyquarterly.com

[42] Ben Charny, "Dell Widens U.S. Computer-Share Lead," *Wall Street Journal*, January 17, 2008, p. B4; Thomas Friedman, *The World Is Flat* (New York: Farrar, Straus, & Giroux, 2005).

[43] Jon Ostrower, "One Year On: The Story of the 787," *Flightglobal*, May 5, 2008, retrieved from www.flightglobal.com; Peter Sanders "Boeing Confronts New Woes in 787 Jet," *Wall Street Journal*, June 25, 2010, p. B1; Gary Walther, "Fly The Dreamy Skies," *Forbes*, March 12, 2012, pp. 104–106.

[44] George Yip, *Total Global Strategy II* (Upper Saddle River, NJ: Prentice Hall, 2003).

[45] Thomas Davenport, Leandro Mule, and John Lucker, "Know What Your Customers Want Before They Do," *Harvard Business Review*, December 2011, pp. 84–92; James Womack and Daniel Jones, *Lean Solutions* (New York: Free Press, 2005).

[46] Capelli (2008).

[47] Barney Gimbel, "Yule Log Jam," *Fortune*, December 13, 2004, pp. 164–170.

[48] Alison Maitland, "Make Sure You Have Your Christmas Stock In," *Financial Times*, December 19, 2005, p. 11.

[49] J. Lynn Lunsford, "Outsourcing at Crux of Boeing Strike," *Wall Street Journal*, September 8, 2008, pp. B1, B4.

[50] Christopher Conkey, "Strapped Cities Outsource Transit Lines," *Wall Street Journal*, July 13, 2009, p. A6; Celeste Pagano, "Proceed with Caution: Avoiding Hazards in Toll Road Privatizations," *St. John's Law Review* 83, no. 1 (2009): 351–394.

[51] Eric Bellman and Nathan Koppel, "More U.S. Legal Work Moves to India's Low-Cost Lawyers," *Wall Street Journal*, September 28, 2005, p. B1; Kazmin (2009).

[52] *The Week* (2011).

[53] Chanda (2008); J. McCarthy, "3.3 Million U.S. Service Jobs to Go Offshore," *Forrester Research, Inc.*, 2002, retrieved from http://www.forrester.com

[54] "To Start Up Here, Companies Hire Over There," *USAToday*, February 11, 2005, pp. 1B–2B.

[55] John Thoburn, Kirsten Sutherland, and Thi Hoa Nguyen, "Globalization and Poverty: Impacts on Households of Employment and Restructuring in the Textiles Industry of Vietnam," *Journal of the Asia Pacific Economy* 12, no. 3 (2007): 345–362.

[56] Ryan Jeltema, "Electrolux Plant Walls Come Tumbling Down," *The Daily News*, June 7, 2007, retrieved from http://www.thedailynews.cc

[57] Lisa Gillespie, "Weighing the Pros and Cons of Outsourcing," *Employee Benefit Adviser*, February 2012, p. 50; L. D. Tyson, "Offshoring: The Pros and Cons for Europe," *BusinessWeek*, December 6, 2004, p. 32.

[58] Michael Mandel, "The Real Cost of Offshoring," *BusinessWeek*, June 18, 2007, p. 29.

[59] Joseph A. Schumpeter, *Capitalism, Socialism, and Democracy* (New York: Harper, 1942).

[60] Tyson (2004).

Chapter 18

[1] Shaoming Zou and S. Tamer Cavusgil, "The GMS: A Broad Conceptualization of Global Marketing Strategy and Its Effect on Firm Performance," *Journal of Marketing* 66 (2002): 40–56.

[2] H. Gatignon, J. Eliashberg, and T. Robertson, "Modeling Multinational Diffusion Patterns: An Efficient Methodology," *Marketing Science* 8 (1989): 231–243.

[3] G. Fowler and M. Marr, "Disney's China Play," *Wall Street Journal*, June 16, 2005, pp. B1, B7.

[4] George Yip, *Total Global Strategy II* (Upper Saddle River, NJ: Prentice Hall, 2003).

[5] David Kaplan and Bill Powell, "General Mills' Global Sweet Spot," *Fortune*, May 23, 2011, pp. 23–25.

[5] Yip (2003); Ellen Byron, "Gillette Sharpens Its Pitch for Expensive Razor," *Wall Street Journal*, October 6, 2008, p. B9.

[7] Roger Calantone, S. Tamer Cavusgil, Jeffrey Schmidt, and Geon-Cheol Shin, "Internationalization and the Dynamics of Product Adaptation—An Empirical Investigation," *Journal of Product Innovation Management* 21 (2004): 185–198.

[8] Kaplan and Powell (2011).

[9] J. Tapper and A. Miller, "'The Simpsons' Exported to Middle East," October 18, 2005, *ABC News*, retrieved from http://abcnews.go.com/wnt

[10] Brian Bremner, "McDonald's Is Loving It in Asia," *BusinessWeek*, January 24, 2007, retrieved from http://www.businessweek.com; Marion Issard, "To Tailor Burgers for France, McDonald's Enlists Baguette," *Wall Street Journal*, February 24, 2012, p. B4.

[11] *The Globe and Mail,* "RIM cuts some BlackBerry prices in India," March 28, 2012, retrieved from www.theglobeandmail.com

[12] Reena Jana, "Inspiration from Emerging Economies," *BusinessWeek*, March 23, 2009, p. 38; Ian Rowley, "Will Japan Fall in Love with Lexus?" *BusinessWeek*, July 11, 2005, p. 49.

[13] Gabriele Suder and David Suder, "Strategic Megabrand Management: Does Global Uncertainty Affect Brands?" *The Journal of Product and Brand Management* 17, no. 7 (2008): 436–445.

[14] Janell Townsend, S. Tamer Cavusgil, and Marietta Baba, "Global Integration of Brands and New Product Development at General Motors," *The Journal of Product Innovation Management* 27, no. 1 (2010): 49–62; Yip (2003).

[15] Douglas Holt, John Quelch, and Earl Taylor, "How Global Brands Compete," *Harvard Business Review* (September 2004), pp. 68–75; Jennifer Rooney, "Forbes Corporate Approval Ratings," *Forbes*, October 24, 2011, pp. 30–32.

[16] Rajshekhar Javalgi, Virginie Pioche Khare, Andrew Gross, and Robert Scherer, "An Application of the Consumer Ethnocentrism Model to French Consumers," *International Business Review* 14 (2005): 325–344.

[17] David Aaker, *Managing Brand Equity* (New York: The Free Press, 1991); James Gregory and Jack Wiechmann, *Branding Across Borders* (Chicago: McGraw-Hill, 2002).

[18] Yip (2003).

[19] Ibid.

[20] "General Motors: 2009 Company Profile Edition 3: Chapter 9 Product Development," *Just-Auto* (September 2009), pp. 28–29; Townsend, Cavusgil, and Baba (2010).

[21] *Proofs*, "Philips Wins International Design Award," January 2012, p. 27; Helen Walters, "IDEA 2009: Designing a Better World," *BusinessWeek*, July 29, 2009, retrieved from http://www.businessweek.com

[22] Matthew B. Myers, "Implications of Pricing Strategy-Venture Strategy Congruence: An Application Using Optimal Models in an International Context," *Journal of Business Research* 57 (2004): 591–690.

[23] Chris Reiter and Edith Balazs, "Daimler's Billion-Dollar Bet on Hungary," *Bloomberg Businessweek*, April 9, 2012, pp. 29–30.

[24] S. Tamer Cavusgil, "Pricing for Global Markets," *Columbia Journal of World Business* (Winter 1996): 66–78.

[25] S. Tamer Cavusgil, "Unraveling the Mystique of Export Pricing," *Business Horizons* 31 (1988): 54–63.

[26] William McDaniel and Edgar Kossack, "The Financial Benefits to Users of Foreign-Trade Zones," *Columbia Journal of World Business* 18 (1983): 33–41.

[27] Cavusgil (1988); Nergiz Dincer and Magda Kandil, "The Effects of Exchange Rate Fluctuations on Exports," *Journal of International Trade & Economic Development* 20, no. 6 (2011): 809–837.

[28] Thomas Pugel and Judith Ugelow, "Transfer Prices and Profit Maximization in Multinational Enterprise Operations," *Journal of International Business Studies* 13 (Spring–Summer 1982): 115–119; Nilufer Usmen, "Transfer Prices: A Financial Perspective," *Journal of International Financial Management & Accounting* 23, no. 1 (2012): 1–22.

[29] Ralph Drtina and Jane Reimers, "Global Transfer Pricing: A Practical Guide for Managers," *S.A.M. Advanced Management Journal* 74, no. 2 (2009): 4–12.

[30] S. Tamer Cavusgil and Ed Sikora, "How Multinationals Can Counter Gray Market Imports," *Columbia Journal of World Business* 23 (1988): 75–86; Reza Ahmadi and B. Rachel Yang, "Parallel Imports: Challenges from Unauthorized Distribution Channels," *Marketing Science* 19 (Summer 2000): 281; Matthew B. Myers, "Incidents of Gray Market Activity Among U.S. Exporters: Occurrences, Characteristics, and Consequences, *Journal of International Business Studies* 30 (1999): 105–126.

[31] Ernst Berndt, "A Primer on the Economics of Re-Importation of Prescription Drugs," *Managerial and Decision Economics* 28 (2007): 415–435; Margaret Kyle, "Strategic Responses to Parallel Trade," *Journal of Economic Analysis & Policy* 11, no. 2 (2011): 1–32.

[32] S. Tamer Cavusgil and Ed Sikora, "How Multinationals Can Counter Gray Market Imports," *Columbia Journal of World Business* 23 (1988): 75–86.

[33] *Marketing Week*, "Global Ad Spend Forecast to Outpace Economic Growth," December 8, 2011, p. 10.

[34] Laurel Wentz and Bradley Johnson, "Top 100 Global Advertisers Heap Their Spending Abroad," *Advertising Age*, November 30, 2009, pp. 1–2.

[35] Macleod (2009).

[36] F. Balfour and D. Kiley, "Ad Agencies Unchained," *BusinessWeek*, April 25, 2005, pp. 50–51.

[37] Yip (2003).

[38] Devon Maylie, "By Foot, by Bike, by Taxi, Nestlé Expands in Africa," *Wall Street Journal*, December 1, 2011, pp. B1, B16.

[39] Linda Shi, Shaoming Zou, J. Chris White, Regina McNally, and S. Tamer Cavusgil, "Executive Insights: Global Account Management Capability," *Journal of International Marketing* 13 (2005): 93–113; Sengun Yeniyurt, S. Tamer Cavusgil, and Tomas Hult, "A Global Market Advantage Framework: The Role of Global Market Knowledge Competencies," *International Business Review* 14 (2005): 1–19.

Chapter 19

[1] Peter Dowling, Marion Festing, and Allen Engle, *International HRM: Managing People in a Multinational Context*, 5th ed. (London: Thomson Learning, 2008).

[2] Ibid.

[3] Ibid.

[4] Jo Johnson, "More Westerners Take Top Posts in India as Locals' Pay Demand Soars," *Financial Times*, May 30, 2007, p. 1.

[5] Dowling, Festing, and Engle (2008).

[6] MSNBC, "Italy Labor Market Reform Moves Ahead," April 4, 2012, retrieved from www.msnbc.msn.com

[7] James Neelankavil, Anil Mathur, and Yong Zhang, "Determinants of Managerial Performance: A Cross-Cultural Comparison of the Perceptions of Middle-Level Managers in Four Countries," *Journal of International Business Studies* 31, no. 1 (2000): 121–141.

[8] Dowling, Festing, and Engle (2008); Anne-Wil Harzing, "Of Bears, Bumble-Bees, and Spiders: The Role of Expatriates in Controlling Foreign Subsidiaries," *Journal of World Business* 36, no. 4 (2008): 366–379.

[9] Anne-Wil Harzing, "Who's in Charge? An Empirical Study of Executive Staffing Practices in Foreign Subsidiaries," *Human Resource Management* 40, no. 2 (2001): 139–145.

[10] Debbie Lovewell, "Employer Profile: World Order," *Employee Benefits*, September 2009, p. 50.

[11] Nanette Byrnes, "Star Search," *BusinessWeek*, October 10, 2005, p. 68; David Pollitt, "Unilever 'Raises the Bar' in Terms of Leadership Performance," *Human Resource Management International Digest* 14, no. 5 (2006): 23–25; Philip Harris, Robert Moran, and Sarah Moran, *Managing Cultural Differences*, 6th ed. (Burlington, MA: Elsevier Buttermann-Heinemann, 2007).

[12] Robert T. Moran and John R. Riesenberger, *The Global Challenge* (London: McGraw-Hill, 1994).

[13] Ben L. Kedia and Akuro Mukherji, "Global Managers: Developing a Mindset for Global Competitiveness," *Journal of World Business* 34, no. 3 (1999): 230–251; Orly Levy, Schon Beechler, Sully Taylor, and Nakiye Boyacigiller, "What We Talk about When We Talk about 'Global Mindset'—Managerial Cognition in Multinational Corporations," *Journal of International Business Studies* 38, no. 2 (2007): 231–258.

[14] Dowling, Festing, and Engle (2008).

[15] Harris, Moran, and Moran (2007).

[16] Jeanne Brett, Kristin Beyfar, and Mary Kern, "Managing Multicultural Teams," *Harvard Business Review* 84 (2007), no. 11: 84–92.

[17] S. Ang, L. Van Dyne, and C. K. S. Koh, "Personality Correlates of the Four Factor Model of Cultural Intelligence," *Group and Organization Management* 31 (2006): 100–123; Brent MacNab, Richard Brislin, and Reginald Worthley, "Experiential Cultural Intelligence Development: Context and Individual Attributes," *International Journal of Human Resource Management* 23, no. 7 (2012): 1320–1341.

[18] Ibid.

[19] Dowling, Festing, and Engle (2008).

[20] Anne-Wil Harzing and Claus Christensen, "Expatriate Failure: Time to Abandon the Concept?" *Career Development International* 9, no. 6/7 (2004): 616–620; Ann Murdoch and Eugene Kaciak, "Culture Shock Re-Visited: What Features of the Polish Culture Most Bother Expatriates in Poland?," *Journal of Applied Business Research* 27 no. 2 (2011): 87–104.

[21] M. Mendenhall, E. Dunbar, and G. Oddou, "Expatriate Selection, Training and Career Pathing: A Review and Critique," *Human Resources Management* 26 (1987): 331–345.

[22] Harris, Moran, and Moran (2007).

[23] Stephen Rhinesmith, *A Manager's Guide to Globalization* (Homewood, IL: Business One Irwin, 1998).

[24] Rosalie Tung, "Expatriate Assignments: Enhancing Success and Minimizing Failure," *Academy of Management Executive* 1 (1987): 117–126.

[25] J. Black, H. Gregersen, and M. Mendenhall, "Toward a Theoretical Framework of Repatriation Adjustment," *Journal of International Business Studies* 23 (1992): 737–760.

[26] Harris, Moran, and Moran (2007).

[27] George Yip, *Total Global Strategy II* (Upper Saddle River, NJ: Prentice Hall, 2003).

[28] Peter Dowling, Denice Welch, and Randall Schuler, *International Human Resource Management*, 3rd ed. (Cincinnati, OH: South-Western, 1999).

[29] Ibid.

[30] Ibid.

[31] Richard Hodgetts and Fred Luthans, *International Management: Culture, Strategy, and Behavior*, 5th ed. (Boston: McGraw-Hill Irwin, 2003).

[32] Ibid.

[33] David Blanchflower, "International Patterns of Union Membership," *British Journal of Industrial Relations* 45, no. 1 (2007): 1–28.

[34] Ibid.; Guglielmo Meardi, "Multinationals' Heaven? Uncovering and Understanding Worker Responses to Multinational Companies in Post-Communist Central Europe," *International Journal of Human Resource Management* 17, no. 8 (2006): 1366–1378.

[35] "Paris in the Spring; Unrest in France," *The Economist*, March 21, 2009, p. 52; Charles Duhigg and David Barboza, "In China, Human Costs Are Built Into an iPad," *New York Times*, January 25, 2012, retrieved from http://www.nytimes.com; Dexter Roberts and Bruce Einhorn, "Using Propaganda to Stop China's Strikes," *Bloomberg Businessweek*, December 19–25, 2011, pp. 15–16.

[36] M. Dubofsky and F. R. Dulles, *Labor in America: A History*, 7th ed. (Wheeling, IL: Harlan Davidson, 2004).

[37] "Business: Membership Required; Trade Unions in China," *The Economist*, August 2, 2008, p. 55; Dexter Roberts, "Waking Up to Their Rights," *BusinessWeek*, August 22–29, 2005, pp. 123–28.

[38] Ying Zhu, Malcolm Warner, and Tongqing Feng, "Employment Relations 'with Chinese Characteristics': The Role of Trade Unions in China," *International Labour Review* 150, no. (2011): 127–143.

[39] John Gennard, "Development of Transnational Collective Bargaining in Europe," *Employee Relations* 31, no. 4 (2009): 341–346; Wenzel Matiaske and Gerd Grözinger, "The Future of Trade Unions in Europe. Part I," *Management Revue* 23, no. 1 (2012): 5–6.

[40] Alberto Alesina and Francesco Giavazzi, *The Future of Europe: Reform or Decline* (Boston: MIT Press, 2006).

[41] David Wessel, "U.S. Firms Eager to Add Foreign Jobs," *Wall Street Journal*, November 22, 2011, p. B1.

[42] Stanley Pignal, John Reed, and Daniel Schafer, "GM Opel Confirms Antwerp Factory Will Shut," *Financial Times*, January 22, 2010, p. 24.

[43] Max Abelson and Ambereen Choudhury, "After Massive Job Cuts, Wall Street's a Different Place," *Bloomberg Businessweek*, December 5–11, 2011, pp. 55–57.

[44] Ashby Monk, "The Knot of Contracts: The Corporate Geography of Legacy Costs," *Economic Geography* 84, no. 2 (2008): 211–235.

[45] Lawrence Koslow and Robert Scarlett, *Global Business* (Houston, TX: Cashman Dudley, 1999).

[46] Richard Boudreaux and Paulo Prada, "Exodus of Workers from Continent Reverses Old Patterns," *Wall Street Journal*, January 14–15, 2012, pp. A1, A8.

[47] C. Mako, P. Csizmadi, and M. Illessy, "Labour Relations in Comparative Perspective," *Journal for East European Management Studies* 11, no. 3 (2006): 267–287.

[48] Jessica Marquez, "Unions' Global End Run," *Workforce Management*, January 30, 2006, pp. 1–4.

[49] John Gennard, "A New Emerging Trend? Cross Border Trade Union Mergers," *Employee Relations* 31, no. 1 (2009): 5–8.

[50] BBC, "South Korea Police Break Up Yoosung Hyundai Strike," May 24, 2011, retrieved from www.bbc.co.uk; Kyong-Ae Choi, "Riot Police Break Up Strike at Hyundai Supplier," *Wall Street Journal*, May 24, 2011, retrieved from www.wsj.com

51 Dowling, Welch, and Schuler (1999); "The Conundrum of the Glass Ceiling," *The Economist*, July 23, 2005, pp. 63–65; Price Waterhouse, *International Assignments: European Policy and Practice 1997/1998* (London: Price Waterhouse, 1997).

52 Grant Thornton International Ltd., "Women in Senior Management: Still Not Enough," *International Business Report 2012*, retrieved from www.gti.com

53 Nancy Adler, *International Dimensions of Organizational Behavior*, 4th ed. (Cincinnati, OH: South-Western, 2002); Harris, Moran, and Moran (2007).

54 Robert T. Moran, Phillip R. Harris, and Sarah V. Moran, *Managing Cultural Differences, Global Leadership Strategies for the 21st Century*, 7th ed. (Oxford, UK: Elsevier, 2007); Jeanine Prime, Karsten Jonsen, Nancy Carter, and Martha Maznevski, "Managers' Perceptions of Women and Men Leaders: A Cross Cultural Comparison," *International Journal of Cross Cultural Management* 8, no. 2 (2008): 171–180.

55 Georges Desvaux, Sandrine Devillard-Hoellinger, and Mary Meaney, "A Business Case for Women," *McKinsey Quarterly*, September 2008, retrieved from www.mckinseyquarterly.com; Lynda Gratton, "Steps That Can Help Women Make It to the Top," *Financial Times*, May 23, 2007, p. 13.

56 *Economist*, "Female Power," January 2, 2010, pp. 49–51; Jasen Lee, "Women in International Business Growing," *Deseret News*, November 8, 2011, retrieved from www.deseretnews.com

57 Ibid.; "Conundrum of the Glass Ceiling" (2005); Ruth Simpson and Afam Ituma, "Transformation and Feminisation: The Masculinity of the MBA and the 'Un-Development' of Men," *Journal of Management Development* 28, no. 4 (2009): 301–316.

58 "Women and the World Economy: A Guide to Womenomics," *Economics*, April 12, 2006, p. 80; Matthew Brannan and Vincenza Priola, "Between a Rock and a Hard Place: Exploring Women's Experience of Participation and Progress in Managerial Careers," *Equal Opportunities International* 28, no. 5 (2009): 378–397.

59 Mercer Human Resource Consulting, "More Females Sent on International Assignment Than Ever Before, Survey Finds," October 12, 2006, retrieved from http://www.mercerhr.com

60 Joanna Barsh and Lareina Yee, "Unlocking the Full Potential of Women at Work," Special Report, April 30, 2012, McKinsey & Co., retrieved from www.mckinsey.com

Chapter 20

1 Peter Yeoh, "Causes of the Global Financial Crisis: Learning from the Competing Insights," International Journal of Disclosure and Governance 7, no. 1 (2010): 42–69.

2 Ernst and Young, "Globalisation Act II: Team Europe Defends Its Goals," results of 2006 survey on the attractiveness of Europe (Paris: Ernst & Young, 2006).

3 Bank for International Settlements, Statistics Division, retrieved from http://www.bis.org

4 Charles Roxburgh, Susan Lund, Richard Dobbs, James Manyika, and Haihao Wu, "The Emerging Equity Gap: Growth and Stability in the New Investor Landscape," December 2011, McKinsey Global Institute, retrieved from www.mckinsey.com/mgi; Richard Murphy, "New Global Hot Spots for Investors," *Fortune*, December 26, 2011, pp. 125–133.

5 K. Lewis, "Trying to Explain Home Bias in Equities and Consumption," *Journal of Economic Literature* 37 (1999): 571–608.

6 Robert Cottrell, "Thinking Big: A Survey of International Banking," *The Economist*, May 20, 2006, survey section.

7 Organisation for Economic Co-operation and Development (OECD), *Pension Markets in Focus*, June 2011, retrieved from http://www.oecd.org

8 Tomoko Yamazaki and Komaki Ito, "Japanese Pensions Plan More Alternative Investments After AIJ," April 23, 2012, retrieved from www.bloomberg.com

9 "Battle of the Bourses," May 27, 2006, *The Economist*, pp. 83–85.

10 Cottrell (2006).

11 Steve Hanke, "When Currencies Falter," *Forbes*, June 8, 2009, p. 106; Michael Sesit and Craig Karmin, "How One Word Haunts the Dollar," *Wall Street Journal*, March 17, 2005, p. C16.

12 IBM, Inc., *2008 Annual Report*, retrieved from http://www.ibm.com

13 Here is an example of how transfer pricing works: Consider an MNE with subsidiaries in three countries. Suppose that subsidiary A operates in country A with high corporate income taxes, and subsidiary B operates in country B, a tax haven. One way to minimize taxes is for subsidiary A to sell merchandise to subsidiary B for a low transfer price. Subsidiary B then resells the merchandise to subsidiary C in the third country at a high transfer price. This results in lower overall taxes for subsidiary A because of its low profits, for subsidiary B because of country B's low tax rates, and for subsidiary C because the high cost of its purchase reduces its profits. While this approach to transferring funds within the MNE is quite common, transfer pricing has some drawbacks. First, while transfer pricing between members of the corporate family is legal when carried out within reasonable limits, governments strongly disapprove of the practice of avoiding tax obligations. Thus, many governments impose policies that restrict transfer pricing. Coca-Cola's Japan subsidiary was fined 15 billion yen for making royalty payments from trademarks and products to its U.S. parent that Japan's National Tax Administration judged as too high. Second, transfer pricing can distort the financial results of foreign subsidiaries. For instance, a subsidiary that is required to charge low prices for its exports may experience unusually low profitability, which harms its performance and can demoralize local staff. Third, some MNEs use artificial transfer prices to hide the poor results of a badly performing subsidiary or achieve other goals aimed at concealing the true performance of the firm.

14 Timor Mehpare and Seyhan Sipahi, "Fast-Food Restaurant Site Selection Factor Evaluation by the Analytic Hierarchy Process," *The Business Review* 4 (2005): 161–167.

15 Here is an illustration of net present value analysis: A U.S.-based MNE is considering an expansion project through its subsidiary in Mexico. The project requires an initial investment of 220 million Mexican pesos (MXP) and has an economic life of five years. The project is expected to generate annual after-tax cash flows of MXP120 million, MXP125 million, MXP150 million, MXP155 million, and MXP200 million, which will be remitted to the parent company during the next five years. The current spot exchange rate is MXP11/$1 and the spot rates are expected to be MXP11.10/$1, MXP11.25/$1, MXP11.50/$1, MXP11.55/$1, and MXP11.75/$1

for the next five years. Assuming that the appropriate discount rate for this project is 10 percent, what is the NPV of the project from the parent company's perspective? Should the MNE accept this project based on its NPV? Let's analyze. The U.S. cash flows of the project can be calculated as follows:

	0	1	2	3	4	5
Mexican peso cash flows	−MXP 220 Million	MXP 120 Million	MXP 125 Million	MXP 150 Million	MXP 155 Million	MXP 200 Million
Prevailing spot exchange rate	MXP 11/$1	MXP 11.10/$1	MXP 11.25/$1	MXP 11.50/$1	MXP 11.55/$1	MXP 11.75/$1
U.S dollar cash flows	−$20,000,000	$10,810,811	$11,111,111	$13,043,478	$13,419,913	$17,021,277

The NPV of the project can be calculated as follows:

$$NPV = -\$20,000,000 + \$10,810,811/(1+0.10)^1 +$$
$$\$11,111,111/(1 + 0.10)^2 + \$13,043,478/(1 + 0.10)^3 +$$
$$\$13,419,913/(1 + 0.10)^4 + \$17,021,277/(1 + 0.10)^5$$
$$NPV = \$28,545,359$$

The MNE can accept the project because it has a positive NPV.

[16] The discount rate used in the NPV analysis of international projects may be higher due to a premium for additional risks involved in doing business internationally. Management may insist on a higher level of required return in the net present value calculation because higher country–political and currency risks indicate a higher probability of venture failure. A firm might apply a 7 percent discount rate to potential investments in Germany and Japan because those countries enjoy political and economic stability. But the same firm might use a 14 percent discount rate for similar potential investments in Pakistan and Russia because those countries experience political and economic turmoil. The higher the discount rate, the higher the projected net cash flows must be for the investment to have a positive net present value contribution. Occasionally, the discount rate for international projects can be lower than for domestic ones. Risk arises from various sources, and management must systematically assess the range of potentially influential factors.

[17] Reshma Kapadia, "The Currency Conundrum," *SmartMoney*, April 2012, pp. 78–82.

[18] Robert Aliber, *Exchange Risk and International Finance* (New York: Wiley, 1979).

[19] International Monetary Fund, "Currency Composition of Official Foreign Exchange Reserves (COFER)," March 30, 2012, retrieved from www.imf.org; Kapadia (2012).

[20] Morten Bech, "FX Volume During the Financial Crisis and Now," Bank for International Settlements, March 2012, retrieved from http://www.bis.org; Anchalee Worrachate and David Goodman, "Currency Trading at $5 Trillion a Day Surpassed Pre-Lehman High, BIS Says," *Bloomberg*, March 12, 2012, retrieved from www.bloomberg.com

[21] Gordon Platt, "World's Best Foreign Exchange Banks 2005," *Global Finance* 19 (2005): 24–33.

[22] Adam Rombel, "The World's Best Internet Banks," *Global Finance* 16 (2002): 37–38.

[23] David Sedgwick, Diana Kurylko, Jamie LaReau, and Rick Kranz, "As Dollar Falls, Automakers Must Adjust Plans," *Automotive News Europe*, March 17, 2008, p. 16.

[24] Ira Iosebashvili, "Capital Flees Russia, Damping Official Hopes Over Putin's Win," *Wall Street Journal*, April 5, 2012, p. A8.

[25] Ariful Hoquea, Felix Chana, and Meher Manzur, "Efficiency of the Foreign Currency Options Market," *Global Finance Journal* 19, no. 2 (2008): 157–170.

[26] Here is a simple example of an option transaction from a familiar context: Say you are in the market to buy a house. You find one that you like, but you are not sure if you want to buy it. At this stage, you opt to put a deposit down to have the seller keep his for-sale house for you for two weeks. Later, if you buy the house, the deposit counts toward the purchase price. If you do not buy the house, you lose your deposit. You have the option to buy the house at an agreed-upon price but not the obligation to do so.

[27] W. Wallace and J. Walsh, "Apples to Apples: Profits Abroad," *Financial Executive*, May–June, 1995, pp. 28–31.

[28] Hank Boerner, "Europe Faces Eagle Eye of US Financial Regulation," *European Business Forum* 21 (2005): 46–49.

[29] Paul Miller and Paul Bahnson, "The Demise of the Drive to Bring International Standard-Setting to the U.S.," *Accounting Today*, February 2012, pp. 16–17.

[30] Computershare, *2003 Annual Report*, retrieved from http://www.computershare.com

[31] Alan J. Auerbach and Martin Feldstein, *Handbook of Public Economics*, 3rd ed. (Amsterdam: North-Holland, 2001); Peter Cohn and Matthew Caminiti, "Corporate Taxes: The Multinational Advantage," *Bloomberg Businessweek*, January 24–30, 2011, p. 31; KPMG International, "Corporate & Indirect Tax Survey 2011," accessed at http://www.kpmg.com/global

[32] Joseph Froomkin and Ira Wender, "Revenue Implications of United States Income Tax Treaties," *National Tax Journal* 7, no. 2 (1954): 177–181.

[33] Peter Coy and Jesse Drucker, "Profits on Overseas Holiday," *Bloomberg Businessweek*, March 21–27, 2011, pp. 64–69; Charles Duhigg and David Kocieniewski, "How Apple Sidesteps Billions in Taxes," *New York Times*, April 29, 2012, p. A1; Timothy Noah, "Bono, Tax Avoider," *Slate*, October 31, 2006, retrieved from http://www.slate.com

[34] Dries Lesage, David McNair, and Mattias Vermeiren, "From Monterrey to Doha: Taxation and Financing for Development," *Development Policy Review* 28, no. 2 (2010): 155–162; Brody Mullins, "Accenture Lobbyists Near Big Win on Securing Tax-Haven Status," *Wall Street Journal*, July 14, 2005, p. A2.

> Author Index

This index includes names of authors cited. For names of companies, see the Company Index. For terms and topics, see the Subject Index. Page references with "e" refer to exhibits. Page references with "n" refer to notes cited by number.

A

Adler, Carlye, 431n
Adolph, G., 244n
Agarwal, S., 333n
Aguiar, M., 267n
Ahmed, M., 95n
Ahuja, Maneet, 227n
Alexander, Philip, 514n
Alon, Ilan, 431n
Amine, Lyn, 326n
Anand, Geeta, 438n
Applegate, Evan, 444n
Armstrong, David, 104n
Athanassakos, G., 22n
Authers, J., 237n

B

Balakrishnan, A., 28n
Balassa, Bela, 220n
Balfour, F., 124n, 252n
Banerjee, Sy, 192n
Banga, Kamini, 473n
Barel, R., 22n
Barnard, Bruce, 75n
Barrett, Paul, 112n
Basu, Choton, 56n
Batson, Andrew, 112n
Baughn, C. Christopher, 361n
Beattie, Alan, 444n
Beckenbauer, Angela, 429n
Belassa, Bela, 220n
Bellman, E., 192n
Bernard, Stephen, 227n
Bertolinia, M., 457n
Bethune, Brian, 412
Bevilacquab, M., 457n
Birkland, Carol, 112n
Blaško, M., 405n
Bomberg, Elizabeth, 218n
Borneman, J., 237n
Bornon, J., 106n
Bottania, E., 457n
Bradsher, Keith, 136n
Braga, C. Primo, 183n
Bray, C., 129n
Briody, Elizabeth K., 104n
Brown, G., 12n
Buck, Trevor, 320n, 361n
Burkitt, Laurie, 431n
Burne, Katy, 227n
Butcher, Dan, 484n
Byrnes, N., 124n

C

Cai, Y., 71n
Callis, Todd, 457
Cameron, Carolynn, 490n
Cameron, Doug, 211n
Campbell, Colin, 136n
Canterbery, E., 106n
Canterbury, Andrew, 326n
Cavusgil, Erin, 56n, 484

Cavusgil, S. Tamer, 56n, 320, 326n, 329, 334, 348, 358n, 372n
Chadee, D., 28n
Chaffin, Joshua, 211n
Chang, Juichuan, 244n
Chao, L., 82n
Chao, Loretta, 431n
Charny, Ben, 412n
Chaturvedi, Anumeha, 464n
Chen, H., 82n
Cheng, Patricia, 484n
Chiang, C. R., 484n
Choo, Stephen, 422n
Chunxia, W., 82n
Clark, D., 237n
Clark, Pilita, 211n
Clothier, M., 22n
Coffin, B., 267n
Colvin, G., 237n
Conger, Jay, 320n
Coopman, Robert, 186n
Coy, P., 207n
Crawford, D., 129n
Crosby, Cindy, 490n
Crosman, Penny, 444n
Crown, J., 211n
Cultice, C., 354n

D

Dadush, Uri, 50n
d'Almeida, J., 333n
Dalton, Matthew, 218n
Dao, T., 361n
Dass, M., 166n
David, K., 88e
Davies, Jerry, 534n
Davis, Bob, 252n
Davis, Ian, 333n
Day, K., 106n
Dayal-Gulati, A., 431n
Dean, Jason, 252n
Delacroix, J., 106n
De Mente, Boye, 93e
Derrick, Stuart, 412n
Dicken, P., 39n
Dickson, D., 293n
Dietz, Meagan, 429n
Dobbs, Richard, 333n, 519n
Doherty, Sharon, 354n
Doorey, David, 504n
Duening, Thomas, 429n
Duhigg, Charles, 136n
Dunning, John, 157

E

Eckert, Barton, 534n
Edmondson, Gail, 15n
Edwards, William, 431n
Efrati, A., 82n
Eichenseher, J., 95n
Einhorn, Bruce, 444n
Elder, M., 166n
Ellinger, A., 82n
Ellouzi, Meriam, 326n
Elvy, C., 59e
Engardio, Pete, 121e, 438n, 444n
Enyinda, Chris, 186n
Epstein, Joseph, 534n
Epstein, K., 211n

Espinoza, J., 397n
Esterl, M., 129n
Evans, Carolyn, 207n

F

Fan, Terence, 56n
Feng, Betty, 320n
Ferraro, Gary, 85
Field, A., 457n
Filatotchev, Igor, 361n
Filipski, Mateusz, 237n
Finkelstein, S., 405n
Finnessy, Randahl, 534n
Fiscus, Philip, 438n
Fletcher, Owen, 136n
Francis, T., 333n
French, Howard, 384n
Friedman, Thomas, 28n, 59e
Fuhrman, Elizabeth, 112n
Fuhrmans, V., 129n
Furness, V., 71n
Fyrwald, E., 82n

G

Gannon, Martin, 91
Gassmann, Oliver, 429n
Gauthier-Villars, D., 211n
Gethard, G., 293n
Gibson, Richard, 431n
Giertz-Mårtenson, Ingrid, 484n
Glass, G., 186n
González-Padron, Tracy, 75
Gordon, R., 98e
Goss, Barry, 514n
Gravel, Julio, 354n
Grontzki, P., 129n
Grossman, L., 4n
Grundy, K., 22n
Gumbel, P., 293n
Gunther, Marc, 464n
Gwynne, P., 82n

H

Hagerty, J., 22n
Hall, Edward T., 88–89, 89n
Hamblen, M., 129n
Hamelin, Nicolas, 326n
Hamprecht, Harald, 405n
Handley, Lucy, 320n
Hannon, D., 75n
Hannon, Paul, 397n
Hartley, R., 22n
Hawser, A., 397n
Heaven, W., 4n
Hemphill, Thomas, 192n
Hesseldahl, Arik, 58e
Hill, Linda, 320n
Hille, K., 71n
Hisrich, Robert, 429n
Hjelt, Paola, 61e
Hofman, D., 59e
Hofstede, Geert, 85, 89–91, 93n
Hohner, Douglas, 444n
Houanye, Paulin, 384n
Houlton, Sarah, 186n

> Company Index

This index includes names of companies and commercial banks.
For names of authors, see the Author Index.
For terms and topics, see the Subject Index.
Page numbers with "e" refer to exhibits.

A

A&W, 429
ABB, 10e, 262
ABN AMRO, 8, 121e, 393e, 449
ABN AMRO Private Banking, 286
Abu Dhabi Investment Authority, 74
Accenture, 26, 425, 442, 446, 448, 506
Accor, 61
Acer, 318
Adams Pressed Metals, 395
Adidas, 60e, 236, 237
Adiento, 484
Advanced Biomedical Devices, 347–348
Aegis, 482e
AES, 177
Agfa-Gevaert, 306
Agricultural Bank of China, 288
AIG (American International Group), 292–293
AIG Financial Products (AIGFP), 292
Airbus, 210–211, 252, 359, 466
Air Canada, 399
Air New Zealand, 399, 426
AJC International, 69
AKM Semiconductor, 58e
AkzoNobel, 385
Alcan, 46, 60e, 123
Alcoa, 17, 157
Alcon, 13
Alenia/Vought, 451e
ALFA, 259e
Al Jazeera English, 425
Allianz SE, 217, 230, 393e
Alps, 440e
Amazon.com, 61, 71, 417, 482, 506
AMD, 84
American Standard, 16
Amul, 263
Amway Corporation, 469
Anheuser-Busch, 65
AOL, 26
Apple, Inc., 35, 57, 58e, 95, 134–136, 208, 257, 315, 414, 427, 438, 467, 470, 499, 506, 531
Arab-Malaysian Merchant Bank, 286
Arcelik, 242
ArcelorMittal, 168, 490
Argos, 71
ARM Holdings, 58e
Asea AB, 235
Asterix, 176
Astra, 259e, 260
AstraZeneca, 146
AT&T, 60e, 416, 520
A.T. Kearney, 10e, 18, 337, 338, 341e, 393, 445
AU Optronics, 440e
Avis, 401, 422
Avon Products, 480
AvtoVAZ, 390
AXA Asia Pacific, 245
Ayala, 259e

B

BAA Limited, 426
Baazee, 9
Bajaj, 17
Bajaj Motors, 267

Bakers Footwear Group, 71
Banco General, 286
Banco Santander, 449
Bangladesh Rural Advancement Committee, 121
Bank of America, 10e, 286
Bank of China, 288
Bank of Nova Scotia, 286
Barclays, 10e, 13, 16, 60, 72, 292
Barrett Farm Foods, 376–377
BASF, 30
Bates Advertising, 342
Bavaria S.A., 385
Baxter International, 60e
Bayer, 30
BBC Worldwide, 415
BBVA, 286, 288, 520
Bechtel Group, 10e, 66e, 262, 425
Bell Laboratories, 418
Bell South, 342
Ben & Jerry's, 422
Benetton, 46, 236, 419, 479, 481
Berkshire Hathaway, 236
Berlitz, 10e
Best Buy, 61, 68, 364, 438
Bharti Airtel, 383
Bharti Enterprises, 191
BHP Billiton, 245
Bill and Melinda Gates Foundation, 16, 186, 264
Bimantara Citra Group, 258
Bimbo, 304
Biogen Idec, 16, 398
Bio-Rad Laboratories Inc., 360e
Black & Decker, 17, 252
Blackberry, 35
Bloomsbury, 305
Blue Dart, 74
Blue Financial Services, 265
BlueLinx Corporation, 261
Bluem, 444e
BMW, 21, 41, 48, 72, 74, 176, 210, 439, 466, 472e, 474, 526
BNP Paribas, 10e, 393e
Body Shop, 419, 420
Boeing, 166, 210–211, 359, 398, 426, 450, 451, 451e, 454
Boeing Fredrickson, 451e
Boeing Winnipeg, 451e
Bombardier, 389
Booz Allen Hamilton, 10e
Booz & Company, 146, 147
Borders, 75
Boston Consulting Group, 242
Boston Scientific, 148
Bottin International, 370
Bouygues, 61, 66e
Bovis Lend Lease, 425
BP, 30, 178, 286, 392e, 426
Brasilcel, 395
Brasil Foods, 242–243
Brilliance China Automotive Holdings Ltd., 439
British Airways, 10e, 26
British American Tobacco, 124
British Wellcome Trust, 16
BroadenGate, 444e
Brown, Boveri & Co., 235
Brunswick Corporation, 343
Buderim Ginger, 376
Budweiser, 65, 418
Burger King, 43, 101, 420, 422
Burns Philip, 376
Business Entrepreneurial Risk Intelligence, 184

C

Cadbury, 95, 395, 471
Cafe Spice, 46
Campbell Soup Company, 8, 385
Canadian Tire, 68
Canamo, 257
C & M Antoniou, 376
Canon, 17, 286, 304, 467, 472e, 518
Capacitor Industries Inc., 68–69
Cap Gemini, 392
Capital One, 60e
Capstone Turbine Corporation, 371
CARE, 16, 57, 121
Cargill, 69, 359
Carlson Wagonlit, 10e
Carrefour, 68, 179, 191, 360, 402, 403, 417, 420, 503
Catcher Technology, 58e
Caterpillar, 13, 17, 30, 152, 235, 306, 340, 373, 386, 455, 479
CBS, 152
Cemex, 13, 177, 242, 264, 520
Century 21 Real Estate, 355
Cerbus Capital Management, 405
China Airlines, 59
China Commercial Aircraft Co., 211
China Construction Bank, 288
China Film Group, 385
China Investment Corporation, 74
China Life, 61
China Mengniu Dairy, 60e
China Minmetals, 201
China Mobile, 13, 60e, 61
China National Petroleum Company, 120
China Netcom, 61
China Oilfield Services, 60e
China Resources Snow Breweries, 253, 385
Chiquita Brands International Inc., 360e, 364
Chrysler, 30, 41, 47e, 159, 286, 404–405
Chugai Pharmaceuticals, 417
CIGNA, 10e, 61
Circuit City, 75
Cirrus Logic, 58e
Cisco Systems, 10e, 26, 40, 66, 252, 427
Citibank, 10e, 288, 524, 525
Citicorp, 72, 393e, 446
CitiFX Interactive, 524
Citigroup, 73, 393
Citroën, 225
Clarks, 455
CNOOC, 61, 244, 385
Coach, 60e
Coca-Cola, 30, 59, 60, 110–112, 117, 124, 152, 166, 199, 252, 265, 305, 312, 360e, 374, 386, 413, 414, 415, 466, 472, 472e
COFCO, 69e
Coles, 482
Colgate-Palmolive, 480
Collegiate Licensing Company, 417e
Compal, 440e
Computershare, 530
ConocoPhillips, 166
Conservation Coffee Alliance, 46
Corning Glass Works, 398
Corus Group, 266, 303
Credit Lyonnais, 286
Crocus Technology, 398
Curad, 326
Curves, 65, 422e
CVO Group, 62

> Subject Index

This index includes terms and topics.
For names of companies, see the Company Index.
For authors cited, see the Author Index.
Page numbers with "e" refer to exhibits.

A

Absolute advantage principle, 138–140
Accounting, 528–533. *See also* Financial
    management
  consolidation of financial statements for
    subsidiaries, 530–531
  harmonization trends, 530
  international taxation, 531–533
  reporting laws as country risk, 182
  transparency in financial reporting, 529–530
Acculturation, 86
Acquisition, 394
Active hedging, 527
Adaptation
  defined, 466
  in marketing, 467e, 468–471
Administrative procedures. *See* Bureaucratic
    procedures
Advanced Biomedical Devices, case study,
    347–348
Advanced economies
  defined, 244
  economic development comparisons,
    245, 248e
  explanation of, 245
  GDP growth rate, 251e
  maps of, 245, 246e–247e
  national characteristics of, 250e
  trade conditions, 249e
Advertising. *See also* Marketing
  culture and, 480–481
  deceptive practices, 113–114
  examples of misuse of language, 99e
  large advertising agencies, 482e
  marketing and distribution laws, 180
  marketing communications adaptation, 364
  media characteristics, country rankings, 481e
  methods, 480–481
  regulatory restrictions on, 469
Africa
  AIDS crisis, 120, 186, 265
  diamond trade, 264–265, 375
  ethical standards in, 118
  FDI success by Huawei, 382–384
  foreign direct investment in, 264–265
  globalization impacts, 47
  healthcare in, 264, 265
  MNE investment in, 39, 47
  oil exports, 47
  poverty levels, 43, 46e, 248, 264–265
  regional economic integration in, 230
African Development Bank, 370
Agents, 67–68
Agreement on Subsidies and Countervailing Mea-
    sures (ASCM), 210
Agricultural industry, 201, 207, 219, 233, 249
AIDS crisis, 120, 186, 245, 265
AIG, case study, 292–293
Airbus, case study, 210–211
Aircraft industry, 210–211
Airline industry, 260, 399
Air transport, 453
All-China Federation of Trade Unions
    (ACFTU), 501
Allowances, in compensation packages, 499
Ambiguity, attitudes toward, 101
Andean Pact, 228–229, 231e, 232

Angola, 47
Antiboycott regulations, 182
Anti-Counterfeiting Trade Agreement
    (ACTA), 203
Antidumping duty, 202
Apocalypse Now (film), 105
Apparel industry, 236–237, 416, 417e, 438, 482–484,
    504
Arab Maghreb Union, 230
Arbitragers, 526
Arbitration, 184
Area studies, defined, 496
Argentina
  foreign debt crisis, 290
  inflation rates (1980-2011), 279e
  IT industry in, 440
Asian Development Bank, 370
Asia Pacific Economic Cooperation (APEC),
    33, 229
Asociación Interamericana de Contabilidad
    (Interamerican Association
    of Accounting), 530
Association of Southeast Asian Nations (ASEAN),
    176, 220e, 229, 231e
Association of Women in International
    Trade, 505
Attitudes and values, 91–92
Austin, Philip, 376
Austrade (Australia), 371
Australia
  as advanced economy, 245
  average import tariff ranking, 198e
  born global firms, 63
  cultural characteristics of, 89, 90, 93–94
Australia and New Zealand Closer Economic Rela-
    tions Agreement (CER), 220e, 229–230
Auto industry
  collaborative ventures, 401–402
  company market share (1989–2012), 47e
  global financial crisis (2008), 159
  global product development, 472–473
  global trends, 159–160
  merger failures, 404–405
  new global challengers in, 266–267
  standardization attempts, 470–471
  Toyota's U.S. plant investment, 396e
  U.S. voluntary export restraints (1980s), 194
  visionary leadership, 303–304

B

Back-office activities (BPO), 439
Balance of payments, 280–281
Balance of trade, 280
Bangalore, India, 26–28, 151
Bank for International Settlements, 289, 527
Banking, international
  bank assets, country rankings, 519e
  Basel III rules, 183
  central banks, 13
  financial market integration, 34–35
  foreign-exchange trading, 525–526
  as growth sector, 9–10, 33, 72
  international loans, 518–520
  microfinancing of entrepreneurs, 264, 265
  online, 38
  post-recession reforms, 181
Banking crisis, 289–290
Bank of England, 288–289
Bank of Japan, 288–289
Banque de France, 288–289
Barrett Farm Foods, case study, 376
Barter, 374

Base remuneration, 499
Belgium
  cultural characteristics of, 90
  EU integration advantages, 230
  government debt as percentage of GDP, 291e
  merchandise trade levels, 7
Benefit packages, 499
Berne Convention for the Protection of Literary and
    Artistic Works, 428
Best Market and Market Update report, 340
Big Mac Index (*The Economist*), 255, 255e
Bilateral trade negotiations, 207
Bill of lading, 365
Boeing
  case study, disputes with Airbus, 210–211
  global sourcing for 787 aircraft, 451e
Bolivia, 177
Bond markets, 286
Bonds, 520
Born global firms
  defined, 14, 62
  emergence of, 54–56, 62–63
  entrepreneurship and, 152
  as focal firms, 62–63
  internationalization of, 358
Bottom of the pyramid (BOP) countries, 473
Boycotts, 178, 182
Brabeck, Peter, 303
Branding, 468, 471–472
Branson, Richard, 88, 403
Brazil
  aircraft industry, 34
  Alcoa's FDI strategy in, 157
  cultural characteristics of, 91
  as emerging market, 18, 242–244
  Harley-Davidson assembly plant in, 21
  health care product sales potential in, 333
  inflation rates (1980-2011), 279e, 280
Bretton Woods Conference, 30, 281–282
Bribery, 115–117, 127–129, 140, 164, 182, 482
BRICs (fast-growth developing economies), 18, 244.
    See also Emerging markets
Brokeback Mountain (film), 106
Buddhism, culture and, 95
Buffett, Warren, 49
Build-operate-transfer (BOT), 425–426
Build-own-transfer venture, 65
Bureaucratic procedures
  as economic development barriers, 248, 257
  as trade barriers, 200
Business format franchising. *See* Franchising
Business process outsourcing (BPO), 439, 446
Buy-back agreements, 374

C

Call centers, 26–28, 253, 443, 446, 448, 449
Call option, 528
CAN (Comunidad Andina de Naciones).
    See Andean Pact
Canada
  antibribery measures, 117
  average import tariff ranking, 198e
  controls on television station ownership,
    233–234
  cultural characteristics of, 89, 93–94
  global financial crisis (2008), 41
  government debt as percentage of GDP, 291e
  government regulatory agencies, 175
  government subsidies, 202
  NAFTA impacts, 19, 226e, 227, 230, 232, 234
  negotiating free trade agreements
    with EU, 236

Trade fairs, 371
Trademarks, 114, 414, 415–416
Trade-Related Aspects of Intellectual Property Rights (TRIPS), 185–186, 428
Trade secrets, 414, 428
Trade surplus, 138
Trade unions. *See* Labor unions
Trading companies, 69–70, 69e
Transaction exposure, 524
Transfer pricing, 477–478, 522, 533
Transformational outsourcing, 446–448
Transition economies, 249
Translation exposure, 524
Transnational strategy, 310–311
Transparency
    defined, 182, 529
    in emerging markets, 257
    in financial reporting, 182–183, 529–530
Transparency International
    corruption, country rankings, 164, 257
Transportation
    history of, 39e
    logistic service providers, 70, 74–75
    in supply-chain management, 453
    technological advances, 29, 39
Travel, as service export, 360
Trends. *See* Future trends; Global Trend
Triandis, Harry, 85
Turkey
    cultural characteristics of, 84, 91
    as emerging market, 242
    inflation rates (1980-2011), 279e
Turnkey contracting, 425
Turnkey contractors, 63, 65

U

UK Trade and Investment, 202, 341e
Uncertainty avoidance, 90
Underdeveloped countries. *See* Developing economies
Underground economy, 42
UNI Global Union, 503
Unintended consequences, of government intervention, 194
United Kingdom
    Airbus subsidies, 210
    cultural characteristics of, 89
    EU integration and, 226, 234
    government subsidies, 202
    manufacturing productivity levels, 147e
    number of world's largest MNEs, 13, 14e
    right to light laws, 200
    total commercial bank assets (2011), 519e
United Nations
    antibribery convention, 117
    on banking and financial reforms, 208
    cost of trade barriers, 196
    Declaration against Corruption and Bribery in International Commercial Transaction, 127
    influence of, 175
    intellectual property multilateral agreements, 428
    on sales of counterfeit pharmaceuticals, 185
    standards harmonization, 530
United Nations Commission on International Trade Law (UNCITRAL)
    Model Law on Electronic Commerce, 183
United Nations Conference on Trade and Development (UNCTAD), 175, 337, 341e, 393
United Nations Convention on Contracts for the International Sale of Goods (CISG), 180
United Nations Convention on the Rights of the Child, 122
United Nations Development Program, 326
United Nations Global Compact, 128
United States
    AIG bailout, 292–293
    apparel industry, 236–237
    average import tariff ranking, 198e

born global firms, 63
cultural characteristics of, 86, 89–90, 93–94
DR-CAFTA impacts, 19
as economic union, 221
ethical standards in, 118
exchange rate fluctuations against dollar, 277e
foreign investment laws, 179
foreign trade zones, 209
franchising statistics, 419e, 421
government debt as percentage of GDP, 291e
Hofstede's comparison to Mexico, 93e
import tariffs, 196, 206
increase in government spending, 172
inflation rates (1980-2011), 279e
manufacturing productivity levels, 147e
NAFTA impacts, 19, 226e, 227, 234
national security measures, 195
number of world's largest MNEs, 13, 14e
sales intensity of U.S.-based manufacturing, 360e
seizure of counterfeited/pirated goods, 115e
SMEs, defined, 14
steel tariffs (2000s), 194
subsidies and support programs, 201
top global brands, 472e
top trading partners of, 364, 365e
total commercial bank assets (2011), 519e
Toyota's U.S. plant investment in, 396e
trade dispute with Mexico, cement imports, 194
trade with Canada, 359
trading companies, 70
voluntary export restraints on Japanese cars (1980s), 194
United States Commercial Service, 329
U.S. Commerce Department, 202, 261, 329, 331, 371
U.S. Committee on Investments, 179
U.S. Congress
    antiboycott regulations, 182
    ban on CNOOC's attempt to buy Unocal, 385
    opposition to Dubai Ports World control of U.S. ports, 179
U.S. Defense Department, 210
U.S. dollar, 73, 255e, 274, 275e, 276, 277e, 281–283, 362, 512, 519
U.S. Financial Accounting Standards Board, 530
U.S. Food and Drug Administration, 436–438
U.S. International Trade Administration, 175, 202, 371
U.S. Justice Department, 182
U.S. Occupational Safety and Health Administration (OSHA), 118
U.S. Securities and Exchange Commission (SEC), 128, 182
U.S. Small Business Administration, 370
U.S. Supreme Court, 173
U.S. Trade Representative, 175, 210
U.S. Treasury Department, 73, 208
Utilitarian approach, to corporate governance, 124

V

Value-added taxes (VATs), 474–475, 531
Value chain, defined, 32
Value-chain activities
    examples of, 48e, 58–59
    globalization impacts on, 32e, 47–48
    suppliers of Apple iPhone components, 58e
    types of international business participants based on, 57–59
Values and attitudes, 91–92
Venezuela
    bureaucracy risks in, 257
    capital flight from, 276
    currency controls, 201
    expropriation of oil industry, 177
    nationalization of cement industry, 177
Vernon, Raymond, 144–145
Vertical integration, 396

Vietnam
    banking industry, 343–344
    competitive advantage of, 151
    footwear industry, 43
    global sourcing and, 443, 445
    Phu My 3 power plant, 426
Violence, as country risk, 178
Virtue approach, to corporate governance, 124
Visionary leadership
    for building global firm, 302–304
    defined, 302
    traits of, 303
Voluntary export restraints (VERs), 194, 199

W

War/insurrection/violence, as country risk, 178
Wholly owned direct investment, 395, 401
Wolverine World Wide, case study, 455–456
Women, in international business, 490, 503–506, 505e
Women Directors on Boards, 505
Working capital, 521–522
World Bank
    overview, 290, 370
    anticorruption measures, 127
    as data source, 341e
    defined, 281
    Ease of Doing Business rankings, 170, 257
    establishment of, 30
    export assistance to SMEs, 361
    financing for telecommunications, 263
    global debt crisis and, 293
    influence of, 175
    New Zealand as business friendly, 150
    people living in poverty, 46e
    poverty thresholds, 43
    tax system transparency, 532
World Bank Doing Business, 341e
World Economic Forum, 179, 263
World Health Organization (WHO), 49, 185
World Intellectual Property Organization (WIPO), 428
World Trade Organization (WTO)
    overview, 5, 30, 175, 219
    Agreement on Subsidies and Countervailing Measures (ASCM), 210
    Airbus/Boeing disputes, 210–211
    antidumping rules, 202, 476
    barrier reduction, 34
    CAP system and, 226
    collapse of Doha Round, 207
    dispute resolution system, 210
    drug patent protections under, 185–186
    effectiveness of, 207
    EU influence with, 231
    pressures on China's fixed exchange rate regime, 456
    prohibition on subsidies that hinder free trade, 201
    Trade-Related Aspects of Intellectual Property Rights (TRIPS), 185–186, 428

Y

Yen (Japan), 275e, 362, 520
Yuan (China), 236, 255, 275e, 456, 525
Yunus, Muhammad, 264
Yu-yung, Chung, 159

Z

Zimbabwe, 177
Zuckerberg, Mark, 2